THE CONFLICT OF LAWS

DICEY, MORRIS AND COLLINS
ON
THE CONFLICT OF LAWS

FIFTEENTH EDITION

UNDER THE GENERAL EDITORSHIP OF

LORD COLLINS OF MAPESBURY
P.C., LL.D., LL.M., F.B.A.

WITH

SPECIALIST EDITORS

VOLUME 1

SWEET & MAXWELL

THOMSON REUTERS

First Edition	1896	By A.V. Dicey
Second Edition	1908	By A.V. Dicey
Third Edition	1922	By A.V. Dicey and A. Berriedale Keith
Fourth Edition	1927	By A. Berriedale Keith
Fifth Edition	1932	By A. Berriedale Keith
Sixth Edition	1949	By J.H.C. Morris and Others
Seventh Edition	1958	By J.H.C. Morris and Others
Eighth Edition	1967	By J.H.C. Morris and Others
Ninth Edition	1973	By J.H.C. Morris and Others
Tenth Edition	1980	By J.H.C. Morris and Others
Eleventh Edition	1987	By Lawrence Collins and Others
Second Impression	1992	By Lawrence Collins and Others
Twelfth Edition	1993	By Lawrence Collins and Others
Second Impression	1994	By Lawrence Collins and Others
Thirteenth Edition	2000	By Lawrence Collins and Others
Fourteenth Edition	2006	By Sir Lawrence Collins and Others
Fifteenth Edition	2012	By Lord Collins of Mapesbury and Others

Published in 2012 by
Sweet & Maxwell
100 Avenue Road, London NW3 3PF
part of Thomson Reuters (Professional) UK Limited
(Registered in England and Wales, Company No. 1679046. Registered office and
address for service: Aldgate House, 33 Aldgate High Street, London EC3N 1DL.)

Computerset by Interactive Sciences Ltd, Gloucester
Printed and bound by CPI Group (UK) Ltd, Croydon, CR0 4YY

No natural forests were destroyed to make this product. Only farmed timber was used
and re-planted.

A CIP catalogue record for this book is available from the British Library.

ISBN: 978-0-414-02453-3

PETER McELEAVY
B.Sc. (Surrey), Ph.D. (Aberdeen)
Of Gray's Inn, Barrister;
Professor of International Family Law, University of Dundee

CAMPBELL McLACHLAN
Q.C., LL.B. (Well.), Ph.D. (London)
Barrister (New Zealand); Professor of Law,
Victoria University of Wellington

C.G.J. MORSE
M.A., B.C.L. (Oxon.)
Of the Middle Temple, Barrister;
Professor of Law, King's College, London

CONTENTS

VOLUME 1

PART ONE
PRELIMINARY MATTERS

Contents

PART TWO

PROCEDURE

PART THREE

JURISDICTION AND FOREIGN JUDGMENTS

Contents

Contents

VOLUME TWO

PART FOUR
FAMILY LAW

Contents

Chapter 21
MENTAL INCAPACITY

PART FIVE
LAW OF PROPERTY

Chapter 22
NATURE AND SITUS OF PROPERTY

Chapter 23
IMMOVABLES

Chapter 24
PARTICULAR TRANSFERS OF MOVABLES

Chapter 25
GOVERNMENTAL ACTS AFFECTING PROPERTY

Chapter 26
ADMINISTRATION OF ESTATES

PART SIX
CORPORATIONS AND INSOLVENCY

Contents

Part Seven
LAW OF OBLIGATIONS

PREFACE

The editorial team continues to have the great responsibility of maintaining the standard of what Lord Goff of Chieveley very generously described in the House of Lords as "the prince of legal textbooks." This is particularly so, given the great reliance on it by the courts. It has been cited in well over 200 judgments of the English courts since the last edition.

As the previous edition noted, Professor Dicey, and even Dr Morris, could not of course have foreseen the huge impact which a supra-national body of law, namely European law, would have on the subject of the conflict of laws. Since the last edition was published in 2006, the EU has demonstrated its intention to legislate for virtually the whole area, and four extremely important Regulations have come into force: The Rome II Regulation, Regulation (EC) 864/2007 of the European Parliament and of the Council on the law applicable to non-contractual obligations; the Rome I Regulation, Regulation (EC) 593/2008 of the European Parliament and of the Council on the law applicable to contractual obligations; the EU Service Regulation, Regulation of the European Parliament and Council (EC) 1393/2007 on the service in the Member States of judicial and extrajudicial documents in civil and commercial matters; and the Maintenance Regulation, Council Regulation (EC) 4/2009 on jurisdiction, applicable law, recognition and enforcement of decisions and co-operation in matters relating to maintenance obligations. The revised Lugano Convention came into force in January 2010.

Since the last edition there have been more than 50 relevant new decisions of the European Court, and more than 1000 decisions of the English courts. The decisions of the European Court include the controversial decision in Case C–185/07 *West Tankers Inc v Allianz SpA (The Front Comor)* [2009] E.C.R. I–663, [2009] 1 A.C. 1138, preventing the English from granting anti-suit injunctions to restrain proceedings in other EU States brought in breach of agreements to arbitrate in London. In addition, the Human Rights Act 1998 and the European Convention have played an increasing role in the areas covered by this work, and account has been taken of them, especially in the area of access to justice in the light of state immunity, and in relation to forum conveniens, and in the area of right to family life in the context of international child abduction.

Much of the work has been re-written and expanded. The main changes are these:

(1) the section on enforceability of foreign public in Chapter 5 has been re-written in the light of the decisions of the Court of Appeal in *Mbasogo v Logo Ltd* and *Islamic Republic of Iran v Barakat Galleries Ltd*;

(2) Chapter 6 contains a new expanded treatment of habitual residence;

(3) Chapter 7 takes account of the impact of the Rome I and Rome II Regulations on issues relating to damages and to limitation of

actions (and now also deals with interest, previously in Chapter 33);

(4) Chapter 8 has been extensively recast and contains for the first time rules for its subject-matter, together with an account of the new EU Service Regulation;

(5) Chapters 11, 12 and 14 have been revised and expanded to take account of the many decisions in the area of jurisdiction and judgments, and also to take account of the new Lugano Convention;

(6) Chapters 11 and 16 have been expanded to take account of the relationship between court proceedings and arbitration;

(7) Chapters 17 and 18 contain expanded treatment of conflict of laws aspects of civil partnership;

(8) Chapters 18 and 19 have been expanded to take account of the Maintenance Regulation;

(9) Chapter 19 contains an account of the 1996 Hague Convention on the Protection of Children, which is not yet in force;

(10) Chapter 29 on trusts now contains five rules instead of the former single rule, including a new rule on constructive and resulting trusts;

(11) Chapter 30 contains a new section on the UNCITRAL Model Law on Cross-Border Insolvency, as implemented in the Cross-Border Insolvency Regulations 2006;

(12) the Rome I Regulation (and other EU legislation) has had a considerable impact on the chapters on movable property (Chapter 24), and on contracts (Chapters 32 and 33), and Chapter 33 in particular has been greatly expanded;

(13) the Rome II Regulation has required very considerable changes to the treatment of torts in the work: Chapter 34 is substantially new and deals with issues common to torts and to other non-contractual obligations; Chapter 35 has been very considerably revised to take account of the Rome II Regulation; and the chapter on restitution has been substantially rewritten as Chapter 36 on unjust enrichment and equitable claims, etc.

Since the last edition, Professor Peter McEleavy and Professor Andrew Dickinson have joined the team. The responsibility of the editors for this edition is as follows: Professor Briggs is responsible for Chapters 2, 3, 4, 9, 12, 14, 24, 26, and 28; Professor Dickinson is responsible for Chapters 33, 34 and 35; Professor Harris is responsible for Chapters 7, 13, 15, 22, 23, 27, 29 and 36; Professor McClean is responsible for Chapters 17 and 18; Professor McEleavy is responsible for Chapters 6, and 19, 20 and 21; Professor McLachlan is responsible for Chapters 8, 16 (jointly with the General Editor) and 37; Professor Morse is responsible for Chapters 30 and 31. In addition to my overall responsibility as General Editor, I am responsible for Chapters 1, 5, 10, 11, 16 (jointly with Professor McLachlan), 25 and 32.

As before, we have had the advantage of much advice and information from friends and colleagues. We should mention especially Professor Francis Reynolds, Aude Fiorini, Maria Hook, Jean McMahon, and Paul Mora. We also acknowledge the administrative assistance of Maria Dolan, and the valuable efforts of the staff of the publisher in maintaining the technical excellence of the book.

This edition endeavours to state the law as at January 1, 2012. Later developments will be dealt with in the first supplement.

Lawrence Collins
September 2012

BIOGRAPHICAL NOTE

ALBERT VENN DICEY, the author of this book, was born on February 4, 1835. He was educated at Balliol College, Oxford, where he took a first in Honour Moderations in 1856 and a first in Greats in 1858; he was also President of the Union. He was elected a Fellow of Trinity College, Oxford, in 1860, and held his Fellowship until his marriage in 1872.

He was called to the Bar by the Inner Temple in 1863 and for some years "devilled" for Sir John Coleridge, afterwards Solicitor-General and Attorney-General. In 1870 he published his first law book, *Parties to Actions*, which (it is interesting to observe) was arranged in the form of rules and illustrations. His practice at the Bar was never very lucrative, though in 1876 he was appointed Junior Counsel to the Commissioners of Inland Revenue, a position which he held until 1890, when he took silk. In 1879 he published his second law book, on Domicil.

From a very early age he was intensely interested in politics. From family tradition and associations he belonged to the Whig as opposed to the Radical wing of the Liberal party. He was a convinced Free Trader. He ardently supported the cause of the North in the American Civil War, and the cause of Italian unity. He disliked the autocratic pretensions of Louis Napoleon and rejoiced in his fall. When Mr Gladstone split the Liberal party in two over the Home Rule question in 1885–1886, Dicey identified himself with the Unionist cause, and was prominent in its support from then until 1921. He wrote many pamphlets against Home Rule, and was an active speaker on Unionist platforms. This—the ruling political passion of his later years—naturally brought him into association with leading Conservative statesmen, whom hitherto he had tended to regard with suspicion. But he never lost his faith in Liberalism. "I am an old, an unconverted, and an impenitent Benthamite" he declared in 1913.

In 1881 the Vinerian Professorship of English law in the University of Oxford fell vacant, and after some hesitation Dicey resolved to become a candidate. He was duly elected in the following year. This Chair, of which Blackstone had been the first occupant, carried with it a Fellowship at All Souls College, and it was here that Dicey's most lasting work was done. He chose as the subject of his inaugural lecture the question "Can English law be taught at the Universities?" to which he replied with a vehement if closely reasoned affirmative. He admitted the immense advantages of reading in chambers, but argued that at the universities "a student can be taught to regard law as a whole, and to consider the relation of one part of English law to another"; that at the universities "can be taught the habit of looking upon law as a series of rules and exceptions, and of carefully marking off the exact limits of ascertained principles." In 1885 he published his *Law of the Constitution*, a book which was based on his Oxford lectures, and made his fame, not only in England but also in France and the United States, as the leading constitutional lawyer of the day. In 1898 he was invited to deliver a course of lectures at the Harvard Law School, the fruit of which was published in 1905 as *Law and Opinion in England*.

His *magnum opus*, however, was *The Conflict of Laws*, at which he was working from 1882 onwards, and which was first published in 1896. In a letter to a friend he declared in 1922 that "a successor of Blackstone should show that of one branch of English Law at least he could speak with authority." Shortly after the publication of the first edition, he thus described the book in a characteristic letter to his friend James Bryce: "In outward look it is like Story. I cannot flatter myself there is much other resemblance. For after reading much on the Conflict of Laws, I am well assured that Story and Savigny have written the only great books on the subject and, considering the state of legal speculation in Story's time and country, I am not sure that his is not the greater achievement of the two. If I had Westlake's knowledge, or if Westlake could have expressed himself as clearly as I can, a considerable book might have been produced. As it is, my clearness makes patent my errors. He has, I must add, acted with great generosity in giving me help when asked for and, if I had had more impudence, I believe I might have asked for and obtained much more. . . . My Introduction I like and some of the appendices. I doubt if there is much else really good which is not to be found in my *Domicil*, but I am tired and not quite a fair judge. Still, my impression is that the 'practical' man will prefer Foote, and the theorist Story or Savigny. What a queer thing life is. Why should I ever have become involved in this conflict of laws?" Four years later he wrote: "It is unlucky that the endless labour expended on the *Conflict of Law* cannot, from the nature of things, ever be visible to my Oxford friends to whom I principally wish, so to speak, to vindicate my work. If they say the labour was misspent, I more than half, though not completely, agree with them. My faith in digests has declined."

In 1907 the University of Oxford conferred on Dicey the degree of Honorary D.C.L., and in 1909 he resigned the Vinerian Chair, having unquestionably brought more lustre to it than any of his predecessors since Blackstone. He still retained his interest in teaching and in the Conflict of Laws, and in the following year All Souls College created especially for him a Lectureship in Private International Law, which he held until 1913. The duties of the post included giving informal instruction as well as lecturing, and he was thus brought into close contact with a number of under-graduates, largely Rhodes scholars, whose society he greatly enjoyed. Many of the Rhodes scholars were Americans, and he felt that his teaching created a new link with the United States. He died on April 7, 1922, at the age of 87, a few days after the publication of the third edition of this book.

J. H. C. M.

BIOGRAPHICAL NOTE

JOHN HUMPHREY CARLILE MORRIS, "whose contribution to the conflict of laws has excelled even that of his great predecessor. A. V. Dicey" (Lord Denning M.R.[1]), the General Editor of the 6th to 10th editions of this book and whose name appeared as co-author from the 8th edition in 1967, was born in 1910. He was an undergraduate of Christ Church, Oxford, and took firsts in the Final Honour School of Jurisprudence and in the B.C.L. and was elected Eldon Scholar. In 1934 he was called to the Bar by Gray's Inn, and following pupillage he practised for a short time in the chambers of Sir Andrew Clark before taking up a Fellowship at Magdalen College, Oxford in 1936, which he retained until his retirement in 1977, when the College elected him to an Honorary Fellowship. From 1951 to 1977 he was Reader in the Conflict of Laws at Oxford University. During that time, and until his death, he achieved and retained a distinction in teaching and scholarship, particularly in the conflict of laws, which earned him worldwide renown and respect and the devotion of generations of his Oxford pupils.

Dicey's great work on the Conflict of Laws, which had, following his death in 1922, suffered a considerable decline, was revived under John Morris' general editorship in 1949. In 1945 he was invited to undertake the sole editorship but (as he put it in the preface to the 6th edition) by October 1946 he felt that the task was beyond his strength and he therefore invited seven learned friends to help him. Those friends were Zelman (later Sir Zelman) Cowen, Rupert (later Sir Rupert) Cross, Otto (later Sir Otto) Kahn-Freund, Dr (later Professor) K. Lipstein, Dr (later Professor) Clive Parry, Mr R.S. Welsh and Professor Ben Wortley. In the preface to the 6th edition he regretted that no practitioner had felt able to accept his invitation to be an editor; but this deficiency was remedied in later editions, among whose editors were two practising barristers (who subsequently became High Court judges, and then members of the Court of Appeal, and one of whom became a distinguished Law Lord) and one practising solicitor (subsequently appointed a High Court judge). His wife, whom, as Jane Kinch, he had married in 1939, was a great support to him and had the unique experience of contributing to the accuracy of the work by reading successive editions aloud to the general editor.

There is no doubt that, even among these distinguished co-editors, it was John Morris' influence as general editor which was paramount in re-establishing the book as the leading work on the subject in the Commonwealth. In succeeding editions the influence of Dicey (from 1967, Dicey and Morris) grew, because under his guidance it kept up with, and anticipated, the great changes in the law caused by the 20th century revolution in communication and travel, and by new social attitudes to family life. As Lord Scarman put it

---

[1] *The Hollandia* [1982] Q.B. 872, 884 (C.A.). See for an appreciation of his life and work, Professor G. Treitel in (1984) 55 B.Y.I.L. p. ix–xiv; Dr P. M. North in (1988) 74 *Proceedings of the British Academy*, pp. 443–482.

in the foreword to an entire issue of the International and Comparative Law Quarterly in 1977 devoted to essays in honour of John Morris, "the depth and range of his learning coupled with his gift of critical analysis brought the flattering consequence that what Dicey said on a point mattered as much to the judges who made the case law as did their case law to the editor of Dicey".[2]

He was also the author of several important articles in the conflict of laws and in property law. Among the most influential in the former field were those on the proper law of contract in 1940, which was co-authored by Professor Cheshire, who acknowledged, however, that it was conceived and written by John Morris[3]; on the choice of law clause in statutes[4]; on family law, especially polygamy[5] and recognition of foreign divorces[6]; on property, especially transfer of chattels[7] and intestate succession to land.[8] No article was more influential than "The Proper Law of a Tort",[9] which had a profound effect on American case law and the American Law Institute Restatement (Second) of the Conflict of Laws.

In addition to his articles and work on this book, John Morris produced four editions of a case-book on the conflict of laws first published in 1939, a book of cases and materials (with Dr P. M. North, now Sir Peter North) in the year of his death, and an influential students' text book on the Conflict of Laws in 1971, the third edition of which was also prohibited in the year of his death. He was editor of three editions of *Theobald on Wills* and the general editor of one edition of *Chitty on Contracts*, as well as co-author (with W. Barton Leach) of a well-known book on the Rule against Perpetuities.

Although he was no seeker of honours, the excellence of his work, and his influence on the law, was marked by a series of distinctions: he was awarded the degree of Doctor of Civil Law by Oxford in 1949; he was elected an Associate Member of the Institute of International Law (1954); Associate Member of the American Academy of Arts and Sciences (1960); Fellow of the British Academy (1966); Honorary Bencher of Gray's Inn (1980); Queen's Counsel (1981). But unlike Dicey, he never became Vinerian Professor at Oxford. As the author (rumoured to be a highly reliable source) of his obituary in *The Times* put it, "in 1964 the Vinerian Chair of English Law at All Souls College fell vacant, and Morris was strongly tipped for the succession. The Chair was offered to him, but to the surprise of his friends and many academic lawyers he declined it. He was devoted to Magdalen, which he served long and faithfully as a Fellow, Clerk to the College and (for one year) as Vice-President and could not bear the thought of migrating to All Souls, for which he had a life-long antipathy." As a result John Morris was entitled to the title of professor only twice, once when he was visiting professor at Harvard Law School in 1950–1951, and latterly when, despite his life-long devotion to

---

[2] (1977) 26 I.C.L.Q. 701.

[3] (1940) 56 L.Q.R. 320, 339. See also (1950) 3 Int. L.Q. 197.

[4] (1946) 62 L.Q.R. 170. See also (1979) 95 L.Q.R. 59.

[5] (1953) 66 Harv. L.Rev. 691, first published in *Festschrift für Martin Wolff* (1952), p. 287.

[6] (1946) 24 Can. Bar Rev. 73; (1952) 29 B.Y.I.L. 283; (1975) 14 I.C.L.Q. 635.

[7] (1945) 22 B.Y.I.L. 232.

[8] (1969) 85 L.Q.R. 339. See also (1937) 18 B.Y.I.L. 32 (renvoi); (1938) 54 L.Q.R. 78 (marriage settlements).

[9] (1951) 64 Harv. L.Rev. 884. See also (1949) 12 M.L.R. 248.

Oxford, he spent a happy year in 1978–1979 as Goodhart Professor at Cambridge University and Fellow of Gonville and Caius College.

He completed work on the last supplement to the 10th edition only a few days before his death on September 29, 1984, and on September 19 he wrote "It is with relief, not untinged with emotion, that I lay down the burden of the task I assumed as long ago as January 1945. I have improved the book—no question about that—and perhaps prevented it from dying a natural death."

L. A. C.

TABLE OF STATUTES

Chapters 1 to 16 will be found in Volume 1; Chapters 17 to 37 will be found in Volume 2.

xxvii

Table of Statutes

Table of Statutes

Table of Statutes

Table of Statutes

TABLE OF CASES

Table of Cases

Table of Cases

Table of Cases

Table of Cases

Table of Cases

Table of Cases

Table of Cases

Table of Cases

Table of Cases

Table of Cases

Table of Cases

Table of Cases

Table of Cases

Table of Cases

Table of Cases

Table of Cases

Table of Cases

Table of Cases

Table of Cases

Table of Cases

Table of Cases

Table of Cases

Table of Cases

Table of Cases

Table of Cases

Table of Cases

Table of Cases

Table of Cases

Table of Cases

Table of Cases

Table of Cases

Table of Cases

Table of Cases

Table of Cases

Table of Cases

Table of Cases

Table of Cases

Table of Cases

Table of Cases

Table of Cases

Table of Cases

Table of Cases

Table of Cases

Table of Cases

Table of Cases

Table of Cases

Table of Cases

Table of Cases

Table of Cases

Table of Cases

Table of Cases

Table of Cases

Table of Cases

Table of Cases

Table of Cases

Table of Cases

Table of Cases

Table of Cases

Table of Cases

Table of Cases

Table of Cases

Table of Cases

Table of Cases

Table of Cases

Table of Cases

Table of Cases

Table of Cases

Table of Cases

Table of Cases

Table of Cases

Table of Cases

Table of Cases

Table of Cases

Table of Cases

Table of Cases

Table of Cases

Table of Cases

Table of Cases

Table of Cases

Table of Cases

Table of Cases

Table of Cases

Table of Cases

Table of Cases

Table of Cases

Table of Cases

Table of Cases

*Decisions of the European Court of Justice are listed below numerically. These decisions are also
included in the preceding alphabetical table.*

Table of Cases

Table of Cases

Table of Cases

Table of Cases

ccciii

Table of Cases

Table of Cases

Table of Cases

Table of Cases

Table of Cases

Table of Cases

TABLE OF STATUTORY INSTRUMENTS

Chapters 1 to 16 will be found in Volume 1; Chapters 17 to 37 will be found in Volume 2.

TABLE OF CIVIL PROCEDURE RULES

Chapters 1 to 16 will be found in Volume 1; Chapters 17 to 37 will be found in Volume 2.

TABLE OF EUROPEAN AND INTERNATIONAL CONVENTIONS AND LEGISLATION

Chapters 1 to 16 will be found in Volume 1; Chapters 17 to 37 will be found in Volume 2.

CONVENTIONS

TABLE OF EC AND EU LEGISLATION

Chapters 1 to 16 will be found in Volume 1; Chapters 17 to 37 will be found in Volume 2.

TABLE OF FOREIGN CASE REFERENCES

Man.L.R.	Manitoba Reports (Canada)
Mass.	Massachusetts Reports (USA)
Md.	Maryland Reports (USA)
Mich.	Michigan Reports (USA)
Milw.	Milward's Ecclesiastical Reports (Ireland)
Minn.	Minnesota Reports (USA)
Misc.	Miscellaneous Reports, New York (USA)
N.B.Eq.	New Brunswick Equity Reports (Canada)
N.B.R.	New Brunswick Reports (Canada)
N.E.	Northeastern Reporter (USA)
N.H.	New Hampshire Reports (USA)
N.Ir.	Northern Ireland Reports
N.J.	New Jersey Reports (USA)
N.L.R.	Natal Law Reports (South Africa)
N.P.D.	Natal Provincial Division (South Africa)
N.S.R.	Nova Scotia Reports (Canada)
N.S.W.L.R.	New South Wales Law Reports (Australia)
N.S.W.R.	New South Wales Reports (Australia)
N.W.	Northwestern Reporter (USA)
N.Y.	New York Court of Appeals Reports (USA)
N.Y.S.	New York Supplement (USA)
N.Z.L.R.	New Zealand Law Reports
O.A.R.	Ontario Appeal Reports (Canada)
O.B. & F.	Ollivier, Bell and Fitzgerald (New Zealand)
Ohio App.	Ohio Appellate Reports (USA)
O.L.R.	Ontario Law Reports (Canada)
O.R.	Ontario Reports (Canada)
P.	Pacific Reporter (USA)
Pa.	Pennsylvania Reports (USA)
Qd.R.	Queensland Reports (Australia)
Q.L.R.	Quebec Law Reports
Qu.K.B.	Quebec Reports King's Bench
Q.R.S.C.	Quebec Reports Superior Court
Que.S.C.	Quebec Superior Court Reports
R.	Session Cases, 4th Series (Rettie) (Scotland)
R. & N.	Rhodesia and Nyasaland Reports
R.F.L.	Reports of Family Law (Canada)
R.I.	Rhode Island Reports (USA)
S.	Session Cases, 1st Series (Shaw) (Scotland)
S.A.	South Africa Law Reports
S.A.R.	South African Republic Supreme Court Reports
Sask.L.R.	Saskatchewan Law Reports (Canada)
S.A.S.R.	South Australian State Reports
S.C.	Session Cases (Scotland)
S.C.	Supreme Court Reports (Cape of Good Hope)
S.C.R.	Canadian Supreme Court Reports
S.E.	Southeastern Reporter (USA)
Sing.L.R.	Singapore Law Reports
S.L.R.	Scottish Law Reporter
S.L.T.	Scots Law Times
So.	Southern Reporter (USA)
S.R.N.S.W.	State Reports New South Wales (Australia)
St.R.Qd.	State Reports Queensland (Australia)
S.W.	Southwestern Reporter (USA)
Terr.L.R.	Territories Law Reports (Canada)
T.P.D.	Transvaal Provincial Division (South Africa)
T.S.	Transvaal Supreme Court (South Africa)
U.C.C.P.	Upper Canada Common Pleas
U.C.Q.B., U.C.R.	Upper Canada Queen's Bench
U.S.	United States Supreme Court Reports
V.L.R.	Victorian Law Reports (Australia)

Table of Foreign Case References

V.R.	Victorian Reports (Australia)
Wall.	Wallace's United States Supreme Court Reports
W.A.L.R.	Western Australian Law Reports
W.A.R.	Western Australia Reports
Wheat	Wheaton's United States Supreme Court Reports
W.I.R.	West Indian Reports
Wis.	Wisconsin Reports (USA)
W.L.D.	Witwatersrand Local Division (South Africa)
W.L.R.	Western Law Reporter (Canada)
W.N.(N.S.W.)	Weekly Notes, New South Wales (Australia)
W.Va.	West Virginia Reports (USA)
W.W. & A'B.	Wyatt, Webb and A'Beckett (Victoria, Australia)
W.W.R.	Western Weekly Reports (Canada)

TABLE OF BOOKS REFERRED TO[1]

Ahern and Binchy	The Rome II Regulation on the Law Applicable to Non-Contractual Obligations (2009)
Anton	Private International Law (3rd ed. 2011, eds Beaumont and McEleavy) (as "Anton")
	Civil Jurisdiction in Scotland (1984)
Bate	Notes on the Doctrine of Renvoi (1904)
Batiffol and Lagarde	Droit International Privé (7th ed. 1981–1983)
Beale	Treatise on the Conflict of Laws (1935)
Blom-Cooper	Bankruptcy in Private International Law (1954)
Born	International Commercial Arbitration (2009)
Bowstead and Reynolds	Agency (19th ed. 2010)
Briggs and Rees	Civil Jurisdiction and Judgments (5th ed. 2009)
Castel and Walker	Canadian Conflict of Laws (6th ed. 2005)
Cavers	The Choice of Law Process (1965)
Chalmers and Guest	Bills of Exchange, Cheques and Promissory Notes (17th ed. 2009)
Cheshire, North and Fawcett	Private International Law (14th ed. 2008)
Collier	Conflict of Laws (3rd ed. 2001)
Collins	Civil Jurisdiction and Judgments Act 1982 (1983) (as "Collins")
	Essays in International Litigation and the Conflict of Laws (1994) (as "Collins, *Essays*")
Cook	Logical and Legal Bases of the Conflict of Laws (1942)
Craig, Park and Paulsson	International Chamber of Commerce Arbitration (3rd ed. 2000)
Currie	Selected Essays on the Conflict of Laws (1963)
de Almeida, Desantes Real, Jenard	Report on the Convention on the accession of the Kingdom of Spain and the Portuguese Republic to the 1968 Convention on jurisdiction and the enforcement of judgments in civil and commercial matters and to the Protocol on its interpretation by the Court of Justice: [1990] O.J. C189/35
Dickinson	The Rome II Regulation (2008)
Ehrenzweig	Treatise on the Conflict of Laws (1962)
Falconbridge	Selected Essays on the Conflict of Laws (2nd ed. 1954)
Fawcett	Declining Jurisdiction in Private International Law (1995)
Fawcett, Harris and Bridge	International Sale of Goods in the Conflict of Laws (2005)
Fawcett and Torremans	Intellectual Property and Private International Law (2nd ed. 2011)
Fentiman	Foreign Law in English Courts (1998)
Fletcher	Insolvency in Private International Law (2nd ed. 2005)
Foote	Private International Law (5th ed. 1925)
Fouchard, Gaillard, Goldman	International Commercial Arbitration (1999, eds Gaillard and Savage)
Giuliano-Lagarde	Report on the Convention on the law applicable to contractual obligations: [1980] O.J. C282/1
Hancock	Torts in the Conflict of Laws (1942)
Harris	The Hague Trusts Convention (2002)
Hartley	Civil Jurisdiction and Judgments (1984)

---

[1] Only books that are cited by the name of the author alone are listed in this table. Where more than one book is listed, the context will indicate which work is being cited.

Table of Books Referred To

Hay, Borchers and Symeonides	Conflict of Laws (5th ed. 2010)
Hertz	Jurisdiction in Contract and Tort under the Brussels Convention (1998)
Jenard	Report on the Convention of 27 September 1968 on jurisdiction and the enforcement of judgments in civil and commercial matters: [1979] O.J. C59/1
Jenard-Möller	Report on the Convention on jurisdiction and the enforcement of judgments in civil and commercial matters done at Lugano on 16 September 1988: [1990] O.J. C189/57
Johnson	Conflict of Laws with special reference to the law of Quebec (1933–1937)
Kaye	Civil Jurisdiction and the Enforcement of Foreign Judgments (1987)
	European Case Law on the Judgments Convention (1998)
	The New Private International Law of Contract of the European Community (1993)
Lalive	The Transfer of Chattels in the Conflict of Laws (1955)
Lando	International Encyclopaedia of Comparative Law, Vol. III, Chapter 24 (1976)
Lauterpacht	Recognition in International Law (1947)
Layton and Mercer	European Civil Practice (2nd ed. 2004)
Lew, Mistelis and Kröll	Comparative International Commercial Arbitration (2003)
Lipstein	Harmonisation of Private International Law by the EEC (1978)
Lorenzen	Selected Articles on the Conflict of Laws (1947)
McClean	International Co-operation in Civil and Criminal Matters (2002)
	Recognition of Family Judgments in the Commonwealth (1983)
McLachlan, Shore and Weiniger	International Investment Arbitration: Substantive Principles (2007)
Mann F.A.	Foreign Affairs in English Courts (1986)
	Further Studies in International Law (1990)
	Legal Aspects of Money (6th ed. Proctor, 2005) (as "Mann")
	Studies in International Law (1973)
Mendelssohn-Bartholdy	Renvoi in Modern English Law (1937)
Morse	Torts in Private International Law (1978)
Moss, Fletcher and Isaacs	The EC Regulation on Insolvency Proceedings (2nd ed. 2009)
Mustill and Boyd	Commercial Arbitration (2nd ed. 1989 and Companion Volume 2001)
Nadelmann	Conflict of Laws: International and Interstate (1972)
Niboyet	Traité de Droit International Privé Français (1944–1951)
North	Contract Conflicts (1982)
	Essays in Private International Law (1993)
Nussbaum	Principles of Private International Law (1943)
Nygh	Autonomy in International Contracts (1999)
Oppenheim	International Law (9th ed. Jennings and Watts, 1992)
Patchett	Recognition of Commercial Judgments and Awards in the Commonwealth (1984)
Petrochilos	Procedural Law in International Arbitration (2004)
Phillimore	Commentaries on International Law (3rd ed. 1879–1889)
Piggott	Foreign Judgments (3rd ed. 1908)
Plender and Wilderspin	The European Private International Law of Obligations (3rd ed. 2009)
Pocar	Explanatory Report on the Convention on jurisdiction and the recognition and enforcement of judgments in civil and commercial matters, signed in Lugano on 30 October 2007 [2009] O.J. C319/1
Poudret and Besson	Comparative Law of International Arbitration (2nd ed. 2007)
Rabel	Conflict of Laws: A Comparative Study (2nd ed. 1958–1964)
Read	Recognition and Enforcement of Foreign Judgments in the Common Law Units of the British Commonwealth (1938)
Redfern and Hunter	International Commercial Arbitration (5th ed. 2009, eds Blacakbay and Partasides)

PART ONE

PRELIMINARY MATTERS

PART ONE deals with matters which are preliminary to the principal topics **I–001** hereafter discussed in this book.

CHAPTER 1 discusses the general nature of the conflict of laws; the interpretation of statutes implementing international conventions; and the operation of statutes in the conflict of laws. It also defines certain geographical and technical terms constantly used in this book, and discusses the determination of the connecting factor.

CHAPTER 2 deals with two matters of great theoretical difficulty, namely, Characterisation and the Incidental Question.

CHAPTER 3 deals with the factor of time in the conflict of laws.

CHAPTER 4 deals with Renvoi or the meaning of the expression "law of a country".

CHAPTER 5 deals with the exclusion of a foreign rule of law on grounds of public policy and with the refusal of English courts to enforce foreign penal, revenue or other public laws or to entertain an action founded on an act of state.

CHAPTER 6 contains the common law rules (as modified by statute) for ascertaining the domicile and residence of a natural person. The domicile and residence of corporations are not dealt with in this chapter but in Chapter 30. Domicile for the purposes of Council Regulation (EC) 44/2001 (the Brussels I Regulation) and the Lugano Convention on jurisdiction and the recognition and enforcement of judgments in civil and commercial matters is dealt with in Chapter 11.

CHAPTER 1

NATURE AND SCOPE OF THE CONFLICT OF LAWS[1]

Introduction. The branch of English law known as the conflict of laws is   **1–001**
that part of the law of England which deals with cases having a foreign
element. By a "foreign element" is meant simply a contact with some system
of law other than English law. Such a contact may exist, for example, because
a contract was made or to be performed in a foreign country, or because a tort
was committed there, or because property was situated there, or because the
parties are not English.[2] In the conflict of laws, a foreign element and a foreign
country[3] mean a non-English element and a country other than England. From
the point of view of the conflict of laws, Scotland and Northern Ireland are for
many purposes as much foreign countries as France or Germany.[4]

If an action is brought in an English court for damages for breach of a   **1–002**
contract made in England between two Englishmen and to be performed in
England, there is no foreign element, the case is not a case in the conflict of
laws, and the English court will naturally apply English internal or domestic
law. But if the contract had been made in Switzerland between two Swiss and
was to be performed in Switzerland, then the case would be (for an English
court, but not for a Swiss court) a case in the conflict of laws, and the English
court would apply Swiss law to most of the matters in dispute before it,[5] just
as a Swiss court would naturally apply Swiss law to all such matters. If we
change the facts once more and assume that the contract was made in
Switzerland between an Englishman and a Swiss but was to be performed in

---

[1] There is an enormous literature on the nature and scope of the subject: see especially Cavers,
The Choice of Law Process (1965); Cavers (1933) 47 Harv. L. Rev. 173, reprinted in *The Choice
of Law* (1985), Ch.1; Cook, *Logical and Legal Bases of the Conflict of Laws* (1942), Chs 1–3;
Cheatham and Reese (1952) 52 Col. L. Rev. 959; Kahn-Freund (1974) *Recueil des Cours*, III, Chs
1 and 2, reprinted as *General Problems in Private International Law*; Kegel (1964) *Recueil des
Cours*, II, 95; Kegel, *International Encyclopedia of Comparative Law*, Vol.III, Ch.3 (1986);
Scoles, Hay, Borchers and Symeonides, Chs 1 and 2.

[2] That is, English by domicile or by residence. There is no such thing as English nationality.

[3] For the meaning of "country," see below, paras 1–065 *et seq.*

[4] The qualification has to be made because (1) England, Scotland and Northern Ireland share
a common court of last resort; (2) many statutes (especially those implementing an international
convention) apply to all three parts of the United Kingdom; (3) Scotland and Northern Ireland are
in a special position as regards (a) jurisdiction in actions *in personam* (see below, Rules 34 and
35) and the reciprocal enforcement of judgments *in personam* (Rule 56); (b) the reciprocal
recognition of divorces (Rule 86), grants of probate (Rule 140) and receiving orders in bankruptcy
(Rule 214); (c) the reciprocal enforcement of maintenance orders (Rule 102(2)); (d) the effect of
bankruptcy as an assignment of the debtor's property (Rule 215) and as a discharge of his
contracts (Rule 220).

[5] Not to all matters, because in an English court matters of procedure are governed by English
domestic law. See Rule 19.

England, then the case is a case in the conflict of laws not only for an English court but also for a Swiss court and indeed for any court in the world in which the contract is litigated and that court will have to decide whether and for what purposes the Swiss or the English elements are the more significant, and apply Swiss or English law accordingly. It is cases of this last type, where the facts are distributed between two or more countries, which give rise to the problem of renvoi, discussed in Chapter 4.

1–003   **Jurisdiction and choice of law.** The questions that arise in conflict of laws cases are of two main types: first, has the English court jurisdiction to determine this case? And secondly, if so, what law should it apply?[6] There may sometimes be a third question, namely, will the English court recognise or enforce a foreign judgment purporting to determine the issue between the parties? Of course this third question arises only if there is a foreign judgment, and thus not in every case. But the first two questions arise in every case with foreign elements, though the answer to one of them may be so obvious that the court is in effect only concerned with the other. The law of every modern country has rules dealing with these questions, called conflict of laws—in contrast to its domestic or internal law.

1–004   The English rules of the conflict of laws differ from those adopted in many continental European countries in one important respect. There are many situations in which, if the English court has jurisdiction, it will apply English domestic law. This is true, for example, of most issues in proceedings for divorce and separation,[7] for the guardianship, custody[8] and adoption[9] of minors, and for the maintenance of wives and children.[10] Conversely, there are many situations in which, if a foreign court has jurisdiction according to English rules of the conflict of laws, its judgment or decree will be recognised in England, regardless of the grounds on which it was based or the choice of law rule which it applied.[11] Thus, in the English conflict of laws, questions of jurisdiction frequently tend to overshadow questions of choice of law. Or, to put it differently, it frequently happens that if the question of jurisdiction (whether of the English or the foreign court) is answered satisfactorily, the question of choice of law does not arise.

1–005   **Justification.** What justification is there for the existence of the conflict of laws? Why should we depart from the rules of our own law and apply those of another system? This is a vital matter on which it is necessary to be clear before we proceed any further. The main justification for the conflict of laws is that it implements the reasonable and legitimate expectations of the parties to a transaction or an occurrence.[12] This can best be seen by considering what would happen if the conflict of laws did not exist.

---

[6] On the increasing significance of jurisdictional issues, see McLachlan (2004) 120 L.Q.R. 580.

[7] See Rule 85(1).

[8] See Rule 106(4).

[9] See below, para.20–099.

[10] See Rule 89(5).

[11] See Rules 43, 44, 88, 90.

[12] See Rheinstein (1944) 19 Tulane L. Rev. 4, 17–24.

Theoretically, it would be possible for English courts, while opening their 1–006
doors to foreigners, to apply English domestic law in all cases.[13] But if they
did so, grave injustice would again be inflicted not only on foreigners but also
on Englishmen. For instance, if two English people married in France in
accordance with the formalities prescribed by French law, but not in accordance with the formalities prescribed by English law, the English court, if it
applied English law to the validity of the marriage, would have to treat the
parties as unmarried persons and their children as illegitimate.

Theoretically, it would be possible for English courts, while opening their 1–007
doors to foreigners and while ready to apply foreign law in appropriate cases,
to refuse to recognise or enforce a foreign judgment determining the issue
between the parties. But if they did so, grave injustice and inconvenience
would result. For instance, if a divorce was granted in a foreign country in
which the parties were settled, and afterwards one of them remarried in
England, he or she might be convicted of bigamy. Or if a plaintiff sued a
defendant in a foreign country for damages for breach of contract or for tort,
and eventually obtained a judgment in his favour, he might find that the
defendant had surreptitiously removed his assets to England, and then would
have to start all over again to enforce his rights.

Comity.[14] It was at one time supposed that the doctrine of comity was a 1–008
sufficient basis for the conflict of laws.[15] Comity is a term of very elastic
content. Sometimes it connotes courtesy or the need for reciprocity; at other
times it is used as a synonym for the rules of public international law.[16] Thus
Diplock L.J. referred to the rules of comity as the "accepted rules of mutual
conduct as between state and state which each state adopts in relation to other
states and expects other states to adopt in relation to itself."[17] Story used it to
mean more than mere courtesy, but something rather less than equivalent to
international law.[18] Dicey was highly critical of the use of comity to explain
the conflict of laws. He said that it was "a singular specimen of confusion of
thought produced by laxity of language."[19] English courts apply, for example,
French law in order to do justice between the parties, and not from any desire

---

[13] But the application by a court of its own law, rather than foreign law, to a wholly foreign
transaction may be regarded by other States as a breach of international law: see below,
para.1–017.

[14] See Collins, in *Reform and Development of Private International Law* (Fawcett ed. 2002),
p.89; Yntema (1966) 65 Mich. L. Rev. 9; F.A. Mann, *Foreign Affairs in English Courts* (1986),
pp.134–137.

[15] Story (1st ed. 1834), pp.33–35.

[16] Oppenheim, *International Law* (9th ed. Jennings and Watts 1992), Vol.1, pp.50–51.

[17] *Buck v Att-Gen* [1965] Ch. 745, 770 (CA).

[18] *cf. Hilton v Guyot*, 159 U.S. 113, 163–164 (1895) (" . . . neither a matter of absolute
obligation, on the one hand, nor of mere courtesy and good will, upon the other"); *Soc Nationale
Industrielle Aérospatiale v US District Court*, 482 U.S. 522, 543 (1987) (" . . . the spirit of
co-operation in which a domestic tribunal approaches the resolution of cases touching the laws
and interests of other sovereign states"). See for an example of comity as courtesy *Aziz v Aziz*
[2007] EWCA Civ 712, [2008] 2 All E.R. 501, at [89]–[90].

[19] 1st ed. 1896, p.10. On September 16, 1896 Sir Frederick Pollock wrote to Dicey about the
first edition of this work, and said: "In particular I rejoice in your summary abolition of the
confusing term *comity*" (Cosgrove, *The Rule of Law: Albert Venn Dicey, Victorian Jurist*, 1980,
p.168). See also Cheshire, North and Fawcett, p.4 ("meaningless or misleading . . . incompatible
with the judicial function"); Wolff, p.15.

to show courtesy to the French Republic, nor even in the hope that if English courts apply French law in appropriate cases, French courts will be encouraged in appropriate cases to apply English law. In the United States recognition of foreign judgments has been said to rest on considerations of comity and reciprocity,[20] but comity has been rejected as the basis for the recognition of foreign judgments in England.[21]

1–009   The concept of comity is increasingly used in common law countries, not as an explanation for the system of the conflict of laws, but as a tool for applying or re-shaping the rules of the conflict of laws. In particular, it is used in a sense which owes much to the rules of public international law, namely respect for the territorial jurisdiction of other States. In *Buck v Att-Gen*[22] Diplock L.J. said that one of the rules of comity was that one State does not purport to exercise jurisdiction over the internal affairs of any other independent State, or to apply measures of coercion to it or to its property, except in accordance with the rules of public international law. He then went on to say that one of the most common applications of that rule was the doctrine of sovereign immunity. When comity is used in this sense, it no longer refers to mere courtesies. It is no doubt in the sense of binding rules of public international law that the expression is used in the cases on state immunity. It was in this sense and in that context that Lord Denning referred to the "comity of nations"[23] and that Cohen L.J. referred to the "principles of comity established by international law."[24]

1–010   Similar language has been used in relation to international civil jurisdiction. In 1886 Lord Coleridge C.J. said that RSC Order 11 (now CPR, r.6.36 and Practice Direction 6B, para.3.1[25]) was enacted to bring English practice "into accordance with well-settled rules of international law, or, at all events, comity."[26] In *Vitkovice Horni a Hutni Tezirstvo v Korner*[27] Lord Radcliffe said that ordinary principles of international comity were invaded by permitting service out of the jurisdiction, and the courts should therefore approach with

---

[20] See Hay, Borchers and Symeonides, pp.1446–1447. *cf. Morguard Investments Ltd v De Savoye* [1990] 3 S.C.R. 1077, 1096–1097 (Sup Ct Can).

[21] *Schibsby v Westenholz* (1870) L.R. 6 Q.B. 155, 159; *Adams v Cape Industries Plc* [1990] Ch. 433, 513 (CA), see below, para.14–007. In many cases on international judicial assistance the courts have emphasised the considerations of comity inherent in the need for international judicial co-operation in obtaining evidence: *State of Minnesota v Philip Morris Inc* [1998] I.L.Pr. 170, 176. *cf. England v Smith* [2001] Ch. 419, at 435 (CA); contrast *Settebello Ltd v Banco Totta and Acores* [1985] 1 W.L.R. 1050, 1057 (CA). For Australia, see *Joyce v Sunland Waterfront (BVI) Ltd* [2011] FCAFC 95, at [57] *et seq.* See, on the United States Supreme Court's use of comity in judicial assistance cases, Collins (2006) 8 Yb. P.I.L. 53, and e.g. *Soc Nationale Industrielle Aérospatiale v US District Court*, 482 U.S. 522, 543 (1987); *Intel Corp v Advanced Micro Devices, Inc*, 542 U.S. 241, 261 *et seq.* (2004). See below, paras 8–074 *et seq.*

[22] [1965] Ch. 745, 770 (CA).

[23] *Rahimtoola v Nizam of Hyderabad* [1958] A.C. 379, 417.

[24] *Krajina v Tass Agency* [1949] 2 All E.R. 274, 280. The same use is found in criminal jurisdiction in international cases: *R. v Treacy* [1971] A.C. 537, at 561–562; *Liangsiriprasert v US Government* [1991] 2 A.C. 225, at 251; *Director of Public Prosecutions v Stonehouse* [1978] A.C. 55, at 77, 82, 93; *R. v Doot* [1973] A.C. 807, at 835; *R. v Smith* [2004] EWCA Crim. 631, [2004] Q.B. 1418.

[25] Rule 34, below.

[26] *Field v Bennett* (1886) 56 L.J.Q.B. 89, at 91.

[27] [1951] A.C. 869, 882. See also *The Brabo* [1949] A.C. 326, 357.

circumspection any request for leave to serve out of the jurisdiction. The same thought was expressed by Scott L.J. in *George Monro Ltd v American Cyanamid Corp*[28]:

"Service out of the jurisdiction at the instance of our courts is necessarily prima facie an interference with the exclusive jurisdiction of the sovereignty of the foreign country where service is to be effected . . . As a matter of international comity it seems to me important to make sure that no such service shall be allowed unless it is clearly within both the letter and the spirit of Or. XI."

More recently, comity has been invoked to justify the caution which is required in the exercise of the power to grant injunctions to restrain proceedings in foreign courts. Both in the Commonwealth and in the United States the courts have been sensitive to the charge that to grant an anti-suit injunction may be contrary to considerations of comity. It used to be emphasised that an anti-suit injunction was directed to the party and not to the foreign court, but it is now recognised that that is not a realistic view. **1–011**

In the *Laker Airways* litigation, British Airways and British Caledonian Airways obtained injunctions in the English courts enjoining the commencement by the liquidator of Laker Airways against them of anti-trust proceedings in the United States. The United States courts enjoined other airlines from taking similar steps in the English courts to frustrate the liquidator's anti-trust proceedings in the United States. In the final phase of this contest between the English and American courts,[29] the House of Lords discharged the English injunctions: in *British Airways Board v Laker Airways Ltd*,[30] Lord Scarman said that an anti-suit injunction was, however disguised and indirect, an interference with the process of justice in the foreign court. More recently, it has been held that comity requires that the English forum should have a sufficient interest in, or connection with, the matter in question to justify the **1–012**

---

[28] [1944] K.B. 432, 437. For a full discussion in the context of judicial jurisdiction see *Spar Aerospace Ltd v American Mobile Satellite Corp* (2002) 220 D.L.R. (4th) 54, 63–66 (Sup Ct Can). See also, in the context of recognition and enforcement of foreign judgments, *Beals v Saldanha*, 2003 SCC 72, (2004) 234 D.L.R. (4th) 1 (Sup Ct Can).

[29] See, e.g. *Laker Airways Ltd v Pan American Airways*, 559 F. Supp. 1124, 1128, *per* Greene J. (DDC 1983) ("It can hardly be said that an order which . . . directs a party not to file further papers in this Court, as did the order of the British court . . . is anything other than a direct interference with the proceedings in this Court."); *British Airways Board v Laker Airways Ltd* [1984] Q.B. 142, at 185–186 (CA) *per* Sir John Donaldson M.R. (" . . . let it be said no less loudly and clearly that neither the English courts nor the English judges entertain any feelings of hostility towards the American anti-trust laws or would ever wish to denigrate that or any other American law. Judicial comity is shorthand for good neighbourliness, common courtesy and mutual respect between those who labour in adjoining judicial vineyards."); *Laker Airways Ltd v Sabena Belgian Airlines*, 731 F. 2d 909, 937 (D.C. Cir. 1984) *per* Wilkey J. ("comity serves our international system like the mortar which cements together a brick house. No one would willingly permit the mortar to crumble or be chipped away for fear of compromising the entire structure.")

[30] [1985] A.C. 58 at 95. See also *Barclays Bank v Homan* [1993] B.C.L.C. 680, 690 (CA); *Phillip Alexander Securities and Futures Ltd v Bamberger* [1997] I.L.Pr. 73, 117 (CA).

indirect interference with the foreign court which such an injunction entails.[31]

1-013   So also, in the exercise of the jurisdiction to grant extra-territorial provisional remedies such as *Mareva* or freezing injunctions, "it is becoming widely accepted that comity between the courts of different countries requires mutual respect for the territorial integrity of each other's jurisdiction."[32] Similarly, the Court of Appeal held that the Charities Act 1993 did not apply to a charity established under Indian law, because as a matter of comity the jurisdiction of the court to control charities could only be exercised in relation to English charities, and any attempt to control foreign charities would be akin to an encroachment upon the sovereignty of a foreign State.[33] In *Masri v Consolidated Contractors International Company SAL (No.2)*[34] the Court of Appeal emphasised that that was why Lord Donaldson MR confirmed that the *Mareva* injunction should not conflict with "the ordinary principles of international law" and that "considerations of comity require the courts of this country to refrain from making orders which infringe the exclusive jurisdiction of the courts of other countries."[35] It was for this reason also that it has been suggested that the extension of the *Mareva* jurisdiction to assets abroad was justifiable in terms of international law and comity provided that the case had some appropriate connection with England, that the court did not purport to affect title to property abroad, and that the court did not seek to control the activities abroad of foreigners who were not subject to the personal jurisdiction of the English court.[36]

1-014   Comity is also invoked in those areas of the conflict of laws which touch on the foreign relations of the United Kingdom, to justify restraint in the application of English law or policy. When the Court of Appeal held that Soviet decrees confiscating property in Russia were to be recognised in England, Scrutton L.J. warned that it would be a serious breach of international comity to postulate that the legislation of a foreign sovereign State was contrary to essential principles of justice and morality.[37]

---

[31] *Soc Nationale Industrielle Aérospatiale v Lee Kui Jak* [1987] A.C. 871, 895 (PC); *Airbus Industrie GIE v Patel* [1999] 1 A.C. 119, 133. See also, e.g. *CSR Ltd v Cigna Insurance Australia Ltd* (1997) 189 C.L.R. 345, 395–396. But the traditional view that the injunction is directed only to the parties is still sometimes expressed: see, e.g. *Turner v Grovit* [2001] UKHL 65, [2002] 1 W.L.R. 107 at [26]; *Through Transport Mutual Insurance Association (Eurasia) Ltd v New India Assurance Co Ltd* [2004] EWCA Civ 1598, [2005] 1 Lloyd's Rep. 67 at [87]–[92]; *OT Africa Line Ltd v Magic Sportswear Corp* [2005] EWCA Civ 710, [2005] 2 Lloyd's Rep. 170 at [36]–[38]. See also, below, para.12–078.

[32] *Crédit Suisse Fides Trust SA v Cuoghi* [1998] Q.B. 818, 827 (CA), *per* Millett L.J.

[33] *Gaudiya Mission v Brahmachary* [1998] Ch. 341 (CA). *cf. Hartford Fire Insurance Co v State of California*, 509 U.S. 764, 817 (1993); *Amchem Products Inc v Workers' Compensation Board* [1993] 1 S.C.R. 897, 934 (Sup Ct Can).

[34] [2008] EWCA Civ 303, [2009] Q.B. 450, at [36]–[39]. See also *Joujou v Masri* [2011] EWCA Civ 746, [47]–[48], [77]–[78].

[35] *Derby & Co Ltd v Weldon (Nos 3 and 4)* [1990] Ch 65, 82.

[36] Collins (1989) 105 L.Q.R. 262, 299.

[37] *Luther v Sagor* [1921] 3 K.B. 532, 558–559 (CA); *cf. Igra v Igra* [1951] P. 404, 412. See also *Fayed v Al-Tajir* [1988] Q.B. 712, 730 (CA). In *Luther v Sagor* the English Court of Appeal had relied on American authority, where it had been said that the rule rested upon "the highest considerations of international comity and expediency": *Oetjen v Central Leather*, 246 U.S. 297, 303–304 (1918). But in 1964 the United States Supreme Court abandoned international law and comity as the basis for the act of state doctrine (*Banco Nacional de Cuba v Sabbatino*, 376 U.S. 398 (1964)) and substituted as its basis the domestic doctrine of separation of powers, reflecting

In *Kuwait Airways Corp v Iraqi Airways Co*[38] the House of Lords held that Iraqi legislation could be disregarded on the ground that it was contrary to international law,[39] but Lord Hope of Craighead emphasised[40] that a judge should be slow to refuse to give effect to the legislation of a foreign State in any sphere in which, according to accepted principles of international law, the foreign State has jurisdiction. Among these accepted principles is that which is founded on the comity of nations. The judge may have an inadequate understanding of the circumstances in which the legislation was passed, and a refusal to recognise it may be embarrassing to the executive, whose function is so far as possible to maintain friendly relations with foreign States.

1–015

It has also been said that it would be a breach of international comity for the English court to enforce a contract, even if otherwise valid under English law, designed to break the laws of a friendly foreign country.[41] And more recently it has been re-affirmed that in the interests of comity the English court should refrain from sitting in judgment on the internal affairs of another State,[42] and from deciding whether a foreign State has been responsible for a breach of its treaty obligations.[43]

1–016

Sometimes, however, the application of foreign law by a municipal court is required by public international law. Thus the United Kingdom may be bound by treaty to provide that its courts will apply foreign law, e.g. under the Hague Convention on the conflict of laws relating to the form of testamentary dispositions, 1961 (given effect by the Wills Act 1963).[44] Or the application by a court of its own law, rather than foreign law, to a wholly foreign transaction may be regarded by other States as a breach of international law.[45]

1–017

Late development in England. Although the conflict of laws has been intensively studied by continental jurists since the 13th century, it is of comparatively recent origin in England.[46] A few rules of the English conflict

1–018

---

the strong sense of the judicial branch that its engagement in the task of passing on the validity of foreign acts of state may hinder the conduct of foreign affairs: see *WS Kirkpatrick & Co v Environmental Tectonics Corp Intl.*, 493 U.S. 400, 404 (1990), *per* Scalia J.

[38] [2002] UKHL 19, [2002] 2 A.C. 883.

[39] See paras 5–052 and 25–011, below.

[40] At [138], citing *Oppenheimer v Cattermole* [1976] AC 249, 277–8, *per* Lord Cross.

[41] *Foster v Driscoll* [1929] 1 K.B. 470, 510 (CA); *Regazzoni v KC Sethia Ltd* [1958] A.C. 301, 327. See also *Ispahani v Bank Melli Iran* [1998] Lloyd's Rep. Bank. 133 (CA), *per* Robert Walker L.J: "international comity is naturally much readier to accept that a country's laws ought to be obeyed within its own territory, than to recognise them as having exorbitant effect." See Collins (1995–6) 6 King's Coll. L.J. 20, and below, paras 5–009; 32–191.

[42] *A Ltd v B Bank* [1997] F.S.R. 165, 172 (CA).

[43] *Westland Helicopters Ltd v Arab Organisation for Industrialisation* [1995] Q.B. 282. See Rule 3.

[44] See Rule 152.

[45] *cf. Midland Bank Plc v Laker Airways Ltd* [1986] Q.B. 689 (CA). For literature on the relationship between private and public international law, see also para.1–089, n.237, below.

[46] For the history of the conflict of laws, see Story, pp.2–20; Westlake, pp.7–22; Wolff, Ch.3; Lorenzen, Ch.7; Beale, Vol.3, pp.1880–1975; Gutzwiller, *Geschichte des Internationalprivatrechts* (1977); Gutzwiller (1929) *Recueil des Cours*, IV, pp.289–400; Meijers (1934) *Recueil des Cours*, III, pp.547–686; Sack, in *Law, A Century of Progress* (1935), Vol.3, pp.342–454 (with special reference to the history in England); Llewelfryn Davies (1937) 18 B.Y.I.L. 49–78; De Nova (1966) *Recueil des Cours*, II, pp.441–477; Lipstein (1972) *Recueil des Cours*, I, pp.104–166.

of laws can be traced back to the late 17th century. But the subject first came into prominence in English courts towards the end of the 18th century, mainly because of conflicts between the laws of England and Scotland. In the 19th century its development was enormously accelerated by the rapid increase in commercial and social intercourse between England and the continent of Europe, and with the British territories overseas. In the 20th century this development has been still further accelerated by the mass movement of populations, stimulated by wars and their aftermath and by technical advances in the means of transport and communications. It has not been easy for the conflict of laws to adapt itself to the changes in social and commercial life which the 20th century has witnessed. Many of its rules were first laid down in the 19th century and seem better suited to 19th century conditions than to those of the 20th century. Obvious examples are furnished until recently by the law of torts[47] and (in spite of recent statutory change[48]) by the common law rules relating to domicile, particularly the rules making it so difficult to shake off a domicile of origin.[49] Remedies for this situation have been sought in the introduction of habitual residence as an alternative to domicile as a jurisdictional or connecting factor,[50] and in a gradual move away from the double actionability rule for foreign torts until its eventual abolition by statute and its replacement by the Rome II Regulation.[51] In the United States the reaction against 19th century ideas has gone much further than it has in England. The "softening of concepts"[52] in the Second Restatement (1971) may be compared with the rigid dogmatism of the First Restatement (1934); and there is an influential school of writers who believe that traditional rules of the conflict of laws have served their purpose, and that they should be scrapped and a fresh start made.[53]

1–019   **Sources.** By far the most significant source of the English conflict of laws today is European Union law. Until the middle of the 20th century, legislative intervention in the conflict of laws was haphazard, sporadic and (compared with the mass of case law) slight and unimportant. Statutes were occasionally passed to remedy some glaring anomaly or injustice,[54] to facilitate the reciprocal enforcement of judgments within the United Kingdom or the Commonwealth or with such foreign States as were prepared to offer reciprocal

---

[47] See below, Ch.35.

[48] Domicile and Matrimonial Proceedings Act 1973, ss.1, 3, 4; see Rules 14–16.

[49] See below, Ch.6, especially Rules 7, 10, 13(2).

[50] See e.g. Rules 30, 82, 83(2), 88(1)(a), 152(1). For the meaning of "connecting factor," see below, paras 1–079 *et seq.*

[51] See *Boys v Chaplin* [1971] A.C. 356; *Red Sea Insurance Co Ltd v Bouygues SA* [1995] 1 A.C. 190 (PC); Private International Law (Miscellaneous Provisions) Act 1995, Pt III; Rome II Regulation below, Ch.35.

[52] This phrase is used by Kahn-Freund (1974) *Recueil des Cours*, III, pp.406–413.

[53] See Currie, *Selected Essays on the Conflict of Laws* (1963); Cavers, *The Choice of Law Process* (1965); Ehrenzweig, especially pp.307–326; Hay, Borchers and Symeonides, Ch.2; Symeonides, *The American Choice-of-Law Revolution: Past, Present and Future* (2006).

[54] e.g. Wills Act 1861; Matrimonial Causes Act 1937, s.13; Law Reform (Miscellaneous Provisions) Act 1949, s.1; Family Allowances and National Insurance Act 1956, s.3 (all of which have since been repealed and replaced by more comprehensive enactments).

treatment,[55] or (on one occasion only) to codify a very small part of the subject.[56] But since the middle of the 20th century there has been an increasing stream of statutes implementing international conventions,[57] and a few very important ones prepared by the Law Commission as part of a thorough-going and well-considered reform of the law.[58]

European law. The Hague Conference. The English rules of the conflict **1–020** of laws were radically affected by conventions negotiated under the auspices of the Hague Conference on Private International Law[59] and then under the auspices of the European Communities, especially the Brussels Convention on jurisdiction and the enforcement of judgments in civil and commercial matters (and the parallel Lugano Convention[60]) and the Rome Convention on the Law Applicable to Contractual Obligations. The European Community became a member of the Hague Conference on April 3, 2007. With the entry into force of the Treaty of Lisbon on December 1, 2009, the European Union replaced and succeeded the European Community as from that date, and it is now the European Union, in place of the Member States, which will become a party to conventions concluded under the auspices of the Hague Conference.[61]

---

[55] e.g. Judgments Extension Act 1868 (repealed by Civil Jurisdiction and Judgments Act 1982); Maintenance Orders (Facilities for Enforcement) Act 1920; Administration of Justice Act 1920, Pt II; Foreign Judgments (Reciprocal Enforcement) Act 1933; Maintenance Orders Act 1950.

[56] Bills of Exchange Act 1882, s.72. For a comprehensive survey see Symeonides, *Codification and Flexibility in Private International Law*, in Brown and Snyder (eds.), *General Reports of the XVIIIth Congress of the International Academy of Comparative Law* (2011).

[57] e.g. Administration of Justice Act 1956, ss.3 and 4 (now Senior Courts Act 1981, ss.21 and 22); Carriage by Air Act 1961; Wills Act 1963; Diplomatic Privileges Act 1964; Carriage of Goods by Road Act 1965; Uniform Laws on International Sales Act 1967; Consular Relations Act 1968; International Organisations Act 1968; Carriage of Goods by Sea Act 1971; Recognition of Divorces and Legal Separations Act 1971 (now Family Law Act 1986, Pt II); Maintenance Orders (Reciprocal Enforcement) Act 1972, Pt II; Carriage by Railway Act 1972 (replaced by International Transport Conventions Act 1983); Arbitration Act 1975 (replaced by Arbitration Act 1996, ss.9 and 100–104); State Immunity Act 1978; Carriage by Air and Road Act 1979; Merchant Shipping Act 1979, ss.14–16 and Sch.3, ss.17–19 and Sch.4 (replaced by Merchant Shipping Act 1995, ss.183–185 and Schs 6 and 7); Civil Jurisdiction and Judgments Act 1982 (as amended by Civil Jurisdiction and Judgments Act 1991); Civil Aviation (Eurocontrol) Act 1983; Child Abduction and Custody Act 1985.

[58] Matrimonial Proceedings (Polygamous Marriages) Act 1972, now Matrimonial Causes Act 1973, s.47; Domicile and Matrimonial Proceedings Act 1973; Matrimonial and Family Proceedings Act 1984, Pt III; Foreign Limitation Periods Act 1984; Family Law Act 1986, Pt I; Family Law Reform Act 1987; Private International Law (Miscellaneous Provisions) Act 1995.

[59] See especially the Hague Conventions on the conflict of laws relating to the form of testamentary dispositions (Wills Act 1963); the recognition of divorces and legal separations (Family Law Act 1986); the taking of evidence abroad in civil or commercial matters (Evidence (Proceedings in Other Jurisdictions) Act 1975); civil aspects of international child abduction (Child Abduction and Custody Act 1985). On the Hague Conventions see North, *Essays in Private International Law* (1993), p.225; Lipstein (1993) 42 I.C.L.Q. 553; TMC Asser Institute, *The Influence of the Hague Conference on Private International Law* (1993); McClean (1992) *Recueil des Cours*, II, p.267; von Overbeck, *ibid.*, 9; Fassberg (1993) Israel L. Rev. 460; *The Hague Conference on Private International Law* (Carrington and Dyer, eds.) in (1994) 57 Law & Contemp. Prob., No.3; McClean, in *E Pluribus Unum* (ed. Borrods 1996), p.205; Fawcett (2000) 53 Curr. Leg. Prob. 303; North (2001) 50 I.C.L.Q. 477.

[60] The revised Lugano Convention (2007) is now in force: see para.11–020, below.

[61] e.g. the Convention on the international recovery of child support and other forms of family maintenance (2007) (not yet in force).

1–021   Today the field of the conflict of laws is increasingly dominated by European Union law,[62] and in particular by Council regulations, which are directly applicable in Member States, including Council Regulation (EC) 44/2001, the "Brussels I Regulation", which for most practical purposes superseded the Brussels and Lugano Conventions;[63] Council Regulation (EC) 2201/2003 on jurisdiction and the recognition and enforcement of judgments in matrimonial matters and in matters of parental responsibility ("Brussels IIa");[64] the insolvency regulation,[65] which regulates jurisdiction in insolvency matters; Council regulations on service of judicial and extra-judicial documents in civil and commercial matters, and on co-operation in the taking of evidence in civil and commercial matters;[66] Regulation (EC) 593/2008 of the European Parliament and of the Council on the law applicable to contractual obligations (Rome I) (the Rome I Regulation);[67] Regulation (EC) 864/2007) of the European Parliament and of the Council on the Law Applicable to Non-Contractual Obligations (the Rome II Regulation).[68]

1–022   The increasing scope of European law will continue. The EU Commission has put forward a proposal for a European bank account preservation order,[69] and the Commission's action plan includes a timetable for the introduction of proposals in relation to these matters: a regulation on the conflict of laws in matters concerning matrimonial property rights, including the question of jurisdiction and mutual recognition, and a regulation on the property consequences of the separation of couples from other types of union; a regulation on limitation periods in cross-border road traffic accidents; a legislative proposal on mutual recognition of the effects of certain civil status documents (e.g. relating to birth, affiliation, adoption, name).

1–023   The European Court has given judgment in more than 200 references[70] in the field of the conflict of laws, mainly on the Brussels Convention and the Brussels I Regulation, but also on the Brussels IIa Regulation and the Rome I and Rome II Regulations. Some of the judgments of the European Court, particularly those in *Turner v Grovit*[71] and *West Tankers Inc v Allianz SpA*[72] which substantially outlaw anti-suit injunctions in relation to proceedings (in

---

[62] See also Dickinson (2005) 1 J. Priv. Int. L. 197; Crawford and Carruthers, 2005 Jur. Rev. 251; Wilderspin and Lewis, 2002 Rev. Crit. 1 and 289; Wilderspin and Rouchard-Joet, 2004 Rev. Crit. 1; Harris (2008) 4 J. Priv. Int. L. 347. See also Barrière Brousse, 2010 *Clunet* 1 on the effect of the Lisbon Treaty.

[63] See especially Chs 11 and 14. For the Commission proposal's for reform of the Brussels I Regulation see COM(2010) 748/3. See also Regulation (EC) 1896/2006 of the European Parliament and of the Council creating a European order for payment procedure; Regulation (EC) 861/2007 of the European Parliament and of the Council establishing a European Small Claims Procedure.

[64] See especially Chs 18 and 19. See also Council Regulation (EC) 4/2009 on jurisdiction, applicable law, recognition and enforcement of decisions and co-operation in matters relating to maintenance obligations.

[65] Council Regulation (EC) 1346/2000.

[66] Respectively Council Regulation (EC) 1348/2000 and Council Regulation (EC) 1206/2001: see Ch.8, below.

[67] See especially Chs 32 and 33.

[68] See especially Chs 34–36.

[69] See para.8–017, n.48.

[70] Now under TFEU, Art.267.

[71] Case C–159/02 [2004] E.C.R. I–3565, [2005] A.C. 101.

[72] Case C–185/07 [2009] E.C.R. I–663, [2009] 1 A.C. 1138.

the latter case even though brought in breach of an obligation to arbitrate in England) in other Member States, and *Owusu v Jackson*[73] which prevents English courts from staying proceedings on *forum conveniens* grounds against persons domiciled in the United Kingdom in favour of non-Member States, have met with considerable criticism and opposition in England.[74]

Human rights.[75] The Human Rights Act 1998 incorporated the European   1–024
Convention on Human Rights into United Kingdom law, and came into force in 2000. Even before then it was held that recognition of a foreign law which offended fundamental rights would be contrary to public policy and a breach of fundamental human rights would displace the rule that foreign acts of state could not be questioned in the English courts.[76] Both the European Court of Justice in Luxembourg and the European Court of Human Rights in Strasbourg have applied the principles in the Human Rights Convention to cases involving the conflict of laws.

The European Court of Justice has said several times in cases involving the   1–025
conflict of laws that fundamental rights form an integral part of the general principles of law whose observance the Court ensures; and that for that purpose, the Court draws inspiration from the constitutional traditions common to the Member States and international instruments for the protection of human rights to which Member States are parties, especially the Human Rights Convention.[77] The European Court of Human Rights has also considered whether Member States have complied with the Convention in dealing with cases involving the conflict of laws. In *Neulinger v Switzerland*[78] the Strasbourg court held that in matters of international child abduction, the obligations imposed by Art.8 of the Convention (right to family life) must be interpreted taking into account, in particular, the Hague Convention on the Civil Aspects of International Child Abduction; the Court was competent to review the procedure followed by domestic courts, in particular to ascertain whether the domestic courts, in applying and interpreting the provisions of the Hague Convention, had secured the guarantees of the Convention and especially those of Art.8. In *Re E (Children) (Abduction: Custody Appeal)*[79] the

---

[73] Case C–281/02 [2005] E.C.R. I–1383, [2005] Q.B. 801.

[74] See below, paras 12–019 *et seq.*

[75] See Fawcett (2007) 56 I.C.L.Q. 1 for a full discussion and also Juratowitch (2007) 3 J. Priv. Int. L. 173; Kinsch, 2011 *Nederlands int. privaatrecht* 19.

[76] See Rules 2 and 3(1) and e.g. *Oppenheimer v Cattermole* [1976] A.C. 249, 278. For recent discussion in the light of the Human Rights Convention see *Berezovsky v Abramovich* [2011] EWCA Civ 153, [2011] 1 C.L.C. 359; *JSC BTA Bank v Ablyazov* [2011] EWHC 202 (Comm.); [2011] 2 All E.R. (Comm.) 10.

[77] e.g. Case C–7/98 *Krombach v Bamberski* [2000] E.C.R. I–1935; [2001] Q.B. 709, [25]; Case C–283/05 *ASML Netherlands BV v Semiconductor Industry Services GmbH (SEMIS)* [2006] E.C.R. I–12041, [26].

[78] [2011] 1 F.L.R. 122, [132]–[133]. See also *Shaw v Hungary* [2011] ECHR 1197, at [68]. See para.19–144, below. On Art.8 and recognition of foreign adoptions see *Wagner v Luxembourg* [2007] ECHR 76240/01 and *Negrepontis-Giannisis v Greece* [2011] ECHR 56759/08, para.20–129, below.

[79] [2011] UKSC 27, [2011] 2 W.L.R. 1326, [26]. See also Case C–400/10 *McB v E* [2011] I.L.Pr. 469: the provisions in the Charter of Fundamental Rights of the European Union relating to respect for private and family life (Art.7) and the right of the child to maintain relationship and contact with parents (Art.24(3)) were taken into account in interpreting the Brussels IIa Regulation.

Supreme Court said that, if the Hague Convention were properly applied, it was unlikely that there would be a violation of the Art.8 rights of the child or of either of the parents.

1-026   The principles in the Human Rights Convention have often been taken into account in conflict of laws cases but they have rarely been decisive. The right of access to justice or right to a fair trial under Art.6 do not in themselves prevent a stay of English proceedings or an injunction to restrain foreign proceedings, but the position may be different if the effect is to deprive a party of any remedy.[80] A foreign judgment which has been obtained in breach of the fundamental right to a fair trial must be refused recognition on public policy grounds.[81] But the rights under Art.6 are not absolute, and so do not affect the right of a State to claim state immunity in accordance with internationally accepted principles.[82] The prohibition of discrimination under Art.14 has been relied on in relation to security for costs to hold that the mere fact that a claimant was non-resident would be an insufficient basis for an order for security.[83]

1-027   **Opinions of jurists.** In the English conflict of laws the courts have been influenced by the opinions of jurists, both foreign and English, to a far greater extent than in most other subjects. The most influential foreign jurists have been Ulrich Huber (1636–1694), who was successively a professor of law and a judge in Friesland; Joseph Story (1779–1845), who was simultaneously a justice of the Supreme Court of the United States and a professor of law at the Harvard Law School; and the 19th century German jurist Friedrich Carl von Savigny.[84]

1-028   **Interpretation of statutes implementing international conventions.**[85] In England, unlike some continental European countries and the United States, international treaties and conventions do not have the force of law merely by reason of having been ratified by the Government, at least in so far as the rights and duties of private persons are concerned. In the United Kingdom, a

---

[80] *cf. Lubbe v Cape Plc* [2000] 1 W.L.R. 1545 (HL); *OT Africa Line Ltd v Hijazy* [2001] 1 Lloyd's Rep. 76. See also *Fiona Trust and Holding Corp v Privalov* [2007] UKHL 40, [2007] Bus. L.R. 1179, [20] (requirement that question be submitted to arbitration not a denial of access to justice under Art.6).

[81] Case C–7/98 *Krombach v Bamberski* [2000] E.C.R. I–1935, [2001] Q.B. 709, para.14–160, below. See, e.g. *WPP Holdings Italy Srl and others v Benatti* [2007] EWCA Civ 263, [2007] 1 W.L.R. 2316, [84]. *cf.* also Case C–14/07 *Ingenieurbüro Michael Weiss und Partner GbR v Industrie-und Handelskammer Berlin* [2008] E.C.R. I–3367 (on Council Regulation (EC) 1348/2000, the Service Regulation, para.8–054, below).

[82] See para.10–003, below.

[83] See *Nasser v United Bank of Kuwait* [2001] EWCA Civ 556, [2002] 1 W.L.R. 1868 and *cf. Relational LLC v Hodges* [2011] EWCA Civ 774. An excessive order might also be contrary to the right to a fair trial under Art.6: *Tolstoy Miloslavsky v United Kingdom* (1995) 20 E.H.R.R. 442.

[84] See, for the more recent influence of refugees from Nazi Germany, Beatson and Zimmermann (eds.), *Jurists Uprooted* (2004), with essays on (among others) Otto Kahn-Freund, Kurt Lipstein, F.A. Mann, and Martin Wolff.

[85] See Gardiner, *Treaty Interpretation*, 2008, Ch.4; F.A. Mann, *Studies in International Law* (1973), pp.614–633; F.A. Mann, *Further Studies in International Law* (1990), pp.270–301; F.A. Mann, *Foreign Affairs in English Courts* (1986), Ch.5; Sinclair (1963) 12 I.C.L.Q. 508, especially pp.525–551; Higgins, in *Effect of Treaties in Domestic Law* (ed. Jacobs and Roberts), 1987, p.123.

treaty provision does not become law until it has been implemented by statute or statutory instrument.[86] There are several legislative techniques for giving the force of law to international conventions. The statute may be based on the convention (the convention itself not being incorporated in the statute) and the statute may[87] or may not[88] indicate in the long title or the preamble that it is intended to give effect to the convention. The statute may incorporate the English text of the convention (or a translation of the French or other language text) in a schedule.[89] Or the statute may incorporate the English and French (or other language) text of the convention in different parts of the schedule, and may contain an express provision that in case of any inconsistency the French version shall prevail.[90] Different principles of interpretation may apply to each of these cases,[91] if only because each technique presents different problems to the courts.

The following principles of interpretation may be deduced from the decisions of the English courts. **1–029**

(1) The purpose of an international convention is to harmonise the laws of **1–030** all contracting States on the particular topic dealt with by the convention. It is therefore very important that the interpretation of the convention should be the same, so far as possible, in all contracting States.[92] This is to some extent a counsel of perfection, because not only are international conventions drafted in a style very different from that of United Kingdom Acts of Parliament, but also English rules for the interpretation of statutes are different from (and usually much stricter than) those applied by courts in continental European countries or even in the United States. English courts have therefore been compelled to relax some of their rules of interpretation when the statute gives effect to an international convention. They will, it has been said, interpret the implementing statute "in a normal manner appropriate for the interpretation of an international convention, unconstrained by technical rules of English law,

---

[86] *Att-Gen for Canada v Att-Gen for Ontario* [1937] A.C. 326 (PC). For modern examples see *British Airways Board v Laker Airways Ltd* [1985] A.C. 58, 83; *JH Rayner (Mincing Lane) Ltd v Department of Trade and Industry* [1990] 2 A.C. 418, 477, 500; *Littrell v Government of the United States (No.2)* [1995] 1 W.L.R. 82 (CA); *R. v Secretary of State for the Home Department, Ex p. Amnesty International, The Times,* December 11, 1998; *Higgs v Minister of National Security* [2000] 2 A.C. 228 (PC).

[87] e.g. Wills Act 1963; Maintenance Orders (Reciprocal Enforcement) Act 1972; Arbitration Act 1975 (replaced by Arbitration Act 1996); State Immunity Act 1978.

[88] e.g. Senior Courts Act 1981, ss.21 and 22; Family Law Act 1986, Pt II (replacing Recognition of Divorces and Legal Separations Act 1971, which did refer to the convention). Although the Evidence (Proceedings in Other Jurisdictions) Act 1975 was passed in order, among other reasons, to enable the UK to ratify the Hague Evidence Convention of 1970, it was held that it is to be construed against the background of previous United Kingdom legislation and not solely by reference to the 1970 Convention: *Re State of Norway's Application (Nos 1 and 2)* [1990] 1 A.C. 723, 796.

[89] e.g. Carriage of Goods by Sea Act 1924 (now repealed) and Carriage of Goods by Sea Act 1971; Diplomatic Privileges Act 1964; Carriage of Goods by Road Act 1965; Uniform Laws on International Sales Act 1967; Consular Relations Act 1968; Carriage of Passengers by Road Act 1974 (now repealed); Merchant Shipping Act 1995, Schs 6 and 7.

[90] e.g. Carriage by Air Act 1961, s.1(2) and Sch.1; Carriage by Air (Supplementary Provisions) Act 1962, s.1(2) and Sch.; Carriage by Air and Road Act 1979, s.1(1) and Sch.1.

[91] *James Buchanan & Co Ltd v Babco Forwarding and Shipping (UK) Ltd* [1978] A.C. 141, 152.

[92] This passage was quoted with approval in *Sidhu v British Airways Plc* [1997] A.C. 430, 444.

or by English legal precedent, but on broad principles of general acceptation."[93] They will also listen to the citation of cases from the courts of other contracting States and will give effect to a prevailing current of foreign opinion on the true construction of the convention.[94] But these are only aids to interpretation, and the value of foreign court decisions will depend on the reputation and standing of the foreign court.[95] On the other hand, the House of Lords has emphatically rejected the notion that in interpreting such a statute the English courts should completely abandon traditional English methods of interpretation, and in particular the notion that, if there is a gap in the convention, English courts are entitled to fill it by judicial legislation.[96]

1–031   (2) If the text of the convention is not incorporated in the statute, is the court entitled to look at the convention? It was at one time supposed that the court could only do so if the statute was ambiguous and if it referred expressly to the convention.[97] But it has become clear that this is not so and that the court can look at the convention, even though it is not expressly referred to in the statute, provided the statute is ambiguous and provided the court is satisfied by extrinsic evidence that the statute was intended to implement the convention. This is because there is a prima facie presumption that Parliament does not intend to act in breach of international law, including specific treaty obligations. But if the statute is unambiguous it must be given effect, whether it carries out the treaty obligations or not.[98] According to Lord Denning M.R., there is no requirement that the statute must be ambiguous[99] and Lord Wilberforce has said that the suggestion that resort to a foreign text is only permissible if the English text is ambiguous "states the rule too techni-

---

[93] *Stag Line Ltd v Foscolo, Mango & Co Ltd* [1932] A.C. 328, 350; *James Buchanan & Co Ltd v Babco Forwarding and Shipping (UK) Ltd,* above, at pp.152, 160, 161; *Ulster-Swift Ltd v Taunton Meat Haulage Ltd* [1977] 1 W.L.R. 625, 628 (CA); *Fothergill v Monarch Airlines Ltd* [1981] A.C. 251, 282, 293; *The Hollandia* [1983] 1 A.C. 565, 572; *The Antares (No.2)* [1986] 2 Lloyd's Rep. 633, 637, affirmed [1987] 1 Lloyd's Rep. 424 (CA).

[94] See e.g. *Corocroft Ltd v Pan American Airways Inc* [1969] 1 Q.B. 616 (CA); *Wilson, Smithett & Cope Ltd v Terruzzi* [1976] Q.B. 683 (CA); *James Buchanan & Co Ltd v Babco Forwarding and Shipping (UK) Ltd,* above, at pp.153–154, 161; *Antwerp United Diamond BVBA v Air Europe* [1996] Q.B. 317, 330–331 (CA); *Sidhu v British Airways Plc* [1997] A.C. 430, 451–453; *Herd v Clyde Helicopters Ltd* [1997] A.C. 534, 553–555. In *Ulster-Swift Ltd v Taunton Meat Haulage Ltd,* above, at pp.631–632, it appeared that no less than 12 different interpretations of the relevant articles of the convention had been adopted by 30 decisions of the courts of six continental European countries, and for that reason the Court of Appeal was not asked to examine them.

[95] *Fothergill v Monarch Airlines Ltd* [1981] A.C. 251, 284, 295. See also *The River Rima* [1988] 1 W.L.R. 758, 765 (HL); *ICI Plc v MAT Transport Ltd* [1987] 1 Lloyd's Rep. 354, 359; *Gatewhite Ltd v Iberia Lineas Aereas* [1990] 1 Q.B. 326, 332–335.

[96] *James Buchanan & Co Ltd v Babco Forwarding and Shipping (UK) Ltd,* above, at pp.153, 156, 160–161. This gap-filling method had been adopted by Lord Denning M.R. in the Court of Appeal: [1977] Q.B. 208, 213–214.

[97] See e.g. *Ellerman Lines Ltd v Murray* [1931] A.C. 126. In *James Buchanan & Co Ltd v Babco Forwarding and Shipping (UK) Ltd,* above, at p.153. Lord Wilberforce said that this oft-cited case was untypical and should no longer be followed.

[98] *Salomon v Commissioners of Customs and Excise* [1967] 2 Q.B. 116, 143–144 (CA); *Post Office v Estuary Radio Ltd* [1968] 2 Q.B. 740, 757 (CA); *cf. IRC v Collco Dealings Ltd* [1962] A.C. 1.

[99] *Salomon v Commissioners of Customs and Excise,* above, at p.141; *The Banco* [1971] P. 137, at p.151; but contrast *R. v Chief Immigration Officer, Heathrow Airport, ex p. Salamat Bibi* [1976] 1 W.L.R. 979, 984 (CA).

cally."[100] In other cases judicial statements of the principle have omitted the preliminary requirement of ambiguity.[101] The differing judicial approaches may be reconciled on the basis that it may only become apparent that the words of the statute are ambiguous (or "loose textured"[102]) after resort to the international convention.

(3) If the convention is expressed in two languages, e.g. English and French, each text being equally authentic, but only the English text is incorporated in the statute, is the court entitled to look at the French text as an aid to its construction? This is a question on which conflicting views have been expressed, but the better opinion would appear to be that the court is so entitled,[103] at any rate if the statute and the English text are ambiguous or "loose-textured". Where a convention is concluded under the auspices of the European Communities, all language versions are equally authentic. There can be no doubt in such cases that the process of interpretation will inevitably involve a comparison between the different language versions.[104]   **1–032**

(4) If the court is required by statute,[105] or decides for itself, to look at the French text of the convention, how should it inform itself of the meaning of the French words? In *Fothergill v Monarch Airlines Ltd*[106] the House of Lords held that it was inappropriate to lay down precise rules, because, as Lord Wilberforce put it, the process of ascertaining the meaning of the foreign language must vary according to the subject matter: the court may use its own knowledge of the foreign language,[107] or it may have resort to such aids as dictionaries, interpreters or expert witnesses,[108] depending on the degree and nature of the difficulty of interpretation.   **1–033**

(5) In construing a purely English statute, the court can have regard to "*travaux préparatoires*" such as reports of Royal Commissions, the Law Commission, committees and the like in order to see what the "mischief" was   **1–034**

---

[100] *James Buchanan & Co Ltd v Babco Forwarding and Shipping (UK) Ltd,* above, at p.152.

[101] e.g. *The Eschersheim* [1976] 1 W.L.R. 430, 436 (HL); *Garland v British Rail Engineering Ltd* [1983] 2 A.C. 751, 771, *per* Lord Diplock (but this may be because he regarded the requirement of ambiguity as implicit). For more orthodox statements see *Fothergill v Monarch Airlines Ltd* [1981] A.C. 251, 299 (Lord Roskill); *Government of Kuwait v Sir Frederick Snow and Partners* [1984] A.C. 426, 435 (Lord Brandon); *JH Rayner (Mincing Lane) Ltd v Department of Trade and Industry* [1990] 2 A.C. 418, 500–502 (Lord Oliver).

[102] *cf. Gatoil International Inc v Arkwright-Boston Manufacturers Mutual Insurance Co* [1985] A.C. 255, 262, *per* Lord Wilberforce.

[103] See *Corocraft Ltd v Pan American Airways Inc* [1969] 1 Q.B. 616 (CA); *Post Office v Estuary Radio Ltd* [1968] 2 Q.B. 740, 760 (CA); *Ulster-Swift Ltd v Taunton Meat Haulage Ltd* [1977] 1 W.L.R. 625, 632 (CA); *James Buchanan & Co Ltd v Babco Forwarding and Shipping (UK) Ltd* [1978] A.C. 141, 152, 161, 166–167; *The Antonis P. Lemos* [1985] A.C. 711, 731; *Silber Ltd v Islander Trucking Ltd* [1985] 2 Lloyd's Rep. 243.

[104] See, e.g. Case 150/80 *Elefanten Schuh GmbH v Jacqmain* [1981] E.C.R. 1671, 1685. *cf.* Collins, *European Community Law in the United Kingdom* (4th ed. 1990), pp.133–134.

[105] e.g. Carriage by Air Act 1961, s.1(2); Carriage by Air (Supplementary Provisions) Act 1962, s.1(2).

[106] [1981] A.C. 251, 273–274, 286, 293–294, 299–300. See also *James Buchanan Co Ltd v Babco Forwarding and Shipping (UK) Ltd* [1978] A.C. 141, 152–153; *Semco Salvage and Marine Pte Ltd v Lancer Navigation Co Ltd* [1997] A.C. 455, 471; *Re Deep Vein Thrombosis and Air Travel Group Litigation* [2005] UKHL 72, [2006] 1 A.C. 495, at [53].

[107] e.g. *Corocraft Ltd v Pan American Airways Inc* [1969] 1 Q.B. 616 (CA) (insertion of "and" in English text).

[108] *cf. The Antonis P Lemos* [1985] A.C. 711, 731.

with which the Act was intended to deal, although, prior to the decision of the House of Lords in *Pepper v Hart*,[109] the court could not take into account direct statements of what the Act was intended or understood to mean nor could it look at the reports of Parliamentary debates in *Hansard*.[110] It has been established by two decisions of the House of Lords that cautious use of *travaux préparatoires* may be made as an aid to interpretation, provided that two conditions are fulfilled: first, that the material is public and accessible; second, that it clearly and indisputably points to a definite legislative intention. In the first case,[111] the House of Lords considered the minutes of the Hague Conference which led to the Hague Protocol to the Warsaw Convention, but was not able to derive much assistance from them. In the second case,[112] the House of Lords resorted to the published proceedings of the conference which led to the Brussels Convention relating to the arrest of sea-going ships to confirm its interpretation of the extent of the Scottish jurisdiction in admiralty.

1–035   As Kerr J. pointed out in *Fothergill v Monarch Airlines Ltd*[113] the modern practice in international conventions is often to replace *travaux préparatoires* by an authoritative report or commentary from an official *rapporteur* to fill in gaps, comment on ambiguities, and generally to enlarge upon matters which cannot conveniently be compressed into the text of the convention. He suggested that it would be highly desirable that statutes implementing international conventions which are supplemented by such a report should expressly provide that the report may be referred to as an aid to interpretation. It was probably as a result of this suggestion that the Civil Jurisdiction and Judgments Act 1982 provided that the court could consider the official reports on the Brussels Convention on jurisdiction and the enforcement of judgments in civil and commercial matters of 1968 in interpreting the Convention and the intra-United Kingdom rules based on it.[114]

1–036   **Statutes and the conflict of laws.**[115] From the point of view of the conflict of laws, statutory provisions may conveniently be divided into six classes:

---

[109] [1993] A.C. 593, where it was held that reference to clear ministerial statements would be permitted where legislation was ambiguous or obscure or otherwise led to absurdity.

[110] *Black-Clawson International Ltd v Papierwerke Waldhof-Aschaffenburg AG* [1975] A.C. 591; *Davis v Johnson* [1979] A.C. 264.

[111] *Fothergill v Monarch Airlines Ltd* [1981] A.C. 251. See also *Sidhu v British Airways Plc* [1997] A.C. 430, 448–449; *Semco Salvage and Marine Pte Ltd v Lancer Navigation Co Ltd* [1997] A.C. 455, 468–469; *Herd v Clyde Helicopters Ltd* [1997] A.C. 534, 552–553; *Re Deep Vein Thrombosis and Air Travel Group Litigation* [2005] UKHL 72, [2006] 1 A.C. 495, at [54].

[112] *Gatoil International Inc v Arkwright-Boston Manufacturers Mutual Insurance Co* [1985] A.C. 255. See also *Hiscox v Outhwaite* [1992] 1 A.C. 562, 593; *MacWilliam Co Inc v Mediterranean Shipping Co SA* [2005] UKHL 11, [2005] 2 A.C. 423.

[113] [1978] Q.B. 108, 119; see also [1981] A.C. 251, 295, *per* Lord Scarman.

[114] ss.3(3) and 3B(2) are superseded for all practical purposes by the Brussels I Regulation and the revised Lugano Convention, which did not require implementation in national law.

[115] There is a substantial literature on this subject, of which the following is only a selection: Morris (1946) 62 L.Q.R. 170; Unger (1967) 83 L.Q.R. 427; Kelly (1969) 18 I.C.L.Q. 249; F.A. Mann (1972–73) 46 B.Y.I.L. 117; Kelly, *Localising Rules in the Conflict of Laws* (1974), especially Ch.5; Kahn-Freund (1974) *Recueil des Cours*, III, pp.234–247; Lipstein (1977) 26 I.C.L.Q. 884; Thomson (1980) 43 M.L.R. 650, 662–668; Forsyth (2005) 1 J. Priv. Int. L. 93; Keyes (2008) 4 J. Priv. Int. L. 1. The reader should be warned that there is no agreement among writers about terminology or even about the categories into which particular statutes fall.

(1) those which lay down a rule of substantive or domestic law without any indication of its application in space; (2) those which lay down a particular or unilateral rule of the conflict of laws purporting to indicate when a rule of substantive or domestic law is applicable; (3) those which lay down a general or multilateral rule of the conflict of laws purporting to indicate what law governs a given question; (4) those containing a limitation in space or otherwise which restricts the scope of a rule of substantive or domestic law (self-limiting statutes); (5) those which apply in the circumstances mentioned in the statute, even though they would not be applicable under the normal rules of the conflict of laws (overriding statutes); and (6) those which do not apply in the circumstances mentioned in the statute, even though they would be applicable under the normal rules of the conflict of laws (self-denying statutes). These categories are by no means mutually exclusive: some statutes may fall within more than one category. Only statutes in categories (2) and (3) above deal *expressis verbis* with the conflict of laws; the rest do not.

(1) *Statutes with no indication of their application in space.* Statutes of this kind are of course by far the most common. They are frequently expressed in general terms without any limitations of space and purport to apply e.g. to "every will," "all contracts," or "any married woman." Obviously, they cannot be read literally, because the Parliament of the United Kingdom does not legislate for the whole world.[116]   1–037

It has often been said that there is a presumption that Parliament does not design its statutes to operate beyond the territorial limits of the United Kingdom.[117] But if this presumption still exists, it is one which is easily rebutted. For instance, it has not prevented the application of the Fatal Accidents Acts to a collision on the high seas off the east coast of the United States between a Panamanian ship manned by a Spanish crew and a Russian trawler manned by Russian sailors, some of whom were drowned.[118] Nor did it prevent the application of the Theft Act 1968 to a theft of crayfish committed by Western Australian fishermen 22 miles off the coast of Western Australia.[119] In other contexts, such as taxation or bankruptcy, it is sometimes   1–038

---

[116] For a recent example see *Lawson v Serco Ltd* [2006] UKHL 3, [2006] I.C.R. 250 at [6], *per* Lord Hoffmann.

[117] See Bennion, *Statutory Interpretation* (5th ed. 2008), s.128(1); *Tomalin v S Pearson & Son Ltd* [1909] 2 K.B. 61, 64 (CA); *Yorke v British and Continental Steamship Co Ltd* (1945) 78 Ll.L.R. 181, 182, 184 (CA); *CEB Draper & Son Ltd v Edward Turner & Son Ltd* [1965] 1 Q.B. 424, 432, 435 (CA), overruled by *Hardwick Game Farm v Suffolk Agricultural Poultry Producers Association* [1969] 2 A.C. 31; *Al Sabah v Grupo Torras SA* [2005] UKPC 1, [2005] 2 A.C. 333, at [13]; *Al-Skeini v Secretary of State for Defence* [2007] UKHL 26, [2008] 1 A.C. 153, at [11], [46]–[51]; *Office of Fair Trading v Lloyds TSB Bank Plc* [2007] UKHL 48, [2008] 1 A.C. 316, at [4]; *Masri v Consolidated Contractors International Company SAL (No.4)* [2008] EWCA Civ 876, [2010] 1 A.C. 90, at [16], *per* Sir Anthony Clarke M.R. and [80], *per* Lawrence Collins L.J., revd. on other grounds [2009] UKHL 43, [2010] 1 A.C. 90; *Serious Organised Crime Agency v Perry* [2010] EWCA Civ 907, [2011] 1 W.L.R. 542; *(No.2)* [2011] EWCA Civ 578. "Extra-territorial" operation in connection with the law of contract sometimes means operation with regard to contracts governed by foreign law: a UK statute of the category under discussion does not normally apply unless the contract is governed by the law of some part of the UK. Contrast overriding and self-denying statutes, below, paras 1–053 *et seq.*

[118] *The Esso Malaysia* [1975] Q.B. 198; *cf. Davidsson v Hill* [1901] 1 K.B. 606. See Collins (1974) 90 L.Q.R. 447.

[119] *Oteri v The Queen* [1976] 1 W.L.R. 1272 (PC).

said that prima facie legislation is applicable only to British subjects or to foreigners who, whether for a long or short time, have made themselves during that time subject to English jurisdiction.[120] But that presumption can be displaced. Thus in *Re Paramount Airways Ltd* [121] it was held that the expression "any person" under s.238 of the Insolvency Act 1986, which enables the administrator or liquidator to apply for an order reversing a transaction entered into by the company with any person at an undervalue, is not subject to any implied limitation as to extra-territorial effect; it applies to any person wherever resident, but the court will not exercise its discretion unless it is satisfied that the defendant has a sufficient connection with England for it to be just and proper to make an order despite the foreign element. So also in *Re Seagull Manufacturing Co Ltd*[122] it was held that s.133 of the Insolvency Act 1986 (which allows the public examination of "any person" in the course of a winding-up) applies to all relevant persons who concern themselves in the affairs of the company, irrespective of whether they were British subjects or within the jurisdiction of the court at the relevant time. This interpretation was justified on the basis that Parliament could not have intended that the section could be evaded by the person leaving the jurisdiction.

1–039   As a typical example of statutes of the first type, s.2 of the Marriage Act 1949 provides that "a marriage solemnized between persons either of whom is under the age of sixteen years shall be void." Obviously, this enactment cannot be read literally so as to apply to all marriages in the world. Obviously, it must be limited in some way, either personally, or territorially, or both. Does it apply to all marriages celebrated in England, or to all marriages between parties domiciled in England, or only to marriages celebrated in England between parties domiciled in England?[123]

1–040   A court, when confronted by a statute of its own law or of foreign law which is expressed in general terms like this, could use one of two methods to determine its scope. The first is to interpret the statute in the light of its purpose and background so as to read into it the limitations which the legislature would have expressed if it had given thought to the matter. This is an artificial method, and perhaps a dangerous one, because *ex hypothesi* the legislature gave no thought to the matter—if it had done so it would have expressed the limitations.[124] The second method is to apply general principles derived from the conflict of laws—i.e. first characterise the question as

---

[120] See *Clark v Oceanic Contractors Inc* [1983] 2 A.C. 130; *Agassi v Robinson* [2006] UKHL 23, [2006] 1 W.L.R. 1380.

[121] [1993] Ch. 223 (CA).

[122] [1993] Ch. 345 (CA). In *Re Seagull Manufacturing Co Ltd (No.2)* [1994] Ch. 91 it was held that the power to make an order under Company Directors Disqualification Act 1986, s.6(1), against "a person" extended to any person, whether or not a British subject, irrespective of where the conduct rendering him unfit to be a director took place. See also *Arab Bank Plc v Merchantile Holdings Ltd* [1994] Ch. 71; *Jyske Bank (Gibraltar) Ltd v Spjeldnaes* [2000] B.C.C. 16; *McIsaac and Wilson, Petrs*, 1995 S.L.T. 498; *Re Doyle* (1993) 112 A.L.R. 653. *cf. Re Drax Holdings Ltd* [2003] EWHC 2743 (Ch.), [2004] 1 W.L.R. 1049. Contrast *Re Sherlock* (1991) 102 A.L.R. 156.

[123] For discussion of the possible scope of the statute and its predecessor, the Age of Marriage Act 1929, see Beckett (1934) 15 B.Y.I.L. 46, 64–65; Morris (1946) 62 L.Q.R. 170–171.

[124] See Unger (1952) 15 M.L.R. 88.

relating to capacity to marry,[125] and then apply the relevant conflict rule to the question so characterised.[126]

In *Pugh v Pugh*,[127] the court adopted both of these methods, and reached **1–041** the surprising conclusion that the section applies to all marriages between parties one at least of whom is domiciled in England, even if the party domiciled in England was over sixteen and the party under sixteen had capacity to marry under the law of her domicile.[128]

(2) *Statutes with a particular choice of law clause.* Conflict rules differ **1–042** from rules of domestic law in that they do not lay down a substantive rule but merely indicate which system of domestic law is applicable. But conflict rules are of two kinds, particular or unilateral and general or multilateral. A statute containing a particular or unilateral conflict rule answers the question, When does the system of law of which the statute forms part apply? A statute containing a general or multilateral conflict rule answers the more general question, What law applies?

A good example of the former type is s.1 of the Marriage (Scotland) Act **1–043** 1977, which provides in subs.(1) that "No person domiciled in Scotland may marry before he attains the age of 16," and in subs.(2) that "A marriage solemnised in Scotland between persons either of whom is under the age of 16 shall be void."[129] This section neatly avoids the strange result which the English court reached in *Pugh v Pugh*.

What should a court do when confronted by a particular or unilateral rule **1–044** in a foreign statute? A court which rejects renvoi[130] might refuse to apply the rule, simply because it is a conflict rule. But quite often the statute can be dissected into (a) a rule of domestic law and (b) a conflict rule indicating when the rule of domestic law is to apply. In such circumstances a court faced with such a foreign statute might justifiably apply (a) but, rejecting renvoi, not (b). But if it did so, it might distort the meaning of the statute and apply it where, under the terms of the statute itself, it is inapplicable. For instance, if an English court had to consider the validity of a marriage celebrated in Austria between a domiciled Scotsman and a domiciled Hungarian girl under the age of sixteen (the marriage being valid by Austrian and Hungarian law), it would, if it dissected s.1 of the Marriage (Scotland) Act 1977 in the manner suggested, presumably hold the marriage void. Yet it is certain that a Scottish court would hold the marriage valid, because the section is expressed to apply only (a) where the party domiciled in Scotland is under the age of sixteen, or (b) where the marriage is solemnised in Scotland. If the English court dissected the section into (a) a rule of Scots domestic law and (b) a particular or

---

[125] For capacity to marry, see Rule 74 and Exceptions thereto.

[126] For characterisation, see Ch.2, below.

[127] [1951] P.482. A marriage was celebrated in Austria between a man domiciled in England and a girl of 15 domiciled in Hungary. The marriage was valid by Austrian and Hungarian law.

[128] A dictum at pp.491–492 suggests that the section would also apply to marriages celebrated in England, regardless of the domicile of the parties. This is entirely in accordance with Exception 2 to Rule 74.

[129] A far less successful particular or unilateral choice of law clause is s.2(3) of the same statute, dealing with marriages within the prohibited degrees.

[130] For renvoi, see Ch.4, below.

unilateral conflict rule indicating when Scots law is to apply, and applied (a) but not (b), it would create a "limping" marriage—that is, a marriage valid in Scotland (and in Austria and Hungary) but void in England. Thus it would seem preferable for the English court to apply s.1 as it stands, and hold the marriage valid.

1–045   Other examples of particular or unilateral choice of law clauses in statutes are the Law Reform (Frustrated Contracts) Act 1943, s.1(1)[131]; the Marriage (Enabling) Act 1960, s.1(3)[132]; the Inheritance (Provision for Family and Dependants) Act 1975, s.1(1)[133]; and the Legitimacy Act 1976, s.1(2).[134]

1–046   The desirability of particular or unilateral choice of law clauses as a legislative technique is strongly criticised by some writers,[135] and equally strongly defended by others.[136]

1–047   (3) *Statutes with a general choice of law clause.* Statutes containing general or multilateral conflict rules are rare in English law, but examples can be found in s.72(1) and (2) of the Bills of Exchange Act 1882[137]; and the Wills Act 1963.[138] They both seek to answer the question "What law applies?"—in the first case to the formal and essential validity of bills of exchange, in the second case to the formal validity of wills. Another example can be constructed from ss.2 and 3 of the Legitimacy Act 1976. Section 2 provides that where the parents of an illegitimate person marry one another, the marriage shall, if the father is at the date of the marriage domiciled in England, render that person, if living, legitimate from the date of the marriage. Taken by itself, this would be a rule of English domestic law coupled with a particular or unilateral conflict rule, purporting to answer the question "When does English law apply?" But s.3 provides that where the parents of an illegitimate person marry one another and the father is not at the time of the marriage domiciled in England but is domiciled in a country by the law of which the illegitimate person became legitimated by virtue of such subsequent marriage, that person, if living, shall in England be recognised as having been so legitimated from the date of the marriage.[139] These two sections, added together, yield a general or multilateral conflict rule to the effect that the law of the father's domicile at the date of the marriage determines whether an illegitimate person is legitimated by the subsequent marriage of his parents.[140]

1–048   On the other hand, it is seldom possible for English courts to do what courts in continental European countries have often done, namely, to derive a general or multilateral conflict rule from a particular or unilateral one contained in a statute. This is because in England the common law is never displaced by a

---

[131] See 14th edition of this work, para.34–021.

[132] See below, para.17–074.

[133] See below, para.27–051.

[134] See below, para.20–027.

[135] Morris (1946) 62 L.Q.R. 170, 172; Unger (1967) 83 L.Q.R. 427, 436–448.

[136] F.A. Mann (1964) 80 L.Q.R. 29, 31; (1972–73) 46 B.Y.I.L. 117, 134; Currie, p.116.

[137] See Rule 240(1) and (2).

[138] See Rule 152.

[139] See Rule 117 and Comment thereto.

[140] See F.A. Mann (1972–73) 46 B.Y.I.L. 117, 118–119; Kahn-Freund (1974) *Recueil des Cours*, III, p.236.

statute unless the statute expressly abolishes the rule of common law.[141] The common law is the rule and the statute is the exception which applies only to the extent expressed therein. Only if there is no common law authority would it be permissible for an English court to derive a multilateral rule from a unilateral one contained in a statute.

(4) *Self-limiting statutes.* A statute may provide that some of its provisions **1–049** apply only to British citizens, or to British ships, or to the capital city, or on Sundays, or during the close season for various classes of game birds, or to certain kinds of employees. Such "self-limiting provisions" as they have been called are clearly not rules of the conflict of laws whether multilateral or unilateral. They limit the application of the statute to certain persons, things, events, times or places connected in a specified way with the country whose legislature enacted the statute. If they are contained in a United Kingdom statute applying to England, they should apply only when it has first been decided that English domestic law applies, unless the statute provides otherwise. If they are contained in a foreign statute, the English court should apply the statute with its self-limiting provisions, otherwise it will distort the meaning of the statute and apply it where, under the terms of the statute itself, it is inapplicable.[142] If an English court finds that a foreign statute is inapplicable because of its self-limiting provisions, it should apply those statutory provisions or common law rules of the foreign law which, under that law, are applicable in that situation.

Section 26 of the Unfair Contract Terms Act 1977 is an example of a self- **1–050** limiting statute. It provides that the limits imposed by the Act on the extent to which a person may exclude or restrict liability by reference to a contract term do not apply to liability arising under a contract of sale which is made by parties whose places of business (or, if they have none, habitual residences) are in the territories of different States, and where the goods are being carried, or will be carried, from the territory of one State to the territory of another; or the acts constituting the offer and acceptance have been done in the territories of different States; or the contract provides for the goods to be delivered to the territory of a State other than that within whose territory those acts were done.

Although the distinction between them is plain enough in principle, it is not **1–051** always easy to distinguish between unilateral conflict rules and self-limiting provisions; nor has any writer succeeded in formulating a satisfactory test for distinguishing between them. One writer suggests that if the statute uses terminology which is recognised in the conflict of laws, such as domicile or

---

[141] For example, s.8(1) of the Legitimacy Act 1926 (the predecessor of s.3 of the Legitimacy Act 1976) was held not to have abolished the common law rule (Rule 116) whereby legitimation by subsequent marriage is governed by the law of the father's domicile at the time of the child's birth and at the time of the subsequent marriage: see below, Rule 117.

[142] *Adamastos Shipping Co v Anglo-Saxon Petroleum Co* [1959] A.C. 133 is not contrary to this submission, because the foreign statute there in question had been incorporated in an English contract and therefore had to be interpreted as part of the contract and not applied as foreign law. The self-limiting provisions of the statute were held by a bare majority of the House of Lords to be inconsistent with the other terms of the contract and therefore had to be rejected in order to make sense of the whole. For the difference between the incorporation of a foreign statute and the application of foreign law, see below, paras 32–056 *et seq.*

place of celebration of a marriage, then it enacts a unilateral conflict rule but if it uses terminology which is not so recognised, such as place of work, then it enacts a self-limiting provision.[143] But this is not entirely satisfactory, because the words used in the statute are surely less significant than the substance of the matter.

1–052   If a statute is expressed in general terms without any self-limiting provisions, courts are sometimes willing to read such provisions into it under the guise of interpreting the statute. This is true whether the statute forms part of the court's own law or of foreign law. This was one reason (not the only one) why the Privy Council, sitting on appeal from the New Zealand Court of Appeal, held that a New Zealand borrower could not take advantage of a Victorian statute which purported to reduce the rate of interest on certain mortgages.[144] It was one reason why an English court held that the general words in s.2 of the Marriage Act 1949 applied only to marriages between parties domiciled in England.[145] It was also one reason why the New York Court of Appeals held that an Ontario statute exonerating the driver of a car from liability for personal injuries to a gratuitous passenger did not apply to a motor accident in Ontario when the parties were New Yorkers: the statute, it was thought, was intended to protect Ontario drivers and their insurance companies, not New York ones.[146] This method of implying self-limiting provisions in statutes is very far from being new. From the 13th century to the middle of the 19th century, i.e. during the era of the statutists, it dominated the theory and practice of the conflict of laws. The meagreness of the results achieved by the statutists should be warning enough to show that it is a method to be used with caution.[147]

1–053   (5) *Overriding statutes.* Statutes of the fifth class are those which must be applied regardless of the normal rules of the conflict of laws, because the statute says so. Since all the examples of overriding statutes to be discussed below are taken from the law of contract, it should be pointed out at the outset of the discussion that, according to standard doctrine in the conflict of laws, a statute does not normally apply to a contract unless it forms part of the governing law of the contract, or unless (being a statute in force in the forum) it is procedural. This was true at common law e.g. of Stamp Acts,[148] statutes affecting the validity of wagering contracts,[149] statutes reducing or otherwise

---

[143] Unger (1967) 83 L.Q.R. 427, 429.

[144] *Mount Albert Borough Council v Australasian etc., Life Assurance Society Ltd* [1938] A.C. 224, 236–239, 243 (PC). cf. *Wanganui-Rangitikei Electric Power Board v Australian Mutual Provident Society* (1934) 50 C.L.R. 581.

[145] *Pugh v Pugh* [1951] P. 482; see above, para.1–041.

[146] *Babcock v Jackson,* 12 N.Y. 2d. 473, 191 N.E. 2d. 279, 284 (1963); see below, para.35–005. This is perhaps the least convincing part of the judgment.

[147] One of the *quaestiones famosissimae* discussed by the statutists was the English rule of primogeniture. They eventually decided that if the English "statute" said that land descended to the eldest son, the statute was real, but if it said that the eldest son succeeded to the land, it was personal. See Beale, Vol.3, pp.1890–1891.

[148] *Royal Exchange Assurance v Vega* [1902] 2 K.B. 384 (CA); *Norske Atlas Insurance Co Ltd v London General Insurance Co Ltd* (1927) 28 Ll.L.R. 104; *Maritime Insurance Co Ltd v Assekuranz Union von 1865* (1935) 52 Ll.L.R. 16.

[149] *Robinson v Bland* (1760) 2 Burr. 1077; *Quarrier v Colston* (1842) 1 Ph. 147; *Saxby v Fulton* [1909] 2 K.B. 208 (CA); and see *Moulis v Owen* [1907] 1 K.B. 746 (CA). See below, Rule 229.

regulating the rate of interest,[150] statutes providing for moratoria[151] or abrogating gold clauses.[152] Overriding statutes are an exception to the general rule that statutes only apply if they form part of the applicable law. One of the main reasons for the overriding character of such legislation is that otherwise the intention of the legislature to regulate certain contractual matters could be frustrated if it were open to the parties to choose some foreign law to govern their contract.[153]

Laws of this kind are referred to as "mandatory rules" or *lois de police* or **1–054** *lois d'application immédiate*.[154] Where such legislation is part of the law of the forum it applies because it is interpreted as applying to all cases within its scope. Thus in contract cases, United Kingdom legislation will be applied to affect a contract governed by foreign law if on its true construction the legislation is intended to override the general principle that legislation relating to contracts is presumed to apply only to contracts governed by the law of a part of the United Kingdom. Article 9(2) of the Rome I Regulation provides that nothing in the Regulation is to restrict the application of the overriding mandatory provisions of the law of the forum.

Mandatory rules which are not part of the law of the forum or of the **1–055** applicable law are not normally applied by the English court.[155] It has, however, been suggested in literature and case law on the continent that the forum may take account of foreign mandatory rules even if they do not form part of the applicable law.[156] This suggestion was reflected in Art.7(1) of the Rome Convention, which provided for the application of the mandatory rules of a country other than that of the forum or the *lex causae* if the situation had a close connection with that country. The United Kingdom exercised its right of reservation to Art.7(1) when it signed the Rome Convention, and accordingly this provision did not come into force in the United Kingdom.[157] The

---

[150] *Mount Albert Borough Council v Australasian, etc., Life Assurance Society Ltd* [1938] A.C. 224 (PC); *Barcelo v Electrolytic Zinc Co of Australasia Ltd* (1932) 48 C.L.R. 391; *Wanganui-Rangitikei Electric Power Board v Australian Mutual Provident Society* (1934) 50 C.L.R. 581.

[151] *Helbert Wagg & Co Ltd, Re* [1956] Ch. 323.

[152] *R. v International Trustee for the Protection of Bondholders AG* [1937] A.C. 500. See below, Rule 262.

[153] *Irish Shipping Ltd v Commercial Union Assurance Co Plc* [1991] 2 Q.B. 206, 220–221 (CA), discussing, but not deciding, the territorial scope of Third Parties (Rights Against Insurers) Act 1930; see para.35–073, below.

[154] Batiffol and Lagarde, Vol.1, pp.425–430, Vol.2, pp.280–281; Mayer and Heuzé, *Droit international privé* (10th ed. 2010), paras 120 *et seq.*; Audit, *Droit international privé* (6th ed. 2010), paras 117 *et seq.*; Bourel and Muir Watt, *Droit international privé* (2007), paras 552 *et seq.*; Fawcett [1990] C.L.J. 44.

[155] *cf. Kleinwort, Sons & Co v Ungarische Baumwolle Industrie AG* [1939] 2 K.B. 678 (CA), subject to a possible exception in the case of illegality under the law of the place of performance, on which see paras 32–097 *et seq.*, below. See also Lipstein, in *Mélanges Zajtay* (1982), pp.357–378.

[156] See Batiffol and Lagarde, Vol.2, pp.280–281; see also Mayer and Heuzé, above, para.122; Audit, above, para.127.

[157] Contracts (Applicable Law) Act 1990, s.2(3). But there were other provisions of the Rome Convention which came into force and which required the application of mandatory foreign rules irrespective of the applicable law (see Art.5(2) on the application, in consumer contracts, of the law of the habitual residence of the consumer) or irrespective of the chosen law (Art.3(3), Art.6(1)).

Rome Convention has been superseded by the Rome I Regulation, Art. 9(3)[158] of which has a more limited provision, that effect may be given to the overriding mandatory provisions of the law of the place of performance.

1–056   A first example of an overriding statute is taken from the Defence Regulations 1939 made under s.3(1) of the Emergency Powers (Defence) Act 1939, which were considered in the leading case of *Boissevain v Weil*.[159] These made it an offence for any British subject (except an authorised dealer) to borrow foreign currency without Treasury permission and consequently made a contract concluded in contravention of this prohibition illegal and void. The defendant, a British subject involuntarily resident in Monaco during the war, borrowed a sum of French francs from the plaintiff, a Dutchman also so resident, and promised to repay him in sterling as soon as the law of England would allow her to do so. In the Court of Appeal Denning L.J. held that the plaintiff could not recover, because the governing law of the contract was English law and therefore the statute applied and rendered it illegal. But the House of Lords held that the statute applied regardless of the governing law of the contract.[160] Of course it was immaterial in this case that the illegality happened to be imposed by a statute. Similar results have been reached when the illegality is imposed by a rule of common law, e.g. the rule that champertous contracts,[161] contracts in restraint of trade[162] or contracts involving trading with the enemy[163] or breaking the laws of a friendly foreign country[164] are illegal.

1–057   Section 204(1) of the Employment Rights Act 1996 provides that "for the purposes of this Act it is immaterial whether the law which (apart from this Act) governs any person's employment is the law of the United Kingdom, or of a part of the United Kingdom, or not."[165] Of course this does not mean that the Act applies to all contracts of employment in the world, regardless of their connection with the United Kingdom. But it does mean that the draftsman, instead of enacting (or leaving it to be assumed) that the Act applies only when the applicable law of the contract of employment is the law of some part of the United Kingdom, has cut across the normal rules of the conflict of laws and laid down his own rules for the application of the Act. His method has two

---

[158] See also Art.3(3) (where all other elements located in a country other than that whose law has been chosen, choice of law does not affect application of provisions of the law of that other country which cannot be derogated from by agreement); Art.6(2) (consumer contracts); Art.8(1) (employment contracts). See Rules 224, 235, 238.

[159] [1949] 1 K.B. 482 (CA); [1950] A.C. 327.

[160] Hence, conversely, if the defendant had not been a British subject, the Defence Regulations would not have applied even if English law had been the law of the contract: the overriding statute also carried its own self-limitation.

[161] *Grell v Levy* (1864) 10 C.B. (N.S.) 73.

[162] *Rousillon v Rousillon* (1880) 14 Ch.D. 351.

[163] *Dynamit AG v Rio Tinto Co* [1918] A.C. 260.

[164] *Regazzoni v KC Sethia Ltd* [1958] A.C. 301.

[165] Employment Rights Act 1996, s.196, provided that certain provisions did not apply where under his contract of employment the employee ordinarily worked outside the United Kingdom. That section was repealed by Employment Relations Act 1999, s.32(3). See *Lawson v Serco Ltd* [2006] UKHL 3, [2006] I.C.R. 250 at [8] *et seq*. See also *Ministry of Defence v Wallis* [2011] EWCA Civ 231, [2011] I.C.R. 617; *Duncombe v Secretary of State for Children, Schools & Families* [2011] UKSC 36, [2011] I.R.L.R. 840; *Ravat v Halliburton Manufacturing & Services Ltd* [2010] CSIH 52, 2010 SC 698. below, Rule 238.

advantages. It prevents the parties evading the Act by choosing foreign law as the governing law of the contract of employment. It also secures the benefits of the Act to employees who work here for foreign employers and whose contracts of employment might well be governed by foreign law. In *Lawson v Serco Ltd*[166] the House of Lords held that the unfair dismissal provisions of the 1996 Act primarily applied where the employee was working in Great Britain at the time of the dismissal (and did not depend on what was contemplated at the time when the contract of employment was made). Where the employee worked in a number of countries (e.g. an airline pilot) the place of employment was his or her base. Where the employee was an expatriate working abroad, the provisions of the 1996 Act would apply if the employment had a strong connection with Great Britain, such as the case where an employee is posted broad by a British employer for the purposes of a business carried on in Great Britain, or where the expatriate employee is operating within what amounts for practical purposes to an extra-territorial British enclave in a foreign country (such as a military base).

Further examples of these overriding or peremptory provisions may be **1–058** taken from the law of consumer protection and from insurance law. The Unfair Contract Terms Act 1977[167] lays down, in the interests of consumers, certain mandatory rules. The parties to certain contracts cannot contract out of these rules[168] and to prevent them from doing so indirectly by agreeing that some foreign law should be the applicable law of their contract, s.27(2) provides that the Act has effect notwithstanding any contract term purporting to apply the law of some country outside the United Kingdom, if either of two conditions laid down in the subsection is satisfied.[169] In *Akai Pty Ltd v People's Insurance Co Ltd*[170] the New South Wales subsidiary of a Japanese multi-national took out with a Singaporean insurance company a policy covering credit risks in Australia. The policy was expressed to be governed by English law and provided for the exclusive jurisdiction of the English courts. Australian insurance legislation invalidated defences which would otherwise be available to the insurers at common law or under the terms of the contract (and which were available under English law), and provided that it applied where the applicable law of the contract was the law of an Australian State: it also provided that where, but for any express choice of foreign law, the applicable law would have been the law of an Australian State, the applicable law was to be regarded as the law of that State. The High Court of Australia held that the effect of the legislation was to override the choice of English law and to invalidate the choice of English jurisdiction, and to enable the insured

---

[166] [2006] UKHL 3, [2006] I.C.R. 250.

[167] The Act repealed and re-enacted (with some modifications) s.55A of the Sale of Goods Act 1893, added by s.5(1) of the Supply of Goods (Implied Terms) Act 1973, but it is much wider in scope. On s.5(1) of the 1973 Act, see F.A. Mann (1974) 90 L.Q.R. 42; (1977) 26 I.C.L.Q. 903. On s.27 of the Act of 1977, see F.A. Mann (1978) 27 I.C.L.Q. 661.

[168] Unless the contract is an "international supply contract" as defined in s.26. That definition follows closely the definition in Uniform Laws on International Sales Act 1967, on which see below, para.33–019.

[169] These are (a) that the term appears to have been imposed wholly or mainly for the purpose of enabling the party imposing it to evade the application of the Act; or (b) that in the making of the contract one party dealt as consumer and was then habitually resident in the United Kingdom and the essential steps necessary for the making of the contract were taken there.

[170] (1996) 188 C.L.R. 418.

to sue in New South Wales so as to prevent the insurer relying on common law and contractual defences. But in subsequent English proceedings by the insurer for a declaration that it was not liable to the insured it was held that the English court's jurisdiction by virtue of the contractual submission was not affected by the decision of the High Court of Australia, and that there was no legal basis for the English court to give effect to the public policy of Australia reflected in its legislation.[171]

1-059   Section 18 of the Third Parties (Rights against Insurers) Act 2010 (not yet in force), provides that except as expressly provided, the application of the Act does not depend on whether there is a connection with a part of the United Kingdom; and in particular it does not depend on (a) whether or not the liability (or the alleged liability) of the insured to the third party was incurred in, or under the law of, England and Wales, Scotland or Northern Ireland; (b) the place of residence or domicile of any of the parties; (c) whether or not the contract of insurance (or a part of it) is governed by the law of England and Wales, Scotland or Northern Ireland; (d) the place where sums due under the contract of insurance are payable.[172]

1-060   Other examples of overriding statutes are furnished by provisions invalidating contractual terms as a sanction for the contravention of statutory requirements, e.g. concerning the disclosure of facts or the adequate disclosure of contractual terms by one party to another. Thus, hire-purchase legislation has been applied in Scotland[173] when the contract was entered into in Scotland, though it was governed by the law of another country. The reason was that the statute was directed against the making of contracts in a form which did not sufficiently safeguard the interests of the economically weaker party. It was also held in Scotland[174] that the provisions of the Truck Act[175] against deductions from wages applied if the deductions were made in Scotland, irrespective of the applicable law of the contract. Section 44 of the Patents Act 1977[176] rendered void certain conditions or terms whereby a patentee abuses his monopoly power by, for example, requiring a customer or a licensee to acquire other products as a condition of the supply of the patented product or of a licence to work the invention. In *Chiron Corp v Organon Teknika Ltd (No.2)*[177] it was held that the section applied to contracts or licences relating to United Kingdom patents, irrespective of whether the contract or licence was governed by English law or foreign law: the object of the legislation was to prevent a person who obtained the privilege of monopoly protection under a United Kingdom patent from enforcing his patent rights if he has abused them. That being the object, it was wholly irrelevant what the applicable law of the contract was; it was the effect of the contract relative to the United Kingdom patent which was decisive.

---

[171] *Akai Pty Ltd v People's Insurance Co Ltd* [1998] 1 Lloyd's Rep. 90; Reynolds [1998] L.M.C.L.Q. 1.

[172] Contrast *Ludgater Holdings Ltd v Gerling Australia Insurance Company Pty Ltd* [2010] NZSC 49, [2010] 3 N.Z.L.R. 713.

[173] *English v Donnelly*, 1958 S.C. 494 (not followed in *Hong Kong Shanghai (Shipping) Ltd v The Cavalry* [1987] H.K.L.R. 287); *cf. Kay's Leasing Corp Pty Ltd v Fletcher* (1964) 116 C.L.R. 124; *Att-Gen's Reference No.1 of 1987* (1987) 47 S.A.S.R. 152.

[174] *Duncan v Motherwell Bridge and Engineering Co Ltd*, 1952 S.C. 131.

[175] Truck Act 1831, ss.2, 3 (since repealed).

[176] Repealed by Competition Act 1998.

[177] [1993] F.S.R. 567 (CA).

All the examples of overriding statutes which have so far been discussed   **1–061**
might be described as crystallised rules of public policy, because they lay
down mandatory rules which the parties cannot contract out of, directly or
indirectly. The remaining examples about to be discussed are taken from the
law of international transport. They all express the public policy which is
inherent in the unification of international transport law. The statutes have this
in common with the other examples, namely, that they apply regardless of the
applicable law of the contract. Section 1(1) of the Carriage by Air Act 1961,
s.1 of the Carriage of Goods by Road Act 1965, s.1(2) of the Carriage of
Goods by Sea Act 1971, and s.183(1) of the Merchant Shipping Act 1995
provide that the provisions of the international conventions set out in the
Schedules to those Acts shall have the force of law in the United Kingdom.[178]
The conventions all contain provisions which determine when they are applicable. These provisions make use of factors quite different from the applicable
law of the contract of carriage. The applicable law of the contract is thus
generally irrelevant in the law of international transport, where the matter is
regulated by an international convention; and the statutory provisions mentioned above apply whether the applicable law of the contract is that of some
part of the United Kingdom or of some foreign country.

Thus in *Corocraft Ltd v Pan American Airways Inc*,[179] a contract was made   **1–062**
in New York between an American consignor and an American airline for the
carriage of diamonds from New York to London. The diamonds were stolen
at London airport by a servant of the carrier. When sued by the consignee for
non-delivery, the carrier argued that the Warsaw Convention set out in the
Carriage by Air Acts did not apply, because the governing law of the contract
was that of New York. This argument was rejected on the ground that the
Convention had been given the force of law in the United Kingdom by
statute.[180] Similarly in *The Hollandia*[181] a machine was shipped from Scotland
to the Dutch West Indies, on a Dutch vessel to the Netherlands, and on a
Norwegian vessel for the remainder of the voyage. The machine was seriously
damaged while being unloaded in the Dutch West Indies. The bill of lading
provided for Dutch law and Dutch jurisdiction, and contained a limitation of
liability, the effect of which was that the liability of the carriers would be
limited to about £250. It was held that the Hague-Visby Rules (the effect of
which was to limit the liability of the carriers to about £11,000), which are
scheduled to the Carriage of Goods by Sea Act 1971 and which have "the
force of law,"[182] applied in proceedings in England notwithstanding the
choice of Dutch law as the governing law.[183] These statutes are therefore

---

[178] See Rule 234. See also International Transport Conventions Act 1983, s.1(1), which does
not schedule the conventions, but whose effect is the same.
[179] [1969] 1 Q.B. 616.
[180] At pp.630–631. The point was not argued in the Court of Appeal.
[181] [1982] Q.B. 872 (CA), affirmed [1983] 1 A.C. 565, on which see F.A. Mann (1983) 99
L.Q.R. 376, (1984) 100 L.Q.R. 369; Jaffey (1984) 100 L.Q.R. 198. See also *The Antares (Nos 1
and 2)* [1987] 1 Lloyd's Rep. 424 (CA), on which see F.A. Mann (1987) 103 L.Q.R. 523.
[182] s.1(3).
[183] In the House of Lords the principal question was the applicability of a clause conferring
jurisdiction on the Dutch courts, and it seems to have been accepted that the Court of Appeal was
right in holding that the 1971 Act overrode the choice of law: see [1983] 1 A.C. 565, 573. The
actual decision would now probably be different: see below, para.12–151.

examples of overriding statutes, because they must be applied regardless of the normal rules of the conflict of laws.

1–063   (6) *Self-denying statutes.* Self-denying statutes are the opposite of overriding statutes: they do not apply in the circumstances where the statute says they shall not apply, even though they would apply under the normal rules of the conflict of laws. The only example of such a statute in English law appears to be s.27(1) of the Unfair Contract Terms Act 1977, which is the converse of s.27(2). Section 27(2) provides, as we have seen,[184] that the Act has effect notwithstanding any contract term purporting to apply the law of some country outside the United Kingdom. Section 27(1)[185] provides that where the applicable law of a contract is the law of any part of the United Kingdom only by choice of the parties (and apart from that choice would be the law of some country outside the United Kingdom), certain provisions of the Act do not operate as part of the law applicable to the contract. Thus, if the applicable law of the contract would have been the law of some foreign country, because the transaction is most closely connected with that system of law, but the parties choose the law of some part of the United Kingdom as the applicable law, the mandatory rules of the Act do not apply to the contract.

1–064   The English and Scottish Law Commissioners explained why it was necessary to include s.27(1) in the Act.[186] They pointed out that the parties to contracts of which the applicable law would otherwise be the law of some country other than England or Scotland often choose English law or Scots law as the applicable law of their contracts, sometimes by an express term to the effect,[187] more often through the medium of an arbitration clause.[188] The effect of imposing the controls contained in the Act in relation to these contracts might well be to discourage foreign businessmen from agreeing to arbitrate their disputes in England or Scotland. The suggestion was that this would strike a heavy blow at the City of London as a centre for international arbitration.[189]

1–065   **Meaning of "country."** This word has from long usage become almost a term of art among English-speaking writers on the conflict of laws, and it is vitally important to appreciate exactly what it means. It was defined by Dicey as "the whole of a territory subject under one sovereign to one body of law." He suggested that a better expression might be "law district": but this phrase has never found much favour with English-speaking writers, who prefer the more familiar word "country." England, Scotland, Northern Ireland, the Isle of Man, Jersey, Guernsey, Alderney, Sark, each British colony, each of the Australian States and each of the Canadian provinces is a separate country in the sense of the conflict of laws, though not one of them is a State known to

---

[184] See above, para.1–058.
[185] As amended by Contracts (Applicable Law) Act 1990, s.5 and Sch.4.
[186] *Second Report on Exemption Clauses*, Law Com. No.69, para.232.
[187] See Rule 222.
[188] See below, paras 32–061 *et seq.*
[189] Dr F.A. Mann criticised the provisions of s.27(1): (1977) 26 I.C.L.Q. 903, 907–909, 911; (1978) 27 I.C.L.Q. 661; but he did not cite the Law Commissions' explanation quoted in the text.

public international law. However, for some purposes larger units than these may constitute countries. Thus, the United Kingdom is one country for the purposes of the law of negotiable instruments,[190] Great Britain is one country for most purposes of the law of companies,[191] Australia is one country for the purposes of the law of marriage[192] and matrimonial causes,[193] and Canada is one country for the purposes of the law of divorce.[194]

Nor is there any doubt that for most purposes of the conflict of laws each **1–066**
State within the United States is a "country." Thus a contract will be governed by the law of New York or Arizona, but not by the law of the United States; and a judgment of the New York State court will be recognised as a New York judgment, and not as an American judgment. In *Adams v Cape Industries Plc*,[195] however, an issue arose as to whether, for the purposes of the enforcement in England of a judgment of a US federal court sitting in Texas, the residence or presence of the judgment debtors in another State of the Union, Illinois, amounted to residence or presence also in the law district in which the federal court sat, namely Texas. The federal court (and not the State court in Texas) had jurisdiction because of the parties' "diversity of citizenship," but it exercised jurisdiction under the rules applicable in the State in which it sat, and (except as regards procedure) it did not apply federal law to the case, but State law. But the federal court was a court established by the United States, and not by the State of Texas. In these circumstances, Scott J. decided that the United States as a whole was the "country" for the purposes of the jurisdiction of the federal court. The Court of Appeal did not find it necessary to decide the question, but indicated that it inclined to the view that Scott J. was correct.[196]

On the other hand, Wales is not a country, because its system of law is **1–067**
the same as that of England. Nor is it necessary that a country in the sense of the conflict of laws should have a separate legislature. For example, the District of Columbia has no such legislature and yet it is a country: and Northern Ireland did not cease to be a country when its legislature was suspended in 1972.[197]

The reader should be warned that although, as mentioned above, "country" **1–068**
has become almost a term of art among English-speaking writers on the conflict of laws, yet the practice of Parliamentary draftsmen is far from uniform. For Parliament, when enacting rules of the conflict of laws, refers sometimes to a "country,"[198] sometimes to a "territory"[199] and sometimes to a "place."[200] This usually causes no confusion, because the meaning is always

---

[190] Bills of Exchange Act 1882.
[191] Companies Act 2006.
[192] Marriage Act 1961 (Aus).
[193] Family Law Act 1975, ss.39(3), 103 (Aus).
[194] Divorce Act R.S.C. 1985, c.D–3, ss.3–5, 13 (Can).
[195] [1990] Ch. 433 (Scott J. and CA).
[196] *ibid.* at pp.484–492 (Scott J.), 550–557 (CA).
[197] Northern Ireland (Temporary Provisions) Act 1972 (repealed by Northern Ireland Act 1998).
[198] e.g. Arbitration Act 1996, s.103(2); Legitimacy Act 1976, s.3; Unfair Contract Terms Act 1977, s.27.
[199] e.g. Wills Act 1963, s.1; Family Law Act 1986, s.49.
[200] e.g. Bills of Exchange Act 1882, s.72; British Nationality Act 1981, s.47(2) (now repealed).

the same. Where it is not the same, Parliament has endeavoured to distinguish the concepts.[201]

1-069　**Meaning of "State."** The word State has various meanings. Whatever may be its meaning in public international law or constitutional law, in this book it means the whole of a territory subject to one sovereign power. Thus, to give some examples, the United Kingdom and Colonies, France, the United States, and each of the independent members of the Commonwealth, whether it does or does not form part of Her Majesty's dominions, is a State. But England, Scotland, New York, Ontario, and New South Wales are not States nor is any British colony or dependent (or overseas) territory.

1-070　A State may or may not coincide with a country in the sense of the conflict of laws. Unitary States like Sweden, the Netherlands and New Zealand, where the law is the same throughout the State, are "countries" in this sense. But composite States like the United Kingdom, the United States, Australia and Canada are not.

1-071　**Meaning of "foreign."** Because of this distinction between "country" and "State," the word "foreign" as used in this book normally means simply "not English." It does not mean foreign in the political sense. Thus the expression "foreign country" means any country except England, and applies as much to Scotland or Northern Ireland as to France or Italy; and the expressions "foreign judgment" and "foreign arbitration award" mean judgments or awards given or made outside England.

1-072　**Geographical expressions.** A writer on the conflict of laws is constantly making use of certain geographical expressions which, it is assumed, are familiar to readers. But since this assumption may not always be well founded, it seems desirable to supply some definitions.[202]

1-073　*England* includes Wales and the town of Berwick-on-Tweed,[203] and adjacent islands, such as the Isle of Wight or Anglesey or Lundy Island,[204] and the territorial waters adjacent thereto.[205]

---

[201] Family Law Act 1986, s.49; Rule 88, below.

[202] See also Interpretation Act 1978, Sch.1, "British Islands", "England", "United Kingdom". The use of the expression "British Isles", which means the same as "British Islands", is now virtually obsolete in statutes.

[203] Wales and Berwick Act 1746, s.3. However, s.4 of the Welsh Language Act 1967 provided that references to "England" in future Acts of Parliament should no longer include Wales: see now Interpretation Act 1978, Sch.3, Pt I. But it seems desirable to adhere to Dicey's definition for reasons of convenience and especially of brevity. It would be cumbersome to have to add "or Wales" after "England" and "or Welsh" after "English" every time those words were used.

[204] See *Harman v Bolt* (1931) 47 T.L.R. 219, with reference to Lundy.

[205] See the Territorial Waters Jurisdiction Act 1878; the Continental Shelf Act 1964, s.1(7), as amended by the Oil and Gas (Enterprise) Act 1982 and Energy Act 2011, and SI 2000/3062. The Orders affecting areas designated by the Continental Shelf Act 1964, s.1(7), no longer apply to those areas which are now within territorial waters as a result of the Territorial Sea Act 1987: SI 1987/1265. The extent of British jurisdiction is a matter to be determined by the Crown, represented by the Secretary of State for Home Affairs, and is properly presented to the court by the Attorney-General: *The Fagernes* [1927] P. 311 (CA). See *R. v Kent Justices, Ex p. Lye* [1967] 2 Q.B. 153; *Post Office v Estuary Radio Ltd* [1968] 2 Q.B. 740 (CA) (Thames Estuary). On the legal status of the sea-bed see *Shetland Salmon Farmers Assn v Crown Estate Commissioners*, 1991 S.L.T. 166.

Great Britain means England as above defined, and Scotland and its **1–074** adjacent territorial waters. It includes the islands of Orkney and Shetland, the Hebrides and Rockall[206] which (in spite of their great distance from the mainland) are part of Scotland. The breadth of the territorial waters of the United Kingdom is now 12 miles.[207]

The United Kingdom means Great Britain and Northern Ireland and their **1–075** adjacent territorial waters.[208] It does not include the Republic of Ireland.[209] Nor for historical reasons does it include the Channel Islands or the Isle of Man.[210]

British Islands means the United Kingdom, the Channel Islands and the Isle **1–076** of Man and their adjacent territorial waters.

The Commonwealth is used in its widest sense to include all territories **1–077** which form part of the dominions of the Crown or which acknowledge the Queen as Head of the Commonwealth, and the territorial waters adjacent thereto.[211] It includes not only the older Dominions but also the Republics and other independent States which, for one reason or another, have ceased to be part of Her Majesty's dominions.[212] It also includes the remaining British Dependent territories.[213] But it does not include the Republic of Ireland.[214]

The United Kingdom is of course part of the Commonwealth as above **1–078** defined. But sometimes it is necessary to distinguish between the United Kingdom and the rest of the Commonwealth. This is done by referring either to "any part of the Commonwealth outside the United Kingdom" or to "the Commonwealth overseas." Either of these expressions as used in this book includes the dependencies of the United Kingdom (i.e. the Channel Islands and the Isle of Man) and the Colonies.

Connecting factors. Like any other legal subject, the conflict of laws has **1–079** its technical terms, some of which must now be explained.

---

[206] Island of Rockall Act 1972, s.1.

[207] Territorial Sea Act 1987, s.1; Territorial Waters Order in Council 1964 (made under the royal prerogative), as amended. See also SI 1991/1722 (Isle of Man); SI 1997/278 (Jersey), as amended by SI 2002/250.

[208] Royal and Parliamentary Titles Act 1927, s.2(1); Interpretation Act 1978, Sch.1. References to Ireland or to the United Kingdom in pre–1922 statutes do not now usually include the Republic of Ireland: see the Irish Free State (Consequential Adaptation of Enactments) Order, S.R.&O. 1923, No.405; and see the Ireland Act 1949. See also Roberts-Wray, *Commonwealth and Colonial Law* (1966), pp.32–35. As to Northern Irish territorial waters, a resident magistrate held that they belong to the Republic of Ireland, but his decision was reversed by the CA: *DPP for Northern Ireland v McNeill* [1975] N.Ir. 177.

[209] Ireland Act 1949, s.1(3).

[210] On the status of the Channel Islands see *Rover International Ltd v Cannon Film Sales Ltd* [1987] 1 W.L.R. 1597; *Chloride Industrial Batteries Ltd v F&W Freight Ltd* [1989] 1 W.L.R. 823 (CA); *Jersey Fishermen's Association Ltd v States of Guernsey* [2007] UKPC 30, [2007] Eur.L.R. 670; *R. (on the application of Barclay) v Secretary of State for Justice* [2009] UKSC 9, [2011] 1 A.C. 464.

[211] See Roberts-Wray, *op. cit.*, pp.1–29, 86–89. The definition there suggested (p.14) seems too complicated for the purposes of this book.

[212] *cf.* British Nationality Act 1981, Sch.3.

[213] *cf.* British Nationality Act 1981, Sch.6.

[214] Ireland Act 1949, s.1(1). Pakistan and South Africa have re-joined the Commonwealth: Pakistan Act 1990; South Africa Act 1995.

The rules of the conflict of laws are, traditionally, expressed in terms of juridical concepts or categories and localising elements or connecting factors.[215] Typical rules of the conflict of laws state that succession to immovables is governed by the law of the *situs*; that the formal validity of a marriage is governed by the law of the place of celebration; and that capacity to marry is governed by the law of each party's antenuptial domicile. In these examples, succession to immovables, formal validity of marriage and capacity to marry are the categories, while *situs*, place of celebration and domicile are the connecting factors.

1–080   The *lex causae* is a convenient shorthand expression denoting the law (usually but not necessarily foreign) which governs the question. It is used in contradistinction to the *lexi fori*, which always means the domestic law of the forum, i.e. (if the forum is English) English law. The *lex causae* may be more specifically denoted by a variety of expressions, usually in Latin, such as the *lex domicilii* (law of the domicile),[216] *lex patriae* (law of the nationality), *lex loci contractus* (law of the country where a contract is made),[217] *lex loci solutionis* (law of the country where a contract is to be performed or where a debt is to be paid),[218] *lex loci delicti* (law of the country where a tort is committed),[219] *lex situs* (law of the country where a thing is situated),[220] *lex loci celebrationis* (law of the country where a marriage is celebrated),[221] *lex loci actus* (law of the country where a legal act takes place), *lex monetae* (law of the country in whose currency a debt or other legal obligation is expressed). The terms of *lex loci disgraziae* (law of the place where a bill of exchange is dishonoured) and *lex loci stabuli* (law of the place where a motor car is garaged) are used only in jest.

1–081   **Determination of the connecting factor.** A fundamental problem in the conflict of laws is whether the connecting factor should be determined by the *lex fori* or by the *lex causae*. Since the determination of the *lex causae* depends on the determination of the connecting factor, it is no longer controversial among learned writers that the connecting factor should be determined by the *lexi fori*.[222] Although the reported cases are mostly concerned

---

[215] This expression (first suggested by Falconbridge) seems the best English equivalent of the French and German technical terms "point de rattachement" and "Anknüpfungspunkt." See Vischer, *International Encyclopedia of Comparative Law*, Vol.III, Ch.4 (1999). On connecting factors generally see *Dell Computer Corp v Union des consommateurs* 2007 SCC 34, (2007) 284 D.L.R. (4th) 577 (Sup Ct Can), [27]–[37].

[216] See Rules 4–16 with reference to the domicile of individuals, and Rule 173 with reference to the domicile of corporations.

[217] As to where a contract is made, see below, para.11–181.

[218] As to where a contract is to be performed, see below, paras 11–197 *et seq.*; 11–277 *et seq.*

[219] See below, paras 35–004 *et seq.*

[220] As to the *situs* of things, see Rule 129.

[221] As to where a marriage is celebrated, see below, paras 17–014 *et seq.*

[222] Many of the writers who discuss the determination of the connecting factor do so in connection with their discussion of the problem of characterisation: see Robertson, pp.104–117; Lorenzen, pp.97–100, 123–127; Falconbridge, pp.129–133. But the two questions are really quite distinct. What is significant for present purposes is that even writers who advocate characterisation in accordance with the *lex causae* admit that the *lex fori* should define the connecting factor: see e.g. Wolff, s.131.

with domicile, it may be assumed that English law has adopted this prevailing opinion, and that, for the purpose of an English conflict rule, the connecting factor will be determined by English law as the *lexi fori*.[223]

The proposition that the *lex fori* determines the connecting factor has two **1–082** related but distinct aspects. The first is that the *lexi fori* defines what it means, e.g. by domicile at common law[224]; the second is that it also determines whether, so defined, the connecting factor links a given issue with one legal system or with another.[225]

For the purposes of an English conflict rule, English law defines what **1–083** domicile means, and also whether a person is or was domiciled in England or in some foreign country. There is therefore nothing to prevent an English court from deciding that, for the purposes e.g. of succession to movables, a Frenchman domiciled in France has acquired an English domicile of choice, even though French law may consider that he has not lost his French domicile,[226] or that an Englishwoman domiciled in England has acquired a domicile of choice in France, even though French law may consider that she has not lost her English domicile.[227] Nor is there anything to prevent an English court from deciding that, for the purposes e.g. of divorce jurisdiction, a man is domiciled in England, even though a Scottish court has recently decided that, for the same purposes, he is domiciled in Scotland.[228]

There are three real exceptions, and one apparent exception, to the proposi- **1–084** tion that for the purposes of an English conflict rule the *lex fori* defines the connecting factor.

The first real exception is concerned with nationality. Nationality is an **1–085** exception to the second of the two aspects of the proposition mentioned above, but not to the first. If the *lex fori* uses nationality as a connecting factor, it must define what it means by nationality, and say, for example, what is to happen when the person concerned has two or more nationalities or none, or is a national of a composite or "plurilegal" State like the United Kingdom, which comprises more than one country.[229] But the *lex fori* can never say whether a person is a national of a foreign State. That can only be done by the law of the State concerned.[230] This is not an exception that has much impor-

---

[223] This passage was approved in *The TS Havprins* [1983] 2 Lloyd's Rep. 356. See also *The Amazonia* [1990] 1 Lloyd's Rep. 236, 240–241 (CA); *Macmillan Inc v Bishopsgate Investment Trust Plc (No.3)* [1996] 1 W.L.R. 387, 392 (CA); *Re Harvard Securities Ltd* [1997] 2 B.C.L.C. 369, 275.

[224] But whether a person is domiciled in a foreign country for the purposes of the Council Regulation (EC) 44/2001 (the Brussels I Regulation) on jurisdiction and the recognition and enforcement of judgments in civil and commercial matters, and for the purposes of the revised Lugano Convention may depend on the law of the foreign country: see below, Rule 30.

[225] Kahn-Freund (1974) *Recueil des Cours*, III, pp.388–395.

[226] *Re Martin* [1900] P. 211 (CA).

[227] *Re Annesley* [1926] Ch. 692; *contra, Re Johnson* [1903] 1 Ch. 821, but this case has been heavily criticised and is no longer law, see below, para.4–015, n.24. See also Rule 8, below.

[228] See *Wilson v Wilson* (1872) 10 M. 573; *Wilson v Wilson* (1872) L.R. 2 P. & D. 435.

[229] In *Re O'Keefe* [1940] Ch. 124 the English judge attempted to do this; he should have left it to the Italian expert witnesses to say what the *lex patriae* meant in the case of a British subject.

[230] *Stoeck v Public Trustee* [1921] 2 Ch. 67, 78, 82; *Re Chamberlain's Settlement* [1921] 2 Ch. 533; *cf. Oppenheimer v Cattermole* [1976] A.C. 249.

tance in the English conflict of laws, because there are very few English conflict rules that are expressed in terms of nationality.[231]

1–086   The second and third real exceptions are provided by legislation. The Family Law Act 1986 provides that if either spouse was domiciled in a foreign country in the sense of that country's law, and it uses the concept of domicile as a ground of jurisdiction, a divorce or legal separation obtained in that country must be recognised in England.[232] The effect of Council Regulation (EC) 44/2001 (the Brussels I Regulation) and of the Lugano Convention is that, where an individual is not domiciled (within the meaning of the Regulation or the Convention) in the United Kingdom, in order to determine whether he is domiciled in another Member State or Convention State, the English court must apply the law of that State.[233]

1–087   The apparent exception arises in connection with the doctrine of renvoi.[234] It can best be understood from an example. Suppose that a person dies intestate domiciled in France in the English sense, but in England in the French sense, leaving movables in England. In order to determine who is entitled to these movables, the English court will refer to French law as the law of the intestate's last domicile but, finding that French law would refer to English law because according to French law he was domiciled in England, it may then proceed to decide the case exactly as a French court would.[235] This is an apparent but not a real exception to the principle that, for the purposes of an English conflict rule, the *lex fori* must determine the connecting factor, because French law is being allowed to determine the question of domicile not for the purposes of an English conflict rule but for the purposes of a French conflict rule. The justification for allowing French law to do so is that it would be intolerable to accept a reference (renvoi) from French to English law if that reference was required by a French conflict rule expressed in terms e.g. of nationality, but not to do so if it was required by a French conflict rule expressed in terms of domicile in the French sense. To draw such a distinction would be to submit to the tyranny of labels.

1–088   **The name of the subject.** The branch of law whose nature we have been considering has been called by various names, of which the two most usual are the conflict of laws and private international law.

1–089   The term "conflict of laws" has won a great deal of authority by reason of its use by Huber, Story, Dicey, Beale and the American Law Institute's Restatements. It is not, however, completely satisfactory because it describes

---

[231] For some rare examples, see Wills Act 1963, s.1, and Rule 152; Family Law Act 1986, s.46(1)(b)(iii), and Rule 88(1)(c). The latter is an example of nationality being used, not as a connecting factor, but as a jurisdictional factor; but the principle is the same.

[232] Family Law Act 1986, s.46(5). This again is an example of domicile being used, not as a connecting factor, but as a jurisdictional factor: but see *Lawrence v Lawrence* [1985] Fam. 106, 133 (CA), *per* Purchas L.J. (a minority view). For recognition of foreign divorces and legal separations, see Rule 88.

[233] Brussels I Regulation, Art.59; Lugano Convention, Art.59. For domicile under the Regulation and the Convention, see Rule 30, below.

[234] For renvoi, see Ch.4, below.

[235] *Re Annesley* [1926] Ch. 692. The evidence of French law in this case was that French law would refer to English law, not because the testatrix was domiciled in England in the French sense, but because she was a British subject; but this was erroneous, see below, para.4–039, n.113.

only that part of the subject which deals with the question of choice of law to the exclusion of the question of jurisdiction, which in England is an essential part of the subject. In civil law countries, the usual title for the subject is private international law, which has been preferred by a number of English writers, notably Westlake and Cheshire. Westlake's view was that the subject falls under international law, denoting "the department which treats of the selection to be made in each action between various national jurisdictions and laws."[236] One obvious objection to this use of the term "international" is that it is a very different employment of the word from its normal meaning in the phrase "international law" which denotes the law governing the relations between States.[237] Another objection is that questions can and do arise just as frequently between the laws of e.g. England and Scotland, Ontario and Quebec, New York and California or Victoria and New South Wales as they do between the laws of e.g. England and France or England and Germany and there is obviously nothing international about questions of the former kind. Wolff[238] observed, however, that since "both titles are used throughout the world and as nobody has found a better one, it hardly seems worth while to devote further thought to this merely terminological issue".

---

[236] Westlake, p.5.
[237] For the relations between public and private international law, see Lipstein (1942) 27 Tr. Grot. Soc. 142; (1944) 29 *ib.* 51; Stevenson (1952) 52 Col.L.Rev. 561; Wortley (1954) *Recueil des Cours*, I, p.245; Hambro (1962) *Recueil des Cours*, I, p.1; Lipstein (1972) *Recueil des Cours*, I, pp.167–194; Kahn-Freund (1974) *Recueil des Cours*, III, pp.165–196; Collier, *Conflict of Laws* (3rd ed. 2001), pp.386–394; McLachlan [1993] Hague Yb. Int. L. 125; Mills, *The Confluence of Public and Private International Law: Justice, Pluralism and Subsidiarity in the International Constitutional Ordering of Private Law* (2009).
[238] p.10.

CHAPTER 2

CHARACTERISATION AND THE INCIDENTAL QUESTION

1. CHARACTERISATION[1]

2–001   THE problem of characterisation, also known as classification,[2] was "discovered" independently and almost simultaneously by the German jurist Kahn[3] and the French jurist Bartin[4] at the end of the 19th century, and was introduced to American lawyers by Lorenzen in 1920[5] and to English lawyers by Beckett in 1934.[6]

2–002   **Nature of the problem.** Characterisation is a fundamental problem in all traditional systems of the conflict of laws, that is to say the systems applicable in England and other European countries. It results from the fact that the rules which have been evolved to deal with choice-of-law problems are expressed in terms of juridical concepts or categories and localising elements or connecting factors.[7] This structure may be illustrated by considering some typical

---

[1] Lorenzen, Chs 4 and 5; Beckett (1934) 15 B.Y.I.L. 46; Unger (1937) 19 Bell Yard 3; Robertson, *Characterisation in the Conflict of Laws* (1940); Falconbridge, Chs 3–5; Cook, Ch.8; Cormack (1941) 14 So. Calif.L.Rev. 221–243; Lederman (1951) 29 Can. Bar Rev. 3, 168; Rabel, Vol.I, pp.47–72; Bland (1957) 6 I.C.L.Q. 10; Inglis (1958) 74 L.Q.R. 493, 503–516; Ehrenzweig in Nadelmann, von Mehren and Hazard (eds.), *XXth Century Comparative and Conflicts Law* (1961), pp.395 *et seq.*; Turpin [1959] *Acta Juridica* 222; Kahn-Freund (1974) *Recueil des Cours*, III, pp.369–382; Dine [1983] Jur. Rev. 73; Forsyth (1998) 114 L.Q.R. 141, Lipstein, *International Encyclopaedia of Comparative Law*, Vol.III, Ch.5 (1999); Lipstein, in *Private International Law in the International Arena—Liber Amicorum Kurt Siehr* (Basedow *et al*. eds. 2000), pp.405–412. For the more extensive Continental literature, see Robertson, pp.xxv–xxix; Lorenzen, Ch.4; and particularly (in addition to citations elsewhere in this chapter) Neuner, *Der Sinn der Internationalprivatrechtlichen Norm* (1932); Meriggi, "Saggio Critico sulle Qualificazioni" (1932) 2 *Rivista Italiana di Diritto Internazionale Privato* 189, French translation in (1933) 28 *Revue de Droit International Privé* 201; Ago (1936) *Recueil des Cours*, IV, p.243; Niederer, *Die Frage der Qualifikation* (1940); Niederer, *Einführung in die allgemeinen Lehren des Internationalen Privatrechts* (2nd ed. 1956), pp.389–391; Wengler, *Festschrift für Martin Wolff* (1952), pp.337 *et seq.*; Rigaux, *La Théorie des Qualifications* (1956), Mistelis, *Charakteriserungen und Qualifikation in Internationalen Privatrecht* (1999).

[2] "Qualification" is the term used by Continental writers.

[3] (1891) 30 Jhering's *Jahrbücher* 1, reprinted in *Abhandlungen* I (1928) 1–123.

[4] (1897) Clunet 225, 466, 720; *cf.* Bartin, *Principes de Droit International Privé* (1930), Vol.I, pp.221–239; Bartin (1930) *Recueil des Cours*, I, p.565.

[5] (1920) 20 Col. L. Rev. 247; reprinted in Lorenzen, Ch.4.

[6] (1934) 15 B.Y.I.L. 46.

[7] For the meaning of "connecting factors," see above, paras 1–079 *et seq.*

rules of the English conflict of laws: "succession to immovables is governed by the law of the *situs*"; "the formal validity of a marriage is governed by the law of the place of celebration"; "capacity to marry is governed by the law of the parties' domicile." In these examples, succession to immovables, formal validity of marriage and capacity to marry are the categories, while *situs*, place of celebration and domicile are the connecting factors.

The problem of characterisation consists in determining which juridical concept or category is appropriate in any given case. Assume, for example, that it is claimed that a marriage is void because the parties did not have the consent of their parents: should this be regarded as falling into the category "formal validity of a marriage" or should one take the view that it comes under "capacity to marry"? The answer could clearly determine the outcome of the case: this would be so if the law of the parties' domicile required them to obtain the consent of their parents, while the law of the place where the marriage was celebrated did not.

2–003

It might seem possible to solve the above problem simply on the basis of normal legal reasoning—though the untutored assumption of most lawyers that parental consent relates to capacity is not in fact the solution adopted by the English courts[8]—but the next problem may seem more difficult. Assume that a testator domiciled in England makes a will disposing of land in Utopia (such will not being made in contemplation of marriage) and subsequently marries. He dies shortly afterwards. Is the will revoked by the marriage? Under the law of England it will be, but we will assume that this is not the case under the law of Utopia. In such a situation, the answer to the question whether the will is revoked could depend on whether the issue is characterised as one relating to succession or to matrimonial law (proprietary consequences of marriage).[9]

2–004

It will be seen from the above examples that the problem of characterisation arises whenever a system of conflict of laws is based on categories and connecting factors. In such a system, it is always necessary to determine which is the appropriate category in any given case. Since the English rules of the conflict of laws are based on categories and connecting factors, there is no way of avoiding the problem, though it may be ameliorated by selecting narrower and more specific categories. Thus the problem set out in the previous paragraph would disappear if there were a category "revocation of a will by subsequent marriage."[10]

2–005

Characterisation and the application of European Regulations. The doctrine of characterisation examined in this chapter is, therefore, a doctrine which is an essential part of the mechanism by which a court chooses which law to apply in cases in which the framework for the decision, and the rules for choice of law, are those of the common law. In cases in which English statutes modify the choice of law rules of common law, the sphere of their

2–006

---

[8] See *Ogden v Ogden* [1908] P. 46 (CA), discussed at para.17–020, below.

[9] It was in these terms that the Court of Appeal analysed the problem in the leading case on the subject, *Re Martin* [1900] P. 211. It concluded that it fell within the category "matrimonial law."

[10] The problem of characterisation can be entirely avoided only by adopting a system of conflict of laws, such as the American doctrine of interest analysis, which does not use categories.

application may also be determined by reference or recourse to the common law of characterisation.

2–007   But where the choice of law rules which the court is directed to apply are those laid down by European Regulation or other European instrument, the question for the court is more usefully understood as one simply of statutory interpretation; and as will be seen at various points throughout this book, the principal canon of that statutory interpretation is that the legislative terms used in European instruments should have a meaning and a sphere of application which is uniform across the Member States. If, for example, an English court has to decide whether the matter before it is one of contractual or non-contractual obligation, in order to determine whether the choice of law rules are those of the Rome I[11] or Rome II[12] Regulation, or neither, the answer is not to be found by asking whether the common law rules of the conflict of laws would regard the issue as contractual, or tortious, or otherwise. The answer is instead to be arrived at by interpreting the statutory language of the Regulations, which is to be done in accordance with the guidance of the European Court of Justice and the principle that the Regulations should be interpreted in the same way, and to the same effect, in all Member States. Although it would be possible to describe the process of determining whether and how the Regulations apply as being a form of characterisation, that is, as a process of allocating the issue before the court to one or another of the potentially-applicable choice of law rules, it is one to be undertaken wholly without reference to the common law of characterisation. It is for this reason better understood as an entirely distinct, self-contained, exercise. It is therefore treated in appropriate detail in the chapters of this book which deal with the specific choice of law rules established by European Regulation. This chapter is therefore principally concerned with the doctrine of characterisation as it operates outside the context of legislative choice of law rules established by European Regulation or analogous instrument.

2–008   **Theories.** The problem of characterisation has given rise to a voluminous literature, much of it highly theoretical.[13] The consequence is that there are almost as many theories as writers and the theories are for the most part so abstract that, when applied to a given case, they can produce almost any result. They appear to have had almost no influence on the practice of the courts in England. For this reason, no attempt will be made to summarise them in detail, though the main features of the most important will be outlined.

2–009   Before doing this, however, we must consider a little more closely what a court does when confronted with a characterisation problem. What exactly is it that is characterised—an issue, a set of facts or a rule of law? Obviously, it can be any of these, depending on the way the court approaches the problem. For example, in one case members of the Court of Appeal referred to

---

[11] Regulation (EC) 593/2008 of the European Parliament and Council, examined in detail in Ch.32 below.

[12] Regulation (EC) 864/2007 of the European Parliament and Council, examined in detail in Chs 34–36 below.

[13] See n.1, above.

characterisation of "the issue",[14] "the question in this action",[15] "the relevant rule of law" and the "juridical concept or category".[16] In the example given above, the court could ask itself whether revocation of a will by subsequent marriage, as an abstract issue, is to be regarded as falling into the area of succession or matrimonial law; alternatively, it could consider how the facts of the case should be characterised. Both these approaches, it is suggested, amount to the same thing. But, as Auld L.J. observed in *Macmillan Inc v Bishopsgate Investment Trust Plc (No.3)*, the characterisation of the issue "requires a parallel exercise in classification of the relevant rule of law."[17] Once it is decided that the issue raised by the proceedings relates to matrimonial law rather than to succession, it logically follows that s.18 of the Wills Act 1837, the relevant provision of English law which deals with the revocation of a will by subsequent marriage, is characterised as a rule of matrimonial law.[18] Alternatively, the court could start by seeking to characterise s.18 of the Wills Act 1837. As will be shown below, this latter procedure can lead to difficulties which do not arise if the court characterises the issue.

The task which most of the writers have set themselves is that of determining which system of law should decide how legal rules and institutions should be characterised. Two main schools of thought have emerged: that favouring the *lex fori* and that favouring the *lex causae*. The various approaches were evaluated by Kahn-Freund, whose assessment was that characterisation in accordance with an "enlightened *lex fori*" was viable though sometimes difficult, that characterisation in accordance with the *lex causae* did not produce harmony, but risked "international dissonance as well as internal inconsistency", and that in some cases there was simply no obviously right answer to be found.[19]   2–010

The great majority of Continental writers follow Kahn and Bartin in thinking that, with certain exceptions,[20] the process of characterisation should be performed in accordance with the domestic law of the forum.[21] If the forum has to characterise a rule or institution of foreign law, it should inquire how the corresponding or most closely analogous rule or institution of its own law is characterised, and apply that characterisation to the foreign institution or rule. The principal argument put forward in favour of this view is that if the foreign law is allowed to determine in what situations it is to be applied, the law of the forum would lose all control over the application of its own   2–011

---

[14] *Macmillan Inc v Bishopsgate Investment Trust Plc (No.3)* [1996] 1 W.L.R. 387, 391 (CA) *per* Staughton L.J.

[15] *ibid.*, at p.393, *per* Staughton L.J.

[16] *ibid.* pp.407 (Auld L.J.) and 417 (Aldous L.J.) respectively.

[17] [1996] 1 W.L.R. 387, 407.

[18] It ought also to follow that any foreign rule which addresses the same issue should be characterised in the same way. See para.2–040.

[19] Kahn-Freund, *General Problems of Private International Law* (1976), pp.223–241.

[20] One of Bartin's exceptions was the characterisation of interests in property as interests in movables or immovables, which he said must be determined by the *lex situs*: (1897) Clunet 250–253. That is still the prevailing view: see Mayer and Heuzé, *Droit international privé* (10th ed. 2010), para.156; Audit, *Droit international privé* (6th ed. 2010), paras 198 *et seq.*; Bourel and Muir Watt, *Droit international privé* (2007), para.391.

[21] Beckett (1934) 15 B.Y.I.L. 46, 49–57; Lorenzen, Ch.4, especially pp.91–93; Robertson, pp.25–38. This theory was adopted in the South African case of *Laconian Marine Enterprises Ltd v Agromar Lineas Ltd*, 1986 (3) S.A. 509, 517–524.

conflicts rules, and would no longer be master in its own home. Several arguments have been advanced against this view. In the first place, it is said that it may result in the forum refusing to apply a rule of foreign law in cases where it would be applicable if its nature were properly appreciated,[22] or in the forum applying a rule of foreign law in cases where according to that law it is not applicable, with the result that the foreign law is distorted, so that the law applied to the case is neither the law of the forum nor the foreign law nor the law of any country whatever. Secondly, this view is said to break down when there is no close analogy in the *lex fori* to an institution or rule of the foreign law.[23] Thus there is no close analogy in English domestic law to the French system of community property, and no close analogy in French domestic law to the English trust. Yet the English and French conflict rules are framed in terms wide enough to accommodate the rights and duties arising from French community property[24] and the English trust[25] respectively.

2–012   Other Continental writers[26] think that the process of characterisation should be performed in accordance with the *lex causae*, that is, the appropriate foreign law. According to Wolff,[27] "every legal rule takes its classification from the legal system to which it belongs." The argument advanced in favour of this view is that to say that the foreign law is to govern, and then not apply its characterisation, is tantamount to not applying it at all. But this view bristles with difficulties, and few writers have adopted it. In the first place, it is arguing in a circle to say that the foreign law governs the process of characterisation before the process of characterisation has led to the selection of the appropriate legal system. Secondly, if there are two potential applicable foreign laws, why should the forum adopt the characterisation of one rather than that of the other?

2–013   The problem with these (and most of the other[28]) theories is that they assume that every legal system contains rules that unambiguously characterise every other rule in that system or, if one prefers, every legal issue. This is simply not true. In some cases, legal systems may give indications regarding the characterisation of rules they contain—for example, a rule may appear under one or another heading in the civil code of a Continental country—but this is certainly not always the case and, in any event, the place of the rule in that part of the code may be the result of accident. Because s.18 of the Wills Act 1837 appears in a statute entitled the "Wills Act," it does not necessarily follow that English law characterises it as relating to succession. Indeed, the Court of Appeal in *Re Martin*[29] did not so characterise it. Furthermore, the fact

---

[22] *Ogden v Ogden* [1908] P. 46 (CA) is sometimes said to be such a case: see below, para. 17–020.

[23] See *The Colorado* [1923] P. 102 (CA). But see Mendelssohn-Bartholdy (1935) 16 B.Y.I.L. 38–39.

[24] *De Nicols v Curlier* [1900] A.C. 21.

[25] Robertson, p.33.

[26] For example, Despagnet (1898) Clunet 253; Wolff, ss.138–157. See, further, Becket *op. cit.* at p.58; Lorenzen, Ch.4, especially pp.94–95 and Robertson, pp.27, 32.

[27] p.154.

[28] Other theories include that of primary and secondary characterisation, according to which one characterises twice—first according to the *lex fori* and then according to the *lex causae*—and a *via media* put forward by Falconbridge. On the former, see Robertson, *passim*, and on the latter, see Falconbridge, Ch.3, especially pp.58–62.

[29] [1900] P. 211.

that a rule of law is characterised in one way for one purpose does not necessarily mean that it should be characterised in the same way for all other purposes.

It follows, therefore, that the characterisation of a rule of law for any **2–014** purpose other than that of the conflict of laws cannot be relied upon for conflicts purposes. However, in the case of a foreign system of law, even such a characterisation will be of use only where the relevant categories in the foreign system of the conflict of laws are the same as those in that of the forum: this means not only that they should have the same name, but that they should mean the same thing. If this is not the case, one is not comparing like with like. As might be expected, this is almost impossible to determine. Moreover, cases in which particular rules of law (or issues) are characterised for the purposes of the conflict of laws are not common.

Examples of characterisation in English law. There are several English **2–015** cases in which questions of characterisation have come before the courts. Thus it has been held that the question whether interests in property are interests in movables or immovables must be determined in accordance with the *lex situs*;[30] that whether the defendant has a defence to a claim for restitution of shares on the basis of bona fide purchase relates to property rather than to restitution;[31] that the English rule that a personal representative can postpone the sale of assets relates to administration and not to succession;[32] that the English rule that a legacy to an attesting witness is void is a rule of essential validity and not of formality;[33] that the English rule as to the burden of proof of testamentary capacity is a rule of procedure and not of substance;[34] and that French rules prohibiting the marriage of minors without the consent of their parents,[35] and Argentine rules permitting marriages to be celebrated by proxy,[36] relate to the formalities of marriage and not to capacity to marry.[37] Unfortunately, however, most of these cases give little indication of the method used by the court to reach its conclusion. The cases which do give such an indication are relatively few in number. They will now be considered in detail.

Re Cohn. The first is *Re Cohn*.[38] This concerned two German women who **2–016** were killed in an air raid in London in circumstances in which it could not be determined which of them died first. One of them, Mrs Oppenheimer, was entitled to movable property under the will of the other, Mrs Cohn, but only

---

[30] *Re Hoyles* [1911] 1 Ch. 179 (CA); below, Rule 128.

[31] *Macmillan Inc v Bishopsgate Investment Trust Plc (No.3)* [1996] 1 W.L.R. 387.

[32] *Re Wilks* [1935] Ch. 645; followed in *Re Kehr* [1952] Ch. 26 (statutory power to appoint trustees of infant's share and statutory powers of maintenance and advancement); see below, para.26–034.

[33] *Re Priest* [1944] Ch. 58. See now Wills Act 1968.

[34] *In the Estate of Fuld (No.3)* [1968] P. 675, 696–697.

[35] *Simonin v Mallac* (1860) 2 Sw. & Tr. 67; *Ogden v Ogden* [1908] P. 46 (CA). See below, paras 17–020 *et seq*.

[36] *Apt v Apt* [1948] P. 83 (CA). See below, para.17–011.

[37] For further examples, see Beckett (1934) 15 B.Y.I.L. 46, 66–81; Falconbridge, pp.73–123; Robertson, pp.164–188, 245–279.

[38] [1945] Ch. 5 (Uthwatt J.).

if she survived the latter. Since Mrs Cohn was domiciled in Germany, succession to her estate was, as far as movable property was concerned, governed by the law of Germany. As the matter was before an English court, however, all questions of procedure, including questions of evidence, were governed by the law of England. The two relevant categories were, therefore, "succession to movable property" and "procedure and evidence." The connecting factor attached to the former was domicile (leading to German law) and that attached to the latter was the place of the action, England.

2–017   Under English law, it was laid down by s.184 of the Law of Property Act 1925 that where two persons die in circumstances rendering it uncertain which of them survived the other, such deaths will, for all purposes affecting the title to property, be presumed to have occurred in order of seniority, and accordingly the younger will be deemed to have survived the elder. If this rule were applicable, Mrs Oppenheimer would be deemed to have survived Mrs Cohn. Under German law, on the other hand, the presumption was that they died simultaneously. The result was that Mrs Oppenheimer could take under the will only if the English presumption were applied.

2–018   The court was thus faced with a problem of characterisation. How did it go about solving it? Interestingly, it did not characterise the concept of survivorship in the abstract. Instead, it looked first at the English provision and decided that it was inapplicable because it was not concerned with proof[39]:

> "The fact proved in this case is that it is impossible to say whether or not Mrs Oppenheimer survived Mrs Cohn. Proof stops there. Section 184 of the Law of Property Act 1925 does not come into the picture at all. It is not part of the law of evidence of the *lex fori*, for the section is not directed to helping in the ascertainment of any fact but contains a rule of substantive law directing a certain presumption to be made in all cases affecting the title to property."

2–019   Having thus characterised the English rule as being part of the law of succession rather than the law of evidence, the judge next turned his attention to the German rule. This was contained in legislation passed in 1939, which amended a provision of the German Civil Code. The latter provision was contained in Book I of the Code, which was entitled "General Principles," and was found under the heading "Natural Persons." His conclusion was that the German rule should also be characterised as falling within the category "succession" rather than "procedure and evidence." His reason was that its "terms and the place in which the repealed article dealing with the same general subject-matter was to be found" made it clear that this was the correct characterisation. The result was that the German rule was applicable and Mrs Oppenheimer did not take under the will.

2–020   What are we to make of this method of solving the problem? The first point to make is that the judge was characterising rules of law, not the general issue. Secondly, there can be little doubt that each rule was characterised independently of the other: the mere fact that the English rule was characterised as relating to succession did not *necessarily* mean that the German rule had to be

---

[39] [1945] Ch. 5, 7–8.

characterised in the same way. On the particular facts of the case this was what actually occurred, but on other facts the result could have been different.[40]

This illustrates one of the potential drawbacks of this approach. What would have happened if the German rule had been contained in a part of the German Civil Code headed "Evidence"? Presumably, the court would have regarded it as being part of the law of procedure and consequently inapplicable. The result would have been that *neither* rule would have applied—a rather awkward situation.[41] Alternatively, the court might have characterised the English rule as being part of the law of evidence. In this case, *both* rules might have been applicable.[42] Having said that, it is improbable that the court would have embarked upon the separate characterisation of the English and German rules without knowing that its doing so would result in the application of one, but only one, of the two rules. If that is correct, the drawback is more theoretical than real.

2–021

There have in fact been cases in which courts have reached absurd results through the application of this method of characterisation. The most notorious is probably a decision of the German Reichsgericht in 1882.[43] In this case, an action was brought in a German court on promissory notes issued in a foreign country and governed by the law of that country. The limitation period had expired under both the foreign law and under German law, so one might have thought that the action was bound to fail. The Reichsgericht, however, held that it could succeed. It reached this surprising conclusion by characterising, not the general question of limitation of actions, but the two rules contained in the foreign system of law and in German law. It concluded that the foreign rule was procedural and therefore inapplicable; the German rule, on the other hand, was characterised as substantive and therefore also inapplicable. The result was that neither applied.[44]

2–022

This brings us to our third point concerning *Re Cohn*. Given that the German rule was clearly of the same nature as the English (it also applied only where it could not be ascertained which person died first) why was it necessary for the English court to characterise it separately? The English court characterised the English rule as relating to succession on the entirely reasonable ground that it was not intended to help the court establish who in fact died first, but laid down a rule on the distribution of property to be followed in cases in which this could not be determined. The German rule did exactly the

2–023

---

[40] See also *Grupo Torras SA v Al-Sabah* [1999] C.L.C. 1469 (reversed on other grounds, [2001] Lloyd's Rep. Banking 36 (CA)) at p.1662, where the rule that Spanish civil proceedings must generally be stayed during the pendency of criminal proceedings was characterised as procedural, partly by reference to the fact that the principles were to be found in the Spanish Procedural Code.

[41] In such a situation it would have been impossible to prove that Mrs Oppenheimer survived Mrs Cohn, nor would there have been any justification for distributing the latter's estate on the assumption that this was the case; consequently, Mrs Oppenheimer would not have been entitled to take under the will.

[42] It could in fact be argued that in such a case the court would be obliged to find, *as a matter of fact*, that Mrs Oppenheimer survived Mrs Cohn. If this were so, the German rule could not come into play, since it applied only where it could not be proved who died first.

[43] *Entscheidungen des Reichsgerichts*, Vol.VII, p.21.

[44] This decision has not been followed in later cases in Germany: see Wolff, p.161, n.1. For further discussion of the way in which statutes of limitation should be characterised, see below, paras 2–042 *et seq.*

same. Surely, there could be no question of characterising it differently. If, through some accident of history, it had been set out in some part of the Code under the heading "Evidence," should this really have made the English court characterise it as procedural? Should it, moreover, have made any difference if it had been established that German courts characterised it as procedural for the purposes of their conflict rule?

2–024　　If one defines a rule of survivorship as a rule which is applicable only in circumstances in which it cannot be ascertained who died first, can one not say that all rules of survivorship are part of the law of succession, rather than the law of evidence? The advantage of such a conclusion, if it had been reached by the court in *Re Cohn*, would have been that the problem would be solved for ever. As it is, however, lawyers in future cases must always, at least in theory, consult experts in the foreign system of law to discover how the foreign rule on survivorship is characterised by the foreign system.

2–025　　**Re Maldonado.** The second case to consider is *Re Maldonado*,[45] which concerned a woman domiciled in Spain who died intestate and without living relatives. She left movable property in England, which was claimed by both the Spanish Government and the British Crown. This raised the question whether the applicable rule was that of Spanish law, which said that it went to the Spanish state, or English law, which said that it escheated to the Crown. This in turn depended on whether it came within the scope of the conflict rule which provides that succession to movables is governed by the law of the deceased's domicile (in which case the Spanish rule would apply) or whether it simply raised a question of ownerless property, *bona vacantia*, in which case it would be covered by the rule that title to property is governed by the law of the place where the property is situated. Since the property in question was in England, this would lead to the application of the English rule.

2–026　　The Court of Appeal held that since, under Spanish law, the Spanish state succeeded to property in such a situation as the final heir (*ultimus heres*), it was entitled to the movables in England. The English rule never came into the picture because the property was never ownerless: on the death of the deceased it passed to the Spanish state. If, on the other hand, the Spanish state had not claimed the property under the law of succession, but on some other basis—for example, as *bona vacantia*—the position would have been different: two earlier cases show that the claim of the British Crown would have been preferred.[46]

2–027　　At first sight, this decision might seem an entirely logical application of the English conflict rule. The truth of the matter is, however, that the difference between the English and Spanish rules was merely verbal. Most legal systems have a rule that the state takes the property of anyone who dies intestate and without heirs. It has been shown by Lipstein[47] that, until the 19th century, this rule was regarded on the Continent (as in England) as a *jus regale*, a prerogative right under public law akin to eminent domain. Then certain German writers put forward the view that in Roman law the state took as heir. This new theory spread rapidly during the middle of the 19th century and was

---

[45] [1954] P. 223 (CA).
[46] *Re Barnett's Trusts* [1902] 1 Ch. 847; *Re Musurus* [1936] 2 All E.R. 1666.
[47] [1954] C.L.J. 22.

adopted in many Continental codes, including the Spanish Civil Code of 1889. The content of the rule was not, however, affected by the change in its theoretical foundation. Today some countries adopt the one theory and some the other, but this appears to have no practical consequences as regards the rules applied, both procedural and substantive.[48]

In view of this, one is entitled to question whether the approach adopted by the Court of Appeal—which again involved characterisation of a rule of law, rather than an issue, and which may be regarded as an application of the theory that characterisation must be determined according to the *lex causae*— was sound. Is it desirable that the right to property in England should depend on a verbal formulation with no real content?   **2–028**

Another difficulty is that this approach gives rise to the same problem as *Re Cohn*: in future cases involving countries other than Spain, lawyers in England will have to discover which theory is adopted by the *lex domicilii*. This may sometimes be hard to discover. Would it not have been better for the court to have recognised that there is a real functional difference between rules of law giving a relative of the intestate the right to succeed and those giving such a right to the state or some other public authority or institution? The former are intended to uphold the presumed wishes of the intestate, while the latter are an expression of governmental power. The English court could then define the English conflict rule with greater precision by ruling that the concept of "succession" as used in the rule does not include a claim of the latter kind.[49]   **2–029**

Adams v National Bank of Greece. It might be thought from what was said above that English courts normally apply foreign law to characterise rules of law belonging to a foreign system. This is what they did in *Re Maldonado* and, less explicitly, in *Re Cohn*. However, these two cases are exceptional: normally English courts look to foreign law only to discover the nature and scope of the foreign rule, not to determine how it (or the general issue) should be characterised.[50]   **2–030**

Adams v National Bank of Greece[51] is a good illustration. In 1927, a Greek bank, the National Mortgage Bank of Greece, issued sterling-denominated mortgage bonds, which were repayable in 1957. The bonds contained a provision that they were governed by English law and they were guaranteed by another Greek bank, the National Bank of Greece. During the war, payment of interest on the bonds ceased and in 1949 Greek legislation provided for a moratorium on all further payments. The bondholders were unable to obtain redress because the Greek banks in question did no business in England and   **2–031**

---

[48] Lipstein, *op. cit.*, pp.25–26.

[49] See below, paras 27–013 *et seq.* The only American cases to have followed *Re Maldonado* appear to be two decisions of the New York Court of Appeals, *Re Utassi's Will*, 15 N.Y. 2d 436, 209 N.E. 2d 65 (1965) and *Khotim v Mikheev*, 41 N.Y. 2d 845, 362 N.E. 2d 253 (1977), but the rule laid down in these cases was subsequently reversed by legislation: see the New York Estates, Powers and Trusts Law, para.4–1.5.

[50] See, for example, *Huntington v Attrill* [1893] A.C. 150 (PC) (especially at p.155); *Ogden v Ogden* [1908] P. 46 (CA); *Re Korvine's Trusts* [1921] 1 Ch. 343; *Re Craven's Estate* [1937] Ch. 423 (better reported in 53 T.L.R. 694); *Apt v Apt* [1948] P. 83 (CA); *US v Inkley* [1989] Q.B. 255 (CA) (especially at p.265).

[51] [1961] A.C. 255.

were not subject to the jurisdiction of the English courts. If the bondholders had sued in Greece, the Greek courts would have applied the moratorium legislation.

2–032 In 1953, however, a Greek law provided for the amalgamation of the National Bank of Greece and a third Greek bank, the Bank of Athens. The new bank was called the National Bank of Greece and Athens. The Greek law provided that the new bank was the universal successor to all the assets and liabilities of the old banks. This meant that the National Bank of Greece and Athens was liable on the bonds, though, of course, the moratorium legislation prevented any action being brought against it in Greece. However, the Bank of Athens had been carrying on business in England and the new amalgamated bank continued to do so. Consequently, it was subject to the jurisdiction of the English courts, and a bondholder, Metliss, brought action in England claiming that it was liable under the guarantee. In *National Bank of Greece and Athens v Metliss*[52] the House of Lords held in favour of Metliss. The moratorium legislation was held to be inapplicable since it purported to alter obligations under a contract and was therefore to be characterised as contractual. Consequently, it could not affect a contract governed by English law.

2–033 Four days after the judgment at first instance was given, the Greek government passed a new law amending the law under which the banks were amalgamated. The new law provided that the amalgamated bank would be the universal successor to all the rights and obligations of the old banks, except obligations, whether as principal or guarantor, under bonds payable in foreign currency. The National Bank of Greece and Athens, which subsequently changed its name to the National Bank of Greece, immediately stopped making payments under the bonds. Another bondholder, Adams, brought new proceedings in the English courts. Did the new law relieve the National Bank of Greece from its liability under the bonds? This depended on how it was characterised. There can be no doubt that the new law was intended by those responsible for its enactment to be characterised as relating to the amalgamation of the banks. If this characterisation had been adopted by the English courts, they would have been obliged to hold that it was applicable in the case before them and that it gave a defence to the banks. The House of Lords, however, rejected this approach and gave judgment for Adams.

2–034 The whole point of the second Greek law was to force the English courts to apply the moratorium rule by re-enacting it as part of the amalgamation legislation. The House of Lords, however, refused to be taken in by this: they took the view that if the effect of the law was to discharge or alter a contractual right, it had to be regarded as contractual, whatever label might be attached to it by its author.[53] The purpose of the Greek law was to relieve the new bank of liability under the bonds and this purpose was not affected by the attempt of the Greek legislator to disguise it as something else.[54]

2–035 This case shows the undesirability of characterising rules of foreign law according to the legal system to which they belong. Attempts by foreign legislatures to force English courts to apply particular rules of law will, of

---

[52] [1958] A.C. 509.
[53] [1961] A.C. 255, at p.274, *per* Viscount Simonds.
[54] See also at p.283, *per* Lord Reid: " . . . we must look at the substance and effect of a foreign law . . . "

course, be rare. But even when there is no deliberate manipulation, there is no reason why the English court should allow foreign law to decide whether a particular rule should be applied in the case before it.

It is apparent that whenever an issue of characterisation arises, the court is **2–036** required to assess the arguments on their individual merits in the particular context, and will endeavour to avoid undue generalisation. The point can be made by reference to two recent decisions on legislative acts done in relation to contractual debts. In *Wight v Eckhardt Marine GmbH*,[55] the Privy Council characterised Bangladeshi statutory rules which provided for the restructuring of the business of an insolvent bank, and which had the effect of extinguishing claims against that bank and creating new claims against a new bank, as relating to the discharge of debts rather than the confiscation of property. They therefore concluded that the debt had been discharged by an act done under its proper law, and that it was not available for admission to proof in the insolvency. By contrast, in *Société Eram Shipping Co Ltd v Hong Kong and Shanghai Banking Corp Ltd*,[56] where an application was made to garnish, and thereby to discharge, a debt which was governed by the law of Hong Kong, the House of Lords held that the English statutory procedure for garnishment[57] of debts could not be applied to a debt owed by a Hong Kong debtor. Lord Hoffmann, in particular, expressed the view[58] that the compulsory discharge of debts by garnishment was akin to the confiscation of property and so was properly a matter for the *lex situs* rather than the *lex contractus*.

In *Through Transport Mutual Assurance Association (Eurasia) Ltd v New India Assurance Co Ltd*[59] the court characterised a direct claim before the Finnish courts and founded on a Finnish statute, brought by the victim of a tort against the liability insurer of the insured person who had caused loss, as contractual in nature, and therefore as a claim which fell within the scope of a contractual obligation to submit claims under the insurance to arbitration. It is unclear whether the construction of a contractual agreement to arbitrate raised a question of characterisation properly so called,[60] but to the extent that it did the court reached its conclusion without being constrained by the view of the matter which would have been taken by a Finnish court.[61]

Equitable claims. It will be apparent from what has been said that there **2–037** may well be a lack of exact correspondence between the internal divisions of English domestic law and those of the conflict of laws. One area in which the problem of characterisation may be seen to be particularly acute is when an

---

[55] [2003] UKPC 37, [2004] 1 A.C. 147.

[56] [2003] UKHL 30, [2004] 1 A.C. 260.

[57] Now known as the Third Party Debt Order procedure: CPR Pt 72, and discussed further below, Ch.24.

[58] At [54].

[59] [2004] EWCA Civ 1598, [2005] 1 Lloyd's Rep. 67 (CA).

[60] Because the question before the court was not one of choice of law to apply to a substantive dispute, but the interpretation of the obligations of an insurance contract which was governed by English domestic law.

[61] For further examples, see *Sweedman v Transport Accident Commission* [2006] HCA 8, (2006) 226 C.L.R. 362 (claim for reimbursement after payment to victim of traffic accident); *Gerling Australia Insurance Co Pty Ltd v Ludgater Holdings Ltd* [2009] NZCA 297, [2010] 2 N.Z.L.R. 145 (direct claim against insurer of tortfeasor).

English court is called upon to deal with a claim which, if it were wholly domestic, would be regarded as equitable. When such a case contains a foreign element, the question arises whether there is a category of issue labelled "equitable issues" for the purpose of choice of law. In some cases, such as where an application is made for specific performance of a contract, it will be clear that the issue is contractual, or contractual in part and procedural in part.[62] In others, such as where it is alleged that a defendant has committed a wrong which corresponds to the equitable wrongs of knowingly receiving trust property, or dishonestly assisting another in a breach of trust, it is arguable that the issue of substantive liability is to be characterised as tortious.[63] In still others, such as where it is alleged that a company director owes duties of loyalty to the company, it is arguable that the issue of substantive liability is to be characterised as falling within the category of issues reserved to the law of incorporation.[64] These instances lend no support to the proposition that the term "equitable" has a discrete role to play in the characterisation of issues for the purpose of choice of law. But other cases, principally Australian, tend to suggest that there may be a category of issues which, being labelled as "equitable", are as such governed by the *lex fori*.[65]

The most persuasive authority tends to suggest that where an obligation which would be equitable in domestic law arises in connection with another legal relationship for which a specific choice of law rule exists, the equitable claim will be characterised as falling within the domain of that other relationship and governed by the same law.[66] It follows that equitable obligations arising between parties to a contract, or to a relationship which is characterised as contractual, for example, will be governed by the *lex contractus*. However, as pointed out above, where obligations owed by one party to the other are governed, for choice of law purposes, by the statutory choice of law rule in the Rome I[67] or Rome II[68] Regulations, the first question will be whether, on its true construction, the Regulation stipulates the choice of law

---

[62] But where the contractual obligation is governed by the choice of law rule imposed by the Rome I Regulation, the question whether the choice of law rule stipulated by the Regulation applies to all or only some of the issues which arise for decision is answered by reference to the Regulation itself, and not by the common law principles of characterisation.

[63] See the analysis in *OJSC Oil Company Yugraneft v Abramovich* [2008] EWHC 2613 (Comm.), though if the dishonest assistance claim had arisen after the Rome II Regulation had come into effect, it is most likely that it, rather than the common law doctrine of characterisation, would have provided the applicable rule for choice of law.

[64] *Base Metal Trading Ltd v Shamurin* [2004] EWCA Civ 1316, [2005] 1 W.L.R. 1157.

[65] See further, below, paras 36–057 *et seq.*, where the cases are discussed; the Australian approach finds little support in England. See generally, Yeo, *Choice of Law for Equitable Doctrines* (2004).

[66] *Murakami v Wiryadi* [2010] NSWCA 7, (2010) 268 A.L.R. 377 (equitable obligations said to arise out of matrimonial property regime governed by the (contractual) law which governed that regime); *Fiona Trust & Holding Corp v Privalov* [2010] EWHC 3199 (Comm.), [148], [153].

[67] Regulation (EC) 593/2007 of the European Parliament and Council, examined in detail in Ch.32 below.

[68] Regulation (EC) 864/2007 of the European Parliament and Council, examined in detail in Chs 34–36 below.

rule which the court must apply. For if the answer is that it does, there is neither room nor need for a separate exercise in characterisation.

Conclusions. In essence, characterisation is a process of refining English   2–038
conflict rules by expressing them with greater precision. If the relevant rule is, for example, "succession to movables is governed by the *lex domicilii* of the deceased," characterisation involves deciding precisely which issues should be governed by the *lex domicilii*. The term "succession" is simply a useful way of referring to the bundle of issues that are regarded as appropriate for determination by the *lex domicilii*. To believe that a term such as "succession" has an objectively defined meaning which exists independently of the purpose for which it is used is mere conceptualism. It is, therefore, pointless to search for the "true" meaning of the term. Moreover, since the purpose of the exercise is to reformulate rules of English law, it is contrary to principle to look to foreign law for the answer. This seems to have been recognised by the English courts. For example, in *Macmillan Inc v Bishopsgate Investment Trust Plc (No.3)*, a recent English case in which the issue of characterisation received extended judicial discussion, Auld L.J. accepted that "the proper approach is to look beyond the formulation of the claim and to identify according to the *lex fori* the true issue or issues thrown up by the claim and the defence."[69]

The way the court should proceed is to consider the rationale of the English   2–039
conflict rule and the purpose of the rule of substantive law to be characterised. On this basis, it can decide whether the conflict rule should be regarded as covering the rule of substantive law.[70] In some cases, the court might conclude that the rule of substantive law should not be regarded as falling within either of the two potentially applicable conflict rules. In this situation, a new conflict rule should be created. As Mance L.J. said in *Raiffeisen Zentralbank Österreich AG v Five Star General Trading LLC*,[71] when dealing with the characterisation of issues:

> "The overall aim is to identify the most appropriate law to govern a particular issue. The classes or categories of issue which the law recognises at the first stage [i.e. for characterisation] are man-made, not natural. They have no inherent value, beyond their purpose in assisting to select the most appropriate law. A mechanistic application, without regard to the consequences, would conflict with the purpose for which they were conceived.

---

[69] [1996] 1 W.L.R. 387, 407 (CA). The decision was discussed and applied by the Court of Appeal in *Raiffeisen Zentralbank Österreich AG v Five Star General Trading LLC* [2001] Q.B. 825 (CA), and in *Haugesund Kommune v Depfa ACS Bank* [2010] EWCA Civ 579, [2012] 2 W.L.R. 199 (characterisation of "capacity" of a corporation to be undertaken in a broad internationalist sense).

[70] This approach borrows from interest analysis, but it is used to develop and refine the traditional English rules of the conflict of laws, not to replace them.

[71] [2001] Q.B. 825 (CA), at [27]. See also *Haugesund Kommune v Depfa ACS Bank* [2010] EWCA Civ 579, [2012] 2 W.L.R. 199 (characterisation of "capacity" of a corporation to be undertaken in a broad internationalist sense).

They may require redefinition or modification, or new categories may have to be recognised ... ".

2–040   Revocation of a will by the subsequent marriage of the testator will serve as an example to demonstrate this methodology. The English rule, which is found in s.18 of the Wills Act 1837, as substituted by s.18 of the Administration of Justice Act 1982, is subject to certain exceptions, one of which is that if it appears from the will that, at the time when it was made, the testator was expecting to be married to a particular person and that he intended that the will should not be revoked by the marriage, it will not be revoked by his marriage to that person.[72] This suggests that the purpose of the rule is to give expression to the presumed intention of the testator: except where the will is made in contemplation of marriage, one might assume that the change of circumstances brought about by the marriage will be such that the average testator would want to make a different disposition of his property. Scottish and French law take a different view. To which testators is it appropriate to apply the English rule? The best way of answering this question is to ask which testators would be most likely deliberately to have refrained from revoking their will because they thought it would be automatically revoked by reason of the English rule. The answer must be: those testators who, at the time of their marriage, thought that their affairs would be governed by English law. This suggests the law of the domicile at the time of marriage, both for movables and immovables.

2–041   This result cannot be attained by characterising the question as relating to succession (essential validity of a will). In such a case, the governing law would be, in the case of movables, the law of the testator's domicile at death and, in the case of immovables, the *lex situs*. If the question is characterised as a matter of matrimonial law, as was done by the Court of Appeal in *Re Martin*,[73] the applicable law would traditionally have been that of the *husband's* domicile at the time of marriage. Where the will is that of a woman, this would be unacceptable today. In Chapter 28 it is suggested that, where the parties to a marriage are domiciled in different countries, the matrimonial property regime should today be determined by the law of the country with which the parties and the marriage have their closest connection.[74] If revocation by subsequent marriage is characterised as being an aspect of the matrimonial property regime, this is the law that would govern. There is, however, an important difference between the matrimonial property regime in general and revocation of a will: the former must be governed by the same system of law for both spouses; the latter need not be. Consequently, there is good reason for regarding it as a special aspect of matrimonial law, with its own choice-of-law rule, the law of the domicile of the testator or testatrix at the time of the marriage. Alternatively, it could be regarded as an independent conflict category in its own right (with the same choice-of-law rule). If the

---

[72] s.18(3).
[73] [1900] P. 211.
[74] See below, para.28–010.

question had been free from authority, the latter would have been the better solution.[75]

If it is correct that the object of characterisation is rules of law, then rules **2–042** which are essentially of the same kind,[76] whether English or foreign, should be characterised in the same way. Examples have already been given of the difficulties caused by the failure of the courts to do this. Statutes of limitation provide a further example, one which also illustrates the defects of mechanical reasoning. The approach of the courts when faced with a question of limitation of actions traditionally was to inquire whether the limitation rule in issue takes away both the right and the remedy or only the remedy. A limitation rule of the former kind would be applied if (and only if) it formed part of the law governing the substance of the matter (the *lex causae*), while a rule of the latter kind was regarded as being procedural and was applicable if (and only if) it was part of the law of the forum.[77] The reasoning behind this distinction was that a rule which extinguished a right was just as much substantive as a rule which created a right, while a rule which left the right intact could only be procedural.[78]

Once it is accepted that characterisation is concerned with the redefinition **2–043** of the English conflict rule, however, this reasoning is seen as artificial. The difference between the two kinds of limitation rule is of little significance for most purposes. Except in a few special situations,[79] it makes no difference to the parties whether the rule is of the one kind or the other. Except in those special situations, a right without a remedy is the same as no right at all. Why should the determination of the governing law depend on such a distinction?

If we apply the methodology suggested above, it becomes apparent that **2–044** there is no justification for regarding any limitation rule as procedural, even if it does not extinguish the substantive right.[80] The rationale of the English conflict rule that matters of procedure are governed by the law of the forum is one of practicality and convenience. This clearly applies to matters such as service of process or courtroom procedure. It does not apply to statutes of limitation: it is no more impractical or inconvenient to apply a foreign

---

[75] See further below, paras 27–088 *et seq.*

[76] In deciding whether rules are essentially the same, one should disregard verbal formulations and consider the function of the rules.

[77] A number of English and foreign rules have been characterised as procedural for this purpose; see *British Linen Co v Drummond* (1830) 10 B. & C. 903; *Don v Lippmann* (1837) 5 Cl. & F. 1 (a Scottish case); *Huber v Steiner* (1835) 2 Bing.N.C. 202; *SA de Prayon v Koppel* (1933) 77 S.J. 800.

[78] But so far as concerns time limitation to institute a claim, since the enactment of Foreign Limitation Periods Act 1984, which declared that limitation was generally to be governed by the *lex causae*, it will be rare that one needs to draw this distinction in relation to the question when proceedings must be instituted. However, where the substantive issue is governed by the choice of law rules imposed by the Rome I or Rome II Regulations (as to which, see above, nn.11 and 12), the Regulation will apply its choice of law rule to the issue of limitation, and the 1984 Act is therefore displaced.

[79] For example, where set-off is pleaded.

[80] See the judgment of La Forest J. in *Tolofson v Jensen* (1994) 120 D.L.R. (4th) 289 (Sup Ct Can).

limitation rule that extinguishes only the remedy than it is to apply one that extinguishes the right as well.[81]

2-045 Besides being wrong in principle, the traditional approach produced unfortunate results. First, it required the practitioner to discover into which category the relevant rule fell. This could not always have been an easy task, especially in the case of a foreign rule. Secondly, in so far as it resulted in the application of the English rule, it could produce injustice, since a foreign debtor might have destroyed his receipts in reliance on the foreign limitation period. Thirdly, it could, as was pointed out above, lead to the absurd result of judgment being given for the plaintiff even though the claim was statute-barred under *both* relevant laws.[82]

2-046 Fortunately, the false turn taken by the English courts was corrected by the Foreign Limitation Periods Act 1984 and the Contracts (Applicable Law) Act 1990,[83] and Rome I Regulation,[84] the effect of which is that the foreign periods of limitation will be applied when the *lex causae* is the foreign law and the English periods when the *lex causae* is English law. It makes no difference whether the law extinguishes both the right and the remedy or the remedy alone.[85] However, characterisation rules based on the same superficial reasoning still exist in the case of other issues, for example s.4 of the Statute of Frauds.[86]

2-047 It is hoped that enough has been said to demonstrate how the problem should be approached. Characterisation has been made needlessly difficult by writers (and judges) who have created a conflict problem within a conflict problem by suggesting that characterisation itself involves a choice of law, that is to say that any court faced with a characterisation problem must first

---

[81] See the dissenting judgments of Mason C.J. and Deane J. in *McKain v Miller & Co* (1991) 174 C.L.R. 1. See, further, Beckett (1934) 15 B.Y.I.L. 46 at p.66; Cook (1933) 42 Yale L.J. 333 at pp.343–344. For a discussion of the general question, see *Classification of Limitation in Private International Law*, Law Com. No.114 (1982).

[82] See above, para.2–020.

[83] Sch.1, Art.10(1)(d).

[84] Regulation (EC) 593/2008 of the European Parliament and Council, Art.15(h), examined in detail in Ch.32 below.

[85] For a fuller discussion of this topic, see below, paras 7–054 *et seq*. Two further examples of uniform characterisation rules are found in s.3 of the Wills Act 1963. The first concerns provisions requiring special formalities to be observed by testators answering a particular description (for example, those under a certain age) and the second concerns provisions that witnesses to the execution of a will must possess certain qualifications. The Wills Act lays down that both classes of provisions are to be characterised as formal requirements, irrespective of how they may be regarded by the legal system of which they are part. It is easy to see that these characterisation rules serve a purpose. The policy behind the Wills Act is to uphold the validity of wills by providing that a will is formally valid if it complies with the requirements of any one of a number of different legal systems (see Rule 143, below). By characterising as formalities the two kinds of provisions mentioned above, the Act brings those provisions under the same regime, thus making it less likely that they will operate to invalidate a will.

[86] *Leroux v Brown* (1852) 12 C.B. 801, discussed below, paras 7–026 *et seq*. This decision was doubted by Willes J. in *Williams v Wheeler* (1806) 8 C.B. (N.S.) 299, 316, and *Gibson v Holland* (1865) L.R. 1 C.P. 1, 8 and condemned by nearly every writer who has discussed it: Beckett (1934) 15 B.Y.I.L. 46, 69–71; Falconbridge, pp.98–105; Robertson, pp.254–255; Cook, pp.229–231; Lorenzen, Ch.11; and see below, para.7–026. Many writers contrast the decision with that of the French Cour de cassation in *Benton v Horeau*, 1880 *Clunet* 480. See also the decision of the Supreme Court of California in *Bernkrant v Fowler*, 55 Cal. 2d 588, 360 P. 2d 906 (1961), discussed below, para.7–028.

decide what law should be applied to decide that problem. Once this idea is rejected, the way lies open for the courts to seek commonsense solutions based on practical considerations.[87]

2. THE INCIDENTAL OR PRELIMINARY QUESTION[88]

THE incidental[89] or preliminary question is a technical problem of consider- **2-048**
able difficulty which was first noticed by academic writers on the Continent.[90] It arises in this way. Suppose that an English court is called upon to decide a question which has foreign elements and, in order to do so, has to consider a subsidiary question which also has foreign elements. Suppose that by the relevant English rule of the conflict of laws the main question is governed by the law of a foreign country. Should the subsidiary question be governed by the English conflict rule appropriate to that question, or should it be governed by the appropriate conflict rule of the foreign system of law governing the main question? An illustration will make this clearer. Suppose[91] that a Greek national domiciled in Greece dies intestate leaving movables in England. By the English conflict of laws rule, succession to his movables is governed by Greek domestic law as the law of his domicile. Suppose that by Greek domestic law the wife of an intestate is entitled to a share of his movables. Such a share is claimed by W on the ground that she was the wife of the intestate. Suppose that the marriage between the intestate and W was celebrated in England and, though perfectly valid by English domestic law (which is the applicable law under the English conflict rule), was formally void by Greek domestic law (which is applicable under the Greek conflict rule)

---

[87] See, e.g. the approach in *Konamaneni v Rolls Royce Industrial Power (India) Ltd* [2002] 1 W.L.R. 1269 at [45]–[50] (determination of law governing right of shareholder to bring derivative action as matter for law of incorporation as opposed to *lex fori*). On whether claims for interest should be regarded as substantive or procedural, or whether rules governing the award of interest are substantive or procedural, see *Maher v Groupama Grand Est* [2009] EWCA Civ 1191, [2010] 1 W.L.R. 1564 (right to claim interest substantive; power to award interest procedural); *Abdel Hadi Abdullah Al Qahtani & Sons Beverage Industry Co v Antliff* [2010] EWHC 1735 (Comm.) (award of interest under Senior Courts Act 1981 s.35A, a procedural matter unaffected by restrictions imposed by the law which governed the substantive claim).

[88] Wengler, *Die Vorfrage im Kollisionenrecht* (1934) 8 *Rabel's Zeitschrift*, 148–251; Wengler, *The Law Applicable to Preliminary (Incidental) Questions* in *International Encyclopedia of Comparative Law*, Vol.III, Ch.7; Melchior, *Die Grundlagen des Deutschen Internationalen Privatrechts* (1932) pp.245–265; Schuz, *Modern Approach to the Incidental Question* (1997); Raape (1934) *Recueil des Cours*, IV, p.405 at pp.485–495; Maury (1936) *Recueil des Cours*, III, p.329 at pp.558–563; De Nova (1966) *Recueil des Cours*, II, p.434 at pp.557–569; Schmidt (1992) *Recueil des Cours*, II, p.305; Breslauer, *The Private International Law of Succession in England, America and Germany* (1937), Ch.4, pp.18–21; Robertson, Ch.6, pp.135–156; Wolff, ss.196–200; Cormack (1941) 14 So. Calif. L. Rev. 243–249; Gotlieb (1955) 33 Can. Bar Rev. 523–555; Rigaux, *La Théorie des Qualifications* (1956), pp.444–467; Louis-Lucas, 1957 *Rev. Crit.*, p.153; Lagarde, 1960 *Rev. Crit.*, p.459; Wengler, 1966 *Rev. Crit.*, pp.165–215; Hartley (1967) 16 I.C.L.Q. 680–691; Gotlieb (1977) 26 I.C.L.Q. 734.

[89] This term is used by Wolff and is considered the most suitable English expression. The French and German terms are "question préalable" and "Vorfrage."

[90] The discovery of the problem is often attributed to the German jurists Melchior and Wengler in 1932–34, but it had in fact been discussed prior to this: see Gotlieb (1977) 26 I.C.L.Q. 734, 735, n.5.

[91] Wolff, p.206.

because no Greek priest was present at the ceremony. Will W's claim to a share in the intestate's movables be determined by the English or the Greek conflict rule?

2–049　　It will be appreciated that this is a fundamental problem that can arise in any conflicts system (at least if it is of the traditional type). It will occur if, but only if, the following three conditions are satisfied. First, the main question must, by the English conflict rule, be governed by the law of some foreign country. Secondly, there must be a subsidiary question involving foreign elements which is capable of arising in its own right and which has a conflict rule of its own available for its determination. Thirdly, the English conflict rule for the determination of the subsidiary question must lead to a different result from the corresponding conflict rule adopted by the country whose law governs the main question.[92]

2–050　　In the past, academic writers have tried to find a general solution, based on logic and theory, that would apply in every case, though they are sharply divided as to what it should be.[93] The main arguments may be illustrated by taking as an example the problem set out above of the Greek dying intestate. According to one view, W should not be permitted to share in the estate because otherwise full effect would not be given to the English conflict rule that succession to the movables is governed by Greek law; according to another view, however, W *should* be permitted to share in the estate because otherwise full effect would not be given to the English conflict rule that the validity of the marriage is governed by English law. Put another way, the first view strives to maintain international harmony (by adopting the same solution as a Greek court would[94]) while the second gives priority to internal harmony (since W would be regarded as the deceased's wife for other purposes).

2–051　　Recently, however, the view has been gaining ground that it is neither possible nor desirable to find a solution which would apply in every case. Rather, each situation should be looked at separately in order to find a solution that produces the best results in that situation. As one writer put it, "there is really no problem of the incidental question, but as many problems as there are cases in which incidental questions can arise."[95] Instead of trying to solve the problem on the basis of general theory, one should consider the practical consequences in each situation. Following this approach, we will now discuss some of the situations in which the problem most commonly occurs.

2–052　　**Bigamy.** At first sight it might be thought that (where no question of polygamy arises) bigamy could not produce a problem in the conflict of laws, since all legal systems prohibit it. The difficulty, however, lies in the fact that, while all relevant systems of law may unite in rejecting bigamy, they may disagree as to whether or not a particular marriage is bigamous. This could

---

[92] *cf.* Robertson, pp.148–149. In order to simplify the discussion in the text, it is assumed that the English conflict rule refers the main question to the law of a foreign country directly and not by way of renvoi (transmission) from the law of another foreign country. Such a case of transmission would involve problems of greater complexity which are discussed by Gotlieb (1955) 33 Can. Bar Rev. 523, 526–528.

[93] See the references in n.88, above.

[94] To this extent, it has something in common with renvoi.

[95] Gotlieb (1955) 33 Can. Bar Rev. 523, 555; for a survey of the various schools of thought, see Gotlieb (1977) 26 I.C.L.Q. 734, 751–760.

occur where one of the parties to the marriage has entered into a previous marriage and, according to the conflict rules of one country, this marriage is valid and subsisting at the time of the second marriage while, according to the conflict rules of the other country, this is not the case. Such a situation could arise where the one regards the first marriage as valid, while the other regards it as void *ab initio*; or where a decree of nullity or divorce is not recognised by the one, but is recognised by the other.

In this situation, the principal question is whether the second marriage is invalid for bigamy. This raises a question of capacity,[96] which is governed (in general[97]) by the law of the parties' domicile. (It will be assumed, for the sake of simplicity, that the parties are both domiciled in the same country.) That law will no doubt say that the second marriage is valid only if neither party to it is a party to an earlier, subsisting marriage. This latter question is the incidental question and the problem then becomes: should one decide the incidental question by the conflict rules of the domicile or by the English conflict rules? 2–053

This problem can arise in two different situations: the first is where the prior marriage is valid and subsisting under the English conflict rules but not under the conflict rules of the domicile (for example, if a prior divorce is not recognised in England but is recognised in the country of the domicile); in the second, the position is reversed and the prior marriage is subsisting according to the conflict rules of the domicile but not according to the English conflict rules. These situations should be distinguished because the consequences of applying the conflict rules of the domicile differ markedly in the two cases: in the first, it will mean that, in English eyes, *both* marriages are valid and subsisting; while in the second, *neither* marriage will be valid and subsisting. 2–054

The Canadian case of *Schwebel v Ungar*[98] is an example of the first situation. Here the wife married her first husband in Hungary, where they were both domiciled, and this marriage was valid under all relevant systems of conflict of laws. Later the couple, who were both Jews, decided to emigrate to Israel. While *en route* to Israel, they were divorced by a Jewish ghet in Italy. This divorce was not recognised by the law of Hungary (where they were still domiciled), nor by the law of Italy, but was recognised by the law of Israel. The parties then acquired a domicile of choice in Israel, where they were regarded as having the status of single persons. Some time later the wife came to Toronto and, while still domiciled in Israel, married her second husband. Beforehand, the parties consulted a rabbi, who told them that it was legal for them to marry. They lived together for a few years and a child was born. Later, however, differences arose between them and the husband brought proceedings for nullity on the ground that the marriage was bigamous. The Supreme Court of Canada, affirming the decision of the Ontario Court of Appeal, held that the marriage was valid. Unfortunately, it is not entirely clear on what ground this conclusion was reached. Under Ontario law, the general rule for the recognition of a foreign divorce was that the divorce must be granted, or recognised, by the courts of the country in which the couple were domiciled 2–055

---

[96] See below, paras 17–082 *et seq.*

[97] For the general rule, and the exceptions, see below, paras 17–058 *et seq.*

[98] (1964) 48 D.L.R. (2d) 644 (Sup Ct Can), affirming (1963) 42 D.L.R. (2d) 622 (Ont CA).

at the time of the divorce. Under this rule, the divorce was invalid. There are, however, passages in the judgments of both courts which suggest that they were prepared to lay down an exception to this general rule to allow the recognition of the divorce on the facts of the case. This exception would presumably be that a divorce will also be recognised in Ontario if it is recognised by the law of the country in which, at any subsequent time, the parties become domiciled.[99] If this was the ground of the decision, the problem of the incidental question did not arise. It is, however, possible that the correct interpretation of the judgment is that the Canadian courts were prepared to uphold the second marriage without recognising the divorce. If this was so, the case is an example of the incidental question.[100]

2–056   If the second view is correct, it means that the courts decided the incidental question (the validity of the divorce) by the conflict rules of Israel, the country whose law governed the main question (the wife's capacity to marry). If this is the correct interpretation of the case—and there are passages in the judgments which suggest that it is[101]—the results are strange. If, before the marriage, the wife had petitioned the Ontario courts for a declaration that the divorce was valid, they would have ruled that it was not. Moreover, if, after the marriage, the first husband had come to Ontario and petitioned for a declaration of status, or a decree of nullity with reference to the first marriage, the courts would have ruled that he was still married. In other words, the wife would, in Ontario eyes, have been monogamously married to two different men at the same time. In spite of these conceptual difficulties, however, this may have been the fairest result on the facts of the case, since the parties had married in good faith and had lived together for some time.[102]

2–057   There is no English case in which the problem has arisen in the same way as in *Schwebel v Ungar*, but there are a number of cases concerning the situation in which the first marriage is no longer subsisting according to English conflict rules but is subsisting according to the conflict rules of the domicile. The first of these is the old case of *Ingham v Sachs*,[103] in which a man domiciled in Austria had divorced his first wife in Berlin and married his second wife in England. The court held[104] that the divorce would be recognised in England, but it was argued that, as it would not be recognised in Austria, he nevertheless lacked capacity to remarry under the law of his domicile. This argument was rejected by the court and the marriage held

---

[99] See (1964) 48 D.L.R. (2d) 644, 649 and (1963) 42 D.L.R. (2d) 622, 634.

[100] This assumes that the question whether the marriage was invalid for bigamy was governed *solely* by the law of the wife's domicile immediately prior to the marriage. It could, however, be argued that the marriage would be valid only if it complied with the law of *both* Israel and Ontario. The latter could be relevant either as the law of the place of celebration (as to which see below paras 17–103 *et seq.*) or as the *lex domicilii* of the second husband (on the basis that he lacked capacity to marry a woman who was a party to a subsisting marriage, a view approved by Simon P. in *Padolecchia v Padolecchia* [1968] P. 314, 336); see further below, para.17–082.

[101] See (1964) 48 D.L.R. (2d) 644, 649 and (1963) 42 D.L.R. (2d) 622, 633.

[102] The real contention between the parties was in fact a dispute regarding the wife's rights in the matrimonial home in Toronto.

[103] (1886) 56 L.T. 920.

[104] On grounds that would not be acceptable today.

valid.[105] A similar argument was, however, accepted in the more modern case of *Padolecchia v Padolecchia*.[106] Here a man domiciled in Italy divorced his first wife in Mexico and married his second wife in England. Sir Jocelyn Simon P. held that, as the divorce would not be recognised by the Italian rules of the conflict of laws, the second marriage was invalid. *Schwebel v Ungar* was approved. However, as the divorce would also not have been recognised under the English conflict rules, the result would (as the court recognised) have been the same whichever approach had been applied.

A case in which the choice of approach *was* decisive was *R. v Brentwood*   **2–058**
Marriage Registrar.[107] Here the husband, an Italian national domiciled in Switzerland, divorced his first wife in Switzerland and then wanted to marry a Spanish national, also domiciled in Switzerland. He could not do this in Switzerland because the Swiss conflict rule on capacity to marry looked to the law of the nationality, and the divorce was not recognised under the Italian conflict rule. The couple came to England to get married but the registrar refused to marry them. An application for mandamus was rejected by the Divisional Court. In this case the problem was complicated by the introduction of renvoi, though the court did not analyse it in these terms. This is because the divorce was valid under both English and Swiss law; it was not recognised under Italian law and this law governed the main question (the husband's capacity) under the Swiss conflict rule. By virtue of the renvoi doctrine the English court was applying Italian law to decide the main question; it was also applying the Italian conflict rule to decide the incidental question.

The results of this decision were in some ways unfortunate. As she was a   **2–059**
Swiss national, the first wife was able to remarry in Switzerland and had done so. But the husband was barred from marriage as long as he retained his Italian nationality. In effect he was in a state of matrimonial limbo: his first marriage was no longer subsisting under either English or Swiss conflict rules but it nevertheless prevented him from remarrying. In spite of this, however, there were arguments in favour of the decision: the parties had no connection with England and came here simply to evade the law of the country in which they were domiciled and in which they intended to live. The case did not really concern England and if the order had been granted it could have been regarded as an interference in the affairs of Switzerland. For these reasons the court said that it would not have exercised its discretion to grant the order even if it had been established that there was no impediment to the marriage.

The solution to the incidental question applied in the *Brentwood Marriage*   **2–060**
Registrar case has, however, been overturned by Parliament. Under s.50 of the Family Law Act 1986, where a decree of divorce or nullity is granted by an English court, or is recognised in England, the fact that the decree would not be recognised elsewhere will not preclude either party to the marriage from remarrying in England, nor will it render the remarriage of either party

---

[105] As the second wife was domiciled in England, the same result would have been reached on the basis of the rule in *Sottomayor v De Barros (No.2)* (1879) 5 P.D. 94 (discussed below, at paras 17–109 *et seq.*), in which case the problem of the incidental question would not have arisen.
[106] [1968] P. 314. See also *In the Marriage of Barriga* (1981) F.L.C. para.91–088.
[107] [1968] 2 Q.B. 956. For a similar decision in Scotland, see *Rojas, Petr.*, 1967 S.L.T. (Sh Ct) 24.

invalid, irrespective of whether the remarriage takes place within or outside the United Kingdom.[108] This solves the problem in the situations covered by the Act;[109] it does not, however, mean that the same solution will apply in the reverse case, that is where the divorce or nullity decree is not recognised in England, but is recognised in the foreign country: it remains to be seen whether *Schwebel v Ungar*[110] will be followed in England.[111]

2–061   **Legitimacy.** The incidental question can occur here if, as will often be the case, the legitimacy of the child depends on the validity of the parents' marriage. The problem then arises whether this latter question should be decided by English conflict rules or by the conflict rules of the country whose law governs the main question. The matter is often complicated by the fact that the question of legitimacy may itself be incidental to a question of succession. Where this is so, an incidental question of the second degree may arise. For the sake of simplicity, however, it will be assumed for the moment that the legitimacy of the child is the principal question; succession will be dealt with separately below.

2–062   Under Rule 113,[112] a child is legitimate in England (1) if he was born in lawful wedlock (i.e. if his parents' marriage was valid under English conflict rules) or (2) if he is legitimate by the law of the domicile of each of his parents at the date of his birth. The latter case includes the situation where he is legitimate under the law of the domicile by reason of the fact that, under the conflict rules of that country (or those countries), his parents' marriage was valid. This means that the child will be legitimate if the parents' marriage is valid either by English conflict rules or by the conflict rules of the parents' domicile. In other words, the incidental question is decided by whichever of the two systems of conflict of laws is more favourable to the child's legitimacy.

2–063   The second alternative may be made clearer if we take as an example a slightly modified version of the facts in *Re Bischoffsheim*.[113] H and W, while domiciled in England,[114] go through a ceremony of marriage in New York. Under English internal law, the marriage is invalid because the parties lack the capacity to marry each other. Under the English conflict rule, this question is

---

[108] This replaces s.7 of the Recognition of Divorces and Legal Separations Act 1971, which was, however, more limited in scope: it applied only to remarriages in the UK after a foreign divorce. For cases (before the 1986 Act) applying the same solution to situations outside the scope of the 1971 Act, see *Perrini v Perrini* [1979] Fam. 84 (remarriage following a foreign decree of nullity) and *Lawrence v Lawrence* [1985] Fam. 106 (CA) (remarriage outside the UK). The decisions in both these cases would have been the same under the 1986 Act.

[109] One situation not covered by the Act to which the same solution should nevertheless be applied is where there is no decree of divorce or nullity, but the first marriage is void *ab initio* under the English rules of the conflict of laws, though it is valid under the foreign rules of the conflict of laws.

[110] See above.

[111] See *Recognition of Foreign Nullity Decrees*, Law Com. No.137 (1984), para.6.60.

[112] See below paras 20–010 *et seq.*

[113] [1948] Ch. 79. This case has been subject to criticism (discussed at paras 20–021 *et seq.*, below) but most of this does not apply to the problem discussed here.

[114] In *Re Bischoffsheim* it was uncertain whether the parties were domiciled in England or in New York, but Romer J. held that the child would be legitimate even if they were domiciled in England.

decided by the law of the domicile and the marriage is therefore invalid in England. Under New York law, on the other hand, the marriage is valid. Let us assume that under the New York conflict rule the validity of the marriage is governed by the internal law of New York.[115] The marriage is therefore valid under the New York conflict rule. After the marriage, H and W acquire a domicile in New York and a child is born to them. Let us assume that the principal question before an English court is whether the child is legitimate.[116] If we refer that question to the law of the parents' domicile at the date of the child's birth (New York law), we find that it depends on the answer to an incidental question, the validity of the marriage. If we decide this incidental question by New York conflict rules, we find that the child is legitimate.[117] If, on the other hand, the marriage had been valid by the English conflict rule and invalid by the New York conflict rule, the first branch of the rule could have been applied and the child would still have been legitimate.

Succession. In general, questions of succession are governed, in the case   **2–064** of movables, by the law of the domicile of the deceased at death and, in the case of immovables, by the *lex situs*.[118] Under this law, the right to share in the estate may depend on whether a person is the wife or child of the deceased (or of some other person). If the principal question is the right to share in the estate, what law should decide these incidental questions?

There is authority to suggest that, in some situations at least, the conflict   **2–065** rules of the *lex successionis* should be applied. In the Australian case of *Haque v Haque*,[119] the deceased, a Moslem who was at all times domiciled in India, married his first wife in India under Islamic law and had two daughters by her. He later went through an Islamic ceremony of marriage in Australia with his second wife. This was valid under Islamic law but did not comply with the formal requirements of Australian law and was consequently invalid under the Australian conflict rule. A son and daughter were born of this union. Subsequently, the second wife was divorced under Islamic law. The husband then died, after making a will leaving his estate to his brother. The High Court of Australia held that the law governing succession to his movables was the law of India, under which Islamic law was to be applied. This grants succession rights, in various shares, to a man's wives, sons and daughters. The High Court held that in order to determine who was the "wife," "son," or "daughter" of the deceased for this purpose, the validity of the deceased's marriages

---

[115] In *Re Bischoffsheim* it was stated by Romer J. that the marriage was valid under New York law but it is unclear whether this meant only under New York internal law or also under the New York conflict rules. It is, however, quite likely that the marriage would have been valid under the New York conflict rules, either on the ground that capacity to marry is governed by the law of the place of celebration or on the ground that, under New York law, the parties were domiciled in New York at the date of the marriage.

[116] In *Re Bischoffsheim* the principal question was actually whether the child could take under an English will. The additional complications raised by this are discussed below, at paras 20–021 *et seq.*

[117] In addition to *Re Bischoffsheim*, authority for this conclusion may be found in *Hashmi v Hashmi* [1972] Fam. 36 and *Seedat's Executors v The Master* 1917 A.D. 302 (South Africa).

[118] See paras 27R–010 *et seq.*, below.

[119] (1962) 108 C.L.R. 230.

had to be decided by Islamic law.[120] Under this, both marriages were valid and, though the second wife was excluded by reason of the divorce, her children could share in the estate together with the first wife and her two daughters.

2–066   This case raised special problems because a system of religious law was involved, but it is likely that the same approach would have been applied even if this had not been the case.[121] This does not, however, mean that the conflict rules of the *lex successionis* will necessarily be applied in all cases, particularly where this would lead to the exclusion of someone regarded by English conflict of laws as the wife or child of the deceased. Thus, for example, it is by no means certain that, in the problem given at the beginning of this discussion,[122] the wife's claim would be rejected, especially if she had lived with her husband in England up until his death.

2–067   **Conclusions.**   Only three areas of the law have been discussed but it is hoped that enough has been said to show both the varied situations in which the problem can arise and the varied considerations that should be taken into account in order to find a solution. In particular, it is suggested that *a priori* reasoning should be avoided and a flexible approach adopted, taking into account policy considerations such as those of favouring legitimacy and upholding the validity of marriages.

---

[120] Unfortunately the court did not consider whether this was the law that would have been applicable under Indian conflict rules, but it is likely that it was. See also *per* Lord Greene M.R. in *Baindail v Baindail* [1946] P. 122, 127 (CA).

[121] See *Re Johnson* [1903] 1 Ch. 821.

[122] See above, para.2–048.

CHAPTER 3

THE TIME FACTOR

THE conflict of laws deals primarily with the application of laws in space. Yet **3–001** as in other branches of law, so in the conflict of laws, problems of time cannot be altogether ignored. There is a considerable continental literature on the time factor in the conflict of laws, and a growing awareness of the problem by English writers,[1] though as might be expected the courts have dealt with it in a somewhat empirical fashion.

Three different types of problem have been primarily identified by writers. **3–002** The time factor may become significant if there is a change in the content of the conflict rule of the forum, or in the content of the connecting factor[2] (for example, where a person's domicile is changed), or in the content of the *lex causae*, that is, the foreign law to which the connecting factor refers. It so happens that the Wills Act 1963[3] furnishes a statutory solution to each type of problem in so far as it may arise in connection with the formal validity of wills. The Act laid down a new conflict rule (or rules) in substitution for earlier rules contained in the Wills Act 1861. In the first place, s.7(2) provides that the Act shall come into force on January 1, 1964; s.7(3) repeals the Wills Act 1861; and s.7(4) provides that the repeal of that Act shall not invalidate a will executed before January 1, 1964. Secondly, s.1 provides that a will shall be treated as properly executed if its execution conformed to the internal law in force in the country where, at the time of its execution or of the testator's death, he was domiciled or had his habitual residence, or in a State of which, at either of those times, he was a national.[4] The section thus indicates the time with reference to which the connecting factors of domicile, habitual residence and nationality must be ascertained. Thirdly, s.6(3) provides that regard shall be had to the formal requirements of a particular law at the time of execution, but that this shall not prevent account being taken of an alteration of law affecting wills executed at that time if the alteration enables the will to be

---

[1] Roubier, *Le Droit Transitoire* (2nd ed. 1960); Gavalda, *Les Conflits dans le temps en droit international privé* (1955); F.A. Mann (1954) 31 B.Y.I.L. 217 (with copious references to continental literature and case law); Grodecki (1959) 35 B.Y.I.L. 58; Spiro (1960) 9 I.C.L.Q. 357; Rabel, Vol.4, pp.503–519; Batiffol and Lagarde, Vol.1, pp.512–524; Lewald (1939) *Recueil des Cours*, III, 5, 94–99; Wengler (1958) *Rabel's Zeitschrift* 535–572; Rigaux (1966) *Recueil des Cours*, I, 333; Kahn-Freund (1974) *Recueil des Cours*, III, 139, 398–403, 441–446; Grodecki, in Lipstein ed., *International Encyclopedia of Comparative Law*, Vol.III, Ch.8 (1975); Pryles (1980) 6 Monash U.L.Rev. 225; Fassberg (1990) 39 I.C.L.Q. 856; (1979) 58 *Annuaire de l'Institut de Droit International*, Vol.I, pp.1–96; *ibid.* Vol.II, pp.179–190; (1981) 59 *Annuaire de l'Institut de Droit International*, Vol.I, pp.285–293; *ibid.* Vol.II, pp.52–115, 246–251.

[2] For the meaning of this expression, see above, para.1–079.

[3] See Rule 152 and Comment thereto.

[4] The Act also permits conformity with the law of the place of execution. But since this is a constant and not a variable connecting factor, it raises no problems as to time.

treated as properly executed. Thus, retrospective alterations in the *lex causae* made after the execution of the will are relevant if they validate but irrelevant if they invalidate the will.

3–003   **Changes in the conflict rule of the forum.** A change in the conflict rule of the forum (which French writers call *le conflit transitoire*) probably does not differ from a change in any other rule of law and its effect must therefore be ascertained in accordance with the familiar English rules of statutory interpretation and of judicial precedent. It is unnecessary to discuss those rules in a work on the conflict of laws, but we must call attention briefly to the different ways in which such changes may occur and to some problems which are peculiar to the conflict of laws.

3–004   In English law such changes may occur in three ways: a statute may alter an earlier statutory rule; a statute may alter an earlier rule of judge-made law; or a judicial decision may reverse an earlier judicial rule, or declare a new one. The Wills Act 1963 (noted above) is an example of the first type, and s.72 of the Bills of Exchange Act 1882 is an example of the second.[5] In each of these cases there is usually no problem, because the statute usually contains precise language indicating when it comes into force and to what extent, if any, it is retrospective. If it does not do so, one is thrown back on the general principles of statutory construction, according to which there is a strong but rebuttable presumption that a statute is not intended to have retrospective effect unless it is procedural or declaratory.[6]

3–005   One curious example may be noted of a statutory provision which was evidently intended to lay down a new conflict rule in substitution for an earlier judge-made rule, but which, because it did not expressly abolish the earlier rule, was held by the courts to leave the old rule subsisting side by side with the new. This is s.8(1) of the Legitimacy Act 1926 (now repealed and replaced by s.3 of the Legitimacy Act 1976). At common law, the question whether an illegitimate child was legitimated by the subsequent marriage of his parents was held to depend on the law of the father's domicile at the date of the child's birth and at the date of the subsequent marriage.[7] Section 8(1) of the Legitimacy Act 1926 provided that where the parents of an illegitimate person marry or have married one another, whether before or after the commencement of the Act, and the father was or is, at the time of the marriage, domiciled in a foreign country by the law of which the illegitimate person became legitimated by virtue of such subsequent marriage, that person, if living, should be recognised as having been so legitimated from the commencement of the Act or from the date of the marriage, whichever last happened, notwithstanding that his father was not at the time of the birth of such person domiciled in a country in which legitimation by subsequent marriage was permitted by law.[8] One may surmise that the framers of this subsection intended to abolish the rule of common law and to make the father's domicile

---

[5] See Rules 240 and 241 and Comment thereto. In *Re Marseilles Extension Railway and Land Co.* (1885) 30 Ch.D. 598 the court in 1885 applied the pre-1882 rules of common law to a bill of exchange drawn, accepted and indorsed before the Act came into force.

[6] Bennion, *Statutory Interpretation* (5th ed. 2008), pp.315 *et seq.*

[7] See Rule 116.

[8] See Rule 117.

at the date of the child's birth irrelevant in future. But they did not use express language to this effect, and so the courts have held that the old rule of common law still exists and can still be resorted to by a litigant if it suits him to do so, as in some situations it does.[9]

Judge-made law is retrospective in operation, whereas statute law is usually **3–006** prospective. Some very strange consequences sometimes follow from a retrospective alteration in a conflict rule of the forum by judicial or legislative action, especially in the field of family relations. Thus, the English conflict rule for the recognition of foreign divorces was radically altered by judicial action in 1953[10] and again in 1967,[11] and by legislative action in 1972[12] and again in 1986.[13] In *Hornett v Hornett*,[14] a man domiciled in England married in 1919 a woman domiciled before her marriage in France. They lived together in France and England until 1924, when the wife obtained a divorce in France. The husband heard about this divorce in 1925. He then resumed cohabitation with his wife in England until 1936, when they parted. No children were born of this cohabitation. In 1969 the husband petitioned for a declaration that the divorce would be recognised in England. Although it could not have been recognised before 1967, the divorce was recognised under the new judge-made rule declared by the House of Lords in that year.[15]

If we alter the facts a little, the consequences of this retrospective alteration **3–007** of the conflict rule are startling:

(a) If children had been born of the resumed cohabitation between the parties after the divorce, would they have been legitimate when born, but rendered illegitimate by the subsequent recognition of the decree?

(b) If the husband had gone through a ceremony of marriage with another woman in 1945, and his second marriage had been annulled for bigamy in 1950, and his second wife had then remarried, would the result of recognising the divorce in 1971 be to invalidate the nullity decree and also the second wife's second marriage?

(c) If the husband had died intestate in 1940, and a share in his property had been distributed to his French wife as his surviving spouse, would she have had to return it when the new conflict rule declared by the House of Lords in 1967 validated her French divorce?[16]

---

[9] See e.g. *Re Askew* [1930] 2 Ch. 259; *Re Hurll* [1952] Ch. 722; see below, paras 20R–048 *et seq.*

[10] *Travers v Holley* [1953] P. 246 (CA); below, para.18–068.

[11] *Indyka v Indyka* [1969] 1 A.C. 33; below, para.18–069.

[12] Recognition of Divorces and Legal Separations Act 1971, repealed and replaced by Family Law Act 1986, Pt II. The provisions of the 1971 Act for recognising divorces obtained in foreign countries outside the British Isles were retrospective: s.10(4).

[13] Family Law Act 1986, Pt II. These provisions are, in general, retrospective: see s.51(1), (2), (3). Part II of the 1986 Act, however, does not now apply to an overseas divorce as regards which provision for its recognition is made by Council Regulation (EC) 2201/2003 (the Brussels IIa Regulation). See below, para.18–093, and Rule 90.

[14] [1971] P. 255. See also *Edward v Edward Estate* [1987] 5 W.W.R. 289 (Sask CA).

[15] *Indyka v Indyka* [1969] 1 A.C. 33.

[16] See the powerful arguments adduced by Latey J. in the court of first instance and by Russell L.J. (dissenting) in the Court of Appeal in *Indyka v Indyka* [1967] P. 233, 244–245, 262–263.

3–008   **Changes in the connecting factor.** From the temporal point of view the connecting factor in a rule of the conflict of laws may be either constant or variable. It may be of such a character that it necessarily refers to a particular moment of time and no other, or it may be liable to change so that further definition is required. For instance, a conflict rule which referred the question of an illegitimate child's legitimation to the law of his father's domicile would be meaningless unless it defined the moment of time at which the father's domicile was relevant. This is achieved by s.3 of the Legitimacy Act 1976, which defines this moment as the time of the father's marriage. Similarly, the simple rule that a person domiciled in a Member State of the European Union which is subject to the Brussels I Regulation,[17] shall be sued in the courts of that State needs to be given greater precision if the defendant's domicile is not constant. Does the court's jurisdiction depend upon the defendant being domiciled in the forum when process is issued or when it is served?[18]

3–009   Examples of constant connecting factors in the English conflict of laws include the *situs* of an immovable, the place where a marriage is celebrated, a will executed, or a tort committed. Examples of varying connecting factors include the *situs* of a movable, the flag of a ship, and the nationality, domicile or residence of an individual.

3–010   The question whether one should refer, e.g. to the law of the father's domicile at the date of the child's birth or at the date of the subsequent marriage in order to discover whether a child has been legitimated is simply a question of formulating the most convenient and just conflict rule, and the time factor, though it cannot be disregarded, is not the dominant consideration.[19] It does not seem to differ in principle from the question whether one should refer to the law of the father's or of the mother's domicile. The question is discussed elsewhere in this book as and when it arises, and here it is only necessary to give the reader a brief outline of the type of problem which requires solution. Should the law of the matrimonial domicile at the time of the marriage or at the time of each subsequent acquisition determine the rights of husband and wife to movable property acquired after the date of their marriage?[20] Is capacity to make a will[21] and is the construction of wills[22] governed by the law of the testator's domicile at the time of making the will or at the time of his death? Is revocation of wills governed by the law of the testator's domicile at the time of his death or at the time of the alleged act of revocation?[23] Is the monogamous or polygamous character of a marriage

---

[17] Council Regulation (EC) 44/2001: see below, para.11–013.

[18] According to *Canada Trust Co v Stolzenberg (No.2)* [2002] 1 A.C. 1 (below, para.11–255), a case decided under the Brussels Convention, it was held that the material date was that of issue, not of service. A related problem arises in relation to the domicile rule in respect of agreements on choice of court under Art.23 of the Brussels I Regulation: is the material date for the determination of a person's domicile that on which the agreement on jurisdiction was made, or that on which the proceedings were instituted? An authoritative answer has not yet been given; see below, para.12–121.

[19] For this reason, it has been doubted whether it is appropriate to treat a change in the connecting factor (which French writers call *le conflit mobile*) as a problem of time in the conflict of laws. See Grodecki (1959) 35 B.Y.I.L. 58.

[20] See Rule 174.

[21] See Rule 151.

[22] See Rule 156.

[23] See Rule 159.

determined once and for all at its inception, or may it change by reason of subsequent events, e.g. a change in the parties' domicile?[24] If chattels are taken from one country to another by someone not the owner and disposed of there to a third party, does the first or the second *lex situs* determine whether the owner loses his title?[25] Since a decision on any of these questions has no relevance to any of the others, it is obviously impossible to formulate a general principle.

Once the time at which the connecting factor must exist has been ascer-   **3–011** tained, an additional problem of time may arise. Is the court, in ascertaining the existence of the connecting factor at the relevant time, confined to scrutinising facts and circumstances which exist at that time or can it take account of facts and circumstances which are subsequent thereto?[26] Again it would appear that it is not possible to formulate a general principle. The relevance or otherwise of subsequent facts and circumstances will vary in the light of the function of the choice of law rule of which the particular connecting factor forms part. Thus in ascertaining the law applicable to a contract, at common law, only facts and circumstances existing at the time the contract was made could be examined.[27] On the other hand when it was necessary to determine whether, at the time of the institution of proceedings for nullity in a foreign country, the petitioner had a real and substantial connection with that country with the result that the foreign nullity decree could be recognised in England, at common law it was possible that events subsequent to the institution of proceedings could be looked at.[28]

Legislative introduction of new choice of law rule. A distinct question   **3–012** arises when legislation imposes a new choice of law rule: the question of the time factor will be simply one of statutory interpretation. It may be generally assumed that the legislation will specify its temporal scope and will, in this sense, answer by legislative *fiat* the question of time which would otherwise arise. In the case of legislation imposing a statutory choice of law rule for contracts, the Rome I Regulation, provided that it applies to contracts made after December 17, 2009:[29] the only question capable of arising is one of pinpointing the precise date on which a contract, resulting from a process of negotiation, is considered to have been made; on this it is to be supposed than an English court would be guided by its own notions of offer and acceptance. In the case of the Rome II Regulation, imposing a statutory choice of law rule

---

[24] See Rule 79.

[25] See Rule 134.

[26] See Pryles (1980) 6 Monash U.L. Rev. 225, 240–242.

[27] *Whitworth Street Estates (Manchester) Ltd v James Miller and Partners Ltd* [1970] A.C. 583. It seems probable that the position was otherwise under the Rome Convention (Contracts (Applicable Law) Act 1990, Sch.1, which applied to contracts made after April 1, 1991), Art.4, and is otherwise under the Rome I Regulation (Regulation (EC) 593/2008, which applies to contracts made after December 17, 2009) Art.4, though the test of being "more closely connected" is not further limited in terms of those facts and matters which may be used to satisfy it.

[28] *Law v Gustin* [1976] Fam. 155, 160. The law relating to the recognition of foreign annulments is now contained in the Family Law Act 1986, Pt II, as modified as to its scope by Council Regulation (EC) 2201/2003 (the Brussels IIa Regulation). The Act does not adopt the test of real and substantial connection. See below, paras 18–092 *et seq.*

[29] Regulation (EC) 593/2008, Art.28.

for non-contractual obligations,[30] the appearance of inconsistency of language as between Arts 31 and 32 was resolved by the European Court, which held that the Regulation applied to events giving rise to damage occurring after January 11, 2009, and that the date on which proceedings were instituted, or on which the court was required to make the choice of law, was immaterial.[31]

3–013   **Changes in the lex causae.** Changes in the *lex causae* present much the most important and difficult problems of time in the conflict of laws, especially when the change purports to have retrospective effect. The overwhelming weight of opinion among writers is that the forum should apply the *lex causae* in its entirety, including its transitional rules. This is certainly the prevailing practice of courts on the continent of Europe. It is probably the prevailing practice of the English courts, although there is one case, *Lynch v Provisional Government of Paraguay*,[32] which is often cited for the contrary proposition. Much confusion has resulted from ambiguous formulations of the conflict rule, and these in turn have suffered from a failure to distinguish between constant and variable connecting factors. If, for example, the forum's conflict rule says that succession to immovables is governed by the *lex situs*, the connecting factor is constant, no further definition is required, and it is natural and proper for courts to apply the *lex situs* as it exists from time to time. But if the forum's conflict rule says that succession to movables is governed by the law of the deceased's domicile, the connecting factor is variable, further definition is required to make the rule more precise, and so the words "at the time of his death" are added in order to define the time at which his domicile is relevant. The effect is to exclude reference to any earlier domicile, but courts have sometimes assumed that the effect is also to exclude changes in the law of the domicile made after the death of the deceased. This assumption, it is submitted, is unnecessary and improper, for the two questions are really quite distinct.

3–014   Although it must be emphasised that the problem is always basically the same, namely, should the forum apply or disregard subsequent changes in the *lex causae*, it will be convenient to deal with it under the following heads, arranged according to subject-matter: (a) succession to immovables; (b) succession to movables; (c) torts; (d) discharge of contracts; (e) legitimation; (f) matrimonial property; (g) validity of marriage. In conclusion, something will be said on (h) the extent to which public policy may occasionally induce the forum to refuse recognition to foreign retrospective laws, and on (i) the time problem in cases where it may be necessary to refer to a foreign law other than the *lex causae* as a *datum* which is relevant to deciding the case.

3–015   (a) *Succession to immovables.* In *Nelson v Bridport*,[33] the King of the Two Sicilies granted land in Sicily to Admiral Nelson for himself and the heirs of his body, with power to appoint a successor. By his will the Admiral devised the land to trustees in trust for his brother W for life with remainders over.

---

[30] Regulation (EC) 864/2007.
[31] Case C–412/10 *Homawoo v GMF Assurances SA* [2012] I.L.Pr. 49.
[32] (1871) L.R. 2 P. & D. 268.
[33] (1846) 8 Beav. 547.

After the Admiral's death, and in the lifetime of W, a law was passed in Sicily abolishing entails and making the persons lawfully in possession of such estates the absolute owners thereof. Taking advantage of this law, W devised the land to his daughter, from whom it was claimed by the remainderman under the Admiral's will. In giving judgment for the defendant, Lord Langdale M.R. took it for granted that he had to apply the law of Sicily as it existed from time to time and not as it was at the time of the Admiral's death or at the time of the original grant.

(b) *Succession to movables.* However, an opposite result was reached in **3–016** *Lynch v Provisional Government of Paraguay.*[34] A testator who had been dictator of Paraguay died domiciled there having by his will left movable property in England to the plaintiff. Two months after his death, but before probate of the will had been granted in England, there was a revolution in Paraguay, and the new Government passed a decree declaring all the testator's property wherever situate to be the property of the State and depriving his will of any validity in England or elsewhere. This decree purported to relate back to the testator's death. The plaintiff applied for a grant of probate as universal legatee under the will. Her application was opposed by the new Government. The Government's opposition was bound to fail, because the decree was penal[35] and because property in England could not be confiscated by a foreign Government.[36] But Lord Penzance, in granting probate to the plaintiff, preferred to rest his judgment on the ground that English law adopts the law of the domicile "as it stands at the time of the death" and does not undertake to give effect to subsequent retrospective changes in that law. In support of this proposition he quoted Story's formulation that succession to movables is governed by the law of the domicile "at the time of the death," without appearing to realise that the last six words were intended to qualify "domicile" and not "law," and that Story was never considering the effect of subsequent retrospective changes in the law.

Lord Penzance's manifest inclination to uphold the will on the peculiar **3–017** facts of the case is understandable, but his wide formulation has been much criticised by writers[37] on the ground that it failed to give effect to the transitional law of the *lex causae*, and appeared to do so irrespective of the content of that law. If, for example, the will had been defective in point of form, e.g. because the law of Paraguay required all wills to be witnessed by a notary public, and after the testator's death it was discovered that a witness, though practising as a notary, was not qualified to do so, and the will had been validated by retrospective legislation in Paraguay, it is hard to suppose that Lord Penzance would have thought it "inconvenient and unjust" to give effect to that legislation.

---

[34] (1871) L.R. 2 P. & D. 268.

[35] *cf. Banco de Vizcaya v Don Alfonso de Borbon y Austria* [1935] 1 K.B. 140; see Rule 3.

[36] See Rule 137. See also *Adams v National Bank of Greece and Athens SA* [1958] 2 Q.B. 59, 76 (affirmed [1961] A.C. 255) and Wengler (1958) *Rabel's Zeitschrift* 563–564, especially n.22.

[37] See F.A. Mann (1954) 31 B.Y.I.L. 217, 234; Grodecki (1959) 35 B.Y.I.L. 58, 67–69, where various interpretations of the decision are discussed.

3-018   The decision was followed without much discussion in *Re Aganoor's Trusts*.[38] In that case, a testatrix died in 1868 domiciled in Padua having by her will given a settled legacy to A for life and if he died without children to B for life and then to B's children living at B's death. This was valid by the Austrian law in force in Padua in 1868; but on September 1, 1871, the Italian Civil Code came into force and forbade trust substitutions, dividing the ownership between the persons in possession on that date and the first persons entitled in remainder who were born or conceived before then. B died in 1891 leaving children. A died in 1894 without children. It was held that the settled legacy was valid and that the change in the law in force in Padua made after the death of the testatrix would be ignored. This result is diametrically opposite to that which was reached in *Nelson v Bridport*.[39]

3-019   If it is true that in succession to movables no account is to be taken of subsequent changes in the *lex causae* made after the death of the testator, that proposition is subject to an important qualification so far as the formal validity of wills is concerned. For, as we have seen,[40] s.6(3) of the Wills Act 1963 provides that retrospective alterations in the *lex causae* made after the execution of the will are relevant in so far as they validate but irrelevant in so far as they invalidate the will. This enactment is not in terms confined to alterations in the law made before the death of the testator, and there seems no reason to read into it words which are not there.

3-020   (c) *Torts*. In *Phillips v Eyre*,[41] an action for assault and false imprisonment was brought in England against the ex-Governor of Jamaica. The acts complained of took place in Jamaica while the defendant was engaged in suppressing a rebellion which had broken out in the island. The acts were illegal by the law of Jamaica as it stood at the time of the tort; but the defendant pleaded that they had been subsequently legalised by an Act of Indemnity passed in Jamaica with retrospective effect. The Court of Exchequer Chamber gave effect to this defence. It follows from this decision that even in 1870 English law had no objection to foreign retrospective legislation as such and what was true in 1870 must be even more true today when retrospective legislation has become a more familiar phenomenon in English domestic law.[42] It must be admitted, however, that the circumstances in *Phillips v Eyre* were rather special, in that the *lex causae* was that of a British colony, there was no difference between the *lex fori* and the *lex causae* except in regard to the Act of Indemnity, and that Act was of a kind familiar to English domestic law. Still, it remains true that the Court of Exchequer Chamber adopted a wholly different approach from that of Lord Penzance in *Lynch's* case.[43]

---

[38] (1895) 64 L.J.Ch. 521; criticised by F.A. Mann (1954) 31 B.Y.I.L. 217, 234; Grodecki (1959) 35 B.Y.I.L. 58, 69–70.

[39] (1846) 8 Beav. 547; above, para.3–015.

[40] See above, para.3–002.

[41] (1870) L.R. 6 Q.B. 1.

[42] Though this will now be subject to the Human Rights Act 1998, which will govern the compatibility of retrospective legislation with the guarantees contained in the European Convention on Human Rights.

[43] (1871) L.R. 2 P. & D. 268.

(d) *Discharge of contracts.* At common law, the discharge of contracts **3–021**
affected the substance of the obligation and therefore normally depended on
the law which governed the contract.[44] The position is the same under the
Rome I Regulation. According to that Regulation the law found applicable to
the contract by reference to the rules of the Regulation governs both matters
of "performance,"[45] and the "various ways of extinguishing obligations."[46]
Numerous common law decisions clearly established that the content of the
rules of the governing law was that which existed from time to time and that
therefore legislation enacted in the country whose law governed the contract
after the date of the contract may have the effect of discharging or modifying
the contractual obligations of the parties.[47] Although the Rome I Regulation
is silent on this question, there would appear to be no doubt that the position
under the Regulation is the same as at common law. A striking example of the
problem at common law, which, it is submitted, would be resolved in the same
way under the Convention is the case of *R. v International Trustee for the
Protection of Bondholders AG*.[48] In February 1917 the British Government
floated a 250 million dollar loan on the New York money market. The capital
was repayable at holder's option either in New York in gold coin of the United
States or in London in sterling at a specified rate of exchange. In 1933 a Joint
Resolution of Congress provided that all gold coin and gold value clauses
attached to obligations expressed in dollars were against public policy and that
all dollar obligations whenever incurred could be discharged upon payment,
dollar for dollar, in any coin or currency which was legal tender at the time of
payment. The bondholders sought to enforce the gold clause according to its
terms. But the House of Lords held that the law governing the contract was the
law of New York and that therefore the gold clause had been abrogated by the
Joint Resolution, with the result that the loan could be repaid in New York in
depreciated paper dollars.

In *Adams v National Bank of Greece and Athens SA*[49] the House of Lords **3–022**
refused to apply a Greek law which purported retrospectively to exonerate a
Greek bank from liability under a contract of guarantee governed by English
law. The House was not unanimous in its reasons for reaching this conclusion;[50] but the main reason seems to have been that since the law applicable
to the contract was English, no Greek law could discharge one party's
obligation thereunder.[51] The same solution would be reached under the provisions of the Rome I Regulation. Since English law governed the contract, that

---

[44] See below, paras 32–008, 32–157 *et seq.*
[45] Regulation (EC) 593/2008, Art.12(1)(b). See below, paras 32–146—32–152.
[46] *ibid.*, Art.12(1)(d). See also Rome Convention, Art.10. See below, paras 32–156 *et seq.*
[47] *Re Chesterman's Trusts* [1923] 2 Ch. 466, 478 (CA); *Perry v Equitable Life Assurance
Society* (1929) 45 T.L.R. 468; *Assicurazioni Generali v Cotran* [1932] A.C. 268 (PC); *De Beéche
v South American Stores Ltd* [1935] A.C. 148; *R. v International Trustee for the Protection of
Bondholders AG* [1937] A.C. 500; *Kornatzki v Oppenheimer* [1937] 4 All E.R. 133; *Kahler v
Midland Bank Ltd* [1950] A.C. 24; *Jabbour v Custodian of Israeli Absentee Property* [1954] 1
W.L.R. 139, 157 (where there was a change of sovereignty in the *locus contractus*); *Re Helbert
Wagg & Co Ltd* [1956] Ch. 323, 341–342.
[48] [1937] A.C. 500. *cf. New Brunswick Ry v British and French Trust Corp* [1939] A.C. 1.
[49] [1961] A.C. 255.
[50] See, for a detailed analysis of the judgments, Grodecki (1961) 24 M.L.R. 701, 706–714.
[51] See, in particular, the judgment of Lord Reid and that of Diplock J. in the court of first
instance: [1958] 2 Q.B. 59.

law would determine whether the obligation of the bank was extinguished,[52] and Greek law could have no effect on the issue.[53] The case is noteworthy in the present context because all five members of the House went out of their way to approve the principle of *Lynch's* case.[54] But only Lord Tucker based his judgment squarely on that decision, and Lord Reid was not satisfied that it should be applied to a case like the one before him. It is submitted that this is the preferable view, and the view which should certainly be adopted in cases falling within the Rome I Regulation.

3–023   In *Wight v Eckhardt Marine GmbH*[55] a contract was made between a claimant and the Bangladeshi branch of a Cayman Islands bank, and was expressed to be governed by Bangladeshi law. When the insolvency of the banking group, of which the individual bank was a part, triggered Bangladeshi legislation, this resulted in the restructuring of business of the bank in Bangladesh, as part of which the contractual rights of the claimant against the bank were extinguished and replaced by rights against a new bank, it was held by the Privy Council that the rights of the claimant against the original bank had ceased to exist, with the result that the claimant had no right to admit to proof in the insolvency of the original bank. In effect the reasoning of the Privy Council was that if a party entered into a contract which was governed by a particular law, it took the risk that the law might be altered to its disadvantage, just as, no doubt, if the *lex contractus* were to be altered in a way which was considered to be beneficial to a contracting party, it would expect to reap the benefit of that alteration.

3–024   (e) *Legitimation.* As we have seen,[56] s.3 of the Legitimacy Act 1976 provides for the recognition in England of a foreign legitimation if the father of the illegitimate person was, at the date of the subsequent marriage, domiciled in a foreign country by whose law the illegitimate person became legitimate by virtue of such marriage.[57] The subsection is confined to legitimation by subsequent marriage and does not extend to other modes and the legitimation is recognised from the date of the marriage, and not from any earlier date. Hence, even if the effect of the foreign *lex causae* is to legitimate the illegitimate person retrospectively from the date of his birth, he cannot be recognised as legitimate in England from that date under s.3 of the Act. But there seems no reason why he should not be recognised in England as having been retrospectively legitimated from the date of his birth under the common law rule,[58] provided his father was domiciled in the foreign country at the date of the illegitimate person's birth as well as at the date of the subsequent marriage, and provided the marriage had this retrospective effect under the

---

[52] Rome I Regulation, Art.12(1)(d). See below, paras 32–156 *et seq.*

[53] It is arguable (though certainly no more than that) that Art.9(3) of the Rome I Regulation might now open the way for Greek law to impinge on the issue. However, as the effect of Greek law was not to make performance of the contract unlawful in Greece, as distinct from its providing that the original contractual obligation was no longer in existence as a matter of Greek law, it is far from clear that Art.9(3) would have any effect. See paras 32–102, below.

[54] [1961] A.C. 255, 275–276, 282, 285, 287.

[55] [2003] UKPC 37, [2004] 1 A.C. 147.

[56] See above, para.3–005.

[57] See Rule 117.

[58] See Rule 126 and above, para.3–005.

foreign law. Scott L.J. in *Re Luck*[59] appeared to think that the effect of legitimation under the common law rule was always retrospective, even in the absence of any retrospective effect in the *lex causae*. But the cases cited by him do not seem to support this view, which appears to be contrary to principle. If the law of France says that an illegitimate person is legitimated as from the date of the marriage, there is no reason why English law should say that he was legitimated as from the date of his birth.

Section 2 of the Legitimacy Act 1976 provides for the legitimation of the child if the father was domiciled in England at the time of the subsequent marriage. Statutes very similar to the English Act are in force in many other countries, including Northern Ireland. None of these statutes contains any provision for recognising a legitimation effected under any of the others except in so far as they refer to legitimation by subsequent marriage. If the father of an illegitimate person marries the mother while domiciled, e.g. in Northern Ireland after the coming into force of the Northern Irish Act, there is of course no difficulty about recognising the legitimation in England under s.3 of the Act of 1976. But if the marriage took place before the coming into force of the Northern Irish Act, and the father was dead, or no longer domiciled in Northern Ireland, when the Northern Irish Act came into force, the child is undoubtedly legitimate in Northern Ireland. But he cannot be recognised as having been legitimated in England under s.3 of the English Act, because it is confined to cases where "the illegitimate person became legitimated by virtue of such subsequent marriage"; and he became legitimated by virtue of the Northern Irish Act, not by virtue of the subsequent marriage. Yet it seems anomalous that a person should be recognised in Northern Ireland but not in England as having been legitimated when the statute law of the two countries is couched in almost identical terms.[60] The solution seems to be to fall back on the English common law rule (which is probably not confined to legitimation by subsequent marriage[61]) and apply the law of the country in which the father was domiciled at the date of the child's birth and the date of the subsequent marriage, as that law stands at the time of the proceedings in England.[62] It is only by giving effect to subsequent changes in the *lex causae* that the anomalous situation referred to above can be avoided. Thus for purposes of British citizenship, a person was deemed to have been legitimated by the subsequent marriage of his parents if, by the law of the place where his father was domiciled at the time of the marriage, the marriage operated immediately *or subsequently* to legitimate him.[63]

3–025

---

[59] [1940] Ch. 864, 898–899 (CA). See below, para.20R–048, n.188.

[60] If the marriage takes place before the commencement of the English Act of 1926 or the Northern Irish Act of 1928, neither Act requires the father to be living at the date of such commencement.

[61] See below, paras 20–062 *et seq.*

[62] *cf. Re Hagerbaum* [1933] I.R. 198. The Australian and New Zealand courts have laid down a much more stringent rule: see below, paras 20–068 *et seq.* The decision in *Heron v National Trustees Executors and Agency Co of Australasia Ltd* [1976] V.R. 733 is consistent with the suggestion in the text; but the case was decided under s.90 of the Australian Marriage Act 1961. The question has not yet arisen in England. See below, paras 20–068 *et seq.*

[63] British Nationality Act 1981, s.47(2) (since repealed).

3–026   (f) *Matrimonial property.* In *Sperling v Sperling*,[64] a husband and wife, domiciled in East Germany, married there in 1954. The marriage was not subject to any community property régime. They emigrated to South Africa in 1957 and acquired a domicile in the Transvaal. In 1965 the East German law was altered with retrospective effect so as to provide for community of acquisitions after marriage. The Appellate Division of the Supreme Court of South Africa held that this retrospective law must receive effect in South Africa. The reference to East German law as the law of the matrimonial domicile meant the whole of its law, including its transitional law, and public policy did not forbid its application.

3–027   (g) *Validity of marriage.* In *Starkowski v Att-Gen*,[65] H1 and W, both Roman Catholics domiciled in Poland, went through a ceremony of marriage in Austria in May 1945 in a Roman Catholic church. They lived together until 1947, when they separated, having acquired a domicile of choice in England. In 1950 W went through a ceremony of marriage in England with H2, a Pole domiciled in England. In May 1945 a purely religious marriage without civil ceremony was void by Austrian law. But in June 1945 a law was passed in Austria retrospectively validating such marriages if they were duly registered. The marriage between H1 and W was registered in 1949, but without W's knowledge or consent, after she had acquired a domicile in England, and after she had separated from H1.[66] The House of Lords held that the Austrian ceremony was valid and the English ceremony was bigamous and void. Lord Reid stated the question to be decided as follows[67]: "Are we to take the law of that place (*sc.* the place of celebration) as it was when the marriage was celebrated, or are we to inquire what the law of that place now is with regard to the formal validity of that marriage?"—a question which he answered by saying "There is no compelling reason why the reference should not be to that law as it is when the problem arises for decision."[68] Lord Cohen distinguished *Lynch*[69] somewhat faintly on the ground that it involved a remotely different subject-matter.[70] Lord Tucker agreed with Barnard J. in the court of first instance[71] that *Lynch* would have been of more assistance if the second ceremony had preceded the registration of the first.[72] But these distinctions seem illusory because, as is shown by Lord Reid's formulation quoted above, the problem was basically the same. The House of Lords adopted a different approach from that of Lord Penzance and (it is submitted) a preferable one.

---

[64] 1975 (3) S.A. 707. To the same effect is *Topolski v The Queen* (1978) 90 D.L.R. (3d) 66, a decision of the Federal Court of Canada. The question has often come before courts in continental Europe: see Grodecki, in Lipstein (ed.), *International Encyclopedia of Comparative Law*, Vol.III, Ch.8, paras 45–48.

[65] [1954] A.C. 155.

[66] Dr F.A. Mann thought that the breakdown of the marriage before the registration of the Austrian ceremony should have led the House of Lords to an opposite conclusion: (1954) 31 B.Y.I.L. 217, 243–245. But this seems unacceptable for the reasons given by Grodecki (1959) 35 B.Y.I.L. 58, 75–76.

[67] [1954] A.C. 155, 170.

[68] [1954] A.C. 155, 172.

[69] (1871) L.R. 2 P. & D. 268.

[70] [1954] A.C. 155, 180.

[71] [1952] P. 135, 144.

[72] [1954] A.C. 155, 175.

(h) *Public policy.* The prevailing practice of the English courts thus seems   **3–028**
to be to apply the *lex causae* as it exists from time to time and to give effect
if need be to retrospective changes therein. But the consequences of giving
effect to retrospective changes in the law are sometimes so extraordinary that
public policy must occasionally impose qualifications and exceptions. There is
an almost complete lack of English authority on this question. The discussion
that follows is therefore highly speculative. It will throw the problem into the
clearest possible relief if we consider some variations on the facts of the
Starkowski case and consider what decision an English court might be
expected to reach.

(1) If the Austrian marriage had been originally valid but had later been   **3–029**
retrospectively invalidated by Austrian legislation, it would seem that, on
grounds of policy, the marriage should be held valid in England. There is,
however, at least one decision of a French court to the opposite effect.[73]

(2) If either party had obtained an English nullity decree annulling the
Austrian marriage for informality before it was registered, it would seem that
foreign retrospective legislation should not be allowed to invalidate the
English nullity decree.[74]

(3) What would the position have been if the English ceremony had   **3–030**
preceded and not followed the registration of the Austrian ceremony? The
majority of the House of Lords expressly left this question open in the
Starkowski case.[75] It is submitted that the English ceremony should have been
held valid. A similar point was decided by the British Columbia Court of
Appeal in *Ambrose v Ambrose*.[76] A wife obtained an interlocutory judgment
for divorce from her first husband in California, where they were domiciled,
on November 25, 1930. This judgment could become final, and so entitle
either party to remarry, at the expiration of one year, either on the application
of either party or on the court's own motion. It was not in fact made final until
1939. Meanwhile in 1935 the wife went through a ceremony of marriage in
the State of Washington with her second husband, who was domiciled in
British Columbia. They lived together in British Columbia until 1956, when
they separated. The wife then took advantage of a Californian statute passed
in 1955 and obtained an order from the Californian court in 1958 which
retrospectively backdated the divorce to November 25, 1931, the earliest date
on which final judgment could have been obtained. The second husband then
petitioned for nullity in British Columbia on the ground that the second
ceremony was bigamous. The court granted a decree. It distinguished *Starkowski v Att-Gen* on two grounds. First, the defect in that case was formal and
could be corrected by the *lex loci celebrationis*, which remained constant
throughout whereas the defect in the instant case related to capacity, a matter
which was governed by the law of the wife's antenuptial domicile: but she

---

[73] *Guerra v Tissander*, Tribunal de Tulle, January 6, 1944, in 1947 *Rev. Crit.* 304. The decision
is approved by Grodecki, in Lipstein (ed.), *International Encyclopedia of Comparative Law*,
Vol.III, Ch.8, para.30; and see para.34(3).

[74] *cf. Starkowski v Att-Gen* [1954] A.C. 155, 172, where Lord Reid, who alone adverted to this
point, expressly refrained from deciding it. See also *Von Lorang v Administrator of Austrian
Property* [1927] A.C. 641, 651.

[75] [1954] A.C. 155, 168, 176, 182.

[76] (1961) 25 D.L.R. (2d) 1 (BCCA); criticised by Castel (1961) 39 Can. Bar Rev. 604; Hartley
(1967) 16 I.C.L.Q. 680, 699–703; Grodecki, *op. cit.*, para.34(1).

ceased to be domiciled in California in 1939, and was therefore domiciled in British Columbia, and not in California, when she obtained her order from the Californian court in 1958. Secondly, in *Starkowski v Att-Gen* the retrospective validation of the Austrian ceremony preceded the English ceremony, whereas in the instant case the Washington ceremony preceded the retrospective validation of the Californian divorce.

3–031　(4) For completeness, it should be observed that if the law which governs a contract were to be altered in a way in which its application would offend English public policy (for example, if a change in the *lex contractus* were to provide that contracts to which members of a religious minority may be party are discharged or are unenforceable by such an individual), the common law would certainly have refused to give effect to such a law, and Art.21 of the Rome I Regulation permits the same reasoning and same conclusion. But though the rule used to reach this conclusion is not confined to cases in which the *lex causae* has undergone a change in content, it will certainly apply where it has.

3–032　(i) *Foreign law as datum.* Finally, attention must be drawn to a problem of time which may arise when, although a particular foreign law is not the *lex causae*, it may nevertheless be necessary to refer to it as a *datum* or fact which is relevant to deciding the case.[77] In this situation it appears that foreign law is applied as it exists at a particular time rather than as it exists from time to time.[78] For example, parties may in a contract incorporate provisions of foreign law as a "shorthand" method of stating contractual terms and conditions.[79] Accordingly it may be necessary to look to that foreign law, not as the law governing the contract, but in order to identify the terms and conditions thus incorporated. In such circumstances the court will look to the content of the foreign law as at the time the contract was made.[80] Conversely the content of the governing law will, as we have seen, in general be determined as it exists from time to time.[81]

---

[77] As to foreign law as datum see below, para.32–056.

[78] See Pryles (1980) 6 Monash U.L. Rev. 225, 234–236 where examples are discussed.

[79] Or, indeed, a body of rules which do not comprise the law of a foreign country: *Halpern v Halpern (Nos 1 and 2)* [2007] EWCA Civ 291, [2008] Q.B. 195.

[80] *Timm v Northumbrian Shipping Co* (1937) 58 Ll.L.R. 45; affirmed [1939] A.C. 397; *Vita Food Products Inc v Unus Shipping Co Ltd* [1939] A.C. 277, 291 (PC). The position is the same under the Rome I Regulation: see below, paras 32–056 *et seq.* where the problem of incorporation by reference is discussed.

[81] See above, para.3–013.

CHAPTER 4

RENVOI[1]

RULE 1—In the Rules and Exceptions in this book the law of a country   4R–001
(e.g. the law of the country where a person is domiciled)
    (1) means, when applied to England, the domestic law of England;
    (2) means, when applied to any foreign country, usually the domestic
    law of that country, sometimes any domestic law which the courts
    of that country would apply to the decision of the case to which the
    Rule refers.

COMMENT

The term "law of a country," e.g. the law of England or the law of Italy is   4–002
ambiguous. It means in its narrower and most usual sense the domestic law of
any country, i.e. the law applied by its courts in cases which contain no foreign
element. It means in its wider sense all the rules, including the rules of the
conflict of laws, which the courts of a country apply.

Until 1995 the subject had attracted rather little judicial attention. But four   4–003
developments have revived interest in the subject. The first comprises a string
of first-instance decisions in England, examining the question whether the
choice of law rule which refers questions of title to tangible movable property
to the *lex situs* is confined to the domestic rules of the lex situs, or includes
principles of choice of law which a court at the *lex situs* would have applied:
as will be shown below, the balance of this authority is against allowing
recourse to the rules of the conflict of laws of the *lex situs*. The second was
the decision of the High Court of Australia in *Neilson v Overseas Projects*

---

[1] The literature on this subject is immense. See Bate, *Notes on the Doctrine of Renvoi* (1904);
Bentwich, *The Law of Domicile in its Relation to Succession and the Doctrine of Renvoi* (1911);
Baty, *Polarized Law* (1914), pp.116 *et seq.*; Mendelssohn-Bartholdy, *Renvoi in Modern English
Law* (1937); Abbott (1908) 24 L.Q.R. 137; Jethro Brown (1909) 25 L.Q.R. 149; Schreiber (1918)
31 Harv.L.R. 523; Morris (1937) 18 B.Y.I.L. 32; Griswold (1938) 51 Harv.L.R. 1165; Cowan
(1938) 87 U. of Penn.L.Rev. 34; Griswold (1939) *ibid.* 257; Cormack (1941) 14 So. Calif. L. Rev.
249–275; Raeburn (1948) 25 B.Y.I.L. 211; Inglis (1958) 74 L.Q.R. 493; Kahn-Freund (1974)
Recueil des Cours, III, pp.431–437; Briggs (1998) 47 I.C.L.Q. 877. The fullest discussion in
English is to be found in Falconbridge, Chs 6–10. For continental literature, see Rabel, Vol.I,
pp.75–90; Lewald (1929) *Recueil des Cours*, IV, p.519; Niboyet, *Traité*, Vol.3, pp.435–487;
Batiffol and Lagarde, Vol.1, pp.491–509; Melchior, *Die Grundlagen des Deutschen Internationalen Privatrechts* (1932), pp.192–245; Franceskakis, *La Théorie du Renvoi* (1958). There
are conflicting decisions on this matter in the New York courts: see *Re Tallmadge*, 181 N.Y. Supp.
336 (1919); *Re Schneider's Estate*, 198 Misc. 1017, 96 N.Y.S. 2d 652 (1950) discussed by Morris
(1951) 4 Int.L.Q. 268, where an attempt is made to reconcile the two cases. These and other
American cases are discussed by Falconbridge, Ch.10.

Corp of Victoria Ltd,[2] on choice of law in tort. The majority of that court interpreted the Australian choice of law rule, which applied the *lex loci delicti commissi*, as meaning (where it was proved[3]) that law which a judge at the *locus delicti* would have applied to the issue. The judgments did not generally favour the proposition that there was a single "doctrine of renvoi", or a uniform approach calling for general acceptance or general rejection of the doctrine of renvoi. Instead, the question was whether the policy which under-pinned the particular rule for choice of law would be better supported, or undermined, by allowing evidence of how a foreign judge would decide the issue if it were before him for decision, and following that choice of law if it were sufficiently proved. To the extent that the approach of the court was to weigh the arguments from the point of principle, it is to be welcomed, though it may also be that the court was influenced by the strictness of the choice of law rule which it was otherwise required to apply.[4] Even so, the judgment demonstrated that a broad and general approach to the doctrine may not be beneficial, and that renvoi may be justified as a tool with which to refine a choice of law rule which the court is otherwise directed to apply. The third is the fact that in claims concerning contractual and non-contractual obligations, the legislative choice of law rules established by European Regulations make specific provision for the exclusion of renvoi. If nothing else, this does serve to focus attention on the scope of the exclusion[5] and on why such exclusion was considered thought to be desirable.

4–004   The fourth came with the clarification from the Supreme Court that the term "renvoi" is properly confined to legal reasoning by which an English court exercises a choice of law to look to the law of a foreign country, in circum-stances in which the courts of that foreign country, seised of the issue in question, would apply a choice of law rule taking them to the law of a country other than their own.[6] That is a renvoi, and the decision for the English court is, in principle, whether to follow this line of reasoning to arrive at its eventual choice of law, or to reject any role for this exercise of looking to the law of another country, and to insist on applying the domestic law of the country originally chosen. All this is quite distinct from the case in which an English court is required to apply French law to an issue, but the evidence of French law is that on the facts of the particular case, perhaps because they are "international", a French court would apply the provisions of an international convention, or what the French court might call "transnational law", rather than French domestic law. For the English court to apply the provisions of the convention, or a body of rules which French law applies to "transnational" cases, is not to admit or allow a renvoi from French law: for one thing, the path of reasoning does not and cannot take the English court to the law of a

---

[2] [2005] HCA 54, (2005) 233 C.L.R. 331.

[3] And where it was not proved to be different, the rule of foreign law in question would be presumed not to differ from the corresponding rule of Australian law.

[4] There is, however, no suggestion in the judgments that this was any part of the motivation of the court.

[5] Because the Regulations apply to contractual and non-contractual obligations; the question of title to property may well be decisive in a claim for relief for breach of such an obligation, but it is not, in itself, a matter which falls within the scope of "obligations".

[6] *Dallah Real Estate and Tourism Holding Co v Ministry of Religious Affairs, Government of Pakistan* [2010] UKSC 46, [2011] 1 A.C. 763, esp. at [123]–[125].

country other than that originally chosen, and for another, the court is simply applying the chapter of French law which French law applies to the facts and matters in question. This is not to be seen as renvoi, but as the ascertainment of the particular rules of French law applicable to the issue in question.

(1) When "country" is England. When any Rule, applied to the circum- **4–005** stances of a given case, directs that the case be determined in accordance with the law of England, then the term "law of England" must mean the domestic law of England. If the term were used in a more general sense and meant whatever law or principle an English court would apply to the case, the Rule would constitute an unmeaning truism; for we are dealing with cases decided by an English court, and any case so decided must be determined in accordance with some law or principle which the English court applies to it. If by the law of England were meant any principle which the English courts would apply to the case, the Rule would afford no guidance whatever.

(2) When "country" is a foreign country. When any Rule applied to the **4–006** circumstances of a given case directs that the case be determined in accordance with the law, e.g. of Italy, then the term "law of Italy" means usually the domestic law of Italy, but sometimes means any system of law which the Italian courts would hold applicable to the particular case. This ambiguity in the expression "law of Italy" gives rise to the difficult problem of renvoi.

Nature of the problem. The problem of renvoi arises whenever a rule of **4–007** the conflict of laws refers to the "law" of a foreign country, but the conflict rule of the foreign country would have referred the question to the "law" of the first country or to the "law" of some third country. The classic illustration is that of the British citizen who dies intestate domiciled in Italy, leaving movables in England. The English conflict rule refers to the law of the domicile (Italian law), but the Italian conflict rule refers to the national law, which may for the moment be assumed to be English law. Here we have a patent conflict of conflict rules involving a reference back (remission) to the forum. Had the intestate been a German instead of a British national we should have had a patent conflict of conflict rules involving a reference on (transmission) to German law. Had the intestate been domiciled in New York in the English sense but in England in the New York sense, and both the English and the New York conflict rules agreed that intestate succession to movables was governed by the law of the domicile, we should have had a latent conflict of conflict rules, arising from the fact that though the English and New York conflict rules were in apparent agreement, they differed in what constitutes domicile.[7]

In these situations, a court might conceivably resolve the ambiguity in three **4–008** different ways.[8]

---

[7] At least two important differences between English and New York rules as to domicile may be suggested: (1) in New York the abandonment of a domicile of choice does not involve the revival of the domicile of origin (contrast Rule 13(2)(ii)); (2) in New York a domicile of origin is more easily displaced by a domicile of choice than it is in England.

[8] Morris (1937) 18 B.Y.I.L. 32, 33; Falconbridge, pp.173–174; First Report of the Private International Law Committee (1954) (Cmd. 9068), para.23.

(a) The court might apply the domestic rule of the foreign country, that is, the law of the foreign country applicable to a purely domestic situation arising therein, without regard to the elements which render the situation a conflict of laws situation for the foreign law. Thus, in the case of a British citizen dying intestate domiciled in Italy, and leaving movables in England, the English court might (if it adopted this method of solution) apply the purely domestic rule of Italian law applicable to Italians, disregarding the fact that the intestate was a British citizen. This method requires proof of the domestic law of the foreign country, but does not require proof of its conflict rules. It has been recommended (*obiter*) by two English judges on the ground that it is "simple and rational,"[9] but rejected in another case after a comprehensive review of the authorities.[10]

4–009   (b) If the conflict rule of the foreign country refers back to the law of the forum or on to the law of a third country, the court might accept the reference and apply the domestic law of the forum or the domestic law of the third country. The former process is technically known as "accepting the renvoi."[11] Thus, in the case of a British citizen dying intestate domiciled in Italy, leaving movables in England, the English court might (if it adopted this method of solution) apply the domestic rule of English law, that is the rule laid down in the Administration of Estates Act 1925 (as amended), disregarding the fact that the intestate was domiciled in Italy. This method requires proof of the conflict rules of the foreign country relating to succession, but does not require proof of the foreign rules about renvoi. It has been adopted by some Continental courts in a number of celebrated cases,[12] and is sometimes enjoined by Continental legislatures,[13] but it is not the current doctrine of the English courts. It may conveniently be called the theory of "partial" or "single" renvoi.

4–010   (c) The court might decide the case in exactly the same way as it would be decided by the foreign court. Thus, in the case of a British citizen dying intestate domiciled in Italy, leaving movables in England, the English court (if it adopted this method of solution) would decide the case as it would be decided by the Italian court. If the Italian court would refer to English "law" and would interpret that reference to mean English domestic law,[14] then the English court would apply English domestic law. If on the other hand the Italian court would refer to English "law" and interpret that reference to mean English conflict of laws, and would "accept the renvoi" from English law and apply Italian domestic law, then the English court would apply Italian domestic law. This method requires proof not only of the conflict rule of the foreign country relating to succession but also of the foreign rules about renvoi. In

---

[9] *Re Annesley* [1926] Ch. 692, 708–709; *Re Askew* [1930] 2 Ch. 259, 278; *cf. Barcelo v Electrolytic Zinc Co of Australasia* (1932) 48 C.L.R. 391, 437.

[10] *Re Ross* [1930] 1 Ch. 377, 402.

[11] This expression must be distinguished from accepting the doctrine of the renvoi, which the forum may do without necessarily accepting the first reference back.

[12] OLG Lübeck, March 21, 1861, 14 Seuffert's Archiv, p.164; *Bigwood v Bigwood* (1881) Belgique Judiciaire, p.758; *L'Affaire Forgo*, 1883 *Clunet* 64; *L'Affaire Soulié*, 1910 *Clunet* 888; Falconbridge, pp.147–149.

[13] e.g. Art.27 of the Introductory Law of the German Civil Code (1900).

[14] Until 1995 this is what the Italian court would have done, but Art.13 of Law No.218 of May 31, 1995 altered Italian law to provide for renvoi in certain cases: see 1996 *Rev. Crit.* 174.

spite of its greater complexity, it seems to represent the present doctrine of the English courts, at least in certain contexts. It may conveniently be called the theory of "total" or "double" renvoi.

Origin and development. The doctrine of renvoi obtained a foothold in   **4–011**
English law through the medium of cases on the formal validity of wills. In that context, three factors favoured its recognition: first, the rigid rule of the English conflict of laws which at that time insisted on compliance with one form and one form only for wills, that of the testator's last domicile;[15] secondly, a more flexible rule in neighbouring European countries (where people of English origin were likely to settle), which allowed compliance with the forms prescribed by either the testator's personal law or the law of the place where the will was made; and thirdly, a judicial bias in favour of upholding wills which admittedly expressed the last wishes of the testator and were defective only in point of form. The fountain-head of authority is *Collier v Rivaz*,[16] where the court had to consider the formal validity of a will and six codicils made by a British subject who died domiciled in Belgium in the English sense, but in England in the Belgian sense because he had not obtained the authorisation of the Belgian Government to establish his domicile in Belgium, as required by Art.13 of the Code Napoleon. The will and two of the codicils were made in local Belgian form and were admitted to probate in England without argument. Four of the codicils were opposed because they were not made in local Belgian form, though they were made in English form. Upon proof that by Belgian law the validity of wills made by foreigners not legally domiciled in Belgium was governed by "the laws of their own country," Sir H. Jenner admitted these codicils to probate, remarking that "the court sitting here to determine it, must consider itself sitting in Belgium under the peculiar circumstances of this case."[17] He did not consider the possibility that a Belgian court might have accepted the renvoi from English law and applied Belgian domestic law.

The fact that the will and the two codicils made in Belgian form were   **4–012**
admitted to probate as well as the four codicils made in English form means that the English conflict rule for the formal validity of wills was interpreted as a rule of alternative reference either to the domestic rules or to the conflict rules of the law of the domicile. For this reason, *Collier v Rivaz* cannot be regarded as an authority favouring the renvoi doctrine as a principle of general application, because according to the doctrine the initial reference is never to the domestic rules of the foreign law. Moreover, a rule of alternative reference, while practicable for the formal validity of wills, is impracticable for the essential (or intrinsic) validity of wills or for intestacy. In such cases the court must choose between the domestic rules and the conflict rules of the foreign

---

[15] The law has since been amended, first by the Wills Act 1861, and now by the Wills Act 1963. See Rule 152.

[16] (1841) 2 Curt. 855; stated below, para.4–039, Illustration 1; discussed by Falconbridge, pp.143–145, 151–152; Abbott (1908) 24 L.Q.R. 143; Schreiber (1918) 31 Harv.L.R. 539–541; Morris (1937) 18 B.Y.I.L. 43–44; Mendelssohn-Bartholdy, pp.58–64. See also *Maltass v Maltass* (1844) 1 Rob. 67, 72; *Frere v Frere* (1847) 5 Notes of Cases 593; *Ross v Ross* (1894) 25 S.C.R. 307.

[17] As to the possible origin of this famous formula, see Falconbridge, pp.190–191.

law. It cannot apply both, for it must decide whether or not the testator had disposing power, whether or not he died intestate, and if he did, who are the next-of-kin.[18] It is one thing to uphold a will if it complies with the formalities prescribed by either the domestic rules or the conflict rules of the law of the domicile. It is quite another thing to allow the next-of-kin entitled under the domestic rules of the law of the domicile to share the property with the next-of-kin entitled under its conflict rules.

4–013   *Collier v Rivaz* was disapproved in *Bremer v Freeman*,[19] where on almost identical facts the Privy Council, on appeal from the Prerogative Court of Canterbury, refused to admit to probate the will of a British subject who died domiciled in France in the English sense, but in England in the French sense (because she had not complied with Art.13), on the ground that it was made in English but not in French form. Since *Bremer v Freeman* is the only English decision on the renvoi doctrine of appellate authority,[20] it would be a very important case if the judgment were unequivocal; but unfortunately the reasoning is so intricate and so ambiguous that it has been claimed as an authority both for[21] and against[22] the doctrine, and few modern lawyers have the patience to unravel its intricacies. The condemnation of *Collier v Rivaz* was, however, expressed in unambiguous terms.

4–014   The decision in *Bremer v Freeman* led to the passing of Lord Kingsdown's Act 1861 which in certain circumstances enabled testators who were British subjects and who were disposing of personal estate to choose between the forms prescribed by no fewer than four systems of law. This extreme indulgence might have been supposed to destroy the argument in favour of interpreting the reference to foreign law as an alternative reference either to its domestic rules or to its conflict rules and it seems likely that Parliament intended to refer only to the former. However, in *In bonis Lacroix*[23] a British subject made two wills in France, one in French form and one in English form, and both were admitted to probate, the latter on the ground that it was made in accordance with the conflict rules of the law of the place where it was made (*lex loci actus*). As in *Collier v Rivaz*, it was necessary to refer to the domestic rules as well as the conflict rules of the foreign law in order to admit both wills to probate.

4–015   In *Re Johnson*,[24] the renvoi doctrine was applied in a case of partial intestacy, and it led to the application of the law of the testatrix' domicile of origin (Malta). But the main ground of the decision was that since the law of the country in which she had established a domicile *animo et facto* (Baden)

---

[18] Falconbridge, p.152.

[19] (1857) 10 Moo. P.C. 306, 374; followed in *Hamilton v Dallas* (1875) 1 Ch.D. 257 (partial intestacy).

[20] By "English decision ... of appellate authority" is meant the decision of a court sitting in England on appeal from a court sitting in England. Decisions of the Privy Council on appeal from Commonwealth courts are purposely excluded.

[21] Jethro Brown (1909) 25 L.Q.R. 149–150; *Re Ross* [1930] 1 Ch. 377, 393–395.

[22] Abbott (1908) 24 L.Q.R. 144; Bate, pp.11–13, 110–111; Mendelssohn-Bartholdy, p.69; Morris (1937) 18 B.Y.I.L. 44–45 *cf.* Falconbridge, pp.152–153, 228.

[23] (1877) 2 P.D. 94.

[24] [1903] 1 Ch. 821; criticised by Dicey (1903) 19 L.Q.R. 244; Pollock (1920) 36 L.Q.R. 92; Bate, pp.19, 115; Abbott (1908) 24 L.Q.R. 144–145; Jethro Brown (1909) 25 L.Q.R. 145; Lorenzen, pp.44–47; Schreiber (1918) 31 Harv.L.R. 544–557; Falconbridge, pp.212, 214; Morris (1937) 18 B.Y.I.L. 45–48.

refused to recognise that she was domiciled there, she had not effectually lost her domicile of origin. This reasoning is inconsistent with the well-settled rule that for the purpose of an English conflict rule domicile means domicile in the English sense,[25] and *Re Johnson* has been subsequently disapproved.[26]

Down to 1926, the few decisions and dicta which recognised the renvoi   **4–016** doctrine were all consistent with a theory of partial or single renvoi. That is to say, the English court first referred to the conflict rules of the relevant foreign law and, where there was a reference back to English law,[27] applied the domestic rules of English law, without considering the possibility that the law of the foreign country might accept the renvoi from English law and apply its own domestic law. In *Re Annesley*,[28] Russell J. introduced the doctrine of double or total renvoi (but without citing any authority or giving any reasons for doing so) and applied French domestic law as the law of the domicile on the ground that a French court would have done so by way of renvoi from English law. He expressed[29] his personal preference for reaching this result by a more direct route, that is, by the application of French domestic law in the first instance without any renvoi at all; but this part of his judgment has not been followed.[30] This theory of double or total renvoi is different from the theory of single or partial renvoi because, by inquiring how the foreign court would decide the case, it envisages the possibility that the foreign court might "accept the renvoi" and apply its own domestic law, as happened in *Re Annesley* and *Re Askew*.[31]

Confusion between the two theories was, however, introduced by an *obiter*   **4–017** *dictum* of the Privy Council in *Kotia v Nahas*,[32] where it was said:

"In the English courts, phrases which refer to the national law of a *propositus* are to be construed, not as referring to the law which the courts of that country would apply in the case of its own national domiciled in its own country with regard (where the situation of the property is relevant) to property in its own country, but to the law which the courts of that country would apply to the particular case of the *propositus*, having regard to what in their view is his domicile (if they consider that to be relevant) and having regard to the situation of the property in question (if they consider that to be relevant)."

This statement was, it is submitted, no more than a dictum, because the Privy Council was considering a clause in the Palestine Succession Ordinance

---

[25] See below, Rule 8.

[26] *Casdagli v Casdagli* [1918] P. 89, 119–120; *Re Annesley* [1926] Ch. 692, 705; *Re Askew* [1930] 2 Ch. 259, 272, where Maugham J. said: "I think the case of *Re Johnson* and the reasons given for that decision by Farwell J. are no longer of authority."

[27] *Re Trufort* (1887) 36 Ch.D. 600 was a case of transmission from the law of the domicile (French law) to the law of the nationality (Swiss law), but the case was complicated by the existence of a treaty between France and Switzerland and of a Swiss judgment in favour of the plaintiff.

[28] [1926] Ch. 692; stated below, para.4–039, Illustration 2.

[29] [1926] Ch. 692, 708–709.

[30] *Re Ross* [1930] 1 Ch. 377, 402. See, however, *Re Askew* [1930] 2 Ch. 259, 278.

[31] [1930] 2 Ch. 259; stated below, para.4–040, Illustration 4.

[32] [1941] A.C. 403, 413.

which expressly provided for partial renvoi in the following terms: "Mulk land shall be distributed in accordance with the national law of the deceased .... Where the national law imports the law of ... the situation of an immovable, the law so imported shall be applied." The Privy Council was sitting on appeal from a Palestine court and was considering a rule of the Palestine conflict of laws which was expressed in statutory form and had no counterpart in the English conflict of laws, and therefore anything said about the English conflict of laws was necessarily *obiter*. But even as a dictum the statement cannot, it is submitted, be considered accurate, because it confuses two different theories, the theory of partial renvoi and the theory of total renvoi, which differ not only in their starting point but also in their result. They differ in their starting point because the former theory does not inquire how the foreign court would decide the case nor consider the possibility that the foreign court might "accept the renvoi" from the law of the forum. They differ in their result because, if the foreign law refers to the law of the forum, that law is invariably applied under the former theory but is not invariably applied under the latter.[33]

4–018   Nevertheless, the dictum of the Privy Council was the principal authority relied upon for the application of the renvoi doctrine in *Re Duke of Wellington*.[34] The testator, who was a British subject domiciled in England, made a Spanish will giving land and movables in Spain to the person who should fulfil two stated qualifications, and made an English will giving all the rest of his property on trust for the person who should fulfil one of the qualifications. At his death there was no person who fulfilled both qualifications, and questions arose as to the devolution of the property in Spain. It appeared that Spanish law, as the *lex situs* of the land, referred questions of succession to the national law of the testator and would not accept the renvoi back to Spanish law. Wynn-Parry J. therefore applied English domestic law and held that the gift in the Spanish will failed for uncertainty and that the Spanish property fell into the residue disposed of by the English will. However, it was nowhere stated that the construction of the Spanish will would have been different in Spanish domestic law and, indeed, if the construction of the Spanish will was the only point at issue, it would seem that English domestic law should have been applied without any reference to Spanish law, because the testator was domiciled in England.[35] One of the counsel engaged in the case furnished the information that by Spanish domestic law the testator could in the circumstances only dispose of half of his property and that the other half passed to his mother as heiress. It may be that this is the explanation of the decision; but it must be admitted that there is no trace of this to be found in the report. Whatever may have been the reason for referring to Spanish law, it is clear that the judge, although he relied mainly on a dictum enunciating a theory of single renvoi, was in fact adopting a theory of double renvoi. Otherwise, there would have been no occasion to inquire whether Spanish law would "accept the renvoi" from English law—an inquiry which occupied much space in the judgment.

---

[33] It is clear that the Palestine Ordinance involved "accepting the renvoi" and not "deciding the case as the national law would decide it." *cf.* the criticisms of Falconbridge, pp.223–225.

[34] [1947] Ch. 506; affirmed on other grounds, [1948] Ch. 118 (CA); stated below, para.4–041, Illustration 6; discussed (1948) 64 L.Q.R. 264, 321; (1948) 11 M.L.R. 232; Falconbridge, pp.229–232.

[35] *Studd v Cook* (1883) 8 App. Cas. 577; Rule 151; (1948) 11 M.L.R. 233–234.

Lord Kingsdown's Act 1861 was repealed and replaced by the Wills Act   **4–019**
1963 which allows an even wider choice of law for the formal validity of
wills. The Act refers throughout to the internal law of the legal systems which
it authorises, thus excluding renvoi.[36] But it does not in terms abolish the old
rule of common law that a will is formally valid if it complies with the
formalities prescribed by the law of the testator's last domicile; and it may be
that a renvoi from this law is still possible.[37]

General conclusion from the cases. The history of the renvoi doctrine in   **4–020**
English law is the history of single instances. The doctrine originated as a
device for mitigating the rigidity of the English conflict rule for the formal
validity of wills. The passing of Lord Kingsdown's Act in 1861 rendered this
mitigation no longer necessary, at any rate in cases where the testator was a
British subject. But the doctrine was applied in cases falling within that Act,
and was extended far beyond its original context to cases of intrinsic validity
of wills and to cases of intestacy. In 1926 the theory underlying the doctrine
underwent a significant change, but no authorities were cited nor reasons
given for making the change.[38] Two of the cases which have been relied on as
establishing the doctrine have been subsequently overruled or dissented
from.[39] In three other cases, the decision would have been the same if the
court had referred to the domestic rules of the foreign law in the first
instance.[40] And in three cases,[41] none of the parties was concerned to argue
that the foreign law meant foreign domestic law. Nevertheless, until the matter
is reviewed by a higher court it must be taken that the theory of double or total
renvoi is the doctrine of the English courts in the situations in which they are
willing to refer to the conflict rules of the foreign law. Hence, if the foreign
law refers to English law and rejects the renvoi doctrine altogether, the result
is that English domestic law is applicable; while if the foreign law refers to
English law and adopts the doctrine of single renvoi, the result is that the
foreign domestic law is applicable.

By contrast, the more recent approach of the High Court of Australia[42]   **4–021**
lends little support to the proposition that the doctrine of renvoi applies in a
single or universal form; and it specifically rejects the terminology of "reference back" or "reference on" to another law. Its point of departure is that the
question for the court seised is the interpretation and application of the choice
of law rules of the forum, and that these are not confined by a rigid doctrine

---

[36] "Internal law" is defined in s.6(1) to mean, in relation to any territory or state, the law which
would apply in a case where no question of the law in force in any other territory or state
arose.

[37] See below, para.27–037.

[38] *Re Annesley* [1926] Ch. 692.

[39] *Collier v Rivaz* (1841) 2 Curt. 855, in *Bremer v Freeman* (1857) 10 Moo. P.C. 306, 374; *Re
Johnson* [1903] 1 Ch. 821, in *Re Annesley* [1926] Ch. 692, 705, and *Re Askew* [1930] 2 Ch. 259,
272.

[40] *Re Annesley* [1926] Ch. 692; *Re Askew* [1930] 2 Ch. 259; *In the Estate of Fuld (No.3)* [1968]
P. 675.

[41] *Re Johnson* [1903] 1 Ch. 821; *Re O'Keefe* [1940] Ch. 124; *Re Duke of Wellington* [1947] Ch.
506. In *Re O'Keefe*, the originating summons did not even suggest the possibility that Italian
domestic law was applicable.

[42] *Neilson v Overseas Projects Corp of Victoria Ltd* [2005] HCA 54, (2005) 223 C.L.R.
331.

of renvoi. Instead, it advocates the refinement of the choice of law rules of the forum by reference to the specific legal context which they regulate, and relegates the doctrine of renvoi to a supporting role which will be invoked where this is appropriate more completely to achieve the goals of the choice of law rule in question.[43]

4–022   **Scope of the doctrine.** The English renvoi doctrine has been applied to the formal[44] and intrinsic[45] validity of wills and to cases of intestate succession.[46] It has been applied when the reference has been to the law of the domicile,[47] the law of the place where a will was made (*lex loci actus*),[48] and the law of the place where an immovable was situated (*lex situs*).[49] Outside the field of succession, it seems to have been applied in England only to legitimation by subsequent marriage.[50] There are indications that it might be applied to the formal validity of marriage,[51] and to capacity to marry.[52] In Canada it has been held applicable to matrimonial property.[53] It no longer applies to the formal validity of wills, at any rate in cases falling within the Wills Act 1963. It does not apply in the field of contract[54] or in relation to torts.[55] It does not seem

---

[43] *cf.* the strikingly similar approach to the doctrine or principle of characterisation put forward by Mance L.J. in *Raiffeisen Zentralbank Österreich AG v Five Star General Trading LLC* [2001] EWCA Civ 68, [2001] Q.B. 825 at [26]–[29].

[44] *Collier v Rivaz* (1841) 2 Curt. 855; *Frere v Frere* (1847) 5 Notes of Cases 593; *In bonis Lacroix* (1877) 2 P.D. 94; *In the goods of Brown-Sequard* (1894) 70 L.T. 811; *In the Estate of Fuld (No.3)* [1968] P. 675; *Ross v Ross* (1894) 25 S.C.R. 307. But under the Wills Act 1963 (Rule 155, below) renvoi is throughout excluded, and the reference is always to the internal law of the foreign country.

[45] *Re Trufort* (1887) 36 Ch. D. 600; *Re Annesley* [1926] Ch. 692; *Re Ross* [1930] 1 Ch. 377; and (perhaps) *Re Duke of Wellington* [1947] Ch. 506.

[46] *Re Johnson* [1903] 1 Ch. 821; *Simmons v Simmons* (1917) 17 S.R.N.S.W. 419, discussed by Morris (1951) 4 Int.L.Q. 244; *Re O'Keefe* [1940] Ch. 124. But see *Re Thom* (1987) 40 D.L.R. (4th) 563 (Man.) where, however, the court seems to have misunderstood renvoi.

[47] *Collier v Rivaz*, above; *Re Trufort*, above; *Re Johnson*, above; *Simmons v Simmons*, above; *Re Annesley*, above; *Re Ross*, above; *Re Askew*, above; *Re O'Keefe*, above; *In the Estate of Fuld (No.3)*, above.

[48] *In bonis Lacroix*, above; *Ross v Ross*, above.

[49] *Re Ross*, above; *Re Duke of Wellington*, above. *cf. Re Bailey* [1985] 2 N.Z.L.R. 656, where it was held applicable to the Inheritance (Provision for Family and Dependants) Act 1975.

[50] *Re Askew*, above.

[51] *Taczanowska v Taczanowski* [1957] P. 301, 305, 318 (CA); below, paras 17–028 *et seq.*

[52] *R. v Brentwood Marriage Registrar* [1968] 2 Q.B. 956. The actual decision in this case would now be different because of s.50 of the Family Law Act 1986: see above, paras 2–060 *et seq.*

[53] *Vladi v Vladi* (1987) 39 D.L.R. (4th) 563 (N.S.). See below, para.4–032.

[54] Where the contract is governed by the Rome I Regulation (Regulation (EC) 593/2008, on which see Ch.32 below), this is provided by Art.20. The rule reproduces Art.15 of the Rome Convention on the Law Applicable to Contractual Obligations (Contracts (Applicable Law) Act 1990, Sch.1). For matters outside the scope of the Regulation, see *Amin Rasheed Shipping Corp v Kuwait Insurance Co* [1984] A.C. 50, 61–62; *Re United Railways of Havana and Regla Warehouses Ltd* [1960] Ch. 52, 96–97, 115; see also *Rosencrantz v Union Contractors Ltd* (1960) 23 D.L.R. (2d) 473 (BC). Dicta to the contrary in *Vita Food Products Inc v Unus Shipping Co* [1939] A.C. 277, 292 (PC) and *Ocean Steamship Co v Queensland State Wheat Board* [1941] 1 K.B. 402 (CA) must be taken to have been overruled.

[55] Where choice of law for the non-contractual obligation is governed by the Rome II Regulation (Regulation (EC) 864/2007, on which see Chs 34–36 below), this is provided by Art.24. For cases not within the domain of the Regulation, see Private International Law (Miscellaneous Provisions) Act 1995, s.9(5). As regards matters which fall outside the scope of the statutory provisions and continue to be governed by the common law, there is no direct

appropriate that the doctrine should be applied to the construction of wills, because that is governed by the law presumably intended by the testator, i.e. prima facie by the law of his domicile,[56] and it must be assumed that the testator would expect the domestic rules of that law to apply.[57]

Even in the sphere in which the doctrine has been most frequently applied, **4–023** namely, succession to movables and immovables, it must be stressed that for every case which supports the doctrine there are hundreds of cases in which the domestic rules of the foreign law have been applied without any reference to its conflict rules, though it must be admitted that most of these can be explained on the ground that no one was concerned to argue that the reference to foreign law included its rules of the conflict of laws.[58] There is therefore as yet no justification for generalising the few English cases on renvoi into a general rule that a reference to foreign "law" always means the conflict rules of the foreign country, and (it is submitted) no justification for the statement that "the English courts have generally, *if not invariably*, meant by 'the law of the country of domicile' the whole law of that country as administered by the courts of that country."[59]

Much of the discussion of the renvoi doctrine has proceeded on the basis **4–024** that the choice lies in all cases between its absolute acceptance and its absolute rejection. The truth would appear to be that in some situations the doctrine is convenient and promotes justice, and that in others it is inconvenient and ought to be rejected.[60] In some cases the doctrine may be a useful means of arriving at a result which is desired for its own sake. For instance, if the court wishes to sustain a marriage which is alleged to be formally invalid, or to promote uniformity of distribution in a case of succession to movables where the deceased left movables in two or more countries, or to avoid conflicts with the *lex situs* in a case of title to land or conflicts with the law of the domicile in a case involving personal status, then the doctrine of

---

English authority. There is Scottish and American authority that renvoi is inapplicable in tort cases: *M'Elroy v M'Allister*, 1949 S.C. 110, 126; *Haumschild v Continental Casualty Co*, 7 Wis. 2d 130, 141–142, 95 N.W. 2d 814, 820 (1959); *Pfau v Trent Aluminium Co*, 55 N.J. 2d 511, 263 A. 2d 129, 136–137 (1970). But in *Neilson v Overseas Projects Corp of Victoria Ltd* [2005] HCA 54, (2005) 223 C.L.R. 331, the High Court of Australia held that it was applicable in the context of the current Australian choice of law rule for overseas torts, which is to apply the *lex loci delicti commissi* to all issues of substance, justifying the conclusion on the basis that to do otherwise would encourage forum shopping [13], would be incoherent [111], would be arbitrary [174, 176], or would be absurd [271].

[56] Rule 156.

[57] See, however, *Re Gansloser* [1952] Ch. 30 (the order made in 1932); and (on one interpretation) *Re Duke of Wellington* [1947] Ch. 506, discussed above, para.4–018. See also *Haji-Ioannou v Frangos* [2009] EWHC 2310 (QB), [2010] 1 All E.R. (Comm.) 303, in which intestate succession to movable property was governed by the law of Monaco, according to the private international law of which state, succession was governed by English law, and a renvoi back to the domestic law of Monaco was accepted. The judge therefore applied Monaco law.

[58] For example, in *Macmillan Inc v Bishopsgate Investment Trust Plc (No.3)* [1996] 1 W.L.R. 387 (CA), a case involving competing claims to shares in a New York company, there was an argument for renvoi, "but mercifully (or sadly, as the case may be)" (at p.405, *per* Staughton L.J.) it was abandoned.

[59] *Re Ross* [1930] 1 Ch. 377, 390 (italics added).

[60] *cf.* Falconbridge, p.141. It may also result in the case being decided as it would be decided in the courts of the natural forum, and by so doing support the general judicial policy against forum shopping: see *Neilson v Overseas Projects Corp of Victoria Ltd*, above.

renvoi may sometimes afford a useful device for achieving the desired result. On the other hand the theoretical and practical difficulties involved in applying the doctrine[61] may on occasion outweigh any advantages it may possess. The doctrine should not therefore be invoked unless the object of the English conflict rule in referring to a foreign law will on balance be better served by construing the reference to mean the conflict rules of that law.

4–025   From the above point of view, and in the light of English legislation which has specifically excluded the doctrine of renvoi, it is thought that the following situations present a relatively strong case for the application of the doctrine:

(a) *Title to land situated abroad.*[62] If the question before the English court is whether a person has acquired a proprietary interest in land situated abroad, the court (so far as it has jurisdiction to deal with the matter at all[63]) will apply the *lex situs*, the law of the place where the land is situated. One of the reasons for applying the *lex situs* is that any adjudication which was contrary to what the *lex situs* had decided or would decide would be in most cases a *brutum fulmen*, since in the last resort the land can only be dealt with in a manner permitted by the *lex situs*. This reason can only be implemented if the *lex situs* is interpreted to mean the law which the *lex situs* would apply.[64] Suppose, for instance, that a British citizen domiciled in England dies intestate leaving land in Spain; and that by Spanish domestic law X is entitled to the land, but that the Spanish courts would apply English domestic law according to which Y is entitled. It would be manifestly useless for an English court to decide that X was entitled to the land, because he could never recover it from Y in Spain.[65] "The meaning of the term 'law of the *situs*' can be ascertained best from a consideration of the reasons underlying the existence of the rule. The primary reason for its existence lies in the fact that the law-making and law-enforcing agencies of the country in which land is situated have exclusive control over such land."[66] However, the Wills Act 1963 excludes renvoi even in the case of immovables so far as the formal validity of wills is concerned.

4–026   (b) *Title to movables situated abroad.*   There is a case, though it is obviously weaker, for interpreting the reference to the *lex situs*, when this is used to determine title to movable property, as being to the law of the *situs* including reference to any law to which the courts at the *situs* can be shown to make reference. On one view, certainty and predictability are enhanced

---

[61] See below, paras 4–033 *et seq.* But *cf. Neilson v Overseas Projects Corp of Victoria Ltd,* above, where the High Court of Australia considered, in that case at least, that the alleged practical difficulties were "not self-evidently true": at [110].

[62] Falconbridge, pp.141, 217–220; Cook, pp.264, 279–280; Lorenzen, p.78.

[63] English courts do not normally try questions of title to foreign land: Rule 131.

[64] Even so, it is far from clear that the rules of the conflict of laws of the *situs* will recognise a foreign judgment concerning title to land, whether or not the adjudicating court reached the answer which the courts of the *situs* would have, and this justification is therefore weak.

[65] For this reason it is submitted that the decision in *Re Ross* [1930] 1 Ch. 377 was correct so far as the immovables were concerned, subject to what is said later (para.4–036) about the difficulty arising from the reference by the foreign law to the national law of a British citizen.

[66] *Re Schneider's Estate*, 198 Misc. 1017, 96 N.Y.S. 2d 652, 656 (1950).

when there is no divergence between what an English court and the courts at the *situs* would have said on the issue of title to a thing which was within the territorial jurisdiction of the *situs*; but on another, reference to the private international law of the *situs* may be haphazard, and is almost bound to be more complicated than simply applying the domestic law of the place where the thing is.

So far as concerns the determination of title to tangible movables, recent **4–027** first instance decisions have demonstrated little enthusiasm either for the application of renvoi or for the suggestion that the approach of the High Court of Australia should be adopted and generalised to apply to English law on choice of law for movables. In *Macmillan Inc v Bishopsgate Investment Trust Plc (No.3)*,[67] it was held that priority of title to intangible movables (registered shares in a New York company) was governed by the *lex loci actus*, in its domestic law sense, excluding the doctrine of renvoi. However, the Court of Appeal rejected the *lex loci actus* in favour of the law of the place of registration of the shares, and no argument was evidently addressed to it on the application of renvoi. In relation to tangible movables, it was said in *Glencore International AG v Metro Trading International Inc*[68] that the question was an open one.

However, in *Islamic Republic of Iran v Berend*,[69] Eady J. declined to apply **4–028** the principle of renvoi in order to determine title to tangible movables in the context of a claim for their return. In *Dornoch Ltd v Westminster International BV*,[70] Tomlinson J. discussed, but did not finally decide, whether the reference to the *lex situs* in questions concerned with title to a ship located in Thailand was a reference to the domestic law of the *situs* or, if its content be proved, to the law including its private international law, though his provisional answer was that the reference was to the domestic law. Though the judge also acknowledged the merits of the approach adopted in *Neilson*, there was no evidence of Thai rules of the conflict of laws before the court, and therefore no material basis to allow him to undertake an analysis of the kind adopted in that case. When the hearing was resumed,[71] it was confirmed that as there was no evidence that a Thai court would do otherwise than apply Thai domestic law to the issue, the issue of renvoi required no further attention. Finally, in *Blue Sky One Ltd v Mahan Air*,[72] Beatson J. rejected any role for renvoi in the determination of the proprietary effect of a mortgage of an aircraft situated overseas.

Even if the foundations on which it rests are not particularly strong, the **4–029** clear balance of opinion at first instance is that where it is necessary to determine the effect of a transaction on the title to movable property, on which issue reference is made to the *lex situs* at the date of the transaction, that

---

[67] [1996] 1 W.L.R. 387.

[68] [2001] 1 Lloyd's Rep. 284, 287. See also *Winkworth v Christie, Manson & Woods Ltd* [1980] Ch. 496, 514.

[69] [2007] EWHC 132 (QB), [2007] 2 All E.R. (Comm.) 132.

[70] [2009] EWHC 889 (Admlty), [2009] 2 Lloyd's Rep. 191.

[71] *Dornoch Ltd v Westminster International BV (No.2)* [2009] EWHC 1782 (Admlty), [2009] 2 Lloyd's Rep. 420.

[72] [2010] EWHC 631 (Comm.), at [157] *et seq.*

reference is to the domestic law only, and that in this sense, renvoi is excluded.[73]

4–030   (c) *Formal validity of marriage.* Factors similar to those which originally favoured the application of the renvoi doctrine as a device for sustaining the formal validity of wills[74] also favour its application as a device for sustaining the formal validity of a marriage celebrated abroad. These factors are, first, a rigid rule of the English conflict of laws which normally requires compliance with the *lex loci celebrationis*[75]; secondly, a more flexible rule in neighbouring European countries (where English people are likely to get married) which allows compliance with either the *lex loci* or the personal law of the parties; and thirdly, a strong judicial bias in favour of the validity of marriage. There is, however, no English[76] case which actually sustains the validity of a marriage on the ground that it was formally valid by the law which the *lex loci celebrationis* would apply. But it is a legitimate inference from *Taczanowska v Taczanowski*[77] that such a marriage would be upheld. This does not mean that a marriage would be held formally invalid for failure to comply with the formalities prescribed by whatever system of domestic law would have been referred to by the conflict rules of the *lex loci celebrationis*. It merely means that a marriage may be formally valid if the parties comply with the formalities prescribed by either the domestic rules of the *lex loci celebrationis* or whatever system of domestic law the *lex loci celebrationis* would apply. Thus, the reference to the *lex loci celebrationis* in the case of formalities of marriage is an alternative reference to either its conflict rules or its domestic rules. It is not a justification for elevating the renvoi doctrine into a rule of general application.

4–031   (d) *Certain cases of transmission.*[78] Where the foreign law referred to by the English court would refer to a second foreign law, and the second foreign law would agree that it was applicable, the case for applying the second foreign law is strong. Thus, if a German national domiciled in Italy died leaving movables in England, and Italian and German law both agreed that German domestic law was applicable because the *propositus* was a German national, it seems that the English court should accept the situation and apply German domestic law. For the practical advantages of deciding the case the

---

[73] This conclusion is stated as a matter of common law principle. The issue has not yet arisen in a case in which choice of law for the actual claim is governed by the Rome II Regulation (Regulation (EC) 864/2007, on which see generally Chs 34–36), such as where the claim is for relief in relation to tortious or otherwise-wrongful interference with property. But as the choice of law rules of Rome II Regulation itself exclude reference to renvoi (Art.24), it is unlikely that the conclusion will diverge from that arrived at in the most recent cases.

[74] See above, para.4–011.

[75] Rule 73.

[76] *Re Lando's Estate*, 112 Minn. 257, 127 N.W. 1125 (1910) is an American decision to this effect. See Lorenzen, pp.55–56, 77–78.

[77] [1957] P. 301, 305, 318; see below, para.4–042, Illustration 7; *cf. Hooper v Hooper* [1959] 1 W.L.R. 1021.

[78] Griswold (1938) 51 Harv.L.R. 1190; Lorenzen, pp.76–77; Bate, pp.112–114; Ehrenzweig, pp.338–340; *cf. Re Trufort* (1887) 36 Ch.D. 600; *R. v Brentwood Marriage Registrar* [1968] 2 Q.B. 956; *Mason v Rose*, 176 F. 2d 486 (2d Cir. 1949).

way the Italian and German courts would decide it (especially if the *propositus* left movables in Italy and Germany as well as in England) seem to outweigh the theoretical disadvantages of this mild form of transmission. If, on the other hand, the second foreign law would not agree that it was applicable, then there seems no reason why it should be applied. Thus, if a Danish national domiciled in Italy died leaving movables in England, and Italian law would apply the law of the nationality, and Danish law would apply the law of the domicile, neither law recognising any renvoi from the other, it seems that the English court should apply Italian domestic law.[79]

The interplay of renvoi and public policy gave rise to an interesting problem in a case on matrimonial property, decided in Nova Scotia, Canada.[80] The Nova Scotia conflict rule (laid down by statute[81]) provided that the governing law was that of the place where the spouses had their last common habitual residence.[82] On the facts of the case, this was Germany. The German conflict rule, however, referred to the law of Iran, the country of which the spouses were nationals. The Nova Scotia court was prepared in principle to apply renvoi and follow the transmission to Iranian law. However, it considered that the application of Iranian matrimonial property law would be contrary to substantial justice (public policy) because it was unfair to women. This raised the question whether it should apply the internal law of Germany or the *lex fori* (which is normally applicable when the relevant provision of foreign law is contrary to public policy). It chose the former on the ground that the rejection of Iranian law did not justify disregarding the original reference to German law.   **4–032**

Difficulties in the application of the doctrine. From what has been said above, it will be clear that the role played by renvoi within the modern conflict of laws is in general controversial, and that the application of the doctrine of total renvoi in particular can give rise to issues of some complexity. In *Barros Mattos Junior v MacDaniels Ltd*[83] the application of renvoi, especially in the form of total renvoi, was considered, in line with the views expressed in this Work, to be something only to be undertaken in exceptional cases. By contrast, the High Court of Australia[84] has expressed a somewhat different point of view, in the context of that country's choice of law rules for overseas torts: it considered that the difficulties said to be created by the doctrine of renvoi were "not self-evidently true".[85] But the High Court also made clear its view that the application of renvoi is to be considered on its individual merits in each separate legal situation in which it proposed to be applied. There may   **4–033**

---

[79] Wolff, p.203.

[80] *Vladi v Vladi* (1987) 39 D.L.R. (4th) 563 (N.S.).

[81] Matrimonial Property Act, S.N.S. 1980, c. 9, s.22(1).

[82] Unlike similar statutes in certain other Canadian provinces, the Nova Scotia Act referred simply to "the law" of the last common habitual residence, not "the internal law." The latter would have excluded the possibility of renvoi.

[83] [2005] EWHC 1323 (Ch.), [2005] I.L.Pr. 630, at [106] *et seq.* (*obiter*, as the particular issue was covered by Private International Law (Miscellaneous Provisions) Act 1995, s.9(5), which excluded the doctrine of renvoi from issues relating to tort).

[84] *Neilson v Overseas Projects Corp of Victoria Ltd* [2005] HCA 54, (2005) 233 C.L.R. 331.

[85] At [110].

therefore be other cases in which the points to be made below have more force than they were considered by the High Court to have in that case.

4-034   (a) *Unpredictability of result.* The doctrine makes everything depend on "the doubtful and conflicting evidence of foreign experts."[86] Moreover, it is peculiar to this theory of renvoi that it requires proof, not only of the foreign choice-of-law rules, but of the foreign rules about renvoi—and there are few matters upon which it is more difficult to obtain reliable information.[87] In Continental countries, decided cases, at least of courts of first instance, are not binding as authorities to be followed, and doctrine changes from decade to decade. Consequently, as Wynn-Parry J. said in *Re Duke of Wellington*,[88] "it would be difficult to imagine a harder task than that which faces me, namely, of expounding for the first time either in this country or in Spain the relevant law of Spain as it would be expounded by the Supreme Court of Spain, which up to the present time has made no pronouncement on the subject, and having to base that exposition on evidence which satisfies me that on this subject there exists a profound cleavage of legal opinion in Spain and two conflicting decisions of courts of inferior jurisdiction." The difficulty is not confined to the judge: it also confronts the lawyer advising his client, for he has to investigate not only the relevant English conflict rule but also (1) the choice-of-law rules of the foreign law; (2) the prevailing theory of renvoi in the foreign country; and (3) the domestic rules of the foreign law. He cannot advise with confidence, because at any of these stages (and particularly the second) he cannot tell what evidence of foreign law may have been collected on the other side.

4-035   The English cases show that the effect of acquiring a domicile in a foreign country may sometimes be to make the foreign domestic law applicable,[89] sometimes English domestic law,[90] sometimes the law of the domicile of origin,[91] and sometimes the law of yet a fourth country.[92] There is no certainty that different results will not be reached in any future case in which the same foreign laws are involved, because foreign law is a question of fact and has to be proved by evidence in each case.[93] Moreover, if the evidence of foreign law is misleading or inadequate, the English court may reach a result which is unreal and unjust to the point of absurdity. Thus, in *Re O'Keefe*[94] the intestate had lived in Italy for the last forty-seven years of her life and was clearly

---

[86] *Re Askew* [1930] 2 Ch. 259, 278. *cf.* Lorenzen, p.127.

[87] See, e.g. *Tezcan v Tezcan* (1992) 87 D.L.R. (4th) 503, 519–521 (BCCA), a case in which, although the foreign law's choice of law rules were proved, its rules on renvoi were not.

[88] [1947] Ch. 506, 515.

[89] *Re Annesley* [1926] Ch. 692; *Re Askew* [1930] 2 Ch. 259.

[90] *Re Ross* [1930] 1 Ch. 377.

[91] *Re Johnson* [1903] 1 Ch. 821; *Re O'Keefe* [1940] Ch. 124.

[92] *Re Trufort* (1887) 36 Ch.D. 600; *R. v Brentwood Marriage Registrar* [1968] 2 Q.B. 956.

[93] See below, Rule 25 (but see the Civil Evidence Act 1972, s.4(2)). In *Simmons v Simmons* (1917) 17 S.R.N.S.W. 419 the NSW court concluded, on expert evidence, that French law does not accept the renvoi, but an opposite conclusion was reached on expert evidence in *Re Annesley* [1926] Ch. 692.

[94] [1940] Ch. 124; stated below, para.4–041, Illustration 5. The short unreserved judgment has given rise to "a flood of writings in all corners of the world, but particularly in Italy": Nadelmann (1969) 17 Am.J.Comp.L. 418, 444. The case recalls the much-criticised decision of Farwell J. in *Re Johnson* [1903] 1 Ch. 821, as to which, see above, para.4–015.

domiciled there. Yet the effect of the total renvoi doctrine was that her movables were distributed not in accordance with the Italian domestic law with which she might be expected to be most familiar, and in reliance on which she may have refrained from making a will, but in accordance with the domestic law of Eire, a political unit which only came into existence during her long sojourn in Italy, of which she was not a citizen, and which she had never visited in her life except for a "short tour" with her father sixty years before her death. The only possible justification for such a result is that it may have enabled the movables in England to devolve in the same way as the movables in Italy. But of course in many cases uniformity of distribution is unattainable so long as some systems of law refer to the national law and others to the law of the domicile. For instance, uniformity of distribution would be impossible on any theory if an Italian national died intestate domiciled in England, for the English and Italian courts would each distribute the movables subject to its control in accordance with its own domestic law.

(b) *The national law of a British citizen.*[95] The most frequent occasion for applying the total renvoi doctrine has been the conflict between English law, which refers to the law of the domicile in succession to movables and in other cases, and the laws of some Continental countries, which refer to the law of the nationality. If the *propositus* is a British or American citizen, the foreign court's reference to his national law is meaningless, for there is no such thing as a "British" or "American" or even a "United Kingdom" law of succession, nor is there any such thing as "English" nationality. If the English court decides for itself how the foreign court might be expected to interpret its reference to the national law of a British citizen, as has been done in some cases, it is not necessarily deciding the case as the foreign court would decide it. Thus in *Re Johnson*[96] and *Re O'Keefe*[97] it was assumed, without any evidence of foreign law, that the national law of a British subject meant the law of his domicile of origin. If, on the other hand, the English court allows the foreign expert witness to assume that the national law of a British citizen is English law, as has been done in other cases, it is basing its decision on a manifestly false premise. Thus, in *Re Ross*[98] the evidence was that "the Italian courts would determine the case on the footing that the English law applicable is that part of the law which would be applicable to an English national (*sic*) domiciled in England." In *Re Askew*,[99] the expert witness stated: "I am informed and believe that John Bertram Askew was an Englishman (*sic*). Therefore English law would be applied by the German court." Of course it can be argued that if the English court seeks to discover what decision the foreign court would reach, the grounds on which the foreign court would

4–036

---

[95] See the valuable discussion in Falconbridge, pp.199–216. *cf.* Cook, pp.239–244.

[96] [1903] 1 Ch. 821, 826: "According to the law of Baden, the legal succession to the property of the deceased of which she has not disposed by will is governed solely by the law of the country of which the testatrix was a subject at the time of her death."

[97] [1940] Ch. 124, 129: "Italian lawyers cannot say what is the meaning of the law of the nationality when there is more than one system of law of the nationality."

[98] [1930] 1 Ch. 377, 404, stated below, para.4–040, Illustration 3.

[99] [1930] 2 Ch. 259, 276.

arrive at its decision are irrelevant. But there is reason to believe that at least the Italian courts do not now interpret the national law of a British citizen to mean either English law or the law of his domicile of origin, but on the contrary interpret it to mean Italian law if he is domiciled in Italy.[100] If this is so, it means that, for this reason also, the cases of *Re Ross* and *Re O'Keefe* are no longer reliable guides.

4–037　　(c) *Circulus inextricabilis.* As we have seen, the effect of applying the doctrine of total renvoi is to make the decision turn on whether the foreign court rejects the renvoi doctrine or adopts a theory of single or partial renvoi. But if the foreign court also adopts the doctrine of total renvoi, then logically no solution is possible at all unless either the English or the foreign court abandons its theory, for otherwise a perpetual *circulus inextricabilis* would be constituted.[101] So far, this difficulty has not yet arisen, because English courts have not yet had occasion to apply their renvoi doctrine to the law of a country which adopts the same doctrine. But it is not inconceivable, for another common law jurisdiction may adopt the principle of total renvoi while using connecting factors which differ in some respect from those of English law. Where this problem arises, the most rational conclusion is that the English court should apply its own law if the issue is remitted back to it from the first-chosen law, as Scrutton L.J. suggested in *Casdagli v Casdagli*[102]:

" . . . it has been argued that if the country of allegiance looks to or sends back the decision to the law of the domicil, and the country of domicil looks to or sends back (*renvoyer*) the decision to the law of nationality, there is an inextricable circle in 'the doctrine of the renvoi' and no result is reached. I do not see that this difficulty is insoluble. If the country of nationality applies the law which the country of domicil would apply to such a case if arising in its Courts, it may well apply its own law as to the subject-matter of dispute, being that which the country of domicil would apply, but not that part of it which would remit the matter to the law of domicil, which part would have spent its operation in the first remittance. The knot may be cut in another way, not so logical, if the country of domicil says 'We are ready to apply the law of nationality, but if the country of nationality chooses to

---

[100] De Nova, *Il Richiamo di Ordinamenti Plurilegislativi: Studio di Diritto Interlocale ed Internazionale Privato* (1940); De Nova, *Il Caso In re O'Keefe e la Determinazione della Lex Patriae di un Cittadino Britannico domiciliato all' Estero*, in *Festschrift für Leo Raape* (Hamburg, 1948); De Nova, 1953 *Rev. Crit.* 143, 147–155; De Nova, 1955 *Rev. Crit.* 1, 15; De Nova (1966) *Recueil des Cours*, II, pp.545–557 (in English); Falconbridge, pp.207–210.

[101] Morris (1937) 18 B.Y.I.L. 37; Falconbridge, pp.175, 179, 183; Lorenzen, p.67. Even writers who approve of the total renvoi doctrine admit that it may produce a *circulus inextricabilis*: Wolff, p.201; Griswold (1938) 51 Harv.L.R. 1192–1193.

[102] [1918] P. 89, 111 (CA). Scrutton L.J.'s dissenting judgment was approved by the House of Lords: [1919] A.C. 145, and was applied by the Privy Council in *Kotia v Nahas* [1941] A.C. 403. It is also consistent with the views expressed by Dr Morris in (1937) 18 B.Y.I.L. 32, 34, where he said that the principle "can never involve more than two crossings of the frontier. Logically, the reference back to the law of the nationality from the *lex domicilii* must be to municipal laws, and not to its private international law with a consequent further reference back, *for the excellent reason that part of its law has spent itself in the first reference*" (emphasis added).

remit the matter to us we will apply the same law as we should apply to our own subjects.' This is the German solution of the difficulty".

In other words, in an English court judicial pragmatism will provide the solution to a problem which has not arisen for direct judicial decision. Once the English court seised of the dispute has applied its rules on choice of law, only to find that this chosen law has remitted the matter back to English law, the English court will apply its own domestic law. A more abstract theoretical possibility, that an endless circle renvoi would arise and would mean that "the English judges and the foreign judges would then continue to bow to each other like the officers at Fontenoy", has nothing whatever to commend it.[103] In *Neilson v Overseas Projects Corp of Victoria Ltd*,[104] the High Court of Australia declined to interpret the evidence before it[105] as leading to the conclusion that a Chinese court would adopt the principle of total renvoi. It therefore did not need to decide what it would have done had the evidence led the court into what was described as a "hall of mirrors".[106] But a fair reading of the judgments suggests that the approach of Scrutton L.J. would have been adopted.

Conclusion. As a purely practical matter it would seem that a court should not undertake the onerous task of trying to ascertain how a foreign court would decide the question, unless the advantages of doing so clearly outweigh the disadvantages. In most situations, the balance of convenience surely lies in interpreting the reference to foreign law to mean its domestic rules. Although the doctrine of renvoi was favoured by Westlake[107] and Dicey,[108] many writers, both English and foreign, are opposed to it. Lorenzen says[109]: "Notwithstanding the great authority of Westlake and Dicey, it may reasonably be hoped that, when the doctrine with all its consequences is squarely presented to the higher English courts, they will not hesitate to reject the decisions of the courts that have lent colour to renvoi in the English law." Indeed, previous editions of this work submitted that such a review was long overdue, plainly implying that the courts should restrict or remove altogether the doctrine from English law. By contrast with this, the High Court of Australia,[110] which was equally free from constraining authority, reached the conclusion that not only were there no significant obstacles to the incorporation of renvoi as an aspect of the *lex causae* for tort claims, but that there were clear advantages in confirming its applicability.

4–038

---

[103] See Private International Law Committee, First Report (1954) Cmd. 9068, para.23(3); Lorenzen, pp.126–127.

[104] [2005] HCA 54, (2005) 233 C.L.R. 331.

[105] Neither on the basis that it was so proved, nor on the footing that in the absence of proof, the Chinese doctrine of renvoi was to the same effect as that of Australian law.

[106] McHugh J. (dissenting) at [39].

[107] Ch.2.

[108] 1st ed., p.77.

[109] Lorenzen, p.53.

[110] *Neilson v Overseas Projects Corp of Victoria Ltd* [2005] HCA 54, (2005) 233 C.L.R. 331.

Illustrations[111]

4–039   1. T, a British subject of Irish domicile of origin and subsequent English domicile of choice, died domiciled in Belgium in the English sense, but not in the Belgain sense because he had not obtained the authorisation of the Belgian Government to establish his domicile in Belgium as required by Art.13 of the Code Napoleon (since repealed). He left a will and six codicils. The will and two of the codicils were executed in the form required by Belgian domestic law. Four of the codicils were executed in the form required by English domestic law but not in the form required by Belgian domestic law. Evidence was given that by Belgian law the succession to foreigners in T's situation was governed by "the laws of their own country." The will and all six codicils were admitted to probate.[112]

2. T, a British subject of English domicile of origin, died domiciled in France in the English sense, but not in the French sense because she had not obtained authority from the French Government to establish her domicile in France as required by Art.13 of the Code Napoleon (since repealed). She left a will which purported to dispose of all her property. By French law, T could only dispose of one-third of her property because she left two children surviving her. Evidence was given that a French court would refer to English law as T's national law and would accept the renvoi back to French law, French domestic law was applied and T's will was only effective to dispose of one-third of her property.[113]

4–040   3. T, a British subject of English domicile of origin, died domiciled in Italy leaving movables in England and Italy and immovables in Italy. By her will T gave her property in England to her niece X and her property in Italy to her grand-nephew Y with usufruct to his mother X for life. T's only son A claimed that by Italian domestic law he was entitled to one-half of her property as his *legitima portio*. The validity of T's will was governed by Italian law as the law of her domicile in respect of movables and by Italian law as the lex situs in respect of immovables. Evidence was given that the Italian courts would refer to English law as the law of T's nationality in respect of both movables and immovables, and would not accept the renvoi back to Italian law. English domestic law applied and A's claim was rejected.[114]

4. A, a British subject of English domicile of origin, separated from his wife, acquired a domicile of choice in Germany, formed an association with a German woman, and had by her a daughter, D. While still domiciled in Germany, A obtained a divorce from his wife in the German court and subsequently married the mother of D. Under the settlement made on the occasion of his first marriage, the proper law of which was English, A had a special power of appointment among the children of any subsequent marriage. A purported to exercise the power in favour of D. By English domestic law, D was illegitimate,[115] but by German domestic law she was legitimated by the subsequent marriage of her parents. Evidence was given that the German courts would refer to English law as the law of A's nationality and would accept the renvoi back to German law. German domestic law applied and D was therefore legitimate and an object of the power.[116]

4–041   5. T, a British subject, who was born in India in 1860, acquired a domicile of choice in Italy in 1890, and lived there until her death intestate in 1937. She left two sisters of the whole blood and a brother and sister of the half blood. T's father was born in 1835 in County Clare and T's domicile of origin was consequently in that part of Ireland which in 1937 was called Eire and is now called the Republic of Ireland. Evidence was given that the Italian courts would refer the succession to T's movables to the law of the country to which she belonged at the time of her death. This was construed to mean the law of Eire, although T was not a citizen of Eire and had never been there in her life except for a short tour with her father in 1878. Hence the brother and

---

[111] All these Illustrations are of the second branch of clause (2) of this Rule, that is, they are all cases in which the law of a foreign country has been interpreted to mean "any domestic law which the courts of that country apply to the decision of the case." Illustrations of the first branch of clause (2) of the Rule, that is, cases in which the law of a foreign country has been interpreted to mean its domestic law, will be found elsewhere in this book.

[112] *Collier v Rivaz* (1841) 2 Curt. 855; see now Wills Act 1963, s.1.

[113] *Re Annesley* [1926] Ch. 692. In fact, French law referred to English law because the testatrix was domiciled in England in the French sense. The evidence of French law was erroneous.

[114] *Re Ross* [1930] 1 Ch. 377.

[115] See Legitimacy Act 1926, s.1(2) (since repealed).

[116] *Re Askew* [1930] 2 Ch. 259.

sister of the half blood were entitled to share equally with the two sisters of the whole blood.[117]

6. T, a British subject domiciled in England, by his Spanish will gave land and movables in Spain to the person who on his death would become Duke of Wellington and Duke of Ciudad Rodrigo. On T's death there was no such person, because the two dukedoms became separated for the first time since 1814. By his English will T gave all the rest of his property to the person who on his death would become Duke of Wellington. For some unexplained reason it was necessary to refer to Spanish law in order to determine the devolution of the Spanish land. Evidence was given that the Spanish courts would refer to English law as the law of T's nationality and would not accept the renvoi back to Spanish law. English domestic law applied and the Spanish land and movables fell into the residue disposed of by the English will.[118]

7. H and W, both Polish nationals domiciled in Poland, marry in Italy in accordance with the **4–042** form prescribed by Polish domestic law, but not in the form prescribed by Italian domestic law. Evidence is given that the Italian courts would recognise a marriage celebrated in Italy in accordance with the forms prescribed by the law of the parties' common nationality. The marriage of H and W is (*semble*) valid.[119]

8. T was domiciled at all material times in Germany. He resided in Ontario between 1940 and 1946, when he became a Canadian citizen and therefore a British subject. He died in 1962, before the Wills Act 1963 came into operation. He left a will and four codicils, two of which were executed in Germany in the form required by English and Ontario law but not in the form required by German law. Evidence was given that a German court would refer in the first instance to the law of Ontario as the national law of the testator and would accept the renvoi back to German law, and would refer in the second instance to German domestic law as the *lex loci actus*. German domestic law was applied and the two codicils were formally invalid.[120]

9. A sculpture discovered in Iran is sold at auction in New York and delivered to the purchaser to France. Subsequently she sends it for sale by an auction house in London. The Iranian government applies to restrain the sale on the ground that it owns the sculpture. The question whether the purchaser acquired title to the sculpture on its delivery to her in France is governed by French law, which means French domestic law without regard to the choice of law rules which a French court would have applied if it had been asked to determine the issue of title acquired by delivery.[121]

10. An aircraft acquired by an English company is leased to an Armenian company and chartered to an Iranian company. While the aircraft is in the Netherlands a mortgage of it is executed in favour of a US company. The validity of the mortgage is determined by Dutch domestic law, according to which it is invalid, even though a Dutch court would have applied English domestic law to the question, according to which the mortgage would have been valid to transfer legal title to the US company.[122]

11. An employee is sent from England to work on a project in China, and is accompanied by his wife. The wife sustains injury by reason of the dangerous condition of the accommodation in which they are quartered and brings proceedings in England against the employer. The claim, and the limitation period within which it has to be commenced, will be determined, in principle at least, by Chinese domestic law, even if it be shown that a Chinese court, seised of the question, would have applied English law to these issues. Were the wife to contend that her claim should be governed by English law, on the footing that England is substantially more closely connected

---

[117] *Re O'Keefe* [1940] Ch. 124. If Italian domestic law had been applied the half-brother and half-sister would each have been entitled to a half share: Italian Civil Code, Book II, Title ii, para. 570, s.2. Thus they would each have got half of what Irish law gave them. Under English domestic law they were entitled to nothing.

[118] *Re Duke of Wellington* [1947] Ch. 506: affirmed on grounds not involving any reference to the law of Spain [1948] Ch. 118 (CA); discussed above, para.4–018.

[119] See *Taczanowska v Taczanowski* [1957] P. 301 (CA), where, however, the marriage was not valid by Polish domestic law and was held valid on another ground. See below, paras 17–028 *et seq.*

[120] *In the Estate of Fuld (No.3)* [1968] P. 675.

[121] *Islamic Repulic of Iran v Berend* [2007] EWHC 132 (QB), [2007] 2 All E.R. (Comm.) 132.

[122] *Blue Sky One Ltd v Mahan Air* [2010] EWHC 631 (Comm.).

to the tort, it is to be doubted whether the fact that a Chinese court would have applied Chinese law would be admissible on that particular issue.[123]

12. A Greek court gives judgment in a civil or commercial matter against F, in favour of H who has a domcile of choice in Monaco. H applies to register the judgment for enforcement in England under Chapter III of the Brussels I Regulation,[124] but dies between the making of the application and the hearing of F's appeal to set registration aside. H's widow, R, applies to be substituted for H as the party entitled to register and enforce the judgment. It is held that her entitlement to do so is determined by Monegasque law, as the law governing succession to H's movable estate, including its rules for choice of law. According to these, R's succession to the judgment was governed by the *lex patriae*, "British law", which a Monegasque court would interpret meaning as English law. A court in Monaco would accept the renvoi from English law to Monegasque law, and therefore the entitlement of R to register the judgment depended on whether she had complied with Monegasque law on acceptance of an inheritance, which she had not.[125]

---

[123] Regulation (EC) 864/2007, Arts 4 and 24. The facts are derived from *Neilson v Overseas Projects Corp of Victoria* [2005] HCA 54, (2005) 233 C.L.R. 331, in which the High Court of Australia, applying the corresponding choice of law rule of Australian common law, applied Australian domestic law on the footing that this is what a Chinese judge would have done.

[124] Regulation (EC) 44/2001, Art.38.

[125] *Haji-Ioannou v Frangos* [2009] EWHC 2310 (QB), [2010] 1 All E.R. (Comm.) 303.

CHAPTER 5

THE EXCLUSION OF FOREIGN LAW

RULE 2—**English courts will not enforce or recognise a right, power, capacity, disability or legal relationship arising under the law of a foreign country, if the enforcement or recognition of such right, power, capacity, disability or legal relationship would be inconsistent with the fundamental public policy of English law.**[1]

5R–001

COMMENT

Rule 2 expresses in very general terms the principle[2] that a foreign law, which is otherwise applicable according to the English rules of the conflict of laws, will not be applied or enforced in England if the law, or the result of its application, is contrary to public policy. "There is abundant authority that an English court will decline to recognise or apply what would otherwise be the appropriate foreign rule of law when to do so would be against English public policy."[3]

5–002

In English domestic law it is now well settled that the doctrine of public policy "should only be invoked in clear cases in which the harm to the public is substantially incontestable, and does not depend upon the idiosyncratic inferences of a few judicial minds."[4] In the conflict of laws it is even more necessary that the doctrine should be kept within proper limits, otherwise the whole basis of the system is liable to be frustrated. "The courts are not free to refuse to enforce a foreign right at the pleasure of the judges, to suit the individual notion of expediency or fairness. They do not close their doors unless help would violate some fundamental principle of justice, some prevalent conception of good morals, some deep-rooted tradition of the common weal."[5] As a result the courts will be slower to invoke public policy in cases

5–003

---

[1] Kahn-Freund, *Selected Writings* (1978), Ch.9; Lloyd, *Public Policy* (1953), Ch.5; Sammartano and Morse, *Public Policy in Transnational Relationships* (1992); Paulsen and Sovern (1956) 56 Col. L.R. 969; Carter (1984) 55 B.Y.I.L. 111, (1993) 42 I.C.L.Q. 1; Bucher (1993) *Recueil des Cours*, II, p.9; Leslie, 1995 Jur. Rev. 477; Enonchong (1996) 45 I.C.L.Q. 633; Meidanis (2005) Eur. L.R. 95; Mills (2008) 4 J. Priv. Int. L. 201.

[2] See *Guardianship Convention Case* (*Netherlands v Sweden*) 1958 I.C.J. Rep. 53, at pp.90–95, *per* Judge Lauterpacht, for a valuable discussion of the role of public policy, and for the conclusion that it is a general principle of law in the field of the conflict of laws.

[3] *Vervaeke v Smith* [1983] 1 A.C. 145, 164, *per* Lord Simon of Glaisdale.

[4] *Fender v St John-Mildmay* [1938] A.C. 1, 12.

[5] *Loucks v Standard Oil Co*, 224 N.Y. 99, 111, 120 N.E. 198, 202 (1918). See *Kuwait Airways Corp v Iraqi Airways Co (Nos 4 and 5)* [2002] UKHL 19, [2002] 2 A.C. 883, at [16], *per* Lord Nicholls of Birkenhead.

involving a foreign element than when a purely municipal legal issue is involved.[6]

5–004　　The doctrine of public policy has assumed far less prominence in the English conflict of laws than have corresponding doctrines in the laws of foreign countries, e.g. France and Germany. One reason for this may be that the courts invariably apply English domestic law in proceedings for divorce[7] and separation,[8] for the guardianship, custody[9] and adoption of minors,[10] and for the maintenance of wives and children.[11] Thus, foreign law is inapplicable in many important departments of family law in which, in foreign countries, its exclusion on grounds of public policy is of frequent occurrence. The doctrine of renvoi,[12] too, sometimes results in the application of English domestic law instead of foreign law; and it should be borne in mind that questions of procedure are governed by English domestic law as the *lex fori*,[13] though the reason for this is not policy but convenience.

5–005　　A distinction should be drawn between the foreign law itself, on the one hand, and the effect of its application on the other.[14] There is, understandably, a reluctance to hold that a foreign law as such is contrary to public policy.[15] "An English court will refuse to apply a law which outrages its sense of justice or decency. But before it exercises such power it must consider the relevant foreign law as a whole."[16] In recent years, influenced by the impact of the European Convention on Human Rights, the House of Lords has indicated that a foreign law should be disregarded if it represents a serious infringement of human rights. In *Oppenheimer v Cattermole*[17] a majority expressed the view, *obiter*, that Nazi nationality decrees depriving absent German Jews of their nationality and confiscating their property fell within this category. As Lord Cross put it, "a law of this sort constitutes so grave an infringement of human rights that the courts of this country ought to refuse to recognise it as a law at all."[18] In *Williams & Humbert Ltd v W&H Trade*

---

[6] *Vervaeke v Smith* [1983] 1 A.C. 145, 164; *Kuwait Airways Corp v Iraqi Airways Co (Nos 4 and 5)* [2002] UKHL 19, [2002] 2 A.C. 883, at [114], *per* Lord Steyn.

[7] Rule 85(1).

[8] *ibid.*

[9] Rule 106(4).

[10] See below, para.20–106.

[11] Rule 89(7).

[12] Rule 1.

[13] Rule 19. Dicey regarded this rule also as an example of public policy (3rd ed., p.37), but it too is better regarded as a fixed rule of law.

[14] *cf.* Regulation (EC) 593/2008 of the European Parliament and of the Council on the law applicable to contractual obligations (Rome I), Art.21 (application of foreign law manifestly incompatible with public policy).

[15] See, e.g. *Luther v Sagor* [1921] 3 K.B. 532, 559 (CA); *Oppenheimer v Cattermole* [1976] A.C. 249, 277–278; *The Playa Larga* [1983] 2 Lloyd's Rep. 171, 190 (CA).

[16] *In the Estate of Fuld (No.3)* [1968] P. 675, 698. See also *Winkworth v Christie, Manson and Woods Ltd* [1980] Ch. 496, 514. On foreign laws licensing prostitution or slavery see *Robinson v Bland* (1760) 2 Burr. 1077, 1084; *Regazzoni v KC Sethia Ltd* [1956] 2 Q.B. 490, 524 (CA); affirmed [1958] A.C. 301. Contrast *Santos v Illidge* (1860) 8 C.B. (N.S.) 861.

[17] [1976] A.C. 249.

[18] At p.278. See also p.283, *per* Lord Salmon. It is not likely that the suggestion in *Frankfurther v WL Exner Ltd* [1947] Ch. 629, 644, that Nazi decrees relating to property in Austria would be recognised, would be followed today.

Marks (Jersey) Ltd[19] it was accepted that in appropriate circumstances the court would disregard a foreign confiscatory decree which offended principles of human rights.

What is usually in question, however, is not the foreign law in the abstract, **5–006** but the results of its enforcement or recognition in England in the concrete case. Thus, the courts may well regard a foreign law which permits polygamy, or the marriage of step-father and step-daughter, as unwise or even immoral. But if such a marriage has taken place under a foreign law according to which it is valid, and especially if children have been born, it may be better to recognise it than to disturb settled family relationships by holding the marriage invalid and the children illegitimate on grounds of public policy. Everything depends upon the nature of the question which arises. Thus, until 1972 no polygamously-married spouse could obtain a divorce from the courts;[20] but the spouses would be treated as married persons and thus incapable of contracting a valid marriage in England;[21] the children would be treated as legitimate;[22] and the wife would be entitled to assert rights of succession and other rights on the footing that she was a wife.[23] Again, to take an improbable but striking example, if a foreign law permitted a bachelor aged fifty to adopt a girl aged seventeen, the courts might hesitate to award the custody of the girl to her adoptive father: but that is no reason for not allowing her to succeed to his property as his "child" on his death intestate.[24] Public policy in such cases is not absolute but relative.

The doctrine of public policy may not only induce a court to refuse to **5–007** enforce or recognise, for example, a contract or a marriage when it would be valid under the applicable foreign law. It may also produce the opposite effect and lead to the enforcement or recognition of, for example, a contract or a marriage which under the applicable foreign law would be invalid. Thus, foreign legislation which invalidates a contract or a marriage may be disregarded if it is penal,[25] or foreign exchange control legislation which affects a contract governed by foreign law, but which is passed, not with the genuine object of protecting the State's economy, but as an "instrument of oppression" may be disregarded on the ground of public policy,[26] and a contract not enforceable under its applicable law may as a result be enforceable in England. On the other hand, the effect of the doctrine of public policy always is to exclude the application of foreign law which would otherwise be applicable. In one case,[27] the doctrine was anomalously applied so as to invoke the application of a foreign law which would otherwise have been inapplicable;

---

[19] [1986] A.C. 368, 428, *per* Lord Templeman. See also *The Playa Larga* [1983] 2 Lloyd's Rep. 171, 190 (CA); *Settebello Ltd v Banco Totta and Acores* [1985] 1 W.L.R. 1050, 1056 (CA).

[20] *Hyde v Hyde* (1866) L.R. 1 P.&D. 130; see now Matrimonial Causes Act 1973, s.47(1), and Rule 82.

[21] *Baindail v Baindail* [1946] P. 122 (CA); see below, para.17–191.

[22] *Bamgbose v Daniel* [1955] A.C. 107 (PC); see below, para.17–193.

[23] *Coleman v Shang* [1961] A.C. 481 (PC); *Shahnaz v Rizwan* [1965] 1 Q.B. 390; *Re Sehota* [1978] 1 W.L.R. 1506; see below, paras 17–197 *et seq.*

[24] See para.20–133, below.

[25] See paras 17–084; 32–157, below.

[26] *Re Helbert Wagg & Co Ltd* [1956] Ch. 323, 351. See also *The Playa Larga* [1983] 2 Lloyd's Rep. 171, 190 (CA), and Carter (1983) 54 B.Y.I.L. 297.

[27] *Lorentzen v Lydden & Co Ltd* [1942] 2 K.B. 202.

but this case has for long been the subject of criticism,[28] and has now been overruled.[29]

5–008   The reservation of public policy in conflict of laws cases is a necessary one, but "no attempt to define the limits of that reservation has ever succeeded."[30] All that can be done, therefore, is to enumerate the cases in which the recognition or enforcement of rights arising under foreign laws has been refused on this ground. It will be found that the doctrine has been principally invoked in two classes of case, namely (1) those involving foreign contracts, and (2) those involving a foreign status.

5–009   **(1) Contracts.**[31] The effect of Art.21 of the Rome I Regulation on the Law Applicable to Contractual Obligations[32] is that the application of a rule of law of any country may be refused if its application is manifestly incompatible with English public policy. At common law English courts refused to enforce champertous contracts,[33] contracts in restraint of trade,[34] contracts entered into under duress or coercion,[35] or contracts involving collusive and corrupt arrangements for a divorce,[36] or trading with the enemy,[37] or breaking the laws of a friendly country,[38] even though such contracts were valid under their applicable law. On the other hand, they have enforced contracts for the loan of money to be spent on gambling abroad,[39] and for foreign loans which contravened the English Moneylenders Acts.[40] In general, it is certainly untrue that contracts governed by a foreign law will not be enforced in England if they are contrary to some rule of the common law which the parties to an

---

[28] *Bank voor Handel en Scheepvaart v Slatford* [1953] 1 Q.B. 248, 263–264.

[29] *Peer International Corp v Termidor Music Publishers Ltd* [2003] EWCA Civ 1156, [2004] Ch. 212.

[30] Westlake, p.51.

[31] For detailed discussion, see Rule 229.

[32] Regulation (EC) 593/2008 of the European Parliament and of the Council.

[33] *Grell v Levy* (1864) 10 C.B. (N.S.) 73. In this case the litigation was to take place in England. cf. *Trendtex Trading Corp v Crédit Suisse* [1980] Q.B. 629, affirmed [1982] A.C. 679. See also *Fraser v Buckle* [1996] 2 I.L.R.M. 34. The principle would not apply to a champertous contract relating to litigation in France or the United States, where champerty is lawful: *Re Trepca Mines Ltd (No.2)* [1963] Ch. 199, 218 (CA). cf. *National Surety Co v Larsen* [1929] 4 D.L.R. 918 (BCCA), where a contract to indemnify bail, valid by the law of Washington where the litigation was pending, was upheld in British Columbia, though such contracts were illegal by British Columbia law.

[34] *Rousillon v Rousillon* (1880) 14 Ch.D. 351; but the case does not amount to a decision on the point. Contrast *Apple Corps Ltd v Apple Computer Inc* [1992] F.S.R. 431 (foreign law on restraint of trade not applicable if contract governed by English law). cf. *Duarte v Black and Decker Corp* [2007] EWHC 2720 (Q.B.), [2008] 1 All E.R. (Comm.) 401 (a case on Rome Convention, Art.16).

[35] *Kaufman v Gerson* [1904] 1 K.B. 591 (CA); but see below, para.32–187.

[36] *Hope v Hope* (1857) 8 De G.M.&G. 731. In this case the divorce was to take place in England. Would the principle apply to a contract to procure a divorce abroad? See *Addison v Brown* [1954] 1 W.L.R. 779.

[37] *Dynamit AG v Rio Tinto Co* [1918] A.C. 260.

[38] *De Wütz v Hendricks* (1824) 2 Bing. 314; *Foster v Driscoll* [1929] 1 K.B. 470 (CA); *Regazzoni v KC Sethia Ltd* [1958] A.C. 301. However, in these cases the contract was governed by English law. See also *Royal Boskalis Westminster NV v Mountain* [1999] Q.B. 674, 692 (CA); *Soleimany v Soleimany* [1999] Q.B. 785, 794 (CA).

[39] *Saxby v Fulton* [1909] 2 K.B. 208 (CA).

[40] *Shrichand v Lacon* (1906) 22 T.L.R. 245.

English contract cannot disregard. Thus, a foreign contract made without consideration will be enforced in England.[41]

(2) Status. Although those incidents of a foreign status which are relevant[42] **5–010** to an issue before a court are normally recognised, an incapacity imposed for reasons which it would be contrary to public policy to enforce is disregarded as a penal incapacity. The courts have thus said or held that incapacities imposed on account of slavery,[43] religion or religious vocation,[44] alien nationality,[45] race,[46] divorce[47] and (perhaps unjustifiably) physical incompetence[48] and prodigality,[49] will be disregarded. Although incapacities imposed for these reasons have traditionally been described as "penal" incapacities, the description is somewhat misleading in that they are not necessarily imposed for a breach of the criminal law, i.e. of a "penal law" such as is referred to in Rule 3(1).[50] However, if this is appreciated, and if it is observed that the

---

[41] *Re Bonacina* [1912] 2 Ch. 394 (CA). As to statutory rules, see above, paras 1–036 *et seq.*

[42] That is to say, indicated as relevant by an English choice of law rule. Since those rules always refer to a territorial system of law, rules existing under, e.g. a person's religious discipline are immaterial unless they are incorporated into the appropriate territorial law: *Re De Wilton* [1900] 2 Ch. 481; *Chetti v Chetti* [1909] P. 67, 78; *R. v Hammersmith Superintendent Registrar of Marriages* [1917] 1 K.B. 634, 643; *Preger v Preger* (1926) 42 T.L.R. 281; *Papadopoulos v Papadopoulos* [1930] P. 55, 64; *MacDougall v Chitnavis*, 1937 S.C. 390, 398, 403, 407. cf. *Re Alison's Trusts* (1874) 31 L.T. 638; *Har-Shefi v Har-Shefi (No.2)* [1953] P. 220; *Cheni v Cheni* [1965] P. 85; *Qureshi v Qureshi* [1972] Fam. 173.

[43] *Smith v Browne & Cooper* (1701) Holt K.B. 495; *Shanley v Harvey* (1762) 2 Eden. 126; *Sommersett's Case* (1771) 20 St. Tr. 1; *Chamberline v Harvey* (1796) 5 Mod. 182; *Forbes v Cochrane* (1824) 2 B.&C. 448. cf. *The Slave Grace* (1827) 2 Hag.Adm. 94; *Stewart v Garnett* (1830) 3 Sim. 398; *Ex p. Rucker* (1834) 3 L.J. Bk. 104; *Santos v Illidge* (1860) 8 C.B. (N.S.) 861.

[44] *Re Metcalfe's Trusts* (1864) 2 De G.J.&S. 122; *Stuart v Prentiss* (1861) 20 U.C.R. 513. cf. *Von Lorang v Administrator of Austrian Property* [1927] A.C. 641, 653.

[45] *Wolff v Oxholm* (1817) 6 M.&S. 92; *Re Fried Krupp AG* [1917] 2 Ch. 188; *Re Askew* [1930] 2 Ch. 259, 275; *Re Helbert Wagg & Co Ltd* [1956] Ch. 323, 345–346.

[46] *Oppenheimer v Cattermole* [1976] A.C. 249, 265, 276–278, 282–283. In *Oppenheimer v Louis Rosenthal Co* [1937] 1 All E.R. 23 (CA) and *Ellinger v Guinness Mahon & Co* [1939] 4 All E.R. 16, the incapacities of Jews in Nazi Germany were taken into account in ordering service out of the jurisdiction under what is now CPR, PD6B, para.3.1. See also *Frankfurther v WL Exner Ltd* [1947] Ch. 629, 636–637; *Novello & Co v Hinrichsen Edition Ltd* [1951] Ch. 595, 604, affirmed on other grounds [1951] Ch. 1026 (CA).

[47] *Scott v Att-Gen* (1886) 11 P.D. 128; *Lundgren v O'Brien (No.2)* [1921] V.L.R. 361; *Pezet v Pezet* (1947) 47 S.R. (N.S.W.) 45, 74. cf. *R. v Brentwood Superintendent Registrar of Marriages* [1968] 2 Q.B. 956, where an inability to remarry was recognised on the basis that an unattractive difference from English law did not make the disability a penal incapacity. *A fortiori* where the foreign prohibition is analogous to an English rule: *Warter v Warter* (1890) 15 P.D. 152; *Le Mesurier v Le Mesurier* (1930) 46 T.L.R. 203. See also *Miller v Teale* (1954) 92 C.L.R. 406; *Hellens v Densmore* (1957) 10 D.L.R. (2d) 561 (Sup Ct Can). Distinguish *Buckle v Buckle* [1956] P.181, which was decided on different grounds. See below, paras 17–084 *et seq.*; 18–142.

[48] *Re Langley's Settlement Trusts* [1962] Ch. 541, 556–557 (CA); criticised by Grodecki (1962) 11 I.C.L.Q. 578; Collier [1962] C.L.J. 36.

[49] *Worms v De Valdor* (1880) 49 L.J. Ch. 261; *Re Selot's Trusts* [1902] 1 Ch. 488. Compare the continental practice: Rabel, Vol.1, p.190.

[50] Infamy is normally a consequence of criminal conviction and there are several American cases where foreign incapacities consequent upon infamy have not been recognised, see Beale, Vol.2, p.657.

present context is one of recognition whilst that of Rule 3(1) is one of enforcement,[51] then no harm attends upon the use of the traditional term.

5–011   Public policy may require that a capacity existing under a foreign law should be disregarded in England[52]: but the circumstances would have to be extreme before such a course becomes justifiable. Thus, the courts recognise the validity of marriages within the prohibited degrees of English law[53] (provided they are valid under the applicable foreign law), but they might refuse to recognise a marriage between persons so closely related that sexual intercourse between them was incestuous by English criminal law,[54] or a marriage with a child below the age of puberty[55] or a marriage with a man suffering from autism and severe impairment of intellectual functioning.[56]

5–012   The mere fact that a foreign status or relationship is unknown to English domestic law is not a ground for refusing to recognise its incidents.[57] Thus, legitimation by subsequent marriage was recognised and given effect to in England long before it became part of English domestic law.[58] The recognition of polygamous marriages is another example.[59]

5–013   **Other cases.** Apart from these two groups of cases, examples of the exclusion of foreign law on the ground of public policy are rare. It has been said that it is a principle of public policy that the courts should give effect to clearly established rules of international law.[60] It has been held that it is not contrary to public policy to recognise a decree of a foreign State expropriating property within its territory merely because it is "confiscatory," i.e. does not provide for compensation.[61] But it may be otherwise if the decree is penal or is discriminatory in such a way as to offend against public policy, or otherwise offends against the principles safeguarding human rights.[62] In *Kuwait Airways Corp v Iraqi Airways Co (Nos 4 and 5)*[63] the House of Lords decided that the court could disregard a foreign law which was plainly contrary to international

---

[51] As to this distinction see *Re Helbert Wagg & Co Ltd* [1956] Ch. 323, 345.

[52] *Cheni v Cheni* [1965] P. 85, 98.

[53] *Re Bozzelli's Settlement* [1902] 1 Ch. 751 (marriage in 1880 with deceased brother's widow); *Re Pozot's Settlement* [1952] 1 All E.R. 1107, 1109 (marriage with step-daughter); *Cheni v Cheni* [1965] P. 85 (marriage between uncle and niece).

[54] See *Brook v Brook* (1861) 9 H.L.C. 193, 227–228; *Cheni v Cheni,* above, at p.97.

[55] In *Mohamed v Knott* [1969] 1 Q.B. 1, a marriage with a girl of 13, valid by Nigerian law, was recognised as valid in England.

[56] *Westminster CC v C* [2008] EWCA Civ 198, [2009] Fam. 11.

[57] *Phrantzes v Argenti* [1960] 2 Q.B. 19; *Shahnaz v Rizwan* [1965] 1 Q.B. 390, 401.

[58] Rule 116.

[59] *Baindail v Baindail* [1946] P. 122 (CA); Rule 80.

[60] *Re Helbert Wagg & Co Ltd* [1956] Ch. 323, 349; *Oppenheimer v Cattermole* [1976] A.C. 249, 278; *Kuwait Airways Corp v Iraqi Airways Co (Nos 4 and 5)* [2002] UKHL 19, [2002] 2 A.C. 883, at [28], *per* Lord Nicholls of Birkenhead.

[61] Cases at para.5–005, above, and *Luther v Sagor* [1921] 3 K.B. 532, 559 (CA); *Princess Paley Olga v Weisz* [1929] 1 K.B. 718 (CA); *cf. Williams & Humbert Ltd v W&H Trade Marks (Jersey) Ltd* [1986] A.C. 368, 427–428.

[62] See especially *Re Helbert Wagg & Co Ltd,* above; *Oppenheimer v Cattermole,* above; *Williams & Humbert Ltd v W&H Trade Marks (Jersey) Ltd,* above; *The Playa Larga* [1983] 2 Lloyd's Rep. 171, 189–190 (CA), and see below, para.25–009, text at n.51.

[63] [2002] UKHL 19, [2002] 2 A.C. 883, below, para.5–052.

law. In that case the breach of international law was flagrant, and its seriousness had been recognised by the international community, including the United Kingdom.

The recognition of a foreign decree of divorce[64] or nullity of marriage[65] or   **5–014**
the enforcement of a foreign judgment *in personam*[66] may be refused on grounds of public policy, but reported instances are rare. There is no general principle that the application of a foreign law is contrary to public policy merely because it operates retrospectively.[67]

Express provision. There are now many statutes, international conventions   **5–015**
and European Union regulations in the field of the conflict of laws which provide for the application of public policy. Many[68] deal with foreign judgments or awards and allow for the non-recognition or non-enforcement on the ground that they are contrary to public policy,[69] or, in an expression originally derived from international conventions in the area, "manifestly" contrary to public policy.[70]

"Residual discretion." In some decisions the judges have stated that the   **5–016**
courts possess a "residual discretion" to refuse to recognise a foreign status[71] conferred or imposed upon a person by the law of his domicile, or a foreign decree of divorce or nullity of marriage[72] granted by a foreign court, if the recognition would be improper or unjust or unconscionable in the circumstances of the particular case. In the first of the cases in which these statements were made it is probable that the court intended to do no more than call

---

[64] See below, paras 18–125 *et seq.*

[65] *ibid.*

[66] See Rule 51, below.

[67] See above, para.3–026.

[68] For exceptions see Foreign Limitation Periods Act 1984, s.2; Regulation (EC) 593/2008 of the European Parliament and of the Council on the law applicable to contractual obligations (Rome I), Art.21; Regulation (EC) 864/2007 of the European Parliament and of the Council on the law applicable to non-contractual obligations (Rome II), Art.26.

[69] Administration of Justice Act 1920, s.9(2)(f); Foreign Judgments (Reciprocal Enforcement) Act 1933, s.4(1)(a)(v); Arbitration Act 1950, s.37(1); Arbitration Act 1996, s.103(3); Adoption and Children Act 2002, s.89(1); Children and Adoption Act 2006, s.9(1).

[70] Family Law Act 1986, s.51(3)(c); State Immunity Act 1978, s.19(1)(a); Civil Aviation Act 1982, s.74A; Civil Partnership Act 2004, s.218; Rome I Regulation, above, Art.21; Rome II Regulation, above, Art.26; Council Regulation (EC) 1346/2000 on Insolvency Proceedings, Art.26; Council Regulation (EC) 44/2001 on jurisdiction and the recognition and enforcement of judgments in civil and commercial matters (the Brussels I Regulation), Art.34; Council Regulation (EC) 2201/2003 concerning jurisdiction and the recognition and enforcement of judgments in matrimonial matters and in matters of parental responsibility (Brussels IIa), Art.22; Council Regulation (EC) 4/2009 on jurisdiction, applicable law, recognition and enforcement of decisions and co-operation in matter relating to maintenance obligations, Art.24; Council Regulation (EU) 1259/2010 implementing enhanced co-operation in the area of the law applicable to divorce and legal separation, Art.12.

[71] *Re Langley's Settlement* [1962] Ch. 541, 555, 557–558 (CA); *Russ v Russ* [1963] P. 87, 100; [1964] P. 315, 327–328, 334, 335 (CA); *Cheni v Cheni* [1965] P. 85, 98; *Qureshi v Qureshi* [1972] Fam. 173, 201.

[72] *Gray v Formosa* [1963] P. 259, 269, 270, 271 (CA); *Lepre v Lepre* [1965] P. 52, 63. As to divorce, see now Family Law Act 1986, s.51(3)(c); *Kendall v Kendall* [1977] Fam. 208; *Chaudhary v Chaudhary* [1985] Fam. 19 (Wood J. and CA), and see below, para.18–125.

attention to the distinction between the recognition of a status and the recognition of its incidents.[73] In the later cases it may be that the courts intended to do no more than refer to the doctrine of public policy and to the analogous doctrine that foreign decrees of divorce and nullity will not be recognised in England if recognition would be contrary to natural justice.[74] But if the courts intended to reduce the whole of the conflict of laws, or even that part of it which is concerned with status, to the level of judicial discretion, it is submitted that this is contrary both to principle and to authority. For, as has been well said, "to state the law in terms of judicial discretion . . . is to admit that no certainty or predictability is attainable in this matter."[75] And again: "the courts might just as well abandon any attempt to formulate and apply defined rules of law if these can be overridden by an undefinable discretion."[76] And, as Lord Hodson said in *Boys v Chaplin*,[77] "rules of law should be defined and adhered to as closely as possible lest they lose themselves in a field of judicial discretion where no secure foothold is to be found by litigants or their advisers."

Illustrations[78]

5–017   1. H, domiciled in South Africa, obtains a divorce from the South African court on the ground of W's adultery, and thereafter remains single. By Roman-Dutch law a decree of divorce does not permit an adulteress to contract another marriage until the remarriage of her husband. W acquires an English domicile and marries H2 in England. The marriage is valid, for although W's marital capacity depends upon the South African decree (for that was the only measure affecting her status as a married woman), the South African provision was penal.[79]

2. A, a French citizen domiciled in France, is a person of full age, but being of extravagant habits is, by a French court of competent jurisdiction, adjudged to be a "prodigal," and is placed under the control of a conseil judiciaire (legal adviser). He is, as a prodigal, incapable of receiving or giving a receipt for his movable property without the consent of such adviser. He becomes entitled to a fund in court in England. The status of a prodigal is unknown to English law. A has a right to receive the fund in court on his own receipt without the consent of his legal adviser because (inter alia) the incapacity is a penal one.[80]

3. A Roman Catholic priest is a citizen of, and domiciled in, a foreign country, under whose law he is, as a priest, incapable of marriage. He marries an English woman in England. The marriage is valid, i.e. English law does not recognise the disability as it is a penal one.[81]

---

[73] *Re Langley's Settlement* [1962] Ch. 541, 554–555 (CA). As to this distinction, see also *Baindail v Baindail* [1946] P. 122, 128 (CA).

[74] See below, para.18–125.

[75] Grodecki (1962) 11 I.C.L.Q. 578, 582.

[76] Nygh (1964) 13 I.C.L.Q. 39, 51.

[77] [1971] A.C. 356, 378.

[78] For Illustrations concerning contracts, see below, paras 32–194 *et seq*.

[79] *Scott v Att-Gen* (1886) 11 P.D. 128, as explained in *Warter v Warter* (1890) 15 P.D. 152, 155.

[80] *Re Selot's Trusts* [1902] 1 Ch. 488; also *Worms v De Valdor* (1880) 49 L.J. Ch. 261. These cases are apparently based on the (untenable) ground that there had been no change of status ([1902] 1 Ch. 492; 49 L.J. Ch. 262), and the penal nature of the French incapacity is a minor ground of decision. In both cases the issue would seem to have been governed by English domestic law; in *Worms v De Valdor* the question was as to the plaintiff's ability to bring an action, which is a question of procedure to be resolved by the *lex fori*; while in *Re Selot's Trusts* the question was capacity to take under the will of a testator who presumably died domiciled in England. In *Re Langley's Settlement Trusts* [1962] Ch. 541, 557, Lord Evershed M.R. declined "to express any final view upon whether all that was said in the two cases . . . was justified."

[81] The marriage would also be valid under the rule in *Sottomayor v De Barros (No.2)* (1879) 5 P.D. 94; see Rule 74, Exception 3, below.

4. A, a German Jew, emigrated to England in 1939 in order to escape persecution by the Nazis. In 1941 a German decree deprived absent Jews of their German nationality and their property. This deprivation would not be recognised in England.[82]

5. In 1954 W, a Belgian national domiciled in Belgium, goes through a ceremony of marriage **5–018** in England with H1. The purpose of the marriage is to enable W to avoid being deported as a prostitute or undesirable alien, and H1 is induced to take part in the ceremony in return for a bribe of £50 and a ticket to South Africa. In March 1970 W goes through another ceremony of marriage with H2, one of the principals in the organisation which has been managing the activities of W as a prostitute. At the wedding party H2 dies of a heart attack, leaving substantial property. Subsequently, W, anxious to establish that she is the widow of H2, petitions the English court for a declaration that her marriage to H1 was null and void on the false ground that she had not consented to it because she was ignorant of the true nature of the ceremony, and in 1971 the petition is dismissed on the ground that W knew the true nature of the ceremony. W goes back to Belgium and obtains a decree from the Belgian courts that the marriage to H1 is a nullity because it was a mock marriage. The Belgian courts decide that although W's plea of lack of consent is *res judicata* by virtue of the decision of the English court, the plea of mock marriage is not barred because it had not been argued in the English proceedings. In 1973 W petitions the English court for a declaration that the Belgian decree of nullity is entitled to recognition. The petition is dismissed because, among other reasons, the English rule that a marriage celebrated in order to acquire nationality is a valid marriage is a rule which reflects a public policy of giving effect to marriages conducted in accordance with the proper formalities whether or not the parties intend to live together; the Belgian judgment reflected a conflicting public policy to the same facts as were finally ascertained by the English court; in any event, public policy precluded recognition of the Belgian decree because it was obtained only after, and because, W's fraudulent petition had been dismissed by the English court.[83]

6. A, a 25-year-old man suffering from autism and severe impairment of intellectual functioning, takes part in a Muslim marriage ceremony to B by telephone while he is in England and B is in Bangladesh. The marriage will not be not recognised. It is inconsistent with English concepts of marriage and A's incapacity renders the marriage sufficiently offensive to the conscience of the English court that it will, on public policy grounds, refuse to recognise it.[84]

Rule 3[85]—English courts have no jurisdiction to entertain an action: 5R–019
(1) for the enforcement, either directly or indirectly, of a penal,[86]

---

[82] *Oppenheimer v Cattermole* [1976] A.C. 249, 265, 276–278, 282–283. It is submitted that the suggestion in *Frankfurther v WL Exner Ltd* [1947] Ch. 629, 644, that such legislation would be recognised as effective with regard to property in the legislating State would not be followed today: see n.18, above.

[83] *Vervaeke v Smith* [1983] 1 A.C. 145.

[84] *Westminster CC v C* [2008] EWCA Civ 198, [2009] Fam. 11.

[85] F.A. Mann, *Foreign Affairs in English Courts* (1986), Chs 9 and 10; Collins (2007) 326 *Recueil des Cours* 11; Baade, in Lipstein (ed.), *International Encyclopedia of Comparative Law*, Vol.III. Ch.12 (1990). See generally *The activities of national judges and the international relations of their State* (Conforti, Rapporteur), *Ann. de l' Institut de droit international*, Vol.65–I, p.327 (1993).

[86] *Folliott v Ogden* (1789) 1 H.Bl. 123, affirmed sub nom. *Ogden v Folliott* (1790) 3 T.R. 326; *Lynch v Provisional Government of Paraguay* (1871) L.R. 2 P.& D. 268, 272; *Huntington v Attrill* [1893] A.C. 150 (PC); *Att-Gen for Canada v Schulze*, (1901) 9 S.L.T. 4; *Raulin v Fischer* [1911] 2 K.B. 93; *Banco de Vizcaya v Don Alfonso de Borbon y Austria* [1935] 1 K.B. 140; *Frankfurther v WL Exner Ltd* [1947] Ch. 629; *Novello & Co v Hinrichsen Edition Ltd* [1951] Ch. 595, affirmed on different grounds [1951] Ch. 1026 (CA); *Re Helbert Wagg & Co Ltd* [1956] Ch. 323, 345; *Schemmer v Property Resources Ltd* [1975] Ch. 273, 288; *Att-Gen of New Zealand v Ortiz* [1984] A.C. 1, 32, 35 (CA), affirmed by HL on different grounds; *Williams & Humbert Ltd v W&H Trade Marks (Jersey) Ltd* [1986] A.C. 368, 428; *US v Inkley* [1989] Q.B. 255, 264; *Islamic Republic of Iran v Barakat Galleries Ltd* [2007] EWCA Civ 1374, [2009] Q.B. 22; *Pocket Kings Ltd v Safenames Ltd* [2009] EWHC 2529 (Ch.), [2010] Ch. 438. *Larkins v NUM* [1985] I.R. 671; *Bank of Ireland v Meeneghan* [1994] 3 I.R. 111; *Gersten v Law Society of New South Wales* [2002] NSWCA 344; *Jamieson v Commissioner for Internal Revenue* [2007] NSWSC 324; Restatement, s.89.

revenue[87] **or other public law**[88] **of a foreign State; or**
(2) founded upon an act of state.[89]

5–020   **General.** There is a well-established and almost universal principle that the
courts of one country will not enforce the penal and revenue laws of another
country. [90] Although the theoretical basis for the Rule is a matter of some

---

[87] *Municipal Council of Sydney v Bull* [1909] 1 K.B. 7; *Cotton v R.* [1914] A.C. 176, 195;
Indian and General Investment Trust Ltd v Borax Consolidated Ltd [1920] 1 K.B. 539, 549; *King
of the Hellenes v Brostrom* (1923) 16 Ll.L.R. 167, 190; *Re Visser* [1928] Ch. 877; *Re Cohen*
[1950] 2 All E.R. 36, 39 (CA); *Peter Buchanan Ltd v McVey* [1954] I.R. 89, [1955] A.C. 516n.;
Government of India v Taylor [1955] A.C. 491; *Metal Industries (Salvage) Ltd v Owners of ST
"Harle"*, 1962 S.L.T. 114; *Rossano v Manufacturers' Life Insurance Co* [1963] 2 Q.B. 352,
376–378; *Brokaw v Seatrain UK Ltd* [1971] 2 Q.B. 476 (CA); *Re Lord Cable* [1977] 1 W.L.R.
7, 13; *Re State of Norway's Application (Nos 1 and 2)* [1990] 1 A.C. 723, 807–809; *QRS 1 ApS
v Frandsen* [1999] 1 W.L.R. 2169 (CA); *USA v Harden* (1963) 41 D.L.R. (2d) 721 (Sup Ct Can);
Stringham v Dubois [1993] 3 W.W.R. 273 (Alta CA); *Commissioner of Taxes v McFarland*, 1965
(1) S.A. 470; *Priestley v Clegg*, 1985 (3) S.A. 955; M. Mann (1954) 3 I.C.L.Q. 465, (1955) 4
I.C.L.Q. 564; Castel (1964) 42 Can. Bar Rev. 277; Smart (1986) 35 I.C.L.Q. 704; Briggs [2001]
Sing.J.L.S. 280; Basedow, *et al.* (2004) 6 Yb. P.I.L. 1. For developments in the United States see
Attorney General of Canada v RJ Reynolds Tobacco Holdings, Inc, 268 F.3d 103 (2d Cir. 2001)
(RICO action by the Canadian Government against American and Canadian tobacco companies
for damages based on lost revenues as a result of their participation in schemes to avoid taxes by
smuggling cigarettes across the Canadian border: complaint was dismissed because the action was
barred by the revenue rule); *Pasquantino v United States*, 544 U.S. 349 (2005) (conviction for
federal wire fraud for scheme to smuggle alcohol into Canada from the United States: by a 5:4
majority, held that the conviction was not barred by revenue rule); *European Community v RJR
Nabisco, Inc*, 424 F.3d 175 (2d Cir. 2005), cert. den 546 U.S. 1092 (2006) (RICO action by the
European Community, Member States, and Colombia against tobacco companies barred by
revenue rule notwithstanding decision of the United States Supreme Court in *Pasquantino v
United States*, above).
[88] *Emperor of Austria v Day* (1861) 3 De G.&F. J. 217, 232, 238, 251; *Huntington v Attrill*
[1893] A.C. 150, 156 (PC); *Government of India v Taylor* [1955] A.C. 491, 511; *R. v Governor
of Pentonville Prison, ex p. Budlong* [1980] 1 W.L.R. 1110, 1125 (DC); *Att-Gen of New Zealand
v Ortiz* [1984] A.C. 1, 20–21 (CA), *per* Lord Denning M.R.; *US v Inkley* [1989] Q.B. 255, 264
(CA); *Camdex International Ltd v Bank of Zambia (No.2)* [1997] C.L.C. 714, 723–724, 736 (CA);
Equatorial Guinea v Bank of Scotland International [2006] UKPC 7; *Mbasogo v Logo Ltd* [2006]
EWCA Civ 1370, [2007] Q.B. 846; *Islamic Republic of Iran v Barakat Galleries Ltd* [2007]
EWCA Civ 1374, [2009] Q.B. 22; *United States Securities and Exchange Commission v
Manterfield* [2009] EWCA Civ 27, [2009] 2 All E.R. 1009; *Pocket Kings Ltd v Safenames Ltd*
[2009] EWHC 2529 (Ch.), [2010] Ch. 438; *Carey Group Plc v AIB Group (UK) Plc* [2011]
EWHC 567 (Ch.); *Att-Gen (UK) v Heinemann Publishers Australia Pty Ltd* (1988) 165 C.L.R. 30,
41–43; F.A. Mann, *Studies in International Law* (1973), p.492; (1962) 11 I.C.L.Q. 481; (1971)
Recueil des Cours, I, p.107, at pp.178–180; *Further Studies in International Law* (1990), pp.355
and 389; Carter [1989] C.L.J. 417; Collins, *Essays*, 118–129; Collins, in *Mélanges Lalive* (1993),
pp.221–230; Verhoeven, *ibid.*, pp.359–373; Collins (2007) 326 *Recueil des Cours* 11.
[89] Holdsworth, *History of English Law*, Vol.14, pp.33–52; Harrison Moore, *Act of State in
English Law* (1906); E.C.S. Wade (1934) 15 B.Y.I.L. 98; Gilmour, 1967 Jur. Rev. 149, [1970]
Public Law 120; Collier [1968] C.L.J. 102; F.A. Mann, *Studies in International Law* (1973),
p.420; (1971) *Recueil des Cours*, I, p.107, at pp.145–156; Singer (1981) 75 A.J.I.L. 283;
Oppenheim, *International Law* (9th ed. Jennings and Watts, 1992), Vol.1, pp.365–376.
[90] *Williams & Humbert Ltd v W&H Trade Marks (Jersey) Ltd* [1986] A.C. 368, 428, *per* Lord
Templeman; *Derby & Co Ltd v Weldon (No.6)* [1990] 1 W.L.R. 1139 (CA), at 1154, *per*
Staughton L.J.

controversy, [91] the best explanation, it is submitted, is that suggested by Lord Keith of Avonholm in *Government of India v Taylor*,[92] that enforcement of such claims is an extension of the sovereign power which imposed the taxes, and "an assertion of sovereign authority by one State within the territory of another, as distinct from a patrimonial claim by a foreign sovereign, is (treaty or convention apart) contrary to all concepts of independent sovereignties." Although it was not necessary to decide the precise theoretical basis for the rule, in *Re State of Norway's Application (Nos 1 and 2)*[93] Lord Goff of Chieveley was inclined to agree with this view. Clause (1) of Rule 3 describes those laws which a foreign State may seek to enforce solely as an exercise of sovereignty, and which "by the law of nations are exclusively assigned to their domestic forum."[94] Whether a foreign law falls within the categories of those laws which the English court will not enforce is a matter for English law. Thus whether the foreign law regards the law in question as a penal law[95] or a revenue law[96] or a public law[97] is irrelevant.

Rule 3 is framed in terms of lack of jurisdiction, and it has frequently been cited by the courts,[98] but claims made within the scope of the Rule have usually been dismissed on the merits or been struck out.[99] This was so even in *Huntington v Attrill*,[100] where the Privy Council used the terminology of jurisdiction, and which was the principal authority for Rule 3 when it was first formulated.[101] In the eleventh edition of this book it was suggested that it is the foreign State which has no international jurisdiction to enforce its law abroad, and the English court will not exercise its own jurisdiction in aid of an excess of jurisdiction by the foreign State. The substance of this view was adopted in *Re State of Norway's Application (Nos 1 and 2)*,[102] but in view of its wide acceptance in judicial decisions, Rule 3 has been retained in its traditional form. **5–021**

This Rule is not affected by the Brussels I Regulation. In *QRS 1 ApS v Frandsen*[103] it was held that a claim by the liquidator of a Danish company **5–022**

---

[91] See F.A. Mann, *Studies in International Law* (1973), pp.495–499.

[92] [1955] A.C. 491, 511. *cf. Att-Gen of New Zealand v Ortiz* [1984] A.C. 1 (CA), at pp.20–21, *per* Lord Denning M.R., at p.32, *per* Ackner L.J.

[93] [1990] 1 A.C. 723, 808. *cf. Att-Gen (UK) v Heinemann Publishers Australia Pty Ltd* (1988) 165 C.L.R. 30, 40–44.

[94] *Huntington v Attrill* [1893] A.C. 150, 156 (PC).

[95] *ibid.*; *Att-Gen of New Zealand v Ortiz* [1984] A.C. 1, 32 (CA), affirmed by HL on different grounds; *US v Inkley* [1989] Q.B. 255, 265 (CA); *Islamic Republic of Iran v Barakat Galleries Ltd* [2007] EWCA Civ 1374, [2009] Q.B. 22, [106].

[96] *Metal Industries (Salvage) Ltd v Owners of ST "Harle"*, 1962 S.L.T. 114, 116.

[97] *Att-Gen (UK) v Heinemann Publishers Australia Pty Ltd* (1988) 165 C.L.R. 30, 46.

[98] See, e.g. *Re Visser*, [1928] Ch. 877, 882; *Government of India v Taylor* [1955] A.C. 491, 507; *Att-Gen of New Zealand v Ortiz* [1984] A.C. 1, 20 (CA); *Williams & Humbert Ltd v W&H Trade Marks (Jersey) Ltd* [1986] A.C. 368, 437.

[99] See, e.g. *Re Visser*, above; *Att-Gen of New Zealand v Ortiz*, above; *Mbasogo v Logo Ltd*, above.

[100] [1893] A.C. 150 (PC).

[101] At p.155. See 1st ed., p.220.

[102] [1990] 1 A.C. 723, 808. See also *Tasarruf Mevduati Sigorta Fonu v Demirel* [2006] EWHC 3354 (Ch.), [2007] 2 All E.R. 815, affd. on other grounds [2007] EWCA Civ 799, [2007] 1 W.L.R. 2508; *Islamic Republic of Iran v Barakat Galleries Ltd* [2007] EWCA Civ 1374, [2009] Q.B. 22, [97].

[103] [1999] 1 W.L.R. 2169 (CA).

against a shareholder in respect of the stripping of its assets was an unenforceable revenue claim, because the only creditors were the Danish tax authorities, who were funding the claim.[104] The claim was a revenue matter within the meaning of the Brussels Convention, and the rule that the English court would not directly or indirectly enforce the revenue laws of another country was not overridden by the Convention (or by the EC Treaty). It was also indicated (*obiter*) that if the Brussels Convention applied, then Rule 3 could not have applied because its effect would have been to impair the operation of the Convention. This suggestion is open to the criticism that Rule 3, as indicated above, is not really a rule of jurisdiction, but a substantive rule of law. In any event, the significance of Rule 3 in the European Union is much lessened by the effect of the EU Directives on mutual assistance between Member States for the recovery of claims relating to taxes, duties and other measure, the current one[105] of which is given effect by the Finance Act 2011.[106]

5–023   Direct enforcement occurs where a foreign State or its nominee seeks to obtain money or property, or other relief, in reliance on the foreign rule in question.[107] But indirect enforcement is also prohibited, for a foreign State cannot be allowed to do indirectly what it cannot do directly. Indirect enforcement is, however, easier to describe than to define. Rule 3(1) relates only to *enforcement*, but it does not prevent *recognition* of a foreign law of the type in question, and it is sometimes difficult to draw the line between an issue involving merely recognition of a foreign law and indirect enforcement of it.

5–024   Where direct or indirect enforcement does not arise, a foreign law of a type falling within Rule 3(1) will be recognised if it is relevant to the issue,[108] and provided it is not contrary to public policy.[109] For example, a contract invalid according to a penal or revenue law of its applicable law, or performance of which is prohibited by a penal law of the place of performance, may be held to be invalid or unenforceable;[110] and the English court will refuse to restrain trustees from acting in compliance with foreign fiscal legislation forming part of the proper law of the trust.[111] Likewise trustees will be entitled to be

---

[104] See below, text at n.113. It is not easy to justify this result from the point of view of policy. See Briggs (1999) 70 B.Y.I.L. 341; Smart (2000) 116 L.Q.R. 360 for criticism. See also Case C–406/09 *Realchemie Nederland BV v Bayer Crop Science AG* [2012] I.L.Pr. 17 (Brussels I Regulation applies to fine payable to the State for breach of injunction in favour of private party in a civil and commercial matter).

[105] Council Directive 2010/24/EU.

[106] s.87, and Sch.25.

[107] *Brokaw v Seatrain UK Ltd* [1971] 2 Q.B. 476, 483 (CA); *Att-Gen of New Zealand v Ortiz* [1984] A.C. 1, 32 (CA), *per* Ackner L.J., affirmed on different grounds: *Williams & Humbert Ltd v W&H Trade Marks (Jersey) Ltd* [1986] A.C. 368, 437.

[108] *Re Emery's Investment Trusts* [1959] Ch. 410; *Regazzoni v KC Sethia Ltd* [1956] 2 Q.B. 490, 515 (CA), affirmed [1958] A.C. 301, 322, 324, 328, 330; *Att-Gen of New Zealand v Ortiz* [1984] A.C. 1, 20 (CA), *per* Lord Denning M.R.

[109] *Re Helbert Wagg & Co Ltd* [1956] Ch. 323, 345–349.

[110] See, e.g. *Foster v Driscoll* [1929] 1 K.B. 470 (CA); *Regazzoni v KC Sethia Ltd*, above. See also, below, Rule 229.

[111] *Re Lord Cable* [1977] 1 W.L.R. 7, 24–25. *cf. Scottish National Orchestra Society Ltd v Thomson's Executor*, 1969 S.L.T. 325; *Bath v British and Malayan Trustees Ltd* [1969] 2 N.S.W.R. 114; *Jones v Borland*, 1969(4) S.A. 29.

indemnified out of an estate in England in respect of such sums which they have been personally compelled to pay abroad in satisfaction of a foreign government's claim for estate duty upon that estate even though the claim would have been unenforceable in this country.[112]

Indirect enforcement occurs where the foreign State (or its nominee) in form seeks a remedy, not based on the foreign rule in question, but which in substance is designed to give it extra-territorial effect; or where a private party raises a defence based on the foreign law in order to vindicate or assert the right of the foreign State. An example of the former is the case of a foreign company in liquidation which seeks to recover from one of its directors assets under his control which the liquidator (appointed by the court at the instance of foreign revenue authorities) would use only for the purpose of satisfying the foreign State's unsatisfied claim for taxes due from the company.[113] On the other hand, in *Williams & Humbert Ltd v W&H Trade Marks (Jersey) Ltd*[114] the Spanish Government expropriated shares in various Spanish companies, and appointed new directors to those companies and their English subsidiaries. The new directors commenced actions in England in the name of their respective companies to recover assets in the hands of former shareholders and alleged to belong to the plaintiff companies. The House of Lords held that the action was not an indirect enforcement of the Spanish decree: it was designed to vindicate the rights of the plaintiff companies, and not to satisfy claims by the Spanish State. Nor, in *Re State of Norway's Application (Nos 1 and 2)*,[115] was it an exercise of extra-territorial sovereignty for a foreign State to seek the assistance of the English court to obtain evidence for the enforcement of its revenue laws in its own country.

5–025

Examples of cases where a private party raises a claim or defence in order to vindicate or assert the rights of a foreign State include the case of a bank which seeks delivery of securities owned by the former King of a foreign country and held by his agent in London in order to deliver them to the foreign State, which had declared all the ex-King's property forfeit on account of his alleged treason;[116] or the case of a debtor who seeks to defeat a claim against him by pleading that the debt has been attached through a garnishee order

5–026

---

[112] *Re Lord Cable* [1977] 1 W.L.R. 7, 15; *Re Reid* (1970) 17 D.L.R. (3d) 199 (BCCA) (not followed in *Stringham v Dubois* [1993] 3 W.W.R. 273 (Alta CA)).

[113] *Peter Buchanan Ltd v McVey* [1954] I.R. 89, [1955] A.C. 516n. (as explained in *Williams & Humbert Ltd v W&H Trade Marks (Jersey) Ltd* [1986] A.C. 368), distinguished in *Ayres v Evans* (1981) 39 A.L.R. 129; *QRS 1 ApS v Frandsen* [1999] 1 W.L.R. 2169 (CA) (criticised Briggs (1999) 70 B.Y.I.L. 341; Smart (2000) 116 L.Q.R. 360); *Priestley v Clegg*, 1985(3) S.A. 955; *Re Tucker* [1988] L.R.C. (Comm.) 995 (Isle of Man).

[114] [1986] A.C. 368 criticised by F.A. Mann, *Further Studies in International Law* (1990), p.389. See also *Air India Ltd v Caribjet Inc* [2002] 1 Lloyd's Rep. 314. *cf. Bank of Ethiopia v National Bank of Egypt and Liguori* [1937] 1 Ch. 513; *Banco de Bilbao v Sancha and Rey* [1938] 2 K.B. 176; *Brown, Gow, Wilson v Beleggings-Societeit NV* (1961) 29 D.L.R. (2d) 673 (Ont).

[115] [1990] 1 A.C. 723, 809.

[116] *Banco de Vizcaya v Don Alfonso de Borbon y Austria* [1935] 1 K.B. 140. Contrast *Kahler v Midland Bank* [1950] A.C. 24, criticised by F.A. Mann, *Studies in International Law* (1973), pp.506–508. Contrast *Carey Group Plc v AIB Group (UK) Plc* [2011] EWHC 567 (Ch.), at [61]–[62] (no injunction to restrain voluntary compliance with Irish public law relating to nationalisation of bank assets), distinguishing *Pocket Kings Ltd v Safenames Ltd* [2009] EWHC 2529 (Ch.), [2010] Ch. 438.

served by or on behalf of a foreign State in respect of tax liabilities;[117] or the case of a shipowner who refuses to hand over goods to their owner because it has received a notice of levy from a foreign government which under its own law has encumbered the goods with a lien in respect of unpaid tax.[118] Where, however, the foreign government has a patrimonial claim,[119] e.g. to the property of unsuccessful revolutionaries or former governments,[120] or where it claims or reclaims property which it has reduced into its possession,[121] the case is not one of enforcement of title, but of recognition, and the claim will be enforced. The foreign State may sue to prevent injury to its property, and in this context it was held in the 19th century that the Emperor of Austria could sue to restrain the manufacture of counterfeit bank notes,[122] and most recently that the Kingdom of Spain had an arguable case (on a striking-out application) that it could sue to restrain the use of forged export licences.[123]

5–027   **Penal laws.** "The common law considers crimes as altogether local, and cognisable and punishable exclusively in the country where they are committed . . . Chief Justice Marshall, in delivering the opinion of the Supreme Court, said: 'The courts of no country execute the penal laws of another'."[124] In *Huntington v Attrill*[125] the Privy Council defined penal to include not only crimes in the strict sense, but "all breaches of public law punishable by pecuniary mulct or otherwise, at the instance of the state government, or someone representing the public" and (adopting the test laid down by the United States Supreme Court[126]) "all suits in favour of the state for the recovery of pecuniary penalties for any violation of statutes for the protection

---

[117] *Rossano v Manufacturers' Life Insurance Co* [1963] 2 Q.B. 352. *cf. Van de Mark v Toronto-Dominion Bank* (1989) 68 O.R. (2d) 379.

[118] *Brokaw v Seatrain UK Ltd* [1971] 2 Q.B. 476 (CA), where on an interpleader the US Government argued unsuccessfully that the effect of the notice of levy should be recognised on the basis that the rule as to non-enforcement of revenue claims applied only to direct actions in courts of law. *cf. Bank of Ireland v Menneghan* [1994] 3 I.R. 111.

[119] *Government of India v Taylor* [1955] A.C. 491, 511, *per* Lord Keith of Avonholm; *Islamic Republic of Iran v Barakat Galleries Ltd* [2007] EWCA Civ 1374, [2009] Q.B. 22, [133]–[136].

[120] e.g. *King of Two Sicilies v Willcox* (1851) 1 Sim.(N.S.) 301; *USA v Prioleau* (1865) 2 H.&M. 559; *USA v McRae* (1867) L.R. 3 Ch.App. 79; *USSR v Belaiew* (1925) 42 T.L.R. 21.

[121] *Islamic Republic of Iran v Barakat Galleries Ltd* [2007] EWCA Civ 1374, [2009] Q.B. 22, [143]–[148].

[122] *Emperor of Austria v Day* (1861) 3 De G.F. & J. 217, 253–254.

[123] *Kingdom of Spain v Christie, Manson & Woods Ltd* [1986] 1 W.L.R. 1120 (discussed in *Associated Newspapers Group Plc v Insert Media Ltd* [1988] 1 W.L.R. 509, 512–513). On the question whether a foreign State may seek to recover assets taken by former rulers or officials see Collins, in *Mélanges Lalive* (1993), pp.221–230; and *cf. Republic of the Philippines v Marcos*, 862 F. 2d 1355 (9th Cir.), cert. den. 490 U.S. 1035 (1988) (where such a claim was permitted) with *Duvalier v Etat haïtien*, Cour de cassation, France, 1990, in 1991 *Clunet* 137 (where the claim was disallowed). The point was not taken in *Republic of Haiti v Duvalier* [1990] 1 Q.B. 202 (CA).

[124] Story, ss.620–621, citing *The Antelope* (1825) 10 Wheat. 66, 123. See also *Folliott v Ogden* (1789) 1 H.B1. 123, 135, *per* Lord Loughborough; *Ogden v Folliott* (1790) 3 T.R. 726, 733, *per* Buller J.

[125] [1893] A.C. 150, 156 (PC).

[126] *Wisconsin v Pelican Insurance Co*, 127 U.S. 265, 292 (1888).

of its revenue or other municipal laws, and to all judgments for such penalties." Thus for this purpose a penal law is a law which punishes[127] or prevents[128] an offence. To come within this principle the law does not have to be part of the criminal code of the foreign country. Thus a law intended to protect the historic heritage of New Zealand by forfeiting historic articles illegally exported was held to be penal;[129] so also in Ireland it was held that the process of sequestration of assets of the National Union of Mineworkers after its civil contempt of court in England was penal in nature.[130] The penalty must normally be exigible by the State,[131] and therefore an action for punitive damages by a private person will not be regarded as penal.[132] But the mere fact that a law contains criminal penalties does not render penal all the other provisions of the law. In *Islamic Republic of Iran v Barakat Galleries Ltd* Iran was not debarred by the penal law rule from recovering ancient artefacts allegedly exported from Iran and belonging to the Iranian State. The Iranian law contained penalties for (inter alia) illegal export, but Iran was relying on provisions which vested title in the State, and these were not penal provisions.[133]

Since "the essential nature and real foundation of a cause of action are not changed by recovering judgment upon it,"[134] the English court will not enforce a foreign criminal judgment.[135]   5–028

Revenue laws. " . . . [T]here is a well recognised rule, which has been enforced for at least 200 years or thereabouts, under which these courts will not collect the taxes of foreign states for the benefit of the sovereigns of those foreign states".[136] This is because "tax gathering is not a matter of contract but of authority and administration as between the State and those within its jurisdiction."[137] Accordingly, the courts do not enforce foreign revenue laws,   5–029

---

[127] *Huntington v Attrill* [1893] A.C. 150 (PC).

[128] *Schemmer v Property Resources Ltd* [1975] Ch. 273, 288.

[129] *Att-Gen of New Zealand v Ortiz* [1984] A.C. 1, 34–35 (CA), *per* Ackner and O'Connor L.JJ., affirmed by HL on different grounds.

[130] *Larkins v NUM* [1985] I.R. 671.

[131] *Huntington v Attrill* [1893] A.C. 150, 157–158.

[132] *SA Consortium General Textiles v Sun and Sand Agencies Ltd* [1978] Q.B. 279, 299–300, 305–306 (CA). But an action for treble damages under United States anti-trust law may be an action for a penalty, since the right to treble damages is granted so that private parties may act as "private attornies-general" to vindicate the anti-trust law: see below, paras 14–022; 14–272 *et seq*. In *Old North State Brewing Co v Newlands Services Inc* [1999] 4 W.W.R. 573 (BCCA) a North Carolina judgment contained an award of treble damages on the basis that the judgment debtor had been found to have committed unfair and deceptive trade practices, and included an award for punitive damages. It was held that the trebling of damages could be equated to exemplary damages under Canadian law, and enforcement of the judgment was not contrary to public policy.

[133] [2007] EWCA Civ 1374, [2009] Q.B. 22, at [111], disapproving *Schemmer v Property Resources Ltd* [1975] Ch. 273 on this point.

[134] *Wisconsin v Pelican Insurance Co*, 127 U.S. 265, 292 (1888).

[135] Rule 42, below.

[136] *Re Visser* [1928] Ch. 877, 884, *per* Tomlin J. See also *King of the Hellenes v Brostrom* (1923) 16 Ll.L.R. 167, 190 at p.193.

[137] *Government of India v Taylor* [1955] A.C. 491, 514.

nor judgments based on foreign revenue claims.[138] In *Government of India v Taylor*[139] Lord Keith of Avonholm accepted that this rule was subject to contrary agreement by treaty or convention, and it has been held that the State of Norway could seek the extradition of its national for offences of false accounting, forgery and theft which were connected with tax offences.[140] In addition, as indicated above,[141] very substantial inroads have been made on Rule 3 in relation to claims in England for the collection of taxes in European Union Member States by the EU Directives relating to mutual assistance in the recovery of taxes and duties.

5–030   The expression "revenue law" has not been defined, but certainly includes a rule requiring a non-contractual payment of money or kind in favour of central or local government. Thus rules imposing an income tax,[142] a capital gains tax,[143] a profits levy,[144] a succession duty,[145] a municipal contribution,[146] a compulsory state insurance scheme contribution,[147] and a customs duty[148] have been characterised as revenue laws; but rules under which a State can recover social security payments[149] or obtain legal aid contributions[150] have not been so characterised. The character to be given exchange control regulations is not clear. Although they may not be revenue laws,[151] it has been

---

[138] On such judgments see, below, Rules 42(1) and 54; *Government of India v Taylor* [1955] A.C. 491, 506; *USA v Harden* (1963) 41 D.L.R. (2d) 721 (Sup Ct Can); *Commissioner of Taxes v MacFarland*, 1965 (1) S.A. 470. *cf. Att-Gen for Canada v Schulze* (1901) 9 S.L.T. 4 (foreign judgment for costs awarded in revenue case). See Stoel (1967) 16 I.C.L.Q. 663.

[139] [1955] A.C. 491, 511.

[140] *R. v Chief Metropolitan Stipendiary Magistrate, Ex p. Secretary of State for the Home Department* [1988] 1 W.L.R. 1204 (DC).

[141] para.5–022.

[142] *Indian and General Investment Trust Co Ltd v Borax Consolidated Ltd* [1920] 1 K.B. 539, 550; *USA v Harden* (1963) 41 D.L.R. (2d) 721 (Sup Ct Can).

[143] *Government of India v Taylor* [1955] A.C. 491.

[144] *Peter Buchanan Ltd v McVey* [1954] I.R. 89, [1955] A.C. 516n.

[145] *Cotton v R.* [1914] A.C. 176, 195 (PC); *Re Visser* [1928] Ch. 877; *Re Lord Cable* [1977] 1 W.L.R. 7, 13; *Bath v British and Malayan Trustees Ltd* [1969] 2 N.S.W.R. 114; *Re Dwelle Estate* (1969) 69 W.W.R. 212 (Alta); *Jones v Borland*, 1969 (4) S.A. 29.

[146] *Municipal Council of Sydney v Bull* [1909] 1 K.B. 7, 12.

[147] *Metal Industries (Salvage) Ltd v Owners of ST "Harle"*, 1962 S.L.T. 114. The point seems to have been overlooked in *The Acrux* [1965] P. 391.

[148] *Holman v Johnson* (1775) 1 Cowp. 341, 343; *cf. Att-Gen for Canada v Schulze*, (1901) 9 S.L.T. 4; *King of the Hellenes v Brostrom* (1923) 16 Ll.L.R. 167, 190; *Regazzoni v KC Sethia Ltd* [1958] A.C. 301, 330.

[149] *Weir v Lohr* (1967) 65 D.L.R. (2d) 717 (Man.). See also Case C–271/00 *Gemeent Steenbergen v Baten* [2002] E.C.R. I–10489: right to recover social assistance payments a "civil matter" under Brussels Convention, Art.1, and not within the scope of "social security" for the purposes of the exclusion in Art.1(3).

[150] *Connor v Connor* [1974] 1 N.Z.L.R. 632. In this case, and in *Weir v Lohr,* above, proceedings by private plaintiffs were held to be maintainable notwithstanding that the fruits of their litigation would be claimed by a foreign State which had paid social security claims or legal aid contributions and of which it was entitled to reimbursement. A direct claim by a foreign State for reimbursement would not be maintainable, it seems, unless it had a contractual or quasi-contractual character: see F.A. Mann (1971) *Recueil des Cours*, I, p.107, at pp.173–175.

[151] *Frankman v Prague Credit Bank* [1948] 1 K.B. 730, 746; *Kahler v Midland Bank* [1950] A.C. 24, 46–47, 57. But export regulations designed to protect foreign exchange were treated as revenue laws in *King of the Hellenes v Brostrom,* above.

doubted (it is submitted, correctly) whether the courts would entertain proceedings under a foreign exchange control regulation for the repatriation of
funds situate in England.[152]

Although it was once said that revenue laws are never recognised abroad,[153]   **5–031**
this proposition had no justification and it is clear that a foreign revenue law
which is part of the applicable law may be recognised.[154] Accordingly where
no question of enforcement arises, foreign revenue laws are applied by the
courts if they are relevant to an issue, although in individual cases such laws
may (like any other foreign rule) have to be disregarded on grounds of public
policy. Thus a contract which violates the customs regulations of the governing law will be treated as invalid in England.

Public laws. As the authorities now stand, the prohibition on the enforce-   **5–032**
ment of "other public law" extends to those laws (other than penal and
revenue laws) which will not be enforced because the claim involves the
exercise or the assertion of a sovereign right, or seeks to enforce governmental interests.[155] It was submitted in earlier editions of this work that the
prohibitions on the enforcement of penal[156] and revenue laws are examples of
a wider principle that a State cannot enforce its public law or its political or
prerogative rights.[157] As Lord Keith of Avonholm put it in *Government of
India v Taylor*,[158] an assertion of sovereign authority by one State within the
territory of another is contrary to all concepts of independent sovereign
authorities.

The prohibition on enforcement of public law has been the subject of two   **5–033**
relatively recent decisions of the Court of Appeal,[159] but has not received the

---

[152] *Re Lord Cable* [1977] 1 W.L.R. 7, 13. See also *Camdex International Ltd v Bank of Zambia
(No.2)* [1997] C.L.C. 714 (CA). *cf. Banco do Brasil v AC Israel Commodity Co*, 12 N.Y. 2d 371,
190 N.E. 2d 235 (1963), cert. den. 376 U.S. 906 (1964); contrast *Banco Frances e Brasileiro v
Doe*, 36 N.Y. 2d 592, 331 N.E. 2d 502, cert. den. 423 U.S. 867 (1975).

[153] See, e.g. *Holman v Johnson* (1775) 1 Cowp. 341, 342. Foreign rules requiring documents
to be stamped as a prerequisite of validity have long been recognised: *Alves v Hodgson* (1797) 7
T.R. 241, 243; *Clegg v Levy* (1812) 3 Camp. 166; *Bristow v Sequeville* (1850) 5 Exch. 275.
Contrast *James v Catherwood* (1823) 3 Dow. & Ry. (K.B.) 190.

[154] See *Re Visser* [1928] 1 Ch. 877; *Government of India v Taylor* [1955] A.C. 491, 505, 513;
Regazzoni v KC Sethia Ltd [1956] 2 Q.B. 490, 515 (CA); affirmed [1958] A.C. 301, 322, 324,
328, 330.

[155] *Islamic Republic of Iran v Barakat Galleries Ltd* [2007] EWCA Civ 1374, [2009] Q.B. 22,
[114]–[126]. That part of Rule 3(1) referring to "other public law" has its origin in the 4th edition
(1927), Rule 54, p.224, when it appeared as "political law," citing *Emperor of Austria v Day and
Kossuth* (1861) 3 De G.F. & J. 217 and distinguishing proprietary rights from claims to enforce
political laws. The expression "political law" was replaced by "other public law" in the 7th
edition (1958), Rule 21, p.159. This was in response (it seems) to criticism of the expression
"political law" by F.A. Mann (1954) 40 Tr. Gro. Soc. 25, reprinted in F. A. Mann, *Studies in
International Law* (1973), p.492 (see at p.500), and by Parker L.J. in *Regazzoni v KC Sethia
(1944) Ltd* [1956] 2 Q.B. 490, 524. The expression "public law", was intended to be equivalent
to "prerogative right", the term used by Dr Mann: see 7th ed., p.162, n.60.

[156] Which were defined in *Huntington v Attrill* [1893] A.C. 150, 156 (PC) to include all
breaches of "public law" punishable by fine or otherwise.

[157] A submission which was approved in *United States v Inkley* [1989] Q.B. 255, 264 (CA).

[158] [1955] A.C. 491, 511, quoted above, para.5–020.

[159] *Mbasogo v Logo Ltd* [2006] EWCA Civ 1370, [2007] Q.B. 846; *Islamic Republic of Iran
v Barakat Galleries Ltd* [2007] EWCA Civ 1374, [2009] Q.B. 22.

direct approval of the House of Lords or the Supreme Court.[160] Until these decisions there was very little authority which dealt directly with the general principle that foreign public laws will not be enforced in the English court. This is, at least partially, explained by the fact that States do not generally seek to enforce their public laws abroad and by the fact that it is often difficult to see to what cause of action such claims could give rise. Thus in *Re Lord Cable*[161] the Indian Government sought to be joined in proceedings for the execution of a will trust, in order that it might argue (inter alia) that the will trustees should remit funds to India in accordance with Indian exchange control legislation. Joinder was refused because, among other grounds, Slade J. was not satisfied that the English court would ever entertain proceedings by a foreign State of which the sole purpose was directly to enforce its exchange control regulations. In that case, the Indian Government sought to be joined so that it could oppose an application by beneficiaries to restrain the trustees from remitting funds to India. But if it had commenced an action itself to require remittance of the funds to India in accordance with the exchange control regulations, it is clear that there would have been no cause of action appropriate to the claim. It is not necessary to assimilate exchange control regulations to revenue laws to arrive at that conclusion. There are no principles of the conflict of laws which deal with public rights of that kind.

5–034 In *Att-Gen of New Zealand v Ortiz*[162] the New Zealand Government sought to recover a valuable Maori carving which had been illegally exported from New Zealand. The carving had been bought by Ortiz and was in the possession of Sotheby's, the auctioneers, for sale on behalf of Ortiz. Under a New Zealand statute historic articles exported without permission were forfeited to the Crown. The defendants resisted the action on two principal grounds, (a) that under New Zealand law the forfeiture was not automatic and did not take effect unless the goods were seized by the authorities (which they had not been), and (b) that the New Zealand statute could not be enforced because it was a penal or public law. Staughton J. decided in favour of the New Zealand Government on the basis that (a) under New Zealand law forfeiture was automatic, and (b) the law was not penal and there was no general category of non-enforceability of foreign public law. In the Court of Appeal his decision was reversed, (a) unanimously on the basis that forfeiture was not automatic, and (b) *per* Lord Denning M.R. on the basis that the statute was a public law which would not be enforced, and *per* Ackner and O'Connor L.JJ. on the basis that it was a penal law. The decision of the Court of Appeal was affirmed by the House of Lords solely on the ground that the New Zealand statute did not provide for automatic forfeiture, and the House of Lords pointed out that the views of the Court of Appeal on the applicability of the principle of non-enforceability of penal or public laws were *obiter*, and that the House, having heard no argument on this aspect, would not express any conclusion on the correctness of the opinions of the Court of Appeal. The view of Staughton J. on the relevant aspect was that the authorities did not support a general

---

[160] The House of Lords gave leave to appeal in *Mbasogo v Logo Ltd*, above, but the appeal was withdrawn when the proceedings were settled in the course of the hearing. Leave to appeal was refused in *Islamic Republic of Iran v Barakat Galleries Ltd*, above.

[161] [1977] 1 W.L.R. 7.

[162] [1982] Q.B. 349, reversed [1984] A.C. 1 (CA and HL).

principle that public laws should not be enforced, and that the better approach was to consider in each individual case whether there was a special ground of public policy which required the law in question not to be enforced. Lord Denning M.R., after a review of the authorities,[163] adopted the view expressed in this work that foreign public laws are not enforceable in this country, because they are acts done in the exercise of sovereign authority which will not be enforced outside the territory of the foreign State. Ackner L.J. did not reach a concluded view, but indicated some support for Staughton J.'s conclusion.

Claims to enforce governmental interests. The issue arose again in Australia and New Zealand in the extensive litigation by the British Government in which it sought to restrain the publication of *Spycatcher*, a book written by Peter Wright, a former member of the British security services. The claim was not directly based on public law. The British Government claimed that the book had drawn on confidential knowledge obtained by Wright while he was an officer of the security services, and that consequently the proposed publication was a breach of fiduciary duty, or a breach of an equitable or contractual obligation of confidence. The High Court of Australia[164] accepted that there was a principle that the court should not enforce foreign public laws, in the sense that the court would not allow the enforcement outside the territory of the foreign sovereign of claims based on or related to the exercise of foreign

    5–035

---

[163] Those which were said to support the general rule include *Don Alonso v Cornero* (1613) Hob. 212 (where it was held that the English court would not enforce a Spanish decree of forfeiture; but the decree was penal and the property concerned was forfeited when it was outside Spain); *King of Italy v De Medici* (1918) 34 T.L.R. 623 (where the court refused to grant an interlocutory injunction at the instance of the Italian Government in respect of the Medici family papers said to have been illegally exported; but the grounds of the decision are not clear). In *Williams & Humbert Ltd v W&H Trade Marks (Jersey) Ltd* [1986] A.C. 368 the defendants to claims by Spanish companies whose shares had been expropriated by the Spanish State sought to resist the claims on the ground (inter alia) that the proceedings were an attempt to enforce a foreign law which was penal or otherwise ought not to be enforced by the court, i.e. that the action was an attempted enforcement of a foreign public law and contrary to public policy. The House of Lords upheld the striking out of this defence on the basis that the action did not amount to enforcement, direct or indirect, of the Spanish decree. For criticism of this decision see F.A. Mann, *Further Studies in International Law* (1990), p.389. For a decision in a related action in the United States see *Williams & Humbert Ltd v W&H Trade Marks (Jersey) Ltd*, 840 F. 2d 73 (DC Cir. 1988). See also *US v Inkley* [1989] Q.B. 255 (CA); *Camdex International Ltd v Bank of Zambia (No.2)* [1997] C.L.C. 714 (CA).

[164] *Att-Gen (UK) v Heinemann Publishers Australia Pty Ltd* (1988) 165 C.L.R. 30, 42–43. Brennan J. agreed with the result, but on the narrow basis that it was contrary to public policy to enforce an obligation of confidence in an action brought for the purpose of protecting the intelligence secrets and political information of a foreign government. In the NSWCA, Street C.J. and Kirby P. accepted that there was a third residual category, but Street C.J. dissented on the basis that such an action should be allowed if the local sovereign supported the claim of the foreign sovereign on the ground that disclosure would harm the public interest: (1987) 10 N.S.W.L.R. 86. For criticism see F.A. Mann (1988) 104 L.Q.R. 497; see also Collier [1989] C.L.J. 33. See also *Evans v European Bank Ltd* [2004] NSWCA 82, (2004) 61 N.S.W.L.R. 75: a receiver appointed by the United States Federal Trade Commission could sue in New South Wales to recover the proceeds of a credit card fraud; the proceedings were not to be characterised as proceedings to secure a governmental interest; *United States Securities and Exchange Commission v Manterfield* [2009] EWCA Civ 27, [2010] 1 W.L.R. 172 (US judgment in favour of SEC for disgorgement of proceeds of fraud enforceable in England). *cf. Republic of Haiti v Duvalier* 1991 *Rev. Crit.* 386.

governmental power. The High Court recognised that it was difficult to identify the foreign laws or rights which fell within the general principle, and suggested that, rather than refer to "public laws" it would be more apt to refer to "public interests" or "governmental interests" to signify that the rule applies to claims enforcing the interests of a foreign sovereign which arise from the exercise of certain powers peculiar to government. Accordingly, the injunction was refused on the ground that the court would not enforce a claim arising out of acts of a foreign State in the exercise of such powers in the pursuit of its national security. The claim for relief arose out of, and was secured by, an exercise of the prerogative of the Crown, in the maintenance of national security, and the right or interest asserted was to be classified as a governmental interest, and not the vindication of private law obligations derived from the fiduciary and contractual relationship between Wright and the British Government. As a result, the action fell within the rule of international law which rendered the claim unenforceable.[165]

5–036   As already noted, in the *Spycatcher* litigation the claim of the British government was at least in form a private law claim for breach of confidence. So also the claims by the Government of Equatorial Guinea in England and in Guernsey arising out of an unsuccessful attempted coup in Equatorial Guinea, in which Simon Mann, a United Kingdom national, was allegedly involved, were based on private law. The President of Equatorial Guinea sued Simon Mann and his companies in England for damage caused by the unsuccessful attempt at revolution, and obtained orders in Guernsey for a bank to give information about the ownership of various companies and bank accounts which the Government had traced.

5–037   On an appeal from Guernsey in relation to an order for production of documents by a bank, the Privy Council decided that the order should be upheld, but (in an opinion written by Lord Bingham and Lord Hoffmann) expressed disquiet at the fact that no argument was addressed, whether to the courts in Guernsey or to the Privy Council, on the question whether the Guernsey court lacked jurisdiction to make the order which it did on the ground that it could be regarded as the enforcement, direct or indirect, of the public law of a foreign State. It was arguable that the claims which the Government said it wished to make in the English proceedings represented an exercise of sovereign authority, namely the preservation of the security of the State and its ruler. Because of its doubts about the justiciability of the claim, and since the same questions in relation to English law were likely to come before the English Court of Appeal, the Privy Council decided that the order should be suspended until the Court of Appeal had decided whether the

---

[165] In New Zealand the Court of Appeal refused an injunction because the material in the book had already entered the public domain, and because it was in the New Zealand public interest that it should be published. Cooke P. seems to have accepted the residual category of "public laws," but considered that the secret service agent's duty of confidentiality should be enforced, at any rate if the local sovereign supported the claim: *Att-Gen (UK) v Wellington Newspapers Ltd* [1988] 1 N.Z.L.R. 129, 173–175. For Canada see *United States v Levy* (1999) 45 O.R. (3d) 129; *United States v Yemec* (2010) 320 D.L.R. (4th) 96 (Ont. CA) (US laws regulating sale of lottery tickets). Whether there is a special rule relating to foreign public law was left open by the United States Supreme Court in *Banco Nacional de Cuba v Sabbatino*, 376 U.S. 398, 414 (1964), and see also *Attorney General of Canada v RJ Reynolds Tobacco Holdings, Inc*, 268 F.3d 103, 134 (2d Cir. 2001).

Government had a cause of action enforceable in English law. In *Mbasogo v Logo Ltd*[166] the Court of Appeal held that the critical question was whether, in bringing a claim, the claimant was doing an act which was of a sovereign character or which was done by virtue of sovereign authority; and whether the claim involved the exercise or assertion of a sovereign right. The alleged losses arose as a result of decisions taken by the claimants to protect the State and citizens of Equatorial Guinea. The defence of a State and its subjects was a paradigm function of government. The special damages claimed by both claimants were in respect of losses incurred as a direct result of their response to the alleged conspiracy. The Court of Appeal said that the appeal could be resolved without adopting the "governmental interest" approach enunciated by the majority of the High Court of Australia in the *Spycatcher* case, and it was not necessary to express a view as to whether that decision would be correct as a matter of English law.

Enforcement of public laws. In the *Equatorial Guinea* case the Court of   **5–038**
Appeal also held[167] that Rule 3(1) accurately reflected English law, including the reference to "other public laws." The question of the enforceability of foreign public laws arose for decision in *Islamic Republic of Iran v Barakat Galleries Ltd*[168] in which the Court of Appeal decided, on preliminary issues, that Iran was not debarred by the penal law/public law rule from recovering ancient artefacts allegedly exported from Iran and vested by legislation in the Iranian State. In the *Iran* decision the Court of Appeal said[169] that the *Equatorial Guinea* case was not in fact a case involving the attempted enforcement of foreign public law, and the ratio was that a claim involving the exercise or assertion of a sovereign right was not justiciable, and that was not far removed from the test adopted by the High Court of Australia in the *Spycatcher* case. The Court of Appeal held that the claim by Iran to the artefacts was a patrimonial claim, i.e. a claim based on its ownership of the artefacts, and not a claim to enforce a foreign public law or to assert sovereign rights.

The Court of Appeal also held, alternatively, that if the claim were to   **5–039**
enforce foreign public law, there was no inflexible rule that the court would not entertain an action whose object was to enforce the public law of another State. There were positive reasons of policy why a claim by a State to recover antiquities which formed part of its national heritage and which otherwise complied with the requirements of private international law. There was international recognition that states should assist one another to prevent the unlawful removal of cultural objects including antiquities. There were a number of international instruments (to some of which the United Kingdom was party) which had the purpose of preventing unlawful dealing in property which was part of the cultural heritage of states.

---

[166] [2006] EWCA Civ 1370, [2007] Q.B. 846. Contrast *Tasarruf Mevduati Sigorta Fonu v Demirel* [2006] EWHC 3354 (Ch.), [2007] 2 All E.R. 815 (affd. on other grounds [2007] EWCA Civ 799, [2007] 1 W.L.R. 2508): claim by State-owned bank as successor to private banks was not a public law claim.

[167] At [51].

[168] [2007] EWCA Civ 1374, [2009] Q.B. 22.

[169] At [123].

5–040   The result of the authorities in the Court of Appeal is that the English court will not enforce a claim based on foreign public law if the claim involves the exercise or assertion of a sovereign right, unless it is contrary to public policy for the claim to be shut out.[170] In the *Iran* case the Court of Appeal also considered what types of public law would be likely to fall within the prohibition. It approved the test suggested by Lord Denning M.R. in *Att-Gen of New Zealand v Ortiz*[171] that the question depended on whether the claim involved acts done by a sovereign *jure imperii*, by virtue of sovereign authority. The Court of Appeal concluded that exchange control legislation,[172] and (perhaps) export restrictions[173] would so fall. In practice probably the most important rules falling within the category are those which authorise governmental interference with private property, whether in the form of requisition, nationalisation or confiscation.

5–041   Where the foreign state has acquired title under its law to property within its jurisdiction in cases not involving compulsory acquisition of title from private parties, there is no reason in principle why the English court should not recognise its title in accordance with the general principle.[174] But where the foreign state has sought to confiscate or attach private property, the state's title will only be recognised in England if it has reduced the property to possession. In *Williams & Humbert Ltd v W & H Trade Marks (Jersey) Ltd* Lord Templeman said that the principle was that "an English court will recognise the compulsory acquisition law of a foreign state and will recognise the change of title to property which has come under the control of the foreign state and will recognise the consequences of that change of title."[175]

5–042   Consequently, the distinction between the two categories of cases, those where the foreign state will be able to claim its property in England even if it has not reduced it into its possession, and those where it may not claim unless it has reduced the property into its possession, depends on the way in which

---

[170] At [125], [154].

[171] [1984] A.C. 1, 20–21.

[172] *Re Lord Cable* [1977] 1 W.L.R. 7 and *Camdex International Ltd v Bank of Zambia* [1997] C.L.C. 714, 724 (Simon Brown L.J.), 734 (Phillips L.J.).

[173] *cf. King of Italy v de Medici* (1918) 34 T.L.R. 623 (claim to Medici archive) and *Spain v Christie Manson & Woods Ltd* [1986] 1 W.L.R. 1120 (claim to painting by Goya), each of which might have raised the question, but did not. See now Council Directive 93/7/EEC of March 15, 1993 on the return of cultural objects unlawfully removed from the territory of a Member State, and SI 1994/501, as amended.

[174] *cf. King of Italy v de Medici* (1918) 34 T.L.R. 623 (archive belonging to Italy); *Gotha City v Sotheby's (No.2)*, *The Times*, October 8, 1998 (Federal Republic of Germany entitled to recover painting originally owned and possessed by the Duke of Saxe-Coburg-Gotha Foundation for Art and Science, and which had been looted); and cases involving claims to assets held by predecessor or revolutionary governments: *King of the Two Sicilies v Willcox* (1851) 1 Sim. (N.S.) 301; *USA v Prioleau* (1865) 2 H.&M. 559; *USSR v Belaiew* (1925) 42 T.L.R. 21; *British Arab Commercial Bank Plc v National Transitional Council of the State of Libya* [2011] EWHC 2274 (Comm.). See also *Brunei Investment Agency v Fidelis Nominees Ltd* [2008] JRC 152 (Royal Court, Jersey). See generally, on recovery of assets by States, Collins (2007) 326 *Recueil des Cours* 11.

[175] [1986] A.C. 368 , 431; and see *Luther v Sagor* [1921] 3 K.B. 532 (CA); *Princess Paley Olga v Weisz* [1929] 1 K.B. 718 (CA) (in each of which the property had been reduced to possession by the Soviet authorities; and contrast *Brokaw v Seatrain UK Ltd* [1971] 2 Q.B. 476, 483 (CA) (revenue claim: notice of levy ineffective because goods not reduced into possession). See F.A. Mann, *Studies in International Law* (1973), pp.503–504.

it has acquired ownership. If it has acquired title under public law by confiscation or compulsory process from the former owner then it will not be able to claim the property in England from the former owner or his successors in title unless it has had possession. If it has taken the property into its possession then its claim will be treated as depending on recognition; if it has not had possession it will be seeking to exercise its sovereign authority.[176]

Act of State. It has been held that the courts will not investigate the **5–043** propriety of an act of the Crown performed in the course of its relations with a foreign State,[177] or enforce any right alleged to have been created by such an act unless that right has been incorporated into English domestic law.[178] Such acts are "acts of state," which, it has been said, "cannot be challenged, controlled or interfered with by municipal courts."[179] This proposition does not mean that an act of state is not recognised by the courts or that it cannot affect private rights existing prior to its commission.[180] Nor does it mean that areas which were once thought to be exclusively within the prerogative power

---

[176] [2009] Q.B. at [148].

[177] *Secretary of State in Council of India v Kamachee Boye Sahaba* (1859) 13 Moo. P.C. 22, 75; *Cook v Sprigg* [1899] A.C. 572, 578 (PC); *Salaman v Secretary of State for India* [1906] 1 K.B. 613 (CA); *Johnstone v Pedlar* [1921] 2 A.C. 262, 290; *Secretary of State for India v Sardar Rustam Khan* [1941] A.C. 356, 372 (PC). cf. *R. v Secretary of State for Foreign and Commonwealth Affairs, ex p. Pirbai, The Times*, October 17, 1985 (CA); *Ex p. Molyneux* [1986] 1 W.L.R. 331; *JH Rayner (Mincing Lane) Ltd v Department of Trade and Industry* [1990] 2 A.C. 418, 499; *R. v Secretary of State for Home Affairs, ex p. Rees-Mogg* [1994] Q.B. 552.

[178] *Nabob of the Carnatic v East India Co* (1793) 2 Ves. 56, 60; *Cook v Sprigg* [1899] A.C. 572, 578 (PC); *West Rand Central Gold Mining Co Ltd v R.* [1905] 2 K.B. 391; *Vajesingji v Secretary of State for India* (1924) L.R. 51 I.A. 357, 360 (PC); *Hoani Te Heuheu Tukino v Aotea District Maori Land Board* [1941] A.C. 308 (PC). See also *Rustomjee v R.* (1876) 2 Q.B.D. 69, 73; *Civilian War Claimants' Association v R.* [1932] A.C. 14; *Republic of Italy v Hambros Bank* [1950] Ch. 314; *Winfat Ltd v Att-Gen of Hong Kong* [1985] A.C. 733 (PC); *JH Rayner (Mincing Lane) Ltd v Department of Trade and Industry* [1990] 2 A.C. 418; *Re International Tin Council* [1989] Ch. 309 (CA); *Arab Monetary Fund v Hashim (No.3)* [1991] 2 A.C. 114; *Littrell v Government of the United States (No.2)* [1995] 1 W.L.R. 82 (CA); *Philipp Brothers v Republic of Sierra Leone* [1995] 1 Lloyd's Rep. 289 (CA); *Lonrho Exports Ltd v Export Credits Guarantee Dept* [1999] Ch. 158.

[179] *Salaman v Secretary of State for India* [1906] 1 K.B. 613, 639 (CA).

[180] *ibid.* at p.640. For example, under the former practice relating to recognition of governments (see below, para.25–004); acceptance by the court of recognition of a foreign régime which had changed the law of the foreign country could have involved an alteration in the court's attitude to private rights existing under the old law: *Luther v Sagor* [1921] 3 K.B. 532 (CA). On the effect of executive statements see *Republic of Somalia v Woodhouse Drake and Carey (Suisse) SA* [1993] Q.B. 54; *Sierra Leone Telecommunications Co Ltd v Barclays Bank Plc* [1998] 2 All E.R. 821; *Kuwait Airways Corp v Iraqi Airways Co (Nos 4 and 5)* [2002] UKHL 19, [2002] 2 A.C. 883; *R. (on the application of Kibris Turk Hava Yollari) v Secretary of State for Transport* [2009] EWHC 1918 (Admin), [2010] 1 All E.R. (Comm.) 253; *British Arab Commercial Bank Plc v National Transitional Council of the State of Libya* [2011] EWHC 2274 (Comm.). See also *Christian v R.* [2006] UKPC 47, [2007] 2 A.C. 400 (executive's statement that a territory is a British colony conclusive); *R. (on the application of HRH Sultan of Pahang) v Secretary of State for the Home Department* [2011] EWCA Civ 616 (executive statement that the Sultan not a head of state); *Att-Gen for Fiji v Robert Jones House Ltd* [1989] 2 N.Z.L.R. 69; and Warbrick (1986) 35 I.C.L.Q. 138; Wilmshurst (1986) 35 I.C.L.Q. 157; and on recognition of States see *Gur Corp v Trust Bank of Africa Ltd* [1987] Q.B. 559 (CA). See generally Lauterpacht, *Recognition in International Law* (1947); Talmon, *Recognition of Governments in International Law* (1998).

of the Crown in the exercise of foreign relations, such as the exercise of diplomatic protection, cannot be the subject of judicial review.[181]

5–044   The expression "act of state" is also used to describe executive acts which are authorised or ratified by the Crown in the exercise of sovereign power.[182] The victim of such an act is in some circumstances denied any redress against the actor because the act, once it has been identified as an act of state, is one which the court has no jurisdiction to examine.[183] The defence can be raised in regard to an act performed outside the United Kingdom and its colonies against the person or property of an alien[184] and is also available in regard to the deportation[185] or internment[186] of an alien of enemy nationality. The defence is probably not available in regard to acts affecting the property in the United Kingdom of a non-resident alien.[187] It is an open question whether the defence can apply to acts performed outside the United Kingdom and its colonies against the person or property of a British citizen.[188] The defence is inapplicable to an act performed within the United Kingdom and its colonies against the person or property of a British citizen[189] or of a non-enemy alien present here.[190]

5–045   The expression "act of state" is also used in connection with the executive and legislative acts of foreign States. The expression is found in several contexts, and it may not be possible to extract a general principle which will apply to all of them. One line of authorities (concerning the rights of inhabitants of ceded territory) indicates that the English courts will not investigate the propriety of an act of a foreign government performed in the course of its

---

[181] *R. (on the application of Abassi) v Secretary of State for Foreign and Commonwealth Affairs* [2002] EWCA Civ 1598, [2003] U.K.H.R.R. 76.

[182] *Nissan v Att-Gen* [1970] A.C. 179, 218, 238.

[183] *The Rolla* (1807) 6 C.Rob. 364, 366; *Buron v Denman* (1848) 2 Exch. 167; *R. v Crewe, ex p. Sekgome* [1910] 2 K.B. 576, 606, 624, 628 (CA); *Sobhuza II v Miller* [1926] A.C. 518 (PC); *Nissan v Att-Gen* [1970] A.C. 179, 216; *Buttes Gas & Oil Co v Hammer (Nos 2 and 3)* [1982] A.C. 888, 930–931.

[184] *Buron v Denman* (1848) 2 Exch. 167.

[185] *Netz v Ede* [1946] Ch. 224. For the deportation of aliens of non-enemy nationality see Immigration Act 1971, s.3(5), as amended by Immigration and Asylum Act 1999.

[186] *R. v Bottrill, ex p. Kuechenmeister* [1947] K.B. 41 (CA).

[187] *cf. Commercial and Estates Company of Egypt v Board of Trade* [1925] 1 K.B. 271, 290 (CA); *Buttes Gas & Oil Co v Hammer* [1975] Q.B. 557, 573 (CA), reversed on other grounds [1982] A.C. 888. It is probable that the Human Rights Act 1998 has removed any doubt. *cf. R. (on the application of Al-Skeini) v Secretary of State for Defence* [2005] EWCA Civ 1609.

[188] This point was left open by the majority of the House of Lords in *Nissan v Att-Gen* [1970] A.C. 179, 221, 226–227, 236 and 240. Lord Reid (at p.213) thought the defence could never apply in regard to a British subject "at least if he is also a citizen of the United Kingdom and Colonies." This category has now been replaced by British citizenship, British Overseas Territories citizenship and British Overseas citizenship and the status of British National Overseas: British Nationality Act 1981, as amended. In *Buttes Gas & Oil Co v Hammer* [1975] Q.B. 557, 573 (reversed on other grounds [1982] A.C. 888) Lord Denning M.R. thought the defence is "probably not available" in the case of a "British subject". In *Al-Jedda v Secretary of State for Defence* [2010] EWCA Civ 758, [2011] 2 W.L.R. 225 (a case involving the internment in Iraq of a British national by the British forces acting under a UN Security Council resolution) Arden L.J. was of the view that the defence applied to British nationals (at [108] *et seq.*); Elias L.J. was of the contrary view (at [192] *et seq.*); Sir John Dyson expressed no view. See also Collier [1968] C.L.J. 102, 115–117; Polack (1963) 26 M.L.R. 138; Kato [1969] Public Law 219; Perreau-Saussine (2007) 78 B.Y.I.L. 176.

[189] *Walker v Baird* [1892] A.C. 491 (PC).

[190] *Johnstone v Pedlar* [1921] 2 A.C. 262.

relations with another State or to enforce any right alleged to have been created by such an act.[191]

In the 19th century[192] it was held that the court could not enquire into a sovereign act done within the territory of the foreign State, and this principle was expressed by the United States Supreme Court[193] in a much quoted dictum which was in turn adopted by the Court of Appeal in England[194]:   **5–046**

> "Every sovereign State is bound to respect the independence of every other sovereign State, and the courts of one country will not sit in judgment on the acts of the government of another done within its own territory."

This principle is sometimes used as an alternative ground for a result which can also be reached by the application of the ordinary rules of the conflict of laws. Thus the executive seizure of property by a foreign sovereign within its territory will not give rise to an action in tort in England, either on the basis of this general principle, or because the act was lawful by the law of the place where it was committed and thus afforded a defence under the second rule in *Phillips v Eyre*.[195] Nor can a former owner challenge title to property acquired from a foreign government which had been confiscated within its own territory, again either on the basis of the general principle or on the basis of the rule that the validity of a confiscatory transfer of title depends on the *lex situs*.[196]   **5–047**

The general principle, however, is not an absolute one. In the first place, the foreign legislative act may be disregarded if it is not applicable under the normal principles of the conflict of laws[197] or if it is contrary to public policy in England.[198] Secondly, there may be circumstances in which foreign legislation may be held by the English court to be unconstitutional under the foreign   **5–048**

---

[191] *Cook v Sprigg* [1899] A.C. 572, 578 (PC); *Vajesingji v Secretary of State for India* (1924) L.R. 51 I.A. 357, 360 (PC); *cf. Johnstone v Pedlar* [1921] 2 A.C. 262, 290.

[192] *Duke of Brunswick v King of Hanover* (1844) 6 Beav. 1, 57–58; affirmed (1848) 2 H.L.C. 1, 17, 19, 21, 22, 24, 27. See also *Blad's Case* (1673) 3 Swan. 603 (PC), and *Blad v Bamfield* (1674) 3 Swan. 604; *Carr v Fracis Times & Co* [1902] A.C. 176, 179–180; *Johnstone v Pedlar* [1921] 2 A.C. 262, 290. See F.A. Mann, *Studies in International Law* (1973), p.420; (1971) *Recueil des Cours*, I, p.107, at pp.148–149; Singer (1981) 75 A.J.I.L. 283; Staker (1987) 58 B.Y.I.L. 151, 234–250; Collins (1995–96) 6 King's Coll. L.J. 20.

[193] *Underhill v Hernandez*, 168 U.S. 250, 252 (1897), affirming (1895) 65 F. 577; *Oetjen v Central Leather Co*, 246 U.S. 297, 304 (1918). See now *Banco Nacional de Cuba v Sabbatino*, 376 U.S. 398 (1964); *First National City Bank v Banco Nacional de Cuba*, 406 U.S. 759 (1972); *Alfred Dunhill of London Inc v Republic of Cuba*, 425 U.S. 682 (1976); Restatement Third, *Foreign Relations Law of the United States* (1987), s.443. In *Kirkpatrick & Co Inc v Environmental Tectonics Corp International*, 493 U.S. 400 (1990), noted by F.A. Mann (1990) 106 L.Q.R. 352, the US Supreme Court held that the act of state doctrine was concerned only with questions involving the validity of acts of foreign sovereigns in their own territory. This decision was applied in *A Ltd v B Bank* [1997] I.L.Pr. 586 (CA).

[194] *Luther v Sagor* [1921] 3 K.B. 532, 548 (CA); *Princess Paley Olga v Weisz* [1929] 1 K.B. 718, 724–725 (CA); *cf. Oppenheimer v Cattermole* [1976] A.C. 249, 282; *Att-Gen (UK) v Heinemann Publishers Australia Pty Ltd* (1988) 165 C.L.R. 30, 40–41.

[195] *Carr v Fracis Times & Co*, above. See below, para.35–006.

[196] *Luther v Sagor; Princess Paley Olga v Weisz*, above. See Rule 137.

[197] e.g. as in *Bank voor Handel en Scheepvaart NV v Slatford* [1953] 1 Q.B. 248; *Peer International Corp v Termidor Music Publishers Ltd* [2003] EWCA Civ 1156, [2004] Ch. 212. See also *Moti v R.* [2011] HCA 50, [46]–[52].

[198] *Re Helbert Wagg & Co Ltd* [1956] Ch. 323; *Oppenheimer v Cattermole* [1976] A.C. 249.

law. But the court will not entertain an action the object of which is to obtain a determination of the constitutionality of the foreign legislation.[199] Thirdly, the act of state doctrine has no application when it is clear that the relevant acts were done outside the foreign sovereign's territory.[200] Fourthly, it has no application in cases where a statute requires investigation of the propriety or the validity of foreign acts of state.[201] Fifthly, it does not apply to all official acts of a foreign State, and in particular it does not apply to acts of officials granting or registering intellectual property rights.[202]

5–049   But although the English court may consider the expressed intention of the foreign legislation and the circumstances in which it was enacted, it will be slow to investigate the motives of the foreign legislator and to question its good faith.[203]

5–050   The extent to which foreign legislation which would otherwise be regarded as valid and applicable may be disregarded on the ground that it is contrary to public international law has been a controversial question. The point first arose in connection with the expropriation of foreign-owned property by States, when the original owners sought to recover their property after it had left the territory of the confiscating State. As more fully developed in Chapter 25, there were differing views. In *The Rose Mary*[204] the Anglo-Iranian Oil Company (later British Petroleum), represented by Sir Hartley Shawcross (former Attorney-General) persuaded the Supreme Court of Aden to hold that the Iranian Government's nationalisation of Anglo-Iranian's oil was invalid by international law. The decision was criticised in England,[205] and the United

---

[199] cf. *A/S Tallinna Laevauhisus v Estonian State SS Line* (1947) 80 Ll.L.R. 99 (CA); *Buck v Att-Gen* [1965] Ch. 745 (CA); *Nuova Safim SpA v Sakura Bank Ltd* [1998] C.L.C. 306, affirmed [1999] C.L.C. 1830 (CA); *Fitzgibbon v Att-Gen* [2005] EWHC 114 (Ch.); *Hunt v T&N Plc* (1993) 109 D.L.R. (4th) 16 (Sup Ct Can); and F.A. Mann, *Studies in International Law* (1973), p.442; (1965) 14 I.C.L.Q. 985 (1971) *Recueil des Cours*, I, p.107, at pp.147–149; Kahn-Freund, in *Festschrift für F.A. Mann* (1977), p.207. The statement in the text was approved in *Dubai Bank Ltd v Galadari (No.5), The Times*, June 26, 1990. Contrast *Al-Jedda v Secretary of State for Defence* [2010] EWCA Civ 758, [2011] 2 W.L.R. 758, at [74], [189] (incidental interpretation and application of foreign constitution not barred). cf. *Total E&P Soudan v Edmonds* [2006] EWHC 1136 (Comm.), affd. [2007] EWCA Civ 50, [2007] C.P. Rep. 20.

[200] *The Playa Larga* [1983] 2 Lloyd's Rep. 171, 194 (CA).

[201] *R. v Bow Street Magistrate, Ex p. Pinochet* [2000] 1 A.C. 61, 106. This decision was subsequently set aside: [2000] 1 A.C. 119. For the final decision see *R. v Bow Street Magistrate, ex p. Pinochet (No.3)* [2000] 1 A.C. 147.

[202] *Lucasfilm Ltd v Ainsworth* [2011] UKSC 39, [2011] 3 W.L.R. 487, [81]–[86], *per* Lord Walker of Gestingthorpe and Lord Collins of Mapesbury.

[203] In *Settebello v Banco Totta and Acores* [1985] 1 W.L.R. 1050 (CA) it was held that the English court would not issue letters rogatory to a foreign court for the purpose of taking evidence on the motives of the Portuguese legislature because it would be contrary to "judicial comity." cf. *Marubeni Hong Kong and South China Ltd v Government of Mongolia* [2004] EWHC 472 (Comm.), [2004] 2 Lloyd's Rep. 198, affirmed [2005] EWCA Civ 395, [2005] 1 W.L.R. 2497.

[204] [1953] 1 W.L.R. 246.

[205] *Re Helbert Wagg & Co Ltd* [1956] Ch. 323, 352. See also *Regazzoni v KC Sethia Ltd* [1956] 2 Q.B. 490, 500, affirmed [1958] A.C. 301, 326; *The Playa Larga* [1983] 2 Lloyd's Rep. 171, 190 (CA); *Williams & Humbert Ltd v W&H Trade Marks (Jersey) Ltd* [1986] A.C. 368, 436; *Kuwait Airways Corp v Iraqi Airways Co* [1995] 1 W.L.R. 1147, 1166 (HL); *Empresa Nacional de Telecomunicaciones SA v Deutsche Bank AG* [2009] EWHC 2579 (QB), [2010] 1 All E.R. (Comm.) 649.

States Supreme Court decided in *Banco Nacional de Cuba v Sabbatino*[206] that the United States courts would not question the validity of a taking of property by a foreign government within its own territory, in the absence of a treaty or other unambiguous agreement, even if were alleged that the taking violated customary international law.

In *Buttes Gas and Oil Co v Hammer (Nos 2 and 3)*[207] the House of Lords   5–051
held that the act of state cases are part of a "more general principle that the courts will not adjudicate on the transactions of foreign sovereign states." This principle, it was said, was not a variety of "act of state" but one of "judicial restraint or abstention" which was not one of discretion but was "inherent in the very nature of the judicial process." In that case the House of Lords stayed claims and counterclaims between two oil companies for defamation and conspiracy because the heart of the case concerned a question of title to a portion of continental shelf in the Middle East to which there were rival claims by the two rulers who had granted the oil companies their respective concessions. It was held that there were no judicial or manageable standards by which the issues could be judged.

The principle stated by Lord Wilberforce was very wide in potential   5–052
scope,[208] and has been relied upon by litigants in many reported cases. Although the principle has been recognised in many such cases, the principle (or a related principle)[209] has only very rarely been applied[210] so

---

[206] 376 U.S. 398 (1964).

[207] [1982] A.C. 888.

[208] See Collins (2002) 51 I.C.L.Q. 485, at 506–508; F.A. Mann, *Foreign Affairs in English Courts* (1986), Ch.4 (whose view, expressed in a handwritten note on his copy of the book, was that "it was the House of Lords which lacked 'judicial restraint'!").

[209] Cases in which *Buttes Gas* was cited, and which the principle, or related principles, were applied include *Westland Helicopters Ltd v Arab Organisation for Industrialisation* [1995] Q.B. 282; *JH Rayner (Mincing Lane) Ltd v Department of Trade and Industry* [1990] 2 A.C. 418; *R. (on the application of Al-Haq) v Secretary of State for Foreign and Commonwealth Affairs* [2009] EWHC 1910 (Admin.); *JSC BTA Bank v Ablyazov (No.4)* [2011] EWHC 202 (Comm.), [2011] 2 All E.R. (Comm.) 10; *Wells Fargo Bank Northwest National Assn v Victoria Aircraft Leasing Ltd (No.2)* [2004] VSC 341; *Petrotimor Companhia de Petroleos SARL v Commonwealth of Australia* (2003) 197 F.L.R. 461 (Full Ct); *Air New Zealand Ltd v Director of Civil Aviation* [2002] 3 N.Z.L.R. 796 (CA). *cf. Settebello v Banco Totta y Acores, The Times*, August 4, 1984, affirmed [1985] 1 W.L.R. 1050; *R. (on the Application of Abassi) v Secretary of State for Foreign and Commonwealth Affairs* [2002] EWCA Civ. 1598, [2003] U.K.H.R.R. 76. *Tajik Aluminium Plant v Ermatov* [2006] EWHC 2374 (Comm.); *Republic of Serbia v ImageSat International NV* [2009] EWHC 2853 (Comm.), [2010] 1 Lloyd's Rep. 324.

[210] It was not applied in *Fayed v Al Tajir* [1988] Q.B. 712, 725 (CA); *Kuwait Airways Corp v Iraqi Airways, Financial Times*, July 17, 1992; *Arab Monetary Fund v Hashim* [1993] 1 Lloyd's Rep. 543, 572, affirmed on this aspect [1996] 1 Lloyd's Rep. 589, 596 (CA); *A Ltd v B Bank* [1997] I.L.Pr. 586 (CA); *R. v Home Secretary, Ex p. Launder (No.2)* [1998] Q.B. 994; *R. v Home Secretary, Ex p. Johnson* [1999] Q.B. 1174; *Re Banco Nacional de Cuba* [2001] 1 W.L.R. 2039; *Mamidoil-Jetoil Greek Petroleum Co SA v Okta Crude Oil Refinery (No.2)* [2003] 2 Lloyd's Rep. 635; *Republic of Ecuador v Occidental Exploration and Production Co* [2005] EWCA Civ 1116, [2006] Q.B. 432; *Re AY Bank Ltd* [2006] EWHC 830 (Ch.), [2006] 2 All E.R. (Comm.) 463; *Korea National Insurance Corp v Allianz Global Corporate and Speciality AG* [2008] EWCA Civ 1355, [2008] 2 C.L.C. 837; *Croatia v Serbia* [2009] EWHC 1559 (Ch.), [2010] Ch. 200; *Yukos Capital SARL v OJSC Rosneft Oil Co* [2011] EWHC 1461 (Comm.), [2011] 2 C.L.C. 129; *Berezovsky v Abramovich* [2011] EWCA Civ 153, [2011] 1 C.L.C. 359; *Att-Gen for England and Wales v R.* [2002] 2 N.Z.L.R. 91 (CA), affirmed sub. nom. *R. v Her Majesty's Att-Gen for England and Wales* [2003] UKPC 22, [2004] 2 N.Z.L.R. 577.

as to render a claim non-justiciable. In *Kuwait Airways Corp v Iraqi Airways Co (Nos 4 and 5)*[211] it was held that a claim for wrongful interference with aircraft in the course of the Iraqi invasion of Kuwait was justiciable notwithstanding that the claim proceeded on the basis that the invasion was contrary to international law: the United Nations Security Council had declared the invasion illegal, called on all Member States not to recognise the invasion, and demanded that Iraq rescind its actions purporting to annex Kuwait. It would be contrary to the international obligations of the United Kingdom were its courts to adopt an approach which was inconsistent with its duty under the United Nations Charter and under the relevant Security Council resolutions. It was held by the House of Lords that the non-justiciability principle did not mean that the judiciary must shut its eyes to a breach of an established principle of international law committed by one State against another when the breach was plain. The standard being applied by the court was clear and manageable. The non-justiciability principle did not mean that the judiciary must shut its eyes to a breach of an established principle of international law committed by one State against another when the breach was plain and acknowledged. In such a case the adjudication problems confronting the English court in *Buttes Gas & Oil Co v Hammer* did not arise. The standard being applied by the court was clear and manageable, and the outcome not in doubt.[212] The English court should give effect to clearly established rules of international law. As nations became ever more interdependent, the need to recognise and adhere to standards of conduct set by international law became ever more important. A breach of international law of such seriousness was a matter of deep concern to the world-wide community of nations. Enforcement or recognition would also be contrary to the United Kingdom's obligations under the United Nations Charter. Enforcement or recognition of the Iraqi law would be manifestly contrary to the public policy of English law.[213] A legislative act by a foreign State which was in flagrant breach of clearly established rules of international law ought not to be recognised as forming part of the *lex situs* of that State.[214]

5-053   In *Lucasfilm Ltd v Ainsworth*[215] the Supreme Court left open the question whether, in the light of the ruling of the European Court in *Owusu v Jackson*[216] that what is now Art.2 of the Brussels I Regulation[217] is mandatory in nature, the non-justiciability principle could be applied in a claim against a defendant domiciled in the United Kingdom, or whether that ruling required that there be a remedy in England. It is suggested that the principle in *Owusu*

---

[211] [2002] UKHL 19, [2002] 2 A.C. 883. See also *R. (on the Application of Abassi) v Secretary of State for Foreign and Commonwealth Affairs* [2002] EWCA Civ 1598, [2003] U.K.H.R.R. 76.

[212] At [25]–[26].

[213] Lord Nicholls of Birkenhead, at [26] *et seq.*, Lord Steyn, at [113] *et seq.*, Lord Hope of Craighead, at [146] *et seq.*

[214] Lord Hope of Craighead, at [148]–[149], approving F.A. Mann (1954) 70 L.Q.R. 181; also in *Further Studies in International Law*, pp.177–183.

[215] [2011] UKSC 39, [2011] 3 W.L.R. 487, at [112]–[114]. See also Scott (2007) 3 J. Priv. Int. L. 309.

[216] Case C–281/02 [2005] ECR I–1383, [2005] Q.B. 801, para.12–019, below.

[217] Domicile as the primary rule of jurisdiction.

v Jackson does not affect the rules relating to matters which have hitherto been regarded as non-justiciable, such as "the transactions of foreign sovereign states" which were held to be non-justiciable in *Buttes Gas and Oil Co v Hammer (No.3)*; and that to require the English court to so adjudicate might put the United Kingdom in breach of international law.

ILLUSTRATIONS

(1) PENAL LAWS

1. X incurs a penalty of £100 for the infringement of the law of a foreign country prohibiting **5–054** the sale of spirits. The penalty is recoverable in the courts of the foreign country in an action for debt brought by an official of the foreign government. X is in England. The proper official brings an action in the High Court for the recovery of the £100. The claim cannot be maintained.[218]

2. Under the law of New York, the director of a trading corporation, who signs certain certificates with regard to the affairs of the corporation knowing such certificates to be false, becomes personally liable for the debts of the corporation. Under this law X, a director of a New York company, becomes liable to A, a creditor, for a debt due from the company. X is in England. A brings an action against X for the debt. *Semble*, X may be made liable.[219]

3. The circumstances are the same as in Illustration 2, except that A has recovered judgment in the court of New York for the debt, and brings an action against X in England on the judgment. *Semble*, the judgment is enforceable.[220]

4. The King of Spain deposits securities with the Westminster Bank in London to the order of a Spanish bank as his agents. A decree by the Constituent Cortes of Spain declares the King to be guilty of treason, and all his assets are ordered to be seized for its own benefit by the Spanish State. The court will not order the delivery up of the securities deposited in England to a nominee of the Spanish Republic.[221]

5. X, a British subject, is charged with fraud in the United States, and is released on bail, on condition that he enters into an "appearance bond" in the sum of $48,000. He is allowed by the United States court to go back to England for a month, but he does not return to the United States, and the United States Government obtains a civil judgment in the United States federal court in Florida on the bond. No action on the Florida judgment can be brought in England because the purpose of the bond was to ensure the presence of X for a criminal prosecution and to exact pecuniary penalties for non-attendance.[222]

(2) REVENUE LAWS

6. Under an Act of Parliament of New South Wales the municipality of Sydney is authorised **5–055** to carry out improvements in the city and to charge the cost to the owners of the property affected. X, an owner of property affected, is resident in England. The council of the municipality brings an action against X for the sum due from him under the New South Wales Act. The claim cannot be maintained.[223]

7. A company registered in England carries on business in India, where it becomes liable to capital gains tax on a sale of its undertaking. The company is wound up in England and the Indian Government lodges a claim in respect of the unpaid tax. The liquidator is justified in rejecting the proof because only liabilities which could have been enforced against the company in England are receivable, and the court would not have enforced the Indian Government's claim.[224]

8. X is the personal representative in England of a Dutch national domiciled at his death in Holland. Under Dutch law duties are payable in respect of his estate. An action is brought by the Queen of Holland against X to recover the sum due. The action fails.[225]

---

[218] *cf. Huntington v Attrill* [1893] A.C. 150 (PC).

[219] *cf. Huntington v Attrill,* above.

[220] *Huntington v Attrill,* above.

[221] *Banco de Vizcaya v Don Alfonso de Borbon y Austria* [1935] 1 K.B. 140.

[222] *US v Inkley* [1989] Q.B. 255 (CA).

[223] *Municipal Council of Sydney v Bull* [1909] 1 K.B. 7.

[224] *Government of India v Taylor* [1955] A.C. 491. It is immaterial where the company is incorporated.

[225] *Re Visser* [1928] Ch. 877.

9. X Co is a Canadian insurance company with a branch in Egypt, which issues policies to A, under which money is due to A. X Co is served with a garnishee order by the Egyptian revenue authorities in respect of tax allegedly due by A to the Egyptian Government. The garnishee order does not afford X Co a defence in proceedings in England to recover the debt, since recognition of the order would constitute indirect enforcement of a foreign revenue law.[226]

10. T dies domiciled in South Africa leaving property in England and South Africa. A is his English executor. X is his South African executor. After payment of United Kingdom duties and debts there is a surplus of assets in A's hands. There are insufficient assets in South Africa to pay South African death duties. A seeks the direction of the court on how to dispose of the assets in his hands. Because the South African Government would be unable to enforce its claim for duties in England, it is A's duty to remit the surplus assets direct to the legatees and not to X.[227]

11. The circumstances are the same as in Illustration 10, except that some of the legatees reside in South Africa, and if these legatees are paid their legacies, they will be answerable to the South African Government to the extent of their legacies for duty on the whole estate. A's duty is to remit the surplus assets to X.[228]

12. X and Y, United States citizens, send some furniture by sea to Z, their son-in-law, who is living in London. The United States Government claim that X and Y owe the United States Treasury money for taxes, and while the ship is on the high seas the United States Treasury serves a notice of levy on the shipowners in respect of unpaid tax demanding surrender of all property belonging to X and Y. The property is not reduced into the possession of the United States Treasury, and Z is entitled to claim the furniture from the shipowners, because to give effect to the claim of the United States Government would be indirect enforcement of a revenue law.[229]

(3) OTHER PUBLIC LAWS

5–056

13. The government of a foreign State passes a decree expropriating certain jewellery belonging to X which is situate within that State at the time of the decree. X brings the jewellery to London, where it is claimed by the foreign government. *Semble*, the claim fails.[230]

14. In furtherance of their agreement for the establishment of an international monopoly, an English company is assigned certain American patents by an American corporation. The United States Government claims the cancellation of the assignment under the Sherman Anti-Trust Act. The claim fails.[231]

15. X bring manuscripts to England from Italy despite a decree of the Italian Government forbidding their export. The decree also grants the Italian State a first option to purchase the manuscripts. X seeks to dispose of them to Y in London, and the Italian Government claims an injunction to prevent such a disposal. *Semble*, the court will not grant an injunction.[232]

16. X brings an ancient Maori carving from New Zealand to England in contravention of a New Zealand statute which provides that historic articles illegally exported shall be forfeited to the Crown. The New Zealand Government brings an action in England against X for the return and delivery up of the carving. The action fails because the Crown has not acquired title under New Zealand law, but also, *per* Lord Denning M.R., because the New Zealand statute is a public law, or, *per* Ackner and O'Connor L.JJ., because it is a penal law.[233]

17. X is a German national resident in France. A state of war exists between Germany and France. The French custodian of enemy property duly appointed under French law, who is entitled thereunder to the control of all X's property, claims the payment to him of a dividend on shares held by X in an English company. *Semble*, the court will not order payment.[234]

18. X is a former member of the British security services, and Y is a publisher. X writes a book about his experiences, and proposes to publish it in (among other countries) Australia. The British Government seeks an injunction against X and Y in Australia to restrain publication. An

---

[226] *Rossano v Manufacturers' Life Insurance Co* [1963] 2 Q.B. 352.

[227] *cf. Jones v Borland*, 1969 (4) S.A. 29.

[228] *cf. Scottish National Orchestra Society Ltd v Thomson's Executor*, 1969 S.L.T. 325.

[229] *Brokaw v Seatrain UK Ltd* [1971] 2 Q.B. 476 (CA).

[230] Suggested by *Don Alonso v Cornero* (1613) Hob. 212; and *Princess Paley Olga v Weisz* [1929] 1 K.B. 718 (CA).

[231] Suggested by *British Nylon Spinners Ltd v ICI Ltd* [1953] Ch. 19 (CA); [1955] Ch. 37.

[232] *cf. King of Italy v De Medici* (1918) 34 T.L.R. 623.

[233] *Att-Gen of New Zealand v Ortiz* [1984] A.C. 1 (CA and HL).

[234] Based on the facts of *Lepage v San Paulo Copper Estates Ltd* [1917] W.N. 216, which, it is submitted, was wrongly decided.

injunction is refused because the purpose of the action by the British Government is to enforce a governmental interest, namely to protect the efficiency of its security service.[235]

19. A & Co obtains a judgment in England against the Bank of Zambia. It seeks a garnishee order absolute in respect of funds held in London by X & Co, the biggest copper producer in Zambia. Under Zambian exchange control law, X & Co is bound to transfer a proportion of the funds to the Bank of Zambia. The garnishee order nisi is set aside. Even if the obligation of X & Co to the Bank of Zambia were a debt (which it is not) attachment of such a debt would be the enforcement of Zambian public law.[236]

20. The United States Securities and Exchange Commission brings proceedings in the United States District Court in Massachusetts, alleging that X and Y fraudulently induced Taiwanese investors to invest approximately $34 million in a fund, and that they misappropriated millions of dollars, withdrawing $8 million of which it was alleged X received $2.35 million. The SEC makes an application to the English court for interim freezing orders in support of its proceedings in Massachusetts. The freezing orders are upheld because the US proceedings are for the disgorgement of the proceeds of fraud, and their return to the investors, and consequently a judgment in those proceedings would not be a penal judgment, or otherwise unenforceable under Rule 3.[237]

21. The head of state of a mineral-rich African republic and the State itself, bring proceedings against X and Y for, inter alia, conspiracy and intentional infliction of harm by unlawful means, alleging that X and Y had conspired in England and elsewhere to overthrow the State's government and seize power by means of a coup which ultimately failed. The claimants claim damages for damage to the State's commercial interests and infrastructure and for costs incurred in investigating the conspiracy, detaining and prosecuting suspects, and increasing security. The head of state also claims general damages for serious anxiety, distress and disruption to his personal life and work. The claims are not justiciable because they are in respect of losses which arose as a result of decisions taken by the claimants to protect the State and its citizens, which could only have been suffered by the governing body of the State, and the claims amount to the exercise of its sovereign power within the jurisdiction of the English court.[238]

(4) ACTS OF STATE

22. A obtains the right to work minerals in the territory of a foreign State from the government of that State. The territory of the foreign State is annexed by the Crown. A claims a declaration that the Crown must respect the concession. The court will not grant such a declaration.[239]   **5–057**

23. X, an officer of the Crown, duly authorised, destroys property of A, a Spanish subject, at a place outside the United Kingdom and Colonies. Spain and the United Kingdom are at peace, and X's act is tortious by the law of the place where it is committed. X's act is an act of state, and the court will not entertain an action by A against X.[240]

24. X is the bodyguard of Y, a foreign potentate, who is on a State visit to England. While attending a civic ceremony Y misunderstands the enthusiasm of the spectators and orders X to shoot at them. X does so, and injures A, who is an innocent bystander. In an action by A, X may not plead act of State.

25. The Sheikh of Araby promulgates a decree which has the effect of depriving X of the right to exploit an oil-rich area and of giving that right to A. X says the decree was "cooked up" by A. A's action for slander is met by a defence of justification and a counterclaim for conspiracy. The claim and the counterclaim will be stayed because the pleadings involve the adjudication of the transactions of foreign States and the issues raised are non-justiciable.[241]

26. A & Co seek to enforce a Swiss arbitration award against AOI, an international organisation formed in 1975 by a treaty between Egypt, Saudi Arabia, Qatar and the United Arab Emirates, with its headquarters and operations in Egypt. After the peace treaty between Egypt and Israel in 1979, the three Member States other than Egypt purport to suspend the operations of AOI and to

---

[235] *Att-Gen (UK) v Heinemann Publishers Australia Pty Ltd* (1988) 165 C.L.R. 30.

[236] *cf. Camdex International Ltd v Bank of Zambia (No.2)* [1997] C.L.C. 714 (CA).

[237] *United States Securities and Exchange Commission v Manterfield* [2009] EWCA Civ 27, [2010] 1 W.L.R. 172.

[238] *Mbasogo v Logo Ltd* [2006] EWCA Civ 1370, [2007] Q.B. 846.

[239] *Cook v Sprigg* [1899] A.C. 572 (PC). See Crown Proceedings Act 1947, s.11(1).

[240] *Buron v Denman* (1848) 2 Exch. 167. See Crown Proceedings Act 1947, ss.2(1) and 11(1).

[241] *Buttes Gas & Oil Co v Hammer (Nos 2 and 3)* [1982] A.C. 888.

set up a liquidation committee. Egypt passes legislation reconstituting the management of AOI. An issue arises as to whether the management appointed pursuant to the Egyptian legislation is properly authorised to represent the AOI. The constitution of AOI is governed by international law, and the authority of the management depended on whether the Egyptian legislation was a justifiable countermeasure in international law, which in turn depended on the issue whether the three States had acted in breach of the treaty setting up the AOI. That was a non-justiciable issue, because it was not open to the English court to determine whether a foreign sovereign State had broken or terminated a treaty.[242] Consequently, the Egyptian-appointed management is not able to adduce proof that it is properly authorised.

27. Iraq invades Kuwait in August 1990, and civil aircraft belonging to Kuwait Airways are seized and removed to Iraq. Iraqi legislation is enacted purporting to dissolve Kuwait Airways and to transfer its assets to Iraqi Airways, which then incorporates the aircraft in its fleet and makes use of them. In an action in England by Kuwait Airways against Iraqi Airways for wrongful interference, it is held that the Iraqi legislation is not capable of recognition in England, because it was exorbitant and contrary to international law.[243]

---

[242] *Westland Helicopters Ltd v Arab Organisation for Industrialisation* [1995] Q.B. 282.
[243] *Kuwait Airways Corp v Iraqi Airways Co (Nos 4 and 5)* [2002] UKHL 19, [2002] 2 A.C. 883.

DOMICILE AND RESIDENCE

1. GENERAL PRINCIPLES

RULE 4—(1) A person[1] is, in general, domiciled in the country in which he is considered by English law to have his permanent home.

(2) A person may sometimes be domiciled in a country although he does not have his permanent home in it.[2]

6R–001

COMMENT

Concepts of domicile. Rules 4 to 16 are concerned with the traditional concept of domicile in English law. In most contexts within the English rules of the conflict of laws, the word "domicile" refers to this concept; but, unfortunately for the clarity of those rules, not in all such contexts. The Brussels I Regulation and the Brussels and Lugano Conventions on jurisdiction and the enforcement of judgments in civil and commercial matters use the notion of the domicile of an individual, without defining it. The necessary definition is provided by the Civil Jurisdiction and Judgments Act 1982, in respect of the Conventions, and by the Civil Jurisdiction and Judgments Order 2001[3] in respect of the Brussels I Regulation, but the resulting concept has little in common, save its name, with the traditional concept.[4] It is to be noted that use of this new concept is not limited to cases falling within the Brussels I Regulation or the Conventions.[5] A further specialised category of domicile has been introduced by the Constitutional Reform and Governance Act 2010, which provides that MPs and most members of the House of Lords shall be deemed to be domiciled in the United Kingdom for purpose of certain tax liabilities.[6]

6–002

---

[1] As to domicile of corporations, see Rule 173.
[2] See Rules 5, 10 and 13 to 16.
[3] SI 2001/3929.
[4] For the new concept, see Rule 30.
[5] e.g. CPR, r.6.31(i); see below, para.11–079.
[6] s.41.

6–003   It is of course the case that in interpreting a contractual document, especially one not governed by English law, the court may attribute to the term "domicile" a popular meaning differing from either of its technical meanings in English law.[7]

6–004   **Permanent home.** The notion which lies at the root of the concept of domicile is that of permanent home. "By domicile we mean home, the permanent home; and if you do not understand your permanent home I am afraid that no illustration drawn from foreign writers or foreign languages will very much help you to it."[8] A person may be said to have his home in a country if he resides in it without any intention of at present removing from it permanently or for an indefinite period. But a person does not cease to have his home in a country merely because he is temporarily resident elsewhere; and a person who has formed the intention of leaving a country does not cease to have his home in it until he acts according to that intention.

6–005   While the notion of permanent home can be explained largely in the light of commonsense principles, the same is certainly not true of domicile. Domicile is "an idea of law"[9] which diverges from the notion of permanent home in two principal respects. In the first place, the elements which are required for the acquisition of a domicile go beyond those required for the acquisition of a permanent home. In order to acquire a domicile of choice in a country a person must intend to reside in it permanently or indefinitely.[10] A person who intends to reside in a country for ten years and no more does not acquire a domicile in it, although he has his home there during the ten years. Again, a person cannot acquire a domicile of choice in a country in which he has never been physically present,[11] but he may well have his permanent home in it if he establishes his family there and intends shortly to join them. Secondly, domicile differs from permanent home in that the law in some cases says that a person is domiciled in a country whether or not he has his permanent home in it. Thus a person may in fact have no home, either because he is a permanent vagrant or because he has abandoned one home and has not yet acquired another; but the law nonetheless attributes a domicile to him.[12] Again, a person may in fact have a permanent home in one country but be domiciled in another because the law denies him or her the capacity of acquiring a domicile. Thus children under sixteen and mentally disordered persons may be domiciled in countries in which they do not have their permanent home.[13]

---

[7] *Cowley v Heatley, The Times*, July 24, 1986 (interpretation of Commonwealth Games Constitution).

[8] *Whicker v Hume* (1858) 7 H.L.C. 124, 160; *cf. Re Craignish* [1892] 3 Ch. 180, 192; *Winans v Att-Gen* [1904] A.C. 287, 288.

[9] *Bell v Kennedy* (1868) L.R. 1 Sc. & Div. 307, 320; *cf. Bergner & Engel Brewing Co v Dreyfus*, 172 Mass. 154, 157, 51 N.E. 531, 532 (1898); *Garthwaite v Garthwaite* [1964] P. 356, 378, 393 (CA).

[10] Rule 10.

[11] *ibid.*

[12] Rule 5.

[13] Rules 15 and 16.

Reform of the law of domicile. The traditional concept of domicile has   **6–006**
received repeated critical attention from law reform agencies in England and
in other countries which have received the English common law.[14] Important
reforms were made by Pt I of the Domicile and Matrimonial Proceedings Act
1973[15] but they were limited to the special rules affecting the domicile of
married women and children. Proposals for a new Code of Domicile made in
1954 by the Private International Law Committee[16] proved abortive, but after
the enactment of reforming legislation in New Zealand[17] and Australia[18] the
English and Scottish Law Commissions published in 1987 a report containing
further proposals for the general reform of the law of domicile.[19] These
inspired a partial, and as a result unsatisfactory, reform of the rules governing
the domicile of children in Scotland.[20] There is, however, no prospect of these
recommendations being implemented in England.

Area of domicile. The object of determining a person's domicile is to   **6–007**
connect him for the purpose of a particular inquiry with some system or rule
of law. To establish this connection it is sufficient to fix the person's domicile
in a "country," that is, in a "territory subject under one sovereign to one body
of law."[21] It is not necessary to show in what part of the country he had his
permanent home.[22] It is also in general necessary to fix a person's domicile in
a particular country, so that it is not sufficient to show that his permanent
home is in a State[23] which contains several countries.[24] Thus a person who
comes to the United Kingdom with the intention of settling in England or
Scotland, or a person who goes to Australia with the intention of settling in
Victoria or New South Wales, does not in the eyes of English law acquire a
domicile in any of the "countries" in question until he effects his intention.
But for some purposes a person may be domiciled in the United Kingdom, or
in Canada or Australia, whether or not the United Kingdom or Canada or
Australia are "countries" within the above definition.[25] This position is

---

[14] See McClean, *Recognition of Family Judgments in the Commonwealth* (1983), Ch.1.

[15] See paras 6–084, 6E–100—6–106, below.

[16] Cmd. 9068 (1954). See Mann (1959) 8 I.C.L.Q. 457.

[17] Domicile Act 1976.

[18] A uniform Domicile Act enacted in the various Australian jurisdictions came into force on July 1, 1982: Victoria, 1978 (amended in 1982 to bring a variant s.8 into line with the text adopted in the other jurisdictions); New South Wales and Northern Territory, 1979; South Australia and Tasmania, 1980; Queensland and Western Australia, 1981; the Commonwealth Parliament in respect of the law of the Commonwealth, the Australian Capital Territory and other Territories (with different numbering of principal sections), 1982.

[19] Law Com. No.168; Scot. Law Cm. No.107. The principal proposals are noted, below, in the context of the detailed examination of the relevant rule.

[20] Family Law (Scotland) Act 2006, s.22. See Maher (2006) S.L.T. 149; McEleavy (2007) 56 I.C.L.Q. 453.

[21] Above, paras 1–065 *et seq.*

[22] *Re Craignish* [1892] 3 Ch. 180, 192; *Arnott v Groom* (1846) 9 D. (Ct of Sess) 142.

[23] Above, paras 1–069—1–070.

[24] *Bell v Kennedy* (1868) L.R. 1 Sc. & Div. 307; *Att-Gen for Alberta v Cook* [1926] A.C. 444, 448–450 (PC); *Gatty v Att-Gen* [1951] P. 444; *Trottier v Rajotte* [1940] 1 D.L.R. 433 (Sup Ct Can); *Johnson v Johnson* [1931] A.D. 391; *Smith v Smith* 1970 (1) S.A. 146. And see Rule 6, below.

[25] See below, paras 6–015—6–016; e.g. where, as in Canada and Australia, divorce is regulated by Federal law.

unsatisfactory and the English and Scottish Law Commissions have recommended the adoption in England of rules based on those in the modern Australian legislation, so that a person who is present in a federal or composite State with the intention to settle in that State for an indefinite period should, if he is not held under the general rules to be domiciled in any country within that State, be domiciled in the country therein with which he is for the time being most closely connected.[26]

6–008 Difficulties sometimes arise when territories are divided or frontiers change.[27] After Ireland was divided in 1921 into Northern Ireland and what is now called the Republic of Ireland, it was held in Ireland that a man could be domiciled in Northern Ireland in 1907[28] or in the Republic in 1898,[29] in each case because he had his home in what subsequently became Northern Ireland and the Republic respectively. In neither of these cases did the court refer to an Order in Council made in pursuance of the Government of Ireland Act 1920, which provides that "for the purpose of determining the domicile of any person, Northern Ireland shall be deemed always to have been a separate part of the United Kingdom."[30] "Separate" in this Order no doubt means "separate from the Republic."

6–009 Domicile is a connection with a locality and not with a group of persons.[31] Thus the House of Lords has rejected the argument that a person could not acquire a domicile in a country merely because he belonged to a group which, by treaty, enjoyed special privileges and some immunity from the jurisdiction of the local courts.[32] The 19th-century cases in which British residents in India were held to have acquired an "Anglo-Indian" domicile proceed in disregard of this principle and are now regarded as anomalous.[33]

ILLUSTRATIONS

6–010 1. D, who is domiciled in England, accepts employment in New Zealand under a contract of service by which he will be obliged to remain in New Zealand for ten years. He accordingly takes his family and belongings to New Zealand and sets up house there intending to return to England after the end of the ten years. Although his home is for the time being in New Zealand, he continues to be domiciled in England.

2. D, who is domiciled in England, intends to emigrate to New South Wales. He sends his family and belongings there, but himself stays behind in England, living in hotels, to wind up his affairs. During this period he continues to be domiciled in England although his home is in New South Wales.

3. D lives in England. He has no settled place of abode, but does not intend ever to leave England. Although he has no home, he is domiciled in England.

---

[26] *The Law of Domicile* (Law Com. No.168), paras 7.1—7.8. *cf.* the uniform Domicile Act in the Australian jurisdictions, s.10.

[27] *Platt v Att-Gen for New South Wales* (1878) 3 App. Cas. 336 (PC) (separation of Queensland from New South Wales); *Evans v Evans* (1960) 2 W.I.R. 246 (separation of Dominica from the Leeward Islands). *cf. Re O'Keefe* [1940] Ch. 124.

[28] *Re M* [1937] N.Ir. 151. *Egan v Egan* [1928] N.Ir. 159 must be regarded as turning on its special facts.

[29] *Re P* [1945] Irish Jurist 17.

[30] S.R. & O. 1922 No.77, art.8.

[31] *Casdagli v Casdagli* [1919] A.C. 145; *Grant v Grant*, 1931 S.C. 238.

[32] *Casdagli v Casdagli*, above.

[33] *Casdagli v Casdagli*, above.

4. D, the descendant of a Scottish family, has a domicile of origin in Jamaica. In 1837 he leaves Jamaica "for good" and comes to Scotland. By 1838 he has not made up his mind whether to settle in Scotland, England or elsewhere. In 1838 he is domiciled in Jamaica although his home is not there.[34]

5. D was born in India in 1860. Her father at the time of her birth retained his Irish domicile of origin. The father's family lived, at his birth, in County Clare which is now in the Republic of Ireland. In 1940 a question arose as to D's domicile of origin. D's domicile of origin was assumed to be in the Republic of Ireland.[35]

6. D was born in 1890. His parents were married in 1907. D's father F was born and lived all his life in County Antrim which is now in Northern Ireland. F was domiciled in Northern Ireland in 1907 within the meaning of the Legitimacy Act (NI) 1928.[36]

RULE 5—No person can be without a domicile.   6R–011

COMMENT

It has been frequently laid down that no person can be without a domicile.[37] **6–012** This Rule is based on the practical necessity of connecting every person with some system of law by which a number of his legal relationships (especially those concerned with private as opposed to public law issues[38]) may be regulated. Where a person is in fact homeless, the law nonetheless attributes a domicile to him in accordance with the Rules contained in this chapter. An independent person who has his permanent home in a country is domiciled in it. If he has no home but resides in a country with the intention of residing permanently in it, he is domiciled in that country.[39] If he has no home and no such intention, he is domiciled in the country of his domicile of origin.[40] If he has his home in the country of his domicile of origin, he continues to be domiciled there until he acquires a domicile of choice in another country.[41] Having acquired such a domicile of choice, he retains it until he abandons it: upon such abandonment, he may acquire a new domicile of choice; if he does not, his domicile of origin revives.[42] It will be seen that these Rules ensure that no person of full age and capacity can be without a domicile. Since the domicile of a dependent person is always either dependent on that of an ascertainable independent person or fixed by law,[43] it follows that no person can be without a domicile.

RULE 6—No person can at the same time for the same purpose have more   6R–013 than one domicile.

---

[34] *Bell v Kennedy* (1868) L.R. 1 Sc. & Div. 307.

[35] *Re O'Keefe* [1940] Ch. 124.

[36] *Re M* [1937] N.Ir. 151. *cf. Re P* [1945] Irish Jurist 17. Contrast *Egan v Egan* [1928] N.Ir. 159, where on very special facts it was held that the *propositus* could elect to be domiciled in either Northern or Southern Ireland.

[37] *Udny v Udny* (1869) L.R. 1 Sc. & Div. 441, 448, 453, 457; *Bell v Kennedy* (1868) L.R. 1 Sc. & Div. 307, 320; *Re Craignish* [1892] 3 Ch. 180, 192.

[38] *Mark v Mark* [2005] UKHL 42, [2006] 1 A.C. 98, at [5], *per* Lord Hope of Craighead.

[39] Rule 4.

[40] Rule 9.

[41] Rules 10 to 12.

[42] Rule 13.

[43] Rules 14 to 16.

Comment

6–014 Since the object of determining a person's domicile is to connect that person with some system or rule of law, it is obvious that, for the purpose of any given inquiry, a person cannot have more than one domicile, and the Rule to this effect is now well established.[44] If a person has two homes in different countries, he is in the absence of a contrary intention domiciled in that country in which he has his principal home.[45]

6–015 It has, however, sometimes been suggested that a person may have different domiciles for different purposes.[46] Such a possibility was the basis of one judgment in the Court of Appeal in *Lawrence v Lawrence*,[47] where Purchas L.J.[48] argued that in certain circumstances, in the context of capacity to re-marry, a person could be treated for that limited purpose as having a domicile other than that which he would possess under the general rules. Less controversial illustrations are to be found in some federal or composite States. So, in Australia, the Family Law Act 1975 provides that divorce proceedings may be instituted if either party "is domiciled in Australia".[49] It was held in *Lloyd v Lloyd*[50] that a similar provision in the Commonwealth Matrimonial Causes Act 1959[51] limiting access to the state courts which then exercised divorce jurisdiction to persons "domiciled in Australia" enabled a person who was domiciled in New South Wales to institute divorce proceedings in Victoria.[52] For the purpose of divorce jurisdiction the parties to the marriage were domiciled in "Australia" though for most other purposes they were domiciled in New South Wales. The expression "domiciled in the United Kingdom" similarly occurs in a number of Acts of the United Kingdom Parliament.[53] It would be possible for English courts to follow the reasoning of *Lloyd v Lloyd* and so to hold that, for the purposes of such Acts, a person could be domiciled in the United Kingdom. This would be a welcome relaxation of the old idea that a person can only have one domicile for all

---

[44] *Udny v Udny* (1869) L.R. 1 Sc. & Div. 441, 448; *Saccharin Corp Ltd v Chemische Fabrik von Heyden* [1911] 2 K.B. 516, 527 (CA); *Garthwaite v Garthwaite* [1964] P. 356, 379 (CA); Khan (1965) 82 S.A.L.J. 147; for early statements of the view that a man could have two domiciles for certain purposes, see *Somerville v Somerville* (1801) 5 Ves. 750, 786; *Re Capdevielle* (1864) 2 H. & C. 985, 1018. *cf.* the New Zealand Domicile Act 1976, s.13: "A person domiciled in a country forming part of a union is also domiciled in that union."

[45] *cf. Forbes v Forbes* (1854) Kay 341, 367. Contrast *Huntley v Gaskell* [1906] A.C. 56.

[46] *Att-Gen v Rowe* (1862) 1 H. & C. 31, 45; *Yelverton v Yelverton* (1859) 1 Sw. & Tr. 574, 585; *cf. Texas v Florida*, 306 U.S. 398, 428–429 (1939); Cook, Ch.7; Pollak (1933) 50 S.A.L.J. 449, 455–456; Reese (1955) 55 Col.L.Rev. 589; Fawcett (1985) Oxford J.L.S. 378.

[47] [1985] Fam. 106.

[48] At pp.132–133.

[49] s.39(3)(b).

[50] [1962] V.R. 70; Cowen and Mendes da Costa (1962) 78 L.Q.R. 62.

[51] s.23(4); and see s.24(1).

[52] In *Lee v Commissioner of Taxation* (1963) 6 F.L.R. 285 the court was inclined to accept the principle for tax purposes. *cf. Re Benko* [1968] S.A.S.R. 243.

[53] e.g. Constitutional Reform and Governance Act 2010, s.41; Human Fertilisation and Embryology Act 2008, s.54; Inheritance Tax Act 1984, ss.18, 48, 267. The last provision requires certain persons not domiciled in the UK to be treated as domiciled there for the purposes of the Act; but this falls short of establishing a separate domicile.

purposes; but it would also raise many problems which are as yet unresolved.[54]

In *Lloyd v Lloyd* there was no doubt that the parties were domiciled in New **6–016** South Wales. It is not clear what the position would have been had they been immigrants who had not yet decided in which of the Australian states they would settle. Is it necessary to establish a domicile in some law-district within Australia before one can be domiciled in Australia?[55] It is not necessary under the reformed law of domicile in force in Australia (and New Zealand);[56] but that is not determinative for an English court which must apply the English law of domicile.[57] If an immigrant husband with an English domicile of origin were to die shortly after obtaining an Australian divorce and before he had decided in which Australian state to settle, there can be no doubt that the English court would hold that he died domiciled in England;[58] but there can equally be little doubt that the divorce would be recognised on the basis that he was domiciled in Australia. The Australian legislation would be taken into account by the English court not to determine the issue of domicile but simply to define the law district or "country" within which a person must be domiciled in the context of the divorce jurisdiction. To this extent, therefore, a person can be domiciled in two different countries for different purposes at the same time.

RULE 7—An existing domicile is presumed to continue until it is proved **6R–017** **that a new domicile has been acquired.**

COMMENT

There is a presumption that a person continues to be domiciled in the country **6–018** in which he is domiciled;[59] or, to put it differently, the burden of proving a change of domicile lies on those who assert it.[60] This presumption varies in strength according to the kind of domicile which is alleged to continue. It is

---

[54] Alternatively flexibility can be integrated within specific conflict of laws rules. In the Maintenance Regulation a subsidiary ground of jurisdiction provides that the Member State of the common domicile of the parties shall be competent (Art.6) where no court of a Member State has jurisdiction under Arts 3–5 of the Regulation. By contrast with Council Regulation (EC) 2201/2003 concerning jurisdiction and the recognition and enforcement of judgments in matrimonial matters and the matters of parental responsibility (the Brussels IIa Regulation), Art.3, this is extended to apply to situations where the parties have their domiciles in different territorial units of the same Member State (Art.2(2)(3)).

[55] cf. *Att-Gen for Alberta v Cook* [1926] A.C. 444, 449–450 (PC) and *Re Benko* [1968] S.A.S.R. 243.

[56] See the uniform Domicile Act of the Australian jurisdictions, s.10; Domicile Act 1976 (New Zealand), s.10.

[57] Rule 8.

[58] For the recommendation of the English and Scottish Law Commissions that would lead to a different conclusion, see above, para.6–007.

[59] *Att-Gen v Rowe* (1862) 1 H. & C. 31, 42; *Bell v Kennedy* (1868) L.R. 1 Sc. & Div. 307, 319; *Re Patience* (1885) 29 Ch.D. 976; *Re De Almeda* (1902) 18 T.L.R. 414 (CA).

[60] *Winans v Att-Gen* [1904] A.C. 287; *Ramsay v Liverpool Royal Infirmary* [1930] A.C. 588; *In the Estate of Fuld (No.3)* [1968] P. 675, 685; *Fremlin v Fremlin* (1913) 16 C.L.R. 212; *Holden v Holden* [1968] N.Ir.7; *Terrassin v Terrassin* [1968] 3 N.S.W.R. 600.

weakest when that domicile is one of dependency[61] and strongest when the domicile is one of origin,[62] for "its character is more enduring, its hold stronger, and less easily shaken off."[63] The presumption is not, however, a legal rule and it has been held that the evidence required will depend on the application of common sense to the particular circumstances.[64] Moreover, it has been suggested that for many people their attachment to a domicile of choice will be as great as to the domicile of origin which they enjoyed originally.[65]

6–019   The courts have offered different formulations of the standard of proof required to rebut the presumption. It is clear that the standard is that adopted in civil proceedings, proof on a balance of probabilities, not that adopted in criminal proceedings, proof beyond reasonable doubt.[66] Although Sir Jocelyn Simon P. said that "the standard of proof goes beyond a mere balance of probabilities"[67] the prevailing view is that of Scarman J.[68] that "two things are clear—first, that unless the judicial conscience is satisfied by evidence of change, the domicile of origin persists; and secondly, that the acquisition of a domicile of choice is a serious matter not to be lightly inferred from slight indications or casual words." Cogent and clear evidence is needed to show that the balance of probabilities has been tipped, and this is true whether the issue is the acquisition or loss of a domicile of choice.[69]

6–020   In 1987 the English and Scottish Law Commissions recommended no change in the rule that the burden of proving the acquisition of a new domicile falls on the person alleging it. They recommended that the normal civil standard of proof on a balance of probabilities should apply in all disputes about domicile and that no higher or different quality of intention should be required when the alleged change of domicile is from one acquired at birth than when it is from any other domicile.[70]

---

[61] See below, paras 6–086—6–087.

[62] See below, para.6–031.

[63] *Winans v Att-Gen*, above, at p.290; *Cyganik v Agulian* [2006] EWCA Civ 129, [2006] 1 F.C.R. 406, at [49]; *cf. Henderson v Henderson* [1967] P. 77, 80.

[64] *Henwood v Barlow Clowes International Ltd* [2008] EWCA Civ 577, [2008] B.P.I.R. 778, at [94], [96] *per* Arden L.J. (the association of a domicile of origin with a person's "native character" will not always be possible; a person may never have had that character or enjoyed any real connection to that place, or he may have disclaimed his intention to live there. Equally the domicile of origin may have revived or the contest may be between two jurisdictions within the same state, so that there may be little difference in terms of the "native character" of such citizens: at [93]).

[65] *ibid.* at [91].

[66] *In the Estate of Fuld (No.3)* [1968] P. 675, 685–686; *Holliday v Musa* [2010] EWCA Civ 335, [2010] 2 F.L.R. 702; *cf. Re Flynn (No.1)* [1968] 1 W.L.R. 103, 115; *Re Edwards* (1969) 113 S.J. 108; *Buswell v IRC* [1974] 1 W.L.R. 1631, 1637 (CA). *cf. Re Cartier* [1952] S.A.S.R. 280, 291, suggesting that a change in a domicile of origin needed to be proved beyond reasonable doubt.

[67] *Henderson v Henderson* [1967] P. 77, 80; *Steadman v Steadman* [1976] A.C. 536, 563.

[68] *In the Estate of Fuld (No.3)*, above, at p.686.

[69] *Irvin v Irvin* [2001] 1 F.L.R. 178; followed in *Re Chow Kam Fai David* [2003] 1205 HKCU 1. See also *Henwood v Barlow Clowes International Ltd* [2008] EWCA Civ 577, [2008] B.P.I.R. 778, at [94].

[70] *The Law of Domicile* (Law Com. No.168), paras 5.4, 5.6, 5.9. *cf.* the uniform Australian Domicile Acts, s.12; New Zealand Domicile Act 1976, s.11.

Rule 8—**For the purposes of an English rule of the conflict of laws, the**   6R–021
question where a person is domiciled is determined according to English
law.

COMMENT

The principle that for the purposes of an English rule of the conflict of laws   6–022
domicile is determined according to English law is now well settled. Thus a
person who is domiciled in England may acquire a domicile of choice in a
foreign country without complying with the formalities required by the law of
that country for the acquisition of a domicile within it.[71] Again, in determining
whether a person who was domiciled abroad has acquired a domicile of choice
in England, the law of the country of the foreign domicile is disregarded.[72] It
is of course perfectly possible for an English rule of the conflict of laws to
make express use of the concept of domicile as understood in a foreign system
of law. The Family Law Act 1986 provides an illustration: s.46 sets out the
grounds for the recognition of overseas divorces, annulments and legal separations by reference (inter alia) to the domicile of one or both parties to the
marriage, and provides that a party is to be treated as domiciled in the relevant
foreign country if he is domiciled there either according to English law or
according to the law of that country in family matters.[73]

    It must be stressed that the principle that domicile is determined according   6–023
to English law only applies "for the purposes of an English rule of the conflict
of laws".[74] Under the renvoi doctrine[75] the court applies the conflict rule of a
foreign country. If that rule is formulated in terms of "domicile," this will
mean "domicile" in the sense of the foreign law. But these are exceptional
situations and do not derogate from the principle that for the purpose of an
English conflict rule domicile is determined according to English law.

ILLUSTRATIONS

1. D, a widow domiciled in England, goes to France and establishes her permanent home there.   6–024
According to the French law, she does not thereby acquire a domicile in France, since she has not
complied with the formalities then[76] required by French law for the acquisition of a domicile in
France. For the purposes of English rules of the conflict of laws, D is domiciled in France.[77]

2. D, who is domiciled in New York, comes to England to perform a contract of service which
will require his presence in England for ten years. He intends to make his home in England during
those ten years, but thereafter to return to New York. By New York law he thereby acquires a

---

[71] *Collier v Rivaz* (1841) 2 Curt. 855; *Bremer v Freeman* (1857) 10 Moo. P.C. 306; *Hamilton
v Dallas* (1975) 1 Ch.D. 257; *Re Annesley* [1926] Ch. 692; *Re Rowan* (1988) 8 I.L.R.M. 65. See
Gillespie v Grant [1992] 6 W.W.R. 599, 610 (Alta).

[72] *Re Martin* [1900] P. 211 (CA). There was no division of opinion in the court on this
point.

[73] See below, para.18–080. See also Civil Partnership Act 2004, s.237.

[74] *cf.* the uniform Australian Domicile Acts, s.4(4), declaring that the Act "has effect to the
exclusion of the application of the laws of any other country relating to any matter dealt with by"
the Act.

[75] Rule 1.

[76] Art.13 of the French Civil Code. This article has since been repealed.

[77] *Re Annesley* [1926] Ch. 692.

domicile of choice in England; by English law he does not. For the purposes of English rules of the conflict of laws, D is not domiciled in England.[78]

3. D, whose domicile of origin is in Florida, acquires a domicile of choice in New York. Forty years later he resolves to leave New York and to settle in California. He sets out for California but dies on his way there in Illinois. By Florida, New York, Californian and Illinois law D died domiciled in New York; by English law he died domiciled in Florida. For the purposes of English rules of the conflict of laws, D died domiciled in Florida.

2. ASCERTAINMENT OF DOMICILE

A. *Domicile of origin*

6R–025   **RULE 9—(1) Every person receives at birth a domicile of origin:**

    (a) A legitimate child born during the lifetime of his father has his domicile of origin in the country in which his father was domiciled at the time of his birth;[79]

    (b) A legitimate child not born during the lifetime of his father, or an illegitimate child, has his domicile of origin in the country in which his mother was domiciled at the time of his birth;[80]

    (c) A foundling has his domicile of origin in the country in which he was found.[81]

(2) A domicile of origin may be changed as a result of adoption or by the issue of a parental order under the Human Fertilisation and Embryology Act 2008, but not otherwise.

COMMENT

6–026   The domicile of origin is a distinctive feature of the English concept of domicile. The English and Scottish Law Commissions, taking the view that the idea of the domicile of origin has "outlived its usefulness," have recommended that the domicile of origin, as a separate type of domicile determined according to a separate set of rules, should disappear from the laws of the United Kingdom. The domicile of a child would be determined in all cases by reference to the new rules recommended by the Law Commissions.[82] Until such time as these recommendations are acted upon, the domicile of origin remains of great importance.

6–027   A domicile of origin is attributed to every person at birth by operation of law.[83] This domicile does not depend on the place where the child is born, nor on the place where his mother or father reside, but on the domicile of the appropriate parent at the time of birth. As a result of this rule, a domicile of

---

[78] *cf. Re Martin* [1900] P. 211, 227 (CA).

[79] *Udny v Udny* (1869) L.R. 1 Sc. & Div. 441; *Somerville v Somerville* (1801) 5 Ves. 750, 787; *Forbes v Forbes* (1854) Kay 341.

[80] *Udny v Udny* (1869) L.R. 1 Sc. & Div. 441, 457; *Re Grove* (1888) 40 Ch.D. 216 (CA); *cf. Urquhart v Butterfield* (1887) 37 Ch.D. 357 (CA).

[81] *cf. Re McKenzie* (1951) 51 S.R.N.S.W. 293. For a New Zealand statutory provision to this effect, see Domicile Act 1976, s.6(6).

[82] *The Law of Domicile* (Law Com. No.168), paras 4.21—4.24. For the recommendations as to the domicile of a child, see below, para.6–098.

[83] *Udny v Udny* (1869) L.R. 1 Sc. & Div. 441, 457.

origin may be transmitted through several generations no member of which has ever resided for any length of time in the country of the domicile of origin.[84]

It is generally accepted that a legitimate child born during the lifetime of his father has his domicile of origin in the country in which his father was domiciled at the time of his birth. But it is, in fact, an open question whether this rule applies to a legitimate child born after the divorce of his parents. It is arguable that such a child should take his mother's domicile at birth. Where the parents are living apart at the time of the birth but are not divorced, different considerations apply. Although a child born of separated parents with different domiciles immediately acquires his mother's domicile as a domicile of dependence under s.4(1) and (2) of the Domicile and Matrimonial Proceedings Act 1973,[85] his domicile of origin will be that of his father. It might seem highly artificial to attribute to a child a domicile of origin which does not then become his effective domicile; but it is a domicile capable of revival throughout his lifetime[86] and its identification could be rendered unduly difficult if it depended upon proof, perhaps many years after the death of both parents, of the date upon which they began to live apart. It is generally assumed, although there is no authority on the point, that a posthumous child takes his mother's domicile at birth. **6–028**

The rule as to the domicile of origin of a foundling is also generally accepted, although there is no direct English authority to support it. The rule also applies to a child who is not strictly speaking a foundling, but about the domicile of whose parents nothing is known.[87] **6–029**

The domicile of a minor child may be changed as a result of adoption or the issue of a parental order under the Human Fertilisation and Embryology Act 2008,[88] or legitimation, or of a change in his parents' domicile.[89] In the case of adoption or by the issue of a parental order, the child acquires a new domicile of origin for he is treated in law as born to the adopters in wedlock,[90] but in the other cases the new domicile which the child gets in this way is a domicile of dependency and not a domicile of origin.[91] Consequently, if the child in later life acquires a domicile of choice and then abandons it without acquiring another, the domicile which will revive[92] will be the domicile of origin, determined in accordance with the present Rule, and not the domicile of dependency imposed as a result of legitimation or of a change in his parents' domicile. **6–030**

A domicile of origin is distinguishable from a domicile of choice in two respects. In the first place, a domicile of origin is more tenacious: in other words, it is more difficult to prove that a person has abandoned his domicile **6–031**

---

[84] *Peal v Peal* (1930) 46 T.L.R. 645 (also reported in [1931] P. 97, but not on this point); *Grant v Grant*, 1931 S.C. 238; *cf. Re O'Keefe* [1940] Ch. 124.

[85] Rule 15, Exception.

[86] Rule 13.

[87] *Re McKenzie* (1951) 51 S.R.N.S.W. 293.

[88] s.54.

[89] Rule 15.

[90] Adoption and Children Act 2002, s.67. See the uniform Domicile Act in the Australian jurisdictions, s.8(3).

[91] *Henderson v Henderson* [1967] P. 77.

[92] Rule 13.

of origin than to prove that he has abandoned a domicile of choice.[93] Secondly, if a person leaves the country of his domicile of origin, intending never to return to it, he continues to be domiciled there until he acquires a domicile of choice in another country.[94] But if a person leaves the country of his domicile of choice, intending never to return to it, he forthwith ceases to be domiciled in that country; and unless and until he acquires a new domicile of choice his domicile of origin revives.[95]

ILLUSTRATIONS

6–032   1. In 1830 A, whose domicile of origin is English, goes to India. He there has a legitimate son, B, who, while resident in India, has a legitimate son, C, who while resident in India, has a legitimate son, D. A, B and C intend to retire to England at the age of sixty, but they all die in India before reaching that age. D's domicile of origin is English.[96]

2. H and W are married and domiciled in Scotland. H dies and W immediately acquires a domicile of choice in England. After she has done this, she gives birth to D, who is H's son. D's domicile of origin is (*semble*) English.

3. D is the illegitimate son of A and B. A is a man domiciled in England; B is a woman domiciled in France. Six months after D's birth, A marries B, thus legitimating D. D's domicile of origin is French.

4. D is the illegitimate child of A and B, both of whom are domiciled in Scotland. D is subsequently adopted in England by C and D, both of whom are domiciled in England. D's domicile of origin is now deemed to be English.[97]

5. D, an illegitimate child, is born in a London hospital. Shortly after his birth his mother disappears. Nothing is known about her domicile. His domicile of origin is English.[98]

6. D is born in England, the legitimate son of F who is domiciled in Scotland. Before D attains the age of sixteen, F acquires a domicile of choice in England. D's domicile of origin is Scottish.[99]

B. *Domicile of choice*

(1) ACQUISITION

6R–033   **RULE 10—Every independent person can acquire a domicile of choice by the combination of residence and intention of permanent or indefinite residence, but not otherwise.**

---

[93] *Jopp v Wood* (1865) 4 D.J. & S. 616; *Douglas v Douglas* (1871) L.R. 12 Eq. 617; *Re Wills-Sandford* (1897) 41 S.J. 366; *Winans v Att-Gen* [1904] A.C. 287, distinguished in *Re Joyce* [1946] I.R. 277; *Huntly v Gaskell* [1906] A.C. 56; *Re James* (1908) 98 L.T. 438; *Ramsay v Liverpool Royal Infirmary* [1930] A.C. 588. *cf. Henwood v Barlow Clowes International Ltd* [2008] EWCA Civ 577, [2008] B.P.I.R. 778.

[94] *Somerville v Somerville* (1801) 5 Ves. 750; *Re Capdevielle* (1864) 2 H. & C. 985; *Bell v Kennedy* (1868) L.R. 1 Sc. & Div. 307; *Aikman v Aikman* (1861) 3 Macq. 854; *Vincent v Buchan* (1889) 16 R. 637; *Grant v Grant*, 1931 S.C. 238; *Vien Estate v Vien Estate* (1988) 49 D.L.R. (4th) 558 (Ont CA).

[95] Rule 13.

[96] *Grant v Grant*, 1931 S.C. 239; *cf. Peal v Peal* (1930) 46 T.L.R. 645, 646 (also reported in [1931] P. 97, but not on this point).

[97] Adoption Act 1976, s.39(1), (5).

[98] *cf. Re McKenzie* (1951) 51 S.R.N.S.W. 293.

[99] *Henderson v Henderson* [1967] P. 77.

COMMENT

Residence.[100] For the purpose of this Rule "residence" means very little **6–034** more than physical presence. But it does mean something more: thus a person is not resident in a country in which he is present "casually or as a traveller."[101] "Residence in a country for the purposes of the law of domicile is physical presence in that country as an inhabitant of it."[102] A person's state of mind may be relevant to the issue whether he is present in a country as a traveller or as an inhabitant; but, subject to this point, residence may be established without any mental element. There is no requirement of *animus residendi*. The distinction between presence as a traveller and presence as an inhabitant helps to reconcile the conflicting views which have been expressed on the question whether a soldier is resident in the barracks in which he is quartered.[103] It is submitted that the answer to this question depends on the facts of each case since the soldier's presence in barracks may approximate to that of a traveller or to that of an inhabitant, according to the circumstances of the case. Of course, a soldier may, and frequently will, lack the intention necessary for the acquisition of a domicile.[104]

It has been suggested[105] that the distinction between an inhabitant and a **6–035** person casually present is of limited value in cases of dual or multiple residence, as a person who retains a residence in his domicile of origin can acquire a domicile of choice in a new country only if the residence established in that country was his "*chief* residence."[106] It is, however, submitted that questions as to the quality of residence are primarily relevant in considering whether the propositus has the *animus manendi*, the intention of permanent or indefinite residence.[107]

It is not, as a matter of law, necessary that the residence should be long in **6–036** point of time:[108] residence for a few days[109] or even for part of a day[110] is enough. Indeed, an immigrant can acquire a domicile immediately upon his arrival in the country in which he intends to settle.[111] The length of the residence is not important in itself: it is only important as evidence of *animus*

---

[100] See further below, paras 6–157 *et seq.*

[101] *Manning v Manning* (1871) L.R. 2 P. & D. 223, 226. The actual decision was not on a point of domicile. *cf.* the New Zealand Domicile Act 1976, s.9(*c*): "he is in that country."

[102] *IRC v Duchess of Portland* [1982] Ch. 314, 318–9. *cf. Re Newcomb*, 192 N.Y. 238, 84 N.E. 950 (1908): "bodily presence as an inhabitant."

[103] See *Re E. R. Smith* (1896) 12 T.L.R. 223; *Sellars v Sellars*, 1942 S.C. 206; *Willar v Willar*, 1954 S.C. 144; *cf.* in another context *Atkinson v Collard* (1885) 16 Q.B.D. 254.

[104] Rule 1.

[105] By Hoffmann J. in *Plummer v IRC* [1988] 1 W.L.R. 292.

[106] An expression used by Lord Westbury in *Udny v Udny* (1869) L.R. 1 Sc. 6 Div. 441. The determination of a "chief residence" will include an assessment of the quality of the residence: *Plummer v IRC* [1988] 1 W.L.R. 292, 295; *Henwood v Barlow Clowes International Ltd* [2008] EWCA Civ 577, [2008] B.P.I.R. 778, at [103].

[107] *Morgan v Cilento* [2004] EWHC 188 (Ch.), [2004] W.T.L.R. 457.

[108] *Bell v Kennedy* (1868) L.R. 1 Sc. & Div. 307, 319; *Stone v Stone* [1958] 1 W.L.R. 1287; *Blackett v Darcy* [2005] NSW L.R. 392.

[109] *Fasbender v Att-Gen* [1922] 2 Ch. 850, 857–858.

[110] *White v Tennant*, 31 W.Va. 790, 8 S.E. 596 (1888); *cf. Miller v Teale* (1954) 92 C.L.R. 406.

[111] *Bell v Kennedy* (1868) L.R. 1 Sc. & Div. 307, 319.

manendi.[112] A person may be resident in a country although he lives in hotels there[113] or in the house of a friend,[114] and although he is staying there for some particular purpose such as conducting business[115] or taking part in legal proceedings.[116] On the other hand, a person spending short periods in a house he owns may be held not to be resident there; he may be there as a visitor and not as an inhabitant.[117]

6–037   Although there is some Commonwealth authority[118] and one English dictum[119] supporting the proposition that a domicile of choice cannot be acquired on the basis of residence which is illegal, it is now settled that in English law the illegality of residence is no bar to the acquisition of a domicile of choice in England.[120] The same would seem to be the case where the issue is the acquisition of a domicile of choice in another country: as Lord Hope of Craighead observed in *Mark v Mark*,[121] as our courts do not apply the public policy of a foreign state, the illegality of the residence under that state's law would not be regarded here as inconsistent with the acquisition of a domicile of choice in that country.

6–038   The English and Scottish Law Commissions have recommended that in the proposed statutory reformulation of the rules as to domicile the term "presence" should be used in place of "residence." They note in particular that a person arriving in a country with the requisite intention should acquire a domicile immediately on arrival.[122]

6–039   **Intention.**[123] The intention which is required for the acquisition of a domicile is the intention to reside permanently or for an unlimited time in a country.[124] "It must be a residence fixed not for a limited period or particular purpose, but general and indefinite in its future contemplation."[125] This intention must be directed exclusively towards one country. Thus a person who leaves the country of his domicile with the intention of settling in one of

---

[112] Rule 11.
[113] *Levene v IRC* [1928] A.C. 217; *Matalon v Matalon* [1952] P. 233; *cf. Gordon v Gordon* [1929] N.Z.L.R. 75.
[114] *Stone v Stone* [1958] 1 W.L.R. 1287.
[115] *IRC v Lysaght* [1928] A.C. 234.
[116] *Matalon v Matalon*, above.
[117] *IRC v Duchess of Portland* [1982] Ch. 314.
[118] *Solomon v Solomon* (1912) 29 W.N. (NSW) 68; *Lim v Lim* [1973] V.R. 370, 372; *In the Marriage of Salacup* (1993) 17 Fam. L.R. 141; *Smith v Smith* 1962 (2) S.A. 930 (where the illegality was principally relevant to the formation of the *animus manendi*). To the contrary are *Jablonowski v Jablonowski* (1972) 28 D.L.R. (3d) 440 (Ont); *Wood v Wood* (1977) 4 R.F.L. (2d) 182 (PEI).
[119] *Puttick v Att-Gen* [1980] Fam. 1, 19.
[120] *Mark v Mark* [2005] UKHL 42, [2006] 1 A.C. 98.
[121] [2005] UKHL 42, [2006] 1 A.C. 98, at [11].
[122] *The Law of Domicile* (Law Com. No.168), para.5.7.
[123] See Fentiman [1991] C.L.J. 445.
[124] *Att-Gen v Pottinger* (1861) 6 H. & N. 733, 747–748; *King v Foxwell* (1876) 3 Ch.D. 518, 520; *Udny v Udny* (1869) L.R. 1 Sc. & Div. 441, 458; *Doucet v Geoghegan* (1878) 9 Ch.D. 441 (CA); *Waddington v Waddington* (1920) 36 T.L.R. 359; *Gulbenkian v Gulbenkian* [1937] 4 All E.R. 618, 626–627.
[125] *Udny v Udny* (1869) L.R. 1 Sc. & Div. 441, 458; *Cramer v Cramer* [1987] 1 F.L.R. 116 (CA). *cf.* the New Zealand Domicile Act 1976, s.9(d): "he intends to live indefinitely in that country," and the Australian uniform Domicile Acts, s.9: "the intention to make his home indefinitely in that country."

several other countries does not acquire a domicile in any of those countries.[126] It is also sometimes said that there must be an intention of leaving the
country of the previous domicile as well as an intention of residing in the
country of the new domicile.[127] It is not necessary to prove an intention to
acquire a domicile: indeed a layman is unlikely to form such a juristic
intent.[128]

A person who determines to spend the rest of his life in a country clearly **6–040**
has the necessary intention even though he does not consider his determination to be irrevocable.[129] It is, however, rare for the *animus manendi* to exist
in this positive form: more frequently a person simply resides in a country
without any intention of leaving it, and such a state of mind may suffice for
the acquisition of a domicile of choice.[130] The fact that a person contemplates
that he might move is not decisive[131]: thus a person who intends to reside in
a country indefinitely may be domiciled there although he envisages the
possibility of returning one day to his native country.[132] If he has in mind the
possibility of such a return should a particular contingency occur, the possibility will be ignored if the contingency is vague and indefinite, for example
making a fortune[133] or suffering some ill-defined deterioration in health;[134] but
if it is a clearly foreseen and reasonably anticipated contingency, for example
the termination of employment,[135] or the offer of an attractive post in the
country of origin,[136] succession to entailed property,[137] a change in the relative
levels of taxation as between two countries,[138] or the death of one's spouse,[139]

---

[126] *Bell v Kennedy* (1868) L.R. 1 Sc. & Div. 307; *Lee v Commissioner of Taxation* (1963) 6
F.L.R. 285.

[127] *Lyall v Paton* (1856) 25 L.J. Ch. 746, 749 (the actual decision would now go the other way
under the doctrine of the revival of the domicile of origin); *cf. Moorhouse v Lord* (1863) 10
H.L.C. 272; *Jopp v Wood* (1865) 4 D.J. & S. 616.

[128] *Re Annesley* [1926] Ch. 692, 701; *Qureshi v Qureshi* [1972] Fam. 173, 191; *IRC v Bullock*
[1976] 1 W.L.R. 1178, 1183 (CA). For a different view, see Cook, pp.203–207.

[129] *Stanley v Bernes* (1830) 3 Hag.Ecc. 373, 437; *Gulbenkian v Gulbenkian* [1937] 4 All E.R.
618; *IRC v Bullock* [1976] 1 W.L.R. 1178, 1185 (CA); *Commissioners of Inland Revenue v
Gordon's Executors* (1850) 12 D. (Ct of Sess) 657, 662.

[130] e.g. *Bell v Bell* [1922] 2 I.R. 152; *cf. Att-Gen v Kent* (1862) 1 H. & C. 12; contrast *Ramsay
v Liverpool Royal Infirmary* [1930] A.C. 588.

[131] *Re Steer* (1858) 3 H. & N. 594; *Att-Gen v Pottinger* (1861) 6 H. & N. 733; *Att-Gen v Kent*
(1862) 1 H. & C. 12; *Drevon v Drevon* (1864) 34 L.J. Ch. 129; *Doucet v Geoghegan* (1878) 9
Ch.D. 441 (CA); *Davis v Adair* [1895] 1 I.R. 379; *Ley v Ley's Executors*, 1951 (3) S.A. 186,
194–195; *Gunn v Gunn* (1956) 2 D.L.R. (2d) 351 (Sask CA).

[132] *Stanley v Bernes* (1830) 3 Hag. Ecc. 373, 438; *Henderson v Henderson* [1967] P. 77, 80–81;
Holliday v Musa [2010] EWCA Civ 335, [2010] 2 F.L.R. 702; *Hyland v Hyland* (1971) 18 F.L.R.
461, 480.

[133] *Doucet v Geoghegan* (1878) 9 Ch.D. 441 (CA); *Henderson v Henderson* [1967] P. 77,
80–81; *In the Estate of Fuld (No.3)* [1968] P. 674, 685; *IRC v Bullock* [1976] 1 W.L.R. 1178, 1186
(CA).

[134] *Re Furse* [1980] 3 All E.R. 838.

[135] *In the Estate of Fuld (No.3)* [1968] P. 674, 684.

[136] *T v L (Att-Gen, notice party)* [2003] I.E.S.C. 59.

[137] *Aikman v Aikman* (1861) 4 L.T. 374, 376 (HL).

[138] *M (C) v M (T) (No.2)* [1990] 2 I.R. 52.

[139] *IRC v Bullock* [1976] 1 W.L.R. 1178 (CA); *cf. Anderson v Laneuville* (1854) 9 Moo. P.C.
325 (death of mistress).

it may prevent the acquisition of a domicile of choice. If a person intends to reside in a country for a fixed period only, he lacks the *animus manendi*, however long that period may be.[140] The same is true where a person intends to reside in a country for an indefinite time but clearly intends to leave the country at some time.[141]

6–041   In deciding whether a person has the intention to reside permanently or indefinitely in a country it is relevant to consider whether he became a naturalised citizen of that country,[142] but it is now[143] settled that this consideration is not decisive as a matter of law: indeed, it cannot well be where it is alleged that a person has acquired a domicile of choice in a country which, together with others, is included in the same State. Thus a person can acquire a domicile of choice in a country without naturalisation[144] and conversely a person does not necessarily acquire a domicile of choice in a country which has granted him naturalisation.[145] "It is not the law either that a change of domicile is a condition of naturalisation, or that naturalisation involves necessarily a change of domicile."[146]

6–042   **No other mode of acquisition.** "A new domicile is not acquired until there is not only a fixed intention of establishing a permanent residence in some other country, but until also this intention has been carried out by actual residence there."[147] Residence without intention is insufficient: this is shown by the many cases in which residence was clearly established and in which the decisions turned solely on the question whether the *propositus* had the necessary intention.[148] Conversely, a domicile cannot be acquired by intention without residence.[149] It follows from this that a domicile cannot be acquired

---

[140] *cf. Att-Gen v Rowe* (1862) 1 H. & C. 31, and the majority view in *Eilon v Eilon*, 1965 (1) S.A. 703 (criticised by Kahn (1965) 82 S.A.L.J. 147). This view is not followed in the United States: Restatement, s.18.

[141] *Jopp v Wood* (1865) 4 D.J. & S. 616; *Qureshi v Qureshi* [1972] Fam. 173; *IRC v Bullock* [1976] 1 W.L.R. 1178 (CA); *O'Mant v O'Mant*, 1947 (1) S.A. 26.

[142] See *D'Etchegoyen v D'Etchegoyen* (1888) 13 P.D. 132, 134; *Qureshi v Qureshi*, above, at p.190; *Sells v Rhodes* (1905) 26 N.Z.L.R. 87; *R. (Haqq) v Knapman* [2003] EWHC 3366 (Admin.). *cf. Bheekhun v Williams* [1999] 2 F.L.R. 229 (CA) (choice of nationality on independence); *Re Chow Kam Fai David* [2003] 1205 HKCU 1 (which of several passports used at relevant time).

[143] For the old view that there must be an intention "*exuere patriam*," see *Moorhouse v Lord* (1863) 10 H.L.C. 272, 283; *Jopp v Wood* (1865) 4 D.J. & S. 616.

[144] *Brunel v Brunel* (1871) L.R. 12 Eq. 298; *Doucet v Geoghegan* (1878) 9 Ch.D. 441 (CA); *Re Grove* (1888) 40 Ch.D. 216 (CA); *Davis v Adair* [1895] 1 I.R. 379; *Bell v Bell* [1922] 2 I.R. 152; *cf. Winans v Att-Gen* [1904] A.C. 287.

[145] *Wahl v Att-Gen* (1932) 147 L.T. 382 (HL); *In the Estate of Fuld (No.3)* [1968] P. 675; *Re Adams* [1967] I.R. 424; *Re Dix* [1951] N.Z.L.R. 642.

[146] *Wahl v Att-Gen*, above, at p.385.

[147] *Bell v Kennedy* (1868) L.R. 1 Sc. & Div. 307, 319.

[148] See especially Rule 11.

[149] *Brown v Smith* (1852) 15 Beav. 444; *Att-Gen v Fitzgerald* (1856) 3 Drew. 610, 616; *In bonis Raffenel* (1863) 3 Sw. & Tr. 49; *Harrison v Harrison* [1953] 1 W.L.R. 865. The rather doubtful case of *Att-Gen v Dunn* (1840) 6 M. & W. 511 can perhaps be explained on the ground that the *propositus* was only present in the new country as a traveller. It was doubted in *Lyall v Paton* (1856) 25 L.J. Ch. 746, as to which see para.6–039, n.127, above.

by merely setting out for the new country: actual arrival there is necessary.[150]

Reform. The English and Scottish Law Commissions have recommended that the intention necessary for the acquisition of a new domicile by an adult should be an intention to settle in the country in question for an indefinite period.[151] Under the draft legislation prepared by the Law Commissions, the term "domicile of choice" would cease to be used; the proposed rules speak simply of the "domicile" possessed by an adult.

6–043

ILLUSTRATIONS

1. D, who is domiciled in England, decides to settle in Scotland. Without breaking up his English home, he goes to Scotland to look for suitable accommodation. He does not thereby acquire a domicile in Scotland, since he is not resident there.

6–044

2. D, who is domiciled in England, determines to settle in Queensland. He sells his house in England, and, taking all his effects with him, embarks for Queensland. He acquires a domicile in Queensland immediately upon his arrival there.[152]

3. D, whose domicile of origin is French, resides in England. He intends to reside in England for an indefinite time but hopes when he has made his fortune to be able to return to France. He is domiciled in England.[153]

4. D, whose domicile of origin is Scottish, goes as a trader to India. He intends ultimately to return to Scotland. He retains his Scottish domicile.[154]

5. D's domicile of origin is in New Jersey. From 1850 to 1860 he works in Russia as a railway contractor. Between 1860 and 1893 he spends a substantial part of each year in England for the sake of his health. From 1893 until his death in 1897 he lives exclusively in England, in spite of his anti-British schemes and sentiments. He has not returned to the United States since his departure therefrom in 1850. He retains his domicile of origin in New Jersey.[155]

6. D's domicile of origin is English. For the last thirty years of his life he lives principally in Scotland, but retains two houses and business interests in England. He makes a Scottish will disposing of his land in Scotland and an English will disposing of the rest of his property. There is evidence that he did not wish to acquire a Scottish domicile as this would restrict his freedom of testation. He is domiciled in England at his death.[156]

7. D's domicile of origin is Scottish. After retiring from work, he lives with his family in Glasgow. When the family moves to Liverpool, he goes with them and lives in Liverpool for the last thirty-five years of his life, partly in lodgings and partly in a house together with other members of his family. He declares that he does not wish to return to Glasgow, but in his will (which is formally valid by Scots but not by English law) he describes himself as "a Glasgow man." He is domiciled in Scotland at his death.[157]

8. D, whose domicile of origin is in South Australia, comes to England in order to read for a law degree. He intends, on the completion of his course, to return to South Australia. He continues, while he is a student, to be domiciled in South Australia.

6–045

---

[150] *Udny v Udny* (1869) L.R. 1 Sc. & Div. 441, 449–450, 453–454, criticising a suggestion in *Munroe v Douglas* (1820) 5 Madd. 379 that a domicile could be acquired *in itinere*.

[151] *The Law of Domicile* (Law Com. No.168), paras 5.8–5.22.

[152] *cf. White v Tennant*, 31 W. Va. 790, 8 S.E. 596 (1888); *Bell v Kennedy* (1868) L.R. 1 Sc. & Div. 307, 319.

[153] *Doucet v Geoghegan* (1878) 9 Ch.D. 441 (CA).

[154] *Jopp v Wood* (1865) 4 D.J. & S. 616; *cf. Browne v Browne* (1917) 36 N.Z.L.R. 425.

[155] *Winans v Att-Gen* [1904] A.C. 287.

[156] *Huntly v Gaskell* [1906] A.C. 56.

[157] *Ramsay v Liverpool Royal Infirmary* [1930] A.C. 588.

9. D, whose domicile of origin is Scottish, comes to England at the age of 30 to accept an appointment in England. The appointment is for an indefinite period, subject to a retiring age of 65. D intends to reside in England until he reaches retiring age and then to return to Scotland. He retains his Scottish domicile.

10. D was born in Nova Scotia with a Nova Scotia domicile of origin in 1910. He came to live in England in 1932 and joined the Royal Air Force. He intended to return to Canada at the end of his service. In 1946 he married an Englishwoman. Although D had hoped to persuade her to make a home in Canada, she was unwilling to leave England. D resolved to live in England so long as his wife was alive, but to return to Nova Scotia on her death. D retained his domicile in Nova Scotia throughout.[158]

11. H was born in the United States, but attended English universities and took an academic post in England in 1965. He married an Englishwoman and was naturalized as a British citizen. In 1974 he took a post in the Netherlands and later divorced his first wife and married a Portuguese woman. He never learned Dutch, read a British newspaper and watched British TV programmes, voted in British general and European elections as an overseas voter, and was a regular contributor to British technical journals. In 1999, he bought a flat in Brighton, he and the wife separated, and he presented a divorce petition in the English courts. He had acquired an English domicile of choice and had never abandoned it; accordingly, he was domiciled in England.[159]

12. H was a Nigerian army officer; W was his fourth wife. H bought a large house near London in which W and their four children lived from 1990, though W visited Nigeria on occasions before 1993. H was in exile in England from 1993 to 1998 when he returned to Nigeria. Permission for W to live in the United Kingdom expired on April 30, 1998, but she was granted indefinite leave to remain in 2002. W petitioned for divorce in the English courts in 2000. In the 12 months preceding the date of the petition, H had spent 47 days in total in England on nine separate visits: he was not habitually resident there. W was both habitually resident and domiciled in England, and the illegality of her residence was no bar to her relying on those facts for the purposes of divorce jurisdiction.[160]

13. D, whose domicile of origin is Cypriot, comes to England at the age of 18. He lives in England for 43 years and builds up a property business. He lives the life of a Greek Cypriot, maintains ties with the country and expresses the wish to return to Cyprus when his business or personal financial situation permit. Late in life he forms a relationship with a Polish woman resident in London and intends to marry her. Notwithstanding the marriage plans he retains his Cypriot domicile of origin at the time of his death.[161]

6R–046   **Rule 11—Any circumstance which is evidence of a person's residence, or of his intention to reside permanently or indefinitely in a country, must be considered in determining whether he has acquired a domicile of choice in that country.**

Comment

6–047   Of the two factors which must be shown in order to prove the acquisition of a domicile of choice, residence rarely causes much difficulty. Residence in a country is in itself some evidence of domicile, and may, in the rare case where no other evidence is available, be decisive.[162] It used to be said that residence

---

[158] *IRC v Bullock* [1976] 1 W.L.R. 1178 (CA); criticised by Carter (1976–1977) 48 B.Y.I.L. 362.

[159] *Irvin v Irvin* [2001] Fam. Law 15, [2001] 1 F.L.R. 178.

[160] *Mark v Mark* [2005] UKHL 42, [2006] 1 A.C. 98.

[161] *Cyganik v Agulian* [2006] EWCA Civ 129, [2006] 1 F.C.R. 406.

[162] e.g. *Re McKenzie* (1951) 51 S.R.N.S.W. 293.

gave rise to a presumption of domicile,[163] but it is doubtful whether this view would still be accepted;[164] and if such a presumption does exist it can easily be rebutted.[165] It is best to regard residence simply as some evidence of *animus manendi*. As such evidence, it increases in cogency with the length of the residence. But whatever the attitude of the law may once have been,[166] it is now settled that "mere length of residence by itself is insufficient evidence from which to infer the *animus*; but the quality of the residence may afford the necessary inference."[167]

Most disputes as to domicile turn on the question of whether the necessary intention accompanied the residence; and this question often involves very complex and intricate issues of fact. This is because "there is no act, no circumstance in a man's life, however trivial it may be in itself, which ought to be left out of consideration in trying the question whether there was an intention to change the domicile. A trivial act might possibly be of more weight with regard to determining this question than an act which was of more importance to a man in his life-time."[168] There is, furthermore, no circumstance or group of circumstances which furnishes any definite criterion of the existence of the intention. A circumstance which is treated as decisive in one case may be disregarded in another, or even relied upon to support a different conclusion.[169]   **6–048**

Thus in some cases[170] long residence in a country has, while in others[171] it has not, given rise to the inference of *animus manendi*; in some cases[172] the purchase of land or the taking of a lease or the building of a house has, while   **6–049**

---

[163] *Bruce v Bruce* (1790) 2 Bos. & Pul. 229; *Bempde v Johnstone* (1796) 3 Ves. 198; *Hodgson v De Beauchesne* (1858) 12 Moo. P.C. 285; *Stanley v Bernes* (1830) 3 Hagg.Ecc. 373; *King v Foxwell* (1876) 3 Ch.D. 518; *Gillis v Gillis* (1874) I.R. 8 Eq. 597; *Munster & Leinster Bank v O'Connor* [1937] I.R. 462.

[164] *M'Lelland v M'Lelland*, 1942 S.C. 502, 510; *Re Ah Hip* [1964] S.A.S.R. 232.

[165] See, for example, *Re Patience* (1885) 29 Ch.D. 976.

[166] In *Re Grove* (1888) 40 Ch.D. 216, 243, Lopes L.J. said that forty-five years' residence gave rise to an "almost irresistible" inference of domicile.

[167] *Ramsay v Liverpool Royal Infirmary* [1930] A.C. 588, 595; cf. *Huntly v Gaskell* [1906] A.C. 56; *In the Marriage of Ferrier-Watson and McElrath* (2000) 26 Fam. L.R. 169.

[168] *Drevon v Drevon* (1864) 34 L.J. Ch. 129, 133.

[169] ibid.

[170] *Att-Gen v Fitzgerald* (1856) 3 Drew 610; *Cockrell v Cockrell* (1856) 25 L.J. Ch. 730; *President of the United States v Drummond* (1864) 33 Beav. 449; *Haldane v Eckford* (1869) L.R. 8 Eq. 631; *Re Grove* (1888) 40 Ch.D. 216 (CA); *Re Eschmann* (1893) 9 T.L.R. 426; *Holliday v Musa* [2010] EWCA Civ 335, [2010] 2 F.L.R. 702; *Haji-Ioannou v Frangos* [2009] EWHC 2310 (QB), [2009] 2 C.L.C. 500; *Lord Advocate v Brown's Trustees*, 1907 S.C. 333; *Moffett v Moffett* [1920] 1 I.R. 57; *Munster & Leinster Bank v O'Connor* [1937] I.R. 462; *Sells v Rhodes* (1905) 26 N.Z.L.R. 87.

[171] *Douglas v Douglas* (1871) L.R. 12 Eq. 617; *Winans v Att-Gen* [1904] A.C. 287; *Ramsay v Liverpool Royal Infirmary* [1930] A.C. 588; *Abraham v Att-Gen* [1934] P. 17; *Aikman v Aikman* (1861) 3 Macq. 854 (HL); *Steel v Steel* (1888) 15 R. 896.

[172] *Curling v Thornton* (1823) 2 Add. 6; *Anderson v Laneuville* (1854) 9 Moo. P.C. 325; *Forbes v Forbes* (1854) Kay 341; *Aitchison v Dixon* (1870) L.R. 10 Eq. 589; *Whicker v Hume* (1858) 7 H.L.C. 124; *Doucet v Geoghegan* (1878) 9 Ch.D. 441 (CA); *Re Craignish* [1892] 3 Ch. 180; *Re Wills-Sandford* (1897) 41 S.J. 366 (as to the land leased); *Fleming v Horniman* (1928) 44 T.L.R. 315; *Boldrini v Boldrini* [1932] P. 9 (CA); *In the Estate of Fuld (No.3)* [1968] P. 675; *Re Flynn (No.1)* [1968] 1 W.L.R. 103; *Sells v Rhodes* (1905) 26 N.Z.L.R. 87; cf. *Re James* (1908) 98 L.T. 438 (retention of land).

in others[173] it has not, given rise to necessary inference; in some cases[174] residence in furnished lodgings or hotels has led to a finding of *animus manendi*, while in others[175] this very mode of residence has been relied upon to negative the intent; in some cases[176] the fact that a person has married a native of the country of the alleged domicile has supported the inference of *animus manendi*, but this fact is clearly not decisive;[177] in some cases, great importance has been attached to the presence of a man's wife and children in a country,[178] but this again is not decisive;[179] in some cases[180] the fact that a person has business interests in a country has been relied on to support a finding of *animus manendi*, while in others[181] the fact that a person went to a country in pursuance of business interests has negatived the intent; and the desire of a person to be buried in a country has in some cases[182] been treated as an important factor, but in others[183] discounted. Many other circumstances

---

[173] *De Bonneval v De Bonneval* (1838) 1 Curt. 856; *Dalhousie v M'Douall* (1840) 7 Cl. & F. 817; *Munro v Munro* (1840) 7 Cl. & F. 842; *Re Wright's Trusts* (1856) 2 K. & J. 595; *Drevon v Drevon* (1864) 34 L.J. Ch. 129; *The Lauderdale Peerage Case* (1885) 10 App. Cas. 692; *Wahl v Att-Gen* (1932) 147 L.T. 382 (HL); *Re Wills-Sandford* (1897) 41 S.J. 366 (as to the land purchased); *Gillis v Gillis* (1874) I.R. 8 Eq. 597; *cf. Wilson v Wilson* (1872) L.R. 2 P. & D. 435 (retention of land).

[174] *Re Craignish* [1892] 3 Ch. 180; *Re Eschmann* (1893) 9 T.L.R. 426; *cf. In the goods of West* (1860) 6 Jur.(N.S.) 831 (retention of furnished room); contrast *Munster & Leinster Bank v O'Connor* [1937] I.R. 462.

[175] *Cochrane v Cochrane* (1847) 9 L.T.(O.S.) 167; *Douglas v Douglas* (1871) L.R. 12 Eq. 617; *Winans v Att-Gen* [1904] A.C. 287; *Arnott v Groom* (1846) 9 D. 142.

[176] *In the goods of James Smith* (1850) 2 Rob.Ecc. 332; *Doucet v Geoghegan* (1878) 9 Ch. D. 441 (CA); *Re Grove* (1888) 40 Ch.D. 216 (CA); *Re Eschmann* (1893) 9 T.L.R. 426; *In the Estate of Fuld (No.3)* [1968] P. 675; *Clarke v Newmarsh* (1836) 14 S. (Ct of Sess) 488; *Moffett v Moffett* [1920] 1 I.R. 57; *Sells v Rhodes* (1905) 26 N.Z.L.R. 87.

[177] *Douglas v Douglas* (1871) L.R. 12 Eq. 617; *Moynihan v Moynihan (No.2)* [1997] 1 F.L.R. 59; *cf. Abraham v Att-Gen* [1934] P. 17; *Re Bethell* (1888) 38 Ch.D. 220; *Cramer v Cramer* [1987] 1 F.L.R. 116 (CA). Similar considerations apply to stable relationships outside marriage: *Spence v Spence*, 1995 S.L.T. 335.

[178] *Forbes v Forbes* (1854) Kay 341; *Platt v Att-Gen for New South Wales* (1878) 3 App. Cas. 336 (PC); *D'Etchegoyen v D'Etchegoyen* (1882) 13 P.D. 132; *Att-Gen v Yule* (1931) 145 L.T. 9 (CA); *Re Ah Hip* [1964] S.A.S.R. 232.

[179] *Abraham v Att-Gen* [1934] P. 17; *cf. Wahl v Att-Gen* (1932) 147 L.T. 382 (HL); *IRC v Bullock* [1976] 1 W.L.R. 1178, 1185 (CA).

[180] *Cockrell v Cockrell* (1856) 25 L.J. Ch. 730; *Re Eschmann* (1893) 9 T.L.R. 426; *Wahl v Att-Gen* (1932) 147 L.T. 382 (HL); *Abraham v Att-Gen* [1934] P. 17; *In the Estate of Fuld (No.3)* [1968] P. 675; *Spurway v Spurway* [1894] 1 I.R. 385; *Brooks v Brooks' Trustees* (1902) 4 F. 1014; affirmed *sub. nom. Huntly v Gaskell* [1906] A.C. 56; *Healy v Healy* [1936] R. & N. 278; *Hyland v Hyland* (1971) 18 F.L.R. 461.

[181] *D'Etchegoyen v D'Etchegoyen* (1882) 13 P.D. 132; *IRC v Cohen* (1937) 21 T.C. 301; *M'Lelland v M'Lelland*, 1942 S.C. 502; *Haque v Haque* (1962) 108 C.L.R. 230; but a person who goes to trade in a country will acquire a domicile in it if he retires there: *Re Sillar* [1956] I.R. 344 *cf. T v L (Att-Gen, notice party)* [2003] I.E.S.C. 59 (temporary tax advantages in living abroad).

[182] *Heath v Samson* (1851) 14 Beav. 441; *Crookenden v Fuller* (1859) 1 Sw. & Tr. 441; *Re de Almeda* (1902) 18 T.L.R. 414 (CA); *Munster & Leinster Bank v O'Connor* [1937] I.R. 462; *Re Adams* [1967] I.R. 424, 449–450; *Reddington v Riach's Executor*, 2002 S.L.T. 537: *cf. Haldane v Eckford* (1869) L.R. 8 Eq. 631 (reinterment of children); *Stevenson v Masson* (1873) L.R. 17 Eq. 78 (sale of grave plot).

[183] *Att-Gen v Wahlstatt* (1864) 3 H. & C. 374; *Platt v Att-Gen for New South Wales* (1878) 3 App. Cas. 336 (PC); *Re Garden* (1895) 11 T.L.R. 167; *Huntly v Gaskell* [1906] A.C. 56; *Bradfield v Swanton* [1931] I.R. 446.

have been taken into account in order to determine whether a person has the necessary intention: for example, the place in which his papers and personal belongings are kept,[184] or in which the bulk of his property or investments are to be found,[185] the form and contents of a will,[186] the exercise of[187] or refusal to exercise[188] political rights such as serving as a member of a legislative body,[189] voting or being registered as a voter or as a resident,[190] the fact of naturalisation,[191] decisions made as to the nationality of children,[192] the education of children,[193] the membership of clubs[194] or of religious or charitable associations,[195] decisions about where to seek employment,[196] the relations between a man and his family,[197] the place where he was divorced[198] (especially where divorce or re-marriage is socially unacceptable in one of the relevant countries[199]), his character,[200] his social habits,[201] learning or not

---

[184] *De Bonneval v De Bonneval* (1838) 1 Curt. 856; *Whicker v Hume* (1858) 7 H.L.C. 124; *Zanelli v Zanelli* (1948) 64 T.L.R. 556 (CA); *Morgan v Cilento* [2004] EWHC 188 (Ch.), [2004] W.T.L.R. 457; *cf. Att-Gen v Wahlstatt* (1864) 3 H & C 374.

[185] *Firebrace v Firebrace* (1878) 4 P.D. 63; *IRC v Bullock* [1976] 1 W.L.R. 1178 (CA); *Cramer v Cramer* [1987] 1 F.L.R. 116 (CA); *North v Skipton Building Society* (unreported, Ch.D., June 7, 2002) (ceasing to pay UK national insurance contributions).

[186] *Curling v Thornton* (1823) 2 Add. 6; *Thornton v Curling* (1824) 8 Sim. 310; *Lyall v Paton* (1856) 25 L.J. Ch. 746 (as to which see para.6–039, n.127, above); *Drevon v Drevon* (1864) 34 L.J. Ch. 129; *Haldane v Eckford* (1869) L.R. 8 Eq. 631; *Doucet v Geoghegan* (1878) 9 Ch.D. 441 (CA); *Re Grove* (1888) 40 Ch.D. 216 (CA); *Re Garden* (1895) 11 T.L.R. 167; *In the Estate of Fuld (No.3)* [1968] P. 675; *IRC v Bullock* [1976] 1 W.L.R. 1178 (CA); *Moffett v Moffett* [1920] 1 I.R. 57; *Sells v Rhodes* (1905) 26 N.Z.L.R. 87; contrast *Bremer v Freeman* (1857) 10 Moo. P.C. 306; *Douglas v Douglas* (1871) L.R. 12 Eq. 617.

[187] *Drevon v Drevon* (1864) 34 L.J. Ch. 129; *Irvin v Irvin* [2001] 1 F.L.R. 178; this factor was held to be of small importance in *De Bonneval v De Bonneval* (1838) 1 Curt. 856.

[188] *IRC v Bullock* [1976] 1 W.L.R. 1178 (CA).

[189] *Re Chow Kam Fai David* [2003] 1205 HKCU 1.

[190] *R v R (Divorce: Jurisdiction: Domicile)* [2006] 1 F.L.R. 389; *Spence v Spence*, 1995 S.L.T. 335.

[191] See above, para.6–041.

[192] *Re Rowan* [1988] I.L.R.M. 65; *Marsh v Marsh*, 2002 S.L.T. (Sh Ct) 87.

[193] *In the goods of West* (1860) 6 Jur.(N.S.) 831; *President of the United States v Drummond* (1864) 33 Beav. 449; *Cramer v Cramer* [1987] 1 F.L.R. 116 (CA); *cf. Re Grove* (1888) 40 Ch.D. 216 (CA) (baptism); *Stevenson v Masson* (1873) L.R. 17 Eq. 78 (making an establishment for children).

[194] *Re Craignish* [1892] 3 Ch. 180 (CA); *Re Sillar* [1956] I.R. 344; *Re Adams* [1967] I.R. 424; *DT v FL* (Irish Sup Ct, November 26, 2003).

[195] *Re de Almeda* (1902) 18 T.L.R. 414 (CA); *Spence v Spence*, 1995 S.L.T. 335 (membership of synagogue and Jewish burial society).

[196] *Irvin v Irvin* [2001] 1 F.L.R. 178.

[197] *Att-Gen v Wahlstatt* (1864) 3 H. & C. 374; *Fleming v Horniman* (1928) 44 T.L.R. 315; *Ramsay v Liverpool Royal Infirmary* [1930] A.C. 588; *cf. Anderson v Laneuville* (1854) 9 Moo. P.C. 325.

[198] *In the Estate of Fuld (No.3)* [1968] P. 675; *M(C) v M(T) (No.2)* [1990] 2 I.R. 52.

[199] *F v F (Divorce: Jurisdiction)* [2009] EWHC 1448 (Fam.), [2009] 2 F.L.R. 1496; *Re Fleming* [1987] I.L.R.M. 638.

[200] *Winans v Att-Gen* [1904] A.C. 287; *Huntly v Gaskell* [1906] A.C. 56; *Ramsay v Liverpool Royal Infirmary* [1930] A.C. 588; contrast *Re Sillar* [1956] I.R. 344.

[201] *Re Craignish* [1892] 3 Ch. 180 (CA); *Re James* (1908) 98 L.T. 438; *Winans v Att-Gen* [1904] A.C. 287; *Moynihan v Moynihan (No.2)* [1997] 1 F.L.R. 59 (living "in the nature of a king" in his place of residence); *Lord Advocate v Brown's Trustees*, 1907 S.C. 333; *B (R) v S (A)* [2002] 2 I.R. 428 (Sup Ct).

learning the local language,[202] and even the way in which he spells his name[203] have all been treated as relevant to the issue of intention. It must be emphasised that this list is not exhaustive: a person's "tastes, habits, conduct, actions, ambitions, health, hopes and projects" are all regarded as "keys to his intention."[204] Thus it is frequently very difficult to determine a person's domicile, and the resulting uncertainty has given rise to criticism and to proposals for reform of the law.[205]

6–050   In determining whether a person has the necessary intention, the court takes into consideration not only the mode but also the place of residence. There is a presumption against the acquisition of a domicile of choice by a person in a country whose religion, manners and customs differ widely from those of his own country.[206] This applies not only to Englishmen or Scotsmen going to e.g. India or China, but also to e.g. Indians or Pakistanis coming to England.[207] But this presumption is rebuttable: there is no rule of law against the acquisition of a domicile of choice by such a person in such a country.[208] Where several countries are included in one State, it is probably easier to prove a change of domicile from one such country to another than from one such country to a politically foreign country.[209]

6–051   Direct declarations of intention call for special comment. The person whose domicile is in question may himself testify as to his intention,[210] but the court will view the evidence of an interested party with suspicion.[211] Declarations of intention made out of court may be given in evidence by way of exception

---

[202] *Irvin v Irvin* [2001] 1 F.L.R. 178; *Marsh v Marsh*, 2002 S.L.T. (Sh Ct) 87.

[203] *Drevon v Drevon* (1864) 34 L.J. Ch. 129; *cf.* as to change of name *Sells v Rhodes* (1905) 26 N.Z.L.R. 87.

[204] *Per* Lord Atkinson in *Casdagli v Casdagli* [1919] A.C. 145, 178, commenting on *Winans v Att-Gen* [1904] A.C. 287.

[205] See below, paras 6–166 *et seq.*

[206] *Maltass v Maltass* (1844) 1 Rob.Ecc. 67; *Casdagli v Casdagli* [1919] A.C. 145; *Steel v Steel* (1888) 15 R. 896 ("Nobody in his senses ever goes to Burmah *sine animo revertendi*," at p.909); *cf. Doucet v Geoghegan* (1878) 9 Ch.D. 441, 453 ("It is well known that everyone who goes to India does so for the express purpose of making money and returning to this country as soon as possible"); *Grant v Grant*, 1931 S.C. 238; *cf. Re Tootal's Trusts* (1882) 23 Ch.D. 532 where it was admitted that an Englishman had not acquired a domicile in China. A similar assumption underlies *Re Bethell* (1888) 38 Ch.D. 220 and *Haque v Haque* (1962) 108 C.L.R. 230.

[207] *Qureshi v Qureshi* [1972] Fam. 173; *Re Ah Chong* (1913) 33 N.Z.L.R. 384 (Chinese in New Zealand).

[208] *Casdagli v Casdagli* [1919] A.C. 145; *Ali v Ali* [1968] P. 564; *Hyland v Hyland* (1971) 18 F.L.R. 461; *F v F (Divorce: Jurisdiction)* [2009] EWHC 1448 (Fam.), [2009] 2 F.L.R. 1496; *Lim v Lim* [1973] V.R. 370; *cf. Lord Advocate v Brown's Trustees*, 1907 S.C. 333.

[209] *Curling v Thornton* (1823) 2 Add. 6, 17; *Whicker v Hume* (1858) 7 H.L.C. 124, 159; *Moorhouse v Lord* (1863) 10 H.L.C. 272, 287; *Winans v Att-Gen* [1904] A.C. 287, 291; *Henwood v Barlow Clowes International Ltd (In Liquidation)* [2008] EWCA Civ 577, [2008] B.P.I.R. 778, at [93]; *Vincent v Buchan* (1889) 16 R. 637; *Fremlin v Fremlin* (1913) 16 C.L.R. 212, 234; *Walton v Walton* [1948] V.L.R. 487; *Gunn v Gunn* (1956) 2 D.L.R. (2d) 351 (Sask CA); *Young v Young* (1959) 21 D.L.R. (2d) 616 (Man CA).

[210] e.g. *Udny v Udny* (1869) L.R. 1 Sc. & Div. 441, 444; *D'Etchegoyen v D'Etchegoyen* (1882) 13 P.D. 132; *White v White* [1950] 4 D.L.R. 474, affirmed [1952] 1 D.L.R. 133 (Man CA).

[211] *Bell v Kennedy* (1868) L.R. 1 Sc. & Div. 307, 313, 322–323; *Re Craignish* [1892] 3 Ch. 180, 190 (CA); *Qureshi v Qureshi* [1972] Fam. 173, 192; *H v H (Validity of Japanese Divorce)* [2006] EWHC 2989 (Fam.), [2007] 1 F.L.R. 1318; *Holliday v Musa* [2010] EWCA Civ 335, [2010] W.T.L.R. 839; *Moncrieff v Moncrieff* [1934] C.P.D. 208; *Young v Young* (1959) 21 D.L.R. (2d) 616 (Man CA).

to the hearsay rule.[212] The weight of such evidence will vary from case to case. To say that declarations as to domicile are "the lowest species of evidence"[213] is probably an exaggeration. The present law has been stated as follows:

"Declarations as to intention are rightly regarded in determining the question of a change of domicile, but they must be examined by considering the persons to whom, the purposes for which, and the circumstances in which they are made, and they must further be fortified and carried into effect by conduct and action consistent with the declared expressions."[214]

Thus in some cases the courts have relied to some extent on declarations of intention in deciding issues as to domicile;[215] indeed, in one case the declaration was decisive.[216] But in other cases the courts have refused to give effect to the declarations on the ground that they were inconsistent with the conduct of the *propositus*:[217] a domicile cannot be acquired[218] or retained[219] by mere declaration. The courts are, in particular, reluctant to give effect to declarations which refer in terms to "domicile" since the declarant is unlikely to have understood the meaning of the word.[220] Declarations which are equivocal have little effect: thus a declaration of intention to reside permanently in the United Kingdom is no evidence of acquisition of a domicile of choice in any of the countries which are included in the United Kingdom;[221] although it might be evidence of the abandonment of a domicile elsewhere.

---

[212] *Bryce v Bryce* [1933] P. 83; *Scappaticci v Att-Gen* [1955] P. 47; *Re Cartier* [1952] S.A.S.R. 280; Cross (1956) 72 L.Q.R. 91, 108; Civil Evidence Act 1995.

[213] *Crookenden v Fuller* (1859) 1 Sw. & Tr. 441, 450; cf. *De Bonneval v De Bonneval* (1838) 1 Curt. 856; *Anderson v Laneuville* (1854) 9 Moo. P.C. 325.

[214] *Ross v Ross* [1930] A.C. 1, 6–7. "Expression" seems to be a misprint for "intention."

[215] *Dalhousie v M'Douall* (1840) 7 Cl. & F. 817; *Munro v Munro* (1840) 7 Cl. & F. 842; *Att-Gen v Fitzgerald* (1856) 3 Drew 610; *In the goods of West* (1860) 6 Jur. (N.S.) 831; *Briggs v Briggs* (1880) 5 P.D. 163; *D'Etchegoyen v D'Etchegoyen* (1882) 13 P.D. 132; *Goulder v Goulder* [1892] P. 240; *Re Eschmann* (1893) 9 T.L.R. 426; *Waddington v Waddington* (1920) 36 T.L.R. 359; *Abraham v Att-Gen* [1934] P. 17; *F v F (Divorce: Jurisdiction)* [2009] EWHC 1448 (Fam.), [2009] 2 F.L.R. 1496; *Gillis v Gillis* (1874) I.R. 8 Eq. 597; *Bell v Bell* [1922] 2 I.R. 152; *Re de Hosson* [1937] I.R. 467; *PL v An tArd Chláraitheoir* [1995] 2 I.L.R.M. 241; *Vincent v Buchan* (1889) 16 R. 637; *Hyland v Hyland* (1971) 18 F.L.R. 461.

[216] *Wilson v Wilson* (1872) L.R. 2 P. & D. 435. In *Wilson v Wilson* (1872) 10 M. 573, the Court of Session reached an opposite conclusion on the same facts; but the husband's evidence though admissible in England was inadmissible in Scotland.

[217] *Att-Gen v Pottinger* (1861) 6 H. & N. 733; *Doucet v Geoghegan* (1878) 9 Ch.D. 441 (CA); *Chaudhary v Chaudhary* [1985] Fam. 19 (no appeal was taken at this point); *Kearly v Kearly* [2009] EWHC 1876 (Fam.), [2010] 1 F.L.R. 619; *Moffett v Moffett* [1920] 1 I.R. 57; *Re Rowan* [1988] I.L.R.M. 65; *M(C) v M(T) (No.2)* [1990] 2 I.R. 456; *T v L (Att-Gen, notice party)* [2003] IESC 59; *Robinson v Robinson's Trustees*, 1934 S.L.T. 183; *Spence v Spence*, 1995 S.L.T. 335; *Re Dix* [1951] N.Z.L.R. 642; as to conflicting declarations see *Fleming v Horniman* (1928) 44 T.L.R. 315; *Terrassin v Terrassin* [1968] 3 N.S.W.R. 600.

[218] *Brown v Smith* (1852) 15 Beav. 444.

[219] *Re Steer* (1858) 3 H. & N. 594; *Doucet v Geoghegan* (1878) 9 Ch.D. 441 (CA); *Re Liddell-Grainger's Will Trusts* (1936) 53 T.L.R. 12; *Moffett v Moffett* [1920] 1 I.R. 57; *Robinson v Robinson's Trustees*, 1934 S.L.T. 183; *Reddington v Riach's Executor*, 2002 S.L.T. 537.

[220] *Re Steer* (1858) 3 H. & N. 594; *Re Annesley* [1926] Ch. 692; *Att-Gen v Yule* (1931) 145 L.T. 9 (CA); *Re Liddell-Grainger's Will Trusts* (1936) 53 T.L.R. 12; *Re Flynn (No.1)* [1968] 1 W.L.R. 103, 111; *Re Adams* [1967] I.R. 424, 448; cf. *Re Sillar* [1956] I.R. 344, 355; *B(R) v S(A)* [2002] 2 I.R. 428 (Sup Ct).

[221] *Wahl v Att-Gen* (1932) 147 L.T. 382 (HL); *Buswell v IRC* [1974] 1 W.L.R. 1631 (CA).

6–052   In order to determine where a person was domiciled at a particular time, the court may take into consideration his conduct after that time.[222] But of course such evidence is not decisive.[223]

6R–053   **Rule 12—Without prejudice to the generality of the foregoing Rule, in determining whether a person intends to reside permanently or indefinitely in a country the court may have regard to:**

     (1) the motive for which he has taken up residence there;

     (2) the fact that the residence was not freely chosen;

     (3) the fact that the residence was precarious.

Comment

6–054   In order that a person may acquire a domicile of choice it has been said that there must be "a residence freely chosen, and not prescribed or dictated by any external necessity, such as the duties of office, the demands of creditors, or the relief from illness."[224] But this must not be understood to mean that only a person who is able to exercise the most perfect freedom of choice can acquire a domicile of choice: indeed, if this were so the acquisition of a domicile of choice would be a rare event. The statement that there must be "a residence freely chosen" is not, in truth, a rigid rule of law: it merely indicates that where the residence is not freely chosen the inference of *animus manendi*, which might otherwise be drawn from the fact of residence, ought not to be drawn from that fact alone.[225] If the necessary intention is proved by other means, it is clear that a domicile of choice can be acquired although the residence is not freely chosen. This may be illustrated by reference to two types of situation.

6–055   In the first type, a person is alleged to lack the *animus manendi* because he has some special motive for coming to, staying in, or leaving a country. One view is that the existence of such a motive negatives the necessary intention.[226] This is true if the existence of the special motive leads to the conclusion that the residence was intended to cease upon the accomplishment of the purpose for which it was taken up.[227] But, apart from such considerations, the predominant view is that the existence of a special motive does not negative, and may indeed help to establish,[228] the necessary intention. Thus a

---

[222] *Bremer v Freeman* (1857) 10 Moo. P.C. 306, 358–359; *Re Grove* (1888) 40 Ch.D. 216 (CA); *Moffett v Moffett* [1920] 1 I.R. 57; *PL v An tArd Chláraitheoir* [1995] 2 I.L.R.M. 241; *Lee v Commissioner of Taxation* (1963) 6 F.L.R. 285.

[223] See *Donaldson v Donaldson* [1949] P. 363, where D was held to be domiciled in Florida at the time of his divorce although he soon afterwards left the United States.

[224] *Udny v Udny* (1869) L.R. 1 Sc. & Div. 441, 458.

[225] *Bempde v Johnstone* (1796) 3 Ves. 198, 201–202.

[226] *White v White* [1950] 4 D.L.R. 474, affd. [1952] 1 D.L.R. 133 (Man CA).

[227] *Re Furse* [1980] 3 All E.R. 838, 844 (residence in England to keep growing children apart from undesirable cousins).

[228] *Somerville v Somerville* (1801) 5 Ves. 750; *De Greuchy v Wills* (1879) 4 C.P.D. 362; *Spurway v Spurway* [1894] 1 I.R. 385.

person who resides in a country in deference to his father's dying injunction,[229] or to his wife's wishes,[230] or in order to marry,[231] or to be with her putative husband,[232] or because the climate suits his troupe of performing chimpanzees,[233] may acquire a domicile there. It is immaterial that the motive is to enjoy a more favourable legal system. Thus a person who resides in a country to evade the rule against accumulations,[234] to achieve freedom of testation,[235] to secure a more favourable tax régime,[236] or to institute[237] or escape from[238] matrimonial proceedings, may acquire a domicile there.

In the second type of situation, a person is alleged to lack the *animus*　**6–056**
manendi because his presence in the country is due to some physical or legal compulsion. Such compulsion may make it improbable that the necessary intent has in fact been formed.[239] But if it is proved that a person wants to be where he is forced to be, there is no rule of law to prevent his acquiring a domicile of choice there.[240]

Another type of situation, which is usually discussed together with the　**6–057**
preceding one, is its converse: a person may lack the *animus manendi* because his residence in a country, though freely chosen, is precarious, that is, liable to be terminated against his will. This danger may well negative the necessary intent as a matter of fact, but it does not as a matter of law prevent the acquisition of a domicile of choice.[241]

The application of these principles may be illustrated with reference to the　**6–058**
following classes of persons:

   1. Prisoners;
   2. Persons liable to deportation;
   3. Refugees and fugitives;
   4. Invalids;
   5. Members of the armed forces;
   6. Employees;
   7. Diplomats.

---

[229] *Somerville v Somerville* (1801) 5 Ves. 750.

[230] *Aitchison v Dixon* (1870) L.R. 10 Eq. 589. *cf. IRC v Bullock* [1976] 1 W.L.R. 1178 (CA), where the husband planned to return to his native country should his wife predecease him.

[231] See *Fasbender v Att-Gen* [1922] 2 Ch. 850 (CA) and contrast *Arnott v Groom* (1846) 9 D. 142. It is arguable that the intention to reside permanently is conditional on the celebration of the marriage and is nullified if that does not take place: *cf. Cramer v Cramer* [1987] 1 F.L.R. 116 (CA).

[232] *Re Cooke's Trusts* (1887) 56 L.T. 737; *Von Lorang v Administrator of Austrian Property* [1927] A.C. 641.

[233] *Wood v Wood* [1957] P. 254 (CA).

[234] *Haldane v Eckford* (1869) L.R. 8 Eq. 631.

[235] *Huntly v Gaskell* [1906] A.C. 56; *cf. Crookenden v Fuller* (1859) 1 Sw. & Tr. 441.

[236] *Spence v Spence*, 1995 S.L.T. 335; *Morgan v Cilento* [2004] EWHC 188 (Ch.), [2004] W.T.L.R. 457.

[237] *Drexel v Drexel* [1916] 1 Ch. 251.

[238] *Firebrace v Firebrace* (1878) 4 P.D. 63.

[239] e.g. *Re Duleep Singh* (1890) 6 T.L.R. 385 (CA).

[240] See especially the cases concerning members of the armed forces, below, paras 6–063 *et seq.*

[241] See especially the cases concerning persons liable to be deported or whose residence permit is liable to be terminated, below.

6–059   **(1) Prisoners.** A prisoner normally retains during imprisonment the domicile which he had at its commencement. Such a person, even if he can be considered to reside where he is imprisoned,[242] is unlikely to intend to reside there permanently or indefinitely.[243] If a prisoner does form such an intention, he acquires a domicile of choice there.[244]

6–060   **(2) Persons liable to deportation.** A person who resides in a country from which he is liable to be deported may lack the *animus manendi* because his residence is precarious.[245] But if in fact he forms the necessary intention, he acquires a domicile of choice. This applies both where he is given permission to reside for an unlimited period but is liable to deportation[246] and also where he is given permission to reside for a limited period which can be extended at the discretion of the authorities of the country in question.[247] Once such a person has acquired a domicile of choice he does not lose it merely because a deportation order has been made against him;[248] he only loses it when he is actually deported.[249] It has even been held that a person who has acquired an English domicile of choice did not lose it by being deported, as he intended to return to this country and as his re-entry would not have been illegal.[250]

6–061   **(3) Refugees and fugitives.** A person who leaves a country as a political refugee, as a fugitive from criminal justice, or in order to evade his creditors, has a special motive for leaving it, but he has no special motive for entering any other particular country, nor is his residence in another country in any sense enforced. The question which causes more difficulty in cases of this kind is whether the fugitive intends to abandon his domicile in the first country: if he does, the acquisition of a new domicile in the second country will readily be assumed. The question is one of fact in each case. If a political refugee intends to return to the country from which he fled as soon as the

---

[242] Contrast *Dunston v Paterson* (1858) 5 C.B.(N.S.) 267 with *Butler v Dolben* (1756) 2 Lee 312.

[243] *Collier v Rivaz* (1841) 2 Curt. 855; *In the goods of Napoleon Bonaparte* (1853) 2 Rob.Ecc. 606, 610; *Burton v Fisher* (1828) Milward's Reps. 183, 191–192; *Moffat v Moffat* (1866) 3 W.W. & A'B. 87; *Whitehouse v Whitehouse* (1900) 21 N.S.W.L.R. Div. 16.

[244] *Stifel v Hopkins*, 477 F. 2d 1116 (6th Cir. 1973); and see *Udny v Udny* (1869) L.R. 1 Sc. & Div. 441, 458.

[245] Illegal residence can be recognised as residence for the purpose of the acquisition of a domicile: above, para.6–037.

[246] *Boldrini v Boldrini* [1932] P. 9 (CA); *Van Rensburg v Ballinger*, 1950 (4) S.A. 427.

[247] *Zanelli v Zanelli* (1948) 64 T.L.R. 556 (CA); *Szechter v Szechter* [1971] P. 286; *Mark v Mark* [2005] UKHL 42, [2006] 1 A.C. 98; *cf. May v May* [1943] 2 All E.R. 146 (residence permitted for a particular purpose); *Hyland v Hyland* (1971) 18 F.L.R. 461; *Lim v Lim* [1973] V.R. 370.

[248] *Cruh v Cruh* [1945] 2 All E.R. 545; *cf. Jablonowski v Jablonowski* (1972) 28 D.L.R. (3d) 440 (Ont) (where the order was made after the institution of the proceedings in question).

[249] *Ex p. Donelly* [1915] W.L.D. 29; *Ex p. Gordon* [1937] W.L.D. 35. See *Mark v Mark* [2005] UKHL 42, [2006] 1 A.C. 98 at [6].

[250] *Thiele v Thiele* (1920) 150 L.T.J. 387; *cf. Ex p. Macleod* [1946] C.P.D. 312; and *Drakensbergpers Bpk v Sharpe*, 1963 (4) S.A. 615, where the re-entry would have been illegal. *Quaere*, whether an English court would take account of the fact that re-entry into a foreign country was illegal under the law of that country: *cf.* above, para.6–037.

political situation changes, he retains his domicile there[251] unless the desired political change is so improbable that his intention is discounted and treated as merely an exile's longing for his native land;[252] but if his intention is not to return to that country even when the political situation has changed, he can acquire a domicile of choice in the country to which he has fled.[253] In the case of a fugitive from criminal justice, the intention to abandon his domicile in the country from which he has fled will readily be assumed, unless perhaps the punishment which he seeks to escape is trivial, or by the law of that country a relatively short period of prescription bars liability to punishment.[254] Similarly, a person who leaves a country to evade his creditors may lose his domicile there;[255] but if he plans to return as soon as he has paid[256] or otherwise got rid of[257] his debts, there is no change of domicile.

(4) Invalids. Conflicting views have been expressed on the question   **6–062** whether a person who resides in a country for the sake of his health acquires a domicile there. Some judges have thought that such a person could not,[258] while others have thought that he might,[259] by such residence acquire a domicile. The two objections to the acquisition of a domicile are that the residence has been taken up for some special motive, and that it may not be freely chosen. But these factors merely make it improbable in fact that a domicile has been acquired:[260] they do not make it impossible in law. A person who is temporarily detained in a country because he is for the time being too ill to be moved, or who goes to a country for the temporary purpose of undergoing a course of medical treatment, clearly does not acquire a domicile of choice there. On the other hand a person who determines to settle in a new country because he believes that he will enjoy better health there may well intend to live there permanently or indefinitely,[261] but of course he does not necessarily have this intention.[262] It has been suggested that a distinction ought to be drawn between persons whose move from one country to another is dictated by immediate danger and those who move simply in order to enjoy

---

[251] *De Bonneval v De Bonneval* (1838) 1 Curt. 856; *Commissioners of Charitable Donations in Ireland v Devereux* (1842) 13 Sim. 14; *Re Lloyd Evans* [1947] Ch. 695; *cf. Cyganik v Agulian* [2006] EWCA Civ 129, [2006] 1 F.C.R. 406.

[252] *cf.* above, para.6–040.

[253] *May v May* [1943] 2 All E.R. 146; *F v F (Divorce: Jurisdiction)* [2009] EWHC 1448 (Fam.), [2009] 2 F.L.R. 1496; *In the Matter of Wu* (1994) F.L.C. 92–477.

[254] *Re Martin* [1900] P. 211 (CA).

[255] *Udny v Udny* (1869) L.R. 1 Sc. & Div. 441; *De Greuchy v Wills* (1879) 4 C.P.D. 362; *Re Robertson* (1885) 2 T.L.R. 178 (CA), but contrast the report of this case in [1885] W.N. 217; *cf. Spurway v Spurway* [1894] 1 I.R. 385; *Briggs v Briggs* (1880) 5 P.D. 163.

[256] *Re Wright's Trusts* (1856) 2 K. & J. 595.

[257] *Pitt v Pitt* (1864) 4 Macq. 627 (HL).

[258] *Moorhouse v Lord* (1863) 10 H.L.C. 272, 283; *Udny v Udny* (1869) L.R. 1 Sc. & Div. 441, 458.

[259] *Hoskins v Matthews* (1855) 8 De G.M. & G. 13, 28–29.

[260] See *Gillis v Gillis* (1874) I.R. 8 Eq. 597.

[261] *Hoskins v Matthews* (1855) 8 De G.M. & G. 13; *Aitchison v Dixon* (1870) L.R. 10 Eq. 589; *Bradford v Swanton* [1931] I.R. 446; *Re Adams* [1967] I.R. 424; *Reddington v Riach's Executor*, 2002 S.L.T. 537.

[262] *Att-Gen v Fitzgerald* (1856) 3 Drew. 610; *Re James* (1908) 98 L.T. 438; *The Lauderdale Peerage Case* (1885) 10 App. Cas. 692, 740; and see *Winans v Att-Gen* [1904] A.C. 287, where, however, this point was not much relied on.

better health.[263] But this, too, appears to be a factual rather than a legal distinction. A person who goes to another country to overcome some immediate danger to his health may well intend to return after the danger has passed; and a person who is mortally ill may well move from one country to another to alleviate his last sufferings, without any intention of breaking up his old home.[264] But if a person is told that he will die in six months if he stays in the country of his present domicile, but will live for ten years if he goes to another country, it is perfectly possible, and indeed likely, that he will form the intention of residing permanently or indefinitely in the second country, and thus acquire a domicile there.

6–063   **(5) Members of the armed forces.** It was at one time thought that a member of the armed forces could not, as a matter of law, acquire a domicile of choice during service:[265] he could not do so where he was stationed because his residence there was enforced, nor elsewhere because his residence in any place was necessarily precarious.[266] This view no longer prevails. It has long been settled that a person can acquire a domicile of choice in a country which he may have to leave on being recalled to active service.[267] It is also clear that a member of the armed forces can, during service, acquire a domicile of choice either in the country in which he is stationed[268] or elsewhere,[269] provided that he has established the necessary residence[270] and formed the necessary intention. Of course, in the great majority of cases a member of the armed forces does not intend to make his permanent home where he is stationed, and retains the domicile which he had on entering service.[271]

---

[263] *Hoskins v Matthews* (1855) 8 De G.M. & G. 13, 28.

[264] e.g. *Att-Gen v Fitzgerald* (1856) 3 Drew. 610; *Haji-Ioannou v Frangos* [2009] EWHC 2310 (QB), [2009] 2 C.L.C. 500; *Re Foote Estate*, 2011 ABCA, [2011] 6 W.W.R. 453.

[265] *Re E.R. Smith* (1896) 12 T.L.R. 223; *Ex p. Cunningham* (1884) 13 Q.B.D. 418, 425 (CA); *Re Macreight* (1885) 30 Ch.D. 165, 168.

[266] See *Craigie v Lewin* (1843) 3 Curt. 435, where a lieutenant in the army of the East India Company was held not to have resumed his Scottish domicile of origin because he was liable to be recalled to India.

[267] *Cockrell v Cockrell* (1856) 25 L.J. Ch. 730; *Att-Gen v Pottinger* (1861) 6 H. & N. 733; *Commissioners of Inland Revenue v Gordon's Executors* (1850) 12 D. 657.

[268] *Donaldson v Donaldson* [1949] P. 363 (which set at rest doubts raised in *Hodgson v De Beauchesne* (1858) 12 Moo. P.C. 285, as to whether a soldier in the British army can acquire a domicile in a politically foreign country); *Cruickshanks v Cruickshanks* [1957] 1 W.L.R. 564, 568; *Clarke v Newmarsh* (1836) 14 S. 488; *Willar v Willar*, 1954 S.C. 144; *Nicol v Nicol*, 1948 (2) S.A. 613, where the conflicting South African decisions on this question are exhaustively discussed; *Ex p. Glass*, 1948 (4) S.A. 379; *Hibbs v Wynne*, 1949 (2) S.A. 10; *Schache v Schache* (1931) 31 S.R.N.S.W. 633; *Cox v Cox* [1945] V.L.R. 105; *Armstead v Armstead* [1954] V.L.R. 733; *Auld v Auld* [1952] V.L.R. 455; *Wilkinson v Wilkinson* [1949] 1 W.W.R. 249 (Alta); *Young v Young* (1959) 21 D.L.R. (2d) 616 (Man CA).

[269] *Baker v Baker* [1945] A.D. 708; *Stone v Stone* [1958] 1 W.L.R. 1287.

[270] See above, para.6–034.

[271] *Tovey v Lindsay* (1813) 1 Dow. 117, 124; *Brown v Smith* (1852) 15 Beav. 444; *Yelverton v Yelverton* (1859) 1 Sw. & Tr. 574; *Firebrace v Firebrace* (1878) 4 P.D. 63; *Re Macreight* (1885) 30 Ch.D. 165; *Att-Gen v Napier* (1851) 6 Exch. 217, 218–219 (in argument); *The Lauderdale Peerage Case* (1885) 10 App. Cas. 692, 739–740; *Cruickshanks v Cruickshanks* [1957] 1 W.L.R. 564; *Sellars v Sellars*, 1942 S.C. 206; *Wilton v Wilton* [1946] 2 D.L.R. 397 (Ont); *McBeth v McBeth* [1954] 1 D.L.R. 590 (BC); *Patterson v Patterson* (1955) 3 D.L.R. (2d) 266 (NS); *Fitzgibbon-Lloyd v Fitzgibbon-Lloyd* [1944] V.L.R. 29.

The law on this topic was at one time obscured by the theory, influenced by **6–064**
the now discredited cases on "Anglo-Indian" domicile, that anyone who
entered the service of a foreign government thereby acquired a domicile in the
foreign country. While a British subject joining the British armed forces
would retain the domicile he had on joining, a foreign recruit would at once
acquire a domicile in some part of the United Kingdom.[272] The theory rested
on an assumption that to serve a foreign government necessarily implies a
duty to reside in the foreign country (which is not necessarily the case in
modern conditions) and on the notion that a man's intentions must be presumed to be consistent with his duty. It is submitted that none of this is good
law. In all issues as to domicile the existence of the *animus manendi* is a
question of fact. A supposed duty to have that intention is immaterial. It has
even been suggested that the existence of a duty tends to negative, rather than
to support, the inference of *animus manendi*.[273]

(6) Employees. A person who goes to a country in pursuance of a contract   **6–065**
of employment is in a position similar to that of a member of the armed forces
in that his residence is in a sense enforced and may, if the contract provided
for his possible removal to another country, be precarious. These factors are
perhaps of less weight in the case of an employee than in the case of a soldier;
an employee always undertakes the duties of his employment of his own free
will and can almost always terminate his employment by giving appropriate
notice. The question whether an employee who is sent to a country intends to
reside there permanently or indefinitely remains in the last resort a question of
fact. There is, for this purpose, no distinction between public servants and
other employees. If such persons go to the country to which they are sent for
the temporary purpose of performing the duties of their office or employment,
they do not acquire a domicile of choice there.[274] But if they go to the country
not merely to work, but also to settle in it, they do acquire a domicile of
choice.[275]

(7) Diplomats. Diplomats are simply a special category of public servants   **6–066**
and their domicile is governed by the same principles. The fiction of extra-
territoriality of embassies does not apply for the purpose of ascertaining the
domicile of a person of this class.[276] Nor is it material that he is to some extent
immune from the jurisdiction of the local courts.[277] It is a question of fact
whether he has formed the intention of residing permanently or indefinitely in

---

[272] *Forbes v Forbes* (1854) Kay 341; *Ex p. Cunningham* (1884) 13 Q.B.D. 418 (CA); *cf.*
Urquhart v Butterfield (1887) 37 Ch.D. 357, 385–386 (CA) as to civil servants.

[273] *Allardice v Onslow* (1864) 33. L.J. Ch. 434, 436.

[274] *Att-Gen v Rowe* (1862) 1 H. & C. 31; *Grant v Grant*, 1931 S.C. 238; *Eilon v Eilon*, 1965
(1) S.A. 703; *Terrassin v Terrassin* [1968] 3 N.S.W.R. 600; *cf. Moncrieff v Moncrieff* [1934]
C.P.D. 208, the reasoning of which is, however, difficult to reconcile with the cases of persons
liable to deportation: see above, para.6–060.

[275] *In the goods of James Smith* (1850) 2 Rob. Ecc. 332; *Commissioners of Inland Revenue v*
Gordon's Executors (1850) 12 D. 657; *Gunn v Gunn* (1956) 2 D.L.R. (2d) 351 (Sask CA);
Waggoner v Waggoner (1956) 2 W.W.R. 74 (Alta); *Russell v Russell* [1935] S.A.S.R. 85.

[276] *Att-Gen v Kent* (1862) 1 H. & C. 12, 28, 29. The fiction was rejected in another context in
Radwan v Radwan (No.1) [1973] Fam. 24.

[277] *cf. Casdagli v Casdagli* [1919] A.C. 145.

the country to which he is sent. Generally, of course, he forms no such intention,[278] but occasionally he may do so and thus acquire a domicile of choice.[279] If a person has acquired a domicile of choice in a country, he does not lose it merely by reason of being appointed to a diplomatic post in that country by the country of his nationality.[280]

ILLUSTRATIONS

(1) PRISONERS

6–067   1. D, whose domicile of origin is Irish, is detained in Belgium as a prisoner of war from 1803 to 1814. He does not thereby acquire a Belgian domicile. He continues to reside in Belgium of his own free will from 1814 to 1829. He acquires a Belgian domicile.[281]

(2) PERSONS LIABLE TO DEPORTATION

6–068   2. D, an Italian, resides in England. Under the Aliens Order 1920, he is liable, in certain circumstances, to be deported. He can acquire a domicile of choice in England.[282]

3. D, an Italian, comes to England and is given permission to reside here for six months. There is evidence that this permission would be readily extended. He can acquire a domicile of choice in England.[283]

4. D, a German, acquires a domicile of choice in England. In 1919 he is repatriated to Germany against his will. He intends to return to England shortly and there is no Home Office order prohibiting his return. He continues to be domiciled in England.[284]

(3) REFUGEES AND FUGITIVES

6–069   5. D, whose domicile of origin is English, acquires a domicile of choice in Belgium. In 1940 he is forced by the German invasion to leave Belgium, and comes to England. He intends to return to Belgium after the end of the German occupation. He continues to be domiciled in Belgium.[285]

6. D, who is domiciled in Germany, comes to England in 1939 as a refugee from Nazi oppression. He does not intend to return to Germany even if the Nazis are overthrown. On forming the intention to reside permanently in England, he acquires an English domicile.[286]

7. D, who is domiciled in France, leaves that country to escape punishment for a crime, and comes to England. By French law, his liability to punishment is extinguished after twenty years. He can, and does, acquire a domicile of choice in England before the expiration of this period.[287]

8. D, who is domiciled in England, goes to France to evade his creditors. He loses his English domicile,[288] unless he intends to pay his debts if and when he can, and then to return to England.[289]

---

[278] e.g. *Udny v Udny* (1869) L.R. 1 Sc. & Div. 441 (as to Colonel Udny's domicile of origin); *Niboyet v Niboyet* (1878) 4 P.D. 1 (CA).

[279] *Naville v Naville*, 1957 (1) S.A. 280; *cf. Heath v Samson* (1851) 14 Beav. 441, where, however, the domicile may have been acquired at a time when the *propositus* held no diplomatic appointment.

[280] *Att-Gen v Kent* (1862) 1 H. & C. 12; *Sharpe v Crispin* (1869) L.R. 1 P. & D. 611.

[281] *Collier v Rivaz* (1841) 2 Curt. 855.

[282] *Boldrini v Boldrini* [1932] P. 9 (CA).

[283] *Zanelli v Zanelli* (1948) 64 T.L.R. 556 (CA).

[284] *Thiele v Thiele* (1920) 150 L.T.J. 387.

[285] *Re Lloyd Evans* [1947] Ch. 695.

[286] *May v May* [1943] 2 All E.R. 146.

[287] *Re Martin* [1900] P. 211 (CA).

[288] *Udny v Udny* (1869) L.R. 1 Sc. & Div. 441.

[289] *Re Wright's Trusts* (1856) 2 K. & J. 595.

(4) INVALIDS

9. D, who is domiciled in England, establishes his home in Italy because he thinks that the   **6–070**
warmer climate there will be good for his health. He acquires a domicile of choice in Italy.[290]

(5) MEMBERS OF THE ARMED FORCES

10. D, an officer on active service in the Royal Air Force, while stationed in Florida forms the   **6–071**
intention of residing there permanently. He acquires a domicile of choice there.[291]

11. D, an American serviceman, determines to settle in England. At the relevant time he is not
stationed in England, but he spends all his leave here. He is domiciled in England.[292]

12. D, whose domicile of origin is English, gets a domicile of dependency in Jersey. He joins
the army and soon afterwards becomes an independent person; but he forms no intention of
settling anywhere. Although he is stationed out of Jersey, he continues to be domiciled
there.[293]

(6) EMPLOYEES

13. D, whose domicile of origin is English, is appointed Chief Justice of Ceylon. He intends   **6–072**
to hold this office until he has earned his pension and then to return to England. He retains his
English domicile.[294]

14. D, whose domicile of origin is in Manitoba, enters into the service of a corporation which
owns cinemas in various provinces of Canada. By way of promotion he is offered, and accepts,
the office of manager of a cinema in Saskatchewan. He accordingly moves to Saskatchewan and
resides there with the intention of residing there for an indefinite period. He acquires a domicile
of choice in Saskatchewan.[295]

(7) DIPLOMATS

15. D, who is domiciled in France, resides for several years in England as French consul. He   **6–073**
does not thereby acquire an English domicile.[296]

16. D, whose domicile of origin is Portuguese, in 1819 comes to England and acquires an
English domicile of choice. In 1857 he is appointed attaché to the Portuguese embassy in
England. He retains his English domicile.[297]

(2) Loss

RULE 13—(1) A person abandons a domicile of choice in a country by   **6R–074**
ceasing to reside there and by ceasing to intend to reside there perma-
nently or indefinitely, and not otherwise.
   (2) When a domicile of choice is abandoned, either
    (i) a new domicile of choice is acquired; or
    (ii) the domicile of origin revives.

COMMENT

A domicile of choice is lost when both the residence and the intention which   **6–075**
must exist for its acquisition are given up.[298] It is not lost merely by giving up

---

[290] *Hoskins v Matthews* (1855) 8 De G.M. & G. 13.

[291] *Donaldson v Donaldson* [1949] P. 363.

[292] *Stone v Stone* [1958] 1 W.L.R. 1287; *cf. Baker v Baker* [1945] A.D. 708.

[293] *Re Macreight* (1885) 30 Ch.D. 165.

[294] *Att-Gen v Rowe* (1862) 1 H. & C. 31.

[295] *Gunn v Gunn* (1956) 2 D.L.R. (2d) 351 (Sask CA).

[296] *Niboyet v Niboyet* (1878) 4 P.D. 1 (CA).

[297] *Att-Gen v Kent* (1862) 1 H. & C. 12.

[298] *Udny v Udny* (1869) L.R. 1 Sc. & Div. 441, 450; e.g. *Fleming v Horniman* (1928) 44 T.L.R.
315; *Bradfield v Swanton* [1931] I.R. 446; *Morgan v Cilento* [2004] EWHC 188 (Ch.), [2004]
W.T.L.R. 457.

the residence[299] nor merely by giving up the intention.[300] It is not necessary to prove a positive intention not to return: it is sufficient to prove merely the absence of an intention to continue to reside.[301] The intention is not considered to have been given up merely because the propositus is dissatisfied with the country of the domicile of choice.[302] In order to show that the intention has been given up, it may be desirable to prove the formation of an intention to reside in another country,[303] but such proof is not essential as a matter of law. Although it has been suggested that residence is given up by "leaving this country or, perhaps more accurately, arriving in another"[304] it is submitted that residence can simply be given up. The view that residence in one country can only be given up by arriving in another seems to be a relic of the discarded doctrine that a domicile of choice cannot be lost by mere abandonment.[305]

6–076   On abandoning a domicile of choice, a person may acquire a new domicile of choice, or he may return to and settle in the country of his domicile of origin. He may also simply abandon his domicile of choice without acquiring a home in another country. It was at one time thought that in such a case the previous domicile was retained until a new one was acquired.[306] But it is now settled that where a person simply abandons a domicile of choice his domicile of origin revives by operation of law.[307] This rule has been much criticised since it may result in a person's being domiciled in a country with which his connection is stale or tenuous and which, indeed, he may never even have visited. It has been abolished in New Zealand and Australia, and replaced by a statutory rule that a domicile continues until a new domicile is acquired.[308] The English and Scottish Law Commissions have proposed similar legislation.[309]

---

[299] *Lyall v Paton* (1856) 25 L.J. Ch. 746, as to which see para.6–039, n.127, above; *Bradford v Young* (1885) 29 Ch.D. 617 (CA); *Thiele v Thiele* (1920) 150 L.T.J. 387; *Re Lloyd Evans* [1947] Ch. 695; *Breuning v Breuning* [2002] EWHC 236 (Fam.), [2002] 1 F.L.R. 888; *cf. Bell v Bell* [1922] 2 I.R. 152, but it is difficult to say in that case that the *propositus* had not also given up the intention.

[300] *In the goods of Raffenel* (1863) 3 Sw. & Tr. 49; *Zanelli v Zanelli* (1948) 64 T.L.R. 556 (CA); *IRC v Duchess of Portland* [1982] Ch. 314. *cf. Plummer v IRC* [1988] 1 W.L.R. 292 where the Rule was criticised *obiter* on the theory that the *propositus* may lose a domicile of choice though continuing to be resident, if his "chief residence" is established elsewhere.

[301] *Re Flynn (No.1)* [1968] 1 W.L.R. 103, 113–115, *per* Megarry J. (*obiter*), approving the wording of the Rule; *Qureshi v Qureshi* [1972] Fam. 173, 191.

[302] *Re Marrett* (1887) 36 Ch.D. 400 (CA).

[303] See *Att-Gen v Gasquet* (1877) 41 J.P. 487; 42 J.P. 346.

[304] *Zanelli v Zanelli* (1948) 64 T.L.R. 556, 557 (CA).

[305] Expressed in *Munroe v Douglas* (1820) 5 Madd. 379, 404. See now *Udny v Udny* (1869) L.R. 1 Sc. & Div. 441.

[306] *Munroe v Douglas*, above. This is still the predominant American view: Restatement, s.19, Comment *b* and Illustration 5.

[307] *Udny v Udny* (1869) L.R. 1 Sc. & Div. 441; *King v Foxwell* (1876) 3 Ch.D. 518; *Harrison v Harrison* [1953] 1 W.L.R. 865; *Re Flynn (No.1)* [1968] 1 W.L.R. 103, 108; *Tee v Tee* [1974] 1 W.L.R. 213 (CA); *Holden v Holden* (1914) 33 N.Z.L.R. 1032; *Ex p. Donelly* [1915] W.L.D. 29; *Ex p. Gordon* [1937] W.L.D. 35; *Strike v Gleich* (1879) O.B. & F. 50.

[308] See, for New Zealand: Domicile Act 1976, s.11; for Australia, the uniform Domicile Acts of the Australian jurisdictions, s.6.

[309] *The Law of Domicile*, para.5.25.

ILLUSTRATIONS

1. D, a German, acquires a domicile of choice in England. In 1919 he is repatriated to Germany,   **6–077**
but intends to return to England as soon as possible and to reside there permanently. He retains
his English domicile.[310]
2. D, whose domicile of origin is English, acquires a domicile of choice in France on marrying
a Frenchman. After her husband's death, she resolves to return to England. She never succeeds
in leaving France. She retains her French domicile.[311]
3. D, whose domicile of origin is Scottish, acquires a domicile of choice in England. Later he
abandons his English domicile and goes to France, but does not acquire a domicile of choice
there. His Scottish domicile of origin revives.[312]
4. D's domicile of origin is English. He emigrates to the United States and in 1953 becomes
a naturalised American citizen and acquires a domicile of choice in New York. In 1960 he moves
to Germany, without at that time losing his domicile of choice. In 1967 he decides to make his
permanent home in England, but does not return to live in England until 1972. His English
domicile of origin revives in 1967.[313]
5. D's domicile of origin is English. At the age of twenty-five he emigrates to the United States,
becomes a naturalised American citizen, and acquires a domicile of choice in New York. He never
revisits England. At the age of sixty-five he decides to leave New York and settle in California.
He sets out for California but dies on his way there in Illinois. He dies domiciled in
England.[314]

C. *Domicile of dependency*

RULE 14—The domicile of a dependent person is, in general, the same as,   **6R–078**
and changes (if at all) with, the domicile of the person on whom he is, as
regards his domicile, legally dependent.

COMMENT

The general principle is that a dependent person has the domicile of the person   **6–079**
on whom he is considered by law to be dependent. The class of dependent
persons was greatly reduced in size by the Domicile and Matrimonial Proceedings Act 1973.[315] It now comprises children who are under sixteen and
unmarried[316] and mentally disordered persons.[317] Previously the age of independence was the age of majority, eighteen years (or, before 1970, twenty-
one[318]) and the class of dependents included all married women.[319] The

---

[310] *Thiele v Thiele* (1920) 150 L.T.J. 387.

[311] *In the goods of Raffenel* (1863) 3 Sw. & Tr. 49 (where the French domicile was one of
dependency).

[312] *Udny v Udny* (1869) L.R. 1 Sc. & Div. 441.

[313] *Tee v Tee* [1974] 1 W.L.R. 213 (CA).

[314] cf. *Nelson v Nelson* [1925] 3 D.L.R. 22 (Alta), where the revival of an inappropriate
domicile of origin was averted by the court's unprincipled use of the concept of nationality; *Re
Foote Estate*, 2009 ABQB 654, at [97], where it was held that the court had a residual authority
to depart from the revival principle and find a person had retained his last domicile of choice
(appeal dismissed, 2011 ABCA 1, [2011] 6 W.W.R. 453).

[315] The Act came into force on January 1, 1974: s.17(5).

[316] Rule 15. A child under 16 can be validly married under some systems of law; see below,
para.17–079.

[317] Rule 16.

[318] See Family Law Reform Act 1969, s.1(1), which effected the reduction; it came into effect
on January 1, 1970.

[319] See below, paras 6–084 *et seq.*

English and Scottish Law Commissions have recommended new statutory rules for determining the domicile of individuals, including children and mentally disordered persons, under which there would be no place for a domicile of dependency as a distinct concept.[320]

6–080   It follows from the general principle that a dependent person cannot acquire a domicile of choice by his own act. Thus although a child under sixteen may have a home separate from that of his parents he cannot acquire an independent domicile unless he is married.

6–081   Where a person is not *sui juris*, but there is no person in existence on whom he is dependent, his domicile cannot for the time being be changed at all. Such is the position of a child without parents or guardians, and probably of a child without parents but with a guardian.[321] The same is also in certain circumstances true of a mentally disordered person.[322]

6–082   Our Rule applies to dependent persons, wherever they are domiciled and whatever is their power under the law of that domicile to acquire a new domicile by their own act. Although it has been suggested that a person's capacity to acquire a new domicile may be governed by the law of his previous domicile, or by the law of the intended new domicile,[323] it is submitted that such capacity is for the purposes of the Rules in this book governed by English law. Any other view is inconsistent with the rule that the question where a person is domiciled must be decided in accordance with English law.[324] Moreover, in dealing with the domicile of Scottish children, English courts have nearly always treated them as dependent persons and have not considered the possibility that by Scots law they might have capacity to acquire a domicile of their own.[325] And in cases on the former dependent domicile of a married woman, it was always assumed that if a woman domiciled in England married a man domiciled abroad,[326] or vice versa,[327] she took his domicile regardless of the foreign law.

6–083   It has been suggested that a domicile of dependency is simply a domicile of choice,[328] but the two kinds of domicile differ in three respects. In the first place, a domicile of choice can, while a domicile of dependency cannot, be abandoned. Secondly, a domicile of dependency is imposed, whereas a domicile of choice is always acquired. Thirdly, it is easier to prove that a formerly

---

[320] *The Law of Domicile* (Law Com. No.168), paras 4.4–4.8 and below, para.6–098. In the reform introduced by the Family Law (Scotland) Act 2006, s.22, a child may in certain circumstances have an independent domicile.

[321] Rule 15(4).

[322] Rule 16.

[323] See *Urquhart v Butterfield* (1887) 37 Ch.D. 357, 380 (CA); *Haque v Haque* (1962) 108 C.L.R. 230, 240—but there the law of the intended new domicile was also the *lex fori*; Graveson (1950) 3 Int.L.Q. 149; Clive, 1966 Jur. Rev. 1, 9–12.

[324] Rule 8.

[325] *Re Beaumont* [1893] 3 Ch. 490; *Att-Gen v Yule* (1931) 145 L.T. 9, 15 (CA); *Henderson v Henderson* [1967] P. 77. See, however, *Urquhart v Butterfield* (1887) 37 Ch.D. 357 (CA). See now Family Law (Scotland) Act 2006, s.22.

[326] e.g. *In the goods of Raffenel* (1863) 3 Sw. & Tr. 49; *Re Cooke's Trusts* (1887) 56 L.T. 737; *Armitage v Att-Gen* [1906] P. 135; *Ogden v Ogden* [1908] P. 46 (CA); *Chapelle v Chapelle* [1950] P. 134; *Lepre v Lepre* [1965] P. 52; *cf. Garthwaite v Garthwaite* [1964] P. 356 (CA).

[327] *Robinson-Scott v Robinson-Scott* [1958] P. 71.

[328] *Udny v Udny* (1869) L.R. 1 Sc. & Div. 441, 457; *Re Wallach* [1950] 1 All E.R. 199, 200.

dependent person has abandoned his last domicile of dependency than it is to prove the abandonment of a domicile of choice.[329]

Married women. Until the coming into effect of the Domicile and Matrimonial Proceedings Act 1973, a married woman was dependent for the purposes of the law of domicile upon her husband. This was the case even if she were a minor; her dependence on her husband prevailed over her dependence on her father. Thus, the domicile of a married woman was the same as, and changed with, the domicile of her husband. That rule, which applied even if the spouses had been living apart and in different countries for many years,[330] reflected social conditions and attitudes of a past age; it was "the last barbarous relic of a wife's servitude."[331] It also produced serious inconvenience in practice, notably in the context of jurisdiction in matrimonial causes, alleviated by special legislative provisions.[332] The rule has been abolished by statute in New Zealand,[333] Australia,[334] the Republic of Ireland[335] and most parts of Canada.[336]

6–084

The domicile of a married woman is now ascertained by reference to the same factors as in the case of any other individual capable of having an independent domicile.[337] The fact of her marriage and the domicile, residence and nationality of her husband will be relevant factors[338] but not determinative of her domicile. Where the spouses are living together, there must be a strong probability of their having the same domicile, but this is an observation of fact and not a rule of law. In appropriate circumstances, such spouses may have different domiciles.

6–085

Termination of dependency. On ceasing to be dependent, a person often continues to be domiciled in the country of his last domicile of dependency. A child reaching the age of sixteen will usually retain the domicile of the appropriate parent as a domicile of choice.[339] But he now has the normal capacity to change his domicile, and such a change may result from acts done during dependency. Cases on the former dependent domicile of married women established that a married woman who settled in a country other than

6–086

---

[329] *Re Cooke's Trusts* (1887) 56 L.T. 737; *Harrison v Harrison* [1953] 1 W.L.R. 865; *Re Scullard* [1957] Ch. 107; *Henderson v Henderson* [1967] P. 77, 82–83; *Arnott v Groom* (1846) 9 D. 142; *Crumpton's Judicial Factor v Finch-Noyes*, 1918 S.C. 378; *Spurway v Spurway* [1894] 1 I.R. 385; *Hyland v Hyland* (1971) 18 F.L.R. 461; *cf. Miller v Teale* (1954) 92 C.L.R. 406.

[330] See e.g. *Re Scullard* [1957] Ch. 107 (separation of 46 years; in different countries for about 30 of those years).

[331] *Gray v Formosa* [1963] P. 259, 267 (CA).

[332] See para.18–002, below.

[333] Domicile Act 1976, s.5.

[334] See the uniform Domicile Acts of the Australian jurisdictions, s.5.

[335] Domicile and Recognition of Foreign Divorces Act 1986. In *M(C) v M(T) (No.2)* [1990] 2 I.R. 52, the dependent domicile of a married woman was held to have been unconstitutional as offending against the principles of equality before the law and of equal rights in marriage (Arts 41 and 42 of the Constitution of Ireland).

[336] e.g. Law and Equity Act 1996, s.60 (British Columbia); Family Law Act 1990, s.64 (Ontario); The Domicile and Habitual Residence Act 1983, s.3 (Manitoba).

[337] Domicile and Matrimonial Proceedings Act 1973, s.1(1).

[338] *cf.* para.6–049, nn.178–179, above, for the corresponding case of the husband's domicile.

[339] *In the goods of Patten* (1860) 6 Jur.(N.S.) 151; *Re Macreight* (1885) 30 Ch.D. 165; *Gulbenkian v Gulbenkian* [1937] 4 All E.R. 618.

that of her husband's domicile could acquire a domicile there as soon as dependency ended, on the death of the husband or a decree absolute of divorce or of nullity of marriage. A widow did not, after becoming a widow, have to establish a new residence or form a new *animus manendi*; it was therefore no bar to the acquisition of a domicile of choice that she never knew of her husband's death.[340] The same result should follow even if the dependent person, having settled in a country, is temporarily absent from it at the time dependency ends.[341]

6–087   Where immediately before January 1, 1974, a woman was married and then had her husband's domicile by dependence, she is treated as retaining that domicile (as a domicile of choice, if it is not also her domicile of origin) unless and until it is changed by acquisition or revival of another domicile either on or after that date.[342] This means that any such married woman who had before 1974 settled in a country other than that of her husband's domicile would acquire a new domicile of choice on January 1, 1974 and without further action on her part.[343] In all other cases, however, the domicile of such a married woman will change only in accordance with the rules for the loss of a domicile of choice[344] or, where her continuing domicile is her domicile of origin, for the acquisition of a domicile of choice.[345] In these latter cases, the wife's history and circumstances before 1974 are treated as irrelevant, with the result that she may be treated as having had, at least for some time after January 1, 1974, what the English and Scottish Law Commissions describe as "a bogus or artificial domicile."[346]

6–088   The Commissions have proposed[347] the replacement of s.1(2) of the Domicile and Matrimonial Proceedings Act 1973 by fresh transitional provisions on the model of the uniform Domicile Acts in the Australian jurisdictions.[348] Under these provisions the proposed statutory rules as to domicile would apply to times before those rules came into force but only for the purpose of determining where, at a time after the rules came into force, a person was domiciled.

ILLUSTRATIONS

6–089   1. D, whose domicile of origin is English, at the age of seventeen travels to Dublin with the intention of making his permanent home there. By English law, D has capacity to acquire a domicile of choice; by Irish law he has not. D is domiciled in the Republic of Ireland.

2. D was born in England with an English domicile of origin in 1930. In 1948, his parents acquired a domicile of choice in South Australia. In 1950, D went to New Zealand with the

---

[340] *Re Scullard* [1957] Ch. 107; *cf. Re Cooke's Trusts* (1887) 56 L.T. 737.

[341] *cf. Harrison v Harrison* [1953] 1 W.L.R. 865, stated as Illustration 2, below.

[342] Domicile and Matrimonial Proceedings Act 1973, s.1(2).

[343] *IRC v Duchess of Portland* [1982] Ch. 314, 319.

[344] i.e. Rule 13, above; *IRC v Duchess of Portland* [1982] Ch. 314, stated as Illustration 3, below; *Breuning v Breuning* [2002] EWHC 236 (Fam.), [2002] 1 F.L.R. 888.

[345] i.e. Rule 10, above.

[346] Working Paper No.88, *The Law of Domicile* (1985), para.8.3.

[347] Report on *The Law of Domicile* (Law Com. No.168), para.8.7.

[348] s.4(1)(2). *cf.* the virtually identical provisions in Domicile Act 1976 (New Zealand), ss.3, 4.

intention of settling there. He continued to entertain this intention until he reached the then age of majority in 1951, but before that time he returned to England for a temporary purpose. As soon as he reached twenty-one he lost his South Australian domicile of dependency.[349]

3. W, whose domicile of origin was in Quebec, married H, domiciled at all material times in England, in 1948. Each year, W spent some 10 or 12 weeks (and H some six weeks) in their house in Quebec; the remainder of the year they lived in their house in England. In 1975, H and W decided that when, at some future time, H retired, they would take up full-time residence in Quebec. On January 1, 1974, W's domicile of dependence in England was deemed to be a domicile of choice there. This domicile was not lost at the time of W's annual visits to Quebec in 1974 or subsequent years; for the purposes of domicile, she remained resident in England.[350]

RULE 15—Subject to the Exception hereinafter mentioned, the domicile of an unmarried child under 16 is determined as follows: 6R–090

(1) the domicile of a legitimate child is, during the lifetime of his father, the same as, and changes with, the domicile of his father;

(2) the domicile of a legitimated child is, from the time at which the legitimation takes effect, during the lifetime of his father, the same as, and changes with, the domicile of his father;

(3) the domicile of an illegitimate child and of a child whose father is dead is, in general, the same as, and changes with, the domicile of his mother;

(4) the domicile of a legitimate or legitimated child without living parents, or of an illegitimate child without a living mother, probably cannot be changed;

(5) the domicile of an adopted child is determined as if he were the legitimate child of the adoptive parent or parents.

(6) the domicile of a child who is the subject of a parental order made under the Human Fertilisation and Embryology Act 2008 is determined as if he were the legitimate child of the persons who obtained the order.

COMMENT

(1) Legitimate children. The rule that the domicile of a legitimate child depends on that of his father is well established.[351] Although the rule has sometimes been criticised,[352] much of the force of those criticisms was removed by the Domicile and Matrimonial Proceedings Act 1973 which introduced important qualifications to the rule. It does not apply to a child   6–091

---

[349] *Harrison v Harrison* [1953] 1 W.L.R. 865. But he did not acquire a domicile of choice in New Zealand on the ground that he had not resided there since coming of age (*sed quaere*).

[350] Domicile and Matrimonial Proceedings Act 1973, s.1(2); *IRC v Duchess of Portland* [1982] Ch. 314.

[351] *Re Duleep Singh* (1890) 6 T.L.R. 385 (CA); *Gulbenkian v Gulbenkian* [1937] 4 All E.R. 618; *Henderson v Henderson* [1967] P. 77; *Spurway v Spurway* [1894] 1 I.R. 385.

[352] *Re P (GE) (An Infant)* [1965] Ch. 568, 589 (CA), though Lord Denning M.R. may have had the rule as to revival of a domicile of origin as much in mind as the present rule; Blaikie, 1984 Jur. Rev. 1.

aged sixteen or over,[353] or to one who is married under that age;[354] nor in some cases in which the parents of the *propositus* are living apart.[355] Parents living together may exceptionally have different domiciles,[356] and it is necessary to have a rule indicating which domicile should be attributed to the child. A child in such a family takes the domicile of the father. That rule must once have seemed an obvious reflection of social and economic realities. It remains the case that most children in such families are economically dependent on their father, but the notion of a child's domicile is arguably more to do with the transmission of cultural norms from parent to child than with economic dependence; the rule is, however, well settled.

There is no English authority to support the view accepted in some American jurisdictions that a child may gain capacity to acquire a domicile by being emancipated or abandoned.[357]

6–092   **(2) Legitimated children.** Although there is no authority on the point, it is submitted that the domicile of a legitimated child is determined as follows: until the time when the legitimation takes effect, his domicile depends on his mother's in accordance with clause (3) of this Rule; when the legitimation takes effect, the child's domicile becomes dependent on his father's, at any rate if the legitimation is due to the marriage of the child's parents;[358] if the parents begin to live apart, the Exception to this Rule will apply; after the father's death, the child's domicile depends once again on his mother's in accordance with clause (3) of this Rule.

6–093   **(3) Illegitimate and fatherless children.** The general rule is that the domicile of an illegitimate or fatherless child depends on that of his mother.[359] But in this case the rule is probably less general in scope than is the rule applying to a child whose domicile depends on that of his father. "The change in the domicile of an infant which ... may follow from a change of domicile on the part of the mother, is not to be regarded as a necessary consequence of a change of the mother's domicile, but as the result of the exercise by her of a power vested in her for the welfare of the infants, which, in their interest, she may abstain from exercising, even when she changes her own domicile."[360] Thus it was held that the remarriage of a widow, which at that time led to her getting a new domicile of dependence, did not of itself affect the domicile of

---

[353] Domicile and Matrimonial Proceedings Act 1973, s.3(1). This provision extends to England and Northern Ireland: s.3(2). In Scotland a child's domicile will follow that of his parents where they have a common domicile and he has a home with one or both. In all other circumstances a child shall be domiciled in the country with which he has for the time being the closest connection, Family Law (Scotland) Act 2006, s.22.

[354] Domicile and Matrimonial Proceedings Act 1973, s.3(1). For New Zealand, see the Domicile Act 1976, s.6(2); for the Australian jurisdictions, the uniform Domicile Acts, s.7.

[355] See the Exception to this Rule, below.

[356] See para.6–085, above.

[357] Restatement, s.22, comment *f*.

[358] As to legitimation by civil partnership see Legitimacy Act 1976, ss.2A, 3(2), see below, para.20–042.

[359] *Potinger v Wightman* (1817) 3 Mer. 67; *Johnstone v Beattie* (1843) 10 Cl. & F. 42, 66, 138; *Arnott v Groom* (1846) 9 D. 142; *Crumpton's Judicial Factor v Finch-Noyes*, 1918 S.C. 378.

[360] *Re Beaumont* [1893] 3 Ch. 490, 496–497.

her children.[361] Similarly if the mother acquires a new domicile of choice (whether or not related to remarriage) but leaves the child behind in the country of the previous domicile she may be said to have abstained from exercising her power of changing the child's domicile.[362] It does not follow as a matter of law that the mother can only change the child's domicile by physically taking the child to the country of the new domicile. There is New Zealand authority for the proposition that the power vested in the mother extends to giving the child a domicile in a country other than that in which the mother is or has been domiciled,[363] but it is difficult to justify so extensive a power, unless it is also given to the father of a legitimate child.[364]

(4) Children without living parents. It is an open question whether the 6–094 domicile of a child without living parents can be changed by his guardian. There is no English authority on this point.[365] It may be that a distinction can be drawn between "natural guardians" (i.e. grandparents), who have the power to change the child's domicile, and others, who do not.[366] Alternatively, it may be that a guardian has power to change the child's domicile to a country in which he is recognised as guardian, but not otherwise.[367] But these are speculative possibilities so far as English law is concerned, and the safest view appears to be that the domicile of a child without living parents cannot be changed. The same rule probably holds good for an illegitimate child whose mother is dead but whose father is alive.

(5) Adopted children. An adopted child is treated in law as the legitimate 6–095 child of his adoptive parent or parents.[368] Accordingly his domicile will be determined in accordance with the appropriate clauses of this Rule and of the Exception thereto, as if he were such a legitimate child.

(6) Children subject of a parental order. A child who is the subject of a 6–096 parental order made under the Human Fertilisation and Embryology Act 2008[369] is treated in law as the legitimate child of the persons who obtained the order.[370] Accordingly his domicile will be determined in accordance with the appropriate clauses of this Rule and of the Exception thereto, as if he were such a legitimate child.

---

[361] *Re Beaumont*, above; *Re G.* [1966] N.Z.L.R. 1028; *cf. Crumpton's Judicial Factor v Finch-Noyes*, 1918, S.C. 378.

[362] *Re Beaumont*, above; *cf. Johnstone v Beattie* (1843) 10 Cl. & F. 42, 138. Although Lord Campbell dissented, he agreed with the majority on this point.

[363] *Re G.* [1966] N.Z.L.R. 1028.

[364] *cf.* Blaikie, 1984 Jur. Rev. 1.

[365] In *Potinger v Wightman* (1817) 3 Mer. 67, the guardian was the child's mother. The case was explained on this ground in *Johnstone v Beattie* (1843) 10 Cl. & F. 42, 66 (in argument).

[366] Restatement, s.22, comment *i*.

[367] This would avoid the difficulty "that a person may be guardian in one place and not in another"; *Douglas v Douglas* (1871) L.R. 12 Eq. 617, 625.

[368] Adoption and Children Act 2002, s.67(1)(5)(6), applying from the date of the adoption as respects things done, or events occurring, on or after the adoption.

[369] s.54.

[370] SI 2010/985, Sch.1, which, inter alia, extends the Adoption and Children Act 2002, s.67 to children subject of a parental order.

6–097　　**Same-sex parents.** Rule 15 is based on a traditional understanding of parenthood whereby a child has a father and a mother. Technological advances and legal reforms now mean that a child can be recognised in law as being the legitimate child of parents of the same sex.[371] This takes the determination of the domicile of such children into unchartered waters, and creates a practical problem where the parents do not share a common domicile. In the case of a child the subject of a parental order, an objective method of choosing between the two parents would be for the child to take the domicile of the parent whose gametes were used to bring about the creation of the embryo.[372] In the absence of any biological link a determination will simply have to be made on the facts of the case. Regard may be paid to the recommendations of the Law Commissions outlined below, which if implemented would provide a framework for solving such cases.[373]

6–098　　**Reform.** The English and Scottish Law Commissions have recommended[374] new statutory rules as to the domicile of children which would replace those stated in Rule 15 and the Exception thereto. Under the proposed rules the domicile of a child (i.e. any person under 16, whether married or unmarried, and whether or not that person was a parent) would be determined as follows. The child would be domiciled in the country with which he was for the time being most closely connected. Where the child's parents were domiciled in the same country and the child had his home with either or both of them, it would be presumed, unless the contrary were shown, that the child was most closely connected with that country. Where the child's parents were not domiciled in the same country and he had his home with one of them, but not with the other, it would similarly be presumed that the child was most closely connected with the country in which the parent with whom he had his home was domiciled. No presumption would apply in cases in which the parents were domiciled in separate countries and the child had a home with both of them; nor in cases where the child had a home with neither parent. For the purposes of these rules, "parent" includes parents who are not married to one another; there would no longer be separate rules applying to legitimate, illegitimate and legitimated children.[375] No change is proposed in the case of adopted children, whose adoptive parents will be the "parents" to whom the rules will refer.

Illustrations

6–099　　1. D, a legitimate child whose father is domiciled in England, is sent, at the age of fourteen, to live with his uncle in France. D's father then acquires a domicile in Ireland. D thereupon gets

---

[371] Adoption and Children Act 2002, s.144(4); Human Fertilisation and Embryology Act 2008, ss.42, 43, 48(6), 54.

[372] Human Fertilisation and Embryology Act 2008, s.54(1)(b).

[373] *cf.* Family Law (Scotland) Act 2006, s.22.

[374] *The Law of Domicile* (Law Com. No.168), Pt IV.

[375] There would be no place for the power of election which seems to be enjoyed at common law by a parent in certain circumstances, i.e. under *Re Beaumont* [1893] 3 Ch. 490 (above, para.6–093).

an Irish domicile and cannot acquire a domicile of choice in France until he reaches the age of sixteen.[376]

2. D was born in 1950, the illegitimate son of A, a woman domiciled in France, and B, a man domiciled in Scotland. In 1955, A acquires a domicile of choice in England. In 1960 B marries A, thus legitimating D. In 1965, B acquires a domicile of choice in New Zealand. D is domiciled from 1950 to 1955 in France from 1955 to 1960 in England; from 1960 to 1965 in Scotland and from 1965 in New Zealand.

3. W and H1 are domiciled in Scotland; they have two legitimate children, D1 and D2. After H1's death, W marries H2; they acquire domiciles of choice in England. W takes D1 to reside with her and H2 in England, but leaves D2 to reside with her aunt in Scotland. D1 gets an English domicile, but D2 continues to be domiciled in Scotland.[377]

4. D is a child whose parents are dead and who is domiciled in Scotland. G, who is also domiciled in Scotland, is appointed D's guardian in Scotland. Subsequently, G acquires an English domicile of choice. *Semble*, D continues to be domiciled in Scotland whether or not he resides with G in England.

Exception—**The domicile of a legitimate or legitimated unmarried child**　　6E–100
under sixteen whose parents are living apart, or were living apart at the
death of the mother, is determined as follows:

(1) **if he has his home with his mother and has no home with his**
father, the domicile of the child is the same as, and changes with,
the domicile of his mother;

(2) **if the preceding clause has applied to him at any time and he has**
not since had a home with his father, the domicile of the child is the
same as, and changes with, the domicile of his mother;

(3) **if at the time of the death of his mother, his domicile was the same**
as that of his mother by virtue of clause (1) or (2), and he has not
since had a home with his father, the domicile of the child is the
domicile his mother last had before she died;

(4) **in any other case, the domicile of the child is the same as, and**
changes with, the domicile of his father.

COMMENT

This Exception states the effect of section 4 of the Domicile and Matrimonial　　6–101
Proceedings Act 1973, which regulates the domicile of a dependent child as
at any time after January 1, 1974, when his father and mother are alive but
living apart, or were living apart at the date of the death of the mother.[378] The
general object of the provision is to create a number of additional cases in
which the domicile of dependency of a child will be that of its mother;
previously existing rules of law to that effect[379] are expressly preserved.[380]

The Exception only applies if the parents are "living apart." That phrase is　　6–102
not defined in the Act, but it clearly connotes something more than the mere

---

[376] See *Spurway v Spurway* [1894] 1 I.R. 385.

[377] See *Re Beaumont* [1893] 3 Ch. 490.

[378] For comparable provisions along similar lines, see Domicile Act 1976 (New Zealand), s.6 and the uniform Domicile Acts of the Australian jurisdictions, s.8. For the proposed replacement of the English provisions, see above, para.6–098. This provision has been repealed in Scotland, Family Law (Scotland) Act 2006, Sch.3, para.1.

[379] e.g. those stated in clause (3) of Rule 15.

[380] Domicile and Matrimonial Proceedings Act 1973, s.4(4).

absence of one spouse from the matrimonial home for a short period. Parents who share a matrimonial home may have different domiciles;[381] if the temporary absence of a father for hospital treatment or on business meant that such parents were "living apart," the domicile of their child would be governed by the Exception and, unless the child were held to retain a home with the absent father, the child's domicile might change with undesirable frequency. It is submitted that parents should not be taken to be "living apart" despite one parent's temporary absence if they continue to belong to the same household.

6–103　　If the parents are living apart, the usual rule that the domicile of dependency of their child under sixteen will be the domicile of the father applies in many cases. It applies when the child's home is with his father, and when the child's last home with either parent was with his father. It also applies if, since the parents began to live apart, the child has had no home with either parent, his home being, for example, with grand-parents, foster-parents, or in a residential institution. But if at any time the child has a home with the mother and has no home with the father, the usual rule is displaced, and the child's domicile of dependency becomes that of the mother.[382] Once the child becomes dependent on the mother for the purposes of domicile, he remains so dependent until he acquires a home with his father.[383] This applies even after the death of the mother, her last domicile continuing to be the child's domicile of dependence.[384]

6–104　　Where the child's domicile follows that of the mother under these statutory provisions, there is no room for the exercise by her of any discretion as to what the child's domicile should be, such as exists at common law in the case of illegitimate and fatherless children.[385] The statutory provisions cease to apply on the death of the father, for the parents are no longer "living apart," and the child's domicile continues to depend on that of the mother by virtue of the common law rules; but it would seem inappropriate in such circumstances for the fact of the father's death to give rise to a discretionary power vested in the mother which she did not enjoy under the statutory rules.

6–105　　In determining whether a child has a home with a parent, it will be relevant to consider not only the amount of time they live together but also the state of the relationships between the child and his parents, matters such as where a young child's toys and possessions are usually kept, and, especially in the case of an older child, the child's own view of the matter.[386] The question is whether the child has a home with a particular person, and not whether he has a home in a particular place. It is possible for a child to have two homes, one with each parent,[387] or one with a parent and one with some other person. Circumstances are so variable that it is dangerous to seek to formulate detailed

---

[381] e.g. *IRC v Bullock* [1976] 1 W.L.R. 1178 (CA) where the matrimonial home was in England but the husband remained domiciled in his native country to which he planned to return if he survived his English wife.

[382] Domicile and Matrimonial Proceedings Act 1973, s.4(2)(a).

[383] *ibid.* s.4(2)(b).

[384] *ibid.* s.4(3).

[385] *Re Beaumont* [1893] 3 Ch. 490; see above, para.6–098.

[386] *cf. Re P (GE) (An Infant)* [1965] Ch. 568, 585 (CA), where a child's ordinary residence was defined in terms of his home.

[387] Domicile and Matrimonial Proceedings Act 1973, s.4(2)(a).

rules. For example, if a child lives most of the year with his mother, spending time with his father only during the school holidays, it may well be that he will be regarded as having his home with his mother. But a child at boarding school, spending the school holidays with one parent will probably be treated as having his home with that parent.[388] A newly-born child remaining for a short period in a maternity hospital will have a home, unless both parents have repudiated him. The existence and terms of any custody or residence order are not determinative, but may be relevant evidence. The same applies to a court order placing the child in the care of the local authority, which does not preclude the possibility of the child having a home with a parent, as where the child is returned home on trial by the authority.

ILLUSTRATIONS

1. In 1973, H, domiciled in Scotland, marries W, domiciled in England. They live together in Scotland and have a child C, born in 1974. In 1975 they separate and W returns to England, intending to remain permanently, and taking C with her. In 1980 W dies, and C goes to live in Scotland, with G, his paternal grandmother. C has had no home with H since the separation between H and W. C is domiciled in Scotland until 1975 and in England from 1975 until 1990, when he attains the age of sixteen and becomes capable of having an independent domicile.[389]   **6–106**

2. The circumstances are the same as in Illustration 1, except that G spends 1982 in Canada visiting another son, and during that period C has a home with H. C then becomes domiciled in Scotland, and retains H's domicile as his domicile of dependency until 1990.[390]

RULE 16—A person lacking mental capacity to make decisions as to his future permanent residence cannot acquire a domicile of choice and, subject to the Exception hereinafter mentioned, retains, while lacking that capacity, the domicile he had when last having that capacity.   **6R–107**

COMMENT

The acquisition and loss of a domicile of choice each require a decision by the *propositus*, the formation or abandonment of the intention of permanent or indefinite residence, the *animus manendi*.[391] It seems necessarily to follow that a person lacking the mental capacity to make the relevant decisions cannot acquire or lose a domicile of choice.   **6–108**

The Rule can be supported by reference to cases which use the language of lunacy, insanity, or unsoundness of mind.[392] Those terms and the associated procedures are no longer part of English law. The Mental Health Act 1983 makes provision for many kinds and degrees of mental disorder and for the   **6–109**

---

[388] See *Re P (GE) (An Infant)*, above; *A, Petitioners*, 1953 S.L.T. (Sh Ct) 45 (continuous care and possession of child for purposes of adoption; test held to be whether the child had his home with petitioners; such a home established despite child's absence for training except at weekends and holiday periods).

[389] Domicile and Matrimonial Proceedings Act 1973, s.4(2)(a), (3).

[390] *ibid.* s.4(3).

[391] See Rules 10 and 13.

[392] *Re Bariatinski* (1843) 13 L.J. Ch. 69, 71 (in argument); *Hepburn v Skirving* (1861) 9 W.R. 764; *Urquhart v Butterfield* (1887) 37 Ch.D. 357 (CA); *Crumpton's Judicial factor v Finch-Noyes*, 1918 S.C. 378; *Rifkin v Rifkin* [1936] W.L.D. 69; *Kertesz v Kertesz* [1954] V.L.R. 195; *cf. Bempde v Johnstone* (1796) 3 Ves. 198.

care and treatment of persons suffering from such disorder. Not all those who suffer from one of the recognised types of mental disorder will lack capacity for the purposes of the Rule. Capacity to take decisions is dealt with in the Mental Capacity Act 2005. Persons lack capacity for the purposes of the 2005 Act if they unable to take particular decisions because of an impairment of, or a disturbance in the functioning of, the mind or brain.[393] Although the language in the 2005 Act is much more sophisticated, the root idea is that found in one of the earliest cases on the domicile of a lunatic: he was "unable to exercise any will".[394]

6–110   Although the Mental Health Act 1983 made provision for dealing with the property and affairs of a mentally disordered person, and these provisions are further developed in the Mental Capacity Act 2005, there is no power to determine the domicile of such a person. Under the 2005 Act the Court of Protection is given power to take decisions on behalf of the person lacking capacity in respect of his property and affairs,[395] and the Act contains a partial list of the types of decision covered by this power.[396] A decision as to where a person is to live in the immediate future is within the scope of the power, but it is thought that a decision about permanent residence, such as is required for the *animus manendi*, is not.

6–111   Where the rule that a mentally disordered person cannot change his domicile applies, it is quite general in scope. Thus it does not seem that such a person's domicile will be changed because he is moved from one country to another by the person in charge of him, or under the direction of the appropriate administrative authority.[397]

6–112   For the purposes of an English rule of the conflict of laws, the question where a person is domiciled is determined according to English law.[398] Accordingly, the fact that a person domiciled in a foreign country has been declared legally insane under the law of that country will not determine, in an English court, the issue of his capacity to acquire a domicile of choice elsewhere.

6–113   **Reform.** The effect of the law as stated in the Rule is to fix the domicile of the mentally disordered person at a certain date; it cannot be changed even if, as may happen in a few cases, he acquires a permanent home in another country. The English and Scottish Law Commissions have recommended[399] new statutory rules as to the domicile of mentally disordered persons, referred to as "adults under disability", which would replace those stated in this Rule and the Exception hereto. Under the proposed rules, an adult lacking the capacity to form the intention necessary for acquiring a domicile would be domiciled in the country with which he was for the time being most closely connected. When that capacity was restored to him, he would retain the

---

[393] Mental Capacity Act 2005, ss.2, 3.
[394] *Urquhart v Butterfield* (1887) 37 Ch.D. 357, 382 (CA).
[395] Mental Capacity Act 2005, s.14.
[396] Mental Capacity Act 2005, s.16.
[397] e.g. under Pt VI of the Mental Health Act 1983.
[398] Rule 8, above.
[399] *The Law of Domicile* (Law Com. No.168), Pt VI.

domicile he had immediately before it was restored, but could of course then acquire a new domicile under the rules applying to adults generally.

ILLUSTRATIONS

1. D, who is domiciled in India, becomes insane and is sent to England. He retains his Indian domicile so long as he remains insane,[400] even although he resides in England as a lunatic for forty-eight years.[401]

6–114

2. D was born in 1859 with a domicile of origin in Barbados. His father died in 1870. Shortly afterwards his mother resumed her domicile of origin in Scotland, taking D with her. D continued to reside in Scotland till 1882, when he became insane and was placed in a Scottish institution. He died in 1916 without having recovered his sanity. From 1870 onwards D was domiciled in Scotland.[402]

3. The circumstances are the same as in Illustration 2, except that D is placed in an English institution from 1882 until his death. D dies domiciled in Scotland.

Exception—**The domicile of a person who never acquires, or who loses as a dependent child, the mental capacity to make decisions as to his future permanent residence is determined, so long as he lacks that capacity, as if he continued to be a dependent child.**

6E–115

COMMENT

The rules as to the domicile of dependent children exist because such children are deemed unable to make responsible and informed decisions as to their long-term future. The ability to make such decisions is acquired through the ordinary processes of development and education. The Exception deals with cases in which the want of capacity is due not to youth but to an impairment of, or a disturbance in the functioning of, the mind or brain.[403]

6–116

ILLUSTRATIONS

1. D is the legitimate child of H, who is domiciled in Portugal. D becomes insane at the age of fifteen and remains insane. When D is twenty-five years old, H acquires a domicile in England. D gets an English domicile.[404]

6–117

2. D, a legitimate minor whose domicile of origin is in New Zealand, becomes insane. After her father's death she is at the age of thirteen sent by her mother to Scotland and placed in an institution there. When D is aged twenty-nine (and still insane) her mother marries a man domiciled in England and so gets an English domicile. There is no evidence of any intention on the mother's part to change D's domicile. D continues to be domiciled in New Zealand.[405]

3. RESIDENCE

Residence is an essential element within domicile, but law-makers now favour connecting or jurisdictional factors which ensure greater priority is accorded

6–118

---

[400] *Hepburn v Skirving* (1861) 9 W.R. 764.

[401] *cf. Bempde v Johnstone* (1976) 3 Ves. 198; *cf. Re Mackenzie* (unreported), referred to in *Re Mackenzie* [1941] Ch. 69, 71, 74.

[402] *Crumpton's Judicial Factor v Finch-Noyes*, 1918 S.C. 378.

[403] See Mental Capacity Act 2005, ss.2, 3.

[404] *cf. Sharpe v Crispin* (1869) L.R. 1 P. & D. 611, especially at p.618.

[405] *Re G* [1966] N.Z.L.R. 1028.

to an individual's factual ties. Formulae include residence, ordinary residence, normal residence or even permanent residence. But it is habitual residence which is the preferred formula for conflict of laws problems.

6–119   **Habitual Residence.**[406] Within the English rules of the conflict of laws habitual residence is present in two separate forms. The traditional interpretation, which is satisfied by residence for settled purposes as part of the regular order of a person's life, applies wherever habitual residence is found in domestic legislation, whilst the European understanding, which looks to a person's permanent or habitual centre of interests, applies where the connecting factor is employed in European Union law. This leaves open the interpretation to be applied where, as in intra-European Union cases of child abduction, an international instrument[407] operates in conjunction with the Brussels IIa Regulation.[408] There has been a reluctance to consider the extension of the European interpretation to such cases,[409] but the integrated manner in which child abduction and jurisdiction in matters relating to parental responsibility are dealt with in the European Union means that distinct interpretations are simply not feasible.[410]

6–120   The two variants of habitual residence have matured in parallel over the course of the last thirty years, but detailed appreciation of European Union habitual residence by domestic courts has only followed the entry into force of the Brussels IIa Regulation. In both contexts the development of the connecting factor has been influenced by case law spanning diverse areas of law. In the case of traditional habitual residence, this has centred on family law matters, in particular the Child Abduction and Custody Act 1985, the Family Law Act 1986 and the Domicile and Matrimonial Proceedings Act 1973, but has also included areas outside the conflict of laws, including social security.[411] As regards European Union habitual residence, the spectrum is broader still, from social security,[412] to tax exemptions,[413] the rules applying to the European civil service,[414] and the framework provisions for the

---

[406] de Winter (1969) *Recueil des Cours* III, 357; Cavers (1972) 21 Am. Univ L. Rev 475; Clive (1997) Jur. Rev. 137; Beaumont and McEleavy, *The Hague Convention on International Child Abduction* (1999) Ch.7; Rogerson (2000) 49 I.C.L.Q. 49; Schuz (2001) 13 C.F.L.Q. 1; Schuz (2001) 11 J. Transnational L. & Policy 2; Goldstein (2005) 65 Revue du Barreau 219.

[407] 1980 Hague Convention on the Civil Aspects of International Child Abduction.

[408] Council Regulation (EC) 2201/2003 concerning jurisdiction and the recognition and enforcement of judgments in matrimonial matters and the matters of parental responsibility, Recital 17.

[409] *Re P-J (Children) (Abduction: Habitual Residence: Consent)* [2009] EWCA Civ 588, [2010] 1 W.L.R. 1237, at [22]. *cf. Re H-K (Children) (Habitual Residence)* [2011] EWCA Civ 1100, [2012] 1 F.L.R. 436 at [17].

[410] Case C–523/07 *Proceedings brought by A* [2009] E.C.R. I–2805 (Opinion of Kokott A.-G.) at [23].

[411] See e.g. SI 1987/1967.

[412] Council Regulation (EC) 1408/71 (social security).

[413] Council Directive 83/182/EEC (tax exemptions).

[414] Staff Regulations of Officials of the European Communities, May 1, 2004 (repatriation expenses; reimbursement of travel expenses on taking up an appointment: see Case T–63/91 *Benzler v Commission* [1992] E.C.R. II–2095).

European arrest warrant,[415] as well as conflict of laws rules.[416]

The two forms of habitual residence are now considered in turn.   **6–121**

RULE 17—(1) Subject to Rule 18, a person is in general habitually   **6R–122**
resident in the country in which he is resident for settled purposes as part
of the regular order of his life for the time being.

(2) A child is in general habitually resident in the country in which he
resides, when the persons who hold parental responsibility have fixed his
residence there for settled purposes as part of the regular order of his life
for the time being.

COMMENT

Introduction. Habitual residence is a concept which has long been asso-   **6–123**
ciated with the Hague Conference on Private International Law. It appears in
many Hague Conventions and therefore English statutes giving effect to them.
One of its first uses at the Hague Conference was in the context of the custody
of children,[417] largely because of the artificiality of the notion of domicile as
applied to young children.[418] No definition of habitual residence has ever been
included in a Hague Convention.[419] This is a matter of deliberate policy, the
aim being to leave the notion free from technical rules. Nevertheless, significant inconsistencies have developed in the interpretation of habitual residence as between different legal systems, particularly in the context of the
1980 Child Abduction Convention.[420]

In the United Kingdom courts have frequently held that the expression is   **6–124**
not to be treated as a term of art, but rather applied according to the ordinary

---

[415] Council Framework Decision of June 13, 2002 [2002] O.J. L190/1; Case C–66/08 *Kozlow-ski* [2008] E.C.R. I–6041.

[416] Brussels IIa Regulation (Council Regulation (EC) 2201/2003); Regulation 864/2007 of the European Parliament and the Council of July 11, 2007 on the Law Applicable to Non-Contractual Obligations (Rome II); Regulation 593/2008 of the European Parliament and the Council of June 17, 2008 on the Law Applicable to Contractual Obligations (Rome I); Council Regulation (EU) 1259/2010 of December 20, 2010 Implementing Enhanced Cooperation in the Area of the Law Applicable to Divorce and Legal Separation.

[417] Convention of June 12, 1902.

[418] See Cavers, above, at p.477; van Hoogstraten (1967) *Recueil des Cours,* III, 343, 359.

[419] Attempts at formulating a definition are regularly made, but have never been successful, for example at the 18th Diplomatic Session in October 1996, see Lagarde, *Explanatory Report on the Convention of 19 October 1996 on Jurisdiction, Applicable Law, Recognition, Enforcement and Co-operation in Respect of Parental Responsibility and Measures for the Protection of Children,* (1998), para.40.

[420] This is most notable in the United States where Federal Courts of Appeals have adopted contrasting interpretations in relation to habitual residence for the purposes of the 1980 Hague Convention. The 6th Circuit has advocated a child centred approach: *Friedrich v Friedrich,* 983 F.2d 1396 (6th Cir. 1993). The 3rd and 8th Circuits have held that reference must in addition paid to the parents' present shared intentions: *Feder v Evans-Feder,* 63 F.3d 217 (3d Cir. 1995); *Silverman v Silverman,* 338 F.3d 886 (8th Cir. 2003). Other Circuits have concentrated on parental intention, finding that there should ordinarily be a settled intention to abandon an existing habitual residence before a new one can be acquired: *Mozes v Mozes,* 239 F.3d 1067 (9th Cir. 2001); *Ruiz v Tenorio,* 392 F.3d 1247 (11th Cir. 2004); *Gitter v Gitter,* 396 F.3d 124 (2d Cir. 2005); *Koch v Koch,* 450 F.3d 703 (7th Cir. 2006).

and natural meaning of the two words it contains,[421] and that habitual residence is a question of fact to be decided by reference to the circumstances of each particular case.[422] These assertions of principle have not, however, deterred the courts from developing rules and guidance as to when habitual residence may or may not be established. In this process reliance has been placed on authorities interpreting "ordinary residence",[423] it being generally accepted that the two connecting factors are interchangeable.[424]

6–125   **Clause (1).** The English approach to the interpretation of habitual residence requires that a person has taken up residence in a country and that he can show a certain commitment to that place, in the form of a settled purpose. The extent of the factual connection and the level of commitment will vary depending on the circumstances of the case. The meaning of the connecting factor may depend on the statutory context in which it is employed.[425]

6–126   *Residence.* Much attention has been focused on the length of residence necessary to establish habituation. In *Re J (A Minor) (Abduction: Custody Rights)*[426] Lord Brandon stated, albeit *obiter*, that an appreciable period of time must be spent in the country in question before a person with a settled intention can acquire a habitual residence there. "Appreciable" in this context is not necessarily given a literal interpretation.[427] Indeed in the case which has been relied upon as a benchmark for the minimum level of residence necessary, it was held that four weeks could suffice where a family had relocated to Australia.[428] In *Nessa v Chief Adjudication Officer*[429] Lord Slynn suggested that in his use of "appreciable" Lord Brandon had meant no more than "residence in fact for a period which shows that the residence has become 'habitual' and, . . . will or is likely to continue to be habitual."[430] In a more recent case, involving a move between European Union Member States, it was

---

[421] *Re J (A Minor) (Abduction: Custody Rights)* [1990] 2 A.C. 562; *Dickson v Dickson* 1990 S.C.L.R. 692; *Findlay v Findlay (No.2)* 1995 S.L.T. 492.

[422] *Re J (A Minor) (Abduction: Custody Rights)* [1990] 2 A.C. 562; *Re M (Minors) (Residence Order: Jurisdiction)* [1993] 1 F.L.R. 495.

[423] See below para.6–160.

[424] *Mark v Mark* [2005] UKHL 42, [2006] 1 A.C. 98 at [33]. *cf. Nessa v Chief Adjudication Officer* [1999] 1 W.L.R. 1937, 1941 (HL), where Lord Slynn stated he was not satisfied the two were always synonymous, rather "each may take a shade of meaning from the context and the object and purpose of the legislation". See *Re P-J (Children) (Abduction: Habitual Residence: Consent)* [2009] EWCA Civ 588, [2010] 1 W.L.R. 1237, at [26].

[425] *Mark v Mark* [2005] UKHL 42, [2006] 1 A.C. 98, at [37].

[426] *sub nom. C v S (A Minor) (Abduction)* [1990] 2 A.C. 562, 578, 579.

[427] *Nessa v Chief Adjudication Officer* [1998] 2 All E.R. 728, 737 (CA).

[428] *Re F (A Minor) (Child Abduction)* [1992] 1 F.L.R. 548 (at the time of the removal of the child the family had actually been in Australia for nearly three months), on which see Lord Slynn in *Nessa v Chief Adjudication Officer* [1999] 1 W.L.R. 1937, 1943 (HL). See also *C v C* [1989] N.I. 252 (45 days in Australia sufficed for a change in habitual residence); *Re A (Abduction: Habitual Residence)* [2007] EWHC 779 (Fam.), [2007] 2 F.L.R. 129 (seven or eight days insufficient).

[429] [1999] 1 W.L.R. 1937 (HL).

[430] *ibid.* p.1942.

found that a period of seven-eight weeks sufficed to establish a habitual residence, and this despite the maintenance of strong links with the former home State and the likely duration of the move being for between three and nine months.[431]

In *Nessa* the issue before the House of Lords was whether a habitual   **6–127** residence could be acquired immediately upon arrival in a country. This was, as a "matter of ordinary language", rejected because the concept was held to imply that actual residence must have endured for a period of time.[432] Lord Slynn nevertheless identified two situations in which a different approach might be required. The first was where for the purpose of making legislation effective a person should not be left without a habitual residence;[433] the second was where a person was returning to resume a former habitual residence.[434]

The factual context in which residence begins and develops is of central   **6–128** importance in the determination of when, if at all, it can be considered to be habitual. In the words of Lord Slynn: "It may be longer where there are doubts. It may be short . . . ."[435] Clear trends are difficult to identify, even as between cases involving similar factual situations. In sabbatical or work placement cases persuasive arguments can be made both that the stay is a temporary absence, with the original habitual residence retained throughout, or, that the original habitual residence is replaced by one in the new State. In *Re S (Minors) (Abduction: Wrongful Retention)*[436] the members of an Israeli family were held to have retained their original habitual residence eight months into a one year stay at a British university. This outcome was subsequently questioned,[437] but a similar result was later achieved in the Court of Appeal,[438] where a mother had taken her children to Wales for a year to improve their English and whilst their home in Spain was being renovated.[439] Conversely it has been found that a habitual residence may change where a

---

[431] *Re S (A Child) (Habitual Residence)* [2009] EWCA Civ 1021, [2010] 1 F.L.R. 1146.

[432] *Nessa v Chief Adjudication Officer* [1999] 1 W.L.R. 1937, 1942 (HL).

[433] *ibid.* p.1942. For example, in the Hague Child Abduction Convention case *Re F (A Minor) (Child Abduction)* [1992] 1 F.L.R. 548, Butler-Sloss L.J. accepted the argument that courts "should not strain to find a lack of habitual residence where, on a broad canvas, the child has settled in a particular country", otherwise the instrument would not apply.

[434] *Nessa v Chief Adjudication Officer* [1999] 1 W.L.R. 1937, 1943 (HL).

[435] *ibid.* p.1943.

[436] [1994] Fam. 70. See also *Rellis v Hart*, 1993 S.L.T. 738.

[437] *D v S (Abduction: Acquiescence)* [2008] EWHC 363 (Fam.), [2008] 2 F.L.R. 293, at [179].

[438] *Re P-J (Children) (Abduction: Habitual Residence: Consent)* [2009] EWCA Civ 588, [2010] 1 W.L.R. 1237. See also *A v P (Habitual Residence)* [2011] EWHC (Fam.) 1530, [2012] 1 F.L.R. 125.

[439] The year in Wales was classified by Ward L.J. as being "extraordinary" at [34]. In a leading US authority an identical result was achieved but by introducing the principle of abandonment— the parents had not jointly agreed that the children's Israeli habitual residence be abandoned during a one-year sabbatical in California: *Mozes v Mozes*, 239 F.3d 1067 (9th Cir. 2001). Other examples of retention during a long absence include: *Re H (Abduction: Habitual Residence: Consent)* [2000] 2 F.L.R. 294 (Swedish habitual residence retained whilst 12 month art course followed in England and Spain) and *C v FC (Brussels II: Free-Standing Application for Parental Responsibility)* [2004] 1 F.L.R. 317 (English habitual residence retained during two year stay in Hong Kong and subsequently nine months in Portugal).

one year sabbatical is undertaken,[440] or even where a stay may last for only six months.[441]

6–129   In certain instances a move may neither be a permanent relocation nor time limited, but a more fluid, open-ended arrangement. In circumstances where residence in a country becomes extended and connections with the former State of residence weaken, it may be difficult to identify the precise moment of loss and acquisition.[442] Subjective considerations may equally influence the character of a move. Where residence in a State is motivated by the desire to bring about a reconciliation with an estranged spouse or partner this may be a relevant factor in determining when the residence can be characterised as habitual; in such circumstances 10 weeks has been found to insufficient,[443] but where a move endured for six months a change of habitual residence did result.[444] In cases where a family has relocated abroad one parent may seek to argue against the acquisition of a new habitual residence on the basis that he was a reluctant participant or that the move was temporary or for exploratory purposes. Such arguments are only likely to prevail where the stay has been short.[445]

6–130   *Settled Purpose.* It has long been established that when assessing whether residence is "habitual" or indeed "ordinary" regard is to be paid to qualitative factors indicating connection and not simply to the length of time which has been spent in the country in question.[446] Lord Brandon in *Re J* referred to a person having a "settled intention".[447] He did not qualify this reference, but, in explaining how an existing habitual residence might be lost on departure,

---

[440] *Re S (A Minor) (Abduction)* [1991] 2 F.L.R. 1; *Re M (Minors) (Residence Order: Jurisdiction)* [1993] 1 F.L.R. 495; *Moran v Moran*, 1997 S.L.T. 541.

[441] *Re R (Abduction: Habitual Residence)* [2003] EWHC (Fam.) 1968, [2004] 1 F.L.R. 216; *Cameron v Cameron*, 1996 S.C. 17. See also *Re B (Minors) (Abduction) (No.2)* [1993] 1 F.L.R. 993. *cf. A v P (Habitual Residence)* [2011] EWHC (Fam.) 1530, [2012] 1 F.L.R. 125. Stays for shorter periods of time have generally not been accepted as leading to a change in habitual residence: *Findlay v Findlay (No.2)*, 1995 S.L.T. 492 (four months). An exception is found in an unreported decision, one which is frequently cited in the United States: *Re Bates (Minor)*, February 23, 1989, transcript, Family Division (three months). It is clear that a vacation will not lead to a change in habitual residence: *Re A (Abduction: Habitual Residence)* [1998] 1 F.L.R. 497. This is so even if the vacation is extended: *Re N (Child Abduction: Habitual Residence)* [1993] 2 F.L.R. 124.

[442] *Re A (Removal outside Jurisdiction: Habitual Residence)* [2011] EWCA Civ 265, [2011] 1 F.L.R. 2025 (the transfer in habitual residence from England to Cameroon was deemed to have occurred over an 18 month period).

[443] *Re B (A Minor) (Child Abduction: Habitual Residence)* [1994] 2 F.L.R. 915. See also *DW v Director-General, Department of Child Safety* [2006] Fam CA 93 (11 weeks insufficient).

[444] *Re B (Minors) (Abduction) (No.2)* [1993] 1 F.L.R. 993.

[445] *Re N (Abduction: Habitual Residence)* [2000] 2 F.L.R. 899 (three months—even though a business and property had been purchased); *cf. Re B (Minors) (Abduction) (No.2)* [1993] 1 F.L.R. 993 (six month trial was sufficient to establish a habitual residence in Germany). Where a person simply has a change of heart about a relocation then this will most likely have to occur very quickly indeed to prevent the finding of an acquisition of a new habitual residence: *Re A (Abduction: Habitual Residence)* [2007] EWHC 779 (Fam.), [2007] 2 F.L.R. 129 (whilst the existing English habitual residence had been lost, eight days was not sufficient to acquire a new one in Washington State).

[446] *Inland Revenue Commissioners v Lysaght* [1928] A.C. 234; *R. v Barnet LBC, Ex p. Shah* [1983] 2 A.C. 309.

[447] *Re J (A Minor) (Abduction: Custody Rights)* [1990] 2 A.C. 562, 579.

he referred to a settled intention to take up "long term residence" in another State.[448] This interpretation, which would promote stability and prevent frequent changes of habitual residence, has received some judicial support.[449] But a clear preference[450] has emerged for the explanation of Lord Scarman in *Ex p. Shah*, in which reference is not made to "long term residence" but simply to residence having "a degree of settled purpose". This allows a very significant degree of flexibility, for there may be one purpose or there may be several, it may be specific or general.[451] The purpose does not require there to be indefinite residence, and it has been held that even to ask whether a family has settled in the sense of "putting down substantial roots" is a misdirection, for this would be to confuse ordinary or habitual residence with domicile.[452] Rather a settled purpose may be effected within a limited period of time if it is part of the regular order of the person's life for the time being. The underlying requirement is that the residence "has a sufficient degree of continuity to be properly described as settled".[453]

"Settled purpose" has been given its natural and ordinary meaning.[454] The **6–131** Court of Appeal has accepted that a habitual residence may be acquired despite the fact the purpose of the move was intended to be fulfilled within a comparatively short duration or indeed that the move was only on a trial basis.[455] This has led in certain instances to habitual residence being construed in a very flexible manner, with even short-term stays abroad capable of resulting in a change of habitual residence.[456]

Factors indicative of a settled purpose or intention to live in a place have **6–132** been taken to include: the sale of a home prior to departure and the purchase of a property in the jurisdiction of destination;[457] the renting of property in

---

[448] *ibid.* p.578.

[449] *A v A (Child Abduction) (Habitual Residence)* [1993] 2 F.L.R. 225; *Re VP (Loss of Child's Habitual Residence)* [2001] 1 F.C.R. 712; *Secretary of State for Work and Pensions v Bhakta* [2006] EWCA Civ 65.

[450] *Al Habtoor v Fotheringham* [2001] EWCA Civ 186, [2001] 1 F.L.R. 951; *LK v Director-General, Dept of Community Services* [2009] HCA 9, (2009) 253 A.L.R. 202. In *Re P-J (Children) (Abduction: Habitual Residence: Consent)* [2009] EWCA Civ 588, [2010] 1 W.L.R. 1237, Ward L.J. at [32] said that *Ex p. Shah* "tells judges nearly all they need to know", whilst it was held by the House of Lords to be the principal authority on habitual residence: *Mark v Mark* [2005] UKHL 42, [2006] 1 A.C. 98, [27].

[451] [1983] 2 A.C. 309, 344. The examples cited by Lord Scarman were: education, business or profession, employment, health, family, or merely love of the place.

[452] *Al Habtoor v Fotheringham* [2001] EWCA Civ 186, [2001] 1 F.L.R. 951, at [38]; *Re P-J (Children) (Abduction: Habitual Residence: Consent)* [2009] EWCA Civ 588, [2010] 1 W.L.R. 1237.

[453] [1983] 2 A.C. 309 at 343.

[454] Insufficient regard has been paid to the context in which Lord Scarman's assessment was delivered, which was whether overseas students who had been in the United Kingdom for three years had acquired an ordinary residence. The respondent local authorities had unsuccessfully argued against such a finding on the basis that the appellants did not have their "real home" in the country.

[455] *Al Habtoor v Fotheringham* [2001] EWCA Civ 186, [2001] 1 F.L.R. 951, at [37].

[456] *Re S (A Child) (Habitual Residence)* [2009] EWCA Civ 1021, [2010] 1 F.L.R. 1146; *Re R (Abduction: Habitual Residence)* [2003] EWHC (Fam.) 1968, [2004] 1 F.L.R. 216; *Cameron v Cameron*, 1996 S.C. 17. See *Re B (Minors) (Abduction) (No.2)* [1993] 1 F.L.R. 993.

[457] e.g. *Re A (Abduction: Consent: Habitual Residence)* [2005] EWHC 2998 (Fam.), [2006] 2 F.L.R. 1. This is not, however, always determinative: *Re N (Abduction: Habitual Residence)* [2000] 2 F.L.R. 899.

that place;[458] the shipping of possessions;[459] or indeed employment.[460] Conversely, factors which might indicate the absence of commitment and settled intention have been taken to include: bringing of divorce proceedings in the former State of residence;[461] retention of a property in that State;[462] as well as failure to organise schooling for dependent children,[463] or to follow up on a school application upon arrival in the destination country.[464]

6–133   Lord Scarman further specified in *Ex p. Shah* that residence must be "voluntarily adopted",[465] a position repeated in *Nessa*.[466] Given the factual nature of habitual residence, it must be questioned whether this can be an absolute rule. Elsewhere it has been accepted that a habitual residence may in certain circumstances be acquired even where residence is involuntary.[467] An analogy may equally be made with child abduction cases, for it has been conceded in case law,[468] and now recognised in the Brussels IIa Regulation,[469] that a wrongfully removed or retained child may eventually become habitually resident in the State of refuge. Occasional attempts have been made to use the voluntariness criterion to challenge the argument that there has been a change in habitual residence. A soldier on a standard military posting did not succeed with such an attempt for he was deemed to have made a voluntary election by virtue of his enlistment.[470] A victim of domestic violence may have been bullied into agreeing to a move, but during nine months in Italy she had acquired a habitual residence there.[471] However, a spouse whose passport was retained by her husband and who was left without funds to return home was held not to be in Bangladesh voluntarily and therefore did not acquire a habitual residence there after 18 months.[472]

6–134   Lord Scarman also held in *Ex p. Shah* that as a point of principle it should not be possible to place reliance on residence which was unlawful.[473] But in

---

[458] *D v D (Custody: Jurisdiction)* [1996] 1 F.L.R. 574.

[459] *Re F (A Minor) (Child Abduction)* [1992] 1 F.L.R. 548; *A v A (Child Abduction)* [1993] 2 F.L.R. 225.

[460] *V v B (A Minor) (Abduction)* [1991] 1 F.L.R. 266; *Re R (Abduction: Habitual Residence)* [2003] EWHC (Fam.) 1968, [2004] 1 F.L.R. 216, but again this is not always determinative: *Re N (Abduction: Habitual Residence)* [2000] 2 F.L.R. 899.

[461] *A v P (Habitual Residence)* [2011] EWHC (Fam.) 1530, [2012] 1 F.L.R. 125.

[462] *Re H (Abduction: Habitual Residence: Consent)* [2000] 2 F.L.R. 294, though this is not always determinative: *Re S (A Child) (Habitual Residence)* [2009] EWCA Civ 1021, [2010] 1 F.L.R. 1146.

[463] *Re N (Abduction: Habitual Residence)* [2000] 2 F.L.R. 899.

[464] *E v E* [2007] EWHC 276 (Fam.), [2007] 1 F.L.R. 1977.

[465] *R. v Barnet LBC, Ex p. Shah* [1983] 2 A.C. 309 at 344.

[466] *Nessa v Chief Adjudication Officer* [1999] 1 W.L.R. 1937.

[467] *Cameron v Cameron*, 1996 S.C. 17.

[468] *Re D (A Child) (Abduction: Foreign Custody Rights)* [2006] UKHL 51, [2007] 1 A.C. 619; *Re B (Abduction: Children's Objections)* [1998] 1 F.L.R. 667 and *Re C (A Child) (Residence and Contact)* [2005] EWHC 2205 (Fam.), [2006] 2 F.L.R. 277.

[469] Art.10.

[470] *Re A (Minors) (Abduction: Habitual Residence)* [1996] 1 W.L.R. 25. It was suggested that an exception might be made where a soldier is posted to a country on active service.

[471] *DT v LBT (Abduction: Domestic Abuse)* [2010] EWHC 3177 (Fam.), [2011] 1 F.L.R. 1215.

[472] *B v H (Habitual Residence: Wardship)* [2002] 1 F.L.R. 388.

[473] *R. v Barnet LBC, Ex p. Shah* [1983] 2 A.C. 309, 344. See also *Puttick v Attorney General* [1980] Fam. 1 and *Cannon v Cannon* [2004] EWCA Civ 1330, [2005] 1 F.L.R. 169 at [55].

Mark v Mark[474] the House of Lords ruled that as a matter of statutory interpretation there was no reason to imply the word "lawfully" into the residence requirement of s.5(2) of the Domicile and Matrimonial Proceedings Act 1973. In divorce jurisdiction the legality of residence can only go to the issue of whether the requisite factual connection has been achieved.[475]

Loss. Loss and acquisition are distinct elements in the assessment of   **6–135** habitual residence in English law. Whilst loss of an existing habitual residence may facilitate subsequent acquisition of a new connection, it is not a prerequisite and there is no principle of abandonment.[476] Ascertainment of whether a habitual residence has been lost will in certain instances be an issue in its own right, for it may determine whether jurisdiction is retained by the English courts,[477] or whether a statute or international instrument is applicable.[478] In contrast to acquisition, loss can be immediate. In the words of Lord Brandon: "A person may cease to be habitually resident in country A in a single day if he or she leaves it with a settled intention not to return to it but to take up long-term residence in country B instead."[479] Moves abroad of lesser duration, or where there is an element of conditionality, can also lead to the immediate loss of an existing habitual residence.[480] Otherwise loss, if it occurs, will be a more gradual process and therefore the precise moment of its occurrence can be difficult to identify.[481]

Absence of Habitual Residence. It is accepted that a person may have no   **6–136** habitual residence. This a direct consequence of Lord Brandon's reasoning in *Re J* that an existing habitual residence may be lost in a day, but an appreciable period of time will be required before a new habitual residence can be acquired.[482] It is also in accordance with the factual nature of the connecting factor. However, the fact that a person may be without a habitual residence

---

[474] [2005] UKHL 42, [2006] 1 A.C. 98. See also *M v M-T* [2005] EWHC 79 (Fam.).

[475] Baroness Hale did acknowledge, at [36], that legality of residence could be a relevant consideration in certain public law matters, notably as regards benefit entitlement or in respect of issues of immigration status: e.g. *Re Abdul Manan* [1971] 1 W.L.R. 859; *R. v Secretary of State for Health* [2009] EWCA Civ 225, [2010] 1 W.L.R. 279 (non-acquisition of ordinary residence by a failed asylum seeker). *cf. Hayward v Hayward* [1995] 12 F.R.N.Z. 498 (unlawful residence lasting 26 months did not prevent a family acquiring a habitual residence in California).

[476] *Re R (Abduction: Habitual Residence)* [2003] EWHC 1968, [2004] 1 F.L.R. 216; *M v M-T* [2005] EWHC 79 (Fam.). See also *SK v KP* [2005] 3 N.Z.L.R. 590; *AS v CS* [2010] 1 I.R. 370. Abandonment has been upheld in certain Federal Circuits in the United States in the interpretation of habitual residence for the purposes of the 1980 Hague Child Abduction Convention: *Mozes v Mozes*, 239 F.3d 1067 (9th Cir. 2001); *Ruiz v Tenorio*, 392 F.3d 1247, 1253 (11th Cir. 2004).

[477] *Al Habtoor v Fotheringham* [2001] EWCA Civ 186, [2001] 1 F.L.R. 951.

[478] *Re J (A Minor) (Abduction: Custody Rights* [1990] 2 A.C. 562.

[479] *ibid.* p.578. This will be the case even if the individual concerned has a change of heart in the immediate aftermath of the move: *Re A (Abduction: Habitual Residence)* [2007] EWHC 779 (Fam.), [2007] 2 F.L.R. 129 (after eight days).

[480] *Al Habtoor v Fotheringham* [2001] EWCA Civ 186, [2001] 1 F.L.R. 951; *Moran v Moran*, 1997 S.L.T. 541.

[481] *Re A (Removal outside Jurisdiction: Habitual Residence)* [2011] EWCA Civ 265, [2011] 1 F.L.R. 2025.

[482] *Re J (A Minor) (Abduction: Custody Rights)*, [1990] 2 A.C. 562 at 578, 579. See *Re M (Minors) (Residence Order: Jurisdiction)* [1993] 1 F.L.R. 495; *Al Habtoor v Fotheringham* [2001] EWCA Civ 186, [2001] 1 F.L.R. 951; *W and B v H (Child Abduction: Surrogacy)* [2002] 1 F.L.R. 1008; *Re A (Abduction: Habitual Residence)* [2007] EWHC 779 (Fam.), [2007] 2 F.L.R. 129.

may mean that there will be no connecting factor to the applicable law in a situation involving a foreign element.[483] In the context of child abduction, it has on occasion been stressed that such an outcome should, if possible, be avoided.[484]

6–137   **Dual Habitual Residences.** Where a person's life is divided between two countries the designation of one place as the habitual residence is potentially artificial.[485] However, the existence of two habitual residences may cause difficulties in the application of conflict of laws rules, particularly those dealing with applicable law. The Court of Appeal has nevertheless accepted, for the purposes of divorce jurisdiction, that a person can have simultaneous habitual residences in two States.[486] The practical significance of this conclusion has, however, been much reduced following the entry into force of the Brussels IIa Regulation, for several Family Division decisions have confirmed that the Regulation does not allow room for duality.[487]

6–138   **Clause (2).** The determination of the habitual residence of children has presented many challenges to the courts, in particular the difficulty of balancing the factual nature of the connecting factor with respect for parental rights.[488] It is accepted that reference must be made to the intention of the parents, or those persons who hold parental responsibility,[489] for they have the right to fix the child's residence.[490] Where residence is taken up in a country

---

[483] *Nessa v Chief Adjudication Officer* [1999] 1 W.L.R. 1937, 1942, 1943.

[484] In *Re F (A Minor) (Child Abduction)* [1992] 1 F.L.R. 548 at 555–556, Butler-Sloss L.J. said that courts " . . . should not strain to find a lack of habitual residence where, on a broad canvas, the child has settled in a particular country." Whilst in *Nessa v Chief Adjudication Officer* [1998] 2 All E.R. 728, at 734 Thorpe L.J. accepted that to ensure the efficiency of the 1980 Convention there might be some: " . . . tendency to find habitual residence established and consequently to lean against the vacuum in transition between the termination of one habitual residence and the acquisition of another." See also *AS v CS* [2010] 1 I.R. 370.

[485] Clive, Jur. Rev., at 144; Cavers, at 483.

[486] *Ikimi v Ikimi* [2001] EWCA Civ 873, [2002] Fam. 72, (CA); see also *Armstrong v Armstrong* [2003] EWHC 777 (Fam.), [2003] 2 F.L.R. 375. It has also been accepted that for tax purposes an individual could have more than one ordinary residence: *Cooper (Surveyor of Taxes) v Cadwallader* [1904] 5 T.C. 101; *Re Norris (Ex p. Reynolds)* (1888) 4 T.L.R. 452; *Pittar v Richardson* (1917) 87 L.J.K.B. 59.

[487] *Marinos v Marinos* [2007] EWHC 2047 (Fam.), [2007] 2 F.L.R. 1018. See also *Re A; HA v MB (Brussels II Revised: Article 11(7) Application)* [2007] EWHC 2016 (Fam.), [2008] 1 F.L.R. 289, at [98]. A person having dual EU nationalities has not though undermined the operation of the divorce jurisdiction rules in the Brussels IIa Regulation: Case C–168/08 *Hadadi v Hadadi* [2009] E.C.R. I–6871.

[488] Different approaches have been advanced in English-speaking jurisdictions as to the most appropriate manner in which the habitual residence of a child should be ascertained. These have been classified as the parental rights model, the dependency model and the child centred model: Schuz (2001) 13 C.F.L.Q. 1; *Punter v Secretary for Justice* [2007] 1 N.Z.F.L.R. 40.

[489] Where children are in care and the relevant local authority has acquired parental responsibility, then regard must be paid to the plans of that body in determining where the children are habitually resident; *Greenwich London BC v S* [2007] EWHC 820 (Fam.), [2007] 2 F.L.R. 154. See *Re JS (Private International Adoption)* [2000] 2 F.L.R. 638. Where the determination of habitual residence concerns an older child his views may be relevant: *AS v CS* [2010] 1 I.R. 370.

[490] *Re M (Minors) (Residence Order: Jurisdiction)* [1993] 1 F.L.R. 495. There has been a reluctance to involve the actual child in the determination process: *Nyachowe v Fielder* [2007] EWCA Civ 1129 (intentions of 12 year old girl did not impact on the determination of where she was habitually resident).

consideration must be given to whether the parents share a settled purpose in respect of the stay.[491] Where a shared settled purpose or common intention is found to exist, then parents and child will acquire a habitual residence once a sufficient period of time is deemed to have elapsed.

In contested cases the parents will invariably advance divergent views on the nature of the move in question. In *Re F (A Minor) (Child Abduction)*[492] the family's trip to Australia was for the father an extended vacation, whilst for the mother it was emigration and the start of new life. The Court of Appeal found that the evidence, in particular the shipping of nineteen packing cases, favoured the mother's case and held that after the passage of nearly three months a habitual residence had been acquired by the child concerned, although Butler-Sloss L.J. added that even a month's residence would have sufficed.   **6–139**

A shared purpose which is lost prior to departure will not suffice,[493] nor will one which fails to crystallise because of reservations held by one of the parents.[494] However, an argument against the acquisition of a new habitual residence which is constructed around one parent's doubts or reluctance about a move, even if made out, is only likely to succeed where the period of time spent in the new country of residence is limited, for once time passes the reluctant participant may be deemed to have endorsed or acquiesced in the move and the factual realities of the child's situation will prevail.[495] Similarly, a shared intention as regards a time limited move, with subsequent return to the State of origin, will not prevent the acquisition of a habitual residence in the destination State should sufficient time be spent there.[496] The sending of a child abroad for the purposes of education is, however, treated as a special case and will not lead to a change in habitual residence.[497]   **6–140**

Where parents have a shared intention to leave their current home State and pursue a settled purpose elsewhere then they and their children will lose their existing habitual residence on departure.[498] Such an outcome will not be altered by one parent having a change of heart very shortly thereafter.[499] The act of moving is central to the process of loss. And so where a child is sent abroad by his parents to be raised by grandparents and resides there for 17   **6–141**

---

[491] *Re G (Abduction: Withdrawal of Proceedings, Acquiescence, Habitual Residence)* [2007] EWHC 2807 (Fam.), [2008] 2 F.L.R. 351.

[492] [1992] 1 F.L.R. 548.

[493] *E v E* [2007] EWHC 276 (Fam.), [2007] 1 F.L.R. 1977 at [42].

[494] *Re N (Abduction: Habitual Residence)* [2000] 2 F.L.R. 899.

[495] *Re A (Wardship: Habitual Residence)* [2006] EWHC 3338 (Fam.), [2007] 1 F.L.R. 1589; *Re T* [2010] EWHC 3177 (Fam.); *Re A (Removal outside Jurisdiction: Habitual Residence)* [2011] EWCA Civ 265, [2011] 1 F.L.R. 2025.

[496] *Re S (A Minor) (Abduction)* [1991] 2 F.L.R. 1; *Re Z (Abduction)* [2008] EWHC (Fam.) 3473, [2009] 2 F.L.R. 298 at [14]; *Watson v Jamieson*, 1998 S.L.T. 180; *Punter v Secretary for Justice* [2007] 1 N.Z.F.L.R. 40. The High Court has adopted a very generous approach where the placement of children overseas is concerned: *Greenwich London BC v S* [2007] EWHC 820 (Fam.), [2007] 2 F.L.R. 154, at [31] (existing habitual residence retained for a period of up to two years, unless there was compelling evidence to the contrary). See also *Re JS (Private International Adoption)* [2000] 2 F.L.R. 638.

[497] *Re P (G.E.) (An Infant)* [1965] Ch 568 (ordinary residence); *P v P* [2006] EWHC 2410 (Fam.), [2007] 2 F.L.R. 439; *B v D (Abduction: Inherent Jurisdiction)* [2008] EWHC 1246 (Fam.), [2009] 1 F.L.R. 1015.

[498] *Al Habtoor v Fotheringham* [2001] EWCA Civ 186, [2001] 1 F.L.R. 951.

[499] *Re A (Abduction: Habitual Residence)* [2007] EWHC 779 (Fam.), [2007] 2 F.L.R. 129.

months becoming habitually resident there, then that habitual residence cannot be lost and the former habitual residence re-acquired if the child's physical residence does not change.[500]

6–142   Where a child has a single parent, or only one parent is in possession of parental responsibility, that parent will in effect control the child's habitual residence, although there is no formal doctrine of dependency and factual circumstances must be respected.[501] And so when a single parent sent her children to stay with the paternal grandparents for a one year period the children were held to have acquired a habitual resident in the grandparents' jurisdiction,[502] but when the parent decided to terminate the arrangement during a period of contact in the country of origin, the children were held to have lost their newly acquired habitual residence forthwith.[503] Where a child is taken from England by a mother with sole parental responsibility in circumstances which might indicate a definitive move, he will nevertheless not lose his English habitual residence immediately upon departure if the mother is not found to have lost her habitual residence at that time.[504]

6–143   *Newborn Children.* The situation of newborn children has proved problematic. Where parents share the same habitual residence at the moment of birth and the child is born in that place it is axiomatic that the child will also be habitually resident there. Where the child is not born in the parent's State of habitual residence the situation is less clear. It has been suggested that the child's habitual residence should simply follow that of the parents,[505] but this risks turning the connecting factor away from its factual origins.[506] In the case of twins born to a surrogate mother in England when the commissioning parents were habitually resident in California, the children were found to be without a habitual residence.[507] Where the parents do not share a common

---

[500] *Re M (Abduction: Habitual Residence)* [1996] 1 F.L.R. 887.

[501] *Re M (Abduction: Habitual Residence)* [1996] 1 F.L.R. 887; *Re M (Minors) (Residence Order: Jurisdiction)* [1993] 1 F.L.R. 495. See also *H v H (Jurisdiction to Grant Wardship)* [2011] EWCA Civ 796, [2012] 1 F.L.R. 23. *cf. B v H (Habitual Residence: Wardship)* [2002] 1 F.L.R. 388.

[502] *cf. Re P-J (Children) (Abduction: Habitual Residence: Consent)* [2009] EWCA Civ 588, [2010] 1 W.L.R. 1237.

[503] *Re M (Minors) (Residence Order: Jurisdiction)* [1993] 1 F.L.R. 495. In the absence of movement it has been very much doubted whether a parent's change of mind can alter a child's existing habitual residence: *Re M (Abduction: Habitual Residence)* [1996] 1 F.L.R. 887.

[504] *Mercredi v Chaffe* [2011] EWCA Civ 272, [2011] 2 F.L.R. 515; *Re B-M (Wardship: Jurisdiction)* [1993] 1 F.L.R. 979; *F v S (Wardship: Jurisdiction)* [1993] 2 F.L.R. 686. See also *Re S (A Child) (Wardship: Peremptory Return)* [2010] EWCA Civ 465, [2010] 2 F.L.R. 1960 at [13], *per* Wall L.J. In *Re S (A Minor) (Custody: Habitual Residence)* [1998] A.C. 750 the removal of the child occurred after the death of the child's mother, who alone held parental responsibility. In these cases the preservation of jurisdiction in the face of a precipitous removal was undoubtedly an underlying factor. For the purposes of European Union law, however, it has been said that the motivation of single parent in leaving a Member State should not be treated as a relevant consideration in the determination of the child's habitual residence: Case C–497/10 PPU *Mercredi v Chaffe* [2012] Fam. 22, opinion of Cruz Villalón A.-G., at [90]–[91]. The Advocate-General's opinion is at [2011] I.L.Pr. 405.

[505] *B v H (Habitual Residence: Wardship)* [2002] 1 F.L.R. 388.

[506] *H v H (Jurisdiction to Grant Wardship)*, above.

[507] *W and B v H (Child Abduction: Surrogacy)* [2002] 1 F.L.R. 1008; see also *Re F (Abduction: Unborn Child)* [2006] EWHC 2199 (Fam.), [2007] 1 F.L.R. 627. *cf. Re KJB and LRB [Adoption]* [2010] N.Z.F.L.R. 97.

habitual residence at the moment of birth, Sir Mark Potter P. suggested that there could be no hard and fast rule.[508] On the facts of that case the child took the mother's habitual residence, which was also the country of birth. In *B v H (Habitual Residence: Wardship)*[509] the child was also deemed to take and retain the mother's English habitual residence, but he was born in Bangladesh and stayed there for almost two years. In that case, the mother's presence in Bangladesh was coerced, but the outcome does not rest easily with the factual nature of habitual residence.

Wrongful Removal/Retention. It has long been established that a parent   **6–144**
cannot change his child's habitual residence without the consent, express or tacit, of the other parent or a court order.[510] This is a rule which, in seeking to deprive abductors of any possible jurisdictional advantage, has undoubtedly emerged for policy reasons.[511] However, it is not absolute, for it has been accepted that a time may come when a child will have to be considered as being habitually resident in the State of refuge.[512] This is equally implicit in Art.10 of the Brussels IIa Regulation,[513] as well as s.41 of the Family Law Act 1986.

RULE 18—(1) In the context of European Union law a person is, in   6R–145 general, habitually resident in the country in which he has established a residence which is his permanent or habitual centre of interests.

(2) A child is habitually resident in the country in which he is resident and has achieved a degree of integration in a social and family environment. The factors relevant to making that determination will vary depending on the age of the child.

COMMENT

Introduction. Habitual residence plays a key role in European Union   **6–146** private international law[514] and is the primary connecting factor in instruments dealing with family law matters.[515] The concept is to be given an

---

[508] *Re G (Abduction: Withdrawal of Proceedings, Acquiescence, Habitual Residence)* [2007] EWHC 2807 (Fam.), [2008] 2 F.L.R. 351.

[509] [2002] 1 F.L.R. 388.

[510] *Re P (GE) (An Infant)* [1965] Ch. 568, 586 (ordinary residence); *Re J (A Minor) (Abduction: Custody Rights)* [1990] 2 A.C. 562, 572, *per* Lord Donaldson M.R.; *Re M (Abduction: Habitual Residence)* [1996] 1 F.L.R. 887.

[511] *Harper v Johnson* [2008] N.Z.F.L.R. 775.

[512] *Re B (Abduction: Children's Objections)* [1998] 1 F.L.R. 667; *Re C (A Child) (Residence and Contact)* [2005] EWHC 2205 (Fam.), [2006] 2 F.L.R. 277; *Re D (A Child) (Abduction: Rights of Custody)* [2006] UKHL 51, [2007] 1 A.C. 619 at [4].

[513] *Re A; HA v MB (Brussels II Revised: Article 11(7) Application)* [2007] EWHC 2016 (Fam.), [2008] 1 F.L.R. 289 at [84].

[514] The connecting factor features in each of: the Brussels I Regulation; Insolvency Regulation; Small Claims Regulation; EPO Regulation and EEO Regulation. For the purposes of the Rome I Regulation (Art.19) and the Rome II Regulation (Art.23) definitions are provided for the habitual residences of: companies and other bodies, corporate or unincorporated, (place of central administration); branches, agencies or other establishments (place of location); and natural persons acting in the course of their business activity (principal place of business).

[515] Brussels IIa Regulation; Maintenance Regulation; and Rome III Regulation.

autonomous interpretation,[516] and regard must always be paid to the objectives of the underlying legislative provision.[517] As yet there has been no specific guidance from the European Court as to how it should be interpreted in respect of adults in a conflict of laws context, although two rulings have considered the situation of children for the purposes of the Brussels IIa Regulation.[518] There is, however, a rich corpus of case law from the European Court interpreting habitual residence and related residence based connecting factors in other areas of European law, most notably as regards social security[519] and European Union civil service allowances.[520] This case law inspired the drafters of the Brussels II Convention,[521] almost certainly the Brussels IIa Regulation[522] and has been relied upon by the Family Division when considering jurisdiction in divorce.[523]

6–147   **Clause (1).** In determining whether a habitual residence has been acquired in a Member State the European Court has identified as relevant such matters as: the person's family situation; the reasons for the move; the length and continuity of the residence; the stability of any employment; and the person's intention such as it appears from all the circumstances.[524] In the European context intention and such factors indicative of connection are not directed towards ascertaining whether a settled purpose of short or long duration underpins a person's actual residence in a Member State,[525] but to determine whether that place can be considered the person's permanent or habitual centre of interests. This standard, which forms the basis of clause (1), is found

---

[516] Case C–523/07 *Proceedings brought by A* [2009] E.C.R. I–2805.

[517] Case C–102/91 *Knoch v Bundesanstalt für Arbeit* [1992] E.C.R. I–4341, at [29]; Case F–126/05 *Borbély v Commission*, January 16, 2007, Civil Service Tribunal of the European Union, [66]; *Marinos v Marinos* [2007] EWHC 2047 (Fam.), [2007] 2 F.L.R. 1018, at [35].

[518] See Clause (2) of this Rule.

[519] Case 76/76 *Di Paolo v Office National de l'Emploi* [1977] E.C.R. 315; C–102/91 *Knoch v Bundesanstalt für Arbeit* [1992] E.C.R. I–4341; Case C–90/97 *Swaddling v Adjudication Officer* [1999] E.C.R. I–1075.

[520] Case T-63/91 *Benzler v Commission* [1992] E.C.R. II-2095; Case C–452/93 *Fernández v Commission* [1994] E.C.R. I–4295; Case T–251/02 *E v Commission* [2004] ECR-SC I-A-359 and II–1643; Case T-298/02 *Romeu v Commission* [2005] E.C.R. II–4599.

[521] Borrás, *Explanatory Report on the Convention* [1998] O.J. C221/27, para.32.

[522] This is evident in the drafters' acceptance of the possibility of a habitual residence being acquired immediately upon arrival in a Member State (*cf.* Case C–90/97 *Swaddling v Adjudication Officer* [1999] E.C.R. I–1075), see European Commission, *Practice Guide for the Application of the New Brussels II Regulation*, 2005, p.15. Art.9 of the Brussels IIa Regulation, which provides for a limited three month continuing jurisdiction where a child moves lawfully between Member States but only upon acquisition of a habitual residence in the new Member State, is only completely effective where a habitual residence is acquired immediately upon arrival, see Case C-497/10 PPU *Mercredi v Chaffe*, opinion of Cruz Villalón A.-G., at [74], above, n.504.

[523] *L-K v K* (No.2) [2006] EWHC 3280 (Fam.), [2007] 2 F.L.R. 729; *Marinos v Marinos* [2007] EWHC 2047 (Fam.), [2007] 2 F.L.R. 1018; *Z v Z (Divorce: Jurisdiction)* [2009] EWHC 2626 (Fam.), [2010] 1 F.L.R. 694.

[524] Case C–90/97 *Swaddling v Adjudication Officer* [1999] E.C.R. I–1075. See Case 76/76 *Di Paolo v Office National de l'Emploi* [1977] E.C.R. 315, at [22]; Case C–216/89 *Reibold v Bundesanstalt für Arbeit* [1990] E.C.R. I–4163; C-102/91 *Knoch v Bundesanstalt für Arbeit* [1992] E.C.R. I–434.

[525] *cf. R. v Barnet LBC Ex p. Shah* [1983] 2 A.C. 309.

in numerous European Court judgments,[526] was highlighted in the Borrás Report[527] and has been accepted by the Family Division for purposes of jurisdiction in divorce.[528] Guidance as to its interpretation may be derived from the explanation of Saggio A.-G. in *Swaddling v Adjudication Officer*, who explained that the conceptual basis of residence in its various manifestations in European legislation is the identification of the Member State to which the person concerned has formed a social attachment which is stronger and more stable than any links he may have with other Member States.[529] In *Z v Z (Divorce: Jurisdiction)*[530] Ryder J. adopted the formulation of a centre of interests of a stable character. This in turn corresponds with the subsequent assessment of the European Court when considering the jurisdiction rules applicable to children in the Brussels IIa Regulation, that the adjective habitual implies residence which has a certain permanence or regularity.[531]

The determination of habitual residence is to be made on the facts of the case with regard paid to all the circumstances which point to a person's real choice of a country as his State of residence.[532] In *Swaddling* the European Court accepted that length of residence was not an intrinsic element of habitual residence;[533] Saggio A.-G.'s opinion was that the United Kingdom was the permanent centre of Mr Swaddling's interests and had been so as soon as he returned to the country after living and working in France.[534] This interpretation of immediate acquisition was applied in *Marinos v Marinos*,[535] the petitioner wife being held to have acquired a habitual residence in the United Kingdom upon her arrival at Heathrow airport, because she was undertaking a planned, purposeful and permanent relocation.

6–148

The priority placed on stability by the European Court means that an established habitual residence, with which connections are maintained, may endure notwithstanding a significant period of time spent working, training or

6–149

---

[526] Case T–63/91 *Benzler v Commission* [1992] E.C.R. II–2095; Case C–452/93 *Fernández v Commission* [1994] E.C.R. I–4295; Case T–298/02 *Romeu v Commission* [2005] E.C.R. II–4599; Case F–129/06 *Roldán v Commission*, September 26, 2007, Civil Service Tribunal of the European Union. In the social security decisions Case 76/76 *Di Paolo v Office National de l'Emploi* [1977] E.C.R. 315 and Case C–90/97 *Swaddling v Adjudication Officer* [1999] E.C.R. I–1075 the European Court referred simply to habitual centre of interests. However, in the light of the context of both judgments, including the opinions of both Advocates-General, this should not be treated as a difference of emphasis.

[527] Borrás, above, n.521, para.32.

[528] *L-K v K* (No.2) [2006] EWHC 3280 (Fam.), [2007] 2 F.L.R. 729, at [36]; *Marinos v Marinos* [2007] EWHC 2047 (Fam.), [2007] 2 F.L.R. 1018, at [18]–[24].

[529] Case C–90/97 *Swaddling v Adjudication Officer* [1999] E.C.R. I–1075, at [18]. See also Case 76/76 *Di Paolo v Office National de l'Emploi* [1977] E.C.R. 315, 331 (opinion of Capotorti A.-G.).

[530] [2009] EWHC 2626 (Fam.), [2010] 1 F.L.R. 694, at [49].

[531] Case C–497/10 PPU *Mercredi v Chaffe* [2012] Fam. 22, at [44].

[532] Case C–90/97 *Swaddling v Adjudication Officer* [1999] E.C.R. I–1075, at [19]; Case C–452/93 *Fernández v Commission* [1994] E.C.R. I–4295, at [22].

[533] Case C–90/97 *Swaddling v Adjudication Officer* [1999] E.C.R. I–1075, at [30]. The length of a person's stay may be used to gauge his intention to make that State the centre of his interests: opinion of Saggio A.-G., at [19].

[534] *ibid.* at [19].

[535] [2007] EWHC 2047 (Fam.), [2007] 2 F.L.R. 1018, at [86]. See also *L-K v K* (No.2) [2006] EWHC 3280 (Fam.), [2007] 2 F.L.R. 729.

studying in another Member State. The Court has emphasised that there is, however, no precise definition as to length of absence.[536] Thus a change in permanent centre of interests and thereby habitual residence did not result when a Finnish employee of a Finnish company on a fixed term contract spent 18 months working in Belgium.[537] Similarly four years of vocational training in Germany were not, in the absence of other relevant factors, considered sufficient to move a young Belgian's centre of interests.[538] In a case concerning social security entitlement it was held that 21 months spent as a language assistant under a university exchange programme did not constitute stable employment.[539] Presence, however, in a Member State for the purposes of study will not always act as a bar to the acquisition of a habitual residence, but such situations will be limited, notably where the period of study was both preceded and followed, almost without interruption, by extended residence in that same State.[540]

6–150   National courts have acknowledged the emphasis placed on stability when applying divorce jurisdiction rules. In a divorce petition involving a British couple, the French Cour de cassation upheld an interpretation of habitual residence based on the transfer of the individual's permanent and habitual centre of interests.[541] On the facts it was found that the petitioner had not intended to affect such a transfer, and so 14 months into an 18 month stay in Provence she had retained her habitual residence in the United Kingdom. In *Z v Z (Divorce: Jurisdiction)*[542] it was held that a residence which ostensibly indicated a stable centre of interests would not automatically be characterised as such, if the parties intended that their stay be temporary. Ryder J. held that a contrary finding would have undesirable policy consequences for international families who relocated on a regular basis.[543]

6–151   *Dual habitual residences.* There is no European Court authority which decides that a person may have more than one habitual residence at any particular moment.[544] In the context of jurisdiction under the Brussels IIa Regulation Family Division authority has adopted the position that a person can have only one habitual residence, relying also on the wording of the

---

[536] C–102/91 *Knoch v Bundesanstalt für Arbeit* [1992] E.C.R. I–4341, at [26].

[537] Case T–259/04 *Koistinen v Commission*, September 27, 2006, Court of First Instance. See Case C–452/93 *Fernández v Commission* [1994] E.C.R. I–4295 (9 months seeking employment in Spain did not terminate an existing Belgian habitual residence). cf. Case T–251/02 *E v Commission* [2004] ECR-SC I-A-359 and II–1643.

[538] Case T–63/91 *Benzler v Commission* [1992] E.C.R. II–2095.

[539] C–102/91 *Knoch v Bundesanstalt für Arbeit* [1992] E.C.R. I–4341, at [25]–[29]. Van Gerven A.-G.'s opinion was that it was scarcely plausible for a temporary teaching post abroad under an academic exchange programme to lead of itself to a change of residence: at [8].

[540] Case C–201/88 *Atala-Palmerini v Commission* [1989] E.C.R. 3109; discussed in Case F–33/09 *Tzvetanova v Commission*, Civil Service Tribunal (First Chamber), March 9, 2010.

[541] *Moore v Moore* [2006] I.L.Pr. 628.

[542] [2009] EWHC 2626 (Fam.), [2010] 1 F.L.R. 694, at [44]. See also *C v S (Divorce: Jurisdiction)* [2010] EWHC 2676 (Fam.), [2011] 2 F.L.R. 19.

[543] e.g. *Olafisoye v Olafisoye* [2010] EWHC 3539 (Fam.), [2011] 2 F.L.R. 553.

[544] The possibility of a person having more than one habitual residence was excluded by Cruz Villalón A.-G. in Case C–497/10 PPU *Mercredi v Chaffe*, at [71], above, n.504.

Regulation in which habitual residence is referred to in the singular.[545] The European Court has, however, accepted that an individual may have a residence with a non-habitual character in a second Member State.[546] This may in certain circumstances be characterised as the place of main professional activity.[547]

Absence of habitual residence. Equally there is no European Court author- **6–152** ity which provides that an adult may be without a habitual residence. In the context of a definitive relocation between Member States the recognition that a new habitual residence may be acquired immediately limits the possibility of this issue arising for consideration.[548] In other situations regard must be paid to the legislative context and a relevant factor will almost certainly be whether a finding of an absence of habitual residence would render a European Union private international law instrument unworkable.[549]

Clause (2). In its first ruling on the interpretation of habitual residence in **6–153** a conflict of laws context, the European Court declined to extend the interpretation given to the habitual residence of adults in the contexts of social security and European Union civil service allowances to children for the purposes of jurisdiction under the Brussels IIa Regulation.[550] Pursuant to the objectives of the jurisdictional rules in the Regulation, the European Court has held that the connecting factor is to be interpreted in the light of the best interests of the child and in particular the criterion of proximity.[551] This

---

[545] *Marinos v Marinos* [2007] EWHC 2047 (Fam.), [2007] 2 F.L.R. 1018, at [40]; *Munro v Munro* [2007] EWHC 3315 (Fam.), [2008] 1 F.L.R. 1613 at [47]; *Z v Z (Divorce : Jurisdiction)* [2009] EWHC 2626 (Fam.), [2010] 1 F.L.R. 694, at [41]; *Olafisoye v Olafisoye* [2010] EWHC 3539 (Fam.), [2011] 2 F.L.R. 553, at [21]; *V v V* [2011] EWHC 1190 (Fam.), [2011] 2 F.L.R. 778, [36]. *cf. M v H (A Child) (Shared Residence Order: Habitual Residence)* [2005] EWHC 1186 (Fam.). See also *C v FC (Brussels II: Free-Standing Application for Parental Responsibility)* [2004] 1 F.L.R. 317.

[546] Case 76/76 *Di Paolo v Office National de l'Emploi* [1977] E.C.R. 315, at [21]. In *Marinos v Marinos* [2007] EWHC 2047 (Fam.), [2007] 2 F.L.R. 1018, at [48], this was adopted and applied with regard to Art.3(1)(a)(vi) of the Brussels IIa Regulation. See *V v V* [2011] EWHC 1190 (Fam.), [2011] 2 F.L.R. 778 at [52]; *C v S (Divorce: Jurisdiction)* [2010] EWHC 2676 (Fam.), [2011] 2 F.L.R. 19.

[547] Case T–251/02 *E v Commission* [2004] ECR-SC I-A-359 and II–1643, at [73], and Case T–259/04 *Koistinen v Commission*, September 27, 2006, Court of First Instance, at [38].

[548] *Marinos v Marinos* [2007] EWHC 2047 (Fam.), [2007] 2 F.L.R. 1018, at [87]–[89]. *cf.* Case C–497/10 PPU *Mercredi v Chaffe*, opinion of Cruz Villalón A.-G., at [71] (above, n.504) as regards situations where a move is followed by residence which is more tentative in nature. In such a context the facts may be such that the existing habitual residence is considered to endure, at least temporarily: *Mercredi v Chaffe* [2011] EWCA Civ 272, [2011] 2 F.L.R. 515. However, in Case C–523/07 *Proceedings brought by A* [2009] E.C.R. I–2805, Kokott A.-G.'s opinion was, at [45], as regards the standard applied to children, that it would be in exceptional cases that during a transitional stage there would be no habitual residence in the former State, whilst the status in the new State had not crystallised into habitual residence.

[549] The possibility of a child being without a habitual residence, accepted in both Case C–523/07 *Proceedings brought by A* [2009] E.C.R. I–2805 and Case C–497/10 PPU *Mercredi v Chaffe* [2012] Fam. 22, is expressly provided for in the Brussels IIa Regulation due to the inclusion of a subsidiary basis of jurisdiction based on presence, Art.13.

[550] The Commission had argued for the same interpretation to be applied: Case C–523/07 *Proceedings brought by A* [2009] E.C.R. I–2805, at [36].

[551] Case C–523/07 *Proceedings brought by A* [2009] E.C.R. I–2805, at [35]; Case C–497/10 PPU *Mercredi v Chaffe* [2012] Fam. 22, at [46]. See Brussels IIa Regulation, Recital 12.

requires a close connection between the child and the designated forum, and to this end there must be actual presence in a Member State, evidence the presence is not in any way temporary or intermittent, and, as set out in Clause (2), some degree of integration by the child in a social and family environment. In *Proceedings brought by A*, Kokott A.-G. spoke of the child's "actual centre of interests" when referring to the latter approach to the interpretation of habitual residence.[552] The European Court has held that relevant factors in the determination of habitual residence include the duration, regularity, conditions and reasons for the stay, the child's nationality, the place and conditions of attendance at school, linguistic knowledge and the family and social relationships of the child in the Member State in question.[553]

6–154   The importance of parental intention in the determination of a child's habitual residence will vary. In *Proceedings brought by A* the European Court stated that the intention of parents to settle with the child in another Member State could, when accompanied by practical steps such as the purchase or lease of a property in that State, constitute an indicator of the transfer of the child's habitual residence. In *Mercredi v Chaffe*,[554] which concerned the removal of an infant child from the United Kingdom to the island of La Réunion by her French mother, who alone had parental responsibility, the emphasis was notably greater. The European Court held that the factors to be considered in determining habitual residence would vary according to the age of the child.[555] In this it drew a distinction between children who had left school, school age children, young children and infants. As a general rule, the environment of a young child will essentially be a family environment determined by reference to the person(s) with whom the child lives and was in fact looked after. An infant, however, will necessarily share the social and family environment of the circle of people on whom he is dependent. On the facts of *Mercredi* this meant the mother's integration in her social and family environment had to be considered. The European Court did not exclude the possibility of mother, and consequently the infant child, acquiring a habitual residence within a few days of their arrival in La Réunion.[556] In arriving at this position the Court's reasoning reiterates the child-centred approach advanced in *Proceedings brought by A*, and it held that as a general rule habitual residence must have a certain duration which reflects an adequate degree of permanence. However, it then noted that the Regulation did not establish a minimum duration for that residence and added that the duration of a stay was only an indicator in the consideration of the permanence of the residence. The European Court then drew on language associated with traditional habitual

---

[552] Case C–523/07 [2009] E.C.R. I–2805, at [38].

[553] *ibid.* at [39].

[554] Case C–497/10 PPU *Mercredi v Chaffe*, above.

[555] In *Proceedings brought by A*, Kokott A.-G.'s opinion had been, at [47], that the relevance of factors may vary according to the age of the child.

[556] In Case C–497/10 PPU *Mercredi v Chaffe,* Cruz Villalón A.-G.'s opinion, at [78] (above, n.504), having considered the application and terms of Art.9 of the Brussels Regulation, was that a lawful removal from one Member State to another Member State which exhibited all the signs of an indefinite, longer-term establishment, should create a presumption of the acquisition of habitual residence in that Member State. However, at [79], he also added that this presumption should in any event still be subject to the assessment propounded in Case C-523/07 *Proceedings brought by A* [2009] E.C.R. I–2805.

residence case law on adults taken from other areas of European law, holding that for a habitual residence to be transferred it was of paramount importance that the person concerned had it in mind to establish there the "permanent or habitual centre of his interests, with the intention that this should be of a lasting character".[557] In making this assessment reference must also be made to the parent's integration, and, it might be implied, his capacity to integrate, for the factors identified by the European Court in *Mercredi* included the mother's geographic and family origins, as well as the languages known to her.[558]

European Union and domestic habitual residence compared. It is in   6–155
respect of adults that the differences between the two interpretations of habitual residence are most marked. The European Court has accepted the possibility of immediate acquisition in the field of benefit entitlement,[559] whilst in the same area of law the House of Lords has re-affirmed the necessity of there being an appreciable period of actual residence, although it acknowledged the possibility of the period of time being short.[560] Furthermore the settled purpose test derived from *Ex p. Shah*[561] has been applied in such a manner that a habitual residence may be lost and acquired with relative ease.[562] Conversely the centre of interests test advanced by the European Court has tended to favour stability and a longer term view of an individual's connections.[563] This means that an existing habitual residence in a Member State may be retained notwithstanding an extended period of time elsewhere, in circumstances where an English court would undoubtedly find that a change of habitual residence had occurred.

As regards children the European Union interpretation must still be treated   6–156
as being in a state of evolution.[564] It is unclear whether the balance between parental intention and a child's factual connections as found in English authorities is exactly replicated in European Court case law. In particular in the case of infants and young children it would appear that the emphasis placed by the European Court on parental intention is such that a habitual residence could be acquired notwithstanding a very limited period of actual residence in the Member State in question.[565]

Residence.[566] The word "residence" has different meanings in different   6–157
branches of the law. It is clear that it must be distinguished from mere presence, the state of being found in a country, but the nature of the distinction

---

[557] Case C–497/10 PPU *Mercredi v Chaffe* [2012] Fam. 22, at [51].
[558] *ibid.* at [55].
[559] Case C–90/97 *Swaddling v Adjudication Officer* [1999] E.C.R. I–1075.
[560] *Nessa v Chief Adjudication Officer* [1999] 1 W.L.R. 1937.
[561] *R. v Barnet LBC, Ex p. Shah* [1983] 2 A.C. 309.
[562] *Re S (A Child) (Habitual Residence)* [2009] EWCA Civ 1021, [2010] 1 F.L.R. 1146; *Re R (Abduction: Habitual Residence)* [2003] EWHC (Fam.) 1968, [2004] 1 F.L.R. 216; *Cameron v Cameron*, 1996 S.C. 17.
[563] Case T–63/91 *Benzler v Commission* [1992] E.C.R. II–2095; Case T–259/04 *Koistinen v Commission*, September 27, 2006, Court of First Instance.
[564] Case C–523/07 *Proceedings brought by A* [2009] E.C.R. I–2805; Case C–497/10 PPU *Mercredi v Chaffe*, above.
[565] Case C–497/10 PPU *Mercredi v Chaffe*, above.
[566] See Farnsworth (1952) 38 Tr. Grot. Soc. 59; McClean (1962) 11 I.C.L.Q. 1153.

and the factors which should be taken into account will vary with the subject-matter.

6–158   It has been suggested that there is now "a rule of construction that prima facie at least residence involves some degree of permanence."[567] This view gains support from Viscount Cave L.C.'s reliance in a taxation context[568] upon the Oxford English Dictionary definition of "reside," "to dwell permanently or for a considerable time, to have one's settled or usual abode. ... " This definition has been influential in those decisions emphasising, in a number of contexts, the need for some degree of permanence.[569] However, the actual case in which Viscount Cave L.C. was delivering his opinion involved a taxpayer who spent only a small part of each year in this country, and stayed in hotels on each visit, but was held to be resident for tax purposes.[570] Decisions in other contexts have recognised residence as having been established without any element of permanence.[571] Mere fleeting or casual presence will, however, not constitute residence.[572]

6–159   For tax purposes, it has been held that the question where a person is resident is one of fact.[573] But the question must nonetheless be "determined on proper legal principles";[574] and for other legal purposes the question has been described as "a mixed question of law and fact."[575] All the circumstances must be taken into account, the weight to be given to the various aspects of the facts varying with the circumstances. So in a matrimonial causes context, the location of the matrimonial home, and the situation of spouse and children was significant;[576] for some purposes it is sufficient to

---

[567] *Brokelmann v Barr* [1971] 2 Q.B. 602, 611–612.

[568] *Levene v IRC* [1928] A.C. 217, 222.

[569] *Re Adoption Application No.52 of 1951* [1952] Ch. 16 (adoption); *Fox v Stirk* [1970] 2 Q.B. 463 (CA) (electoral registration qualifications); *Brokelmann v Barr* [1971] 2 Q.B. 602 (exemptions from customs duty); *Williams v Horsham DC* [2004] EWCA Civ 39, [2004] 3 All E.R. 30 ("main residence" for Council tax purposes). See also *Grace v The Commissioners for Her Majesty's Revenue & Customs* [2009] EWCA Civ 1082, [2009] S.T.C. 2707.

[570] *Levene v IRC* [1928] A.C. 217. See the companion case, *IRC v Lysaght* [1928] A.C. 234. Residence at a house for approximately fifty days a year was sufficient for that place to constitute a "usual residence" for the purposes of service under CPR r.6.9(2): *Varsani v Relfo Ltd* [2010] EWCA Civ 560, [2011] 1 W.L.R. 1402. Regard must be paid to the nature or quality of the use of the premises, which in the latter case were occupied permanently by the defendant's family. *cf. Cherney v Deripaska* [2007] EWHC 965 (Comm.), [2007] 2 All E.R. (Comm) 785, where the quality of residence of a Russian oligarch at his London property was "intermittent and generally fleeting". See also *OJSC Oil Company Yugraneft (in liquidation) v Abramovich* [2008] EWHC 2613 (Comm.).

[571] e.g. *Matalon v Matalon* [1952] P. 233 (judicial separation).

[572] *Manning v Manning* (1871) L.R. 2 P. & D. 223; *Armytage v Armytage* [1898] P. 178; *Sinclair v Sinclair* [1968] P. 189 (CA). *cf.* Resolution (72) 1 of the Committee of Ministers of the Council of Europe on the Standardisation of the Legal Concepts of "Domicile" and of "Residence," Annex, Rule 8: "A man has a residence in a country ... if he dwells there for a certain period of time."

[573] *IRC v Lysaght* [1928] A.C. 234. See also *Grace v The Commissioners for Her Majesty's Revenue & Customs* [2009] EWCA Civ 1082, [2009] S.T.C. 2707; *R. (on the application of Davies) v Commissioners for Her Majesty's Revenue & Customs* [2010] EWCA Civ 83, [2010] S.T.C. 860.

[574] *Pickles v Foulsham* (1923) 9 Tax Cas. 261, 274 (the passage does not appear in the report at [1923] 2 K.B. 413).

[575] *Sinclair v Sinclair* [1968] P. 189, 213 (CA).

[576] *Sinclair v Sinclair*, above, at p.232.

describe a person as resident where he works, while for other purposes this is not sufficient;[577] in some contexts a man may be said to be resident where he sleeps, but this will not be an appropriate criterion in others.[578]

It is possible to be resident in a country despite a temporary absence;[579] and, at least in some contexts, to have two or more residences.[580]

Ordinary residence. It has sometimes been said that "ordinary residence" means nothing more or less than "residence,"[581] but it is submitted that the better view is that the adjective does add something,[582] an element of continuity, order, or settled purpose.   **6–160**

So, in a tax context, it has been said that ordinary residence "connotes residence in a place with some degree of continuity and apart from accidental or temporary absences"[583] and that "if it has any definite meaning I should say it means according to the way in which a man's life is usually ordered."[584] In the context of entitlement to educational awards, it was held that ordinary residence refers to a person's abode in a particular place or country which he has adopted voluntarily and for settled purposes as part of the regular order of his life for the time being, whether of short or long duration.[585] It is not essential to ordinary residence that it should be for a commercial or any other specific purpose.[586]   **6–161**

It was held in the context of jurisdiction in matrimonial causes that a person who habitually lives in a country may continue to be ordinarily resident there while he is actually resident in another country, e.g. during a prolonged stay in the second country for business or professional purposes; and that a wife who accompanies her husband on such occasions may similarly retain her   **6–162**

---

[577] Contrast *Ablett v Basham* (1856) 5 E. & B. 1019 (indorsement of writ of summons) with *Haslope v Thorne* (1813) 1 M. & S. 103 (affidavit to hold bail).

[578] Contrast *R. v Vice-Chancellor of Oxford University* (1872) L.R. 7 Q.B. 471 (membership of university body) with *Walcot v Botfield* (1854) Kay 534 (condition of residence imposed in will); *cf. Re Brauch* [1978] Ch. 316 (CA) (bankruptcy; a case on ordinary residence).

[579] *Dasent v Dasent* (1850) 1 Rob.Eccl. 800, 803; *Fox v Stirk* [1970] 2 Q.B. 463, 475 (CA).

[580] *IRC v Lysaght* [1928] A.C. 234; *Sinclair v Sinclair* [1968] P. 189, 232 (CA); *R. (on the application of Sunderland City Council) v South Tyneside* [2011] EWHC 2355 (Admin).

[581] *Levene v IRC* [1928] A.C. 217, at p.225 *per* Viscount Cave, L.C.; *Hopkins v Hopkins* [1951] P. 116, 112 (matrimonial jurisdiction); *Lowry v Lowry* [1952] P. 252, 255 (magistrates' matrimonial jurisdiction).

[582] *Re Erskine* (1893) 10 T.L.R. 32 (CA); *Re Bright* (1901) 18 T.L.R. 37 (CA) (bankruptcy cases); *Levene v IRC* [1928] A.C. 217, 232 *per* Lord Warrington; *IRC v Lysaght* [1928] A.C. 234, 243, 248 *per* Lords Sumner and Buckmaster (tax cases); *Stransky v Stransky* [1954] P. 428, 437 (matrimonial jurisdiction); *R. v Barnet LBC, Ex p. Nilish Shah* [1982] Q.B. 688 (CA) at pp.722–723 *per* Eveleigh L.J., at pp.729–30 *per* Templeman L.J. (entitlement to educational awards); *R. v Secretary of State for Health* [2009] EWCA Civ 225, [2010] 1 W.L.R. 279 (entitlement to free NHS treatment); *R. (on the application of M) v Hammersmith and Fulham LBC* [2011] EWCA Civ 77 (responsibility for the social care of a mentally ill person).

[583] *Levene v IRC* [1928] A.C. 217, 225. In the Income and Corporation Taxes Act 1988, s.334, ordinary residence is contrasted with occasional residence; see *Reed (Inspector of Taxes) v Clark* [1986] Ch. 1, decided under identical provisions in earlier legislation.

[584] *Levene v IRC*, above, at p.232. *cf. Thomson v Minister of National Revenue* [1946] 1 D.L.R. 689 (Sup Ct Can); Farnsworth (1951) 67 L.Q.R. 32.

[585] *R. v Barnet LBC, Ex p. Nilish Shah* [1983] 2 A.C. 309.

[586] *Re Brauch* [1978] Ch. 316 (CA).

ordinary residence in the first country.[587] On the other hand, ordinary residence in the first country will cease when the original connection with it is completely severed, e.g. if the persons in question decide to emigrate to the second country and dispose of their home in the first.[588] The fact that a person keeps a home available for immediate occupation in a country is evidence of ordinary residence there;[589] but it is probably not a necessary condition of ordinary residence. Thus a person may be ordinarily resident in a country although he has no home in it at all but lives in hotels.[590] And it is submitted that a person who lets his house for a short period while he is away for business or professional purposes remains ordinarily resident where that house is.

6–163   Ordinary residence can be changed in a day.[591] For certain purposes at least a person may be ordinarily resident in two or more countries.[592] It has been held in immigration cases that a person who is in a country illegally cannot be ordinarily resident there; s.50(5) of the British Nationality Act 1981 expressly provides that a person is not to be treated as ordinarily resident in the United Kingdom for the purposes of that Act at a time when he is there in breach of the immigration laws,[593] but the legality of a person's residence is completely irrelevant for tax purposes.[594]

6–164   It has been said[595] that a child of tender years "who cannot decide for himself where to live" is ordinarily resident in his parents' matrimonial home;[596] and that this ordinary residence cannot be changed by one parent without the consent of the other. If the parents are living apart and the child is, by agreement between them, living with one of them, he is ordinarily resident in the home of that one and his ordinary residence is not changed merely because the other parent takes the child away from that home.[597] Similar considerations will apply in the case of a mentally handicapped person

---

[587] *Stransky v Stransky* [1954] P. 428; *Lewis v Lewis* [1956] 1 W.L.R. 200. *cf. Casey v Casey*, 1968 S.L.T. 56 (wife's visit to seek reconciliation with separated husband did not interrupt ordinary residence). Contrast *R. v Lancashire CC, Ex p. Huddleston* [1986] 2 All E.R. 941 (CA) (ordinary residence broken by prolonged, albeit not permanent, residence abroad).

[588] *Hopkins v Hopkins* [1951] P. 116; *cf. Macrae v Macrae* [1949] P. 397 (CA). Contrast *Levene v IRC* [1928] A.C. 217.

[589] As in *Stransky v Stransky* and *Lewis v Lewis*, above.

[590] As in the *Lysaght* and *Levene* cases, above. See also *Re Bright* (1903) 19 T.L.R. 203 (CA); *Re Brauch* [1978] Ch. 316 (CA). *cf. Re Norris* (1888) 4 T.L.R. 452 (CA) (hotel room taken on long-term basis for use as required).

[591] *Macrae v Macrae* [1949] P. 397, 403 (CA).

[592] *Re Norris* (1888) 4 T.L.R. 452 (CA); *Cooper v Cadwalader* (1904) 5 Tax Cas. 201; *Pittar v Richardson* (1917) 87 L.J.K.B. 59, 61; *Britto v Secretary of State for the Home Department* [1984] Imm. A.R. 93; *R. v Nottinghamshire CC, Ex p. Jain* [1989] C.O.D. 442 (DC).

[593] *Re Abdul Manan* [1971] 1 W.L.R. 859 (CA); *R. v Governor of Pentonville Prison, Ex p. Azam* [1974] A.C. 18; *R. v Secretary of State for the Home Department, Ex p. Margueritte* [1983] Q.B. 180 (CA) (see *R. v Barnet LBC, Ex p. Shah* [1983] 2 A.C. 309, 343); *Mark v Mark* [2005] UKHL 42, [2006] 1 A.C. 98 at [32]; *R v Secretary of State for Health* [2009] EWCA Civ 225, [2010] 1 W.L.R. 279 (an asylum seeker cannot be ordinarily resident for the purposes of free NHS treatment); *cf.* para.6–134. *cf. Trotter v Trotter* (1992) 90 D.L.R. (4th) 554 (Ont) (person on visitor's permit and lacking landed immigrant status could become habitually resident), applied in *Alexiou v Alexiou* (1996) 41 Alta. L.R. (3d) 90 (in context of divorce jurisdiction).

[594] *Mark v Mark* [2005] UKHL 42, [2006] 1 A.C. 98 at [31].

[595] *Re P (GE) (An Infant)* [1965] Ch. 568, 585–586 (CA).

[596] "Even if he is away at boarding school," which may be in another country.

[597] The domicile of the child may be changed: see Exception to Rule 15.

incapable of making an independent decision as to where to live and totally dependent upon a parent or guardian; he will be ordinarily resident with that person, though a second ordinary residence (for example during a stay in an institution) may also be acquired.[598]

ILLUSTRATIONS

1. N was born in Bangladesh and did not leave that country until 1994, although her husband **6–165** had lived in the United Kingdom from 1962 until 1975, when he died. N had the right of abode in the United Kingdom and arrived there on August 22, 1994. She applied four days later for income support, a benefit available to persons habitually resident in the United Kingdom. At the relevant date she was not habitually resident in the United Kingdom.[599]

2. C was born in Western Australia to British parents who were unmarried. In March 1990, M returned to England with C, intending to make England her permanent home. Under the law of Western Australia, M alone had custody rights. C's habitual residence depended on that of M and C's habitual residence in Western Australia was lost immediately when M left.[600]

3. C was born in 1992 to M an Englishwoman, as a result of a relationship between M and F who was from Dubai. In 1999 it was agreed that T, M, and M's husband and the three children of that marriage, all of whom were living in England, would go to live in Dubai, substantially at F's expense. The arrangement broke down and M returned to England, without C, after a few months. M had become habitually resident in Dubai on her arrival there, but had resumed an habitual residence in England on her return. Her unilateral action could not affect the habitual residence of C, which remained in Dubai.[601]

4. M, who was from Wales, and F, who was Spanish, married in 1995 and lived in Spain with their five children until 2007. It was then agreed that M would spend a year in the United Kingdom with the children for the purposes of their schooling. In June 2008, towards the end of the stay, M announced her intention to remain and divorce F. A subsequent reconciliation in Spain failed and M took the children back to the United Kingdom. The original stay had not led to a change in the children's habitual residence, their ordered way of life was Spanish.[602]

5. H and W had lived in Greece with their children between late 2002 and early 2007. During this time W worked part-time as a flight attendant, based at London Heathrow, and studied part-time in England to qualify as a solicitor. On January 31, 2007 W took the children back to England and on February 1 she issued a petition for divorce. Whilst W may have spent slightly more time in Greece than England or elsewhere, the habitual centre of her interests was held, from September 2004 at least, to be in England because this was where her current and planned future career was located. Alternatively, were her centre of interest to have been in Greece where her children lived, by undertaking a planned, purposeful and permanent relocation between Member States she immediately acquired an English habitual residence on arrival in the country on January 31, 2007.[603]

4. DOMICILE, RESIDENCE AND NATIONALITY

The concept of domicile remains of importance in the rules of the conflict of **6–166** laws prevailing in common law countries. But its pre-eminence has been lost, almost certainly for good. Despite reforms made by statute, or proposed by law reform agencies, in the law of domicile with the object of removing its

---

[598] *R. v London Borough of Waltham Forest, Ex p. Vale, The Times*, February 25, 1985; *R. v Kent CC, Ex p. S* [2000] 1 F.L.R. 155.

[599] *Nessa v Chief Adjudication Officer* [1999] 1 W.L.R. 1937 (HL).

[600] *Re J (A Minor) (Abduction: Custody Rights)* [1990] 2 A.C. 562.

[601] *Al Habtoor v Fotheringham* [2001] EWCA Civ 186, [2001] 1 F.L.R. 951.

[602] *Re P-J (Children) (Abduction: Habitual Residence: Consent)* [2009] EWCA Civ 588, [2010] 1 W.L.R. 1237.

[603] *Marinos v Marinos* [2007] EWHC 2047 (Fam.), [2007] 2 F.L.R. 1018.

less satisfactory features, it is residence based connecting factors which are favoured in the international and regional instruments which dominate contemporary conflict of laws. This is particularly the case within the European Union where habitual residence is used both in matters of jurisdiction and choice of law, with only limited reliance placed on nationality and domicile.

6–167   **Domicile and nationality.**[604] Until the beginning of the 19th century domicile was universally regarded as the personal law for purposes of the conflict of laws. The change from domicile to nationality on the continent of Europe started in France with the promulgation of the Code Napoleon in 1804. One of the principal objects of the codifiers was to substitute a uniform law throughout the whole of France for the different *coutumes* of the French provinces. In matters of personal status these *coutumes* applied to persons domiciled within the province, wherever they happened to be. It was natural that the new uniform law should apply to Frenchmen everywhere, and art.3(1) of the Civil Code provided that "the laws governing the status and capacity of persons govern Frenchmen even though they are residing in foreign countries." No provision was expressly made for the converse case of foreigners residing in France, but the French courts held that in matters of status and capacity they too were governed by their national law. The provisions of the French code were adopted in Belgium and Luxembourg, and similar provisions were contained in the Austrian code of 1811 and the Dutch code of 1829.

6–168   The change from domicile to nationality on the continent of Europe was accelerated by Mancini's famous lecture delivered at the University of Turin in 1851. Under Mancini's influence, art.6 of the Italian Civil Code (1865) provided that "the status and capacity of persons and family relations are governed by the laws of the nation to which they belong." Mancini's ideas proved extremely influential outside Italy too, and in the second half of the 19th century the principle of nationality replaced that of domicile in code after code in continental Europe, although domicile was often retained in specific contexts. The result is that the nations of the world have become divided in their definition of the personal law; and it is this fact more than any other which has traditionally impeded international agreement on uniform rules of the conflict of laws. What then are the arguments in favour of nationality and domicile as the personal law?

6–169   The advocates of nationality claim that it is more stable than domicile because nationality cannot be changed without the formal consent of the State of new nationality. But this would be "through the sacrifice of a man's personal freedom to adopt the legal system of his own choice."[605]

6–170   It is also claimed that nationality is easier to ascertain than domicile because a change of nationality involves a formal act of naturalisation and does not depend on the subjective intentions of the *propositus*. This is undoubtedly true, though there may be difficult cases of double nationality or of statelessness. But it does not follow that the most easily ascertained law is

---

[604] Nadelmann (1969) 17 Am.J. Comp. Law 418; de Winter (1969) *Recueil des Cours* III, p.347; Law Com. No.48, (1972) paras 19–26.
[605] Anton, para.7.06.

the most appropriate law. Many immigrants who have no intention of returning to their country of origin do not trouble to apply for naturalisation.

The decisive consideration for countries like the United Kingdom, the   **6–171**
United States, Australia and Canada is that, save in a very few respects, there
is no such thing as United Kingdom, American, Australian or Canadian law.
Since the object of referring matters of status and capacity to the personal law
is to connect a man with some one legal system for many legal purposes,
nationality breaks down altogether if the State contains more than one country
in the sense of the conflict of laws.[606] International conventions commonly
contain provisions seeking to resolve this problem; they may leave it to the
law of the nationality to determine the territorial unit whose law is to govern,
or rely on some other connecting factor to make that determination.[607] The
matter may also be addressed in implementing legislation.[608]

The replacement of domicile? The increased reliance on habitual resi-   **6–172**
dence as the primary connecting factor in contemporary conflict of laws
instruments and proposals, particularly within the European Union, raises the
question whether this factually orientated concept is capable of being the
personal law. Apart from being acceptable to lawyers of both the common law
and civil law traditions, the strength of habitual residence lies in its flexibility,
a characteristic particularly valued in the regulation of jurisdiction. But an
advantage for purposes of jurisdiction is conversely a potential disadvantage
in matters of choice of law. Where issues of status and capacity are implicated,
repeated changes in an individual's personal law are apt to create uncertainty
as well as undesirable results, most notably if a person is living in a country
which upholds values that differ markedly to those of his homeland.[609] In this
context it can be understood why in their 1987 Report, the Law Commissions
did not recommend the replacement of domicile as the general connecting
factor in English law, for it offers a level of stability which cannot be
guaranteed by habitual residence.[610]

---

[606] See *Re O'Keefe* [1940] Ch. 124, and above, para.4–035.
[607] e.g. the Hague Convention on Matrimonial Property Regimes, Art.16 (prepared in 1976).
[608] Mental Capacity Act 2005, Sch.3, Pt.2, para.8.
[609] Law Com. No.107 (1987) para.3.6.
[610] *ibid.* para.3.12.

PART TWO

PROCEDURE

CHAPTER 7 deals with procedural questions, including the distinction **II–001** between matters of substance and matters of procedure, remedies and process, evidence, set-off and counterclaim, priorities, damages, statutes of limitation, and interest.

CHAPTER 8 deals with a number of significant procedural issues which arise in the conduct of international litigation: injunctions to restrain removal or dissipation of assets before judgment (*Mareva* injunctions or freezing injunctions), international judicial assistance in relation to service of process and the taking of evidence abroad, and the taking of security for costs.

CHAPTER 9 deals with the mode of proving foreign law.

CHAPTER 7

SUBSTANCE AND PROCEDURE

RULE 19—All matters of procedure are governed by the domestic law of the country to which the court wherein any legal proceedings are taken belongs (*lex fori*).   7R–001

COMMENT

The principle that procedure is governed by the *lex fori* is of general applica-   7–002
tion and universally admitted.[1] In a body of Rules such as those contained in
this book, which state the principles enforced by an English court, the maxim
that procedure is governed by the *lex fori* means in effect that it is governed
by the ordinary law of England without any reference to any foreign law
whatever. Thus the English court will always apply its own rules of procedure,
and will, moreover, refuse to apply any foreign rule which in its view is
procedural.[2] In deciding whether a foreign rule is procedural, the court refers
to the foreign law in order to determine whether the rule is of such a nature
as to be procedural in the English sense.[3]

While procedure is governed by the *lex fori*, matters of substance are   7–003
governed by the law to which the court is directed by its choice of law rule
(*lex causae*).[4] Dicey wrote that English lawyers gave "the widest possible
extension to the meaning of the term 'procedure.' "[5] As a matter of history,
this is true[6]; and a court may, even today, be tempted to extend the meaning
of "procedure" in order to evade an unsatisfactory choice of law rule.[7] But in
general the attitude expressed by Dicey has fallen into disfavour precisely
because it tends to frustrate the purposes of choice of law rules. It has also
been affected by the entry into force of harmonised European choice of law
rules which require certain matters to be classified as substantive.[8] Thus some

---

[1] Ailes (1941) 39 Mich.L.Rev. 392.

[2] e.g. *Hansen v Dixon* (1906) 23 T.L.R. 56. Rule 19 was applied and the text was cited with approval in *De Gortari v Smithwick* [2000] 1 I.L.R.M. 463 (Sup Ct).

[3] *Huber v Steiner* (1835) 2 Bing. N.C. 202; *cf. Société Anonyme Metallurgique de Prayon v Koppel* (1933) 77 S.J. 800; Beckett (1934) 15 B.Y.I.L. 46, 75; Robertson, pp.248–253; Cook, p.224; above, Ch.2.

[4] *Huber v Steiner* (1835) 2 Bing.N.C. 202, 210; *Harding v Wealands* [2006] UKHL 32, [2007] 2 A.C. 1; *AK Investment CJSC v Kyrgyz Mobil Tel Ltd* [2011] UKPC 7, [2011] 4 All E.R. 1027, at [105].

[5] 1st ed., p.712.

[6] *cf.* Lorenzen, pp.339–340.

[7] e.g. *Grant v McAuliffe*, 41 Cal. 2d 859, 246 P. 2d 944 (1953); *Kilberg v Northeast Airlines Inc*, 9 N.Y. 2d 34, 172 N.E. 2d 526 (1961); Currie, Ch.3.

[8] See below, paras 7–006 *et seq.*

questions which were at one time thought of wholly in terms of procedure are now considered to be procedural in some of their aspects only. The development of the law as to limitation periods[9] and damages[10] illustrates this process.

7-004   The difficulty in applying this Rule lies in discriminating between rules of procedure and rules of substance. The distinction is by no means clear-cut. In drawing it, regard should be had in each case to the purpose for which the distinction is being used and to the consequences of the decision in the instant context.[11] The rule under examination must be considered as a whole, without giving undue weight to the verbal formula selected by previous judges or by the draftsman of a statute to introduce the rule. So, the words "where proceedings are taken in any court . . . " have been held to introduce a rule of substance.[12] The mechanistic approach, sometimes found in English cases, of relying on the classification of the introductory verbal formula as used in a quite different statute,[13] or of accepting a classification as procedural or substantive made for some purpose quite unrelated to the conflict of laws,[14] is now discredited. The distinction may have to be drawn in one place for the purpose of this Rule but in another place for the purpose of the rule that statutes affecting procedure are, while statutes affecting substance are not, presumed to have retrospective effect. This is not to say that the distinction may not be drawn in the same place for many purposes: it is merely to deny that it must necessarily be drawn in the same place for all purposes. The primary object of this Rule is to obviate the inconvenience of conducting the trial of a case containing foreign elements in a manner with which the court is unfamiliar. In principle, therefore, if it is possible to apply a foreign rule, or to refrain from applying an English rule, without causing any such inconvenience,[15] those rules should not necessarily, for the purpose of this Rule, be classified as procedural.[16]

---

[9] See below, paras 7–054 *et seq.*

[10] See below, paras 7–043—7–053 *et seq.*

[11] Falconbridge, p.304; *Block Bros Realty Ltd v Mollard* (1981) 122 D.L.R. (3d) 323 (BCCA). See Panagopoulos (2005) 1 J. Priv. Int. L. 69.

[12] *Shrichand & Co v Lacon* (1906) 22 T.L.R. 245. Similarly, a rule which provides that a person "may not bring proceedings for the recovery of damages" unless certain conditions are satisfied has been construed as a rule of substance: *Sherwood v Webb* (1992) 28 N.S.W.L.R. 251. See also *James Hardie & Co Pty Ltd v Hall* (1998) 43 N.S.W.L.R. 554.

[13] e.g. *Moulis v Owen* [1907] 1 K.B. 746, 753 (CA); *Hill v William Hill (Park Lane) Ltd* [1949] A.C. 530, 579, where decisions under the Gaming Acts 1845 and 1892 were influenced by the earlier classification of the same formula ("No action shall be brought . . . ") in the Statute of Frauds 1677, s.4. *cf. Toronto-Dominion Bank v Martin* [1985] 4 W.W.R. 557 (Sask.); *Horseshoe Club Operating Co v Bath* [1998] 3 W.W.R. 128 (BC).

[14] e.g. *Leroux v Brown* (1852) 12 C.B. 801, 827. *cf.* Cook, Ch.6.

[15] And consistently with precedent.

[16] *Bateman & Litman Real Estate Ltd v Big T Motel Ltd* (1964) 44 D.L.R. (2d) 474, affirmed 49 D.L.R. (2d) 480 (Sask CA), citing the corresponding text in the 7th edition of this work. See also *Shaik Sahied bin Abdullah Bajerai v Sockalingam Chettiar* [1933] A.C. 342, 346 (PC); *The Zollverein* (1856) Swab. 96, 98; *Nihalchand Navalchand v McMullan* [1934] 1 K.B. 171 (CA) as explained in (1935) 16 B.Y.I.L. 210; *Merchants Bank of Canada v Elliot* [1918] 1 W.W.R. 698 (an English case of which there is only a Canadian report); *Monterosso Shipping Co Ltd v International Transport Workers Federation* [1982] I.C.R. 675, 681–682 (CA).

Nonetheless, in *John Pfeiffer Pty Ltd v Rogerson*[17] the High Court of **7–005** Australia considered the English common law understanding of matter of "procedure" to be overly broad and capable of undermining the faithful application of the *lex causae*.[18] It adopted a broader understanding of what constitute matters of substance and stated that "matters that affect the existence, extent or enforceability of the rights or duties of the parties to an action are matters that, on their face, appear to be concerned with issues of substance".[19] In *Harding v Wealands*,[20] however, the House of Lords restated the orthodox approach in English law[21] and overruled the majority decision of the Court of Appeal, which had followed the Australian authorities which narrowed the meaning of the term "procedure".[22]

Rome I and Rome II Regulations. Today, the exercise of distinguishing **7–006** between matters of substance and procedure in England has been significantly affected by the entry into force of harmonised European rules on the scope of application of the *lex causae*, which will be considered in more detail below.

A number of matters dealt with in this chapter are affected by the Rome I **7–007** Regulation on the Law Applicable to Contractual Obligations.[23] Its relevance here is that a number of its provisions extend the scope of the application of the *lex causae*, the law governing the contract, to cover some issues which under the common law position reflected in the Rule are matters of procedure governed by the *lex fori*. These provisions, noted at appropriate places in this chapter but more fully considered in Chapter 32, concern remedies for breach of contract, including assessment of damages,[24] and certain matters of evidence: proof of a contract[25] and provisions of the law of contract as to the burden of proof and presumptions of law.[26]

Similarly, the Rome II Regulation on the Law Applicable to Non-Con- **7–008** tractual Obligations[27] contains provisions on these matters.[28] Again, these are

---

[17] (2000) 203 C.L.R. 503.

[18] On the dichotomy between substance and procedure in Australian law, see Davis, in Berryman and Bigwood (eds.), *The Law of Remedies: New Directions in the Common Law* (2010), Ch.19. See also Keyes (2010) 8 Torts L.J. 201.

[19] (2000) 203 C.L.R. 503, 543.

[20] [2006] UKHL 32, [2007] 2 A.C. 1.

[21] Following *Boys v Chaplin* [1971] A.C. 356. This applies in relation to areas of law not harmonised across the EU.

[22] The decision in *Harding v Wealands* itself would now be different: see below, para.7–050.

[23] Regulation (EC) 593/2008 of the European Parliament and of the Council on the law applicable to contractual obligations (Rome I): [2008] O.J. L177/6 (with corrigendum: [2009] O.J. L307/87) applies to contracts concluded on or after December 17, 2009. It supersedes the Rome Convention on the Law Applicable to Contractual Obligations 1980, given effect in English law by the Contracts (Applicable Law) Act 1990.

[24] Rome I Regulation, Art.12(1)(c); see below, paras 32–153 *et seq.*

[25] Rome I Regulation, Art.18; see below, para.32–131.

[26] Rome I Regulation, Art.18; see below, para.32–034. See also Art.12(1)(d) of the Rome I Regulation (Art.10(1)(d) of the Rome Convention) on limitation of actions.

[27] Regulation (EC) 864/2007 of the European Parliament and of the Council on the Law Applicable to Non-Contractual Obligations ([2007] O.J. L199/40), which entered into force on January 11, 2009. See Ch.32, below.

[28] Notably in Arts 15 and 22.

considered at appropriate places in the chapter but more fully discussed in Chapters 34 to 36.[29]

7–009   Hence, for matters falling within the scope of the Rome I and II Regulations, the key consideration is as to whether the law applicable on the substance also applies to the issue in question.[30] Although the Rome I and II Regulations exclude matters of evidence and procedure,[31] they also contain rules on the scope of the governing law.[32] Since the Regulations must be applied uniformly, the dichotomy between rules of substance and procedure in respect of those Regulations will ultimately be resolved by European autonomous rules. Accordingly, it is essential to appreciate that the principles established at common law[33] as to the distinction between matters of substance and matters of procedure may not apply where the Rome I or Rome II Regulation is applicable.

7–010   In the sections below, the common law principles will be examined first. They must be read subject to the impact of the Rome I and II Regulations. The common law principles will apply in respect of matters that are not the subject of harmonisation at EU level.[34]

7–011   **(1) Nature of remedy and method of enforcement.** As a matter of English common law, the nature of the remedy is a matter of procedure to be determined by the *lex fori*.[35] Thus if the claimant is by the *lex causae* entitled only to damages but is by English law entitled to specific relief, the latter type of remedy is available in England.[36] Conversely, an English court will not grant specific relief where to do so is contrary to the principles of English law: thus no injunction can be obtained in England for breach of negative stipulations in a foreign contract of service if such an injunction would in effect amount to specific enforcement of the contract.[37] Again, a remedy which is discretionary according to English law cannot be demanded as of right in an English court merely because this is possible according to the *lex causae*.

7–012   Generally speaking the common law principle that the forum grants its own remedies in respect of wrongs governed by a foreign law only applies if two conditions are satisfied. First, the *lex causae* must give the claimant some

---

[29] On remedies for breach of non-contractual obligations, including the assessment of damages, see Art.15; on proof of a non-contractual obligation, see Art.22(2); on burdens of proof and presumptions of law, see Art.22(1).

[30] On the impact of the Rome I and Rome II Regulations on the dichotomy between substance and procedure, see Illmer (2009) 28 C.J.Q. 237; see also Briggs (2009) 125 L.Q.R. 191, at 195. On the application of the distinction between substance and procedure to the Rome II Regulation, see Schoeman [2010] L.M.C.L.Q. 81.

[31] See Rome I Regulation, Art.1(3) (subject to Art.18); Rome II Regulation, Art.1(3) (subject to Arts 21 and 22).

[32] Rome I Regulation, Art.12; Rome II Regulation, Art.15.

[33] Including rules in English statutes.

[34] Although they may, of course, be modified in some respects by domestic legislation.

[35] *Flack v Holm* (1820) 1 J. & W. 405; *De la Vega v Vianna* (1830) 1 B. & Ad. 284; *Liverpool Marine Credit Co v Hunter* (1868) L.R. 3 Ch. App. 479, 486; *Harding v Wealands* [2006] UKHL 32, [2007] 2 A.C. 1; *Fiona Trust & Holding Corp v Privalov* [2010] EWHC 3199 (Comm.), at [155].

[36] *Baschet v London Illustrated Standard Co* [1900] 1 Ch.73; *Boys v Chaplin* [1971] A.C. 356, 394.

[37] cf. *Warner Brothers Pictures Inc v Nelson* [1937] 1 K.B. 209; where, however, this point was not discussed.

remedy against the defendant in respect of a wrong similar in character to that alleged in the English proceedings.[38] Secondly, the English remedy sought must "harmonise with the right according to its nature and extent as fixed by the foreign law."[39] Thus English remedies will be refused if they are so different from those provided by the *lex causae* as "to make the right sought to be enforced a different right."[40] Although an action in England will not fail merely because the claim is unknown to English law, it will fail if English law has no appropriate remedy for giving effect to the claimant's alleged foreign right.[41]

The method of enforcing a judgment is a matter of procedure.[42] The *lex fori* **7–013** determines what property of the defendant is available to satisfy the judgment, and in what order. Thus if the *lex causae* provides that mortgage debts are to be satisfied primarily out of the mortgaged property, this does not prevent the forum from ordering the satisfaction of such debts out of the debtor's property generally.[43] But if the *lex causae* provided that only the mortgaged property was liable for the debt, this would amount to a rule of substance to the effect that by the *lex causae* the "debtor" was under no personal liability. Such a rule would, therefore, be applied by the forum.[44] Conversely, a court would not apply a rule of its own domestic law protecting the debtor from personal liability where the *lex causae* imposed such liability upon him.[45]

These common law principles are substantially eroded by the Rome I and **7–014** Rome II Regulations, which determine, for matters within their scope, the law applicable to contractual and non-contractual obligations, respectively. In the case of a contract, the principle that the nature of the remedy is a matter for the *lex fori* is affected by the provisions of the Rome I Regulation. The law applicable to a contract by virtue of Arts 3 to 8 and 14 of the Regulation[46] governs, within the limits of the powers conferred on the court by its procedural law,[47] the consequences of a total or partial breach of obligations, including the assessment of damages in so far as it is governed by rules of law.[48]

A similar principle is to be found in the Rome II Regulation. Article 15(c) **7–015** stipulates that "the existence, the nature and the assessment of damage or the

---

[38] *McMillan v Canadian Northern Ry Co* [1923] A.C. 120 (PC).

[39] *Phrantzes v Argenti* [1960] 2 Q.B. 19, 35.

[40] At p.36.

[41] ibid.; *Khalij Commercial Bank Ltd v Woods* (1985) 17 D.L.R. (4th) 358 (Ont).

[42] *Minister of Public Works of Kuwait v Sir Frederick Snow and Partners* [1983] 1 W.L.R. 818, 829 (CA).

[43] cf. *Northern Trusts Co v McLean* [1926] 3 D.L.R. 93 (Ont CA); *243930 Alberta Ltd v Wickham* (1987) 61 O.R. (2d) 731.

[44] *Melan v Fitzjames* (1797) 1 Bos. & P. 138 is perhaps distinguishable from *De la Vega v Vianna* (1830) 1 B. & Ad. 284 along the lines suggested in the text.

[45] *Canadian Acceptance Corp Ltd v Matte* (1957) 9 D.L.R. (2d) 304 (Sask CA); *Sigurdson v Farrow* (1981) 121 D.L.R. (3d) 183 (Alta). cf. *243930 Alberta Ltd v Wickham* (1987) 61 O.R. (2d) 731 where provisions virtually identical to those classified as substantive in *Canadian Acceptance Corp Ltd v Matte* (1957) 9 D.L.R. (2d) 304 (Sask CA) and *Sigurdson v Farrow* (1981) 121 D.L.R. (3d) 183 (Alta) were held to be procedural.

[46] Compare Contracts (Applicable Law) Act 1990, s.2 and Sch.1, Arts 3 to 6 and 12.

[47] i.e. the forum court is not required to make an order unknown to its legal system.

[48] Rome I Regulation, Art.12(1)(c); compare Contracts (Applicable Law) Act 1990, s.2 and Sch.1, Art.10(1)(c). See further, below, paras 32–153 *et seq.*

remedy claimed" are to be determined by the governing law of the non-contractual obligation. Furthermore, pursuant to Art.15(d), an English court should apply the law governing the non-contractual obligation "within the limits of powers conferred on the court by its procedural law, the measures which a court may take to prevent or terminate injury or damage or to ensure the provision of compensation." Article 15(d) does not, accordingly, require English courts to create remedies unknown in English law or procedures for the granting and enforcement of such remedies. In the event that an English court cannot award the remedy stipulated by the *lex causae*, it is likely, however, to strive to invoke the most analogous remedy or procedure available in English law.[49]

7–016   Equitable doctrines may give rise to particular difficulties of classification in the conflict of laws,[50] for example as to the classification of tracing. This involves identification of property or its value when it has changed its form through mixture or substitution. It could be argued that tracing should be classified as procedural, since "In truth, tracing is a process of identifying assets; it belongs to the realm of evidence. It tells us nothing about the legal or equitable rights to the assets traced."[51] Nevertheless, tracing will be an essential step in the bringing of substantive actions in the law of property, trusts and restitution. The better view is that it should be treated as substantive and governed by the law applicable to the claimant's cause of action.[52] It is further suggested that the *lex causae* should also apply insofar as the cause of action falls within the ambit of the Rome I or II Regulations, since it is that law that determines the rights of the parties and the remedies to which they are entitled and it would be curious for tracing, which may be a pre-requisite to bringing the action and obtaining relief, to be subject to a different law.

It is suggested that the question of whether a constructive trust arises is substantive.[53] A court should apply, in principle, the law governing the cause of action which is said to give rise to the trust.[54] The same approach should be adopted where a constructive trust is imposed pursuant to the breach of a non-contractual obligation under the Rome II Regulation.[55]

7–017   **(2) Parties.** In determining who are the proper parties to proceedings, the first question is whether the claimant or defendant is the sort of person or body

---

[49] Dickinson, *The Rome II Regulation* (2008), para.14.34.

[50] See paras 34–083 and 36–057 *et seq.* below; Yeo, *Choice of Law for Equitable Doctrines* (2004), Ch.4. In principle, equitable doctrines should be incorporated within established, analogous legal categories wherever possible: *Fiona Trust & Holding Corp v Privalov* [2010] EWHC 3199 (Comm.), at [153].

[51] *Foskett v McKeown* [2001] 1 A.C. 102, 113, *per* Lord Steyn.

[52] See *Chase Manhattan v Israel-British Bank* [1981] Ch. 105; *El Ajou v Dollar Land Holdings Plc* [1993] 3 All E.R. 717, reversed (but not on this issue) [1994] 2 All E.R. 685; Harris (2003) 63 B.Y.I.L. 65; Panagopoulos (1998) 6 R.L.R. 73; Yeo, *op. cit.*, pp.133–134; below, paras 29–056 and 34–096 *et seq.*

[53] See *Chase Manhattan v Israel-British Bank* [1981] Ch. 105, at p.127 *(obiter)*.

[54] Yeo, *op. cit.*, pp.127–8. However, the position may be more complex where the governing law does not know the concept of the constructive trust. See below, paras 29R–075 *et seq.*; and 36–080 *et seq.*

[55] See further below, paras 36–080 *et seq.*

that can be made a party to litigation.[56] This is a question for the *lex fori*.[57] Thus proceedings could not be commenced in England in the name of a dead man, even though this was possible by the *lex causae*.[58] The same applies, *mutatis mutandis*, and subject to statutory exceptions,[59] to actions by and against dissolved companies,[60] though the question whether a company has been dissolved must be decided by reference to the law of the place of incorporation.[61] Again, a foreign body which does not have legal personality and which does not carry on business in England cannot, as such, sue or be sued in England.[62] There is, however, no reason why a foreign entity which enjoys legal personality under the law of the country where it is established should not be able to participate in proceedings in England even though it has not been expressly incorporated. "The courts of one country give recognition, by a comity of nations, to a legal personality created by the law of another country."[63] In *Bumper Development Corp v Commissioner of Police for the Metropolis*[64] an Indian temple, which was recognised as having legal personality under Indian law, was permitted to sue in English proceedings, notwithstanding the fact that the temple, which was "little more than a pile of stones",[65] lacked the basic characteristics of a legal person under English law. Similarly, in *Oxnard Financing SA v Rahn*[66] it was decided that a partnership which, though not a corporation, had legal personality under Swiss law could be sued in England either by reference to the partnership name or by reference to the names of its members.

Assuming that a claimant is capable of suing in the above sense, the next question is whether he is the proper claimant in the particular action before the court.[67] Clearly he is not if by the *lex causae* the right which he is seeking to

7–018

---

[56] The distinct questions raised by jurisdictional immunities are considered in Ch.10 and are not determined by the rules of substance and procedure; but *cf. Garsec Pty Ltd v Sultan of Brunei* [2008] NSWCA 211, 250 A.L.R. 682; see also *Fleming v Marshall* [2011] NSWCA 86, at [99].

[57] *Oxnard Financing SA v Rahn* [1998] 1 W.L.R. 1465 (CA).

[58] *Banque Internationale de Commerce de Petrograd v Goukassow* [1923] 2 K.B. 682, reversed on other grounds [1925] A.C. 150.

[59] See *Russian & English Bank v Baring Brothers & Co Ltd* [1936] A.C. 405; *cf.* below, paras 30–057 *et seq.*

[60] *Banque Internationale de Commerce de Petrograd v Goukassow* [1923] 2 K.B. 682 (CA), revd. on other grounds: [1925] A.C. 150; *Deutsche Bank v Banque des Marchands de Moscou* (1932) 158 L.T. 364 (CA).

[61] *Lazard Bros & Co v Midland Bank Ltd* [1933] A.C. 289; *cf.* paras 30–010 *et seq.*, below.

[62] *Von Hellfeld v Rechnitzer* [1914] 1 Ch. 748.

[63] *Chaff v Hay Acquisition Committee v JA Hemptill and Sons Pty Ltd* (1947) 74 C.L.R. 375, 390, *per* McTiernan J. (cited with approval by Lord Templeman in *Arab Monetary Fund v Hashim (No 3)* [1991] 2 A.C. 114, 162). See also *Skyline Associates v Small* (1975) 56 D.L.R. (3d) 471 (BCCA); *International Association of Science and Technology for Development v Hamza* (1995) 122 D.L.R. (4th) 92 (Alta CA).

[64] [1991] 1 W.L.R. 1362 (CA).

[65] [1991] 1 W.L.R. 1362, 1371, *per* Purchas L.J.

[66] [1998] 1 W.L.R. 1465 (CA).

[67] The *obiter dictum* of Lord Diplock in *Bankers Trust International Ltd v Todd Shipyards Corp* [1981] A.C. 221, 235 (PC) that "any question as to who is entitled to bring a particular kind of proceeding in an English court . . . is a question of jurisdiction . . . to be decided by English law as the *lex fori*" cannot be supported, and must be confined to the special context of maritime liens. See below, para.7–041.

enforce did not vest in him but in someone else.[68] If the right is vested in him, further problems may arise from rules of the *lex causae* or of the *lex fori* to the effect that the claimant may not sue in his own name or in his own name alone, but must sue in the name of some third party, or in the name of himself and of a third party jointly. The authorities are divided on the question whether rules requiring the assignee of a debt to sue in the name of, or together with, the assignor are substantive or procedural. The authorities which support the view that such rules are procedural[69] can all be explained on other grounds; and the authorities which treat the matter as substantive[70] can be supported on the ground that the application of foreign rules of this kind will not, in general, cause any procedural inconvenience to the court. The principal object of such rules appears to be to protect the debtor; and if the *lex causae* does not give him such protection it is hard to see why he should have it when he is sued in England.

7–019   In some cases, the claimant claims to be entitled to sue in England in a representative capacity, relying on an appointment made under foreign law. As Parker J. observed in *Kamouh v Associated Electrical Industries International Ltd*,[71] two conflicting principles can be found, "first, that [the English] courts should as a matter of comity give effect to the curator's or tuteur's right under foreign law to sue in his own name; second, that municipal procedure should be applied." The first principle applies in the case of trustees in bankruptcy,[72] liquidators,[73] receivers,[74] administrators of alien enemy property,[75] and curators of mentally disordered persons (though in this last case the curator should join the mentally disordered person, suing by his next friend, as co-claimant).[76] But the second principle, precluding the claimant from relying on

---

[68] *Ross v Sinhjee* (1891) 19 R. 31; Hancock, p.124; *Lucas v Coupal* [1931] 1 D.L.R. 391 (Ont); Falconbridge, pp.120–123; *cf. Hartmann v Konig* (1933) 50 T.L.R. 114 (HL). The identification of the parties to an arbitration agreement is a matter of substance: see *Peterson Farms Inc v C&M Farming Ltd* [2004] EWHC 121 (Comm.), [2004] 1 Lloyd's Rep. 603.

[69] In *Wolff v Oxholm* (1817) 6 M. & S. 92 English law was both the *lex fori* and the *lex causae*. In *Jeffery v M'Taggart* (1817) 6 M. & S. 126 and *Barber v Mexican Land Co* (1899) 16 T.L.R. 127 the *leges causae* were not intended to have extraterritorial effect. In *Regas Ltd v Plotkins* (1961) 29 D.L.R. (2d) 282 (Sup Ct Can) the *lex fori* was also the proper law of the debt; and it is arguable that the action succeeded on the ground that the assignee was also the original creditor and sued as such: see p.287 and (1959) 22 D.L.R. (2d) 169, 174.

[70] *Innes v Dunlop* (1800) 8 T.R. 595; *O'Callaghan v Thomond* (1810) 3 Taunt. 82; *cf. Trimbey v Vignier* (1834) 1 Bing. N.C. 151.

[71] [1980] Q.B. 199, 206.

[72] *Smith v Buchanan* (1800) 1 East 6, 11; *O'Callaghan v Thomond* (1810) 3 Taunt. 82; *Alivon v Furnival* (1834) 1 Cr.M. & R. 277, 296; *Macaulay v Guaranty Trust Co of New York* (1927) 44 T.L.R. 99; *Obers v Paton's Trustees* (1897) 24 R. 719; *Kamouh v Associated Electrical Industries International Ltd* [1980] Q.B. 199, 206. See Rule 216.

[73] *Bank of Ethiopia v National Bank of Egypt and Liguori* [1937] Ch. 513, 524. *cf. North Australian Territory Co v Goldsbrough Mort & Co* (1889) 61 L.T. 716. See Rule 179.

[74] *Schemmer v Property Resources Ltd* [1975] Ch. 273, especially at p.287; *Macaulay v Guaranty Trust Co. of New York* (1927) 44 T.L.R. 99, which was, however, treated as a bankruptcy case; *Re Young* [1955] Qd.R. 254; *Kamouh v Associated Electrical Industries International Ltd.* [1980] Q.B. 199, 206; *White v Verkouille* [1990] 2 Qd.R. 191. *cf. Perry v Zissis* [1977] 1 Lloyd's Rep. 607, 615 (CA). See Rule 180.

[75] *Lepage v San Paulo Copper Estates Ltd* [1917] W.N. 216.

[76] *Didisheim v London and Westminster Bank* [1900] 2 Ch. 15 (CA); *Pélégrin v Coutts & Co* [1915] 1 Ch. 696; *Kamouh v Associated Electrical Industries International Ltd* [1980] Q.B. 199, 206; *Re S.* [1951] N.Z.L.R. 122. See Rules 124 and 125.

his foreign appointment, applies to administrators of deceased persons,[77] and to administrators of absentees' property.[78]

The final question is whether the person sued is the proper defendant to the action. In some foreign systems of law a defendant cannot be sued unless and until some other person has been sued first. For instance, in some foreign systems a creditor cannot sue an individual partner until he has first sued the firm and its assets have been exhausted, or cannot sue a surety until he has first sued the principal debtor. Such rules are in sharp contrast to the rule of English law that any partner may be sued alone for the whole of the partnership debts, or that a surety may be sued without joining the principal debtor. The question is whether such a rule of foreign law is substantive or procedural. If the *lex causae* regards the defendant as under no liability whatever unless other persons are sued first, the rule is substantive and must be applied in English proceedings.[79] If on the other hand the *lex causae* regards the defendant as liable, but makes his liability conditional on other persons being sued first, then the rule is procedural and is ignored in English proceedings.[80]   **7–020**

These principles are modified where the Rome II Regulation applies.[81] Article 15(a) applies the *lex causae* to "the determination of persons who may be held liable for acts performed by them."[82] This would apparently also encompass the question of capacity to incur liability.[83] Article 15(e) provides that the question whether "a right to claim damages or a remedy may be transferred, including by inheritance"[84] is determined by the law applicable to the non-contractual obligation.[85] That law also applies to determine the persons entitled to compensation for damage sustained personally;[86] and the liability for the acts of another person.[87]   **7–021**

---

[77] *Carter and Crost's Case* (1585) Godb. 33; *Tourton v Flower* (1735) 3 P. Will. 369, 370; *New York Breweries Co Ltd v Att-Gen* [1899] A.C. 62; *Finnegan v Cementation Co Ltd* [1953] 1 Q.B. 688 (CA); *Kamouh v Associated Electrical Industries International Ltd* [1980] Q.B. 199, 206. See Rule 144.

[78] *Kamouh v Associated Electrical Industries International Ltd* [1980] Q.B. 199.

[79] *General Steam Navigation Co v Guillou* (1843) 11 M. & W. 877; *The Mary Moxham* (1876) 1 P.D. 107 (CA).

[80] *General Steam Navigation Co v Guillou* (1843) 11 M. & W. 877; *Bullock v Caird* (1875) L.R. 10 Q.B. 276; *Re Doetsch* [1896] 2 Ch. 836; *Subbotovsky v Waung* [1968] 3 N.S.W.R. 216, affirmed on other grounds sub nom. *Waung v Subbotovsky* [1968] 3 N.S.W.R. 499; (1969) 121 C.L.R. 337; *Johnson Matthey & Wallace Ltd v Alloush* (1984) 135 N.L.J. 1012 (CA). For criticism see Wolff, p.240; Rabel, Vol.2, pp.118–119; Anton, para.27.13. See also *OJSC Oil Co Yugraneft v Abramovich* [2008] EWHC 2613 (Comm.), at [298].

[81] See Hay (2007) 4 Eu. L.F. 137; Beaumont and Tang (2008) 12 Edin.L.Rev. 131.

[82] On whether a direct action may be brought by an injured party in a road accident against the insurer of the allegedly negligent driver, see Rome II Regulation, Art.18. See also *Maher v Groupama Grand Est* [2009] EWCA Civ 1191, [2010] 1 W.L.R. 1564, [2010] 2 All E.R. 455.

[83] See also Recital (12). See further Dickinson, *The Rome II Regulation* (2008), paras 14.09–14.12. Contrast Rome I Regulation, Art.1(2)(a).

[84] But the question of who inherits that right is a matter of the law of succession and so outside the ambit of the Regulation: Art.1(2)(b).

[85] But it is conceivable that some such rules, e.g. the English rules on champerty may be regarded as an aspect of English public policy capable of overriding the *lex causae* in an English court. Conversely, where English law applies, it has been suggested that the English rules on champerty would not need necessarily be intended to apply to claims governed by English law that are brought in a foreign court: Dickinson, *The Rome II Regulation*, para.14.40.

[86] Art.15(f).

[87] Art.15(g).

7–022   **(3) Evidence.** "The law of evidence," it has been said, "is the *lex fori* which governs the courts. Whether a witness is competent or not; whether a certain matter requires to be proved by writing or not; whether certain evidence proves a certain fact or not; that is to be determined by the law of the country where the question arises, where the remedy is sought to be enforced and where the court sits to enforce it."[88] On the other hand, "it is not everything that appears in a treatise on the law of evidence that is to be classified internationally as adjective law, but only provisions of a technical or procedural character—for instance rules as to the admissibility of hearsay evidence or what matters may be noticed judicially."[89] Thus the *lex causae* generally determines what are the facts in issue;[90] and it may do so by providing that no evidence need, or may, be given as to certain matters, for instance as to compliance, or failure to comply with, certain formalities of a marriage ceremony. Such provisions are substantive.[91] On the other hand, as a general rule, the *lex fori* determines how the facts in issue must be proved.[92] In the context of English proceedings, whether or not a document is privileged is to be determined by English law; the fact that under a foreign law the document is not privileged or that the privilege that existed is deemed to have been waived is irrelevant.[93]

7–023   Exceptions to this general rule may be provided by legislation.[94] A contract or an act intended to have legal effect may be proved by any mode of proof recognised in English law or by any of the laws referred to in Art.11 of the Rome I Regulation,[95] under which that contract or act is formally valid, provided that a mode of proof recognised by a foreign law is only available in English proceedings if it can be administered by English law.[96] Similar provisions are contained in the Rome II Regulation.[97]

The following problems in the law of evidence call for special consideration.

7–024   *Admissibility.* Questions as to the admissibility of evidence are decided (subject to the impact of the Rome I and II Regulations) in accordance with the *lex fori*.[98] Thus, at common law, a document may be received as evidence

---

[88] *Bain v Whitehaven and Furness Junction Ry* (1850) 3 H.L.C. 1, 19.

[89] *Mahadervan v Mahadervan* [1964] P. 233, 243.

[90] *The Gaetano and Maria* (1882) 7 P.D. 137 (CA).

[91] *Mahadervan v Mahadervan*, above, distinguished in *Dubai Bank Ltd v Galadari (No.5), The Times*, June 26, 1990, where the text was cited with approval.

[92] See *Loutchansky v Times Newspapers Ltd (Nos 2 to 5)* [2001] EWCA Civ 1805, [2002] Q.B. 783, at [86].

[93] *Bourns Inc v Raychem Corp (No.3)* [1999] C.L.C. 1029 (CA).

[94] See, e.g. *McAllister v General Medical Council* [1993] A.C. 388 (PC) in which it was held that, by virtue of the Medical Act 1983 and the rules made under it, proceedings before the Professional Conduct Committee of the General Medical Council were governed by English law, even in a case where the Committee sat in Scotland.

[95] Compare Contracts (Applicable Law) Act 1990, Sch.1, Art.9.

[96] Rome I Regulation, Art.18(2); compare Contracts (Applicable Law) Act 1990, s.2 and Sch.1, Art.14(2). See below, para.32–131.

[97] See Arts 21 and 22(2).

[98] *Yates v Thomson* (1835) 3 Cl. & F. 544; *Bain v Whitehaven and Furness Junction Ry* (1850) 3 H.L.C. 1.

by the English court although it is inadmissible by the *lex causae*.[99] Conversely, copies of foreign documents, though admissible by the *lex causae*, are inadmissible in England,[100] unless they comply with the English rules as to the admissibility of secondary evidence of documents.[101] The latter rule is now subject to a statutory exception. Under the Evidence (Foreign, Dominion and Colonial Documents) Act 1933,[102] the Crown has power to make Orders in Council providing, inter alia, that official and properly authenticated copies of foreign public registers shall be admissible in the United Kingdom to prove the contents of such registers.[103]

A distinction has been drawn between extrinsic evidence adduced to interpret a written document, e.g. a contract, and extrinsic evidence adduced to add to, vary or contradict its terms. The admissibility of the former is a question of interpretation, governed in the case of a contract by its applicable law.[104] The admissibility of the latter is a question of evidence, governed, subject to the possible effect of the Rome I and II Regulations, by the *lex fori*.[105] Thus in *St Pierre v South American Stores Ltd*[106] a question arose as to the meaning of the covenant to pay rent contained in a lease of land in Chile and governed by Chilean law. It was held that evidence of negotiations prior to the contract and of subsequent writings was admissible, although it was inadmissible by English law. On the other hand, in *Korner v Witkowitzer*[107] the plaintiff sued to recover arrears of pension under a contract governed by Czech law. In order to obtain leave to serve notice of the writ out of the jurisdiction he had to prove that the contract was broken in England. It was held by Denning L.J. that evidence of an oral agreement whereby the plaintiff was to receive his pension in the country in which he might be living when it accrued was inadmissible, since this would be to vary the terms of the written agreement. Although matters of evidence and procedure are generally outside the scope of the Rome I Regulation, Art.18(2) provides that a contract or an act intended to have legal effect may be proved by any means of proof recognised by the law of the forum or by any of the laws which govern formal validity under the Regulation, provided that the mode of proof can be administered in the

7–025

---

[99] *Bristow v Sequeville* (1850) 5 Exch. 275; contrast *Alves v Hodgson* (1797) 7 T.R. 241 and *Clegg v Levy* (1812) 3 Camp. 166, where the document was not merely inadmissible by the *lex causae* but an utter nullity.

[100] *Appleton v Braybrook* (1817) 6 M. & S. 34; *Brown v Thornton* (1837) 6 Ad. & E. 185; *Finlay v Finlay* (1862) 31 L.J.P. 149.

[101] As in *Roe v Roe* (1916) 115 L.T. 792; *Brown v Brown* (1917) 116 L.T. 702; see also *Abbott v Abbott* (1860) 4 Sw. & Tr. 254.

[102] As amended by s.5 of the Oaths and Evidence (Overseas Authorities and Countries) Act 1963, which abolished the requirement of reciprocity.

[103] For existing orders, see *Halsbury's Statutory Instruments*, Vol.8 (2006 issue), paras 10 *et seq*. See also *Motture v Motture* [1955] 1 W.L.R. 1066.

[104] Rome I Regulation, Art.12(1)(a); compare Contracts (Applicable Law) Act 1990, Sch.1, Art.10(1)(a). The same position obtained at common law: *St Pierre v South American Stores Ltd* [1937] 1 All E.R. 206, 209; affirmed [1937] 3 All E.R. 349 (CA). *cf. Re Barker* [1995] 2 V.R. 439 (in which it was held that whether a German will was intended to affect an earlier Australian will was to be determined by the *lex fori* rather than the *lex domicilii*).

[105] *Korner v Witkowitzer* [1950] 2 K.B. 128, 162–163 (CA); affirmed sub nom. *Vitkovice v Korner* [1951] A.C. 869.

[106] See above.

[107] See above; see also *Australian Zircon Nl v Austpac Resources Nl* [2010] WASC 166, at [69].

forum.[108] It is submitted, though with some hesitation, that this will in some cases render admissible evidence of the type declared inadmissible under English law in *Korner v Witkowitzer*. Similar principles are applicable under the Rome II Regulation, insofar as a party may seek to admit evidence to prove or disprove the existence of a non-contractual obligation.[109]

7–026   *Requirement of written evidence.*[110] Section 4 of the Statute of Frauds 1677 provided that "no action shall be brought" on a number of contracts unless the agreement, or a note or memorandum thereof, was in writing. Section 4 now applies only to contracts of guarantee. It was held in *Leroux v Brown*[111] that s.4 contained a rule of procedure and therefore prevented the enforcement in England of an oral contract governed by French law which could have been sued upon in France. This decision has been severely criticised by writers[112] on the ground that no serious procedural inconvenience would be caused by admitting oral evidence of a contract within s.4: indeed the court is bound to admit such evidence if the contract is not set up for the purpose of enforcement but as a defence. To characterise the section as procedural merely because it says "no action shall be brought" is to regard the form of the section as more important than its substance. To characterise it as procedural for the purposes of the conflict of laws merely because it had previously been characterised as procedural for some purposes of English domestic law is to lose sight of the purpose of the characterisation.

7–027   The decision was judicially doubted[113] and the court once refused (on somewhat specious reasoning) to apply s.4 to a French contract relating to English land,[114] but it has twice been approved *obiter* in the House of Lords[115] and the Court of Appeal, having considered the earlier criticisms, has declared itself unwilling to disturb the decision.[116] Mustill L.J., with whom Woolf L.J. agreed, declared the reasoning in *Leroux v Brown* to be "unassailable," and noted that Parliament had not taken the opportunity presented by two amendments to the Statute of Frauds to limit its effect to contracts governed by English law; only the House of Lords could overturn the decision. Purchas L.J. similarly declared himself unwilling to disturb it.[117]

---

[108] Compare Contracts (Applicable Law) Act 1990, Sch.1, Art.14(2).

[109] See Art.22(2) of the Rome II Regulation.

[110] On the position in the US, see Restatement, s.141.

[111] (1852) 12 C.B. 801; the same result was reached in *Acebal v Levy* (1834) 10 Bing. 376, but it was not argued in that case that the contract was governed by foreign law.

[112] Falconbridge, pp.98–102; Robertson, p.255; Beckett (1934) 15 B.Y.I.L. 46, 69–71; Cook, pp.229–231.

[113] *Williams v Wheeler* (1860) 8 C.B.(N.S.) 299, 316; *Gibson v Holland* (1865) L.R. 1 C.P. 1, 8; *Rawley v Rawley* (1876) 1 Q.B.D. 460, 461.

[114] *Re De Nicols (No.2)* [1900] 2 Ch. 410; see below, paras 28–021 *et seq.*

[115] *Maddison v Alderson* (1883) 8 App. Cas. 467, 474; *Morris v Baron & Co.* [1918] A.C. 1, 15.

[116] *Irvani v G and H Montage GmbH* [1990] 1 W.L.R. 667 (CA) where the Statute of Frauds was, however, ultimately held inapplicable on the facts.

[117] Section 179 of the Trade Union and Labour Relations (Consolidation) Act 1992 provides that in certain cases a collective agreement "shall be conclusively presumed not to have been intended by the parties to be a legally enforceable contract" unless it is in writing and contains a provision declaring that the parties did intend to enter into a legally enforceable contract. In *Monterosso Shipping Co Ltd v International Transport Workers' Federation* [1982] I.C.R. 675 (CA), the Court of Appeal held that the predecessor of s.179 contained a substantive and not

Very different from the approach of the Court of Common Pleas in *Leroux*   **7–028**
v Brown was that of the Supreme Court of California in *Bernkrant v*
Fowler.[118] There the court refused to apply the Californian Statute of Frauds
to an oral Nevada contract on the ground that, having regard to "the scope of
the statute in the light of applicable principles of the conflict of laws," it did
not apply to foreign contracts. The court stressed the "basic policy of upholding the expectations of the parties by enforcing contracts valid under the only
law apparently applicable," and the lack of any "interest" which California
might have in applying its statute to a foreign contract. In *Tipperary Develop-*
ments Pty Ltd v The State of Western Australia,[119] the Western Australian
Court of Appeal held that the Statute of Frauds was to be treated as substantive and that, following the decision in *John Pfeiffer Pty Ltd v Roger-*
son,[120] the decision in *Leroux v Brown* no longer represented the law in
Australia.[121]

Difficult problems may arise where both the *lex causae* and the *lex fori*   **7–029**
contain provisions analogous to the Statute of Frauds which differ from each
other in the stringency of their requirements. Questions of this kind have not
yet arisen for decision in England. It is not impossible that the court might, in
the circumstances of a particular case, decide that the rule of the *lex causae* is
substantive, whereas the rule of the *lex fori* is procedural,[122] in which case
both rules would prima facie be applicable. Conversely, it might be decided
that the rule of the *lex causae* is procedural and the forum's rule substantive,
in which case strict logic might suggest that neither should apply; and indeed
a lower court in New York once reached this absurd result.[123] However, given
that the purpose of classification is to determine the proper scope of the
forum's conflict rules,[124] there should be no question of an English court
seeking to classify the Statute of Frauds differently from analogous foreign
rules; either the English rule and the analogous rule of the *lex causae* are both
procedural, in which case the English rule is applicable, or they are both
substantive and the *lex causae* governs.

---

merely a procedural rule. May L.J. distinguished the cases on the Statutes of Frauds and the
Limitation Acts, where the statutory language and context were different (at p.685); Lord
Denning M.R. declared (at pp.681–682) the reasoning in those cases to be unsatisfactory, the true
distinction in the present context being between the existence of a contract (a question of
substantive law) and remedies for breach (a procedural question). See further *Star City Pty Ltd*
v Tan Hong Woon [2002] 2 Sing.L.R. 22. Under the Rome I Regulation, remedies for breach will
now be treated as substantive (Art.12(1)(c)).

[118] 55 Cal. 2d 588, 360 P. 2d 906 (1961). For comment see Cavers in *Perspectives of Law* (ed.
Pound, Griswold and Sutherland), pp.38–68. See also *Intercontinental Planning Ltd v Daystrom*
Inc, 300 N.Y.S. 2d 817, 248 N.E. 2d 576 (1969). Other jurisdictions in the United States adopt
different approaches, e.g. that statutes of frauds should always be classed as substantive (*Muccilli*
v Huff's Boys' Store Inc, 12 Ariz.App. 584, 473 P. 2d 786 (1970)).

[119] [2009] WASCA 126, (2009) 258 A.L.R. 124.

[120] (2000) 203 C.L.R. 503. The *Pfeiffer* decision has not been followed in England: *Harding v*
Wealands [2006] UKHL 32, [2007] 2 A.C. 1.

[121] However, as the proper law of the contract was Western Australian law, it made no
difference on the facts.

[122] In cases falling outside the ambit of the Rome I and II Regulations.

[123] *Marie v Garrison*, 13 Abb. N.C. 210 (1883); criticised by Lorenzen, p.339, n.59; *cf.* Cook,
pp.225–228. See also Harris (2004) 57 Curr. Leg. Prob. 305, 308–312.

[124] See Ch.2.

7–030   In England, the effect of *Leroux v Brown* has been greatly reduced by the Rome I Regulation, Art.18(2),[125] which allows the proof of a contract by reference to the law governing the issue of formal validity as an alternative to the law of the forum. The better view is that s.4 of the Statute of Frauds should be classified as an English rule of formal validity for the purposes of the Regulation. The practical effect of this is that *Leroux v Brown* will not apply in cases falling within the ambit of harmonised European choice of law rules.

7–031   Section 53(1)(b) of the Law of Property Act 1925, re-enacting s.7 of the Statute of Frauds, provides that "a declaration of trust respecting any land . . . must be manifested and proved by some writing." There is support for the view that this enactment contains a rule of procedure[126] but it is doubtful whether this still represents the law.[127] There is, as yet, no authority on the question whether requirements of written evidence imposed by other statutes are substantive or procedural.

7–032   *Witnesses.* Whether a witness is competent[128] or compellable, or whether he can claim privilege,[129] all appear to be questions for the *lex fori*.[130] Of course, if, as is often the case, questions of competence, compellability or privilege depend on the matrimonial status of a witness, the question of status must be referred to the appropriate *lex causae* before the English rule of evidence can be applied.

7–033   *Functions of judge and jury.* Two questions arise in determining the functions of judge and jury: whether, in a given case, there should be trial by jury at all; and, if so, what are the respective functions of judge and jury. It is submitted that both these questions must be left exclusively to the *lex fori*

---

[125] Compare Contracts (Applicable Law) Act 1990, Sch.1, Art.14(2). See further, below, para.32–131. Similarly, in respect of non-contractual obligations, Art.22(2) of the Rome II Regulation states that: "Acts intended to have legal effect may be proved by any mode of proof recognised by the law of the forum or by any of the laws referred to in Art.21 under which that act is formally valid, provided that such mode of proof can be administered by the forum."

[126] An *obiter dictum* in *Rochefoucauld v Boustead* [1897] 1 Ch. 196, 207 (CA).

[127] It is not immediately clear whether rules relating to the formal validity of a trust fall within the ambit of the Hague Trusts Convention, enacted into English law by the Recognition of Trusts Act 1987, or are excluded as preliminary matters (Art.4 of the Convention). If they are within the Convention's scope, it is also unclear whether the law applicable to the trust applies pursuant to Art.8 of the Convention. The Official Report by von Overbeck comments that "Article 8 deals with substantive issues without expressly excluding issues of form" (para.82, p.388). It has been argued that formality rules that are specific to the law of trusts (as opposed to e.g. rules as to the formal validity of a will containing a trust, which are not trusts specific) fall within the Convention's ambit and are, in principle, governed by the law applicable to the trust: see Harris, *The Hague Trusts Convention*, pp.272–274. See also below, para.29–038.

[128] *Bain v Whitehaven & Furness Junction Ry* (1850) 3 H.L.C. 1, 19.

[129] For privilege claims under the Evidence (Proceedings in Other Jurisdictions) Act 1975, see below, para.8–104.

[130] A dictum in *Re Atherton* [1912] 2 K.B. 251, 255–256 is contrary to the proposition in the text, but the actual decision turned on the interpretation of s.17(1) of the Bankruptcy Act 1883 (now repealed). *cf. F F Seeley Nominees Pty Ltd v El Ar Initiations (UK) Ltd* (1990) 96 A.L.R. 468 (S Austr) (privilege against self-incrimination; offence under foreign law).

since they involve issues of procedural convenience, and, it may be added, of public policy.[131]

Burden of proof. Although there is some authority for the proposition that, **7–034** at common law, questions relating to the burden of proof are matters for the *lex fori*,[132] there is much to be said for treating them as substantive, for the outcome of a case can depend on where the burden of proof lies. As Lorenzen says,[133] "the statement that courts should enforce foreign substantive rights but not foreign procedural laws has no justifiable basis if the so-called procedural law would normally affect the outcome of the litigation." This is reflected in the Restatement proposition that where the primary purpose of the rule as to burden of proof in the *lex causae* is to affect decision of the issue rather than to regulate the conduct of the trial, it will be applied in preference to the rule in the *lex fori*.[134] This principle has been applied in many contexts, including some American cases on the burden of proving or disproving contributory negligence,[135] and the burden of proving that an insurer was given notice of an accident.[136]

In the case of a contract, the law governing the contract under the Rome I **7–035** Regulation applies to the extent that it contains, in the law of contract as opposed to the law of procedure, rules which determine the burden of proof.[137] The Rome II Regulation contains a similar provision for rules which determine the burden of proof that are contained in the law which governs a non-contractual obligation.[138]

Presumptions. In order to determine whether presumptions are rules of **7–036** substance or rules of procedure, it is necessary to distinguish between three kinds of presumptions: presumptions of fact, and irrebuttable and rebuttable presumptions of law. Presumptions of fact arise when, on proof of certain basic facts, the trier of fact may, but need not, find the existence of a presumed fact. Presumptions of fact have, strictly speaking, no legal effect at all, and need not be considered here. So far as presumptions of law are concerned, there is a statutory rule that, in the case of a contract, the law governing the contract under the Rome I Regulation applies to the extent that it contains, in the law of contract as opposed to the law of procedure, rules which raise

---

[131] See Hancock, pp.148–153, who would leave the second question to the *lex causae*. On the effects of Art.15(d) of the Rome II Regulation, see Dickinson, *The Rome II Regulation*, para.14.34.

[132] *The Roberta* (1937) 58 Ll.L.R. 159, 177; *In the Estate of Fuld (No.3)* [1968] P. 675, 696–697; *Fiona Trust & Holding Corp v Privalov* [2010] EWHC 3199 (Comm.), at [94]. The law in Scotland is the same: Anton, para.27–17, citing *Mackenzie v Hall* (1854) 17 D. 164.

[133] Lorenzen, p.134.

[134] s.133; and see Annot., 35 A.L.R. 3d 289.

[135] *Fitzpatrick v International Ry* 252 N.Y. 127, 169 N.E. 112 (1929). See Restatement, s.133, Illustrations 2–4. Contributory negligence was treated as substantive in *Dawson v Broughton* (2007) 151 So. J. 1167 (Manchester County Court).

[136] *Peterson v Warren* 31 Wis. 2d 547, 143 N.W. 2d 560 (1966).

[137] Art.18(1); compare Contracts (Applicable Law) Act 1990, s.2 and Sch.1, Art.14(1). See below, para.32–034.

[138] Art.22(1).

presumptions of law.[139] No distinction is drawn in this provision between presumptions of law which are rebuttable and those which are irrebuttable; it appears to apply to both categories. A similar provision in the Rome II Regulation applies the presumptions of law that are contained in the law applicable to a non-contractual obligation, as opposed to the rules of procedure.[140] The distinction does, however, need to be observed in considering the position at common law. Irrebuttable presumptions of law arise when, on proof of the basic facts, the trier of fact must find the presumed fact in any event.[141] An example is the presumption of survivorship contained in s.184 of the Law of Property Act 1925. It is now generally agreed that, even for the purposes of domestic law, irrebuttable presumptions of law are rules of substance, and this is also true for the purpose of the conflict of laws.[142] Rebuttable presumptions of law arise when, on proof of the basic facts, the trier of fact must find the presumed fact unless the contrary is proved. For the purpose of the conflict of laws they must be further subdivided into those which apply only in certain contexts, and those which apply in all types of case. Examples of the first type are the presumptions of resulting trust, advancement, satisfaction and ademption, and the presumptions contained in s.2 of the Perpetuities and Accumulations Act 1964 to the effect that a female under the age of twelve or over the age of fifty-five cannot have a child. All these are thought to be so closely connected with the existence of substantive rights that they ought to be characterised as rules of substance.[143]

7–037   Examples of the second type of presumptions are the presumptions of marriage,[144] legitimacy,[145] and death, which apply (although not always in precisely the same way) to all types of case. It is uncertain whether such presumptions are rules of substance or rules of procedure. In cases involving presumptions of marriage the courts have applied the *lex causae* whenever that law was proved;[146] and a dictum on the subject treats such a presumption as a rule of substance.[147] But where it is sought to base a presumption on cohabitation in a number of different countries, whose laws on the subject differ, the forum may have no option but to apply its own rule.[148] There is no

---

[139] Rome I Regulation, Art.18(1); compare Contracts (Applicable Law) Act 1990, s.2 and Sch.1, Art.14(1).

[140] Art.22(1).

[141] *cf. Cross and Tapper on Evidence* (12th ed. 2010), Ch.3.

[142] *Re Cohn* [1945] Ch. 5; *Fiona Trust & Holding Corp v Privalov* [2010] EWHC 3199 (Comm.), at [98].

[143] Thus it was assumed in *Stevenson v Masson* (1873) L.R. 17 Eq. 78 that the presumption of ademption was a rule of substance; *cf.* Wolff, s.221, who also explains *Re Cohn*, above, on this ground.

[144] See below paras 17–047 *et seq.*

[145] Much weakened by s.26 of the Family Law Reform Act 1969.

[146] *Hill v Hibbit* (1870) 25 L.T. 183; *De Thoren v Att-Gen* (1876) 1 App. Cas. 686. In *Re Shephard* [1904] 1 Ch. 456, *Re Taplin* [1937] 3 All E.R. 105 and *Mahadervan v Mahadervan* [1964] P. 233 the court applied the English rule—but there was no evidence of a different rule of the *lex causae*. In *Leong Sow Nom v Chin Yee You* [1934] 3 W.W.R. 686 (BC) (discussed by Falconbridge, pp.314–315) the court refused to apply its own presumptions even though there was no evidence of the *lex causae*.

[147] *Mahadervan v Mahadervan* [1964] P. 233, 242.

[148] *cf.* below, paras 17–048 *et seq.*

direct authority on the question whether the common law presumptions of legitimacy and death are rules of substance or of procedure.

Estoppel.[149]   For the purposes of English domestic law, estoppel is some-   **7–038**
times said to be a rule of evidence.[150] Whether, for the purpose of this Rule, it should be regarded as a rule of substance or as a rule of procedure is an entirely open question, the answer to which may well vary with the type of estoppel under consideration.[151] Thus the question whether a principal is estopped from denying his agent's authority to deal with a third party proba- bly depends on the *lex causae*.[152] On the other hand, the question precisely when an estoppel by record arises probably depends on the *lex fori*,[153] although, of course that law may distinguish for this purpose between the effect of foreign and domestic judgments.[154]

(4) Set-off and counterclaim. Set-off is of two kinds. It may be a claim   **7–039**
of a certain kind which the defendant has against the claimant and which can conveniently be tried together with the claim against the defendant. The question whether a set-off of this kind can be raised in an action is one of procedure for the *lex fori*.[155] A set-off may, on the other hand, amount to an equity directly attaching to the claim[156] and operate in partial or total extinc- tion thereof; an example is the *compensation de plein droit* of French law.[157] The question whether a set-off of this kind exists is one of substance for the *lex causae*, i.e. the law governing the claim which the defendant asserts has been discharged in whole or in part.[158] A counterclaim is a claim by the defendant which, though not operative by way of set-off, can conveniently be tried together with the claim against the defendant. The question whether a

---

[149] For discussion of this paragraph in the previous edition of this work, see *Dornoch Ltd v Westminster International BV* [2009] EWHC 1782 (Admlty), [2009] 2 Lloyd's Rep. 420, at [21].

[150] *Low v Bouverie* [1891] 3 Ch. 82, 105 (CA). See generally *Cross and Tapper on Evidence* (12th ed. 2010), pp.85–108.

[151] See Yeo, *Choice of Law for Equitable Doctrines* (2004), pp.134–6.

[152] See below, paras 33–436 *et seq.*; *cf. Allen v Hay* (1922) 69 D.L.R. 193 (Sup Ct Can), suggesting that estoppel by conduct is a rule of substance for the present purpose. A dictum in *Cuthbertson v Cuthbertson* [1952] 4 D.L.R. 814, 818 (Ont.) may perhaps suggest the contrary.

[153] *Vervaeke v Smith* [1983] 1 A.C. 146, 162 (estoppel *per rem judicatam* based on an English judgment). The statement in *Carl Zeiss Stiftung v Rayner & Keeler Ltd. (No.2)* [1967] 1 A.C. 853, 919 that "estoppel is a matter for the *lex fori*" was made in this context and should, it is submitted, be restricted to it. See also Illustration 8, below, para.7–077.

[154] Rules 42, 48 and especially paras 14–122 *et seq.*, below.

[155] *Meyer v Dresser* (1864) 16 C.B. (N.S.) 646. See also Case C–341/93 *Danvaern Production A/S v Schuhfabriken Otterbeck GmbH & Co* [1995] E.C.R. I–2053.

[156] See *Holmes v Kidd* (1858) 3 H. & N. 891, and contrast *Re Overend, Gurney & Co* (1868) L.R. 6 Eq. 344.

[157] See Rabel, Vol.3 (2nd ed.), pp.474–475; Wolff, pp.233–234.

[158] See *MacFarlane v Norris* (1862) 2 B. & S. 783, where, however, there does not appear to have been any conflict between the *lex fori* and the *lex causae; Meridien BIAO Bank GmbH v Bank of New York* [1997] 1 Lloyd's Rep. 437 (CA); *cf. Allen v Kemble* (1848) 6 Moo. P.C. 314, but in this case the *lex fori* was also the *lex causae; Rouquette v Overmann* (1875) L.R. 10 Q.B. 525, 540–541. In *Maspons v Mildred, Goyeneche & Co* (1882) 9 Q.B.D. 530 (CA), affirmed without reference to this point (1883) 8 App.Cas. 874, it is not clear whether English law was applied as *lex fori* or as *lex causae*: the contract sued upon was governed by English law. See Wood, *English and International Set-Off* (1989), Ch.23.

claim can be raised by way of counterclaim is one of procedure for the *lex fori*.[159]

7–040   These principles are affected, for matters within its ambit, by the Rome I Regulation.[160] Article 17 provides that: "Where the right to set-off is not agreed by the parties, set-off shall be governed by the law applicable to the claim against which the right to set-off is asserted." A set-off amounting to an equity attaching directly to the claim will fall within the ambit of Art.17. Beyond that, the ambit of Art.17 is not immediately clear. The better view is that it does not affect the question of whether a claim which the defendant has against the defendant can be tried together with the claimant's claim against the defendant, this being a matter of procedure outside the ambit of the Regulation. Similarly, the question of whether a counterclaim may be brought is best regarded as procedural and outside the ambit of Art.17.

7–041   **(5) Priorities.** The priorities as between claimants to a limited fund which is being distributed by a court are governed by the *lex fori*.[161] The existence and quantification of each creditor's claim is of course a matter for the *lex causae* of the claim,[162] but once the claims are established the *lex fori* determines priorities, for the court "is primarily concerned in doing even-handed justice between competing creditors whose respective claims to be a creditor may have arisen under a whole variety of different and, it may be, conflicting systems of national law."[163] The principle is well established;[164] a creditor can neither gain priority by virtue of a special rule in the foreign law governing his claim[165] nor lose priority by virtue of such a rule.[166] In order to assign a foreign claim to the appropriate class in the order of priorities under the *lex fori*, the court will examine the events on which the claim was founded

---

[159] *South African Republic v Compagnie Franco-Belge du Chemin de Fer du Nord* [1897] 2 Ch. 487 (CA).

[160] See Hellner, in Ferrari and Leible (eds), *The Rome I Regulation* (2009), Ch.14. There was no such provision in the Rome Convention. Nor is there any such provision in the Rome II Regulation.

[161] *Bankers Trust International Ltd v Todd Shipyards Corp (The Halcyon Isle)* [1981] A.C. 221 (P.C.).

[162] *The Colorado* [1923] P. 102 (CA), as explained in *The Zigurds* [1932] P. 113 and *Bankers Trust International Ltd v Todd Shipyards Corp (The Halcyon Isle)*, above.

[163] *Bankers Trust International Ltd v Todd Shipyards Corp (The Halcyon Isle)* [1981] A.C. 221, 230–231 (PC). The principle that priorities are governed by the *lex fori* is equally applicable in cases where all the competing claims are governed by the same (foreign) *lex causae: Fournier v The Ship "Margaret Z"* [1999] 3 N.Z.L.R. 111.

[164] *The Milford* (1858) Swa. 362, approved in *The Tagus* [1903] P. 44; *The Jonathan Goodhue* (1859) Swa. 524; *The Union* (1860) Lush. 128; *Maspons v Mildred, Goyeneche & Co* (1882) 9 Q.B.D. 530 (CA), affirmed without reference to this point (1883) 8 App. Cas. 874; *Re Kloebe* (1884) 28 Ch.D. 175; *Canada Deposit Insurance Corp v Canadian Commercial Bank* (1994) 121 D.L.R. (4th) 360 (Alta). *cf. Clark v Bowring*, 1908 S.C. 1168; *Todd Shipyards Corp v Altema Compania Maritima SA (The Ioannis Daskalelis)* (1972) 32 D.L.R. (3d) 571 (Sup Ct Can), disapproved in *Bankers Trust International Ltd v Todd Shipyards Corp (The Halcyon Isle)* [1981] A.C. 221 (PC); *JP Morgan Chase Bank v Mystras Maritime Corp* [2008] FCA 399, (2008) 305 D.L.R. (4th) 442 (appeal dismissed without consideration of this point: 2010 FC 1053). But, on recent legislative developments in Canada, see *World Fuel Services Corporation v The Ship "Nordems"* [2011] FCA 73.

[165] e.g. *Pardo v Bingham* (1868) L.R. 6 Eq. 485.

[166] e.g. *Ex p. Melbourn* (1870) L.R. 6 Ch. App. 64. Contrast *Cook v Gregson* (1854) 2 Drew. 286 (foreign asset administered according to the priorities under the foreign law).

and give the claim the priority to which it would be entitled under the *lex fori* if those events had occurred within the territorial jurisdiction of the court.[167]

The principle that priorities are governed by the *lex fori* is not, however, a universal one.[168] Thus it is probable that the priority of competing assignments of a debt is governed by the law applicable to the debt.[169] It is possible, also, that the priority of claims against foreign land is governed by the *lex situs*.[170]   **7–042**

(6) Damages.[171] The common law rules on the assessment of damages have been very largely qualified by the Rome I and II Regulations, which determine, respectively, the law applicable to contractual and non-contractual obligations.[172] The common law cases remain relevant to matters falling outside the ambit of the Rome I and II Regulations, including defamation.[173]   **7–043**

Contractual obligations. It was clear[174] that, at common law, the law relating to damages was partly procedural and partly substantive.[175] A distinction was drawn between remoteness[176] and heads of damage, which were questions of substance governed by the *lex causae*, and measure or quantification of damages, which was a question of procedure governed by the *lex fori*.[177] The former included the question in respect of what items of loss the claimant could recover compensation. The latter included the method to be   **7–044**

---

[167] *Bankers Trust International Ltd. v Todd Shipyards Corp (The Halcyon Isle)* [1981] A.C. 221 (PC); followed in *The Ship "Betty Ott" v General Bills Ltd* [1992] 1 N.Z.L.R. 655 (CA), which cited with approval the equivalent paragraph of text in the 11th ed.

[168] The statutory exception in Maritime Conventions Act 1911, s.7 (apportionment of salvage) was repealed by Merchant Shipping Act 1995, s.314, Sch.12.

[169] Rule 135. Questions as to the priority of competing assignments must be distinguished from questions as to the validity of competing assignments: contrast, at common law, *Kelly v Selwyn* [1905] 2 Ch. 117, with *Republica de Guatemala v Nunez* (1926) 42 T.L.R. 625; [1927] 1 K.B. 669 (CA). See, in respect of the Rome I Regulation, Arts 14 and 27(2). See also Bridge (2009) 125 L.Q.R. 671; Hartley (2011) 60 I.C.L.Q. 29; Mollmann [2011] L.M.C.L.Q. 262; Verhagen and Van Dongen (2010) 6 J. Priv. Int. L. 1. See further below, paras 24R–050 *et seq.*

[170] See *Norton v Florence Land and Public Works Co* (1877) 7 Ch.D. 332.

[171] The question of interest is dealt with separately in Rule 20, below.

[172] For matters within their respective ambits. See further, for damages in contract, below, paras 32–153 *et seq.*; for damages in tort, below, paras 34–056 *et seq.*

[173] Which is excluded from the ambit of the Rome I Regulation (Art.1(2)(g)). It is also excluded by Private International Law (Miscellaneous Provisions) Act 1995, Pt III, s.13.

[174] Despite earlier dicta to the contrary e.g. in *Kremezi v Ridgway* [1949] 1 All E.R. 662, 664; *Kohnke v Karger* [1951] 2 K.B. 670, 677.

[175] *Boys v Chaplin* [1971] A.C. 356, 379.

[176] See, at common law, the judgment of Pilcher J. in *D'Almeida Araujo Lda v Sir Frederick Becker and Co Ltd* [1953] 2 Q.B. 329, following *Livesley v Horst Co* [1925] 1 D.L.R. 159 (Sup Ct Can) and *Cheshire*, 4th ed., pp.659–660, in treating remoteness as substantive. The proposition that remoteness or heads of damage are governed by the *lex causae* was supported by a number of cases in which it was held that the question whether a debt carries interest depends on the governing law of the debt: see Rule 20, below.

[177] This distinction was recognised in *Boys v Chaplin*, above, and was equally applicable at common law to contracts.

used in assessing the monetary compensation which the defendant must pay in respect of those items of loss for which he was liable.[178]

7–045   In the case of contracts, the assessment of damages is now a matter for the *lex causae*,[179] at least insofar as it is governed by rules of law. This is the effect of the Rome I Regulation:[180] the law applicable to a contract by virtue of Arts 3 to 8 and 14 of the Regulation governs, within the limits of the powers conferred on the court by its procedural law, the consequences of a total or partial breach of obligations, including the assessment of damages so far as it is governed by rules of law.[181] Hence, a rule of the *lex causae* limiting the amount of compensation payable would be applied under the Regulation. The same is true of rules of the governing law of the contract on remoteness of damages. The assessment of damages (insofar as it is not subject to rules of law) will be governed by the *lex fori*.

7–046   *Non-contractual obligations.* The position in respect of non-contractual obligations has been significantly affected by the entry into force of the Rome II Regulation. Prior to its entry into force, the common law position that questions of heads of damages are substantive applied to actions in tort as well as to actions in contract.[182] Thus in *Boys v Chaplin*,[183] a majority of the House of Lords held that the question whether damages were recoverable for pain and suffering was a question of substance.[184] In a number of Scots cases in which it was held that no claim for *solatium* could be maintained in Scotland by the spouse or near relative of a person killed in a country by whose law no such claim was recognised.[185] The proposition that the quantification of damages was governed by the *lex fori* at common law was illustrated by the fact that in an English court damages must be assessed once and for all except

---

[178] In *King v T. Tunnock Ltd*, 2000 S.L.T. 744, the Court of Session (Inner House) decided that, in the context of a claim for compensation under the Commercial Agents (Council Directive) Regulations (SI 1993/3053), which implement Council Directive (EC) 653/86, the principles of French law on which the Directive's compensation system is based, rather than the common law rules governing the quantification of damages, are relevant for determining the level of compensation to which the claimant might be entitled.

[179] See Carruthers (2004) 53 I.C.L.Q. 691.

[180] Compare Contracts (Applicable Law) Act 1990, s.2 and Sch.1, Arts 3 to 6 and 12.

[181] Rome I Regulation, Art.12(1)(c); compare Contracts (Applicable Law) Act 1990, s.2 and Sch.1, Art.10(1)(c). See below, para.32–153 *et seq*.

[182] This distinction was recognised in *Boys v Chaplin*, above, *per* Lord Hodson at p.379, *per* Lord Guest at pp.381–382, *per* Lord Wilberforce at p.393, *per* Lord Pearson at p.395. See, to the same effect, *Breavington v Godleman* (1988) 169 C.L.R. 41; *Waterhouse v Australian Broadcasting Corp* (1989) 86 A.C.T.R. 1, 19. See also *Edmunds v Simmonds* [2001] 1 W.L.R. 1003; *Hulse v Chambers* [2001] 1 W.L.R. 2386; *Harding v Wealands* [2006] UKHL 32, [2007] 2 A.C. 1.

[183] [1971] A.C. 356, *per* Lord Hodson at p.379, *per* Lord Wilberforce at p.393, *per* Lord Pearson at pp.394–395. The dissentients were Lord Guest at p.382, and Lord Donovan at p.383. This principle has been applied for the purposes of Private International Law (Miscellaneous Provisions) Act 1995, Part III: see *Edmunds v Simmonds* [2001] 1 W.L.R. 1003; *Hulse v Chambers* [2001] 1 W.L.R. 2386.

[184] The proposition that remoteness or heads of damage are governed by the *lex causae* was supported by a number of cases in which it was held that the question whether a debt carries interest depends on the governing law of the debt: see Rule 20, below.

[185] *Kendrick v Burnett* (1897) 25 R. 82; *Naftalin v LMS*, 1933 S.C. 259; *M'Elroy v M'Allister*, 1949 S.C. 110; contrast *Kemp v Piper* [1971] S.A.S.R. 25.

in cases where provisional damages are awarded in a personal injuries case.[186] An English court has no power to award periodical payments by way of damages, nor to increase an award of damages if the injuries become aggravated after a final judgment has been delivered. These rules would undoubtedly have been applied even though different rules might exist in the *lex causae*.[187]

Although these proposition could be stated straightforwardly, it was not always clear on which side of the line certain issues fell. Statutory provisions limiting a defendant's liability proved particularly problematic. The majority of the High Court of Australia in *Stevens v Head*,[188] held that a provision in the Motor Accidents Act 1988 of New South Wales which limited the amount of damages which could be recovered in respect of non-economic loss was procedural as it did not touch the heads of liability in respect of which damages might be awarded, but simply related to the quantification of damages.[189] A much narrower view of the ambit of procedure was, however, adopted by the High Court of Australia in *John Pfeiffer Pty Ltd v Rogerson*.[190] The plaintiff sued his employer in the Australian Capital Territory (ACT) in relation to injury suffered in an accident at work in New South Wales. In the ACT damages were assessed at A$30,000 plus out of pocket expenses; under the Workers' Compensation Act 1987 (NSW) damages would have been limited to a considerably lesser sum. The High Court of Australia reconsidered the rule laid down in *Stevens v Head*[191] and decided that the NSW provision, which placed a cap on damages, was a substantive rule. A majority of the High Court of Australia[192] went further and indicated that *all* questions about the amount of damages that may be recovered ought to be treated as substantive issues.[193]

7–047

The classification of statutory ceilings on damages was examined in England in *Harding v Wealands*.[194] A claim arose out of a motor accident in New

7–048

---

[186] Senior Courts Act 1981, s.32A (as inserted by Administration of Justice Act 1982, s.6; s.6(3) of which was repealed by Statute Law (Repeals) Act 2004, Sch.1(1)(4) para.1).

[187] *Kohnke v Karger* [1951] 2 K.B. 670; *Boys v Chaplin* [1971] A.C. 356, 394.

[188] (1993) 176 C.L.R. 433. For criticism of the decision see Opeskin (1993) 109 L.Q.R. 533.

[189] See also *Somers v Fournier* (2002) 214 D.L.R. (4th) 611 (Ont. C.A.).

[190] (2000) 203 C.L.R. 503. For a comparative analysis of the classification of financial remedies in tort, see Gray (2008) 4 J. Priv. Int. L. 279.

[191] (1993) 176 C.L.R. 433.

[192] At p.651, *per* Gleeson C.J., Gaudron, McHugh, Gummow and Hayne J.J.

[193] Although this was a case confined to intra-Australian conflicts. In *Régie National des Usines Renault v Zhang* (2002) 187 A.L.R. 1, the High Court left open the question whether this approach should be extended to foreign torts. Compare the judgment of Mason C.J. in *Stevens v Head* (1993) 176 C.L.R. 433, 448–451. See also *Tolofson v Jensen* [1994] 3 S.C.R. 1022, (1994) 120 DLR (4th) 289, 321, where La Forest J. said that the primary purpose of classifying a rule as substantive or procedural is "to determine which rules will make the machinery of the forum court run smoothly as distinguished from those determinative of the rights of both parties".

[194] [2006] UKHL 32, [2007] 2 A.C. 1. For discussion, see Scott [2007] L.M.C.L.Q. 44; Beaumont and Tang (2008) 12 Edin. L.Rev. 131. For a United States perspective on the decision, see Weintraub (2007) 42 Tex. Int. L.J. 311. The case involved consideration of the ambit of Private International Law (Miscellaneous Provisions) Act 1995, s.14. In *Re T&N Ltd* [2005] EWHC 2990 (Ch.), at [70] and [87], [2006] 1 W.L.R. 1792, David Richards J. stated that the meaning of the word "procedure" should be the same for the purposes of the common law choice of law rules in tort and the 1995 Act.

South Wales. Section 5 of the Motor Accidents Compensation Act 1999 (NSW) contains provisions for the maximum compensation payable by a defendant for financial loss, loss of earnings and preventing interest being paid for certain types of financial loss. The majority of the Court of Appeal decided that the decision in *Boys v Chaplin* did not require it to conclude that only the question of the availability of heads of damages was substantive and that all other matters, such as maximum limits on damages, were procedural. The Court of Appeal cited with approval the High Court of Australia's decision in *John Pfeiffer Pty Ltd v Rogerson* and held that "procedure" should be narrowly confined to matters that related to the manner and conduct of the proceedings and all other provisions or rules were to be classified as substantive. The House of Lords, however, reversed the decision and held that the narrower view of the ambit of procedure adopted by the High Court of Australia in *John Pfeiffer Pty Ltd v Rogerson* did not apply in England.[195] The effect of *Boys v Chaplin* was that all matters relating to the quantification of damages were to be treated as procedural. The meaning of the word "procedure" was the same under the Private International Law (Miscellaneous Provisions) Act 1995, Part III[196] as at common law. Lord Hoffmann construed dicta in a 19th century case, *Cope v Doherty*,[197] as standing for the proposition that where a statute of limitation imposes a contractual term limiting the obligation to pay damages, this is to be treated as "an express limitation upon the substantive liabilities."[198] He held that where a statutory provision limiting liability does not operate as an imposed contractual term, such a provision should be classified as procedural. Hence, Lord Hoffmann observed[199] that the court "was right in *Caltex Singapore Pte Ltd v BP Shipping Ltd*[200] to treat a modern limitation statute . . . as a procedural provision, limiting the remedy rather than the substantive right . . . ". The result was that the statutory provision imposing a ceiling on compensation was not applied.

7-049 For matters within its scope, the classification of damages for non-contractual obligations, including torts and delicts, as substantive and procedural is now determined in England by the Rome II Regulation. Although the Regulation excludes matters of procedure from its ambit,[201] it equally contains provisions on the scope of the law governing the non-contractual obligation.[202] The ambit of these provisions will be determined uniformly and autonomously for all Regulation States. The Regulation treats a significantly broader range of issues as substantive than the prior law. Hence, it may be of

---

[195] See also *Re T&N Ltd* [2005] EWHC 2990 (Ch.), at [75], [2006] 1 W.L.R. 1792. Contrast *McNeilly v Imbree* [2007] NSWCA 156.

[196] s.14(3)(b).

[197] (1858) 4 K. & J. 367, 384–5, and (1858) 2 De G. & J. 614, 623.

[198] At [46], relying on the judgment of Street C.J. in *Allan J Panozza & Co Pty Ltd v Allied Interstate (Qld) Pty Ltd* [1976] 2 N.S.W.L.R. 192, 196–7. The actual decision in *Cope v Doherty* had long been obsolete: see *The Amalia* (1863) 1 Moo. P.C. (N.S.) 471.

[199] At [47].

[200] [1996] 1 Lloyd's Rep. 286. This decision was overruled on other grounds in *The Herceg Novi* [1998] 4 All E.R. 238 (CA). See also Merchant Shipping Act 1995, s.185 (as amended by Merchant Shipping and Maritime Security Act 1997, s.15; SI 1998/1258; SI 2004/1273).

[201] Art.1(3).

[202] Art.15.

critical importance to determine whether a damages claim falls within the ambit of the Rome II Regulation.[203]

Article 15(b)[204] of the Regulation applies the governing law to "the grounds for exemption from liability, any limitation of liability and any division of liability." Article 15(c) provides that "the nature and assessment of damage"[205] is a matter for the law applicable to the non-contractual obligation. Hence, the availability of particular heads of damages is to be treated as a substantive matter.[206] The same is true of rules of remoteness. In relation to the "assessment of damages", Art.15(c) reverses the effect of *Boys v Chaplin*.[207] Moreover, if the facts of *Harding v Wealands* were to arise today, it would lead to a different outcome.[208] Rules imposing a statutory ceiling on the level of damages affect the assessment of those damages and are to be treated as substantive, so that such rules of the *lex causae* would be applied in England. The application of the *lex causae* is not limited to compensatory damages.[209] More generally, it appears that the English courts should endeavour to consider the rules of the *lex causae* together with relevant judicial practices and guidelines as to their application, so as to endeavour to apply the law of damages to reflect, as accurately as possible, the level of damages that would actually be awarded in the courts of the country whose law is applicable.[210]

7–050

Article 15(d) states that the *lex causae* applies "within the limits of powers conferred on the court by its procedural law" to "the measures which a court may take to prevent or terminate injury or damage or to ensure the provision of compensation". This constitutes a qualified reference to the *lex causae*, which should be applied provided that the remedy in question is known

7–051

---

[203] The European Court has held that the Regulation applies only to events giving rise to damage occurring after January 11, 2009 and that the date on which the proceedings seeking compensation for damage were brought or the date on which the applicable law was determined by the court seised do not affect the applicability of the Regulation: see Case C–412/10 *Homawoo v GMF Assurance SA* [2012] I.L.Pr. 49. See also Schoeman [2010] L.M.C.L.Q. 81.

[204] On the limitation of liability of ship owners under international conventions and their relationship to the Rome II Regulation, see Tsimplis (2010) 16 J.I.M.L. 289; [2011] L.M.C.L.Q. 307.

[205] The word "damage" rather than "damages" is used. On this issue, see Dickinson, *The Rome II Regulation*, para.14.20.

[206] Recital (33) of the Regulation provides that: "According to the current national rules on compensation awarded to victims of road traffic accidents, when quantifying damages for personal injury in cases in which the accident takes place in a State other than that of the habitual residence of the victim, the court seised should take into account all the relevant actual circumstances of the specific victim, including in particular the actual losses and cost of after-care and medical attention."

[207] At least to the extent that application of that law does not infringe an overriding mandatory rule of English law (Art.16) or is not manifestly incompatible with the public policy of the forum (Art.26). On the problems of awarding exemplary or punitive anti-trust damages under the Rome II Regulation, see Danov (2008) 29 E.C.L.R. 430.

[208] It is conceivable that ceilings on damages would fall within Art.15(b) as a "limitation of liability"; but this make no difference in practice. See also Schoeman (2011) 7 J. Priv. Int. L. 361, 388–392.

[209] In respect of punitive damages, see also Recital (32) and Art.26.

[210] Dickinson, *The Rome II Regulation*, para.14.19; *cf.* Rushworth and Scott [2008] L.M.C.L.Q. 274, 294.

according to English law and that it is not unduly burdensome for the English court to grant it.[211]

7–052   The governing law may be disapplied under the Rome II Regulation if it is manifestly incompatible with public policy[212] or if there is an overriding mandatory provision of English law.[213] In some cases, this may in practice negate the classification of the issue as substantive. In *Roerig v Valiant Trawlers Ltd*,[214] the court considered the nature of s.4 of the Fatal Accidents Act 1976, which states that "in assessing damages in respect of a person's death in an action under this Act, benefits which have accrued or will or may accrue to any person from his estate or otherwise as a result of his death shall be disregarded." It classified the issue as procedural[215] and hence not subject to the choice of law rules in the Private International Law (Miscellaneous Provisions Act) 1995, Part III.[216] In principle, the issue of whether other benefits received on death should be taken into account in assessing damages should henceforth be determined under the Rome II Regulation by the *lex causae*.[217] The Court of Appeal in *Roerig v Valiant Trawlers Ltd* also held, however that, as a matter of statutory construction, "it is a part of the law which the English court must apply to actions brought under this particular statute".[218] This might suggest that s.4 of the 1976 Act should be regarded as an overriding mandatory provision of English law so that it is nonetheless to be applied, for matters within its ambit, irrespective of the governing law. The better view, however, is that issues relating to the assessment of damages should be determined by the *lex causae*, in accordance with Art.15. Under the Rome I Regulation,[219] "overriding mandatory provisions" are narrowly defined as "provisions the respect for which is regarded as crucial by a country for safeguarding its public interests, such as its political, social or economic organisation, to such an extent that they are applicable to any situation falling within their scope, irrespective of the law otherwise applicable to the contract under this Regulation." It is doubtful whether s.4 of the 1976 Act would fall within a restrictive concept of overriding mandatory provisions under the Regulation.

---

[211] Compare Art.12(1)(c) of the Rome I Regulation.

[212] Recital (32) and Art.26.

[213] Art.16.

[214] [2002] EWCA Civ 21, [2002] 1 W.L.R 2304.

[215] In light of the decision of the House of Lords in *Harding v Wealands* [2006] UKHL 32, [2007] 2 A.C. 1, this almost certainly represented the position at common law and under the 1995 Act. See also *Cox v Ergo Versicherung AG* [2011] EWHC 2806 (QB), [2012] R.T.R. 11. Contrast the approach in Australia, where in *BHP Billiton Ltd v Schultz* [2004] HCA 61, at [251], the issue was treated as substantive; and, to similar effect, *Zardo v Ivancic* (2001) 161 F.L.R. 228, at [19].

[216] See s.14(3)(b) of the 1995 Act.

[217] Rome II Regulation, Art.15(c).

[218] *per* Waller L.J., at [29]. See also *Harding v Wealands* [2004] EWCA Civ 1735, [2005] 1 W.L.R. 1539, at [48]. The point was not considered by the House of Lords: [2006] UKHL 32, [2007] 2 A.C. 1. See also *Cox v Ergo Versicherung AG* [2011] EWHC 2806 (QB), [2012] R.T.R. 11, at [29].

[219] Although there is no such definition in the Rome II Regulation, it is almost certain that the same meaning will be adopted for that purpose: see Rome I Regulation, Recital (7).

These rules of the Rome II Regulation apply not only to tort claims, but also   7–053
to obligations arising out of unjust enrichment,[220] as well as to *negotiorum
gestio*[221] and *culpa in contrahendo.*[222]

(7) Statutes of limitation. Where proceedings in England concern a matter   7–054
which is under English choice of law rules to be governed by English law, i.e.
English law is both the *lex fori* and the *lex causae*, nothing turns upon the
classification of the English statute of limitations which is applicable in any
event. Where the *lex causae* is that of a foreign country difficult questions can
arise. The classification of limitation periods in England has undergone
considerable changes and has been greatly simplified,[223] first by the Foreign
Limitation Periods Act 1984 and then by the Rome I[224] and II Regulations.
This section considers first the position at common law and then considers the
impact of the Foreign Limitation Periods Act 1984. It then examines the
further changes brought about by the Rome I and II Regulations.[225]

The position at common law. At common law, a distinction was drawn   7–055
between two kinds of statutes of limitation: those which merely bar a remedy
and those which extinguish a right.[226] Statutes of the former kind were
procedural, while statutes of the latter kind were substantive. This common
law rule was well-established, although it was subjected to searching judicial
criticism, doubting whether the distinction between "right" and "remedy"
provided an acceptable basis on which to proceed.[227] In general, the English
law as to limitation of actions was regarded as procedural at common law,[228]
but ss.3(2) and 17 of the Limitation Act 1980 were probably substantive since
they expressly extinguish the title of the former owner.[229]

---

[220] Art.10.

[221] Art.11.

[222] Art.12.

[223] For the process of reform in Australia see the Law Reform Commission's Report No.58 on
choice of law and *Gardner v Wallace* (1995) 184 C.L.R. 95, which examines the drafting and
effect of the uniform legislation which was enacted in response to the report.

[224] And, prior to the entry into force of the Rome I Regulation, by the Rome Convention.

[225] As well as a miscellany of other rules imposing time limits falling outside the scope of the
Foreign Limitation Periods Act 1984.

[226] *Phillips v Eyre* (1870) L.R. 6 Q.B. 1, 29 (Exch. Ch.); *Black-Clawson Ltd v Papierwerke
Waldhof-Aschaffenberg AG* [1975] A.C. 591, 630; *Higgins v Ewing's Trustees*, 1925 S.C. 440,
449; *McKain v RW Miller & Co (South Australia) Pty Ltd* (1991) 174 C.L.R. 1 (High Ct
Australia). cf. *Chase Securities Corp v Donaldson* (1945) 325 U.S. 304, 313.

[227] See the dissenting judgments in *McKain v RW Miller & Co (South Australia) Pty Ltd*,
above. See also *Tolofson v Jensen*, above; *Clark v Naqvi* (1990) 63 D.L.R. (4th) 361 (NBCA);
Michalski v Olson [1998] 3 W.W.R. 37 (Man CA).

[228] *Williams v Jones* (1811) 13 East 439; *Ruckmaboye v Mottichund* (1851) 8 Moo. P.C. 4;
Commonwealth of Australia v Dixon (1988) 13 N.S.W.L.R. 601; *Byrnes v Groote Eylandt Mining
Co Pty Ltd* (1990) 19 N.S.W.L.R. 13; *Clark v Naqvi* (1990) 63 D.L.R. (4th) 361 (NBCA).

[229] Sometimes a statute creates an entirely new right of action unknown to the common law and
at the same time imposes a shorter period of limitation than that applicable under the general law.
An example is the Civil Liability (Contribution) Act 1978; where a person becomes entitled to a
right to recover contribution under s.1 of that Act the limitation period is two years (Limitation
Act 1980, s.10, as amended by SI 2011/1133, Pt 3, reg.23). There is Scottish, Australian and
American authority in favour of the view that such special periods of limitation are substantive
even though they are contained in a different statute from that creating the right: *Goodman v LNW
Ry* (1877) 14 S.L.R. 449; *M'Elroy v M'Allister*, 1949 S.C. 110, 125–128, 137; *Maxwell v Murphy*
(1957) 96 C.L.R. 261; *The Harrisburg*, 119 U.S. 199 (1886); cf. *Bournias v Atlantic Maritime Co,*

7–056   The *lex causae* and the *lex fori* might differ not only in their periods of
limitation but also in the nature of their limitation provisions. In considering
foreign rules as to limitation the English courts traditionally applied their own
classification based on the distinction between barring a right and extinguishing a remedy. The position resulting from this approach, can be illustrated by
reference to the different situations which can arise: (i) if the statutes of
limitation of the *lex causae* and of the *lex fori* were both procedural, an action
would fail if it were brought after the period of limitation of the *lex fori* had
expired although that of the *lex causae* had not yet expired;[230] but would
succeed if the period of limitation of the *lex fori* had not yet expired although
that of the *lex causae* has expired.[231] This in effect enabled a party to enlarge
his rights by suing in England in circumstances where the limitation period of
the *lex causae* had expired and the English limitation period had not. It could
thus create incentives to forum shopping and might cause injustice to a debtor
who, in reliance of the *lex causae*, had destroyed his receipts.[232] (ii) If the
statute of limitation of the *lex causae* was substantive but that of the *lex fori*
was procedural, the *lex fori* would probably apply if its period of limitation
was shorter than that of the *lex causae* on the ground that it was inconvenient
for the *forum* to hear what it considered to be stale claims.[233] But once a
substantive period of limitation of the *lex causae* had expired, no action could
be maintained even though a procedural period of limitation imposed by the
lex fori had not yet expired: in such a case there was simply no right left to
be enforced.[234] (iii) If the statutes of limitation of the *lex causae* and of the *lex
fori* were both substantive, it is probable that the same results would have
followed as in the case just considered.[235] (iv) If the statute of the *lex causae*
was procedural and that of the *lex fori* substantive, strict logic might suggest
that neither applied, so that the claim remained perpetually enforceable. A

---

220 F. 2d 152 (2d Cir. 1955); contrast *Kerr v Palfrey* [1970] V.R. 825. See also *Davis v Mills*, 194
U.S. 451 (1904); Restatement, s.143, comment *c*.

[230] *Don v Lippmann* (1837) 5 Cl. & F. 1, where it is, however, not clear whether Scots law was
applied as *lex fori* or as the law of the debtor's residence; *Dupleix v De Roven* (1705) 2 Vern. 540
supports the proposition in the text but was not decided on the principles here discussed; see also
Re Lorillard [1922] 2 Ch. 638 (CA); *Allard v Charbonneau* [1953] 2 D.L.R. 442 (Ont CA).

[231] *Huber v Steiner* (1835) 2 Bing. N.C. 202; *Harris v Quine* (1869) L.R. 4 Q.B. 653, approved
in *Re Low* [1894] 1 Ch. 147, 162 (CA) and *Black-Clawson International Ltd v Papierwerke
Waldhof-Aschaffenburg AG* [1975] A.C. 591; *Alliance Bank of Simla v Carey* (1880) 5 C.P.D. 429;
Finch v Finch (1876) 45 L.J. Ch. 816; *Société Anonyme Métallurgique de Prayon v Koppel* (1933)
77 S.J. 800; *Carvell v Wallace* (1873) 9 N.S.R. 165; *Bondholders Securities Corporation v
Manville* [1933] 4 D.L.R. 699 (Sask CA); *Waung v Subbotovsky* (1969) 121 C.L.R. 337; *Pederson
v Young* (1964) 110 C.L.R. 162; *Scotland v Bargen* (1982) 39 A.L.R. 644; *McKain v RW Miller
& Co (South Australia) Pty Ltd* (1991) 174 C.L.R. 1 (High Ct Australia).

[232] Wolff, s.219. See the dissenting judgments in *McKain v RW Miller & Co (South Australia)
Pty Ltd*, above.

[233] *British Linen Co v Drummond* (1830) 10 B. & C. 903 (see p.909, n.(*c*) for the substantive
nature of the Scots rule there under discussion). This case was approved in *Fergusson v Fyffe*
(1841) 8 Cl. & F. 121. See, to similar effect, *C(DH) v T(DH)* (1987) 11 R.F.L. 147 (N.S.). *cf.
Lopez v Burslem* (1843) 4 Moo. P.C. 300.

[234] Thus in *Harris v Quine* (1869) L.R. 4 Q.B. 653, 658 it was said that the decision would have
gone the other way had the Manx statute of limitations been substantive; *cf.* similar dicta in *Huber
v Steiner* (1835) 2 Bing. N.C. 202, 210.*cf.* also *Black-Clawson International Ltd v Papierwerke
Waldhof-Aschaffenburg AG* [1975] A.C. 591.

[235] *cf. Kuhne & Nagel AG Zurich v APA Distributors Pty Ltd*, 1981(3) S.A. 536 (W.), applying
the *lex causae* in preference to the *lex fori* in such a case.

notorious decision of the German Supreme Court once actually reached this absurd result.[236] But writers have suggested various ways of escape from this dilemma,[237] and it seems probable that a court would have applied one statute or the other. Nonetheless, it is apparent that the common law approach had the potential to create uncertainty and to permit actions to be brought in England which could not be brought in the courts whose law governed on the substance, or vice-versa.

The traditional common law approach was thrown into some doubt by   **7–057**
decisions in Australia and Canada.[238] In *John Pfeiffer Pty Ltd v Rogerson*,[239] the High Court of Australia indicated (*obiter*) that, at common law, statutes of limitation are substantive, rather than procedural. Subsequently, in *Neilson v Overseas Projects Corporation of Victoria Ltd*,[240] the High Court of Australia applied the limitation period of the law applicable to the tort.[241] In *Tolofson v Jensen*,[242] the Supreme Court of Canada rejected the traditional common law classification of statutes of limitation and the distinction between right and remedy on which it is based and held that statutes of limitation are to be classified as substantive. This approach was confirmed in *Castillo v Castillo*.[243] The Supreme Court applied a one-year limitation period under the law applicable to the tort, Californian law, despite a provision of Alberta law which provided that Alberta limitation law (which had a two-year period) should apply "notwithstanding that, in accordance with conflict of law rules, the claim will be adjudicated under the substantive law of another jurisdiction."[244] A majority of the Supreme Court of Canada held that this provision had no application because the claim was already time-barred when the action was brought.[245]

Under the Foreign Limitation Periods Act 1984.[246] The Act was based on   **7–058**
the recommendations of the Law Commission.[247] It adopts the general

---

[236] (1882) 7 R.G.Z. 21. More recent German decisions have refused to follow this precedent. See also the decision of the South African Supreme Court of Appeal in *Society of Lloyd's v Price* [2006] SCA 87; Forsyth (2006) 2 J. Priv. Int. L. 425; Harder (2011) 60 I.C.L.Q. 659.

[237] Beckett (1934) 15 B.Y.I.L. 46, 76–77; Cook, pp.220 *et seq.*; Falconbridge, pp.292–295.

[238] By this time, the Foreign Limitation Periods Act 1984 had entered into force in England and largely replaced the common law rules.

[239] (2000) 203 C.L.R. 503.

[240] [2005] HCA 54, (2005) 223 C.L.R. 331.

[241] The High Court of Australia went on to invoke the doctrine of *renvoi*. See further Harder (2011) 60 I.C.L.Q. 659.

[242] [1994] 3 S.C.R. 1022. *Tolofson v Jensen* was distinguished by the Supreme Court of Canada in *Yugraneft Corp v Rexx Management Corp*, 2010 SCC 19, [2010] 1 S.C.R. 649, at [14]–[40], in the context of the enforcement of a foreign arbitral award in Alberta.

[243] 2005 SCC 83, (2005) 260 D.L.R. (4th) 439. For discussion, see Walker (2006) 43 C.B.L.J. 487.

[244] Limitations Act 2000, s.12.

[245] See also *Roy v North American Leisure Group Inc* (2004) 246 D.L.R. (4th) 306 (Ont CA).

[246] As amended by Law Applicable to Non-Contractual Obligations (England and Wales and Northern Ireland) Regulations SI 2008/2986; Law Applicable to Contractual Obligations (England and Wales and Northern Ireland) Regulations SI 2009/3064; Cross-Border Mediation (EU Directive) Regulations SI 2011/1133, Pt 3, reg.29. Sections 1, 2 and 4 of the 1984 Act do not apply where the Rome I or Rome II Regulation is applicable: see s.8 of the 1984 Act.

[247] *Classification of Limitation in Private International Law*, Law Com. No.114 (1982). For commentaries on the Act, see Carter (1985) 101 L.Q.R. 68; Stone [1985] L.M.C.L.Q. 497.

principle,[248] subject to an exception based on public policy, that the limitation rules of the *lex causae* are to be applied in actions in England,[249] even if those rules do not lay down any limitation period for the claim.[250] English limitation rules are not to be applied unless English law is the *lex causae* or one of two *leges causae* governing the matter.[251] The double actionability rule as to foreign torts, which applies to defamation claims,[252] illustrates the case of two *leges causae*.[253] In such a case the limitation rules of the law both of England and of the relevant foreign country will apply and the expiry of either limitation period will bar the action. The applicable provisions of the foreign *lex causae* are defined to include both procedural and substantive rules with respect to a limitation period,[254] but any renvoi is excluded[255] and the English court must disregard any rule under which a limitation period is or may be extended or interrupted in respect of the absence of a party from any specified jurisdiction or country.[256] If the foreign *lex causae* confers a discretion, an English court must so far as is practicable exercise that discretion in the manner in which it is exercised in comparable cases by the courts of the foreign country.[257] English law as the *lex fori* does, however, determine whether, and the time at which, proceedings have been commenced;[258] that is, the *terminus ad quem* of the limitation period prescribed by a foreign *lex causae* is to be determined by English law.[259]

7–059   To the general principle, there is one major exception. The principle is not to be applied to the extent that it conflicts with English public policy.[260] Where there is such a conflict, s.1 of the Act does not apply.[261] The effect is that the issue is then governed by the common law principles, under which the

---

[248] The Act does not affect any action commenced in England before October 1, 1985, the date on which it was brought into force, nor any matter in respect of which the limitation period would, apart from the Act, have expired before that date: see s.7(3). It is, however, immaterial that the event giving rise to the action occurred before October 1985: *Jones v Trollope Colls Cementation Overseas Ltd, The Times,* January 26, 1990 (CA).

[249] The same principle applies to arbitrations whose seat is in England: Arbitration Act 1996, s.13. See Hill (1997) 46 I.C.L.Q. 274, 297. For the analogous position in Scotland under Prescription and Limitation (Scotland) Act 1973, s.23A(1), see *Kleinwort Benson Ltd v Glasgow City Council (No.3),* 2002 S.L.T. 1190.

[250] *Dubai Bank Ltd v Abbas* [1998] I.L.Pr. 391.

[251] s.1(2).

[252] Defamation is excluded from the ambit of the Rome I Regulation by Art.1(2)(g); and from the ambit of the Private International Law (Miscellaneous Provisions) Act 1995 by s.13. See below, paras 35R–099 *et seq.*

[253] See also *Metall und Rohstoff AG v Donaldson, Lufkin and Jenrette Inc* [1990] Q.B. 391 (CA); *Re ERAS EIL Actions* [1992] 1 Lloyd's Rep. 570 (CA). For the application of s.1(2) in a different factual context see *Gotha City v Sotheby's, The Times,* October 8, 1998.

[254] s.4.

[255] ss.1(5), 4(2).

[256] s.2(3); but rules relating to extensions, etc., for other reasons, e.g. infancy, are applicable: s.4(1)(a).

[257] s.1(4).

[258] s.1(3). See *Barros Mattos Jnr v MacDaniels Ltd* [2005] EWHC 1323 (Ch.), [2005] I.L.Pr. 630, at [131].

[259] Including Limitation Act 1980, s.35, in relation to claims by way of set-off, counterclaims, and to the addition or substitution of new claims or parties: s.1(3).

[260] s.2(1). See also s.1A on the extension of limitation periods because of mediation of certain cross-border disputes, inserted by SI 2011/1133, Pt 3, reg.29.

[261] *ibid.*

limitation periods prescribed by English law as the *lex fori* will be applied. It is declared that there is a conflict with public policy to the extent that undue hardship would be caused to a person who is, or might be, a party.[262] A finding of "undue hardship" must depend on all the circumstances of the particular case; it was found present where defendants had agreed to an extension of time which turned out to be ineffectual under the foreign *lex causae*[263] and in a case involving a foreign limitation period of only 12 months, where the plaintiff had spent some time in hospital and had been led to believe that her claim would be met.[264] In a dispute involving competing claims to personal property, it has been held (*obiter*) that it would be contrary to public policy to allow a foreign limitation rule to be relied upon by a thief or by any transferee of stolen property other than a purchaser in good faith.[265] It has also been suggested that a foreign limitation period may be disapplied in a situation where the action has become time barred as a consequence of the defendant's deliberate concealment of relevant facts.[266] However, the mere fact that the foreign limitation period is shorter than the English period does not, without more, give rise to "undue hardship".[267] Similarly, it is not contrary to public policy to apply a foreign limitation period under s.1 simply on the ground that the foreign law does not have an equivalent of s.33 of the Limitation Act 1980 (under which the limitation period may be disapplied in certain circumstances).[268] If within the foreign limitation period the claimant acquires all the material required for bringing the action, it is not contrary to public policy to apply the foreign rule even if he is only a few days late in commencing proceedings.[269] The exception may also be relied upon in cases where the foreign *lex causae* does not lay down a limitation period at all or where the foreign limitation period is significantly longer than that under English law; in appropriate circumstances the English court might decline to apply the foreign rule, holding that the action must fail. In any case in which a claim is made for equitable relief, and the claim is not statute-barred, the English courts have a discretion to withhold relief, for example on the grounds of acquiescence or laches;[270] the Act does not prevent the exercise of this discretion but does require the court to have regard to the provisions of the foreign *lex causae*.[271]

In *Harley v Smith*,[272] Foskett J. reviewed the authorities on the meaning and scope of the "undue hardship" exception. He stated[273] that the previous **7–060**

---

[262] s.2(2). See Law Com. No.114 (1982), paras 4.44–4.48 for a discussion of possible cases of hardship.

[263] *The Komninos S* [1990] 1 Lloyd's Rep. 541 (reversed but not on this point, [1991] 1 Lloyd's Rep. 370 (CA)).

[264] *Jones v Trollope Colls Cementation Overseas Ltd, The Times*, January 26, 1990 (CA).

[265] See *Gotha City v Sotheby's, The Times*, October 8, 1998.

[266] *ibid.*

[267] *Durham v T&N Noble Plc*, May 1, 1996 (unreported).

[268] *Connelly v RTZ Corporation Plc (No.3)* [1999] C.L.C. 533. See also Limitation Act 1980, s.33A on extension of time because of mediation of certain cross-border disputes, inserted by SI 2011/1133, Pt 3, reg.26.

[269] *Arab Monetary Fund v Hashim* [1996] 1 Lloyd's Rep. 589 (CA).

[270] See Yeo, *Choice of Law for Equitable Doctrines* (2004), pp.131–2.

[271] s.4(3).

[272] [2009] EWHC 56 (QB), [2009] 1 Lloyd's Rep. 359.

[273] At [94].

authorities established three propositions: (i) that the mere fact that the foreign limitation period is less generous than the equivalent English period is insufficient to trigger s.2(2); (ii) the claimant must satisfy the court that he would suffer particular hardship on the facts of the case; and (iii) that in considering (ii), the focus is on the claimant's interests rather than a balancing exercise between the interests of the claimant on the one hand and the defendant on the other. The Court of Appeal upheld the decision[274] and specifically endorsed this statement of the law.[275] It found, however, that the judge had erroneously applied the test that he had correctly stated in two respects. First, the undue hardship must be caused by the foreign limitation period itself and not by allegedly erroneous legal advice as to what that limitation period was. Second, any uncertainty as to the applicable limitation period in the foreign law would normally be irrelevant, since it would encourage a claimant to bring proceedings sooner rather than later to avoid the risk of being out of time.[276]

7–061   *The impact of the Rome I and II Regulations.* The Rome I and II Regulations both contain provisions on the law applicable to limitation periods. Sections 1, 2 and 4 of the Foreign Limitation Periods Act 1984 are disapplied where the Rome I or Rome II Regulation applies.[277]

7–062   *Rome I Regulation.* The law applicable to a contract by virtue of Arts 3 to 8 and 14 of the Rome I Regulation,[278] governs prescription and the limitation of actions.[279] This application of the *lex causae*[280] achieves the same result as the Foreign Limitation Periods Act 1984.[281] The application of the governing law under the Rome I Regulation may be refused if its application would be manifestly[282] incompatible with English public policy,[283] whereas under the 1984 Act the relevant public policy is indicated by the "undue hardship" provision of the 1984 Act.[284]

---

[274] [2010] EWCA Civ 78, [2010] C.P. Rep. 33.

[275] Whilst it agreed that the limitation period had not expired, it concluded, however, that the judge was wrong to say that the "undue hardship" exception would otherwise have been triggered and varied the order to that extent.

[276] See also *OJSC Oil Co Yugraneft v Abramovich* [2008] EWHC 2613 (Comm.), at [318]–[324].

[277] Foreign Limitation Periods Act 1984, s.8; SI 2008/2986; SI 2009/3064. This includes cases involving conflicts solely between the laws of different parts of the United Kingdom or between one or more parts of the United Kingdom and Gibraltar. s.1A on extension of time because of mediation of certain cross-border disputes, inserted by SI 2011/1133, Pt 3, reg.29, is not subject to s.8.

[278] Compare Contract (Applicable Law) Act 1990, Sch.1, Arts 3–6 and 12.

[279] Rome I Regulation, Art.12(1)(d); compare Contracts (Applicable Law) Act 1990, Sch.1, Art.10(1)(d). See below, paras 32–156 *et seq.*

[280] As with the 1984 Act, the doctrine of *renvoi* is excluded: see Rome I Regulation, Art.20 (compare Rome Convention, Art.15).

[281] But applies instead of the Foreign Limitation Periods Act 1984: see s.8 of the 1984 Act.

[282] The word "manifestly" is not used in s.2 of the 1984 Act.

[283] Rome I Regulation, Art.21. See also Recital (37). Compare Contracts (Applicable Law) Act 1990 Sch.1, Art.16.

[284] i.e. s.2(2), considered above. See below, para.32–161; and Dickinson, *The Rome II Regulation*, para.14.49 (in respect of the equivalent provision in Art.26 of the Rome II Regulation, suggesting it is more restrictive than s.2(2) of the 1984 Act.)

A possible difference between the Rome I Regulation and the 1984 Act **7–063**
concerns equitable relief such as laches and acquiescence. Section 4(3) of the
1984 Act preserves the application of such relief even where a foreign law
applies, although the English court must have regard to any relevant rules of
the foreign law. By contrast, Art.12(1)(d) of the Rome I Regulation simply
refers all questions of prescription and limitation to the *lex causae*. It is
unlikely that the English rules on discretionary equitable relief can be
regarded as overriding mandatory provisions of the forum[285] and so it would
appear that they cannot be applied in an English court if a foreign law governs
the contract.

Rome II Regulation. Similarly, the law applicable to a non-contractual **7–064**
obligation by virtue of Arts 4 to 14 of the Rome II Regulation governs "the
manner in which an obligation may be extinguished and rules of prescription
and limitation, including rules relating to the commencement, interruption and
suspension of a period of prescription or limitation."[286] Again, the application
of the *lex causae* achieves the same result as the Foreign Limitation Periods
Act 1984.[287] The application of the governing law under the Rome II Regulation may be refused if its application would be manifestly incompatible with
English public policy.[288]

As with the Rome I Regulation, however, it would seem that s.4(3) of the **7–065**
1984 Act preserving the application of English rules on equitable relief cannot
be applied where a foreign law is applicable under the Rome II Regulation.[289]
Furthermore, in extending the application of the *lex causae* to rules relating to
the commencement of the period of limitation or prescription, the Rome II
Regulation adopts a different approach to that in s.1(3) of the 1984 Act, which
applies the law of the forum to this matter.[290] Hence, if the limitation period
does not run under the relevant foreign law until, for example, a claimant
reaches a specified age of majority or becomes aware of the facts which give
rise to a claim, such provisions should be applied in the English courts.
Beyond that, however, it may be thought that rules on when an action is
deemed to have begun in an English court[291] and rules relating to the
introduction of new claims or the amendment of a statement of case in a
pending action should be classified as procedural in nature and hence outside

---

[285] For the purposes of Art.9(2).

[286] Art.15(h).

[287] But the 1984 Act gives way to the Rome II Regulation: see s.8 of the 1984 Act.

[288] Art.26 and Recital (32). See Dickinson, *The Rome II Regulation*, para.14.49, suggesting that
the public policy provisions in the Rome II Regulation are more restrictive than those in s.2(2)
of the 1984 Act.

[289] *ibid.*

[290] The rules of the Rome II Regulation prevail.

[291] Compare *Vogler v Szendroi* (2008) 290 D.L.R. (4th) 642 (N.S.C.A.), in which the Nova
Scotia Court of Appeal declined to apply provisions of the governing law, the law of Wyoming,
stating that an action is commenced by filing process with the court and if service has not been
effected within sixty days, the action is not deemed to have been commenced until the date of
service. The Nova Scotia Court of Appeal held that the Wyoming rule was procedural, since it
determined the manner in which proceedings were to be instigated, and did not concern the rights
of the plaintiff. Of course, the decision can, at most, only be of oblique relevance in England and
certainly cannot determine the correct construction of European Regulations.

the scope of the Rome II Regulation.[292] If so, then s.1(3) of the 1984 Act will remain applicable to that extent.

7–066   Section 2(3) of the 1984 Act requires an English court to disregard rules of the *lex causae* allowing the limitation period to be extended or interrupted in respect of the absence of a party to the action or proceedings from any specified jurisdiction or country. By contrast, the Rome II Regulation applies the *lex causae* to the "interruption" of a limitation period. Insofar as there is an overlap between these provisions, those in the Rome II Regulation prevail. It may, however, be that rules on the interruption of a limitation period designed to reflect the difficulties of serving a defendant who is outside the jurisdiction should be regarded as procedural and so outside the scope of the Rome II Regulation, with the result that s.2(3) of the 1984 Act still applies.[293]

7–067   *Other rules imposing time-limits.* There are two questions raising issues similar to those arising in connection with statutes of limitations which can be considered here. They do not concern limitation periods and are not within the scope of the 1984 Act.

7–068   First, there are certain legal rights which must be exercised within a reasonable time, for example, the right to repudiate a marriage settlement made during minority or the right to rescind a contract for misrepresentation. The *lex fori* might differ from the *lex causae* in its method of calculating what was a reasonable time: thus under one system time might run from the making of the contract and under the other from the time when the party purporting to rescind discovered his rights. It seems that such matters should be determined by the *lex causae* since the relevant rules operate, if at all, so as wholly to extinguish the right to rescind; and since the application of foreign rules will not cause any procedural inconvenience.[294]

7–069   Where the case falls within the scope of the Rome I Regulation, the matter is governed by the applicable law, which is declared to govern "the various ways of extinguishing obligations, and prescription and limitation of actions."[295] Secondly, a contract may itself provide a period of limitation shorter than that imposed by the general law. Such a provision, which is analogous to one limiting or agreeing damages,[296] will also be governed by the applicable law.[297]

7–070   Where the case falls within the scope of the Rome II Regulation, the law governing the non-contractual obligation applies to the manner in which an obligation may be extinguished and rules of prescription and limitation, including rules relating to the commencement, interruption and suspension of

---

[292] Art.1(3) of the Rome II Regulation. On the issues raised by s.35 of the Limitation Act 1980, see Dickinson, *The Rome II Regulation*, paras 14.51–14.52.

[293] See Dickinson, *The Rome II Regulation*, para.14.49.

[294] See, to similar effect, Law Com. No.114 (1982), paras 4.52–4.53.

[295] Rome I Regulation, Art.12(1)(d); compare Contracts (Applicable Law) Act 1990, Sch.1, Art.10(1)(d).

[296] *cf. Godard v Gray* (1870) L.R. 6 Q.B. 139, 147–148.

[297] *cf. Allan J Panozza & Co Pty Ltd v Allied Interstate (Qld) Pty Ltd* [1976] 2 N.S.W.L.R. 192 (NSWCA) (contractual term requiring notice of any loss to be given to carrier within five days was held to be procedural).

a period of prescription or limitation."[298] In the event that the parties reach their own agreement on a shorter limitation than that imposed by the general law, in principle, such a provision will also be governed by the applicable law.[299]

(8) Miscellaneous cases. It has been suggested that the question whether   7–071
a debtor is entitled to contribution from a co-debtor is governed by the *lex fori* as it "depends not upon contract but upon equity."[300] But it is hard to see why the forum should always apply its own views of "equity" to such a question. The *lex causae* is applied in most circumstances as a result of the Rome I Regulation. The effect of Art.16 of the Rome I Regulation is that where several persons are subject to the same contractual claim and one of them has satisfied the creditor, the law governing the debtor's obligation towards the creditor also governs the debtor's right to claim recourse from the other debtor.[301] The other debtors may rely on the defences they had against the creditor to the extent allowed by the law governing their obligations towards the creditor.[302] The Rome II Regulation also treats claims for contributions as substantive.[303] The law applicable to the debtor's non-contractual obligation towards the creditor shall determine whether the creditor may demand compensation from the other debtors.[304]

The question whether a civil action can be brought in respect of acts constituting a crime before criminal proceedings have been taken in the matter is one of procedure.[305]

In *Somers v Fournier*[306] the Ontario Court of Appeal held that the issue of   7–072
litigation costs was a procedural matter. It is clear that rules on the conduct of the parties prior to the instigation of proceedings, for example on providing

---

[298] Foreign Limitation Periods Act 1984, s.8.

[299] The parties' freedom to choose the governing law is limited by Art.14 of the Rome II Regulation; but there is no provision in the Rome II Regulation otherwise limiting their power to shorten the applicable limitation period.

[300] *American Surety Co of New York v Wrightson* (1910) 103 L.T. 663, 665; *Arab Monetary Fund v Hashim (No.9)*, *The Times*, October 11, 1994; *Petroleo Brasiliero SA v Mellitus Shipping Inc* [2001] EWCA Civ 418, [2001] 2 Lloyd's Rep. 203. See also Yeo, *op. cit.* above, n.270, pp.129–130.

[301] As opposed to choice of law rules applicable to unjust enrichment.

[302] See also Art.15, which treats subrogation as substantive. It provides that: "Where a person (the creditor) has a contractual claim against another (the debtor) and a third person has a duty to satisfy the creditor, or has in fact satisfied the creditor in discharge of that duty, the law which governs the third person's duty to satisfy the creditor shall determine whether and to what extent the third person is entitled to exercise against the debtor the rights which the creditor had against the debtor under the law governing their relationship." Compare Contracts (Applicable Law) Act 1990, Sch.1, Art.13. See also Rome I Regulation, Art.14 (compare Contracts (Applicable Law) Act 1990, Sch.1, Art.12).

[303] Nor does there seem any convincing reason why the substantive classification of claims for contributions under the Rome I and II Regulations should be negated by treating the Civil Liability (Contribution) Act 1978 as an overriding mandatory provision of the forum.

[304] Art.20. Again, this applies the law applicable to the contractual obligation between the creditor and debtor rather than rules of unjust enrichment. On subrogation (also treated as substantive under the Rome II Regulation) see Art.19.

[305] *Scott v Seymour* (1862) 1 H. & C. 219. See also *OJSC Oil Co Yugraneft v Abramovich* [2008] EWHC 2613 (Comm.), at [298].

[306] (2002) 214 D.L.R. (4th) 611.

notice before action, or on the need for a meeting between the parties before starting proceedings, are procedural.[307]

7-073   There is virtually no English authority[308] on the question whether the rules which determine whether an action lies at the suit of, or against, the representatives of a deceased person are substantive or procedural. The predominant American view is that these rules are substantive.[309] The related question whether the death of a human being gives rise to an action at the suit of a third party who has suffered loss as a result of the death is also one of substance.[310] In *Matthews v Ministry of Defence*[311] the House of Lords, in a case not involving a foreign element, treated a rule exempting the defendant from liability for death or personal injury as substantive. Lord Millett recognised that in drawing the dividing line between substance and procedure, "it is best to avoid a formalistic approach and inquire whether the rule which bars the claim is of general application and independent of the facts which found the claim."[312]

7-074   Prior to the advent of the Rome II Regulation, opinion was divided on the question whether the rules which determine the tortious liability of spouses towards one another were substantive or procedural.[313] In English domestic law, s.1(1) of the Law Reform (Husband and Wife) Act 1962 provides that "the parties to a marriage shall have the like right of action in tort against each other as if they were not married."[314] Article 1(2)(a) of the Rome II Regulation excludes "non-contractual obligations arising out of family relationships and relationships deemed by the law applicable to such relationships to have comparable effects including maintenance obligations."[315] Although the ambit of this exclusion is not certain,[316] it may apply to an action for compensation for damage caused by late payment of a maintenance obligation.[317] Otherwise, however, it would appear that the question of whether actions in tort between spouses are permitted is within the ambit of the

---

[307] This is the case in Australia, notwithstanding the broader approach to the classification of matters as substantive adopted there since *John Pfeiffer Pty Ltd v Rogerson* (2000) 203 C.L.R. 503, 543 than is applied in England. This is because, the rights and duties of the parties are unaffected: *Hamilton v Merck & Co Inc* [2006] NSWCA 55, (2006) 230 A.L.R. 156, (2006) 66 N.S.W.L.R. 48. See also *Hodgson v Dimbola Pty Ltd* [2009] ACTSC 59, at [24]; *Kok v Sheppard* [2009] NSWSC 1262, at [35]–[43]; *RACQ Insurance Ltd v Wilkins* [2009] QSC 365.

[308] An *obiter dictum* in *Batthyany v Walford* (1887) 36 Ch.D. 269, 278 may suggest that the question is one of procedure.

[309] Restatement, s.124, Illustration 2, and s.167; Currie, Ch.3; and see below, para.34–062.

[310] *Kendrick v Burnett* (1897) 25 R. 82, 89; *cf. Naftalin v LMS*, 1933 S.C. 259; *M'Elroy v M'Allister*, 1949 S.C. 110. See below, para.34–061.

[311] [2003] UKHL 4, [2003] 1 A.C. 1163.

[312] At [79].

[313] Wolff, s.222, and Hancock, pp.235–236 regarded these rules as substantive; but see also Hancock (1962) 29 U. of Chic. L. Rev. 237, commenting on *Haumschild v Continental Casualty Co*, 7 Wis. 2d 130, 95 N.W. 2d 814 (1959), where the court found it unnecessary to determine whether such rules were substantive or procedural. Kahn-Freund (1952) 15 M.L.R. 133 showed that in English domestic law the rules were partly substantive and partly procedural. See the discussion at para.7–058 of the 14th ed. of this work.

[314] The power to stay proceedings in s.1(2) would appear to be procedural.

[315] See also Recital (10).

[316] See below, para.34–029.

[317] See the Explanatory Memorandum to the Commission Proposal COM(2003) 0427 final, commentary on Art.1.

Regulation, and governed by the *lex causae*,[318] with the effect that s.1(1) of the Law Reform (Husband and Wife) Act 1962 is applicable only where the governing law of the non-contractual obligation is English law.[319]

ILLUSTRATIONS

(1) NATURE OF REMEDY AND METHOD OF ENFORCEMENT

1. A and X are domiciled in Greece, A is the daughter of X. A, who has just been married, claims that by Greek law X is under an obligation to provide her with a dowry. A's claim is dismissed, not because it is unknown to English law, but because by Greek law the amount of the dowry is within the discretion of the court and varies in accordance with X's wealth and social position and the number of his children, and with A's behaviour. English law therefore has no remedy for giving effect to Greek law.[320]

2. In 2012, A concludes a contract to sell goods to B. The contract is specifically enforceable according to the *lex causae* but not by English law. B is entitled to specific performance.[321]

7–075

(2) PARTIES

3. A company which was incorporated in Russia is dissolved by a Russian decree. This decree is recognised in England, so that, according to English law, the company ceases to exist. The decree is not recognised in France so that, according to French law, the company continues to exist. An action cannot be maintained in England in the name of the company to recover a debt governed by French law.[322]

4. Y in Ireland obtains a judgment against X which he subsequently assigns to A. By an Irish statute such assignments are permitted and the assignees are entitled to sue in their own names. By English law, an assignee can only sue the debtor by joining the assignor as a party to the action. A can sue X in his own name in England.[323]

5. K had a claim against A & Co. for £100,000. In November 1973 he left his residence in Paris and disappeared. In February 1974 a court in Lebanon appointed X as administrator of K's property, K being declared an absentee. In Lebanese law, X could pursue K's claim, suing in his own name. In English law, unless an absent claimant is presumed dead there is no way in which another can sue on his behalf. X's action in England is dismissed.[324]

6. In 2012, A, an English resident employee of B Co., an English company, is involved in a road traffic accident in France during the course of his employment, in which he negligently injures C, a French resident. The *lex causae* determines whether B Co. is liable for the acts of A.[325]

7–076

(3) EVIDENCE

7. M, domiciled in Germany, by will leaves movable property to her daughter D, also domiciled in Germany, if D survives M. M and D are killed in England in circumstances rendering it uncertain which of them survived the other. By English law, D is, for all purposes affecting the title to property, deemed to have survived M. By German law, M and D are presumed to have died

7–077

---

[318] *ibid.*, commentary on Art.11 of the Commission Proposal.

[319] This is on the basis that the question falls within Art.15(b) of the Regulation, which applies the *lex causae* to "the grounds for exemption from liability, any limitation of liability and any division of liability."

[320] *Phrantzes v Argenti* [1960] 2 Q.B. 19.

[321] Rome I Regulation, Art.12(1)(c). The matter might be different if the English courts were not procedurally competent to enforce a particular type of contract or if specific enforcement of the contract in question (e.g. a contract of employment) was manifestly incompatible with English public policy (Art.21).

[322] *Banque Internationale de Commerce de Petrograd v Goukassow* [1923] 2 K.B. 682 (CA); reversed on other grounds [1925] A.C. 150.

[323] *O'Callaghan v Thomond* (1810) 3 Taunt. 82.

[324] *Kamouh v Associated Electrical Industries International Ltd.* [1980] Q.B. 199.

[325] Rome II Regulation, Art.15(g).

simultaneously. Both these rules are rules of substance so that the German rule applies and D takes no interest under M's will.[326]

8. W divorces H in England on the ground of his adultery with Q and subsequently publishes abroad the statement that H has committed adultery with Q. Under the law of the place of publication, H could, in a defamation action against W, give evidence in disproof of the alleged adultery with Q; in English domestic law an estoppel by record would prevent him from giving such evidence.[327] The estoppel by record would (*semble*) operate in an action in England on the alleged foreign tort.[328]

9. A sues X for personal injuries inflicted by X upon A in New York. By New York law, A can only succeed if he can prove that he was not guilty of contributory negligence. By English law, X's liability is reduced if he can show that A was guilty of contributory negligence. The burden of proving that he was not guilty of contributory negligence is on A.[329]

(4) Set-Off and Counterclaim

7–078   10. X contracts with A for the carriage of goods from Klaipėda to London. The contract is governed by Lithuanian law. Part of the goods is not shipped, and X deducts £5,000, the value of that part, from the freight due under the contract. A sues X for freight in England. Lithuanian law determines whether X is entitled to set off the £5,000 against the freight due to A in the English proceedings.[330]

(5) Priorities

7–079   11. In an action *in rem* in England against a French ship, claims are made by A, the holder of a French *hypothèque*, and by B, an English necessaries man. By French law, necessaries men have priority over holders of *hypothèques*. By English law, necessaries men are postponed to mortgagees of a ship. A has priority over B. French law governs the existence and scope of A's claim, but English law determines priorities, and the proper classification for those purposes, of the *hypothèque*.[331]

12. In an action *in rem* in England against a foreign ship, claims are made by A, a New York necessaries man, and by B, a mortgagee of the ship. By English law necessaries men are postponed to mortgagees. By the law of the United States, necessaries men have a maritime lien and enjoy priority over mortgagees. The court will not recognise A's claim to a maritime lien, for had the repairs carried out by A been executed in England no maritime lien would have been created. Accordingly B has priority.[332]

(6) Damages

7–080   13. A is injured in a road accident in Malta as a result of X's negligence. A and X are British servicemen ordinarily resident in England and temporarily stationed in Malta. By Maltese law A could only recover damages for financial loss directly suffered, expenses, and loss of wages—in this case, £53. By English law, he could also recover damages for pain and suffering—in this case, a further £2,250. English law applies and A can recover £2,303.[333]

---

[326] *Re Cohn* [1945] Ch. 5.

[327] *Cross and Tapper on Evidence* (12th ed. 2010), pp.85 *et seq.*

[328] The matter falls outside the ambit of the Rome II Regulation (Art.1(2)(g)) and the Private International Law (Miscellaneous Provisions) Act 1995, Part III, so that the common law choice of law rules remain applicable.

[329] Rome II Regulation, Art.22(1); *cf. Fitzpatrick v International Ry*, 252 N.Y. 127, 169 N.E. 112 (1929); *Central Vermont Ry v White*, 238 U.S. 507 (1914); *Dawson v Broughton* (2007) 151 So. J. 1167 (Manchester County Court).

[330] Rome I Regulation, Art.17; *cf. Meyer v Dresser* (1864) 12 C.B. (N.S.) 646.

[331] *The Colorado* [1923] P. 102 (CA) as interpreted in *Bankers Trust International Ltd v Todd Shipyards Corporation* (*The Halcyon Isle*) [1981] A.C. 221 (PC).

[332] *Bankers Trust International Ltd v Todd Shipyards Corporation* (*The Halcyon Isle*) [1981] A.C. 221 (PC). *cf. Todd Shipyards Corporation v Altema Compania Maritima SA* (*The Ioannis Daskalelis*) (1972) 32 D.L.R. (3d) 571 (Sup Ct Can); *JP Morgan Chase Bank v Mystras Maritime Corp* [2008] FCA 399, (2008) 305 D.L.R. (4th) 44 (appeal dismissed without consideration of this point: 2010 FC 1053).

[333] English law applies pursuant to Rome II Regulation, Art.4(2) and the availability of particular heads of damages is substantive under Art.15(c). Heads of damage were also classified as substantive at common law: *Boys v Chaplin* [1971] A.C. 356 (on which these facts are based).

14. In 2012, H and W are involved in a traffic accident in New South Wales in which H is severely injured. The law applicable to the tort, New South Wales law, contains statutory provisions specifying the maximum sum of damages which may be awarded to W. Such provisions are substantive, so that the limits laid down by New South Wales must be applied.[334]

15. In 2012, the widow of a person killed in an accident in 2010 brings a claim as a dependant of the deceased. The law of a foreign state, State X, is applicable to the tort. It states that, in assessing the level of damages to be awarded to the claimant, other benefits conferred upon the widow as a result of the death should be taken into account. The law of the forum provides in s.4 of the Fatal Accidents Act 1976 that such other benefits should be disregarded in assessing the level of damages. The rule of State X is to be regarded as one of substance and applied on the facts of the case;[335] and *sembles*.4 of the Fatal Accidents Act 1976 is inapplicable.[336]

(7) LIMITATION OF ACTIONS

16. X is indebted to A under a contract governed by Scots law. By that law, A's right is **7–081** extinguished after 40 years. By English law, A's remedy is barred after six years. After 10 years, A sues X in England. The action may proceed.[337]

17. The facts are as in Illustration 16, except that A commences his action after 25 years, having given X to understand many years before that no action would be brought. The Scottish limitation rule will apply unless its application would be manifestly incompatible with public policy.[338]

18. A is defamed in a foreign country by X. A sues X in England. The claim is statute-barred by English law but not by the *lex loci delicti*. The action fails.[339]

19. A is injured in a road accident in Pakistan caused by the negligence of an employee of X & Co. Immediately after the accident A is flown to Germany where she spends seven months in hospital. In correspondence with A, a representative of X & Co suggests that A's claim will be settled. A starts proceedings in England within the three-year limitation period laid down by English law, but after the expiry of the one-year limitation period under Pakistani law. The rule of Pakistani law, according to which A's claim is time-barred, is disapplied on the ground that, in the circumstances, its application would cause undue hardship.[340]

20. Three ex-employees bring an action in negligence against a Saudi company and one of its employees in respect of personal injuries suffered in Saudi waters in the course of their employment as divers. It is asserted that under Art.222 of the Saudi Labour Law, the claimants had only one year from the date of the incident, alternatively the termination of their work relationship, to lodge their claims. This provision is inapplicable on the facts and the claim is not

---

[334] This is the effect of Art.15 of the Rome II Regulation, so that the decision in *Harding v Wealands* [2006] UKHL 32, [2007] 2 A.C. 1, which treated the matter as procedural, would be decidedly differently if the facts arose today.

[335] Rome II Regulation, Art.15. Prior to the entry into force of the Regulation, s.4 of the Fatal Accidents Act would have been classified as procedural: *Roerig v Valiant Trawlers Ltd* [2002] EWCA Civ 21, [2002] 1 W.L.R. 2304 (CA).

[336] This depends upon whether s.4 of the Fatal Accidents Act 1976 is an overriding mandatory provision of the forum, applicable pursuant to Rome II Regulation, Art.16. See above, para.7–052; *Roerig v Valiant Trawlers Ltd* [2002] EWCA Civ 21, [2002] 1 W.L.R. 2304 (CA), at [29]; *Harding v Wealands* [2004] EWCA Civ 1735, [2005] 1 W.L.R. 1539, at [48] (the issue was not considered by the House of Lords on appeal in *Harding*: [2006] UKHL 32, [2007] 3 A.C. 1); *Cox v Ergo Versicherung AG* [2011] EWHC 2806 (QB), [2012] R.T.R. 11.

[337] Rome I Regulation, Art.12(1)(d); SI 2009/3064, Reg.5. Contrast the prior position at common law: *British Linen Co v Drummond* (1830) 10 B. & C. 903.

[338] Rome I Regulation, Art.21; SI 2009/3064, Reg.4. The Regulation's rules prevail over those in ss.1, 2 and 4 of the Foreign Limitation Periods Act 1984 (see s.8 of the 1984 Act).

[339] Defamation falls outside the ambit of the Rome II Regulation (Art.1(2)(g)) and the Private International Law (Miscellaneous Provisions) Act 1995, Part III (s.13), so that the common law choice of law rules remain applicable. The limitation period is determined in accordance with Foreign Limitation Periods Act 1984, s.1(2); *cf. M'Elroy v M'Allister* 1949 S.C. 110.

[340] *Jones v Trollope Colls Cementation Overseas Ltd, The Times*, January 26, 1990 (CA). If the facts were to arise today, the relevant question would be whether application of the *lex causae* is manifestly incompatible with English public policy: see Rome II Regulation, Art.26. This applies rather than s.2 of the 1984 Act (see s.8 of the 1984 Act).

time-barred by Saudi law; but, even if it had been applicable, this would not have been manifestly incompatible with English public policy.[341]

INTEREST[342]

7R–082   **RULE 20—(1) The liability to pay contractual interest and the rate of such interest payable in respect of a debt, e.g. in respect of a loan, are, in general,[343] determined by the law applicable to the contract under which the debt is incurred, e.g. by the law applicable to the contract under which the loan is made.[344]**

(2) The liability to pay interest as damages for non-payment of a debt is determined by the law applicable to the contract or non-contractual obligation under which the debt is incurred.[345] *Semble*, the rate of such interest is, in general, determined by English law;[346] but (*semble*) the rate of such interest is determined by the law applicable to the non-

---

[341] Under Rome II Regulation, Art.26; see further Foreign Limitation Periods Act 1984, s.8. *cf. Harley v Smith* [2009] EWHC 56 (QB), [2009] 1 Lloyd's Rep. 359, decided on the basis of the prior choice of law rules, and concluding that the Saudi law would not have caused undue hardship within the meaning of the 1984 Act, s.2(2).

[342] Law Com. No.124, *Foreign Money Liabilities* (1983), paras 2.27–2.33, 3.50–3.57; Law Com. Working Paper No.80, *Foreign Money Liabilities* (1981), paras 4.1–4.28; Guest, in Rose (ed.), *Lex Mercatoria: Essays in Honour of Francis Reynolds* (2000), p.271.

[343] Subject to Late Payment of Commercial Debts (Interest) Act 1998, s.12, below, paras 7–090 *et seq.*

[344] Rome I Regulation, Art.12(1)(b) (adopting the same position as the Rome Convention, Art.10(1)(b)). See also *Bodily v Bellamy* (1760) 2 Burr. 1094; *Dewar v Span* (1789) 3 T.R. 425; *Harvey v Archbold* (1825) 3 B. & C. 626; *Anon* (1825) 3 Bing. 193; *Re Tyre, Ex p. Guillebert* (1837) 2 Deac. 509; *Chili Republic v RMS Packet Co* (1895) 11 T.L.R. 203; *Société des Hôtels Le Touquet Paris-Plage v Cummings* [1922] 1 K.B. 451 (CA); *Shaik Sahied v Sockalingam Chettiar* [1933] A.C. 342 (PC); *Mount Albert BC v Australasian, etc., Assurance Society Ltd* [1938] A.C. 224 (PC); *Midland International Trade Services v Sudairy, Financial Times*, May 2, 1990; *Lesotho Highlands Development Authority v Impregilo SpA* [2002] EWHC 2435 (Comm.), [2003] 1 All E.R. (Comm.) 22, affirmed, [2003] EWCA Civ 1159, [2003] 2 Lloyd's Rep. 497, reversed on other grounds, [2005] UKHL 43, [2006] 1 A.C. 221, [2005] 3 W.L.R. 129, [2005] 3 All E.R. 789; *Rogers v Markel Corp* [2004] EWHC 1375 (QB); *Cloyes v Chapman* (1876) 27 U.C.C.P. 22; *Stuart and Stuart Ltd v Boswell* (1916) 50 N.S.R. 16; *Livesley v Clemens Horst Co* [1925] 1 D.L.R. 159 (Sup Ct Can); *Montreal Trust Co v Stanrock Uranium Mines Ltd* (1965) 53 D.L.R. (2d) 594 (Ont); *Re Savage's Estate* (1908) 29 N.L.R. 397; *Barcelo v Electrolytic Zinc Co etc., Ltd* (1932) 48 C.L.R. 391; *Wanganui etc., Board v Australian Mutual Provident Society* (1934) 50 C.L.R. 581.

[345] Rome I Regulation, Art.12(1)(c) (adopting the same position as the Rome Convention, Art.10(1)(c)); see also *Miliangos v George Frank (Textiles) Ltd (No.2)* [1977] Q.B. 489, 497; *Lesotho Highlands Development Authority v Impregilo SpA*, above; but see *Helmsing Schiffahrts GmbH v Malta Drydocks Corp* [1977] 2 Lloyd's Rep. 444, 449–450. See also *Maher v Groupama Grand Est* [2009] EWCA Civ 1191, [2010] 1 W.L.R. 1564 (a case on tort); *cf. Midland International Trade Services v Sudairy, Financial Times*, May 2, 1990, followed in *Kuwait Oil Tanker Co SAK v Al Bader, The Independent*, January 11, 1999, a case on tort reversed in part, but without expressing a concluded view on the point, [2002] 2 All E.R. (Comm.), 271, 339–244 (CA): see below, paras 7–098 *et seq.*

[346] *Miliangos v George Frank (Textiles) Ltd (No.2)* [1977] Q.B. 489, 497; *Lesotho Highlands Development Authority v Impregilo SpA*, above; *Rogers v Markel Corp*, above, but see *Helmsing Schiffahrts GmbH v Malta Drydocks Corp* [1977] 2 Lloyd's Rep. 444, 449–450. In *The Pacific Colocotronis* [1981] 2 Lloyd's Rep. 40, 45–47 (CA) the rate of interest was determined by English law which was the *lex fori* and the law which governed the contract and no observations were made on this point.

contractual obligation where the Rome II Regulation (Regulation (EC) 864/2007) applies.

(3) The rate of interest awarded by virtue of clause (2) of the Rule is a matter for the discretion of the court pursuant to s.35A of the Senior Courts Act 1981,[347] and in the exercise of that discretion the court will, prima facie, award the rate applicable to the currency in which the debt is expressed.[348]

COMMENT

Interest may be payable either by virtue of an express or implied term of a contract or by way of damages.[349] Clause (1) of the Rule is concerned with the former situation, clauses (2) and (3) with the latter. Clause (3) of the Rule will also apply to the determination of the rate of interest in cases falling within clause (1) of the Rule when English law is the law which governs the contract.   7-083

The right to, and rate of, interest may also be affected by the provisions of the Late Payment of Commercial Debts (Interest) Act 1998. The effect of this statute in cases involving a conflict of laws is discussed in the Comment to clause (1) of the Rule.[350]   7-084

Subject to that Act, the Rule states the effect of the common law and, it is submitted, the position in cases falling within the Rome I and II Regulations.   7-085

Where the Rome I Regulation applies, then for the purposes of Rule 20(1) and (2) the law applicable to the relevant contract will be determined by the rules contained in the Regulation.[351] Article 12(1) of the Regulation,[352] which deals with the scope of the applicable law,[353] does not expressly identify interest as an issue to be governed by the applicable law. However, whether interest is payable by way of an express or implied term of a contract should be regarded as being related to the content of the obligation to be performed   7-086

---

[347] Supreme Court Act 1981 was renamed Senior Courts Act 1981: Constitutional Reform Act 2005, s.59 and Sch.11, in force October 1, 2009.

[348] *Miliangos v George Frank (Textiles) Ltd (No.2)*, above; *Helmsing Schiffahrts GmbH v Malta Drydocks Corporation*, above; *The Pacific Colocotronis*, above; *Lesotho Highlands Development Authority v Impregilo SpA*, above; *Rogers v Markel Corp*, above; *Maher v Groupama Grand Est* [2009] EWCA Civ 1191, [2010] 1 W.L.R. 1564.

[349] For the difference between contractual interest and interest by way of damages for breach of contract, see *Arnott v Redfern* (1826) 3 Bing. 353, a case which established this distinction although it was subsequently not followed on the point of law which it decided. See *McGregor on Damages* (18th ed. 2010), Ch.15; *Chitty on Contracts* (30th ed. 2009), Vol.1, paras 26–167 *et seq.*, Vol.2, paras 38–264 *et seq.* In *Arnott v Redfern*, above, the court arrived at the conclusion that English law was no different from Scots law. It is therefore no authority on the question of interest in the conflict of laws. The conclusion may, in the light of the subsequent case law, have been erroneous, but that does not affect the issue.

[350] See below, paras 7–090 *et seq.*

[351] See below, Rules 222 and 223.

[352] Compare Contracts (Applicable Law) Act 1990, Sch.1, Art.10(1).

[353] See below, Rule 227.

under the contract and thus within the scope of Art.12(1)(b)[354] which submits the question of "performance" to the applicable law.[355] As far as interest by way of damages is concerned, the question can be regarded as being within the scope of "the consequences of a total or partial breach of obligations," etc. for the purposes of Art.12(1)(c)[356] so that the same conclusion follows.[357] In any event, the list of matters referred to in Art.12(1) is not exhaustive so that even if questions relating to interest are treated as independent questions, an English court would be justified in submitting the question of whether there is liability to pay contractual interest or interest by way of damages in contract to the law applicable to the contract.[358] For non-contractual obligations falling within the ambit of the Rome II Regulation, the governing law will be determined in accordance with the rules specified therein.[359] Article 15 of the Regulation applies the *lex causae* to determine the right to damages and the assessment thereof.[360] Although Art.15 does not expressly refer to interest, it seems clear that it encompasses questions of entitlement to interest.

7–087   The submission that the rate of interest payable as damages is governed by the *lex fori* is more tentative. Where the Rome II Regulation applies, however, the better view appears to be that the rate of interest is determined by the *lex causae*. In principle, there is a very strong argument for adopting the same approach in respect of the Rome I Regulation; but as will be seen below, rates of interest have been treated in England as procedural after the entry into force of the Rome Convention, which contained substantially the same relevant wording as the Rome I Regulation on this point. These issues are further in the discussion of clause (2) of the Rule below.

7–088   The position in relation to contractual obligations will be considered first. The position in relation to tortious obligations[361] will be considered below.[362]

7–089   **Clause (1) of the Rule.** If interest is payable on a loan or any other debt, otherwise than by way of damages, it must be so under the law which governs the contract between the parties. Whatever law, therefore, governs the contract must determine all questions relating to interest. Thus, whether an express undertaking to pay interest is lawful or whether it is made invalid wholly or partly by legislation referring to usury or money-lending depends on the question whether that legislation forms part of the law applicable to the

---

[354] Compare Contracts (Applicable Law) Act 1990, Sch.1, Art.10(1)(b).

[355] Below, paras 32–146 *et seq.*

[356] Compare Contracts (Applicable Law) Act 1990, Sch.1, Art.10(1)(c).

[357] Below, paras 32–153 *et seq. cf. Lesotho Highlands Development Authority v Impregilo SpA* [2002] EWHC 2435 (Comm.), [2003] 1 All E.R. (Comm.) 22, affirmed, [2003] EWCA Civ 1159, [2003] 2 Lloyd's Rep. 49, reversed on other grounds, [2005] UKHL 43, [2006] 1 A.C. 221, [2005] 3 W.L.R. 129, [2005] 3 All E.R. 789.

[358] Compare, in respect of the Rome Convention, Giuliano-Lagarde, p.32; below, para.32–142.

[359] Arts 4–14.

[360] Art.15(c). See also Art.15(d).

[361] The Rome II Regulation also applies to other non-contractual obligations within its ambit.

[362] At paras 7–108 *et seq.*

contract.[363] That law decides whether an undertaking to pay interest can and must be implied, and also determines the rate of interest so payable, including the question of compound interest or of interest on interest.[364] The law applicable to the contract will govern the liability to pay interest even if it is not the law of the country where the debt is to be paid or the loan repaid. Thus, if a local authority in New Zealand raises a loan from an insurance company in the Australian State of Victoria, and undertakes to pay interest in Victoria, the law applicable to the contract of loan (which is secured by a charge on the local rates in New Zealand) will be the law of New Zealand. Legislation reducing the rate of interest in Victoria will therefore not affect the contract, although it was enacted in the country in which the contract was to be performed.[365]

Late Payment of Commercial Debts (Interest) Act 1998. This Act[366]   **7–090**
makes provision with respect to interest on the late payment of certain debts. Part I of the Act provides that it is an implied term in a contract for the supply of goods of services[367] where the purchaser and the supplier are each acting in the course of a business,[368] other than an "excepted contract",[369] that any "qualifying debt"[370] created by the contract carries simple interest described as "statutory interest",[371] subject to, and in accordance with, Pt I of the Act,[372] the rate of such interest to be prescribed by order.[373] Part II of the Act sets out

---

[363] Rome I Regulation, Art.12(1)(b); compare Rome Convention, Art.10(1)(b); see *Shamil Bank of Bahrain v Beximico Pharmaceuticals Ltd* [2004] EWCA Civ 19, [2004] 1 W.L.R. 1784; *Shrichand v Lacon* (1906) 22 T.L.R. 245; *Associated Loan Co v Callaghan* (1957) 9 D.L.R. (2d) 559 (Ont CA); *Rosencrantz v Union Contractors Ltd* (1960) 23 D.L.R. (2d) 473 (BC); *cf.* Restatement, s.203. This should include interest payable under the governing law from the moment of the commencement of the proceedings, for if that law determines the existence of a right to claim interest, it should also determine the extent of that right. See Wolff, s.230.

[364] *Montreal Trust Co v Stanrock Uranium Mines Ltd* (1965) 53 D.L.R. (2d) 594 (Ont). *cf. Kuwait Oil Tanker Co SAK v Al Bader* [2002] 2 All E.R. (Comm.) 271 (CA).

[365] *Mount Albert BC v Australasian, etc., Assurance Society* [1938] A.C. 224 (PC); see also *Barcelo v Electrolytic Zinc Co etc., Ltd* (1932) 48 C.L.R. 391; *Wanganui etc., Board v Australian Mutual Provident Society* (1934) 50 C.L.R. 581. As to the position where payment of interest is illegal by the law of the place of payment, see below, paras 32–097 *et seq.*

[366] As amended by Late Payment of Commercial Debts Regulations 2002 (SI 2002/1674), partially implementing Directive 2000/35/EC of the European Parliament and of the Council of June 29, 2000 on combating late payment in commercial transactions ([2000] O.J. L200/35), fully in force from August 7, 2000.

[367] Defined as a contract of sale of goods or a contract other than a contract of sale of goods by which a person, for a consideration that is, or includes, a money consideration, does any, or any combination, of the following things: transferring or agreeing to transfer to another the property in goods; bailing or agreeing to bail goods to another by way of hire or, in Scotland, hiring or agreeing to hire goods to another; and agreeing to carry out a service: Late Payment of Commercial Debts (Interest) Act 1998, s.2(2), (3), (7). A contract of service or apprenticeship is not a contract for the supply of goods or services: *ibid.* s.2(4).

[368] ss.1(1), 2(1), (2), (3), (7), 12(3).

[369] Defined as a consumer credit agreement within the meaning of the Consumer Credit Act 1974, a contract intended to operate by way of mortgage, pledge, charge or other security, and any other contract specified in an order made by the Secretary of State: *ibid.* s.2(5), (6), (7).

[370] *ibid.* ss.1(1), 3(1).

[371] *ibid.* s.1(2).

[372] *ibid.* s.(1).

[373] *ibid.* s.6. The current rate of interest is 8 per cent over the official dealing rate per annum: SI 2002/1675.

the circumstances in which it is permissible to oust or vary this right to statutory interest by appropriate contract terms.[374]

7–091 According to the general principles set out above, the provisions of the 1998 Act as to the right to, and the rate of, statutory interest should only apply where English law is the law applicable to the contract. However, these general principles are modified by a specific provision in the Act which addresses the operation of the Act in cases involving a conflict of laws.[375]

7–092 According to s.12(1) of the Act, the provisions of the Act do not have effect in relation to a contract governed by the law of a part of the United Kingdom by choice of the parties if: (a) there is no significant connection between the contract and that part of the United Kingdom; and (b) but for that choice the applicable law would be a foreign law, defined as the law of a country outside the United Kingdom.[376] This appears to mean that if the parties have, e.g. chosen English law to govern the contract in accordance with Art.3(1) of the Rome I Regulation,[377] but there is no significant connection between the contract and England, and, but for that choice of English law, the contract would, according to Art.4 of the Rome I Regulation,[378] be governed by the law of a country outside the United Kingdom, e.g. that of France, the provisions of the 1998 Act will not apply.[379] Such would appear to be the case even if the contract did have a significant connection with a part of the United Kingdom other than that whose law has been chosen in the contract since the subsection, in terms, requires the absence of a significant connection with the part whose law has been chosen.[380] On the other hand, the Act will apply where English law is chosen but, apart from that, the contract would be governed by the law of a country outside the United Kingdom, if there is, nevertheless, a significant connection between the contract and England. It is apparent, accordingly, that s.12(1) of the 1998 Act envisages that a contract may have a "significant connection"[381] with the part of the United Kingdom whose law has been chosen even though, under Art.4 of the Rome I Regulation,[382] the applicable law in the absence of choice would have been a country outside the United Kingdom.[383]

7–093 The Act is silent as to the factors which may be found to give rise to a significant connection and whether such a connection does, or does not, exist will depend on the circumstances of the particular case. It is likely, however, that such a connection may be constituted, e.g. in a contract of sale, where English law is chosen and England is either the place of business of the purchaser or the place where the purchase price is to be paid, but apart from that choice of law, the contract would be governed by the law of France,

---

[374] *ibid.* ss.7–10.

[375] *cf.* Unfair Contract Terms Act 1977, s.27, below, paras 33–024 *et seq.*, 33–158 *et seq.*

[376] Late Payment of Commercial Debts (Interest) Act 1998, s.12(3). *cf.* Unfair Contract Terms Act 1977, s.27(1) below, paras 33–026 and 33–160.

[377] See below, Rule 222.

[378] See below, Rule 223.

[379] *cf. Surzur Overseas Ltd v Ocean Reliance Shipping Co Ltd* [1997] C.L.Y. 906, below, para.33–026.

[380] Late Payment of Commercial Debts (Interest) Act 1998, s.12(1)(a).

[381] *ibid.*

[382] See below, Rule 223.

[383] Compare Contracts (Applicable Law) Act 1990, Sch.1, Arts 3 and 4.

pursuant to Art.4(1)(a)[384] of the Rome I Regulation because France is the country in which the seller's place of business is situated.[385]

Finally, the provisions of the 1998 Act appear to apply if the law of one part **7–094** of the United Kingdom is chosen in the contract, but, were it not for that choice, the applicable law would be the law of another part of the United Kingdom. This conclusion appears to follow irrespective of whether a significant connection between the contract and the part of the United Kingdom whose law has been chosen does, or does not, exist, because s.12(1) only applies where, in the absence of choice, the contract would be governed by a foreign law and foreign law is defined as the law of a country outside the United Kingdom.[386]

Section 12(2) of the 1998 Act contains a provision designed to prevent **7–095** avoidance of the provisions of the Act.[387] It provides that the Act has effect in relation to a contract governed by a foreign law by choice of the parties if: (a) but for that choice, the applicable law would be the law of a part of the United Kingdom; and (b) there is no significant connection between the contract and any other country other than that part of the United Kingdom. Thus, if, e.g. a contract contains a choice of the law of France which accords with Art.3(1) of the Rome I Regulation,[388] but were it not for that choice, the applicable law would, under Art.4 of the Rome I Regulation, be English law, the Act will apply unless the contract has a significant connection with a country other than England. That connection may be with the country whose law has been chosen, that of France in this example, or with a different foreign country, e.g. Italy, or even with a part of the United Kingdom other than England, e.g. Scotland. For although the expression "country" is not defined in the 1998 Act, it seems clear that it includes the different parts of the United Kingdom in s.12(2) since the subsection expressly refers to "any country other than *that part of the United Kingdom*",[389] whose law has been chosen, a form of words which is, in the above example, apt to include Scotland. Again, what will be found to constitute a significant connection for these purposes will depend on the circumstances of the particular case. It is, however, clear that although the contract has its closest connection[390] with the law of a particular part of the United Kingdom, the contract may, nevertheless, have a significant connection with a country other than that part of the United Kingdom.[391]

Section 12(2) only controls the avoidance of the 1998 Act by a choice of a **7–096** foreign law, i.e. the law of a country outside the United Kingdom.[392] Where, however, an issue arises in English proceedings involving a contract which contains a choice of the law of a different part of the United Kingdom, the Act

---

[384] See below, Rule 223.

[385] Compare Contracts (Applicable Law) Act 1990, Sch.1, Art.4(2).

[386] Late Payment of Commercial Debts (Interest) Act 1998, s.12(3).

[387] *cf.* Unfair Contract Terms Act 1977, s.27(2), below, paras 33–024 *et seq.*, 33–158 *et seq.*

[388] below, Rule 222.

[389] Emphasis added. *cf.* s.12(3) defining foreign law as the law of a country outside the *United Kingdom* (emphasis added).

[390] See below, Rule 223(4).

[391] *cf.* s.12(1), above, paras 7–092 *et seq.*

[392] Late Payment of Commercial Debts (Interest) Act 1998, s.12(3).

appears to apply on general principles,[393] unless the circumstances envisaged in s.12(1) are present.[394] The Act would further appear to apply where the contract contains no choice of law, but because of Art.4 of the Rome I Regulation,[395] the applicable law is the law of a part of the United Kingdom.[396]

7–097   Clause (1) of this Rule points out the general principle of the conflict of laws that liability to pay contractual interest and the rate of such interest is determined by the law applicable to the contract.[397] This principle may thus be modified where the contract is governed by a foreign law as a result of the choice of the parties since if s.12(2) of the 1998 Act applies, the parties may not "contract out" of the Act.

7–098   **Clause (2) of the Rule.** Clause (2) of the Rule requires that a distinction be drawn between the question of the law governing the right to interest payable by way of damages, and the law which governs the rate at which any interest so payable is to be paid.[398] It is submitted that the existence of a right to claim interest is properly classified as a substantive matter and thus should be referred to the *lex causae* of the relevant claim. This accords with modern developments in which the courts have considered the right to damages as an issue of substance to be determined by the *lex causae*[399] and with the approach in the Rome I[400] and II Regulations.[401] By contrast, it is also tentatively submitted that English law as the *lex fori* determines the rate at which interest is payable since this has been regarded as a procedural matter at common law and after the entry into force of the Rome Convention; although the issue is beset by uncertainty under the Rome I Regulation and, as will be seen below, the better view is that rates of interest are to be classified as substantive under the Rome II Regulation.[402]

7–099   Although there is one decision to the contrary, the better view, on principle, it is submitted, is that in respect of claims for interest as damages, the right to claim such interest was, at common law, governed by the law which is

---

[393] Rule 224.

[394] See above, paras 7–092 *et seq.*

[395] See below, Rule 223.

[396] *ibid.*

[397] See above, para.7–089. A debt does not carry statutory interest if, or to the extent that, it consists of a sum to which a right to interest or to charge interest applies by virtue of a statute other than the 1998 Act: Late Payment of Commercial Debts (Interest) Act 1998, s.3(2).

[398] In cases falling outside the ambit of the Rome II Regulation.

[399] Rome I Regulation, Art.12(1)(c); compare Contracts (Applicable Law) Act 1990, Sch.1, Art.10(1)(c). See, in relation to the prior, non-harmonised rules of English law, *D'Almeida Araujo Lda v Sir Frederick Becker & Co Ltd* [1953] 2 Q.B. 329, following *Livesley v Clemens Horst Co* [1925] 1 D.L.R. 159 (Sup Ct Can); *Boys v Chaplin* [1971] A.C. 356, 379, 392–393, 394–395; *Harding v Wealands* [2006] UKHL 32, [2007] 2 A.C. 1. See, however, *NV Handel J. Smits v English Exporters Ltd* [1955] 2 Lloyd's Rep. 69, 72. See above, paras 7–044 and 7–046 *et seq.*

[400] Art.12(1)(c).

[401] Art.15.

[402] The Rome II Regulation applies the *lex causae* to the assessment of damages (Art.15(c)). The Rome I Regulation applies the governing law of the contract to the "assessment of damages in so far as it is governed by rules of law" (Art.12(1)(c)). Both Regulations, however, exclude matters of procedure (Rome I, Art.1(3); Rome II, Art.1(3)) and a key question is whether this excludes questions as to the rate of interest on damages.

applicable to the contract.[403] It is also submitted that the same view should be taken in cases which fall within the Rome I Regulation. Since this right belongs to "the consequences of a total or partial breach of obligations" it should properly be regarded as falling within Art.12(1)(c) of the Regulation[404] and, as such, governed by the applicable law.[405]

Although it is submitted that the foregoing propositions are correct in principle, it cannot be said that they are supported by conclusive authority. As regards the common law position, *Miliangos v George Frank Textiles Ltd (No.2)*[406] is authority for the proposition that in respect of claims for interest as damages in contract, the right to claim such interest is governed by the law applicable to the contract, though the rate of interest to be awarded is a matter for the *lex fori*, since "while you look to the proper law of the contract to see whether there is a right to recover interest by way of damages, you look to the *lex fori* to decide how much."[407] But in *Helmsing Schiffahrts GmbH v Malta Drydocks Corp*,[408] a case in which English law was the governing law and the *lex fori*, Kerr J. preferred the view that the rate of interest was governed by the law applicable to the contract as being "more consonant with principle," though he also intimated that the point required further consideration at a higher level. The Law Commission subsequently examined the issue and concluded that the view of Bristow J. was to be preferred to that of Kerr J.[409]

7–100

However, in *Midland International Trade Services v Sudairy*,[410] Hobhouse J. held that s.35A of what is now the Senior Courts Act 1981 which confers a discretionary power on the court to award interest was procedural rather than substantive in nature and was thus always applicable in English proceedings irrespective of the applicable law.[411] In *Lesotho Highlands Development*

7–101

---

[403] *Miliangos v George Frank (Textiles) Ltd (No.2)* [1977] Q.B. 489, 496–497; *Helmsing Schiffahrts GmbH v Malta Drydocks Corp* [1977] 2 Lloyd's Rep. 444, 449–450. See also *Manners v Pearson & Son* [1898] 1 Ch.581, 588 (CA); *Société des Hôtels Le Touquet Paris-Plage v Cummings* [1922] 1 K.B. 451, 460 (CA). In *BP Exploration Co (Libya) Ltd v Hunt (No.2)* [1979] 1 W.L.R. 783, affirmed [1981] 1 W.L.R. 232 (CA), [1983] 2 A.C. 352, English law as the law governing the contract was applied to a claim for interest in respect of a restitutionary award under the Law Reform (Frustrated Contracts) Act 1943.

[404] Compare Contracts (Applicable Law) Act 1990, Sch.1, Art.10(1)(c).

[405] See *Lesotho Highlands Development Authority v Impregilio SpA* [2003] EWCA Civ 1159, [2003] 2 Lloyd's Rep. 497, at [45], reversed on other grounds, [2005] UKHL 43, [2006] 1 A.C. 221.

[406] See above.

[407] At 497, endorsing the submission to this effect in the 6th ed. of this book, at p.708.

[408] [1977] 2 Lloyd's Rep. 444, 449. Kerr J. preferred the view to this effect expressed in the 9th edition of this work (p.868) and the 10th edition (pp.905–906).

[409] Law Com. No.124 (1983), paras 2.32, 3.55. The Law Commission's arguments are developed more fully in Working Paper No.80 (1981), paras 4.22–4.27.

[410] *Financial Times*, May 2, 1990, followed in *Kuwait Oil Tanker Co SAK v Al Bader, The Independent*, January 11, 1999, a case on tort, reversed in part, but without expressing a concluded view on the point, [2002] 2 All E.R. (Comm.) 271, 339–444. As to interest as damages in tort, see below, para.7–108 *et seq*.

[411] Despite holding that s.35A of the Senior Courts Act 1981 was procedural, Moore-Bick J. in *Kuwait Oil Tanker Co SAK v Al Bader*, above, recognised the force of the argument that the existence of a right to recover interest is a matter for the proper law of the contract. While the Court of Appeal acknowledged ([2002] 2 All E.R. (Comm.) 271, 343) "the force of Hobhouse J.'s reasoning as an analysis of the nature and origins of the English court's general power to award interest", it went on to say (*ibid.*) that "it is also right to observe that the creation of that power

Authority v Impregilo SpA,[412] at first instance, Morison J. preferred the view expressed in *Miliangos v George Frank Textiles Ltd (No.2)*[413] to that expressed by Hobhouse J. in *Midland International Trade Services v Sudairy*.[414] The Court of Appeal affirmed the decision of Morison J.[415] The Court of Appeal found it unnecessary, however, to decide whether s.35A of the Senior Courts Act 1981 was procedural or substantive, but held, nonetheless, that where the applicable law confers a substantive right to interest, the unpaid party is entitled, as a substantive right, to interest from the time when payment is contractually due and in such circumstances there was no room for any discretionary procedural power to award interest. Additionally, the Court of Appeal recognised that "by Art.10(1)(c) of the Rome Convention. . . . the consequences of a breach of contract, which must surely include questions relating to the entitlement to interest if sums are wrongfully withheld by a party in breach, are to be determined by the applicable law of the contract."[416] Upon further appeal, the House of Lords reversed the decision of the Court of Appeal[417] without expressing any view on the issue under discussion. In the opinion of the House, the case was concerned with the power of arbitrators to award interest. This was governed by s.49(3)[418] of the Arbitration Act 1996 which is applicable unless otherwise agreed by the parties[419] and no such agreement had been made.

7–102   In *Maher v Groupama Grand Est*,[420] the court considered Rule 20[421] in a tort case under Private International Law (Miscellaneous Provisions) Act 1995, Part III. It held that the availability of a claim for interest on damages should be regarded as a substantive issue. It concluded, however, that Senior Courts Act 1981, s.35A created a remedy exercised at the court's discretion rather than a substantive right to interest and, therefore, although the existence of a legal right to claim interest was to be determined by French law as the *lex causae*, whether or not such a substantive right existed, an award of interest under s.35A was to be classified as a procedural matter governed by English law as the *lex fori*. The court endorsed the view of

---

creates a right in a claimant to claim interest, which right is recognized and consistently given effect on the basis that it represents compensation to the claimant for having been kept out of money to which he has been held entitled". Additionally, the Court of Appeal expressed no view on the question of whether the right to claim interest by way of damages belonged to the "consequences of breach" for the purposes of Art.10(1)(c) of the Rome Convention since no argument had been heard on the point. *cf. Zebrarise Ltd v De Nieffe* [2004] EWHC 1842 (Comm.), [2005] 1 Lloyd's Rep. 154, at [46]. Compare Art.12(1)(c) of the Rome I Regulation.

[412] [2002] EWHC 2435 (Comm.), [2003] 1 All E.R. (Comm.) 22, affirmed, [2003] EWCA Civ 1159, [2003] 2 Lloyd's Rep. 497, reversed on other grounds, [2005] UKHL 43, [2006] 1 A.C. 221, [2005] 3 W.L.R. 129, [2005] 3 All E.R. 789.

[413] See above. This view was also expressed in the then current edition of this work: see 13th edition, Rule 196(2).

[414] See above.

[415] See above.

[416] See above, at [45]. The same principles would apply pursuant to Art.12(1)(c) of the Rome I Regulation, which subjects "the consequences of a total or partial breach of obligations" to the law applicable to the contract.

[417] See above.

[418] See below, para.37–088.

[419] Arbitration Act 1996, s.49(2).

[420] [2009] EWCA Civ 1191, [2010] 1 W.L.R. 1564, [2010] 2 All E.R. 455.

[421] Rule 226 of the 14th edition of this work.

Hobhouse J. in *Midland International Trade Services v Sudairy.*[422] In exercising its discretion the court might well take into account any relevant provisions of the *lex causae* relating to the recovery of interest but the English principles of assessment are sufficiently flexible to allow the court to fix an appropriate rate, having due regard to any relevant provisions of the governing law relating to the recovery of interest.[423] Despite the complexities of the case law in this area, it is suggested that the approach of the Court of Appeal in *Maher* will henceforth be followed, at least where the relevant choice of law rules have not been harmonised at EU level.

The Court of Appeal in *Maher* made no reference to the position under the   **7–103**
Rome I Regulation. After the entry into force of the Rome Convention, it was held in the Court of Appeal[424] and at first instance[425] that the *lex fori* determines the rate of interest claimed as damages for breach of contract. This is despite Art.10(1)(c) of the Convention stipulating that the law governing the contract shall apply "within the limits of the powers conferred on the court by its procedural law [to] . . . the assessment of damages in so far as it is governed by rules of law". In principle, therefore, the same approach should apply under the Rome I Regulation,[426] which contains a similar provision on the scope of the law governing the contract in Art.12(1)(c). The matter cannot be free from doubt, however, the essential question being how widely the exclusion of matters of evidence and procedure in the Rome I Regulation should be construed. It is suggested below that the *lex causae* should determine the rate of interest under the Rome II Regulation, even though this creates an unfortunate dichotomy between the Rome I and II Regulation. The European Court may yet rule that the issue of rates of interest falls within the scope of the Rome I Regulation and is subject to the applicable law of the contract.[427] But on the state of the English authorities at present, it would

---

[422] It preferred Hobhouse J.'s views to *dicta* of the Court of Appeal in *Kuwait Oil Tanker SAK v Al Bader*, above.

[423] See also *Abdel Hadi Abdallah Al Qahtani & Sons Beverage Industry Co v Antliff* [2010] EWHC 1735 (Comm.), at [59]; and *Knight v Axa Assurances* [2009] EWHC 1900 (Q.B.), [2009] Lloyd's Rep. I.R. 667.

[424] *Lesotho Highlands Development Authority v Impregilo SpA* [2003] EWCA Civ 1159, [2003] 2 Lloyd's Rep. 497, at [50], expressly adopting the reasoning in this paragraph; reversed on other grounds, without reference to the point, [2005] UKHL 43, [2006] 1 A.C. 221.

[425] *Rogers v Markel Corp* [2004] EWHC 1375 (QB) (without express reference to the Rome Convention); see also [2004] EWHC 2046 (QB).

[426] The Rome I Regulation does not apply to matters of procedure: Art.1(3); the same as true under the Rome Convention: Art.1(2)(h).

[427] Pursuant to Art.12(1)(c) of the Rome I Regulation—insofar as the rate of interest is determined by rules of law of the *lex causae*. See also Case C–127/03 *Commission v Trendsoft*, July 8, 2004, where the European Community concluded with the defendant a contract for the implementation of a project entitled "client requirements definition improvement". The sum paid in advance to the defendant exceeded its expenditure and the Commission sought to recover the excess paid. The contract was governed by Irish law and the European Court applied Irish law to determine the rate of interest. See further Case C–315/03 *Commission v Huhtamaki Dourdan SA*, May 12, 2005, where a contract was entered into pursuant to Council Decision 94/571/EC of July 27, 1994 adopting a specific research and technological development, including demonstration, in the field of industrial and materials technologies. The Court held that the rate of interest on a debt was to be treated as substantive. See also Anton, para.27.51, recognising the uncertainty but considering it "likely" in the light of these two European Court decisions in a different context that the European Court will treat rates of interest as substantive under the Rome I and II Regulations.

appear that rates of interest were a procedural matter under the Rome Convention; and there would appear to be insufficient justification to classify them any differently under the Rome I Regulation.

7–104   Hence, it is submitted that the right to claim interest as damages in contract is a substantive question for the law which governs the contract and if it confers a substantive right to a remedy, that will be upheld by the English courts. The view may legitimately be taken on the state of the current authorities that the rate of such interest as is available under the applicable law is a matter of procedure determined by the *lex fori*. In any event, the court's remedial power to award interest under s.35A of the Senior Courts Act 1981 may be exercised even where English law is not the *lex causae*.

7–105   Nevertheless, to say that the *lex fori* determines the rate of interest does not necessarily mean that the applicable rate will be the domestic English rate; and to say that the applicable law determines the rate of interest does not necessarily mean that, if English law is the applicable law, the applicable rate will be the domestic English rate.[428] This is because the rate which will be awarded by the English court is governed by s.35A of the Senior Courts Act 1981 which confers a general judicial discretion as to simple interest. The principles governing the exercise of this discretion, which are discussed in the comment to clause (3) of the Rule, are sufficiently flexible to enable the court to arrive at an appropriate rate, whether English or foreign.[429]

7–106   Interest payable on an English judgment debt would appear to be always governed by the *lex fori*.[430] This is equally true if the English court gives a judgment expressed in a foreign currency.[431]

7–107   **Bills of exchange.** It is also established that, where interest is claimed by

---

[428] See *The Pacific Colocotronis* [1981] 2 Lloyd's Rep. 40 (CA), where, applying English law, the Court of Appeal applied a US dollar rate and not a sterling rate to a contract in US dollars with a judgment in US dollars. And see *Swiss Bank Corp v State of New South Wales* (1993–94) 33 N.S.W.L.R. 63.

[429] *Maher v Groupama Grand Est* [2009] EWCA Civ 1191, [2010] 1 W.L.R. 1564.

[430] See Judgments Act 1838, ss.17, 18, as amended by Administration of Justice Act 1970, s.44 and SI 1998/2940. For interest payable on foreign judgments, see Foreign Judgments (Reciprocal Enforcement) Act 1933, s.2(6); Civil Jurisdiction and Judgments Act 1982, s.7 (as amended by SI 2009/3131 reg.8). For interest on foreign arbitration awards, see *Dalmia Dairy Industries Ltd v National Bank of Pakistan* [1978] 2 Lloyd's Rep. 223, 272–276, 301–303 (CA). This paragraph was cited with approval in *Gater Assets Ltd v Nak Naftogaz Ukrainiy (No.3)* [2008] EWHC 1108 (Comm.), [2008] 2 Lloyd's Rep. 295, at [19].

[431] Administration of Justice Act 1970, s.44A, inserted by Private International Law (Miscellaneous Provisions) Act 1995, s.1(1) (in force from November 1, 1996, SI 1996/2515). According to s.44A, where a judgment is given for a sum expressed in a currency other than sterling and the judgment debt in one to which Judgments Act 1838, s.17 applies, the court may order that the interest rate applicable to the debt shall be such rate as the court thinks fit. The section implements recommendations of the Law Commission: Law Com. No.124 (1983), paras 4.1–4.15. For county court orders, see County Courts Act 1984, s.74(5A), inserted by Private International Law (Miscellaneous Provisions) Act 1995, s.2. For the power of arbitrators to award interest on arbitration awards, see Arbitration Act 1996, s.49, the provisions of which are applicable irrespective of whether the award is expressed in sterling or in a foreign currency. See generally *Lesotho Highlands Development Authority v Impregilo SpA* [2005] UKHL 43, [2006] 1 A.C. 221.

reason of the dishonour of a bill of exchange, the law governing the contract must be applied to determine entitlement to interest.[432]

Claims in tort.[433] In relation to claims in tort, at common law there was old **7–108** authority which suggested that, in such cases, interest by way of damages was awarded in accordance with the law of the place where the tort was committed (*lex loci delicti*).[434] Subsequently, however, it was held at first instance, by Moore-Bick J., that s.35A of the Senior Courts Act 1981 was procedural rather than substantive in nature in the context of tort liability at common law and that therefore the right to claim interest as damages in English proceedings was governed by s.35A[435] rather than by the "double actionability" choice of law rule which was then applicable to torts.[436] In the same case, Moore-Bick J. preferred the view that the power to make an award of compound interest also depended on the *lex fori*.[437] But in respect of each claim he also considered the position under the relevant choice of law rule lest he be wrong in the view he preferred. In these circumstances, the Court of Appeal found it unnecessary to express a concluded view either on the proper characterisation of s.35A or on the law applicable to the right to claim compound interest.[438]

In *Maher v Groupama Grand Est*,[439] the court held that the availability of **7–109** a claim for interest on damages was a substantive issue[440] and subject to the

---

[432] See below, para.33–353; *Cooper v Waldegrave* (1840) 2 Beav. 282; *Karafarin Bank v Dara* [2009] EWHC 3265 (Comm.), [2010] 1 Lloyd's Rep. 236l; Falconbridge, pp.333 *et seq.*, p.361. The law applicable to contractual interest payable on a bill of exchange (see Bills of Exchange Act 1882, s.9(1)(a)) is not necessarily identical with that governing interest payable by reason of dishonour (s.57), but the *lex fori* as such is not applicable in either case.

[433] The Rome II Regulation also applies to other non-contractual obligations (including obligations arising out of unjust enrichment) for matters within its ambit.

[434] *Ekins v East India Co* (1717) 1 P. Wms. 935. This case can also be interpreted as an authority that the law governing a restitutionary claim governs the rate of interest.

[435] *Kuwait Oil Tanker Co SAK v Al Bader, The Independent*, January 11, 1999, reversed in part, without expressing a concluded view on this point, [2002] 2 All E.R. (Comm.) 271, 339–344 (CA). In this case Moore-Bick J. preferred the view expressed by Hobhouse J. in *Midland International Trade Services v Sudairy, Financial Times*, May 2, 1990, above, para.7–101, to that which was expressed in the 12th ed. of this work.

[436] *ibid.* See *Phillips v Eyre* (1870) L.R. 6 Q.B. 1; *Boys v Chaplin* [1971] A.C. 356; *Red Sea Insurance Co Ltd v Bouygues SA* [1995] 1 A.C. 190, below, paras 35–004 *et seq.* On the basis of this so-called "double actionability" rule (still applicable to defamation claims), a claimant would have no right to interest unless he could claim it both under English law and under the *lex loci delicti*. Outside the context of defamation, choice of law in tort is now governed, for maters within its ambit, by the Rome II Regulation (which largely superseded the statutory rules in the Private International Law (Miscellaneous Provisions) Act 1995, Pt III that had, in turn, largely replaced the common law). Defamation falls outside the ambit of the Rome II Regulation (Art.1(2)(g)) and the 1995 Act (s.13). For the power of arbitrators to award interest, see Arbitration Act 1996, above, para.7–101; below, para.37–088.

[437] Applying *Wallersteiner v Moir (No.2)* [1975] Q.B. 373 (CA); *Westdeutsche Landesbank Girozentrale v Islington London Borough Council* [1969] A.C. 669. Senior Courts Act 1981, s.35A, only permits an award of simple interest.

[438] [2000] 2 All E.R. (Comm.) 271, 339–344 (CA). For defamation and related claims see above n.435 and below, Rule 256.

[439] [2009] EWCA Civ 1191, [2010] 1 W.L.R. 1564.

[440] In *Lesotho Highland Development Authority v Impregilo SpA* [2002] EWHC 2435 (Comm.), [2003] 1 All E.R. (Comm.) 22, Morison J. stated that the right to claim interest as damages in tort should be characterised as a substantive issue which fell within the choice of law rules contained in Pt III of the Private International Law (Miscellaneous Provisions) Act 1995 and

law applicable to the tort under the Private International Law (Miscellaneous Provisions) Act 1995,[441] Part III.[442] The court held[443] that rate of interests was to be determined by English law,[444] referring to the view of Hobhouse J. in *Midland International Trade Services v Sudairy*.[445] It went on to hold that in exercising its discretion the court might take into account any relevant provisions of the governing law of the tort, French law, on the recovery of interest. The court made no reference to the position under the Rome II Regulation, so the case is not conclusive on the proper approach to interest under the Regulation.[446]

7–110   For matters within its ambit, the current position depends upon the proper interpretation of the Rome II Regulation,[447] and in particular on whether the right to claim interest by way of damages is to be regarded as falling within the ambit of Art.15 of the Regulation and hence to be determined by the law applicable to the non-contractual obligation. Article 15(c) applies the law applicable to the non-contractual obligation to determine "the existence, the nature and the assessment of damage or the remedy claimed". Article 15(d) applies the same law, within the limits of powers conferred on the court by its procedural law:[448] "[to] the measures which a court may take to ensure the provision of compensation." It is submitted that the right to claim interest by way of damages in a claim in tort is within the ambit of Art.15 and is not, in any sense, a procedural question for the law of the forum. Accordingly, whether there is such a right depends on the law which is found to apply to the tort.

7–111   The position in relation to the law which determines the rate of interest under the Rome II Regulation is uncertain. As seen above, there is a conflict of authority on the point in relation to contractual claims for interest as damages. It is, however, tentatively suggested above that the law of the forum determines the rate of interest on contractual damages for matters falling within the ambit of the Rome I Regulation. In principle, the classification of rates of interest should be the same under the Rome I and II Regulation. Indeed, the Rome I Regulation expressly states that the substantive scope and

---

not as a procedural issue excluded by s.14(3)(b). That case was not concerned with tort and although the Court of Appeal in affirming the decision of Morison J. noted the latter's statement, no observations were made on the point: see [2003] EWCA Civ 1159, [2003] 2 Lloyd's Rep. 497, at [22]. In reversing the Court of Appeal the House of Lords made no reference to the question: [2005] UKHL 43, [2006] 1 A.C. 221. See also *Harding v Wealands* [2006] UKHL 32, [2007] 2 A.C. 1. See further Law Com. No.124, *Foreign Money Liabilities* (1983), paras 2.30, 3.51; Law Com. Working Paper No.80, *Foreign Money Liabilities* (1981), para.4.11.

[441] Which excludes matters of procedure: s.14(3)(b).

[442] It also considered the decision in *Somers v Fournier* (2002) 214 D.L.R. (4th) 611 (Ont. C.A.), where it was held that the right to claim pre-judgment interest in a tort action is a matter of substance not procedure.

[443] At [33], [37], [40]–[43].

[444] *cf. Ekins v East India Co* (1717) 1 P.Wms. 395 where interest was awarded at the rate prevailing in the East Indies, the *lex loci delicti*.

[445] See above.

[446] See also *Abdel Hadi Abdallah Al Qahtani & Sons Beverage Industry Co v Antliff* [2010] EWHC 1735 (Comm.), at [59].

[447] See below, Chs 34 and 35. See also Ch.36 on obligations arising out of unjust enrichment.

[448] There appears to be no reason why an English court would normally not be procedurally competent to apply the rate of interest of the *lex causae*.

the provisions of the Regulation should be consistent with those of the Rome II Regulation.[449]

Article 1(3) of the Rome II Regulation states that it shall not apply to evidence and procedure.[450] Article 1(3) of the Rome I Regulation also excludes evidence and procedure.[451] It should follow that the classification of matters as procedural should be the same in respect of both Regulations. Even so, it is notable that the wording of Art.15 of the Rome II Regulation on the scope of the *lex causae* is in somewhat broader terms than Art.12(1)(c) of the Rome I Regulation.[452] Article 15(c) applies to "the existence, the nature and the assessment of damage or the remedy claimed." The intention for issues relating to the assessment of damages to be determined by the *lex causae* is clear. It might be argued that the rate of interest upon damages goes to, or is intrinsically linked with, the assessment of the overall amount which the claimant can recover in respect of a damages claim. It may be that the exclusion of evidence and procedure should be construed narrowly,[453] at least insofar as it relates to damages.

7–112

It would be unsatisfactory for the meaning and scope of the exclusions of evidence and procedure in the Rome I and II Regulations to differ.[454] At least on the present state of the English authorities, however, rates of interest have been regarded as procedural even after the advent of the Rome Convention;[455] and there is no compelling reason to lead to a different conclusion in respect of substantially identical wording on the scope of the governing law in the Rome I Regulation. The ambit of the exclusion of evidence and procedure in both the Rome I and Rome II Regulations may well be subject to elaboration by the European Court in due course and it is to be hoped that rates of interest will be classified in the same manner for the purposes of both Regulations. Until then, it is tentatively suggested that the rate of interest on damages in respect of tortious obligations[456] is governed by the *lex causae*.[457]

7–113

Clause (3) of the Rule. Clause (3) of the Rule applies where the rate of interest is governed by English law by virtue of clause (2) of the Rule or, where the case falls within clause (1) of the Rule, English law is the law which

7–114

---

[449] Recital (7) of the Rome I Regulation. The Rome II Regulation, however, contains no such provision. It pre-dates the Rome I Regulation and contains no similar provision in respect of similar wording contained in the Rome Convention.

[450] Without prejudice to Arts 21 and 22 on formal validity and burden of proof, respectively.

[451] Art.1(3), without prejudice to Art.18.

[452] Art.12(1)(c) of the Rome I Regulation applies "within the limits of the powers conferred on the court by its procedural law," to "the assessment of damages in so far as it is governed by rules of law."

[453] See Dickinson, *The Rome II Regulation*, paras 14.54–14.62.

[454] Even though the provisions on the scope of the governing law do differ.

[455] *Lesotho Highlands Development Authority v Impregilo SpA* [2003] EWCA Civ 1159, [2003] 2 Lloyd's Rep. 497, at [50], expressly adopting the reasoning in this paragraph, reversed on other grounds, without reference to the point, [2005] UKHL 43, [2006] 1 A.C. 221. See also *Rogers v Markel Corp* [2004] EWHC 1375 (QB) (without express reference to the Rome Convention) and further proceedings: [2004] EWHC 2046 (QB).

[456] And other non-contractual obligations falling within the ambit of the Rome II Regulation.

[457] But that the matter cannot be regarded as settled.

governs the relevant contract. It has been held that the court's discretion to award interest under s.35A of the Senior Courts Act 1981 is a remedy to be exercised in accordance with the _lex fori_.[458]

7–115   If a debt is payable to a foreign creditor or in a foreign currency, difficult questions may arise especially given that an English court can give judgment for an amount expressed in foreign currency[459] and can also calculate the amount of recoverable damages in a foreign currency.[460] This Comment is concerned with illustrating the principles which the court may apply in exercising its discretion under s.35A of the Senior Courts Act 1981 as to what the appropriate rate of interest will be if the debt is payable in a foreign currency. Although there does not appear to be any recent decision on the rate of interest to be applied if a debt payable in pounds sterling is payable abroad, it is submitted that similar principles will apply in such cases.

7–116   Prima facie, where there is a contract which specifies the currency which has to be paid, the rate of interest payable is that applicable to the currency and to the ensuing judgment if the judgment is also in that currency.[461] For example if US dollars is the currency of the contract and judgment is in US dollars, it would be, in general, inappropriate to award interest at the sterling rate[462] for to do so would overcompensate or possibly undercompensate the creditor depending upon the movement in exchange rates.[463] This much appears from the decision of the Court of Appeal in _The Pacific Coloco-tronis_[464] and the reasoning of Bristow J. in _Miliangos v George Frank (Textiles) Ltd (No.2)_,[465] although in the latter case the principle was stated to be applicable without the important qualification that it was only of a prima facie character. Also important in both of these cases was the fact that the creditor's currency corresponded to that which was appropriate under the prima facie principle. However, it may be that the creditor, having been kept out of his money, is unable to borrow in the currency of account and may accordingly, reasonably and forseeably, need to borrow in his own currency in his own country. If that is the case, the rate applicable should be the rate at which a loan in that currency was normally obtainable in that country, with the consequence that the prima facie rule is displaced.[466] On this analysis[467] it is

---

[458] See, in particular, _Maher v Groupama Grand Est_ [2009] EWCA Civ. 1191, [2010] 1 W.L.R. 1564, [2010] 2 All E.R. 455; above, para.7.109. But see the discussion of the effect of the Rome II Regulation (above, para.7–110 _et seq._), where it is tentatively suggested that the rate of interest is a matter for the _lex causae_. See generally paras 7–098—7–113, above.

[459] _Miliangos v George Frank (Textiles) Ltd_ [1976] A.C. 443. See Rule 261, below.

[460] _The Despina R._; _Services Europe Atlantique Sud v Stockholm Rederiaktiebolag Svea_ [1979] A.C. 685. See Rule 260, below.

[461] _Miliangos v George Frank (Textiles) Ltd (No.2)_ [1977] Q.B. 489; _The Pacific Colocotronis_ [1981] 2 Lloyd's Rep. 40, 45–47 (CA); _Empresa Cubana Importadora de Alimentos v Octavia Shipping Co SA_ [1986] 1 Lloyd's Rep. 273, 292; _Rogers v Markel Corp_ [2004] EWHC 1375 (QB), and also [2004] EWHC 2046 (QB); Law Com. No.124 (1983), para.2.33.

[462] _The Pacific Colocotronis_, above; _Rogers v Markel Corp_, above.

[463] _cf._ Bowles and Phillips (1976) 39 M.L.R. 196.

[464] [1981] 2 Lloyd's Rep. 40, 45–47.

[465] [1977] Q.B. 489.

[466] _Helmsing Schiffahrts GmbH v Malta Drydocks Corporation_ [1977] 2 Lloyd's Rep. 444; _The Pacific Colocotronis_ [1981] 2 Lloyd's Rep. 40, 45–47 (CA).

[467] This seems to emerge from _The Pacific Colocotronis_, above.

possible to reconcile *Miliangos v George Frank (Textiles) Ltd (No.2)*[468] with *Helmsing Schiffahrts GmbH v Malta Drydocks Corp*,[469] in which Kerr J., while accepting generally the reasoning of Bristow J., was nevertheless not prepared to accept the latter's approach as a "rule of thumb." For in *Helmsing Schiffahrts GmbH v Malta Drydocks Corporation*[470] there was evidence that the German creditors could not borrow, or could not be reasonably expected to borrow, Maltese pounds and being, in consequence, required to borrow Deutschmarks, were entitled to interest at the German rate. The position may, however, be different in a situation where the creditor can borrow in his own country, in the currency of the contract. In that event the creditor may, as against the debtor, be entitled to borrow in the currency of payment and the rate applicable will be that applied to the currency of account in the creditor's country.[471]

ILLUSTRATIONS

1. X borrows money from A in India. The loan is repayable in India. Whether and what interest is payable is determined by the law of India.[472] **7–117**

2. X, a businessman carrying on business in England, agrees in London to pay A commission for services to be rendered by A in Scotland. A debt of £200 is due under the contract from X to A. Whether the debt carries interest by virtue of an implied term in the contract, and at what rate, is to be determined by the law of England which is the law which governs the contract.[473]

3. X owes a debt of $20,000 to A in New York pursuant to a contract concluded in 2010. The debt remains unpaid until 2011 when A sues X in England. The contract is governed by New York law. If A obtains judgment against X, New York law will determine whether A can claim interest as damages against X;[474] but *semble*, English law will determine at what rate he can claim interest on the judgment debt.[475]

4. In 2005, A, an English claimant, suffered personal injury in a road traffic accident in France in which the driver of the other vehicle was killed. A brought a claim for damages against the defendant, the French insurer of the deceased French driver. The existence of a legal right to claim

---

[468] See above.

[469] See above.

[470] *ibid.*

[471] *cf. BP Exploration Co (Libya) Ltd v Hunt (No.2)* [1979] 1 W.L.R. 783, affirmed [1981] 1 W.L.R. 232 (CA), [1983] 2 A.C. 352. Here a British plaintiff was awarded damages in US dollars, the interest payable thereon being calculated by reference to the London Eurodollar market: [1979] 1 W.L.R. 783, 849. See also *Cia Barca de Panama SA v George Wimpey & Co Ltd* [1980] 1 Lloyd's Rep. 598, 615–617 (CA). In *Empresa Cubana Importadora de Alimentos v Octavia Shipping Co SA* [1986] 1 Lloyd's Rep. 273, 292, a Cuban plaintiff with a claim in Cuban pesos was awarded interest at the Cuban rate. *cf. Rogers v Markel Corp*, above (rate applicable to US dollar debt was English base rate plus 2 per cent).

[472] Rome I Regulation, Art.12(1)(b); compare Rome Convention, Art.10(1)(b). See *Graham v Keble* (1820) 2 Bli. 126. Compare *Thompson v Powles* (1828) 2 Sim. 194 with *Fergusson v Fyffe* (1841) 8 Cl. & F. 121.

[473] Rome I Regulation, Art.12(1)(b) and SI 2009/3064, Reg.5; compare Rome Convention, Art.10(1)(b). See *Arnott v Redfern* (1825) 2 C. & P. 88; (1826) 3 Bing. 353; compare *Connor v Bellamont* (1742) 2 Atk. 382; and *Saunders v Drake* (1742) 2 Atk. 465 (legacy by testator domiciled in Jamaica; rate of interest according to law of Jamaica).

[474] Rome I Regulation, Arts 12(1)(b) and (c); *Lesotho Highlands Development Authority v Impregilo SpA* [2003] EWCA Civ 1159, [2003] 2 Lloyd's Rep. 497, at [50], reversed on other grounds, without reference to the point, [2005] UKHL 43, [2006] 1 A.C. 221. See also *Rogers v Markel Corp* [2004] EWHC 1375 (QB) (without express reference to the Rome Convention) and further proceedings: [2004] EWHC 2046 (QB).

[475] Art.1(3).

interest was[476] a substantive matter determined by French law as the *lex causae*; but whether such a substantive right existed or not an award of interest under s.35A of the Senior Courts Act 1981 was a procedural matter, governed by English law as the *lex fori*, although in exercising its discretion the court might take into account any relevant provisions of French law relating to the recovery of interest.[477]

5. X, English buyers, owe a sum in Swiss francs to A, Swiss sellers, for the price of goods sold. Swiss law is the law applicable to the contract and the price is payable in 1971 in Switzerland. In 1972 A brings an action against X for the price. Sterling having depreciated in terms of Swiss francs, A claims, and in 1975 obtains judgment in Swiss francs or the sterling equivalent at the date of payment. Under Swiss law, interest is payable by way of damages. A is entitled to interest from 1971 to 1975 at the rate at which Swiss francs could be borrowed in Switzerland.[478] *Semble*, if the price had been expressed in United States dollars or in pounds sterling, the proper rate of interest would have been that at which a loan could have been obtained in Switzerland in those currencies respectively.

---

[476] And would be if the same facts arose today.

[477] *Maher v Groupama Grand Est* [2009] EWCA Civ 1191, [2010] 1 W.L.R. 1564. It is, however, tentatively suggested above that the rate of interest should be treated as substantive under the Rome II Regulation if the facts were to occur today.

[478] Rome I Regulation, Art.12(1)(c); compare Rome Convention, Art.10(1)(c); *Miliangos v George Frank (Textiles) Ltd (No.2)* [1977] Q.B. 489. But see *Midland International Trade Services Ltd v Sudairy, Financial Times*, May 2, 1990.

CHAPTER 8

INTERNATIONAL LITIGATION: PROTECTIVE MEASURES AND JUDICIAL ASSISTANCE

1. FREEZING INJUNCTIONS

RULE 21—(1) Where the court has jurisdiction over the substance of the case, it may exceptionally grant a freezing injunction (and any relief ancillary to such a measure) in respect of the respondent's property or assets outside England (whether prior to judgment or in aid of its execution). 8R–001

Provided that such a measure shall not normally affect any person outside England other than the respondent, nor shall it normally prevent any third party from complying with his obligations in respect of the respondent's property under the foreign law applicable to it.[1]

(2) Where the court does not exercise jurisdiction over the substance of the case, it may grant a freezing injunction or other interim relief in support of proceedings pending or contemplated in the courts of another country, in particular where the respondent or his property or assets are in England.

Provided that the court may refuse to grant such a measure when it is inexpedient to do so, having considered the potential for conflict with the foreign court exercising jurisdiction over the substance.[2]

COMMENT

Questions of international litigation procedure which arise in the course of litigation in the English courts are of increasing importance.[3] The issues dealt 8–002

---

[1] *Babanaft International Co SA v Bassatne* [1990] Ch. 13 (CA); *Derby & Co Ltd v Weldon* [1990] Ch. 48 (CA); *(Nos 3 & 4)* [1990] Ch. 65 (CA); *Bank of China v NBM LLC* [2001] EWCA Civ 1933, [2002] 1 W.L.R. 844; *Masri v Consolidated Contractors International Co SAL (No.2)* [2008] EWCA Civ. 303, [2009] Q.B. 450.

[2] Civil Jurisdiction and Judgments Act 1982, s.25; Council Regulation (EC) 44/2001, [2001] O.J./L12/1 (Brussels I Regulation), Art.31; Case C–391/95 *Van Uden Maritime BV v Firma Deco-Line* [1998] E.C.R. I–7091, [1999] Q.B. 1225; *Republic of Haiti v Duvalier* [1990] 1 Q.B. 202 (CA); *Crédit Suisse Fides Trust SA v Cuoghi* [1998] 1 Q.B. 818 (CA); *Motorola Credit Corp v Uzan (No.2)* [2003] EWCA Civ 752, [2004] 1 W.L.R. 113; *Banco Nacional de Comercio Exterior SNC v Empresa de Telecommunicaciones de Cuba SA* [2007] EWCA Civ 662, [2008] 1 W.L.R. 1936.

[3] See generally Collins, *Essays;* McLachlan (2004) 120 L.Q.R. 580; Fentiman, *International Commercial Litigation* (2010), Ch.17.

with here are concerned with either (a) the reach of the court's interim enforcement jurisdiction in respect of persons or property abroad (freezing injunctions); or (b) the use of international judicial assistance as between English courts and foreign courts or agencies in the prosecution of a case (freezing injunctions and other interim relief, service of process and taking of evidence abroad). International judicial assistance may be treated as a major function of the conflict of laws.[4] It is a subject of increasing international co-operation, both within the European Union and internationally (where the principal international conventions have been framed under the aegis of the Hague Conference on Private International Law). This Chapter therefore deals in turn with (1) freezing injunctions; (2) service of process; and (3) taking of evidence abroad. For convenience, this Chapter also deals with (4) the application of the English rules on security for costs to a non-resident claimant.

8–003   **The legal character of the freezing injunction.** Relaxation of exchange controls and the development of electronic banking have made the international transfer of funds easy and almost instantaneous. These developments have led to a much greater attention to the need for interim protection to ensure the enforceability of judgments and to prevent defendants from frustrating their effectiveness by moving funds from one country to another.[5] Provisional and protective measures have two main objects: the first is to ensure that, pending final determination of a dispute, the status quo will be maintained; a second, and related, object is to protect the ultimate judgment of the court by preventing the defendant from disposing of assets pending final determination of the proceedings. The first object is achieved in English law by the interlocutory injunction, and by similar orders in other systems of law; the second object is achieved in England by a special form of interim injunction originally known as the *Mareva* injunction[6] and now called the freezing injunction,[7] and in countries not following the English system by judicial attachments of assets.

8–004   *Development of English remedy.* Before 1975 there was no effective procedure available in England whereby a claimant could seize the assets of a defendant before obtaining judgment. Until the 19th century the process of "foreign attachment" was available as part of the custom of London, but it fell into disuse after it was decided by the House of Lords that it was not available

---

[4] Schlosser (2000) 284 *Recueil des Cours* 9; McClean, *International Co-operation in Civil and Criminal Matters* (2002).

[5] See generally on protective measures in international cases Collins (1992) *Recueil des Cours*, III, p.9, reprinted in Collins, *Essays*, p.1; Fallon (1993) 7 Rev. dr. Univ. Libre Bruxelles 43; Vareilles-Sommières, 1996 *Rev. Crit.* 397; Bermann (1997) 35 Col. J. Tr. L. 553; Maher and Rodger (1999) 48 I.C.L.Q. 302; Gerhard, 1999 Rev. suisse de dr. eur. 97; Schlosser (2000) 284 *Receuil des Cours* 9, pp.157–199; Aird (2002) 51 I.C.L.Q. 155. See also International Law Association, Committee on International Civil and Commercial Litigation, *Provisional and Protective Measures in International Litigation*, Second Interim Report, 1996.

[6] After one of the first two cases in which this injunction was developed: *Mareva Compania Naviera SA v International Bulk Carriers SA* [1975] 2 Lloyd's Rep. 509 (CA).

[7] CPR, r.25.1(1)(f).

where the garnishee was (as it frequently would be) a corporation.[8] Nor was it thought possible for a creditor to obtain an injunction to restrain the alleged debtor from parting with his property.[9]

From 1975, however, the English courts developed a practice whereby the court could grant an interlocutory injunction to restrain a defendant from disposing of or dealing with his assets.[10] In two cases[11] in that year the Court of Appeal, in each case with Lord Denning M.R. presiding, decided that such an injunction could be granted to restrain a foreign defendant from removing its assets from the jurisdiction. The injunction, as subsequently developed and extended, became known as the *Mareva* injunction, after the second of the cases. The practice has since been followed in Canada,[12] Australia[13] and New Zealand.[14] **8–005**

In 1981 the practice was given statutory authority by s.37(3) of the Senior Courts Act 1981,[15] which confirmed that the power of the court to grant an interlocutory injunction restraining a party to any proceedings from removing from the jurisdiction, or otherwise dealing with assets located within the jurisdiction, is exercisable whether or not that party is domiciled, resident or present within the jurisdiction. Section 37(3) did not turn the *Mareva* or **8–006**

---

[8] *Mayor and Aldermen of the City of London v London Joint Stock Bank* (1881) 6 App.Cas. 393. See *Rasu Maritima SA v Pertamina* [1978] Q.B. 644, 657–658 (CA). For the history of foreign attachment in the US see *Ownbey v Morgan*, 256 U.S. 94 (1921), and the severe limitations imposed by *Shaffer v Heitner*, 433 U.S. 186 (1977). In *Grupo Mexicano de Desarrollo SA v Alliance Bond Fund Inc*, 527 U.S. 308 (1999), the United States Supreme Court decided by a bare majority that the United States federal courts had no power to grant an interlocutory injunction to restrain a defendant from disposing of its assets pending the determination of an action. See also *Credit Agricole Indosuez v Rossiyskiy Kredit Bank*, 94 N.Y. 2d 541 (NY Ct App. 2000), and Collins (1999) 115 L.Q.R. 601. In Case C–398/92 *Mund & Fester v Hatrex Internationaal Transport* [1994] E.C.R. I–467 it was held that the rule in the German Code of Civil Procedure that an attachment could be granted automatically in cases where a judgment was to be enforced abroad (whereas in other cases it could only be granted where enforcement would be impossible or substantially more difficult) was discriminatory, and therefore contrary to what is now Art.18 of the Treaty on the Functioning of the European Union (TFEU).

[9] *Lister & Co v Stubbs* (1890) 45 Ch.D. 1, 14 (CA) and other cases discussed in *Rasu Maritima SA v Pertamina*, above, at 659–660, *per* Lord Denning M.R.; *The Siskina v Distos Compania Naviera SA* [1979] A.C. 210, 260, *per* Lord Hailsham; *Derby & Co Ltd v Weldon (Nos 3 & 4)* [1990] Ch. 65, 88–89, *per* Neill L.J. See also Report of the Committee on the Enforcement of Judgment Debts, 1969, Cmnd. 3909.

[10] For a full and excellent account see Gee, *Commercial Injunctions* (5th ed. 2004).

[11] *Nippon Yusen Kaisha v Karageorgis* [1975] 1 W.L.R. 1093 (CA); *Mareva Compania Naviera SA v International Bulkcarriers SA* [1975] 2 Lloyd's Rep. 509 (CA). The injunction extends not only to the removal of assets, but also to their dissipation: *Rahman (Prince Abdul) bin Turki al Sudairy v Abu-Taha* [1980] 1 W.L.R. 1268 (CA); CPR, r.25.1(1)(f)(ii).

[12] *Chitel v Rothbart* (1982) 141 D.L.R. (3d) 268 (Ont CA); and other cases referred to by Walker, *Castel and Walker, Canadian Conflict of Laws* (6th ed. 2005), para.6.9 and Pitel and Valentine (2006) 2 J. Priv. Int. L. 339. For the special problems of the practice in a federal system see *Aetna Financial Services Ltd v Feigelmann* [1985] 1 S.C.R. 2.

[13] See, e.g. *Riley McKay Pty Ltd v McKay* [1982] 1 N.S.W.L.R. 264; *Hiero Pty Ltd v Somers* (1983) 47 A.L.R. 605; *Devlin v Collins* (1984) 37 S.A.S.R. 98; *Perth Mint v Mickelberg (No.2)* [1985] W.A.R. 117; *Pearce v Waterhouse* [1986] V.R. 603; *Jackson v Sterling Industries Ltd* (1987) 162 C.L.R. 612; *Cardile v LED Builders Pty Ltd* (1999) 198 C.L.R. 380; Nygh, *Conflict of Laws in Australia* (8th ed. 2010, Davies, Bell and Brereton), para. 4.17–4.29.

[14] *Hunt v BP Exploration (Libya) Ltd* [1980] 1 N.Z.L.R. 104.

[15] This removed doubts which had been expressed in some of the early cases. See also *Bekhor & Co Ltd v Bilton* [1981] Q.B. 923, 936 (CA); *The Siskina v Distos Compania Naviera SA* [1979] A.C. 210, 261; *Walsh v Deloitte & Touche Inc* [2001] UKPC 58, at [9].

freezing injunction into a statutory remedy; it assumed that the remedy existed, and tacitly endorsed its validity.[16] Consequently, s.37(3) does not inhibit the extension of the freezing injunction jurisdiction by the court.[17]

8–007   *In personam relief.* The description of an injunction as a freezing injunction is a convenient label to describe an injunction restraining the removal or disposal of assets in which the claimant claims no proprietary interest, and strictly it should be distinguished from cases in which the claimant seeks to trace assets.[18] Thus, if the claim relates to a particular fund or to a particular piece of property, the injunction might relate only to that fund or property. So also, an injunction in relation to a proprietary claim to a particular fund would not in principle be subject to the normal proviso in a freezing injunction allowing the use of the money for normal business purposes or for legal fees.[19] But the court retains a discretion in such cases to allow funds to be used for legal costs or living expenses, where the defendant has at least an arguable case for denying that the funds belong to the claimant.[20]

8–008   In order to obtain a freezing injunction the claimant must show that he has at least a good arguable case on the merits,[21] and that there is a real risk that a judgment would be unsatisfied if the injunction were not granted.[22] The fundamental principle underlying the jurisdiction is that, within the limits of its powers, no court should permit a defendant to take action which has the effect that subsequent orders of the court are rendered less effective than would otherwise be the case.[23]

8–009   Although Lord Denning M.R. expressed the view that a freezing injunction operated *in rem*,[24] it does not operate as an attachment on property as such, but is relief *in personam*, restraining the owner of the assets from dealing with them. Accordingly, it does not achieve priority over the security interests of

---

[16] *Mercedes Benz AG v Leiduck* [1996] A.C. 284, 299 (PC).

[17] See *Babanaft International Co SA v Bassatne* [1990] Ch. 13, 26 (CA).

[18] See *A v C* [1981] Q.B. 956n; *PCW (Underwriting Agencies) Ltd v Dixon* [1983] 2 All E.R. 158; *Aetna Financial Services Ltd v Feigelmann* [1985] 1 S.C.R. 2, 13; *cf. Bankers Trust Co v Shapira* [1980] 1 W.L.R. 1274 (CA); *Republic of Haiti v Duvalier* [1990] 1 Q.B. 202, 214 (CA); *Mercedes Benz v Leiduck* [1996] A.C. 284, 300 (PC).

[19] *Polly Peck International Plc v Nadir* [1992] 4 All E.R. 769, 784 (CA).

[20] Gee, above, n.10, pp.630–631; see *Ostrich Farming Corp v Ketchell*, December 10, 1997 (CA).

[21] *Rasu Maritima SA v Pertamina* [1978] Q.B. 644 (CA); *Ninemia Corp v Trave GmbH* [1983] 1 W.L.R. 1412 (CA); *Derby & Co Ltd v Weldon* [1990] Ch. 48, 57–58 (CA). Since the application is made without notice (*Ex p.*), full and frank disclosure of relevant matters must be made. For the effect of failure to disclose related proceedings in other jurisdictions see *Behbehani v Salem* [1989] 1 W.L.R. 723 (CA).

[22] *Third Chandris Shipping Corp v Unimarine SA* [1979] Q.B. 654 (CA); *Ninemia Corp v Trave GmbH* [1983] 1 W.L.R. 1412 (CA); *Patterson v BTR Engineering (Aust) Ltd* (1989) 18 N.S.W.L.R. 319.

[23] *Derby & Co Ltd v Weldon (Nos 3 & 4)* [1990] Ch. 65; *The Coral Rose (No.1)* [1991] 1 Lloyd's Rep. 563 (CA); *Atlas Maritime Co SA v Avalon Maritime Ltd (No.3)* [1991] 1 W.L.R. 917 (CA). It is not necessary to show that the defendant intends to evade the effect of a judgment, and the test is an objective one, namely whether there is a real risk that the judgment will remain unsatisfied if injunctive relief is refused: *Ketchum International Plc v Group Public Relations Holdings Ltd* [1997] 1 W.L.R. 4, 13 (CA).

[24] *Z Ltd v A-Z* [1982] Q.B. 558, 573 (CA), said to have been *per incuriam* in *Att-Gen v Times Newspapers Ltd* [1992] 1 A.C. 191, 215, *per* Lord Ackner.

third parties,[25] nor does it give the claimant security rights in priority to other creditors.[26] Consequently, a defendant will normally be allowed to make payments to his creditors in the normal course of business.[27] The injunction must not be used so as to amount to an instrument of oppression which would bring about the cessation of ordinary trading and the court must look at all the circumstances of the case in deciding whether, and to what extent, the injunction should be varied in order to allow the defendant to make payments.[28] Almost invariably the court will require the claimant to give undertakings protecting the defendant in the event that it is held that the order should not have been made.[29]

It has been held by the Court of Appeal that a freezing injunction will not   **8–010** be granted in relation to a cause of action which will accrue, but has not yet accrued.[30] In *Mercedes Benz AG v Leiduck*,[31] however, Lord Nicholls of Birkenhead, in a dissenting opinion on an aspect not dealt with by the majority, doubted the correctness of the principal authorities to this effect. He considered that in such a case there was no reason in principle why an anticipatory injunction could not be granted, and preferred the Australian authority in that sense.[32]

Ancillary orders. There are two important ways in which the jurisdiction is   **8–011** made effective. First, the court may make ancillary orders in aid of the injunction to enable the claimant to obtain disclosure of documents or information from a defendant concerning his assets,[33] and even an ancillary order restraining a defendant from leaving the jurisdiction and requiring him to deliver up his passport.[34]

---

[25] *Cretanor Maritime Co Ltd v Irish Marine Management Ltd* [1978] 1 W.L.R. 966 (CA).

[26] *Iraqi Ministry of Defence v Arcepey Shipping Co SA (The Angel Bell)* [1981] Q.B. 65; *Bekhor & Co Ltd v Bilton* [1981] Q.B. 923, 942 (CA); *Derby & Co Ltd v Weldon* [1990] Ch. 65, 76 (CA); *Mercedes Benz v Leiduck* [1996] A.C. 284, 300 (PC); *Fourie v Le Roux* [2007] UKHL 1, [2007] 1 W.L.R. 320, at [2]; *Aetna Financial Services Ltd v Feigelmann* [1985] 1 S.C.R. 2, 26; *Jackson v Sterling Industries Ltd* (1987) 162 C.L.R. 612, 618, 621.

[27] The *"Angel Bell* variation", established in *Iraqi Ministry of Defence v Arcepey Shipping Co SA* [1981] Q.B. 65. See also *Admiral Shipping v Portlink Ferries Ltd* [1984] 2 Lloyd's Rep. 166 (CA); *Avant Petroleum Inc v Gatoil Overseas Inc* [1986] 2 Lloyd's Rep. 236 (CA).

[28] *The Coral Rose* [1991] 1 Lloyd's Rep. 563 (CA); *Atlas Maritime Co SA v Avalon Maritime Ltd (No.3)* [1991] 1 W.L.R. 917 (CA).

[29] See model form of order in CPR PD25A.

[30] *The Veracruz I* [1992] 1 Lloyd's Rep. 353 (CA), criticised by Collins (1992) 108 L.Q.R. 175; *The P* [1992] 1 Lloyd's Rep. 470; *Zucker v Tyndall Holdings Plc* [1992] 1 W.L.R. 1127 (CA); *Re Q's Estate* [1999] 1 Lloyd's Rep. 931; *The Capaz Duckling* [2007] EWHC 1630 (Comm.), [2008] 1 Lloyd's Rep. 54.

[31] [1996] A.C. 284, 312 (PC). See Collins (1996) 112 L.Q.R. 28.

[32] *Patterson v BTR Engineering (Australia) Ltd* (1989) 18 N.S.W.L.R. 319 (NSWCA).

[33] See, e.g. *A v C* [1981] Q.B. 956; *Bekhor & Co Ltd v Bilton* [1981] Q.B. 923 (CA); *House of Spring Gardens Ltd v Waite* [1985] F.S.R. 173 (CA); *Bank of Crete SA v Koskotas* [1991] 2 Lloyd's Rep. 587 (CA); *(No.2)* [1992] 1 W.L.R. 919. As to privilege against self-incrimination in such cases see *Sociedade Nacional de Combustiveis de Angola UEE v Lundqvist* [1991] 2 Q.B. 310 (CA); *cf. Den Norske Bank ASA v Antonatos* [1999] Q.B. 271 (CA).

[34] *Bayer AG v Winter* [1986] 1 W.L.R. 497 (CA), applied in *Re Oriental Credit* [1988] Ch. 204; *O'Neill v O'Keeffe* [2002] 2 I.R. 1. For the remedy of an order for the issue of a writ prohibiting a debtor from leaving the realm (*ne exeat regno*), where his absence will materially prejudice the claimant in the prosecution of the action see *Felton v Callis* [1969] 1 Q.B. 200; *Lipkin Gorman v Cass, The Times*, May 29, 1985; *Ali v Naseem, The Times*, October 3, 2003. It has been held that this writ may issue in aid of a freezing injunction (*Al Nakhel for Contracting & Trading Ltd v*

8–012 *Effect on third parties.* Secondly, a third party, such as a bank with which the defendant has an account, is guilty of contempt of court if it knowingly assists in a breach of the order, i.e. if knowing the terms of the injunction it wilfully assists the defendant to disobey.[35] This is so whether or not the defendant has been served with or knows of the order, because the third party would be guilty of conduct which knowingly interferes with the administration of justice by causing the order of the court to be disobeyed.[36]

8–013 **International aspects of freezing injunctions.** The specific characteristics of the freezing injunction as it has developed in English law provide essential context for analysis of the international applications of such orders. The ensuing paragraphs of this section will deal with the two questions of the conflict of laws which have arisen relating to freezing injunctions: (a) the territorial scope of such orders in relation to property and persons outside England—the so-called worldwide freezing injunction (Rule 21(1)); and (b) the jurisdiction of the English court to grant freezing injunctions and other interim relief in support of proceedings on the merits in foreign courts (Rule 21(2)). The first question is one of the scope of the court's enforcement jurisdiction. The second introduces a specific form of jurisdiction, limited to provisional, including protective measures, in order to provide international judicial assistance to foreign courts. Both measures constitute different means of addressing the central problem of provisional measures in international litigation namely, how to ensure that a judicial determination on the merits is not frustrated and that assets out of which a judgment may be satisfied are not dissipated, where the defendant's assets may well be found in a country other than that in which the substantive proceedings are taking place. In the first form of measure, the English court (in this context usually, but not invariably, the court deciding the merits) seeks to extend the operation of its interim orders to assets abroad. In the second form of measure, the English court (not being the court deciding the merits) intervenes with the sole purpose of

---

Lowe [1986] Q.B. 235; *cf. Thaya v Thaya* [1987] 2 F.L.R. 142) but the better view is that it may not be issued solely for the purpose of enforcing a freezing injunction, and that in such a case the appropriate remedy is an injunction to restrain the defendant from leaving the jurisdiction: *Allied Arab Bank v Hajjar* [1988] Q.B. 787; *Kuwait Airways Corp v Iraqi Airways Co* [2010] EWCA Civ 741 (post-judgment order against the Director General of the defendant company—a non-resident non-party—pending swearing of an affidavit of disclosure of assets, reinforced by an order requiring delivery up of his passport to the Tipstaff, and granting the Tipstaff powers of search and seizure). See also *Morris v Murjani* [1996] 1 W.L.R. 848 (CA) (court has power under Insolvency Act 1986, s.333, to issue injunction to prevent bankrupt from leaving country). See Gee, *op cit.*, para.8–005, n.10, pp.651–656; Harpum [1986] C.L.J. 189; Anderson (1987) 103 L.Q.R. 246; Andrews [1988] C.L.J. 364.

[35] *Z Ltd v A–Z* [1982] Q.B. 558 (CA). The standard form order contains a warning to this effect: CPR PD25A, Annex. Exceptionally, the order may be made directly against a third party, where the defendant has an interest in, or control over, the asset going beyond an actual or potential cause of action against the third party: *Yukos Capital Sarl v OJSC Rosneft Oil Co* [2010] EWHC 784 (Comm.), [2011] 1 All E.R. (Comm.) 172 and the cases there cited.

[36] *ibid.* at 578, *per* Eveleigh L.J., approved in *Att-Gen v Times Newspapers Ltd* [1992] 1 A.C. 191. But the third party owes no additional common law duty of care to the claimant if it negligently fails to prevent the transfer of assets contrary to the terms of the freezing injunction. There can be no voluntary assumption of responsibility arising from the obligation to comply with an order of the court: *Customs & Excise Commissioners v Barclays Bank Plc* [2006] UKHL 28, [2007] 1 A.C. 181.

preserving assets pending a final determination on the merits elsewhere. The worldwide freezing injunction is entirely a creature of English judicial development. The power to grant interim measures in aid of foreign proceedings, on the other hand, had to be conferred by Parliament, initially pursuant to European law obligations under the Conventions (and now the Brussels I Regulation). That power has now been extended in support of proceedings in countries to which the Brussels I Regulation and the Conventions do not apply.

Clause (1) of the Rule. Worldwide freezing injunctions.[37] The freezing injunction was developed in order to prevent the removal of assets from the jurisdiction, and it was assumed by Parliament[38] and held by the Court of Appeal[39] that the exercise of the freezing injunction jurisdiction was limited to assets within the jurisdiction. In several Commonwealth jurisdictions, however, this limitation on the scope of freezing injunctions was not accepted.[40]   **8–014**

In a series of decisions of the Court of Appeal in 1988 it was held, reversing previous practice, that freezing injunctions and ancillary disclosure orders could be granted in relation to assets abroad. First, in *Babanaft International Co SA v Bassatne*[41] an injunction was granted, after judgment in a fraud action, restraining the judgment debtors from disposing of any of their assets worldwide. Secondly, in *Republic of Haiti v Duvalier*[42] an injunction was granted (in aid of proceedings pending in France) restraining the defendants from dealing with their assets wherever situated and requiring the defendants to disclose information relating to their assets worldwide. Thirdly, in two decisions in *Derby & Co Ltd v Weldon*[43] it was held that a pre-judgment freezing injunction and ancillary disclosure could be granted in relation to assets worldwide in the course of litigation pending in England, irrespective of whether the defendant had assets in England.[44]   **8–015**

---

[37] See Collins (1989) 105 L.Q.R. 262, reprinted in Collins, *Essays*, p.189; Andrews [1989] C.L.J. 199; Hogan (1989) 17 Eur. L. Rev. 191; Malek and Lewis [1990] L.M.C.L.Q. 88; Kaye (1990) 9 Civ.J.Q. 12; Capper (1991) 54 M.L.R. 329; Rogers [1991] L.M.C.L.Q. 231. For earlier discussion see Collins (1981) 1 Yb. Eur. L. 249; McLachlan (1987) 36 I.C.L.Q. 669, 674–676.

[38] Senior Courts Act 1981. s.37(3), para.8–006, above.

[39] *Ashtiani v Kashi* [1987] Q.B. 888 (CA). See also *The Bhoja Trader* [1981] 2 Lloyd's Rep. 256 (CA); *cf. Allied Arab Bank v Hajjar* [1988] Q.B. 787, 796; *Reilly v Fryer* [1988] 2 F.T.L.R. 69 (CA). Contrast *Re A Company* [1985] B.C.L.C. 333 (CA); *Bayer AG v Winter* [1986] 2 F.T.L.R. 111, 112.

[40] *Ballabil Holdings Pty Ltd v Hospital Products Ltd* (1985) 1 N.S.W.L.R. 155; *Coombs & Barei Construction Pty Ltd v Dynasty Pty Ltd* (1986) 42 S.A.S.R. 413; *Yandil Holdings Pty Ltd v Insurance Co of North America* (1987) 7 N.S.W.L.R. 571; *National Australia Bank v Dessau* [1988] V.R. 521; *Banco Ambrosiano Holdings SA v Dunkeld Ranching Ltd* (1987) 85 Alta. R. 278 (CA) (but contrast *Zellers Inc v Doobay* [1989] 3 W.W.R. 497 (BC)); *Mooney v Orr* [1995] 1 W.W.R. 517 (BC); *Asean Resources Ltd v Ka Wah International Merchant Finance Ltd* [1987] L.R.C. (Comm.) 835. See also *Deutsche Bank AG v Murtagh* [1995] 1 I.L.R.M. 381; *Bennett Entreprises Inc v Lipton* [1999] 1 I.L.R.M. 81.

[41] [1990] Ch. 13 (CA), stated below, para.8–118, Illustration 3.

[42] [1990] 1 Q.B. 202 (CA), stated below, Illustration 4.

[43] [1990] Ch. 48 (CA); (*Nos 3 & 4*) [1990] Ch. 65 (CA), see below, Illustration 5. See also *Ghoth v Ghoth* [1992] 2 All E.R. 920 (CA).

[44] Before these cases it was often said that a plaintiff who sought *Mareva* relief must give grounds for a belief that the defendant had assets within the jurisdiction. That this was the normal case did not mean that it was a necessary pre-condition: [1990] Ch. at 77–80.

8-016   It was subsequently held in *Derby Co Ltd v Weldon (No.6)*[45] that the
jurisdiction could be exercised to order the transfer of assets from one foreign
jurisdiction to another, or to restrain the transfer of assets from one foreign
jurisdiction to another, or to order the return to England of assets from a
foreign jurisdiction. But it was emphasised that these were highly exceptional
orders, and in that decision the order was limited to restraining the return to
Switzerland (where, according to the evidence, the English order might not be
recognised) of deposits made outside Switzerland by Swiss banks acting on
the instructions of the defendants.

8-017   The basis for the development of the worldwide freezing injunction was the
recognition that the freezing injunction operates *in personam*, and that where
the defendant is personally subject to the jurisdiction of the court, an injunction may be granted in appropriate circumstances to control his activities
abroad.[46] Although exceptional or special circumstances must be present to
justify a worldwide injunction, that does not mean more than that the court
should go no further than necessity dictates, and that in the first instance it
should look to assets within the jurisdiction.[47] The court with jurisdiction over
the substance of the matter has jurisdiction to grant any ancillary order,
whether before or after judgment and irrespective of whether or not the
Brussels I Regulation or the Lugano Convention applies.[48]

8-018   *Post-judgment freezing injunctions.* A worldwide freezing injunction will
more readily be granted after final judgment has been obtained against the
defendant, or if the claim is a proprietary claim.[49] Once the English court has

---

[45] [1990] 1 W.L.R. 1139.

[46] *Babanaft International Co SA v Bassatne* [1990] Ch. 13, at 38, 41 (CA); *Derby & Co Ltd v
Weldon (No.6)* [1990] 1 W.L.R. 1139, 1149 (CA); *Crédit Suisse Fides Trust SA v Cuoghi* [1998]
Q.B. 818, 826 (CA). See Kerr, *Injunctions* (6th ed. Paterson, 1927), p.11, and (among many other
examples) *Acrow (Automation) Ltd v Rex Chainbelt Inc* [1971] 1 W.L.R. 1676 (CA); *Att-Gen v
Barker* [1990] 3 All E.R. 257 (CA). For the territorial scope of *Anton Piller* orders (the "search
and seizure" orders sanctioned by *Anton Piller KG v Manufacturing Processes Ltd* [1976] Ch. 55
(CA)) *cf. Cook Industries v Galliher* [1979] Ch. 439; and contrast *Protector Alarms Ltd v Maxim
Alarms Ltd* [1978] F.S.R. 442; *Altertext Inc v Advanced Data Communications Ltd* [1985] 1
W.L.R. 457. The *Anton Piller* jurisdiction is given statutory authority by Civil Procedure Act
1997, s.7, which is limited to premises within the jurisdiction: s.7(3); but, by analogy with Senior
Courts Act 1981, s.37(3), it is not likely to preclude the extension of the jurisdiction by the court:
see above, para.8–006. Orders under Civil Procedure Act 1997, s.7, are now called "search
orders": CPR, r.25.1(1)(h).

[47] *Derby & Co Ltd v Weldon (Nos 3 & 4)* [1990] Ch. 65, 79 (CA).

[48] *Masri v Consolidated Contractors International Co SAL (No.2)* [2008] EWCA Civ. 303,
[2009] Q.B. 450, applying Case C–391/95 *Van Uden Maritime BV v Firma Deco-Line* [1998]
ECR I–7091, [1999] Q.B. 1225 and Case C–99/96 *Mietz v Intership Yachting Sneek BV* [1999]
ECR I–2277. Under the European Commission Proposal for a revised Brussels I Regulation
(COM(2010) 748) this would be expressly confirmed. See, to like effect, draft Art.6 of European
Commission Proposal for a Regulation creating a European Account Preservation Order (COM
(2011) 445), which would confer primary jurisdiction to grant such orders on the court hearing
the substance of the matter, and provide that the courts of the State where the bank account is
located shall have jurisdiction to issue such an order for enforcement only in that state.

[49] See, e.g. *Republic of Haiti v Duvalier* [1990] 1 Q.B. 202, at 213–214, *per* Staughton L.J.
(CA). After judgment, a disclosure order relating to assets worldwide may be made as part of the
enforcement process: *Interpool Ltd v Galani* [1988] Q.B. 738 (CA); see also CPR, r.71.2. *cf.
Maclaine Watson Co Ltd v International Tin Council (No.2)* [1989] Ch. 286 (CA); *Gidrxslme
Shipping Co Ltd v Tantomar Transportes Maritimos Ltd* [1995] 1 W.L.R. 295; *Yandil Holdings
Pty Ltd v Insurance Co of North America* (1987) 7 N.S.W.L.R. 571.

rendered judgment on the merits, it is not limited in granting freezing injunctions or other orders which are designed to assist in its enforcement by the terms of Art.31 of the Brussels I Regulation or the Lugano Convention, since the latter is solely concerned with the grant of provisional measures by a court other than that dealing with the substance of the matter.[50]

Effect in English action. It may be appropriate to make a worldwide order   **8–019** even if it will not be recognised by the courts of the country where the assets are situated,[51] since the English court may still make its order effective by striking out the defence if the defendant disobeys the order.[52]

Worldwide disclosure orders. Worldwide injunctions almost invariably pro-   **8–020** vide for disclosure of assets outside the jurisdiction. In those cases where an effective order can be made, it is likely to be the disclosure order which will be the most useful in practical terms. If proper disclosure is made of assets abroad, the claimant will be in a position to make an application in the relevant foreign court for an attachment. The practical consequence is that in such cases it is really the injunction which is ancillary to the disclosure order, rather than the traditional relationship in which it was the disclosure order which was ancillary to the injunction. For the disclosure order will be the main remedy in England, and the injunction will, in the words of Nicholls L.J.[53] be a "holding" injunction, to give the claimant time to apply to the relevant foreign court for appropriate orders of attachment or the like.[54]

Supervision of foreign relief. The practice in relation to worldwide injunc-   **8–021** tions is subject to two important limitations. First, in order to prevent harassment of the defendant and unnecessary multiplicity of actions, the claimant must normally undertake not to make use of information disclosed under the order in foreign proceedings or seek to enforce the order abroad, without the

---

[50] *Masri v Consolidated Contractors International Co SAL (No.2)* [2008] EWCA Civ 303, [2009] Q.B. 450. For the limitations of Art.31 see the comment to clause (2) of the Rule below.

[51] For enforcement in France see *Stolzenberg v Daimler Chrysler Canada Inc* (Cass. Civ. I, July 30, 2003) [2005] I.L.Pr. 266, 2005 *Clunet* 112 (note Cuniberti); and in Switzerland see *Motorola Credit Corp v Uzan* BGE 129 III 626 (Swiss Fed. Sup. Ct.); Weibel, *Enforcement of English Freezing Orders ("Mareva Injunctions") in Switzerland* (2005), at pp.100 *et seq.*

[52] *Derby & Co Ltd v Weldon (Nos 3 & 4)* [1990] Ch. at 81.

[53] *Babanaft International Co SA v Bassatne* [1990] Ch. at 41.

[54] See Collins (1989) 105 L.Q.R. 262, 297 (and in Collins, *Essays*, at p.223), on which see *Grupo Torras SA v Sheikh Fahad Mohammed Al-Sabah*, unreported, February 16, 1994 (CA), *per* Steyn L.J. See also *Crédit Suisse Fides Trust SA v Cuoghi* [1998] Q.B. 818, 827–828 (CA). See also McLachlan (1998) 47 I.C.L.Q. 3. The information provided pursuant to such a disclosure order may be used to police compliance with the freezing injunction, including in contempt proceedings. If an undertaking not to do so has been given, the court will release the applicant from the undertaking where it is just and convenient in order to police compliance with the injunction: *Dadourian Group International Inc v Simms (No.2)* [2006] EWCA Civ 1745, [2007] 1 W.L.R. 2967. Under draft Art.2(b) of the European Commission Proposal for a revised Brussels I Regulation (COM(2010) 748), it would be expressly provided that provisional including protective measures "shall include protective orders aimed at obtaining information and evidence". Recital (22) confirms that such measures do not include non-protective measures, such as "ordering the hearing of a witness for the purpose of enabling the applicant to decide whether to bring a case."

permission of the English court.[55] Permission will be granted on the basis of the following eight guidelines.[56] First, the grant of permission should be just and convenient for the purpose of ensuring the effectiveness of the order, whilst not being oppressive to the parties to the English proceedings or to third parties who may be joined to the foreign proceedings. Second, permission may be granted on terms, including as to costs and as to the form of the foreign proceedings. Third, the interests of the applicant should be balanced against the interests of the other parties to the proceedings and any new party likely to be joined to the foreign proceedings. Fourth, permission should not normally be given in terms that would enable the applicant to obtain relief in the foreign proceedings which is superior to the relief given by the order (in particular by conferring a security interest which might accord the applicant priority to other creditors in the event of the defendant's insolvency). Fifth, the evidence in support of the application for permission should contain all necessary information, including as to the foreign law and proposed procedure and as to the assets in the relevant foreign country. Sixth, the applicant must show that there is a real prospect that such assets are located within the jurisdiction of the foreign court in question. Seventh, there must be evidence of a risk of dissipation of the assets in question. Eighth, normally the application should be made on notice to the respondent. But in cases of urgency, where it is just to do so, permission may be given without notice to the respondent, provided he has the earliest possible opportunity for an inter partes hearing.

8–022 *Effect on third parties abroad.* The second limitation on the scope of the worldwide injunction is that what has become known as "the *Babanaft* proviso" has been inserted in such orders in order to make it clear that the English court is not purporting to make third parties abroad subject to the contempt powers of the English court. It has already been seen[57] that a third party who, knowing of a freezing injunction, assists in the breach of the order (e.g. a bank allowing payments to be made by the defendant) is guilty of that type of contempt of court which consists in the interference with the administration of justice. But if the third party is wholly outside the jurisdiction of the court, the third party is either not to be regarded as being in contempt or it would involve an excess of jurisdiction to seek to punish the third party for that contempt.[58]

8–023 In principle, if the defendant has an account with a foreign branch of an English bank, the bank (being a bank resident in England) will, after service

---

[55] *Babanaft International Co SA v Bassatne* [1990] Ch. at 41, 47; *Republic of Haiti v Duvalier* [1990] 1 Q.B. at 217; *Derby & Co Ltd v Weldon* [1990] Ch. at 55–56, 60; *Tate Access Floors Inc v Boswell* [1991] Ch. 512, 525; *Re Bank of Credit and Commerce International SA* [1994] 1 W.L.R. 708 (CA); *Dadourian Group International Inc v Simms* [2005] EWHC 268 (Ch.), [2005] 2 All E.R. 651 (real prospect that there are assets in foreign jurisdiction).

[56] This paragraph summarises the effect of the guidelines laid down by the Court of Appeal in *Dadourian Group International Inc v Simms (Practice Note)* [2006] EWCA Civ 399, [2006] 1 W.L.R. 2499.

[57] See para.8–012, above.

[58] *Derby & Co Ltd v Weldon (Nos 3 & 4)* [1990] Ch. 65, at 82, *per* Lord Donaldson M.R. See Collins (1989) 105 L.Q.R. at 281–286, or Collins, *Essays*, pp.208–212.

of the order, be required not to allow withdrawals from the foreign branch.[59] If the defendant has an account with the head office of, or a branch of, a foreign bank which also has a branch in London, the position is more controversial,[60] and it was accepted that there was a risk that (in the absence of a variation to the order) the bank might be in contempt if the head office or foreign branch allowed withdrawals.[61] But the Commercial Court Guide[62] makes it clear that, as regards freezing injunctions in respect of assets outside the jurisdiction, the order should normally incorporate wording to enable overseas branches of banks which have offices within the jurisdiction to comply with what they reasonably believe to be their obligations under the laws of the country where the assets are located or under the applicable law of the contract relating to such assets. The current wording of the *Babanaft* proviso in the standard form order[63] is as follows:

"Persons outside England and Wales   8–024

(1) Except as provided in paragraph (2) below, the terms of this order do not affect or concern anyone outside the jurisdiction of this court.

(2) The terms of this order will affect the following persons in a country or state outside the jurisdiction of this court—

(a) the Respondent or his officer or agent appointed by power of attorney;

(b) any person who—

(i) is subject to the jurisdiction of this court;

(ii) has been given written notice of this order at his residence or place of business within the jurisdiction of this court; and

(iii) is able to prevent acts or omissions outside the jurisdiction of this court which constitute or assist in a breach of the terms of this order; and

(c) any other person, only to the extent that this order is declared enforceable by or is enforced by a court in that country or state.

Assets located outside England and Wales

Nothing in this order shall, in respect of assets located outside England and Wales, prevent any third party from complying with—

(1) what it reasonably believes to be its obligations, contractual or otherwise, under the laws and obligations of the country or state in

---

[59] *Securities and Investments Board v Pantell* [1990] Ch. 426, 433.

[60] Collins (1989) 105 L.Q.R. 262, 284–286 (reprinted in Collins, *Essays*, pp.211–212).

[61] *Baltic Shipping Co v Transatlantic Shipping Ltd* [1995] 1 Lloyd's Rep. 673; *Bank of China v NBM LLC* [2001] EWCA Civ 1933, [2002] 1 W.L.R. 844.

[62] para.F15.10 (2011).

[63] Commercial Court Guide (2011), App. 5. See Gee, *op. cit.* para.8–005, n.10, pp.569–570 for variation in the light of *Bank of China v NBM LLC* [2001] EWCA Civ 1933, [2002] 1 W.L.R. 844.

which those assets are situated or under the proper law of any contract between itself and the Respondent; and

(2) any orders of the courts of that country or state, provided that reasonable notice of any application for such an order is given to the Applicant's solicitors."

8–025 **Clause (2) of the Rule. Interim relief in aid of foreign proceedings.** Where the English court has jurisdiction over the substance of a case, it also plainly has jurisdiction to grant interim measures to preserve the position pending adjudication of the merits.[64] If proceedings are pending, or are contemplated, in a foreign country, the claimant may wish to preserve its position by seeking interim relief in England. For example, it may be only in England that there are assets available to satisfy a judgment granted in the foreign country to whose jurisdiction the defendant is amenable, and the claimant may be advised to seek a freezing injunction to prevent the defendant from making itself judgment-proof. There is thus obvious practical good sense in ensuring that the courts at the place where the defendant's assets are situate are empowered to grant provisional measures in aid of foreign proceedings on the merits, even where such courts would otherwise have no original jurisdiction over the defendant.

8–026 *European law provision.* This was well recognised by the framers of the Brussels Convention, who made provision (in Art.24 of the Convention) for a court which did not have jurisdiction over the merits of the claim to have jurisdiction to order provisional and protective measures. The provision is reproduced in the Brussels I Regulation as Art.31 (and the corresponding Art.31 of the revised Lugano Convention) in these terms:

"Application may be made to the courts of a Member State for such provisional, including protective, measures as may be available under the law of that State, even if, under this Regulation, the courts of another Member State have jurisdiction as to the substance of the matter."

8–027 In anticipation of the accession of the United Kingdom to the Brussels Convention, and also to deal with the unsatisfactory state of English law as it had developed, s.25(1) of the Civil Jurisdiction and Judgments Act 1982 ("the 1982 Act") was enacted to empower the High Court to grant interim relief where proceedings within the scope of the Brussels Convention (and later the original and revised Lugano Conventions and the Regulation) had been or were to be commenced in another Contracting State.

8–028 In addition, s.24 of the 1982 Act gives the court power to grant interim relief where the jurisdiction of the English court over the substance of the matter is doubtful. The court may therefore grant such relief where an issue remains to be decided about the jurisdiction of the court over the substance of the matter.

---

[64] This obvious point is expressly confirmed in Case C–391/95 *Van Uden Maritime BV v Firma Deco-Line* [1998] E.C.R. I–7091, [1999] Q.B. 1225, [19], [22] and in Case C–99/96 *Mietz v Intership Yachting Sneek BV* [1999] E.C.R. I–2277, [41].

Development of English law. Section 25 was brought into force on January   **8–029**
1, 1987 as regards proceedings in other Brussels Convention States, and on
January 31, 1992 as regards original Lugano Convention States but it was not
until 1997 that the power in s.25(3) to apply it to other States was exercised,
thus filling a serious gap in English law which had been recognised in the
1970s and with which s.25 was intended to deal. In *The Siskina*[65] plaintiff
cargo-owners had a claim against a one-ship Panamanian company for damages for wrongful detention of their cargo in Cyprus. After discharge of the
cargo the defendants' only asset, their ship, sank and their underwriters in
London were due to pay the insurance proceeds there. The bills of lading
provided that the courts of Genoa, Italy, would have exclusive jurisdiction
over cargo claims. The plaintiffs sought to assert jurisdiction in England on
the basis that their claim for a freezing injunction was an injunction "sought
ordering the defendant to do or refrain from doing anything within the
jurisdiction" (i.e. not to remove or dispose of the insurance proceeds pending
the outcome of the Genoese proceedings) within the meaning of what is now
CPR, PD6B, para.3.1(2), Rule 34, clause (2). The House of Lords held that the
English court had no jurisdiction to grant such an injunction against foreign
defendants otherwise than in support of a cause of action in respect of which
the defendant was amenable to the jurisdiction.

In *Mercedes Benz AG v Leiduck*,[66] the Privy Council held that the Hong   **8–030**
Kong court had no power under RSC Order 11, r.1(1) (now CPR, PD6B,
para.3.1) to restrain a foreign defendant from disposing of shares in a Hong
Kong company pending a civil fraud action against him in Monaco. In that
case the Privy Council drew a distinction between two questions. The first was
one of jurisdiction: whether, even if the court had power to grant a freezing
injunction in aid of foreign proceedings, RSC Order 11, r.1(1) authorised
service of proceedings on a foreign defendant. The second issue was whether,
questions of service apart, the court had power to grant a free-standing
injunction to restrain the disposition of the defendants' assets pending adjudication of the substance of the claim in a foreign court. The Privy Council held,
by a majority, that the purpose of RSC Order 11 was to give jurisdiction to the
court to adjudicate on a claim advanced in an action or matter, and an
application for a freezing injunction alone was not an action or matter which
would decide and give effect to rights. There was therefore no mechanism to
allow service out of the jurisdiction on the defendant. Accordingly, it was not
necessary to decide the second question. But Lord Nicholls of Birkenhead
delivered a powerful dissenting opinion: he thought that *The Siskina*, to the
extent that it held that the right to obtain an interlocutory injunction was

---

[65] [1979] A.C. 210 (reversing the majority decision of the Court of Appeal: Lord Denning M.R. described it as the most disappointing reversal of his career: *Due Process of Law* (1980), p.141). See also *Perry v Zissis* [1977] 1 Lloyd's Rep. 607, 616 (CA); *Rowland v Gulfpac (No.1)* [1999] Lloyd's Rep. Bank. 86; *Re Q's Estate* [1999] 1 Lloyd's Rep. 931; *Walsh v Deloitte & Touche Inc* [2001] UKPC 58, at [10]; *Caudron v Air Zaire* [1986] I.L.R.M. 10 (distinguished in *McKenna v H(E)* [2002] 1 I.R. 72); *Meespierson (Bahamas)Ltd v Grupo Torras SA* [2000] 1 L.R.C. 627 (Bahamas CA). See Collins, *Essays*, pp.30–34.

[66] [1996] A.C. 284 (PC), criticised Collins (1996) 112 L.Q.R. 28. See also *Amoco (UK) Exploration Co v British American Offshore Ltd* [1999] 2 Lloyd's Rep. 772.

dependant on there being an existing cause of action justiciable in England, was no longer good law.[67]

8–031   *Extension of interim relief to other foreign proceedings.* The power to extend s.25 to non-Convention States was exercised in 1997 by means of an Order in Council under s.25(3) of the 1982 Act. This order, which came into effect on April 1, 1997, extended the power to grant interim relief so as to make it exercisable in relation to (a) proceedings otherwise than in a Brussels or Lugano Contracting State and (b) proceedings whose subject-matter was not within the scope of the Brussels Convention as determined by Art.1 thereof.[68] The effect of *The Siskina* and *Mercedes Benz AG v Leiduck* was reversed by amending RSC Order 11, r.1(1) by a provision in what is now CPR, PD6B, para.3.1(5), that permission to serve a claim form out of the jurisdiction may be given where a claim is made for an interim remedy under s.25(1) of the 1982 Act.[69]

Section 25, as amended,[70] now provides that the court has power to grant interim relief where proceedings have been or are to be commenced in a Brussels or Lugano Convention State or a Brussels I Regulation State.[71] But by s.25(2) the court is empowered to refuse to grant the relief "if, in the opinion of the court, the fact that the court has no jurisdiction apart from this section in relation to the subject-matter of the proceedings in question makes it inexpedient for the court to grant it."

8–032   *Matters excluded from interim relief.* For the purposes of s.25 "interim relief" means interim relief of any kind which the court has power to grant in proceedings relating to matters within its jurisdiction other than (a) a warrant for the arrest of property, or (b) provision for obtaining evidence.[72] Consequently, the arrest of ships in admiralty proceedings *in rem* is outside the scope of the section; obtaining evidence is excluded because provision is made for obtaining evidence for foreign courts by the Evidence (Proceedings in Other Jurisdictions) Act 1975 (giving effect to the Hague Convention on the Taking

---

[67] In Jersey (a major centre for offshore funds) the Court of Appeal applied the reasoning of Lord Nicholls of Birkenhead on the second issue and held that where the Jersey court had *in personam* jurisdiction over the defendant (by virtue of its submission to the jurisdiction) it could grant a *Mareva* injunction in aid of foreign proceedings: *Solvalub Ltd v Match Investments Ltd* [1998] I.L.Pr. 419.

[68] SI 1997/302. Thus, for example, s.25 was held applicable in principle (though not on the facts) in support of foreign matrimonial proceedings in *Rhode v Rhode* [2007] EWHC 496 (Fam.), [2007] 2 F.L.R. 971 and *N v R* [2008] EWHC 1347 (Fam.), [2009] 2 F.L.R. 342. Section 25 does not, however, apply in support of arbitration proceedings, nor in support of foreign judicial proceedings which are themselves only for interim relief in aid of arbitration. It requires foreign judicial proceedings on the substance of the matter: *ETI Euro Telecom International NV v Republic of Bolivia* [2008] EWCA Civ 880, [2008] 1 W.L.R. 665. For the separate provisional measures regime in support of arbitration see paras 16–084—16–086 below.

[69] This paragraph provides the exclusive means by which the court may commence a claim for interim measures in aid of proceedings in a foreign court, where the jurisdiction of the court is only engaged by virtue of s.25 of the 1982 Act: *Belletti v Morici* [2009] EWHC 2316 (Comm.), [2010] 1 All E.R. (Comm.) 412; *Linsen International Ltd v Humpuss Sea Transport Pte Ltd* [2011] EWHC 2339 (Comm), [2011] 2 Lloyd's Rep. 663.

[70] See most recently SI 2001/3929, arts.1(b), 4; and Sch.2, para.10(a)(i), (b)(i).

[71] Or a Maintenance Regulation State.

[72] s.25(7).

of Evidence Abroad in Civil or Commercial Matters);[73] but s.25 can be used to preserve evidence (as in an *Anton Piller* order[74]) or to obtain information about the location of assets.[75]

Definition of provisional, including protective, measures. The European   **8–033**
Court has held[76] that the expression "provisional, including protective, measures" in what is now Art.31 of the Regulation is to be given an autonomous interpretation, and means measures which are intended to maintain the status quo in order to protect rights pending their final adjudication. In *Van Uden Maritime BV v Firma Deco-Line*[77] the European Court considered the controversial question[78] whether an interim order requiring payment on account of a claim (in that case a contractual claim) is to be classified as a provisional measure within the meaning of Art.24 of the Brussels Convention. It accepted that an interim payment may be necessary to ensure the efficacy of the decision on the substance. But it recognised that such an order may pre-empt the decision on the substance, and that if the plaintiff could obtain it at the court of his domicile (as has happened in France) the jurisdictional rules of the Brussels Convention could be circumvented. Accordingly, an interim payment of a contractual consideration did not constitute a provisional measure within the meaning of Art.24 unless, first, repayment to the defendant of the sum awarded was guaranteed if the plaintiff was ultimately unsuccessful on the substance, and, second, the measure sought related only to specific assets of the defendant located or to be located within the territorial jurisdiction of the court to which the application for provisional measures was made. In *St Paul Dairy Industries NV v Unibel Exser BVBA*[79] the European Court ruled that an application for a witness to be heard before the proceedings, with the aim of enabling the applicant to decide whether to bring a case, was not a provisional or protective measure for the purposes of Art.24 of the 1968 Convention. The aim of Art.24 was to avoid loss caused by delays inherent in international proceedings, and to preserve the status quo. The application in question did

---

[73] See below, paras 8–093 *et seq.* for the 1975 Act. See Case C–104/03 *St Paul Dairy Industries NV v Unibel Exser BVBA* [2005] E.C.R. I–3481.

[74] Now called a "search order": CPR, r.25.1(1)(h).

[75] See Gee, *op. cit.* para.8–006, n.10, p.171, referring to an unreported decision in the *Republic of Haiti v Duvalier* litigation.

[76] Case C–261/90 *Reichert v Dresdner Bank (No.2)* [1992] E.C.R. I–2149.

[77] Case C–391/95 [1998] E.C.R. I–7091, [1999] 2 Q.B. 1225; and see also Case C–99/96 *Mietz v Intership Yachting Sneek BV* [1999] E.C.R. I–2277. *cf. Wermuth v Wermuth* [2003] EWCA Civ 50, [2003] 1 W.L.R. 942 (matrimonial proceedings); *Comet Group Plc v Unika Computer SA* [2004] I.L.Pr. 10. The European Commission has reported the to the Council of Ministers (COM(2009) 174 final, April 21, 2009, para.3.6) that provisional measures remained an area where diversity in the national procedural laws of the Member States made the free circulation of such measures difficult. The Commission said that it was not clear (a) whether ex parte orders could be recognised and enforced on the basis of the Regulation if the defendant had the opportunity to contest the measure subsequently; (b) whether orders for the hearing of a witness for the purpose of enabling the applicant to decide whether to bring a case were enforceable abroad; (c) how the concept in the *Van Uden* case of the real connecting link between the subject matter of the measure sought and the territorial jurisdiction should be interpreted.

[78] See Collins, *Essays*, pp.37–39.

[79] Case C–104/03 [2005] E.C.R. I–3481. *cf.* 1982 Act, s.25(7). Contrast the preservation of evidence: *cf. Miles Platt Ltd v Townroe Ltd* [2003] EWCA Civ 145, [2003] 1 All E.R. (Comm.) 561.

not pursue those aims, and the order sought could circumvent the jurisdictional rules of the 1968 Convention, and lead to a multiplicity of proceedings, and could also circumvent the rules for the taking of evidence in Council Regulation (EC) 1206/2001 on co-operation between the courts of the Member States in the taking of evidence in civil or commercial matters.[80]

8–034   *Inexpediency and scope of s.25 jurisdiction.* On an application for interim relief under s.25, the court should first consider whether the facts would warrant the relief sought if the substantive proceedings had been brought in England.[81] However, in addition, on an application for interim relief under s.25, the court may refuse to grant the relief if, in the opinion of the court, the fact that the court has no independent jurisdiction in relation to the subject-matter of the proceedings makes it inexpedient for the court to grant it.

The Court of Appeal in *Motorola Credit Corp v Uzan (No.2)*[82] said that there were five particular considerations which had to be borne in mind in relation to the question whether it was inexpedient to make an order under s.25: first, whether the making of the order would interfere with the management of the case in the primary court, e.g. where the English order would be inconsistent with an order in the primary court or would overlap[83] with it; secondly, whether it was the policy of the court in the primary jurisdiction not itself to make worldwide freezing/disclosure orders; thirdly, whether there was a danger that the orders made would give rise to disharmony or confusion and/or the risk of conflicting, inconsistent or overlapping orders in other jurisdctions, in particular the courts of the State where the person to be enjoined resided or where the assets affected were located; fourthly, whether at the time the order was sought there was likely to be a potential conflict as to jurisdiction making it inappropriate and inexpedient to make a worldwide order; fifthly, whether, in a case where jurisdiction was resisted and disobedience was to be expected, the court would be making an order which it could not enforce.

8–035   Where the foreign court determining the substance of the case is prevented from granting effective interim relief only on grounds of lack of jurisdiction, that factor is likely to be a powerful indication that the English court should be prepared to intervene. Where, however, the foreign court has jurisdiction to grant such relief but has refused to do so on the merits or for other substantial reasons, the English court is likely to judge it inexpedient to grant such relief itself.[84]

8–036   *Real connecting link.* The European Court has ruled that the grant of provisional or protective measures under what is now Art.31 of the Brussels

---

[80] See below, paras 8–075 *et seq.*

[81] *Refco Inc v Eastern Trading Co* [1999] 1 Lloyd's Rep. 159 (CA); *Kensington International Ltd v Congo* [2007] EWCA Civ 1128, [2008] 1 W.L.R. 1144.

[82] [2003] EWCA Civ 752, [2004] 1 W.L.R. 113, at [115].

[83] On which see *Indosuez International Finance BV v National Reserve Bank* [2002] EWHC 774 (Comm.); *Ryan v Friction Dynamics Ltd* [2001] C.P. Rep. 75. See also *State of Brunei Darussalam v Bolkiah, The Times,* September 5, 2000.

[84] *Motorola Credit Corp v Uzan (No.2)* [2003] EWCA Civ 752, [2004] 1 W.L.R. 113, at [119], discussing the effect of *Refco Inc v Eastern Trading Co* [1999] 1 Lloyd's Rep. 159 (CA) and *Crédit Suisse Fides Trust SA v Cuoghi* [1998] 1 Q.B. 818 (CA).

I Regulation is conditional upon the existence of a real connecting link between the subject-matter of the measures sought and the territorial jurisdiction of the state before whose court the measures are sought.[85] The question that arises, both in cases where the Brussels I Regulation or the Lugano Convention applies and in cases where they do not and the court must be guided solely by the language of s.25 of the 1982 Act, is what degree of connection is required between the measures sought and the territorial jurisdiction of the state before whose court such measures are sought.[86]

This question has now been considered by the English courts in several **8–037** cases. It is submitted, both on authority and in principle, that the court may properly grant interim relief under s.25 in particular where either: (a) there are assets of the defendant in England which may be enjoined (or documents in England which may be disclosed), in which event the court's jurisdiction to grant interim relief is (save in exceptional cases) limited to the assets or property in England; or, (b) the defendant is present in England and thus properly amenable to the enforcement jurisdiction of the English court in respect of asset freezing injunctions or other *in personam* orders addressed to him. Since the jurisdiction under s.25 is exercised in cases where the English court is not the court dealing with the substance of the matter, and since therefore the court need have no basis for the exercise of original jurisdiction, it is submitted that (save in exceptional cases) it is proper that it should confine its grant of interim relief in aid of foreign court proceedings to situations in which the court has a clear basis for the exercise of enforcement jurisdiction directly over the property in question or the person of the defendant.

Property in England. The first and most direct connecting link is that the **8–038** defendant has property in England, the disposal of which may be restrained by a freezing injunction. As the European Court observed in *Van Uden,* "the courts of the place . . . where the assets subject to the measures sought are located are those best able to assess the circumstances which may lead to the grant or refusal of the measures sought or to the laying down of procedures and conditions which the plaintiff must observe in order to guarantee the provisional and protective character of the measures authorised."[87] The consequence of this is that, where the defendant is not present or resident in England, the court will normally limit the scope of any freezing injunction granted under s.25 to the defendant's assets in England. Thus, in *Banco Nacional de Comercio Exterior SNC v Empresa de Telecommunicaciones de*

---

[85] Case C–391/95 *Van Uden Maritime BV v Firma Deco-Line* [1998] E.C.R. I–7091, [1999] Q.B. 1225, at [48].

[86] McLachlan (1998) 47 I.C.L.Q. 3, 12–19; Merrett [2008] L.M.C.L.Q. 71; Johnson [2008] C.J.Q. 433; Fentiman, *International Commercial Litigation* (2010), paras 17.76–17.175, Hartley (2010) 126 L.Q.R. 194; Dickinson (2010) 6 J.Priv.Int. L. 519.

[87] Case C–391/95 *Van Uden Maritime BV v Firma Deco-Line* [1998] E.C.R. I–7091, [1999] Q.B. 1225, at [39], following Case 125/79 *Denilauler v Snc Couchet Frères* [1980] E.C.R. 1553, at [16], and, to like effect, *Crédit Suisse Fides Trust SA v Cuoghi* [1998] 1 Q.B. 818, 827 per Millett L.J.

Cuba SA,[88] the Court of Appeal refused to grant worldwide relief under s.25 on the ground that the defendant was not resident in England; the English assets were already protected by a domestic freezing injunction; and "[t]here is therefore no connecting link at all between the subject matter of the measure sought and the territorial jurisdiction of this court."[89] Previously, in *Motorola Credit Corp v Uzan (No.2),*[90] the Court of Appeal had left undisturbed a worldwide order against a non-resident defendant. However, the Court was much influenced by the fact that that defendant had very substantial assets in England (which would also provide the court with the means of enforcing its order if disobeyed) and the case was "an apparently serious case of inter-national fraud."[91] It is submitted that, following *Banco Nacional,* this aspect of the *Uzan* decision can only be justified on the ground of the presence of both of these elements.

8–039   *Presence of defendant in England.* An alternative ground for the application of the English court's jurisdiction to worldwide assets under s.25 will be where the order is sought *in personam* against the defendant who is present in England. Thus, in *Crédit Suisse Fides Trust SA v Cuoghi*[92] substantive proceedings for civil fraud were pending in Switzerland (a party to the Lugano Convention) against a defendant who was resident and domiciled in England. The plaintiffs applied to the English court under s.25(1)[93] for a worldwide freezing injunction and an ancillary disclosure order relating to assets world-wide, in aid of the Swiss proceedings. Refusing an application to confine the injunction and disclosure order to assets in England, the Court of Appeal held that it was not "inexpedient" to grant the relief in the light of the facts that the defendant was domiciled in England, the Swiss court had no jurisdiction (under Swiss law) to make such an order against a non-resident, and there was no reason to believe that the Swiss court would not welcome assistance from the courts of the country where the defendant was resident.[94]

8–040   *Other connections: the special case of fraud.* Beyond the two connecting links set out above, there may exceptionally be other cases in which there is

---

[88] [2007] EWCA Civ 662, [2008] 1 W.L.R. 1936; and see also *SanDisk Corp v Koninklijke Philips Electronics NV* [2007] EWHC 332 (Ch.), [2007] Bus.L.R. 705 (worldwide relief refused because neither assets nor defendant in England); and *Mobil Cerro Negro Ltd v Petroleos de Venezuela SA* [2008] EWHC 532 (Comm.), [2008] 1 Lloyd's Rep. 684 (considerations of comity point strongly against granting such an order against a non-resident defendant in the absence of assets in England).

[89] *ibid.* at [29].

[90] [2003] EWCA Civ 752, [2004] 1 W.L.R. 113.

[91] *ibid.* at [128]. This aspect of the decision has been criticised by Johnson [2008] C.J.Q. 433 and Hartley (2010) 126 L.Q.R. 194.

[92] [1998] Q.B. 818 (CA), not following *S T Bautrading v Nordling* [1997] 3 All E.R. 718 (CA). *cf. Republic of Haiti v Duvalier* [1990] 1 Q.B. 202, 216–217 (CA).

[93] Although the defendant was domiciled in England, the effect of Art.21 of the Lugano Convention was that the prior Swiss proceedings deprived the English court of jurisdiction over the substance of the claim: see below, Rule 38(4).

[94] In *Motorola Credit Corp v Uzan (No.2)* [2003] EWCA Civ 752, [2004] 1 W.L.R. 113, at [125]–[127], the Court of Appeal set aside a worldwide order against the second and third defendants, who were non-resident, on the ground that the court's order could not be made effective against them and on the ground of comity, but maintained the order against the resident fourth defendant.

a sufficient connection with England to justify the making of an order in relation to the defendant's worldwide assets. The English courts have been astute to ensure that this possibility is left open, particularly in cases of international fraud. Thus, as has been seen, the Court of Appeal maintained such a worldwide order against a defendant to an international fraud case with very substantial assets in England in *Motorola Credit Corp v Uzan (No.2)*.[95] Earlier, in *Republic of Haiti v Duvalier*,[96] the Court made such an order against a non-resident defendant in support of substantive fraud proceedings in France. The case went to the very edge of what is permissible, but may perhaps be justified on the basis that the defendant had solicitors in England, who could be treated as his agents, and the relevant information relating to the defendant's worldwide assets was in England.[97]

Interim relief where proceedings stayed. A claimant may commence an   **8–041**
action *in personam* or *in rem* in England in a case where (apart from the Brussels I Regulation or the Lugano Convention) the defendant may be entitled to a stay of the proceedings, either as a matter of discretion (e.g. on the ground that some other court is the appropriate forum, or that there is a jurisdiction clause providing for the exclusive jurisdiction of the courts of another country) or as a matter of right, such as where the defendant is entitled to a mandatory stay under the Arbitration Act 1996.[98] Where the stay is discretionary, the court may allow the injunction to remain in force as a condition of the stay.[99]

Admiralty relief in rem. The freezing injunction is a remedy *in personam*   **8–042**
designed to ensure the effectiveness of the final judgment which the claimant seeks. In Admiralty procedings *in rem* the *res* may be arrested by the court and kept in the custody of the Admiralty Marshal until it is released. Where a claim *in rem* is brought against a ship or other property and the property is arrested or other security is given to prevent arrest or obtain release from arrest, the question arises whether the arrested property or other security may be retained even if the proceedings are stayed on the ground that the dispute ought to be decided by another tribunal, e.g. under the inherent jurisdiction of the court[100] or under Arts 23 and 27 to 28 of the Brussels I Regulation and the

---

[95] [2003] EWCA Civ 752, [2004] 1 W.L.R. 113.

[96] [1990] 1 Q.B. 202 (CA).

[97] Collins (1989) 105 L.Q.R. 262, 281; though the information could have been obtained (without the need for a worldwide freezing injunction) under the principle in *Norwich Pharmacal Co v Customs and Excise Commissioners* [1974] A.C. 133, see further below at 8–073).

[98] As to which see below páras 16–084—16–086.

[99] *cf. Spiliada Maritime Corp v Cansulex Ltd* [1987] A.C. 460, 483; *The Rena K* [1979] Q.B. 377, 407. In *Phonogram Ltd v Def American Inc, The Times*, October 7, 1994, it was held that the court had power to grant an interim injunction in English proceedings which had been stayed because of parallel proceedings in California, but the power would only be exercised in an unusual case because otherwise it might pre-empt the ruling of the foreign court. See also *Law v Garrett* (1878) 8 Ch.D. 26, 38 (CA). In *Walsh v Deloitte & Touche Inc* [2001] UKPC 58, at [21]–[22], the Privy Council accepted that a claimant might bring an action in the Bahamas to obtain interim relief, and then obtain a stay in order to proceed with the substantive action in Ontario.

[100] Rule 38(1).

Lugano Convention,[101] or under s.9 of the Arbitration Act 1996.[102] The position is now regulated[103] by s.26 of the Civil Jurisdiction and Judgments Act 1982 and s.11 of the Arbitration Act 1996. Their combined effect is that where the court stays or dismisses Admiralty proceedings on the ground that the dispute should be submitted to the determination of the courts of another part of the United Kingdom or of an overseas country, or stays the proceedings on the ground that the dispute should be submitted to arbitration, the court may order that property arrested be retained as security for the satisfaction of any judgment or award, or order that the stay or dismissal of the proceedings be conditional on the provision of equivalent security.

8–043 These provisions are similar to (but not identical with) Art.7 of the Brussels Arrest Convention of 1952, which provides that if the court within whose jurisdiction a ship has been arrested does not have jurisdiction to decide upon the merits, the bail or other security given to procure its release shall provide that it is given as security for the satisfaction of any judgment which may eventually be pronounced by a court having jurisdiction to decide upon the merits. It was held in *The Nordglimt*[104] that s.26 of the 1982 Act should be construed so as to conform to the provisions of the Brussels Arrest Convention. Consequently it was said (*obiter*) that s.26 applied even if proceedings were struck out for want of jurisdiction, rather than stayed or dismissed. It was also held that s.26 applied where the foreign proceedings or arbitration proceedings had already been commenced at the time of the institution of the proceedings in England.[105]

8–044 Both s.26 of the 1982 Act and s.11 of the Arbitration Act 1996 contemplate that where Admiralty proceedings are stayed or dismissed on the ground that the dispute should be submitted to the determination of the courts of a foreign country or to arbitration, the court may order either (a) that the ship be retained as security for the satisfaction of any ultimate judgment, or by the foreign court award by the arbitral tribunal or (b) that the stay or dismissal be conditional on the provision of equivalent security for the satisfaction of the judgment or award.

8–045 The question has arisen whether it is possible for the court to make the second form of order in cases where the court is obliged to order a stay or decline jurisdiction. The court is obliged to order a stay or decline jurisdiction

---

[101] Rules 38(4) and 39(3).

[102] Rule 65.

[103] Before s.26 of the 1982 Act came into force in 1984, the question had been raised in a number of cases involving arbitration clauses, in which somewhat artificial distinctions had been drawn between security for the action *in rem*, and security for the arbitration: see *The Golden Trader* [1975] Q.B. 348; *The Rena K* [1979] Q.B. 377; *The Andria* [1984] Q.B. 477 (CA); *The Tuyuti* [1984] Q.B. 838 (CA); cf. *The Bazias 3* [1993] Q.B. 673, 680–681 (CA).

[104] [1988] Q.B. 183, overruled on other grounds in *Republic of India v India Steamship Co Ltd (No.2)* [1998] A.C. 878. See also *Clipper Shipping Co Ltd v San Vincente Partners*, 1989 S.L.T. 204. For the practice see *The Emre II* [1989] 2 Lloyd's Rep. 182; *The Sylt* [1991] 1 Lloyd's Rep. 240; *The Bazias 3* [1993] Q.B. 673 (CA).

[105] See also *The Jalamatsya* [1987] 2 Lloyd's Rep. 164, followed in *Allonah Pty Ltd v The Amanda N* (1989) 90 A.L.R. 391. In *The Silver Athens (No.2)* [1986] 2 Lloyd's Rep. 583 it was held that where proceedings had already been stayed before an arrest was effected, an application could be made for the stay to be lifted in order to arrest the vessel and to apply for an order that the security be retained.

where the parties have agreed to submit their disputes to arbitration[106] or where they have agreed to the jurisdiction of the courts of a Member State or a Convention State, or where proceedings have first been commenced in such a country.[107] In *The World Star*[108] it was held that, where the court is required to make an order staying the proceedings under what is now s.9 of the Arbitration Act 1996, the court cannot make the second form of order, i.e. to attach conditions to the grant of a stay. The reason is that the essence of such a condition is that if it is not complied with the stay is removed and the proceedings continue. But where a stay is mandatory, the court has no power to remove the stay;[109] and the same would apply if the court is under a duty to decline jurisdiction under the Regulation or the Convention.[110] It is not, however, necessary to resolve the apparent inconsistency between the provisions of s.26 of the 1982 Act and s.11 of the Arbitration Act 1996 and the mandatory provisions of the Regulation and the Convention and the New York Convention. The same practical result is reached by the first form of order, namely to retain the vessel as security. This is through the use of the discretion of the court to release the vessel from arrest.[111] That power is normally exercised only if security is provided by guarantee or otherwise for the claim, interest and costs.[112] Neither the retention of the vessel nor the exercise of the discretion to release it upon provision of equivalent security involves the imposition of a condition,[113] and if the owner of the vessel which has been arrested wishes to secure its release, it will in practice have no alternative but to provide equivalent security.

Interim relief in aid of enforcement of foreign judgment. Where it is sought to recognise or enforce a foreign judgment in England, the court also has power to grant interim relief. Where that judgment was rendered by a court in a state to which the Brussels I Regulation or the Lugano Convention applies, Art.47 specifically provides that nothing is to prevent the applicant from availing himself of provisional, including protective, measures in accordance with the law of the Member or Convention State requested without a declaration of enforceability. Pursuant to this provision, while the nature and availability of such relief is a matter of national procedural law in the requested state, there is a strong presumption in favour of relief being granted.[114] However, the court may only grant domestic relief, and may not grant a worldwide order.[115] If an application in aid of the enforcement of a foreign judgment is otherwise made under s.25 of the 1982 Act, the court will

        8–046

---

[106] Arbitration Act 1996, s.9, which is not limited (as was Arbitration Act 1975, s.1) to international cases: Rule 65.

[107] Rules 39(3) and 38(4).

[108] [1986] 2 Lloyd's Rep. 274, decided on 1982 Act, s.26, before it was amended by the Arbitration Act 1996 to remove arbitration from its scope. For the position prior to the 1982 Act, see *The Rena K* [1979] Q.B. 377, 400; *cf. The Tuyuti* [1984] Q.B. 838, 849 (CA).

[109] Mustill and Boyd, p.341.

[110] See Hartley (1989) 105 L.Q.R. 640, 656–660.

[111] CPR 61.8(4).

[112] *The Bazias 3* [1993] Q.B. 673 (CA).

[113] *cf. The Tuyuti* [1984] Q.B. 838, 849 (CA).

[114] Case 119/84 *Capelloni v Pelkmans* [1985] E.C.R. 3147.

[115] *Banco Nacional de Comercio Exterior SNC v Empresa de Telecommunicaciones de Cuba SA* [2007] EWCA Civ 662, [2008] 1 W.L.R. 1936.

adopt the same approach in jurisdictional terms to determining whether it is expedient to grant the order as it would pre-judgment.[116]

2. SERVICE OF PROCESS

8R–047   **RULE 22**—**(1) The question whether process must be served abroad is a matter for the law of the forum (*lex fori*).**[117]

(2) Where process is to be served abroad, it may be so served:

(a) by any method provided by:

(i) Regulation (EC) 1393/2007 on the service in the Member States of judicial and extrajudicial documents in civil or commercial matters ("the EU Service Regulation") where it applies;[118] or,

(ii) the Hague Convention on the service abroad of judicial and extra-judicial documents in civil or commercial matters 1965 ("the Hague Service Convention") or any other applicable convention where it applies;[119] or,

(iii) to the extent that there is no such convention in force, either by service through diplomatic or consular channels;[120] or, in the case of Commonwealth states, the Isle of Man and the Channel Islands and British overseas territories, by personal service;[121] or,

(b) by any method permitted by the law of the country where service is to be effected.[122]

(3) No process may be served in a manner which is contrary to the law of the country where service is effected.[123]

COMMENT

8–048   **The function of service of process in international cases.** As will be seen in Chapter 11, the service of originating process is not a mere administrative step. The general principle set out in Rule 29 is that the Court has jurisdiction over a defendant if and only if he is served with process in England or abroad in the circumstances authorised by, and in the manner prescribed by, statute or statutory order. Where the Brussels I Regulation or the Lugano Convention applies, service does not found jurisdiction, but nevertheless a failure to effect service of originating process may preclude enforcement of a subsequent default judgment.[124] For these reasons, it is of great importance to ensure that the defendant has been properly served.

---

[116] *ibid.*

[117] See further Rule 29 below and the authorities there cited.

[118] CPR, r.6.41; for text see [2007] O.J. L324/ 79, and PD6B.

[119] CPR, r.6.42(1); for text of the Hague Service Convention: Cmnd. 3968 and *http://www.hcch.net.*

[120] CPR, r.6.42(2).

[121] CPR, r.6.42(3)

[122] CPR, r.6.40(3)(c).

[123] CPR, r.6.40(4); *The Sky One* [1988] 1 Lloyd's Rep. 238.

[124] Art.34(2) Brussels I Regulation; see para.14–169 below.

The jurisdictional implications of service of process. Service of process 8–049
also seeks to subject the defendant to the power of the court, as an organ of
the State. As such, it is an exercise of sovereignty. Thus, in *Cookney v
Anderson*, Lord Westbury L.C. observed:[125]

> "The right of administering justice is the attribute of sovereignty, and all
> persons within the dominions of a sovereign are within his allegiance and
> under his protection. If, therefore, one sovereign causes process to be
> served in the territory of another, and summons a foreign subject to his
> Court of Justice, it is in fact an invasion of sovereignty, and would be
> unjustifiable, unless done with consent."

This basic premise underpins the specific international arrangements for the
service of process abroad, enumerated in Rule 22 and analysed further below.
But it has tended to be obscured in England by the fact that, in the common
law tradition, whilst the writ was the command of the sovereign, the responsibility for actual service of the writ rested on the party, and not on the court.
Thus, traditionally, the court took no part in effecting service of the proceedings.[126] It followed, therefore, that, when the court did permit service of
process outside its jurisdiction, it was left to the claimant to effect service.
Therefore, the court did not of necessity become involved in seeking the
assistance of foreign authorities, unless so moved by the claimant in cases
where official intervention was required in the country where service was to
be effected. Other countries in the common law tradition, both in the Commonwealth and in the United States, took the same approach. By the same
token, common law countries traditionally had no objection to the direct
service of foreign process on their territory by the claimant or his agent.[127] By
contrast, in the civil law tradition, service of process is of its nature a public
judicial act. Thus, when executed abroad, it, by definition, requires the
co-operation of the official authorities in the foreign country. For this reason,
the conclusion of international arrangements for service of process has
achieved greater importance in dealings with civil law countries.

Clause (1) of the Rule. *Lex fori* determines whether service abroad 8–050
required. Clause (1) of the Rule sets out the rule applicable to determination
of the question whether service abroad is required. Although there is no
express English authority confirming this approach, it is submitted that it
underlies Rule 29, and is consistent with the authorities there cited. The point
has become an important one in determining the application of international

---

[125] (1863) 1 De G. J. & S. 365, 46 E.R. 146; and see, to like effect, *George Munro Ltd v
American Cyanamid and Chemical Corp* [1944] 1 K.B. 432, 437 (CA); *Afro Continental Nigeria
v Meridian Shipping Co SA (The Vrontados)* [1982] 2 Lloyd's Rep. 241, 245 (CA); *Molins Plc
v G.D. S.p.A.* [2000] 1 W.L.R. 1741, [40] (CA); *Bayat v Cecil* [2011] EWCA Civ 135, [2011] 1
W.L.R. 3086, [61]–[64].

[126] By CPR, r.6.4, this is no longer the general rule in England. On the contrary, the court will
serve the claim form except where (a) a rule or practice direction provides that the claimant must
serve it; (b) the claimant notifies the court that the claimant wishes to serve it; or (c) the court
orders or directs otherwise.

[127] Harwood (1961) 10 I.C.L.Q. 284, 288; McClean & Patchett, *The Recognition and Enforcement of Judgments and Orders and the Service of Process within the Commonwealth: a Further
Report* (1977), paras 8.12 and 8.58.

conventions for the service of process, notably the Hague Service Convention. In *Volkswagenwerk AG v Schlunk*,[128] the United States Supreme Court held that, although the provisions of that Convention were mandatory, in the sense that, whenever there was occasion to transmit a document abroad to a state party to the Convention, the methods of service provided for or permitted in the Convention had to be employed, nevertheless it was for the *lex fori* to determine when such service abroad was required. If service could properly, under the *lex fori,* be effected locally, the provisions of the Convention would not be engaged. This decision was not received uncritically,[129] and may, if not checked in some cases, lead to abuse and injustice, especially where the form of service does not necessarily lead to notice to the defendant, or otherwise subverts the carefully negotiated terms of international agreements designed to protect the rights of nationals subjected to foreign process.[130] However, it is submitted that the general principle is sound and widely-accepted. The States parties to the Convention took the same view in 2009, when they re-affirmed the view "that the Service Convention is of a non-mandatory but exclusive character".[131] These terms are to be understood in the following way:[132]

> "The language [in Art. 1] 'where there is occasion to transmit' is under-stood as meaning that the Service Convention is non-mandatory in the sense that it is a matter for the *lex fori* to determine whether a document must be transmitted for service abroad. The use of the word 'shall' is understood as meaning that the Service Convention is exclusive, in the sense that once the law of the forum has determined that a document must be transmitted abroad for service, the channels of transmission expressly available or otherwise permissible under the Hague Service Convention are the *only* channels that may be used."

It follows that, where the defendant may properly be served in England, no international question will arise. The circumstances in which this may properly be done are a question for English law as the *lex fori* and are set out in Chapter 11 of this work.[133] Two specific modes of local service, however, have a particular potential for abuse, when applied to foreign defendants: (a) in England: service by an alternative method (formerly called substituted service) under CPR, r.6.15; and (b) in some civil law countries: fictitious service on a state official. The general principle has, therefore, been qualified in respect of these modes of service by judicial determination.

8–051   *Service by an alternative method.* CPR, r.6.15 provides that "[w]here it appears to the court that there is a good reason to authorise service by a method or at a place not otherwise permitted by this Part, the court may make

---

[128] 486 U.S. 694 (1988).

[129] See McClean, *International Co-operation in Civil and Criminal Matters* (2002) pp.47–55 and the references there cited.

[130] See the limitations on the principle in English law set out in paras 8–051—8–052 below.

[131] Hague Conference on Private International Law, Special Commission Conclusions and Recommendations (2009), para.12.

[132] Hague Conference on Private International Law, Special Commission, Prel. Doc. No.10, para.6.

[133] Paras 11R–101—11–123 below.

an order permitting service by an alternative method or at an alternative place." Nevertheless, this provision for service by an alternative method may not be used to outflank the provisions of international agreements for the service of process abroad, if the effect of such an order would be to subvert those agreements. The desire to find a faster method of service locally on a foreign defendant is not a good reason to order substituted service.[134]

Fictitious service on local state official. The law of some civil law countries   8–052
permits a form of fictitious "service" on a foreign defendant by leaving the relevant document at the office of an official in the forum state (a *notification au parquet*). Although that official is then expected to take steps to bring the document to the attention of the defendant, service is treated as complete, and time begins to run, regardless of when the defendant receives actual notice of the proceedings.[135] In England it has been held that such a provision cannot circumvent the requirements of the EU Service Regulation, even if the law of the country of origin deems service on a court official in that state to be good service on the foreign party. Once it has been determined that the Regulation applies, the validity and date of service fall to be determined by the Regulation.[136] It is submitted that this reasoning is equally applicable to service pursuant to other international agreements to which the United Kingdom is party.

Clause (2) of the Rule. Modes of service abroad. Once English law, as the   8–053
lex fori, has determined that process must be served abroad, clause (2) sets out the various means by which such service may be effected in their order of priority. These are now conveniently enumerated in CPR, rr.6.40–6.42 and in PD6B. They consist of: (a) the EU Service Regulation, which makes provision for the service of judicial and extra-judicial documents within the European Union;[137] (b) the Hague Service Convention, which is the most important international convention on the subject, and any other applicable convention; (c) where no such arrangements are applicable, either by British consular or foreign diplomatic channels, or, in the case of Commonwealth countries and island and overseas territories, by personal service; or (d) by any other method permitted in the country where service is to be effected.

---

[134] *Knauf UK GmbH v British Gypsum Ltd* [2001] EWCA Civ 1570, [2002] 1 W.L.R. 907, [47]. *cf. Department of Civil Aviation of the Kyrgyz Republic v Finrep GmbH* [2006] EWHC 1722 (Comm.), [2006] 2 C.L.C. 402 (substituted service of an arbitration application, made in the context of an arbitration with its seat in England, on the party's English solicitors who had acted in the arbitration); *Marconi Communications International Ltd v PT Pan Indonesia Bank Ltd TBK* [2004] EWHC 129 (Comm.), [2004] 1 Lloyd's Rep. 594 (substituted service on the defendant's solicitors in England following evidence of extensive and deliberate delay in effecting service abroad).

[135] McClean, *International Co-operation in Civil and Criminal Matters* (2002), pp. 23–25; Schlosser (2000) 284 *Recueil des Cours* 9, 107–110.

[136] *Tavoulareas v Tsavliris* [2004] EWCA Civ 48, [2004] 1 Lloyd's Rep. 445.

[137] The text of the Regulation is reproduced in PD6B. Art.20 provides that this Regulation shall prevail over other provisions in bilateral or multilateral agreements or arrangements concluded by Member States, though it does not preclude Member States from maintaining or concluding agreements or arrangements to expedite further or simplify the transmission of documents, provided they are compatible with the Regulation.

8–054   **The EU Service Regulation.** European Parliament and Council Regulation (EC) 1393/2007 on the service in the Member States of judicial and extra-judicial documents in civil and commercial matters (service of documents) took effect from November 13, 2008.[138] The Regulation makes comprehensive provision for service of process in civil and commercial matters[139] within European Union states,[140] whenever a judicial document has to be transmitted from one Member State to another for service there.[141]

8–055   *Transmission and service of judicial documents through receiving agencies.* The Regulation establishes a comprehensive and decentralised network of transmission and receiving agencies in Member States, which are charged with the task of arranging for the service of judicial documents.[142] The Regulation greatly simplifies the procedure for transmission. It permits transmission "by any appropriate means provided that the content of the document received is true and faithful to that of the document forwarded and that all information in it is easily legible",[143] and provides a standard form of request.[144] The receiving agency must send the transmitting agency a standard form receipt within seven days.[145] It is obliged to effect service as soon as possible, and in any event within one month.[146] It is to carry out service "either in accordance with the law of the Member State addressed or by a particular method requested by the transmitting agency, unless that method is incompatible with the law of that Member State."[147] The date of service is determined according to the law of the Member State addressed.[148] However,

---

[138] [2007] O.J. L324/79. The text is also reproduced in PD6B. The Regulation repeals and replaces Council Regulation (EC) 1348/2000: Art.25.

[139] The Regulation does not add its own definition of "civil and commercial matters" beyond providing in Art.1(1) that "it shall not extend in particular to revenue, customs or administrative matters or to liability of the State for actions or omissions in the exercise of state authority (*acta iure imperii*)". It is submitted that the expression should be defined consistently with other provisions of European law, notably the Brussels I Regulation (as to which see below paras.11–029—11–034). In *Re Anderson Owen Ltd* [2009] EWHC 2837 (Ch.), [2011] I.L.Pr. 165, Norris J considered *obiter,* in the context of an insolvency proceeding under the Insolvency Rules 1986, that the Service Regulation should be construed consistently with the EC Insolvency Regulation 1346/2000, with the consequence that the Service Regulation would apply to some proceedings which were "insolvency proceedings" for the purpose of the Insolvency Rules 1986 (despite the terms of I.R. r.12.12(1)), but not to others.

[140] In the case of Denmark, the terms of the Regulation are applicable by virtue of a declaration made by Denmark ([2008] O.J. L331/21), pursuant to a parallel convention that it had entered into with the European Community: [2005] O.J. L300/55.

[141] Where the defendant has given in writing the business address of a European lawyer within an EEA state as the address for service of process, or the European lawyer has notified the claimant that he is instructed to accept service on behalf of the defendant, service may be effected at that address: CPR, r.6.7(3), giving effect to SI 1978/1910.

[142] Ch.II, s.1. Full details of these agencies are maintained by the European Commission on the website of the European Judicial Atlas: *http://ec.europa.eu/justice_home/judicialatlascivil/html/ ds_information_en.htm?countrySession=3&.*

In exceptional circumstances, Member States may also use consular or diplomatic channels to forward judicial documents to receiving agencies: Art.12.

[143] Art.4(2).

[144] Art.4(3) & Annex I.

[145] Art.6(1).

[146] Art.7(2).

[147] Art.7(1).

[148] Art.9(1).

"where according to the law of a Member State a document has to be served within a particular period, the date to be taken into account with respect to the applicant shall be that determined by the law of that Member State."[149] Once service has been effected, the receiving agency will return a certificate of service in standard form.[150]

Translation requirements. The documents to be served must be either in a language which the addressee understands, or in the official language of place in the Member State addressed where service is to be effected; and service may be refused if this requirement is not complied with.[151] In *Ingenieurbüro Michael Weiss und Partner GbR v Industrie-und Handelskammer Berlin*[152] the European Court considered the interpretation of the translation requirements in the case of documents instituting proceedings. It held that the term "document to be served" meant the document or documents which must be served on the defendant in due time in order to enable him to assert his rights in legal proceedings in the State of transmission. Such a document must make it possible to identify with a degree of certainty at the very least the subject-matter of the claim and the cause of action as well as the summons to appear before the court or, depending on the nature of the pending proceedings, to be aware that it was possible to appeal. Documents which had a purely evidential function and were not necessary for the purpose of understanding the subject-matter of the claim and the cause of action did not form an integral part of the document instituting the proceedings. It was for the national court to determine whether the content of the document instituting the proceedings was sufficient to enable the defendant to assert his rights or whether it was necessary for the party instituting the proceedings to remedy the fact that a necessary annex had not been translated. The fact that the addressee of a document served had agreed in a contract concluded with the applicant in the course of his business that correspondence was to be conducted in the language of the Member State of transmission did not give rise to a presumption of knowledge of that language, but was evidence which the court might take into account in determining whether that addressee understood the language of the Member State of transmission. But where the addressee concluded a contract in the course of his business in which he agreed that correspondence was to be conducted in the language of the Member State of transmission and the annexes concerned that correspondence and were written in the agreed language, the addressee could not rely on Art.8(1) to refuse to accept the documents.

8–056

---

[149] Art.9(2). The United Kingdom has stated that it intends to derogate from these provisions on the basis that the complexities of its law on time-limits and limitation periods would only be exacerbated by this Article.

[150] Art.10.

[151] Art.8. Where the requisite translation has been omitted, and the defendant refuses service on that ground, the claimant may remedy that defect by supplying a translation, provided that he does so as soon as possible: Case C–443/03 *Leffler v Berlin Chemie AG* [2005] E.C.R. I–9611.

[152] Case C–14/07 [2008] E.C.R. I–3367. The case was decided under Art.8 of the prior Regulation 1348/2000, but the Court's reasoning is equally applicable under the current Regulation.

8–057   *Service by other means.* The Regulation also makes provision for service in other Member States by three other means: (a) directly through the diplomatic or consular agents of the requesting state;[153] (b) by post—using registered letter with acknowledgement of receipt or equivalent;[154] and, (c) "directly through the judicial officers, officials or other competent persons of the Member State addressed where such direct service is permitted under the law of such State."[155] These alternatives are of considerable potential practical significance. The Regulation imposes no hierarchy between the various methods of service provided. Service by any one of the permitted methods will be valid.[156] However, their application is limited in two respects. In the first place, Member States are free to notify their opposition to service by diplomatic agents or by direct service. Full details of these declarations are available electronically on the European Judicial Network.[157] Many countries in the civil law tradition object to service through diplomatic channels, save where the addressee is a national of the requesting state.[158] Practice in relation to direct service is not uniform. In some civil law countries, such as France, such service is permitted, and there is an established practice of service through the office of huissier or official process server. In other states, no such direct service is permitted.[159] Service by post presents obvious practical advantages, and there is no provision for Member States to object to such service. However, its effectiveness, where the defendant does not enter an appearance will depend upon satisfactory evidence of acknowledgement of receipt (see the next paragraph).

8–058   *Defendant not entering an appearance.* The importance of ensuring correct service is underlined by Article 19, which makes provision for the case where service has been transmitted to another Member State under the provisions of the Regulation and the defendant has not entered an appearance. In such a case, judgment may not be entered until it is established that either "(a) the document was served by a method prescribed by the internal law of the Member State addressed for the service of documents in domestic actions upon persons who are within its territory; or (b) the document was actually delivered to the defendant or to his residence by another method provided for by this Regulation; and that in either of these cases the service or the delivery was effected in sufficient time to enable the defendant to defend."[160] There is additional provision for Member States to declare that a default judgment may be entered even if no certificate of service or delivery has been received if the document has been transmitted by one of the methods allowed under the

---

[153] Art.13.

[154] Art.14.

[155] Art.15.

[156] Case C–473/04 *Plumex v Young Sports N. V.* [2006] E.C.R. I–1417.

[157] Art.23(3). The website address is above at n.142.

[158] The United Kingdom has indicated that it has no objection to service by diplomatic or consular agents.

[159] The United Kingdom has entered an objection to direct service under the Regulation in England and Wales and Northern Ireland (but not in Scotland). This objection is surprising in view of the traditional permissive approach of the common law in relation to the service of foreign process in England, see para.8–049 above and the references there cited.

[160] Art.19(1).

Regulation; a period of at least six months has elapsed; and every reasonable effort has been made to obtain a certificate of service.[161]

Service of extrajudicial documents. The Regulation also permits transmis-   **8–059** sion of extrajudicial documents in accordance with its provisions.[162] In *Roda Golf & Beach Resort SL*[163] the clerk of a Spanish court had refused to serve, in the absence of legal proceedings, addressees in the United Kingdom and Ireland with a notarial act terminating a number of contracts for the sale of immovable property. The refusal was on the ground that no legal proceedings were in train. The European Court held that the concept of "extrajudicial document" was a Community law concept. A document could be regarded as an extrajudicial document even if there were no connection with current or contemplated legal proceedings, if the judicial co-operation governed by the Regulation had cross-border implications and was necessary for the proper functioning of the internal market. The service of a notarial act falls within that definition.

The Hague Service Convention. Where service is to be effected in a   **8–060** country outside the scope of the EU Service Regulation, the major multilateral convention dealing with service of process in civil and commercial matters is the Hague Service Convention,[164] to which the United Kingdom is a party. There are more than 60 Contracting States, and they include many of the United Kingdom's major trading partners outside the European Union, includ- ing China, Japan, Russia, and the United States of America. The text and mechanisms of the Hague Convention have a number of similar features to the EU Service Regulation (the latter drew heavily on the practical experience of European States with operation of the Hague Convention). Both instruments have as their objective to simplify and expedite the process by which judicial and extrajudicial documents may be served abroad. But, in contrast to the decentralised system of the EU Service Regulation, the Hague Service Con- vention adopts as its primary means of transmission a system of Central Authorities in each Contracting State, which bear the responsibility of arrang- ing for the service of documents in the State addressed.[165]

Service in Hague Convention countries by other means. The Hague Service   **8–061** Convention also permits service by other means: (a) directly by diplomatic or consular officers of the state of origin;[166] (b) by post;[167] (c) directly through the judicial officers or other competent persons of the state of destination.[168] But, in the case of method (a) the state of destination may declare that it objects to such service unless the document is to be served on a national of the

---

[161] Art.19(2). This provision is applicable in the United Kingdom.
[162] Art.16.
[163] Case C–14/08 [2009] E.C.R. I–5439.
[164] Hague Conference on Private International Law, *Practical Handbook on the Operation of the Hague Service Convention* (2006); McClean, *International Co-operation in Civil and Crimi- nal Matters* (2002), pp.23–55.
[165] Arts.2–5.
[166] Art.8.
[167] Art.10(a).
[168] Arts 10(b) & (c).

state of origin. Methods (b) and (c) are only available provided that the state of destination does not object. Art.21(2)(a) requires each Contracting State to notify the depositary of its opposition to the use of methods of transmission pursuant to Arts 8 and 10. It is submitted that such notification is conclusive as to whether these alternative methods of service have been excluded in the relevant state of destination.[169]

8–062   *Defendant not entering an appearance.* The Hague Service Convention (like the EU Service Regulation, which adopted the Hague model), incorporates some important protections for defendants against the risk of the entry of a default judgment without proper notice of the proceedings. Article 15(1) provides that a default judgment shall not be entered until it is established that process was served by a method prescribed by the internal law of the State addressed for the service of documents in domestic actions upon persons who are within its territory, or that it was actually delivered to the defendant or to his residence by another method provided for in the Convention, in either case in sufficient time to enable the defendant to defend. By declaration under Article 15(2), Contracting States may, despite this provision, permit a judge to enter judgment, even if these conditions have not been fulfilled, provided that process was served by one of the Convention methods; not less than six months have elapsed; and every reasonable effort has been made to obtain a certificate of service.[170]

8–063   **Service under other conventions.** Although, for practical purposes, the EU Service Regulation and the Hague Service Convention now cover the majority of countries with which the United Kingdom has international arrangements for the service of process, there remains nevertheless a small number of countries where there are bilateral treaty arrangements, but the co-Contracting State is not subject to the EU Service Regulation or party to the Hague Service Convention.[171] In cases where the arrangements overlap,

---

[169] The suggestion *obiter* in *Fonexco Group Ltd v Manches* [2010] EWHC 493 (QB) that a provision of national law in the state of destination disallowing service by post could apply even where the relevant state had not notified its objection under the Convention is contrary to the principle of certainty underlying the requirement of Art.21(2)(a) (not referred to in the judgment) and should not be followed.

[170] The United Kingdom has made such a declaration. Full details of declarations made under the Hague Service Convention are maintained by the Permanent Bureau and may be accessed at the website of the Hague Conference. For practice under this provision see Hague Conference on Private International Law, *Practical Handbook on the Operation of the Hague Service Convention* (2006); McClean, *International Co-operation in Civil and Criminal Matters* (2002), pp.40–43.

[171] States with whom the United Kingdom has subsisting bilateral conventions, who are not also party to the Hague Service Convention are Algeria (2007, Cmd. 6927); Austria (1932, Cmd. 4007); Iraq (1936, Cmd. 5369); Lebanon (1922, Cmd. 1661, extended by declaration 1952); and the United Arab Emirates (2008, Cmd. 7535). In addition, Art.1(2) of Protocol 1 to the Lugano Convention permits public officers of the respective states to transmit documents for service directly between them, unless the state of destination has filed a declaration of objection. Otherwise, Art.1(1) provides that service is to be effected in accordance with procedures in conventions and agreements in force between the relevant States. The effect of Art.1(1), in the case of Switzerland, is to make service under the Hague Service Convention the mandatory method of service: *Phillips v Symes (No.3)* [2008] UKHL 1, [2008] 1 W.L.R. 180; *Bentinck v Bentinck* [2007] EWCA Civ 175, [2007] 2 F.L.R. 1.

Art.20 of the EU Service Regulation provides that it shall prevail over other provisions in bilateral or multilateral agreements or arrangements concluded by Member States, though it does not preclude Member States from maintaining or concluding agreements or arrangements to expedite further or simplify the transmission of documents, provided they are compatible with the Regulation. By contrast, Art.25 of the Hague Service Convention provides that the Convention shall not derogate from other conventions entered into by the Contracting Parties. Whilst therefore the provisions of any applicable bilateral treaty arrangement should be checked, since the majority (though not all) of the United Kingdom's bilateral treaties governing service of process originate from the early 20th century, it is unlikely that they will afford more efficient means of service of process than the EU Service Regulation or the Hague Service Convention where either of the latter are available. But they may do so, and where they do, service effected by such means will be valid.[172]

Service in the absence of treaty arrangements. Where there exists no **8–064** treaty arrangement in force with the state in which service is to be effected, and where that state is not subject to the EU Service Regulation, the following modes of service must be considered. First, as provided in Rule 22(2)(b) (CPR, r.6.40(3)(c)), service may always be effected by any method permitted by the law of the country where service is to be effected. Where service is to be effected in a Commonwealth country, the Isle of Man and the Channel Islands or in a British overseas territory, service of process may be effected by personal service.[173] That follows from the common law approach to service as being the responsibility of the parties and carries with it the further consequence that there is no objection to personal service of foreign process on the territory of Commonwealth countries. In civil law countries, however, in cases where there exists no other lawful provision for the service of foreign process, it will be necessary to effect service through diplomatic channels.[174] In such cases, there are two possibilities. First, it may be possible to serve documents through a British consular officer in the relevant country.[175] However, although this method of service is well-recognised in international law, many states (particularly civil law states) only permit such service on their territories where the defendant is a national of the originating state. Otherwise, it will be necessary to proceed by way of a letter of request issued from the English court and addressed to the judicial authorities of the state where service is to be effected.[176]

Compliance with the law in the place of service. The overriding require- **8–065** ment in effecting service of English process in a foreign country is that no

---

[172] *Debt Collection London Ltd v SK Slavia Praha-Fotbal AS* [2009] EWHC 2726, [2010] 1 All E.R. (Comm.) 902 (QB). It is not essential that such a convention has been notified to the European Commission under Art.20(3) of the EU Service Regulation for service under the convention to be valid: *ibid.* (affd. on other grounds [2010] EWCA Civ 1250, [2011] 1 W.L.R. 866).

[173] Rule 22(2)(a)(iii), CPR, r.6.42(3).

[174] Rule 22(2)(a)(iii), CPR, r.6.42(2).

[175] CPR, r.6.42(2)(b); Art.5, Vienna Convention on Consular Relations 1965 (which has the force of law in the United Kingdom pursuant to Consular Relations Act 1968, s.1(1)).

[176] CPR, r.6.42(2)(a). The procedure is set out in CPR, r.6.43.

process may be served in a manner which is contrary to the law of the country where service is to be effected.[177] However, in truly exceptional cases, the English court may take action to remedy a defect in service under the law of the country in which service was to be effected. So, in *Phillips v Symes (No.3)*,[178] where a misunderstanding caused an essential document to be omitted from a bundle of documents served in Switzerland (though a translation was included), the House of Lords held that what is now CPR, r.6.16 could be used to dispense with service, even though in that case the effect was to make the English court the one first seised for the purposes of jurisdiction under the Lugano Convention. So, too, in *Olafsson v Gissurarson (No.2)*,[179] where the claim form and associated documents were served by personal service in Iceland; they were read and understood by the addressee but Icelandic law was not complied with as he was not asked to sign a receipt for the documents. The applicable limitation period had now expired, but the Court of Appeal applied what is now CPR, r.6.16, noting that doing so would not subvert the provisions of the Convention.

8–066   **Service of foreign process in England.** There is no objection in English law to the use of the consular channel, nor to service by post. Foreign parties are also free to effect service through the agency of an English solicitor. Where the document originates in a Regulation State, the procedures will be those laid down in the Service Regulation. Where the document to be served originates in a Contracting State to the Hague Convention, the Central Authority[180] will act, and these official channels will also respond to requests under bilateral Civil Procedure Conventions or, in practice, in other cases from foreign judicial, consular or diplomatic sources.[181]

3. OBTAINING EVIDENCE ABROAD

8R–067   RULE 23—**(1) The obligations of parties to a case pending before the court in respect of disclosure and evidence are governed by the law of the forum (*lex fori*).**[182]

(2) Save in accordance with the procedures set out in clause (3) below, the court has no power to compel a third party who is outside the United Kingdom to provide evidence; nor (save in exceptional cases) will it compel a third party to produce documents which are outside the United Kingdom.[183]

---

[177] Rule 22(3), CPR, 6.40(4); *The Sky One* [1988] 1 Lloyd's Rep. 238 (CA); *Bentinck v Bentinck* [2007] EWCA Civ 175, [2007] 2 F.L.R. 1. *cf. Habib Bank Ltd v Central Bank of Sudan* [2006] EWHC 1767 (Comm.), [2007] 1 W.L.R. 470 (proper to authorise personal service in Sudan, which though not provided for in Sudanese law did not contravene that law).

[178] [2008] UKHL 1, [2008] 1 W.L.R. 180.

[179] [2008] EWCA Civ 152, [2008] 1 W.L.R. 2016.

[180] The Senior Master, Royal Courts of Justice. There are additional authorities ("other authorities" under Art.18(1)) in the various parts of the United Kingdom.

[181] For procedure, see CPR, rr.6.48 to 6.52.

[182] *The Heidberg* [1993] 2 Lloyd's Rep. 324; *Masri v Consolidated Contractors International (UK) Ltd (No.4)* [2008] EWCA Civ 876, [2010] 1 A.C. 90 (reversed [2009] UKHL 43, [2010] 1 A.C. 90, but not on this point).

[183] *Masri v Consolidated Contractors International (UK) Ltd (No.4)* [2009] UKHL 43, [2010] 1 A.C. 90; *Mackinnon v Donaldson, Lufkin & Jenrette Securities Corp* [1986] Ch. 482.

(3) Where, for the purpose of a case pending before the court, either party desires to obtain evidence abroad from a third party (whether by way of witness testimony or the production of documents), the court may:

    (a) **issue a request under Regulation (EC) 1206/2001 on co-operation between the courts of the Regulation States in the taking of evidence in civil or commercial matters ("the EU Evidence Regulation") where it applies;[184] or,**

    (b) **issue a letter of request under the Hague Convention on the Taking of Evidence Abroad in Civil and Commercial Matters 1970 ("the Hague Evidence Convention") where it applies,[185] or other convention in force; or,**

    (c) **order the taking of evidence by a diplomatic officer, consular agent, commissioner or examiner, to the extent that this is permitted by the state where the evidence is to be taken;[186] or,**

    (d) **issue a letter of request to the foreign court, to the extent that no convention is in force.[187]**

(4) Nothing in this Rule prevents a party from obtaining evidence from a third party abroad without compulsion of law, provided that this is not contrary to the law of the place where the evidence is to be obtained; or from making direct application to a foreign court for assistance, save where such application would be unconscionable.[188]

(5) The court may order the taking of evidence (but not discovery of documents) in England in aid of foreign civil proceedings at the request of a foreign court or tribunal under the Evidence (Proceedings in Other Jurisdictions) Act 1975 ("the 1975 Act").[189]

COMMENT

In countries in the common law tradition the preparation of a case for trial is   **8–068** the private responsibility of the parties. The taking of evidence by a foreign consul or commissioner for the purposes of foreign court proceedings will in such countries meet with no legal objection and require few if any preliminary

---

[184] [2001] O.J. L174/1. Full details of the implementation of the Regulation in Member States are found at: *http://ec.europa.eu/justice_home/judicialatlascivil/html/te_information_en.htm.* The Regulation does not apply to Denmark. Accordingly, as between Denmark and the other Member States, the Hague Evidence Convention applies.

[185] Cmnd. 3991. The text together with useful information about the operation of the Convention is available on the website of the Hague Conference.

[186] CPR, r.34.13(4)

[187] CPR, r.34.13(1A).

[188] *South Carolina Insurance Co v Assurantie Maatshappij "De Zeven Provincien" NV* [1987] A.C. 24; *Joyce v Sunland Waterfront (BVI) Ltd* [2011] FCAFC 95, 195 F.C.R. 213 (evidence taken voluntarily by video-link).

[189] *Re Westinghouse Uranium Contract Litigation MDL Docket No.235 (Nos 1 and 2)* [1978] A.C. 547; *State of Minnesota v Philip Morris Inc* [1998] I.L. Pr. 170 (CA); *First American Corp v Zayed* [1999] 1 W.L.R. 1154 (CA).

formalities. Many civil law countries view the obtaining of evidence as part of the judicial function, and the actions of agents of a foreign court may be seen as offending the sovereignty of the State in its judicial aspect. If evidence is to be obtained in such countries official intervention will normally be required, though bilateral and multilateral civil procedure conventions may exist to regulate and simplify the procedures.

8–069 The provisions of Rule 23 reflect these basic distinctions in approach.[190] Clause (1) deals with the obligations of the parties to English litigation, which are, in principle, governed by the *lex fori*, irrespective of whether they, or the evidence or documents in question, are located in England or abroad. By contrast, as clause (2) confirms, the powers of the English court to compel third parties to provide evidence for use in English proceedings are, in general, strictly territorially limited. As a consequence, when evidence is required from a third party outside England which cannot be obtained voluntarily, it will be necessary to use one of the methods specified in clause (3). Where the third party will provide evidence voluntarily, clause (4) confirms that such evidence may be taken in a foreign country, provided that this is not contrary to the law of that country. Alternatively, it may in some cases be possible to make direct application to the courts of the foreign country for assistance. Finally, clause (5) confirms that the English court has generous powers to assist foreign courts in the taking of evidence in England. The limits on those powers will be examined further below in the comment on that clause.

8–070 **Clause (1) of the Rule. *Lex fori* governs the parties' evidence obligations.** Clause (1) embodies the basic principle that a party to litigation in England "must play according to the local rules."[191] Thus the same obligations in relation to the disclosure of documents and evidence apply, whether the party, or the documents or evidence, are in England or abroad. Any other approach would create an unacceptable inequality of treatment as between the parties.[192] In *Masri v Consolidated Contractors International (UK) Ltd (No.4)*[193] the Court of Appeal emphasised that the EU Evidence Regulation only applies where a request is made by a court in one Member State either to take evidence in another Member State or that a court in that State should itself take evidence. An order under CPR, r.71.2 against a judgment debtor in English proceedings, requiring him to provide evidence to the English court as to nature and location of his assets, did not fall within the EU Evidence Regulation, no such request being made.

8–071 It follows that, although the court retains discretion in cases of real risk, the court will not generally excuse a party from compliance with its obligations

---

[190] See generally McClean, *International Co-operation in Civil and Criminal Matters* (2002) Chs 3, 4; McLachlan (1998) 47 I.C.L.Q. 3.

[191] *Mackinnon v Donaldson, Lufkin & Jenrette Securities Corp* [1986] Ch. 482, 494 (*per* Hoffmann J.), applied in *The Heidberg* [1993] 2 Lloyd's Rep. 324.

[192] McLachlan (1998) 47 I.C.L.Q. 3.

[193] [2008] EWCA Civ 876, [2010] 1 A.C. 90, reversed [2009] UKHL 43, [2010] 1 A.C. 90, but not on this point. See Rushworth [2009] L.M.C.L.Q. 196.

to the court on the ground that to do so would infringe foreign law or expose him to penal sanctions in a foreign country.[194]

Clause (2) of the Rule. English court's powers to compel production of   8–072
evidence from third parties territorially limited. The position in relation to the production of evidence is quite different where it is sought to compel production from persons who are not parties to the litigation. In that event, the court is exercising a purely enforcement jurisdiction. As such, its powers are (save in wholly exceptional circumstances) limited to persons who are within the court's territorial jurisdiction. In *Masri v Consolidated Contractors International (UK) Ltd (No.4)*[195] the House of Lords confirmed that the service of a writ of subpoena under s.36 of the Senior Courts Act 1981 was only possible in respect of persons in one of the parts of the United Kingdom. No rule of court could require an ordinary witness outside the jurisdiction to attend for examination within the jurisdiction. The House examined the scope of CPR, r.71.2 which enables a judgment creditor to apply for an order requiring a judgment debtor, or if a judgment debtor is a company or other corporation, an officer of that body, to attend court to provide information about the judgment debtor's means or other matters needed for the enforcement of a judgment or order. Distinguishing *Re Seagull Manufacturing Co Ltd*[196] the House held that an order under CPR, r.71.2 could not be made against third parties abroad (including the non-resident officers of a corporation). Its scope was, however, not limited to assets within the jurisdiction.

Further, the use of a witness summons for the production of documents   8–073
abroad, even if served on a person within the jurisdiction,[197] or the making of an order for the inspection of books under s.7 of the Bankers' Books Evidence Act 1879[198] in respect of such documents, is an infringement of the sovereignty of the foreign State, which can only be justified in exceptional cases of urgent necessity.[199] The same principles apply where the English court is asked to make an order for disclosure of documents against someone who is joined as a defendant solely for that purpose,[200] since, although in form this

---

[194] *Morris v Banque Arabe et Internationale d'Investissement SA* [2001] I.L.Pr. 37; *Masri v Consolidated Contractors International Co SAL* [2008] EWHC 2492 (Comm.); *Masri v Consolidated Contractors International Co SAL* [2011] EWHC 409 (Comm.), reversed in part [2011] EWCA Civ 746 but not on this point; *Michael Wilson & Partners Ltd v Nicholls* [2008] NSWSC 1230, (2008) 74 N.S.W.L.R. 218. The same principle is enunciated in *Brannigan v Davison* [1997] A.C. 238 (PC) and *Spencer v The Queen* [1985] 2 S.C.R. 278 (public law cases).

[195] [2009] UKHL 43, [2010] 1 A.C. 90.

[196] [1993] Ch. 345 (CA) (public examination of a company director on an insolvency). An order under s.236 Insolvency Act 1986 may be made in respect of documents located abroad, since this is expressly authorised by Parliament, and the courts will not therefore require proof of exceptional circumstances: *Re Mid East Trading Ltd* [1998] 1 All E.R. 577 (CA).

[197] CPR, r.34.2(1)(b).

[198] *Mackinnon v Donaldson, Lufkin & Jenrette Securities Corp* [1986] Ch. 482.

[199] *London and Counties Securities Ltd v Caplan* (unreported, May 26, 1978); *R. v Grossman* (1981) 73 Cr.App.R. 302 (CA).

[200] Under the principle in *Norwich Pharmacal Co v Customs and Excise Commissioners* [1974] A.C. 133 and *Bankers Trust Co v Shapira* [1980] 1 W.L.R. 1274 (CA). See *Mercantile Group (Europe) AG v Aiyela* [1994] Q.B. 366 (CA).

involves disclosure by a party, in substance it is an order against a third party.[201]

8–074   **Clause (3) of the Rule. Judicial assistance in obtaining evidence abroad from third parties.** Where it is necessary to obtain evidence under compulsion from a third party who is outside the jurisdiction, it will be necessary to seek international judicial assistance. Clause (3) of the Rule enumerates the various arrangements pursuant to which such assistance may be obtained. Those are: (a) the EU Evidence Regulation, where the evidence is sought from a Member State; (b) the Hague Evidence Convention, where the evidence is sought from a Contracting State; (c) the taking of evidence before a British consular officer or an examiner appointed by the court, to the extent that this is permitted by the state where the evidence is to be given; and, failing all of the above, (d) the issue of a letter of request seeking the assistance of the foreign court.

8–075   **EU Evidence Regulation.** The taking of evidence in other Member States of the European Union (other than Denmark) is facilitated by Council Regulation (EC) 1206/2001 of May 28, 2001 on co-operation between the courts of the Member States in the taking of evidence in civil or commercial matters ("the EU Evidence Regulation"),[202] which came into force on January 1, 2004. The EU Evidence Regulation builds on the Hague Convention of 1970, a major difference being that the Regulation provides for the direct transmission of requests from court to court, dispensing with the device of Central Authorities, though preserving a limited role for what are termed "central bodies".[203] The EU Evidence Regulation prevails over other provisions contained in bilateral or multilateral agreements or arrangements concluded by the Member States and in particular the Hague Convention.[204] The EU Evidence Regulation applies in civil or commercial matters where the court of a Member State, in accordance with the provisions of the law of that State, requests (a) the competent court of another Member State to take evidence; or (b) to take evidence directly in another Member State.[205] A request may not be made to obtain evidence which is not intended for use in judicial proceedings, commenced or contemplated.[206] Requests are to be transmitted by the

---

[201] *Mackinnon v Donaldson, Lufkin & Jenrette Securities Corp* [1986] Ch. 482. *cf. Fusco v O'Dea* [1994] 2 I.L.R.M. 389 (Sup Ct).

[202] [2001] O.J. L174. A Manual containing comprehensive information about procedures under the Regulation in each Member State is to be found on the website of the European Judicial Network. For the procedure for taking evidence in England, see CPR, r.34.24.

[203] Art.3.

[204] Art.21(1).

[205] Art.1(1). In Case C–175/06 *Tedesco v Tomasoni Fittings SrL* [2007] E.C.R. I–07929 (later removed from court register), Kokott A-G delivered an opinion on July 18, 2007 to the effect that measures for the preservation and collection of evidence (such as seizure of counterfeit goods under the Italian Industrial Property Code) constituted a request for the taking of evidence coming within the scope of Art.1, which the competent court of a Regulation State must execute at the request of a court from another Regulation State. On the question whether the Regulation is the exclusive means of obtaining evidence between Regulation States see Nuyts, 2007 *Rev. Crit.* 53.

[206] Art.1(2); *Dendron GmbH v Regents of the University of California* [2004] EWHC 589 (Ch.), [2005] 1 W.L.R. 200.

court before which the proceedings are commenced or contemplated, "the requesting court", directly to the competent court of another Member State, "the requested court", for the taking of evidence.[207] Each Member State specifies the courts competent for the performance of taking of evidence under the Regulation, indicating the territorial and, where appropriate, the special jurisdiction of those courts.[208]

The EU Evidence Regulation contains an Annex of Forms which specify the detailed information to be provided.[209] Requests and other communications sent under the Regulation must be in the official language of the requested State or, if there are several official languages in that State, in the official language or one of the official languages of the place where the requested taking of evidence is to be performed, or in another language which the requested State has indicated it can accept.[210] Requests and other communications are to be transmitted by the swiftest possible means which the requested State has indicated it can accept: in many cases this will include electronic means. The only essential requirement is that the document is received accurately, reflects the content of the document forwarded and that all information in it is legible.[211]

8–076

A request for the taking of evidence by the requested court must be executed without delay and, at the latest, within 90 days of receipt of the request.[212] The requested court is to execute the request in accordance with the law of its Member State.[213] If, however, the requesting court asks for the request to be executed in accordance with a special procedure provided for by the law of its Member State, the requested court must comply unless the special procedure is incompatible with the law of the Member State of the requested court or major practical difficulties prevent compliance.[214] Similar provisions apply where the requesting court asks the requested court to use communications technology at the performance of the taking of evidence, in particular by using videoconferencing or teleconferencing.[215] Charges are payable only in special circumstances, e.g. involving a special procedure, expert evidence, or the use of communications technology.[216] Where necessary, in executing a request the requested court is to apply the appropriate coercive measures in the instances and to the extent as are provided for by the law of the requested State for the execution of a request made for the same purpose by its national authorities or one of the parties.[217] If the requested court is not in a position to execute the request within 90 days of receipt, it must inform the requesting court, giving reasons.[218]

8–077

---

[207] Art.2(1).

[208] Art.2(2). In England, these are the Foreign Process Section of the Royal Courts of Justice and courts in Birmingham, Bristol, Cardiff, Leeds and Manchester.

[209] See also Art.4(1).

[210] Art.5.

[211] Art.6.

[212] Art.10(1). For the presence and participation of the parties and representatives of the requesting court, see Arts 11, 12.

[213] Art.10(2).

[214] Art.10(3).

[215] Art.10(4).

[216] Art.18.

[217] Art.13.

[218] Art.15.

8–078   Where the request involves testimony by a witness, it is not to be executed when the person concerned claims the right to refuse to give evidence or to be prohibited from giving evidence (a) under the law of the requested State; or (b) under the law of the requesting State, where that right has been specified in the request, or, if need be, at the instance of the requested court, has been confirmed by the requesting court.[219] The only other grounds on which the execution of a request may be refused are that (a) the request does not fall within the scope of the EU Evidence Regulation; or (b) the execution of the request under the law of the requested State does not fall within the functions of the judiciary; or (c) the requesting court fails to repair the omissions in an incomplete request within 30 days of being asked to do so; or (d) a deposit or advance in respect of expert evidence is not made within 60 days after the requested court has requested one.[220] (No deposit or advance may be required for the taking of ordinary witness evidence[221]). Execution may not be refused by the requested court solely on the ground that under the law of the requested State a court of that State has exclusive jurisdiction over the subject matter of the action or that the law of that State would not admit the right of action on it.[222]

8–079   The EU Evidence Regulation includes novel provisions as to the taking by the requesting court itself of evidence on the territory of another Member State.[223] In this type of case, the request is submitted to the designated central body of the requested State. The direct taking of evidence may only take place if it can be performed on a voluntary basis without the need for coercive measures.

8–080   **The Hague Evidence Convention.** Where the EU Evidence Convention does not apply, the major international convention for the taking of evidence abroad is the Hague Evidence Convention. The United Kingdom is one of more than 50 Contracting States to this Convention. Other Contracting States outside the European Union include many of the United Kingdom's major trading partners, including China, India, Russia and the United States.[224] The Hague Evidence Convention establishes a clear and centralised mechanism for the provision of international judicial assistance in the taking of evidence abroad. Chapter I of the Convention is concerned with the Letters of Request procedure and applies to Letters issued by the judicial authorities of a Contracting State in civil or commercial matters to obtain evidence intended for use in judicial proceedings, commenced or contemplated.[225] The request can cover a variety of forms of evidence, including oral testimony and the

---

[219] Art.14(1).
[220] Art.14(2).
[221] Art.18(3); Case C–283/09 *Werynski v Mediatel 4B spólka z o.o.* [2011] 2 W.L.R. 1316.
[222] Art.14(4).
[223] Art.17.
[224] Full details of the Contracting States may be found on the website of the Hague Conference.
[225] Art.1. Private arbitral tribunals are not included: *Commerce and Industry Insurance Co of Canada v Certain Underwriters at Lloyd's of London* [2002] 1 W.L.R. 1323.

inspection of documents or other property,[226] and is sent to a Central Authority designated for the purposes of the Convention in the country in which the evidence is to be taken.[227] The Convention does not exclude the use of other methods of obtaining evidence provided for under the national law of the State in which the evidence is sought.[228]

Non-exclusive character. In *Société Nationale Industrielle Aérospatiale v US District Court for the Southern District of Iowa*[229] the United States Supreme Court held that the Hague Convention does not provide an exclusive or mandatory set of procedures, nor even a preferred set of procedures to which first resort must always be had. The court did, however, recognise the need for considerations of comity to be addressed before orders were made which would be regarded by the foreign State concerned as an infringement of its sovereignty.[230] The English court has taken a similar approach, confirming an order for discovery against a French company despite an argument that first resort should have been had either to the Hague Convention or to the bilateral Civil Procedure Convention between the United Kingdom and France.[231] The Contracting States have not been able to reach a consensus on the question whether the Convention has a mandatory character.[232]   **8–081**

Application to discovery. Under Art.23 of the Convention, inserted at the proposal of the United Kingdom, a reservation is permitted. A Contracting State may declare "that it will not execute Letters of Request issued for the purpose of obtaining pre-trial discovery of documents as known in Common Law countries." It is now recognised amongst delegates at the Hague Conference that this Article was poorly drafted. It also seems that the authors of the Convention failed to address important questions as to the relationship between a reservation under Art.23 and the primary provisions of the Convention which is concerned with "evidence" and "other judicial acts," concepts which few of the signatory States would regard as including the more extensive forms of discovery procedures. The phrase "pre-trial discovery of documents as known in Common Law countries" obscures significant differences   **8–082**

---

[226] See Art.3(1)(f)(g). The appointment of a technical expert to assist the court is not within the scope of the Hague Convention: *Sté Luxguard v Sté SN Sitaco* [1996] I.L.Pr. 5 (Cr d'app., Versailles, 1993) (exploring relationship between that Convention and Brussels Convention of 1968). A Special Commission of the Hague Conference on Private International Law of February 2009 took the view (at para.55) that the use of video conferencing was consistent with the provisions of The Hague Evidence Convention (but *cf.* Davis (2007) 55 Am. J. Comp. L. 205).

[227] In the UK, as in most countries, the Central Authority and other relevant authorities are the same as those acting in respect of the Hague Service Convention.

[228] Art.27(c).

[229] 482 U.S. 522 (1987).

[230] See Slomanson (1988) 37 I.C.L.Q. 391; Born and Hoing (1990) 24 Int.L. 393; McClean, *International Co-operation in Civil and Criminal Matters* (2002), pp.133–143.

[231] *The Heidberg* [1993] 2 Lloyd's Rep. 324.

[232] Hague Conference on Private International Law, *The mandatory/non-mandatory character of the Evidence Convention* (Prel. Doc. No.10, December 2008); Conclusions and Recommendations of the Special Commission (February 2009), para.53.

between the procedures available in countries following the practice contained in what is now Pt 31 of the Civil Procedure Rules 1998 and the much more extensive procedures available in many jurisdictions in the United States which can include wide-ranging requests for non-parties to the action to make oral depositions or to produce documents[233] which may not necessarily be relevant to the issues but could possibly assist the plaintiff to formulate allegations against the defendant. The United Kingdom's reservation under Art.23 contains a statement of its intended scope, which is reflected in the Evidence (Proceedings in Other Jurisdictions) Act 1975.[234] A number of other Contracting States have revised their own reservations to incorporate this statement.[235]

8-083 *Taking evidence in Hague Convention countries by other means.* Chapter II of the Convention is concerned with the Taking of Evidence by Diplomatic Officers, Consular Agents and Commissioners. Diplomatic agents and consular officers may take the evidence of nationals of the State they represent without seeking prior permission from the authorities of the State in which they serve; a Contracting State may however declare that prior permission is required in these cases.[236] Where diplomats or consuls wish to take the evidence of other persons, or where a commissioner is appointed to take any evidence, prior permission is required (and may be given subject to conditions) unless the Contracting State concerned has made a declaration waiving this requirement.[237] A Contracting State may declare its willingness to make available appropriate assistance to obtain the evidence by compulsion in any of these cases.[238]

8-084 **Taking evidence under bilateral conventions.** In addition to the above multilateral arrangements, the United Kingdom has also concluded bilateral civil procedure conventions with a number of countries, which deal inter alia with the taking of evidence.[239] In the light of the overriding character of the EU Evidence Regulation as between Member States,[240] those bilateral conventions with continuing relevance for the taking of evidence abroad will be

---

[233] And, indeed, other forms of information; Art.23 refers only to the discovery *of documents.*

[234] s.2(4): see below, para.8–103.

[235] See Collins (1986) 35 I.C.L.Q. 765 (reprinted in Collins, *Essays*, p.289) and the Report of the Special Commission of the Hague Conference on the operation of the Convention, *Actes et Documents* of the Fourteenth Session, 420–1. A Special Commission of the Hague Conference on Private International Law in 2009 recommended (at para.51) that States which have made a general, non-particularised declaration under Art.23 revisit their declaration taking into account terms such as those contained in the United Kingdom declaration or in Art.16 of the Additional Protocol of 1984 to the Inter-American Convention on the Taking of Evidence Abroad.

[236] Art.15.

[237] Arts 16, 17.

[238] Art.18.

[239] A list of these conventions in force is maintained by the Foreign & Commonwealth Office: *http://www.fco.gov.uk/en/publications-and-documents/treaties/lists-treaties/bilateral-civil-procedure.*

[240] para.8–075 above.

those with non-Member States, where either the requested state is not party to the Hague Evidence Convention or where the bilateral convention provides enhanced means for the taking of evidence abroad. Many of the bilateral conventions provide for the taking of evidence by consular agent or special examiner in addition to the use of the letter of request procedure, procedures which can present substantial practical advantages.[241]

Obtaining evidence abroad by other means. Even in those cases in which neither the EU Evidence Regulation nor the Hague Evidence Convention is applicable, English law makes ample provision enabling parties to English proceedings to obtain evidence abroad. The powers given are exercised with the greatest discretion,[242] partly because of the sensitivities of other countries but also to avoid unnecessary expense, delay and inconvenience. For these reasons the English courts are reluctant to grant applications by a claimant (who has chosen to sue in England) for evidence, especially his own evidence, to be taken abroad.[243] In appropriate circumstances, however, the court will exercise its powers. For example, in *News International Plc v Clinger*,[244] an order was made on the plaintiff's application for cross-examination of a defendant before an examiner (the judge himself) in Israel in support of a freezing injunction. The taking of evidence before an examiner was allowed by the terms of the relevant bilateral civil procedure convention, and it was held that this included evidence on an interlocutory issue.[245] **8–085**

The same reluctance will not be applied on a defendant's application. There may be circumstances in which, while England is an appropriate forum, the practical realities are such that unless the defendant can give evidence abroad he will be unable to defend the action. To avoid such oppression and unfairness, the court will exercise its powers to enable the evidence to be taken abroad.[246] **8–086**

Depositions abroad. The court will require to be satisfied that the witness cannot attend for examination in England, as a result of proven ill-health[247] or, in some cases, the disproportionate cost of travel,[248] and that the witness has **8–087**

---

[241] An analytical table of the procedures provided under bilateral conventions is at McClean *op. cit.*, p.106. Since 2002, the United Kingdom has also concluded bilateral civil procedure conventions with Algeria (2006, Cmd.6927) and the United Arab Emirates (2006, Cmd.7535), neither of which states are yet party to the Hague Evidence Convention, providing for the taking of evidence under letter of request only. For an example of a case where the relevant bilateral convention provided for the taking of evidence by special examiner see *News International Plc v Clinger*, unreported, August 16, 1996, Ch. D.

[242] *Settebello Ltd v Banco Totta & Acores* [1985] 1 W.L.R. 1050 (CA).

[243] e.g. *Berdan v Greenwood* (1880) 20 Ch.D. 764n. (CA), stated as Illustration 8, below.

[244] unreported, August 16, 1996, Ch.D.

[245] The defendant's attendance would be voluntary, despite the fact that his failure to attend would mean that his affidavit evidence would not be used in evidence under CPR, r.32.7.

[246] *Ross v Woodford* [1894] 1 Ch. 38, stated as Illustration 9, para.8–120, below. *cf. Re A Debtor (No.2283 of 1976)* [1979] 1 All E.R. 434 (CA).

[247] *Berdan v Greenwood*, above; *Haynes v Haynes* (1962) 35 D.L.R. (2d) 602 (BC).

[248] *Wong Doo v Kana Bhana* [1973] N.Z.L.R. 1455 (CA).

material evidence to give.[249] Where the credibility of the witness is especially important, and particularly where there is an issue as to his identity,[250] the court will not make an order depriving the claimant of the opportunity to test the evidence by cross-examination in open court.[251]

8–088 The court acts under its general power to order depositions to be taken before an examiner, with appropriate disclosure of documents before the examination takes place.[252] A number of different procedures are available when the person to be examined is out of the jurisdiction. That most generally available involves the issue of a Letter of Request to the judicial authorities of the foreign country asking the foreign court to take or cause to be taken the required evidence. The Letter may be accompanied by interrogatories and may request that cross-examination be permitted. A second procedure entails the appointment of a special examiner to take the evidence abroad; this is only available if the government of the foreign country allows such examinations,[253] and only a few States will make available the assistance of their courts to grant measures of compulsion should the witness be unwilling to appear before the examiner. Finally, a British consul may be appointed to act as a special examiner, either in accordance with a Civil Procedure Convention with the relevant foreign country or with the consent of the Foreign Secretary.[254] Where a person is to have his evidence taken outside the jurisdiction, he may be examined on oath or affirmation or otherwise in accordance with the procedure of the country where the examination is to take place.[255] Although the court normally acts under what was Order 39 of the Rules of the Supreme Court,[256] and is now Rule 34.13 of the Civil Procedure Rules 1998, the power to issue a Letter of Request derives from the inherent jurisdiction. So, for example, even if no order could be made to require a company to produce documents (because any such order must be part of one for the examination of a witness and a company cannot attend to give oral evidence), the court had power to make whatever *request* of a foreign court (which did not involve the making of an *order*) was desirable in the interests of justice and to which the foreign court would be likely to be receptive (e.g. because the request came within the broad terms of the Hague Convention, in which "evidence" is not defined).

8–089 In exercising its discretion, an English court will issue a Letter of Request seeking to have a person not a party to the proceedings produce documents or give oral evidence abroad only in circumstances in which the person concerned would have been required to do so in England; and the principles

---

[249] *Hardie Rubber Co Pty Ltd v General Tire and Rubber Co* (1973) 129 C.L.R. 521; *Lucas Industries Ltd v Chloride Batteries Australia Ltd* (1978) 45 F.L.R. 160. *cf. Ehrmann v Ehrmann* [1896] 2 Ch. 611 (CA) (insufficient that evidence would "bolster" other evidence).

[250] *Nadin v Bassett* (1884) 25 Ch.D. 21 (CA).

[251] *Hardie Rubber Co Pty Ltd v General Tire and Rubber Co* (1973) 129 C.L.R. 521 (difficulties of conducting cross-examination in Japan). In particular circumstances, the English judge may appoint himself as special examiner to hear evidence abroad: *Peer International Corp v Termidor Music Publishers Ltd* [2005] EWHC 1048 (Ch.).

[252] CPR, r.34.8.

[253] CPR, r.34.13(4). CPR, r.34.13 does not apply if the proposed deponent is in another Member State.

[254] CPR, r.PD34A, para.5.8.

[255] CPR, r.34.13(5).

[256] *Panayiotou v Sony Music Entertainment (UK) Ltd* [1994] Ch. 142.

governing the issue of an outgoing Letter of Request are the same as those governing the giving of effect to an incoming request.[257]

Intra-United Kingdom requests. Where evidence is to be obtained from **8–090** another part of the United Kingdom, the same procedures are available as in the case of a politically foreign country. The sensitivities surrounding the issue of state sovereignty are, of course, absent but the English court will nonetheless exercise care before approving an order. So, when a Letter of Request is to be addressed to a court in another part of the United Kingdom, the English court as the requesting court will itself examine the proposed request to see if it is one which meets the requirements of the requested court[258] such as those laid down by the House of Lords in *Re Westinghouse Uranium Contract Litigation MDL Docket No.235.*[259]

Clause (4) of the Rule. Obtaining evidence directly in a foreign country. **8–091** It is a principle of English civil procedure that a party obtains by his own means the evidence he needs to support his case. The means used may include the taking in foreign countries of any steps which may lawfully be taken there.[260] This may include the making of a direct application to a foreign court for a procedural remedy available under the law of that court, for example an extensive order for discovery which a United States court may make under its own procedural rules even if the evidence is intended for use in English proceedings.[261] However the English court may restrain the use of foreign procedures where their use would be unconscionable, as where it was proposed to take pre-trial depositions from persons whom it was proposed to call (and who were willing to act) as witnesses in the English trial.[262] United States courts may assist litigants in cases before foreign tribunals by ordering discovery under a federal statutory provision[263] which enables a district court to order a person living within its district to give his testimony or statement or to produce a document or other thing for use in a proceeding in a foreign or international tribunal.[264] The order may be made not only in response to a request made by such a tribunal but also on the application of any interested

---

[257] *Panayiotou v Sony Music Entertainment (UK) Ltd* [1994] Ch. 142; *Charman v Charman* [2005] EWCA Civ 1606, [2006] 1 W.L.R. 1053. However, in the context of ancillary relief in divorce proceedings, the court may issue a Letter of Request in respect of "conjectural" documents: *ibid.* See also *Mackinnon v Donaldson, Lufkin and Jenrette Securities Corp* [1986] Ch. 482; *Re Mid East Trading Ltd* [1998] 1 All E.R. 577 (CA).

[258] *Stewart v Callaghan*, 1996 S.L.T. (Sh Ct) 12.

[259] [1978] A.C. 547 (see below, para. 8–105).

[260] *Joyce v Sunland Waterfront (BVI) Ltd* [2011] FCAFC 95, 195 F.C.R. 213, permitting the taking of evidence voluntarily by video-link from a witness in the UAE, where the evidence was the that such a mode of evidence collection in aid of foreign proceedings was not unlawful there and the s.47A Federal Court of Australia Act 1976 (Cth) expressly contemplated the taking of evidence abroad by this means.

[261] *South Carolina Insurance Co v Assurantie Maatschappij "De Zeven Provincien" NV* [1987] A.C. 24.

[262] *Omega Croup Holdings Ltd v Kozeny* [2002] C.L.C. 132.

[263] 28 U.S.C., s.1782.

[264] *Euromepa SA v R. Esmerian Inc*, 154 F. 3d 24 (2d Cir. 1998) (no likelihood of evidence being used in foreign jurisdiction; assistance refused); *Intel Corp v Advanced Micro Devices Inc*, 542 U.S. 241 (2004) (European Commission a "tribunal" when adjudicating).

person.[265] This power may be exercised even where the material sought is not discoverable under the law of the foreign jurisdiction.[266] No prior application to the foreign court is required,[267] but the court will guard against applications which would cause offence to the foreign court[268] or are vehicles for harassment.[269] This power is not intended to provide discovery of documents maintained within the foreign forum.[270] There is no settled position on whether it applies to arbitration proceedings.[271] The English court will not restrain a party from taking such steps in a foreign country unless they amount to unconscionable conduct interfering with the due process of the English court or invade the legal or equitable rights of another party.[272]

8–092 As between the different parts of the United Kingdom, the same principles no doubt obtain, but the requested court might well give closer attention to the question whether a similar remedy were available in the part in which the principal action was to be heard. So, in ordering disclosure of documents in Scotland to assist a party to an English patent action, the Inner House of the Court of Session noted that it might not serve the ends of justice to do what would not be done by the court in which the main proceedings were in train.[273]

8–093 **Clause (5) of the Rule. Obtaining evidence in England for use in another jurisdiction.** In many cases it is possible for evidence to be taken in England for use in foreign proceedings. This may occur with or without the involvement of the authorities of this country.

8–094 *Taking evidence without the assistance of the English court.* There is no objection in English law to the taking of evidence required for use in foreign proceedings without the intervention or permission of an English court or official agency. Such intervention will be required if measures of compulsion are required against an unwilling witness. However, the oath may only be administered in England with lawful authority. A person appointed by a court or other judicial authority of a foreign country does have power to administer oaths in the United Kingdom for the purpose of taking evidence in civil

---

[265] *Intel Corp v Advanced Micro Devices Inc*, 542 U.S. 241 (2004).

[266] *Intel Corp v Advanced Micro Devices Inc*, 542 U.S. 241 (2004).

[267] *Re Application of Malev Hungarian Airlines*, 964 F. 2d 97 (2d Cir. 1992), cert. den. sub nom. *United Technologies International v Malev Hungarian Airlines*, 506 U.S. 861 (1992).

[268] *Re Application of Bayer AG*, 146 F. 3d 188 (3d Cir. 1998).

[269] *Re Request for Assistance from Ministry of Legal Affairs of Trinidad and Tobago*, 848 F. 2d 1151 (11th Cir. 1988).

[270] *Re Application of Sarrio SA for Assistance before Foreign Tribunal* [1996] I.L.Pr. 564 (S.D.N.Y. 1995) (but point reserved on appeal: 119 F. 3d 143 (2d Cir. 1997)); *Four Pillars Enterprises Co v Avery Dennison Corp*, 308 F.3d 1075, 1079–80 (9th Cir. 2002) (also inconclusive).

[271] *National Broadcasting Co v Bear Stearns & Co*, 165 F. 3d 184 (2d Cir. 1999); *Re Norfolk Southern Corp*, 626 F. Supp. 2d 882 (N.D. III 2009) (*contra*); *cf. Re Babcock Borsig AG*, 583 F. Supp. 2d 233 (D. Mass. 2008) (*pro*). See Fellas (2007) 23 Arb.Int. 379; Knöfel (2009) 5 J. Priv. Int. L. 281; Beale, Lugar & Schwarz (2011) 47 Stanford J.I.L. 51.

[272] *South Carolina Insurance Co v Assurantie Maatshappij "De Zeven Provincien" NV* [1987] A.C. 24.

[273] *Union Carbide Corp v BP Chemicals Ltd*, 1995 S.L.T. 972.

proceedings carried on under the law of that foreign country,[274] and a foreign diplomatic agent or consular officer has a general power to administer oaths in accordance with the law of the country he represents.[275]

Taking evidence by order of the High Court. The High Court may order the **8–095** taking of evidence in England at the request of a foreign court or tribunal under the Evidence (Proceedings in Other Jurisdictions) Act 1975.[276] There is no inherent jurisdiction; the only powers available to the courts in this context are those set out in the Act.[277] Within the limits set by the Act, "it is the duty and pleasure of the [English] court to give all such assistance as it can to the requesting court".[278] Although the Act was passed to enable the United Kingdom to ratify the Hague Convention on the Taking of Evidence Abroad in Civil or Commercial Matters 1970, it does not reproduce the provisions of the Convention. The Act contains additional material, notably in relation to criminal proceedings,[279] and is drafted so as to apply to all requests for assistance whether or not made under the Convention.

The requirements of the Act in cases concerning foreign civil proceedings **8–096** are as follows. When an application is made to the High Court under the Act,[280] the court must be satisfied that the application is made in pursuance of a request issued by or on behalf of a court or tribunal exercising jurisdiction in another part of the United Kingdom or in a country or territory outside the United Kingdom,[281] or by the European Court.[282] The court must be satisfied that the evidence is to be obtained for the purposes of civil proceedings which have either been instituted before the requesting court or whose institution before that court is contemplated.[283] The request will be refused where the foreign proceedings have been settled or discontinued.[284] The court may not order any steps to be taken unless they are steps which could be required to be taken by way of obtaining evidence for the purposes of civil proceedings in the English court.[285]

Civil proceedings. For this purpose, "civil proceedings" includes all the **8–097** procedural steps taken in the course of the proceedings from their institution up to and including their completion, including, if the procedural system of

---

[274] Oaths and Evidence (Overseas Authorities and Countries) Act 1963, s.1.

[275] Consular Relations Act 1968, s.10(1).

[276] For procedure see CPR, rr.34.16–34.21.

[277] *Boeing Co v PPG Industries Inc* [1988] 3 All E.R. 839 (CA); *Re Pan American Airways Inc's Application* [1992] Q.B. 854 (CA).

[278] *United States of America v Philip Morris Inc* [2004] EWCA Civ 330 at [16]; *Re Westinghouse Uranium Contract Litigation MDL Docket No.235* [1978] A.C. 547 (CA and HL), especially *per* Lord Denning at 560; *Securities and Exchange Commission v Credit Bancorp*, unreported, Q.B.D., February 20, 2001; *Genira Trade & Finance Inc v Refco Capital Markets Ltd* [2001] EWCA Civ 1733; *Gredd v Arpad Busson* [2003] EWHC 3001 (QB); *British America Tobacco Australia Services Ltd v Eubanks* [2004] NSWCA 158, (2004) 60 N.S.W.L.R. 483.

[279] Now contained in the Crime (International Co-operation) Act 2003.

[280] See CPR PD34A, para.6.

[281] s.1(a).

[282] Evidence (European Court) Order 1976 (SI 1976/428) made under s.6 of the Act.

[283] s.1(b).

[284] *Re International Power Industries Inc* [1985] B.C.L.C. 128.

[285] s.2(3).

the requesting court provides for such procedures, the examination of witnesses or the production of documents for the purpose of enabling a party to ascertain whether there exists admissible evidence to support his own case or to contradict that of his opponent. The power of the High Court to make orders in respect of pre-trial phases of foreign litigation is, however, limited by the other provisions of the Act.[286] In the absence of evidence to the contrary, the High Court will accept the statement by the requesting court as to the nature of the proceedings.[287]

8–098   The civil proceedings have to be "proceedings in any civil or commercial matter."[288] Given that there is in this context no internationally acceptable definition of a "civil or commercial matter," the English court must satisfy itself that the proceedings concern a civil or commercial matter under the laws of both the requesting and requested countries.[289] For the purposes of English law, "proceedings in any civil matter" includes all proceedings other than criminal proceedings, and "proceedings in any commercial matter" fall within "proceedings in any civil matter." So far as the law of a requesting country is concerned, reference is to be made to the law and practice of that country, having regard to the manner in which classification is ordinarily made in that country.[290] This approach may be contrasted with that taken by a Special Commission of the Hague Conference in April 1989, that it was desirable that the words "civil and commercial" should be interpreted in an autonomous manner, without reference exclusively either to the law of the requesting country or to the law of the requested country, or to both laws cumulatively. The Commission recognised that there existed in international practice a "grey area" between private and public law. Developments in practice had led bankruptcy, insurance and employment to be treated as within "civil and commercial matters" but most countries excluded tax matters.[291] In English law, fiscal matters are properly within the category of "civil and commercial," and a request by a foreign country for assistance in obtaining evidence to be used in the enforcement of revenue law of that country in proceedings before the courts of that country does not constitute direct or indirect enforcement of the revenue law of a foreign State.[292]

8–099   *Evidence.* The Act is concerned with the process by which "evidence" is to be obtained. It has already been noted that few of the authors of the Hague Convention would regard the term "evidence" as including all the material capable of being gathered in the extensive forms of pre-trial discovery found

---

[286] See s.2; *Re Westinghouse Uranium Contract Litigation MDL Docket No.235* [1978] A.C. 547, 633–4.

[287] *ibid.*, at p.634.

[288] s.9(1).

[289] *Re State of Norway's Application (Nos. 1 and 2)* [1990] 1 A.C. 723, where the history of UK legislation since the Foreign Tribunals Evidence Act 1856 is examined. See F.A. Mann (1989) 105 L.Q.R. 341.

[290] *ibid.*

[291] See the Report of the Work of the Commission, pp.26–27, noted F.A. Mann (1990) 106 L.Q.R. 354 (but *quaere* whether Mann is justified in describing the opinion of the 1989 Special Commission as an "authentic interpretation"). *cf.* Szladits, "Structure and the Divisions of the Law," *Int.Encyc.Comp. L.*, Vol.II, Ch.2, discussed in *Re State of Norway's Application (Nos 1 and 2)*, above, and Lipstein (1990) 39 I.C.L.Q. 120.

[292] *Re State of Norway's Application (Nos 1 and 2)* [1990] 1 A.C. 723; *cf.* Rule 3(1).

in United States jurisdictions. A Letter of Request seeking such material may be seeking both evidence, which would be admissible at trial, and other material which though relevant to issues in the case would be inadmissible as evidence. This distinction is related to that drawn in cases under earlier legislation[293] between "direct" evidence and "indirect" material sought by way of discovery. The English court can only order the taking of evidence, and must decline to assist a foreign court if its Letter of Request is solely seeking material of the "indirect" variety.[294] The issue whether the order sought is for an illegitimate investigation rather than to obtain evidence to be adduced at trial is to be determined principally by reference to the terms of the letter of request, but the court will consider the evidence before it as a whole. Particularly pertinent will be the stage at which the order is sought and the extent to which the party seeking the order is able to demonstrate that the information sought is relevant to issues in the foreign proceedings in the sense of being capable of being adduced at trial in support of those issues; statements in a letter of request to the effect that evidence is sought for use at trial are relevant but not conclusive. In the case of requests emanating from the United States, the court will take into account anything in the evidence before it that indicates that the party that obtained the order for the letter of request and the judge in the United States who authorised the issue of the letter of request appreciated and took into account the differences between United States and English procedural rules.[295]

The English courts are, however, anxious to assist foreign courts wherever possible, and in *State of Minnesota v Philip Morris Inc*,[296] Lord Woolf M.R. indicated that the benefit of any doubt should be given to the applicant; in that case the breadth of the proposed questioning made the Letter of Request irremediable. The judge at first instance had made an order with a limitation that the scope of the questioning was to be limited "only to elicit evidence admissible at trial", and Scottish courts have followed a similar practice where this would enable the request to be accepted.[297] This practice was fully

8–100

---

[293] i.e. the Foreign Tribunals Evidence Act 1856 (which remains in force in some Commonwealth jurisdictions): *Burchard v Macfarlane* [1891] 2 Q.B. 241 (CA); *Radio Corp of America v Rauland Corp* [1956] 1 Q.B. 618; *Re Scholnick and Bank of Nova Scotia* (1987) 59 O.R. (2d) 538.

[294] *Re Westinghouse Uranium Contract Litigation MDL Docket No.235* [1978] A.C. 547 at p.610; *Lord Advocate, Ptr*, 1998 S.C. 87.

[295] *Genira Trade & Finance Inc v Refco Capital Markets Ltd* [2001] EWCA Civ 1733, [2002] C.L.C. 301; *Gredd v Arpad Busson* [2003] EWHC 3001 (QB), followed in *British American Tobacco Australia Services Ltd v Eubanks* [2004] NSWCA 158, (2004) 60 N.S.W.L.R. 483. In Canada, the courts will scrutinise the foreign request in order to be satisfied that the evidence requested is relevant, necessary, not otherwise obtainable, not contrary to public policy, identified with reasonable specificity and not unduly burdensome: *Friction Division Products Inc v El Du Pont de Nemours & Co (No.2)* (1986) 32 D.L.R. (4th) 105; *Fecht v Deloitte & Touche* (1996) 28 O.R. (3d) 188, aff'd. (1997) 32 O.R. (3d) 417 (Ont. CA); *OPSEU Pension Trust Fund v Clark* (2006) 270 D.L.R. (4th) 429 (Ont. CA); *Presbyterian Church of Sudan v Rybiak* (2006) 275 D.L.R. (4th) 512 (Ont. CA). See generally Pengelley (2006) 85 Can.B.Rev. 345.

[296] [1998] I.L.Pr. 170 (CA). See also *First American Corp v Zayed* [1999] 1 W.L.R. 1154 (CA).

[297] *Lord Advocate, Ptr*, 1993 S.C. 638 where the court also specified the presence of a legal representative of the witness who could object to unacceptable questions.

examined by the Court of Appeal in *Golden Eagle Refinery Co Inc v Associated International Insurance Co*,[298] where the Letter of Request was found to have a dual or hybrid purpose: to seek testimony for use at trial and also to make enquiries as to discovery which were unknown in English procedure. The Court of Appeal rejected an argument that the mere presence of the second purpose deprived the English court of jurisdiction to make any order under the 1975 Act. It did however adopt a set of conditions to be included in the court's order. These conditions, which have become known as "the *Golden Eagle* conditions" are designed to ensure that the examination is not used for the purposes of an enquiry wider than the gathering of evidence. They are that the examination of the witnesses shall be for the purpose only of eliciting and recording testimony appropriate to be given at the trial, and that no question may be asked of the witness that in the opinion of the examiner is not a question of the nature that could properly be asked by counsel examining a witness in chief at a trial held before the High Court. The court also requires an undertaking that the testimony taken be immediately transmitted to the foreign court and be made available to all parties to the proceedings.

8–101   The distinction between the legitimate gathering of evidence and mere "fishing", important in the case of requests for the production of documents, is less easy to apply in the case of oral testimony. As the Court of Appeal has observed, if oral evidence is being sought for the purpose of use at trial and if there is good reason to believe that the intended witness has knowledge of matters in issue so as to be likely to be able to give relevant evidence, the application cannot be regarded as mere "fishing".[299] The English court will, however, bear in mind the need to protect intended witnesses from an oppressive request.[300]

8–102   *The court's powers.* The High Court has wide powers in giving effect to the application for assistance. It may make such provision for obtaining evidence in England as appears appropriate for giving effect to the request in pursuance of which the application is made.[301] It may, in particular, make provision for the examination of witnesses, either orally or in writing;[302] for the production of documents; for the inspection, photographing, preservation, custody or detention of any property; for the taking of samples of any property and the carrying out of any experiments on or with any property; for the medical examination of any person; and for the taking and testing of samples of blood from any person.[303] The court normally appoints a practising lawyer to conduct the examination, but exceptionally, for example where the facts of the case are such that there is likely to be a need for authoritative rulings to be

---

[298] CA, unreported, February 19, 1998. See *Securities and Exchange Commission v Credit Bancorp Ltd*, QBD, unreported, February 20, 2001; *Genira Trade & Finance Inc v Refco Capital Markets Ltd* [2001] EWCA Civ 1733, [2002] C.L.C. 301.

[299] *First American Corp v Zayed* [1999] 1 W.L.R. 1154 (CA), applied in *Honda Giken Kogyou Kabushiki Kaisha v KJM Superbikes Ltd* [2007] EWCA Civ 313, [2007] C.P. Rep. 28.

[300] *ibid.*

[301] s.2(1). See *Lord Advocate v Sheriffs*, 1978 S.C. 56, 61.

[302] See CPR, r.34.18 as to the appointment of an examiner (applying CPR, rr.34.9, 34.10 and 34.14); *R. v Rathbone, Ex p. Dikko* [1985] Q.B. 630.

[303] s.2(2).

made in the course of the examination, the court will order that the examination be conducted by English counsel before a High Court judge.[304] A request made by a foreign court as to the manner of taking evidence should be allowed unless what is proposed is so contrary to established English procedures that it ought not to be permitted.[305] The High Court will not seek to determine in advance whether the evidence sought is relevant to the issues likely to arise in the foreign proceedings, this being a matter for the requesting court.[306] The High Court may not, however, require any particular steps to be taken unless they are steps which can be required to be taken by way of obtaining evidence for the purposes of civil proceedings (of any description) in the High Court; but unsworn testimony may be received if the foreign court so requests.[307] Thus interrogatories cannot be administered under the Act in England to a corporation as such, even though this is possible by the *lex causae* or by the domestic law of the requesting court.[308] An order requiring a corporation to produce documents must similarly be made in the English form, i.e. that the corporation should "by its proper officer" attend and produce the documents.[309] Conversely, the court cannot make an order for the taking of evidence for use in foreign proceedings except in accordance with the Act, even if the particular evidence sought could have been obtained under the rules relating to corresponding proceedings in the English courts.[310] The court may not make an order under the Act binding on the Crown or on any person in his capacity as an officer or servant of the Crown.[311]

Under the Act, the court may not require a person to state what documents **8–103** relevant to the foreign proceedings are in his possession, custody or power, or to produce any documents other than particular documents specified in the court's order as being documents appearing to the court to be, or to be likely to be, in his possession, custody or power.[312] "Fishing" arises where what is sought is not evidence as such, but information which may lead to a line of enquiry which would disclose evidence; it is a search, a roving enquiry, for material in the hope of being able to raise allegations of fact.[313] For this reason, the statutory reference to "particular documents specified in the order" is to be given a strict construction. It is not sufficient to refer to a class

---

[304] As was done in *United States of America v Philip Morris Inc* [2003] EWHC 3028 (Comm.), affirmed [2004] EWCA Civ 330.

[305] *J Barber and Sons v Lloyd's Underwriters* [1987] Q.B. 103 (videotaping the making of depositions); *Harris v Baker* (1986) 42 S.A.S.R. 316 (request that evidence be taken before court reporter).

[306] *Re Westinghouse Uranium Contract Litigation MDL Docket No.235* [1978] A.C. 547 at p.654; *Re Asbestos Insurance Coverage Cases* [1985] 1 W.L.R. 331 at p.339 (HL); *Friction Division Products Inc v EI du Pont de Nemours & Co Inc (No.2)* (1986) 32 D.L.R. (4th) 105, 116 (Ont).

[307] s.2(3), which applies to both oral and documentary evidence: *Re Westinghouse Uranium Contract Litigation MDL Docket No.235*, above at p.634.

[308] *Penn-Texas Corp v Murat Anstalt* [1964] 1 Q.B. 40 (CA) (decided under an earlier statute).

[309] *Penn-Taxas Corp v Murat Anstalt (No.2)* [1964] 2 Q.B. 647 (CA).

[310] *Re Westinghouse Uranium Contract Litigation MDL Docket No.235*, above, at p.610.

[311] s.9(4); *Re Pan American Airways Inc's Application* [1992] Q.B. 854 (CA).

[312] s.2(4); *Charman v Charman* [2005] EWCA Civ 1606, [2006] 1 W.L.R. 1053.

[313] *Re State of Norway's Application (No.1)* [1990] 1 A.C. 723 (CA); affirmed on other grounds (HL).

of documents (e.g. "all bank statements for 1984"); the order must refer to individual documents or a specific group of documents (e.g. "monthly statements for 1984 relating to the current account at X & Co's Bank").[314] There must be evidence that the documents actually exist and are likely to be in the respondent's possession; mere conjecture is not enough.[315] If a request for assistance is framed too widely, it may be possible for the English court to order partial compliance with the request, striking out the impermissible material; but the English court will not undertake the task of redrafting the request.[316]

8–104   It is however possible under the Act to order the production of documents by a third party even though this is not ancillary to the oral examination of that party as a witness, provided they are sought for use at the trial and not as part of a pre-trial discovery process.[317] A witness whose evidence is to be taken by virtue of an order under the Act may claim any privilege existing in English law[318] or in the law of the foreign country from which the request emanated.[319] Assistance will therefore be refused where a duty of confidentiality placed upon a party to a particular relationship, for example a banker or financial adviser in his relationship with a customer, is regarded, under English law or the law of the foreign country, as outweighing the duty to give all relevant information to the court.[320] A party to the foreign proceedings in which the foreign court issued the letters rogatory which are being executed under the Act has standing to apply to set aside an ex parte order giving effect to the letters rogatory, even if he is not a person to whom the order is addressed.[321]

8–105   *Sovereign interests.* The court's powers under the Act are discretionary.[322] In the interests of comity, it will wish to assist by giving effect to the foreign

---

[314] The examples are given by Lord Fraser in *Re Asbestos Insurance Coverage Cases* [1985] 1 W.L.R. 331 at pp.337–338 (HL). See also *Boeing Co v PPG Industries Inc* [1988] 3 All E.R. 839 (CA); *Genira Trade & Finance Inc v Refco Capital Markets Ltd* [2001] EWCA Civ 1733.

[315] *Re Asbestos Insurance Coverage Cases* [1985] 1 W.L.R. 331, 338 (HL).

[316] cf. *Re Westinghouse Uranium Contract Litigation MDL Docket No.235*, above and *Re State of Norway's Application*, above.

[317] *Re Westinghouse Uranium Contract Litigation MDL Docket No.235*, above, at p.654; cf. the position under the Foreign Tribunals Evidence Act 1856; *Burchard v Macfarlane* [1891] 2 Q.B. 241 (CA).

[318] s.3(1)(a). See e.g. *Re Sarah Getty Trust* [1985] Q.B. 956; *United States of America v Philip Morris Inc* [2004] EWCA Civ 330; *Re Mulroney and Coates* (1986) 27 D.L.R. (4th) 118 (Ont) (Crown privilege).

[319] s.3(1)(b): e.g. the privilege under the Fifth Amendment to the US Constitution; *Re Westinghouse Uranium Contract Litigation MDL Docket No.235*, above. cf. *Appeal Enterprises Ltd v First National Bank of Chicago* (1984) 46 O.R. (2d) 590 (privilege under foreign law only available to local residents did not avail resident of requested country, assistance not depending on "precise reciprocity").

[320] *Re State of Norway's Application (No.1)* [1990] 1 A.C. 723 (CA); affirmed on other grounds (HL).

[321] *Boeing Co v PPG Industries Inc* [1988] 3 All E.R. 839 (CA).

[322] For the exercise of the discretion in the case of expert witnesses, see *Seyfang v GD Searle & Co* [1973] Q.B. 148 (under the Foreign Tribunals Evidence Act 1856); *Novell Inc v MCB Enterprises* [2001] 1 I.R. 608 (Sup Ct; under the Foreign Tribunals Evidence Act 1856, still in force in Ireland).

court's request[323] "unless it is driven to the clear conclusion that it cannot properly do so."[324] In the *Westinghouse* case, the English court received a request seeking pretrial discovery in connection with anti-trust proceedings in the United States. The House of Lords took note of the view of the United Kingdom Government that the wide investigatory procedures under United States anti-trust legislation against persons outside the United States who were not United States citizens constituted an infringement on the proper jurisdiction and sovereignty of the United Kingdom. It was held that possible prejudice to the sovereignty of the United Kingdom could be taken into account by the English court in exercising its discretion.[325] The Protection of Trading Interests Act 1980[326] which was enacted primarily in the context of hostility to the United States' anti-trust jurisdiction provides that the English court must refuse to make an order in response to a foreign court's request if it is shown that the request infringes the jurisdiction of the United Kingdom or is otherwise prejudicial to the sovereignty of the United Kingdom. A certificate signed by or on behalf of the Secretary of State to the effect that the request is such an infringement or is so prejudicial is conclusive,[327] but such a certificate is not an essential prerequisite.[328]

The Secretary of State may also give directions for prohibiting compliance **8–106** with certain orders of foreign courts or authorities requiring any person in the United Kingdom to produce any commercial document not within the territorial jurisdiction of the foreign country, or to provide commercial information compiled from such documents, or to publish any such document or information.[329] A direction may be given if it appears to the Secretary of State that a requirement infringes the jurisdiction of the United Kingdom or is otherwise prejudicial to the sovereignty of the United Kingdom, or if compliance with it would be prejudicial to the security or foreign relations of the United Kingdom.[330] Except in cases where the requirement is concerned only with the publication of documents or information, a direction may also be given if the requirement is not for the purposes of actual or contemplated civil proceedings or actual criminal proceedings in the foreign country, or if it is

---

[323] *Re Westinghouse Uranium Contract Litigation MDL Docket No.235*, above at p.560 (CA) and at p.618.

[324] *Re State of Norway's Application (No.1)*, above. So, too, in Canada, a request will be refused as contrary to Canadian public policy where it infringes Canada's sovereign interests: *Presbyterian Church of Sudan v Rybiak* (2006) 275 D.L.R. (4th) 512 (Ont. CA); *Morgan, Lewis & Bockius LLP v Gauthier* (2006) 82 O.R. (3d) 189.

[325] *cf.* Art.12(b) of Hague Convention on the Taking of Evidence Abroad 1970. See *Fullmer v Cape York Cattle Co* [1987] 1 Qd.R. 6 (issue raised, but not resolved, whether a court might properly refuse to assist a foreign court in connection with litigation concerning title to land in the country of the requested court).

[326] Extending powers conferred in carriage by sea cases in Shipping Contracts and Commercial Documents Act 1964 (repealed).

[327] Protection of Trading Interests Act 1980, s.4.

[328] *Re State of Norway's Application (No.1)*, above.

[329] Protection of Trading Interests Act 1980, s.2(1). The direction may be given in anticipation of the imposition of a requirement by a foreign court or authority. See the orders considered in *British Airways Board v Laker Airways Ltd* [1985] A.C. 58. "Document" includes data storage devices; s.2(6).

[330] Protection of Trading Interests Act 1980, s.2(2).

wholly or mainly for the purposes of obtaining pre-trial discovery of documents.[331] It is an offence knowingly to contravene any such direction.[332]

8–107　　*Assistance to overseas regulatory authorities.* The Secretary of State for Trade and Industry has wide powers to obtain information under s.447 of the Companies Act 1985.[333] The Companies Act 1989 enables this information to be disclosed to an overseas regulatory authority[334] to assist it in the exercise of its regulatory functions.[335] The 1989 Act also gave new powers to examine persons on oath and to require the production of documents and the giving of other assistance; these powers may be exercised whenever the Secretary of State considers that there is good reason for their exercise in response to a request for assistance from an overseas authority.[336] There are exemptions on the ground of legal professional privilege,[337] and restrictions on the disclosure of the information obtained under these powers.[338] These powers complement the growing international network of Memoranda of Understanding between regulatory bodies.[339]

8–108　　*Legalisation.* The practice of legalisation, which involves the official attestation of the origins of a document, can be an unnecessary source of delay in international litigation and other transactions. The Hague Convention Abolishing the Requirement of Legalisation for Foreign Public Documents 1961, to which the United Kingdom and many other countries are party, applies to public documents[340] which have been executed in the territory of one Contracting State and which have to be produced in the territory of another Contracting State. Any requirement that a diplomatic or consular agent should certify the authenticity of the signature, the capacity in which the signatory acted, or the identity of any stamp or seal on a document is abolished.[341] Instead a simple certificate, or "apostille," in a prescribed form issued by the competent authority of the State from which the document originates (in the United Kingdom, the Foreign and Commonwealth Office) suffices.[342]

---

[331] *ibid.* s.2(3).

[332] *ibid.* s.3(1).

[333] As substituted by the Companies (Audit, Investigations and Community Enterprise) Act 2004, s.21, and amended by the Companies Act 2006, s.1038(2).

[334] Defined in Companies Act 1989, s.82(2), as amended by SI 2001/3649, art.76(1),(2); SI 2005/1433, reg.2(3), Sch.3, para.1, and Criminal Justice Act 1993, s.79(13), Sch.5, Pt I, para.16.

[335] Companies Act 1985, s.449(2), Sch.15D, para.39 as substituted and inserted by Companies (Audit, Investigations and Community Enterprise) Act 2004, s.25(1), Sch.2, Pt 3, paras 16, 18, 25.

[336] Companies Act 1989, s.83.

[337] *ibid.* s.83(5).

[338] *ibid.* ss.86, 87 as amended.

[339] See McClean, *International Co-operation in Civil and Criminal Matters* (2002), pp.335–339.

[340] Defined in Art.1(2) as including court and administrative documents, notarial acts and official certificates placed on documents signed by a person in his private capacity.

[341] Arts 1, 2.

[342] See Art.4 and the annexed Model Certificate.

4. SECURITY FOR COSTS

RULE 24—(1) Security for costs may be ordered against a non-resident   **8R–109**
claimant (or appellant on appeal[343]) if it is just to do so and either an
enactment so permits or one of the following conditions applies:[344]

   (a) the claimant is resident outside the jurisdiction, but not resident in
        a state to which the Brussels I Regulation or the Lugano Conven-
        tion applies;[345] or,

   (b) the claimant is a company or other body corporate (whether
        incorporated inside or outside Great Britain) and there is reason
        to believe it will be unable to pay the defendant's costs if ordered
        to do so;[346] or,

   (c) the claimant changed his address since the claim was commenced
        with a view to evading the consequences of the litigation;[347] or
        failed to give an address in the claim form or gave an incorrect
        address;[348] or has taken steps in relation to his assets that would
        make it difficult to enforce an order for costs against him;[349] or

   (d) the claimant is acting as a nominal claimant (other than as a
        representative claimant under CPR, Pt 19) and there is reason to
        believe that he will be unable to pay the defendant's costs if
        ordered to do so;[350]

Provided however that the Court will not order security for costs where
this is precluded by the terms of an international convention to which the
United Kingdom is a party.[351]

(2) In exercising its discretion whether to order security for costs
against a non-resident claimant, the court will pay particular regard to
the ease of enforcement of a judgment for costs in countries where the
claimant has assets.[352]

COMMENT

The institution of English civil procedure pursuant to which a court may   **8–110**
require a claimant (or an appellant on appeal) to provide security for the
defendant's costs as a condition of being allowed to proceed with his action

---

[343] CPR, r.25.15; *Dar International FEF Co v Aon Ltd* [2003] EWCA Civ 1833, [2004] 1 W.L.R. 1395.

[344] CPR, r.25.13(1).

[345] CPR, r.25.13(2)(a); *Longstaff International Ltd v Baker & McKenzie* [2004] EWHC 1852 (Ch.), [2004] 1 W.L.R. 2917.

[346] CPR, r.25.13(2)(c).

[347] CPR, r.25.13(2)(d); the change of address need not be from that given in the claim form: *Aoun v Bahri* [2002] EWHC 29 (Comm.), [2002] 3 All E.R. 182.

[348] CPR, r.25.13(2)(e).

[349] CPR, r.25.13(2)(g). It is not necessary to show that the claimant's actions were intended to make enforcement difficult: *Aoun v Bahri* [2002] EWHC 29 (Comm.), [2002] 3 All E.R. 182.

[350] CPR, r.25.13(2)(f). An undertaking by another person to pay costs is immaterial: *Longstaff International Ltd v Baker & McKenzie* [2004] EWHC 1852 (Ch.), [2004] 1 W.L.R. 2917.

[351] For details of these conventions, see para.8–116, below.

[352] *Nasser v United Bank of Kuwait* [2001] EWCA Civ 556, [2002] 1 W.L.R. 1868; *Al-Koronky v Time-Life Entertainment Group Ltd* [2006] EWCA Civ 1123.

is designed to ensure that a successful defendant will have a fund available within the jurisdiction against which he can enforce a judgment for costs.[353] The High Court will exercise this power only when the circumstances make it just to do so. Security for costs is dealt with in this work in view of the fact that the English rules had, and to some extent still have, a particular application when the claimant is not resident in England. Thus, whilst specifying generally the grounds for the award of security for costs, Rule 24 deals in particular with three private international law questions: (a) the relevance of the residence of the claimant as a ground for awarding security (clause (1)(a)); (b) the effect of international conventions upon the ability to order security (proviso to clause (1)); and (c) the relevance of the enforceability of a costs judgment upon the grant of security (clause (2)).

8–111   **Clause (1) of the Rule. Relevance of residence of the claimant.** Clause (1)(a), following CPR, r.25.13(2)(a), draws a sharp distinction between a claimant who is resident in a Brussels I Regulation or Lugano Convention State and claimants from other States. The old rules had simply applied an inflexible rule that every claimant ordinarily resident abroad had to provide security.[354] However, in the light of a decision of the European Court in *Mund & Fester v Hatrex Internationaal Transport*,[355] that a not dissimilar German practice involved covert discrimination contrary to what is now Art.18 of the TFEU unless it could be justified by objective circumstance, the Court of Appeal held that the English practice based on the ordinary residence of the plaintiff must similarly be regarded as covertly discriminatory on grounds of nationality.[356] As a result, the rules were redrafted so that the mere fact of foreign residence is not a ground for awarding security at all where the claimant is resident in Europe and subject to one of the three major civil jurisdiction instruments.

8–112   Where the claimant is resident elsewhere, the award of security has now become a matter of discretion. But the retention of a rule providing that foreign residence may be a ground for the award of security in non-European cases has been held not to offend the anti-discrimination or access to court provisions of human rights instruments,[357] provided that the circumstances in which security is awarded are objectively justifiable, because substantial difficulties or extra costs would likely be involved for the defendant in recovering any costs judgment against the foreign claimant. In these circumstances, consideration of the enforceability of any costs judgment in a country

---

[353] *Porzelack KG v Porzelack (UK) Ltd* [1987] 1 W.L.R. 420, 422.

[354] *Aeronave SpA v Westland Charters Ltd* [1971] 1 W.L.R. 1445 (CA).

[355] Case C–398/92 [1994] E.C.R. I–467.

[356] *Fitzgerald v Williams* [1996] Q.B. 657 (CA), not following *Berkeley Administration Inc v McClelland* [1990] 2 Q.B. 407 (CA).

[357] *Nasser v United Bank of Kuwait* [2001] EWCA Civ 556, [2002] 1 W.L.R. 1868. The European Commission of Human Rights rejected as manifestly ill-founded an application challenging an award of security against a non-resident appellant under Art.6(1) of the European Convention on Human Rights: App No.14551/89 *JR and WA v United Kingdom* (April 12, 1989). Similar applications have been rejected under s.15(1) of the Canadian Charter of Rights and Freedoms: *Crothers v Simpson Sears Ltd* (1988) 51 D.L.R. (4th) 529; *Lapierre v Barrette* (1988) 59 D.L.R. (4th) 200 (Que CA); and under the Irish Constitution: *Salih v General Accident Fire and Life Assurance Corp Ltd* [1987] I.R. 628.

in which the claimant has assets (clause (2) of the Rule, as to which see the Comment below) will be particularly important.

Factors in the exercise of the discretion. The discretion of the court extends **8–113** to ordering security as against a claimant resident abroad even where there is a co-claimant resident in England,[358] though this power was formerly thought not to exist.[359] It may be relevant in considering the exercise of this discretion that the English claimant is a wholly-owned subsidiary of the foreign claimant; the distinct legal entity enjoyed by the subsidiary may be outweighed by the commercial realities. Where there are co-claimants in England and abroad, and there is a reasonable prospect of unsuccessful claimants each being ordered to bear an *aliquot* share of the costs, it may be appropriate to order the claimants resident abroad to provide security only for a proportion of the costs, but each case must be considered on its own facts.[360] If an English claimant has been made a party unnecessarily or improperly, perhaps in the hope of evading an order for security for costs, the court will order that he cease to be a party[361] and security for costs may then be required.[362] No order will be made if the claimant shows that he has substantial property within the jurisdiction which could be made available to satisfy any order as to costs.[363] It has been held that an order will not be made against a Crown servant resident abroad in order to carry out his official duties,[364] but these cases are best understood as illustrations of the court's discretion. An order can be made against a foreign sovereign.[365] An order can be made if the claimant goes to live abroad after the issue of process, and can include past as well as future costs.[366] The fact that the claimant is compelled to take proceedings in England, e.g. because of an English jurisdiction clause[367] in a contract, is not a sufficient reason for not ordering him to give security. If the defendant admits liability, the claimant will not be ordered to give security for costs,[368] even if the defendant counterclaims.[369]

---

[358] *Slazengers Ltd v Seaspeed Ferries International Ltd* [1988] 1 W.L.R. 221 (CA); *The Alpha* [1991] 2 Lloyd's Rep. 52 (CA).

[359] *Winthorp v Royal Exchange Assurance Co* (1755) Dick. 282; *D'Hormusgee v Grey* (1882) 10 Q.B.D. 13.

[360] *Slazengers Ltd v Seaspeed Ferries International Ltd* [1988] 1 W.L.R. 221 (CA); *The Alpha* [1991] 2 Lloyd's Rep. 52 (CA).

[361] CPR, r.19.3.

[362] *Jones v Gurney* [1913] W.N. 72.

[363] *Hamburger v Poetting* (1882) 47 L.T. 249; *Re Apollinaris Co's Trade Marks* [1891] 1 Ch. 1 (CA); *Kevorkian v Burney (No.2)* [1937] 4 All E.R. 468 (CA). Contrast *Ebrard v Gassier* (1884) 28 Ch. D. 232 (CA); *Clarke v Barber* (1890) 6 T.L.R. 256, where the property was not considered sufficiently substantial.

[364] *Colebrook v Jones* (1751) Dick. 154 (consul); *Evelyn v Chippendale* (1839) 9 Sim. 497 (colonial harbourmaster).

[365] *Republic of Costa Rica v Erlanger* (1876) 3 Ch.D. 62 (CA); *The Newbattle* (1885) 10 P.D. 33 (CA); *Duff Development Co v Government of Kelantan* (1925) 41 T.L.R. 375; *Ministère de la Culture et de la Communication de France v Lieb, The Times*, December 24, 1981.

[366] *Massey v Allen* (1879) 12 Ch.D. 807; *Caldwell v Sumpters* [1972] Ch. 478, reversed on other grounds *ibid.* (CA).

[367] *Aeronave SPA v Westland Charters Ltd* [1971] 1 W.L.R. 1445 (CA).

[368] *De St Martin v Davis & Co* [1884] W.N. 86.

[369] *Winterfield v Bradnum* (1878) 3 Q.B.D. 324 (CA).

8–114   *Identification of true claimant.* It is a cardinal principle that a defendant resident abroad is never ordered to give security for costs, not even if the claimant is also resident abroad.[370] But it is not always easy to determine whether a person is in substance in the position of a plaintiff or a defendant. The courts look at the substance of the matter and not merely at the form, and regard any person who assumes the position of an actor in the proceeding in question as a claimant,[371] and any person who is really defending himself against attack as a defendant.[372] If the defendant brings a counterclaim which arises out of an independent cause of action and is really in the nature of a cross-action, or which is pursued after the claim has been determined, he may be ordered to give security;[373] but if the counterclaim arises out of the same transaction and is in substance in the nature of a defence to the proceedings, security will not be ordered.[374] But the matter is one for the discretion of the court and each case must depend on its own merits.[375] "The principle seems to be that where a defendant counter-attacks on the same front on which he is being attacked by the plaintiff, it will be regarded as a defensive manoeuvre. But if he opens a counter-attack on a different front, even to relieve pressure on the front attacked by the plaintiff, he is in danger of an order for security for costs."[376] So a defendant in interpleader proceedings, or proceedings analogous thereto, can be ordered to give security for costs if he is in substance a claimant.[377] But if both claimants to the thing in dispute are resident abroad, the court is reluctant to make an order against one and not against the other.[378]

8–115   *Security for costs in arbitrations.* Unless the parties have agreed otherwise, an arbitral tribunal has the power to order a claimant to provide security for the costs of the arbitration.[379] However, this power cannot be exercised on the ground that the claimant is an individual ordinarily resident outside the United Kingdom or a corporation or association incorporated or formed under the law of a country outside the United Kingdom or whose central management and

---

[370] *Naamlooze Vennootschap v Bank of England* [1948] 1 All E.R. 465 (CA).

[371] See, e.g. *Apollinaris Co v Wilson* (1886) 31 Ch.D. 632 (CA); *Re Pretoria Pietersburg Ry* [1904] 2 Ch. 359 (claimant in a winding up); *Duff Development Co v Government of Kelantan* (1925) 41 T.L.R. 375 (party to an arbitration asking that an arbitrator be ordered to state a special case).

[372] See, e.g. *Re Percy and Kelly Nickel etc. Co* (1876) 2 Ch.D. 531 (shareholder opposing creditor's winding up petition); *Re Miller's Patent* (1894) 70 L.T. 270 (owner of patent resisting petition for revocation); *Re La Société Anonyme des Verreries de l'Etoile* [1893] W.N. 119 (same for trade mark); *Re B (Infants)* [1965] 1 W.L.R. 946 (motion by husband to vary custody order in favour of wife); *Visco v Minter* [1969] P. 82.

[373] *Sykes v Sacerdoti* (1885) 15 Q.B.D. 423 (CA); *Lake v Haseltine* (1885) 55 L.J.Q.B. 205; *cf. The Julia Fisher* (1877) 2 P.D. 115.

[374] *Mapleson v Masini* (1879) 5 Q.B.D. 144; *Neck v Taylor* [1893] 1 Q.B. 560 (CA).

[375] *New Fenix Compagnie etc. v General Accident etc. Corp* [1911] 2 K.B. 619 (CA).

[376] *Visco v Minter* [1969] P. 82, 85.

[377] *Tomlinson v Land and Finance Corp Ltd* (1884) 14 Q.B.D. 539 (CA); *Tudor Furnishers Ltd v Montague & Co* [1950] Ch.113.

[378] *Belmonte v Aynard* (1879) 4 C.P.D. 221, 352 (CA); *Maatschappij voor Fondsenbezit v Shell Transport and Trading Co* [1923] 2 K.B. 166 (CA); *cf. Tudor Furnishers Ltd v Montague & Co*, above.

[379] Arbitration Act 1996, s.38(2)(3).

control is exercised outside the United Kingdom.[380] It was formerly the case that the court itself could intervene to order security for costs in an arbitration but this power was removed by the Arbitration Act 1996.[381]

Proviso to clause (1). International conventions. Insofar as international   **8–116** conventions make it easier to enforce a judgment for costs in another country, they reduce the need for ordering security. Many conventions have a more direct effect in excluding the power to order security for costs. For example Chapter III of the Hague Convention on Civil Procedure of 1954 and its successor Chapter II of the Convention on International Access to Justice of 1980[382] prohibit any requirement of security, by reason only of their foreign nationality or residence, from persons (including legal persons) habitually resident in a Contracting State who are plaintiffs or parties intervening before the courts of another Contracting State. The United Kingdom is not a party to either convention but comparable provisions are found in a number of bilateral conventions on civil procedure.[383] Another type of provision, found in conventions dealing with a particular subject-matter, prohibits any requirement of security in cases falling within the scope of the convention. This type of provision is found in a number of conventions to which the United Kingdom is party: the Geneva Convention on the Contract for the International Carriage of Goods by Road,[384] the Geneva Convention on the Contract for the International Carriage of Passengers and Luggage,[385] the Convention concerning International Carriage by Rail,[386] and the Hague Convention on the Civil Aspects of International Child Abduction.[387] The Paris, Brussels and Vienna Conventions on Third Party Liability in the Field of Nuclear Energy each contain a general provision that "this Convention shall be applied without any discrimination based on nationality, domicile or residence".[388] Yet other conventions contain more limited provisions, prohibiting the requirement of security for costs on certain specified grounds. Article 51 of the Brussels I Regulation and Lugano Convention prohibits the requirement of security on the ground of foreign nationality, domicile or residence of a party who in one Member or Convention State applies for the enforcement of a judgment in another Member or Convention State. This exclusion is already given effect in English law by virtue of Rule 24(1)(a).

---

[380] *ibid.* s.38(3). See the Department of Trade and Industry's Advisory Committee on International Commercial Arbitration Law's Report on the Arbitration Bill (February 1996), especially pp.44–45 and 76–77.

[381] Repealing Arbitration Act 1950, s.12(6)(a) and reversing the effect of *SA Coppée Lavalin NV v Ken-Ren Chemicals and Fertilizers Ltd* [1995] 1 A.C. 38. The ability of the court to order security in the enforcement of arbitral awards under the New York Convention 1958 is discussed below at para.16–146.

[382] Art.17 of the 1954 Convention, based solely on nationality; Art.14 of the 1980 Convention, adding considerations of residence.

[383] e.g. Convention on Security for Costs and Judicial Assistance of April 15, 1936 between UK and France, Art.3.

[384] The "CMR Convention", Art.31(5); see Carriage of Goods by Road Act 1965.

[385] The "CVR Convention", Art.21(5); see Carriage of Passengers by Road Act 1974.

[386] The "COTIF Convention", Art.18(4); see International Transport Conventions Act 1983.

[387] Art.22; see Child Abduction and Custody Act 1985.

[388] Paris Convention 1960, Art.14(a); Brussels Convention 1962, Art.12(3); Vienna Convention 1963, Art.13.

8–117   **Clause (2) of the Rule. Relevance of enforceability of costs judgment.**
An important consideration in the practice under the current rules is the ease
with which judgments for costs can be enforced in the country in which the
claimant has assets. If a non-resident claimant has assets in England,[389] or if
a judgment for costs can be readily enforced in the country in which the
claimant has assets, use of the power to order security will normally be
inappropriate. Within the United Kingdom, the effect of the Civil Jurisdiction
and Judgments Act 1982 is that such judgments given by an English court can
very easily be enforced in other parts of the United Kingdom. Security will
only be ordered against claimants resident in other such parts if there are
special circumstances such as the insolvency of the claimant company.[390] For
similar reasons the residence of the claimant in a State to which the Brussels
I Regulation or the Lugano Convention applies cannot be relied upon as a
reason for making an order, for in such countries enforcement is similarly
readily available;[391] but where the claimant is a company an alternative
ground for an order is that that the claimant is a company or other body
(whether incorporated inside or outside Great Britain) and there is reason to
believe that it will be unable to pay the defendant's costs if ordered to do so.[392]
Where a judgment for costs would be enforced in a country to which Pt II of
the Administration of Justice Act 1920 or Pt I of the Foreign Judgments
(Reciprocal Enforcement) Act 1933 has been extended by Order in Council,
the position is rather different: the procedure for enforcement in such cases is
not automatic, and may involve a contest in the foreign country, and the court
will weigh the circumstances before deciding whether to order security for
costs. If it appears that the judgment can be enforced almost as easily as in
England, no security will be ordered,[393] but it will be otherwise if there may
be difficulty and delay.[394] The Court of Appeal in *Nasser v United Bank of
Kuwait*[395] noted the distinction drawn between claimants against whom a
claim can be enforced under the Brussels or original Lugano Conventions and
other claimants. However, other countries, such as Commonwealth countries
and, despite the absence of any treaty, the United States (the relevant country
in the instant case), were countries in which the enforcement of judgments
presented little difficulty but could involve further proceedings. The absence
of reciprocal arrangements for enforcement could not justify an inference that
enforcement would not be possible. Where substantial difficulties or extra
costs were likely, an order for security for costs could be objectively
justifiable.[396]

---

[389] *Longstaff International Ltd v Baker & McKenzie* [2004] EWHC 1852 (Ch.), [2004] 1
W.L.R. 2917.

[390] *DSQ Property Co Ltd v Lotus Cars Ltd* [1987] 1 W.L.R. 127 (Northern Ireland company)
(under the former rules).

[391] See CPR, r.25.13(2)(b)(ii).

[392] CPR, r.25.13(2)(c). See *Chequepoint SARL v McClelland* [1997] Q.B. 51 (CA) (under
former rules; order against French company upheld.

[393] *Thune v London Properties* [1990] 1 W.L.R. 562 (CA) (enforceability in Norway) (under
the former rules).

[394] *Lonkar v JO Simms,* CA, unreported, January 28, 1998 (India) (under the former rules).

[395] [2001] EWCA Civ 556, [2002] 1 All E.R. 401 (CA).

[396] *Al-Koronky v Time-Life Entertainment Group Ltd* [2006] EWCA Civ 1123, [2006] C.P. Rep.
47.

ILLUSTRATIONS

(1) FREEZING INJUNCTIONS

1. A & Co, Japanese shipowners, let three ships on charter to X and Y, who fail to pay the hire **8–118**
and cannot be traced. They have funds in bank accounts in London. The court will issue an
injunction, on the application of A & Co., restraining X and Y from removing any of their assets
from the jurisdiction.[397]

2. X & Co, a Panamanian company, own a vessel, which they let on charter. On the failure of
the charterers to pay the charter freight in full, X & Co. cause the vessel to be arrested in Cyprus
by order of the courts of Cyprus and the cargo is unloaded. Subsequently the vessel sinks and
becomes a total loss. X & Co claim against their insurers, London underwriters. The bills of
lading contain a clause conferring exclusive jurisdiction on the Italian courts. The cargo-owners
commence an action in the High Court against X & Co, alleging breach of duty or of contract.
The court may issue an injunction restraining X & Co from removing the insurance moneys from
the jurisdiction if the cargo-owners have commenced, or are to commence, proceedings in
Italy.[398]

3. A, a Panamanian company, obtains a judgment in England for $15 million against X and Y
Lebanese nationals, one of whom lives mainly in Switzerland and the other mainly in Greece.
They carry on business through a network of companies incorporated in such places as Panama,
Liberia and the Dutch Antilles. The court grants a freezing injunction in aid of enforcement of the
English judgment extending to assets outside the jurisdiction.[399]

4. The Republic of Haiti commences proceedings in France to recover more than $20 million
alleged embezzled by former President "Baby Doc" Duvalier. English solicitors for Duvalier hold
assets on his behalf in various countries and hold information in England about those assets. The
court grants a worldwide freezing injunction in aid of the French proceedings, and the English
solicitors are ordered to disclose the nature, location and value of Duvalier's assets known to
them.[400]

5. A brings an action in England against X and Y, individuals, and Z, a Luxembourg
corporation, for conspiracy and fraudulent breach of fiduciary duty. The court grants a freezing
injunction over X and Y's foreign assets and appoints a receiver of the assets of Z.[401]

6. A & Co sues X (who is resident and domiciled in England), alleging that X had participated
in the fraudulent misappropriation of A & Co's funds by Y, a former employee of A & Co. A &
Co applies in England for a worldwide freezing injunction, and an associated disclosure order, in
aid of the Swiss proceedings. Although similar relief is not available under Swiss procedure, the
English court may grant it because the defendant is domiciled in England.[402]

(2) JUDICIAL ASSISTANCE: SERVICE OF PROCESS

7. A obtained the leave of the court to serve process out of the jurisdiction on X at a stated **8–119**
address in Lugano or elsewhere in Switzerland. X applied for service to be set aside on the
grounds that personal service by the agent of a foreign plaintiff without the leave of the Swiss
authorities was a criminal offence under the Swiss Penal Code. The court set the service aside.
In the circumstances, and despite the expiry of both the writ and the relevant limitation period,
the court renewed the validity of the writ for four months to allow other modes of service to be
used.[403]

(3) JUDICIAL ASSISTANCE: OBTAINING EVIDENCE ABROAD

8. A brings an action in England against B, claiming commission due under a contract **8–120**
concerning the supply of rifles to the Russian Government. A is resident at Bucharest and applies
for an order that his evidence be taken there. He suffers from heart disease and claims that the

---

[397] *Nippon Yusen Kaisha v Karageorgis* [1975] 1 W.L.R. 1093 (CA).

[398] These are the facts of *The Siskina v Distos Compania Naviera SA* [1979] A.C. 210, the
effect of which is reversed by Civil Jurisdiction and Judgments Act 1982, s.25(1).

[399] *Babanaft International Co SA v Bassatne* [1990] Ch. 13 (CA).

[400] *Republic of Haiti v Duvalier* [1990] 1 Q.B. 202 (CA). The action in France was subsequently dismissed: 1991 *Clunet* 137.

[401] *Derby & Co Ltd v Weldon (Nos 3 & 4)* [1990] Ch. 65 (CA).

[402] *Crédit Suisse Fides Trust SA v Cuoghi* [1998] Q.B. 818 (CA).

[403] *The Sky One* [1988] 1 Lloyd's Rep. 238 (CA).

cross-Channel sea crossing could endanger his life had he to attend in London. A's evidence will be crucial and cross-examination will be important to B's case. The application is refused.[404]

9. A brings an action in England against B on an alleged contract to transfer shares in a South African company. The contract is made while B was temporarily resident in England; he is still so resident when the writ was issued. B subsequently returns to his permanent home in Johannesburg. He wishes to defend the action but cannot afford another journey to England. B applies for an order enabling his evidence to be taken in South Africa. It is granted.[405]

10. Letters of request from a court in Virginia seek production of a series of specified documents and of any memoranda, correspondence or other documents relating thereto. An order will be made in respect of the specified documents only.[406]

11. Letters of request from a Californian court seek the production of written instructions from the plaintiff or his agents to obtain specified insurance policies. There is no evidence that written instructions existed. No order for the production of the documents will be made.[407]

12. Letters of request from a court in Virginia seek an order that A should give evidence and that B & Co should produce specified documents. A claims privilege against self-incrimination under s.14(1) of the Civil Evidence Act 1968. B & Co claim privilege against self-incrimination under the Fifth Amendment to the United States Constitution. Both claims will be upheld and no order made.[408]

13. Letters of request from a court in Norway issued, with the concurrence of both parties, in proceedings brought to challenge a tax assessment sought an order that A and B, English bankers, should give evidence. No order was made owing to the unacceptable width of the questions sought to be asked, and, in the circumstances, to respect the bankers' duty of confidentiality. Second, more narrowly drawn, letters of request were received. An order was made, the proceedings being civil proceedings under both English and Norwegian law; the request did not amount to an attempt to enforce the revenue law of Norway.[409]

14. A, an English judgment creditor, seeks an order under CPR, r.71 for the examination of B, an officer of the judgment debtor. B is not present or resident in England. No order can be made or served outside the jurisdiction. The English court has no jurisdiction to compel a foreign witness to give evidence in England.[410]

(4) Security for costs

8–121   15. P, ordinarily resident in the Irish Republic, commences proceedings in England against D claiming damages for fraudulent misrepresentation in connection with investments in works of art. D seeks an order for security for costs. To make such an order would amount to covert discrimination on grounds of nationality contrary to what is now Art.18 of the TFEU, unless it could be justified by objective circumstances relating to difficulties in obtaining enforcement of any judgment as to costs. As Ireland is a Member State of the Brussels I Regulation, enforcement there presents no difficulty and no order will be made.[411]

16. P, a French company ordinarily resident in France, brings an action for defamation against D. D seeks an order for security for costs, alleging the impecuniosity of P. The circumstances alleged are such that were P. an English company, an order for security would be made under CPR, r.25.13(2)(c). To make a similar order against a French company would involve no discrimination and so would not offend against the TFEU. An order will be made.[412]

17. N brought proceedings in England against U. They were struck out but N appealed. U sought an order for security for costs against N who was resident in the United States, which was

---

[404] *Berdan v Greenwood* (1880) 20 Ch.D. 764n. (CA).

[405] *Ross v Woodford* [1894] 1 Ch. 38.

[406] Evidence (Proceedings in Other Jurisdictions) Act 1975, s.2(4)(b); *Re Westinghouse Uranium Contract Litigation MDL Docket No.235* [1978] A.C. 547.

[407] *Re Asbestos Insurance Coverage Cases* [1985] 1 W.L.R. 331 (HL).

[408] Evidence (Proceedings in Other Jurisdictions) Act 1975, s.3; *Re Westinghouse Uranium Contract Litigation MDL Docket No.235*, above.

[409] *Re State of Norway's Application (Nos 1 and 2)* [1990] 1 A.C. 723.

[410] *Masri v Consolidated Contractors International (UK) Ltd (No.4)* [2009] UKHL 43, [2010] 1 A.C. 90.

[411] *Fitzgerald v Williams* [1996] Q.B. 657 (CA) following Case C–398/92 *Mund & Fester v Hatrex Internationaal Transport* [1994] E.C.R. I–467.

[412] *Chequepoint SARL v McClelland* [1997] Q.B. 51 (CA), distinguishing *Fitzgerald v Williams* [1996] Q.B. 657 (CA).

not a party to any convention with the United Kingdom for the enforcement of orders. The power to award security for costs against an individual resident in a country not party to an applicable enforcement convention could only be exercised on objectively justified grounds relating to obstacles to, or the burden of, enforcement in the context of the particular individual or country concerned. Enforcement of an English judgment for costs in the United States would be likely to involve a significantly greater burden in terms of costs and delay than an enforcement of a costs order in England or a State party to an enforcement convention, and in the circumstances an order for security was justified.[413]

---

[413] *Nasser v United Bank of Kuwait* [2001] EWCA Civ 556, [2002] 1 W.L.R. 1868.

CHAPTER 9

PROOF OF FOREIGN LAW[1]

9R–001   **RULE 25—(1) In any case to which foreign law applies, that law must be pleaded and proved as a fact to the satisfaction of the judge by expert evidence or sometimes by certain other means.**

    (2) In the absence of satisfactory evidence of foreign law, the court will apply English law to such a case.[2]

COMMENT

9–002   **(1) Foreign law a fact.** The principle that, in an English[3] court, foreign law is a matter of fact has long been well established:[4] it must be pleaded, and it must be proved: these requirements are examined in detail below. It follows that a representation of foreign law is a representation of fact for the purposes of the law of misrepresentation,[5] and a finding upon foreign law made by arbitrators is a finding of fact which may not form the basis of an appeal on a point of law under s.69 of the Arbitration Act 1996.[6] It is also said to follow that it the parties elect not to prove the content of foreign law, a case will be decided by the application of English domestic law as though the case were a wholly domestic one, and this is generally true.[7] But in recent years there have been increasing signs that this cannot invariably follow, and in cases

---

[1] Fentiman, *Foreign Law in English Courts* (1998); Geeroms, *Foreign Law in Civil Litigation* (2004).

[2] This Rule was explicitly approved in *Bumper Development Corp v Commissioner of Police of the Metropolis* [1991] 1 W.L.R. 1362, 1369 (CA). However, for qualifications to the absolute form of the Rule, see further below, para.9–026.

[3] In certain foreign jurisdictions, the principle that *curia novit ius* requires the court to discover and apply a foreign law which its rules of the conflict of laws make applicable. This may create substantial difficulty in practice. See, e.g. *Re Claim Against Croatian Branch of Slovenian Bank* [1998] I.L.Pr. 269 (German Fed Sup Ct, 1996), but see generally, on the procedure in foreign courts, Geeroms, *op. cit*, n.1, above); Rühl (2007) 71 *RabelsZ* 59.

[4] *Fremoult v Dedire* (1718) 1 P. Wms. 429; *Mostyn v Fabrigas* (1774) 1 Cowp. 161, 174; *Nelson v Bridport* (1845) 8 Beav. 527; *Bankers and Shippers Insurance Co of New York v Liverpool Marine and General Insurance Co Ltd* (1926) 24 Ll.L.R. 85, 93 (HL); *Ottoman Bank of Nicosia v Chakarian (No.2)* [1938] A.C. 260, 279 (PC); *A/S Tallinna Laevauhisus v Estonian State Steamship Line* (1947) 80 Ll.L.R. 99, 107, 113 (CA); *Glencore International AG v Metro Trading International Inc* [2001] 1 Lloyd's Rep. 284.

[5] *André et Cie SA v Ets. Michel Blanc et Fils* [1977] 2 Lloyd's Rep. 166; *PT Royal Bali Leisure v Hutchinson & Co Trust Co Ltd* [2004] EWHC 1014 (Ch.), at [123].

[6] *Egmatra v Marco* [1999] 1 Lloyd's Rep. 862; *Reliance Industries Ltd v Enron Oil and Gas (India) Ltd* [2002] 1 All E.R. (Comm.) 59 (where Indian law assumed to be same as English law, so English law applied by default, appeal not on a question of law for purpose of Arbitration Act 1996 s.82).

[7] See below, para.9–011.

where it would be wholly artificial to apply rules of English law to an issue governed by foreign law, a court may simply regard a party who has pleaded but who has failed to prove foreign law with sufficient specificity as will allow an English court simply to apply it, as having failed to establish his case without regard to the corresponding principle of English domestic law.[8]

(i) *Foreign law must be pleaded.* The general rule is that if a party wishes **9–003** to rely on a foreign law he must plead it in the same way as any other fact.[9] Unless this is done, the court will in principle decide a case containing foreign elements as though it were a purely domestic English case.[10] There is, however, a statutory exception to this principle. If a case is governed by the law of some Commonwealth country, the court may order that law to be ascertained under the British Law Ascertainment Act 1859[11] if it regards such ascertainment as "necessary or expedient for the proper disposal of" the action. Orders for the ascertainment of a foreign law under this Act have been made at the court's own motion although the foreign law was not pleaded.[12]

(ii) *Foreign law must be proved.* English courts take judicial notice of the **9–004** law of England and of notorious facts, but not of foreign law.[13] Consequently, foreign law must be proved[14] in each case: it cannot be deduced from previous English decisions in which the same rule of foreign law has been before the court,[15] although such decisions may be admissible in evidence for the

---

[8] *Shaker v Al-Bedrawi* [2002] EWCA Civ 1452, [2003] Ch. 350 (CA) (provisions of Companies Act 1985); *Damberg v Damberg* [2001] NSWCA 87, (2001) 52 N.S.W.L.R. 492 (fiscal laws); see further below, para.9–026.

[9] *King of Spain v Machado* (1827) 4 Russ. 225, 239; *Ascherberg, Hopwood & Crew Ltd v Casa Musicale Sonzogno* [1971] 1 W.L.R. 173, 1128 (CA).

[10] See below, para.9–025. It is open to a party to allege the incorporation of provisions of a non-English law into a contract, though this may not make (and if the incorporation is not of the law of a State, but of some non-State system of rules, will not make) the incorporated "law" the *lex contractus*. The incorporation must be of specific provisions or rules, as distinct from a general invocation of general religious or other principles: *Shamil Bank of Bahrein EC v Beximco Pharmaceuticals Ltd* [2004] EWCA Civ 19, [2004] 1 W.L.R. 1784 ("subject to the principles of the Glorious Sharia" ineffective); *Halpern v Halpern (Nos 1 & 2)* [2007] EWCA Civ 291, [2008] Q.B. 195 (Jewish law not available for selection as *lex contractus*). If the court is asked to enforce provisions of such systems as terms of the contract, they must be proved in the normal way.

[11] See below, para.9–023.

[12] *Topham v Duke of Portland* (1863) 1 De G.J. & S. 517, varied, but without reference to this point sub nom. *Duke of Portland v Topham* (1864) 11 H.L.C. 32; *Eglinton v Lamb* (1867) 15 L.T. 657.

[13] *Fremoult v Dedire* (1718) 1 P.Wms. 429; *Nelson v Bridport* (1845) 8 Beav. 527; *Lloyd v Guibert* (1865) L.R. 1 Q.B. 115, 129; *Neilson v Overseas Projects Corp of Victoria Ltd* [2005] HCA 54, (2005) 223 C.L.R. 331, at [115].

[14] *Ganer v Lanesborough* (1790) Peake 25; *Brenan and Galen's Case* (1847) 10 Q.B. 492, 498; *Bumper Development Corp v Commissioner of Police of the Metropolis* [1991] 1 W.L.R. 1362, 1368 (CA); *Macnamara v Hatteras (Owners)* [1931] I.R. 73, 337; [1933] I.R. 675. Where a foreign law confers a discretion on the foreign court administering it, evidence may be given as to the manner in which that foreign court exercises that discretion: *National Mutual Holdings Pty Ltd v Sentry Corp* (1989) 87 A.L.R. 539, 556.

[15] *M'Cormick v Garnett* (1854) 5 D.M. & G. 278; *Re Marseilles Extension Railway and Land Co* (1885) 30 Ch.D. 598, 602; *Lazard Brothers & Co v Midland Bank Ltd* [1933] A.C. 289, 297–298; *Schnaider v Jaffe* (1916) 7 C.P.D. 696. This principle was lost sight of in *Simons v Simons* [1939] 1 K.B. 490, 495, and in *Re Sebba* [1959] Ch. 166.

purpose of proving foreign law.[16] Indeed, it is perfectly possible for the English court to reach different conclusions in different cases as to the effect of a given rule of foreign law.[17]

9–005   In the following exceptional cases, foreign law need not be proved:

(a) Foreign law need not be proved where a statute expressly provides that it shall be judicially noticed.[18]

(b) Foreign law may sometimes be judicially noticed as a notorious fact: thus judicial notice has been taken of the fact that roulette is not unlawful in Monte Carlo.[19] On the other hand, it has been held that judicial notice could not on this ground be taken of the fact that continental lawyers adopt a more liberal attitude than English lawyers towards the construction of documents, since this fact is not notorious.[20]

9–006   (c) The court may take judicial notice of a foreign law if its content is, at least in part, determined by a rule of English law, and if, according to English law, the foreign law is the same as, or substantially similar to, English law. Thus it was and is, though of little contemporary relevance, a rule of English law that settlers from the United Kingdom carry with them to a new colony, which before their arrival had no civilised system of law, the common law of England and English statutory law, in so far as it is applicable to the conditions prevailing in the colony.[21] The court can take judicial notice of the common law of such a colony,[22] and can decide, as a matter of law, whether a given English statute applies to the colony.[23] Of course, this principle does not enable the court to take judicial notice of laws passed by the legislature of the colony.[24]

9–007   (d) An appellate court which has jurisdiction to determine appeals from the courts of several countries takes judicial notice of the laws of any of those countries when it hears an appeal from a court in any one of them. Thus the UK Supreme Court, when hearing an English or Northern Irish appeal, takes judicial notice of Scots law;[25] and conversely, when hearing a Scottish appeal,

---

[16] Civil Evidence Act 1972, s.4(2), below, para.9–021.

[17] *Lazard Brothers & Co v Midland Bank Ltd* [1933] A.C. 289; *Ottoman Bank of Nicosia v Chakarian* [1938] A.C. 260 (PC). This possibility is recognised in Civil Evidence Act 1972, s.4(2) proviso. According to *Neilson v Overseas Projects Corp of Victoria Ltd* [2005] HCA 54, (2005) 223 C.L.R. 331, at [115], dealing with the position at common law, "decisions about the content of foreign law create no precedent".

[18] See Maintenance Orders Act 1950, s.22(2); cf. *Knight v Knight* [1925] 2 D.L.R. 467, 469 (Man.); and Civil Evidence Act 1972, s.4(2), below, para.9–021.

[19] *Saxby v Fulton* [1909] 2 K.B. 208, 211; cf. *Harold Meyers Travel Service Ltd v Magid* (1975) 60 D.L.R. (3d) 42, 44, affirmed on other grounds (1977) 77 D.L.R. (3d) 32 (Ont CA); *Re Turner* [1906] W.N. 27, where judicial notice was taken of the fact that the laws of the different States of the German Empire varied considerably.

[20] *Hartmann v Konig* (1933) 50 T.L.R. 114, 117 (HL).

[21] *Cooper v Stuart* (1889) 14 App. Cas. 286, 291–292 (PC); *Terrell v Secretary of State for the Colonies* [1953] 2 Q.B. 482, 492; Halsbury, *Laws of England* (5th ed. 2009), vol.13, para.867; Roberts-Wray, *Commonwealth and Colonial Law* (1966), pp.539–557.

[22] *Limerick v Limerick* (1863) 4 Sw. & Tr. 252, 253. cf. *Re Nesbitt* (1844) 14 L.J.M.C. 30, 32, where judicial notice was taken of the fact that the common law of England prevailed in Ireland.

[23] e.g. *Terrell v Secretary of State for the Colonies* [1953] 2 Q.B. 482.

[24] For proof of Colonial statutes, see para.9–022, below.

[25] *De Thoren v Att-Gen* (1876) 1 App. Cas. 686; *Elliot v Joicey* [1935] A.C. 209, 236; *MacShannon v Rockware Glass Ltd* [1978] A.C. 795, 815, 821.

the Court takes judicial notice of English or Northern Irish law.[26] Similarly, the Supreme Court of Canada takes judicial notice of the laws of all the Provinces when it hears an appeal from any one of them.[27] It seems that the same principle applies to the Judicial Committee of the Privy Council.[28] In these cases, the foreign law, which was a matter of fact in the courts below, becomes a matter of law on appeal.

(e) Foreign law need not be proved if it is admitted.[29] Such admission may be express but may also occur where a party, by his pleading (now called statement of case), is deemed by the applicable procedural rules to admit the foreign law upon which his opponent has relied.[30]

9–008

(f) The court may decide a question of foreign law without proof if it is requested to do so by both parties. But except in cases concerning the interpretation of foreign statutes, the courts are reluctant to take this course.[31] The issue arose in acute form before the High Court of Australia in *Neilson v Overseas Projects Corp of Victoria Ltd*,[32] where the rule of foreign statute law which was admitted permitted, but did not require, the foreign court to act in a particular manner. On the questions whether the evidence before the High Court was sufficient to prove how that rule of foreign law would be interpreted, or (if not) whether it was open to the Australian court to interpret it in accordance with the rules of construction which would have applied if it had been an Australian statute cast in the same terms, there was a divergence of view with no single answer commanding a clear majority.[33]

(g) In a few cases, the courts have determined questions of foreign law although, so far as one can see from the reports, no evidence of the foreign law was given. Thus in *Re Cohn*[34] the court construed and applied a section of the

9–009

---

[26] *Douglas v Brown* (1831) 2 Dow. & Cl. 171 (HL); *Cooper v Cooper* (1888) 13 App. Cas. 88.

[27] *Logan v Lee* (1907) 39 S.C.R. 311; *Canadian Pacific Ry v Parent* [1917] A.C. 195, 201 (PC); *Pettkus v Becker* (1980) 117 D.L.R. (3d) 257, 278 (Sup Ct Can).

[28] However, in *Oakley v Osiris Trustees Ltd* [2008] UKPC 2, [2009] W.T.L.R. 461, the Privy Council preferred to leave this question open. *cf.* British Law Ascertainment Act 1859, s.4; below, para.9–023.

[29] e.g. in *Moulis v Owen* [1907] 1 K.B. 746 (CA) it was admitted that a wagering contract was lawful by French law; *cf. The Torni* [1932] P. 27 and 78 (CA) where the text of a Palestine Ordinance was admitted.

[30] *Prowse v European and American Steam Shipping Co* (1860) 13 Moo. P.C. 484 (plea in confession and avoidance); *cf.* CPR, rr.16.5(3) and 16.7.

[31] *Beatty v Beatty* [1924] 1 K.B. 807 (CA) where the court was helped by a deposition made by a foreign lawyer for the purposes of the case but not used at the trial; as to the interpretation of foreign statutes, see *F&K Jabbour v Custodian of Israeli Absentee Property* [1954] 1 W.L.R. 139, 147–148; *Re Marshall* [1957] Ch. 507 (CA); *Islamic Republic of Iran v Berend* [2007] EWHC 132 (QB), [2007] 2 All E.R. (Comm.) 132, [35]. *cf. Re Sebba* [1959] Ch. 166; *Wilson, Smithett & Cope Ltd v Terruzzi* [1976] Q.B. 683, 692; below, paras 9–018 *et seq.*

[32] [2005] HCA 54, (2005) 223 C.L.R. 331.

[33] The proposition that rules of statutory construction are rules of law on which the *lex fori* will be applied unless the content of foreign law is proved to be different, which was accepted by Callinan and Heydon JJ., appears to be practical, but involves the risk of applying a foreign statutory rule in a manner which would not be adopted by the foreign court if it were trying the case. Kirby J. disparaged such an approach as "guesswork", and McHugh J. also rejected it. The majority neither explicitly approved nor disapproved the approach of Callinan and Heydon JJ., finding that on the evidence it was "inevitable" that the rule of foreign law would be interpreted in the same way as an Australian court would have read it.

[34] [1945] Ch. 5.

German Civil Code which was not proved, and as to the effect of which no evidence was given. Again, the courts have in a number of cases applied colonial laws without proof.[35]

9–010 Although foreign law is a question of fact, it is "a question of fact of a peculiar kind." Thus in *Parkasho v Singh*[36] a Divisional Court reversed a manifestly erroneous decision by magistrates on a question of foreign law, while recognising that appellate courts are slow to interfere with trial courts on a question of fact. Likewise, in *King v Brandywine Reinsurance Co*,[37] the Court of Appeal reaffirmed the "special" character of findings of foreign law as questions of fact, holding that it was entitled to reverse the findings of the trial judge on the law of New York, especially as the actual question of New York law was one as to the construction of commercial documents.[38] But generally, an appellate court, which will not have had not had the opportunity to put questions to the expert witness of foreign law, will be slow to substitute its opinion for that of the trial judge.[39]

9–011 The treatment of foreign law as a question of fact to be pleaded and proved by either or both of the parties means that the question of the applicability of foreign law in a case involving the conflict of laws may ultimately depend, in England, on the rules of procedure and evidence since it is to that legal category that the question belongs once this approach is accepted.[40] The consequences may be illustrated by an example. According to the Rome I Regulation on the Law Applicable to Contractual Obligations,[41] a "contract shall be governed by the law chosen by the parties."[42] A contract which becomes the subject of English litigation may contain an express choice of foreign law. Although the language of the Rome I Regulation may suggest that the court is bound to apply the foreign law chosen, the rules of the Regulation are expressed, subject to a limited exception,[43] not to apply to matters of

---

[35] e.g. *Re Baker's Trusts* (1871) L.R. 13 Eq. 168; *Re Barlow's Will* (1887) 36 Ch.D. 287 (CA); *Roe v Roe* (1916) 115 L.T. 792; *L. (orse B) v L* (1919) 36 T.L.R. 148; *Bonhote v Bonhote* [1920] W.N. 142. The colonial laws in these cases might have been proved under the Colonial Laws Validity Act 1865, s.6 or under the Evidence (Colonial Statutes) Act 1907 (para.9–022, below) but these Acts are not mentioned in the reports.

[36] [1968] P. 233, 250; approved in *Dalmia Dairy Industries Ltd v National Bank of Pakistan* [1978] 2 Lloyd's Rep. 223, 286 (CA); *The Amazonia* [1990] 1 Lloyd's Rep. 236 (CA); *Bumper Development Corp v Commissioner of Police of the Metropolis* [1991] 1 W.L.R. 1362, 1370 (CA); *Abu Dhabi Investment Co v H Clarkson & Co Ltd* [2006] EWHC 1252 (Comm.); *James Hardie & Co Ltd v Hall* (1998) 43 N.S.W.L.R. 554, 573–574 (CA).

[37] [2005] EWCA Civ 235, [2005] 1 Lloyd's Rep. 655 (*obiter*, as the judge's conclusion was not disturbed).

[38] For the significance of this, see below, n.100.

[39] *Dallah Estate and Tourism Holding Co v Ministry of Religious Affairs, Government of Pakistan* [2009] EWCA Civ 755, [28]–[29], affirmed without reference to this point: [2010] UKSC 46, [2011] 1 A.C. 783.

[40] For the practical reasons why parties might not plead and prove foreign law, see Fentiman, above, n.1, Ch.5. See also *Muduroglu Ltd v TC Ziraat Bankasi* [1986] 1 Q.B. 1225, 1246 (CA).

[41] Regulation (EC) 593/2008. The Rome I Regulation superseded the Rome Convention on the Law Applicable to Contractual Obligations, given force in the United Kingdom by Contracts (Applicable Law) Act 1990, but for present purposes the Regulation reproduces the material provisions of the Convention. See below, para.32–011.

[42] Art.3(1). See below, Rule 222.

[43] See Art.18.

evidence and procedure[44]: and it is apparently the case that whether a particular rule belongs to this category is a matter for the law of the forum.[45] If neither party relies on the chosen foreign law, the case will be decided exclusively by reference to English law since the procedural or evidential nature of the English rule concerning pleading and proof of foreign law is untouched by the Regulation.[46] The same result ensued in cases involving contracts governed by foreign law at common law which were also decided exclusively by reference to English law since neither party saw fit to plead or prove a foreign law which was of undoubted relevance according to normal rules of the conflict of laws.[47]

(2) To be proved to the satisfaction of the judge. Formerly, questions of foreign law had to be submitted to the jury. This rule was altered by statute, so that now questions of foreign law are decided by the judge alone.[48] This rule applies to criminal trials.[49]

9–012

(3) Mode of proof[50]

(i) *Expert evidence.* It is now well settled that foreign law must, in general, be proved by expert evidence.[51] Foreign law cannot be proved merely by

9–013

---

[44] Art.1(3).

[45] According to the Giuliano-Lagarde Report, [1980] O.J. C282/35–36, this was so for the predecessor of the Rome I Regulation, the Rome Convention on the Law Applicable to Contractual Obligations, given force in the United Kingdom by Contracts (Applicable Law) Act 1990. The general principle of legal certainty and stability should ensure that the answer is the same for the Rome I Regulation. Art.30 of the Rome II Regulation (Regulation (EC) 864/2007, as to which, see generally Chs 34–36) requires the European Commission to report on the effects of the way or ways in which foreign law is treated in the Member States, and the extent to which the courts apply foreign law in practice under the Rome II Regulation.

[46] Art.3(2) of the Regulation (below, para.32–011) enables the parties to change the law originally chosen to apply to the contract. According to Giuliano-Lagarde, p.18, if "the choice of law is made or changed in the course of proceedings the question arises as to the limits within which the choice or change can be effective. However, the question falls within the ambit of the national law of procedure, and can be settled only in accordance with that law." This observation reinforces the view of the English approach expressed in the text. For analysis of the role of Rule 25 in the context of the Rome Convention, see Fentiman, above, n.1, pp.80–97.

[47] e.g. *Aluminium Industrie Vaassen BV v Romalpa Aluminium Ltd* [1976] 1 W.L.R. 676 (CA). See below, paras 33–029 *et seq.*

[48] Originally Administration of Justice Act 1920, s.15. For the High Court see Senior Courts Act 1981, s.69(5); for county courts see County Courts Act 1984, s.68; for all other courts, including the Crown Court, the original provision presumably remains in force.

[49] *R. v Hammer* [1923] 2 K.B. 786.

[50] See generally *MCC Proceeds Inc v Bishopsgate Investment Trust Plc (No.4)* [1999] C.L.C. 418 (CA). For analysis of the method of proof, and consideration of alternative approaches, see Fentiman, above, n.1, pp.173–264.

[51] *Baron de Bode's Case* (1845) 8 Q.B. 208, 246–267; *Nelson v Bridport* (1845) 8 Beav. 527, 536; *The Earldom of Perth* (1846) 2 H.L.C. 865, 873; *Castrique v Imrie* (1870) L.R. 4 H.L. 414, 430; *Sussex Peerage Case* (1844) 11 Cl. & F. 85, 115; *Bumper Development Corp v Commissioner of Police of the Metropolis* [1991] 1 W.L.R. 1362, 1368 (CA) ("trite law"); *O'Callaghan v O'Sullivan* [1925] 1 I.R. 90, 119. The earlier view, that expert evidence was not sufficient to prove foreign written laws (last expressed by Lord Campbell in the *Sussex Peerage Case* (above) at pp.114–115) has now clearly been abandoned.

putting the text of a foreign enactment before the court, nor merely by citing foreign decisions or books of authority.[52] Such materials can only be brought before the court as part of the evidence of an expert witness,[53] since without his assistance the court cannot evaluate or interpret them. This may be especially important (even if the ultimate task of the judge is made little easier) when the foreign law in question is found in a number of sources whose relationship to each other is not easily understood or explained,[54] or in cases in which the essence of the foreign law is that a local judge will inform himself as to what the material principles of religious[55] law require in circumstances in which he is not bound to follow previous decisions, even his own, and there is no tradition of textbook writing.[56]

9–014 No precise or comprehensive answer can be given to the question who, for this purpose, is a competent expert.[57] A judge or legal practitioner[58] from the foreign country is always competent. But in civil proceedings there is no longer any rule of law (if indeed there ever was) that the expert witness must have practised, or at least be entitled to practise, in the foreign country. For s.4(1) of the Civil Evidence Act 1972[59] provides that "it is hereby declared that in civil proceedings a person who is suitably qualified to do so on account of his knowledge or experience is competent to give expert evidence as to [foreign law[60]] irrespective of whether he has acted or is entitled to act as a legal practitioner [in the foreign country]."[61] Under these principles, which are probably declaratory of the law,[62] a former practitioner in the foreign

---

[52] *Nelson v Bridport* (1845) 8 Beav. 527, 542; *Buerger v New York Life Assurance Co* (1927) 96 L.J.K.B. 930, 940, 942 (CA); *Bumper Development Corp v Commissioner of Police of the Metropolis* [1991] 1 W.L.R. 1362, 1371 (CA); cf. *Callwood v Callwood* [1960] A.C. 659 (PC).

[53] *Bumper Development Corp v Commissioner of Police of the Metropolis, ibid.,* Glencore *International AG v Metro Trading International Inc* [2001] 1 Lloyd's Rep. 284; *Dymocks Franchise Systems (NSW) Pty Ltd v Todd* [2002] UKPC 50, [2004] 1 N.Z.L.R. 289, [2002] 2 All E.R. (Comm.) 849 (PC). But for trenchant criticism of this traditional methodology, see *Bodum USA Inc v La Cafetière Inc*, 621 F. 3d 624 (7th Cir. 2010).

[54] *Harley v Smith* [2010] EWCA Civ 78, approving [2009] EWHC 56 (QB), [2009] 1 Lloyd's Rep. 359 (Saudi legislative decrees and Shari'a principles).

[55] This being applied as part of Saudi Arabian law, and not as the *lex causae* in its own right.

[56] *Abdel Hadi Abdullah Al Qahtani & Sons Beverage Industry Co v Antliff* [2010] EWHC 1735 (Comm.) (Saudi law).

[57] *Glencore International AG v Metro Trading International Inc*, above, at pp.299–300; *R. v Okolie, The Times*, June 16, 2000 (CA) (general employee of foreign company alleged to be victim of crime not competent to give expert evidence of foreign criminal law). Falconbridge, Ch.47: as to probate matters, see Non-Contentious Probate Rules 1987 (SI 1987/2024), r.19.

[58] This would presumably include a person such as a notary public: cf. *In the Goods of Whitelegg* [1899] P. 267.

[59] This gives effect to the Seventeenth Report of the Law Reform Committee, Cmnd. 4489 (1970).

[60] Including Scots and Northern Irish law.

[61] See *Associated Shipping Services Ltd v Department of Private Affairs of HH Sheikh Zayed Bin Sultan Al-Nahayan, Financial Times*, July 31, 1990 (CA). In *Bristow v Sequeville* (1850) 5 Exch. 275, 277, it was held that a person who had studied the law of a foreign country but who had never practised there was not competent. This case was followed in *In the Goods of Bonelli* (1875) 1 P.D. 69 and *Re Turner* [1906] W.N. 27 but is rendered obsolete by s.4(1).

[62] *Clyne v Federal Commissioner of Taxation (No.2)* (1981) 57 F.L.R. 198, 203.

country may be competent,[63] as may be a person who is entitled to practise in the foreign country but who has not done so,[64] a person who although he has neither practised nor been entitled to practise in the foreign country, has practised in a second foreign country whose law is the same as that of the first,[65] and a person who although having no knowledge or experience of the foreign law based on study or practice has nevertheless become conversant with a point of foreign law through work involving contact with that foreign law.[66] There can be no doubt also, that an academic lawyer who has specialised in the law of the foreign country is competent[67] and it is common for such persons to supply expert evidence.[68] In principle, a witness may be competent although he is not a lawyer of any kind providing that, by virtue of his profession or calling, he has acquired a practical knowledge of a foreign law,[69] though such persons will, of course, only be regarded as experts in that

---

[63] *Re Duke of Wellington* [1947] Ch. 506, 514–515; *Re Banque des Marchands de Moscou* [1958] Ch. 182; *Rossano v Manufacturers' Life Insurance Co* [1963] 2 Q.B. 352, 373; *Kertesz v Kertesz* [1954] V.L.R. 195; *Etler v Kertesz* (1960) 26 D.L.R. (2d) 209 (Ont CA). Tsarist lawyers who practised law before the 1917 Revolution were often allowed to give evidence of Soviet law although they had no practical experience of it. See, e.g. *Russian Commercial and Industrial Bank v Comptoir d'Escompte de Mulhouse* [1925] A.C. 112; *Employers Liability Co v Sedgwick, Collins & Co* [1927] A.C. 95; *Buerger v New York Life Assurance Co* (1927) 96 L.J.K.B. 930 (CA). But the evidence of Soviet lawyers was preferred if available: *Lazard Brothers & Co v Midland Bank Ltd* [1933] A.C. 289, 299.

[64] *Barford v Barford* [1918] P. 140; *Perlak Petroleum Maatschappij v Deen* [1924] 1 K.B. 111 (CA). *cf. Etler v Kertesz* (1960) 26 D.L.R. (2d) 209 (Ont CA), where the witness had only practised in the foreign country for a brief period but had for many years been entitled to do so.

[65] *Reinblatt v Gold* (1928) Que.R. 45 K.B. 136; affirmed [1929] S.C.R. 74; also reported on another point [1929] 1 D.L.R. 959 (Sup Ct Can). The authorities conflict as to whether an English barrister who has acquired a knowledge of foreign law through practice before the Privy Council is competent: see *Wilson v Wilson* [1903] P. 157 (competent); *Cartwright v Cartwright* (1878) 26 W.R. 684 (not competent).

[66] *Associated Shipping Services Ltd v Department of Private Affairs of HH Sheikh Zayed Bin Sultan Al-Nahayan, Financial Times,* July 31, 1990 (CA) (lawyer employed as legal adviser to defendant competent expert on question whether defendant an independent juridical entity).

[67] *Brailey v Rhodesia Consolidated Ltd* [1910] 2 Ch. 95 (Reader in Roman-Dutch law to the Council of Legal Education); *cf. Dalrymple v Dalrymple* (1811) 2 Hagg. Con. 54, 81 ("learned professors"). An English solicitor who had never practised in Chile but who had considerable experience of its laws was held competent in *In the Goods of Whitelegg* [1899] P. 267.

[68] e.g. *Bodley Head v Flegon* [1972] 1 W.L.R. 680; *R. v Registrar-General of Births, Deaths and Marriages, Ex. p. Minhas* [1977] Q.B. 1; *X AG v A Bank* [1983] 2 All E.R. 464; *PT Royal Bali Leisure v Hutchinson & Co Trust Co Ltd* [2004] EWHC 1014 (Ch.).

[69] e.g. Governor of a Colony (*Cooper-King v Cooper-King* [1900] P. 65); ambassador (*In the Goods of Oldenburg* (1884) 9 P.D. 234); embassy official (*In the Goods of Dost Aly Khan* (1880) 6 P.D. 6); vice-consul (*Lacon v Higgins* (1822) Dow & Ry. N.P. 38); bishop (*Sussex Peerage Case* (1844) 11 Cl. & F. 85; *R. v Naoum* (1911) 24 O.L.R. 306 (CA)); parish priests (*R. v Savage* (1876) 13 Cox C.C. 178 (not competent); *R. v Ilich* [1935] N.Z.L.R. 90; *Saari v Nykanen* [1944] 4 D.L.R. 619 (Ont) (competent)); merchant (*Vander Donckt v Thellusson* (1849) 8 C.B. 812, though it has been said that the court may refuse to admit the evidence of such a witness where that of a qualified lawyer is readily available: *Direct Winters Transport v Duplate Canada Ltd* (1962) 32 D.L.R. (2d) 278 (Ont), disapproved in *Clyne v Federal Commissioner of Taxation (No.2)* (1981) 57 F.L.R. 198, 202–203); bank manager (*De Beéche v South American Stores Ltd* [1935] A.C. 148; *Ajami v Comptroller of Customs* [1954] 1 W.L.R. 1405 (PC), followed in *Associated Shipping Services Ltd v Department of Private Affairs of HH Sheikh Zayed Bin Sultan Al-Nahayan, Financial Times,* July 31, 1990 (CA) where, however, the witness was a lawyer not an expert in the foreign law by virtue of study or qualification, but as a result of experience through work; police officer (*Guerin v Proulx* (1982) 37 O.R. (2d) 558).

part of the foreign law with which they are bound, by virtue of their profession or calling, to be familiar. In practice, however, there will be few cases in the modern law where it will be necessary to rely on the expert evidence of such persons[70]: for it is safe to assume that, almost invariably, such evidence will be obtained from a legal practitioner or an academic lawyer with the relevant expertise. It is, of course, a truism that a person who has no special knowledge of foreign law is not competent.[71] And it is equally a truism that just because a witness is technically competent, his lack of plausibility[72] or independence may severely weaken the credibility of the evidence which he purports to give.[73]

9–015   (ii) *Use of foreign sources.* An English court will not conduct its own researches into foreign law;[74] in the common law system, "the trial is not an inquisition into the content of relevant foreign law any more than it is an inquisition into other factual issues that the parties tender for decision by the court".[75] But if an expert witness refers to foreign statutes, decisions or books, the court is entitled to look at them as part of his evidence.[76] But the court is not entitled to go beyond this: thus if a witness cites a passage from a foreign law-book he does not put the whole book in evidence since he does not necessarily regard the whole book as accurate.[77] Similarly, if the witness cites a section from a foreign code or a passage from a foreign decision the court will not look at other sections of the code or at other parts of the decision without the aid of the witness, since they may have been abrogated by subsequent legislation.

9–016   If the evidence of the expert witness as to the effect of the sources quoted by him is uncontradicted, "it has been repeatedly said that the court should be reluctant to reject it,"[78] and it has been held that where each party's expert witness agrees on the meaning and effect of the foreign law, the court is not

---

[70] For examples see *Guerin v Proulx,* above; *Associated Shipping Services Ltd v Department of Private Affairs of HH Sheikh Zayed Bin Sultan Al-Nahayan,* above.

[71] e.g. *R. v Povey* (1852) Dears. 32; *R. v Naguib* [1917] 1 K.B. 359; *Perlak Petroleum Maatschappij v Deen* [1924] 1 K.B. 111 (CA); *Clyne v Federal Commissioner of Taxation (No.2)* 57 F.L.R. 198.

[72] *Dornoch Ltd v Westminster International BV* [2009] EWHC 1782 (Admlty), [2009] 2 Lloyd's Rep. 191, [49].

[73] *Debt Collect London Ltd v SK Slavia Praha Fotbal AS* [2010] EWCA Civ 1250, [2011] 1 W.L.R. 866, [31]–[36].

[74] *Di Sora v Phillipps* (1863) 10 H.L.C. 624, 640; *Bumper Development Corp v Commissioner of Police of the Metropolis* [1991] 1 W.L.R. 1362, 1369 (CA), approving the proposition in the text.

[75] *Neilson v Overseas Projects Corp of Victoria Ltd* [2005] HCA 54, (2005) 223 C.L.R. 331, at [118].

[76] *Nelson v Bridport* (1845) 8 Beav. 527, 541; *Concha v Murietta* (1889) 40 Ch.D. 543 (CA); *Lazard Brothers & Co v Midland Bank Ltd* [1933] A.C. 289, 298; *Bumper Development Corp v Commissioner of Police of the Metropolis*, above.

[77] *Nelson v Bridport* (1845) 8 Beav. 527, 542; *Waung v Subbotovsky* [1968] 3 N.S.W.R. 261, 499.

[78] *Sharif v Azad* [1967] 1 Q.B. 605, 616 (CA). See *Buerger v New York Life Assurance Co* (1927) 96 L.J.K.B. 930, 941 (CA); *Koechlin & Cie v Kestenbaum* [1927] 1 K.B. 616, 622, reversed on appeal but not on this point: [1927] 1 K.B. 889, 895 (CA); *Re Banque des Marchands de Moscou* [1958] Ch. 192; *Rossano v Manufacturers' Life Insurance Co* [1963] 2 Q.B. 352; *O'Callaghan v O'Sullivan* [1925] 1 I.R. 90, 119; *Macnamara v Hatteras (Owners)* [1933] I.R. 675, 695, 699; *Etler v Kertesz* (1960) 26 D.L.R. (2d) 209 (Ont CA).

entitled to reject such agreed evidence, at least on the basis of its own research into foreign law.[79] But while the court will normally accept such evidence it will not do so if it is "obviously false,"[80] "obscure,"[81] "extravagant,"[82] lacking in obvious "objectivity and impartiality",[83] or "patently absurd,"[84] or if "he never applied his mind to the real point of law",[85] or if "the matters stated by [the expert] did not support his conclusion according to any stated or implied process of reasoning";[86] or if the relevant foreign court would not employ the reasoning of the expert even if it agreed with the conclusion.[87] In such cases the court may reject the evidence and examine the foreign sources to form its own conclusion as to their effect. Or, in other words, a court is not inhibited from "using its own intelligence as on any other question of evidence".[88] Similarly, the court may reject an expert's opinion as to the meaning of a foreign statute if it is inconsistent with the text or the English translation and is not justified by reference to any special rule of construction of the foreign law.[89] It should, however, be noted in this connection that quite simple words may well be terms of art in a foreign statute.[90]

If the evidence of several expert witnesses conflicts as to the effect of foreign sources, the court is entitled, and indeed bound, to look at those sources in order itself to decide between the conflicting testimony.[91] Similarly, **9–017**

---

[79] *Bumper Development Corp v Commissioner of Police of the Metropolis* [1991] 1 W.L.R. 1362 (CA).

[80] *O'Callaghan v O'Sullivan* [1925] 1 I.R. 90, 119.

[81] *Allen v Hay* (1922) 69 D.L.R. 193, 195–196 (Sup Ct Can).

[82] *Buerger v New York Life Assurance Co* (1927) 96 L.J.K.B. 930, 941 (CA).

[83] *Debt Collect London Ltd v SK Slavia Praha Fotbal AS* [2010] EWCA Civ 1250, [2011] 1 W.L.R. 866, [33], [36].

[84] *A/S Tallinna Laevauhisus v Estonian State Steamship Line* (1947) 80 Ll.L.R. 99, 108 (CA).

[85] *Re Valentine's Settlement* [1965] Ch. 831, 855 (CA), *per* Salmon L.J., dissenting; *cf. Callwood v Callwood* [1960] A.C. 659 (PC).

[86] *Associated Shipping Services Ltd v Department of Private Affairs of HH Sheikh Zayed Bin Sultan Al-Nahayan, Financial Times,* July 31, 1990 (CA).

[87] *Macmillan Inc v Bishopsgate Investment Trust Plc (No.3)* [1995] 1 W.L.R. 978, 1009; the decision to reject the expert evidence was approved in *MCC Proceeds Inc v Bishopsgate Investment Trust Plc (No.4)* [1999] C.L.C. 418 (CA).

[88] *A/S Tallinna Laevauhisus v Estonian State Steamship Line* (1947) 80 Ll. L. R. 99, 107 (CA); *Glencore International AG v Metro Trading International Inc,* above, at p.300; *Catalyst Recycling Ltd v Nickelhütte Aue GmbH* [2008] EWCA Civ 541, [49]–[52].

[89] *A/S Tallinna Laevauhisus v Estonian State Steamship Line,* above.

[90] e.g. "kindred" and "incidental" in *Camille and Henry Dreyfus Foundation Inc v IRC* [1954] Ch. 672, 692 (CA); affirmed [1956] A.C. 39.

[91] *Dalrymple v Dalrymple* (1811) 2 Hagg.Con. 54; *Trimbey v Vignier* (1834) 1 Bing. N.C. 151; *Devaux v Steele* (1840) 6 Bing. N.C. 360; *Nelson v Bridport* (1845) 8 Beav. 527, 537; *Bremer v Freeman* (1857) 10 Moo. P.C. 306; *Concha v Murietta* (1889) 40 Ch.D. 543 (CA); *Guaranty Trust Corporation of New York v Hannay* [1918] 2 K.B. 623 (CA); *Russian Commercial and Industrial Bank v Comptoir d'Escompte de Mulhouse* [1923] 2 K.B. 630, reversed [1925] A.C. 112 on the ground that the Court of Appeal had misinterpreted the foreign law; *Princess Paley Olga v Weisz* [1929] 1 K.B. 718 (CA); *Re Duke of Wellington* [1947] Ch. 506; *In the Estate of Fuld (No.3)* [1968] P. 675, 700–703; *Dubai Bank Ltd v Galadari (No.5), The Times,* June 26, 1990; *Bumper Development Corp v Commissioner of Police of the Metropolis* [1991] 1 W.L.R. 1362, 1369–1370 (CA), expressly approving the proposition in the text; *MCC Proceeds Inc v Bishopsgate Investment Trust Plc (No.4)* [1999] C.L.C. 418 (CA); *Shiblaq v Sadikoglu* [2004] EWHC 1890 (Comm.), [2004] 2 All E.R. (Comm.) 596; *Arros Invest Ltd v Nishanov* [2004] EWHC 576 (Ch.), [2004] I.L.Pr. 366. *Kolbin and Sons v Kinnear,* 1930 S.C. 724; *Macnamara v Hatteras (Owners)* [1933] I.R. 675, 699–700.

where the evidence of expert witnesses as to the constitutionality or *vires* of foreign legislation conflicts, it seems that the court can determine the question,[92] provided at any rate that it is one which, according to the foreign law, is determinable by ordinary judicial proceedings.[93] In addition the territory of what was once a single country may be divided, for instance in times of revolution or civil war, or as a result of enemy occupation; and the question may then arise which of two legislatures or systems of courts has the right to determine the law of any given part of that territory. In this situation, the problem to be resolved is not one of proof of foreign law but rather that of identifying the appropriate law-maker. The evidence of expert witnesses is irrelevant on the latter issue which is discussed elsewhere in this work.[94] Once, of course, the appropriate law-maker has been identified, the question of proving what the content of the law handed down by that law-maker actually is will have to be determined by reference to the evidence of an appropriately qualified expert.

9–018   Since the effect of foreign sources is primarily a matter for the expert witness, it is desirable, when proving a foreign statute, also to obtain evidence as to its interpretation.[95] It may happen, however, that the text of a foreign statute is admitted, or that it is proved without expert evidence under the Evidence (Colonial Statutes) Act 1907,[96] or that the expert fails to give any evidence as to its interpretation. In such cases, the court can put its own construction on the foreign statute.[97] The court may also undertake this task at the express request of the parties.[98] In all these cases the court acts on the assumption that the foreign rules of construction are the same as those of English law.[99]

9–019   The function of the expert witness in relation to the interpretation of foreign statutes must be contrasted with his function in relation to the construction of foreign documents. In the former case, the expert tells the court what the

---

[92] *King of the Hellenes v Brostrom* (1923) 16 Ll.L.R. 167, 190, 192; *Re Amand* [1941] 2 K.B. 239; *Re Amand (No.2)* [1942] 1 K.B. 445; *A/S Tallinna Laevauhisus v Estonian State Steamship Line* (1947) 80 Ll.L.R. 99, 114 (CA); *Dubai Bank Ltd v Galadari (No.5), The Times*, June 26, 1990; F.A. Mann, *Studies in International Law* (1973), pp.444–449.

[93] Lipstein (1967) 42 B.Y.I.L. 265. It has been said to be doubtful whether the court can determine such a question if in the foreign country it cannot be decided by a court at all (as in Switzerland) or only by a special constitutional court (as in Germany). See Kahn-Freund, *Festschrift für FA Mann* (1977), pp.207–225.

[94] See below, para.25–004. For special provisions relating to corporations, see Foreign Corporations Act 1991, discussed below, para.30–015.

[95] *Baron de Bode's Case* (1845) 8 Q.B. 208, 251, 265–266; *Castrique v Imrie* (1870) L.R. 4 HL 414, 430; *Higgins v Ewing's Trustees*, 1925 S.C. 440; *Allen v Standard Trusts Co* (1919) 49 D.L.R. 399 (Man).

[96] See below, para.9–022.

[97] e.g. *Prowse v European and American Steam Shipping Co* (1860) 13 Moo. P.C. 484; *Papadopoulos v Papadopoulos* [1930] P. 55; *The Torni* [1932] P. 78 (CA); *Jasiewicz v Jasiewicz* [1962] 1 W.L.R. 1426; *Mahadervan v Mahadervan* [1964] P. 233.

[98] See above, para.9–008, n.31.

[99] *F&K Jabbour v Custodian of Israeli Absentee Property* [1954] 1 W.L.R. 139, 147–148. This approach was expressly adopted in *Neilson v Overseas Projects Corp of Victoria Ltd* [2005] HCA 54, (2005) 223 C.L.R. 331 by Callinan J., and expressly approved by Heydon J.; but it was expressly rejected by McHugh and Kirby JJ. The majority (Gleeson C.J., Gummow and Hayne JJ.) was able to reach its conclusion on the footing, denied by the other four judges, that the evidence of foreign law before the court was sufficient to answer the question which arose for decision without the need to rely on any such assumption as the basis for decision.

statute means, explaining his opinion, if necessary, by reference to foreign rules of construction. In the latter case, the expert merely proves the foreign rules of construction, and the court itself, in the light of these rules, determines the meaning of the documents.[100] Where a document which is to be construed by English law incorporates the words of a foreign statute as part of its terms, the court construes the document without reference to foreign rules of construction,[101] unless the parties to the document intend it to be construed in accordance with such foreign rules.[102]

Considerable weight is usually given to the decisions of foreign courts as evidence of foreign law,[103] though such decisions can only, it seems, be referred to if referred to in the evidence of an expert witness[104] and, further, must be interpreted in the light on the meaning attributed to the decisions by the expert rather than according to the court's independent research involving material not referred to by the expert.[105] But the court is not bound to apply a foreign decision if it is satisfied, as a result of all the evidence, that the decision does not accurately represent the foreign law.[106] Where foreign decisions conflict, the court may be asked to decide between them, even though in the foreign country the question still remains to be authoritatively settled.[107] **9–020**

(iii) *Other modes of proof.* Under certain statutes, proof of foreign law may sometimes be dispensed with. **9–021**

---

[100] *Trotter v Trotter* (1828) 4 Bli.(N.S.) 502; *King of Spain v Machado* (1827) 4 Russ. 225, 239–240; *Rouyer Guillet & Cie v Rouyer Guillet & Co Ltd* [1949] 1 All E.R. 244 (CA); *Mount Cook (Northland) Ltd v Swedish Motors Ltd* [1986] 1 N.Z.L.R. 720, 727. This sentence was approved in *Toomey (of Syndicate 2021) v Banco Vitalico de España SA de Seguros y Reaseguros* [2003] EWHC 1102 (Comm.) at [37] (affirmed without reference to this point: [2004] EWCA Civ 662); *Evialis SA v SIAT* [2003] EWHC 863 (Comm.), [2003] 2 Lloyd's Rep. 337 at [44]; *cf. Svenska Petroleum Exploration AB v Republic of Lithuania* [2005] EWHC 2437 (Comm.), [2006] 1 Lloyd's Rep. 181, [29] (affd. without reference to this point, [2006] EWCA Civ 1529, [2007] Q.B. 886). For further authority confirming that the proper role of the expert is to prove the rules of construction of foreign law but not to assume the court's function in applying those rules, see *King v Brandywine Reinsurance Co* [2005] EWCA Civ 235, [2005] 1 Lloyd's Rep. 655; *Rendell v Combined Insurance Co of America* [2005] EWHC 678 (Comm.).

[101] *Dobell v Steamship Rossmore Co* [1895] 2 Q.B. 408 (CA); *cf.*, paras 32–058 *et seq.*, below.

[102] See *Stafford Allen and Sons Ltd v Pacific Steam Navigation Co* [1956] 1 W.L.R. 629 (CA).

[103] *Beatty v Beatty* [1924] 1 K.B. 807 (CA); *Re Annesley* [1926] Ch. 692; *Bankers and Shippers Insurance Co of New York v Liverpool Marine and General Insurance Co Ltd* (1926) 24 Ll.L.R. 85 (HL); *In the Estate of Fuld (No.3)* [1968] P. 675, 701–702; *Law Debenture Trust Corp Plc v Elektrim SA* [2009] EWHC 1801 (Ch.), [100].

[104] *Bumper Development Corp v Commissioner of Police of the Metropolis* [1991] 1 W.L.R. 1362, 1370–1371 (CA).

[105] *ibid.*

[106] *Guaranty Trust Corp of New York v Hannay* [1918] 2 K.B. 623 (CA); *Callwood v Callwood* [1960] A.C. 659 (PC).

[107] *Re Duke of Wellington* [1947] Ch. 506; *Breen v Breen* [1964] P. 144. See also *JP Morgan Chase Bank v Lanner (The)* (2008) 305 D.L.R. (4th) 442 (difficulty presented by disagreement between US Circuit Courts of Appeal); *Blue Sky One Ltd v Mahan Air* [2010] EWHC 631 (Comm.), [88] (lack of decisive guidance from Supreme Court of Iran, requiring judge to "determine the trajectory" of Iranian law); *Abdel Hadi Abdullah Al Qahtani & Sons Beverage Industry Co v Antliff* [2010] EWHC 1735 (Comm.) (Saudi law).

By the Civil Evidence Act 1972, section 4(2),[108] where, whether before or after the passing of that act, any question of foreign law[109] has been determined in civil or criminal proceedings at first instance in the High Court, the Crown Court, a court of quarter sessions[110] or the county palatine Courts of Chancery of Lancaster or Durham,[111] or in any appeal therefrom, or in the Privy Council on appeal from any court outside the United Kingdom,[112] then any finding made or decision given on that question is admissible in evidence in any civil proceedings, and the foreign law shall be taken to be in accordance with that finding or decision unless the contrary is proved. The finding or decision as to foreign law must be reported or recorded in citable form, which means that it must be reported or recorded in writing in a report, transcript or other document which could be cited as an authority in legal proceedings in England if the question had been one of English law.[113] Except with the permission of the court, a party may not adduce any such finding or decision as evidence of foreign law unless he has in accordance with rules of court notified every other party of his intention to do so.[114] The subsection does not apply if the subsequent proceedings are before a court which can take judicial notice of the foreign law. Thus a determination of a point of Scots law by the High Court or the Court of Appeal is not even prima facie evidence of that point in subsequent proceedings before the Supreme Court. Nor is the determination prima facie binding if there are conflicting findings or decisions on the same question.[115]

9–022   By the Evidence (Colonial Statutes) Act 1907,[116] copies of laws made by the legislature of any "British possession,"[117] if purporting to be printed by the government printer of the "British possession," can be received in evidence in the United Kingdom without proof that the copies were so printed. Under this Act, the text of such laws can be proved without expert evidence;[118] but the court may require expert evidence to show that the alleged law is still in force.[119] The Act continues to apply to the legislation of many Commonwealth countries which are no longer part of Her Majesty's dominions, e.g. because they have become republics.[120]

---

[108] This gives effect to the Seventeenth Report of the Law Reform Committee, Cmnd. 4489 (1970), para.64; *cf. Phoenix Marine Inc v China Ocean Shipping Co* [1999] 1 Lloyd's Rep. 682.

[109] Including Scots or Northern Irish law.

[110] Courts of quarter sessions were abolished by the Courts Act 1971, s.3.

[111] These courts were abolished on their merger with the High Court: *ibid.* ss.41, 57(3)(b).

[112] Civil Evidence Act 1972, s.4(4).

[113] s.4(5).

[114] s.4(3).

[115] s.4(2), proviso.

[116] For a similar, but less general, provision, see Colonial Laws Validity Act 1865, s.6. See also Isle of Man Act 1979, s.12(1).

[117] i.e. "any part of [Her] Majesty's dominions exclusive of the United Kingdom ... ": s.1(3).

[118] *Taylor v Taylor* [1923] W.N. 65; *Waterfield v Waterfield* (1929) 73 S.J. 300; *Papadopoulos v Papadopoulos* [1930] P. 55. See also the cases cited above, para.9–009.

[119] *Brown v Brown* (1917) 116 L.T. 702; *R. v Governor of Brixton Prison, ex p. Shuter* [1960] 2 Q.B. 89; *Jasiewicz v Jasiewicz* [1962] 1 W.L.R. 1426.

[120] This is the effect of provisions in Acts of the UK Parliament for the continuation of existing laws in relation to such countries when they cease to form part of Her Majesty's dominions: *Jasiewicz v Jasiewicz* [1962] 1 W.L.R. 1426.

By the British Law Ascertainment Act 1859, a court in any part of Her **9–023** Majesty's dominions may, if it thinks necessary or expedient for the proper disposal of an action, state a case for the opinion of a court in any other part of Her Majesty's dominions in order to ascertain the view of that court as to the law applicable to the facts of the case stated.[121] The Act continues to apply to many Commonwealth countries which are no longer part of Her Majesty's dominions.[122] The court may take advantage of the provisions of the Act of its own motion[123] and may, on the other hand, refuse to state a case on request if it is satisfied that it already has enough evidence of the foreign law.[124] The court has a complete discretion whether or not to state a case.[125] There are very few reported cases in which it has done so, because the procedure is expensive and involves delay. The opinion of the foreign court is binding on the English court now that the power of submitting such opinion to the jury as evidence of the foreign law[126] has become obsolete.[127] But the opinion is not binding on the Supreme Court if it was given by a court over which it exercises appellate jurisdiction; and similarly the opinion of a court over which the Privy Council exercises appellate jurisdiction does not bind the Privy Council.[128]

Although statutory provision was made for the application of similar **9–024** procedures to the ascertainment of the law of foreign countries outside the Commonwealth, no international conventions to this end were ever concluded.[129] However, a multilateral convention serving the same purposes was signed in London in 1968. The European Convention on Information on Foreign Law[130] came into effect in the following year; the great majority of Member States of the Council of Europe, including the United Kingdom, have ratified the Convention. Where proceedings have actually been instituted, a judicial authority in any Contracting State may make a request for information under the Convention.[131] The request must state the nature of the case, the questions on which information concerning the law of the requested State is desired, and the facts necessary both for the proper understanding of the request and for the formulation of an exact and precise reply.[132] The request must be for information as to law and procedure in civil and commercial fields, or as to judicial organisation, but other matters may be raised if they are incidental to primary questions falling within that area.[133] The request is transmitted through designated national liaison organs,[134] and a reply may be

---

[121] s.1.

[122] For the reason given above.

[123] See above, para.9–003.

[124] *MacDougall v Chitnavis*, 1937 S.C. 390, 407–408.

[125] *Lord v Colvin* (1860) 1 Dr. & Sm. 24.

[126] s.3.

[127] See above, para.9–012; *MacDougall v Chitnavis*, 1937 S.C. 390, 400.

[128] s.4; *De Thoren v Att-Gen* (1876) 1 App. Cas. 686.

[129] See Foreign Law Ascertainment Act 1861, repealed in 1973.

[130] For text, see Treaty Series No.117 (1969) (Cmnd. 4229); Rodger & Van Doorn (1997) 46 I.C.L.Q. 151.

[131] Art.3(1).

[132] Art.4(1)(2).

[133] Arts 1(1), 4(3).

[134] The UK has designated the Legal and Executive Branch of the Foreign and Commonwealth Office.

prepared by the liaison organ of the requested State, or by an official or private body or an individual qualified lawyer on its behalf.[135] The information given in the reply does not bind the judicial authority from which the request emanated.[136] No provision has been made in English rules of court as to the practice under this Convention.[137] Despite this, there are signs that direct court-to-court co-operation may provide a new avenue for the ascertainment of foreign law, with the result in a court in one jurisdiction may be asked to, and may, entertain proceedings whose purpose is to obtain an authoritative statement of foreign law for use in local proceedings. An English court has given such a judgment in response to proceedings brought before it to ascertain English law for the purpose of proceedings before the courts in Singapore;[138] and the courts in New South Wales may refer cases directly to courts in certain other countries for a ruling on a question of foreign law.[139]

9–025   **(4) Burden of proof.** The burden of proving foreign law lies on the party who bases his claim or defence on it.[140] If that party adduces no evidence, or insufficient evidence, of the foreign law, the court applies English law.[141] This principle is sometimes expressed in the form that foreign law is presumed to be the same as English law until the contrary is proved.[142] But this mode of expression has given rise to uneasiness in certain cases. Thus in one case the court refused to apply the presumption of similarity where the foreign law was not based on the common law,[143] and in others it has been doubted whether the court was entitled to presume that the foreign law was the same as the statute

---

[135] Art.6(1)(2).

[136] Art.8.

[137] See Layton & Mercer, para.8–014, for the suggestion that an English court may take advantage of the provisions of this Convention under its powers to issue letters of request for the taking of evidence abroad (as to which see above, paras 8–074 *et seq.*) or under the court's inherent jurisdiction. See also Fentiman, above, n.1, pp.239–244; *cf. Panayiotou v Sony Music Entertainment (UK) Ltd* [1994] Ch. 142, 149–150.

[138] *Westacre Investments Inc v Yugoimport SDPR* [2008] EWHC 801 (Comm), [2009] 1 All E.R. (Comm.) 780.

[139] Spigelman (2011) 127 L.Q.R. 208; Bell (2011) 85 A.L.J. 562.

[140] *Brown v Gracey* (1821) Dow. & Ry.N.P. 41n.; *Dynamit AG v Rio Tinto Co* [1918] A.C. 260, 295, 301; *Guaranty Trust Co of New York v Hannay* [1918] 2 K.B. 623, 655 (CA); *Schapiro v Schapiro* [1904] T.S. 673; *Rodden v Whatlings Ltd*, 1961 S.C. 132; *Furlong v Burns & Co Ltd* (1964) 43 D.L.R. (2d) 689 (Ont); *Morgardshammar v Radomski & Co Ltd* (1983) 145 D.L.R. (3d) 111 (Ont), appeal dismissed (1984) 5 D.L.R. (4th) 576 (Ont CA). For the burden of proving the law applicable to the tort, if it is a foreign law, in actions on foreign torts, see Fentiman, above, pp.97–106; see also below, para.35–121.

[141] *Lloyd v Guibert* (1865) L.R. 1 Q.B. 115, 129; *Nouvelle Banque de l'Union v Ayton* (1891) 7 T.L.R. 377; *Hartmann v Konig* (1933) 50 T.L.R. 114, 117 (HL); *Re Tank of Oslo* [1940] 1 All E.R. 40, 42 (CA); *Re Parana Plantations Ltd* [1946] 2 All E.R. 214, 217–218; *Szechter v Szechter* [1971] P. 286, 296; *Concord Trust v Law Debenture Trust Corp Plc* [2005] UKHL 27, [2005] 1 W.L.R. 1591 at [44]. *cf. Pickering v Stephenson* (1872) L.R. 14 Eq. 322. *Ward v Dey* (1849) 1 Rob.Ecc. 759 appears to be based on this principle.

[142] e.g. *Dynamit A.G. v Rio Tinto Co* [1918] A.C. 260, 295; *The Parchim* [1918] A.C. 157, 161 (PC); *The Colorado* [1923] P. 102, 111 (CA); *Casey v Casey* [1949] P. 420, 430 (CA); *University of Glasgow v The Economist, The Times*, July 13, 1990.

[143] *Guépratte v Young* (1851) 4 De G. & Sm. 217.

law of the forum.[144] In view of these difficulties it is better to abandon the terminology of presumption, and simply to say that where foreign law is not proved, the court applies English law.[145]

Even so, there will still be cases in which the application of English law, whether because the party seeking to have foreign law applied has pleaded foreign law but has failed to prove its content to the satisfaction of the court, or because the parties have tacitly agreed not to seek to prove the content of foreign law and have the *lex fori* applied by default, will be just too strained or artificial to be appropriate. However, although recent authorities demonstrate that there are cases in which neither the presumption of similarity nor the default application of the *lex fori* will be suitable for the disposition of the case, they do not yet offer precise guidance as to when this point will be reached. The most striking illustrations have been from the Australian courts. On the one hand, they have refused to presume that German tax law was identical to Australian law and have concluded that in the absence of proof of the content of a provision of German tax law, the claim before the court simply failed.[146] On the other, it was accepted that Liberian law on ship registration and ownership was essentially the same as Australian law, which would therefore be applied to an issue properly governed by Liberian law;[147] and it was even accepted that in the absence of proof that the canons of statutory construction of Chinese law differed from those of Australian law, Australian canons of construction should be applied to draw out the meaning of a Chinese statutory rule.[148]

9–026

The recent practice of the English courts also suggests that the default application of English law where foreign law is not proved, is not unqualified, and is more likely to be challenged where the rule of English law is statutory[149] rather than being a rule of the common law. In principle, an English statute may not be applied to a matter governed by a foreign law, in circumstances where that foreign law has not been proved, if the English statutory rule appears to state a rule of purely domestic law, or where the wording of the statute would need to be adapted or changed in order to be made applicable to facts which do not otherwise fall within it. The proposition that the gist of a statute may be extracted from its precise wording, and then applied to a case which is not governed by English law but for which the content of the applicable law has not been proved, on the basis that states a rule of "general application", is dubious and probably wrong. For example, Part 15 of the Companies Act 2006 does not apply to companies incorporated under some

9–027

---

[144] *Purdom v Pavey* (1896) 26 S.C.R. 412, 417; *Schnaider v Jaffe* (1916) 7 C.P.D. 696; *cf. The Ship "Mercury Bell" v Amosin* (1986) 27 D.L.R. (4th) 641 (FCA).

[145] See Fentiman, above, pp.147–148.

[146] *Damberg v Damberg* [2001] NSWCA 87, (2001) 52 N.S.W.L.R. 492.

[147] *Tisand Pty Ltd v Owners of the Ship MV Cape Morton* (2005) 219 A.L.R. 48 (on the footing that both countries' laws were derived from an international convention).

[148] *Neilson v Overseas Projects Corp of Victoria Ltd* [2005] HCA 54, (2005) 233 C.L.R. 331. See also *National Auto-Class Supplies (Australia) Pty Ltd v Nielsen & Moller Autoglass (NSW) Pty Ltd (No.8)* [2007] FCA 1625, (presumption of similarity is "not inflexible"); *TS Production LLC v Drew Pictures Pty Ltd* [2008] FCAFC 194, (2008) 252 A.L.R. 1 (presumption of similarity applicable if "reliable"); *Nicholls v Michael Wilson & Partners Ltd* [2010] NSWCA 222, (2010) 243 F.L.R. 177; and see McComish (2007) 31 Melb.U.L.Rev. 400.

[149] At least, where the statute deals with specialist subject matter, as distinct from laying down more generally applicable norms.

other law. The Court of Appeal was unwilling to generalise from it to produce or invent a rule of "English law" which would be applicable to an issue otherwise governed by Pennsylvanian law which had not been proved.[150] A claim based on a contract pleaded as governed by the law of Saudi Arabia was simply struck out as disclosing no ground for bringing the claim;[151] and in a case in which foreign law was pleaded and proved, but one point overlooked and not proved, the court refused to allow the gap in the case to be filled by applying English law.[152]

9–028   On the other hand, the Unfair Contract Terms Act 1977 was applied to a contract pleaded as being governed by either Danish or Norwegian law, but without there being evidence before the court to show that the *lex contractus* contained provisions to similar effect.[153] English law was also applied, in default of pleading and proof of Polish law, to serve as the basis for establishing the content of notional legal advice which formed part of the analysis of liability, despite the evident artificiality of so doing.[154]

9–029   The conclusion is that there are cases in which the default application of a rule of English law is simply too problematic to be appropriate, but that apart from the fact that a court should not 'invent' a rule of English law to be applied in default of proof of foreign law, no sharp line exists to define the limits of the principle that in default of sufficient proof, foreign law will be taken to be the same as English law.

9–030   There is one established exception to this rule. In a trial for bigamy, the validity of the first marriage may depend on a rule of foreign law. In such a case, the prosecution must prove that the marriage is valid according to that law. If no evidence of foreign law is given, the court will not apply English law but will direct an acquittal.[155] However, as has been shown above, it may be that the true principle is considerably broader than this, and that in cases where it would be wholly artificial to apply rules of English law to a claim governed by foreign law, a court may simply regard a party who has pleaded but failed to prove foreign law as having failed to establish his case without regard to the corresponding principle of English domestic law.

---

[150] *Shaker v Al-Bedrawi* [2002] EWCA Civ 1452, [2003] Ch. 350.

[151] *Global Multimedia International Ltd v Ara Media Services* [2006] EWHC 3107 (Ch.), [2007] 1 All E.R. (Comm.) 1160. The effect of the decision may be mis-stated in *Royal Bank of Scotland Plc v Davidson* [2009] CSOH 134, 2010 S.L.T. 92 (though the case shows Scots law to impose a more demanding requirement as to pleading and statement of foreign law in the pleadings).

[152] *Tamil Nadu Electricity Board v St CMS Electricity Co Ltd* [2007] EWHC 1713 (Comm.), [2008] 2 Lloyd's Rep. 484.

[153] *Balmoral Group Ltd v Borealis UK Ltd* [2006] EWHC 1900 (Comm.), [2006] 2 C.L.C. 220.

[154] *Law Debenture Trust Corp Plc v Elektrim SA* [2009] EWHC 1801 (Ch.).

[155] *cf. R. v Naguib* [1917] 1 K.B. 359 where a marriage under foreign law was relied on by the defence. As to proof of foreign marriage, see Fentiman, above, pp.226–230, and below, paras 17–039 *et seq.*

PART THREE

JURISDICTION AND FOREIGN JUDGMENTS

PART THREE deals with the jurisdiction of the court in claims *in personam* **III–001**
and in claims *in rem*, the enforcement of foreign judgments, and with arbitration and the enforcement of foreign awards.

CHAPTER 10 deals with the jurisdictional immunities of foreign States,
foreign diplomats and consuls and members of international organisations.

CHAPTER 11 deals with the jurisdiction of the court in claims *in personam*
under the common law, under the Civil Procedure Rules and under Council
Regulation (EC) 44/2001 (the Brussels I Regulation) and the Lugano Convention on jurisdiction and the recognition and enforcement of judgments in civil
and commercial matters.

CHAPTER 12 deals with the jurisdiction of the court to stay proceedings
when it is necessary to prevent injustice, with *lis alibi pendens* under the
Brussels I Regulation and the Lugano Convention, with injunctions to restrain
foreign proceedings (anti-suit injunctions), and the effect in England of a
contractual provision that all disputes between the parties are to be referred to
the jurisdiction of the courts of a specified country.

CHAPTER 13 deals with the jurisdiction of the High Court in Admiralty
claims *in rem*.

CHAPTER 14 deals with the enforcement and recognition in England of **III–002**
foreign judgments *in personam* and *in rem*, and in particular with the jurisdiction of foreign courts to give such judgments, and with the defences that may
be raised in England against their enforcement or recognition. It states the
rules contained in the common law, in the Administration of Justice Act 1920
(which deals with the reciprocal enforcement of judgments between the
United Kingdom and certain countries of the Commonwealth overseas), in
the Foreign Judgments (Reciprocal Enforcement) Act 1933 (which deals with
the reciprocal enforcement of judgments between the United Kingdom and
certain other countries) and in the Civil Jurisdiction and Judgments Order
2001 and the Civil Jurisdiction and Judgments Act 1982, which deal with the
reciprocal enforcement of judgments between the United Kingdom and the
other States which are subject to the Brussels I Regulation and to the Lugano
Convention; and Pt II of the 1982 Act which deals with the reciprocal
enforcement of judgments within the United Kingdom.

CHAPTER 15 deals with the jurisdiction of English courts and the enforce- **III–003**
ment and recognition of foreign judgments in certain cases arising out of
multilateral conventions, to which special rules apply.

CHAPTER 16 deals with the law governing arbitration agreements and
arbitration procedure; with the duty of the court to stay proceedings brought
in England by a party to a submission to arbitration and its power to enjoin
proceedings brought in foreign courts in breach of arbitration agreements; the
enforcement in England of foreign arbitration awards at common law, under

the Arbitration Act 1996, under the Administration of Justice Act 1920 and the Foreign Judgments (Reciprocal Enforcement) Act 1933 and under the Arbitration (International Investment Disputes) Act 1966.

III–004   The jurisdiction of English and foreign courts in matrimonial causes;[1] guardianship, custody and maintenance of minors;[2] legitimacy, legitimation and adoption;[3] adults with incapacity;[4] the administration of estates of deceased persons;[5] succession;[6] the winding up of companies;[7] and bankruptcy,[8] are not dealt with in this Part but in the Chapters respectively dealing with these subjects.

---

[1] See Ch.18, below.
[2] See Ch.19, below.
[3] See Ch.20, below.
[4] See Ch.21, below.
[5] See Ch.26, below.
[6] See Ch.27, below.
[7] See Ch.30, below.
[8] See Ch.31, below.

CHAPTER 10

JURISDICTIONAL IMMUNITIES

RULE 26[1]—Subject to the Exceptions hereinafter mentioned, a foreign State is immune from the jurisdiction of the English courts.　10R–001

COMMENT

Introductory. The basic principle, confirmed by s.1(1) of the State Immunity Act 1978, and now subject to far-reaching statutory exceptions, is that a foreign State is immune from the jurisdiction of the courts of the United Kingdom. In the words of Lord Atkin (described by Lord Denning M.R. as a "classic restatement"[2]) "the courts of a country will not implead a foreign sovereign, that is, they will not by their process make him against his will a party to legal proceedings, whether the proceedings involve process against his person or seek to recover from him specific property or damages."[3] The immunity is derived ultimately from the rules of public international law,[4] and from the maxim of that law, *par in parem non habet imperium*. The relevant rules became part of the English common law,[5] and are now reflected in the State Immunity Act 1978.　10–002

State immunity and human rights. Since 2001 the European Court of Human Rights has decided several cases on the compatibility of the principles　10–003

---

[1] There is a very considerable literature on the subject of State immunity: see, in particular, Fox, *Law of State Immunity* (2nd ed. 2008); Schreuer, *State Immunity: Some Recent Developments* (1988), with extensive bibliography at pp.177–189; Hafner, Kohen and Breau (eds.), *State Practice Regarding State Immunities* (2006). Brownlie, *Principles of Public International Law* (7th ed. 2008), Ch.16; Oppenheim, *International Law* (9th ed. Jennings and Watts, 1992), pp.341–363; Brownlie, *Ann. de l'Institut de droit international*, Vol.62–I, p.13 (1987), *ibid.* Vol.63–I, p.13 (1989); Lauterpacht (1951) 28 B.Y.I.L. 220; Sinclair (1980) *Recueil des Cours*, II, p.113; Trooboff (1986) *Recueil des Cours*, V, p.235; Greig (1989) 38 I.C.L.Q. 243 and 560. For the recognition and enforcement in England of foreign judgments against foreign States, see below, Rule 45, and *NML Capital Ltd v Argentina* [2011] UKSC 31, [2011] 2 A.C. 495.

[2] *Trendtex Trading Corporation v Central Bank of Nigeria* [1977] Q.B. 529, 555 (CA).

[3] *The Cristina* [1938] A.C. 485, 490. *cf. The Parlement Belge* (1880) 5 P.D. 197, 207, 214–215 (CA). See on immunity from taxation *R. v IRC, Ex p. Camacq Corp* [1990] 1 W.L.R. 191 (CA).

[4] In *Jurisdictional Immunities of the State (Germany v Italy)* (pending) Germany has brought proceedings in the International Court of Justice claiming that, by allowing claims to be brought in Italian courts arising out of acts by German forces in the Second World War (and by declaring Greek judgments, arising out of similar occurrences, enforceable in Italy) Italy had failed to respect Germany's immunity under international law.

[5] *The Cristina* [1938] A.C. 485, 490; *Trendtex Trading Corporation v Central Bank of Nigeria* [1977] Q.B. 529, 553–554, 567–569, 578–579 (CA).

of state immunity under international law with the right of access to court under Art.6(1) of the European Convention on Human Rights.[6] The European Court of Human Rights held that, whilst a limitation on the right of access to court must pursue a legitimate aim and must be proportionate, the grant of state immunity in civil proceedings pursued the legitimate aim of complying with international law to promote comity and good relations between States through respect for another State's sovereignty; and measures taken which reflected generally recognised rules of public international law could not in principle be regarded as imposing a disproportionate restriction on the right of access to a court. Just as the right of access to a court was an inherent part of the guarantee of a fair trial, so some restrictions on access were inherent, such as those limitations generally accepted by the community of nations as part of the doctrine of state immunity. In *Al-Adsani v United Kingdom*,[7] in which there had been a civil claim in England for damages arising out of alleged torture, the Court, in a decision by a majority of nine to eight, noted the growing recognition of the overriding importance of the prohibition of torture, but did not find that it was established that there was already acceptance in international law of the proposition that States were not entitled to immunity in respect of civil claims for damages for alleged torture committed outside the forum State.[8] In *McElhinney v Ireland*[9] the Court noted the trend towards limiting state immunity in respect of personal injury caused within the forum State, but also noted that Ireland was not alone in holding that immunity attached to such actions in respect of torts committed by *acta jure imperii.* Accordingly, it was not possible, in the current state of development of international law, to conclude that Irish law conflicted with the principles of international law. In *Fogarty v United Kingdom*[10] the Court noted that there

---

[6] See *McElhinney v Ireland* (2002) 34 E.H.R.R. 322; *Al-Adsani v United Kingdom* (2002) 34 E.H.R.R. 273; *Fogarty v United Kingdom* (2002) 34 E.H.R.R. 302; *Cudak v Lithuania* (2010) 51 E.H.R.R. 15; *Sabeh El Leil v France* [2011] ECHR 1055. See Kloth, *Immunities and the Right of Access to Court under Article 6 of the European Convention on Human Rights* (2010); Garnett (2002) 118 L.Q.R. 367; Voyiakis (2003) 52 I.C.L.Q. 297; Lloyd Jones (2003) 52 I.C.L.Q. 463; Xiaodong Yang (2003) 74 B.Y.I.L. 333; McGregor (2006) 55 I.C.LQ. 437. In Case C–292/05 *Lechouritou v Dimosio tis Omospondiakis Dimokratias tis Germanias* [2007] E.C.R. I–1519 the European Court did not find it necessary to decide the question whether state immunity was compatible with the right of a claimant to sue in the State of the defendant's domicile under Art.2 of what is now the Brussels I Regulation. In *Grovit v Nederlandsche Bank* [2005] EWHC 2944 (QB), [2006] 1 W.L.R. 3323, affd. on different grounds [2007] EWCA Civ 953, [2008] 1 W.L.R. 51 state immunity was held to be compatible with the Brussels I Regulation.

[7] (2002) 34 E.H.R.R. 273 (arising out of *Al-Adsani v Government of Kuwait (No.2)*, *The Times*, March 29, 1996, 107 Int. L.R. 536 (CA)).

[8] The decision was applied in *Jones v Ministry of Interior of Saudi Arabia* [2006] UKHL 26, [2007] 1 A.C. 270, but Lord Bingham and Lord Hoffmann expressed doubts as to whether Art.6 of the European Convention on Human Rights was engaged by the grant of immunity under international law: see [14] and [64]. See also *Holland v Lampen-Wolfe* [2000] 1 W.L.R. 1573, 1588; *AIG Capital Partners, Inc v Republic of Kazakhstan* [2005] EWHC 2239 (Comm.), [2006] 1 W.L.R. 1420; *Grovit v Nederlandsche Bank* [2005] EWHC 2944 (QB), [2006] 1 W.L.R. 3323, affd. on different grounds [2007] EWCA Civ 953, [2008] 1 W.L.R. 51; *Entico Corp Ltd v United Nations Educational Scientific and Cultural Association* [2008] EWHC 531 (Comm.), [2008] 1 Lloyd's Rep. 673.

[9] (2002) 34 E.H.R.R. 322 (arising out of *McElhinney v Williams* [1996] 1 I.L.R.M. 276).

[10] (2002) 34 E.H.R.R. 302.

appeared to be a trend limiting state immunity in employment-related disputes; but international practice was divided on the question whether immunity applied to employment in a mission or embassy, and the level of employees to which it applied. The case related to alleged discrimination in the employment process, and might involve sensitive and confidential issues relating to the diplomatic and organisational policy of a foreign State, and the Court was not aware of any trend towards relaxation of state immunity in such cases. But in *Cudak v Lithuania*[11] the Grand Chamber decided that the Art.6 rights of a Lithuanian secretary and switchboard operator at the Polish embassy in Vilnius had been violated by the Lithuanian courts' refusal to exercise jurisdiction over Poland in her claim for unfair dismissal. Immunity pursed a legitimate aim, but the grant of immunity was disproportionate in the light of the growing consensus that there was no immunity for employment claims by non-nationals.

History.   In the 19th century and for much of the 20th century the   **10–004**
"absolute" rule of immunity prevailed, whereby foreign States and sovereigns were accorded immunity for all activities, whether governmental or commercial. But the increase in state trading in the 20th century led a number of countries to develop a distinction, generally called the "restrictive" theory, between acts of government, *acta jure imperii*, and acts of a commercial nature, *acta jure gestionis*.[12] Under the restrictive theory, States were immune in respect of acts of government but not in respect of commercial acts. An early attempt to exclude immunity in the case of ships and cargoes owned or operated by States for commercial purposes, the Brussels Convention of 1926, achieved only limited support, and was not ratified by the United Kingdom until 1979. The enormous increase in state trading after the Second World War led the United States Department of State to announce, in 1952, its adherence to the restrictive theory,[13] and the distinction between governmental and commercial acts was applied by the United States courts[14] and was in 1976 enacted in federal legislation.[15] In 1972 a European Convention on State Immunity, severely restricting the scope of immunity, was concluded under the auspices of the Council of Europe, and came into force in 1976.[16]

---

[11] (2010) 51 E.H.R.R. 15. See also *Sabeh El Leil v France* [2011] ECHR 1055.

[12] See Lauterpacht (1951) 28 B.Y.I.L. 220, 222–226.

[13] In the "Tate letter," quoted in Whiteman, *Digest of International Law*, Vol.6, pp.569–571.

[14] See, e.g. *Victory Transport Inc v Comisaria General de Abastesimientos y Transportes*, 336 F.2d 354 (2d Cir. 1964), cert.den. 381 U.S. 934 (1965).

[15] Foreign Sovereign Immunities Act 1976, text in (1976) 15 Int. Leg. Mat. 1388, with amendments *ibid.* (1989), Vol.28, p.396.

[16] For text see Cmnd. 7742. See Sinclair (1973) 22 I.C.L.Q. 254. The Convention came into force for the United Kingdom on October 4, 1979. Following work by the International Law Commission, *Report of Working Group on Jurisdictional Immunities of States and their Property* (1999), in 2004 the General Assembly of the United Nations adopted the UN Convention on Jurisdictional Immunities of States and their Property (text in (2005) 44 Int. Leg. Mat. 803), and invited States to become parties to it. The Convention restricts immunity in line with current international practice, and will come into force after there have been ratifications by 30 States. On the UN Convention see Fox, *op. cit.* n.1, Ch.12. For the use of the UN Convention as indicative of contemporary international law see *Jones v Ministry of Interior of Saudi Arabia* [2006] UKHL 26, [2007] 1 A.C. 270, [8]; *NML Capital Ltd v Argentina* [2011] UKSC 31, [2011] 2 A.C. 495, [126]; *Cudak v Lithuania* (2010) 51 E.H.R.R. 15, [66]–[67].

10–005   In the United Kingdom the courts applied the absolute theory[17] both in relation to actions *in rem* against trading ships[18] and actions *in personam* involving trading activities,[19] but in 1975 the Privy Council held that a foreign government was not entitled to claim immunity in an action *in rem* against a vessel used for trading purposes,[20] and in 1977 the Court of Appeal held, by a majority, that a State was not entitled to immunity in respect of commercial transactions.[21] In 1981, after the law had been altered by statute, the House of Lords confirmed that the restrictive theory of immunity applied at common law.[22]

10–006   **State Immunity Act 1978.**[23]   The law of state immunity in the United Kingdom is now regulated by the State Immunity Act 1978, which introduced or confirmed a number of major exceptions to the basic rule of immunity, and was designed in part to implement the European Convention on State Immunity.[24] The principal provisions of the Act do not apply to proceedings in respect of matters that occurred before it came into force in 1978.[25] The Act is to be construed against the background of generally recognised principles of public international law.[26] In *Jones v Ministry of Interior of Saudi Arabia*[27]

---

[17] Subject to certain possible exceptions, such as actions relating to trust funds and immovable property: see 9th ed. of this work at pp.143–144.

[18] *The Porto Alexandre* [1920] P. 30 (CA). *cf. The Cristina* [1938] A.C. 485, 490 (*per* Lord Atkin), 512 (*per* Lord Wright).

[19] *Compania Mercantil Argentina v US Shipping Board* (1924) 40 T.L.R. 601 (CA); *Kahan v Pakistan Federation* [1951] 2 K.B. 1003 (CA); *Baccus SRL v Servicio Nacional del Trigo* [1957] 1 Q.B. 438 (CA).

[20] *The Philippine Admiral* [1977] A.C. 373, approving dicta of Lord Maugham in *The Cristina* [1938] A.C. 485, 519–520.

[21] *Trendtex Trading Corp v Central Bank of Nigeria* [1977] Q.B. 529 (CA); *Hispano Americana Mercantile SA v Central Bank of Nigeria* [1979] 2 Lloyd's Rep. 277 (CA). For earlier formulations of Lord Denning see *Rahimtoola v Nizam of Hyderabad* [1958] A.C. 379, 422–423 and *Thai-Europe Tapioca Service Ltd v Government of Pakistan* [1975] 1 W.L.R. 1485, 1491–1492 (CA). For similar developments in Ireland, Canada, New Zealand and South Africa see *Government of Canada v Employment Appeals Tribunal* [1992] I.L.R.M. 325 (Sup Ct); *McElhinney v Williams* [1996] 1 I.L.R.M. 276 (Sup Ct); *Adams v DPP* [2001] 2 I.L.R.M. 401 (Sup Ct); *Zodiac International Products Inc v Polish People's Republic* (1977) 81 D.L.R. (3d) 656 (Qu CA); *The Ship "Atra" v Lorac Transport Ltd* (1986) 28 D.L.R. (4th) 309 (Fed CA); *Reid v Republic of Nauru* [1993] 1 V.R. 251; *Reef Shipping Co Ltd v The Ship "Fua Kavenga"* [1987] 1 N.Z.L.R. 550; *Governor of Pitcairn v Sutton* [1995] 1 N.Z.L.R. 426 (CA); *Controller and Auditor-General v Davison* [1996] 2 N.Z.L.R. 278 (CA); *Inter-Science Research and Development Services Pty Ltd v Republica de Moçambique*, 1980 (2) S.A. 111.

[22] *The I Congreso del Partido* [1983] 1 A.C. 244. See also *Alcom Ltd v Republic of Colombia* [1984] A.C. 580; *Planmount v Republic of Zaire* [1981] 1 All E.R. 1110. On the history see *Jones v Ministry of Interior of Saudi Arabia* [2006] UKHL 26, [2007] 1 A.C. 270, at [8]; *NML Capital Ltd v Argentina* [2011] UKSC 31, [2011] 2 A.C. 495, [8]–[12].

[23] See F.A. Mann, *Further Studies in International Law* (1990), p.302; Delaume (1979) 73 A.J.I.L. 185. Similar legislation has been enacted in South Africa (Foreign States Immunities Act 1981), in Canada (State Immunity Act 1982), and in Australia (Foreign State Immunities Act 1985; see Law Reform Commission, Report No.24, 1984).

[24] See above, n.16.

[25] See *Sengupta v Republic of India* [1983] I.C.R. 221 (EAT).

[26] *Alcom v Republic of Colombia* [1984] A.C. 580, 597.

[27] [2006] UKHL 26, [2007] 1 A.C. 270. See also *Al-Adsani v Government of Kuwait, The Times,* March 29, 1996; 107 Int. L.R. 536 (CA), applying *Argentine Republic v Amerada Hess Shipping Corp,* 488 U.S. 428 (1989) and *Siderman de Blake v Republic of Argentina,* 965 F.2d 699 (9th Cir. 1992). See also *Bouzari v Iran* (2004) 243 D.L.R. (4th) 406 (Ont CA); *Kazemi*

the House of Lords held that, although international law condemned and prohibited the practice of torture and had established a universal criminal jurisdiction over alleged torturers that operated as an exception to state immunity, no such universal jurisdiction had yet been recognised in respect of civil proceedings which would allow a victim of torture to seek compensation in the United Kingdom courts in respect of acts committed elsewhere.

It is important to note that the 1978 Act lays down a number of *exceptions*   **10–007** to the immunity of a foreign State. It does not *confer* jurisdiction on the English courts which they would otherwise not have, and the Act expressly provides that the method of service on foreign States laid down by the Act does not affect any rules of court whereby leave is required for the service of process outside the jurisdiction.[28] Thus the exception relating to commercial transactions does not relieve the claimant of the necessity of bringing an appropriate case within the provisions of CPR, r.6.36, and PD6B, para.3.1, or of the Brussels I Regulation or the Lugano Convention (discussed in Ch.11), unless (for example) the defendant is a foreign State which has submitted to the jurisdiction or is a separate entity with a branch in England. In this respect the 1978 Act[29] differs from its United States counterpart, the Foreign Sovereign Immunities Act 1976, which enacts rules of personal jurisdiction over foreign States.

Meaning of State. The immunity from suit applies to any foreign or   **10–008** Commonwealth State other than the United Kingdom, and it applies not only to the State itself but also to the sovereign of the State in his public capacity,[30] to the government of the State, and any department of its government.[31] In *Jones v Ministry of Interior of Saudi Arabia*[32] it was held that the immunity extends to officials in relation to acts, even if they are unauthorised, for which the State is internationally responsible. The foreign State is entitled to claim

---

(Estate) v Iran (2011) 330 DLR (4th) 1 (Que.). Contrast *R. v Bow Street Magistrate, Ex p. Pinochet (No.3)* [2000] 1 A.C. 147, where it was held that there is no immunity from criminal jurisdiction in respect of acts of torture for which a former head of State is alleged to be responsible. See generally Bröhmer, *State Immunity and the Violation of Human Rights* (1997); Caplan (2003) 97 A.J.I.L. 741; Focarelli (2005) 54 I.C.L.Q. 951.

[28] s.12(7).

[29] The European Convention on State Immunity laid down jurisdictional links, but they were not enacted in the 1978 Act.

[30] The sovereign in his personal capacity is assimilated to the head of a diplomatic mission, with certain modifications (in particular, immunities and privileges are not to be subject to restrictions by reference to nationality or residence): State Immunity Act 1978, s.20. See also *Bank of Credit and Commerce International (Overseas) Ltd v Price Waterhouse* [1997] 4 All E.R. 108 (third party notice against Ruler of Abu Dhabi, who was also President of the United Arab Emirates; held he was entitled to immunities of head of diplomatic mission, and not to State immunity: although he was acting in his public capacity *vis-à-vis* Abu Dhabi (which is a constituent territory of the United Arab Emirates), he was not acting in a public capacity on behalf of the United Arab Emirates); *Thor Shipping A/S v The Ship "Al Duhail"* [2008] FCA 1842, (2008) 252 A.L.R. 20. See *Aziz v Aziz* [2007] EWCA Civ 712, [2008] 2 All E.R. 501 for an unsuccessful application by a head of State to have judgments edited to remove references to himself on the ground that they amounted to an attack on his dignity. On the position of former heads of State see *R. v Bow Street Magistrate, Ex p. Pinochet (No.3)* [2000] 1 A.C. 147. See generally Watts (1994) *Recueil des Cours*, III, 9. See also *Democratic Republic of Congo v Belgium (Case concerning the Arrest Warrant of 11 April 2000)*, 2002 I.C.J. Rep. 1, at 20–24.

[31] State Immunity Act 1978, s.14(1).

[32] [2006] UKHL 26, [2007] 1 A.C. 270.

immunity for its servants as it could if sued itself, and its right to immunity cannot be circumvented by suing its servants or agents.[33]

10–009   An entity (referred to in the Act as a "separate entity") which is distinct from the executive organs of the government of the State and is capable of suing or being sued is entitled to immunity only if (a) the proceedings relate to anything done by it in the exercise of sovereign authority and (b) the circumstances are such that a State would have been immune.[34] There is no express requirement that such a separate entity be owned or controlled by the foreign State, but it would be a considerable extension of the doctrine of immunity to apply the notion of separate entity to *any* agent of the foreign State, and it is therefore suggested that a separate entity not owned or controlled by the State is not capable of acting in the exercise of sovereign authority.[35] For a separate entity to be immune, there are two requirements. The first is that the proceedings must relate to something "done by it in the exercise of sovereign authority."[36] This requirement is by its terms additional to the second requirement, namely that the circumstances must be such that a State would have been immune. In *Kuwait Airways Corp v Iraqi Airways Co*[37] it was held that acts "done by it in the exercise of sovereign authority" meant *acta jure imperii* in the sense in which that expression had been adopted by

---

[33] *Twycross v Dreyfus* (1877) 5 Ch. D. 605; *Zoernsch v Waldock* [1964] 1 W.L.R. 675; *Propend Finance Pty Ltd v Sing, The Times*, May 2, 1997 (1997) 111 Int. L.R. 611; *R. v Bow Street Metropolitan Stipendiary Magistrate, Ex p. Pinochet Ugarte (No.3)* [2000] 1 AC 147, 269, 285–286; *Holland v Lampen-Wolfe* [2000] 1 W.L.R. 1573, 1583; *Schmidt v Home Secretary of the Government of the United Kingdom* [1997] 2 I.R. 121 (Sup. Ct.); *Jaffe v Miller* (1993) 13 OR (3d) 745, 758–759; *University of Calgary v Colorado School of Mines* [1996] 2 W.W.R. 596 (Alta); *Herbage v Meese*, 747 F. Supp. 60 (DDC 1990), affirmed 946 F. 2d 1564 (DC Cir. 1991); UN Convention, Art.2(1)(b)(iv) (State includes "representatives of the state acting in that capacity"). See also *Prosecutor v Blaskic* (1997) 110 Int. L.R. 607, 707 (Appeals Chamber of the International Criminal Tribunal for the Former Yugoslavia); *Democratic Republic of Congo v Belgium (Case concerning the Arrest Warrant of 11 April 2000)*, 2002 I.C.J. Rep. 1, at 20–24. In *Samantar v Yousuf*, 130 S.Ct. 2278 (2010) the U.S. Supreme Court decided that the former Prime Minister of Somalia was not immune under the Foreign Sovereign Immunities Act in a claim brought by Somalis who claimed that he had authorised torture and killing of the claimants or their relatives. It was held that a State official is not to be regarded as an "agency or instrumentality" of the State. But whether the official was entitled to immunity under the common law, and whether he had other valid defences to the charges against him, were matters to be addressed by the District Court on remand.
[34] State Immunity Act 1978, s.14(1)–(2). Separate entity includes a State's central bank or other monetary authority, to whose property special rules apply: see below, para.10–016. See *PT Garuda Indonesia Ltd v Australian Competition and Consumer Commission* [2011] FCAFC 52, (2011) 277 A.L.R. 67 (corporation a separate entity of a foreign State for the purposes of the Australian Foreign States Immunities Act if corporation is acting for or being used by the foreign State as its means to achieve some purpose or end of that State; whether or not the foreign State owns or exerts day-to-day management control over corporation not determinative).
[35] In *Kuwait Airways Corp v Iraqi Airways Co* [1995] 1 W.L.R. 1147, 1158 (HL) it was said (*obiter*) that it was probable that the expressions "any entity" and "separate entity" were intended to refer to an entity or separate entity of a State. In Canada it has been held that for the purposes of the Canadian State Immunity Act 1985 (" 'agency of a foreign state' means any legal entity that is an organ of the foreign state but that is separate from the foreign state") a bank which assisted a United States undercover agent to entrap an arms dealer was "an organ of the foreign State": *Walker v Bank of New York* (1994) 111 D.L.R. (4th) 186 (Ont CA); *sed quaere*.
[36] This additional requirement derives from Art.27(2) of the European Convention, where it appears as "acts performed by the entity in the exercise of sovereign authority (*acta jure imperii*)." See *Kuwait Airways Corp v Iraqi Airways, Financial Times*, July 17, 1992.
[37] [1995] 1 W.L.R. 1147, 1156 (HL) see below, para.10–033.

English law from public international law, i.e. governmental acts, as opposed to acts which any private citizen could perform. In the case of acts done by a separate entity, they are not *acta jure imperii* simply because they are done on the directions of the State or because their purpose is to serve the interests of the State, since they may not possess the character of a governmental act.[38]

Even where a State is not immune because one of the exceptions applies, its property (except that used for commercial purposes) is immune from process of execution,[39] but the property (of whatever kind) of a separate entity (other than a central bank) would be subject in such circumstances to execution if the proceedings did not relate to something done by it in the exercise of sovereign authority. Further, a number of the exceptions laid down in the Act are narrowly defined, and the additional requirement that the proceedings relate to something done in the exercise of sovereign authority may widen some of the exceptions in relation to a separate entity. Thus, a State is not immune as respects proceedings relating to a contract of employment, but this exception is subject to a number of qualifications.[40] If the defendant were a separate entity, it would not be immune even if the qualifications would have applied to a defendant State, because in normal circumstances such proceedings would not relate to something done in the exercise of sovereign authority. **10–010**

The immunities granted to States may be extended by Order in Council to any constituent territory of a federal State, and in the absence of such an Order a constituent territory is treated as a separate entity.[41] **10–011**

A certificate by or on behalf of the Secretary of State is conclusive evidence on any question whether any country is a State, whether any territory is a constituent territory of a federal State or as to the person or persons to be regarded as the head or government of a State.[42] **10–012**

---

[38] Lord Goff of Chieveley gave as an example *Arango v Guzman Travel Advisers Corp*, 621 F. 2d 137 (5th Cir. 1980), in which Dominicana (the national airline of the Dominican Republic) was held entitled to plead sovereign immunity under the United States Foreign Sovereign Immunities Act 1976, on the ground that it was impressed into service by Dominican immigration officials, acting pursuant to the country's laws, to perform the functions which led to the plaintiff being re-routed. See *Koo Golden East Mongolia v Bank of Nova Scotia* [2007] EWCA Civ 1443, [2008] Q.B. 717 (State bank entered into contract in exercise of sovereign authority); *The Altair* [2008] EWHC 612 (Comm.), [2008] 2 Lloyd's Rep. 90 (Grain Board of Iraq; entry into salvage agreement not a sovereign act); *Wilhelm Finance Inc v Ente Administrador Del Astillero Rio Santiago* [2009] EWHC 1074 (Comm.), [2009] 1 C.L.C. 867 (State-owned shipyard a separate entity); *Pocket Kings Ltd v Safenames Ltd* [2009] EWHC 2529 (Ch.), [2010] 2 W.L.R. 1110 (Commonwealth of Kentucky, in exercising its powers to regulate gambling in Kentucky, not acting in the exercise of the sovereign authority of the United States). See generally Dickinson (2009) 10 Bus. L. Int. 97.

[39] See below, paras 10–014 *et seq.*

[40] See below, para.10–038.

[41] s.14(5)–(6). See SI 1979/457 (Austria); SI 1993/2809 (Germany). The Commonwealth of Kentucky, to which the State Immunity Act 1978 has not been extended, is not entitled to immunity as a State: *Pocket Kings Ltd v Safenames Ltd* [2009] EWHC 2529 (Ch.), [2010] 2 W.L.R. 1110.

[42] s.21(a). The certificate is not susceptible to judicial review: *R. v Secretary of State for Foreign Affairs, Ex p. Trawnik, The Times*, February 21, 1986 (CA). See *R. (on the application of Sultan of Pahang) v Secretary of State for the Home Department* [2011] EWCA Civ 616 (immigration case: conclusive certificate by Foreign Secretary that Pahang was a constituent territory of the Federation of Malaysia and that Sultan, who had previously been Supreme Head of the Federation, was not Head of State). See also *R. (on the application of Alamieyeseigha) v Crown Prosecution Service* [2005] EWHC 2704 (Admin.).

10–013   **Property.** The immunity protects a foreign State not only in direct proceedings against it *in personam* but also in indirect proceedings against property which is in its possession or control or in which it claims an interest.[43] Thus if a foreign State has an interest in property situated within the jurisdiction, whether proprietary, possessory or of some lesser nature, a claim which affects its interest will be stayed, even though it is not brought against it personally, but is, e.g. a claim *in rem* against a ship[44] or a claim *in personam* against its bailee[45] or agent.[46] The rule is not limited to ownership, and applies to lesser interests which may not merely be not proprietary but not even possessory, so that it applies to property under the control of the foreign State,[47] and perhaps also to property in respect of which it has no beneficial interest but only the legal title.[48] The 1978 Act provides that the court may entertain proceedings against a person other than a State notwithstanding that the proceedings relate to property in its possession or control, or in which it claims an interest, if the State would not have been immune had the proceedings been brought against it, or, in the case where the State merely claims an interest, if the claim is neither admitted nor supported by prima facie evidence.[49]

10–014   **Execution.** A foreign State is also immune from the processes of execution.[50] The 1978 Act provides that relief shall not be given against a State by way of injunction[51] or order for specific performance or for the recovery of land or other property, and that the property of a State shall not be subject to any process for the enforcement of a judgment[52] or arbitration award or, in an action *in rem*, for its arrest, detention or sale.[53] In Scotland it has been held that the immunity did not prevent the assumption of jurisdiction *in personam*

---

[43] This was the rule at common law (see, e.g. *The Cristina* [1938] A.C. 485, 490, 507) and is implicit in the 1978 Act: see ss.2(4)(b), 6 and 10. "Property" includes a credit balance on a bank account: *Alcom v Republic of Colombia* [1984] A.C. 580, 602.

[44] *The Parlement Belge* (1880) 5 P.D. 197 (CA); *The Jupiter* [1924] P. 236 (CA); *The Cristina* [1938] A.C. 485; *The Arantzazu Mendi* [1939] A.C. 256.

[45] *USA and Republic of France v Dollfus Mieg et cie. and Bank of England* [1952] A.C. 582.

[46] *Rahimtoola v Nizam of Hyderabad* [1958] A.C. 379.

[47] *The Cristina* [1938] A.C. 485; *The Arantzazu Mendi* [1939] A.C. 256.

[48] *Rahimtoola v Nizam of Hyderabad* [1958] A.C. 379, 403, *per* Lord Reid.

[49] s.6(4). *cf. Juan Ysmael & Co Inc v Indonesian Government* [1955] A.C. 72, 89–90 (PC); *Rahimtoola v Nizam of Hyderabad* [1958] A.C. 379, 410; *Shearson Lehman Brothers Inc v Maclaine Watson & Co Ltd* [1988] 1 W.L.R. 16, 29–31 (HL); *Australian Federation of Islamic Councils Inc v Westpac Banking Corp* (1989) 17 N.S.W.L.R. 623.

[50] See Fox, *Law of State Immunity* (2nd ed. 2008), Ch.18; Crawford (1981) 75 A.J.I.L. 820; Byers (1995) 44 I.C.L.Q. 882.

[51] See *Soleh Boneh International Ltd v Government of Uganda* [1993] 2 Lloyd's Rep. 208 (CA) (order for provision of security for arbitral award not an injunction for this purpose).

[52] By RSC Ord.46, r.6(4)(iii) (in CPR, Sch.1), where judgment on failure to acknowledge service has been entered against a State, before execution can issue, evidence must be produced that the State has been served in accordance with CPR, r.40.10 (below, n.78) and that the judgment has taken effect. Provision is made for a Master or district judge to inform the Foreign and Commonwealth Office before execution can issue against a foreign or Commonwealth state: *Supreme Court Practice* (1999), para.46/2/15 (not reproduced in the current *Civil Procedure* (2011).

[53] s.13(2). This immunity applies to a State's central bank or other monetary authority even if it is a "separate entity": s.14(4).

over a foreign State, where the jurisdiction was based on the presence of immovable property owned by the State, even if the property itself (the United States Consulate-General in Edinburgh) was not subject to process of execution.[54] *In personam* jurisdiction based on the possession of immovable property in Scotland does not (by contrast with arrestment of movables) involve any taking of possession, or interference with the right to dispose, of the property. If any such taking were involved, the result could not be justified.

The immunity from injunctive relief and execution is distinct from immunity from suit and applies even if one of the jurisdictional exceptions applies. Thus even though a State is not immune as respects proceedings relating to a commercial transaction, the State cannot be enjoined from breach of the contract.[55] But the immunity from injunctive relief and execution is subject to two important exceptions. First, such relief may be given or process may be issued with the written consent (which may be contained in a prior agreement) of the State.[56] It has been held that a waiver of immunity in relation to property will allow a freezing injunction to be made against a foreign State, but that a contractual waiver of immunity from execution will not be regarded as extending to diplomatic premises.[57] Secondly, the immunity from process does not prevent the issue of any process in respect of property which is for the time being in use or intended for use for commercial purposes.[58] "Commercial purposes" means[59] the purposes of those transactions which are defined as "commercial transactions" in s.3(3) and which are discussed below in connection with Exception 2 to this Rule. Thus execution cannot issue against a credit balance on a bank account kept by a foreign State for the purpose of meeting the ordinary expenditure of its embassy; but it may issue where the account was earmarked for the discharge of liabilities incurred in commercial transactions.[60] A judgment against the State cannot be enforced

10–015

---

[54] *Forth Tugs Ltd v Wilmington Trust Co*, 1987 S.L.T. 153.

[55] *ETI Euro Telecom International NV v Republic of Bolivia* [2008] EWCA Civ 880, [2008] 1 W.L.R. 665, at [113].

[56] s.13(3). A submission merely to the jurisdiction is not to be regarded as a consent to execution: *ibid. cf. Arab Banking Corp. v International Tin Council* (1986) 77 Int.L.R. 1. In *Sabah Shipyard (Pakistan) Ltd v Islamic Republic of Pakistan* [2002] EWCA Civ 1643, [2003] 2 Lloyd's Rep. 571, waiver of immunity in a contractual submission to the English jurisdiction was held to extend to an anti-suit injunction restraining proceedings in Pakistan.

[57] *A Co Ltd v Republic of X* [1990] 2 Lloyd's Rep. 520 (criticised on the latter point by F.A. Mann (1991) 107 L.Q.R. 362).

[58] s.13(4). But this exception does not apply, otherwise than in actions *in rem*, to States which are parties to the European Convention on State Immunity unless the process is for enforcing a judgment which is not subject to appeal or (if a default judgment) liable to be set aside, and the State has made a declaration under Art.24 of the Convention (which provides that a contracting State may declare that its courts shall be entitled to entertain proceedings against contracting States to the extent that its courts are entitled to entertain proceedings against non-contracting States), or the process is for enforcing an arbitral award: *ibid.* The certificate of the Secretary of State as to whether a State is a party to the European Convention or has made a declaration under Art.24 is conclusive: s.21(c).

[59] s.17(1).

[60] *Alcom v Republic of Colombia* [1984] A.C. 580, 604. See also *Orascom Telecom Holding SAE v Republic of Chad* [2008] EWHC 1841 (Comm.), [2008] 2 Lloyd's Rep. 396; *Servaas Inc v Rafidain Bank* [2011] EWCA Civ 1256.

against the assets of a separate entity even if those assets would not be immune from execution in an action against the separate entity.[61]

10–016   A central bank or other monetary authority is accorded special treatment under the Act.[62] If it is not distinct from the executive organs of the State and not capable of suing or being sued, it will be on precisely the same footing as a State, but if (as is more likely to be the case) it is a separate entity within the meaning of the Act, it will differ from other separate entities in the following respects: first, even if it is not entitled to immunity from suit, its property will normally be immune from execution because the property of a central bank or other monetary authority, irrespective of whether it is a separate entity, is not regarded as in use or intended for use for commercial purposes;[63] secondly, it is specifically provided that where a central bank or other monetary authority is a separate entity it is entitled to immunity from injunctive relief and execution as if it were a State.[64] In practice, therefore, the property of a State's central bank will only be liable to process of execution if it has waived, in writing, its immunity from execution.[65]

10–017   The head of a State's diplomatic mission in the United Kingdom (or the person for the time being performing his functions) is deemed to have authority to give, on behalf of the State, consent to execution,[66] and the certificate of any such person to the effect that any property is not in use or intended for use by or on behalf of the State for commercial purposes shall be accepted as sufficient evidence of that fact unless the contrary is proved.[67]

10–018   **Procedure.** When a question of immunity is raised, then the question whether a State is or is not immune under the 1978 Act must be decided as a preliminary issue before the substantive action can proceed.[68]

10–019   The court must give effect to the immunity conferred by the Act even though the State does not appear in the proceedings in question.[69] The Act

---

[61] *AIG Capital Partners Inc v Republic of Kazakhstan* [2005] EWHC 2239, [2006] 1 W.L.R. 1420; followed in *Continental Transfert Technique Ltd v Federal Government of Nigeria* [2009] EWHC 2898 (Comm.). The position is different if the entity has no separate legal existence: *Kensington International Ltd v Congo* [2005] EWHC 2684 (Comm.), [2006] 2 B.C.L.C. 296.

[62] See Blair [1998] C.L.J. 374.

[63] s.14(4). See *AIC Ltd v Federal Government of Nigeria* [2003] EWHC 1357 (QB); *AIG Capital Partners Inc v Republic of Kazakhstan* [2005] EWHC 2239 (Comm.), [2006] 1 W.L.R. 1420 (also holding that the restriction on enforcement on the property of a central bank is compliant with European Convention on Human Rights: above, para.10–003).

[64] *ibid.* It is also entitled to immunity from penalty in respect of failure to disclose or produce documents or information, as to which see para.10–021, below.

[65] s.13(3). See *Servaas Inc v Rafidain Bank* [2011] EWCA Civ 1256.

[66] s.13(5). But any other duly authorised representative would also have authority.

[67] s.13(5).

[68] *JH Rayner (Mincing Lane) Ltd v Department of Trade and Industry* [1989] Ch. 72, 194–195, 252 (CA), affirmed without reference to this point [1990] 2 A.C. 418; *ETI Euro Telecom International NV v Republic of Bolivia* [2008] EWCA Civ 880, [2008] 1 W.L.R. 665, at [110], [128]; *A Co Ltd v Republic of X* [1990] 2 Lloyd's Rep. 520, 525. cf. *Advisory Opinion on the Difference Relating to Immunity from Legal Process of a Special Rapporteur of the Commission on Human Rights*, 1999 I.C.J. Rep. 62, para.63 (questions of immunity must be expeditiously decided *in limine litis*). A claim to immunity should be heard in public: *Harb v King Fahd Bin Abdul Aziz* [2005] EWCA Civ 632.

[69] s.1(2). See *United Arab Emirates v Abdelghafar* [1995] I.C.R. 65 (EAT); *Mauritius Tourism Promotion Authority v Wong Min* [2008] UKEAT 0185/08/2411 (EAT).

provides for a method of service on a State by transmission through the Foreign and Commonwealth Office to the Ministry of Foreign Affairs of the State.[70] As indicated above[71] the claimant is not thereby relieved of the need to bring the case within one of the heads of CPR, PD6B, para.3.1 in cases in which they apply.[72] A State which appears in proceedings cannot thereafter object that service was not properly effected upon it.[73] Service by transmission through the Foreign and Commonwealth Office is not necessary if the State has agreed to a different method of service,[74] and in such a case permission to serve out of the jurisdiction is required only if the defendant State is not a State to which the Brussels I Regulation applies (or is not a Lugano Convention State)[75] and the place designated for service by the agreement is outside the jurisdiction.[76]

No judgment in default may be given against a State unless it is proved that service has been properly effected and the time for acknowledgment of service has expired.[77] A copy of a default judgment is to be transmitted through the Foreign and Commonwealth Office to the Ministry of Foreign Affairs of the State, and the time for applying to have the judgment set aside begins to run two months after receipt of the copy judgment.[78]   **10–020**

As regards disclosure of documents, the Act provides that no penalty by way of committal or fine is to be imposed in respect of any failure or refusal by a State to disclose or provide any document or other information in proceedings to which it is a party.[79]   **10–021**

Miscellaneous. Provision may be made, by Order in Council, to restrict or extend the immunities of a State under the Act if (as the case may be) they exceed those accorded by the law of that State to the United Kingdom, or are less than those required by any international agreement to which that State and the United Kingdom are parties.[80]   **10–022**

---

[70] s.12(1). See *Kuwait Airways Corp v Iraqi Airways Co* [1995] 1 W.L.R. 1147 (HL): service by the Foreign and Commonwealth Office on the Iraqi embassy was insufficient. See also *Westminster City Council v Iran* [1986] 1 W.L.R. 979. Service is deemed to be effected on receipt at the Ministry. When service is effected in this way, the time for acknowledgment of service is two months: s.12(2). See also CPR, r.6.44. This procedure applies to an application under CPR, r.62.18 to enforce an arbitral award: *Norsk Hydro ASA v State Property Fund of Ukraine* [2002] EWHC 2120 (Comm.), [2009] Bus. L.R. 558.

[71] See above, para.10–007.

[72] s.12(7).

[73] s.12(3).

[74] s.12(6).

[75] See below, paras 11–188 *et seq.*

[76] See CPR, PD6B, para.3.1(6)(d); below, paras 11–013; 12–146—12–148.

[77] s.12(4); CPR PD12, para.4.4.

[78] s.12(5). See also CPR, r.40.10 and CPR PD6B, para.6.5. See *Crescent Oil and Shipping Services Ltd v Importang UEE* [1998] 1 W.L.R. 919 (no alternative contractual method can be agreed).

[79] s.13(1). No doubt the court could draw appropriate inferences from the failure to give discovery, or even strike out its defence. See also Art.18 of the European Convention.

[80] s.15(1). There are no such orders in force. An order was made in relation to the USSR, which was replaced by an order which required notice to a consular officer of applications for warrants of arrest in an action *in rem* against a ship owned by Russia, the Ukraine and Georgia or cargo aboard it, and prevented execution against ships or cargo owned by them. It had been held, after the break-up of the Soviet Union, that the order relating to the USSR did not apply to the Russian Federation, even though the United Kingdom Government regards it as continuing the legal

10–023   The 1978 Act does not affect immunities under the Diplomatic Privileges Act 1964 or the Consular Relations Act 1968.[81] It does not apply to proceedings relating to anything done by or relating to the armed forces of a State while present in the United Kingdom, and has effect subject to the Visiting Forces Act 1952.[82] It does not apply to proceedings to which s.17(6) of the Nuclear Installations Act 1965 applies,[83] and Pt I of the 1978 Act does not apply to criminal proceedings.[84]

ILLUSTRATIONS

10–024   1. A, an English company, is granted a concession by the Government of Ruritania to work mines in Ruritania. The Government repudiates the contract, and A brings an action for damages in England. The court has no jurisdiction.[85]

2. A's assets in Ruritania are confiscated by the Government of Ruritania. A brings an action in England for damages. The court has no jurisdiction.[86]

3. A claims damages for a libel published in England in the official newspaper of the Government of Ruritania, which owns and runs the newspaper. The court has no jurisdiction.[87]

4. The circumstances are the same as in Illustration 3, except that the newspaper is published by a department which is separate from the executive organs of the Government and is capable of suing and being sued. The court has jurisdiction.[88]

5. A, an English bank, lends money under a loan agreement to the State of Ruritania, with a guarantee by the Central Bank of Ruritania, which is a separate entity distinct from the State. The contract contains an express submission to the jurisdiction of the English courts. The State defaults on the loan. The court has jurisdiction over the State under Exception 1 below and over the Central Bank because it is a separate entity and the proceedings do not relate to something done by it in the exercise of sovereign authority in circumstances in which the State would be immune.[89] The court gives judgment for A against both defendants. The State has a stock of grain in London in the name of its Ministry of Agriculture, which is in the process of selling the stock. The Central Bank has sterling deposits with the Bank of England. A may levy execution against the grain, because it is intended for use for commercial purposes,[90] but not against the sterling deposits,[91] unless there has been written consent in the loan agreement or otherwise to execution against the property of the State.[92]

10–025   6. In August 1990 Iraq invaded Kuwait. On the orders of the Iraqi government civil aircraft belonging to Kuwait Airways were flown by Iraqi Airways to Iraq, and then incorporated into the Iraqi Airways fleet and used for its own flights. Iraqi Airways is a separate entity. It is immune from suit in respect of the taking of the aircraft and their removal from Kuwait to Iraq because

---

personality of the former Soviet Union (*Coreck Maritime GmbH v Sevrybokholodflot*, 1994 S.L.T. 983) nor to the Republic of the Ukraine, even though the United Kingdom Government regards it (and the other former Soviet Republics) as successor States to the USSR (*The Giuseppe di Vittorio* [1998] 1 Lloyd's Rep. 136 (CA)). The order was repealed by SI 1999/668.

[81] s.16(1). See *Alcom Ltd v Republic of Colombia* [1984] A.C. 580; *A Co Ltd v Republic of X* [1990] 2 Lloyd's Rep. 520.

[82] s.16(2). See *Holland v Lampen-Wolfe* [2001] 1 W.L.R. 157 (HL); *United States v Nolan* [2009] I.R.L.R. 923 (EAT).

[83] s.16(3). See below, para.15–052.

[84] s.16(4).

[85] State Immunity Act 1978, s.1(1).

[86] *ibid.* s.1(1).

[87] *ibid.* s.1(1).

[88] *ibid.* s.14(2). Contrast *Krajina v Tass Agency* [1949] 2 All E.R. 274 (CA), decided at common law.

[89] State Immunity Act 1978, s.14(2). *cf. Trendtex Trading Corp v Central Bank of Nigeria* [1977] Q.B. 529 (CA), decided at common law.

[90] *ibid.* s.13(4).

[91] *ibid.* s.14(4).

[92] *ibid.* s.13(3).

that conduct constituted an exercise of governmental power by the State of Iraq. But it is not immune in respect of the subsequent retention and use of the aircraft because they were not acts done in the exercise of sovereign authority, but were acts done by Iraqi Airways in consequence of the vesting in it of the aircraft by Iraqi legislative decree.[93]

7. A, a French company, is the owner of sixty-four gold bars deposited in a French bank at Limoges. In 1944 the bars are looted by German troops and taken to Germany, but recovered in the following year by allied troops. They are then deposited in the Bank of England on behalf of the Governments of the United Kingdom, France and the United States. A sues the bank claiming delivery of the bars and damages for their detention. The bank moves to stay the proceedings on the ground that they implead two foreign sovereign States which decline to submit to the jurisdiction. It is then discovered that the bank had sold thirteen of the bars by mistake. The action is allowed to proceed in respect of the thirteen bars because the bank by its own act had determined the bailment, but is stayed as regards the fifty-one bars.[94]

8. A, the Nizam of Hyderabad, has funds on deposit with a London bank. X, the Finance Minister of Hyderabad, is one of the persons entitled to operate the account. When Indian troops are invading Hyderabad, X, acting in the supposed interests of A, but without actual authority from A to do so, transfers the account into the name of Y, the High Commissioner of Pakistan in the United Kingdom. Y receives the account as agent for Pakistan and on the instructions of the Foreign Minister thereof. A sues X, Y (who has ceased to be High Commissioner but who has not yet accounted to Pakistan) and the bank, claiming the money. Y asks for a stay on the ground that the action impleads the State of Pakistan, although that State claims no beneficial interest in the money. The court has no jurisdiction, because the fund is in the legal control of the State of Pakistan.[95]

9. A, a Philippines company, charters a ship to the Indonesian Government for the carriage of troops, legal possession of the ship remaining with A. A's agent, who has (as the Indonesian Government knows) no authority from A to do so, purports to sell the ship to the Government. A brings an action *in rem* against the ship claiming possession as owner. The court has jurisdiction because the Indonesian Government's title to the ship is manifestly defective.[96]

10. A's ship is run down and damaged on the high seas by a ship owned and operated by the Government of Ruritania as a troop-carrier. A brings an action *in rem* in England against the ship for damages. The court has no jurisdiction, because the ship is not in use or intended for use for commercial purposes.[97]

10–026

11. A obtains a default judgment against the Republic of Colombia for goods sold and delivered. The embassy of the Republic maintains a current account with a bank in London in the name of the Republic. The account is used for the normal expenses of the embassy. A obtains a garnishee order nisi attaching the bank account. The garnishee order is set aside because the debt represented by the credit balance on the account is not property which is "in use or intended for use for commercial purposes."[98]

12. The Government of Ruritania enters into a barter agreement, whereby it buys a quantity of rice from A, an English company, and agrees to supply cocoa and coffee in return, and to make up the difference by paying additional sums. The agreement contains a term that the Government

---

[93] *Kuwait Airways Corp v Iraqi Airways Co* [1995] 1 W.L.R. 1147 (HL). Subsequently it was held that the decision giving Iraqi Airways the benefit of immunity had been procured by fraud: *Kuwait Airways Corp v Iraqi Airways Co (No.2)* [2001] 1 W.L.R. 428; *Kuwait Airways Corp v Iraqi Airways Co* [2003] EWHC 31 (Comm.), [2003] 1 Lloyd's Rep. 448; *Kuwait Airways Corp v Iraqi Airways Co* [2005] EWHC 2524 (Comm.).

[94] These are the facts of *USA and Republic of France v Dollfus Mieg et cie and Bank of England* [1952] A.C. 582, which, it seems, would be decided in the same way under the 1978 Act.

[95] These are the facts of *Rahimtoola v Nizam of Hyderabad* [1958] A.C. 379, which, it seems, would be decided in the same way today.

[96] These are the facts of *Juan Ysmael & Co Inc v Indonesian Government* [1955] A.C. 72 (PC), which would be decided in the same way today: s.6(4) of the 1978 Act. Contrast Illustration to Exception 10, para.10–057, below.

[97] State Immunity Act 1978, s.10(2).

[98] State Immunity Act 1978, s.13(2)(b), (4); *Alcom v Republic of Colombia* [1984] A.C. 580.

waives whatever defence it may have of sovereign immunity for itself and its property. When the Government fails to make up the difference, A obtains leave to issue and serve a writ outside the jurisdiction, and is granted an *ex parte* freezing injunction, which is confirmed *inter partes*. The waiver amounts to an agreement that the property of the State can be made the subject of a freezing injunction, but it is discharged to the extent that it affects diplomatic premises.[99]

13. A enters into a contract to supply machinery to the Government of Iraq. When the Government repudiates the contract, A sues in England. Meanwhile, the British embassy in Baghdad has been closed down, and Iraq has broken off diplomatic relations with the United Kingdom; but the Iraqi embassy in London continues to function and is recognised as a diplomatic mission. A purports to serve the writ on the Iraqi embassy, and it is received by an accredited diplomat. The court has jurisdiction under Exception 2 below, but the service is ineffective.[100]

10E–027   *Exception 1—A State is not immune as respects proceedings in respect of which it has submitted to the jurisdiction of the courts of the United Kingdom.*[101]

Comment

10–028   At common law, sovereign immunity could be waived by or on behalf of the foreign State,[102] but waiver had to have taken place at the time the court was asked to exercise jurisdiction[103] and could not be constituted by, or inferred from, a prior contract to submit to the jurisdiction of the court or to arbitration.[104] The Act, however, has made a far-reaching and beneficial change by providing expressly that a State may submit (a) after the dispute giving rise to the proceedings has arisen or (b) by a prior written agreement.[105] Whether a contractual provision amounts to a submission is a question of construction. In *NML Capital Ltd v Argentina*[106] bonds (which were governed by New York law) issued by Argentina contained a "waiver and jurisdiction" clause which provided that a judgment on the bonds could be enforced in any courts to the

---

[99] *A Co Ltd v Republic of X* [1990] 2 Lloyd's Rep. 520.

[100] *ibid.* s.12(1). *cf. Kuwait Airways Corp v Iraqi Airways Co* [1995] 1 W.L.R. 1147 (HL).

[101] s.2(1). For other specific statutory provisions for waiver see paras 15–015; 15–028, below.

[102] See Cohn (1958) 34 B.Y.I.L. 260.

[103] *Mighell v Sultan of Johore* [1894] 1 Q.B. 149 (CA); *Duff Development Co v Government of Kelantan* [1924] A.C. 797; *Kahan v Pakistan Federation* [1951] 2 K.B. 1003 (CA); *A Co Ltd v Republic of X* [1990] 2 Lloyd's Rep. 520 (criticised by F.A. Mann (1991) 107 L.Q.R. 362). See *NML Capital Ltd v Argentina* [2011] UKSC 31, [2011] 2 A.C. 495, at [125].

[104] *Duff Development Co v Government of Kelantan,* above; *Kahan v Pakistan Federation,* above; *Baccus SRL v Servicio Nacional del Trigo* [1957] 1 Q.B. 438 (CA); *Compania Mercantil Argentina v United States Shipping Board* (1924) 93 L.J.K.B. 816 (CA). Contrast *Standard Chartered Bank v International Tin Council* [1987] 1 W.L.R. 641; but see *A Co Ltd v Republic of X* [1990] 2 Lloyd's Rep. 520.

[105] s.2(2). But a provision in an agreement that it is to be governed by the law of the United Kingdom is not of itself a submission: *ibid.* The agreement need not necessarily be between the parties to the litigation, since the submission may be constituted by an international agreement: s.17(2).

[106] [2011] UKSC 31, [2011] 2 A.C. 495. See also *A Company Ltd v Republic of X* [1990] 2 Lloyd's Rep. 520.

jurisdiction of which Argentina was or might be subject, and that Argentina agreed that, to the extent it was entitled in any jurisdiction to immunity, it waived any such immunity. There was no specific reference to the English court. It was held that the clause was an effective submission to an action at common law to enforce a New York judgment on the bonds. In addition, a State will be deemed to have submitted if it has instituted the proceedings;[107] or if it has intervened or taken any steps in the proceedings, unless the intervention has been made or the steps taken (a) for the purpose only of claiming immunity or asserting an interest in property in circumstances such that the State would have been entitled to immunity if the proceedings had been brought against it, or (b) in ignorance of facts entitling it to immunity (if those facts could not reasonably have been ascertained) and immunity is claimed as soon as reasonably practicable.[108] Whether any other steps taken in the proceedings will amount to a submission will depend on general principles discussed in Chapter 11.[109]

Once a foreign State has waived its immunity, it will be treated just like any other litigant in such matters as security for costs[110] and disclosure of documents,[111] but the Act provides that no penalty by way of committal or fine shall be imposed in respect of any failure or refusal by or on behalf of a State to disclose or produce any document or other information for the purpose of proceedings to which it is a party.[112]   **10–029**

A submission in respect of any proceedings extends to any appeal, but not to a counterclaim unless it arises out of the same legal relationship or facts as the claim.[113] A submission to jurisdiction is not a submission to execution, but process of execution may be issued with the written consent of the State.[114]   **10–030**

The head of State's diplomatic mission in the United Kingdom, or the person for the time being performing his functions, is deemed to have authority to submit to proceedings on behalf of the State; and any person who has entered into a contract on behalf and with the authority of a State is   **10–031**

---

[107] s.2(3)(a).

[108] ss.2(3)(b), 2(4) and 2(5). See also *Propend Finance Pty Ltd v Sing, The Times*, May 2, 1997, 111 Int. L.R. 611 (CA). For cases of alleged mistake see *The Jassy* [1906] P. 270; *Baccus SRL v Servicio Nacional del Trigo* [1957] 1 Q.B. 438 (CA); *Aziz v Republic of Yemen* [2005] EWCA Civ 745.

[109] See below, Rule 32. See *Kuwait Airways Corp v Iraqi Airways Co* [1995] 1 Lloyd's Rep. 32 (CA) (reversed in part on other grounds: see [1995] 1 W.L.R. 1147, 1164 (HL)); *cf. Jaffe v Miller* (1993) 13 O.R. (3d) 745 (Ont CA); *Robinson v Kuwait Liaison Office* (1997) 145 A.L.R. 68. See also *London Branch of the Nigerian Universities Commission v Bastians* [1995] I.C.R. 358 (EAT).

[110] *Republic of Costa Rica v Erlanger* (1876) 3 Ch.D. 62 (CA); *The Newbattle* (1885) 10 P.D. 33 (CA); *Ministère de la Culture v Lieb, The Times*, December 24, 1981. But *cf.* Art.17 of the European Convention.

[111] *United States of America v Wagner* (1867) L.R. 2 Ch. App. 582; *South African Republic v Compagnie Franco-Belge du Chemin de Fer du Nord* [1898] 1 Ch. 190, 195.

[112] s.13(1). See para.10–021, above.

[113] s.2(6). *cf. Sultan of Johore v Bendahar* [1952] A.C. 318 (PC) (appeal); *South African Republic v Compagnie Franco-Belge du Chemin de Fer du Nord* [1897] 2 Ch. 487 (CA); [1898] 1 Ch. 190 (counterclaim); *USSR v Belaiew* (1925) 42 T.L.R. 21 (counterclaim); *United States v Friedland* (1999) 182 D.L.R. (4th) 614 (Ont CA) (counterclaim).

[114] s.13(3), see above, para.10–015, n.56.

deemed to have authority to submit on its behalf in respect of proceedings arising out of the contract.[115]

10E–032   *Exception 2*—**A State is not immune as respects proceedings relating to (a) a commercial transaction entered into by the State; or (b) an obligation of the State which by virtue of a contract (whether a commercial transaction or not) falls to be performed wholly or partly in the United Kingdom.**[116]

COMMENT

10–033   This extremely important Exception applies to proceedings relating to two quite separate classes of transaction. The first is the commercial transaction, which is defined as (a) any contract for the supply of goods or services; (b) any loan or other transaction for the provision of finance (and any guarantee or indemnity in respect thereof or of any other financial obligation); and (c) any other transaction or activity (whether of a commercial, industrial, financial, professional or other similar character) into which a State enters or in which it engages otherwise than in the exercise of sovereign authority. Thus, for example, contracts for the purchase or sale of goods required for public purposes, such as arms, are within the Exception. Contracts for the supply of goods and services, and financial transactions, are likely to comprise the vast majority of commercial transactions, and it is not therefore likely that it will frequently be necessary to consider what other transactions a State may enter into "otherwise than in the exercise of sovereign authority."[117] In *NML Capital Ltd v Argentina*[118] it was held by a majority that proceedings for the enforcement of a foreign judgment entered in respect of a commercial transaction are not themselves proceedings "relating to a commercial transaction." The expression "in the exercise of sovereign authority" refers to the concept of *acta jure imperii* in public international law, and in *Kuwait Airways Corp v Iraqi Airways Co*[119] it was said that the ultimate test of what constitutes an

---

[115] s.2(7). See *Malaysian Industrial Development Authority v Jeyasingham* [1998] I.C.R. 307 (EAT). *cf. Donegal International Ltd v Republic of Zambia* [2007] EWHC 197 (Comm.), [2007] 1 Lloyd's Rep. 397 (authority of Minister).

[116] s.3(1).

[117] In *Svenska Petroleum Exploration AB v Lithuania (No.2)* [2006] EWCA Civ 1529, [2008] Q.B. 886 the Court of Appeal left open the question whether a joint venture agreement between a State organisation and a private investor to exploit a commercial opportunity relating to the State's natural resources on a profit-sharing basis was to be regarded as a commercial transaction for the purposes of the State Immunity Act 1978, s.3(3)(c). *cf. PASC v US Defence Dept* [1992] 2 S.C.R. 50, (1992) 91 D.L.R. (4th) 449; *Bedessee Imports Ltd v Guyana Sugar Corp* (2010) 329 DLR (4th) 382 (Ont.).

[118] [2011] UKSC 31, [2011] 2 A.C. 495, approving on this point *AIC Ltd v Federal Government of Nigeria* [2003] EWHC 1357 (QB); *Svenska Petroleum Exploration AB v Republic of Lithuania (No.2)* [2005] EWHC 2437 (Comm.), 2006] 1 Lloyd's Rep. 181, affd, [2006] EWCA Civ 1529, [2006] Q.B. 886.

[119] [1995] 1 W.L.R. 1147, 1156 (HL), *per* Lord Goff of Chieveley, applying *The I Congreso del Partido* [1983] 1 A.C. 244 and *Alcom v Republic of Colombia* [1984] A.C. 580. Subsequently it was held that the decision giving Iraqi Airways the benefit of immunity had been procured by fraud: see above, para.10–025, n.93.

act *jure imperii* is whether the act in question is of its own character a governmental act, as opposed to an act which any private citizen can perform.[120]

The second category is proceedings relating to an obligation of the State **10–034** which falls to be performed wholly or partly in the United Kingdom.[121] This Exception applies whether or not the transaction is a commercial one, and whether or not the contract was made in the United Kingdom,[122] but it does not apply if each of the three following conditions is met: the contract is not a commercial transaction (as defined above), the contract was made in the territory of the State concerned, and the obligation in question is governed by its administrative law.[123] The notion of the contract being governed by administrative law is derived from Art.4(2)(c) of the European Convention on State Immunity, and is a notion which is foreign to the common law, although it is widespread in civil law countries, where it comprises a large variety of contracts concluded by the State, including concessions and state loans. Whether a contract is governed by its administrative law would (*semble*) fall to be determined by that country's law, at any rate if the contract is not governed by English law.

It must be emphasised that neither of these categories *confers* jurisdiction **10–035** on the English court. If the State does not submit to the jurisdiction, then even if the transaction is a commercial one, or the obligation in question falls to be performed in the United Kingdom, the requirements of CPR, r.6.36 and PD6B, para.3.1, or of the Brussels I Regulation, or of the Lugano Convention, must be satisfied before the English court will have jurisdiction.[124]

---

[120] For the position at common law see *Littrell v Government of the United States (No.2)* [1995] 1 W.L.R. 82 (CA), where it was held, in an action based on allegedly negligent treatment of a member of the US airforce at a US military hospital in England, that the activity of providing medical treatment to members of the armed forces at a base was an activity *jure imperii*; *Holland v Lampen-Wolfe* [2000] 1 W.L.R. 1573 (HL), where, in an action for libel by an American civilian employed to teach courses at US bases in Europe, it was held that an unfavourable report by an educational services officer on the plaintiff's teaching was part of a State's sovereign function of maintaining its armed forces, and the publication of the memorandum in the course of the defendant's supervision of such provision was an act within the sovereign authority of the US so as to attract immunity. These were cases at common law, since the 1978 Act does not apply to proceedings in relation to the armed forces of a foreign State in the UK: s.16(2). See also *Arab Republic of Egypt v Gamal Eldin* [1996] I.C.R. 13 (EAT); *McElhinney v Williams* [1996] 1 I.L.R.M. 276 (Sup Ct) (immunity for acts of member of British forces on checkpoint duty in Northern Ireland). *cf. United States v Public Service Alliance of Canada* [1992] 2 S.C.R. 50 ("commercial activity"); *Saudi Arabia v Nelson*, 507 U.S. 349 (1993), ("based upon a commercial activity carried on in the United States by the foreign state": action for personal injuries sustained in Saudi Arabia by plaintiff who had been recruited in the US not so based); *Republic of Argentina v Weltover, Inc*, 504 U.S. 607 (1992) ("action . . . based upon an act outside the territory of the United States in connection with a commercial activity of the foreign state elsewhere and that act causes a direct effect in the United States": State subject to US jurisdiction for breach of contract claim on failure to pay bonds payable in New York).

[121] *cf.* the position under the Brussels I Regulation and the Lugano Convention, see below, paras 11–277 *et seq.*

[122] It is not necessary that the State be a party to the contract, if it has some secondary liability: *JH Rayner (Mincing Lane) Ltd v Department of Trade and Industry* [1989] Ch. 72, 194–195, 222, 252 (CA), affirmed on other grounds [1990] 2 A.C. 418 (HL).

[123] s.3(2).

[124] See above, para.10–007.

This Exception does not apply (i) if the parties to the dispute are States or have otherwise agreed in writing,[125] or (ii) if the proceedings relate to a contract of employment.[126]

ILLUSTRATION

10–036   A, an English company, enters into a contract, governed by English law, to supply arms to the Government of Ruritania. When the Government repudiates the contract, A sues in England. The court has jurisdiction because the contract is one for the supply of goods.[127]

10E–037   ***Exception 3—A State is not immune as respects proceedings relating to a contract of employment between the State and an individual where (a) the contract was made in the United Kingdom or (b) the work is to be wholly or partly performed in the United Kingdom.***[128]

COMMENT

10–038   This Exception does not apply if either (a) at the time the proceedings are brought, the employee is a national of the State concerned, or (b) if at the time the contract was made the employee was neither a national of, nor habitually resident in, the United Kingdom;[129] but in each of those cases the Exception *does* apply where the work is for an office, agency or establishment maintained in the United Kingdom for commercial purposes[130] unless, at the time the contract was made, the employee was habitually resident in the State concerned. Nor does the Exception apply if the parties to the contract have agreed in writing that the courts of the United Kingdom shall not have jurisdiction;[131] but the parties cannot effectively agree that the courts shall not have jurisdiction where the law of the United Kingdom requires the proceedings to be brought before a court of the United Kingdom.[132] This Exception does not apply to proceedings concerning the employment of members of a diplomatic mission or of a consular post.[133]

---

[125] s.3(2).

[126] s.3(3).

[127] s.3(3)(a).

[128] s.4(1). See Fox, *Law of State Immunity* (2nd ed. 2008), pp.547–550; Garnett (1997) 64 I.C.L.Q. 81; Garnett (2005) 54 I.C.L.Q. 705; Pingel, 2005 *Rev. Crit.* 1115. "Proceedings relating to a contract of employment" include proceedings in relation to statutory rights and duties arising out of the contract of employment: s.4(6). For the common law position see *Sengupta v Republic of India* [1983] I.C.R. 221 (EAT); *Reid v Republic of Nauru* [1993] 1 V.R. 251; *Governor of Pitcairn v Sutton* [1995] 1 N.Z.L.R. 426.

[129] s.4(2)(a)–(b). For meaning of national of the United Kingdom see s.4(5), as amended.

[130] See s.17(1) for meaning of this expression.

[131] s.4(2)(c).

[132] s.4(4). See Employment Rights Act 1996, s.203. *cf.* Brussels I Regulation, Art.21, and Lugano Convention, Art.21, below, para.12–117.

[133] s.16(1)(a).

ILLUSTRATIONS

1. A, a British citizen, is employed by the Government of Ruritania on a five-year contract, **10–039**
made in England, to manage its tourist office in London. He is dismissed after one year and sues
the Government for damages. The court has jurisdiction.[134]

2. The facts are the same as in Illustration 1, except that A is a national of Ruritania who is
resident in England. The court has jurisdiction because the work is for an establishment maintained for commercial purposes.[135]

3. The facts are the same as in Illustration 2, except that when the contract is executed A is
habitually resident in Ruritania. The court has no jurisdiction.[136]

Exception 4—A State is not immune as respects proceedings in respect of **10E–040**
(a) death or personal injury or (b) damage to or loss of tangible property,
in each case where it was caused by an act or omission in the United
Kingdom.[137]

ILLUSTRATION

A's tug, whilst at anchor in a fog off Dover, is run down and damaged by the Ostend-Dover **10–041**
packet which carries mail as well as passengers and cargo and is owned by the King of the
Belgians and operated by his servants. A brings an action for damages against the Kingdom of
Belgium. The court has jurisdiction.[138]

Exception 5—A State is not immune as respects proceedings relating to **10E–042**
any interest of the State in, or its possession or use of, immovable
property in the United Kingdom, or any obligation of the State arising
therefrom.[139]

COMMENT

This Exception does not apply to proceedings concerning title to, or posses- **10–043**
sion of, property used for the purposes of the State's diplomatic mission.[140]
Proceedings for breach of covenant in a lease are not proceedings concerning
title or possession.[141]

ILLUSTRATIONS

1. A leases premises in Oxford Street, London, to the Government of Ruritania. The premises **10–044**
are to be used as a tourist office. The Government falls into arrears with its payment of rent. A
sues for arrears of rent and for possession. The court has jurisdiction.[142]

---

[134] s.4(1).

[135] ss.4(2)(a) and 4(3).

[136] ss.4(2)(a) and 4(3).

[137] s.5. See *Schreiber v Canada (Att-Gen)* (2002) 216 D.L.R. (4th) 513 (Sup Ct Can) on the
origin of the exception for death and personal injury.

[138] s.5. Contrast *The Parlement Belge* (1880) 5 P.D. 197 (CA), an action *in rem* decided at
common law.

[139] s.6(1). *cf. The Charkieh* (1873) L.R. 4 Adm. & Ecc. 59, 97; *Sultan of Johore v Bendahar*
[1952] A.C. 318 (PC); *Thai-Europe Tapioca Service Ltd v Government of Pakistan* [1975] 1
W.L.R. 1485, 1490–1491 (CA).

[140] s.16(1)(b).

[141] *Intpro Properties (UK) Ltd v Sauvel* [1983] Q.B. 1019 (CA).

[142] s.6(1).

2. A leases a flat in Kensington to the French Government for use as a private residence for a member of the French embassy and his family. In breach of a covenant in the lease A is denied access to the flat when A seeks to enter to carry out repairs necessitated by dry rot in the premises. After the flat has been vacated, A claims damages against the French Government for the loss caused as a result of the refusal to permit entry. The court has jurisdiction. The action does not concern title or possession, and the premises were not used "for the purposes of a diplomatic mission" because they were used primarily as a private residence.[143]

10E–045 *Exception 6—A State is not immune as respects proceedings relating to an interest arising by way of succession, gift or bona vacantia in movable or immovable property, nor does any interest of a State in property prevent exercise of any jurisdiction relating to the estates of the deceased persons or persons of unsound mind or to insolvency, the winding up of companies or the administration of trusts.*[144]

COMMENT

10–046 Prior to the Act it was recognised that the Chancery Division had jurisdiction to distribute a trust fund among the beneficiaries, notwithstanding the entitlement of a foreign sovereign to an interest therein,[145] and that the Companies Court had jurisdiction to wind up a company, even though a foreign sovereign might be interested in any surplus assets.[146] The effect of Exception 6 is that a foreign State which is a creditor of an insolvent company cannot claim its debts in priority to other creditors, since a winding up order does not of itself affect the property of the State, i.e. the chose in action represented by a bank deposit.[147]

10–047 Although the Act provides that a State's interest in property will not prevent the exercise of jurisdiction relating to the administration of trusts, it seems that a foreign State cannot be made liable as a trustee, unless one of the other Exceptions is applicable.[148]

10E–048 *Exception 7—A State is not immune as respects proceedings relating to:*

   (a) **any patent, trademark, design or plant breeders' rights belonging to the State, and registered or protected in the United Kingdom or for which the State has applied in the United Kingdom;**

   (b) **an alleged infringement by the State in the United Kingdom of any patent, trade mark, design, plant breeders' rights or copyright; or**

   (c) **the right to use a trade or business name in the United Kingdom.**[149]

---

[143] *Intpro Properties (UK) Ltd v Sauvel,* above.

[144] s.6(2)–(3).

[145] See *Rahimtoola v Nizam of Hyderabad* [1958] A.C. 379, 397, 398, 401, 408, 420.

[146] *Re Russian Bank for Foreign Trade* [1933] Ch. 745, 769–770.

[147] *Re Rafidain Bank* [1992] B.C.L.C. 301.

[148] *Rahimtoola v Nizam of Hyderabad* [1958] A.C. 379, 401, 408. But see *Duke of Brunswick v King of Hanover* (1848) 2 H.L.C. 1, 25 and *cf. Gladstone v Musurus Bey* (1862) 1 H. & M. 495, 503.

[149] s.7.

Exception **8—A State is not immune as respects proceedings relating to its**   10E–049
membership of a body corporate, an unincorporated body or a partner-
ship which (a) has members other than States, and (b) is incorporated or
constituted under the law of the United Kingdom or is controlled from or
has its principal place of business in the United Kingdom, being proceed-
ings arising between the State and the body or its other members or, as
the case may be, between the State and the other partners, unless provi-
sion to the contrary has been made by agreement in writing or by the
instrument establishing the body or partnership.[150]

Exception **9—Where a State has agreed in writing to submit a dispute**   10E–050
which has arisen, or may arise, to arbitration, it is not immune as respects
proceedings in the courts of the United Kingdom which relate to the
arbitration, except (a) where contrary provision is made or (b) where the
arbitration agreement is between States.[151]

COMMENT

This Exception applies to proceedings relating to the arbitration, including   10–051
proceedings to enforce the arbitration agreement or for review of an award. In
Svenska Petroleum Exploration AB v Lithuania (No.2)[152] it was held that this
Exception applies to applications for leave to enforce an award as a judgment.
The Court of Appeal said that arbitration was a consensual procedure and the
principle underlying this Exception was that if a State has submitted to
arbitration, it rendered itself amenable to such process as might be necessary
to render the arbitration effective. An application under the Arbitration Act
1996, s.101(2), for leave to enforce an award as a judgment was the final stage
in rendering the arbitral procedure effective.

Exception **10—In admiralty proceedings (or proceedings on any claim**   10E–052
which could be made the subject of admiralty proceedings) a State is not
immune as respects:
   (a) **an action *in rem* against a ship belonging to that State, or an action**
       ***in personam* for enforcing a claim in connection with such a ship,**
       if, at the time when the cause of action arose, the ship was in use
       or intended for use for commercial purposes;[153] **or**
   (b) **an action *in rem* against a cargo belonging to that State if both the**
       cargo and the ship carrying it were, at the time when the cause of
       action arose, in use or intended for use for commercial purposes;
       or an action *in personam* for enforcing a claim in connection with

---

[150] s.8. On the application of this provision to very unusual circumstances see *Maclaine Watson
& Co Ltd v International Tin Council* [1989] Ch. 253, 282–283 (CA), affirmed on other grounds
[1990] 2 A.C. 418.
[151] s.9.
[152] [2005] EWHC 2437 (Comm.), [2006] 1 Lloyd's Rep. 181, affd. [2006] EWCA Civ 1529,
[2008] Q.B. 886; applied in *The Altair* [2008] EWHC 612 (Comm.), [2008] 2 Lloyd's Rep.
90.
[153] s.10(2).

such a cargo if the ship carrying it was then in use or intended for use for commercial purposes.[154]

COMMENT

10–053   At common law there was a division of judicial opinion on the question whether a ship owned by a foreign sovereign but used for ordinary commercial purposes was immune from the jurisdiction,[155] but the modern authorities were against such an immunity.[156] Section 10 of the Act of 1978 enacts, broadly, the principle that ships or cargoes owned[157] by a foreign State in use, or intended for use, for commercial purposes[158] are not immune.

10–054   Where proceedings *in rem* are brought against a sister ship to enforce a claim in connection with another ship,[159] the Exception does not apply as regards the sister ship unless, at the time when the cause of action relating to that other ship arose, both ships were in use or intended for use for commercial purposes.[160]

10–055   If the proceedings are *in personam* to enforce a claim in connection with a cargo carried on a ship in use for commercial purposes, it seems that Exception (b) above applies whether or not the cargo is in use or intended for use for commercial purposes.

10–056   If the State in question is a party to the Brussels Convention for the Unification of Certain Rules Concerning the Immunity of State-owned Ships of 1926, and the claim relates to the operation of, or the carriage of cargo or passengers on, a ship owned or operated by that State, or the carriage of cargo owned by that State on any other ship, Exceptions 2 to 4 above do not apply.[161]

ILLUSTRATION

10–057   The Government of the Philippines sells a ship, the *Philippine Admiral*, to X by a contract whereby X has possession and control but the Government retains title until the price is paid in full. Before the price is paid in full, X, which operates the ship for commercial purposes, charters the ship to A. At the time of the charterparty and immediately thereafter the ship is under repair. X falls into arrears with the instalments under the sale contract and cancels the charterparty. A, the charterer, and B, ship repairers, bring an action *in rem* against the ship for breach of

---

[154] s.10(4).

[155] See *The Porto Alexandre* [1920] P. 30 (CA); *The Cristina* [1938] A.C. 485; *Zarine v Owners of SS Ramava* [1924] I.R. 148; *Flota Maritima Browning de Cuba SA v Republic of Cuba* [1962] S.C.R. 598.

[156] In *The Philippine Admiral* [1977] A.C. 373 (approved in *The I Congreso del Partido* [1983] 1 A.C. 244) the Privy Council followed the views expressed by the majority in *The Cristina* [1938] A.C. 485 that no immunity could be claimed for vessels used only for commercial purposes. See also *Thai-Europe Tapioca Service Ltd v Government of Pakistan* [1975] 1 W.L.R. 1485, 1491 (CA).

[157] Or in its possession or control or in which it claims an interest: s.10(5).

[158] For meaning of commercial purposes see s.17(1).

[159] Under the Senior Courts Act 1981, s.21(4), as to which see below, paras 13–009 *et seq.*

[160] s.10(3).

[161] s.10(6).

charterparty and for repair charges respectively. The Government continues to own the ship. The court has jurisdiction because the ship was in commercial use.[162]

Exception **11—A State is not immune as respects proceedings relating to its liability for value added tax, customs duty, agricultural levy, or rates in respects of premises occupied by it for commercial purposes.**[163]   10E–058

RULE 27—**Subject to certain qualifications, English courts have no jurisdiction to entertain an action or other proceeding against any person entitled to immunity under the Diplomatic Privileges Act 1964 or the Consular Relations Act 1968.**[164]   10R–059

COMMENT

In its judgments in the *Diplomatic and Consular Staff* (*United States v Iran*) cases the International Court of Justice re-affirmed that the principles of diplomatic and consular immunity were deep-rooted in international law; the institution of diplomacy, with its concomitant privileges and immunities, had withheld the test of centuries, and the unimpeded conduct of consular relations had been established since ancient times; every State which maintained diplomatic or consular relations was under an obligation to recognise the imperative obligations, now codified in the Vienna Convention on Diplomatic Relations of 1961 and the Vienna Convention on Consular Relations of 1963.[165] The privileges and immunities conferred by international law have been recognised at common law for centuries.[166]   10–060

Diplomats. Subject to a number of qualifications, which will be discussed below, no ambassador, High Commissioner or other head of a diplomatic mission duly accredited by another State to the Court of St James, and no member of his staff, can be sued or impleaded in an English court, nor can his property be seized. This immunity from suit was formerly secured by the Diplomatic Privileges Act 1708, which has always been treated as declaratory of the common law.[167] It was repealed and replaced by the Diplomatic   10–061

---

[162] *ibid.* s.10(2). These are the facts of *The Philippine Admiral* [1977] A.C. 373 (PC), decided at common law. Contrast Illustration 10 to Rule 26, above.

[163] s.11. This list is exhaustive of the taxes in respect of which there is no immunity: s.16(5).

[164] Brownlie, *Principles of Public International Law* (7th ed. 2008), Ch.17; Oppenheim, *International Law* (9th ed. Jennings and Watts, 1992), pp.1090–1105, 1142–1149; Denza, *Diplomatic Law* (3rd ed. 2008); Brown (1988) 37 I.C.L.Q. 53. See also Diplomatic Relations and Immunities Act 1967 (Rep. of Ireland); Diplomatic Privileges and Immunities Act 1967 and Consular Privileges and Immunities Act 1972 (Aus.); Foreign Missions and International Organizations Act 1991 (Can.); Diplomatic Privileges and Immunities Act 1968, ss.3–7, 13–18 (NZ). For the immunities of a Head of State, his family and servants see State Immunity Act 1978, s.20 and above, para.10–008, n.30.

[165] 1979 I.C.J. Rep. 7, at 19–20; 1980 I.C.J. Rep. 3, at 42.

[166] See, e.g. *Engelke v Musmann* [1928] A.C. 433, 459 *per* Lord Phillimore.

[167] For the circumstances in which it was passed, see *Taylor v Best* (1854) C.B. 487, 491–493.

359

Privileges Act 1964, which gives effect to the Vienna Convention on Diplomatic Relations (1961).[168] Section 1 of the Act provides that the following provisions of the Act shall have effect in substitution for any previous enactment or rule of law; and s.2 enacts those articles of the Convention[169] which are set out in Schedule 1 as part of the law of the United Kingdom. Hence, much of the old case law is now only of historical interest. The articles of the Convention will no doubt be interpreted so as to secure the greatest possible measure of conformity with the law of other parties to the Convention.[170]

10–062   The Act authorises the withdrawal of immunity from the diplomatic mission of a State which fails to accord proper immunity to Her Majesty's mission in that State.[171] Conversely, the United Kingdom has reciprocal arrangements with certain States whereby their diplomatic missions are granted more extensive immunities than those provided by the Convention. The Act makes provision for continuing these arrangements.[172]

10–063   The most important single change effected by the Convention in the law of the United Kingdom is that it abolished the principle of absolute immunity: diplomatic immunity, even that of the head of mission himself, is now only qualified. The Convention divides persons entitled to diplomatic immunity into three categories[173]: (1) "diplomatic agents," namely, the head of the mission and members of his diplomatic staff; (2) "members of the administrative and technical staff," e.g. persons employed in secretarial, clerical and communications duties, such as typists, translators and coding clerks; and (3) "members of the service staff," namely, members of the staff of the mission in its domestic service, such as cooks, cleaners, porters and chauffeurs.

10–064   (1) Provided that they are not nationals of nor permanently resident in the receiving State, diplomatic agents enjoy complete immunity from criminal jurisdiction, and immunity from civil and administrative jurisdiction and from execution except in three cases:

(a) a real action relating to private immovable property situated in the United Kingdom (unless it is held on behalf of the sending State for the purposes of the mission);[174]

(b) an action relating to succession in which the diplomatic agent is involved as executor, administrator or beneficiary as a private person;

---

[168] For a commentary on the Act and the Convention, see Buckley (1965–1966) 41 B.Y.I.L. 321. See also Denza, *Diplomatic Law* (3rd ed. 2008); Satow, *Diplomatic Practice* (6th ed. Roberts, 2009).

[169] Cmnd. 2565.

[170] See above, para.1–030.

[171] s.3(1).

[172] s.7(1).

[173] Sch.1, Art.1.

[174] "Real action," a term taken from the civil law, signifies "an action where ownership or possession of immovable property is claimed" (Satow, *Diplomatic Practice* (6th ed. Roberts, 2009), para.9.17); *Intpro Properties (UK) Ltd v Sauvel* [1983] Q.B. 1019 (CA); see also Denza, *Diplomatic Law* (3rd ed. 2008), pp.291–294. On immunity of property used for diplomatic purposes see also *Alcom Ltd v Republic of Colombia* [1984] A.C. 580; *Westminster City Council v Iran* [1986] 1 W.L.R. 979; *A Co Ltd v Republic of X* [1990] 2 Lloyd's Rep. 520. See also Diplomatic and Consular Premises Act 1987; *R. v Secretary of State of Foreign and Commonwealth Affairs, Ex p. Samuel, The Times,* August 17, 1989, (1989) 83 Int.L.R. 232 (CA).

(c) an action relating to any professional or commercial activity exercised by the diplomatic agent in the United Kingdom outside his official functions.[175]

A like immunity is conferred on the members of the family of a diplomatic agent forming part of his household, unless they are nationals of the receiving State,[176] i.e. British citizens, British Overseas Territories citizens, British Overseas citizens and British Nationals (Overseas).[177] **10–065**

(2) The members of the administrative and technical staff of the mission, together with the members of their families forming part of their respective households, provided they are not nationals of nor permanently resident in the receiving State, enjoy a like immunity, but with the important qualification that immunity from civil and administrative jurisdiction does not extend to acts performed outside the course of their duties.[178] Thus members of the administrative and technical staff are not immune from the making of interim care orders in respect of their children, even if the order cannot be enforced effectively.[179] **10–066**

(3) The members of the service staff of the mission, provided they are not nationals of nor permanently resident in the receiving State, only enjoy immunity from jurisdiction in respect of acts performed in the course of their duties.[180] **10–067**

Thus, the difference between the immunity of (1) diplomatic agents and that of (2) administrative and technical staff is that the latter is confined to acts performed in the course of their official duties so far as civil (but not criminal) jurisdiction is concerned. The differences between the immunity of (2) administrative and technical staff and that of (3) service staff are that the latter does not extend to members of their families, nor, as regards criminal jurisdiction, to acts performed outside the course of their duties. **10–068**

Private servants of members of the mission (who are not employees of the sending State) enjoy immunity only to the extent admitted by the receiving State.[181] Diplomatic agents who are nationals of or permanently resident in the receiving State only enjoy immunity from jurisdiction in respect of official acts performed in the exercise of their functions, except in so far as additional immunities may be granted by the receiving State.[182] Other members of the staff of the mission and private servants who are nationals of or permanently resident in the receiving State enjoy immunities only to the extent admitted by the United Kingdom as receiving State; but the receiving State must exercise its jurisdiction over those persons in such a manner as not to interfere unduly with the performance of the functions of the mission.[183] The "extent admitted by the receiving State" and the "additional immunities" here referred to mean **10–069**

---

[175] Diplomatic Privileges Act 1964, Sch.1, Art.31.

[176] *ibid.* Art.37(1). See *Re C* [1959] Ch. 363; *R. v Guildhall Magistrates' Court, Ex p. Jarrett-Thorpe, The Times,* October 6, 1977; O'Keefe (1976) 25 I.C.L.Q. 329.

[177] s.2(2) of the Act; British Nationality Act 1981, s.51(3).

[178] Sch.1, Art.37(2). See Whomersley (1992) 41 I.C.L.Q. 848.

[179] *Re B (A Child) (Care proceedings: Diplomatic Immunity)* [2002] EWHC 1751 (Fam.), [2003] Fam. 16 (embassy driver: allegations of abuse of daughter).

[180] *ibid.* Art.37(3).

[181] Diplomatic Privileges Act 1964, Sch.1, Art.37(4), Art.1(h).

[182] *ibid.* Art.38(1).

[183] *ibid.* Art.38(2).

such as may be specified by Order in Council.[184] Orders in Council provide that a person who is a member of the mission of specified independent countries of the Commonwealth, or the Republic of Ireland, or who is a private servant of such a member, and is a citizen of that country and also a British citizen,[185] shall be entitled to the same privileges and immunities as he would have been entitled to if he were not a British citizen, etc.[186]

10–070   Every person entitled to immunity from jurisdiction enjoys it from the moment he enters the territory of the receiving State to take up his post or, if he is already there, from the moment when his appointment is notified to the appropriate Ministry of the receiving State.[187] In the former case it is not also necessary that his appointment be notified to, or accepted by, the department of the Secretary of State concerned.[188] He enjoys the immunity even if he only became entitled to it after the commencement of the proceedings.[189] When his functions come to an end, his immunity normally ceases at the moment when he leaves the country, or on the expiry of a reasonable period in which to do so; except in the case of acts performed in the exercise of his functions, when it continues to subsist.[190] But if the proceedings are commenced before his immunity ceases, and have not been struck out, the proceedings may continue after his immunity ceases.[191] If he dies, the members of his family continue to enjoy any immunity to which they were entitled until the expiry of a reasonable period in which to leave the country.[192] The running of any limitation period is suspended during such time as the defendant enjoys diplomatic immunity.[193]

10–071   The Convention deals with immunity from the jurisdiction "of the receiving State." It does not deal with immunity from the jurisdiction of any other State.[194] There is only one reported English case[195] in which such immunity has been discussed. In that case the plaintiff sought leave to serve notice of the writ out of the jurisdiction on the Venezuelan Ambassador to France. His

---

[184] s.2(6) of the Act.

[185] Or the other classes of citizenship, above, para.10–065.

[186] SI 1999/670.

[187] Sch.1, Art.39(1) and s.2(2) of the Act.

[188] *R. v Home Secretary, Ex p. Bagga* [1991] 1 Q.B. 485 (CA), doubting *R. v Governor of Pentonville Prison, Ex p. Teja* [1971] 2 Q.B. 274; *R. v Lambeth Justices, Ex p. Yusufu* [1985] Crim.L.R. 510; *R. v Governor of Pentonville Prison, Ex p. Osman (No.2), The Times*, January 5, 1989. These were immigration or extradition cases. See also Brown (1988) 37 I.C.L.Q. 53, 54–59.

[189] *Ghosh v D'Rozario* [1963] 1 Q.B. 106 (CA).

[190] Diplomatic Privileges Act 1964, Sch.1, Art.39(2). *cf. Musurus Bey v Gadban* [1894] 2 Q.B. 352 (CA); *Zoernsch v Waldock* [1964] 1 W.L.R. 675; *Re Regina & Palacios* (1984) 45 O.R. (2d) 269. *cf. Re P (Children Act: Diplomatic Immunity)* [1998] 1 F.L.R. 624 and *Re P (Diplomatic Immunity: Jurisdiction), ibid.* 1026. See also *R. v Bow Street Magistrate, Ex p. Pinochet (No.3)* [2000] 1 A.C. 147, 255–257, 269–270.

[191] *Shaw v Shaw* [1979] Fam. 62 (divorce petition).

[192] Diplomatic Privileges Act 1964, Sch.1, Art.39(3).

[193] *Musurus Bey v Gadban* [1894] 2 Q.B. 352 (CA).

[194] Except in the one case of a diplomatic agent passing through the territory of one State in order to take up or return to a post in another State or to return to his own country: Art.40. It has been held, in a criminal case, that Art.40 is not limited to cases of mere transit: *R. v Guildhall Magistrates' Court, Ex p. Jarrett-Thorpe, The Times*, October 6, 1977. But *cf. R. v Governor of Pentonville Prison, Ex p. Teja* [1971] 2 Q.B. 274. See Brown (1988) 37 I.C.L.Q. 53, 59–63.

[195] *New Chile Gold Mining Co v Blanco* (1888) 4 T.L.R. 346. *cf. Rush v Rush* [1920] P. 242 (CA), where the point was not argued.

application was refused on the ground that the case did not fall within the terms of RSC Order 11, r.1 (now CPR, r.6.36, and PD6B, para.3.1); and conflicting views were expressed on the question whether the proposed defendant was entitled to diplomatic immunity.

Foreign consuls. Foreign consuls and members of their staffs are not within the terms of the Vienna Convention on Diplomatic Relations. It appears to be accepted that they were entitled to immunity from suit at common law in respect of their official acts, but not in respect of their private acts.[196] This is confirmed by the Consular Relations Act 1968, which enacts as part of the law of the United Kingdom those articles of the Vienna Convention on Consular Relations (1963) which are set out in the Schedule.[197] Under that Convention, consular officers and consular employees[198] are not amenable to jurisdiction in respect of acts performed in the exercise of consular functions, except in civil actions (a) arising out of a contract made by the consular officer or consular employee in which he did not contract expressly or impliedly as an agent of the sending State, or (b) by a third party for damage arising from an accident in the United Kingdom caused by a vehicle, vessel or aircraft.[199] A third exception is contained in the Consular Conventions Act 1949, which makes provision for the grant of probate or letters of administration to foreign consular officers in respect of foreign nationals dying possessed of property in the United Kingdom,[200] and deprives them of any immunity in respect of any act done in connection with any such grant.[201] 　　　**10–072**

The Consular Relations Act 1968[202] also empowers the Crown by Order in Council[203] to confer consular immunities on (a) persons in the service of countries of the Commonwealth or of the Republic of Ireland, holding offices involving the performance of duties substantially corresponding to those which, in the case of a foreign sovereign power, would be performed by a consular officer; and (b) any person recognised by the United Kingdom Government as the chief representative in the United Kingdom of a State or province of a country within the Commonwealth. 　　　**10–073**

Waiver. Diplomatic and consular immunity may be waived by the sending State[204] and a waiver by the head or acting head of the mission is deemed to 　　　**10–074**

---

[196] See *Engelke v Musmann* [1928] A.C. 433, 437–438; *S v Penrose*, 1966 (1) S.A. 5; noted in (1966) 83 S.A.L.J. 126; *cf. R. v Jiminez-Paez* (1993) 98 Cr.App.R. 239 (CA). See also Beckett (1944) 21 B.Y.I.L. 34; Lee and Shipley, *Consular Law and Practice* (3rd ed. 2008), Chs 29–31; Parry, *British Digest of International Law* (1965), Vol.8, pp.141–166.

[197] s.1(1). For the full text see Cmnd. 5219.

[198] For definitions, see Sch.1, Art.1(d) and (e).

[199] *ibid.* Art.43; see also Arts 53, 57, 58, 71.

[200] See below, para.26–016.

[201] s.3, which applies to States specified by Order in Council under s.6(1).

[202] s.12, as substituted by the Diplomatic and other Privileges Act 1971, Sch.

[203] See SI 1985/1983.

[204] Diplomatic Privileges Act 1964, Sch.1, Art.32(1); Consular Relations Act 1968, Sch.1, Art.45(1). See generally *Propend Finance Pty Ltd v Sing, The Times*, May 2, 1997, 111 Int. L.R. 611 (CA).

be a waiver by that State.²⁰⁵ Waiver must always be express, except that the initiation of proceedings precludes the claimant from invoking immunity from jurisdiction in respect of any counterclaims directly connected with the principal claim.²⁰⁶ Thus the court has no jurisdiction to entertain a counterclaim for damages for libel or slander in an action by a head of mission for breach of contract.²⁰⁷ Waiver of immunity from jurisdiction in civil or administrative proceedings does not imply waiver of immunity in respect of the execution of the judgment, for which a separate waiver is required.²⁰⁸ Waiver is not defined, but in both Acts the expression is derived from international conventions, and it should not therefore be given the narrow scope it had at common law.²⁰⁹

10–075   **Evidence.** If in any proceedings any question arises whether or not any person is entitled to diplomatic or consular immunity, a certificate issued by or under the authority of the Secretary of State stating any fact relating to that question is conclusive evidence of that fact.²¹⁰ The Foreign and Commonwealth Office is notified of the appointments, arrivals and departure of the staff of diplomatic missions and consular posts.²¹¹ The notification will normally indicate the category and the nationality and residence of the person concerned.

ILLUSTRATIONS

10–076   1. X, a member of the diplomatic staff of a foreign embassy, is the tenant of a private house in Hampstead. X can be sued by the landlord for possession on the expiry of the lease.²¹²

---

²⁰⁵ Diplomatic Privileges Act 1964, s.2(3); Consular Relations Act 1968, s.1(5). At common law it was doubtful whether the head of the mission could waive his own immunity without the authority of the sending State (on which see *Re Republic of Bolivia Exploration Syndicate Ltd* [1914] 1 Ch. 139; *Re Suarez* [1918] 1 Ch. 176, 191; Parry, *Digest of International Law* (1965), Vol.7, pp.872–875) but s.2(3) of the Diplomatic Privileges Act 1964 appears to render unnecessary an investigation whether a waiver by the head of the mission has the sanction of the sending State.
²⁰⁶ Diplomatic Privileges Act 1964, Sch.1, Art.32(2) and (3); Consular Relations Act 1968, Sch.1, Art.45(2) and (3).
²⁰⁷ *cf. High Commissioner for India v Ghosh* [1960] 1 Q.B. 134 (CA), decided at common law. See Simmonds (1960) 9 I.C.L.Q. 334.
²⁰⁸ Diplomatic Privileges Act 1964, Sch.1, Art.32(4); Consular Relations Act 1968, Sch.1, Art.45(4). *cf. Re Suarez* [1917] 2 Ch. 131, decided at common law.
²⁰⁹ In *A Co Ltd v Republic of X* [1990] 2 Lloyd's Rep. 520 (criticised by F.A. Mann (1991) 107 L.Q.R. 362) it was held (applying the obsolete rule on State immunity: para.10–028, text at n.104, above) that immunity from execution over diplomatic property could not be waived by contract, but only by an undertaking or consent given to the court when the court was asked to exercise jurisdiction. But this condition is not required by the Vienna Convention nor by the 1964 Act and the authorities to this effect were convincingly criticised by Cohn (1958) 34 B.Y.I.L. 260. See also *NML Capital Ltd v Argentina* [2011] UKSC 31, [2011] 2 A.C. 495. [125]. *cf. Standard Chartered Bank v International Tin Council* [1987] 1 W.L.R. 641.
²¹⁰ Diplomatic Privileges Act 1964, s.4; Consular Relations Act 1968, s.11.
²¹¹ See Vienna Convention on Diplomatic Relations, Art.10 and Vienna Convention on Consular Relations, Art.24 (neither Article is scheduled to the relevant Act). But notification is not a condition of immunity: above, para.10–070, n.188.
²¹² Diplomatic Privileges Act 1964, Sch.1, Art.31(1)(a). Contrast *Engelke v Musmann* [1928] A.C. 433, decided at common law.

2. T dies intestate and letters of administration to his estate are granted to X. X is subsequently appointed ambassador of a foreign State accredited to the Court of St James. A, claiming to be one of T's next-of-kin, begins an administration action against X, asking for an account and that T's estate may be administered by the court. The court has jurisdiction.[213]

3. X, the ambassador of a foreign State, is a partner in a London publishing firm. He can be sued for partnership debts.[214]

4. W brings an action *in rem* against a yacht registered in the name of her husband H, claiming that it had been bought with money belonging to her. The yacht is laid up in an English yacht yard, and is in the possession and control of H. H is on the diplomatic staff of a foreign embassy. H appears under protest and moves to have the writ set aside. The court will set it aside, for W's action does not fall within any of the exceptions to H's diplomatic immunity.[215]

5. A is injured in a motor accident caused by the negligence of X, the chauffeur to a foreign ambassador, and a member of the service staff of the mission, who was driving the ambassador's car. X is not a British citizen. If X was at the time of the accident on an official journey, he is not liable to pay damages to A; but if he was on a frolic of his own, he is so liable.[216] In neither case is the ambassador vicariously liable.[217]   **10–077**

6. X, the Ruritanian consul in Manchester, refuses a visa to A, and subsequently without justification describes A to newspaper reporters as a disreputable person. The court has jurisdiction to entertain an action by A against X for defamation, but not in respect of the refusal of the visa, which is an act performed in the exercise of consular functions.[218]

7. A, the High Commissioner for India, brings an action against X claiming damages for breach of contract. X counterclaims for damages for slander. The court has no jurisdiction to hear X's counterclaim, which is ordered to be struck out.[219]

8. X, a member of the administrative and technical staff of the Indian High Commission, is prosecuted for obtaining a railway ticket by false pretences. At the committal proceedings X's solicitor purports to waive his immunity. Nothing is said about it at the trial, and X is convicted. Three months later, the High Commissioner for India writes a letter to the Commonwealth Relations Office waiving X's immunity. X appeals against his conviction, which is quashed. The alleged waiver by his solicitor is inoperative because it was made without authority. The alleged waiver by the High Commissioner is inoperative because it did not purport to be retrospective.[220]

RULE 28—Subject to certain qualifications, English courts have no jurisdiction to entertain an action or other proceeding against an international organisation or its officials specially protected by or under statute.[221]   **10R–078**

---

[213] Diplomatic Privileges Act 1964, Sch.1, Art.31(1)(b). Contrast *Re Suarez* [1917] 2 Ch. 131; [1918] 1 Ch. 176 (CA), decided at common law.

[214] Diplomatic Privileges Act 1964, Sch.1, Art.31(1)(c). Contrast *Magdalena Steam Navigation Co v Martin* (1859) 2 E. & E. 94, decided at common law.

[215] *cf. The Amazone* [1940] P. 40 (CA).

[216] Diplomatic Privileges Act 1964, Sch.1, Art.37(3).

[217] *ibid.* Art.31(1). As to the liability of the insurance company, see *Dickinson v Del Solar* [1930] 1 K.B. 376.

[218] Consular Relations Act 1968, Sch.1, Art.43. *cf. Princess Zizianoff v Bigelow* (Cour de cassation, France) (1927–1928) 4 Int.L.R. 384.

[219] *High Commissioner for India v Ghosh* [1960] 1 Q.B. 134 (CA).

[220] *R. v Madan* [1961] 2 Q.B. 1 (CCA). Even if the High Commissioner's letter did purport to be retrospective, it is difficult to see how the court could have had jurisdiction to try X.

[221] International Organisations Acts 1968 and 1981; Commonwealth Secretariat Act 1966; Arbitration (International Investment Disputes) Act 1966; International Monetary Fund Act 1979; Multilateral Investment Guarantee Agency Act 1988; International Criminal Court Act 2001; International Development Act 2002; International Organisations Act 2005. See also Diplomatic Relations and Immunities Act 1967, ss.7–49 (Rep of Ireland); International Organisations (Privileges and Immunities) Act 1963 (Aus); Foreign Missions and International Organizations Act 1991 (Can); Diplomatic Privileges and Immunities Act, 1968, ss.8–12 (NZ).

Comment

10–079   There has been a proliferation of international organisations established by States under public international law, particularly since the Second World War.[222] In 1949 the International Court of Justice, in its famous advisory opinion in the *Reparation for Injuries* case, declared that the United Nations was an international person, i.e. a subject of international law and capable of possessing international rights and duties.[223] But the International Court also accepted that not all its rights and duties must be on the international plane, any more than all the rights and duties of a State must be. Accordingly, many international organisations enter into private law transactions, but generally their constitutive instruments provide for immunities and privileges.[224] Since 1944 there has been provision in United Kingdom legislation for the conferment of immunities and privileges, and of the legal capacities of a body corporate, on international organisations.[225]

10–080   Following the financial collapse of the International Tin Council in 1985 there were several years of extensive litigation in proceedings by creditors against the International Tin Council and its members. The International Tin Council was an organisation established in 1954, whose members in 1985 included 23 States (including the United Kingdom) and the EEC, and whose headquarters were in London. The main action against the Member States and the EEC failed on the ground that it was the International Tin Council, and not its members, which had contracted with the plaintiffs, and that, since it had been established in English law as a separate legal person, only it was liable on the contracts, and its members were not so liable. The question whether the International Tin Council's constitutive instrument (the Sixth International Tin Agreement) constituted it the agent for its members as undisclosed principals was not justiciable, but even if it were justiciable, the International Tin Council was not acting as agent. It was also held that a receiver should not be appointed to enforce in its name any rights it might have for contribution from its members, because such a claim would be a claim under the Sixth International Tin Agreement and would not be justiciable.[226]

10–081   In the course of this litigation it was held that apart from legislation an international organisation has no immunity at common law analogous to that of a State.[227] Kerr L.J. referred to an argument made on behalf of the International Tin Council in the course of proceedings in New York that it was entitled to sovereign immunity as "astonishing,"[228] and a similar claim to

---

[222] See generally Bowett, *Law of International Institutions* (6th ed. Sands and Klein, 2009); Seidl-Hohenveldern, *Corporations in and under International Law* (1987), Pt II.

[223] 1949 I.C.J. Rep. 174, at 179.

[224] See Jenks, *International Immunities* (1961).

[225] For the history see *JH Rayner (Mincing Lane) Ltd v Department of Trade and Industry* [1989] Ch. 72, 143–146 (CA), [1990] 2 A.C. 418, 483–484, 494–495; Marston (1991) 40 I.C.L.Q. 403.

[226] *JH Rayner (Mincing Lane) Ltd v Department of Trade and Industry* [1990] 2 A.C. 418.

[227] *Standard Chartered Bank v International Tin Council* [1987] 1 W.L.R. 641, 647–648; *Maclaine Watson & Co Ltd v International Tin Council (No.3), The Times*, June 27, 1988.

[228] [1989] Ch. at 172.

immunity made by the EEC was described by him as "ill-judged and untenable."[229]

The International Organisations Act 1968, which repealed and replaced the **10–082** International Organisations (Immunities and Privileges) Act 1950, empowers the Crown by Order in Council to confer immunity from suit and legal process in the United Kingdom upon any international organisation[230] of which the United Kingdom is a member;[231] to confer the like immunity from suit and legal process as is accorded to the head of a diplomatic mission upon representatives to the organisation or representatives on, or members of, any of its organs, committees or other subordinate bodies, upon specified high officers of the organisation and persons employed by or serving as experts or as persons engaged on missions for the organisation;[232] and to confer a limited immunity from suit, extending only to things done or omitted to be done in the course of the performance of official duties, upon specified subordinate officers and servants of the organisation.[233] No such immunity may be conferred upon any person as the representative of Her Majesty's Government in the United Kingdom or as a member of his staff.[234]

The Act further provides for the conferring of immunity from suit on the **10–083** judges, registrars and other officers of any international tribunal, or parties to

---

[229] *ibid.* at 203; and see 252–253 *per* Ralph Gibson L.J. But in *Arab Monetary Fund v Hashim* [1993] 1 Lloyd's Rep. 543, 573–574, reversed in part on other grounds [1996] 1 Lloyd's Rep. 589 (CA), it was held that the director-general of an international organisation (of which the United Kingdom was not a member) was entitled to immunity from suit at common law (incorporating customary international law) in respect of his official acts, but the defendant was not entitled to immunity in a fraud action by the organisation because the alleged acts of fraud could not be regarded as official acts, and the bringing of suit by the organisation necessarily involved a waiver of immunity.

[230] Including organisations composed of Commonwealth States: International Organisations Act 1968, s.1(1), as amended by International Organisations Act 1981, s.1. See, e.g. SI 1974/1260 (UN Specialized Agencies), applied in *Entico Corp Ltd v United Nations Educational Scientific and Cultural Association* [2008] EWHC 531 (Comm.), [2008] 1 Lloyd's Rep. 673.

[231] s.1(1), (2)(b) and Sch.1, Pt I, para.1. See s.4 for conferment of legal capacity on international organisations of which the United Kingdom is not a member and which maintain establishments in the United Kingdom pursuant to an agreement with the United Kingdom. No provision is made for immunity of such organisations or of other international organisations of which the United Kingdom is not a member, except that s.4A (added by the International Organisations Act 1981, s.2) enables immunities to be conferred on international commodity organisations of which the United Kingdom is not a member. *cf.* International Sugar Organisation Act 1973. In *Arab Monetary Fund v Hashim (No.3)* [1991] 2 A.C. 114 (on which see F.A. Mann (1991) 107 L.Q.R. 357; Marston [1991] C.L.J. 218) it was held that an international organisation, of which the United Kingdom was not a member, and which had its headquarters in the United Arab Emirates under whose law it was given legal personality, had capacity to sue in England even though legal capacity had not been conferred upon it in English law: the conferment of legal personality by the UAE created a corporate body which the English court recognised. See also F.A. Mann (1967) 42 B.Y.I.L. 145, 171–174 (also in *Studies in International Law* (1973), pp.586–589); Jenks, *International Immunities* (1961), pp.32–34.

[232] s.1(2)(c) and Sch.1, Pt II, para.9. This immunity extends to the members of the official staff of such representatives, provided they are recognised as holding a rank equivalent to that of diplomatic agent (s.1(4) and Sch.1, Pt IV, para.20); and to the members of the family forming part of the household of such representatives, high officers, and members of their official staffs holding diplomatic rank (*ibid.* para.23(1), (2) and (3)).

[233] s.1(2)(d) and Sch.1, Pt III, para.14. This immunity extends to members of the technical and administrative staff of such representatives (s.1(4) and Sch.1, Pt IV, para.21) and to members of their families forming part of their households (*ibid.* para.23(4)).

[234] s.1(6)(b).

any proceedings before any such tribunal, and their advocates and witnesses;[235] and on representatives of foreign and Commonwealth States and their official staffs attending conferences in the United Kingdom.[236]

10–084   If in any proceedings a question arises whether any person is or is not entitled to any immunity, a certificate issued by or under the authority of the Secretary of State stating any fact relating to that question is conclusive evidence of that fact.[237]

10–085   Orders in Council made under the International Organisations (Immunities and Privileges) Act 1950 continue in force notwithstanding the repeal of that Act.[238] Orders in Council have been made applying the 1968 Act and its predecessor to many international organisations, from the United Nations and its specialised agencies to a number of organisations dealing with limited and highly technical matters.[239]

10–086   In the *International Tin Council* litigation it was held that immunity from "suit and legal process" (a phrase occurring in Sch.1 to the 1968 Act as well as in the Order in Council relating to the International Tin Council) embraced all forms of adjudicative and enforcement jurisdiction, and clearly included proceedings to wind up the organisation. Nor were winding-up proceedings within the exception to immunity in the Order in Council relating to the enforcement of an arbitration award, but were rather an alternative method of recovering the debt. Accordingly, for this reason (among others) there was no jurisdiction to wind up the organisation.[240]

10–087   The privileges and immunities of the European Union and its officials are provided by Art.343 of the Treaty on the Functioning of the European Union (TFEU) and the Protocol of April 8, 1965 on the privileges and immunities of

---

[235] s.5(1), (2).

[236] s.6, as amended by International Organisations Act 1981, s.1(3). S.5A (added by International Organisations Act 1981, s.3) enables immunities to be conferred on representatives (whether of governments or not) attending conferences convened in the United Kingdom by international organisations.

[237] International Organisations Act 1968, s.8. See also *Zoernsch v Waldock* [1964] 1 W.L.R. 675.

[238] International Organisations Act 1968, s.12(5).

[239] For the organisations on which immunities have been conferred see Halsbury, *Laws of England*, 4th ed., reissue, Vol.18(2), para.917.

[240] *Re International Tin Council* [1987] Ch. 419, 452–456; affirmed [1989] Ch. 309, 331–334 (CA). See also *Shearson Lehman Brothers Inc v Maclaine Watson & Co Ltd (No.2)* [1988] 1 W.L.R. 16 (HL) and *Maclaine Watson & Co Ltd v International Tin Council (No.2)* [1989] Ch. 286 (CA) (inviolability of archives: the International Tin Council sought, unsuccessfully, to prevent production by third parties of documents emanating from it, and to resist an order for production in proceedings in respect of the enforcement of an arbitral award); *Amalgamated Metal Trading Ltd v Department of Trade and Industry, The Times*, March 21, 1989 (misrepresentation claim against Member States and EEC); Case C–241/87 *Maclaine Watson & Co Ltd v Council and Commission* [1990] E.C.R. 1797 (claims for damages in European Court: opinion of Darmon A.-G. on admissibility); *Standard Chartered Bank v International Tin Council* [1987] 1 W.L.R. 641 (contractual waiver of immunity from suit effective); *Arab Banking Corp v International Tin Council* (1986) 77 Int.L.R. 1 (waiver of immunity from suit not a waiver of immunity from *Mareva* injunction); *International Tin Council v Amalgamet Inc*, 524 N.Y.S. 2d 971, affirmed 529 N.Y.S. 2d 983 (App.Div. 1988). See also *Mukoro v European Bank for Reconstruction and Development* [1994] I.C.R. 897 (EAT) for immunity from proceedings in industrial tribunal under Race Relations Act 1976.

the European Union as amended (Protocol No.7 to the TFEU).[241] These take effect under the European Communities Act 1972.[242] But subject to special provisions for members of the European Parliament (and for judges of the European Court of Justice in Protocol No.3 on the Statute of the Court of Justice) there is no immunity from suit. It was held that the European Economic Community (now the European Union) was not entitled to any immunity from legal process analogous to that of a foreign State, even though it exercises powers which are analogous to those of sovereign States, such as the right to receive and send diplomatic missions and the power to enter into treaties. There is no basis for such immunity from suit in the European Union treaties, or in the law of the United Kingdom, or in customary international law.[243]

The International Monetary Fund Act 1979[244] and the International Development Act 2002[245] empower the Crown by Order in Council to make provision for the carrying into effect of the agreements relating to the immunities of international financial organisations (the International Monetary Fund, the World Bank, the International Finance Corporation and the International Development Association) and their officers and employees.   **10–088**

The Commonwealth Secretariat Act 1966 provides that the Commonwealth Secretariat shall have immunity from suit and legal process except in respect of a civil action for damage caused by a motor-vehicle belonging to or operated on behalf of the Secretariat or in respect of a motor traffic offence involving such a motor-vehicle; and in respect of arbitration proceedings relating to any written contract entered into by or on behalf of the Secretariat. It also provides that any senior officer of the Secretariat who is recognised as such by the Secretary of State and who is a citizen of an independent country of the Commonwealth, and any member of his family forming part of his household, other than a member who is a British citizen[246] only, shall, if permanently resident outside the United Kingdom, have the like privileges and immunities as are accorded by law to a diplomatic agent and the members of his family; and that every other officer and servant of the Secretariat shall have immunity from suit and legal process in respect of acts or omissions of his in the course of the performance of official duties, except in respect of a civil action for damage caused by a motor-vehicle belonging to or driven by him, or in respect of a motor traffic offence involving such a vehicle.[247]   **10–089**

The Arbitration (International Investment Disputes) Act 1966 provides that the International Centre for the Settlement of Investment Disputes shall enjoy immunity from all legal process; and that the chairman and members of its   **10–090**

---

[241] See also International Organisations Act 1968, s.4B (added by International Organisations Act 2005) (power to confer immunity on bodies established under Titles V and VI of the Treaty on European Union).

[242] s.2(1).

[243] *JH Rayner (Mincing Lane) Ltd v Department of Trade and Industry* [1989] Ch. 72, 196–203, 252–253 (CA), affirmed on other grounds [1990] 2 A.C. 418. International Organisations Act 1968, s.4B (inserted by International Organisations Act 2005) makes provision for the conferment of immunities on certain bodies established under the Treaty on European Union.

[244] s.5(1).

[245] s.12. See also Multilateral Investment Guarantee Agency Act 1988, s.3.

[246] Or the other classes of citizenship, above, para.10–065.

[247] s.1(2) and Sch., paras 1, 5, 6 and 10(1).

Administrative Council, conciliators, arbitrators, officers and employees of its Secretariat, and parties to conciliation and arbitration proceedings and their advocates and witnesses shall enjoy immunity from legal process with respect to acts performed by them in the exercise of their functions.[248]

10–091   The possibility of waiver of the immunities thereby conferred is specifically provided for by the Orders in Council[249] made under the International Organisations Act 1968 and earlier legislation, by the Commonwealth Secretariat Act 1966[250] and by the Arbitration (International Investment Disputes) Act 1966.[251]

---

[248] s.4(1) and Sch., Arts 20, 21(a) and 22.
[249] See above, para.10–085. See *Standard Chartered Bank v International Tin Council* [1987] 1 W.L.R. 641.
[250] s.1(2) and Sch., para.8.
[251] Sch.1, Arts 20 and 21(a).

JURISDICTION IN CLAIMS IN PERSONAM

1. GENERAL PRINCIPLE

RULE 29[1]—(1) Subject to clause (2), the court has jurisdiction to entertain a claim *in personam* if, and only if, the defendant is served with process in England or abroad in the circumstances authorised by, and in the manner prescribed by, statute or statutory order.

(2) Where a claim relates to a civil or commercial matter within the meaning of (a) Council Regulation (EC) 44/2001 on jurisdiction and the recognition and enforcement of judgments in civil and commercial matters ("the Brussels I Regulation"[2] or "the Regulation") or (b) the Lugano Convention on jurisdiction and the recognition and enforcement of judgments in civil and commercial matters (the "Lugano Convention," or "the Convention"[3]) the court has jurisdiction to entertain a claim *in personam* solely in accordance with the provisions of the Brussels I Regulation and the Lugano Convention.

11R–001

COMMENT

Claim in personam. A claim *in personam* may be defined positively as a claim brought against a person to compel him to do a particular thing, e.g. the payment of a debt or of damages for a breach of contract or for tort, or the specific performance of a contract; or to compel him not to do something, e.g. when an injunction is sought. A claim *in personam* may be negatively

11–002

---

[1] The Rules in this Chapter must be read subject to the Rules in Ch.10. As to the power of the court to stay proceedings, see below, Ch.12. On jurisdiction in the United States see Hay, Borchers and Symeonides, Chs 5 to 10; Restatement, ss.26–52.

[2] [2001] O.J. L12, as amended by Corrigendum [2001] O.J. L307; Commission Regulation (EC) 280/2009 [2009] O.J. L93/13; Commission Regulation (EU) 416/2010 [2010] O.J. L119/7, and the Act concerning the conditions of accession of the Czech Republic, etc.: [2003] O.J. L236.

[3] Text in [2007] O.J. L339.

described as any claim which is not an Admiralty claim *in rem*, a probate claim, or an administration claim. It may be well, though hardly necessary, to add that a claim *in personam* does not include a proceeding for divorce or judicial separation, or for a declaration of nullity of marriage or of legitimacy, or a proceeding in bankruptcy or regarding the custody of children, or an application to set aside an arbitral award.

11–003   **Service of process.** Clause (1) of this Rule expresses the general principle that in England service of process is the foundation of the court's jurisdiction to entertain a claim *in personam*. Every action commences with the issue of a claim form.[4] When process cannot legally be served upon a defendant, the court can exercise no jurisdiction over him. In proceedings *in personam* the converse of this statement holds good, and whenever a defendant can be legally served with process, then the court, on service being effected, has jurisdiction to entertain a claim against him. Hence in proceedings *in personam* (and subject to the effect of the Brussels I Regulation and the Lugano Convention) the rules as to service define the limits of the court's jurisdiction. The methods of service are laid down by the Civil Procedure Rules 1998 ("CPR"), and provision is made for substituted service (now called "service by an alternative method") on individual defendants where personal service cannot be effected.[5]

11–004   **The Brussels Convention and the Lugano Convention.**[6] Prior to the Civil Jurisdiction and Judgments Act 1982 ("the 1982 Act") coming into full force on January 1, 1987 the position in England, broadly, was that the court had jurisdiction over (a) persons who were present in England at the time of service of process, and (b) in certain specified cases over persons who were outside England. In the latter case it was generally (except for certain cases mainly arising under international conventions) necessary for the permission of the court to be obtained for issue of process and its service outside the jurisdiction. In each case the exercise of the court's jurisdiction was subject to a discretion: in the former case it was subject to the discretion to stay the proceedings under Rule 38; in the latter case the issue and service of process out of the jurisdiction was subject to the discretion of the court.

11–005   In 1968 the six original members of the European Economic Community entered into a Convention on jurisdiction and the recognition and enforcement of judgments in civil and commercial matters ("the Brussels Convention"). The position following the incorporation of the Brussels Convention and the Lugano Convention by the 1982 Act (as amended by the Civil Jurisdiction and

---

[4] See CPR, Pt 7. The claim form replaces what in the High Court was known as a writ and an originating summons.

[5] CPR, Pt 6.

[6] On the Brussels I Regulation and the Brussels and Lugano Conventions see generally Layton and Mercer, *European Civil Practice* (2nd ed. 2004); Briggs and Rees, *Civil Jurisdiction and Judgments* (5th ed. 2009); Collins, *Civil Jurisdiction and Judgments Act 1982* (1983); Hartley, *Civil Jurisdiction and Judgments* (1984); Kaye, *Civil Jurisdiction and Enforcement of Foreign Judgments* (1987); Magnus, Mankowski (eds.), *Brussels I Regulation* (2007); Gaudemet-Tallon, *Compétence et exécution des jugements en Europe* (4th ed. 2010); Droz and Gaudemet-Tallon, 2001 *Rev. Crit.* 601; Weser, *Convention communautaire sur la compétence judiciaire et l'exécu-tion des décisions* (1975).

Judgments Act 1991, "the 1991 Act") was substantially different. The mere presence of the defendant in England was no longer a sufficient basis of jurisdiction if he was domiciled in another part of the United Kingdom or in another Contracting State, and where the Conventions conferred jurisdiction on the English court its discretion not to exercise it was severely curtailed.[7] Similar, but not identical, rules were introduced by Sch.4 to the 1982 Act for intra-United Kingdom cases.[8]

The original purpose of the Brussels Convention was to facilitate the **11–006** enforcement of judgments between the Contracting States, but both the Brussels Convention and the original Lugano Convention also provided a detailed set of rules dealing with the circumstances in which courts in the Contracting States might exercise jurisdiction in matters within the scope of the Conventions. The approach of the Conventions was quite different from that of the United Kingdom bilateral conventions governing the recognition and enforcement of foreign judgments. Those conventions, which took effect in the United Kingdom through the Foreign Judgments (Reciprocal Enforcement) Act 1933,[9] did not regulate the circumstances in which the court which was originally seised might exercise jurisdiction: they merely told the enforcing court in which circumstances the jurisdiction of the original court had to be recognised, and they allowed the enforcing court to investigate whether the original court had international jurisdiction. This is frequently called a system of "indirect" rules of jurisdiction, which do not affect the courts of the State in which the action is originally brought, and only become relevant at the stage of enforcement.

By contrast, the Brussels Convention and the Lugano Convention laid down **11–007** a very elaborate system of jurisdictional rules, to which the court in which the action is originally brought had to adhere—this is a system of "direct" rules of jurisdiction. The primary basis of jurisdiction under the Conventions over those "domiciled" in a Contracting State was the "domicile" of the defendant. The Conventions did not define domicile, and left its determination to national law; corporations were to be treated as domiciled where they had their seat, but the determination of the seat was also left to national law.[10] In addition to the courts of the domicile of the defendant, there were other special bases of jurisdiction, such as the place of performance of a contractual obligation and the place of a tort, and there were certain areas of exclusive jurisdiction which displaced the domicile. Provision was also made for submission to jurisdiction by contract or by appearance, and for certain other procedural matters, including *lis alibi pendens* and jurisdiction to order provisional measures.

The origins of the Brussels Convention lay in the notion that the ideals of **11–008** the European Economic Community would be furthered by the greater facilitation of the enforcement of judgments between the Member States. Negotiations for the Convention began in 1959. It was signed in 1968 and entered into force for the original Contracting States (Belgium, Federal Republic of Germany, France, Italy, Luxembourg, Netherlands) in 1973. In 1971 they entered

---

[7] See below, paras 11–028; 12–019 *et seq.*
[8] See below, para.11–071.
[9] See below, Rule 54.
[10] See 1982 Act, ss.41 to 46, below, Rule 30.

into a Protocol conferring jurisdiction on the European Court to interpret the Brussels Convention, and the Protocol entered into force in 1975. In 1978 the United Kingdom, the Republic of Ireland and Denmark entered into an Accession Convention with the original Contracting States ("the 1978 Accession Convention"). The 1978 Accession Convention contained some important modifications of the Brussels Convention.

11–009   Conventions were signed in 1982 for the accession of Greece ("the 1982 Accession Convention"),[11] in 1989 for the accession of Spain and Portugal ("the 1989 Accession Convention"),[12] and in 1996 for the accession of Austria, Finland and Sweden.[13] The 1989 Accession Convention (also known as the San Sebastian Convention) made a number of substantive changes.[14] The Brussels Convention as amended by the Accession Conventions came into force between the United Kingdom and all the Contracting States.

11–010   The original Lugano Convention was opened for signature in 1988. It was adopted by the 12 Member States of the European Communities and by the six Member States of the European Free Trade Association (EFTA) (Austria, Finland, Iceland, Norway, Sweden and Switzerland). The accession of Poland took effect in 2000. Following the enlargement of the European Union and the adoption of the Brussels I Regulation, the original Lugano Convention applied only to Iceland, Norway and Switzerland.

11–011   The purpose of the original Lugano Convention was to strengthen the economic co-operation between the European Communities and EFTA. Negotiations proceeded from 1985 on the drafting of what was then called a parallel Convention to the Brussels Convention. The United Kingdom ratified the Lugano Convention in 1991, and it came into force for the United Kingdom in 1992. The original Lugano Convention was substantially[15] the same as the Brussels Convention as amended by the 1978 Accession Convention and the 1989 Accession Convention. An important distinction between the Brussels Convention and the Lugano Convention was that the European Court had no jurisdiction to give preliminary rulings on the interpretation of the Lugano Convention: the EFTA Member States would not have accepted that the European Court, an institution of the European Communities, should have jurisdiction to rule on the Lugano Convention. Instead, the Second Protocol to the Lugano Convention and two accompanying Declarations made by the signatory States contained special provisions designed to lead to uniformity of interpretation both as between national courts and between the two Convention systems.

11–012   Both the Brussels Convention and the 1978 Accession Convention were the subject of substantial reports which were sent to the governments concerned at the same time as the draft Conventions. The reports were, respectively, by M. Jenard (the rapporteur of the working party for the Brussels Convention)

---

[11] The text of the 1982 Accession Convention is in [1982] O.J. L388, with Report by Evrigenis and Kerameus at [1986] O.J. C298/1; and in Collins, p.251.

[12] [1989] O.J. L285, with report by de Almeida Cruz, Desantes Real and Jenard [1990] O.J. C189/35.

[13] [1997] O.J. C15.

[14] The Lugano Convention was negotiated before the 1989 Accession Convention and the variations from the original Brussels Convention were substantially derived from the Lugano Convention.

[15] But not quite identical (see especially Arts 5(1), 16(1), 17(5)).

and Professor Schlosser (the rapporteur of the working party for the 1978 Accession Convention). The original Lugano Convention was the subject of a report by M. Jenard and Mr Möller (a Finnish judge) which was submitted to the Member States of the European Communities and of EFTA before the diplomatic conference at Lugano in 1988. Each of these reports (and the reports on the 1982 and 1989 Accession Conventions) had a special status in relation to the interpretation of the Conventions.[16] They are also relevant to the interpretation of the Brussels I Regulation and the revised Lugano Convention, most of the provisions of which are derived from the Brussels and original Lugano Conventions.

Brussels I Regulation. The Brussels I Regulation came into force on   **11–013** March 1, 2002,[17] and applies to all the Member States of the European Union, with the exception of Denmark. Denmark opted out of the Brussels I Regulation, and the Brussels Convention continued to apply to it. But with effect from July 1, 2007 the Brussels I Regulation applies to Denmark by virtue of a parallel agreement.[18] The Brussels I Regulation supersedes the Brussels Convention,[19] and it also superseded (except as regards Iceland, Norway and Switzerland) the original Lugano Convention.

The background to the Brussels I Regulation was that in December 1997   **11–014** the Council of the European Union instructed an ad hoc working party comprised of representatives of all Member States and of the EFTA States which were parties to the Lugano Convention to work on parallel revision of the Brussels and Lugano Conventions. The new Art.65 of the EC Treaty (now Art.81, TFEU) was introduced by the Treaty of Amsterdam, which came into effect in May 1999. Article 65 provided that measures in the field of judicial co-operation in civil matters having cross-border implications, to be taken in accordance with Art.69 and insofar as necessary for the proper functioning of the internal market, were to include (among other things) improving and simplifying the recognition and enforcement of judgments in civil and commercial cases, and promoting the compatibility of the rules applicable in the Member States concerning the conflict of laws and of jurisdiction. By Art.67, during the transitional period of five years following the entry into force of the Treaty of Amsterdam, the Council was to act unanimously on a proposal from

---

[16] The Jenard and the Schlosser reports are at [1979] O.J. C59 and are hereinafter cited as "Jenard" and "Schlosser." The Jenard-Möller report on the original Lugano Convention is at [1990] O.J. C189/57. These reports, and also the reports on the 1982 Accession Convention by Evrigenis and Kerameus and on the 1989 Accession Convention by de Almeida Cruz, Desantes Real and Jenard (above, n.11), are also in Butterworths, *International Litigation Handbook* (2nd ed. Dickinson *et al.*), ss.[3035], [3047], [3070], [3048], and [3052], respectively. The Scottish Committee on Jurisdiction and Enforcement under the Chairmanship of Lord Maxwell published a report ("the Maxwell Report") in 1980 on (inter alia) the practical aspects of the implementation of the Brussels Convention. On the history of the Brussels Convention see Jenard, p.3; Schlosser, paras 1–3; Maxwell Report, paras 1.9–1.15.

[17] On the transitional provisions of the Brussels I Regulation, see *Advent Capital Plc v GN Ellinas Imports-Exports Ltd* [2005] EWHC 1242 (Comm.), [2005] 2 Lloyd's Rep. 607.

[18] [2006] O.J. L120/22; SI 2001/3929, art.3A (providing that the Brussels I Regulation shall have effect as regards Denmark in accordance with the Agreement), added by SI 2007/1655.

[19] The Brussels Convention continues to apply to certain dependencies of France (French overseas territories, now called overseas collectivities) and the Netherlands (Aruba).

the Commission or on the initiative of a Member State and after consulting the European Parliament.

11–015   By Art.3 of the Protocol on the position of the United Kingdom and Ireland, the United Kingdom and Ireland had the power to notify the President of the Council, within three months after a proposal or initiative had been presented to the Council pursuant to what became Title IV of the EC Treaty, that they wished to take part in the adoption and application of any such proposed measure. Denmark opted out of Title IV. In March 1999 the United Kingdom and Ireland indicated their intention to adopt Community instruments in relation to judicial co-operation in civil matters.

11–016   In July 1999 a proposal was made[20] in which the Commission converted its previous proposals for reform of the Brussels Convention into a proposal for a Council Regulation. The Brussels I Regulation was adopted on December 22, 2000.

11–017   Because the Brussels I Regulation is directly applicable in the United Kingdom by virtue of s.2(1) of the European Communities Act 1972, there is no implementing United Kingdom legislation, with the exception of those matters which are left by the Regulation to national law, such as the ascertainment of domicile,[21] and which are the subject of statutory order.[22] The Regulation uses the expression "Member State" (which is, however, defined to mean Member States of what is now the European Union with the exception of Denmark[23]) to refer to the States which are subject to it.

11–018   **Revised Lugano Convention.** In 1997 the Council of the European Union set up a working party of experts to work on amendments to the Brussels Convention and the original Lugano Convention in parallel. Although the proposal for a Council Regulation to replace the Brussels Convention proceeded from a proposal in July 1999 to its approval in December 2000, the revised Lugano Convention was held up because the European Commission took the view that, when the Amsterdam Treaty came into force in 1999, the conclusion of a revised Lugano Convention fell entirely within the sphere of the exclusive competence of the Community, and outside the competence of the Member States. The question of competence was referred by the Council to the European Court.

11–019   The European Court gave an opinion[24] that the conclusion of the new Lugano Convention fell entirely within the sphere of exclusive competence of the European Community. Where common rules had been adopted, the Member States no longer had the right, acting individually or collectively, to undertake obligations with non-Member States which affected those rules. In

---

[20] See European Commission, *Proposal for a Council Regulation (EC) on jurisdiction and the recognition and enforcement of judgments in civil and commercial matters*, with explanatory memorandum: COM (1999) 348 final; [1999] O.J. C376.

[21] See below, Rule 30.

[22] SI 2001/3929, Sch.1. See Sch.2 for amendment of 1982 Act, Sch.4 on allocation of intra-UK legislation: see below, para.11–071.

[23] Art.1(3). For all practical purposes, however, Denmark may be regarded as a "Member State" for the purposes of the Brussels I Regulation: para.11–013, above.

[24] Opinion 1/03 *Competence of the Community to conclude the new Lugano Convention on jurisdiction and the recognition and enforcement of judgments (Opinion pursuant to Article 300 EC)* [2006] E.C.R. I–1145.

such a case, the Community had exclusive competence to conclude international agreements. Given the unified and coherent system of rules on jurisdiction for which the Brussels I Regulation provided, any international agreement also establishing a unified system of rules on conflict of jurisdiction such as that established by the Regulation was capable of affecting those rules of jurisdiction. The new Lugano Convention affected the uniform and consistent application of the Community rules on jurisdiction and the proper functioning of the system established by those rules. Accordingly, the Community had exclusive competence to conclude the new Lugano Convention.[25]

The revised Lugano Convention[26] entered into force between the Member   **11–020**
States of the European Union (including Denmark) and Norway on January 1, 2010, and is now also in force for Iceland and Switzerland. Iceland, Norway and Switzerland will be referred to as "Convention States."[27] The original Lugano Convention was given effect by the 1982 Act[28] but the view has been taken that it is not necessary to incorporate the revised Lugano Convention into United Kingdom law because it is a treaty concluded by the European Union which takes direct effect in the United Kingdom, and requires legislation only to the extent of consequential matters arising out of the Convention, and matters which are left by the Convention to national law. The 1982 Act, as amended, deals with such consequential matters[29] as allocation of jurisdiction within the United Kingdom[30] and with matters which are left by the Convention to national law.[31]

Principal differences between the Brussels and original Lugano Con-   **11–021**
ventions and the Brussels I Regulation. The main changes introduced by the Brussels I Regulation were these: (1) The Regulation contains new autonomous rules for the domicile of companies.[32] (2) In the Regulation, an autonomous definition of the place of performance is provided for contracts for the sale of goods and the provision of services.[33] (3) The Regulation confirms that the place of the harmful event in jurisdiction in tort and delict extends to the place where the harmful event "may occur."[34] (4) There are changes to the provisions on insurance[35] and consumer contracts[36] and new provision is made for employment contracts.[37] (5) In relation to jurisdiction in disputes relating to immovable property, the exception to the court of the *situs* for short

---

[25] See Borrás (2006) 8 Yb. P.I.L. 37.
[26] [2007] O.J. L339/1. See the Pocar Report [2009] O.J. C319/1; Pocar (2008) 10 Yb. P.I.L. 1.
[27] It is also open to accession by other States: Art. 70, subject to the conditions in Art.72.
[28] It was set out in Sch.3C, inserted by the 1991 Act, and repealed by SI 2009/3131.
[29] See, e.g. ss.5A, 6A, 7–8, 11A, 14, 48.
[30] s.10.
[31] see ss.41A, 43A, 44A.
[32] Art.60.
[33] Art.5(1)(b), (c).
[34] Art.5(3).
[35] Arts 9(1)(b), 13(5), 14.
[36] Arts 15(1)(c), 15(3).
[37] Arts 18–21.

tenancies is an amalgam[38] of the differing provisions in the Brussels Convention and the original Lugano Convention. (6) The Regulation confirms the effectiveness of non-exclusive jurisdiction agreements.[39] (7) The Regulation contains a definition of seisin for the purposes of the *lis pendens* provisions.[40] An important effect of the rules being enacted in a Council Regulation is that references to the European Court are no longer to be under a separate Protocol, (as they were in the Brussels Convention regime), but will be under Art.267, TFEU.

11–022   **Proposals for amendment of the Brussels I Regulation.** Art.73 of the Brussels I Regulation provided that within five years of its entry into force the European Commission was to present to the European Parliament, the Council and the European Economic and Social Committee a report on the application of the Regulation, accompanied, if need be, by proposals for adaptations to it. The European Commission made the report in 2009.[41] The report was prepared on the basis of a general study ("the Heidelberg Report") commissioned by the European Commission. The Commission Report was accompanied by a Green Paper which was intended to launch a broad consultation on possible ways to improve the Regulation with respect to the points raised in the Report.[42] The more important points are noted at the appropriate places in this work, but they included these. First, the Commission proposed that the jurisdictional rules of the Regulation be extended to defendants domiciled in non-Member States.[43] The Report suggested that the absence of common rules determining jurisdiction against third State defendants might jeopardise the application of mandatory Community legislation, for example on consumer protection, commercial agents, data protection or product liability. Second, the Commission noted that problems were caused by there being no uniform rule for the validity of jurisdiction agreements, with the result that a choice of court agreement might be considered valid in one Member State and invalid in another.[44] Third, the Commission drew attention to the problems caused in the area of *lis pendens* by actions for negative declarations in intellectual property cases, and in cases involving corporate loans and in competition cases.[45] Fourth, the Commission considered that the diversity in the national procedural laws of the Member States relating to provisional measures made the free circulation of such measures difficult.[46] Fifthly, the Commission drew

---

[38] Art.22(1).

[39] Art.23(1).

[40] Art.30.

[41] COM(2009) 174, April 21, 2009. See Dickinson (2010) 12 Yb. P.I.L. 247; Briggs [2011] L.M.C.L.Q. 157. See also draft Report of the Committee on Legal Affairs of the European Parliament: 2010/0384 (COD), June 28, 2011; opinion of the European Economic and Social Committee [2011] O.J.C218/78; UK Ministry of Justice, Consultation Paper, *Revision of the Brussels I Regulation —How should the United Kingdom approach the negotiations*, CP18/10 (2010).

[42] COM(2009) 175, April 21, 2009.

[43] This proposal is rejected in the draft Report of the Committee on Legal Affairs of the European Parliament, above.

[44] See below, para.12–130.

[45] See below, para.12–063.

[46] See below, para.8–033, n.77.

attention to the difficulties caused by the exception of arbitration from the scope of the Regulation.[47] In December 2010 the Commission published a proposal for a new Regulation implementing these proposals.[48]

European Order for Payment Procedure. Regulation (EC) 1896/2006 of   **11–023**
the European Parliament and of the Council creating a European order for payment procedure (which applies to the United Kingdom and Ireland, but not to Denmark) provides for the application to a court for an order for payment in the case of claims for a specific amount.[49] Jurisdiction is to be determined in accordance with the relevant rules of the Brussels I Regulation.[50] But in the case of claims against a consumer, for a purpose which could be regarded as being outside his trade or profession, only the courts of the Member State in which the defendant is domiciled will have jurisdiction.[51] The defendant is to be advised of his options to pay the amount indicated in the order or oppose the order by lodging with the court of origin a statement of opposition.[52] The procedure in England is regulated by section I of Part 78 of the Civil Procedure Rules.[53]

European Small Claims Procedure. Regulation (EC) 861/2007 of the   **11–024**
European Parliament and of the Council (in force January 1, 2009) establishes a European Small Claims Procedure, and applies in the United Kingdom and Ireland, but not in Denmark.[54] It applies in cross-border cases to civil and commercial matters, whatever the nature of the court or a tribunal, where the value of a claim does not exceed €2,000.[55] For the purposes of the Regulation a cross-border case is one in which at least one of the parties is domiciled or habitually resident in a Member State other than the Member State of the court or tribunal seised, and domicile is to be determined in accordance with Arts 59 and 60 of the Brussels I Regulation.[56] The body of the Regulation does not deal expressly with the grounds of jurisdiction, but it is apparent from Annex 1, which sets out the claim form, that the tribunal must have jurisdiction in accordance with the rules of the Brussels I Regulation.[57] The procedure in England is regulated by section II of Part 78 of the Civil Procedure Rules.[58]

---

[47] See below, paras 11–046 *et seq*. See also the Green Paper of the House of Lords European Union Committee, Sub-committee E (Law and Institutions, under the chairmanship of Lord Mance), July 27, 2009, which is particularly supportive of proposals to increase the effectiveness of jurisdiction and arbitration agreements.

[48] COM (2010) 748/3.

[49] [2006] O.J. L399/1. See Lopez de Tejada 2007 *Rev. Crit.* 717.

[50] Art.6(1).

[51] Art.6(2).

[52] Art.12.

[53] CPR, rr.78.2–78.11.

[54] [2007] O.J. L199/1.

[55] Art.2.

[56] Art.3. On domicile see paras 11R–077 *et seq*., below.

[57] Annex 1, Form A, para.4.

[58] CPR, rr.78.12–78.22.

11–025   **Mediation in civil and commercial matters.** Directive 2008/52/EC of the European Parliament and of the Council of May 21, 2008[59] on certain aspects of mediation in civil and commercial matters is designed to facilitate access to alternative dispute resolution and to promote the amicable settlement of disputes by encouraging the use of mediation and by ensuring a balanced relationship between mediation and judicial proceedings. It applies to all civil and commercial matters (including family law), but not to revenue, customs or administrative matters or to the liability of the State for acts and omissions in the exercise of State authority (*acta iure imperii*).[60] It requires the content of an agreement resulting from mediation which has been made enforceable in a Member State to be recognised and declared enforceable in the other Member States in accordance with applicable Community or national law,[61] Section III of Part 78 of the Civil Procedure Rules was introduced to deal with this obligation.[62]

11–026   **Hague Conference developments.** In 1993 the Hague Conference on Private International Law decided to open negotiations for the conclusion of a worldwide convention on jurisdiction and the enforcement of judgments, but the negotiations did not meet with success.[63] Instead in 2005 a more limited Hague Convention on Choice of Court Agreements was adopted and opened for signature. It is not in force.[64]

11–027   ***Forum conveniens.*** In *Effer SpA v Kantner*[65] the European Court emphasised that the rules on jurisdiction in the Brussels Convention were designed in part to confer jurisdiction on the national court which was best qualified to determine a dispute. But it also recognised that the application of the jurisdictional rules might lead to a claim being subject to the jurisdiction of a court which does not have the closest connection with the dispute.[66]

11–028   The question therefore arose whether the English court had a discretion to decline jurisdiction or stay an action on the ground that the courts of another State were the more appropriate forum. It was accepted that the jurisdictional rules of the Brussels Convention were not subject to a discretion in the national court to stay an action on the basis that the courts of some other Convention State were the more appropriate forum.[67] But there was for some time uncertainty as to whether the court could stay proceedings brought in England under the Brussels Convention (and the Brussels I Regulation) rules on the ground that the courts of a non-Convention State (or non-Member

---

[59] [2008] O.J. L136/3. It does not apply to Denmark.

[60] Art.2.

[61] Art.6.

[62] Especially CPR, rr.78.23, 78.25. See also SI 2011/1133.

[63] See McClean, in *Reform and Development of Private International Law* (Fawcett ed., 2002), p.255; O'Brian (2003) 66 M.L.R. 491.

[64] See below, para.12–101.

[65] Case 38/81 [1982] E.C.R. 825, 834.

[66] Case C–282/92 *Custom Made Commercial Ltd v Stawa Metallbau GmbH* [1994] E.C.R. I–2913.

[67] See below, paras 11–249, 12–019 *et seq.*; *Aiglon Ltd v Gau Shan Co Ltd* [1993] 1 Lloyd's Rep. 164; and Schlosser, paras 76–81; Layton and Mercer, Vol.1, pp.373–374; Kaye, pp.269, 1244.

State) were more appropriate.[68] But in *Owusu v Jackson*[69] the European Court confirmed that a court having jurisdiction under the Brussels Convention could not apply the *forum non conveniens* doctrine to decline jurisdiction, even in favour of a non-Convention State. It held that application of the doctrine would undermine the predictability of the rules of jurisdiction laid down by the Convention. There is no doubt that the same conclusion applies in the case of the Brussels I Regulation. This question is dealt with more fully in connection with Rule 38.

Sphere of application of the Brussels I Regulation and the Lugano Convention. Civil and commercial matters. Article 1 of the Regulation (and of the Convention) provides that it is to apply in civil and commercial matters whatever the nature of the court or tribunal and that it is not to extend, in particular, to revenue, customs or administrative matters. In addition it is specifically provided that it is not to apply to the status or legal capacity of natural persons; rights in property arising out of a matrimonial relationship; wills and succession; bankruptcy, proceedings relating to the winding-up of insolvent companies or other legal persons, judicial arrangements, compositions and analogous proceedings, social security; or arbitration. In civil law countries "civil" law (which includes commercial law) is generally contrasted with "public" law. The term "civil and commercial" is not a term of art in the United Kingdom, although it appears as early as the Foreign Tribunals Evidence Act 1856, and the United Kingdom is party to several bilateral treaties with some of the Member States for the recognition and enforcement of judgments in "civil and commercial matters"[70] and to Hague Conventions which are similarly limited.[71] In the original Brussels Convention States there is a well-developed separate corpus of law dealing with the activities of public bodies acting in the exercise of public functions. It is claims by and against these authorities in relation to those functions which are effectively excluded by the general words of Art.1. But the precise boundaries of civil and public law differ even in the civil law countries and therefore the question arose at an early stage in the life of the Brussels Convention as to what system of law was to be applied to solve any difficulties of classification.

In a consistent series of decisions of the European Court, commencing in 1976 in the *Eurocontrol* case,[72] the Court held that the concept must be given

11–029

11–030

---

[68] See *Re Harrods (Buenos Aires) Ltd* [1992] Ch. 72 (CA), in which a reference by the House of Lords to the European Court was withdrawn when the case was settled.

[69] Case C–281/02 [2005] E.C.R. I–1383, [2005] Q.B. 801, on which see paras 12–019 *et seq.* See also, e.g. *Catalyst Investment Group Ltd v Lewinsohn* [2009] EWHC 1964 (Ch.), [2010] Ch. 218; *Skype Technologies SA v Joltid Ltd* [2009] EWHC 2783 (Ch.), [2011] I.L.Pr. 103; *UBS AG v HSH Nordbank* [2009] EWCA Civ 585, [2009] 1 Lloyd's Rep. 272, [103]. See generally Kruger, *Civil Jurisdiction Rules of the EU and their impact on third States* (2008).

[70] With Austria (SI 1962/1339); Belgium (S.R. O. 1936 No.1169); France (S.R. O. 1936 No.609); Germany (SI 1961/1199); Italy (SI 1973/1894); *cf.* Norway (SI 1962/636) ("civil matters"). The European Court held that the meaning of the expression may be different in a bilateral convention from its meaning in the Brussels Convention: Joined Cases 9 and 10/77 *Bavaria and Germanair v Eurocontrol* [1977] E.C.R. 1517.

[71] Service Abroad of Judicial and Extrajudicial Documents in Civil or Commercial Matters (1965); Taking of Evidence Abroad in Civil or Commercial Matters (1970), on which see *Re State of Norway's Application (Nos 1 & 2)* [1990] 1 A.C. 723, criticised by F.A. Mann (1989) 105 L.Q.R. 341.

[72] Case 29/76 *LTU GmbH v Eurocontrol* [1976] E.C.R. 1541.

an independent meaning in the light of "the objectives and scheme of the Convention" and "the general principles which stem from the corpus of the national legal systems."[73] This case concerned a claim for route charges levied on aircraft owners by Eurocontrol, an international organisation set up by treaty. The Court held that judgments in favour of such a body might be within the scope of the Brussels Convention, but not where the public authority was acting in the exercise of its powers. Thus in *Netherlands State v Rüffer*[74] the European Court held that an action for the recovery of the costs involved in the removal of a wreck in a public waterway, administered by the State pursuant to an international obligation and in its capacity as a public authority in the administration of that waterway, was not a civil or commercial matter. In *Sonntag v Waidmann*[75] the European Court held that, even if it were joined to criminal proceedings, a civil action for compensation for injury following a criminal act was civil in nature; and that the activity of a school teacher in a state school while supervising pupils during a school trip did not constitute an exercise of public authority. So also these claims have been held to be within the concept of civil or commercial matters: an action by a public authority against a man for recovery of sums paid as social assistance to his ex-wife and child;[76] a claim to statutory subrogation by the State against the parents of the recipients of education grants governed by civil law;[77] an action between private parties for the reimbursement of customs duties paid by the claimant;[78] a fine payable to the State for breach of an injunction in a civil and commercial matter.[79]

11–031   In *Lechouritou v Dimosio tis Omospondiakis Dimokratias tis Germanias*[80] a reference was made in proceedings by Greek nationals resident in Greece

---

[73] [1976] E.C.R. at p.1552. See also Joined Cases 9 and 10/77 *Bavaria and Germanair v Eurocontrol* [1977] E.C.R. 1517; Case 133/78 *Gourdain v Nadler* [1979] E.C.R. 733; Case 814/79 *Netherlands State v Rüffer* [1980] E.C.R. 3807; Case C–172/91 *Sonntag v Waidmann* [1993] E.C.R. I–1963; Case C–266/01 *Préservatrice Foncière TIARD Cie d'Assurances v Netherlands* [2003] E.C.R. I–4867.

[74] Case 814/79 [1980] E.C.R. 3807. In Case C–167/00 *Verein für Konsumenteninformation v Henkel* [2002] E.C.R. I–8111 an action by a consumer protection organisation to prevent traders from using unfair contract terms was held to be a civil matter: the consumer protection organisation was a private body, and the subject-matter of the proceedings was not an exercise of public powers, since the proceedings did not concern the exercise of powers derogating from the rules of law applicable to relations between private individuals, but concerned the prohibition on the use of unfair terms in contracts with consumers. *cf. R. v Harrow Crown Court, Ex p. UNIC Centre SARL* [2000] 1 W.L.R. 2112, where it was held that proceedings against a French company under the Trade Marks Act 1994 by the trading standards service for forfeiture of counterfeit jeans were in a civil matter: the local authority did not have a duty to bring such proceedings, nor any exclusive status to bring them, and the relief enured to the benefit of private individuals. Contrast *Criminal Assets Bureau v JWPL* [2007] IEHC 177, [2008] I.L.Pr. 298 (Irish High Ct.) See, on the impact of Art.1 on environmental claims, Betlem and Bernasconi (2006) 122 L.Q.R. 124.

[75] Case C–172/91 [1993] E.C.R. I–1963. See also *Grovit v Nederlandsche Bank* [2005] EWHC 2944, [2006] 1 W.L.R. 3323 (QB), affd. [2007] EWCA Civ 953, [2008] 1 W.L.R. 51.

[76] Case C–271/00 *Gemeent Steenbergen v Baten* [2002] E.C.R. I–10489.

[77] Case C–433/01 *Freistaat Bayern v Blijdenstein* [2004] E.C.R. I–981.

[78] Case C–265/02 *Frahuil SA v Assitalia SpA* [2004] E.C.R. I–1543.

[79] Case C–406/09 *Realchemie Nederland v Bayer CropScience AG* [2012] I.L.Pr. 17.

[80] Case C–292/05 [2007] E.C.R. I–1519. *cf.* Case C–435/06 *C* [2007] E.C.R. I–10141, [2008] Fam. 27 (Council Regulation (EC) 2201/2003, Art.1, is to be interpreted to the effect that a single decision ordering that a child be taken into care and placed outside his original home in a foster family is covered by the term "civil matters").

against Germany for compensation for damage which the plaintiffs had suffered on account of acts perpetrated by the German armed forces and of which their parents were victims at the time of the occupation of Greece during the Second World War, namely the massacre of civilians by soldiers in the German armed forces in 1943 in Kalavrita. The European Court ruled that "civil matters" did not cover a legal action brought by natural persons in a Convention State against another Convention State for compensation in respect of the loss or damage suffered by the successors of the victims of acts perpetrated by armed forces in the course of warfare in the territory of the first State. Operations conducted by armed forces were one of the characteristic emanations of State sovereignty, and were inextricably linked to foreign and defence policy. The action for damages therefore resulted from the exercise of public powers on the part of the State concerned on the date when those acts were perpetrated, irrespective of whether those acts were lawful.

Article 1(1) of each instrument provides expressly that it "shall not extend, **11–032** in particular, to revenue, customs or administrative matters." This provision was added by the 1978 Accession Convention following the request of the United Kingdom in the accession negotiations. The exclusion of revenue and customs matters reflects the general principle found in most countries that foreign tax laws will not be enforced.[81] In *Préservatrice Foncière TIARD Cie d'Assurances v Netherlands*[82] it was held that the exclusion for customs matters did not extend to a claim by which the State sought to enforce a guarantee for the payment of a customs liability, where the legal relationship between the State and the guarantor did not entail the exercise by the State of powers going beyond those existing under private law relationships, even if the guarantor raised in the proceedings an issue as to the existence and scope of the liability to customs duty.

In most of the Member States and in the EFTA countries claims relating to **11–033** the exercise of powers by public authorities are usually within the jurisdiction of special administrative courts. But the exclusion of "administrative matters" from the Brussels I Regulation and the Lugano Convention does not relate to the tribunal in which the claim is brought or by which the judgment is given. It relates to the nature of the legal relationship between the parties or the subject-matter of the action.[83]

It is settled that maintenance claims are covered by the Brussels I Regula- **11–034** tion and the Lugano Convention. They are within the concept of "civil matters," they are not excluded by Art.1(2), and Art.5(2) makes specific provision for such claims.[84] It is likely that claims for damages caused by restrictive practices or unfair competition, which often have public law elements, come within the scope of the Regulation and the Convention. Finally,

---

[81] See above, paras 5–029 *et seq.* See *QRS 1 ApS v Frandsen* [1999] 1 W.L.R. 2169 (CA): the rule that the English court will not directly or indirectly enforce the revenue laws of another country is not overridden by Art.1. But see above, para.5–029 for the Council Directives on mutual assistance for the recovery of claims relating to certain taxes and duties.

[82] Case C–266/01 [2003] E.C.R. I–4867.

[83] *LTU GmbH v Eurocontrol*, above; *Netherlands State v Rüffer*, above; *cf. Re Senator Hanseatische Verwaltungsgesellschaft mbH* [1997] 1 W.L.R. 515 (CA); *Bank of Scotland v IMRO*, 1989 S.L.T. 432; *Short v Ireland* [1996] IESC 8, [1996] 2 I.R. 188.

[84] See Case 120/79 *De Cavel v De Cavel (No.2)* [1980] E.C.R. 731; Case C–220/95 *Van den Boogaard v Laumen* [1997] E.C.R. I–1147, [1997] Q.B. 759.

they apply to labour or employment law claims (which in some countries are not regarded as part of the civil law), at least to the extent that they are not claims by or against public authorities in some capacity other than as employer.[85]

11–035   **Matters expressly excluded from the scope of the Brussels I Regulation and the Lugano Convention.** Article 1(2) excludes, as has been seen, four general categories from the scope of the Regulation and the Convention: (1) status; (2) bankruptcy; (3) social security; and (4) arbitration. These categories were originally excluded from the scope of the Brussels Convention for two main reasons: first, to exclude one category which fell within the borderland of civil and public law, namely social security; secondly, to exclude those cases where there was a great disparity between the Contracting States in relation both to substantive law and private international law, particularly where there were other conventions in force or in draft; it was thought that to bring these areas within the scope of the Brussels Convention might interfere with the unification process being pursued in the European Communities.[86]

11–036   *Status or legal capacity of natural persons.*[87] The most important area excluded by this provision is divorce, but it also excludes judgments relating to voidability and nullity of marriage, judicial separation, death, status and legal capacity of minors, legal representation of mental patients, nationality or domicile of individuals, custody and adoption of children, guardianship. But they are only excluded if the proceedings deal directly with these questions. If they arise only in an incidental fashion the case will not be excluded from the scope of the Regulation and the Convention. The fact that a proceeding or judgment deals with matters which fall outside their scope will not prevent orders which do fall within it from being enforced.[88] Maintenance orders, in relation both to spouses and to children, are within the Regulation and the Convention.[89]

11–037   *Rights in property arising out of a matrimonial relationship ("régimes matrimoniaux").* This exception is considered in a later chapter.[90]

11–038   *Wills and succession.* Matters relating to wills and succession were excluded because it was thought that the divergence in laws, especially in the relevant rules of private international law, among the original Brussels Convention States was so great that it would be premature to include them before

---

[85] Case 25/79 *Sanicentral v Collin* [1979] E.C.R. 3423, 3429; Case 133/81 *Ivenel v Schwab* [1982] E.C.R. 1891. See now also the Brussels I Regulation and the Lugano Convention, Arts 18–21.

[86] See Jenard, p.10.

[87] In 1998 the members of the EU concluded a Convention on jurisdiction and the recognition and enforcement of judgments in matrimonial matters: [1998] O.J. C221/1. It did not come into force, but became the basis for Council Regulation (EC) 1347/2000 (now superseded by Council Regulation (EC) 2201/2003), below, paras 18–005 *et seq.*

[88] See Case 120/79 *De Cavel v De Cavel (No.2)* [1980] E.C.R. 731.

[89] See below, Rules 89, 102, 111.

[90] See below, paras 18–177 *et seq.*

the rules of private international law had been unified.[91] The expression "wills and succession" covers all claims to testate or intestate succession, including disputes as to validity or interpretation of wills setting up trusts; but disputes concerning the relations of the trustee with persons other than beneficiaries may come within the scope of the Regulation and the Convention.[92]

Bankruptcy, etc. This exclusion extends to bankruptcy, proceedings relating   **11–039**
to the winding-up of insolvent companies or other legal persons, judicial
arrangements, compositions and analogous proceedings. Bankruptcy was
excluded because of the great disparities in national practice between the
original Brussels Convention States, because of its proximity to public law,
and because a draft Bankruptcy Convention was being considered by the
Community.[93] In *Gourdain v Nadler*[94] the European Court held that for
proceedings to be excluded on the basis that they concerned bankruptcy, etc.,
it was necessary that they must derive directly from the bankruptcy or
winding-up and be closely connected with the bankruptcy proceedings. Thus
a claim by an English liquidator against the directors of a company for
fraudulent trading under s.213 of the Insolvency Act 1986 would be outside
the scope of the Brussels I Regulation and the Lugano Convention. But an
action by a liquidator to recover debts due to an insolvent company would not
be excluded, since the claim in no sense relates to bankruptcy.[95] Nor would a
claim against directors for breach of duty be excluded, even if the company is
subject to insolvency proceedings in another Member State or Convention
State.[96]

Social security. Social security was excluded because in some countries it   **11–040**
was a matter of public law and in others it fell within the borderline area
between private law and public law; in some countries it was within the
jurisdiction of the ordinary courts, and in others within the jurisdiction of
administrative tribunals, and sometimes both.[97] What is social security
depends on Community law, and encompasses the matters covered by Regulation (EC) 883/2004 of the European Parliament and the Council.[98] The
exclusion of social security concerns only disputes arising out of the relationship between the administration and employers and employees, and not cases

---

[91] See Jenard, p.11.

[92] Under Art.5(6), below, Rule 35, clause (6); see Schlosser, para.52. See also Case 25/81 *CHW v GJH* [1982] E.C.R. 1189, where a question was raised (but not decided) as to whether an application for the return of a "codicil" was excluded from the scope of the Brussels Convention as relating to wills and succession. See also *Re Hayward* [1997] Ch. 45.

[93] For the subsequent history see Fletcher, *Insolvency in Private International Law* (2nd ed. 2005), Ch.7.

[94] Case 133/78 [1979] E.C.R. 733, 744. See also *UBS AG v Omni Holding AG* [2000] 1 W.L.R. 916; *Oakley v Ultra Vehicle Design Ltd* [2005] EWHC 872 (Ch.), [2005] I.L.Pr. 747.

[95] This passage was approved in *Re Hayward* [1997] Ch. 45, 54.

[96] *Grupo Torras SA v Sheikh Fahad Mohammed Al-Sabah* [1995] 1 Lloyd's Rep. 374, 400, affirmed on other grounds [1996] 1 Lloyd's Rep. 7 (CA). Contrast *Firswood Ltd v Petra Bank* [1996] C.L.C. 608 (CA). *cf. Soc Rewah France v Walczak* (France, Cr. Cass, May 5, 2004) 2005 *Rev. Crit.* 104, note Bureau, also in [2005] I.L.Pr. 503.

[97] Jenard, p.12.

[98] On the application of social security rules to employed persons and their families moving within the EU.

where the administration exercises a direct right of action against a third party liable for injury or is subrogated to the rights of a victim insured by it, because it is then acting under the rules of private law.[99]

11–041 *Arbitration.* Article 1(2)(d) of the Brussels I Regulation (and of the Lugano Convention) provides that it is not to apply to "arbitration."[100] Arbitration was excluded from the Brussels Convention because of the other international instruments in force or in contemplation dealing with the subject.[101] The Jenard Report indicated that the Brussels Convention did not apply to the recognition and enforcement of arbitral awards; nor did it determine the jurisdiction of courts in respect of litigation relating to arbitration, for example, proceedings to set aside an arbitral award, or deal with the recognition of judgments given in such proceedings.[102] But the Report gave no further elucidation. In the course of the negotiations which led to the 1978 Accession Convention, the United Kingdom took the view[103] that the exclusion covered all disputes which the parties had agreed should be settled by arbitration, including any secondary disputes connected with the arbitration. The original Brussels Convention States, on the other hand, thought that it had a narrower purpose, namely to exclude proceedings in national courts which related to arbitration proceedings which were contemplated, or were in progress, or had concluded. It was agreed that no amendment should be made to the original text, and that the new Contracting States could deal with the problem in their implementing legislation.[104] It is clear from the Schlosser Report that most of the discussion concerned the question whether the exclusion of arbitration from the scope of the Brussels Convention meant that Contracting States could refuse to enforce judgments given by foreign courts in proceedings brought in breach of arbitration agreements.[105]

11–042 *Schlosser and Evrigenis-Kerameus Reports.* The Schlosser Report also indicated that the Brussels Convention did not apply to court proceedings which were ancillary to arbitration proceedings, such as the appointment or dismissal of arbitrators, the fixing of the place of arbitration, or the extension

---

[99] Case C–271/00 *Gemeent Steenbergen v Baten* [2002] E.C.R. I–10527, adopting Jenard Report, pp.1, 12, 13 and the Schlosser Report, para.60.

[100] Regulation (EC) 1896/2006 of the European Parliament and of the Council creating a European order for payment procedure does not have an arbitration exception in Art.2, by contrast with Art.2 of Regulation (EC) 861/2007 of the European Parliament and of the Council establishing a European Small Claims Procedure.

[101] Jenard Report, p.13. The exclusion of "arbitration" is not an exclusion of arbitral proceedings as such, but of court proceedings relating to arbitration: *ETI Euro Telecom International NV v Republic of Bolivia* [2008] EWCA Civ 880, [2008] 1 W.L.R. 665, [82].

[102] *ibid.* p.13. See also Schlosser, para.65.

[103] A committee was appointed by the Lord Chancellor and the Secretary of State for Scotland in March 1972 under the chairmanship of Lord Kilbrandon to advise the United Kingdom Government on any adjustments which it might be necessary or desirable to negotiate with a view to enabling the United Kingdom to accede to the Brussels Convention. The committee reported that it was a matter of some importance to the United Kingdom that the exclusion of arbitration should be understood in the widest sense: *Report of the Committee on the European Judgments Convention* (October 1973), para.72 (unpublished): see *Youell v La Réunion Aérienne* [2009] EWCA Civ 175, [2009] 1 Lloyd's Rep. 586, at [26].

[104] Schlosser, para.61.

[105] See *ibid.* para.62, and below, paras 14–208 *et seq.*

of time limits; nor to a judgment determining whether an arbitration agreement was valid or not. The Evrigenis-Kerameus Report on the 1982 Accession Convention[106] drew a distinction between proceedings which were directly concerned with arbitration and proceedings which only incidentally raised the arbitration agreement. Proceedings which were directly concerned with arbitration as the principal issue, e.g. the establishment of the tribunal, annulment or the recognition of the validity or defectiveness of an award, were outside the Brussels Convention. But the verification, as an incidental question, of the validity of an arbitration agreement which was relied on by a litigant in order to contest the jurisdiction of the court before which he was being sued pursuant to the Brussels Convention, fell within the scope of the Convention.

The Marc Rich case. In *Marc Rich & Co AG v Società Italiana Impianti PA*   **11–043** *(The Atlantic Emperor)*[107] Italian sellers sold a cargo of crude oil to Swiss buyers. The contract was made by an exchange of telexes, one of which (from the buyers) contained a provision for English law and London arbitration. But the Italian sellers did not reply to the telex. Following delivery the buyers alleged that the oil had been contaminated with water. The Italian sellers sued the Swiss buyers in the Italian courts claiming a declaration that they were not liable to the buyers and denying that they were bound by the arbitration clause contained in the telex. The Swiss buyers commenced an arbitration, claiming damages, and sought in English proceedings the appointment of an arbitrator, and the Italian sellers argued that under Art.21 of the Brussels Convention (equivalent to Art.27 of the Brussels I Regulation) they were entitled to a stay because the Italian proceedings had priority. In the first reference from a United Kingdom court on the Brussels Convention, the European Court held[108] that, by excluding arbitration from the scope of the Brussels Convention on the ground that it was already covered by international conventions, the Contracting States intended to exclude arbitration "in its entirety", including proceedings brought before national courts. The appointment by a court of an arbitrator was covered by the exclusion because it was a measure adopted by the State as part of the process of setting arbitration proceedings in motion. The Court said that this conclusion was corroborated by the Schlosser Report,[109] according to which the Brussels Convention did not apply to court proceedings which were ancillary to arbitration proceedings, such as the appointment or dismissal of arbitrators. This was so even if the judicial proceedings necessarily involved the question of the existence or validity of an arbitration agreement. The test for determining whether the proceedings were outside the scope of the exclusion was the nature of the subject-matter

---

[106] [1986] O.J. C298/1, at p.10, para.35.

[107] [1989] 1 Lloyd's Rep. 548 (Hirst J. and CA).

[108] Case C–190/89 [1991] E.C.R. I–3855. The Swiss buyers contested the jurisdiction of the Italian courts, but after their objection was dismissed they defended the case on the merits, and were refused an injunction in England to restrain the Italian proceedings because they had submitted to the Italian jurisdiction: *The Atlantic Emperor (No.2)* [1992] 1 Lloyd's Rep. 624 (CA).

[109] para.64. Professor Schlosser changed his views and submitted (as did M. Jenard) an opinion on behalf of the Italian sellers: published at (1991) 7 Arb. Int. 227 and 243. The Court also relied on the Evrigenis-Kerameus Report on the 1982 Accession Convention, above.

of the proceedings. If the subject-matter of the proceedings was the appointment of an arbitrator, the fact that the court had to resolve a preliminary issue as to the existence or validity of the arbitration agreement did not justify the application of the Convention; and it would be contrary to the principle of legal certainty for the applicability of the Convention to vary according to whether there was a preliminary issue.

11–044   The actual ruling in that case was the narrow one that the exclusion of arbitration in what is now Art.1(2)(d) of the Brussels I Regulation extends to proceedings before a national court concerning the appointment of an arbitrator, even if the existence or validity of an arbitration agreement is a preliminary issue in that litigation.[110] In a second case before the European Court, *Van Uden Maritime BV v Deco-Line*,[111] one of the questions was whether the jurisdiction of a national court to order provisional measures in support of arbitration was within the scope of the Brussels Convention, or excluded by the arbitration exception. The Court held that proceedings to obtain provisional measures in aid of arbitration were not excluded. After referring to the views of the Schlosser Report, the Court said that the critical question was the nature of the rights which the proceedings sought to protect. Where the subject-matter of the application for provisional measures related to a question which fell within the scope *ratione materiae* of the Brussels Convention, the Convention was applicable even if arbitration proceedings had been, or were to be, commenced on the substance of the case. The Court also said that where the parties had validly excluded the jurisdiction of the courts in disputes arising under a contract and had referred the dispute to arbitration, there were no courts which had jurisdiction under the Convention as to the substance of the case.

11–045   Consequently both cases emphasise that the applicability of the arbitration exception depends on the subject-matter of the proceedings. In *West Tankers Inc v Allianz SpA (The Front Comor)*[112] a vessel was chartered to an Italian company under a charterparty containing a London arbitration clause. It collided with a jetty in Sicily owned by the charterer. The charterer's insurers, relying on their rights of subrogation under the Italian Civil Code, commenced proceedings in Syracuse against the owners for the money which they had paid to their insured. The owners commenced proceedings against the insurers in England for a declaration that the insurers were bound by the arbitration clause and for an injunction to restrain the Italian proceedings. For reasons which will be developed below,[113] the European Court ruled that it was incompatible with the Brussels I Regulation for a court of a Member State to

---

[110] See generally Hascher (1996) 12 Arb. Int. 233, (1997) 13 Arb. Int. 33; Van Houtte (1997) 13 Arb.Int. 85. *cf. Lexmar Corp v Nordisk Skibsrederforensig* [1997] 1 Lloyd's Rep. 289 (although matters relating to security for costs in an arbitration were within the exclusion, proceedings to enforce a letter of undertaking securing costs in arbitration were not within exclusion).

[111] Case C–391/95 [1998] E.C.R. I–7091, [1999] Q.B. 1225.

[112] Case C–185/07 [2009] E.C.R. I–663, [2009] 1 A.C. 1138; on a reference from the House of Lords *sub nom. West Tankers Inc v Ras Riunione Adriatica di Sicurta SpA (The Front Comor)* [2007] UKHL 4, [2007] 1 Lloyd's Rep. 391; below, para.16–096. See also *DHL GBS (UK) Ltd v Fallimento Finmatica SpA* [2009] EWHC 291 (Comm.), [2009] 1 Lloyd's Rep. 430.

[113] paras 16–092 *et seq.*

make an order to restrain a person from commencing or continuing proceedings before the courts of another Member State on the ground that such proceedings would be contrary to an arbitration agreement. But, as regards the scope of the arbitration exclusion, the European Court accepted that the English proceedings as a whole, which sought declaratory as well as injunctive relief, did not come within the scope of the Brussels I Regulation because their subject matter was arbitration. The proceedings before the Italian court, however, came within the scope of the Regulation, and consequently the effect of the arbitration agreement, including its validity, was an incidental question, which also came within the scope of the Regulation.[114] Consequently it was the Italian court which had the exclusive power under the Regulation to rule on the effect of the arbitration agreement on its jurisdiction.

Plainly, therefore, judicial proceedings to determine the existence or validity of an arbitration agreement are within the exclusion.[115] It is clear from the Jenard Report[116] and the Schlosser Report[117] that the recognition and enforcement of arbitral awards will be outside the scope of the Regulation and the Convention. It was held that a French judgment making a French award enforceable was not entitled to enforcement under the Brussels Convention for that reason.[118] Other examples of cases within the exclusion are proceedings claiming that an arbitration agreement is invalid,[119] or proceedings to enjoin an arbitration in a Member State on the basis of an English jurisdiction agreement.[120] The mere fact that there are arbitration proceedings pending abroad will not deprive the court of jurisdiction.[121]   **11–046**

Two further controversial questions have arisen in this context. The first question is whether a judgment deciding that an arbitration agreement is valid, or invalid or ineffective, is entitled to recognition under the Regulation or the Convention. The second question is whether a decision of a court in another Member State or Convention State that there is no valid arbitration agreement, or giving judgment in disregard of what English law would regard as a valid   **11–047**

---

[114] At [26], citing the Evrigenis and Kerameus report on the 1982 Accession Convention, above, text at n.106.

[115] The *West Tankers* case itself; *Through Transport Mutual Insurance Association (Eurasia) Ltd v New India Assurance Co Ltd* [2004] EWCA Civ 1598, [2005] 1 Lloyd's Rep. 67, approving *The Ivan Zagubanski* [2002] 1 Lloyd's Rep. 106. See also *The Lake Avery* [1997] 1 Lloyd's Rep. 540; *Sovarex SA v Alvarez SA* [2011] EWHC 1661 (Comm.), [2011] 2 Lloyd's Rep. 320. Contrast *Vale do Rio Doce Navegaçao SA v Shanghai Bao Steel Ocean Shipping Co Ltd* [2000] 2 Lloyd's Rep. 1 (claim for declaration against brokers that their principals bound by arbitration agreement not within exception).

[116] p.13, referred to with approval in Case C–190/89 *Marc Rich & Co AG v Soc Italiana Impianti PA* [1991] E.C.R. I–3855, 3900.

[117] para.65(c), referred to with approval in Case C–391/95 *Van Uden Maritime BV v Firma Deco-Line* [1998] E.C.R. I–7091, [1999] Q.B. 1225, para.32.

[118] *ABCI v Banque Franco-Tunisienne* [1996] 1 Lloyd's Rep. 495; affirmed on other aspects [1997] 1 Lloyd's Rep. 531 (CA). See Hascher (1996) 12 Arb. Int. 233, who suggests that the decision is supportable on the basis that the French order was not in fact a judgment on the award, but simply an execution order.

[119] *A v B* [2006] EWHC 2006 (Comm.), [2007] 1 Lloyd's Rep. 237.

[120] *Claxton Engineering v TXM (No.2)* [2011] EWHC 345 (Comm.), [2011] 1 Lloyd's Rep. 510.

[121] *Youell v La Réunion Aérienne* [2009] EWCA Civ 175, [2009] 1 Lloyd's Rep. 586 (fact that claims made in legal proceedings are the mirror image of claims made in an arbitration does not engage the arbitration exception).

arbitration agreement, is entitled to recognition or enforcement under the Regulation or the Convention. These questions are considered below in connection with the recognition and enforcement of foreign judgments.[122]

11–048   *Proposals for change.* The European Commission has recognised that the current legal framework does not sufficiently protect the effectiveness of arbitration agreements in the EU. The Commission has accepted that the ruling in the *West Tankers* case creates a real risk of the abuse of litigation tactics and has put forward proposals for changes to the Brussels I Regulation as part of the general review of the Regulation.[123] It has put forward a solution designed to ensure that a national court should stay its proceedings in favour of the courts of the seat of the arbitration, or in favour of the arbitral tribunal.[124]

11–049   **Ancillary claims and provisional measures.** It is clear that applications for provisional measures, such as preservation of property or interim injunctions, are within the scope of the Regulation and the Convention[125] and it is equally clear that provisional orders for interim payments, e.g. in respect of damages or of maintenance, are also within them.[126] The European Court has recognised that procedures authorising provisional and protective measures are found in the legal systems of the Brussels Convention States; but the grant of these measures requires special care on the part of the national court and detailed knowledge of the actual circumstances in which the measures are to take effect; the courts of the State where the assets subject to the measures sought are located are those best able to assess the need for the measures and the conditions on which they are to be granted; it was for this reason that Art.24 of the Brussels Convention (now Art.31 of the Regulation and the Lugano Convention) allowed applications for provisional and protective measures to be made to the courts of a Convention State even if, under the Convention, the courts of another Convention State had jurisdiction as to the substance of the matter.[127] Where a case involves some aspects which are within the Regulation and the Convention and others which are not, those aspects which are within them are severable. But if the ancillary claims are concerned essentially with a matter which is excluded from the scope of the Regulation and the Convention, the ancillary claims themselves are outside their scope.[128]

---

[122] Below, paras 14–206 *et seq.*

[123] Below, para.16–097.

[124] COM (2010) 748 Final, para.3.1.4. See also Report to the European Parliament, etc. on the application of the Brussels I Regulation, April 21, 2009 (COM (2009) 174, para.3.7; Green Paper, April 21, 2009 (COM (2009) 175, para.7; Hess, Pfeiffer, Schlosser, *The Brussels I Regulation (EC) No 44/2001* (2008), at paras 106–136. A draft report of the Committee on Legal Affairs of the European Parliament proposes that the exclusion of arbitration should be widened to include judicial procedures ruling on the validity or extent of arbitral competence as a principal issue or as an incidental or preliminary question. 2010/0383(COD), p.13, and also pp.6, 9.

[125] See Art.31, above, paras 8–026 *et seq.*; Case 143/78 *De Cavel v De Cavel (No.1)* [1979] E.C.R. 1055; *Babanaft International Co SA v Bassatne* [1990] Ch. 13, 29–32 (CA).

[126] Case 120/79 *De Cavel v De Cavel (No.2)* [1980] E.C.R. 731.

[127] Case 125/79 *Denilauler v SNC Couchet Frères* [1980] E.C.R. 1553, 1570.

[128] Case 143/78 *De Cavel v De Cavel (No.1)* [1979] E.C.R. 1055; Case 25/81 *CHW v GJH* [1982] E.C.R. 1189; Case 120/79 *De Cavel v De Cavel (No.2)* [1980] E.C.R. 731.

Application of the Brussels I Regulation and the Lugano Convention   **11–050**
and relationship with other international instruments. Generally the Regulation and the Convention apply where the defendant is domiciled in a
Member State or a Convention State, even if the claimant is not so domiciled,
and as a general rule the place where the claimant is domiciled is not relevant
for the purpose of applying the jurisdictional rules of the Regulation or the
Convention.[129]

By Art.4(1) of the Regulation (and the Convention), if the defendant is not   **11–051**
domiciled in a Member State (or Convention State), the jurisdiction of the
courts of that Member State (or Convention State) is determined by the law of
that State. Consequently, in England the jurisdictional rules in what was RSC
Order 11, r.1(1) and which are now contained in CPR, r.36.6 and Practice
Direction 6B, apply to defendants domiciled outside the Member States or
Convention States.[130] But the Regulation and the Convention apply to defendants outside the Member and Convention States where Art.22 (exclusive
jurisdiction) or Art.23 (jurisdiction agreements) apply.[131]

Chapter VII of the Regulation deals (as do the equivalent provisions of Title   **11–052**
VII of the Convention[132]) with its relationship with other conventions. Art.69
provides that the existing treaties (mainly bilateral) on the recognition and
enforcement of judgments are to be superseded, including those in force
between the United Kingdom and other Member States, to the extent that the
Regulation applies to the subject-matter of the specific conventions.[133]

Article 71[134] deals with other treaties governing jurisdiction or the recogni-   **11–053**
tion and enforcement of judgments, and provides in Art.71(1): "This Regulation shall not affect any conventions to which the Member States are parties
and which in relation to particular matters, govern jurisdiction or the recognition or enforcement of judgments." By Art.71(2), with a view to its uniform
interpretation, Art.71(1) is to be interpreted so that (as regards the assumption
of jurisdiction) (a) the Regulation is not to prevent a court of a Member State
which is a party to a convention on a particular matter from assuming
jurisdiction in accordance with it, even if the defendant is domiciled in another
Member State which is not a party; (b) where the defendant is domiciled in

---

[129] Case C–412/98 *Universal General Insurance Co (UGIC) v Group Josi Reinsurance Co SA*
[2000] E.C.R. I–5925, [2001] 1 Q.B. 68.

[130] The Commission has proposed that this provision be removed, and that the Regulation
should apply to defendants domiciled in any part of the world: see para.11–022, above.

[131] In addition, entities domiciled outside Member or Convention States, but with branches
there, will be regarded as domiciled in there for the purposes of the rules on insurance contracts,
consumer contracts and employment contracts: see para.11–097, below. There are also provisions
to ensure that Art.4(1) does not apply in Member States to defendants domiciled in Convention
States, and vice versa: Brussels I Regulation, Art.71; Lugano Convention, Art.64.

[132] For the inter-relationship of the Regulation and the Lugano Convention, see Lugano
Convention, Art.64; Jenard-Möller, pp.67–68.

[133] See Joined Cases 9 and 10/77 *Bavaria and Germanair v Eurocontrol* [1977] E.C.R. 1517;
and Art.70(1).

[134] See also Lugano Convention, Art.67, and Protocol No.3, para.1. Section 9(1) of the 1982
Act (as amended by the 1991 Act and by SI 2001/3929) provides that the relevant provisions of
Title VII of the Convention shall have effect in relation to any statutory provision implementing
any such other convention in the United Kingdom, and in relation to any rule of law so far as it
has the effect of so implementing any such other convention.

another Member State and does not enter an appearance, the court must examine whether it has jurisdiction and whether the defendant has had an opportunity to arrange for his defence.[135]

11–054   The United Kingdom is a party to several such conventions, which are discussed in Chapters 13 (jurisdiction *in rem*) and 15 (international conventions). Some of the conventions lay down direct rules of jurisdiction which are different from those of the Regulation and the Convention, including such bases as diverse as that of the court of the place of destination under the Warsaw Convention on international carriage by air or the arrest of a ship under the Brussels Convention (1952) on arrest of seagoing ships.

11–055   The effect of these provisions is that, notwithstanding the normal jurisdictional rules of the Regulation and the Convention, the English court may exercise jurisdiction in accordance with the provisions of international conventions to which the United Kingdom is a party, such as the Brussels Arrest Convention and the Brussels Collision Convention of 1952.[136] The effect of Art.71(2) of the Regulation (and Art.67 of the Convention) is that in these cases the court which is entitled to exercise jurisdiction under the treaty may do so and its judgment will be enforced in another Member State or Convention State even if the defendant is domiciled in that other State and that other State is not a party to the relevant international convention. Article 67(4) of the Lugano Convention allows the Convention State in which recognition or enforcement of a judgment is sought to refuse recognition or enforcement if that State is not a party to the convention in question and the person against whom recognition or enforcement is sought is domiciled in that State.[137]

11–056   It does not follow that, where a specialised convention is applicable, the Regulation and the Convention are entirely superseded. Thus the Brussels Arrest Convention contains rules on jurisdiction, but no rules on *lis alibi pendens*. Accordingly, the *lis pendens*[138] provisions of the Regulation and the Lugano Convention apply, because their rules are excluded "solely in relation to questions governed by a specialised convention."[139] But a provision in bills of lading for the exclusive jurisdiction of German courts has been held not to deprive the English court of jurisdiction under the Brussels Arrest Convention, even though the Arrest Convention had no provision equivalent to what

---

[135] Under Art.26, below, paras 11–075 *et seq*. This includes jurisdiction under an international convention: Case C–148/03 *Nürnberger Allgemeine Versicherungs AG v Portbridge Transport International BV* [2004] E.C.R. I–1023, [2005] 1 Lloyd's Rep. 592.

[136] *The Deichland* [1990] 1 Q.B. 361 (CA); *The Po* [1991] 2 Lloyd's Rep. 206 (CA); *The Nordglimt* [1988] Q.B. 183; *The Anna H* [1995] 1 Lloyd's Rep. 11 (CA) and see also *The Netty* [1981] 2 Lloyd's Rep. 57; *Clipper Shipping Co Ltd v San Vincente Partners*, 1989 S.L.T. 204.

[137] For other provisions in relation to recognition and enforcement of judgments see below, Rule 53.

[138] Rule 38(4).

[139] Case C–406/92 *The Tatry* [1994] E.C.R. I–5439, 5471, [1999] Q.B. 515, 533. The same conclusion had been reached in *The Nordglimt* [1988] Q.B. 183 and *The Linda* [1988] 1 Lloyd's Rep. 175. Contrast *Deaville v Aeroflot Russian International Airlines* [1997] 2 Lloyd's Rep. 67 (Warsaw Convention); *Pearce v Ove Arup Partnership Ltd* [2000] Ch. 403, 441–442 (CA) (Berne Convention). See also below, paras 13–034 *et seq*. and *Andrea Merzario Ltd v Internationale Spedition Leitner Gesellschaft GmbH* [2001] EWCA Civ 61, [2001] 1 Lloyd's Rep. 490, disapproving *Frans Maas Logistics (UK) Ltd v CDR Trucking BV* [1999] 2 Lloyd's Rep. 179.

is now Art.23 of the Brussels I Regulation giving effect to jurisdiction clauses.[140] That is because to deprive the English court of jurisdiction would involve a conflict between the jurisdictional provisions of the Arrest Convention and the Regulation; in such cases the specialised convention prevails.[141] But the European Court has held[142] that the application of specialised conventions under Art.71 cannot compromise the principles which underlie judicial co-operation in civil and commercial matters in the European Union, such as the principles in the Brussels I Regulation of (inter alia) predictability as to the courts having jurisdiction and therefore legal certainty for litigants and the minimisation of the risk of concurrent proceedings. Consequently, Art.71 cannot be interpreted to mean that, in a field covered by the Regulation, a specialised convention, such as the Convention on the Contract for the International Carriage of Goods by Road 1956 (CMR), may lead to results which are less favourable for achieving sound operation of the internal market than the results to which the Regulation's provisions lead. Accordingly the Court ruled that the effect of Art.71 was that the rules governing jurisdiction, recognition and enforcement which were laid down by a convention on a particular matter, such as the *lis pendens* rule set out in Art.31(2) of the CMR, and the rule relating to enforceability in Art.31(3) of the CMR, applied, provided that they were highly predictable, facilitated the sound administration of justice and enabled the risk of concurrent proceedings to be minimised and that they ensured, under conditions at least as favourable as those provided for by the Regulation, the free movement of judgments in civil and commercial matters and mutual trust in the administration of justice in the European Union.

Direct applicability of the Brussels I Regulation and the Lugano Convention.　**11–057**
The 1982 Act brought into effect for the United Kingdom the rules of jurisdiction provided for by the Brussels Convention, as amended by the Accession Convention of 1978, and applied similar (but not identical) rules for allocating jurisdiction as between the constituent parts of the United Kingdom.[143] It also provided for the recognition and enforcement of judgments emanating from other Convention States, and introduced a revised system for the enforcement of judgments given by courts of one part of the United Kingdom in other parts. Amendments to the 1982 Act and its schedules came into force in 1989 to take account of the 1982 Accession Convention (Greece) and in 1991 to take account of the 1989 Accession Convention. The Civil Jurisdiction and Judgments Act 1991 was enacted to amend the 1982 Act in order to give effect to the original Lugano Convention.

---

[140] See below, Rule 39.
[141] *The Bergen* [1997] 1 Lloyd's Rep. 380. A stay of proceedings was subsequently granted: *The Bergen (No.2)* [1997] 2 Lloyd's Rep. 710.
[142] Case C–533/08 *TNT Express Nederland BV v AXA Versicherung AG* [2010] I.L.Pr. 663.
[143] The 1982 Act also introduced a new system of jurisdictional rules in Scotland: Sch.8, on which see *Tehrani v Secretary of State for the Home Department (Scotland)* [2006] UKHL 47, [2007] 1 A.C. 521, at [37]–[44]. For the special position of Gibraltar see SI 1997/2602, and below, Rule 56(3).

11–058   The Brussels I Regulation is directly applicable in the United Kingdom by virtue of s.2(1) of the European Communities Act 1972. The Civil Jurisdiction and Judgments Order 2001[144] ("the 2001 Order") was made under the European Communities Act 1972, s.2(2), to deal with certain matters of implementation, including matters left by the Regulation to national law, such as the determination of the domicile of individuals. It has already been seen[145] that because the revised Lugano Convention was entered into by the European Union on behalf of the Member States, the United Kingdom Government has taken the view that incorporating legislation is unnecessary. The 1982 Act has been amended to deal with consequential matters and matters left to national law.

11–059   As a result of the introduction of the Brussels/Lugano regime in the United Kingdom there will be three sets of basic rules of jurisdiction in the United Kingdom: one set for cases within the Regulation and the Convention (mainly, but not only, where the defendant is domiciled in another Member State or Convention State); a second set, similar but not identical to the first, where the defendant is domiciled in another part of the United Kingdom; and a third set, substantially different from the first two, where the defendant is not domiciled in a Member State or a Convention State.

11–060   The Regulation and the Convention supersede any inconsistent prior legislation. This may have some unexpected results going beyond amendment of the existing general rules relating to jurisdiction and judgments. Thus the effect of the original Art.17 of the Brussels Convention was that where parties, one of whom was domiciled in a Convention State, agreed that a court in a Convention State was to have jurisdiction, that court would have exclusive jurisdiction. The effect of the unamended[146] version of Art.17 was that where it applied the jurisdiction of the courts of the defendant's domicile was wholly ousted, if another court had been chosen. The law of the United Kingdom contains provisions which prevent parties from contracting out of the jurisdiction of United Kingdom courts. Thus s.203 of the Employment Rights Act 1996 (as amended) is intended to prevent an English employee of a German company from effectively agreeing that any claims brought by the employee should be brought in a German court. There are similar laws in other countries.

11–061   But the effect of the decision of the European Court in *Sanicentral GmbH v Collin*[147] was that an agreement under the unamended Art.17 to oust the jurisdiction of the local court in favour of the courts of another Convention State had to be given effect notwithstanding the mandatory nature of the employment legislation of the local law. The European Court held that employment disputes came within the Brussels Convention, and that a jurisdiction clause in a contract between a French worker and a German employer

---

[144] SI 2001/3929. The Order (as amended) also applies the Brussels I Regulation to Denmark following the 2005 Agreement whereby the provisions of the Brussels I Regulation are applied to Denmark: Art.3A, and para.11–013, above.

[145] para.11–020.

[146] Special provision is now made for jurisdiction clauses in employment contracts: See Brussels I Regulation, Art.21; Lugano Convention, Art.21; below, para.12–132.

[147] Case 25/79 [1979] E.C.R. 3423.

conferring jurisdiction on a German court deprived the French courts of jurisdiction, notwithstanding that the jurisdiction clause was void by French law when it was entered into (before the Convention came into force in 1973). The effect of the decision is far-reaching. The Court disclaimed any intention on the part of the Convention to affect rules of substantive law, but held that "in matters of civil jurisdiction, the national procedural laws applicable to the cases concerned are set aside in the matters governed by the Convention in favour of the provisions thereof."[148]

Interpretation of the Brussels I Regulation and the Lugano Conven-   **11–062**
tion. All language versions of the Regulation, and of the Convention[149] are equally authentic. Consequently, the court will be able to consider the foreign language texts of the Regulation and the Convention and the official reports on the three Conventions may be resorted to for the purpose of interpretation. The United Kingdom court is entitled, and bound, to look at the texts in other languages where a problem of interpretation arises. There is therefore no room for a rule in this context that the other language versions may be resorted to only in the case of ambiguity in the English text. The English versions of the Regulation and the Convention are only one of the authentic versions, and resort may be had to the others for the purposes of interpretation. A striking example of this occurred when the European Court held, basing itself on the French text of Art.18[150] of the Brussels Convention, that an appearance to contest the jurisdiction was not to be regarded as a submission even if at the same time the defendant pleaded to the merits in the alternative. The other language texts required the protest to be solely to contest the jurisdiction if it was to escape being a voluntary submission, but the Court preferred the French text as being more in keeping with the objectives and spirit of the Brussels Convention.[151]

Because the Regulation and the Convention are not incorporated by legisla-   **11–063**
tion, there is no statutory provision equivalent to that in the 1982 Act in relation to the Brussels Convention[152] whereby the successive reports on the Brussels Convention (and the Accession Conventions) may be considered in ascertaining the meaning of the instruments. But there is no doubt that the provisions in the 1982 Act are declaratory of international law and European law, and that the reports remain a valuable aid to interpretation and have been so used by the European Court and by national courts since the inception of the Brussels/Lugano regime.

References to the European Court. There have been more than 200   **11–064**
rulings by the European Court on the Brussels Convention and the Brussels I

---

[148] At p.3429; *cf.* Case 150/80 *Elefanten Schuh GmbH v Jacqmain* [1981] E.C.R. 1671.
[149] Art.79.
[150] Now Art.24 of the Brussels I Regulation and the Lugano Convention.
[151] Case 150/80 *Elefanten Schuh GmbH v Jacqmain* [1981] E.C.R. 1671, 1685. See also Case 38/81 *Effer SpA v Kantner* [1982] E.C.R. 825, 834; Case C–305/88 *Isabelle Lancray SA v Peters und Sickert KG* [1990] E.C.R. I–2725.
[152] s.3(3).

Regulation. References to the European Court under the Brussels Convention were governed by a protocol to the Convention. References on the interpretation of the Brussels I Regulation were governed by the EC Treaty but until the Lisbon Treaty came into force in 2009 the power of national courts to make references to the European Court on the interpretation of the Regulation was limited to courts or tribunals of a Member State against whose decisions there was no judicial remedy under national law. But since the Lisbon Treaty[153] references are governed by what is now Art.267 of the Treaty on the Functioning of the European Union (TFEU). Under Art.267, the European Court has jurisdiction to give preliminary rulings concerning the interpretation of acts of the European Union institutions, such as the Regulation. Where a question of interpretation is raised, a national court may, if it considers that a decision on the question is necessary to enable it to give judgment, request the Court to give a ruling, and where any such question is raised in a case pending before a court against whose decisions there is no judicial remedy under national law, that court must bring the matter before the European Court.[154]

11–065   The mere fact that one of the parties contends that the dispute gives rise to a question of interpretation does not mean that the English court is bound to consider that a true question of interpretation arises. If the English court considers that there is no room for reasonable doubt as to the interpretation and that the matter would be equally obvious in the courts of the other States it need not make a reference; but the court must bear in mind that the different language versions are equally authentic and that interpretation involves a comparison of the different language versions; in a clear case, however, the English court may refrain from making a reference.[155] The normal practice on references to the European Court, that the national court should not refer hypothetical questions and should find the relevant facts first, applies to references in relation to the Regulation.[156]

11–066   The European Court has held that, because the Brussels I Regulation sought to retain the structure and basic principles of the Brussels Convention, provisions in the Regulation are to be interpreted in accordance with its jurisprudence on the Convention.[157] Consequently, almost all of the extensive case law of the European Court on the Brussels Convention will apply to the interpretation of the Regulation. The European Court emphasised that the

---

[153] See C–278/09 *Martinez v MGN Ltd* [2009] E.C.R. I–11099 (jurisdiction declined because Art.267 not in force).

[154] For interpretation of the intra-UK provisions in 1982 Act, Sch.4, see below, para. 11–071.

[155] See, e.g. *Jordan Grand Prix Ltd v Baltic Insurance Group* [1999] 2 W.L.R. 134, 140 (HL) (*acte clair*) and *cf.* on the exercise of discretion, *The Nile Rhapsody* [1994] 1 Lloyd's Rep. 382 (CA); *Jarrett v Barclays Bank Plc* [1999] Q.B. 1 (CA).

[156] See C–111/01 *Gantner Electronic GmbH v Basch Exploitatie Maatschappij BV* [2003] E.C.R. I–4207.

[157] Case C–533/07 *Falco Privatstiftung v Weller-Lindhorst* [2009] E.C.R. I–3327, [2010] Bus. L.R. 210; C–167/08 *Draka NK Cables v Omnipol Ltd* [2009] E.C.R. I–3477; Case C–189/08 *Zuid-Chemie BV v Philippo's Mineralenfabriek NV/SA* [2009] E.C.R. I–6917; Case C–292/08 *German Graphics Graphische Maschinen GmbH v van der Schee* [2009] E.C.R. I–8421; Case C–406/09 *Realchemie Nederland v Bayer CropScience AG* [2012] I.L.Pr. 17; and Brussels I Regulation, recital (19).

Brussels Convention was to be interpreted by reference to its principles and objectives; thus the Court took into account the purposes of the simplification of formalities regarding the reciprocal recognition and enforcement of judgments and of strengthening the legal protection of persons within the European Communities.[158] The Court has encouraged uniformity in the Member States by interpreting most provisions of the instruments which have come before it according to an autonomous interpretation, rather than by a purely national interpretation.

This is because a common problem has been whether terms are to be interpreted according to national law (usually that of the *lex fori*) or according to an independent concept. In a few cases the instrument itself supplies the answer by referring to national law, or by supplying a definition itself. But more commonly the instruments are silent. The Court has almost invariably interpreted terms in accordance with an independent concept:[159] e.g. "civil and commercial matters" in Art.1;[160] "place of performance"[161] and "contract" in Art.5(1)(a);[162] "sale of goods" and "provision of services" in Art.5(1)(b);[163] place where goods "delivered" in Art.5(1)(b);[164] "maintenance" in Art.5(2)[165] "matters relating to tort, delict or quasi-delict" in Art.5(3);[166] "place where the

11–067

---

[158] Among many others see Case 33/78 *Somafer SA v Saar-Ferngas AG* [1978] E.C.R. 2183; Case 144/86 *Gubisch Maschinenfabrik AG v Palumbo* [1987] E.C.R. 4861; Case C–351/89 *Overseas Union Insurance Ltd v New Hampshire Insurance Co* [1991] E.C.R. I–3317, [1992] Q.B. 434. On the principle of "legal certainty" see, e.g. Case 38/81 *Effer SpA v Kantner* [1982] E.C.R. 825, 834; Case C–190/89 *Marc Rich & Co AG v Soc Italiana Impianti PA* [1991] E.C.R. I–3855.

[159] See Newton, *Uniform Interpretation of the Brussels and Lugano Conventions* (2002). For criticism see Audit, 2004 *Clunet* 789.

[160] Case 29/76 *LTU GmbH v Eurocontrol* [1976] E.C.R. 1541; Joined Cases 9 and 10/77 *Bavaria and Germanair v Eurocontrol* [1977] E.C.R. 1517; Case 133/78 *Gourdain v Nadler* [1979] E.C.R. 733; Case 814/79 *Netherlands State v Rüffer* [1980] E.C.R. 3807; Case C–172/91 *Sonntag v Waidmann* [1993] E.C.R. I–1963; Case C–167/00 *Verein für Konsumenteninformation v Henkel* [2002] E.C.R. I–8111; Case C–271/00 *Gemeent Steenbergen v Baten* [2002] E.C.R. I–10527; Case C–433/01 *Freistaat Bayern v Blijdenstein* [2004] E.C.R. I–981; Case C–343/04 *Land Oberösterreich v CEZ a.s.* [2006] E.C.R. I–4557; C–292/05 *Lechouritou v Dimosio tis Omospondiakis Dimokratias tis Germanias* [2007] E.C.R I–1519.

[161] Case C–204/08 *Rehder v Air Baltic Corp* [2009] E.C.R. I–6073.

[162] Case 34/82 *Peters v ZNAV* [1983] E.C.R. 787; Case 9/87 *Arcado v Haviland SA* [1988] E.C.R. 1539; Case C–26/91 *Soc Jakob Handte et cie GmbH v TMCS* [1993] E.C.R. I–3967; Case C–51/97 *Réunion européenne SA v Spliethoff's Bevrachtingskantoor BV* [1998] E.C.R. I–6511; Case C–334/00 *Fonderie Officine Meccaniche SpA v HWS GmbH* [2002] E.C.R. I–7357; Case C–167/00 *Verein für Konsumenteninformation v Henkel* [2002] E.C.R. I–8111; Case C–265/02 *Frahuil SA v Assitalia SpA* [2004] E.C.R. I–1543; Case C–27/02 *Engler v Janus Versand GmbH* [2005] E.C.R. I–481.

[163] C–381/08 *Car Trim GmbH v Key Safety Systems Srl* [2010] E.C.R. I–1255; Case C–533/07 *Falco Privatstiftung v Weller-Lindhorst* [2009] E.C.R. I–3327; Case C–19/09 *Wood Floor Solutions Andreas Domberger GmbH v Silva Trade SA* [2010] 1 W.L.R. 1900.

[164] Case C–386/05 *Color Drack GmbH v Lexx International Vertriebs GmbH* [2007] E.C.R. I–3699, [2010] 1 W.L.R. 1909.

[165] Case C–433/01 *Freistaat Bayern v Blijdenstein* [2004] E.C.R. I–981.

[166] Case 189/87 *Kalfelis v Schröder* [1988] E.C.R. 5565; Case C–261/90 *Reichert v Dresdner Bank (No.2)* [1992] E.C.R. I–2149; Case C–334/00 *Fonderie Officine Meccaniche SpA v HWS GmbH* [2002] E.C.R. I–7357; Case C–96/00 *Gabriel v Schlank & Schick GmbH* [2002] E.C.R. I–6367; Case C–167/00 *Verein für Konsumenteninformation v Henkel* [2002] E.C.R. I–8111; Case C–27/02 *Engler v Janus Versand GmbH* [2005] E.C.R. I–481.

harmful event occurred" in Art.5(3);[167] "contract," "consumer" and "instalment credit terms" in Art.15;[168] "rights *in rem* in immovable property"[169] and "tenancies of immovable property"[170] in Art.22(1); "proceedings concerned with registration or validity of patents" in Art.22(4);[171] "proceedings concerned with the enforcement of judgments" in Art.22(5);[172] whether there has been an agreement on jurisdiction under Art.23;[173] "provisional, including protective measures" in Art.31;[174] "ordinary appeal" in Arts 37 and 46;[175] and "party" in Art.43(1).[176] But where the reference is to procedural concepts the tendency towards an autonomous interpretation is less marked.[177]

11–068   The object of interpreting the terms autonomously is to ensure that the instruments are fully effective, and to ensure their uniform application, so as to avoid as far as possible multiplication of the bases of jurisdiction in relation to the same legal relationship and to reinforce legal protection by allowing the plaintiff easily to identify the court before which he may bring an action and the defendant reasonably to foresee the court before which he may be sued.[178] These objects have been used to justify an avoidance of an excessively liberal interpretation of the expression "harmful event" in Art.5(3)[179] and have justified an autonomous, rather than a national, interpretation of Art.5(5) on the meaning of "branch, agency or other establishment."[180] The Court has held that the exceptions to Art.2, which gives primacy to the court of the domicile, which is the basic jurisdictional rule, are to be construed strictly,[181]

---

[167] Case 21/76 *Bier v Mines de Potasse d'Alsace SA* [1976] E.C.R. 1735, [1978] Q.B. 708; and e.g. Case C–189/08 *Zuid-Chemie BV v Philippo's Mineralenfabriek NV/SA* [2009] E.C.R. I–6917.

[168] See Case C–89/91 *Shearson Lehman Hutton Inc v TVB* [1993] E.C.R. I–139; Case 150/77 *Société Bertrand v Paul Ott KG* [1978] E.C.R. 1431; Case C–99/96 *Mietz v Intership Yachting Sneek BV* [1999] E.C.R. I–2277; Case C–96/00 *Gabriel v Schlank & Schick GmbH* [2002] E.C.R. I–6367; Case C–167/00 *Verein für Konsumenteninformation v Henkel* [2002] E.C.R. I–8111; Case C–27/02 *Engler v Janus Versand GmbH* [2005] E.C.R. I–481.

[169] Case 115/88 *Reichert v Dresdner Bank* [1990] E.C.R. I–27; Case C–343/04 *Land Oberösterreich v CEZ a.s.* [2006] E.C.R. I–4557.

[170] Case 73/77 *Sanders v Van der Putte* [1977] E.C.R. 2383.

[171] See Case 288/82 *Duijnstee v Goderbauer* [1983] E.C.R. 3663; Case C–4/03 *Gesellschaft für Antriebstechnik mbH & Co KG v Lamellen und Kupplungsbau Beteiligungs KG* [2007] E.C.R. I–6509.

[172] See Case C–261/90 *Reichert v Dresdner Bank (No.2)*, above.

[173] Many of the cases on Brussels Convention, Art.17 (Regulation, Art.23) from Case 24/76 *Salotti v RÜWA* [1976] E.C.R. 1831 to (especially) Case 214/89 *Powell Duffryn Plc v Petereit* [1992] E.C.R. I–1745.

[174] See Case C–261/90 *Reichert v Dresdner Bank (No.2)*, above.

[175] Case C–43/77 *Industrial Diamond Supplies v Riva* [1977] E.C.R. 2175.

[176] Case C–167/08 *Draka NK Cables v Omnipol Ltd* [2009] E.C.R. I–3477.

[177] See Case 365/88 *Kongress Agentur Hagen GmbH v Zeehaghe BV* [1990] E.C.R. I–1845; Case 56/79 *Zelger v Salinitri* [1980] E.C.R. 89; Case 148/84 *Deutsche Genossenschaftsbank v Brasserie du Pêcheur SA* [1985] E.C.R. 1981; Case 145/86 *Hoffmann v Krieg* [1988] E.C.R. 645. But contrast Case 144/86 *Gubisch Maschinenfabrik AG v Palumbo* [1987] E.C.R. 4861.

[178] Case C–125/92 *Mulox IBC Ltd v Geels* [1993] E.C.R. I–4075; Case C–383/95 *Rutten v Cross Medical Ltd* [1997] E.C.R. I–1000, [1997] I.C.R. 715; Case C–295/95 *Farrell v Long* [1997] E.C.R. I–1683, [1997] Q.B. 842.

[179] Case 220/88 *Dumez France SA v Hessische Landesbank* [1990] E.C.R. I–49.

[180] Case 33/78 *Somafer SA v Saar-Ferngas AG* [1978] E.C.R. 2183.

[181] See, e.g. Case 189/87 *Kalfelis v Schröder* [1988] E.C.R. 5565; Case 32/88 *Six Constructions Ltd v Humbert* [1989] E.C.R. 341; Case 220/88 *Dumez France SA v Hessische Landesbank* [1990] E.C.R. I–49; Case C–89/91 *Shearson Lehman Hutton Inc v TVB* [1993] E.C.R. I–139;

particularly those rules (Art.22 on exclusive jurisdiction, and Art.23 on prorogation) which altogether exclude the jurisdiction of the court of the domicile.[182] Those provisions which safeguard the procedural rights of the defendant are to be interpreted liberally.[183]

The Lugano Convention: special provisions. It was necessary to make special provision for interpretation of the original Lugano Convention, because the European Court has no jurisdiction to interpret the Lugano Convention[184] and because the EFTA Member States would not have accepted a new régime under which an institution of the Communities on which they were not represented would rule, as a court of last resort, on the Lugano Convention. Nor was it desirable to create a new court for that purpose, since that would have created the possibility of conflicting rulings.[185]   **11–069**

Broadly following the equivalent Protocol to the original Lugano Convention, Protocol No.2 to the revised Lugano Convention provides that any court applying and interpreting the Convention shall pay due account to the principles laid down by any relevant decision concerning the relevant of the original Lugano Convention, the Brussels I Regulation and the Brussels Convention rendered by the States bound by the Convention and by the European Court.[186] The non-EU parties to the Lugano Convention are entitled to submit observations to the European Court on references concerning the Lugano Convention or the Brussels I Regulation.[187] By Art.3, the European Commission is to set up a system of exchange of information concerning relevant judgments delivered pursuant to the revised Lugano Convention as well as relevant judgments under the original Lugano Convention, the Brussels Convention and the Brussels I Regulation. No doubt the Jenard-Möller Report on the original Lugano Convention will remain an important aid to interpretation to the extent that it deals with matters which are still relevant to the new Brussels/Lugano regime. The Pocar Report on the revised Lugano Convention[188] is very full, and indicates that its purpose is to provide courts with a point of reference to clarify the meaning of the revised Lugano Convention and facilitate its uniform application.[189]   **11–070**

Case C–269/95 *Benincasa v Dentalkit Srl* [1997] E.C.R. I–3767; Case C–51/97 *Réunion européenne SA v Spliethoff's Bevrachtingskantoor BV* [1998] E.C.R. I–6511; Case C–98/06 *Freeport Plc v Arnoldsson* [2007] E.C.R. I–839.

[182] Case 24/76 *Salotti v RÜWA* [1976] E.C.R. 1831; Case 25/76 *Galeries Segoura Sprl v Bonakdarian* [1976] E.C.R. 1851; Case 73/77 *Sanders v Van der Putte* [1977] E.C.R. 2383; Case 115/88 *Reichert v Dresdner Bank* [1990] E.C.R. I–27; Case C–292/93 *Lieber v Göbel* [1994] E.C.R. I–2535; Case 8/98 *Dansommer v Götz* [2000] E.C.R. I–393.

[183] Case 150/80 *Elefanten Schuh GmbH v Jacqmain* [1981] E.C.R. 1671; Case 166/80 *Klomps v Michel* [1981] E.C.R. 1593. *cf.* Case 125/79 *Denilauler v SNC Couchet Frères* [1980] E.C.R. 1553.

[184] It is not possible to obtain a ruling on the Lugano Convention by the use of what is now Art.267, TFEU: *Agnew v Lansförsakringsbolagens AB* [1997] 4 All E.R. 937 (CA), affirmed on other aspects [2001] 1 A.C. 223. On interpretation of the Lugano Convention, see Tebbens (2001) 3 Yb. Priv. Int. L. 1.

[185] Jenard-Möller, para.110.

[186] Art.1.

[187] Art.2.

[188] para.11–020, n.26, above.

[189] para.3.

11–071   **Intra-United Kingdom cases.** Prior to the 1982 Act, service of process in English proceedings on individuals who were not in England, but were in Scotland or Northern Ireland, normally depended on whether the case was covered by a relevant head of jurisdiction under what was then RSC Order 11, r.1(1). Schedule 4 to the 1982 Act introduced rules for the assumption of jurisdiction in intra-United Kingdom cases, which were similar to, but not identical with, the provisions of the Brussels Convention. Since the coming into force of the Brussels I Regulation, a new Sch.4 has been introduced,[190] which is modelled upon, but is not identical with, the provisions of the Regulation. The differences will be mentioned at the appropriate points, but the main differences are these. First, Rule 3(a) (the equivalent of Art.5(1)) does not contain the partial definition of the place of performance.[191] Second, Sch.4 does not contain special provision for insurance contracts.[192] Third, Rule 4 (the equivalent of Art.22(2)) in relation to proceedings which have as their object a decision of a company organ is not exclusive.[193] Fourth, Rule 12 on jurisdiction agreements does not contain any formal requirements, and allows the chosen court to decline jurisdiction, by contrast with the Regulation.[194]

11–072   It should also be noted that in relation to intra-United Kingdom jurisdiction and Scottish rules of jurisdiction,[195] the 1982 Act provides[196] that, in determining any question as to the meaning or effect of any provision in Sch.4 and of any provision in Sch.8, regard is to be had to any relevant principles laid down by, and any relevant decision of, the European Court in connection with the Brussels Convention and the Brussels I Regulation, and to the reports on the Brussels Convention and the Accession Conventions. In *Kleinwort Benson Ltd v City of Glasgow DC*[197] the European Court held that it had no jurisdiction to interpret provisions in Sch.4 to the 1982 Act. Sch.4 took the Brussels Convention as a model only, and did not wholly reproduce its terms. The Court also referred to the fact that Sch.4 could be modified (pursuant to s.47 of the 1982 Act) to produce divergence from the corresponding provision of the Brussels Convention as interpreted by the European Court; in cases under the Brussels Convention, s.3 of the 1982 Act required the United Kingdom court to determine them in accordance with the principles laid down by, and any relevant decision of, the European Court; by contrast, in cases under Sch.4, s.16(3)(a) merely provided that "regard" should be had to such principles and decisions. Accordingly, any replies given by the European Court to the English court would be purely advisory, since the interpretation would not be binding on the English court.[198] To give such replies would have been to

---

[190] SI 2001/3929, Sch.2, para.4.
[191] Rule 35(2), below.
[192] Rule 35(13), below.
[193] Rule 35(17), below.
[194] Rule 39, below.
[195] See *Tehrani v Secretary of State for the Home Department (Scotland)* [2006] UKHL 47, [2007] 1 A.C. 521, at [37]–[44].
[196] ss.16(3), 20(5), as amended by the 2001 Order, Sch.2. See also SI 1997/2602 (Gibraltar).
[197] Case C–346/93 [1995] E.C.R. I–615, [1996] Q.B. 57.
[198] In *Kleinwort Benson Ltd v Glasgow City Council* [1999] 1 A.C. 153 Lord Goff of Chieveley and Lord Clyde adverted to, but did not decide, the question whether in a Sch.4 case it might not be possible to adopt a broader concept of contractual obligation under Art.5(1) (on which see paras 11–268 *et seq.*, below) than existed in European law.

alter the function of the Court under the 1971 Protocol, namely that of a court whose judgments were binding.

Method of challenge to jurisdiction. A defendant who has been served with process and wishes to challenge the jurisdiction of the English court should file an acknowledgment of service and apply, within 14 days (or 28 days in the Commercial Court) after filing an acknowledgment of service, for service to be set aside or other appropriate relief.[199] If the defendant files an acknowledgment of service, and does not make an application within the specified period, he is to be treated as having accepted that the court has jurisdiction to try the claim.[200] Where the defendant does not challenge the *existence* of jurisdiction but wishes to persuade the court not to exercise it, e.g. because, in a case not covered by the Regulation or the Lugano Convention, England is not the *forum conveniens* or there is an agreement between the parties conferring jurisdiction on the courts of another country,[201] he should apply under Pt 11 of the Civil Procedure Rules for a stay of the English proceedings and not for process to be set aside,[202] as an application to stay proceedings is not a challenge to the jurisdiction of the court.[203]   **11–073**

The Civil Procedure Rules provide that, upon the failure of an application for a declaration that the court has no jurisdiction or that its jurisdiction should not be exercised, the acknowledgment of service will cease to have effect and the defendant has a further period in which to file a further acknowledgment of service; and if the further acknowledgment of service is filed the defendant is treated as having accepted that the court has jurisdiction to try the claim.[204]   **11–074**

Examination by the court of its jurisdiction. Normally an English court is not required of its own motion to consider whether it has jurisdiction, although where a plaintiff seeks permission to serve a defendant out of the jurisdiction under Rule 34, i.e. CPR, r.6.36, and Practice Direction 6B, para.3.1, he has to satisfy the court that England is the proper place in which to bring the claim.[205] But there are some cases where the court itself must, as a result of express provisions of the Regulation or the Convention, declare of   **11–075**

---

[199] CPR, rr.11(4) and 58.7(2). It is not necessary that service of the application be made within the period: *Carmel Exporters (Sales) Ltd v Sealand Services Ltd* [1981] 1 W.L.R. 1068; *Broken Hill Pty Co Ltd v Xenakis* [1982] 2 Lloyd's Rep. 304 (decided under the RSC). The court has power to order disclosure of documents on the application, but the power will be exercised rarely: *Canada Trust Co v Stolzenberg* [1995] 1 W.L.R. 1582 (CA); *Rome v Punjab National Bank (No.1)* [1989] 2 Lloyd's Rep. 424; *Bank of Credit and Commerce International SA v Al-Kaylani* [1999] I.L.Pr. 278. See below, para.11–128, for the effect of this procedure.

[200] CPR, r.11(5). Permission may be given to make the application after the period has expired: *Sawyer v Atari Interactive Inc* [2005] EWHC 2351 (Ch.), [2006] I.L.Pr. 129 (applying authorities on earlier version of the rule).

[201] See Rules 38 and 39.

[202] See *The Fehmarn* [1958] 1 W.L.R. 159, 161 (CA); *The Eleftheria* [1970] P. 94, 98.

[203] *Bankers Trust Co v Galadari* [1986] 2 Lloyd's Rep. 446, 449 (CA). But see *The Sydney Express* [1988] 2 Lloyd's Rep. 257.

[204] CPR, r.11(7). But even if the defendant does not file the further acknowledgment of service and takes no further part, any resulting default judgment will be enforceable in other Member States or Convention States: see below, paras 14–222; 14–229.

[205] CPR, r.6.37(3).

its own motion that it has no jurisdiction. The effect of Arts 25 and 26[206] is that the English court must do so in the following two cases: first, where the claim is principally concerned with a matter over which the courts of another Member (or Convention) State have exclusive jurisdiction by virtue of Art.22; secondly, where the defendant is domiciled in another Member State or Convention State and does not enter an appearance, and the English court does not have jurisdiction under the Regulation or the Convention.[207]

11–076   If the defendant fails to give notice of intention to defend, a default judgment may not be entered unless it is shown that the defendant was properly served.[208] The Civil Procedure Rules give effect to these require-ments by: (a) requiring a claimant who intends to serve a claim form out of the jurisdiction to file with the claim form a notice containing a statement of the grounds on which the claimant is entitled to serve the claim form out of the jurisdiction, and to serve the notice with the claim form;[209] (b) requiring, before judgment in default of notice of filing of acknowledgment of service is entered on a claim form served out of the jurisdiction without permission or served within the jurisdiction on a defendant domiciled in another part of the United Kingdom or in a Member State or Convention State, an application supported by evidence that the claim is one which the court has power to hear and decide, that no other court has exclusive jurisdiction under the 1982 Act or the Lugano Convention or the Regulation, and that the claim has been properly served in accordance with Art.20 of Sch.1 to the 1982 Act, para.15 of Sch.4 to the 1982 Act, or Art.26 of the Regulation or the Convention.[210]

2. DOMICILE

11R–077   **RULE 30—(1) For the purposes of Rules 34 to 37 the domicile of an individual is determined as follows:**
  (a) **an individual is domiciled in the United Kingdom (or a particular part of the United Kingdom) if he is resident in, and the nature and circumstances of his residence indicate that he has a sub-stantial connection with, the United Kingdom (or that part);[211]**
  (b) **an individual is domiciled in a particular place in the United Kingdom if he is domiciled in the part of the United Kingdom in which that place is situated and is resident in that place;[212]**
  (c) **an individual who is not domiciled in the United Kingdom in accordance with paragraph (a) of this clause is domiciled in**

---

[206] These provisions apply, in modified form, in intra-UK cases. See also Case 288/82 *Duijnstee v Goderbauer* [1983] E.C.R. 3663; *Coin Controls Ltd v Suzo International (UK) Ltd* [1999] Ch. 33.

[207] Art.26(1). This includes jurisdiction under an international convention: Case C–148/03 *Nürnberger Allgemeine Versicherungs AG v Portbridge Transport International BV* [2004] E.C.R. I–1023, [2005] 1 Lloyd's Rep. 592.

[208] *cf.* Art.26(2); *Noirhomme v Walklate* [1992] 1 Lloyd's Rep. 427.

[209] CPR, r.6.34(1); CPR 6PDB, para. 2.1; CPR PD7A, para.3.5; practice form N510.

[210] CPR, r.12.10(b)(i), (ii), PD12, para.4.3.

[211] SI 2001/3929, Sch.1, para.9(2), (3) (Brussels I Regulation); 1982 Act, s.41A(2), (3) (Lugano Convention).

[212] SI 2001/3929, Sch.1, para.9(4) (Regulation); 1982 Act, s.41A(4) (Lugano Convention).

another Member State or Convention State if by the law of that State he is domiciled in that State;[213]

(d) an individual is domiciled in a State other than a Member State or Convention State if he is resident in, and the nature and circumstances of his residence indicate that he has a substantial connection with, that State.[214]

(2) For the purposes of jurisdiction under the Brussels I Regulation and the Lugano Convention, a company or other legal person or association of natural or legal persons is domiciled in the place where it has its (a) statutory seat, or (b) central administration, or (c) principal place of business.[215] In this clause "statutory seat" means the registered office or, where there is no such office anywhere, the place under the law of which the formation took place.[216]

(3) For the purposes of intra-United Kingdom jurisdiction under Schedule 4 to the 1982 Act, a corporation or association is domiciled at its seat,[217] which for those purposes[218] shall be determined as follows:

(a) a corporation or association has its seat in the United Kingdom if either (i) it was incorporated under the law of a part of the United Kingdom or (ii) its central management and control is exercised in the United Kingdom;[219]

(b) a corporation or association has its seat in a particular part of the United Kingdom (or in a particular place in the United Kingdom) if it has its seat in the United Kingdom and (i) it has its registered office or other official address in that part (or that place), or (ii) its central management and control is exercised in that part (or that place), or (iii) it has a place of business in that part (or that place);[220]

(c) a corporation or association has its seat in a State other than the United Kingdom if (i) it was incorporated under the law of that State and has its registered office or other official address there or (ii) its central management and control is exercised in that State, provided that it shall not be regarded as having its seat in a Member State or Convention State if by the law of that State it does not have its seat there.[221]

---

[213] Regulation, Art.59(2); Lugano Convention, Art.59(2).

[214] SI 2001/3929, Sch.1, para.9(7) (Regulation); 1982 Act, s.41A(7) (Lugano Convention).

[215] Regulation, Art.60(1); Lugano Convention, Art.60(1). On the meaning of principal place of business see *King v Crown Energy Trading AG* [2003] EWHC 163 (Comm.), [2003] I.L.Pr. 489.

[216] Regulation, Art.60(2); Lugano Convention, Art.60(2). For the special rules (in connection with insurance and consumer contracts and employment contracts) relating to branches of persons who would otherwise be regarded as domiciled outside the UK see SI 2001/3929, para.11 (Brussels I Regulation); 1982 Act, s.44A (Lugano Convention) and below, paras 11–340; 11–364; 11–371.

[217] s.42(1).

[218] For the seat of a corporation for the purposes of Art.22(2) and 1982 Act, Sch.4, Rule 11 (exclusive jurisdiction) see ss.43 and 43A and SI 2001/3929, para.10, and below, para.11–384.

[219] s.42(3).

[220] s.42(4), (5).

[221] s.42(6), (7).

(4) For the purposes of jurisdiction under Rule 34, a company is domiciled in England if it has its registered office in England or its central management and control is exercised in that part.[222]

COMMENT

11–078   The concept of domicile under the Brussels I Regulation, the Lugano Convention and the 1982 Act is relevant in several contexts, to determine whether a person is domiciled in one of the Member States or Convention States;[223] whether a person is domiciled outside the Member States or Convention States;[224] whether a person is domiciled outside a particular Member State or Convention State;[225] whether a person is domiciled in a particular place;[226] whether a person is domiciled in a part of the United Kingdom, and, if so, which part.[227]

11–079   "Domicile" was not defined in the Brussels Convention. This was so because among other reasons it was thought that a new uniform definition of domicile properly belonged in a convention on uniform law rather than in a jurisdiction and judgments convention.[228] In the original Brussels Convention States the domicile of an individual was close to the notion of habitual residence, although its meaning differed somewhat as between the States.[229] In the case of corporations, the Brussels Convention assimilated domicile to the "seat", but the original Brussels Convention States had differing approaches to the determination of the seat, some preferring the "siège réel" or effective seat, and others the "siège statutaire" or law of incorporation. Consequently the Brussels Convention limited itself to providing rules regulating what law would determine the domicile of an individual or corporation for the purposes of the Convention, and the original Lugano Convention contained identical provisions.

The concept of "seat" of a corporation has no precise equivalent in the law of the United Kingdom (where the domicile of a corporation is the place of its incorporation)[230] and it was necessary to provide expressly in the 1982 Act for the determination of the domicile of corporations and associations. This was effected in s.42, which provided for the purposes of the Brussels Convention that a corporation or association had its seat in the United Kingdom if and only if (a) it was incorporated or formed under the law of a part of the United Kingdom and had its registered office or some other official address in the

---

[222] This is the effect of CPR, r.6.31(i).

[223] Arts 2(1), 3, 4(2), 5, 6, 9(1), 12, 13(3), 15(1), 16(1), 17, 23(1), 26(1), 43(5).

[224] Arts 4(1), 9(2), 13(4), 23(3).

[225] Art.51.

[226] Arts 5(2), 6(1), 39(2).

[227] 1982 Act, Sch.4. See, e.g. *Davenport v Corinthian Motor Policies at Lloyd's*, 1991 S.L.T. 774.

[228] Jenard, pp.15–16.

[229] Schlosser, para.73. The Regulation and Convention concepts of domicile are adopted for non-Convention cases under CPR, r.6.36, and PD6B, para.3.1: see CPR, r.6.31(i).

[230] See below, Rule 173.

404

United Kingdom or (b) its central management and control was exercised in the United Kingdom.[231]

The Regulation and the Convention contain, in Art.59, the same provision on the domicile of individuals as the Brussels Convention. But Art.60 of the Regulation (and the Lugano Convention) introduces a new autonomous rule for the ascertainment of the domicile of companies, etc. Such an entity is domiciled at the place where it has its (a) statutory seat, or (b) central administration, or (c) principal place of business. Article 60(2) provides that for the purposes of the United Kingdom and Ireland "statutory seat" means the registered office, or, where there is no such office anywhere, the place of incorporation or, where there is no such place anywhere, the place under the law of which the formation took place.

Clause (1) of the Rule. *Individuals.* Article 59 of the Regulation (and the Convention) provides (as does the corresponding Art.52 of the Brussels and the original Lugano Conventions) that in order to determine whether a party is domiciled in the Member or Convention State whose courts are seised of the matter, the court is to apply its internal law. If a party is not domiciled in the State whose courts are seised of the matter, then, in order to determine whether the party is domiciled in another Member or Convention State, the court is to apply the law of that other State. **11–080**

The application of the domicile rule in the Brussels Convention to the common law of domicile[232] in the United Kingdom as it stood prior to the 1982 Act would have produced a serious imbalance, because the traditional concept of domicile with its emphasis on permanent home would have excluded many persons settled, but not domiciled, in the United Kingdom from the provisions of the Brussels Convention, and included many persons settled outside, but domiciled within, the United Kingdom. Accordingly, it was agreed in the negotiations for accession to the Brussels Convention that the United Kingdom (and the Republic of Ireland) would include in their legislation for the purposes of the Convention a definition of domicile which would reflect more the concept of domicile as understood in the original Contracting States. This was effected in the 1982 Act by a definition of domicile of individuals based on a combination of residence in, and substantial connection with, the United Kingdom. Identical provisions were introduced for the purposes of the Brussels I Regulation and the revised Lugano Convention.[233] **11–081**

The main differences between this concept of domicile and the concept at common law are that there is no question of the need for a "permanent home" under the jurisdictional scheme; the concept of domicile of origin has no role under the jurisdictional scheme; under the jurisdictional scheme it will be possible for a person to have more than one domicile, whereas at common law only one domicile is possible. At common law the question where a person is domiciled depends on English law as the *lex fori*, whereas under the Regulation/Convention scheme the United Kingdom court must apply the law of **11–082**

---

[231] 1982 Act, s.42(2). On the meaning of "central management and control" see below, para.30–006.

[232] See above, Ch.6.

[233] SI 2001/3929, Sch.1, para.9; 1982 Act, s.41A.

another Member State or Convention State to determine whether a party is domiciled in that State.

11–083   The first principle in Art.59 of the Regulation and the Convention is that in order to determine whether an individual is domiciled in the Member State or Convention State whose courts are seised of the matter, the court is to apply its internal law.[234] When a court in the United Kingdom is the court seised, the relevant internal law is that an individual is domiciled in the United Kingdom if and only if he is resident in the United Kingdom and the nature and circumstances of his residence indicate that he has a substantial connection with the United Kingdom.[235] In the case of an individual who is resident in the United Kingdom and has been so for the last three months or more, the requirement of substantial connection is presumed to be fulfilled unless the contrary is proved.[236] "Residence" is not defined but it indicates some degree of permanence or continuity.[237]

11–084   If a party is not domiciled in the State whose courts are seised of the matter, then, in order to determine whether the party is domiciled in another Member State or Convention State, the court is to apply the law of that other State.[238] This provision did not require specific treatment in the United Kingdom legislation because under the Regulation and the Lugano Convention (which are directly applicable) the United Kingdom court will apply the law of the relevant Member State or Convention State. The Regulation and the Convention lay down no rules for determining the domicile of a person who is not domiciled in a Member State or Convention State. An individual is domiciled in a State other than a Member State or a Convention State if and only if he is resident in that State and the nature and circumstances of his residence indicate that he has a substantial connection with that State.[239]

11–085   It is frequently necessary to determine the "place" of an individual's domicile, or the part of the United Kingdom in which he is domiciled. An individual is domiciled in a particular place in the United Kingdom if, and only if, he is (a) domiciled in the part of the United Kingdom in which that place is situated; and (b) resident in that place.[240] He is domiciled in a

---

[234] Art.59(1).

[235] SI 2001/3929, Sch.1, para.9(2); 1982 Act, s.41A(2).

[236] SI 2001/3929, Sch.1, para.9(6); 1982 Act, s.41A(6). The critical date for the determination of domicile is the date of issue of proceedings: *Canada Trust Co v Stolzenberg (No.2)* [2000] UKHL 51, [2002] 1 A.C. 1. Consequently, where proceedings were issued against a defendant domiciled in England at the date of issue, other defendants could be added under Art.6(1) (in that case, of the original Lugano Convention) even if, by the time the process was served on the additional defendants, that person was no longer domiciled in England. *cf. Petrotrade Inc v Smith* [1998] 2 All E.R. 346 (enforced presence as a result of bail conditions on arrest not residence).

[237] *Bank of Dubai Ltd v Abbas* [1997] I.L.Pr. 308 (CA); *Royal & Sun Alliance Insurance Plc v MK Digital FZE (Cyprus) Ltd* [2006] EWCA Civ 629, [2006] 2 Lloyd's Rep. 110; *High Tech International AG v Deripaska* [2006] EWHC 3276 (QB), [2007] E.M.L.R. 15; *Cherney v Deripaska* [2007] EWHC 965 (Comm.), [2007] 2 All E.R. (Comm.) 785; *OJSC Oil Company Yugraneft v Abramovich* [2008] EWHC (Comm.) 2613.

[238] Brussels I Regulation, Art.59(2); Lugano Convention, Art.59(2).

[239] SI 2001/3929, Sch.1, para.9(7); 1982 Act, s.41A(7). The presumption based on three months' residence does not apply to this case.

[240] SI 2001/3929, Sch.1, para.9(4); 1982 Act, s.41A(4).

particular part of the United Kingdom if, and only if, (a) he is resident in that part; and (b) the nature and circumstances of his residence indicate that he has a substantial connection with that part,[241] but if he is domiciled in the United Kingdom and has no substantial connection with any particular part, he is to be treated as domiciled in the part of the United Kingdom in which he is resident.[242] The latter provision deals with the case where a person has ties with the United Kingdom but does not stay long at any place.

It will be apparent from the above that a person may be domiciled in more **11–086** than one Member State or Convention State. The United Kingdom legislation seeks to answer the questions (a) whether an individual is domiciled in the United Kingdom and (b) whether an individual is domiciled in a State other than a Member State or a Convention State. It does not answer the question whether he is domiciled in another Member State or Convention State, since that question depends, by Art.59(2) of the Regulation and the Convention, on the law of that other State.

This may be illustrated by the case of a person, who is from New York by **11–087** origin, and who lives both in Paris and London. He is on a visit to New York. May he be sued in a contract dispute in England (a) on the basis of service on him out of the jurisdiction under Rule 34, clause (4), i.e. CPR, PD6B, para.3.1(6), on the theory that the contract is governed by English law,[243] or (b) on the basis of the Regulation rules by virtue of his domicile in the United Kingdom?[244] If he is domiciled in a Member State, CPR, PD6B, para.3.1(6) cannot be applied under the Regulation. The English court will have first to decide whether he is domiciled in the United Kingdom; this will turn on whether he is resident in the United Kingdom and whether the nature and circumstances of his residence indicate that he has a substantial connection with the United Kingdom and, in particular, with England (which will be presumed in each case from three months' residence). If he is so domiciled, then he may be sued in England on the basis of the Brussels I Regulation and intra-United Kingdom rules. If he is not so domiciled, then he may object to the jurisdiction on the basis that he is domiciled in France and must be sued there: in that case the court will apply French law to determine his domicile. If he is not domiciled in the United Kingdom or France, then the English court may exercise jurisdiction. But if he is domiciled in the United Kingdom under the 2001 Order,[245] it will be no answer for him to say that he is also domiciled in France under French law, because the English court will be able to exercise jurisdiction unless a French court is first seised.[246]

Clauses (2), (3), and (4) of the Rule. Corporations and associations. The **11–088** Brussels I Regulation and the Lugano Convention do not indicate what corporate bodies are included within the expression "or other legal person or

---

[241] SI 2001/3929, Sch.1, para.9(3); 1982 Act, s.41A(3).
[242] SI 2001/3929, Sch.1, para.9(5); 1982 Act, s.41A(5).
[243] See below, Rule 34(6).
[244] See below, Rule 35(1).
[245] SI 2001/3929, Sch.1, para.9.
[246] Arts 27 and 28: see below, Rule 38(4).

association of natural or legal persons." There can be little doubt that the expression should be given an autonomous interpretation.

11–089   Schlosser[247] suggests that the similar expression in what is now Art.22(2) of the Regulation and the Convention applies to partnerships established under United Kingdom law, and the other language versions of the Regulation and the Convention use expressions which are apt to include partnerships. In *Phillips v Symes*[248] it was held that the expression included English partnerships. In Scotland it was assumed that a Lloyd's syndicate was an association for this purpose.[249] There is no doubt that the new form of legal entity (the LLP) established by the Limited Liability Partnerships Act 2000 is an association for this purpose. The 2000 Act provides[250] that regulations may make provision about "overseas limited liability partnerships", and such a partnership is defined as a body incorporated or otherwise established outside the United Kingdom and having such connection with the United Kingdom and such other features, as regulations may prescribe.[251] The Rules in this chapter apply to LLPs.[252]

11–090   The autonomous rule for the ascertainment of the domicile of companies, etc. in Art.60 of the Regulation and the Convention is that such an entity is domiciled at the place where it has (a) its statutory seat, or (b) its central administration, or (c) its principal place of business. Article 60(2) provides that for the purposes of the United Kingdom and Ireland "statutory seat" means the registered office, or, where there is no such office anywhere, the place of incorporation or, where there is no such place anywhere, the place under the law of which the formation took place. Principal "place" of business must connote some degree of permanence.[253]

11–091   Thus a Panamanian company with its principal place of business in Switzerland and its central administration in the United Kingdom will be domiciled in all three countries. It was held that a Bermudian holding company, which was resident for tax purposes in Canada because its central management and control was in Canada, was nevertheless arguably domiciled in the United Kingdom because the entirety of the administration took place in London, those members of the Board who undertook management responsibilities were in London, and management instructions were given from London.[254]

---

[247] para.162.

[248] [2002] 1 W.L.R. 853. *cf.* 1982 Act, s.50 (Scottish partnerships).

[249] *Davenport v Corinthian Motor Policies at Lloyd's*, 1991 S.L.T. 774. A Lloyd's syndicate is, in law, a body of persons each of whom accepts personal liability to the extent of his "line" but who is not responsible for any other members of the syndicate.

[250] s.15.

[251] s.14(3). See generally *Palmer's Limited Liability Partnership Law* (2nd ed. Morse *et al.* 2011), paras A1–61—A1–65.

[252] For provisions on service see SI 2009/1804, reg.75, and CPR, r.6.9. See *Palmer's Limited Liability Partnership Law*, above, para.A1–104.

[253] *cf. The Theodohos* [1977] 2 Lloyd's Rep. 428; *South India Shipping Corp Ltd v Export-Import bank of Korea* [1985] 1 W.L.R. 858 (CA).

[254] *889457 Alberta Inc v Katanga Mining Ltd* [2008] EWHC 2679 (Comm.), [2009] 1 B.C.L.C. 189. See also *Ministry of Defence and Support of the Armed Forces of Iran v FAZ Aviation Ltd* [2007] EWHC 1042 (Comm.), [2007] I.L.Pr. 538; *Masri v Consolidated Contractors International (UK) Ltd* [2008] EWCA Civ 303, [2009] Q.B. 450.

But that provision does not apply to the determination of the seat for the   **11–092**
purposes of Art.22(2),[255] which assigns exclusive jurisdiction in certain disputes relating to companies, etc. to the State where the seat is situated. For the
purposes of the determination of the seat under that provision, Art.22(2)
provides that the court is to apply its rules of private international law. In the
United Kingdom the relevant rule[256] is that the entity has its seat in the United
Kingdom if it was incorporated or formed under the law of a part of the United
Kingdom, or its central management and control is exercised in the
United Kingdom; and it has its seat in a Member State or Convention State
other than the United Kingdom if it was incorporated or formed under the law
of that State, or its central management and control[257] is exercised in that
State; but it is not to be regarded as having its seat in a Member State or
Convention State other than the United Kingdom if it has its seat in the United
Kingdom, or if it is shown that the courts of that other State would not regard
it for the purposes of Art.22(2) as having its seat there.

The Companies Act 2006 makes provision for foreign companies with   **11–093**
branches or places of business in Great Britain to file with the Registrar of
Companies the name and address of a person authorised to accept process,[258]
and under the Civil Procedure Rules service may be effected at any place of
business of the company within the jurisdiction.[259] These provisions are
considered below in the context of service, and of the question whether (at
least in cases not covered by the Regulation or the Lugano Convention) there
must be a relationship between the claim and the branch or place of business.[260] But under the Regulation/Convention scheme, such a company is not
domiciled in the Untied Kingdom unless its central administration or principal
place of business is situated there. Thus for a French company to be capable
of being sued in England or Scotland one of the other heads of jurisdiction
will have to be applicable, e.g. Art.5(5) of the Regulation, which confers
jurisdiction, in relation to disputes arising out of the operations of a branch, on
the courts of the place of the branch.

Domicile of companies for the purposes of intra-United Kingdom jurisdic-   **11–094**
tion. Section 42 of the 1982 Act, which defines the domicile of companies for
the purposes of the 1982 Act, applies for the purposes of Sch.4. The effect is
that determination of the domicile of companies depends on the provisions of
s.42 of the 1982 Act rather than the somewhat different provisions of Art.60
of the Regulation and the Convention.[261]

Section 42 of the 1982 Act provides that a corporation or association has its   **11–095**
seat in the United Kingdom if and only if (a) it was incorporated or formed
under the law of a part of the United Kingdom and has its registered office or

---

[255] See below, para.11–384.
[256] SI 2001/3929, Sch.1, para.10; 1982 Act, s.43A.
[257] On the meaning of "central management and control" see para.30–006.
[258] Companies Act 2006, ss.1139–1142.
[259] CPR, r.6.9.
[260] See below, para.11–117.
[261] But it does not apply for the purposes of Rules 4 and 11(b) (proceedings contemplated by
Regulation, Art.22(5)): s.42(2).

some other official address in the United Kingdom or (b) its central management and control is exercised in the United Kingdom.[262]

11–096   *Domicile of companies for the purposes of Rule 34.* Rule 34 deals with those cases in which permission to serve proceedings out of the jurisdiction may be given under CPR, r.6.36 and PD6B, para.3.1. Several of those provisions may involve an issue of domicile: para.3.1(1) (jurisdiction based on the domicile of the defendant: clause (1) of Rule 34); para.3.1(13) (administration of person domiciled in England: clause (13)); and para.3.1(17) (revenue claims against a defendant domiciled in England: clause (17)). CPR, r.6.31(i) provides that domicile is to be determined (i) in relation to a Convention territory, in accordance with ss.41–46 of the 1982 Act; and (ii) in relation to a Member State, in accordance with the Brussels I Regulation and the Civil Jurisdiction and Judgments Order 2001, Sch.1, paras 9–12. The effect is to apply the Regulation/Convention rules, including the autonomous definition for companies.[263]

11–097   *Additional provisions relating to insurance contracts, consumer contracts and employment contracts.* The Regulation and the Convention[264] provide that, in the case of insurance and consumer contracts, a person who is not domiciled in a Member State or Convention State is deemed to be domiciled in such a State in which it has a branch in connection with disputes arising out of the operations of that branch. They contain similar provisions in relation to the domicile of employers in employment contract disputes.[265] Although these provisions apply both to individuals and companies they are likely to be of practical relevance mainly in relation to corporate defendants.

11–098   The 2001 Order[266] and s.44A of the 1982 Act confirm that for the purposes of these provisions, a person who is deemed for the purposes of the Regulation and the Convention to be domiciled in the United Kingdom, shall be treated as so domiciled, and as domiciled in the part of the United Kingdom in which the branch, agency or establishment in question is situated.

11–099   **Trusts.** Article 60(3) of the Regulation and the Convention (which was added to the Brussels Convention by the 1978 Accession Convention) provides that in order to determine whether a trust is domiciled in the Member State (or Convention State) whose courts are seised of the matter[267] the court shall apply its rules of private international law. The relevant rules of private international law in the United Kingdom are that a trust is domiciled in the United Kingdom if and only if it is domiciled in a part of the United Kingdom. It is domiciled in a part of the United Kingdom if and only if the system of

---

[262] 1982 Act, s.42(2).

[263] It is not clear why there is a reference to the 2001 Order, Sch.1, para.10, since this deals with the determination of the seat for the purposes of Art.22.

[264] Arts 9(2) and 15(2).

[265] Art.18(2).

[266] SI 2001/3929, Sch.1, para.11.

[267] See Art.5(6), below, para.11–304.

law of that part is the system of law with which the trust has its closest and most real connection.[268]

1. X, an individual, has lived at all material times in London. For the purposes of the Brussels I Regulation and the Lugano Convention the State in which he is domiciled is the United Kingdom and the part of the United Kingdom in which he is domiciled is England.[269]

2. X, an individual, is staying in London but his home and his work are in Edinburgh. For the purposes of the Regulations and the Convention the State in which he is domiciled is the United Kingdom and the part of the United Kingdom in which he is domiciled is Scotland.[270]

3. X, an individual, has residences both in New York and Geneva. He has a substantial connection with New York, and by Swiss law he is domiciled in Switzerland. X is domiciled both in New York and in Switzerland.[271]

4. X Ltd, a company incorporated under the Companies Act 2006, has its registered office in London, and its central administration is in Bermuda. Its seat (and therefore its domicile) is in the United Kingdom (and the part of the United Kingdom in which it has its seat and domicile is England) and also in Bermuda.[272]

5. X Ltd, a company incorporated under the Companies Act 2006, has its registered office in Edinburgh, its principal place of business in London and a branch in Belfast. Its seat (and domicile) is in the United Kingdom, and also in Scotland, England and Northern Ireland.[273]

6. X NV, a Dutch company, has its statutory seat in Rotterdam, and its central administration is in London. Its statutory seat (and domicile) is in the Netherlands and also in the United Kingdom (and the part of the United Kingdom in which it has its seat and domicile is England).[274]

7. X Ltd, a Panamanian company, has German directors and its central administration is in Germany. It has its statutory seat (and domicile) in Panama, and is also domiciled in Germany.[275]

8. X Inc, a New York insurance company, has a branch in London, but its central administration and principal place of business is in New York. It has its statutory seat (and its domicile) in New York,[276] except that for the purposes of the insurance provisions of the Regulation it is deemed to be domiciled in the United Kingdom (and in England) in relation to disputes arising out of the operations of the branch.[277]

11–100

3. RULES RELATING TO JURISDICTION

A. *Where the Brussels I Regulation and the Lugano Convention do not apply or where the defendant is not domiciled in the United Kingdom or any part thereof or in any other State which is a Member State or a Convention State*

RULE 31—The court has jurisdiction, subject to Rules 36 and 37 (exclusive jurisdiction under the Brussels I Regulation and the Lugano Convention) and Rules 60 and 61 (international conventions) to entertain a claim

11R–101

---

[268] SI 2001/3929, Sch.1, para.12; 1982 Act, s.45(3).

[269] SI 2001/3929, Sch.1, paras 9(2),(3); s.41A(2), (3).

[270] *ibid.*

[271] 1982 Act, s.41(7); Lugano Convention, Art.59(2).

[272] 1982 Act, s.42(3), (4), (6).

[273] ss.42(3)(a). If the Regulation rules had been applied, X Ltd would not be domiciled in Northern Ireland.

[274] Regulation, Art.60(1); 1982 Act, s.42(4).

[275] Regulation, Art.60(1); *cf. The Deichland* [1990] 1 Q.B. 361 (CA).

[276] 1982 Act, s.42(6).

[277] SI 2001/3929, Sch.1, para.11; 1982 Act, s.44A, see below, para.11–340.

in personam **against a defendant (other than a person domiciled or deemed to be domiciled in another Member State or in a Convention State[278] or in Scotland or Northern Ireland) who is present in England[279] and duly served there with process.**

COMMENT

11–102   As has been seen above, the foundation of jurisdiction *in personam* is service of process. Until the 1982 Act came into force the English court, subject to certain exceptions deriving from rules contained in international conventions which are referred to in Rule 60 below, had jurisdiction over any person who could be served with process in England even if he was only temporarily present in England. Following the incorporation of the Brussels Convention by the 1982 Act the position became significantly different, and this head of jurisdiction was branded as an "exorbitant jurisdiction."[280] Article 3(2) of the Brussels Convention provided that the rule of English law which enables jurisdiction to be founded on service on the defendant during his temporary presence may not be applied as against any person domiciled in a Contracting State other than the United Kingdom. The Brussels I Regulation and the Lugano Convention contain identical provisions. The effect of the provisions relating to jurisdiction within the United Kingdom in Sch.4 to the 1982 Act is that, in general, jurisdiction based on mere presence cannot be applied as regards defendants domiciled in Scotland and Northern Ireland.

11–103   It should be noted, however, that where a case falls outside the scope of the Regulation and the Convention[281] this Rule will apply even if the defendant is domiciled in a Member State or Convention State or in another part of the United Kingdom. But, as regards cases within the scope of the Regulation or the Convention, it will apply only to defendants not domiciled in any of the Member States or Convention States. Art.4[282] of each of the Regulation and the Convention provides that where the defendant is not domiciled in a Member State (or Convention State), the jurisdiction of the courts of the Member State or Convention State shall be determined by the law of that State. This includes its "exorbitant" rules of jurisdiction.

11–104   But Art.4 of the Regulation[283] and the Convention is expressly subject to Art.22, which provides that in five circumstances the courts of specified Member States or Convention States shall have exclusive jurisdiction

---

[278] For Member States and Convention States see above, paras 11–013, 11–020.

[279] For this purpose a person on board a ship of the Royal Navy, wherever situate, is considered as being in England, and CPR, r.6.36 and PD6B, para.3.1, i.e. Rule 34, is inapplicable to him: *Seagrove v Parks* [1891] 1 Q.B. 551. For the continuing requirement of presence within the jurisdiction, see para.11–106, below.

[280] See Schlosser, para.86.

[281] As to which see above, paras 11–029 *et seq.*

[282] On which see *Re Harrods (Buenos Aires) Ltd* [1992] Ch. 72, 100 (CA); *Balkanbank v Taher (No.2)* [1995] 1 W.L.R. 1067, 1074 (CA); *Haji-Ioannou v Frangos* [1999] 2 Lloyd's Rep. 337 (CA).

[283] Art.4 is also subject to Art.23, as to which see para.11–105.

"regardless of domicile". These cases are discussed in connection with Rules 36[284] and 131[285] and it is sufficient at this point to indicate that the English court will not have jurisdiction, even as regards a non-domiciliary of any Member State or Convention State,[286] in the following cases: (1) in proceedings which have as their object rights *in rem* in, or tenancies of, immovable property, where the property is situated in another Member State or Convention State; (2) in proceedings which have as their object the validity of the constitution, the nullity or the dissolution of companies or other legal persons or associations of natural or legal persons, or the validity of the decisions of their organs,[287] where the company, legal person or association has its seat in another Member State or Convention State; (3) in proceedings which have as their object the validity of entries in public registers, where the register is kept in another Member State or Convention State; (4) in proceedings concerned with the registration or validity of patents, trade marks, designs or other similar rights required to be deposited, where the deposit or registration has been applied for or taken place (or deemed to have taken place) in another Member State or Convention State; (5) in proceedings concerned with the enforcement of judgments, where the judgment has been or is to be enforced in another Member State or Convention State.

Article 23 of the Regulation (and of the Convention) contains rules relating to clauses conferring jurisdiction on the courts of a Member State or Convention State, which are discussed in detail below.[288] Where they apply the chosen court or courts will have exclusive jurisdiction.[289] If one at least of the parties is domiciled in a Member State or Convention State, the English court will not have jurisdiction under this Rule if the parties have validly conferred exclusive jurisdiction[290] on the courts of another Member State or Convention State. If neither of the parties is domiciled in a Member State or Convention State and the parties have conferred jurisdiction on the courts of a Member State or Convention State other than the United Kingdom the English court may not exercise jurisdiction unless the chosen court has declined jurisdiction.[291]   **11–105**

Rule 31 is also subject to Rules 60 and 61, which deal with jurisdiction under international conventions incorporated by statute. Under these conventions presence is not a sufficient basis of jurisdiction.

The jurisdiction under this Rule remains operative even if the defendant leaves the country, so far as the original claim is concerned, but the claimant cannot amend by adding a new claim unless permission to serve the amended claim form out of the jurisdiction is obtainable.[292]   **11–106**

---

[284] See below, para.11R–408.
[285] See below, para.23R–022.
[286] Even if he purports to submit to the jurisdiction: Art.24.
[287] Art.22(2).
[288] See below, Rule 39.
[289] Art.23(1) also makes provision for non-exclusive jurisdiction agreements.
[290] See Rule 39(3), below.
[291] In such a case it may be that the English court would initially assume jurisdiction under this Rule, subject to an application for a stay under Rule 38.
[292] See para.11–149, below; Restatement, s.26.

11–107   The application of this Rule differs according as to whether the defendant is an individual, a partnership firm, or a corporation.

11–108   *Individuals.* Any individual who is present in England is liable to be served with process in proceedings *in personam*, however short may be the period for which he is present in England. Thus an American who has flown from New York to London and intends to leave on the same day is liable to be served with process in proceedings brought to recover a debt due to the claimant incurred by the American and payable in New York. No doubt in some cases the exercise of such a jurisdiction may be exorbitant,[293] and it has been contended that process cannot rightly be served on a foreigner who is not strictly speaking resident in England.[294] But temporary presence as a basis of jurisdiction was emphatically affirmed by the Court of Appeal[295] and has the support of weighty dicta by Lord Russell of Killowen.[296] The history of English procedure bears out this view; the right of an English court to entertain an action depended originally upon a defendant being served in England with the King's writ, and this again was only part of the general doctrine that any person whilst in England owed at least temporary allegiance to the King. But the court has a discretion to refuse to entertain proceedings if to do so might work injustice, where, for example, the claim is contested and the case has no connection with England.[297]

11–109   As will be seen below, a foreign corporation or partnership firm which carries on business in England is amenable to the jurisdiction of the court. The question therefore arises whether the court has jurisdiction to entertain proceedings *in personam* against an individual who is not in England, but who carries on business in England. The effect of CPR, r.6.9(2) is that an individual foreigner trading within the jurisdiction but resident outside the jurisdiction may be served with process at his place of business within the jurisdiction. It had been held under the wording as it was prior to amendment of the Rules of the Supreme Court as from 1987 that the rules relating to service on a

---

[293] The United States Supreme Court has held that the transient jurisdiction rule, as it is called in the United States, is not contrary to the due process clause of the Constitution: *Burnham v Superior Court of California*, 495 US 604 (1990) (an inter-State, and not an international, case) on which see Collins (1991) 107 L.Q.R. 10; Hay, 1990 U.Ill.L.Rev. 593. *cf. Richman v Ben-Tovim*, 2007 2 S.A. 283; and see generally Oppong (2007) 3 J. Priv. Int. L. 321.

[294] See also Ehrenzweig, 65 Yale L.J. 289 (1956).

[295] *Colt Industries Inc v Sarlie* [1966] 1 W.L.R. 440 (CA); *Maharanee of Baroda v Wildenstein* [1972] 2 Q.B. 283 (CA). Annex I to the Regulation assumes that the rule is part of English law, and it was accepted as such in *Adams v Cape Industries Plc* [1990] Ch. 433, 518 (CA).

[296] See *Carrick v Hancock* (1895) 12 T.L.R. 59, 60. See also *Forbes v Simmons* (1914) 20 D.L.R. 100 (Alta); *Laurie v Carroll* (1958) 98 C.L.R. 310, 323. Where a man has been brought by force of law from one Canadian province to another, or from one Australian State to another, service of process on him in the second province or State has been held to be good: *Doyle v Doyle* (1974) 52 D.L.R. (3d) 143 (Newf.); *John Sanderson Ltd v Giddings* [1976] V.R. 421; *Baldry v Jackson* [1976] 1 N.S.W.L.R. 19, affirmed on different grounds [1976] 2 N.S.W.L.R. 415. Should, however, a foreigner be fraudulently enticed within the jurisdiction, that may be a good reason for setting aside service: see *Stein v Valkenhuysen* (1858) E.B. E. 65; *Watkins v North American Lands, etc. Co* (1904) 20 T.L.R. 534 (HL); *Perrett v Robinson* [1985] 1 Qd.R. 83.

[297] See Rule 38, below.

partnership (which allow service at the principal place of business within the jurisdiction) did not apply to an individual trading as a firm who resided out of the jurisdiction but who carried on business within the jurisdiction through a branch.[298] This anomalous distinction between foreign individual traders and foreign partnerships has been removed. But it would seem that if the foreigner carries on business in his own name this jurisdiction cannot be exercised.[299] This is not likely to be of practical importance since it is not easy to envisage a cause of action arising out of the operation of the business which would not come within one of the heads of jurisdiction under CPR, r.6.36 and PD6B, para.3.1 i.e. Rule 34.

The Civil Procedure Rules provide for a number of alternative methods of service within the jurisdiction.[300] The methods include: personal service, i.e. leaving the document with the person to be served; service by first class post to the usual or last known residence of the person to be served; service through a document exchange or by fax. In previous editions of this work[301] it was said that in such cases the defendant had to be in England when the process was served, and it was so held in *Chellaram v Chellaram (No.2)*.[302] But this decision was disapproved by the Court of Appeal in *City & Country Properties Ltd v Kamali*,[303] in which it was held that there is not, or is no longer, any fundamental principle that the defendant must be in England at the time of service. The decision of the Court of Appeal has been criticised on the ground that it makes the fundamental rules on service out of the jurisdiction optional or redundant in a significant number of cases.[304]　　**11–110**

A similar question arises in relation to what was once called substituted service and is now known as service by an alternative method.[305] Under the practice prior to the Civil Procedure Rules, the general principle was that an order for substituted service within the jurisdiction could not be made against a person outside the jurisdiction.[306] The current Rules contains no specific provision for service by an alternative method on defendants outside the jurisdiction, but it is suggested that alternative service within the jurisdiction should not be ordered unless the case is one which is otherwise suitable for an　　**11–111**

---

[298] *St Gobain, etc. v Hoyermann's Agency* [1893] 2 Q.B. 96 (CA).

[299] Cases cited [1893] 2 Q.B. at p.103.

[300] CPR, Pt 6 and Practice Direction 6A.

[301] 13th ed. 2000, para.11–084; 14th ed. 2006, para.11–105.

[302] [2002] EWHC 632 (Ch.), [2002] All E.R. 17. *cf. Barclays Bank of Swaziland Ltd v Hahn* [1989] 1 W.L.R. 506 (HL); *India Videogram Ltd v Patel* [1991] 1 W.L.R. 173; *Cadogan Properties Ltd v Mount Eden Land Ltd* [2000] I.L.Pr. 722 (CA).

[303] [2006] EWCA Civ 1879, [2007] 1 W.L.R. 1219, applying *Rolph v Zolan* [1993] 1 W.L.R. 1305 (CA) (a decision on the former County Court Rules).

[304] Briggs and Rees, para.5.03; Briggs (2007) 78 B.Y.I.L. 600. See now *SSL International Plc v TTK LIG Ltd* [2011] EWCA Civ 1170, [2012] 1 All E.R. (Comm.) 429, in which the Court of Appeal endorsed (at [57]) the general statement of principle in *Chellaram v Chellaram (No.2)* and reaffirmed that it is a general principle of the common law that absent specific provision (as in the rules for service out of the jurisdiction) the courts only exercise jurisdiction against those subject to, i.e. within, the jurisdiction.

[305] CPR, r.6.15.

[306] See *Porter v Freudenberg* [1915] 1 K.B. 857, in the light of the decisions of the High Court of Australia in *Laurie v Carroll* (1958) 98 C.L.R. 310, and of the Court of Appeal in *Myerson v Martin* [1979] 1 W.L.R. 1390 (CA).

order for service outside the jurisdiction, and there is good reason for alternative service within the jurisdiction.[307]

11–112   *Partnerships.*[308] The effect of the Civil Procedure Rules is that claims against partners who carried on business within the jurisdiction[309] when the cause of action arose must normally be brought in the partnership name, and the proceedings may be served on a partner or on a person who, at the time of service, has the control or management of the partnership business at its principal place of business, or (where personal service is not effected) at the usual or last known address of a partner, or at the principal or last known place of business of the partnership.[310] The effect is to extend the jurisdiction of the court over defendants who are absent from England.

11–113   *Corporations.*[311] In the case of a company registered in England under the Companies Act, or any other Act, no difficulty concerning service arises. Even if the company is formed to carry on business abroad, nevertheless it is present in England by virtue of its incorporation here, and service of process can always be effected by leaving it at, or sending it by post to, the registered office of the company in England.[312] If a company registered in Scotland carries on business in England, process of any court in England may be served[313] on it by leaving it at or sending it by post to the principal place of business of the company in England, addressed to the manager or head officer there, and a copy of the process must be sent to the registered office in Scotland.[314] In addition, under the Civil Procedure Rules, a company registered in England may be served at its principal office,[315] or at any place of business within the jurisdiction which has a real connection with the claim.[316]

---

[307] See generally on service by an alternative method and the exercise of the power to dispense with service in international cases: *Knauf UK GmbH v British Gypsum Ltd* [2001] EWCA Civ 1570, [2002] 1 W.L.R. 907; *BAS Capital Funding Corp v Medfinco Ltd* [2003] EWHC 1798 (Ch.), [2004] 1 Lloyd's Rep. 652; *Shiblaq v Sadikoglu* [2004] EWHC 1890 (Comm.); *Habib Bank Ltd v Central Bank of Sudan* [2006] EWHC 1767 (Comm.), [2007] 1 W.L.R. 470; *Phillips v Symes (No.3)* [2008] UKHL 1, [2008] 1 W.L.R. 180; *Olafsson v Gissurarson (No.2)* [2008] EWCA Civ 152, [2008] 1 W.L.R. 2016; *Bayat v Cecil* [2011] EWCA Civ 135, [2011] 1 W.L.R. 3086.

[308] On the question whether a foreign entity is a corporation or a partnership, see *Von Hellfeld v Rechnitzer* [1914] 1 Ch. 748 (CA); *Oxnard Financing SA v Rahn* [1998] 1 W.L.R. 1496 (CA). For limited liability partnerships see n.316, below.

[309] Of any nationality: *Worcester, etc. Banking Co v Firbank* [1984] 1 Q.B. 784, (CA).

[310] CPR, rr.6.5(3)(c), 6.9(2), PD7A, para.5A.

[311] See generally Fawcett (1988) 37 I.C.L.Q. 645.

[312] s.1139. See *Addis Ltd v Berkeley Supplies Ltd* [1964] 1 W.L.R. 943.

[313] But *jurisdiction*, as distinct from service, will depend on the modified version of the Brussels I Regulation in 1982 Act, Sch.4, as substituted by SI 2001/3929, Sch.2, para.4.

[314] s.1139(4).

[315] Where process is addressed to the company itself, rather than to the person named as authorised to accept service, the service is irregular, but may be cured under what is now CPR, r.3.10: *Boocock v Hilton International Co* [1993] 1 W.L.R. 1065 (CA).

[316] CPR, rr.6.3(2)(b), 6.9. SI 2009/1804, reg.75 provides that the service provisions relating to companies apply as modified to limited liability partnerships, and CPR, r.6.9 provides for service on the principal office, or at any place of business within the jurisdiction which has a real connection with the claim.

The position with regard to foreign companies following the implementa- **11–114**
tion in 1992 of the 11th Company Law Directive[317] is as follows. By s.1046
of the Companies Act 2006 regulations may be made requiring overseas
companies to register particulars, which must (by s.1056) include particulars
identifying every person resident in the United Kingdom authorised to accept
service of documents on behalf of the company, or a statement that there is no
such person.[318] By s.1139(2) process may be served on an overseas company
whose particulars are registered (a) by leaving it at, or sending it by post to,
the registered address of any person resident in the United Kingdom who is
authorised to accept service of documents on the company's behalf, or (b) if
there is no such person, or if any such person refuses service or service cannot
for any other reason be effected, by leaving it at or sending by post to any
place of business[319] of the company in the United Kingdom.

Under the Civil Procedure Rules[320] service on a company may be effected, **11–115**
in addition to the methods of service under the Companies Act 2006, by any
method permitted under CPR Part 6, which includes leaving process with a
person holding a senior position within the company[321] or at any place within
the jurisdiction where the company carries on its business and which has a real
connection with the claim.[322] But the provision in CPR, r. 6.5(3)(b) for service
on "a person holding a senior position within [a] company or corporation"
does not apply if the company or corporation does not carry on business and
is not present within the jurisdiction.[323]

If the company has ceased to carry on business in England, process cannot **11–116**
be served by leaving it at a former place of business.[324] But it may be served
on a person authorised to accept service, even if he is no longer present or
resident in England, by being addressed to him and left at the address last
notified.[325]

These provisions are exclusively concerned with *service*. If the foreign **11–117**
company is domiciled in a Member State or Convention State, *jurisdiction*
will depend on the provisions of the Regulation or the Convention. In cases
outside the scope of the Regulation and the Convention, if a foreign company
has a branch in England, it may be served in England under CPR, r.6.9 even

---

[317] Directive 89/666/EC [1989] OJ L395/36.

[318] See SI 2008/3000, reg.10. There is no procedure by which a name can be withdrawn from
the file without the substitution of a fresh one, but it appears from *South India Shipping Corp Ltd
v Export-Import Bank of Korea* [1985] 1 W.L.R. 585 (CA) that a foreign company persuaded the
Registrar of Companies to remove its file on the ground that it had registered in error.

[319] On the meaning of "place of business" see *Saab v Saudi American Bank* [1999] 1 W.L.R.
1861 (CA).

[320] CPR, r. 6.3(2). See also *Sea Assets Ltd v PT Garuda Indonesia* [2000] 4 All E.R. 371: the
method of service under what is now Companies Act 2006, is not exclusive, and the alternative
methods under CPR Pt 6 are not *ultra vires*.

[321] CPR, r.6.5(3)(b).

[322] CPR, r.6.9(2).

[323] *SSL International Plc v TTK LIG Ltd* [2011] EWCA Civ 1170, deciding that the pre-CPR
decisions still represent the law: *Okura Co Ltd v Forsbacka Jernverks A/B* [1914] 1 K.B. 715
(CA); *The Theodohos* [1977] 2 Lloyd's Rep. 428; and *The Vrontados* [1982] 2 Lloyd's Rep 241
(CA).

[324] *Deverall v Grant Advertising Inc* [1955] Ch. 111 (CA).

[325] *Rome v Punjab National Bank (No.2)* [1989] 1 W.L.R. 1211 (CA).

if the claim has no connection with the branch or with England. The cause of action may be quite independent,[326] but the lack of connection of the claim with the branch or place of business in England may be a ground for a stay under Rule 38.[327] Where, however, a foreign company has its domicile[328] in a Member State or a Convention State, the court must have jurisdiction under one of the provisions of the Regulation or the Convention.[329]

11–118 The expression "place of business" is not defined in the Companies Act 2006 or in the Civil Procedure Rules, but it includes a share transfer or share registration office[330] and therefore has a wide meaning. It is clear that, as at common law, the "place" of business must be a fixed and definite one;[331] the activity must have been carried on for a sufficient time for it to be characterised as a business, but nine days were held sufficient in one case at common law.[332] It is not necessary that the activity within the jurisdiction should constitute a substantial part of, or be incidental to, the main objects of the foreign company. In *South India Shipping Corp Ltd v Export-Import Bank of Korea*[333] a foreign bank was held to have been duly served at a place in England where it conducted external relations with other banks and carried out preliminary work in relation to granting or obtaining loans, but where it did not conclude any banking transactions.

11–119 The business must be that of the corporation. The normal case will be a branch of a foreign corporation, where there will be no doubt that the place of business is that of the corporation.[334] In the overwhelming majority of cases, the corporation will comply with the filing requirements of the Companies Act 2006, and service can be effected in accordance with the provisions of the Act. Accordingly in practice a real problem will normally only arise where the corporation's business is alleged to be carried on by a representative or agent, who is not an officer or employee of the corporation, and who may act as a

---

[326] See *South India Shipping Corp Ltd v Export-Import Bank of Korea* [1985] 1 W.L.R. 585 (CA), and older authorities, including *Haggin v Comptoir d'Escompte de Paris* (1889) 23 Q.B.D. 519 (CA); *La Bourgogne* [1899] A.C. 431; *Logan v Bank of Scotland (No.1)* [1904] 2 K.B. 495 (CA); *A/S Dampskib Hercules v Grand Trunk Pacific Ry of Canada* [1912] 1 K.B. 222 (CA); *Saab v Saudi American Bank* [1999] 1 W.L.R. 1861, 1871 (CA).

[327] *Logan v Bank of Scotland (No.2)* [1906] 1 K.B. 152–153; *First National Bank of Boston v Union Bank of Switzerland* [1990] 1 Lloyd's Rep. 32 (CA); contrast *European Asian Bank v Punjab Bank* [1982] 2 Lloyd's Rep. 356 (CA).

[328] For the meaning of domicile of companies, see above, paras 11–088 *et seq.*

[329] e.g. Art.5(5), see below, para.11–297.

[330] s.698; *The Madrid* [1937] P. 40; *cf. A/S Dampskib Hercules v Grand Trunk Pacific Ry of Canada* [1912] 1 K.B. 222 (CA); and contrast *Badcock v Cumberland Gap Co* [1893] 1 Ch. 362, decided at common law.

[331] *The Theodohos* [1977] 2 Lloyd's Rep. 428; *Saccharin Corporation Ltd v Chemische Fabrik AG* [1911] 2 K.B. 516 (CA); *Okura Co Ltd v Forsbacka Jernverks A/B* [1914] 1 K.B. 715 (CA).

[332] See *Dunlop Pneumatic Tyre Co Ltd v AG Cudell Co* [1902] 1 K.B. 342 (CA), where the place of business was a stand at an exhibition.

[333] [1985] 1 W.L.R. 585 (CA), stated below, para.11–123, Illustration 12. Contrast *National Commercial Bank v Wimborne* (1979) 11 N.S.W.L.R. 156 (local correspondent bank not place of business of foreign bank).

[334] e.g. *South India Shipping Corp Ltd v Export-Import Bank of Korea* [1985] 1 W.L.R. 585 (CA); *cf. Newby v Van Oppen Co* (1872) L.R. 7 Q.B. 293; *Haggin v Comptoir d'Escompte de Paris* (1889) 23 Q.B.D. 519 (CA).

representative or agent for other corporations in addition. Service may be effected on the representative or agent if the business is that of the corporation, and not solely the business of the representative or agent who acts for it in England. Where the representative or agent has power to make contracts on behalf of the foreign corporation and displays its name on his premises, there will be little difficulty in establishing that the place of business is that of the corporation.[335]

In *Adams v Cape Industries Plc*[336] the Court of Appeal, in a case involving **11–120** the presence or residence of a corporation in a foreign country for the purpose of the enforcement of a foreign judgment, undertook an exhaustive examination of the old authorities on the presence of a corporation at common law. It concluded that, although the power to contract was of great importance, it was not the only factor, and that the question whether the representative had been carrying on the foreign corporation's business or had been doing no more than carry on his own business would necessitate an investigation of the functions he had been performing and all aspects of the relationship between him and the corporation, including the following: (a) whether or not the fixed place of business from which the representative operated was originally acquired for the purpose of enabling him to act on behalf of the corporation; (b) whether the corporation had directly reimbursed him for (i) the cost of his accommodation at the fixed place of business; (ii) the cost of his staff; (c) what other contribution, if any, the overseas corporation made to the financing of the business carried on by the representative; (d) whether the representative was remunerated by reference to transactions, e.g. by commission, or by fixed regular payments or in some other way; (e) what degree of control the corporation exercised over the running of the business conducted by the representative; (f) whether the representative reserved part of his accommodation or part of his staff for conducting business related to the corporation; (g) whether the representative displayed the corporation's name at his premises or on his stationery, and if so, whether he did so in such a way as to indicate that he was a representative of the corporation; (h) what business, if any, the representative transacted as principal exclusively on his own behalf; (i) whether the representative made contracts with customers or other third parties in the name of the corporation, or otherwise in such manner as to bind it; (j) if so, whether the representative required specific authority in advance before binding the corporation to contractual obligations. But the presence of a power to contract on behalf of the foreign corporation was not an exclusive or necessary condition, although it was of great importance and was the principal test.[337]

---

[335] *Saccharin Corporation Ltd v Chemische Fabrik AG* [1911] 2 K.B. 516 (CA); contrast *Okura Co Ltd v Forsbacka Jernverks A/B* [1914] 1 K.B. 715 (CA). See also *Rakusens Ltd v Baser Ambalaj Plastik Sanayi Ticaret AS* [2001] EWCA Civ 1820, [2002] 1 B.C.L.C. 104; *Harrods Ltd v Dow Jones & Co Inc* [2003] EWHC 1162 (QB).

[336] [1990] Ch. 433, 523–531 (CA). See *SSL International Plc v TTK LIG Ltd* [2011] EWCA Civ 1170, [2012] 1 All E.R. (Comm.) 429 (holding of occasional board meetings not carrying on of business).

[337] [1990] Ch. 433, 531.

Illustrations

(1) Individuals

11–121   1. A, an American company, brings proceedings against X, an American, in respect of a debt incurred in New York and serves process on X while X is staying for a few days in a London hotel. The court has jurisdiction.[338]

2. A Co issues proceedings against its tenant, X, for arrears of rent and service charges. The claim form is served by post at X's last known place of business in England while he is temporarily abroad. Service is effective.[339]

(2) Partnerships

11–122   3. Y and Z are residing in Natal. They carry on business under the firm name of X & Co both in Natal and England. A sues X & Co upon a promissory note made by Y and Z in Cape Town and payable at their London office, and A brings proceedings against them in the name of X & Co The court has jurisdiction.[340]

4. A brings proceedings against X & Co, a New York firm carrying on business in New York and having no place of business in England. The three partners of X & Co are all in the United States. The court has no jurisdiction.[341]

(3) Corporations

11–123   5. X & Co is a Saudi bank. It establishes a branch in England and registers N, who is resident in England, as the person authorised to accept service. A has a claim against X & Co which arises (in part) out of the business of the branch. A commences proceedings against X & Co, and serves process on N. The court has jurisdiction.[342]

6. The facts are as in Illustration 6, except that the claim has no connection with the branch, and the claim form is served by leaving it at the branch. The court has jurisdiction.[343]

7. The facts are as in Illustration 7, except that X & Co is a French bank. Service is valid, but the court has no jurisdiction unless the case falls within one of the clauses of Rule 35.

8. X & Co is a Panamanian ship-owning company, which has no place of business in England. N, its president, resides in London. A brings proceedings against X & Co for damage to cargo and serves process on N. The court has no jurisdiction.[344]

9. X & Co is a Japanese corporation which manufactures goods in Japan. It employs N as sole agent in England. N rents an office in London and is paid by commission. He has authority to make contracts for the sale of X & Co's goods. He delivers the goods out of stocks in his office or under his control at public wharves in London. He also acts as agent for another foreign corporation. A brings proceedings against X & Co claiming damages for breach of contract and serves process on X & Co by leaving a copy at N's office. The court has jurisdiction.[345]

10. X & Co is a Korean corporation which manufactures steel in Korea. It employs N & Co as its sole agents in the United Kingdom. N & Co also act as agents for other corporations and carry on business as merchants on their own account. They have no general authority to make contracts on behalf of X & Co but obtain orders and submit them to X & Co for approval. X &

---

[338] *Colt Industries Inc v Sarlie* [1966] 1 W.L.R. 440 (CA).

[339] *City & Country Properties Ltd v Kamali* [2006] EWCA Civ 1879, [2007] 1 W.L.R. 1219. That X was only temporarily abroad was significant: see *SSL International Plc v TTK LIG Ltd* [2011] EWCA Civ 1170, [2012] 1 All E.R. (Comm.) 429 at [56]. See para.11–110, above.

[340] *Worcester, etc., Banking Co v Firbank* [1894] 1 Q.B. 784 (CA); CPR, rr.6.5(3)(c), 6.9(2), PD7A, para.5A.

[341] *cf. Von Hellfeld v Rechnitzer* [1914] 1 Ch. 748 (CA).

[342] Companies Act 2006, s.1139(2); *Saab v Saudi American Bank* [1999] 1 W.L.R. 1861 (CA).

[343] CPR, rr.6.3(2); 6.9. But the defendant may apply for a stay of proceedings: see Rule 38.

[344] *The Theodohos* [1977] 2 Lloyd's Rep. 428.

[345] Companies Act 2006, s.1139. In this and the succeeding Illustrations it is assumed that X & Co is not registered as an overseas company under Part 34 of the Companies Act 2006. *cf. Saccharin Corporation Ltd v Chemische Fabrik AG* [1911] 2 K.B. 516 (CA).

Co ships the steel direct to purchasers in England. N & Co receive payment from the purchasers and remit the amount to X & Co less their agreed commission. A brings proceedings against X & Co claiming damages for breach of contract and serves X & Co at N & Co's office. The court has no jurisdiction.[346]

11. X & Co is a Japanese shipping company. It employs N as agent in London for the booking of freight and issue of passenger tickets. N is paid by commission and has no concern with the management of X & Co The only name appearing on the door of his office is his own name, but on the window of the ground floor his name is exhibited as agent for X & Co and other shipping companies. A brings proceedings against X & Co claiming damages in respect of a collision in which one of X & Co's ships was involved. The court has no jurisdiction.[347]

12. X & Co, a Korean bank with its main business in Korea, gives a guarantee to A & Co, an Indian corporation, whereby X & Co guarantees the repayment to A & Co of advance payments made by A & Co to N & Co, a Korean company, in connection with shipbuilding contracts entered into between A & Co and N & Co The transaction has no connection with England. When N & Co defaults, A & Co commences proceedings in 1984 in England against X & Co and serves process on the London office of X & Co The representative office had been registered under Part X of the Companies Act 1948 (now Part 34 of the Companies Act 2006) but the registration was deleted in 1983. The representative office does not conclude any banking transactions in London, but it has premises and staff, it conducts external relations with other banks and financial institutions, and carries out preliminary work in relation to granting or obtaining loans. Process is validly served because these activities make the representative office a place of business within what is now s.1139(2) of the Companies Act 2006.[348]

13. A Ltd and B Ltd sue X Ltd, an Indian company, for breach of contract. X Ltd is a joint venture company in which A Ltd holds 50 per cent of the shares and has the right to appoint half of the board. Occasional board meetings are held in London. A Ltd and B Ltd purport to serve X Ltd by serving one of its directors (who was an A Ltd appointee). Service is bad, because (a) the facility to serve a company by serving an officer does not apply if the company does not have a place of business in England, and (b) the holding of occasional board meetings does not amount to carrying on business within the jurisdiction.[349]

RULE 32—Subject to Rule 36, the court has jurisdiction to entertain a claim *in personam* against a person who submits to the jurisdiction of the court.   11R–124

COMMENT

A person who would not otherwise be subject to the jurisdiction of the court may preclude himself by his own conduct from objecting to the jurisdiction, and thus give the court an authority over him which, but for his submission, it would not possess. This principle is also expressed in Art.24 of the Brussels I Regulation and of the Lugano Convention.[350]   11–125

A person who begins proceedings in general gives the court jurisdiction to entertain a counterclaim against him which may extend to cases in which, if separate proceedings were to be brought, permission to serve process under   11–126

---

[346] *Okura Co Ltd v Forsbacka Jernverks A/B* [1914] 1 K.B. 715 (CA).

[347] cf. *The Lalandia* [1933] P. 56.

[348] *South India Shipping Corp Ltd v Export-Import Bank of Korea* [1985] 1 W.L.R. 585 (CA).

[349] *SSL International Plc v TTK LIG Ltd* [2011] EWCA Civ 1170, [2012] 1 All E.R. (Comm.) 429.

[350] See below, Rule 35, clause (22).

CPR, r.6.36 and PD6B, para.3.1, i.e. Rule 34, might not be obtainable.[351] Although it is sometimes said that it is not necessary that the counterclaim be related to the claim,[352] the true principle is that a counterclaim is allowed so that justice can be done as between the parties.[353] In English law this principle is given effect by the rule that the court may require a counterclaim to be disposed of separately.[354]

11–127   A person who appears voluntarily after service on him submits to the jurisdiction, even though he is out of England at the time of issue and service of the process. He may, for instance, instruct his solicitor to accept service on his behalf; and the Civil Procedure Rules provide that where a solicitor is authorised to accept service on behalf of a party, in principle process must be served on the solicitor.[355] But the solicitor may accept service of proceedings on the basis that the defendant remains free to contest the jurisdiction in the same way as if the claimant had obtained permission to serve abroad and had effected service abroad.[356] If the defendant instructs his solicitor to accept service and the solicitor communicates those instructions to the claimant, the defendant will be regarded as having submitted, even if the instructions are withdrawn.[357]

---

[351] *Republic of Liberia v Gulf Oceanic Inc* [1985] 1 Lloyd's Rep. 539, 544, 547 (CA); *Metal Scrap Trade Corp Ltd v Kate Shipping Co Ltd* [1990] 1 W.L.R. 115, 130 (HL); *Balkanbank v Taher (No.2)* [1995] 1 W.L.R. 1067 (CA) (application for worldwide freezing injunction under 1982 Act, s.25 an "action" for purposes of defendant's counterclaim); *Glencore International AG v Exter Shipping Ltd* [2002] EWCA Civ 528, [2002] All E.R. (Comm.) 1; *Marketmaker Technology Ltd v CMC Group Plc* [2008] EWHC 1556 (QB); *AK Investment CJSC v Kyrgyz Mobil Tel Ltd* [2011] UKPC 7, [2011] 4 All E.R. 1027. See also *Derby Co Ltd v Larsson* [1976] 1 W.L.R. 202, 205 (HL). It has been held that a defendant added on the application, not of the plaintiff, but of other defendants, was entitled to counterclaim against a foreign plaintiff notwithstanding that it would not have been possible to obtain leave to serve the plaintiff under what is now CPR, r.6.36 and PD6B, para.3.1, i.e. Rule 34, if the plaintiff had been sued in a separate action: *Union Bank of the Middle East v Clapham* (1981) 125 S.J. 862 (CA); *sed quaere. cf. Soc Commerciale de Réassurance v Eras International Ltd (No.2)* [1995] 2 All E.R. 78 (foreign plaintiff may be subject to claim by third party). Appearance as claimant in interpleader proceedings has been held not to be a submission to the jurisdiction (*Eschger Co v Morrison, Kekewich Co* (1890) 6 T.L.R. 145 (CA)), but this will depend on the circumstances; see also *Commonwealth of Australia v Peacekeeper International FZC UAE* [2008] EWHC 1220 (QB).

[352] See, e.g. Restatement, s.34.

[353] *Griendtoveen v Hamlyn Co* (1892) 8 T.L.R. 231; *Factories Insurance Co Ltd v Anglo-Scottish General Commercial Insurance Co Ltd* (1913) 29 T.L.R. 312. See also *South African Republic v Compagnie Franco-Belge du Chemin de Fer du Nord* [1897] 2 Ch. 487, 492 (CA), [1898] 1 Ch. 190; *High Commissioner for India v Ghosh* [1960] 1 Q.B. 134, 141 (CA) (state immunity cases, now governed by State Immunity Act 1978, s.2(6), which expressly provides that the counterclaim must arise out of the same legal relationship or facts as the claim); *National Commercial Bank v Wimborne* (1979) 11 N.S.W.L.R. 156, 169–176, approved in *Marlborough Harbour Board v Charter Travel Co* (1989) 18 N.S.W.L.R. 223, 232. See now Art.6(3), Brussels I Regulation and Lugano Convention.

[354] CPR, r.3.1(2)(e); r.20.9. *cf. Republic of Liberia v Gulf Oceanic Inc* [1985] 1 Lloyd's Rep. 539 (CA); *Metal Scrap Trade Corp v Kate Shipping Co Ltd* [1990] 1 W.L.R. 115 (HL).

[355] CPR, r.6.7. An agreement to accept service is not *per se* a waiver in advance of any irregularity (such as failure to serve in time): *Caribbean Gold Ltd v Alga Shipping Ltd* [1993] 1 W.L.R. 1100. On acceptance of service induced by misrepresentation, see *Beecham Group Plc v Norton Healthcare Ltd* [1997] F.S.R. 81, 88.

[356] *Sphere Drake Insurance Plc v Gunes Sikorta* [1988] 1 Lloyd's Rep. 139 (CA).

[357] *Manta Line v Sofianites* [1984] 1 Lloyd's Rep. 14 (CA). *cf. Carmel Exporters (Sales) Ltd v Sea-Land Services Inc* [1981] 1 W.L.R. 1068, 1077–1078; *Broken Hill Pty Co Ltd v Xenakis* [1982] 2 Lloyd's Rep. 304.

A defendant who wishes to dispute the jurisdiction of the court to try the **11–128** claim, or to argue that the court should not exercise its jurisdiction, must file an acknowledgment of service and apply to the court for an order declaring that it has no jurisdiction or should not exercise any jurisdiction which it may have.[358] The application must be made within 14 days (or 28 days in the Commercial Court) after filing an acknowledgment of service.[359] It is provided that a defendant who acknowledges service does not, by doing so, lose any right to dispute the court's jurisdiction, unless he fails to make an application within the period specified for making the application.[360] If the court does not make a declaration that it has no jurisdiction or will not exercise its jurisdiction, the acknowledgment of service ceases to have effect and the defendant has a further period in which to file a further acknowledgment of service; if the defendant then files a further acknowledgment of service, he is to be treated as having accepted that the court has jurisdiction to try the claim.[361] These rules give expression to the general principle that a person who appears merely to contest the jurisdiction of the court does not thereby submit.[362]

In order to establish that the defendant has, by his conduct in the proceed-   **11–129** ings, submitted or waived his objection to the jurisdiction, it must be shown that he has taken some step which is only necessary or only useful if the objection has been waived or never been entertained at all.[363] In *Jameel v Dow Jones & Co Inc*[364] it was held that, even if the defendant had submitted to the jurisdiction, it could apply for proceedings to be struck out as an abuse of the process on the ground that there had been no real and substantial tort within the jurisdiction.

---

[358] A defendant who files an acknowledgment of service indicating that he intends to defend the claim but not that he intends to dispute the jurisdiction thereby submits: *Global Multimedia International Ltd v ARA Media Services* [2006] EWHC 3612 (Ch.), [2007] 1 All E.R. (Comm.) 1160.

[359] CPR, rr.11(1), (4); 58.7(2). On the power of the court to extend the time limit see above, para.11–073.

[360] CPR, r.11(3), (5). *cf. The Messiniaki Tolmi* [1984] 1 Lloyd's Rep. 266 (CA). A request for an extension of time to file a defence will not prevent an application under CPR, r.11(1): *ISC Technologies Ltd v Radcliffe*, December 7, 1990, unreported, cited in *Kurz v Stella Musical GmbH* [1992] Ch. 196; *SMAY Investments Ltd v Sachdev* [2003] EWHC 474 (Ch.), [2003] 1 W.L.R. 1973.

[361] CPR, r.11(7), (8). RSC, Ord.12, r.8, which was replaced by CPR, r.11, did not apply to applications for a stay of proceedings (as distinct from applications to set aside service), and it was held that an application for a stay of proceedings was not to be regarded as a submission if it were made as an alternative to an application for the proceedings to be set aside on the basis that the court had no jurisdiction: *Williams & Glyn's Bank v Astro Dinamico* [1984] 1 W.L.R. 438 (HL). It has also been held that an application for a stay under what is now Arbitration Act 1996, s.9, see below, Rule 65, is not a submission: *Finnish Marine Co Ltd v Protective National Insurance Co* [1990] 1 Q.B. 1078.

[362] *Re Dulles' Settlement (No.2)* [1951] Ch. 842 (CA).

[363] *Rein v Stein* (1892) 66 L.T. 469, 471, *per* Cave J., affirmed [1892] 1 Q.B. 753, approved in *Williams & Glyn's Bank v Astro Dinamico* [1984] 1 W.L.R. 438, 444 (HL); *Advent Capital Plc v GN Ellinas Imports-Exports Ltd* [2005] EWHC 1242 (Comm.), [2005] 2 Lloyd's Rep. 607; *Air Nauru v Niue Airlines Ltd* [1993] 2 N.Z.L.R. 632; *cf. Laurie v Carroll* (1958) 98 C.L.R. 310, 335–336.

[364] [2005] EWCA Civ 75, [2005] Q.B. 946.

11–130   Submission has been inferred when the defendant applied to strike out part of the claim.[365] It has also been inferred when the defendant filed affidavits and appeared through counsel to argue the merits[366] on the claimant's application for an injunction; or when the defendant consented *inter partes* to the continuance of a freezing injunction without reserving his right to contest the jurisdiction;[367] or when he sought to set aside a committal order and gave an undertaking and submitted evidence;[368] when he moved to set aside a default judgment and at the same time applied for an order that the plaintiff deliver a statement of claim;[369] and when he applied for an order for security for costs.[370] The clear trend of the modern authorities is that the defendant will not be regarded as having submitted by making an application in the proceedings, provided that he has specifically reserved his objection to the jurisdiction.[371]

11–131   Submission may also be inferred from the terms of a contract. At common law, the mere agreement of the parties that the court was to have jurisdiction to determine disputes arising out of a contract between them was insufficient by itself to give the court jurisdiction, because the defendant could not be legally served with process if he was out of England.[372] But if one party to the contract nominated an agent resident in England to accept service of process on his behalf, he was deemed to submit to the jurisdiction, and service could be effected on the agent in accordance with the contract.[373] This rule of the common law is confirmed by CPR, r.6.11,[374] which gives effect to the

---

[365] *The Messiniaki Tolmi* [1984] 1 Lloyd's Rep. 266 (CA).

[366] *Boyle v Sacker* (1888) 39 Ch.D. 249 (CA). But not merely where the purpose was to seek to have a freezing injunction discharged: *Obikoga v Silvernorth Ltd, The Times*, July 6, 1983.

[367] *Esal Ltd v Pujara* [1989] 2 Lloyd's Rep. 479 (CA), distinguishing *Obikoga v Silvernorth Ltd, The Times*, July 6, 1983. *cf. The Xing Su Hai* [1995] 2 Lloyd's Rep. 15 (compliance with disclosure order not a submission when made subject to reservation as to jurisdiction). A party who appears to challenge a freezing injunction obtained without notice does not thereby waive his right to contest jurisdiction unless as part of those proceedings he agrees to an order regulating his position until the trial of the action: *SMAY Investments Ltd v Sachdev* [2003] EWHC 474 (Ch.), [2003] 1 W.L.R. 1973.

[368] *Marketmaker Technology Ltd v CMC Group Plc* [2008] EWHC 1556 (QB).

[369] *Fry v Moore* (1889) 23 Q.B.D. 395 (CA). *cf. Ngcobo v Thor Chemical Holdings Ltd, The Times*, November 10, 1995 (CA) (service of defence after leave to appeal given from judge's refusal to stay: appeal struck out); *Williams v Society of Lloyd's* [1994] 1 V.R. 274 (request for particulars not a submission).

[370] *Lhoneux Limon Co v Hong Kong Banking Corporation* (1886) 33 Ch.D. 446. But the position will be different if he makes it clear that the application is without prejudice to the objection to the jurisdiction and if the application is limited to the costs of the challenge to the jurisdiction: see *Hewden Stuart Heavy Cranes Ltd v Leo Gottwald*, unreported, 1992 (CA) (a case on what is now Art.24, Brussels I Regulation, below, paras 11R–397 *et seq.*); *cf. Catalyst Research Corp v Medtronic Inc* (1982) 131 D.L.R. (3d) 767 (Fed CA).

[371] *Williams & Glyn's Bank v Astro Dinamico*, above; *Esal Ltd v Pujara*, above; *Catalyst Research Corp v Medtronic Inc*, above.

[372] See *British Wagon Co v Gray* [1896] 1 Q.B. 35 (CA). The actual decision would now be different because of CPR, PD6B, para.3.1(6)(d)): see Rule 39(1).

[373] *Tharsis Sulphur Co v Société des Métaux* (1889) 58 L.J.Q.B. 435; *Montgomery Jones Co v Liebenthal Co* [1898] 1 Q.B. 487 (CA); *Reversionary Interest Society Ltd v Locking* [1928] W.N. 227.

[374] Previously RSC, Ord.10, r.3.

principle that the parties to a contract may agree that the court shall have jurisdiction to determine any dispute between them, and also provides machinery for serving the process in the manner laid down in the contract.[375] But there is an important distinction between the case where the mode of serving the process specified in the contract involves service in England, and the case where it involves service abroad. In the former case, service may be effected as of right without special leave. But in the latter case permission must be obtained for the service of process out of England, unless of course the defendant submits to the jurisdiction in some other way; but permission will normally be granted under CPR, PD6B, para.3.1(6)(d), i.e. Rule 34(4), and under any other clause of Rule 34 which may be applicable.[376]

In *Employers' Liability Assurance Corporation v Sedgwick, Collins Co*,[377]   **11–132** three members of the House of Lords suggested that an overseas company which files the name and address of a person authorised to accept service[378] thereby submits to the jurisdiction of the English courts. But to say that a corporation which, under the threat of a heavy fine, files with the Registrar of Companies the name of a person authorised to accept service of process on its behalf thereby submits to the jurisdiction seems even more artificial than saying that a corporation which establishes a place of business in England is deemed to be present in England. For this reason the jurisdiction of the court over foreign corporations is discussed in connection with Rule 31[379] and not in connection with Rule 32. There is perhaps more justification for saying that a foreign partnership which carries on business in England thereby submits to the jurisdiction[380] since in this case no question of a penalty arises. But for reasons of convenience this case also is discussed in connection with Rule 31[381] in order that all the cases on carrying on business in England may be considered together.

The principle of submission can give the court jurisdiction only to the   **11–133** extent of removing objections thereto which are purely personal to the party submitting, as, for example, that he has not been duly served with process.[382] Submission cannot give the court jurisdiction to entertain proceedings which in itself lies beyond the competence or authority of the court. Thus, even as regards defendants who are not domiciled in a Member State or a Convention State, submission cannot confer jurisdiction on the English court where the

---

[375] An ad hoc agreement, not expressly contemplated by CPR, r.6.11, will also be effective: *Kenneth Allison Ltd v Limehouse Co* [1992] 2 A.C. 105.

[376] See below, Rule 39(1) and, e.g. *The Chaparral* [1968] 2 Lloyd's Rep. 158 (CA); *The Vikfrost* [1980] 1 Lloyd's Rep. 560 (CA).

[377] [1927] A.C. 95, 104, 107, 114–115.

[378] See above, para.11–113.

[379] See above, paras 11–114 *et seq.* But *cf. Mitsui & Co Ltd v Nexen Petroleum UK Ltd* [2005] EWHC 625 (Ch.), [2005] 3 All E.R. 511.

[380] *Hobbs v Australian Press Association* [1933] 1 K.B. 1, 18 (CA).

[381] See above, para.11–112.

[382] For the purposes of amendment of statements of case to add new claims, a foreign defendant who submits should be treated as a party who only came into the proceedings by virtue of service out of the jurisdiction. Accordingly, a new claim can only be added if it is such that, independently of the original claim, permission would be granted to serve out of the jurisdiction: *Beecham Group Ltd v Norton Healthcare Ltd* [1997] F.S.R. 81.

courts of another Member State or Convention State have exclusive jurisdiction under Art.22.[383] The principle of submission does not apply to a suit for divorce[384] or nullity; nor (*semble*) does it apply to proceedings relating to foreign land which the court has no jurisdiction to try;[385] nor to proceedings in magistrates' courts which derive their jurisdiction from statute.[386]

ILLUSTRATIONS

11–134   1. A, an English bank, sues X & Co and Y & Co, Panamanian companies with their management in New York. X & Co and Y & Co apply for a declaration that the English court has no jurisdiction, and at the same time apply for a stay on the ground that England is not the appropriate forum. The application for a stay is not a submission to the jurisdiction or a waiver of the objection to the jurisdiction because the application for a stay is not inconsistent with the protest to the jurisdiction.[387]
     2. A, a US company, sues X & Co, a Panamanian company, in England. X & Co applies for a declaration that the court has no jurisdiction, and makes a separate application for security for its costs of its jurisdictional application. The application for security for costs is not a submission.[388]
     3. A Co and B sue, among other persons, X Ltd, an Indian company for deceit and breach of contract, and obtain a worldwide freezing injunction. X Ltd files an acknowledgment of service indicating an intention to defend, and before the time for challenging jurisdiction expires, applies to set aside the freezing injunction. X Ltd does not thereby submit.[389]
     4. X & Co is a Delaware corporation carrying on business in Pennsylvania and having no place of business in England. A is a company with a registered office in Glasgow, carrying on business in England. There is a contract between A and X & Co which provides that the parties submit to the jurisdiction of the High Court and that N of London should be the agent of X & Co to accept service of process on its behalf. A brings an action against X & Co for breach of contract. Process is served upon N. The court has jurisdiction.[390]

11R–135   **Rule 33—The court has jurisdiction to entertain proceedings if each claim made therein is one which the court has power to determine notwithstanding that the person against whom the claim is made is not in England or that the facts giving rise to the claim did not occur in England.**[391]

COMMENT

11–136   This Rule is based on CPR, r.6.33(3). Before the 1982 Act it was the only case in which a writ could be served without permission on a defendant out of

---

[383] See below, Rule 36. But the jurisdiction agreement provisions of Art.23 of the Regulation and of the Convention, which also apply in certain circumstances where a defendant is not domiciled in a Member State or Convention State, are subject to the principle of submission: Case 150/80 *Elefanten Schuh GmbH v Jacqmain* [1981] E.C.R. 1671.

[384] Domicile and Matrimonial Proceedings Act 1973, s.5(2)(3).

[385] Rule 130.

[386] *Forsyth v Forsyth* [1948] P. 125, 136 (CA).

[387] *cf. Williams & Glyn's Bank v Astro Dinamico* [1984] 1 W.L.R. 438 (HL).

[388] *cf. Hewden Stuart Heavy Cranes Ltd v Leo Gottwald*, unreported, 1992 (CA) (a case on what is now Art.24, Brussels I Regulation).

[389] *SMAY Investments Ltd v Sachdev* [2003] EWHC 474 (Ch.), [2003] 1 W.L.R. 1973.

[390] *cf. Tharsis Sulphur Co v Société des Métaux* (1889) 58 L.J.Q.B. 435.

[391] CPR, r.6.33(3).

England in an action *in personam* (as opposed, e.g. to a petition in a matrimonial cause[392]). This provision of the CPR is derived from RSC, Ord. 11, r.1(2), which was originally introduced in 1965 to implement the Civil Aviation (Eurocontrol) Act 1962, which was enacted to give effect to the Brussels Convention of December 13, 1960, on co-operation for the safety of air navigation.[393] In its original form it applied so as to give a right to serve proceedings abroad without the permission of the court if "by virtue of an enactment" the court had power to hear and determine the claim notwithstanding that the person against whom the claim is made was not within the jurisdiction of the court or that the wrongful act, neglect or default giving rise to the claim did not take place within its jurisdiction. The expression "by virtue of an enactment" does not appear in the current version of the provision in CPR, r.6.33(3), but there is no doubt that it is intended to cover the same ground as its predecessors. It applies to actions brought under other legislation implementing international conventions, which are discussed in Chapter 15. It also applies to claims brought under the Protection of Trading Interests Act 1980 in relation to "clawback" awards of multiple damages made by foreign courts.[394] Rule 33 applies to these cases even if the defendant is domiciled in a Member State or Convention State. In the case of the statutes implementing international conventions this is because Art.71 of the Brussels I Regulation and Art.67 of the Lugano Convention[395] allow United Kingdom courts to assume jurisdiction in accordance with multilateral conventions governing jurisdiction in particular matters notwithstanding that the defendant is domiciled in a Member State or Convention State, whether or not it is a party to the multilateral convention. Proceedings under the Protection of Trading Interests Act 1980 are probably outside the scope of the Regulation and the Convention since it is doubtful whether claims of the type contemplated by the 1980 Act can be classified as civil or commercial matters.

11–137   To be within Rule 33 an enactment must, if it does not use the precise wording in the Rule, at least indicate on its face that it is expressly contemplating proceedings against persons who are not within the jurisdiction of the court, or where the wrongful act, neglect or default giving rise to the claim did not take place within the jurisdiction. It is not enough that the enactment gives a remedy in general cases without any express contemplation of a foreign element.[396]

11–138   Under this Rule, as under Rules 31 and 32, the court exercises jurisdiction *ex debito justitiae* and not, as it does under Rule 34, a discretionary jurisdiction. Where service may be made out of the jurisdiction under this Rule, it is not open to the claimant to rely on Rule 34 if for some reason the jurisdictional requirements under this Rule cannot be met.[397]

---

[392] See below, para.18–015.

[393] Text in Cmnd. 1373.

[394] See below, Rule 59.

[395] See above, para.11–053.

[396] *Re Harrods (Buenos Aires) Ltd (No.2)* [1992] Ch. 72, 116 (Companies Act 1985), applied in *Re Banco Nacional de Cuba* [2001] 1 W.L.R. 2039 (Insolvency Act 1986).

[397] *cf. Arctic Electronics Co (UK) Ltd v McGregor Sea Air Services Ltd* [1985] 2 Lloyd's Rep. 510.

11R–139   RULE 34—The court has jurisdiction to entertain a claim *in personam* against a defendant (other than a person domiciled or deemed to be domiciled in another State to which the Brussels I Regulation applies or in another State party to the Lugano Convention[398] or in Scotland or Northern Ireland) who is not in England at the time for the service of process whenever it assumes jurisdiction in any of the cases mentioned in this Rule.[399]

COMMENT

11–140   If the defendant is not in England and served there with process and does not submit to the jurisdiction, the court has no jurisdiction at common law to entertain a claim *in personam* against him. But this common law principle was modified, first by ss.18 and 19 of the Common Law Procedure Act 1852, and later by the Rules of the Supreme Court, Order 11. Rule 6.20 of the new Civil Procedure Rules, replaced RSC Order 11, r.1 in 2000. Now the only relevant rule is CPR, r.6.36, which provides that the claimant may serve a claim form out of the jurisdiction with the permission of the court if any of the grounds set out in paragraph 3.1 of Practice Direction 6B apply. Consequently the heads of jurisdiction, which have a very long history in the rules of court since the 19th century, have now been relegated to para.3.1 of Practice Direction 6B ("PD6B"), under which the court has a discretionary power in a number of cases, corresponding to the 20 clauses of this Rule, to permit service of process[400] on a defendant irrespective of nationality who is out of England. Before these various cases are stated and discussed, the following general points should be noted.

11–141   (1) There is an essential difference between the jurisdiction exercised by the court when the defendant is in England (Rule 31) or when he submits to the jurisdiction (Rule 32) and its jurisdiction when the action comes under any of the clauses of Rule 34. Under Rules 31 and 32, the jurisdiction of the court is not discretionary;[401] the claimant has a right to demand that it shall be

---

[398] Rule 34 has no application also, even as respects persons not domiciled in a Member State or in a Convention State, if Rules 35(15) and 36(1) (immovable property) or Rules 35(20) and 37 (jurisdiction agreements) apply.

[399] CPR, 6.36 and PD6B, para.3.1; Collins, Essays, p.226. On service of orders made in proceedings see CPR, r.6.38(2) and *Union Bank of Finland v Lelakis* [1997] 1 W.L.R. 590 (CA); *Masri v Consolidated Contractors International Co SAL (No.4)* [2009] UKHL 43, [201] 1 A.C. 90.

[400] Service must be effected exactly where authorised; thus service in Hong Kong in lieu of Japan is a nullity: *Bonnell v Preston* (1908) 24 T.L.R. 756 (CA). Process may not be served abroad in a manner which is contrary to the law of the foreign country: CPR, r.6.40(4), but the court retains a discretion under CPR, r.3.10 to waive the irregularity: *The Sky One* [1988] 1 Lloyd's Rep. 238; *The Anna* [1994] 2 Lloyd's Rep. 379; *National Commercial Bank v Hague* [1994] C.L.C. 230 (CA); contrast *The Goldean Mariner* [1989] 2 Lloyd's Rep. 390, 398, affirmed [1990] 2 Lloyd's Rep. 215 (CA); *The Oinoussin Pride* [1991] 1 Lloyd's Rep. 126. Permission to serve out of the jurisdiction may be granted retrospectively: *National Justice Compania Naviera v Prudential Assurance Co Ltd (No.2)* [2000] 1 W.L.R. 603 (CA). The court probably has power to dispense with service: *cf. Bas Capital Funding Corp v Medfinco Ltd* [2003] EWHC 1798 (Ch), [2004] 1 Lloyd's Rep 652, [163]–[168], [216]; *Olafsson v Gissurarson (No.2)* [2008] EWCA Civ 152, [2008] 1 W.L.R. 2016, [64].

[401] But it is discretionary in cases to which CPR, r.6.11, applies: see para.11–131.

exercised, though the court has a discretion to stay the action to prevent injustice.[402] But under Rule 34, the jurisdiction of the court is essentially discretionary, for the court may, if it sees fit, decline to allow the service of process, and thus decline to exercise its jurisdiction.

(2) Four cardinal points have been emphasised in the decided cases.[403] **11–142** First, the court ought to be cautious in allowing process to be served on a foreigner out of England. This has frequently been said to be because service out of the jurisdiction is an interference with the sovereignty of other countries,[404] although today all countries exercise a degree of jurisdiction over persons abroad. Secondly, if there is any doubt in the construction of any of the heads of jurisdiction, that doubt ought to be resolved in favour of the defendant. Thirdly, since the application for permission is made without notice to the defendant, a full and fair disclosure of all relevant facts ought to be made.[405] Fourthly, the court will refuse permission if the case is within the letter but outside the spirit of the Rule.[406]

(3) In exercising its jurisdiction under Rule 34 the court will consider, inter **11–143** alia, whether England is the *forum conveniens*. This principle has been

---

[402] See Rule 38. Although a stay of proceedings is the normal remedy, the court has power to strike out or dismiss the action in appropriate circumstances: *Haji-Ioannou v Frangos* [1999] 2 Lloyd's Rep. 337 (CA).

[403] See, especially for the first three points, *Societe Generale de Paris v Dreyfus Bros* (1885) 29 Ch.D. 239, 242–243; (1887) 37 Ch.D. 215, 224, 225 (CA); *The Hagen* [1908] P. 189, 201 (CA); *Re Schintz* [1926] Ch. 710, 716–717 (CA).

[404] See, e.g. *George Monro Ltd v American Cyanamid Corp* [1944] K.B. 432, 437 (CA); *The Brabo* [1949] A.C. 326, 357; *Mackender v Feldia* [1967] 2 Q.B. 590, 599 (CA); *Derby & Co Ltd v Larsson* [1976] 1 W.L.R. 202, 204 (HL); *The Sky One* [1988] 1 Lloyd's Rep. 238, 241 (CA). Lord Diplock expressed the view that the jurisdiction under RSC Ord.11 was an exorbitant one, which ran counter to comity since it was a wider jurisdiction than was recognised in English law as being possessed by courts of foreign countries: *The Siskina v Distos Compania Naviera SA* [1979] A.C. 210, 254; *Amin Rasheed Shipping Corp v Kuwait Insurance Co Ltd* [1984] A.C. 50, 65; and see also *The Alexandros P* [1986] Q.B. 464, 478; *Insurance Co of Ireland v Strombus International Insurance* [1985] 2 Lloyd's Rep. 138, 146 (CA); *Spiliada Maritime Corp v Cansulex Ltd* [1987] A.C. 460, 481; *Agar v Hyde* (2000) 201 C.L.R. 552, 570. But it is suggested that the jurisdiction exercised under Rule 34 is not exorbitant, since it is similar to the jurisdiction exercised by many countries, and is also in many respects similar to the rules in the Regulation and the Lugano Convention: see Collins (1991) 107 L.Q.R. 10, 13–14.

[405] See also *Ellinger v Guinness Mahon & Co* [1939] 4 All E.R. 16; *Macaulay (Tweeds) Ltd v Independent Harris Tweed Producers Ltd* [1961] R.P.C. 184, 193–196; *The Nimrod* [1973] 2 Lloyd's Rep. 91, 95; *GAF Corporation v Amchem Products Inc* [1975] 1 Lloyd's Rep. 601, 607–608; *The Hida Maru* [1981] 2 Lloyd's Rep. 510 (CA); *Electric Furnace Co v Selas Corp of America* [1987] R.P.C. 23 (CA); *The Volvox Hollandia* [1988] 2 Lloyd's Rep. 361, 372 (CA); *Trafalgar Tours Ltd v Henry* [1990] 2 Lloyd's Rep. 298 (CA); *Newtherapeutics Ltd v Katz* [1991] Ch. 226; *The Olib* [1991] 2 Lloyd's Rep. 108; *ABCI v Banque Franco-Tunisienne* [1996] 1 Lloyd's Rep. 485, affirmed [1997] 1 Lloyd's Rep. 531 (CA); *ANCAP v Ridgley Shipping Inc* [1996] 1 Lloyd's Rep. 570; *Konamaneni v Rolls-Royce Industrial Power (India) Ltd* [2002] 1 W.L.R. 1269; *Marubeni Hong Kong and South China Ltd v Mongolian Government* [2002] 2 All E.R. (Comm.) 873; *BAS Capital Funding Corp v Medfinco Ltd* [2003] EWHC 1798 (Ch.), [2004] 1 Lloyd's Rep. 652; *Pakistan v Zardari* [2006] EWHC 2411 (Comm.), [2006] 2 C.L.C. 667. There is a continuing duty of disclosure after the order is made: *Network Telecom (Europe) Ltd v Telephone Systems International Inc* [2003] EWHC 2890 (Q.B.), [2004] 1 All E.R. (Comm.) 418.

[406] *Johnson v Taylor Bros* [1920] A.C. 144, 153; *Rosler v Hilbery* [1925] Ch. 250, 259–260 (CA); *George Monro Ltd v American Cyanamid Corp* [1944] K.B. 432, 437, 442 (CA); *Beck v Value Capital Ltd (No.2)* [1975] 1 W.L.R. 6; affirmed [1976] 1 W.L.R. 572n. (CA); *Sharab v Al-Saud* [2009] EWCA Civ 353, [2009] 1 Lloyd's Rep. 160, [35].

established since the 19th century,[407] and finds its modern expression in the speeches of Lord Wilberforce in *Amin Rasheed Shipping Corp v Kuwait Insurance Co*[408] and of Lord Goff of Chieveley in *Spiliada Maritime Corp v Cansulex Ltd*.[409] The claimant must show good reasons why service on a foreign defendant should be permitted, and in considering this question the court must take into account the nature of the dispute, the legal and practical issues involved, such questions as local knowledge, availability of witnesses and their evidence, and expense. The fundamental question (as it is in cases of staying of actions on *forum non conveniens* grounds[410]) is to identify the forum in which the case can suitably be tried for the interests of all the parties and for the ends of justice. To justify the exercise of the discretion, the claimant has to show that England is clearly the appropriate forum for the trial of the action.[411] In practice, the defendant should identify the issues which are appropriate to be tried in the foreign court.[412]

11-144   Where the defendant is present in a country which has the civil law system it is wrong for the English court to compare the relative efficiency of the civil law and common law procedures for the determination of disputed facts, or to compare the reputation and standing of the foreign court with the English court.[413] But the court may take into account that there is a risk that the claimant will be deprived of a fair trial in the foreign country, especially for political or racial reasons.[414] Where the claimant has acted reasonably in commencing proceedings in England, and has not acted unreasonably in failing to commence proceedings in the foreign jurisdiction, and would be met by a time bar in the foreign jurisdiction if permission to serve outside the jurisdiction were to be set aside, the court may make it a condition of setting aside permission that the defendant should waive the time bar in the foreign proceedings.[415] If the parties have agreed that the dispute between them shall

---

[407] See Rule 38(3).

[408] [1984] A.C. 50.

[409] [1987] A.C. 460.

[410] See Rule 38(1), (2).

[411] [1987] A.C. at 480–482. See also *The Handgate* [1987] 1 Lloyd's Rep. 142 (CA); *Islamic Arab Insurance Co v Saudi Egyptian American Reinsurance Co* [1987] 1 Lloyd's Rep. 315 (CA); *EI du Pont de Nemours v Agnew* [1987] 2 Lloyd's Rep. 585, 588–589 (CA); *Roneleigh Ltd v MII Exports Inc* [1989] 1 W.L.R. 619 (CA); *Metall und Rohstoff AG v Donaldson Lufkin & Jenrette Inc* [1990] 1 Q.B. 391, 482–489 (CA); *The Goldean Mariner* [1989] 2 Lloyd's Rep. 390; affirmed [1990] 2 Lloyd's Rep. 215 (CA); *The Oinoussian Pride* [1991] 1 Lloyd's Rep. 126; *Bank of Baroda v Vysya Bank Ltd* [1994] 2 Lloyd's Rep. 87; *McConnell Dowell Constructors Ltd v Lloyd's Syndicate 396* [1988] 2 N.Z.L.R. 257. In jurisdictions, such as New Zealand and Canada, where service outside the jurisdiction is allowed without leave in specified circumstances, the court retains its discretion to set aside service on the application of the defendant: see *Kuwait Asia Bank EC v National Mutual Life Nominees Ltd* [1991] 1 A.C. 187, 217 (PC); and other cases cited para.12–053, n.260.

[412] *Limit (No.3) Ltd v PDV Insurance Co* [2005] EWCA Civ 383, [73]; *Sawyer v Atari Interactive Inc* [2005] EWHC 2351 (Ch.), [2006] I.L.Pr. 129.

[413] *Amin Rasheed Shipping Corp v Kuwait Insurance Co* [1984] A.C. 50, 65.

[414] *Oppenheimer v Louis Rosenthal & Co* [1937] 1 All E.R. 23 (CA); *Ellinger v Guinness Mahon & Co* [1939] 4 All E.R. 16; *Cherney v Deripaska* [2007] EWHC 965 (Comm.), [2007] 2 All E.R. (Comm.) 785; *OJSC Oil Company Yugraneft v Abramovich* [2008] EWHC (Comm.) 2613; *AK Investment CJSC v Kyrgyz Mobil Tel* [2011] UKPC 7, [2011] 4 All E.R. 1027, [89]–[102], where the authorities are fully discussed. See also below, paras 12–040—12–041.

[415] *Spiliada Maritime Corp v Cansulex Ltd* [1987] A.C. at 483–484.

be referred to the exclusive jurisdiction of a foreign court[416] or to arbitration,[417] permission will normally be refused.

(4) CPR, r.6.37(3) provides that the court will not give permission unless　**11–145**
satisfied that England is the proper place in which to bring the claim. This
provision imposes on the claimant the burden of showing good reason why
service should in the circumstances be permitted on a foreign defendant.[418]

The claimant must show that he has a cause of action against the defendant　**11–146**
and that the case falls within one of the heads of jurisdiction in Rule 34. In
Seaconsar Far East Ltd v Bank Markazi Iran[419] the House of Lords, resolving
earlier inconsistent authorities, considered the question of the standard of
proof which the claimant had to discharge on these questions, and the relationship of the strength of the claimant's case to the issue of *forum conveniens*. It
was held that the standard of proof in respect of the cause of action was
whether, on the affidavit evidence, there was a serious question to be tried, i.e.
a substantial question of fact or law, or both, which the claimant bona fide
desired to have tried. CPR, r.6.37(1)(b) now requires the claimant to adduce
evidence stating that he believes his claim has "a reasonable prospect of
success." It has been held that this threshold is the same as if the claimant
were resisting an application by the defendant for summary judgment.[420]

The standard to be applied in considering whether the jurisdiction of the　**11–147**
court had been sufficiently established under one or more of the heads of what
is now PD6B, para.3.1 was that of the good arguable case.[421] In *Canada Trust
Co v Stolzenberg (No.2)*[422] Waller L.J. pointed out that there may be contested
issues which go both to jurisdiction and to the very matter to be argued at the
trial, e.g. the existence of a contract, or issues which go purely to jurisdiction,
e.g. the domicile of a defendant. The question before the court is one which
is normally decided on affidavits from both sides and without full disclosure
and/or cross-examination, and the power to order a preliminary issue on
jurisdiction will seldom be used because trials on jurisdiction issues are to be

---

[416] *Re Schintz* [1926] Ch. 710 (CA); *Mackender v Feldia* [1967] 2 Q.B. 590 (CA). Contrast
Ellinger v Guinness Mahon & Co [1939] 4 All E.R. 16; *Evans Marshall & Co Ltd v Bertola SA*
[1973] 1 W.L.R. 349 (CA); *Re Jogia (A Bankrupt)* [1988] 1 W.L.R. 484. See Rule 32(2).

[417] *A&B v C&D* [1982] 1 Lloyd's Rep. 166, affirmed sub nom. *Qatar Petroleum v Shell
International Petroleum* [1983] 2 Lloyd's Rep. 35 (CA).

[418] *Amin Rasheed Shipping Corp v Kuwait Insurance Co* [1984] A.C. 50, 72; see also *GAF
Corporation v Amchem Products Inc* [1975] 1 Lloyd's Rep. 601, 609 (CA).

[419] [1994] 1 A.C. 438.

[420] *AK Investment CJSC v Kyrgyz Mobil Tel Ltd* [2011] UKPC 7, [2011] 4 All E.R. 1027, [71];
Carvill America Inc v Camperdown UK Ltd [2005] EWCA Civ 645, [2005] 2 Lloyd's Rep. 457.
See also *De Molestina v Ponton* [2002] 1 Lloyd's Rep. 271; *MRG (Japan) Ltd v Engelhard Metals
Japan Ltd* [2004] 1 Lloyd's Rep. 731; *Swiss Reinsurance Co Ltd v United India Insurance Co*
[2002] EWHC 741 (Comm.), [2004] I.L.Pr. 53. But there may be no practical difference between
that test and the previous test: *Sawyer v Atari Interactive Inc* [2005] EWHC 2351 (Ch.), [2006]
I.L.Pr. 129; *Pakistan v Zardari* [2006] EWHC 2411 (Comm.), [2006] 2 C.L.C. 667. See also
Hague v Nam Tai Electronics Inc [2008] UKPC 13, [2008] B.C.C. 295.

[421] See *Vitkovice Horni a Hutni Tezirstvo v Korner* [1951] A.C. 869. As regards the relevant
date for the existence of the factual circumstances to be taken into account see *ISC Technologies
Inc v Guerin* [1992] 2 Lloyd's Rep. 430 and *BMG Trading Ltd v McKay* [1998] I.L.Pr. 691
(CA).

[422] [1998] 1 W.L.R. 547, 555–556 (CA), affirmed [2002] 1 A.C. 1. See also *Bols Distilleries
v Superior Yacht Services* [2005] UKPC 45, [2007] 1 W.L.R. 12, [26]–[28]. The test propounded
by Waller L.J. has given rise to some difficulty: see, e.g. *Cecil v Bayat* [2010] EWHC 641
(Comm.), [32]–[37].

strongly discouraged. The court must be concerned not even to appear to express some concluded view as to the merits, e.g. as to whether the contract existed or not. "Good arguable case" reflects in that context that one side has a much better argument on the material available. It is the concept which the phrase reflects on which it is important to concentrate, i.e. of the court being satisfied or as satisfied as it can be having regard to the limitations which an interlocutory process imposes that factors exist which allow the court to take jurisdiction. But if the applicability of PD6B, para.3.1 depends on a question of law or construction, there is no room for the application of the test of good arguable case: the court must decide the question on the application to set aside.[423]

11–148   In *Seaconsar Far East Ltd v Bank Markazi Iran* the House of Lords also considered the relationship between the standard of proof on the existence of the cause of action and the principle of *forum conveniens*. It disapproved the view that they were inter-related in the sense that the more conspicuous the presence of one element the less consistent with the demands of justice that the other should also be conspicuous.[424] A case particularly strong on the merits could not compensate for a weak case on *forum conveniens*; and a very strong connection with the English forum could not justify a weak case on the merits, if a stronger case on the merits would otherwise be required. The two elements are separate and distinct. The invocation of the principle of *forum conveniens* springs from the often expressed anxiety that great care should be taken in bringing before the English court a foreigner who owes no allegiance here. But if jurisdiction is established under Rule 34, and it is also established that England is the *forum conveniens*, there is no good reason why any particular degree of cogency should be required in relation to the merits of the claimant's case.[425]

11–149   (5) Proceedings may fall at the same time within more than one of the clauses of Rule 34.[426] Thus a claim for the breach of a contract made in England falls within clause (6), but if the contract be a contract concerning land in England, the action falls also within clause (11). But if proceedings fall within one or more of the clauses it is not permissible to litigate any other cause of action which does not fall within one of the clauses.[427] It has been

---

[423] *EF Hutton & Co (London) Ltd v Mofarrij* [1989] 1 W.L.R. 488 (CA); *cf. The Brabo* [1949] A.C. 326; *BP Exploration Co (Libya) Ltd v Hunt* [1976] 1 W.L.R. 786; *The Delfini* [1990] 1 Lloyd's Rep. 252 (CA); *Kuwait Asia Bank EC v National Mutual Life Nominees Ltd* [1991] 1 A.C. 187 (PC). Contrast *Unilever Plc v Gillette (UK) Ltd* [1989] R.P.C. 583, 602 (CA). See also *Chellaram v Chellaram (No.2)* [2002] EWHC 632 (Ch.), [2002] 3 All E.R. 17; *AK Investment CJSC v Kyrgyz Mobil Tel Ltd* [2011] UKPC 7, [2011] 4 All E.R. 1027 (but perhaps not where the application raises a controversial question of law in a developing area, especially when the facts have not been found: at [84]) and *cf. Marubeni Hong Kong and South China Ltd v Mongolian Government* [2002] 2 All E.R. (Comm.) 873.

[424] *Soc Commerciale de Reassurance v Eras International Ltd* [1992] 1 Lloyd's Rep. 570, 588 (CA), *per* Mustill L.J.

[425] [1994] 1 A.C. at 456.

[426] *Tassell v Hallen* [1892] 1 Q.B. 321, 323–325.

[427] *Holland v Leslie* [1894] 2 Q.B. 450 (CA); *Waterhouse v Reid* [1938] 1 K.B. 743 (CA); *The Siskina v Distos Compania Naviera SA* [1979] A.C. 210, 255; *Donohue v Armco Inc* [2002] 1 All E.R. 749, 757–758 (HL). *cf. Beck v Value Capital Ltd (No.2)* [1975] 1 W.L.R. 6; affirmed [1976] 1 W.L.R. 572n. (CA); *Tricon Industries Pty Ltd v Abel Lemon & Co Pty Ltd* [1988] 2 Qd.R. 464; *Australian Iron & Steel Pty v Jumbo (Curacao) NV* (1988) 14 N.S.W.L.R. 507; *David Syme & Co Ltd v Grey* (1992) 38 F.C.R. 303.

held that where permission to serve out of the jurisdiction is based on one cause of action it cannot be treated as permission based on some other cause of action;[428] nor, if a claim has been put forward on one legal basis, can the claimant subsequently justify permission on another legal basis.[429] But the Supreme Court has held[430] that the cases which are authority for those propositions have been superseded by the "overriding objective" of the Civil Procedure Rules to enable the court to deal with cases justly, and that this involves saving expense and ensuring that cases are dealt with expeditiously. The court has power to grant permission to amend and dispense with re-service.

(6) A defendant who wishes to contest the jurisdiction of the court, either on the ground that the case is not within Rule 34, or that the case is not a proper one for the exercise of the discretion, should acknowledge service of the proceedings, and, within 14 days (28 days in the Commercial Court) after filing an acknowledgment of service, apply to the court for an order declaring that it has no jurisdiction.[431]   **11–150**

Brussels I Regulation, Lugano Convention and intra-United Kingdom jurisdiction. As has been seen,[432] there are a number of cases in which exclusive jurisdiction may be vested in the courts of other Member States or Convention States even though the defendant is not domiciled in a Member State, or in a Convention State. In such a case the English court would not be able to exercise jurisdiction under Rule 34. This will be a rare case since it is not easy to envisage any but the most unlikely circumstances which would both give exclusive jurisdiction to the courts of another Member or Convention State under Art.22 of the Regulation or the Convention, and also found jurisdiction in England under Rule 34. Cases in which exclusive jurisdiction is given to the courts of a Member or Convention State under Art.23 and which also come within Rule 34 are easier to imagine. In such cases the English court would not be entitled to assume jurisdiction under, for example, Rule 34, clause (6), on the basis that the contract is governed by English law. But even apart from the Regulation and the Convention the English court would be reluctant to assume jurisdiction in such a case.[433] Similar considerations apply where the defendant is domiciled in Scotland or Northern Ireland. But the cases of overlap are likely to be even rarer because Rule 12 in Sch.4 to the 1982 Act does not attribute conclusive effect to jurisdiction clauses.[434]   **11–151**

---

[428] *Parker v Schuller* (1901) 17 T.L.R. 299 (CA).

[429] *Metall und Rohstoff AG v Donaldson Lufkin & Jenrette Inc* [1990] 1 Q.B. 391, 436 (CA). See also *Excess Insurance Co Ltd v Astra SA Insurance and Reinsurance Co* [1997] C.L.C. 160 (CA).

[430] *NML Capital Ltd v Republic of Argentina* [2011] UKSC 31, [2011] 3 W.L.R. 273. This holding was *obiter* because the case concerned the grounds on which the claimants relied for an exception to state immunity, and there are no procedural rules analogous to those in CPR, Pt 6.

[431] CPR, r.11(1), (2), (4); r.58.7. See para.11–073.

[432] para.11–104.

[433] para.11–144, n.416.

[434] para.12–144.

11–152   Conversely there will be a number of rare cases in which a defendant domiciled in another Member State or in another Convention State or in Scotland or Northern Ireland may be sued under Rule 34. These will include cases outside the scope of the Regulation and the Convention because they are not civil or commercial matters or are otherwise excluded by Art.1 of the Regulation or the Convention. Examples would be claims to enforce arbitral awards and revenue claims. Both are excluded by Art.1 of the Regulation and the Convention from their scope, and both may found jurisdiction under Rule 34[435] over persons not present in England and who are domiciled in another Member State or in another Convention State or in Scotland or Northern Ireland.

11–153   In the rare cases in which Rule 34 will apply to defendants domiciled in Scotland or Northern Ireland, r.6.37(4) provides that if it appears to the court that the claimant may also be entitled to a remedy in Scotland or Northern Ireland the court, in deciding whether to grant permission, shall compare the cost and convenience of proceeding there or in England, and (where that is relevant) to the powers and jurisdiction of the Sheriff Court in Scotland or the county court or courts of summary jurisdiction in Northern Ireland. The object of this rule is to protect persons living in Scotland or Northern Ireland from the inconvenience of an action which, though it might be brought in England, would cause them unnecessary cost. It is not an additional ground for giving permission to serve out of the jurisdiction, but an additional obstacle that the claimant has to surmount.[436]

11R–154   **(1) The court may assume jurisdiction if a claim is made for a remedy against a person domiciled in England.**[437]

COMMENT

11–155   In this clause, which before an amendment to RSC Order 11, r.1(1) in 1983 applied to persons domiciled or ordinarily resident in England, the expression "domiciled" is to be determined[438] (i) in relation to a Lugano Convention State, in accordance with ss.41 to 46 of the 1982 Act, and (ii) in relation to a Member State, in accordance with the Regulation and paras 9 to 12 of Sch.1 to the Civil Jurisdiction and Judgments Order 2001.[439] The clause applies not only to individuals but also to partnerships and bodies corporate.[440] The term "remedy" in this clause includes the recovery of a debt, or of damages in an action for breach of contract or tort,[441] or an injunction requiring an act

---

[435] Clauses (10) and (17).
[436] See *Tottenham v Barry* (1879) 12 Ch.D. 797; *Kinahan v Kinahan* (1890) 45 Ch.D. 78; *Washburn, etc., Co v Cunard Co* (1889) 5 T.L.R. 592; *Re De Penny* [1891] 2 Ch. 63; *Williams v Cartwright* [1895] 1 Q.B. 142 (CA); *Macaulay (Tweeds) Ltd v Independent Harris Tweed Producers Ltd* [1961] R.P.C. 184, 192–193.
[437] CPR, r.6.36 and PD6B, para.3.1(1).
[438] CPR, r.6.31(i). See Rule 30.
[439] SI 2001/3929.
[440] See Interpretation Act 1978, Sch.1.
[441] See *Hadad v Bruce* (1892) 8 T.L.R. 409.

abroad.[442] Hence domicile in England is of itself a ground of jurisdiction against a defendant who might otherwise, on account of his absence from England, be exempt from the jurisdiction of the court. If he is domiciled in England he would be put in the same position as a person who is in this country.[443]

This head of Rule 34 is likely to be of little practical significance, since **11–156** permission to serve process outside the jurisdiction on a defendant domiciled in England is required only in cases falling outside the scope of the Regulation and the Convention. If the case falls within the Regulation or the Convention (or within the intra-United Kingdom provisions of Sch.4 to the 1982 Act) permission to serve out of the jurisdiction is not required.[444]

(2) The court may assume jurisdiction if a claim is made for an injunction **11R–157** **ordering the defendant to do or refrain from doing an act in England.**[445]

COMMENT

The injunction need not be the only relief sought, but it must be the substantial **11–158** relief sought: permission will be refused if the claim for an injunction is not made bona fide, but merely to bring the case within the clause.[446] Permission will also be refused if a foreign court can more conveniently deal with the question,[447] or if there is no real ground to anticipate repetition of the action complained of,[448] or if the injunction cannot be made effective in England.[449] To come within this clause the injunction sought in the action has to be part of the substantive relief to which the claimant's cause of action entitles him, e.g. an injunction to restrain a threatened breach of contract.[450]

ILLUSTRATIONS

1. X, who is resident in New York, sends cards to A in London, through the post-office and **11–159** otherwise, containing libellous and defamatory matter. A brings proceedings claiming an injunction to restrain X from sending such post-cards, and also claiming damages. The court may assume jurisdiction.[451]

---

[442] *Re Liddell's Settlement* [1936] Ch. 365 (CA).

[443] *ibid.* at p.374.

[444] See Rule 35, clause (1).

[445] CPR, r.6.36 and PD6B, para.3.1(2).

[446] Compare *Watson v Daily Record* [1907] 1 K.B. 853 (CA); *De Bernales v New York Herald* (1893) 68 L.T. 658; [1893] 2 Q.B. 97n. (CA); *Alexander & Co v Valentine & Sons* (1908) 25 T.L.R. 29 (CA); *GAF Corp v Amchem Products Inc* [1975] 1 Lloyd's Rep. 601, 605–606; *Joynt v McCrum* [1899] 1 I.R. 217.

[447] *Societe Generale de Paris v Dreyfus* (1885) 29 Ch.D. 239; (1887) 37 Ch.D. 215 (CA); *Kinahan v Kinahan* (1890) 45 Ch.D. 78; *Re De Penny* [1891] 2 Ch. 63; *Rosler v Hilbery* [1925] Ch. 250 (CA).

[448] *De Bernales v New York Herald* (1893) 68 L.T. 658; [1893] 2 Q.B. 97n. (CA). Compare *Watson v Daily Record Ltd* [1907] 1 K.B. 853 (CA), and contrast *Alexander & Co v Valentine & Sons* (1908) 25 T.L.R. 29.

[449] See *Marshall v Marshall* (1888) 38 Ch.D. 330 (CA).

[450] *James North & Sons Ltd v North Cape Textiles Ltd* [1984] 1 W.L.R. 1428 (CA).

[451] *cf. Tozier v Hawkins* (1885) 15 Q.B.D. 650, 680 (CA); *Dunlop Rubber Co v Dunlop* [1921] 1 A.C. 367. See also *Alexander & Co v Valentine & Sons* (1908) 25 T.L.R. 29.

2. X & Co carry on business in South Africa. X & Co at Manchester infringe A's trade mark. A brings proceedings to restrain infringement. The court may assume jurisdiction.[452]

3. X resides in New York, and there contracts with A & Co, an English company, to perform certain services in South Africa at a salary. He goes to South Africa, but returns thence before he has fully performed his contract. A & Co refuse to pay X part of the salary which he claims. X threatens a petition for the winding-up of A & Co. A & Co bring proceedings against X, claiming (1) rescission of contract, (2) return of moneys paid, (3) injunction to restrain X from presenting the petition. The court may assume jurisdiction.[453]

4. N, a trader in England, orders goods from X, a manufacturer in Illinois. X addresses the goods to N in England and delivers them to the Chicago post office by which they are forwarded to England. The goods are manufactured by X according to an invention protected by an English patent. Proceedings are brought by A, the patentee, against X, claiming an injunction against infringement of patent. The court has no jurisdiction, because the sale and delivery of the goods by X was complete when he delivered them to the post office in Chicago.[454]

11R–160   **(3) The court may assume jurisdiction if a claim is made against someone on whom the claim form has been or will be served and (a) there is between the claimant and that person a real issue which it is reasonable for the court to try and (b) the claimant wishes to serve the claim form on another person who is a necessary or proper party to that claim.[455]**

(4) The court may assume jurisdiction if the claim is an additional claim under CPR Part 20 and the person to be served is a necessary or proper party to the claim or additional claim.[456]

COMMENT

11–161   It may be necessary or proper that a claimant, A, should make not only one person, X, but also some other person, Y, defendant in the proceedings. This is so, for example, where X and Y are joint debtors,[457] or where A has a claim, alternatively, either against X or Y, or where otherwise the claims can be conveniently disposed of in the same proceedings.[458] This clause originally required X to be served within the jurisdiction but is not now so limited. It allows Y to be joined in the proceedings even though Y could not be served under any of the other clauses of this Rule if he had been sued alone, e.g. proceedings for a tort committed abroad.[459] But because the cause of action may have no connection with England, especial care is required before

---

[452] *cf. Re Burland's Trade Mark* (1889) 41 Ch.D. 542. Contrast *Marshall v Marshall* (1888) 38 Ch.D. 330 (CA).

[453] *cf. Lisbon Berlyn Gold Fields v Heddle* (1885) 52 L.T. 796.

[454] *cf. Badische Anilin und Soda Fabrik v Basle Chemical Works, Bindschedler* [1898] A.C. 200.

[455] CPR, r.6.36 and PD6B, para.3.1(3). See *United Film Distribution Ltd v Chhabria* [2001] EWCA Civ 416, [2001] 2 All E.R. (Comm.) 865 (CA); *The Baltic Flame* [2001] EWCA Civ 418, [2001] 2 Lloyd's Rep. 203 (CA); *Carvill America Inc v Camperdown UK Ltd* [2005] EWCA Civ 645, [2005] 2 Lloyd's Rep. 457; *OT Africa Line Ltd v Magic Sportswear Corp* [2005] EWCA Civ 710, [2005] 2 Lloyd's Rep 170. See also *Analog Devices BV v Zurich Insurance Co* [2002] 1 I.R. 272 (Sup Ct); *McCarthy v Pillay* [2003] 1 I.R. 592 (Sup Ct).

[456] CPR, r.6.36 and PD6B, para.3.1(4). See Takahashi (2002) 51 I.C.L.Q. 127.

[457] If one joint debtor is outside the jurisdiction he need not be joined in proceedings against the other or others: *Wilson, Sons & Co v Balcarres Brook SS Co* [1893] 1 Q.B. 422 (CA).

[458] CPR, r.7.3.

[459] *Williams v Cartwright* [1895] 1 Q.B. 142, 145, 148 (CA); *The Duc d'Aumale* [1903] P. 18 (CA).

permission to serve out of the jurisdiction will be allowed.[460] In particular, the court should not grant permission under this clause as a matter of course merely because not to do so would mean that more than one set of proceedings would be required.[461]

In order that the court may have jurisdiction within clause (3) the following conditions must be fulfilled: **11–162**

(1) X has been or will be served. Service may be in England as of right, or abroad with permission under r.6.36 and PD6B, para.3.1, i.e. Rule 34, or abroad as of right under CPR, r.6.33(3). Where X is outside the jurisdiction and instructs solicitors to accept service on his behalf within the jurisdiction, A may join Y under this clause.[462]   **11–163**

(2) A must satisfy the court by written evidence that there is between A and X a real issue which it is reasonable for the court to try.[463] The mere fact that X is sued only for the purpose of bringing in Y is not fatal to the application for permission to serve Y out of the jurisdiction.[464] It is a factor in the exercise of the discretion and not an element in the question whether the action is "properly brought" against X, provided that there is a viable claim against X.[465] But the action is not "properly brought" against X if it is bound to fail.[466] Thus permission will not be granted if X has a complete answer to the claim by A,[467] or if Y has a complete answer.[468] But permission may be granted if the causes of action are alternative, so that the claim against one of them will ultimately fail.[469] If the question is whether the claim against X is bound to fail on a question of law it should be decided on the application for   **11–164**

---

[460] *The Brabo* [1949] A.C. 326, 328; *Multinational Gas Co v Multinational Gas Services Ltd* [1983] Ch. 258, 271 (CA); *Arab Monetary Fund v Hashim (No.4)* [1992] 1 W.L.R. 553, 557, affirmed [1992] 1 W.L.R. 1176 (CA); *AK Investment CJSC v Kyrgyz Mobil Tel Ltd* [2011] UKPC 7, [2011] 4 All E.R. 1027. See also Piggott, *Foreign Judgments and Jurisdiction* (3rd ed. 1910), Pt.III, p.238.

[461] *AK Investment CJSC v Kyrgyz Mobil Tel Ltd* [2011] UKPC 7, [2011] 4 All E.R. 1027; *The Goldean Mariner* [1990] 2 Lloyd's Rep. 215 (CA).

[462] *The Benarty (No.1)* [1983] 1 Lloyd's Rep. 361 (CA), distinguishing *John Russell & Co Ltd v Cayzer, Irvine & Co Ltd* [1916] 2 A.C. 298; followed, with some misgivings, in *Amanuel v Alexandros Shipping Co* [1986] Q.B. 464. A mere submission by X, without service of process on him then or thereafter, may not be sufficient to allow service on Y.

[463] CPR, PD6B, para.3.1(3)(a), derived from *Ellinger v Guinness, Mahon & Co* [1939] 4 All E.R. 16, 22. See also *Soc Commerciale Reassurance v Eras International Ltd* [1992] 1 Lloyd's Rep. 570 (CA); *The Ines* [1993] 2 Lloyd's Rep. 492; *The Xing Su Hai* [1995] 2 Lloyd's Rep. 15; *The Flecha* [1999] 1 Lloyd's Rep. 612.

[464] *The Brabo* [1949] A.C. 326, 338–9; *Derby & Co Ltd v Larsson* [1976] 1 W.L.R. 202, 203 (HL); *AK Investment CJSC v Kyrgyz Mobil Tel Ltd* [2011] UKPC 7, [2011] 4 All E.R. 1027, [76]. *cf. Multinational Gas Co v Multinational Gas Services Ltd* [1983] Ch. 258 (CA).

[465] *AK Investment CJSC v Kyrgyz Mobil Tel Ltd*, above, [76]–[79].

[466] *The Brabo*, above, 338–9; *AK Investment CJSC v Kyrgyz Mobil Tel Ltd*, above, at [80]. See also *Multinational Gas Co v Multinational Gas Services Ltd*, above, at 273–274.

[467] *The Brabo* [1949] A.C. 326; *Witted v Galbraith* [1893] 1 Q.B. 577 (CA); *Flower v Rose & Co* (1891) 7 T.L.R. 280.

[468] *Multinational Gas Co v Multinational Gas Services Ltd* [1983] Ch. 258 (CA); *Kuwait Asia Bank EC v National Mutual Life Nominees Ltd* [1991] 1 A.C. 187 (PC); *DSQ Property Co Ltd v Lotus Cars Ltd, The Times*, June 28, 1990 (CA) (in which both X and Y had a complete answer); *Barings Plc v Coopers & Lybrand* [1997] I.L.Pr. 12 (CA). But the fact that Y would have a complete answer if sued in the courts for the place where he is domiciled is not of itself a sufficient reason to refuse joinder: *The Baltic Flame* [2001] EWCA Civ 418, [2001] 1 Lloyd's Rep. 203 (CA).

[469] *Massey v Heynes* (1888) 21 Q.B.D. 330 (CA).

permission to serve Y (or on the application to discharge the order granting permission), but not where there is an exceptionally difficult and doubtful point of law.[470]

11–165   (3) Y, who is out of England, must be either a necessary or proper party to the proceedings. If Y is a proper party it is not also a requirement that he be a necessary party; but if adding Y is likely in practice to achieve no potential advantage for the claimant, it would not ordinarily be a proper case for service out of the jurisdiction.[471] The question whether Y is a proper party to proceedings against X depends on this: supposing both X and Y had been in England, would they both have been proper parties to the proceedings? If they would, and only one of them, X, is in this country, then Y is a proper party and permission may be given to serve him out of the jurisdiction.[472] Y will be a proper party if the claims against X and Y involve one investigation.[473] It is not necessary that the alleged liability of Y be joint or several with that of X.[474]

11–166   In the rare cases falling outside the intra-United Kingdom provisions of the 1982 Act, clause (3) applies to a defendant domiciled or ordinarily resident in Scotland or Northern Ireland;[475] and CPR, r.6.37(4)(b)(i), which requires the court to have regard to the comparative cost and convenience of proceeding there or in England, applies to such a case.[476]

11–167   Additional claims are counterclaims and what used to be known as third party claims. An additional claim is defined by the Civil Procedure Rules[477] to mean any claim other than a claim by a claimant against a defendant, and includes (a) a counterclaim by a defendant against the claimant or against the claimant and some other person; (b) an additional claim by a defendant against any person (whether or not already a party) for contribution or indemnity or some other remedy; and (c) where a claim has been made against

---

[470] *The Brabo*, above, at 341, *per* Lord Porter; 351, *per* Lord du Parcq, and contrast Lord Simonds at 348; *AK Investment CJSC v Kyrgyz Mobil Tel Ltd*, above at [86].

[471] *Electric Furnace Co v Selas Corp of America* [1987] R.P.C. 23, 32–33 (CA).

[472] *Massey v Heynes* (1888) 21 Q.B.D. 330, 338 (CA); *Lightowler v Lightowler* [1884] W.N. 8; *The Elton* [1891] P. 265; *The Duc d'Aumale* [1903] P. 18 (CA); *Oesterreichische Export, etc. Co v British Indemnity Co Ltd* [1914] 2 K.B. 747 (CA); *Macaulay (Tweeds) Ltd v Independent Harris Tweed Producers Ltd* [1961] R.P.C. 184; *Qatar Petroleum v Shell International Petroleum* [1983] 2 Lloyd's Rep. 35 (CA); *The Goldean Mariner* [1989] 2 Lloyd's Rep. 390, 395 (approving the statement in the text); affirmed [1990] 2 Lloyd's Rep. 215 (CA). See also *Aiglon Ltd v Gau Shan & Co Ltd* [1993] 1 Lloyd's Rep. 164; *C Inc v L* [2001] 2 Lloyd's Rep. 459.

[473] *Massey v Heynes & Co* at 338, applied in *The Baltic Flame* [2001] EWCA Civ 418, [2001] C.L.C. 1151 at [33] and in *Carvill America Inc v Camperdown UK Ltd* [2005] EWCA Civ 645; [2005] 1 C.L.C. 845 at [48], where Clarke L.J. also used, or approved, in this connection the expressions "closely bound up" and "a common thread": at [46], [49]. See *AK Investment CJSC v Kyrgyz Mobil Tel Ltd*, above at [87].

[474] See, e.g. *Oesterreichische Export, etc., Co v British Indemnity Co Ltd* [1914] 2 K.B. 747 (CA); *Bank of NSW v Commonwealth Steel Co Ltd* [1983] 1 N.S.W.L.R. 69.

[475] See *Washburn, etc., Co v Cunard Co & Parkes* (1889) 5 T.L.R. 592; *Croft v King* [1893] 1 Q.B. 419; *Williams v Cartwright* [1895] 1 Q.B. 142 (CA); *Oesterreichische Export, etc., Co v British Indemnity Co Ltd* [1914] 2 K.B. 747 (CA).

[476] *Washburn, etc., Co v Cunard Co & Parkes* (1889) 5 T.L.R. 592; *Williams v Cartwright* [1895] 1 Q.B. 142 (CA); *Macaulay (Tweeds) Ltd v Independent Harris Tweed Producers Ltd* [1961] R.P.C. 184, 192–193.

[477] CPR, r.20.2.

a person who is not already a party, any additional claim made by that person against any other person (whether or not already a party).

It seems that it would apply not only where the defendant seeks a direct remedy against a foreign third party, but also (as under the former version of clause (3)) where the defendant adds a new foreign defendant to a counter-claim against the claimant.[478] **11–168**

ILLUSTRATIONS

1. X, on instructions from Y, enters, as agent for Y, into a contract with A. Y repudiates the contract. A brings proceedings against X, who is in England, for breach of warranty that X was authorised to contract for Y, who is in New York, and has an alternative claim against Y if X was authorised to contract for him. The court may assume jurisdiction to entertain an action against Y as co-defendant with X.[479] **11–169**

2. A & Co, an American company, own a patent for barbed wire. Y, carrying on business in Japan, buys from N, in America, wire which is an infringement of A & Co's patent. X & Co, an English shipping company, carry the wire for Y and land it at Liverpool for transhipment to Y in Japan. A & Co bring proceedings against X & Co to obtain an injunction against their dealing with the wire. A & Co apply for permission to add Y and serve Y in Japan. The court may assume jurisdiction.[480]

3. A brings proceedings for deceit against X and Y in respect of a fraud jointly committed by them in London. X is in England. Y is domiciled in New York. X has been served with process, and Y is a necessary and proper party to the proceedings. The court may assume jurisdiction.[481]

4. A brings proceedings against X, residing in England, who supplied him with defective goods, and applies for permission to serve Y, residing in the United States, who designed the goods. The court may assume jurisdiction.[482]

5. A & Co, a Liberian corporation, through its liquidator sues, alleging negligence and breach of duty, X & Co, an English company, Y and others (directors of A & Co), all resident abroad, and Z & Co and others, foreign companies who own the shares in A & Co. X & Co and Y and the other directors are not in a position to satisfy the substantial claim, and the predominant (but not the sole) purpose of suing X & Co is to enable A & Co to join the parties outside the jurisdiction. But as a matter of English company law Y and the other directors and Z & Co and the other shareholders are not liable to A & Co. Although the proceedings are "properly brought" against X & Co, notwithstanding the predominant purpose of joining the foreign defendants, Y and the other directors and Z & Co and the other shareholders are not "proper parties" because the proceedings against them are bound to fail.[483] **11–170**

6. A Co, a Kyrgyz mobile telephone company, seeks to enforce a Kyrgyz judgment by proceedings in the Isle of Man against X Ltd, Y Ltd, and Z Ltd, incorporated in the Isle of Man. A Co was originally owned by X Ltd, Y Ltd and Z Ltd, and the effect of the Kyrgyz proceedings is to divest them of ownership. They counterclaim against A Co. for (inter alia) a declaration and damages on the basis that the Kyrgyz judgment was obtained by fraud, and obtain permission to join 13 additional defendants to the counterclaim and serve them out of the jurisdiction. Six of those additional defendants to the counterclaim (including companies incorporated in the British Virgin Islands, Russia and the Kyrgyz Republic) apply for an order setting aside service out of the jurisdiction. The counterclaims against the additional defendants raise causes of action which involve allegations that X Ltd, Y Ltd and Z Ltd were unlawfully deprived of their interest in A Co and that the Kyrgyz judgment was obtained by fraud. The counterclaim is "properly brought" against A Co and the six defendants to counterclaim are "proper parties" to the counterclaim

---

[478] *Derby & Co Ltd v Larsson* [1976] 1 W.L.R. 202 (HL).

[479] *Massey v Heynes* (1888) 21 Q.B.D. 330 (CA).

[480] cf. *Washburn, etc., Co v Cunard Co & Parkes* (1889) 5 T.L.R. 592.

[481] cf. *Williams v Cartwright* [1895] 1 Q.B. 142 (CA).

[482] *The Manchester Courage* [1973] 1 Lloyd's Rep. 386; see also *Adastra Aviation Ltd v Airparts (NZ) Ltd* [1964] N.Z.L.R. 393; *Pratt v Rural Aviaton Ltd* [1969] N.Z.L.R. 46.

[483] *Multinational Gas Co v Multinational Gas Services Ltd* [1983] Ch. 258 (CA).

because the claims against A Co and the claims against six defendants to counterclaim involve a single investigation.[484]

7. A brings proceedings against X, residing in the United States, who supplied him with defective goods, and obtains permission to serve him abroad. X is served and defends the proceedings. X applies for permission to serve an additional claim (previously called third party proceedings) against Y, who supplied him with the goods. The court may assume jurisdiction.

11R–171   **(5) The court may assume jurisdiction if a claim is made for an interim remedy under section 25 of the Civil Jurisdiction and Judgments Act 1982.**[485]

Comment

11–172   In *The Siskina*[486] the House of Lords held that clause (2) of Rule 34 could not be used to found an action, or obtain interim relief, when the only claimed basis of jurisdiction was an interlocutory injunction to restrain a defendant from removing his assets out of the jurisdiction.[487] The same result was reached by the Privy Council in *Mercedes Benz AG v Leiduck*,[488] on the basis that clause (2) applied only to claims advanced in an action and for relief founded on a right asserted by the claimant in that action, to be enforced ultimately through the medium of a judgment given by the court in that action. A *Mareva* injunction in support of proceedings in a foreign court was not such a claim, and therefore service of process claiming a *Mareva* injunction only did not fall within clause (2).

11–173   Under the Brussels I Regulation and the Lugano Convention the courts of a relevant State may exercise jurisdiction to grant interim relief of this kind even though the courts of another relevant State have jurisdiction over the substance of the matter,[489] and s.25(1) of the 1982 Act gives the English court power to grant interim relief in such cases within the scope of the Regulation and the Convention and in intra-United Kingdom cases. This power has been extended under s.25(3) to give the court power to grant interim relief so as to make it exercisable in relation (inter alia) to proceedings commenced or to be commenced in States to which the Regulation and the Convention do not apply or to proceedings outside the scope of the Regulation and the Convention. Consequently, the effect of the decisions in *The Siskina* and *Mercedes Benz AG v Leiduck* was reversed.

11–174   A claim form for an interim remedy under s.25 may be served out of the jurisdiction with the permission of the court. On an application for interim relief under s.25 of the 1982 Act, the court may refuse to grant the relief if,

---

[484] *AK Investment CJSC v Kyrgyz Mobil Tel Ltd* [2011] UKPC 7, [2011] 4 All E.R. 1027 (where the facts were more complicated).

[485] CPR, r.6.36 and PD6B, para.3.1(5).

[486] *The Siskina v Distos Compania Naviera* [1979] A.C. 210; followed in *Caudron v Air Zaire* [1986] I.L.R.M. 10 (distinguished in *McKenna v H(E)* [2002] 1 I.R. 72); *Suncorp Realty Inc v PLN Investments, Inc* (1985) 23 D.L.R. (4th) 83 (Man); cf. *Perry v Zissis* [1977] 1 Lloyd's Rep. 607 (CA). See para.8–029; and Collins, *Essays*, pp.30–34.

[487] A *Mareva* injunction (after *Mareva Naviera SA v International Bulkcarriers SA* [1975] 2 Lloyd's Rep. 509 (CA)), as to which see paras 8–005 *et seq*. The Civil Procedure Rules now call it a freezing injunction.

[488] [1996] A.C. 284 (PC).

[489] Art.31; Rule 35, clause (23).

in the opinion of the court, the fact that the court has no independent jurisdiction in relation to the subject-matter of the proceedings makes it inexpedient for the court to grant it.[490]

ILLUSTRATION

X & Co, a Panamanian company, own a vessel, which they let on charter. On the failure of the charterers to pay the freight in full, X & Co cause the vessel to be arrested in Cyprus by order of the courts of Cyprus and the cargo is unloaded. Subsequently the vessel sinks and becomes a total loss. X & Co claim against their insurers, London underwriters. The cargo-owners commence proceedings in the High Court against X & Co, alleging breach of duty or of contract. The court may issue an injunction restraining X & Co from removing the insurance moneys from the jurisdiction.[491]   **11–175**

(6) The court may assume jurisdiction if the claim is made in respect of a contract where the contract   **11R–176**
    (i) was made in England, or
    (ii) was made by or through an agent trading or residing in England, or
    (iii) is governed by English law, or
    (iv) contains a term to the effect that the court shall have jurisdiction to determine any claim in respect of the contract.[492]

COMMENT

This clause applies to four cases: (i) where a contract is made in England; (ii) where a contract is made by or through an agent trading or residing in England; (iii) where a contract is governed by English law; (iv) where a contract contains a submission to the jurisdiction of the English court. These cases are, of course, to be read disjunctively, i.e. it is sufficient if the claimant can bring his case within any one of them.[493] The claimant must have a good arguable case that the conditions of clause (6) are fulfilled, namely that there was a contract and that, e.g. it was made in England, and must also show that there is a serious issue to be tried on the merits of the claim.[494] It includes an alleged contract, provided the claimant shows an arguable case that one existed.[495]   **11–177**

---

[490] s.25(2) on which see *Motorola Credit Corp v Uzan (No.2)* [2003] EWCA Civ 752, [2004] 1 W.L.R. 113, and other cases cited at paras 8–034 *et seq.*

[491] CPR, r.6.36 and PD6B, para.3.1(6); 1982 Act, s.25(1), reversing the effect of *The Siskina v Distos Compania Naviera SA* [1979] A.C. 210.

[492] CPR, r.6.36 and PD6B, para.3.1(6).

[493] *Wansborough Paper Co Ltd v Laughland* [1920] W.N. 344 (CA).

[494] *Seaconsar Far East Ltd v Bank Markazi Iran* [1994] 1 A.C. 438, 454–455. See, e.g. *Maritrop Trading Corp v Guangzhou Ocean Shipping Co* [1998] C.L.C. 224.

[495] *Hemelryck v William Lyall Shipbuilding Co Ltd* [1921] 1 A.C. 698 (PC); *Cromie v Moore* [1936] 2 All E.R. 177 (CA); *Vitkovice Horni A Hutni Tezirstvo v Korner* [1951] A.C. 869: *Britannia Steamship Insurance Assn v Ausonia Assicurazioni SpA* [1984] 2 Lloyd's Rep. 98 (CA); *The Parouth* [1982] 2 Lloyd's Rep. 351 (CA); *Egon Oldendorff v Libera Corp* [1995] 2 Lloyd's Rep. 64; see above, para.11–148.

11–178   A "contract" in the previous versions of this clause has been held to include a quasi-contract,[496] and a covenant in a declaration of trust,[497] but not the mere holding of an office of director without a contract of employment.[498]

11–179   Under the version of this clause in RSC Order 11, r.1(1)(1)(d) the power to grant permission under this clause referred to a claim brought "to enforce, rescind, dissolve, annul or otherwise affect" a contract. It is now necessary only that the claim be made "in respect of a contract," and it is not likely that the authorities[499] on the application of RSC Order 11 will be of much assistance in interpreting the new version. Clause (6) applies to a claim that a contract is valid;[500] to a claim that a contract has been frustrated;[501] and to a claim for an injunction to restrain foreign proceedings in breach of an arbitration agreement governed by English law.[502] But it does not apply to a claim for inducement of breach of contract.[503] It has been held that it does not apply to interpleader proceedings brought by charterers to determine whether charterparty hire should be paid to owners or owners' assignees: it is concerned with a claim which the claimant wished to bring, not with a claim which might be brought against a claimant, and with claims asserted by claimants, and not with claims asserted against claimants.[504]

11–180   It has been held[505] that if, on the claimant's own showing, no such contract as he alleges was made with the defendant, permission will not be granted under this clause, but specific provision has been introduced to allow permission to be given in proceedings for such a declaration.[506]

11–181   **(i) Where a contract is made in England.** If the parties enter into negotiations by correspondence from different countries, the contract is made where the letter of acceptance is posted.[507] But in commercial transactions today communication by telephone, telex, fax and electronic mail is much more common than by post. It is now well established, following the decision

---

[496] *Bowling v Cox* [1926] A.C. 751 (PC); *Rousou's Trustee v Rousou* [1955] 1 W.L.R. 545; *Re Jogia (A Bankrupt)* [1988] 1 W.L.R. 484; *The Kurnia Dewi* [1997] 1 Lloyd's Rep. 552; *Durra v Bank of NSW* [1940] V.L.R. 170; *Earthworks Ltd v FT Eastment & Sons Ltd* [1966] V.R. 24. A claim under statute for harbour dues is not a contractual or quasi-contractual claim for the purposes of clause (6): *Carlingford Harbour Commissioners v Everard & Sons Ltd* [1985] I.R. 50, following *Shipsey v British and South American Steam Navigation Co Ltd* [1936] I.R. 65.

[497] *Official Solicitor v Stype Investments Ltd* [1983] 1 W.L.R. 214.

[498] *Newtherapeutics Ltd v Katz* [1991] Ch. 226.

[499] See cases in the 13th ed., para.11–154. See also *ABCI v Banque Franco-Tunisienne* [2003] EWCA Civ 205 (CA), [2003] 2 Lloyd's Rep 146.

[500] *cf. Gulf Bank KSC v Mitsubishi Heavy Industries Ltd* [1994] 1 Lloyd's Rep. 323.

[501] *cf. BP Exploration Co (Libya) Ltd v Hunt* [1976] 1 W.L.R. 788; *Gulf Bank KSC v Mitsubishi Heavy Industries Ltd* [1994] 1 Lloyd's Rep. 323.

[502] *cf. Schiffahrtgesellschaft Detlev von Appen GmbH v Voest Alpine Intertrading GmbH* [1997] 2 Lloyd's Rep. 279 (CA).

[503] *cf. EF Hutton & Co (London) Ltd v Mofarrij* [1989] 1 W.L.R. 488, 494 (CA). Contrast *South Adelaide Football Club v Fitzroy Football Club* (1988) 92 F.L.R. 117.

[504] *Cool Carriers AB v HSBC Bank USA* [2001] 2 Lloyd's Rep. 22.

[505] *Finnish Marine Insurance Co Ltd v Protective National Insurance Co* [1990] 1 Q.B. 1078.

[506] CPR, r.6.36 and PD6B, para.3.1(8), clause (8) of this Rule.

[507] *Wansborough Paper Co Ltd v Laughland* [1920] W.N. 344 (CA); *Benaim v Debono* [1924] A.C. 514, 520 (PC); *Clarke v Harper and Robinson* [1938] N.Ir. 162; *Williams v Society of Lloyd's* [1994] 1 V.R. 274. See also *Cowan v O'Connor* (1888) 20 Q.B.D. 640; *Lewis Construction Co Ltd v M Tichauer SA* [1966] V.R. 341.

of the Court of Appeal in *Entores v Miles Far East Corporation*[508] (which was approved by the House of Lords[509]) that if the parties use "instantaneous" means of communication such as telephone, fax or electronic mail,[510] the contract is made where the acceptance is communicated to the offeror. It has been held that if a contract made in England contains a submission to arbitration in a foreign country, an action in England at common law to enforce the foreign arbitration award is within this part of the clause.[511] The contract must actually be made in England as that phrase is understood in English law. It is not sufficient if it merely says that it shall be deemed to be so made, though this may be sufficient to make it one which is governed by English law.[512] A contract may be made in England within the meaning of this clause although it was preceded by a less formal agreement made abroad,[513] or if it was originally made in England, but amended abroad.[514]

**(ii) Where a contract is made by or through an agent trading or   11–182
residing in England.** The clause says "by or through" an agent, not "by" an agent. Hence the case is within the clause, although the agent has no authority to make contracts on behalf of his foreign principal, but only has authority to obtain orders and transmit them to his principal for acceptance or rejection.[515] This part of the clause is designed to bring within Rule 34 foreigners who transact business in England by or through agents, and consequently it does not apply where the agent's principal is the claimant. Hence a claimant cannot invoke clause (6)(ii) where the contract was made by or through his agent.[516]

If proceedings are brought by consignees of a cargo against foreign ship-   11–183
owners under the bills of lading, the case is not within this part of the clause if the charterparty (but not the bills of lading) was made by or through agents of the shipowners in England, even though it refers to the bills of lading and was made by charterers acting on behalf of the consignees.[517] It may be otherwise, however, if the charterers are identical with the consignees.

---

[508] [1955] 2 Q.B. 327 (CA); *Gill & Duffus Landauer v London Export Corp* [1982] 2 Lloyd's Rep. 627; *Kelly v Cruise Catering Ltd* [1994] 2 I.L.R.M. 394; *Hampstead Meats Pty Ltd v Emerson and Yates Pty Ltd* [1967] S.A.S.R. 109; *Express Airways v Port Augusta Air Services* [1980] Qd. 543; *Mendelson-Zeller Co Inc v T&C Providores Pty Ltd* [1981] 1 N.S.W.L.R. 366; *Re Modern Fashions Ltd* (1969) 8 D.L.R. (3d) 590 (Man); *McDonald & Sons Ltd v Export Packers Co Ltd* (1979) 95 D.L.R. (3d) 174 (BC); *Eastern Power Ltd v Azienda Communale Energia e Ambiente* [2001] I.L. Pr. 55 (Ont CA).

[509] *Brinkibon Ltd v Stahag Stahl* [1983] 2 A.C. 34. See also *Apple Corps Ltd v Apple Computer Inc* [2004] EWHC 768 (Ch.), [2004] I.L.Pr. 597. *cf. Bank of Baroda v Vysya Bank Ltd* [1994] 2 Lloyd's Rep. 87; *Chunilal v Merrill Lynch International Inc* [2010] EWHC 1467 (Comm.).

[510] But the place of receipt of electronic mail is a concept by no means free from difficulty. See *Dow Jones & Co Inc v Gutnick* [2002] HCA 56, (2003) 210 C.L.R. 575.

[511] *Bremer Oeltransport v Drewry* [1933] 1 K.B. 753 (CA). See para.16–105. But see now CPR, r.6.36 and PD6B, para.3.1(10), clause (10), below.

[512] See Rule 223 and *cf. British Controlled Oilfields Ltd v Stagg* [1921] W.N. 319.

[513] *Gibbon v Commerz und Creditbank AG* [1958] 2 Lloyd's Rep. 113.

[514] *Sharab v Al-Saud* [2009] EWCA Civ 353, [2009] 1 Lloyd's Rep. 160.

[515] *National Mortgage and Agency Co of NZ Ltd v Gosselin* (1922) 38 T.L.R. 832 (CA); *cf. BHP Petroleum Pty Ltd v Oil Basins Ltd* [1985] V.R. 725; affirmed [1985] V.R. 756.

[516] *Union International Insurance Co Ltd v Jubilee Insurance Co Ltd* [1991] 1 W.L.R. 415.

[517] *The Metamorphosis* [1953] 1 W.L.R. 543.

11-184   Rule 6.12 of the Civil Procedure Rules provides an alternative method of service if the conditions laid down in clause (6)(ii) of Rule 34 are satisfied together with two other conditions, namely, that the contract was made in England with or through the defendant's agent, and that the agent's authority has not been terminated or he is still in business relations with his principal. This method is to issue proceedings against the principal, and serve process with permission of the court on the agent in England.

11-185   When an order under CPR, r.6.12 has been obtained, the proceedings are served on the agent, and copies are sent to the defendant. The procedure is essentially discretionary, not normally to be resorted to when there is no difficulty in proceeding under Rule 34. It is more appropriate in a case where the foreign principal has a general agent doing large business for him in England than where the foreign principal makes a single contract through a broker.

11-186   **(iii) Where a contract is governed by English law.** The rules for ascertaining the governing law of a contract are considered in Rules 221 to 223.[518] The Rome I Regulation on the law applicable to contractual obligations will be applied to determine whether a contract by its terms or by implication is governed by English law for the purposes of this clause.[519]

11-187   Although the fact that a contract is governed by English law is an important factor in the exercise of the discretion under this head in favour of the English forum,[520] it is not conclusive. This head of jurisdiction was described as exorbitant in *Amin Rasheed Shipping Corp v Kuwait Insurance Co*,[521] where the House of Lords held that in the circumstances it was not appropriate for the English court to determine a dispute involving a marine insurance policy governed by English law when the Kuwaiti courts were the *forum conveniens*. Until that decision it was generally thought that the fact that a contract was governed by English law was in itself sufficient to justify leave. But now the claimant has a heavier burden. In *Amin Rasheed* Lord Diplock suggested[522] that, in order to justify leave under this head, the plaintiff had to show that justice could not be obtained by him in the foreign court, or could only be obtained at excessive cost, delay or inconvenience. But it was subsequently held that Lord Diplock was merely giving examples, and was not providing an exhaustive list, of the relevant factors.[523] The court has to consider all factors, and the fact that English law is the applicable law may be of great importance,

---

[518] Several important cases on the common law rules as to the ascertainment of the governing law were decided under clause (6) of Rule 34, the most important modern example of which was *Amin Rasheed Shipping Corp v Kuwait Insurance Co* [1984] A.C. 50.

[519] Most of the English cases on the Rome Convention mentioned in Ch.32 involved questions of jurisdiction. See *Bank of Baroda v Vysya Bank Ltd* [1994] 2 Lloyd's Rep. 87; *Egon Oldendorff v Libera Corp* [1995] 2 Lloyd's Rep. 64, stated below, Illustration 11; *Marconi Communications International Ltd v PT Pan Indonesia Bank Ltd TBK* [2005] EWCA Civ 422, [2007] 2 Lloyd's Rep. 72.

[520] *BP Exploration Co (Libya) v Hunt* [1976] 3 All E.R. 879, 893, as explained in *The Elli 2* [1985] 1 Lloyd's Rep. 107, 118 (CA).

[521] [1984] A.C. 50, 65, Illustration 7, below. It is regarded as exorbitant in civil law countries; see Schlosser, para.87.

[522] [1984] A.C. at 68.

[523] *Spiliada Maritime Corp v Cansulex Ltd* [1987] A.C. 460, 480, approving *The Elli 2* [1985] 1 Lloyd's Rep. 107 (CA).

or it may be of little consequence as seen in the context of the whole case.[524] Thus if there is likely to be no dispute on matters of law or construction, or if the law of the foreign forum is substantially the same as English law, the fact that English law is the applicable law will be of little weight. But where an issue of English public policy arises in relation to a contract which is (or may be) governed by English law, it is desirable that it should be decided by the English court;[525] conversely, where the foreign court may apply its own public policy to defeat a claim based on a contract governed by English law, that too is a reason for the English court taking jurisdiction.[526] If the claimant has alternative remedies in contract and tort upon the same facts, he can choose his remedy.[527]

(iv) Where a contract contains a term to the effect that the court shall **11–188** **have jurisdiction to determine any claim in respect of the contract.** This clause had its origin in 1920,[528] when it was introduced to allow service out of the jurisdiction in cases where there was a contractual submission but where no other head of RSC Order 11, r.1(1) was applicable. It is dealt with more fully in connection with Rule 39(1) on jurisdiction clauses which confer jurisdiction on English courts.[529]

ILLUSTRATIONS

(1) CONTRACT MADE IN ENGLAND

1. X, by letter posted in New York, orders goods from A in England. A accepts the order by **11–189** letter posted in England. The contract is made in England and the court may assume jurisdiction.[530]

2. A in London sends an offer by telex to buy goods to X in Tokyo. X accepts the offer in a similar manner. The contract is made in England and the court may assume jurisdiction.[531]

3. X in Delhi sends by telex an offer to sell goods to A is London. A accepts the offer by sending a telex to Delhi. The contract is made in Delhi and the court has no jurisdiction.[532]

4. A charterparty made in London between A, a Swedish firm of shipowners, and X, who resides in Spain, contains a clause providing for the submission of disputes to arbitration in Stockholm. Under an arbitration conducted in Stockholm in pursuance of this clause, an award is made against X of £20,000 payable in English currency. A brings proceedings against X to

---

[524] [1987] A.C. at 481, 486; *Sawyer v Atari Interactive Inc* [2005] EWHC 2351 (Ch.), [2006] I.L.Pr. 129; *Novus Aviation Limited v Onur Air Tasimacilik AS* [2009] EWCA Civ 122, [2009] 1 Lloyd's Rep. 576; *Stonebridge Underwriting Ltd v Ontario Municipal Insurance Exchange* [2010] EWHC 2279 (Comm.), [2011] Lloyd's Rep I.R. 171; *Wright v Deccan Chargers Sporting Ventures Ltd* [2011] EWHC 1307 (QB); *Mujur Bakat SDN Bhd v Uni Asia General Insurance Bhd* [2011] EWHC 643 (Comm.), [2011] Lloyd's Rep. I.R. 465; *Faraday Reinsurance Co Ltd v Howden North America Inc* [2011] EWHC 2837 (Comm.).

[525] *El du Pont de Nemours v Agnew* [1987] 2 Lloyd's Rep. 585 (CA); *Mitsubishi Corp v Alafouzos* [1988] 1 Lloyd's Rep. 191.

[526] *The Magnum* [1989] 1 Lloyd's Rep. 47 (CA).

[527] *Matthews v Kuwait Bechtel Corporation* [1959] 2 Q.B. 57 (CA), stated below, Illustration 6.

[528] To reverse the decision in *British Wagon Co v Gray* [1896] 1 Q.B. 35 (CA).

[529] See paras 12–147 *et seq.*

[530] *cf. Wansborough Paper Co Ltd v Laughland* [1920] W.N. 344 (CA).

[531] *cf. Entores Ltd v Miles Far East Corporation* [1955] 2 Q.B. 327 (CA).

[532] *cf. Brinkibon Ltd v Stahag Stahl* [1983] 2 A.C. 34.

enforce the award. The court may assume jurisdiction because the contract containing the submission to arbitration was made in England.[533]

(2) CONTRACT MADE BY OR THROUGH AN AGENT TRADING OR RESIDING IN ENGLAND

11–190　　5. X, who resides and carries on business in Canada, employs N, who resides and carries on business in England, as his agent to obtain orders for goods and submit them to X in Canada for acceptance or rejection. N has no authority to make contracts on X's behalf. N obtains an order from A and submits it to X, who accepts it. A brings proceedings against X for breach of warranty. The court may assume jurisdiction.[534]

(3) CONTRACT GOVERNED BY ENGLISH LAW

11–191　　6. A is employed by X & Co in Kuwait under a contract governed by English law. He sustains personal injuries in Kuwait in the course of his employment there. He brings proceedings against X & Co in England for breach of an implied term in the contract of service. The court may assume jurisdiction.[535]

7. X & Co, a Kuwaiti insurance company, issues a policy insuring a vessel owned by A & Co, a Liberian corporation. The policy is based on the form scheduled to the Marine Insurance Act 1906. The vessel is seized by the Saudi Arabian authorities and A & Co claims under the policy for constructive total loss. X & Co claims that the vessel was engaged in smuggling and that accordingly the exclusion in the policy relating to infringement of customs regulations applies. The court has jurisdiction because the policy is governed by English law. But the court will not exercise its jurisdiction because the Kuwaiti courts are the *forum conveniens* in the circumstances of the case.[536]

8. A & Co, Liberian shipowners, chartered a ship to Y & Co, an Indian company, for the carriage of a cargo of sulphur from Vancouver, Canada, to Indian ports. X & Co, a Canadian company, sold the sulphur to Y & Co, and bills of lading, expressed to be governed by English law, were issued to and accepted by X & Co. A & Co allege that the cargo of sulphur was wet and caused severe corrosion of the ship, and claim under the contract of carriage contained in, or evidenced by, the bills of lading. The court assumes jurisdiction (even though much of the factual dispute relates to events in British Columbia), particularly because there has been extensive litigation in England arising out of a similar shipment on another ship owned by different shipowners, which had been settled, but in the course of which an enormous amount of factual and scientific evidence had been collected; the owners' insurers and solicitors are the same in both sets of litigation; and there is a dispute as to the effect under English law of the bill of lading contract and as to the nature of the obligations under the contract in respect of dangerous cargo.[537]

9. A & Co, a Japanese company, agrees to build a bulk carrier for Y & Co, a Greek company, which is owned by X, a Greek shipowner. The shipbuilding contract is governed by English law, and provides for arbitration in London. X signs a performance guarantee, which contains no express choice of law. X alleges that the guarantee is illegal and contrary to English public policy because it was drafted in such a way as to mislead the Japanese authorities about the price in order to obtain an export licence. The guarantee is governed by English law, and the court will exercise its jurisdiction against X because it is highly desirable that the issue of English public policy should be decided by the English court.[538]

10. A & Co, a German partnership, agrees with X & Co, a Japanese company, that X & Co will charter to A & Co two bulk carriers to be built for X & Co in Japan. The charter contains a London arbitration clause. The court has jurisdiction because the charter is governed by English law under Rule 222.[539]

---

[533] *cf. Bremer Oeltransport GmbH v Drewry* [1933] 1 K.B. 753 (CA). The Brussels I Regulation and the Lugano Convention do not apply to the enforcement of arbitral awards: paras 11–041 *et seq.* See now clause (10), below.

[534] *cf. National Mortgage and Agency Co of NZ Ltd v Gosselin* (1922) 38 T.L.R. 832 (CA).

[535] *Matthews v Kuwait Bechtel Corp* [1959] 2 Q.B. 57 (CA).

[536] *Amin Rasheed Shipping Corp v Kuwait Insurance Co* [1984] A.C. 50.

[537] *Spiliada Maritime Corp v Cansulex Ltd* [1987] A.C. 460.

[538] *Mitsubishi Corp v Alafouzos* [1988] 1 Lloyd's Rep. 191 (a pre-Brussels Convention case).

[539] *Egon Oldendorff v Libera Corp* [1995] 2 Lloyd's Rep. 64.

11. A Co, a Bahamian company, is part of a group which carries on business dealing with and trading in commercial aircraft from offices in Switzerland and the Lebanon. It enters into a contract with X Co, a Turkish airline company, under which X Co would lease aircraft to Z Co, a Saudi airline, through the exclusive agency of A Co. The contract between A Co and X Co is expressly governed by English law and is in English. X Co subsequently deals directly with Z Co and A Co claims damages from X Co for failure to pay commissions to A Co. The English court has jurisdiction and will exercise it. Although there are no factual connections with England, the dispute has no factual connection with Turkey, and England is the appropriate forum.[540]

(4) CONTRACT CONTAINS A TERM TO THE EFFECT THAT THE COURT SHALL HAVE JURISDICTION

12. A contract is made abroad (and governed by foreign law) between A & Co, a Japanese company, and X & Co, an American company, whereby A & Co agree to tow X & Co's oil rig from Venice, Louisiana, to Ravenna, Italy. The contract provides that "any dispute arising must be treated before the London court of justice." The tug and tow are forced to take refuge in Tampa, Florida, each alleging that this was the other's fault. X & Co bring proceedings against A & Co in Florida, and A & Co bring an action against X & Co in England. The court may assume jurisdiction.[541]   **11–192**

(7) The court may assume jurisdiction if the claim is made in respect of a breach of contract committed in England.[542]   11R–193

COMMENT

A contract may be broken in one of three ways, namely, by express repudiation, implied repudiation or failure to perform.   **11–194**

Breach by express repudiation occurs when one party informs the other that he no longer intends to perform the contract. If X who is abroad writes a letter of repudiation to A in England, the breach is not committed in England.[543] On the other hand, if X who is abroad sends his agent to England, or writes to his agent who is in England, instructing him to repudiate the contract, and the agent does so, e.g. by letter posted in England to A in England, then the breach is committed in England.[544]

Breach by implied repudiation occurs when one party does an act which is inconsistent with his performance of the contract, for instance, when X promises to sell a house to A but sells it to B instead. Although there is no authority on the point, the breach in such a case presumably occurs where the inconsistent act is done. This principle would appear to apply wherever the contractual obligation consists in an omission rather than an act, e.g. an   **11–195**

---

[540] *Novus Aviation Limited v Onur Air Tasimacilik AS* [2009] EWCA Civ 122, [2009] 1 Lloyd's Rep. 576.

[541] *cf. The Chaparral* [1968] 2 Lloyd's Rep. 158 (CA). For the sequel in the American courts, see *M/S Bremen v Zapata Offshore Co*, 407 U.S. 1 (1972); [1972] 2 Lloyd's Rep. 315; Collins, *Essays*, p.253; Kahn-Freund (1977) 26 I.C.L.Q. 825, 845–848.

[542] CPR, r.6.36 and PD6B, para.3.1(7). It has been held that for the purposes of a predecessor of this clause, contract includes quasi-contract: *McFee Engineering Pty Ltd v CBS Construction Pty Ltd* (1980) 28 A.L.R. 339. For restitutionary claims, see clause (16), below.

[543] *Cherry v Thompson* (1872) L.R. 7 Q.B. 573, 579; *Holland v Bennett* [1902] 1 K.B. 867 (CA), both approved in *Martin v Stout* [1925] A.C. 359, 368–369 (PC); *Atlantic Underwriting Agencies Ltd v Compagnia di Assicurazione di Milano* [1979] 2 Lloyd's Rep. 240; *Safran v Chani* [1970] 1 N.S.W.L.R. 70; *Stanley Kerr Holdings Pty Ltd v Gibor Textile Enterprises Ltd* [1978] 2 N.S.W.L.R. 372.

[544] *Mutzenbecher v La Aseguradora Espanola* [1906] 1 K.B. 254 (CA); *Oppenheimer v Louis Rosenthal & Co AG* [1937] 1 All E.R. 23 (CA).

obligation not to sell certain goods in England. The clause would apply if the goods were sold there.

11–196   If a contract is broken in England by express or implied repudiation, it would seem to be immaterial, for the purposes of clause (7) whether or not the contract was to be performed in England. Formerly the rule referred to a contract which "according to the terms thereof ought to be performed in England"; but there are no such words in the operative part of the present rule.

11–197   The normal form of breach is the failure of one party to perform one or more of his obligations under the contract. In such a case it is not necessary that the whole contract was to be performed in England by both the parties thereto, but it is necessary that some part of it was to be performed in England and that there has been a breach of that part.[545] It is not sufficient if the contract or part of it might be performed either in England or abroad; it is necessary that the contract or part of it was to be performed in England and not elsewhere.[546] The contract need not contain an express term providing for performance in England.[547] It is enough if the court can gather that this was the intention of the parties by construing the contract in the light of the surrounding circumstances, including the course of dealing between the parties.[548] In most of the reported cases, the breach complained of was the failure to pay money, a matter in which it is especially difficult to determine the place of performance in the absence of an express term in the contract.[549] "The general rule is that where no place of payment is specified, either expressly or by implication, the debtor must seek out his creditor."[550] But this is only a general rule[551] and, as stated, it only applies where no place of payment is expressed *or implied* in the contract. It certainly does not mean that a creditor can confer jurisdiction on the English court merely by taking up his residence in England after the making of the contract.[552]

11–198   If the contract is for the sale of goods by a seller in England to a buyer abroad, it will, in the absence of a contractual term to the contrary, be easy to

---

[545] *Rein v Stein* [1892] 1 Q.B. 753 (CA).

[546] *Bell & Co v Antwerp London and Brazil Line* [1891] 1 Q.B. 103 (CA); *The Eider* [1893] P. 119 (CA); *Comber v Leyland* [1898] A.C. 524; *Cuban Atlantic Sugar Sales Corporation v Compania de Vapores San Elefterio Lda* [1960] 1 Q.B. 187. *cf. BHP Petroleum Pty Ltd v Oil Basins Ltd* [1985] V.R. 725; affirmed [1985] V.R. 756.

[547] *Reynolds v Coleman* (1887) 36 Ch.D. 453 (CA), decided at a time when the clause referred to a contract which "according to the terms thereof" ought to be performed in England.

[548] The course of dealing was stressed in the following cases: *Rein v Stein* [1892] 1 Q.B. 753 (CA); *Fry & Co v Raggio* (1891) 40 W.R. 120; *Charles Duval & Co Ltd v Gans* [1904] 2 K.B. 685 (CA); *O'Mara Ltd v Dodd* [1912] 2 I.R. 55; *Shallay Holdings Pty Ltd v Griffith Co-operative Society Ltd* [1983] 1 V.R. 760.

[549] See also Law Commission, *Report on Council of Europe Convention on Place of Payment of Money Liabilities* (1972), Law Com. No.109 (1981), p.28.

[550] *The Eider* [1893] P. 119, 136–137 (CA). See also *Bank of Scotland v Seitz*, 1990 S.L.T. 584 (a case on the Brussels Convention).

[551] *Deutsche Ruckversicherung AG v La Fondaria Assicurazioni SpA* [2001] 2 Lloyd's Rep. 621; *Earthworks Ltd v FT Eastment & Sons Ltd* [1966] V.R. 24; *BP Australia Ltd v Wales* [1982] Qd.R. 386.

[552] *Malik v Narodni Banka Ceskoslovenska* [1946] 2 All E.R. 663 (CA); *cf. Fessard v Mugnier* (1865) 18 C.B. (N.S.) 286.

infer that the buyer's obligation was to pay for the goods in England.[553] The same is the case if a principal in England sends goods to an agent abroad to be sold by him on commission.[554] But it is otherwise if, on the true construction of the contract, the only duty of the foreign agent is to sell the goods and remit the proceeds to England from abroad in a specified manner, because it will be inferred that his duty is at an end when he makes the remittance.[555] If a foreign principal appoints an agent in England to sell his goods on commission, it is usually inferred that the commission is payable in England.[556] In such a case, the fact that the agent claims an account of sales does not take the case out of the clause.[557]

The duties of the seller of goods under a c.i.f. contract are to ship the goods   **11–199**
and deliver the shipping documents to the buyer. It is not his duty to deliver the goods to the buyer.[558] Consequently, if the foreign seller ships goods which are found to be defective upon their arrival in England,[559] or if he fails to ship them at all, the breach is not committed in England within the meaning of the clause.

In a contract of service, wages or salary would normally be payable where   **11–200**
the service is to be performed, in the absence of an express or implied term in the contract.[560] But if the servant is employed in only a nominal or consultative capacity, and is free to reside where he likes, his salary may be payable in England, if that is where he decides to live.[561] In a contract for services, it may be possible to infer that the fee or commission is payable at the contractor's usual place of business, even if the work is to be performed abroad.[562]

The fact that the contract provides for payment to be made in English   **11–201**
currency has sometimes been held to yield the inference that payment was to be made in England,[563] but this is by no means a decisive consideration.[564] Conversely, the fact that payment is to be made in foreign currency does not necessarily mean that England was not to be the place of payment.[565] No

---

[553] *Robey & Co v Snaefell Mining Co Ltd* (1887) 20 Q.B.D. 152; *Hassall v Lawrence* (1887) 4 T.L.R. 23; *Fry & Co v Raggio* (1891) 40 W.R. 120; *O'Mara Ltd v Dodd* [1912] 2 I.R. 55.

[554] *Rein v Stein* [1892] 1 Q.B. 753 (CA); *Charles Duval & Co Ltd v Gans* [1904] 2 K.B. 685 (CA).

[555] *Comber v Leyland* [1898] A.C. 524, a case "of a somewhat special character", *per* Stirling L.J. in *Charles Duval & Co Ltd v Gans* [1904] 2 K.B. 685, 691 (CA).

[556] *Hoerter v Hanover, etc., Works* (1893) 10 T.L.R. 103 (CA); *International Corporation Ltd v Besser Manufacturing Co* [1950] 1 K.B. 488 (CA).

[557] *ibid.*

[558] See *Clemens Horst Co v Biddell* [1912] A.C. 18, approving the dissenting judgment of Kennedy L.J. in the CA [1911] 1 K.B. 214.

[559] *Crozier Stephens & Co v Auerbach* [1908] 2 K.B. 161 (CA); *Cordova Land Co Ltd v Victor Bros Inc* [1966] 1 W.L.R. 793.

[560] See *Malik v Narodni Banka Ceskoslovenska* [1946] 2 All E.R. 663 (CA).

[561] *Vitkovice Horni A Hutni Tezirstvo v Korner* [1951] A.C. 869.

[562] *Thompson v Palmer* [1893] 2 Q.B. 80 (CA); *International Power and Engineering Consultants Ltd v Clark* (1964) 43 D.L.R. (2d) 394 (BCCA). Contrast *Auckland Receivers Ltd v Diners Club* [1985] 2 N.S.W.L.R. 652.

[563] *Fry & Co v Raggio* (1891) 40 W.R. 120.

[564] *Bremer Oeltransport GmbH v Drewry* [1933] 1 K.B. 753 (CA).

[565] *Rein v Stein* [1892] 1 Q.B. 753 (CA); *Drexel v Drexel* [1916] 1 Ch. 251; *Vitkovice Horni A Huni Tezirstvo v Korner* [1951] A.C. 869.

inference as to the place of payment can properly be drawn from the fact that the contract contains a gold clause.[566]

11–202   If money is due under a compromise of a disputed claim, it is usually inferred that the money is payable where litigation is pending or would probably have taken place.[567]

An implied warranty of authority has been held to have been broken where the warranty was relied on.[568]

11–203   If the contract is governed by a foreign applicable law, the applicable law of the contract will determine where money due thereunder is payable.[569]

Illustrations

11–204   1. X, who resides in Toronto, is the owner of a New York newspaper. He employs A to act as London correspondent for the newspaper's European edition. He writes a letter from Naples to A in England, wrongfully dismissing him. The court has no jurisdiction by reason of the letter of repudiation.[570] But it would have jurisdiction if the letter was followed by non-payment of salary, because of the concluding words of the clause.

2. By a contract made in the Canary Islands X & Co, a Brazilian insurance company, appoint A, a London insurance agent, to act as their exclusive agent for five years for insurance business in the United Kingdom, and her overseas Colonies and Dominions, in continental Europe (except Spain, Portugal and Turkey) and in the United States. After one year X & Co send their agent-general to England with instructions to terminate A's appointment. The agent-general does so by letter posted in London to A in England. A brings proceedings against X & Co for breach of contract. The court may assume jurisdiction.[571]

3. A, an American citizen resident in England, and X, an American citizen resident in the United States, agree that if A will transfer certain patents to X, X will transfer to A 500 shares in an English company. A transfers the patents but X refuses to transfer the shares. The court may assume jurisdiction.[572]

11–205   4. X & Co, a Panamanian company, charter a ship from A & Co, English shipowners, to load a cargo in London and proceed therewith to Rio de Janeiro and Santos. The charterparty provides that the freight shall be paid as to part at the ports of discharge and as to the balance in London, and that all lighterage at ports of discharge shall be at charterers' risk and expense. A & Co, having paid the lighterage at the ports of discharge, bring proceedings against X & Co for reimbursement. The court has no jurisdiction.[573]

5. A ship belonging to X & Co, Liberian shipowners, while on passage from New York to Bremen is stranded on the Wolf Rock, i.e. outside English territorial waters. A contract is made between the master and the agents of A & Co and B & Co, Swedish and German salvage companies, whereby the salvage companies agree to salve the ship and tow it to Falmouth for repairs in return for 50 per cent, of its value when salved. The contract provides for payment of the salvage money to B & Co, the German company, no place of payment being specified. It is

---

[566] *Vitkovice Horni A Hutni Tezirstvo v Korner*, below.

[567] *Golden v Darlow* (1891) 8 T.L.R. 57 (CA); *Anger v Vasnier* (1902) 18 T.L.R. 596 (CA).

[568] *The Piraeus* [1974] 2 Lloyd's Rep. 266 (CA).

[569] *cf. Malik v Narodni Banka Ceskoslovenska* [1946] 2 All E.R. 663 (CA); *Vitkovice Horni A Hutni Tezirstvo v Korner* [1951] A.C. 869; and see *ibid.* sub nom. *Korner v Witkowitzer* [1950] 2 K.B. 128, esp. at pp.159–161. See now Rome I Regulation, Art.12(1)(b).

[570] *cf. Holland v Bennett* [1902] 1 K.B. 867 (CA), following *Cherry v Thompson* (1872) L.R. 7 Q.E. 573, 579 (promise in Germany to marry in Germany, repudiated by letter sent from Germany to England: held, broken in Germany). Contrast *Cooper v Knight* (1901) 17 T.L.R. 299 (CA) (promise in England to marry in England, repudiated by letter sent from Belgium to England: held, broken in England).

[571] *cf. Mutzenbecher v La Aseguradora Espanola* [1906] 1 K.B. 254 (CA); *cf. Oppenheimer v Louis Rosenthal & Co AG* [1937] 1 All E.R. 23 (CA).

[572] *Reynolds v Coleman* (1887) 36 Ch.D. 453 (CA).

[573] *cf. Bell & Co v Antwerp London and Brazil Line* [1891] 1 Q.B. 103 (CA).

orally agreed between the agents of the two salvage companies that A & Co will receive half the salvage money. Disputes arise as to the value of the ship when salved, and A & Co bring proceedings against X & Co for their share. The court has no jurisdiction.[574]

6. X & Co, a Manx company, order a boiler and machinery to be supplied by A & Co in England and delivered to X & Co's mine in the Isle of Man for £585 A & Co accept and execute the order. In proceedings by A & Co for non-payment of the price, the court may assume jurisdiction.[575]

7. A sends goods from England to X, his agent in Brazil, X contracts with A to sell the goods and remit the proceeds to England by first-class bank bills. X sells the goods but keeps the proceeds. The court has no jurisdiction, because X can perform his part of the contract by posting the bills from Brazil.[576]

11–206

8. By a contract made in New York, A & Co, wine shippers in London, appoint X, a firm of New York wine merchants, their sole agents for the sale of champagne in the United States, Canada and Cuba. The contract does not state where the champagne is to be paid for, but the course of dealing between the parties is for X to pay by drafts on a London bank. The court may assume jurisdiction.[577]

9. By a contract made in the United States X & Co, an American company, appoint A & Co, an English company, their sole agents for the sale of X & Co's products in England and the countries of continental Europe, and agree to pay A & Co a commission of 15 per cent on all products sold. A & Co bring proceedings against X & Co claiming an account of all sales effected by them and payment of commission on such sales. The court may assume jurisdiction.[578]

10. A, a Czech, is employed by X & Co, a Czech bank, as manager of the bank's foreign exchange department. His contract of employment provides for salary to be paid in Czech crowns. In August 1939 A goes to Switzerland, partly on leave and partly to safeguard the bank's deposit of gold there in the event of war. A then proceeds to England. In proceedings by A for nonpayment of salary, the court has no jurisdiction.[579]

11–207

11. By a contract made in Czechoslovakia in 1929 X & Co, a Czech company, agrees to pay a pension to A, a Czech, one of the directors of X & Co, on his retirement. The contract provides for payment in Czech crowns. It is agreed between the parties that A shall be entitled to live where he likes and to be paid his pension in the place where he resides. A retires in 1938, and by another contract X & Co agrees to retain his services in a consultative capacity in Switzerland, France or England at A's option, and to pay him a salary of £2,000 a year in addition to his pension. A retires to England. In proceedings by A for non-payment of his pension and salary, the court may assume jurisdiction.[580]

12. A, a Newcastle mining engineer, is engaged by X to design and superintend the construction of docks which X is to build in Russia for the Russian Government. A brings proceedings against X for non-payment of his commission and travelling expenses to Russia. The court may assume jurisdiction.[581]

13. A bill of exchange is drawn by A in London on X and accepted by X in London, "payable at the C.M. Bank, Kandy." In proceedings by A for non-payment the court may assume jurisdiction, because under s.19 of the Bills of Exchange Act 1882 an acceptance payable at a particular place is a general acceptance unless it expressly states that the bill is to be paid there only and not elsewhere.[582]

---

[574] *cf. The Eider* [1893] P. 119 (CA), where the stranding occurred and the contract was made in English territorial waters. At that date the fact that a contract was made in England did not bring a case within clause (6), above.

[575] *Robey & Co v Snaefell Mining Co Ltd* (1887) 20 Q.B.D. 152.

[576] *Comber v Leyland* [1898] A.C. 524.

[577] *Charles Duval & Co Ltd v Gans* [1904] 2 K.B. 685 (CA).

[578] *International Corporation Ltd v Besser Manufacturing Co* [1950] 1 K.B. 488 (CA).

[579] *Malik v Narodni Banka Ceskoslovenska* [1946] 2 All E.R. 663 (CA). The Czech Republic is now subject to the Brussels I Regulation.

[580] *Vitkovice Horni A Hutni Tezirstyo v Korner* [1951] A.C. 869. The Czech Republic is now subject to the Brussels I Regulation.

[581] *cf. Thompson v Palmer* [1893] 2 Q.B. 80 (CA). *cf. International Power and Engineering Consultants Ltd v Clark* (1964) 43 D.L.R. (2d) 394 (BCCA).

[582] *Ex. p. Hayward* (1887) 3 T.L.R. 687.

11R–208   **(8) The court may assume jurisdiction if the claim is made for a declaration that no contract exists where, if the contract were found to exist, it would comply with the conditions in clause (6).**[583]

Comment

11–209   It had been held, in relation to the predecessor of clause (6), that if, on the claimant's own showing, no contract was made with the defendant, then permission could not be granted under clause (6).[584] Accordingly if the claimant was seeking a declaration that there was no contract, then the court would have no jurisdiction, whereas if the other party had brought the converse claim for a declaration that there was a contract, the court would have jurisdiction. Clause (8) now allows what would be an essentially contractual dispute to be determined in England if the requisite English connections exist, and jurisdiction does not depend on which party seeks the declaration.

Illustration

11–210   A, a Singaporean insurance company, seeks a declaration that it is not bound by reinsurance contracts to indemnify X, a United States insurance company, because the brokers who purportedly placed the reinsurance on behalf of X had no authority from A. If the reinsurance contracts had been validly placed they would be governed by English law. The court has jurisdiction.[585]

11R–211   **(9) The court may assume jurisdiction if the claim is made in tort where the damage was sustained in England, or the damage sustained resulted from an act committed within England.**[586]

Comment

11–212   The choice of law rules for tort are fully considered elsewhere.[587] Until the amendment of RSC, Order 11, r.1(1) in 1987 jurisdiction could be assumed under this clause only if the action was "founded on a tort committed within the jurisdiction." As both the Privy Council[588] and the Supreme Court of Canada[589] have pointed out, the competing theories for the determination of the place of a tort have been that (i) all ingredients of the cause of action

---

[583] CPR, r.6.36 and PD6B, para.3.1(8).

[584] *Finnish Marine Insurance Co Ltd v Protective National Insurance Co* [1990] Q.B. 1078.

[585] CPR, r.6.36 and PD6B, para.3.1(8), reversing the effect of *Finnish Marine Insurance Co Ltd v Protective National Insurance Co* [1990] Q.B. 1078.

[586] CPR, r.6.36 and PD6B, para.3.1(9). See generally *Transnational Tort Litigation: Jurisdictional Principles*, ed. McLachlan and Nygh (1996).

[587] Chap.35.

[588] *Distillers Co Ltd v Thompson* [1971] A.C. 458.

[589] *Moran v Pyle National (Canada) Ltd* (1973) 43 D.L.R. (3d) 239. In this case, discussed by Collins (1975) 24 I.C.L.Q. 325, the court held, in a product liability case where the plaintiff had suffered injury in one province from a product negligently made in another province, that the province where the harm had occurred could exercise jurisdiction. It was extended to purely economic loss in *Skyrotors v Carrière Technical Industries* (1979) 102 D.L.R. (3d) 323 (Ont); see also *Ichi Canada Ltd v Yamauchi Rubber Industry Co* (1983) 144 D.L.R. (3d) 533 (BCCA).

must have occurred within the jurisdiction, or (ii) the last ingredient, the event which completes a cause of action, must have occurred within the jurisdiction, or (iii) the act which the defendant committed must have occurred within the jurisdiction.

In *Distillers Co Ltd v Thompson*[590] the Privy Council adopted the test of the place where in substance the act or omission occurred which gave the plaintiff his cause of action. So that where the essence of the complaint was failure to warn the consumer of the dangers of a product (rather than the faulty manufacture of the product) the cause of action was held to have arisen at the place where the failure to warn occurred;[591] and the torts of negligent and fraudulent misrepresentation, where the negligent or fraudulent statement was communicated from one country to another, were held to have been committed where the statement was received and acted upon.[592] Prior to the adoption of that test, but consistently with it, it had been held that the tort of defamation was committed where the defamatory statements were published and not where they were posted or uttered.[593]

11–213

The current version of this clause was adopted originally in order to bring the tort provision of RSC, Order 11, r.1(1) into line with the Brussels Convention and intra-United Kingdom provisions.[594] These provisions (and those of the Judgments Regulation and the Lugano Convention) grant jurisdiction to the courts of "the place where the harmful event occurred" and this expression was interpreted by the European Court in 1976[595] to grant alternative jurisdiction to the courts of the places, if different, (a) where the damage occurred, and (b) where the event which gave rise to the damage occurred. Clause (9) accordingly applies where the claim is founded on a tort, and (a) the damage was sustained within the jurisdiction, or (b) the damage sustained resulted from an act committed within the jurisdiction.

11–214

---

[590] [1971] A.C. 458 (PC). This decision related to a differently formulated rule in NSW, but it was applied to the former English rule in *Diamond v Bank of London and Montreal Ltd* [1979] Q.B. 333 (CA); *Castree v Squibb & Sons Ltd* [1980] 1 W.L.R. 1248 (CA); *Multinational Gas Co v Multinational Gas Services Ltd* [1983] Ch. 258 (CA); *cf. Russell v Woolworth & Co*, 1982 S.C. 20; *Kirkcaldy DC v Household Manufacturing Ltd*, 1987 S.L.T. 617; *Scott Lithgow Ltd v GEC Electrical Projects Ltd*, 1992 S.L.T. 244 (cases on Scots law prior to the 1982 Act); *FFSB Ltd v Seward & Kissel LLP* [2007] UKPC 16. The Supreme Court of Ireland held that there is jurisdiction (for the purposes of the unamended clause (9)) if "any significant element" has occurred within the jurisdiction: *Grehan v Medical Inc* [1986] I.R. 528, 541–542.

[591] *Distillers Co Ltd v Thompson*, above; Collins, *Essays*, pp 234–237; *Castree v Squibb & Sons Ltd*, above; *Buttigeig v Universal Terminal and Stevedoring Corp* [1972] V.R. 626; *My v Toyota Motor Co Ltd* [1977] 2 N.Z.L.R. 113.

[592] *Multinational Gas Co v Multinational Gas Services Ltd* [1983] Ch. 258 (CA); *The Albaforth* [1984] 2 Lloyd's Rep. 91 (CA); *Original Blouse Co Ltd v Bruck Mills Ltd* (1963) 42 D.L.R. (2d) 174 (BC); *Petersen v A/B Bahco* (1980) 107 D.L.R. (3d) 49 (BC); *Canadian Commercial Bank v Carpenter* (1990) 62 D.L.R. (4th) 734 (BCCA); *National Bank of Canada v Clifford Chance* (1996) 30 O.R. (3d) 746; *Pei v Bank Bumiputra Malaysia Berhad* (1998) 41 O.R. (3d) 39. Contrast *Cordova Land Co Ltd v Victor Bros Inc* [1966] 1 W.L.R. 793 (CA). *cf. Minster Investments Ltd v Hyundai Precision and Industry Co Ltd* [1988] 2 Lloyd's Rep. 621; but see *Domicrest Ltd v Swiss Bank Corp* [1999] Q.B. 547, para.11–289.

[593] *Bata v Bata* [1948] W.N. 366 (CA); *Jenner v Sun Oil Co* [1952] 2 D.L.R. 526 (Ont); *Pindling v NBC* (1984) 14 D.L.R. (4th) 391 (Ont); *cf. Bree v Marescaux* (1881) 7 Q.B.D. 434. For libel on the internet see below, para.11–219.

[594] See Rule 35, clause (3).

[595] Case 21/76 *Bier v Mines de Potasse d'Alsace SA* [1976] E.C.R. 1735; [1978] Q.B. 708. For later developments see Rule 35, clause (3).

11–215   In *Metall und Rohstoff AG v Donaldson Lufkin & Jenrette Inc*[596] the Court of Appeal posed the question of what law is to be applied in resolving whether the claim is "founded on a tort" (the then expression: now "made in tort"), and answered it in part by citing a statement in the eleventh edition of this work that the question concerned the interpretation of a connecting factor, which would always be answered in accordance with the English rules of the conflict of laws.[597] Accordingly, relying exclusively on principles of English law, the Court of Appeal decided that claims based on constructive trust, or procuring a breach of trust, were not claims based on tort.[598]

11–216   Damage sustained within the jurisdiction must refer to recoverable damage, including recoverable economic loss. In Canada and Australia, similar wording has been held to apply to consequential pecuniary damage sustained in the forum flowing from physical injury caused outside the forum,[599] and these decisions have been followed in England.[600] The fact that the centre of the claimant's business is within the jurisdiction does not necessarily mean that the economic damage is sustained there.[601] In the second part of the formula, "an act committed within the jurisdiction" also extends to negligent omissions such as a failure to give adequate warning about the dangers of a product. In the *Metall und Rohstoff* case it was held that, for the purposes of each part of the formula, it is not necessary that all of the damage be sustained within the jurisdiction, or that all of the acts be committed within the jurisdiction. Some significant damage must have occurred in England; or the damage (wherever sustained) must result from substantial and efficacious acts committed within the jurisdiction, irrespective of whether or not other substantial and efficacious acts have been committed elsewhere.[602]

11–217   By contrast, however, with Art.5(3) of the Brussels I Regulation and the Lugano Convention, the exercise of jurisdiction under clause (9) is discretionary, and the court must consider what is the *forum conveniens*. In principle the jurisdiction where the tort is committed is prima facie the natural forum for the determination of the dispute: "If the substance of an alleged tort is committed within a certain jurisdiction, it is not easy to imagine what other

---

[596] [1990] 1 Q.B. 391 (CA), overruled in *Lonrho Plc v Fayed* [1992] 1 A.C. 448 on other aspects.

[597] At pp.437, 441.

[598] At pp.473–474, 480–481. *cf. Suncorp Realty Inc v PLN Investments Inc* (1985) 23 D.L.R. (4th) 83 (Man) (action to set aside fraudulent conveyance not an action in tort).

[599] *Skyrotors Ltd v Carrière Technical Industries* (1979) 102 D.L.R. (3d) 323 (Ont); *Vile v von Wendt* (1979) 103 D.L.R. (3d) 356 (Ont CA); *Poirier v Williston* (1980) 113 D.L.R. (3d) 252; app. dismissed (1981) 118 D.L.R. (3d) 576 (Ont CA); *Muscutt v Courcelles* (2002) 213 D.L.R. (4th) 577, [28] (Ont CA); *Challenor v Douglas* [1983] 2 N.S.W.L.R. 405; *Girgis v Flaherty* [1984] 1 N.S.W.L.R. 56; affirmed sub nom *Flaherty v Girgis* (1985) 4 N.S.W.L.R. 248; *Heilbrunn v Lightwood Plc* [2007] FCA 433.

[600] *Booth v Phillips* [2004] EWHC 1437 (Comm.), [2004] 1 W.L.R. 3292 (dependency of English widow in claim arising out of death of husband in Egypt: damage in England). See also *Cooley v Ramsey* [2008] EWHC 129 (QB), [2008] I.L.Pr. 345: English claimant seriously injured in a traffic accident in New South Wales while working in Australia; held, the English court had jurisdiction in damages claim, because the pain and suffering, and loss of income and amenities of life, was damage sustained within the jurisdiction: *sed quaere*.

[601] *Soc Commerciale Réassurance v Eras International Ltd* [1992] 1 Lloyd's Rep. 570 (CA); *Bastone & Firminger Ltd v Nasima Enterprises (Nigeria) Ltd* [1996] C.L.C. 1902. Contrast *Skyrotors Ltd v Carrière Technical Industries Ltd* (1979) 102 D.L.R. (3d) 323 (Ont).

[602] [1990] 1 Q.B. 391, 437 (CA).

facts could displace the conclusion that the courts of that jurisdiction are the natural forum."[603] But where the acts or omissions occur, and the damage is sustained, in different countries, the *forum conveniens* may depend on the extent to which the issues are likely to relate to liability or to damage, and the relative importance of the place of acting and the place of damage from the point of view of the convenience of the parties and of witnesses and the other factors which the court takes into account in the exercise of the discretion under Rule 34.[604]

In *Berezovsky v Michaels*[605] an influential American business magazine **11–218** called "Forbes" published an article alleging that the first plaintiff, a Russian businessman, was a leader of organised crime and corruption in Russia, and that the second plaintiff, another Russian businessman, was his criminal associate. Sales of the issue of the magazine were 785,000 in the United States and Canada, 1,900 in England, and 13 in Russia. Each of the plaintiffs was a frequent visitor to England, and each sought leave to serve English proceedings, which claimed relief only in respect of publication in England, against the editors and publishers in the United States. It was held that the publication in England of an internationally disseminated libel was a separate tort so as to permit the bringing of an action in England. The burden was on the plaintiffs to prove that England was clearly the appropriate forum, but regard was to be had to the principle that the jurisdiction in which a tort was committed was prima facie the natural forum for the dispute.

In that case the magazine was published in England through distribution of **11–219** the magazine and also through its availability on the internet. The consequences of publication of allegedly defamatory material on the internet have been considered in several recent decisions, the effect of which is that where an article is posted on a web server outside England, but is accessed in England, publication takes place in England.[606]

---

[603] *The Albaforth* [1984] 2 Lloyd's Rep. 91, 96 (CA), *per* Robert Goff L.J., applied in *Metall und Rohstoff AG v Donaldson Lufkin & Jenrette Inc* [1990] 1 Q.B. 391, 484 (CA). See also *Electric Furnace Co v Selas Corp of America* [1987] R.P.C. 23, 35 (CA); *ISC Technologies Ltd v Guerin* [1992] 2 Lloyd's Rep. 430; *Schapira v Ahronson* [1998] I.L.Pr. 587 (CA); *Lewis v King* [2004] EWCA Civ 1329, [2005] I.L.Pr. 185; *Bangoura v Washington Post* (2005) 258 D.L.R. (4th) 341 (Ont CA); *Barrick Gold Corp v Lopehandia* (2004) 71 O.R. (3d) 416 (CA).

[604] See above, para.11–143.

[605] [2000] 1 W.L.R. 1004 (HL).

[606] *Jameel v Dow Jones & Co Inc* [2005] EWCA Civ 75, [2005] Q.B. 946, at [48]; see also *Loutchansky v Times Newspapers Ltd (Nos 2 to 5)* [2001] EWCA Civ 1805, [2002] Q.B. 783, at [58]–[59]; *Harrods Ltd v Dow Jones & Co Inc* [2003] EWHC 1162 (QB). In *Dow Jones & Co Inc v Gutnick* [2002] HCA 56, (2003) 210 C.L.R. 575 the alleged libel was contained in a publication called Barron's Online. The editorial offices were in New York, and the material was transferred to a computer in New Jersey, and loaded onto servers in New Jersey. It was accessed in (among other places) Melbourne. Under the Victoria rules service out of the jurisdiction was permissible if the proceeding was founded on a tort committed in Victoria, or if it was brought in respect of damage suffered wholly or partly in Victoria. Although it was said that the tort of defamation will ordinarily be the place where the material is available in comprehensible form, it was not necessary to decide where the tort was committed, because in any event damage to reputation had occurred in Victoria: at [44], [46]–[47] (*per* Gleeson C.J., McHugh, Gummow, and Hayne JJ.), [100] (*per* Kirby J.). On the exercise of discretion in such cases, see *Berezovsky v Michaels*, above; *Chadha v Dow Jones & Co Inc* [1999] E.M.L.R. 724; *Lewis v King* [2004] EWCA Civ 1329, [2005] I.L.Pr. 185; *Harrods Ltd v Dow Jones & Co Inc*, above; *Metropolitan International Schools Ltd v Designtechnica Corp* [2009] EWHC 1765 (QB), [2011] 1 W.L.R.

If the claimant has a cause of action in both contract and tort he can elect to sue in either (or both) and may apply for permission under clause (6), (7) or (9), at his option.[607]

Illustrations

11–220   1. A brings proceedings against X & Co, an American company, for a libel contained in X & Co's French and Belgian newspapers, of which only a few copies have been sold in England. A has no connection whatsoever with England, and has only taken up residence here for the purposes of the libel claim. His real complaint is the publication of the libel in France and Belgium. The court will not exercise jurisdiction.[608]

2. A is a businessman living in Melbourne, Victoria, Australia. X Inc, whose editorial offices are in New York, publishes the *Wall Street Journal* newspaper and *Barron's* magazine. It operates a subscription service whereby subscribers can access these publications on X Inc's website, Xinc.com. Editorial material is sent by computer to a site operated by X Inc in New Jersey, where it is loaded onto six servers maintained by it in New Jersey. Publication takes place in Victoria, when the material is downloaded by a subscriber and not when it is uploaded onto the servers in New Jersey and becomes available.[609]

3. A and B are Russian businessmen. X Co, a United States publishing company, publishes a magazine, an article in which claims that A is a leader of organised crime and corruption in Russia, and that B is his associate. Sales of the issue of the magazine are 785,000 in the United States, 1,900 in England and 13 in Russia. The court has jurisdiction in respect of the publication in England, and England is the prima facie natural forum as the jurisdiction in which the tort is committed.[610]

4. A is a Saudi businessman. X Co is the publisher of a United States newspaper. A claims that an article posted by X Co on a website in the United States, which is available to subscribers in England, implies that he was or is suspected of having been involved in funding a terrorist organisation. X Co claims that only five subscribers in England had accessed the internet version of the article, and A accepts that was minimal publication in England. There is no real and substantial tort in England, and the court will not exercise jurisdiction.[611]

5. Under a contract made in New York and governed by its law, X & Co, an American company, sell rat poison to A & Co, an English company. It is agreed that the property shall pass in New York. X & Co omit to warn A & Co that the poison is dangerous unless certain precautions are taken. An English farmer who purchases the rat poison from A & Co in England suffers losses to his livestock in consequence of using it, and A & Co are compelled to compensate him. A & Co bring proceedings in tort for negligence against X & Co. The court has jurisdiction because the damage was sustained in England.[612]

6. X & Co, a Canadian company, manufactures and sells in Canada to Y & Co, its English wholly owned subsidiary, a drug the principal ingredient of which is obtained in bulk from German manufacturers. The drug is intended for resale in England. X & Co does not warn either Y & Co or potential purchasers, in the printed matter supplied with the drug, of the harmful effect on a foetus if the drug is taken by a pregnant mother. A, whose mother has purchased the drug

---

1743. On "libel tourism" see Hartley (2010) 59 I.C.L.Q. 25. *cf. Soc Castellblanch v Soc Champagne Louis Roderer* (France, Cr. Cass., December 9, 2003), 2004 *Rev. Crit.* 632, note Cachard; 2004 *Clunet* 872, note Huet (trade mark infringement).

[607] *Matthews v Kuwait Bechtel Corporation* [1959] 2 Q.B. 57 (CA).

[608] *cf. Kroch v Rossell et Cie* [1937] 1 All E.R. 725 (CA); contrast *Buttes Gas and Oil Co v Hammer* [1971] 3 All E.R. 1025 (CA). See also *Pillai v Sarkar, The Times*, July 21, 1994. For the different position under the Brussels I Regulation and the Lugano Convention, see paras 11–288 *et seq.*

[609] *Dow Jones & Co Inc v Gutnick* [2002] HCA 56, (2003) 210 C.L.R. 575.

[610] *Berezovsky v Michaels* [2000] 1 W.L.R.1004 (HL).

[611] *cf. Jameel v Dow Jones & Co Inc* [2005] EWCA Civ 75, [2005] Q.B. 946 (not a jurisdiction case).

[612] *cf. George Monro Ltd v American Cyanamid and Chemical Corporation* [1944] K.B. 432 (CA), decided under the previous version of clause (9), where it was held that even if the tort had been committed in England, the discretion would be exercised against the plaintiff.

in England, is born with defective eyesight and without arms. A brings proceedings for negligence against X & Co for failure to warn his mother of the dangers of taking the drug while pregnant. The court may assume jurisdiction under this clause because the damage was sustained in England and it resulted from an act (negligent failure to warn) within the jurisdiction.[613]

7. Circular letters containing a libel on A are posted by X in New York to addresses in England.   **11–221** The court may assume jurisdiction.[614]

8. A, a London commodity broker, wishes to purchase a consignment of sugar from US brokers acting for undisclosed principals. In fact the sugar does not exist and the transaction is not completed. A alleges that an employee of X Ltd, a Nassau bank, had confirmed to him in London by telephone and telex that the sugar was available and the US brokers were able to undertake the sale. In A's proceedings for negligent and fraudulent misrepresentation, the court has jurisdiction but will not exercise it because A does not have a good arguable case on the merits.[615]

9. A & Co, a Swiss company, trades on the London Metal Exchange with X & Co, an English company carrying on business as metal brokers, whose immediate parent company is Y & Co, an American company, and whose ultimate holding company is Z & Co, another American company. A & Co's chief aluminium trader, with the assistance of X & Co's employees, trades fraudulently. The fraud is discovered by X & Co, Y & Co, and Z & Co and X & Co (in breach of its contract with A & Co, and on the instruction of Y & Co and Z & Co) closes out A & Co's accounts and seizes metal warrants belonging to A & Co which X & Co had held as security for advances. A & Co are awarded substantial damages against X & Co, but recover only a small proportion because X & Co is insolvent. The court has jurisdiction in proceedings against Y & Co and Z & Co for inducement of breach of contract. Although the acts alleged against Y & Co and Z & Co of inducing or procuring a breach of contract had in the main taken place in New York, it was the breaches of contract by X & Co which had caused A & Co substantial damage in England and in substance the tort was committed in England.[616]

(10) The court may assume jurisdiction if the claim is brought to enforce   11R–222 any judgment or arbitral award.[617]

COMMENT

This clause was introduced in 1983 to fill a gap which had been revealed in   **11–223** cases where judgment creditors sought to enforce at common law judgments emanating from countries whose judgments were not capable of registration in England. Where enforcement by registration is possible,[618] the *in personam* jurisdiction of the English court over the defendant is irrelevant.[619] But where it was not possible (e.g. in the case of a judgment of a United States court) the remedy open to a judgment creditor who wished to proceed against assets in England was an action *in personam* at common law against the judgment debtor. Where the judgment debtor was in England at the date of service of the writ, the English court had jurisdiction.[620] But where the judgment debtor was outside England, and was not domiciled there, he could not be served with the

---

[613] *cf. Distillers Co Ltd v Thompson* [1971] A.C. 458 (PC). The court would also have jurisdiction over X Ltd under clause (3) in an action against Y Ltd.

[614] *cf. Bata v Bata* [1948] W.N. 366 (CA).

[615] *cf. Diamond v Bank of London & Montreal Ltd* [1979] Q.B. 333 (CA).

[616] *Metall und Rohstoff AG v Donaldson Lufkin and Jenrette Inc* [1990] 1 Q.B. 391 (CA). The decision was overruled in *Lonrho Plc v Fayed* [1992] 1 A.C. 448 on other aspects.

[617] CPR, r.6.36 and PD6B, para.3.1(10).

[618] Under the Administration of Justice Act 1920, Foreign Judgments (Reciprocal Enforcement) Act 1933, and the Civil Jurisdiction and Judgments Act 1982, Pts I and II.

[619] *cf. Hunt v BP Exploration Co (Libya) Ltd* (1980) 144 C.L.R. 565; *Hunt v BP Exploration Co (Libya) Ltd* [1980] 1 N.Z.L.R. 104.

[620] As in *Colt Industries Inc v Sarlie (No.1)* [1966] 1 W.L.R. 440 (CA).

writ and there was no basis for service out of the jurisdiction even though he had assets in England which could be attached to satisfy the judgment.[621] Clause (10) remedies this defect and allows service abroad on the judgment debtor in proceedings at common law to enforce a foreign judgment or award.[622] The claimant does not have to show that there are assets in England available for execution.[623] But an application for the examination of the foreign officer of a judgment debtor is not within clause (10)[624] and clause (10) does not justify service out of the jurisdiction of process designed to enforce a judgment which has not yet been obtained but which may be obtained in the future.[625]

ILLUSTRATION

11–224   1. A, an Englishman, obtains a judgment in California against X, a resident of California, who never comes to England, but who owns property in England. The court may assume jurisdiction by A in proceedings against X to enforce the judgment at common law.[626]

2. A Co, a Turkish banking institution, obtains a Turkish judgment against X, a former director of banks to which A Co is the successor, in connection with X's alleged misappropriation of bank assets. X has no identifiable assets in England. A Co may obtain permission to serve X out of the jurisdiction in an action on the judgment without having to show that X has assets in England.[627]

11R–225   **(11) The court may assume jurisdiction if the whole subject-matter of the claim relates to property located within England.**[628]

COMMENT

11–226   Clause (11) reproduces the combined effect of what is now CPR, r.6.36 and PD6B, para.3.1(11), which is a considerably simplified and much wider version of its predecessors in the Rules of the Supreme Court, which dealt separately with proceedings relating to land situate in England, and the perpetuation of testimony relating to land; to claims for rectification of

---

[621] *Perry v Zissis* [1977] 1 Lloyd's Rep. 607 (CA). In *Nominal Defendant v Motor Vehicle Insurance Trust of W Australia* (1983) 81 F.L.R. 29 it was held that a foreign judgment could be enforced under clause (6); *sed quaere*. The court followed, but doubted the correctness of, the dictum in *Grant v Easton* (1883) 13 Q.B.D. 302, 303 that liability on a foreign judgment arises upon an implied contract to pay the amount of the judgment. But *Grant v Easton* was not a case on service out of the jurisdiction.

[622] See, e.g. *Midland International Trade Services Ltd v Sudairy, Financial Times*, May 2, 1990.

[623] *Tasarruf Mevduati Sigorta Fonu v Demirel* [2006] EWHC 3354 (Ch.), [2007] 2 All E.R. 815, affirmed [2007] EWCA Civ 799, [2007] 1 W.L.R. 2508. This decision appears not to have been cited in an unreserved judgment to the opposite effect, *Linsen International Ltd v Humpuss Transportasi Kimia* [2011] EWCA Civ 1042: see *Parbulk II AS v PT Humpuss Intermoda Transportasi TBK* [2011] EWHC 3143 (Comm.), at [80]).

[624] *Masri v Consolidated Contractors International Co SAL (No.4)* [2009] UKHL 43, [2010] 1 A.C. 90.

[625] *Mercedes Benz AG v Leiduck* [1996] A.C. 284 (PC).

[626] Contrast *Perry v Zissis*, above, decided before clause (10) was introduced.

[627] *Tasarruf Mevduati Sigorta Fonu v Demirel* [2007] EWCA Civ 799, [2007] 1 W.L.R. 2508.

[628] CPR, r.6.36 and PD6B, para.3.1(11).

instruments relating to land in England; to claims relating to debts secured on immovable property in England; and claims relating to rights in movable property in England.

In *Re Banco Nacional de Cuba*[629] it was held that the new rule was not to   **11–227**
be construed as confined to claims relating to the ownership or possession of property. It extended to any claim for relief, whether for damages or otherwise, so long as it was related to property located within the jurisdiction. Since the exercise of the jurisdiction was discretionary, the court would consider in each case whether the character and closeness of the relationship with England was such that the jurisdiction against foreigners abroad should be exercised.

ILLUSTRATIONS

1. X, as beneficial owner, conveyed to A by way of mortgage his interest in movables under   **11–228**
an English marriage settlement, in order to secure a loan and the interest payable on it. Both X
and A were then resident in England, but X is now residing in Australia. A issues proceedings
against X claiming an account of the sum due under the mortgage deed and enforcement of
payment of that sum by foreclosure or sale, and applies to the court for leave to serve the
summons on X in Australia. The court may allow service.[630]

2. A & Co, bankers, carrying on business in England, claim as against X, residing in Panama,
a declaration that they are entitled to a charge on certain policies of life insurance deposited with
them, and that the charge may be enforced by foreclosure. The court may assume
jurisdiction.[631]

3. A, having obtained judgment against X for £2,000 obtains an order charging the judgment
debt with interest on X's shares in a public company in England. X is resident in America. In
order to enforce the charge A institutes proceedings asking for the sale of the shares. The court
may assume jurisdiction.[632]

4. Land in Surrey, held in the names of three companies, has been purchased on behalf of the
former Prime Minister of a foreign government and her husband with funds allegedly derived
from bribes and secret commissions. The Government claims that it is beneficially entitled to the
proceeds of sale of the estate. The claim relates to disputes over funds representing property in
England. The court may assume jurisdiction.[633]

**(12) The court may assume jurisdiction if the claim is made for any   11R–229
remedy which might be obtained in proceedings to execute the trusts of a
written instrument, where the trusts ought to be executed according to
English law, and the person on whom the claim form is to be served is a
trustee of the trusts.**[634]

COMMENT

This clause confers jurisdiction in proceedings against trustees to execute a   **11–230**
written trust governed by English law. Before its amendment in 1983 this

---

[629] [2001] 1 W.L.R. 2039. See also *Pakistan v Zardari* [2006] EWHC 2411 (Comm.), [2006]
2 C.L.C. 667 (constructive trust claim to land in England); *Ashton Investments v OJSC Russian
Aluminium* [2006] EWHC 2545 (Comm.), [2007] 1 Lloyd's Rep. 311 (confidential information
within the jurisdiction).

[630] Contrast *Hughes v Oxenham* [1913] 1 Ch. 254 (CA), which was decided before the rules
were amended to cover proceedings to enforce charges.

[631] Contrast *Deutsche National Bank v Paul* [1898] 1 Ch. 283, decided under the old rules.

[632] Contrast *Kolchmann v Meurice* [1903] 1 K.B. 534.

[633] *Pakistan v Zardari* [2006] EWHC 2411 (Comm.), [2006] 2 C.L.C. 667.

[634] CPR, r.6.36 and PD6B, para.3.1(12).

clause related to the execution of trusts "as to property situate within the jurisdiction" and it had been held[635] that the clause did not apply when a trustee of stock sold it in breach of trust before leaving England, so that, where at the time of leave being given to serve him there was no property in England subject to the trust, service was set aside. This decision was criticised on the ground that the relevant date for determining the situation of the property was the date of accrual of the cause of action,[636] but the decision is now obsolete. In *Chellaram v Chellaram (No.2)*[637] it was held that the critical date for determining the law applicable to the trust was the date when permission to serve out of the jurisdiction was sought, and not the date when the cause of action arose.

Illustration

11–231   X is sole trustee of an English settlement. Under the trusts of the settlement, A is beneficially entitled to stock. X sells the stock and leaves England, and has not returned there. There is no other property in England which is subject to the trusts of the settlement. The court has jurisdiction to entertain proceedings by A for execution of the trusts of the settlement.[638]

11R–232   **(13) The court may assume jurisdiction if the claim is made for any remedy which might be obtained in proceedings for the administration of the estate of a person who died domiciled[639] in England.[640]**

11R–233   **(14) The court may assume jurisdiction if the claim is a probate claim or a claim for the rectification of a will.[641]**

Comment

11–234   Probate proceedings are claims for the grant of probate or letters of administration, or the revocation of such a grant, or for a decree pronouncing for or against the validity of an alleged will.[642]

11R–235   **(15) The court may assume jurisdiction if the claim is made against the defendant as constructive trustee where the defendant's alleged liability arises out of acts committed within England.[643]**

---

[635] *Winter v Winter* [1894] 1 Ch. 421.
[636] *Official Solicitor v Stype Investments Ltd* [1983] 1 W.L.R. 214.
[637] [2002] EWHC 632 (Ch.), [2002] 3 All E.R. 17.
[638] Contrast *Winter v Winter* [1894] 1 Ch. 421, decided under the former version of this clause.
[639] For determination of domicile in this context, see CPR, r.6.31(i).
[640] CPR, r.6.36 and PD6B, para.3.1(13).
[641] CPR, r.6.36 and PD6B, para.3.1(14).
[642] CPR, r.57.1(2). For rectification of wills, see CPR, r.57.12.
[643] CPR, r.6.36 and PD6B, para.3.1(15).

(16) The court may assume jurisdiction if a claim is made for restitution where the defendant's alleged liability arises out of acts committed within England.[644]   11R–236

COMMENT

A claim against a defendant as constructive trustee normally arises in one of three situations. The first is where a person receives for his benefit trust property transferred to him in breach of trust; he is liable as a constructive trustee if he received it with notice, actual or constructive, that it was trust property and that the transfer to him was a breach of trust, or subsequently discovered the facts. The second is where a person receives trust property lawfully and then misappropriates it or otherwise deals with it in a manner inconsistent with the trust. The third is where a person dishonestly assists in the furtherance of a fraudulent and dishonest breach of trust.[645] The first and second categories were often referred to as "knowing receipt" cases, and the third as "knowing assistance", and are referred to today as "recipient liability" and "accessory liability".[646] Clause (15) was added in 1990 after it had been held that a claim based on constructive trust (in each of the three categories) was not founded on a tort for the purposes of clause (9).[647] In *NABB Brothers International Ltd v Lloyds Bank International (Guernsey) Ltd*[648] it was said (*obiter*) that a proprietary claim to funds in an offshore bank account was a claim against the defendant as constructive trustee for the purposes of clause (15) even where the liability of the defendant to restore the property was not dependent on knowing receipt; and was also a claim in restitution for the purposes of clause (16)[649] even though it was not based on unjust enrichment.   11–237

There has been a division of judicial opinion as to the extent to which the relevant acts necessary to establish liability must occur in England in order to bring the case within clause (15). In a case on a previous version of clause (16), when it provided that the acts done in England could be those of the defendant or another person, Millett J. held that the clause only applied if all the acts necessary to impose liability were committed in England; and that clause (15) therefore applied to knowing participation by acts in a fraudulent breach of trust committed in England, but not knowing receipt abroad of the proceeds of such fraud.[650] In subsequent proceedings in the same litigation, Hoffmann J. suggested, *obiter*, that this was too narrow a view and that clause   11–238

---

[644] CPR, r.6.36 and PD6B, para.3.1(16). See *Cecil v Bayat* [2010] EWHC 641 (Comm.) (quantum meruit) (appeal allowed on other grounds *sub nom. Bayat v Cecil* [2011] EWCA Civ 135).

[645] See, e.g. *Agip (Africa) Ltd v Jackson* [1990] Ch. 265, 291–293; affirmed [1991] Ch. 547 (CA). See also *Ghana Commercial Bank v C, The Times*, March 3, 1997.

[646] See *Royal Brunei Airlines Sdn Bhd v Tan* [1995] 2 A.C. 378 (PC).

[647] *Metall und Rohstoff AG v Donaldson Lufkin & Jenrette Inc* [1990] 1 Q.B. 391, 473–474 (CA). See also *DSQ Property Co Ltd v Lotus Car Sales Ltd, The Times*, June 28, 1990 (CA).

[648] [2005] EWHC 405 (Ch.), [2005] I.L.Pr. 506

[649] See also *Douglas v Hello!* [2003] EWCA Civ 139, [2003] E.M.L.R. 28 (action for breach of confidence); *Astrazeneca UK Ltd v Albemarle International Corp* [2010] EWHC 1028 (Comm.), [2010] 2 Lloyd's Rep. 61 (duress).

[650] *ISC Technologies Ltd v Radcliffe*, December 7, 1990, unreported (Millett J.).

(15) was primarily designed for a foreign entity which had not participated in the fraud but had been used as a receptacle for the proceeds.[651] The latter view was followed by Knox J. in *Polly Peck International Plc v Nadir*.[652] He held that a construction of clause (15) which required all the acts constituting the alleged constructive trust to have been committed in England would empty it of nearly all its practical utility. It was sufficient if some, at least, of the acts which gave rise to the claim (but not necessarily the acquisition of knowledge) had occurred in England. The decision was reversed by the Court of Appeal on other grounds, but Hoffmann L.J. said that he adhered to the view which he had expressed in *ISC Technologies Ltd v Guerin*.

11–239   In *NABB Brothers International Ltd v Lloyds Bank International (Guernsey) Ltd*[653] the view was expressed (*obiter*) that there must be some link between acts committed within the jurisdiction and the defendant, but those acts did not have to be those of the defendant: if the principal fraudster gives instructions for money in London to be paid abroad to a knowing recipient, it is not necessary for jurisdictional purposes that the recipient should have done anything in London for clause (15) to apply. In most cases the principal fraudster will be subject to the jurisdiction under another head, and there will be jurisdiction over the accessory party under the necessary and proper party provision of clause (3). The jurisdiction is not exorbitant, because in each case the claimant will have to show as against the foreign defendant that England is clearly the appropriate forum.

ILLUSTRATION

Land in Surrey, held in the names of three companies, has been purchased on behalf of the former Prime Minister of a foreign government and her husband with funds allegedly derived from bribes and secret commissions. The Government claims that it is beneficially entitled to the proceeds of sale of the estate. The companies are constructive trustees on the basis of knowing receipt of the proceeds of the bribes, and a substantial part of the acts giving rise to liability took place within the jurisdiction, the acquisition of the land in England with allegedly corrupt funds.[654]

11R–240   **(17) The court may assume jurisdiction if the claim is made by the Commissioners for H.M. Revenue and Customs relating to duties or taxes against a defendant not domiciled in Scotland or Northern Ireland.**[655]

11R–241   **(18) The court may assume jurisdiction if the claim is made by a party to proceedings for an order that the court exercise its powers under s.51 of the Senior Courts Act 1981 to make a costs order in favour of or against a person who is not a party to those proceedings.**[656]

---

[651] *ISC Technologies Ltd v Guerin* [1992] 2 Lloyd's Rep. 430.
[652] *The Independent*, September 2, 1992; reversed on other grounds, *The Times*, March 22, 1993 (CA). See also *Nycal (UK) Ltd v Lacey* [1994] C.L.C. 12. *cf. Cronos Containers NV v Palatin* [2002] EWHC 2819 (Comm.), [2003] I.L.Pr. 283 (a case on what is now Art.5(3) of the Brussels I Regulation).
[653] [2005] EWHC 405 (Ch.), [2005] I.L.Pr. 506. See also *Pakistan v Zardari* [2006] EWHC 2411 (Comm.), [2006] 2 C.L.C. 667. *cf. Dexter v Harley, The Times*, April 2, 2001 (a case on what is now Brussels I Regulation, Art.5(3)).
[654] *cf. Pakistan v Zardari* [2006] EWHC 2411 (Comm.), [2006] 2 C.L.C. 667.
[655] CPR, r.6.36 and PD6B, para.3.1(17).
[656] CPR, r.6.36 and PD6B, para.3.1(18).

COMMENT

Section 51 of the Senior Courts Act 1981 provides that the award of costs is   **11–242**
in the discretion of the court. It was held by the House of Lords that the power
includes a power to award costs against a person who is not a party to the
proceedings.[657] There was some doubt as to how this power could be exercised against a person outside the jurisdiction. It was held that permission
could be sought under the former Rules of the Supreme Court to serve the
non-party with the application to make him liable for the costs, but the Court
of Appeal drew attention to a possible gap in the new Civil Procedure Rules,
Rule 48.2 of which contains a procedure for making the non-party a party to
the proceedings for the purposes of the costs application, but which contained
no provision for service out of the jurisdiction of the application, and provision was made for this case.[658]

ILLUSTRATION

A, an English bank, brings proceedings for possession of a house in Chelsea occupied by X, who   **11–243**
is domiciled in England. She defends the proceedings on the ground that she has an equitable
interest in the house because of promises made to her by her second husband. After a trial her
defence is rejected. The bank seeks an order for costs from her first husband, who is in the United
States, and who has funded her defence. The court has jurisdiction under clause (18).[659]

**(19) The court may assume jurisdiction if a claim is (a) in the nature of   11R–244
salvage and any part of the services took place within England; or (b) to
enforce a claim under s.153, 154, 175 or 176A of the Merchant Shipping
Act 1995.**[660]

COMMENT

A salvage claim is a non-contractual claim arising under maritime law. The   **11–245**
sections of the Merchant Shipping Act 1995 deal with claims in connection
with oil pollution.

**(20) The court may assume jurisdiction if a claim is made (a) under an   11R–246
enactment which allows proceedings to be brought and those proceedings
are not covered by any of the other grounds in Rule 34; or (b) under the
Directive of the Council of the European Communities dated March 15,
1976, 76/308/EEC, where service is to be effected in a Member State of the
European Union.**[661]

---

[657] *Aiden Shipping Co, Ltd v Interbulk Ltd* [1986] A.C. 965.
[658] *National Justice Co Naviera SA v Prudential Assurance Co Ltd (No.2)* [2000] 1 W.L.R. 603
(CA).
[659] Based on the facts of *Locabail (UK) Ltd v Bayfield Properties Ltd (No.3)* [2000] 2 Costs
L.R. 169.
[660] CPR, r.6.36 and PD6B, para.3.1(19).
[661] CPR, r.6.36 and 6PD6B, para.3.1(20).

Comment

This clause formerly referred in terms to the legislation which it was intended to cover,[662] but no longer does so, apart from the reference to Council Directive 76/308/EEC, which relates to claims by HM Customs and Excise for sums due under the European Agricultural Guidance and Guarantee Fund and for agricultural levies and customs duties.

B. *Where the defendant is domiciled in a Member State, in a Convention State, or in Scotland or Northern Ireland*

11R–247   **Rule 35—Subject to Rules 36 and 37 (exclusive jurisdiction under the Brussels I Regulation and the Lugano Convention), 60 and 61 (international conventions) and 38(3) (*lis alibi pendens*) the court has jurisdiction to entertain a claim *in personam* in a civil or commercial matter falling within the scope of the Regulation or the Convention in the cases mentioned in this Rule.**

Comment

11–248   This Rule deals with the heads of *in personam* jurisdiction under the Brussels I Regulation and the Lugano Convention, and the similar, but not identical, counterpart in Sch.4 to the 1982 Act, which allocates jurisdiction within the United Kingdom in relation to matters within the scope of the Regulation. Although the heading of this section refers to the domicile of the defendant, several qualifications have to be made to it. First, even if the defendant is domiciled in a Member State, or a Convention State, the jurisdictional rules discussed here do not apply if the case is outside the scope of the Regulation or the Convention.[663] Matters which are outside their scope or excluded from Sch.4 will be governed by Rules 31 to 34. Secondly, the provisions relating to exclusive jurisdiction[664] (and the corresponding provisions of Sch.4) are not confined to cases where the defendant is domiciled in a Member State or Convention State (or in a particular part of the United Kingdom). Thirdly, Art.23 of the Regulation (and of the Convention) confers jurisdiction on the court chosen by a jurisdiction agreement where one of the parties is domiciled in a Member State or a Convention State, and that party may not necessarily be the defendant.[665] Fourthly, powers[666] under the Regulation and the Convention (given effect by s.25 of the 1982 Act) to grant interim remedies may be exercised where proceedings on the substance of the matter are in another

---

[662] In their current form (and in the order in which they appeared in RSC, Ord 11, r.1(1), and the former CPR, r.6.20) they are: Nuclear Installations Act 1965; Social Security Contributions and Benefits Act 1992; Drug Trafficking Act 1994; Proceeds of Crime Act 2002; Inheritance (Provision for Family and Dependants) Act 1975; Immigration (Carriers' Liability) Act 1987; Immigration and Asylum Act 1999, Pt.II; Immigration Act 1971; Financial Services and Markets Act 2000; Pensions Act 1995; Pensions Act 2004.
[663] See paras 11–029 *et seq.*
[664] See Rule 36.
[665] See Rule 39(3).
[666] Art.31.

Member State or Convention State, irrespective of the domicile of the defendant.

It is important to note that the jurisdiction under this Rule is not subject to **11–249** the discretion of the court even as regards defendants to be served outside England. By CPR, r.6.33 service of process out of the jurisdiction is permissible without the permission of the court if the claim is one to which the Regulation or the Convention or the intra-United Kingdom rules apply.[667] There is no room for the application of discretionary *forum conveniens* principles as between Member States or Convention States.[668] A defendant who wishes to dispute the jurisdiction of the court may apply for an order declaring that it has no jurisdiction, and also for an order setting aside service.[669] The European Court has held that it is for the national court to determine the standard of proof required to establish that the conditions for the establishment of jurisdiction under the Regulation are satisfied, provided that they do not impair its effectiveness.[670] In England it has been held that the standard to be applied in considering whether the jurisdiction of the court has been established for the purposes of the Regulation is the same as that under Rule 34, i.e. a good arguable case.[671] The more stringent test of balance of probabilities might require the trial of an issue and involve great expense and delay. Although jurisdictional issues are very important, they ought generally to be decided with due despatch without hearing oral evidence.[672]

Allocation of jurisdiction within the United Kingdom. The primary rule **11–250** of jurisdiction in the Regulation is that a defendant domiciled in a Member State is to be sued in the courts of that State. Because the United Kingdom is not a unitary State for the purposes of civil jurisdiction it was necessary to allocate jurisdiction as between its constituent parts. But instead of confining itself to determining in which part of the United Kingdom a party is domiciled, the 1982 Act goes much further in laying down rules for determining jurisdiction in cases where the parties are domiciled in different parts of the

---

[667] The only exception is CPR, r.6.36 and PD6B, para.3.1(5), which requires permission for the service of a claim form for an interim remedy under s.25(1) of the 1982 Act: see para.8–031.

[668] See para.11–028, and paras 12–019 *et seq.*

[669] CPR, r.11(1), (6). If the defendant is to be served out of the jurisdiction the claim form (and the particulars of claim, if contained in a separate document) must be endorsed with a statement that the court has power under the 1982 Act or the Regulation to deal with the claim and that no proceedings based on the same claim are pending between the parties in another part of the United Kingdom or another Member or Convention State: CPR, r.34(1); CPR, PD6B, para.2.1; PD7A, para.3.5; Form N510. See *DSG International Sourcing Ltd v Universal Media Corp (Slovakia) SRO* [2011] EWHC 1116 (Comm.), [2011] I.L.Pr. 698. On the effect of non-compliance with the requirement in CPR, r.6.34(1) to state the grounds for entitlement to serve the claim form out of the jurisdiction, see *Trustor AB v Barclays Bank Plc, The Times,* November 22, 2000.

[670] Case C–68/93 *Shevill v Presse Alliance* [1995] E.C.R. I–415, [1995] 2 A.C. 18.

[671] See *Canada Trust Co v Stolzenberg (No.2)* [1998] 1 W.L.R. 547 (CA) (affirmed [2002] 1 A.C. 1, 13), applying *Tesam Distribution Ltd v Schuh Mode Team GmbH* [1990] I.L.Pr. 149 (CA) and *Mölnlycke AB v Procter & Gamble Ltd,* [1992] 1 W.L.R. 1112 (CA), in the light of *Seaconsar Far East Ltd v Bank Markazi Iran* [1994] 1 A.C. 438. See also *Bols Distilleries v Superior Yacht Services* [2005] UKPC 45, [2007] 1 W.L.R. 12, at [28]; *WPP Holdings Italy SRL v Benatti* [2007] EWCA Civ 263, [2007] 1 W.L.R. 2316, at [41]; *Kolden Holdings Ltd v Rodette Commerce Ltd* [2008] EWCA Civ 10, [2008] Bus. L.R. 1051, at [49]–[52]; *Masri v Consolidated Contractors International Company SAL (No.2)* [2008] EWCA Civ 303, [2009] Q.B. 450, at [88].

[672] *Canada Trust Co v Stolzenberg (No.2)* [2002] 1 A.C. 1, 13, *per* Lord Steyn.

United Kingdom. These rules are set out in Sch.4 to the 1982 Act: they were originally modelled closely on those in the Brussels Convention, and are now modelled on the Brussels I Regulation, but they are not identical with the rules in the Regulation.[673] They apply where (a) the subject-matter of the proceedings is within the scope of the Regulation as determined by Art.1 (whether or not it has effect in relation to the proceedings) and (b) the defendant is domiciled in the United Kingdom or the proceedings are of a kind mentioned in Art.22 (exclusive jurisdiction).[674] Where, in a case to which the Regulation applies, the courts of the United Kingdom have jurisdiction as the Member State in which the defendant is domiciled, Sch.4 determines in which part of the United Kingdom the defendant must be sued. Similarly, the reference in Art.22 is to the courts of "the Member State" in which the property is situate, the company has its seat, the register is kept, etc. In these cases too it is necessary to allocate the resulting jurisdiction. Where the defendant is not domiciled in the United Kingdom and Art.22 does not apply, the problem of intra-United Kingdom jurisdiction will rarely arise in relation to the Regulation. Allocation is irrelevant in relation to those provisions[675] which give jurisdiction to a "place" and it will be that part of the United Kingdom in which that place is situated which will be the relevant part of the United Kingdom for the purposes of jurisdiction. Where the Regulation refers to a "court"[676] in which proceedings are pending it will be the law district in which the relevant court is situated which will be the court with jurisdiction.

11–251   There are two further cases which require allocation. First, Art.5(6) gives jurisdiction in actions against settlors, trustees or beneficiaries to the courts of the Member State in which the trust is domiciled. Any proceedings which by virtue of Art.5(6) are brought in the United Kingdom are to be brought in the courts of the part of the United Kingdom in which the trust is domiciled.[677] Secondly, Art.16(1) allows a consumer to bring proceedings in the courts of the State in which he is domiciled. Any proceedings which, by virtue of Art.16(1) are brought in the United Kingdom by a consumer on the ground that he is himself domiciled there, are to be brought in the court for the part of the United Kingdom in which he is domiciled.[678]

11–252   The primary rule of jurisdiction in Sch.4 is, like that in the Regulation and the Convention, the domicile of the defendant, but there are differences between Sch.4 and the Regulation equivalent in the other heads of jurisdiction. Certain types of proceeding are excluded from the operation of Sch.4.[679] Most of these are cases which would fall outside the Regulation scheme, but

---

[673] The European Court has no jurisdiction to give preliminary rulings on the interpretation of Sch.4 to the 1982 Act: Case C–346/93 *Kleinwort Benson Ltd v City of Glasgow DC* [1995] E.C.R. I–615, [1996] Q.B. 57 above, para.11–072.

[674] 1982 Act, s.16(1).

[675] Arts 5(1), (2), (3), (5) and 6(1).

[676] Arts 5(4), (7), 6(2), (3) and 7.

[677] SI 2001/3929, Sch.1, para.7(2), below, para.11–304.

[678] *ibid.*, para.7(3), below, clause (14). See also para.11(2) for the allocation of domicile in the case of insurers domiciled outside the Member States, but with a branch in Member State, and in the equivalent case for consumer contracts and employment contracts. See 1982 Act, ss.10(2), (3) and 44A(2) for the position under the Lugano Convention.

[679] See Sch.5.

there are others, such as (a) winding-up of solvent companies or (b) proceedings concerned with registration of patents, etc., which are within the Regulation and the Convention but outside Sch.4. The former is excluded because it was not appropriate to apply the standard tests for seats of companies in the intra-United Kingdom context, where place of incorporation is the only appropriate test for the winding-up of domestic companies. Proceedings relating to registration of patents, etc., are excluded because the principle of Art.22(4) cannot be applied to allocate jurisdiction between courts in the United Kingdom since the registers of patents, trade marks and designs are all situated in London. The main differences between the Regulation and the new Sch.4 are as follows. Rule 3(a) reproduces Art.5(1) of the Brussels Convention on jurisdiction in matters relating to a contract, and not the new version in Art.5(1) of the Regulation. Rule 3(h) of Sch.4 confers jurisdiction on the courts of the part of the United Kingdom in which property is situated in proceedings (a) concerning a debt secured on immovable property or (b) which are brought in connection with proprietary or possessory rights, or security rights in relation to movable property.[680] The provisions of Arts 8 to 14 relating to jurisdiction in matters relating to insurance are entirely deleted. It would follow from this that, in proceedings between an insurer and an insured, they must be brought in the court which has jurisdiction under the general Regulation scheme. A number of other differences of detail are noted at the appropriate points when the corresponding provisions of the Regulation are discussed.[681]

ILLUSTRATIONS

1. A resides in London. While on a visit to France he is injured as a result of the negligence **11–253** of X, who is domiciled in France. The court has no jurisdiction in proceedings by A against X.

2. A resides in London. While X, who is domiciled in France, is on a visit to England he negligently injures A. The court has jurisdiction in proceedings by A against X.[682]

3. A resides in London. While A and X, who is domiciled in England, are on a trip to France, A is injured as a result of the negligence of X. The court has jurisdiction in proceedings by A against X.[683]

4. The facts are as in Illustration 3, except that X is domiciled in Scotland. The court has no jurisdiction.[684]

5. A resides in London. While A and X, who are domiciled in Scotland, are driving in England A is injured as a result of the negligence of X. The court has jurisdiction.[685]

(1) The court has jurisdiction if the claim is made against a person domiciled in England.[686]　　**11R–254**

---

[680] See below, clause (7).

[681] See especially Rule 4 (decisions of organs of companies), below, para.11–379; Rule 12 (jurisdiction agreements: removal of formal requirement; subject to mandatory legislation) below, para.12–144.

[682] Brussels I Regulation, Art.5(3).

[683] *ibid.*, Art.2.

[684] Sch.4, Rule 2.

[685] *ibid.*, Rule 3(c).

[686] Brussels I Regulation, Art.2; 1982 Act, Sch.4, Rule 2.

COMMENT

11–255 The basic principle of the Regulation and Convention schemes (which is also reflected in the intra-United Kingdom provisions of Sch.4) is that persons domiciled in a Member State or a Convention State may be sued there, and may be sued in another Member State or Convention State only by virtue of the special rules of jurisdiction in the Regulation and the Convention. The primary rule of domicile as the basis of jurisdiction is set out in Art.2 which provides that persons domiciled in a Member State or Convention State (as the case may be) shall, whatever their nationality, be sued in the courts of that State. In *Canada Trust Co v Stolzenberg (No.2)*[687] it was held that the critical date for testing whether the defendant was domiciled in England for the purposes of Art.2 (in that case, of the original Lugano Convention) was the date of the *issue* of proceedings rather than the date of service.[688]

11–256 Article 2 is expressly subject to the other provisions of the Regulation and the Convention; but the overriding importance of the principal rule of domicile was the starting point of the European Court's interpretation of the scope of the special jurisdictions under the Brussels Convention and then the Regulation, because the basis of the system of jurisdiction "is the general conferment of jurisdiction on the court of the defendant's domicile"[689] and "it is in accord with the objective of the [Regulation] to avoid a wide and multifarious interpretation of the exceptions to the general rule of jurisdiction contained in Article 2."[690]

11–257 It is the domicile of the defendant which is crucial for the purposes of jurisdiction. Only rarely is the domicile of the claimant relevant.[691] If the defendant is not domiciled in a Member State or Convention State, normally[692] Rules 31 to 34 apply. Article 3(1) provides that persons domiciled in a Member State or Convention State may be sued in the courts of another Member State or Convention State only by virtue of the rules set out in Arts 5 to 24 of the Regulation. Annex I contains a (non-exhaustive) catalogue of jurisdictional rules which may not be invoked against domiciliaries of Member (and Convention) States. Strictly, this provision is not necessary and is merely declaratory, because Art.3(1) makes it clear that domiciliaries may only be sued in the circumstances set out in the Regulation and the Convention. The rule in English law which is in effect branded as exorbitant is the rule allowing the exercise of jurisdiction over an individual by virtue of his mere presence at the time of the service of process.[693] But in practice the operation of this much-criticised rule does not today work inconvenience or injustice, since, in the case of a genuinely contested claim, the courts have

---

[687] [2002] 1 A.C. 1.

[688] *cf.* Art.30 (for purpose of *lis pendens* principles court is seised on issue of proceedings).

[689] Case 12/76 *Industrie Tessili Italiana Como v Dunlop AG* [1976] E.C.R. 1473, 1485. Generally, the Regulation and Convention schemes are hostile to jurisdiction being vested in the claimant's domicile: see Case C–220/88 *Dumez France v Hessische Landesbank* [1990] E.C.R. I–49, 79.

[690] Case 33/78 *Somafer SA v Saar-Ferngas AG* [1978] E.C.R. 2183, 2191.

[691] See Art.5(2) (domicile of maintenance creditor); Art.9(1)(b) (domicile of policyholder, etc); Art.16(1) (domicile of consumer).

[692] For exceptions see Arts 9(2), 15(2), 22, and 23.

[693] Rule 31.

come to accept that a stay of the proceedings will be granted if they have no real connection with England.[694]

Even if the defendant is domiciled in England, the court will not be able to assume jurisdiction in the following cases: (a) where the courts of another Member State or Convention State have exclusive jurisdiction pursuant to Art.22 of the Regulation or the Convention;[695] (b) where the courts of Scotland or Northern Ireland have exclusive jurisdiction pursuant to Rule 11 of Sch.4;[696] (c) where the parties have agreed that the courts of another Member State or Convention State or of Scotland or Northern Ireland shall have jurisdiction pursuant to the terms of Art.23 or Rule 12 of Sch.4;[697] (d) where proceedings involving the same cause of action have already been commenced in the courts of another Member State or Convention State. In the latter case the court has no discretion (as it has if the proceedings are pending in Scotland or Northern Ireland) to assume jurisdiction.[698]

11–258

ILLUSTRATIONS

1. X, who resides in and is domiciled in France, is an art dealer. A is an Indian princess. X in France sells and delivers a picture to A for cash and represents that it was painted by the French artist Boucher. A is later advised that the picture was not painted by Boucher and issues a writ claiming rescission and damages. X is served at Ascot races during his temporary visit to England. Service will be set aside.[699]

2. A & Co, an American company, brings an action against X, who is domiciled in Switzerland, in respect of a debt incurred in New York, and serves X while X is staying for a few days at a London hotel. Service will be set aside.[700]

3. The facts are as in Illustration 2, except that X is domiciled in New York. The court has jurisdiction.[701]

4. The facts are as in Illustration 2, except that X is domiciled in Scotland. Service will be set aside.[702]

11–259

(2)(a) **The court has jurisdiction, subject to clauses (13), (14) and (15) of this Rule, in matters relating to a contract, if England is the place of performance of the obligation in question.[703]**

  (b) **For the purpose of sub-clause (a), and unless otherwise agreed, the place of performance of the obligation in question shall be England if, in the case of the sale of goods, England was the place where, under the contract, the goods were delivered or should have been delivered; and in the case of the provision of**

11R–260

---

[694] Rule 38.

[695] Rules 36 and 131.

[696] *ibid.*

[697] Rule 39(3).

[698] Rule 38.

[699] Brussels I Regulation, Art.3. Contrast *Maharanee of Baroda v Wildenstein* [1972] 2 Q.B. 283 (CA).

[700] Lugano Convention, Art.3. Contrast *Colt Industries v Sarlie* [1966] 1 W.L.R. 440 (CA).

[701] Brussels I Regulation, Art.4.

[702] 1982 Act, Sch.4, Rule 2.

[703] Art.5(1)(a). See generally Hertz, *Jurisdiction in Contract and Tort under the Brussels Convention* (1998); Hill (1995) 44 I.C.L.Q. 591; Kennett (1995) 15 Yb. Eur. L. 193; Takahashi (2002) 27 Eur. L.R. 530; Zheng Tang (2008) 4 J. Priv. Int. L.35.

**services, England was the place where, under the contract, the
services were provided or should have been provided.**[704]

   (c) **Where the defendant is domiciled in Scotland or Northern Ireland, the court has jurisdiction, subject to clauses (13) and (15)
of this Rule, in matters relating to a contract, if England is the
place of performance of the obligation in question.**[705]

Comment

11–261   **Introduction.** Article 5(1) is the basic rule for contract claims against a
defendant domiciled in another Member State or Convention State, although
special provision is made in Arts 8 to 21 for insurance contracts, consumer
contracts and employment contracts, which are the subject of clauses (13),
(14) and (15) of this Rule.

11–262   Under the Brussels Convention (and the original Lugano Convention) "the
obligation in question" whose place of performance must be in England was
the obligation which is the basis of the action. The European Court held
consistently that it was for the court before which the matter was brought to
establish whether the place of performance was situate within its territorial
jurisdiction, and that it must for that purpose determine in accordance with its
own rules of the conflict of laws what was the law applicable to the relationship, and define, in accordance with that law, the place of performance of the
contractual obligation in question.[706] The operation of Art.5(1) of the Brussels
Convention (and of the original Lugano Convention), as interpreted by the
European Court, gave rise to criticism,[707] in particular because (especially
where the obligation sued on was a payment obligation) it tended to give
jurisdiction to the courts of the claimant's domicile, and did not fulfil the
original expectation that it would give jurisdiction to the courts of the country
which had the closest connection with the dispute.

11–263   Consequently, Art.5(1)(b) of the Brussels I Regulation (and of the revised
Lugano Convention)[708] makes special provision for an autonomous definition
of the place of performance of the obligation in the case of the sale of goods
and the provision of services. Article 5(1)(b) provides that for the purposes of
Art.5(1), unless otherwise agreed, the place of performance of the obligation
in question shall be, in the case of the sale of goods, the place in a Member
State where, under the contract, the goods were delivered or should have been
delivered; and in the case of the provision of services, the place in a Member
State where, under the contract, the services were provided or should have
been provided. In other types of contract the basic rule in Art.5(1)(a)
applies.[709] The reason for the change is to prevent an unpaid seller routinely

---

[704] Art.5(1)(b).

[705] 1982 Act, Sch.4, Rule 3(a).

[706] See below, paras 11–274 *et seq.*

[707] See e.g. Hill (1995) 44 I.C.L.Q. 591; Ancel (2001) 3 Yb. Priv. Int. L. 101, 108–110. See
Case C–288/92 *Custom Made Commercial Ltd v Stawa Metallbau GmbH* [1994] E.C.R. I–2913
(German court had jurisdiction in action by German seller against English buyer for the
price).

[708] But not the intra-UK provision in Rule 3(a), 1982 Act, Sch.4, on which see, e.g. *Universal
Steels Ltd v Skanska Construction UK Ltd* [2003] ScotCS 271; *J.S. Swan (Printing) Ltd v Kall
Kwik UK Ltd,* [2009] CSOH 99, 2009 S.C.L.R. 688.

[709] Art.5(1)(c). See generally Rodger, 2001 Jur. Rev. 59 and 69.

being able to sue in its own courts on the footing that the law governing the contract of sale requires payment to be made at the seller's place of residence. The European Court has held[710] that Art.5(1)(a) is to be interpreted in accordance with the jurisprudence on Art.5(1) of the Brussels Convention, in particular its jurisprudence on the relevant obligation and the determination of the place of performance.

Article 5(1) of the Brussels Convention (and Art.5(1) of the original   **11–264** Lugano Convention, but in slightly different terms) made special provision for individual contracts of employment. The Brussels I Regulation and the revised Lugano Convention have no special provisions for employment contracts in Art.5(1), but contain new and more extensive provisions in s.5 (Arts 18 to 21), which are dealt with in connection with clause (15) below.

The changes made by the Brussels I Regulation to the basic rule in contract   **11–265** jurisdiction have not been adopted for the purposes of intra-United Kingdom jurisdiction. Rule 3(a) in Sch.4 to the 1982 Act[711] contains the same rule as the original Brussels Convention, and simply gives jurisdiction to the courts for the place of performance of the obligation in question.

In England, jurisdiction over persons not present, domiciled or resident   **11–266** within England may be exercised in non-Regulation and non-Convention cases in contractual matters (a) where the contract was made within the jurisdiction, or (b) where the contract was made by or through an agent trading or residing within the jurisdiction, or (c) where the contract is by its terms, or by implication, governed by English law or (d) for a breach of contract committed within the jurisdiction; and (e) where there is a contractual choice of English jurisdiction.[712] The Regulation and Convention rules are significantly different. There is no provision corresponding to (a), (b) or (c). Although (d) has some superficial similarity to the Regulation/Convention rule, it differs from it in at least one important respect. Under the English rule it is possible to envisage a breach in England of a contractual obligation to be performed elsewhere, e.g. by express or implied repudiation.[713] Under the Regulation and the Convention, however, jurisdiction is conferred on the place of performance of the obligation in question and not on the place of the breach.

It should be noted also that there are special provisions for contractual   **11–267** claims (especially debts secured on immovable property) connected with actions in matters relating to rights *in rem* in immovable property, and for claims connected with tenancies.[714]

Contract. Article 5(1) confers jurisdiction "in matters relating to a con-   **11–268** tract, in the courts for the place of performance of the obligation in question". This provision relates to contractual claims (*"en matière contractuelle"*). Whether a matter relates to a contract will not usually give rise to difficulty. There is a sufficiently common core on the meaning of contract to result in the

---

[710] Case C–533/07 *Falco Privatstiftung v Weller-Lindhorst* [2009] E.C.R. I–3327.
[711] As substituted by SI 2001/3929, Sch.2. Sch.4 to the 1982 Act, unlike the Brussels I Regulation, contains no special provision for insurance contracts: see Rule 35(15).
[712] See above, Rule 34(4), (5).
[713] para.11–196.
[714] Arts 6(4) and 22(1); 1982 Act, Sch.4, Rules 5(d) and 11(a).

term being given an autonomous interpretation. The European Court has confirmed[715] that the concept of "matters relating to a contract" is to be regarded as an independent concept, and is not to be tested simply by reference to national law. In *Arcado Sprl v Haviland*[716] a Belgian court asked the European Court whether proceedings relating to the repudiation of a commercial agency agreement and the payment of commission under it were proceedings in matters relating to a contract within Art.5(1). Under Belgian law (as under English law) it was clear that such proceedings were for breach of contract and for sums due under contract, but a doubt appears to have arisen because in France there have been suggestions that a claim for breach of contract in bad faith may be delictual in nature.[717] The European Court answered that there is no doubt that a claim for commission is contractual because it finds its basis in the agreement; and similarly a claim for compensation is contractual in nature because its basis is the failure to comply with a contractual obligation.

11–269   In *Soc Handte et Cie GmbH v TMCS*[718] the plaintiffs were a French company which had bought metal-polishing machines from a Swiss company. It fitted to the machines a suction system sold and installed by a French company. That system had been manufactured by a German company. Under French law the plaintiffs' claim against the German manufacturer that the equipment was unfit for its purpose was contractual in nature, even though there was no contract directly between the plaintiffs and the German company. The then prevailing theory in French law was that the intermediate buyer transmitted to the sub-buyer his contractual rights against the manufacturer. The European Court held that such a claim was not contractual for the purpose of Art.5(1). Article 5(1) only applies to cases in which there is an agreement freely entered[719] into between the parties, and in most of the Brussels Conven-

---

[715] Case 34/82 *Peters v ZNAV* [1983] E.C.R. 987; Case 9/87 *Arcado Sprl v Haviland SA* [1988] E.C.R. 1539; Case C–26/91 *Soc Jacob Handte et Cie GmbH v TMCS* [1992] E.C.R. I–3967; Case C–51/97 *Réunion européenne SA v Spliethoff's Bevrachtingskantoor BV* [1998] E.C.R. I–6511; Case C–334/00 *Fonderie Officine Meccaniche SpA v HWS GmbH* [2002] E.C.R. I–7357; Case C–167/00 *Verein für Konsumentenininformation v Henkel* [2002] E.C.R. I–8111; Case C–265/02 *Frahuil SA v Assitalia SpA* [2004] E.C.R. I–1543; Case C–27/02 *Engler v Janus Versand GmbH* [2005] E.C.R. I–481. See also, in relation to 1982 Act, Sch.4, Rule 5(1), *Bank of Scotland v IMRO*, 1989 S.L.T. 432, criticised by Mennie, 1990 S.L.T. (News) 1 (doubted whether obligations arising under bank's membership of self-regulating scheme were contractual in nature); *Engdiv Ltd v G Percy Trentham Ltd*, 1990 S.L.T. 617 (claim for contribution by architects against main contractors held a matter relating to a contract between main contractors and owners); *WPP Holdings Italy SRL v Benatti* [2007] EWCA Civ 263, [2007] 1 W.L.R. 2316 (claim by a third party under the Contracts (Rights of Third Parties) Act 1999 held matter relating to a contract). On unilateral obligations see Maher, 2002 Jur. Rev. 317.

[716] See above.

[717] See Allwood (1988) 16 Eur. L. Rev. 366.

[718] See above. *cf.* Case C–265/02 *Frahuil SA v Assitalia SpA*, above (Art.5(1) does not apply to claim by guarantor of customs duties against owner of goods who did not authorise guarantee). Contrast Case C–27/02 *Engler v Janus Versand GmbH* [2005] E.C.R. I–481, [2005] I.L.Pr. 83 (offer of prize by trader capable of constituting contractual obligation when accepted).

[719] For the use of this test to determine whether the parties were in a contractual relationship, see Case C–51/97 *Réunion européenne SA v Spliethoff's Bevrachtingskantoor BV* [1998] E.C.R. I–6511, [2000] Q.B. 690; Case C–334/00 *Fonderie Officine Meccaniche Tacconi SpA v Heinrich Wagner Sinto Maschinenfabrik* [2002] E.C.R. I–7357; Case C–265/02 *Frahuil SA v Assitalia SpA* [2004] E.C.R. I–1543; Case C–27/02 *Engler v Janus Versand GmbH* [2005] E.C.R. I–481; Case C–98/06 *Freeport plc v Arnoldsson* [2007] E.C.R. I–839, [2008] Q.B. 634.

tion States such a claim would not have been regarded as contractual. Similarly, it was held that although a claim by a consignee (or its insurer) against the carrier who has issued a bill of lading may be contractual, a claim against a carrier who is not in a contractual relationship with the consignee is not within Art.5(1).[720]

In *Kleinwort Benson Ltd v Glasgow City Council*[721] the House of Lords **11–270** held by a majority (Lords Nicholls and Mustill dissenting) that a claim for restitution of money paid under a purported contract which was void did not fall within the intra-United Kingdom version of Art.5(1),[722] as it was not a matter "relating to a contract."[723] A claim fell within Art.5(1) if it could properly be said to be based upon a particular contractual obligation, the place of performance of which was within the jurisdiction of the court. Where the claim was for the recovery of money paid under a supposed contract which in law never existed, it was impossible to say that the claim for the recovery of the money was based upon a particular contractual obligation. A claim to restitution based upon the principle of unjust enrichment did not *per se* fall within Art.5(1). It was not necessary to hold that a claim to restitution could never fall within Art.5(1). Very exceptionally, there might be particular circumstances in which it could properly be said that the claim in question, although a claim to restitution, was nevertheless based on a contractual obligation and fell within Art.5(1). Lord Goff left open the question whether Art.5(1) applied to a claim for the recovery of money paid under a valid contract on the ground of failure of consideration following the defendant's breach.

The question has arisen in England whether an action to avoid an insurance **11–271** or re-insurance contract on the ground of misrepresentation or non-disclosure is a matter "relating to a contract" for the purposes of Art.5(1), and whether the duty of good faith can be the "obligation in question". These questions arise because the proceedings are based on breach of the duty of good faith owed to the insurer or re-insurer, and it is controversial as a matter of English law whether the duty of good faith is properly to be regarded as a contractual obligation or as an equitable obligation under the general law. It was held by the House of Lords in *Agnew v Länsförsäkringsbolagens AB*[724] that a claim to set aside a contract for non-disclosure was a matter relating to a contract. It was also held (by a majority, with Lords Hope of Craighead and Millett dissenting) that pre-contractual obligations fell within Art.5(1); that the "obligation in question" was apt to comprise the defendant's obligations to make a fair presentation of the risk, not to misrepresent it and to disclose material facts; that those obligations were to be performed in London, and the English

---

[720] Case C–51/97 *Réunion européenne SA v Spliethoff's Bevrachtingskantoor BV* [1998] E.C.R. I–6511.

[721] [1999] 1 A.C. 153. See also *Ferguson v Shipbuilders Ltd v Voith Hydro GmbH & Co AG*, 2000 S.L.T. 229.

[722] Sch.4, 1982 Act. The European Court refused to give a ruling in the proceedings: see above, para.11–072.

[723] Nor was it a matter "relating to a tort or delict" within Art.5(3): see below, para.11–285.

[724] [2001] 1 A.C. 223. See also *Alfred Dunhill Ltd v Diffusion Internationale de Maroquinerie de Prestige SARL* [2001] C.L.C. 949: a claim for damages for misrepresentation alleged to have induced a contract is not a matter "relating to a contract," applying [2001] 1 A.C. at 252–253, *per* Lord Hope of Craighead (a dissenting speech, but not on this point).

court had jurisdiction under Art.5(1). It is by no means clear on what basis the majority distinguished the *Kleinwort Benson* case, except perhaps that the *Kleinwort Benson* concerned a void contract.[725]

11–272   But in *Fonderie Officine Meccaniche SpA v HWS GmbH*,[726] the European Court held that an action in Italy based on the breach of the obligation to act in good faith in negotiations was a matter relating to tort, delict or quasi-delict and not contract. Article 5(1) did not require a contract to have been concluded, but it was essential, for Art.5(3) to apply, to identify an obligation, since the jurisdiction of the national court was determined by the place of performance of the obligation in question. Article 5(1) did not apply where there was no obligation freely assumed by one party to the other. The obligation to make good damage allegedly caused by the unjustified breaking off of negotiations could derive only from breach of rules of law, in particular the rule which required the parties to act in good faith in negotiations with a view to the formation of a contract.

11–273   The jurisdiction under Art.5(1) may be invoked even if the existence of the contract is denied by the defendant. In *Effer SpA v Kantner*[727] the dispositive holding was that the plaintiff may invoke this jurisdiction "even when the existence of the contract on which the claim is based is in dispute between the parties." It has been held that this is so even where it is the claimant who denies the existence of the contractual relationship and seeks a negative declaration that he is not bound by any obligation, and it is the defendant who asserts there is a contractual obligation,[728] but this must be regarded as doubtful.[729] The mere allegation of a contract is not enough to found jurisdiction: service may be set aside if there is no basis for the existence of a contract, i.e. no serious question which calls for a trial.[730]

11–274   **The obligation in question.** Subject to the special provision for contracts for the sale of goods and supply of services in the Brussels I Regulation and the Lugano Convention,[731] "the obligation in question" whose place of performance must be in England is the obligation which is the basis of the

---

[725] See Lord Woolf M.R. at p.242.

[726] Case C–334/00 [2002] E.C.R. I–7357.

[727] Case 38/81 [1982] E.C.R. 825. See also Case 73/77 *Sanders v Van der Putte* [1977] E.C.R. 2383 (jurisdiction under Brussels Convention, Art.16(1), in dispute over existence of lease); Case C–27/02 *Engler v Janus Versand GmbH* [2005] E.C.R. I–481, [2005] I.L.Pr. 83. *cf.* Case C–269/95 *Benincasa v Dentalkit Srl* [1997] E.C.R. I–3767 (jurisdiction clause effective under Brussels Convention, Art.17 where party resisting its application claims contract is void).

[728] *Boss Group Ltd v Boss France SA* [1997] 1 W.L.R. 351 (CA). *cf. Fisher v Unione Italiana de Riassicurazione SpA* [1998] C.L.C. 682; also Batiffol and Lagarde, Vol.2, pp.475–476; *Soc I.S.I. v Soc C.P.A.V.*, Cour de cassation, France, in 1983 *Rev. Crit.* 516, note Gaudemet-Tallon. See also the position under CPR, r.6.36 and PD6B, para.3.1(8), above, para.11–209.

[729] The decision was, however, mentioned with apparent approval by Lord Clyde in *Kleinwort Benson Ltd v Glasgow City Council* [1999] 1 A.C. 153, 182. In *Agnew v Länsförsäkringbolagens AB* [2001] 1 A.C. 223, 258, Lord Hope approved the decision, but Lord Millett (at 264) said it was doubtful. See also *USF Ltd v Aquatechnology Hanson NV/SA* [2001] 1 All E.R. (Comm.) 856.

[730] *Tesam Distribution Ltd v Schuh Mode Team GmbH* [1990] I.L.Pr. 149 (CA), applied in *Rank Film Distributors Ltd v Lanterna Editrice Srl* [1992] I.L.Pr. 58; *New England Reinsurance Corp v Messoghios Insurance Co SA* [1992] 2 Lloyd's Rep. 251 (CA).

[731] Many of the cases establishing the general principles on the operation of Art.5(1) were decided under the Brussels Convention, and relate to contracts for the sale of goods or the supply of services.

action. In *De Bloos Sprl v Bouyer SA*[732] the European Court held that the "obligation" in Art.5(1) was the contractual obligation which formed the basis of the legal proceedings;[733] where the plaintiff seeks damages for faulty performance or non-performance of a contractual obligation, it is the latter obligation which is the relevant obligation for the purposes of Art.5(1). But as regards compensation for termination, it was for the national court to decide whether the obligation to pay it was a separate independent contractual obligation or whether it merely replaced the unperformed contractual obligation.[734] This decision gave rise to considerable practical problems in cases of exclusive agency or distribution contracts where the defendant had repudiated a contract containing obligations to be performed in more than one country. In *Ivenel v Schwab*[735] (a case concerned with a claim by a commission agent employed under a contract of employment) the European Court modified its approach to deal with a case involving mutual obligations to be performed in different countries. It held that in such a case the relevant obligation was the obligation which was characteristic of the contract. This was a concept borrowed from the Rome Convention on the Law Applicable to Contractual Obligations and now contained in the Rome I Regulation.[736]

But in *Shenavai v Kreischer*[737] the Court held that the decision in *Ivenel v Schwab* was limited to contracts of employment.[738] In other cases it is not necessary or appropriate to identify the obligation which characterises the contract. Accordingly, in such cases regard should be had solely to the contractual obligations whose performance was sought. The court said that where a dispute is concerned with a number of obligations arising under the contract, the court before which the matter is brought will be guided by the maxim *accessorium sequitur principale*, i.e. where various obligations are at issue, it will be the principal obligation which will determine jurisdiction. Thus in *Medway Packaging Ltd v Meurer Maschinen GmbH*[739] the English distributor of German machinery could sue in England for the German manufacturer's repudiation because the principal obligation which was the basis of the proceedings was the obligation to give reasonable notice of termination, which was performable in England at the distributor's place of business. Similarly, in *Union Transport Plc v Continental Lines SA*[740] English

11–275

---

[732] Case 14/76 [1976] E.C.R. 1497.

[733] This is so even if it leads to a claim being subject to the jurisdiction of a court which does not have the closest connection with the dispute: Case C–288/92 *Custom Made Commercial Ltd v Stawa Metallbau GmbH* [1994] E.C.R. I–2913; *Boss Group Ltd v Boss France SA* [1997] I W.L.R. 351 (CA).

[734] In England it is the latter: *cf. Photo Production Ltd v Securicor Transport Ltd* [1980] A.C. 827, 849, *per* Lord Diplock, whose dicta, it is suggested, do not affect this conclusion. See *Medway Packaging Ltd v Meurer Maschinen GmbH* [1990] 1 Lloyd's Rep. 383, 389, affirmed [1990] 2 Lloyd's Rep. 112 (CA).

[735] Case 133/81 [1982] E.C.R. 1891.

[736] See Rule 223.

[737] Case 266/85 [1987] E.C.R. 239.

[738] For which special provision is now made: see, below, paras 11–369 *et seq.* See also *Mercury Publicity Ltd v Wolfgang Loerke GmbH* [1993] I.L.Pr 142 (CA).

[739] [1990] 2 Lloyd's Rep. 112 (CA). See also *Carl Stuart Ltd v Biotrace* [1993] I.L.R.M. 633; *Bio-Medical Research Ltd v Delatex SA* [2000] I.L.Pr. 23 (Irish High Ct). On distribution agreements in the context of Art.5(1) see Hertz, *Jurisdiction in Contract and Tort under the Brussels Convention* (1998), pp.132–138.

[740] [1992] 1 W.L.R. 15 (HL).

charterers could sue Belgian shipowners in London in a claim arising out of the shipowners' failure to ship a cargo of telegraph poles from Florida to Bangladesh. The relevant obligation was the obligation to nominate a vessel for the voyage charter, and the place of performance of that obligation was in London. In *Source Ltd v TUV Rheinland Holding AG*[741] the plaintiffs, an English company, engaged a German company to conduct quality control inspections in the Far East of goods which the plaintiffs were proposing to import into England from suppliers in Hong Kong and Taiwan. When the plaintiffs received complaints about the quality of the goods, they instituted proceedings in England against the German company. It was held that the principal obligation of the contract was the inspection of the goods in the Far East and not the delivery of reports in England, and accordingly the English court did not have jurisdiction under Art.5(1).

11–276   This approach, however, is inapplicable in cases where no single obligation can be regarded as principal. In *Leathertex Divisione Sintetici SpA v Bodetex BVBA*[742] proceedings were brought in Belgium against an Italian company for arrears of commission and compensation in lieu of notice of termination of an agency contract. The Belgian court held that the obligation to give notice and, in the event of failure to give notice, to pay compensation was to be performed in Belgium, but that the obligation to pay commission was to be performed in Italy under the principle that debts are payable at the residence of the creditor. Accordingly it asked the European Court whether both claims under the two separate obligations (neither of which was accessory to the other) could be brought in Belgium as the place of performance of one of them. The effect of the European Court's ruling is that a court does not have jurisdiction to hear the whole of an action founded on two obligations of equal rank arising from the same contract when, acording to the conflict rules of the State where that court is situated, one of those obligations is to be performed in that State and the other in another Member State.

11–277   **Place of performance.** Once the relevant contractual obligation has been determined, the next problem is what law determines where it is to be performed.[743] In *Industrie Tessili Italiana Como v Dunlop AG*[744] the European

---

[741] [1998] Q.B. 54 (CA). See also *AIG Group (UK) Ltd v The Ethniki* [2000] 2 All E.R. 566 (CA); *WH Martin Ltd v Feldbinder GmbH* [1998] I.L.Pr. 794. The principal obligation may be an implied term: *Raiffeisen Zentralbank Oesterreich AG v National Bank of Greece SA* [1999] 1 Lloyd's Rep. 408.

[742] Case C–420/97 [1999] E.C.R. I–6747. See also *AIG Group (UK) Ltd v The Ethniki* [2000] 2 All E.R. 566 (CA); *Ferguson v Shipbuilders Ltd v Voith Hydro GmbH & Co AG*, 2000 S.L.T. 229.

[743] Where the place of performance is in dispute, the claimant must show a good arguable case that England is the place of performance: *Mercury Publicity Ltd v Wolfgang Loerke GmbH* [1993] I.L.Pr. 142 (CA); *WPP Holdings Italy SRL v Benatti* [2007] EWCA Civ 263, [2007] 1 W.L.R. 2316. Many of the earlier English and Scottish cases on the place of performance are obsolete following the amendment of Art.5(1) effected in the Brussels I Regulation and the revised Lugano Convention. For more recent cases see *WPP Holdings Italy SRL v Benatti* [2007] EWCA Civ 263, [2007] 1 W.L.R. 2316; *Commercial Marine Piling Ltd v Pierse Contracting Ltd* [2009] EWHC 2241 (TCC), [2009] 2 Lloyd's Rep 659; *Gard Marine & Energy Ltd v Tunnicliffe* [2009] EWHC 2388 (Comm.), [2010] Lloyd's Rep. I.R. 62, affd. [2010] EWCA Civ 1052, [2011] I.L.Pr. 134.

[744] Case 12/76 [1976] E.C.R. 1473, applied in *Domicrest Ltd v Swiss Bank Corp* [1999] Q.B. 548. See also Case 133/81 *Ivenel v Schwab*, above. See also Case C–288/92 *Custom Made*

Court held that it is for the court before which the matter is brought to establish whether the place of performance is situated within its territorial jurisdiction, and that it must for that purpose determine in accordance with its own rules of the conflict of laws what is the law applicable to the legal relationship in question, and define, in accordance with that law, the place of performance of the contractual obligation in question.

In *GIE Groupe Concorde v The Master of the Vessel "Suhadiwarno Pan-*   **11–278**
jan"[745] the European Court reaffirmed that the place of performance of the obligation is to be determined in accordance with the law governing the obligation in question according to the conflict of laws rules of the court seised. The Court recognised that it had adopted a different approach in the case of contracts of employment, where it had ruled that the place of performance should be determined by reference to uniform criteria, which led to the choice of the place where the employee actually performed the work covered by the contract: *Mulox IBC v Geels*.[746] But that depended on the peculiar characteristics of the contract of employment, which had been reflected in the 1989 Accession Convention. The principle of legal certainty was one of the objectives of the Brussels Convention, and that principle required that the jurisdictional rules which derogated from the basic principle of domicile should be interpreted in such a way as to enable a normally well-informed defendant reasonably to foresee before which courts, other than those of the State in which he was domiciled, he may be sued. The Rome Convention had standardised the relevant conflict rules. Accordingly it was not appropriate to adopt the formula suggested by the French Cour de cassation that the place of performance of the obligation should be determined by seeking to establish, in the light of the relationship creating the obligation and the circumstances of the case, the place where performance actually took place or should have taken place, without reference to the law governing the obligation.

The European Court has considered in two Brussels Convention cases the   **11–279**
question whether the parties may confer jurisdiction on the courts of what is now a Member State by specifying that the performance of the obligation is deemed to be due there. The result of the cases is that a choice of the place of performance is effective for the purposes of Art.5(1), but it must be a place where the obligation is capable of being performed. In *Zelger v Salinitri (No.1)*[747] the European Court held that if the parties to the contract are permitted by the law applicable to the contract, subject to any conditions imposed by that law, to specify the place of performance of an obligation

---

Commercial Ltd v Stawa Metallbau GmbH [1994] E.C.R. I–2913 (German court had jurisdiction in action by German seller against English buyer for the price). The obligation may be a negative one, and it will then be necessary to identify the country in which the defendant was obliged not to act: cf. *USF Ltd v Aquatechnology Hanson NV/SA* [2001] 1 All E.R. (Comm.) 856; *Kenburn Waste Management Ltd v Bergmann* [2002] EWCA Civ 98, [2002] F.S.R. 711 (CA). But in Case C–256/00 *Besix SA v WABAG* [2002] E.C.R. I–1699, [2003] 1 W.L.R. 1113, the European Court held that where the negative obligation had no geographical limitation, the place of performance could not be regarded as being in every Brussels Convention State, and consequently Art.5(1) did not apply. In those circumstances only the court of the domicile would have jurisdiction.

[745] Case C–440/97 [1999] E.C.R. I–6307.

[746] Case C–125/92 [1993] E.C.R. I–4075. See also Case C–37/00 *Weber v Universal Ogden Services Ltd* [2002] E.C.R. I–2013, [2002] Q.B. 1189; C–437/00 *Pugliese v Finmeccanica SpA* [2003] E.C.R. I–4867.

[747] Case 56/79 [1980] E.C.R. 89.

without satisfying any special condition of form, an agreement (even an oral agreement) on the place of performance of the obligation is sufficient to found jurisdiction in that place under Art.5(1). In the *MSG* case[748] the European Court acknowledged that the parties are free to agree on a place of performance for contractual obligations which differs from that which would be determined under the law applicable to the contract. But it held that they are nevertheless not entitled, with the sole aim of specifying the courts having jurisdiction, to designate a place of performance having no real connection with the reality of the contract at which the obligations arising under the contract could not be performed in accordance with the terms of the contract. Article 5(1)(b) of the Brussels I Regulation (and the Lugano Convention) provides that the new rules on place of performance of contracts for the sale of goods and provision of services are subject to agreement to the contrary.

11–280   **Sale of goods and contracts for services.** Article 5(1)(b) of the Regulation (and the Convention) provides that, for the purposes of Art.5(1), and unless otherwise agreed, the place of performance of the obligation in question shall be: in the case of the sale of goods, the place in a Member (or Convention) State where, under the contract, the goods were delivered or should have been delivered; and, in the case of the provision of services, the place in a Member (or Convention) State where, under the contract, the services were provided or should have been provided. The following points should be noted. First, Art.5(1)(b) recognises that the parties can agree that a different place shall be regarded as the place of performance of the obligation in question. Secondly, it will in international sale of goods cases tend to remove jurisdiction from England as the domicile of the seller. Thirdly, there will be contracts, such as those distribution contracts where the distributor acquires title to the goods, which may fall into both categories.[749]

11–281   The European Court has considered the new provision for sale of goods and the provision of services in several cases from which the following propositions can be derived. First, the categories of sale of goods and provision of services are to be given an autonomous meaning. Consequently, it was held in *Car Trim GmbH v KeySafety Systems SRL*[750] that whether a contract was for the sale of goods or for the provision of services depended on its characteristic obligation: in that case where the purpose of contracts was the supply of goods to be manufactured or produced and, even though the purchaser had specified requirements with regard to the provision, fabrication and delivery of the components to be produced, the purchaser had not supplied the materials and the supplier was responsible for the quality of the goods and their compliance with the contract, the contracts were to be classified as a sale of goods within the meaning of Art.5(1)(b). In *Falco Privatstiftung v Weller-Lindhorst*[751] it

---

[748] Case C–106/95 *Mainschiffahrts-Genossenschaft v Les Gravières Rhénanes Sarl* [1997] E.C.R. I–911, [1997] Q.B. 731; see also *7E Communications v Vertex Antennentechnik* [2007] EWCA Civ 140, [2007] 1 W.L.R. 2175; *Morley v Reiter Engineering GmbH & Co KG* [2011] EWHC 2798 (QB). See para.12–140.

[749] *cf. Print Concept GmbH v GEW (EC) Ltd* [2002] C.L.C. 382 (CA), distributorship contract treated as contract of sale for choice of law purposes.

[750] Case C–381/08 [2010] 2 All E.R. (Comm.) 770.

[751] Case C–533/07 [2009] E.C.R. I–3327, [2010] Bus. L.R. 210. *cf. Crucial Music Corp v Klondyke Management AG* [2007] EWHC 1782 (Ch.), [2007] I.L.Pr. 733.

was held that a contract under which the owner of an intellectual property right grants its contractual partner the right to use the right in return for remuneration was not a contract for the provision of services within the meaning of Art.5(1)(b). The concept of service implied, at the least, that the party who provided the service carried out a particular activity in return for remuneration. A licence was not such a contract, because the only obligation which the owner of the right granted undertook was not to challenge the use of that right. The owner of an intellectual property right did not perform any service in granting a right to use that property and undertook merely to permit the licensee to exploit that right freely. Second, the place of delivery of goods and the place of provision of services is to be determined on an autonomous basis.[752] Thus in the case of sale of goods, the place where the goods were or should have been delivered pursuant to the contract must be determined on the basis of the provisions of the contract; in order to verify whether the place of delivery is determined "under the contract", the national court seised must take account of all the relevant terms and clauses of that contract which are capable of clearly identifying that place, including terms and clauses which are generally recognised and applied through the usages of international trade or commerce, such as the Incoterms drawn up by the International Chamber of Commerce; if it is impossible to determine the place of delivery on that basis, without referring to the substantive law applicable to the contract, the place of delivery is the place where the physical transfer of the goods took place, as a result of which the purchaser obtained, or should have obtained, actual power of disposal over those goods at the final destination of the sales transaction.[753] Where there are several places of delivery of the goods the "place of performance" is the place with the closest linking factor between the contract and the court having jurisdiction and, as a general rule, it will be at the place of the principal delivery, which must be determined on the basis of economic criteria.[754] So also where there is more than one place for the provision of services, the relevant place will be the place of the main provision of services, which is to be deduced, so far as possible, from the contract

---

[752] Case C–386/05 *Color Drack GmbH v Lexx International Vertriebs GmbH* [2007] E.C.R. I–3699, [2010] 1 W.L.R. 1909; Case C–381/08 *Car Trim GmbH v KeySafety Systems SRL* [2010] 2 All E.R. (Comm.) 770 (sale of goods); Case C–204/08 *Rehder v Air Baltic Corporation* [2009] E.C.R. I–6073, [2010] Bus. L.R. 549; Case C–19/09 *Wood Floor Solutions Andreas Domberger GmbH v Silva Trade SA* [2010] 1 W.L.R. 1900 (provision of services).

[753] Case C–87/10 *Electrosteel Europe SA v Edil Centro SpA* [2011] I.L.Pr. 589. In *Scottish & Newcastle International Ltd v Othon Ghalanos Ltd* [2008] UKHL 11, [2008] Bus. L.R. 583 it was held that the place of delivery in an FOB contract for the sale of cider to Limassol, Cyprus, was Liverpool, from which the goods were shipped, and where the sellers had performed all their obligations. Accordingly the English court had jurisdiction in a claim by the sellers for the price.

[754] Case C–386/05 *Color Drack GmbH v Lexx International Vertriebs GmbH* [2007] E.C.R. I–3699, [2010] 1 W.L.R. 1909. This was a case where there were several places of delivery in one Member State, but it has been held that the principle is applicable to cases involving a potential place of performance in more than one State: Case C–204/08 *Rehder v Air Baltic Corporation* [2009] E.C.R. I–6073, [2010] Bus. L.R. 549, at [35]; Case C–19/09 *Wood Floor Solutions Andreas Domberger GmbH v Silva Trade SA* [2010] 1 W.L.R. 1900 (both provision of services cases).

itself.[755] In *Wood Floor Solutions Andreas Domberger GmbH v Silva Trade SA*[756] the European Court ruled, in the case of a contract of agency, that if the provisions of the contract do not enable the place of the main provision of services to be determined, either because they provide for several places where services are provided, or because they do not expressly provide for any specific place where services are to be provided, but the agent has already provided such services, it is appropriate, in the alternative, to take account of the place where he has in fact for the most part carried out his activities in the performance of the contract, provided that the provision of services in that place is not contrary to the parties' intentions as it appears from the provisions of the contract. For that purpose, the factual aspects of the case may be taken into consideration, in particular, the time spent in those places and the importance of the activities carried out there. If the place of the main provision of services cannot be determined on the basis of the provisions of the contract itself or its actual performance, the place must be identified by another means which respects the objectives of predictability and proximity. For that purpose, it will be necessary to consider, as the place of the main provision of the services provided by a commercial agent, the place where the agent is domiciled, which can always be identified with certainty and is therefore predictable, and also has a link of proximity with the dispute since the agent will in all likelihood provide a substantial part of his services there.

11–282　　The relevant services are those of the party who performs the obligation which characterises the contract.[757]

ILLUSTRATIONS

11–283　　1. A in England sells goods to X for delivery in France. By English law the due place of payment of the price is England, and (in the circumstances of the case) by French law the due place of payment is France. The contract of sale is governed by English law. In proceedings by A against X for the price, the court has no jurisdiction.[758]

2. X & Co, a German company, appoints A to be the exclusive distributor of its machines in England. X & Co repudiates the agreement and, in breach of the agreement, sells its machinery to Y & Co. The court has jurisdiction in proceedings by A against X & Co for damages.[759]

3. A & Co, an English company, buys the business of L Ltd from its receiver. L Ltd had previously appointed X & Co, a French company, as the distributor of L Ltd's products in France. After A & Co buys the business of L Ltd, A & Co, appoints a new French distributor. X & Co complains that this is a breach of its distribution agreement. A & Co brings proceedings in England for a declaration that it was not in a contractual relationship with X & Co. The court had jurisdiction, even though A & Co claimed there is no contract, because if there had been a

---

[755] Case C–19/09 *Wood Floor Solutions Andreas Domberger GmbH v Silva Trade SA* [2010] 1 W.L.R. 1900, [38]. In Case C–204/08 *Rehder v Air Baltic Corporation* [2009] E.C.R. I–6073, [2010] Bus. L.R. 549 it was held that in the case of air passenger transport, the claimant had a choice between the courts of the place of departure and those of arrival. *cf. WPP Holdings Italy SRL v Benatti* [2007] EWCA Civ 263, [2007] 1 W.L.R. 2316

[756] Above.

[757] Case C–19/09 *Wood Floor Solutions Andreas Domberger GmbH v Silva Trade SA* [2010] 1 W.L.R. 1900.

[758] Regulation, Art.5(1)(b). Contrast Case 12/76 *Industrie Tessili Italiana Como v Dunlop AG* [1976] E.C.R. 1473.

[759] *ibid. cf. Medway Packaging Ltd v Meurer Maschinen GmbH* [1990] 2 Lloyd's Rep. 112 (CA).

contract, it was to be performed in England by delivery of the products to X & Co in England, and the negative obligations not to supply others extended to England as well as France.[760]

4. A & Co agrees to buy promotional goods from suppliers in Hong Kong and Taiwan for importation and resale in England. A & Co engages X & Co, a German company, to conduct quality control inspections of the goods in the Far East prior to payment by A & Co for the goods. X & Co sends reports on the goods to A & Co in England, and supplies certificates of quality to the sellers to enable them to obtain payment from A & Co When A & Co receives complaints about the quality of the goods, it brings proceedings in England against X & Co. The court has no jurisdiction because the principal contractual obligation of X & Co was the inspection of goods in the Far East rather than the supply of reports to A & Co in England.[761]

5. A & Co, an English company, concludes with X & Co, a Belgian company, a voyage charter of a vessel to be nominated by X & Co for the carriage of a cargo of telegraph poles from Florida to Bangladesh. A dispute arises, as a result of which X & Co informs A & Co that it is no longer interested in lifting the cargo. A & Co sues for breach of charterparty. The court has jurisdiction, because the obligation in question is the obligation to nominate a vessel, and the place of performance of that obligation is England.[762]

6. B & Co, an Italian company, is part of a group of companies of which A & Co, an English company, is the parent company. B & Co engages X, an Italian, as a consultant to advise the group on business opportunities in Italy. A & Co and B & Co claim that, in breach of contract and of his fiduciary duties, X failed to disclose to A & Co's chairman his interests in companies in relation to which he has advised. A & Co's claim is in contract, as a third party beneficiary, and the place of performance of the obligation in question, the duty to disclose, is in England, and the court has jurisdiction.[763]

7. A & Co sell 11 containers of cider to X & Co, a Cypriot company. The contract is an FOB contract with shipment from Liverpool, but the place of delivery is stated on the printed form to be Limassol, Cyprus. In action for the price, the English court has jurisdiction because the obligation was to ship at Liverpool, and the reference to Limassol did not make it the contractually agreed place of delivery, since it was merely a reference to the place of physical delivery in the context of through or mixed transport.[764]

(3) The court has jurisdiction, in matters relating to tort, if England is the place where the harmful event occurred,[765] i.e. if England is the place where the damage occurred or where the event which gave rise to the damage occurred.[766]   11R–284

COMMENT

By Art.5(3) of the Brussels I Regulation and the Lugano Convention jurisdiction is conferred in matters "relating to tort, delict or quasi-delict on the courts   11–285

---

[760] *Boss Group Ltd v Boss France SA* [1997] 1 W.L.R. 351 (CA).

[761] Regulation, Art.5(1)(b). *cf. Source Ltd v TUV Rheinland Holding AG* [1998] Q.B. 54 (CA).

[762] *Union Transport Plc v Continental Lines SA* [1992] 1 W.L.R. 15 (HL).

[763] *cf. WPP Holdings Italy SRL v Benatti* [2007] EWCA Civ 263, [2007] 1 W.L.R. 2316 (where the facts were more complex).

[764] *Scottish & Newcastle International Ltd v Othon Ghalanos Ltd* [2008] UKHL 11, [2008] Bus. L.R. 583.

[765] Brussels I Regulation, Art.5(3); Lugano Convention, Art.5(3); 1982 Act, Sch.4, Rule 3(c).

[766] Case 21/76 *Bier v Mines de Potasse d'Alsace SA* [1976] E.C.R. 1735, [1978] Q.B. 708. Art.5(3) of the Brussels I Regulation is to be interpreted in the same way as Brussels Convention, Art.5(3): Case C–189/08 *Zuid-Chemie BV v Philippo's Mineralenfabriek NV/SA* [2009] E.C.R. I–6917, [19]. See generally *Transnational Tort Litigation: Jurisdictional Principles*, eds. McLachlan and Nygh (1996).

of the place where "the harmful event occurred."[767] In *Kalfelis v Schröder*[768] the European Court held that the expression "matters relating to tort, delict or quasi-delict" should not be interpreted solely by reference to national law, but should be regarded as an autonomous concept which "covers all actions which seek to establish the liability of a defendant and which are not related to a 'contract' within the meaning of Article 5(1)."[769] It was also held that where a national court had jurisdiction over an action in so far as it was based on tort or delict it did not for that reason alone have jurisdiction in relation to other types of claim. It has been decided that in those cases in English law where a claim may be based alternatively in contract and in tort,[770] the claim will be regarded for the purposes of the Conventions as being contractual in nature, and that Clause (3) will not be available as a head of jurisdiction.[771]

11–286   Most of the original parties to the Brussels Convention had a form of jurisdiction in tort matters equivalent to Art.5(3); the draftsmen of the Brussels Convention deliberately left open the question whether the relevant "place" was the place of the wrongful act or the place where the damage occurred if they were different places. The tendency of the English case law on the equivalent provision in RSC Order 11 had been to look to the place

---

[767] Art.5(3) of the Regulation and the Convention and Rule 3(c) in Sch.4 to the 1982 Act also apply where the harmful event "may occur." In *Equitas Ltd v Wave City Shipping Co Ltd* [2005] EWHC 923 (Comm.) it was held that Art.5(3) applied to a claim for a declaration that no wrong had been committed.

[768] Case 189/87 [1988] E.C.R. 5565. See also Case C–51/97 *Réunion européenne SA v Spliethoff's Bevrachtingskantoor BV* [1998] E.C.R. I–6511; Case C–96/00 *Gabriel v Schlank & Schick GmbH* [2002] E.C.R. I–6367; Case C–334/00 *Fonderie Officine Meccaniche SpA v HWS GmbH* [2002] E.C.R. I–7357 (action for breach of obligation to act in good faith in negotiations); Case C–167/00 *Verein für Konsumenteninformation v Henkel* [2002] E.C.R. I–8111 (action by consumer protection organisation to prevent trader from imposing unfair terms within Art.5(3)). *cf.* Case C–18/02 *Danmarks Rederiforening v LO Landsorganisationen i Sverige* [2004] E.C.R. I–1417.

[769] At p.5585. This must be read in context, and does not include a claim for restitution: *Kleinwort Benson Ltd v Glasgow City Council* [1999] 1 A.C. 153, 167. See also Case C–261/90 *Reichert v Dresdner Bank (No.2)* [1992] E.C.R. I–2149 (action to set aside transaction in fraud of creditor not within Art.5(3)); Case 814/79 *Netherlands State v Rüffer* [1980] E.C.R. 3807, 3832–3835, per Warner AG; *Mölnlycke AB v Procter & Gamble Ltd (No.4)* [1992] R.P.C. 21 (CA) (patent infringement); Case C–18/02 *Danmarks Rederiforening v LO Landsorganisationen i Sverige* [2004] E.C.R. I–1417 (proceedings in connection with industrial action within Art.5(3)); Joined Cases C–509/09 and C–161/00 *eDate Advertising GmbH v X* [2012] I.L.Pr. 163 (rights of personality or privacy). In *Davenport v Corinthian Motor Policies at Lloyd's*, 1991 S.L.T. 774, it was held that for the purposes of what is now 1982 Act, Sch.4, Rule 3(c), a statutory claim against an insurer for payment of a judgment by the insured is not based on tort or delict. But in *Hewden Tower Cranes Ltd v Wolfkran GmbH* [2007] EWHC 857 (TCC), [2007] 2 Lloyd's Rep. 138 it was held that a claim for contribution under Civil Liability (Contribution) Act 1978 was within Art.5(3). *cf. Kitechnology BV v Unicor GmbH Plastmaschinen* [1995] F.S.R. 765 (CA) (breach of confidence: not decided whether within Art.5(3)). Art 5(3) applies to a claim in constructive trust based on wrongdoing: *Casio Computer Co Ltd v Sayo* [2001] I.L.Pr. 694 (CA); *Dexter v Harley, The Times*, April 2, 2001. See also *Compagnie Commercial André, SA v Artibell Shipping Co Ltd*, 1999 S.L.T. 1051.

[770] See, e.g. *Matthews v Kuwait Bechtel* [1959] 2 Q.B. 57 (CA).

[771] See *Source Ltd v TUV Rheinland Holding AG* [1998] Q.B. 54 (CA); *Mazur Media Ltd v Mazur Media GmbH* [2004] EWHC 1566 (Ch.), [2004] 1 W.L.R. 2966; *Burke v Uvex Sports GmbH* [2005] 4 I.R. 452 (Irish High Ct). Contrast *Domicrest Ltd v Swiss Bank Corp* [1999] Q.B. 548; *William Grant & Sons International Ltd v Marie-Brizard & Roger International SA*, 1998 S.C. 536. This will not normally make much practical difference, as the place of the tort will usually be the same as the place of performance of the obligation.

where in substance the act or omission occurred which gave rise to the cause of action.[772] The point arose for decision under Art.5(3) of the Brussels Convention in the European Court in *Bier v Mines de Potasse d'Alsace*.[773] The European Court held that the "place" was to be determined, not by the diverging solutions of national law, but by an autonomous interpretation and that the meaning of the expression "place where the harmful event occurred" in Art.5(3) must be interpreted so that the plaintiff has an option to commence proceedings either at the place where the damage occurred or at the place of the event giving rise to it.

The place of damage connotes the place where the physical damage is done   **11–287** or the recoverable economic loss is actually suffered. Even though in one sense a claimant may suffer economic loss at the place of its business, that is not of itself sufficient to confer jurisdiction on that place, for otherwise the place of business of the claimant would almost automatically become another basis of jurisdiction.[774] In particular, a claimant cannot confer jurisdiction on the court of his domicile by alleging that, by suffering economic loss there, he was the victim of a harmful act committed abroad. Thus French companies, whose German subsidiaries had been made insolvent as a result of the alleged negligence of German banks in relation to a property development in Germany, could not sue the German banks in France. The fact that the French companies had experienced financial repercussions in France and had ascertained their loss there did not give the the the French court jurisdiction.[775] So also an Italian who claimed that the wrongful conduct of employees of Lloyds Bank in England had led to his arrest in England and seizure of promissory notes could not sue in Italy for the exchange value of the promissory notes and for damage to his reputation. The jurisdiction could not be interpreted so extensively as to encompass any place where the adverse consequences of an event which had already caused actual damage elsewhere could be felt.[776] A consignee of goods who complains that the goods were delivered in a damaged state may sue in the country where the damage occurred or where the event occurred which gave rise to the damage. But the place of damage is not the place of final delivery or the place where the damage was ascertained. To allow the consignee to sue in those places would in effect attribute jurisdiction

---

[772] See above, para.11–213. CPR, PD6B, para.3.1(9), Rule 34, clause (9), adopts the same solution as the Regulation and the Convention.

[773] Case 21/76 [1976] E.C.R. 1735, [1978] Q.B. 708.

[774] *cf.* Warner A.-G. in Case 814/79 *Netherlands State v Rüffer* [1980] E.C.R. 3807, 3836; Case C–18/02 *Danmarks Rederiforening v LO Landsorganisationen i Sverige* [2004] E.C.R. I–1417 (action concerning legality of industrial action).

[775] Case C–220/88 *Dumez France v Hessische Landesbank* [1990] E.C.R. I–49. See also Case C–168/02 *Kronhofer v Maier* [2004] E.C.R. I–6009.

[776] Case C–364/93 *Marinari v Lloyds Bank Plc* [1995] E.C.R. I–2719, [1996] Q.B. 217. See also, e.g., *Bank of Tokyo-Mitsubishi Ltd v Baskan Gida Sanayi Ve Pazarlama AS* [2004] EWHC 945 (Ch.), [2004] 2 Lloyd's Rep. 395; *London Helicopters Ltd v Heliportugal LDA-INAC* [2006] EWHC 108, [2006] 1 All E.R. (Comm.) 595; *SanDisk Corp v Koninklijke Philips Electronics NV* [2007] EWHC 332 (Ch.), [2007] Bus. L.R. 705; *The Seaward Quest* [2007] EWHC 1460 (Comm.), [2007] 2 Lloyd's Rep. 308; *Dolphin Maritime and Aviation Ltd v Sveriges Angfartygs Assurans Forening* [2009] EWHC 716 (Comm.), [2009] 2 Lloyd's Rep. 123; *Future Investments SA v Federation Internationale de Football Assn* [2010] EWHC 1019 (Ch.), [2010] I.L.Pr. 630. *cf. Kitechnology BV v Unicor GmbH Plastmaschinen* [1995] F.S.R. 765 (CA); *Modus Vivendi Ltd v British Products Sanmex Co Ltd* [1996] F.S.R. 790.

to the place of the plaintiff's domicile. The place where the damage arose is the place where the carrier was to deliver the goods.[777] The place where the damage occurred must not be confused with the place where the event which damaged the product itself occurred. The place where the damage occurred is the place where the event which gave rise to the damage produces its harmful effects, that is to say, the place where the damage caused by the defective product actually manifests itself.[778]

11–288   The concept of "the place of the event giving rise" to the damage has received little elucidation from the European Court. In *Shevill v Press Alliance*[779] the Court considered the question of the appropriate jurisdiction in the case of an action in England by plaintiffs established respectively in England, France and Belgium in respect of an alleged libel published in a French newspaper with a small circulation in England. The European Court held that the victim of a libel by a newspaper article distributed in several Convention States may bring an action for damages against the publisher either before the courts of the Convention State of the place where the publisher of the defamatory publication is established, which will have jurisdiction to award damages for all the harm caused by the defamation; or before the courts of each Convention State in which the publication was distributed and where the victim claims to have suffered injury to his reputation, which will have jurisdiction to rule solely in respect of the harm caused in the State of the court seised. It also held that the criteria for assessing whether the event in question is harmful and the evidence required of the existence and extent of the harm alleged by the victim of the defamation were not governed by the Brussels Convention but by the substantive law determined by the national conflict of laws rules of the court seised, provided that the effectiveness of the Brussels Convention was not thereby impaired. Subsequently the House of Lords, applying this ruling, held that, where English law presumes that the publication of a defamatory statement is harmful to the person defamed without specific proof of damage, that is sufficient for the application of Art.5(3).[780]

11–289   In that case the place of the event giving rise to the damage was said to be the place where the publisher was established, since that was the place where the harmful event originated and from which the libel was issued and put into

---

[777] Case C–51/97 *Réunion européenne SA v Spliethoff's Bevrachingskantoor BV* [1998] E.C.R. I–6511. *cf. Henderson v Jaouen* [2002] EWCA Civ 75, [2002] 1 W.L.R. 2971 (CA) (deterioration in England of injury suffered in France does not make England the place where damage occurred); *Dolphin Maritime and Aviation Ltd v Sveriges Angfartygs Assurans Forening* [2009] EWHC 716 (Comm.), [2009] 2 Lloyd's Rep. 123 (place where benefit should have been received was place where damage occurred).

[778] Case C–189/08 *Zuid-Chemie BV v Philippo's Mineralenfabriek NV/SA* [2009] E.C.R. I–6917.

[779] Case C–68/93 [1995] E.C.R. I–415, [1995] 2 A.C. 18. See also Case C–18/02 *Danmarks Rederiforening v LO Landsorganisationen i Sverige*, above. See also *Mecklermedia Corp v D.C. Congress GmbH* [1998] Ch. 40; *Future Investments SA v Federation Internationale de Football Assn* [2010] EWHC 1019 (Ch.), [2010] I.L.Pr. 630; *Murray v Times Newspapers Ltd* [1997] 3 I.R. 97 (Sup Ct); *Ewins v Carlton UK Television Ltd* [1997] 2 I.L.R.M. 223; *Hunter v Gerald Duckworth & Co* [2000] I.L. Pr. 229 (Irish High Ct). On "libel tourism" see Hartley (2010) 59 I.C.L.Q. 25.

[780] [1996] A.C. 959.

circulation. In *Domicrest Ltd v Swiss Bank Corp*[781] it was held that, for the purposes of Art.5(3), in an action for negligent misstatement the place where the harmful event giving rise to the damage occurs is, by analogy with defamation, the place where the misstatement originated and that the place where the misstatement is received and relied upon is likely to be the place where the damage occurs.

In *eDate Advertising GmbH v X*[782] the decision in *Shevill v Presse Alliance*   **11–290** was adapted to apply to actions in Germany and France to restrain the publication on internet sites operated, respectively, by an Austrian company and an English newspaper. In the former case the plaintiff complained of the publication of his criminal conviction for murder, and in the latter case a French actor and his father complained of infringement of privacy in connection of reports of the actor's private life. It was held that a person who claims that his rights of personality have been infringed has the option of bringing an action for liability, in respect of all the damage caused, either before the courts of the Member State in which the publisher of that content is established or before the courts of the Member State in which the centre of his interests is based. That person may also, instead of an action for liability in respect of all the damage caused, bring his action before the courts of each Member State in the territory of which content placed online is or has been accessible. Those courts have jurisdiction only in respect of the damage caused in the territory of the Member State of the court seised. The Court accepted that the placing online of content on a website was to be distinguished from the regional distribution of media such as printed matter in that it is intended, in principle, to ensure the ubiquity of that content. Consequently, the internet reduced the usefulness of the criterion relating to distribution, because the scope of the distribution of content placed online was in principle universal, and it was not always possible, on a technical level, to quantify that distribution with certainty and accuracy in relation to a particular Member State or, therefore, to assess the damage caused exclusively within that Member State. As a result a person who has suffered an infringement of a "personality right" by means of the internet could bring an action in one forum in respect of all of the damage caused, depending on the place in which the damage caused in the European Union by that infringement occurred. The impact which material placed online was liable to have on an individual's personality rights might best be

---

[781] [1999] Q.B. 548, not following *Minster Investment Ltd v Hyundai Precision and Industry Ltd* [1988] 2 Lloyd's Rep. 621. See also *Source Ltd v TUV Rheinland Holding Ltd* [1998] Q.B. 54; *Waterford Wedgwood Ltd v David Nagli Ltd* [1998] F.S.R. 92; *Raiffeisen Zentral Bank Osterreich AG v Tranos* [2001] I.L.Pr. 85; *ABCI v Banque Franco-Tunisienne* [2003] EWCA Civ 205, [2003] 2 Lloyd's Rep. 395; *Bank of Tokyo-Mitsubishi Ltd v Baskan Gida Sanayi Ve Pazarlama AS* [2004] EWHC 945 (Ch.), [2004] 2 Lloyd's Rep. 395, at [182]–[185]; *London Helicopters Ltd v Heliportugal LDA-INAC* [2006] EWHC 108, [2006] 1 All E.R. (Comm.) 595; *Newsat Holdings Ltd v Zani* [2006] EWHC 342 (Comm.), [2006] 1 Lloyd's Rep. 707; *The Seaward Quest* [2007] EWHC 1460 (Comm.), [2007] 2 Lloyd's Rep. 308; *Casey v Ingersoll-Rand Sales Co Ltd* [1997] 2 I.R. 115. In *Cronos Containers NV v Palatin* [2002] EWHC 2819 (Comm.), [2003] I.L.Pr. 283 it was held that where a defendant procures the payment of money by a third party from a foreign bank account into his account in England, rather than the claimant's account, and used the money, the English court had jurisdiction under Art.5(3) on the basis that knowing assistance of a fraud took place in England, or the defendants converted the property to their own use in England.
[782] Joined Cases C–509/09 and C–161/00 [2012] I.L.Pr. 163.

assessed by the court of the place where the alleged victim had his centre of interests, which corresponded in general to his habitual residence. But a person might also have the centre of his interests in a Member State in which he did not habitually reside, in so far as other factors, such as the pursuit of a professional activity, might establish the existence of a particularly close link with that State. The jurisdiction of the court of the place where the alleged victim had the centre of his interests was in accordance with the aim of predictability of the rules governing jurisdiction also with regard to the defendant, given that the publisher of harmful content was, at the time at which that content was placed online, in a position to know the centres of interests of the persons who were the subject of that content. The centre-of-interests criterion allowed both the applicant easily to identify the court in which he could sue and the defendant reasonably to foresee before which court he might be sued.

11–291   **Threatened wrongs.** Article 5(3) of the Regulation (and of the Convention) confers jurisdiction on the courts of the place where the harmful event occurred "or may occur," and Rule 3(c) of Sch.4 to the 1982 Act also confers jurisdiction for threatened wrongs. Article 5(3) of the Brussels Convention was silent on the point, but in *Verein für Konsumenteninformation v Henkel*[783] the European Court (relying on the Schlosser Report,[784] and on the clarification of Art.5(3) by the Brussels I Regulation) held that Art.5(3) of the Brussels Convention applied to an action to prevent the occurrence of damage.

ILLUSTRATIONS

11–292   1. A brings proceedings against X & Co, a French company with its seat in France, for libel contained in X & Co's French newspaper, of which only a few copies have been sold in England. The court has jurisdiction, but only in respect of damage to A's reputation resulting from publication of the copies in England.[785]

2. X & Co, a German company, manufacture in Germany a motor car with faulty brakes. The motor car fails in England, injuring A, the driver, who cannot work at his business in London for several months. A brings proceedings for negligence against X & Co. The court has jurisdiction.

3. The facts are as in Illustration 2, except that the accident occurs in Germany. The fact that A suffers economic loss to his business in England does not give the court jurisdiction.

4. X & Co, an English company, manufacture in England a motor car with faulty brakes. A, a Frenchman, buys it in France and is injured in an accident when the brakes fail. A brings proceedings against X & Co. The court has jurisdiction.[786]

5. A & Co is an English company which supplies electronic goods. In a telephone conversation, an officer of X & Co, a Swiss bank, assures the agent of A & Co in England that it would be safe to release goods to a buyer on receipt of payment orders from the bank. In reliance on the assurance, A & Co releases goods to the buyer, who is unable to pay, and X & Co refuses to honour the payment orders because it does not have funds from the buyer. In proceedings by A

---

[783] Case C–167/00 [2002] E.C.R. I–8111. See also Case C–18/02 *Danmarks Rederiforening v LO Landsorganisationen i Sverige*, above. For a similar view see *Bonnier Media Ltd v Greg Lloyd Smith*, 2002 S.C.L.R. 977 (OH).

[784] para.134.

[785] Case C–68/93 *Shevill v Presse Alliance SA* [1995] E.C.R. 1–415, [1995] 2 A.C. 18. *cf. Kroch v Rossell et Cie* [1937] 1 All E.R. 725 (CA), where the court did not exercise jurisdiction because A's real complaint related to the damage to his reputation in France and Belgium.

[786] Brussels I Regulation, Art.2.

& Co against X & Co for negligent misrepresentation, it is held that the court has no jurisdiction because the place where the harmful event giving rise to damage occurred was the place where the misstatement occurred, in Switzerland, and not the place (England) where it was received and acted upon.[787]

6. A & Co carry on business in England under the name "Harrods." X & Co, a French company, threaten to open a shop in London called "Harrods." (*Semble*) the court has jurisdiction under this clause in an action by A & Co to restrain the passing-off and trademark infringement.

7. A & Co, an English fertiliser company, buys from B & Co, another English company, a product used for the manufacture of fertiliser. B & Co orders it to be manufactured by X & Co, a Belgian company. The product is defective, and A & Co sues X & Co in England. The English court has jurisdiction because the "place where the harmful event occurred" is A & Co's factory in England where the defective product is processed, causing substantial damage to the end product.[788]

(4) A criminal court has jurisdiction to make an order for damages or restitution in criminal proceedings against a defendant domiciled in another Member State or Convention State or in Scotland or Northern Ireland. 11R–293

COMMENT

This clause, which is based on Art.5(4) of the Regulation and the Convention, is included here for the sake of completeness since claims for restitution in criminal proceedings are outside the scope of this work.[789] 11–294

(5) The court has jurisdiction to determine a dispute arising out of the operations of a branch, agency or other establishment, if the branch, agency or other establishment is situated in England.[790] 11R–295

COMMENT

Article 5(5) of the Regulation (and the Convention) confers jurisdiction in relation to a "dispute arising out of the operations of a branch, agency or other establishment" on the courts of the place where the branch, agency or other establishment is situated.[791] It relates only to defendants domiciled in a Member State or Convention State, i.e. companies or firms with their seat in 11–296

---

[787] *Domicrest Ltd v Swiss Bank Corp* [1999] Q.B. 548.

[788] Case C–189/08 *Zuid-Chemie BV v Philippo's Mineralenfabriek NV/SA* [2009] E.C.R. I–6917.

[789] Art.5(4) (which is reproduced in 1982 Act. Sch.4, Rule 3(d)) is based on the idea, reflected in the legal systems of the original Brussels Convention States, that the right to obtain compensation for damage suffered following behaviour contrary to criminal law is generally recognised as being civil in nature: Case C–172/91 *Sonntag v Waidmann* [1993] E.C.R. 1–1963. See also *Haji-Ioannou v Frangos* [1999] 2 Lloyd's Rep. 337 (CA). See also Case C–7/98 *Krombach v Bamberski* [1999] E.C.R. I–1935 (jurisdictional basis of criminal proceedings irrelevant).

[790] Brussels I Regulation, Art.5(5); Lugano Convention, Art.5(5); 1982 Act, Sch.4, Rule 3(e). See Fawcett (1984) 9 Eur.L.Rev. 326.

[791] Art.5(5) concerns the branch, etc. operations of the defendant. A claimant cannot confer jurisdiction on the court by relying on the presence of the *claimant's* branch: *New Hampshire Insurance Co v Strabag Bau* [1990] 2 Lloyd's Rep. 61, 68; affirmed on other grounds [1992] 1 Lloyd's Rep. 361 (CA).

another Member State or Convention State or in Scotland or Northern Ireland and a branch in England. Companies with their seats outside the Member States or Convention States but with a branch in England fall within Rule 31.[792] But an insurer not domiciled in a Member State or a Convention State but which has a branch, agency or other establishment there is, in disputes arising out of the operations of the branch, agency or establishment, deemed to be domiciled in that State.[793] Similar provision is made in relation to suppliers of goods and services in consumer contracts,[794] and in relation to employers.[795]

11–297   Two main questions arise. First, what is a "branch, agency or other establishment"? Secondly, what disputes arise out of its operations? On the first question, it is clear that the concept must be interpreted by autonomous standards and not by purely national notions.[796] The obvious case of a branch bearing the same business name and staffed by the employees of the main undertaking needs no comment. In two cases the European Court has declined to extend the concept of a branch to distributors or sales agents for goods of foreign companies. In *De Bloos Sprl v Bouyer SA*[797] the Court held that one of the essential characteristics of the concept of branch or agency was the fact of being subject to the direction and control of the parent body; that the concept of "establishment" should be interpreted in a similar way, and that an exclusive distributor was therefore not a "branch," etc., of the manufacturer. In *Blanckaert and Willems PVBA v Trost*[798] the Court held that an independent commercial agent who merely negotiates business, who is free to arrange his own work and decide what proportion of his time to devote to the interests of the undertaking which he agrees to represent, who may represent at the same time several firms competing in the same manufacturing marketing sector, and who merely transmits orders to the parent undertaking without being involved in either their terms or their execution does not have the character of a branch, agency, or other establishment within the meaning of Art.5(5).

11–298   In addition to the element of direction and control the Court has required the element of the "appearance of permanency". In *Somafer SA v Saar-Ferngas AG*[799] the European Court held that the concept of branch, agency or other establishment implies a place of business which has the appearance of permanency, such as the extension of a parent body, so that third parties do not have to deal directly with such parent body but may transact business at the place of business constituting the extension. An important point which was raised but not decided in the *Somafer* case was whether the defendants were estopped from denying that they had an establishment in Germany by virtue of their letterhead which indicated that they had an office there. Advocate General Mayras thought that, having regard to the special nature of the

---

[792] paras 11–113 *et seq.*

[793] Art.9(2).

[794] Art.15(2). See below, clauses (13), (14) and (15).

[795] Art.18(2).

[796] See Case 33/78 *Somafer SA v Saar-Ferngas AG* [1978] E.C.R. 2183, 2190.

[797] Case 14/76 [1976] E.C.R. 1497.

[798] Case 139/80 [1981] E.C.R. 819, applied in *New Hampshire Insurance Co v Strabag Bau* [1990] 2 Lloyd's Rep. 61, 69; affirmed on other grounds [1992] 1 Lloyd's Rep. 361 (CA). Contrast *Latchin v General Mediterranean Holdings SA* [2002] C.L.C. 330.

[799] Case 33/78 [1978] E.C.R. 2183.

jurisdiction under Art.5(5), appearances should be disregarded and the realities considered; it was for third parties who wished to rely on Art.5(5) to adduce evidence that the entity which they wished to bring before the national court was in fact subject to the control and direction of the parent company. But in *SAR Schotte GmbH v Parfums Rothschild SARL*[800] the European Court held that, where the letterhead of a German company appeared to indicate that it was acting as a place of business of a French company, a third party which did business with it was entitled to rely on the appearance thus created. Accordingly the German court had jurisdiction over the French company because the dispute arose out of the operations of the establishment in Germany. This was so even though the French company maintained no dependent branch, agency or other establishment. What established jurisdiction in Germany was that the French company pursued its activities there through a German company (which, in the unusual circumstances of the case, was its parent company) with the same name and identical management which negotiated and conducted business in the name of the French subsidiary and which was used by the French subsidiary as an extension of itself.

The second question will be whether the claim arises out of the operations of the branch, agency or other establishment. In *Somafer SA v Saar-Ferngas AG* the European Court explained that the concept of operations included matters relating to the rights and contractual and non-contractual obligations concerning the actual management of the branch, agency, or other establishment itself, such as those relating to the situation of its building or the local engagement of staff to work there. It also included those relating to undertakings which had been entered into at the place of business in the name of the parent body and which had to be performed in the State where the place of business was established and also actions concerning torts arising from the activities in which it had engaged.   **11–299**

The wording of Art.5(5) suggests that it grants jurisdiction to the courts of the place of the branch in relation to any contract entered into by it. In *Somafer SA v Saar-Ferngas AG* the European Court seemed to limit the jurisdiction to cases where performance is to take place in the same Convention State as the branch. That would have meant that Art.5(5) adds little to Art.5(1) in matters relating to contract. But in *Lloyd's Register of Shipping v Soc Campenon Bernard*[801] the Court held that it is not a pre-condition of jurisdiction under Art.5(5) that the obligations entered into by the branch in the name of its parent body were to be performed in the State in which the branch is situated. Accordingly, in *Anton Durbeck GmbH v Den Norske Bank ASA*[802] it was held that in claims in tort as well as in contract all that was necessary to establish jurisdiction under Art.5(5) was such nexus between the operations of the branch and the dispute as rendered it natural to describe the dispute as one which had arisen out of the operations of the branch. It was not necessary to establish in addition that the activities of the branch had produced the harmful event within the jurisdiction of the court.   **11–300**

---

[800] Case 218/86 [1987] E.C.R. 4905.
[801] Case C–439/93 [1995] E.C.R. I–961. See also *Re A Counterclaim under Italian law* [1995] I.L.Pr. 133 (German Fed Sup Ct, 1993).
[802] [2003] EWCA Civ 147, [2003] Q.B. 1160 (CA).

It may be that an essential element of this jurisdiction is that it is designed for the benefit of third parties, and not for intra-company or intra-firm disputes.[803]

ILLUSTRATIONS

11–301   1. X & Co is a French bank with a branch in London. Through the London branch it employs A to act as its manager in London. X & Co repudiates the contract, and A brings proceedings in London against X & Co. The court has jurisdiction.

2. X & Co is a German manufacturing company. It appoints Y, who is domiciled in England and has an office in London, as its non-exclusive agent for England. Y does not have authority to bind X & Co. Y agrees with A, who is domiciled in England, that X & Co will sell a quantity of its products to A for delivery in France. X & Co repudiates the agreement purportedly made by Y. The court does not have jurisdiction, since Y's office is not a branch of X & Co.[804]

11R–302   **(6) The court has jurisdiction if the claim is made against a person as settlor, trustee or beneficiary of a trust created by the operation of a statute, or by a written instrument, or created orally and evidenced in writing, if the trust is domiciled in England,[805] or, in the case of a trust instrument and where relations between settlor, trustee or beneficiary or their rights or obligations under the trust are involved, if the trust instrument confers jurisdiction on the English court.[806]**

COMMENT

11–303   Article 5(6) was first introduced by the 1978 Accession Convention to provide for jurisdiction over a person sued as a settlor, trustee or beneficiary of a trust created by the operation of a statute, or by a written instrument, or created orally and evidenced in writing, in the courts of the Convention State in which the trust is domiciled.[807] A claim is made against a beneficiary for the purposes of this clause if the claim is that the beneficiary has been overpaid. But a person who is not a trustee but has powers of appointment under a trust is not a trustee for the purposes of this clause.[808] The phrase "created by the operation of a statute, or by a written instrument, or created orally and evidenced in writing" is intended to indicate that the rules apply only to cases in which a trust has been expressly constituted or for which provision is made by statute—it does not include "constructive" or implied trusts.[809] Nor will it apply to testamentary trusts or to trustees in bankruptcy.[810] Article 5(6) is intended only to deal with disputes relating to the internal relationships of the

---

[803] *cf.* Reischl A.-G. in Case 14/76 *De Bloos Sprl v Bouyer SA* [1976] E.C.R. 1497, 1519 and in Case 139/80 *Blanckaert and Willems PVBA v Trost* [1981] E.C.R. 819, 838.

[804] Cases at para.11–297, above.

[805] Art.5(6); 1982 Act. Sch.4, Rule 3(f).

[806] Brussels I Regulation, Art.23(4); Lugano Convention, Art.23(4).

[807] It is wider than clause (12) of Rule 34, i.e. CPR, PD6B, para.3.1(12), above.

[808] *Gómez v Gómez-Monche Vives* [2008] EWCA Civ 1065, [2009] Ch. 245.

[809] Schlosser, para.117; *Gómez v Gómez-Monche Vives* [2008] EWCA Civ 1065, [2009] Ch. 245.

[810] Art.1, exclusion of wills and succession, bankruptcy. On trust deeds for creditors and marriage contract trusts see Maxwell Report, para.5.63.

trust, e.g. disputes between beneficiaries and trustees, and not to its external relations, e.g. the enforcement by third parties of contracts made by a trustee.[811] In *Chellaram v Chellaram (No.2)*[812] it was held that the critical date for determining the law applicable to the trust was the date when the proceedings were commenced, and not the date when the cause of action arose.

Whether a trust is domiciled in the Member State or Convention State **11–304** whose courts are seised, depends on its rules of private international law.[813] A trust is domiciled in the United Kingdom if the trust has its closest and most real connection with a system of law of one of the constituent parts of the United Kingdom and any proceedings which are brought in the United Kingdom by virtue of Art.5(6) are to be brought in the part of the United Kingdom in which the trust is domiciled.[814] The effect of these provisions is that the English court will have jurisdiction if the trust is governed by English law, and where the governing law of the trust had been expressly chosen by the parties, this would almost always be the system of law with which the trust had its closest and most real connection for the purposes of determining its domicile within the meaning of Art.5(6).[815]

Subject to other provisions of the Regulation and the Convention for **11–305** exclusive jurisdiction,[816] the English court will have exclusive jurisdiction in an action concerning relations between settlor, trustee or beneficiary or their rights or obligations under a trust instrument if the trust instrument confers jurisdiction on the English courts.[817]

ILLUSTRATIONS

1. A, who is domiciled in England, is a beneficiary under a trust expressed to be governed by **11–306** English law. X, who is domiciled in France, is a trustee. A brings proceedings against X. The court has jurisdiction.[818]

2. The facts are as Illustration 1, except that the trust is governed by Bermuda law. The court has no jurisdiction.

3. A trust deed governed by Bermuda law provides that all disputes arising out of it shall be submitted to the jurisdiction of the English court. A dispute arises concerning the right of X, a trustee domiciled in France, to charge for his professional services. The court has jurisdiction.[819]

4. A, B, and C bring proceedings in England against, inter alia, X, who is domiciled in Spain, alleging that she is liable for breaches of a trust declared by a written declaration of trust which expressly states that English law is the proper law, in that she received income and capital paid to her by the trustees as a volunteer to which she was not entitled as a beneficiary, and that, as the donee of a fiduciary power conferred by the declaration of trust, she had not been entitled to appoint herself as "appointor." The English court has jurisdiction in the claim for breach of trust

---

[811] Schlosser, para.120.

[812] [2002] EWHC 632 (Ch.), [2002] 3 All E.R. 17.

[813] Art.60(3).

[814] 1982 Act, ss.10(2) and 45; SI 2001/3929, Sch.1, paras 7(2) and 12.

[815] *Gómez v Gómez-Monche Vives*, above. See also *Chellaram v Chellaram (No.2)* [2002] 3 All E.R. 17.

[816] This may arise especially if settled land is involved.

[817] Art.23(4); *cf.* 1982 Act, Sch.4, Rule 12(2).

[818] Regulation, Art.5(6).

[819] Art.23(4).

against X as "beneficiary" because the trust is domiciled in England by virtue of the choice of English law, but not in the claim as "appointor" because it is not a claim against her as trustee.[820]

11R–307   **(7) The court has jurisdiction over a defendant domiciled in Scotland or Northern Ireland in proceedings (a) concerning a debt secured on immovable property, or (b) which are brought to assert, declare or determine proprietary or possessory rights, or rights of security, in or over movable property, or to obtain authority to dispose of movable property, if the property is situated in England.[821]**

COMMENT

11–308   This is a head of jurisdiction conferred by Rule 3(h) of Sch.4 to the 1982 Act and has no directly corresponding provision in the jurisdictional rules of the Regulation or the Convention.[822]

ILLUSTRATION

11–309   X, who is domiciled in Scotland, borrows money from A, who is domiciled in Scotland, under an agreement which charges (inter alia) shares in a public company in England. A institutes proceedings in England to enforce the charge. The court has jurisdiction.

11R–310   **(8) The court, in cases where it has jurisdiction in an action relating to liability from the use or operation of a ship, has jurisdiction over claims for limitation of such liability.[823]**

COMMENT

11–311   A claim for limitation of liability allows a shipowner and others who incur liability in connection with a ship to limit their liability to a specific amount based on the tonnage of the ship. In England a claim for limitation of liability is brought against a potential claimant, or by way of counterclaim. The purpose of this clause which originally was added by the 1978 Accession Convention, and applies also in intra-United Kingdom cases, is to allow limitation claims to be brought in the court of the domicile of the shipowner, or, e.g. in the court of the place where the harmful event occurred[824] or where the ship (or sister ship) has been arrested. But if the claimants have already

---

[820] *Gómez v Gómez-Monche Vives*, above.

[821] 1982 Act, Sch.4, Rule 3(h).

[822] But *cf.* Art.6(4).

[823] Brussels I Regulation, Art.7; Lugano Convention, Art.7; 1982 Act, Sch.4, Rule 6.

[824] See *The Falstria* [1988] 1 Lloyd's Rep. 495. *cf. The Volvox Hollandia* [1988] 2 Lloyd's Rep. 361 (CA).

brought proceedings in another Member State or Convention State, the claim for limitation would have to be made by way of counterclaim abroad.[825]

**(9) The court has jurisdiction, where a defendant is domiciled in England   11R–312
over a co-defendant who is domiciled in another Member State or Convention State or in another part of the United Kingdom, if the claims are so closely connected that it is expedient to hear and determine them together to avoid the risk of irreconcilable judgments resulting from separate proceedings.**[826]

Article 6(1) of the Brussels I Regulation (and of the Lugano Convention)   11–313
provides (as does Art.6(1) of the Lugano Convention) that a person domiciled in a Member State (or Convention State) may also be sued, where he is one of a number of defendants, in the courts for the place where one of them is domiciled,[827] provided that the claims are so closely connected[828] that it is expedient to hear and determine them together to avoid the risk of irreconcilable judgments resulting from separate proceedings.[829] Article 6(1) has been the subject of several decisions of the European Court, not all of which are easily reconcilable, and some of which have been criticised in harsh terms by academic writers, and most recently in less harsh terms by the Advocate-General.[830]

Article 6(1) in its original form was adopted in order to prevent the handing   11–314
down in the Brussels Convention States of judgments which were irreconcilable with one another.[831] In *Kalfelis v Schröder*[832] the European Court held that there must be a connection between the claims made against each of the defendants, and the nature of that connection is to be given a uniform interpretation: Art.6(1) applies where the proceedings brought against the various defendants are related when the proceedings are instituted, i.e. where it is expedient to hear and determine them together in order to avoid the risk of irreconcilable judgments resulting from separate proceedings. The effect of the decision was enshrined[833] in the Brussels I Regulation (and the revised Lugano Convention), which (like Rule 5(a) in Sch.4 to the 1982 Act) adds the words "provided the claims are so closely connected that it is expedient to hear and determine them together to avoid the risk of irreconcilable judgments

---

[825] See also CPR, r.61.11 and Practice Direction, para.10.18.

[826] Brussels I Regulation, Art.6(1); Lugano Convention, Art.6(1). See Tang (2009) 34 Eur. L. Rev. 80.

[827] At the time the proceedings are instituted: *Canada Trust Co v Stolzenberg (No.2)* [2002] 1 A.C. 1; *Petrotrade Inc v Smith* [1999] 1 W.L.R. 457.

[828] This may include alternative or contingent claims: *FKI Engineeering Ltd v De Wind Holdings Ltd* [2008] EWCA Civ 316, [2009] 1 All E.R. (Comm.) 118.

[829] It has been held that Art.6(1) may be used to found jurisdiction against a Greek domiciliary, where the defendant domiciled in England has been sued in separate proceedings: *Masri v Consolidated Contractors International (UK) Ltd* [2005] EWCA Civ 1436, [2006] 1 Lloyd's Rep. 391: *sed quaere*.

[830] See Briggs and Rees, paras 2.202 *et seq.*; Trstenjak A.-G. in Case C–145/10 *Painer v Standard VerlagsGmbH*, December 1, 2011, at [78], [85].

[831] Jenard, p.26.

[832] Case C–189/87 [1988] E.C.R. 5565.

[833] Case C–98/06 *Freeport Plc v Arnoldsson* [2007] E.C.R. I–839, [2008] Q.B. 634, at [41].

resulting from separate proceedings".[834] It is for the national court to assess whether the risk exists.[835]

11–315   Article 6(1) refers to the "courts for the place" of the local defendant's domicile, and not to the court of the State of the domicile. The High Court's jurisdiction[836] is not local and it will have jurisdiction under this clause whenever the defendant is domiciled in England. Although this head of jurisdiction fulfils a function similar to the "necessary or proper party" provisions of CPR, PD6B, para.3.1(4), i.e. Rule 34, clause (3),[837] it is narrower in scope than the latter. In *Canada Trust Co v Stolzenberg (No.2)*[838] it was held that the critical date for the determination of the domicile of the defendant domiciled in England (sometimes called the anchor defendant) is the date of the issue of proceedings against him, and other defendants can be added under this clause even if he subsequently becomes domiciled outside England. It is not necessary for there to be prior service on the defendant domiciled in England.

11–316   In *Kalfelis v Schröder* the European Court, confirming the view of the Jenard Report,[839] held that Art.6(1) did not apply where the action was brought "solely with the object of ousting the jurisdiction of the courts of the State in which the defendant is domiciled,"[840] and this was repeated in subsequent rulings.[841] But in *Freeport Plc v Arnoldsson*[842] the Court ruled that Art.6(1) applied where claims brought against different defendants are connected when the proceedings are instituted, that is to say, where it is expedient

---

[834] On the relationship between Art.6(1) and the references to irreconcilable judgments in Art.28 (stays of related proceedings, paras 12–073 *et seq.* below) and Art.34(3) (non-recognition of judgments, paras 14–235 *et seq.* below) see the contrasting views of Léger A.-G. in Case C–539/03 *Roche Nederland BV v Primus* [2006] E.C.R. I–6535, at [71] *et seq.* and Trstenjak A.-G. in Case C–145/10 *Painer v Standard VerlagsGmbH* at [58]–[71] (the judgment of the Court, December 1, 2011, does not address the question). See also *Gard Marine & Energy Ltd v Tunnicliffe* [2010] EWCA Civ 1052, [2011] Bus. L. R. 839, [25] *et seq.*

[835] *Kalfelis v Schröder*, above, at [12]; and, e.g. Case C–98/06 *Freeport Plc v Arnoldsson* [2007] E.C.R. I–839, [2008] Q.B. 634, at [41]. See *Aiglon Ltd v Gau Shan Co Ltd* [1993] 1 Lloyd's Rep. 164; *Gascoine v Pyrah* [1994] I.L.Pr. 82 (CA); *Fort Dodge Animal Health Ltd v Akzo Nobel NV* [1998] F.S.R. 222 (CA); *Société Commerciale de Réassurance v Eras International Ltd (No.2)* [1995] 2 All E.R. 278; *Casio Computer Co Ltd v Sayo* [2001] EWCA Civ 661, [2001] I.L.Pr. 694; *Latchin v General Mediterranean Holdings SA* [2002] C.L.C. 330; *Andrew Weir Shipping Ltd v Wartsila UK Ltd* [2004] EWHC 1284 (Comm.), [2004] 2 Lloyd's Rep. 377; *ET Plus SA v Welter* [2005] EWHC 2115 (Comm.), [2006] 1 Lloyd's Rep. 251; *FKI Engineering Ltd v Dewind Holdings Ltd* [2008] EWCA Civ 316, [2009] 1 All E.R. (Comm.) 118; *Gard Marine & Energy Ltd v Tunnicliffe* [2010] EWCA Civ 1052, [2011] Bus. L. R. 839; *Compagnie Commercial André, SA v Artibell Shipping Co Ltd,* 1999 S.L.T. 1051; *Gannon v B&I Steampacket Co* [1993] 2 I.R. 359 (Sup Ct); *Daly v Irish Group Travel Ltd* [2007] I.R. 423 (High Ct.).

[836] The jurisdiction of county courts is local.

[837] See above, para.11R–160.

[838] [2002] 1 A.C. 1.

[839] Jenard Report, p.26.

[840] [1988] E.C.R. 5565, at 5583. Art.6(2), below paras 11R–324, has express wording to similar effect.

[841] Case C–51/97 *Réunion européenne SA v Splithoff's Bevrachtingskantoor BV* [1998] E.C.R. I–6511, [2000] Q.B. 690, [47]; Case C–103/05 *Reisch Montage AG v Kiesel Baumaschinen Handels GmbH* [2006] E.C.R. I–6827, [32].

[842] Case C–98/06 [2007] E.C.R. I–839, [2008] Q.B. 634, at [54], not following the opinion of Mengozzi A.-G., or its previous rulings, most recently in Case C–103/05 *Reisch Montage AG v Kiesel Baumaschinen Handels GmbH*, above.

to hear and determine them together to avoid the risk of irreconcilable judgments resulting from separate proceedings; and there is no further need to establish separately that the claims were not brought with the sole object of ousting the jurisdiction of the courts of the Member State where one of the defendants is domiciled. Nevertheless the European Court has continued to say that Art.6(1) cannot be applied so as to allow an applicant to make a claim against a number of defendants with the sole object of ousting the jurisdiction of the courts of the State where one of those defendants is domiciled.[843]

The next matter on which there have been inconsistent decisions of the European Court is the relationship which is required between the causes of action or claims against the defendant domiciled in the State in which the proceedings are brought and the defendant outside that State. In *Réunion européenne SA v Splithoff's Bevrachtingskantoor BV*[844] the European Court indicated that for the purposes of Art.6(1) claims in contract and in tort could not be regarded as connected. The basis for that view appears to have been that in such a case there was no risk of irreconcilable judgments. So also in *Roche Nederland BV v Primus*[845] it was held that Art.6(1) did not apply to claims for patent infringement against various European companies in the Roche group where the infringements were not the same and the patents were governed by the law of the State in which it had been granted.   **11–317**

But the former decision is no longer good law, and the latter decision has been doubted. In *Freeport Plc v Arnoldsson*[846] the plaintiff in Swedish proceedings claimed a success fee from a Swedish company and its English parent for work done in connection with the transfer to the English company of a factory shop in Sweden. The Swedish subsidiary was incorporated subsequently, and took over the shop. The claim against the English company was in contract, but it was contended that the claim, if any, against the Swedish subsidiary could only be non-contractual in nature. The European Court ruled that where one of the defendants was domiciled in a Member State, the fact that claims brought against a number of defendants had different legal bases did not preclude the application of Art.6(1).[847] Most recently, in a case involving infringement of copyright in several Member   **11–318**

---

[843] Case C–145/10 *Painer v Standard VerlagsGmbH*, December 1, 2011, at [78].

[844] Case C–51/97 [1998] E.C.R. I–6511, [2000] Q.B. 690, at [50]. This dictum formed no part of the operative part of the ruling. Neither defendant was domiciled in the forum. The decision was doubted by the Court of Appeal in *Watson v First Choice Holidays and Flights Ltd* [2001] 2 Lloyd's Rep. 339 (CA), which made a reference to the European Court on the point, but the reference was withdrawn when the case was settled.

[845] Case C–539/03 [2006] E.C.R. I–6535.

[846] Case C–98/06 [2007] E.C.R. I–839, [2008] Q.B. 634, applied in Case C–145/10 *Painer v Standard VerlagsGmbH*, December 1, 2011.

[847] The Court said that *Réunion européenne*, above, was to be distinguished. That case concerned Arts 5(1) and (3), and concerned overlapping special jurisdiction based on Art.5(3) to hear an action in tort or delict and special jurisdiction to hear an action based in contract, on the ground that there was a connection between the two actions. It related to an action brought before a court in a Member State where none of the defendants to the main proceedings was domiciled, and it was in the context of Art.5(3) that the Court was able to conclude that two claims in one action, directed against different defendants and based in one instance on contractual liability and in the other on liability in tort or delict could not be regarded as connected. To accept that jurisdiction based on Art.5, which constituted special jurisdiction limited to an exhaustive list of cases, could serve as the basis on which to hear other actions would undermine the scheme of the Brussels I Regulation.

States, the Advocate General criticised *Roche Nederland BV v Primus*, and the Court ruled that the application of Art.6(1) was not precluded solely because actions against several defendants for substantially identical copyright infringements were brought on national legal grounds which varied according to the Member States concerned. It was for the national court to assess, in the light of all the elements of the case, whether there was a risk of irreconcilable judgments if those actions were determined separately.[848]

11–319   The next question is the relevance of the merits of the claim against the defendant domiciled in the State in which proceedings are brought. In *Reisch Montage AG v Kiesel Baumaschinen Handels GmbH*[849] the action was brought in Austria against an Austrian-domiciled individual for recovery of a debt and against a German company, which had guaranteed repayment. After these proceedings were instituted the Austrian court dismissed the proceedings against the individual because bankruptcy proceedings were pending against him, and that the action was therefore inadmissible as against him. The question was whether that meant that there was no jurisdiction under Art.6(1) as against the German company on the basis that there were no grounds for bringing the claim against the Austrian-domiciled defendant. The European Court ruled that that Art.6(1) of the Regulation could not be interpreted in such a way as to make its application dependent on the effects of domestic rules. Consequently, Art.6(1) may be relied on in the context of an action brought in a Member State against a defendant domiciled in that State and a co-defendant domiciled in another Member State even when the action is regarded under a national provision as inadmissible from the time it is brought in relation to the first defendant.

11–320   But it does not follow that there is jurisdiction under Art.6(1) even if the claim against the anchor defendant must fail. In *Freeport Plc v Arnoldsson*[850] the European Court did not rule on the question put by the national court, as to whether the likelihood of success of an action against a party before the courts of the State where he is domiciled is relevant in the determination of whether there is a risk of irreconcilable judgments for the purposes of Art.6(1). Under English law the claimant has to show that there is a real issue on the merits that the court may reasonably be asked to try as to the liability of the additional defendant domiciled in England.[851] If there is no serious issue to be tried against either the anchor defendant or the additional defendant, then there is no risk of irreconcilable judgments.[852]

---

[848] Case C–145/10 *Painer v Standard VerlagsGmbH*, December 1, 2011, at [84], *per* Trstenjak A.-G.

[849] Case C–103/05 [2006] E.C.R. I–6827.

[850] Case C–98/06 [2007] E.C.R. I–839, [2008] Q.B. 634. Mengozzi A.-G.'s opinion on that point was that that assessment may also include an evaluation of the likelihood that the claim brought against the defendant who is domiciled in the forum Member State will succeed. That evaluation will be of real practical relevance for the purpose of excluding the risk of irreconcilable judgments only if that claim proves to be manifestly inadmissible or unfounded in all respects.

[851] *The Rewia* [1991] 2 Lloyd's Rep. 325, 329 (CA); *Cooper Tire & Rubber Company Europe Ltd v Dow Deutschland Inc* [2010] EWCA Civ 864, [2010] Bus. L. R. 1697; *FKI Engineeering Ltd v De Wind Holdings Ltd* [2008] EWCA Civ 316, [2009] 1 All E.R. (Comm.) 118; *Gannon v B&I Steampacket Co Ltd* [1993] 2 I.R. 359 (Sup. Ct.).

[852] *Brown v Innovatorone Plc* [2010] EWHC 2281 (Comm.), [2011] I.L.Pr. 118.

There must be a good arguable case that the court of the domicile is validly   **11–321**
seised of the claim. Thus if X is domiciled in England, but has agreed with A
that the courts of France are to have exclusive jurisdiction over disputes
between them, A cannot use Art.6(1) to justify bringing an action in England
against X and adding Y and Z, domiciled in Germany, as additional defendants. If the additional defendant has a contract with the claimant providing
for the exclusive jurisdiction of another court, then the provisions of Art.23 of
the Brussels I Regulation would supersede those of Art.6(1) and the chosen
court would continue to have exclusive jurisdiction.[853]

An important limitation on the scope of Art.6(1) has been imposed by the   **11–322**
ruling of the European Court in *GlaxoSmithkline v Rouard*.[854] An Austrian
court asked whether Art.6(1) was applicable to an action brought by an
employee against two companies established in different Member States
which he considered to have been his joint employers. The European Court
ruled that Art.6(1) could not be applied to a dispute falling under the special
jurisdictional rules in s.5 of Ch.II applicable to individual contracts of
employment.[855] That conclusion was said to be supported by the consideration
that the sound administration of justice would imply that any possibility of
relying on Art.6(1) should be open, as in the case of counter-claims, both to
employees and to employers. Such an application of Art.6(1) could give rise
to consequences contrary to the objective of protection, which the insertion of
a specific section for contracts of employment sought specifically to ensure.
Reliance by an employer on Art.6(1) could deprive the employee of the
protection afforded to him by Art.20(1) under which proceedings can be
brought against an employee only in the courts of the Member State in which
he is domiciled.[856]

ILLUSTRATIONS

1. A enters into a contract with X, who is domiciled in England and Y, who is domiciled in   **11–323**
France, whereby A is to perform services for X and Y in the Republic of Ireland. X and Y
repudiate the contract. A brings proceedings against X in England, and seeks to join Y. The court
has jurisdiction over Y.

2. A & Co sues X & Co, domiciled in England, and Y & Co, its US parent company, alleging
that X & Co and Y & Co have infringed A & Co's patent for disposable nappies. A & Co seek
to join Z GmbH, a German subsidiary of Y & Co. Its primary purpose in joining Z GmbH is to
obtain discovery of documents in its possession. Jurisdiction may be taken under Art.5(3), i.e.
clause (3), but not (*semble*) under Art.6(1) where the predominant purpose is to obtain
discovery.[857]

3. A is chased by a security guard while he on holiday at a resort in Spain, and suffers injuries.
A sues X & Co, the English package holiday organiser, for breach of contract on the basis of

---

[853] See *Hough v P&O Containers Ltd* [1999] Q.B. 834 (a case on Art.6(2), below). See also
Droz, para.92. *cf. Soc Berlit Staudt v Cie d'assurances l'Alsacienne*, French Cour de cassation,
1989, in 1991 *Clunet* 155; See also *Deforche SA v Tomacrau SA* [2007] I.L.Pr. 367 (French Cour
de cassation, 2006).

[854] Case C–462/06 [2008] E.C.R. I–3965, [2008] I.C.R. 1375 (criticised by Harris (2008) 124
L.Q.R. 523).

[855] See paras 11–369 *et seq.* below.

[856] See below, para.11–372.

[857] *Mölnlycke AB v Procter & Gamble Ltd* [1992] 1 W.L.R. 1112 (CA), *per* Dillon L.J. (Woolf
and Leggatt L.JJ. expressed no view).

implied terms as to the safety of the resort and the standard of training and supervision of staff. He also joins Y & Co, the Spanish company managing the resort, claiming that it was negligent in training and supervising the guard, and in relation to the premises. *Semble*, Y & Co may be joined under Art. 6(1), notwithstanding that the claim against X & Co is in contract and the claim against Y & Co is in tort.[858]

11R–324   (10) The court has jurisdiction, where a defendant is sued in proceedings in England, to determine a third party claim[859] by the defendant against a person domiciled in another Member State or Convention State or in another part of the United Kingdom, unless the proceedings were instituted in order to deprive the third party of the jurisdiction of the courts of the country which would otherwise be competent to determine the claim against him.[860]

COMMENT

11–325   The English text of Art.6(2) provides for jurisdiction in proceedings on a warranty or guarantee or other third party proceedings[861] in the court seised of the original proceedings unless they were instituted solely with the object of removing the third party from the jurisdiction of the court which would otherwise be competent. The *"demande en garantie"* is equivalent to a claim for indemnity, and this provision deals with what in England is regulated by what was previously known as third party procedure and are now called additional claims.[862] A third party may be sued in England, even if England has little connection with the claim against the third party, e.g. if the jurisdiction of the court over the original action is derived from a contract between the claimant and defendant. An attempt is made to prevent abuse of this head of jurisdiction by providing that it is not to apply if the original proceedings were brought solely with the object of removing the third party from the jurisdiction which would otherwise have been competent. In *GIE Réunion Européenne v Zurich España*[863] the European Court held that there was an inherent relationship between an action brought against an insurer seeking indemnification for

---

[858] *Watson v First Choice Holidays and Flights Ltd* [2001] 1 Lloyd's Rep. 339 (CA). See Case C–98/06 *Freeport Plc v Arnoldsson* [2007] E.C.R. I–839.

[859] A third party claim is now described as an additional claim (CPR, r.20.2). In *National Justice Compania Naviera SA v Prudential Assurance Co Ltd (No.2)* [2000] 1 W.L.R. 603 (CA) it was held that a non-party to litigation domiciled in a Brussels Convention State could be made liable for costs under the Senior Courts Act 1981, s.51, either on the basis that the application did not involve "suing" him within Art.2, or if it did, that he was being sued as a third party under Art.6(2).

[860] Brussels I Regulation, Art.6(2); Lugano Convention, Art.6(2); 1982 Act, Sch.4, Rule 5(b).

[861] *"une demande en garantie ou . . . une demande en intervention."*

[862] CPR, Pt 20. See e.g. *Kinnear v Falcon Films NV* [1996] 1 W.L.R. 920; *Waterford Wedgwood Plc v David Nagli Ltd* [1998] F.S.R. 92; *Caltex Trading Pte Ltd v Metro Trading International Plc* [1999] 2 Lloyd's Rep. 724; *Knauf UK GmbH v British Gypsum Ltd (No.2)* [2002] EWHC 739 (Comm.), [2002] 2 Lloyd's Rep. 416. Foreign third parties may now be joined as necessary or proper parties to an English proceeding under CPR, r.6.36 and PD6B, para.3.1(4), Rule 34, clause (3), above.

[863] Case C–77/04 [2005] E.C.R. I–4509. For further proceedings see *GIE Réunion Européenne v Zurich Seguros* [2007] I.L.Pr. 301 (French Cour de cassation, 2006). The special provisions for third party proceedings in insurance matters do not apply to proceedings between insurers: below, para.11–345, n.908.

the consequences of an insured event and proceedings whereby that insurer seeks contribution from another insurer. The Court said that it is for the national court seised of the original claim to ascertain the existence of a connection between the two sets of proceedings, in the sense that it must satisfy itself that the third-party proceedings do not seek to remove the defendant from the jurisdiction of the court which would be competent in the case. Article 6(2) does not require the existence of any connection other than that which is sufficient to establish that the choice of forum does not amount to an abuse.[864]

But the European Court also emphasised that Art.6(2) merely determined **11–326** which court had jurisdiction, and the national court could apply its own procedural rules.[865] Thus in *Kongress Agentur Hagen GmbH v Zeehaghe BV*[866] the European Court confirmed that Art.6(2) applied if the national court had jurisdiction over the defendant in the plaintiff's original claim, irrespective of the domicile of the original defendant. In that case jurisdiction over the defendant had been taken on the basis of Art.5(1). It was also held that Art.6(2) does not *require* the national court to exercise jurisdiction against the third party, and it may apply its own procedural rules in order to determine whether the action is admissible, provided that the effectiveness of what is now the Regulation is not impaired, and, in particular, that leave to bring the claim on the guarantee is not refused on the ground that the third party resides or is domiciled in a State other than that of the court seised of the original proceedings.

In England the court has a wide discretion under the Civil Procedure Rules **11–327** to dismiss or strike out what are now called additional claims. But the effect of the decision of the European Court is that the third party proceedings cannot be set aside solely on the ground of the delay which would be caused by the fact that the third party is domiciled in another Member State or Convention State.[867]

If the third party has an agreement with the defendant providing for the **11–328** jurisdiction of the courts of another Member State (or Convention State), the agreement will be given effect under Art.23 of the Regulation (or of the Convention)[868] in priority to Art.6(2).[869]

ILLUSTRATIONS

1. A buys a French machine for delivery in England from X, who is domiciled in France and **11–329** who bought it from Y, who is also domiciled in France. The machine is faulty and A brings proceedings in England against X. X may join Y.[870]

---

[864] At [31]–[32].

[865] At [34].

[866] Case C–365/88 [1990] E.C.R. I–1845. It would seem to follow that jurisdiction under Art.6(2) is available even if the defendant in the original claim is domiciled outside the Member States or Convention States and is sued on an "exorbitant" ground (such as mere presence) under Art.4: *cf.* Kaye, p.648; *Veenbrink v Banque Internationale pour l'Afrique Occidentale*, French Cour de cassation, 1992, in 1993 *Clunet* 151, note Huet.

[867] See Lenz A.-G. [1990] E.C.R. I–1845, 1858.

[868] See below, Rule 39(3).

[869] *Hough v P&O Containers Ltd* [1999] Q.B. 834. *cf. Soc de Groot Nijkerk v Soc Rhenania*, 1993 *Clunet* 151 (French Cour de cassation, 1992).

[870] Case C–365/88 *Kongress Agentur Hagen GmbH v Zeehaghe BV* [1990] E.C.R. I–1845.

2. The facts are as in Illustration 1, except that the machinery was bought and delivered in France. When A brings proceedings in England against X, X (who would not otherwise be subject to the jurisdiction) submits to the jurisdiction. *Semble*, X may join Y.

3. The facts are as in Illustration 2, except that X submits to the jurisdiction as part of a collusive plan between A and X to procure that X may join Y in the English proceedings. The court has no jurisdiction.

4. The facts are as in Illustration 1, except that X's claim against Y is time-barred under French law. The court may set aside the claim against Y.

5. A film actor was injured in an accident while making a film in Spain, and subsequently died in hospital in Madrid. His administrators sued the film company, and the producer and director of the film. The defendants were able to join the Spanish orthopaedic surgeon and the Spanish hospital as third parties claiming contribution under the Civil Liability (Contribution) Act 1978 and damages for breach of contract allegedly concluded between the defendants and the hospital for treatment of the actor.[871]

6. A is injured while working for X & Co, an English company, as an electrician on board one of its ships while it was undergoing repairs in a German shipyard. A sues X & Co in England for negligence and breach of statutory duty. The repairs were being done by Y & Co pursuant to a contract which was governed by German law and provided for the jurisdiction of the Hamburg courts. The English court has no jurisdiction over X & Co's third party claim against Y & Co because the jurisdiction agreement provisions of Art.23 of the Regulation[872] take priority over the third party jurisdiction under Art.6(2).[873]

11R–330   **(11) The court has jurisdiction, where a claimant domiciled in another Member State or Convention State or in Scotland or Northern Ireland sues in England, to determine a counterclaim arising from the same contract or facts on which the original claim was based.[874]**

COMMENT

11–331   Article 6(3) provides that a person domiciled in a Member State (or, as the case may be, in a Convention State) may be sued on a counterclaim,[875] arising from the same contract or facts on which the original claim was based, in the court in which the original claim is pending. This is similar to the English rule of jurisdiction that a claimant submits to counterclaims.[876] In Art.6(3) the

---

[871] *Kinnear v Falcon Films NV* [1996] 1 W.L.R. 920.

[872] para.12–119.

[873] *Hough v P&O Containers Ltd* [1999] Q.B. 834.

[874] Brussels I Regulation, Art.6(3); Lugano Convention, Art.6(3); 1982 Act, Sch.4, Rule 5(c).

[875] *"une demande reconventionnelle"*—which is not quite the same as a counterclaim since it does not have to be brought in the same action: see Anton, paras 8.331–8.332, on the Scots procedure of reconvention. Art.6(3) does not regulate the circumstances when a set-off (as distinct from a counterclaim) may be raised. That is a matter for national law: Case C–341/93 *Danvaern Productions A/S v Schuhfabriken Otterbeck GmbH & Co* [1995] E.C.R. I–2053. Nor does it allow an additional party to be joined by counterclaim: cf. *Jordan Grand Prix Ltd v Baltic Insurance Group* [1999] 2 A.C. 127 (a case on what is now Art.12(2) of the Regulation); *Bank of Tokyo-Mitsubishi Ltd v Baskan Gida Sanayi Ve Pazarlama AS* [2004] EWHC 945 (Ch.), [2004] 2 Lloyd's Rep. 395, at [189].

[876] para.11–126. On the special problems raised by set-off or counterclaim when the parties have entered into an agreement providing for the exclusive jurisdiction of the courts of Member States or Convention States see Case 23/78 *Meeth v Glacetal Sàri* [1978] E.C.R. 2133; Case 48/84 *Spitzley v Sommer Exploitation SA* [1985] E.C.R. 787. See also *Hough v P&O Containers Ltd* [1999] Q.B. 834 (on Art.6(2), above). cf. *Aectra Refining & Marketing Inc v Exmar NV* [1994] 1 W.L.R. 1634, 1649–1651 (CA) (arbitration). See also *Dollfus Mieg et Cie v CWD International Ltd, The Times*, April 19, 2003.

requirement that the claims be related is expressed in the following way: the counterclaim must (a) "arise" (b) from the same contract or (c) from the same facts (d) on which the original claim was "based." These requirements are stricter than a requirement that the matters merely be "related."

ILLUSTRATION

A & Co, a German company, buys a paper-making machine from X, who is domiciled in England, the price to be payable in Germany. When the machine fails, A & Co refuses to pay and sues X in England for damages. X counterclaims for the unpaid price. The court has jurisdiction.   **11–332**

(12) The court has jurisdiction in matters relating to a contract, if the action may be combined with an action against the same defendant in matters relating to rights *in rem* in immovable property situated in England.   **11R–333**

COMMENT

This clause is based on Art.6(4) of the Brussels I Regulation and of the Lugano Convention. It is primarily concerned with actions to recover secured debts and to enforce the security, and is considered below in connection with clause (15).[877] There is an equivalent provision in Sch.4, Rule 5(d), to the 1982 Act.   **11–334**

(13) In matters relating to insurance (but not as regards defendants domiciled in Scotland or Northern Ireland[878])   **11R–335**
    (1) the court has jurisdiction in an action against an insurer:
        (i) if the insurer is domiciled in England;[879] or
        (ii) in disputes arising out of the operations of its branch, agency or other establishment, if the branch, agency or other establishment is in England;[880] or
        (iii) if the policyholder, the insured or a beneficiary is domiciled in England;[881]
        (iv) if the insurer is a co-insurer, and proceedings are brought in England against the leading insurer;[882] or
        (v) in the case of liability insurance or insurance of immovable property, if the harmful event occurred in England;[883] or
        (vi) in a third party claim by the insured in the case of liability insurance, where the insured has been sued in England;[884] or

---

[877] *cf.* clause (7), above.
[878] There is no equivalent in Sch.4 of the provisions relating to insurance in the Regulation. Proceedings relating to insurance contracts will therefore fall within the other provisions of Sch.4, especially Rule 3(a). See below, para.11–354.
[879] Brussels I Regulation, Art.9(1)(a); Lugano Convention, Art.9(1)(a).
[880] Arts 8, 5(5).
[881] Art.9(1)(b).
[882] Art.9(1)(c).
[883] Art.10.
[884] Art.11(1).

  (vii) **in the case of a counterclaim against the insurer, if the insurer has commenced proceedings in England arising from the same contract or facts;**[885] **or**
  (viii) **if the insurer has entered into an agreement conferring jurisdiction on the English court;**[886]
(2) **the court has jurisdiction over a policyholder, insured or beneficiary:**
  (i) **if he is domiciled in England;**[887] **or**
  (ii) **in the case of a counterclaim, if he has commenced proceedings in England arising from the same contract or facts;**[888] **or**
  (iii) **in the case of the policyholder or insured, where a direct action has been brought against the insurer in England and the law governing direct actions permits the policyholder or insured to be joined;**[889] **or**
  (iv) **if the parties have conferred jurisdiction on the English court by agreement,**
  (a) where the agreement was entered into after the dispute arose;[890] **or**
  (b) where the policyholder and insurer were both domiciled or habitually resident in England when the agreement was entered into;[891] **or**
  (c) where the agreement relates to certain insurance covering loss of or damage to, or liability arising out of the operation of, ships, aircraft or cargoes, and to all large risks as defined in Council Directive 73/239/EEC as amended.[892]

COMMENT

11–336 The draftsmen of the Brussels Convention made special provision for insurance in order to protect policyholders.[893] In the negotiations for accession, the United Kingdom sought to adapt the Convention to meet the needs of the London insurance market; in particular, the United Kingdom stressed that the nature of the London market was such that a large proportion of its business was with policyholders outside the Community; and that a large proportion was insurance of "large risks" with substantial industrial and commercial

---

[885] Arts 12(2), 6(3).
[886] Art.13(2).
[887] Art.12(1).
[888] Art.12(2).
[889] Art.11(3).
[890] Art.13(1).
[891] Art.13(3).
[892] Arts 13(5), 14.
[893] See Case 201/82 *Gerling v Treasury Administration* [1983] E.C.R. 2503, 2516; Case C–112/03 *Société financière et industrielle du Peloux v Axa Belgium* [2005] I.L.Pr. 432. But this does not extend to persons (such as other insurers) for whom such protection is not justified: Case C–412/98 *Universal General Insurance Co (UGIC) v Group Josi Reinsurance Co S.A.* [2000] E.C.R. I–5925, [2001] 1 Q.B. 68; Case C–77/04 *GIE Réunion Européenne v Zurich España* [2005] E.C.R. I–459.

concerns; neither of these groups needed the special protection of the Convention rules. The special position of the United Kingdom did result in some changes to the Convention, but these were not of a very far-reaching character, and did not much mitigate the problems of forum-shopping to which the insurance provisions give rise.[894]

The main changes made by the Regulation (and also contained in the revised Lugano Convention) to the insurance provisions are these. First, an insurer domiciled in a Member or Convention State may be sued in another such State, not only (as in the Brussels Convention) where the policyholder is domiciled, but also, in the case of actions brought by the policyholder, the insured or a beneficiary, in the courts where the claimant is domiciled: Art.9(1)(b). Secondly, Art.13(5) and Art.14 allow the jurisdiction provisions to be excluded by agreement in the case, not only of the particular risks referred to in the Brussels Convention, but also in respect of all "large risks" as defined in Council Directive 73/239 as amended by 88/357 and 90/618, and as they may be amended in the future.   **11–337**

The provisions discussed here apply "in matters relating to insurance." The expression is not defined, but the 1978 Accession Convention was negotiated on the basis that it did not apply to reinsurance, and the Schlosser Report said that reinsurance contracts could not be equated with insurance contracts, and that accordingly these provisions did not apply to reinsurance contracts.[895] In *Universal General Insurance Co (UGIC) v Group Josi Reinsurance Co SA*[896] the European Court confirmed that reinsurance contracts were not covered by the insurance provisions of the Brussels Convention. The object of those provisions was to protect the weaker party to a contract of insurance. The rules protecting a party deemed to be economically weaker and less experienced in legal matters should not be extended to persons for whom that protection was not justified. No particular protection was justified in the relationship between a reinsured and reinsurer, since both parties were professionals in the insurance sector. The House of Lords had come to the same conclusion in *Agnew v Länsförsäkringsbolagens AB*.[897]   **11–338**

Where there is doubt whether a contract is one of insurance, the national court (and ultimately the European Court) will have to apply an autonomous, rather than a national, interpretation. In *New Hampshire Insurance Co v Strabag Bau AG*[898] the Court of Appeal rejected an argument[899] that what was on its face an insurance contract should not be so regarded for the purposes of these provisions because it was made between commercial concerns. It was held that the expression "matters relating to insurance" meant what it said and was not restricted to insurance for domestic or private purposes.   **11–339**

---

[894] See Kerr (1978) Law Soc Gaz. 1190; Collins, p.68.

[895] Schlosser, para.151; *Citadel Insurance Co v Atlantic Union Insurance Co SA* [1982] 2 Lloyd's Rep. 543, 549 (CA). Whether it applied to reinsurance was raised, but not decided, in Case C–351/89 *Overseas Union Insurance Ltd v New Hampshire Insurance Co* [1991] E.C.R. I–3317, [1992] Q.B. 434. See also Rule 237.

[896] Case C–412/98 [2000] E.C.R. I–5925, [2001] 1 Q.B. 68.

[897] [2001] 1 A.C. 223.

[898] [1992] 1 Lloyd's Rep. 361 (CA).

[899] Based by analogy on Case 150/77 *Société Bertrand v Paul Ott KG* [1978] E.C.R. 1431, below, para.11–357.

11–340   The complex effect of these provisions is summarised in clause (13). In addition to the heads of jurisdiction set out there, the defendant can also confer jurisdiction on the English court by submission under Art.24.[900] The provisions apply only where the defendant is domiciled in a Member State or in a Convention State, and where the defendant is not so domiciled Rules 31 to 32 and 34 will apply. This is subject to one important qualification. An insurer who is not domiciled in a Member State or Convention State but has a branch, agency or other establishment in one of the Member States or Convention States shall, in disputes arising out of the operations of the branch, etc., be deemed to be domiciled in that State.[901] A person who is deemed to be domiciled in the United Kingdom as a result is to be treated as domiciled in the part of the United Kingdom in which the branch, etc., is situate.[902] Thus for the purposes of the provisions on insurance a United States insurance company with branches in London, Paris and Geneva will be deemed to be domiciled in England, France and Switzerland.

11–341   **Policyholder, insured and beneficiary.** The insurance provisions of the Regulation and the Convention distinguish between policyholder, insured and beneficiary. The purpose of these expressions is to distinguish between the original party to the contract of insurance (*"preneur d'assurance"*) who may not necessarily be the same person as the insured or beneficiary. The practical effect of these distinctions is considerable, particularly when the benefit of the policy is assigned or transmitted with goods, or when the beneficiary is different from the person who takes out the policy.

11–342   **General scope.** An insurer domiciled in a Member State or Convention State may be sued: (1) in the courts of the State where he is domiciled, or (2) in the Member State or Convention State in which the policyholder or the insured or a beneficiary is domiciled, or (3) if he is a co-insurer, in the courts of the State in which proceedings are brought against the leading insurer.[903]

11–343   Leading insurer is not defined, and Art.9(1) does not impose an obligation for proceedings to be concentrated in one court. There is nothing in theory to prevent a policyholder from suing the various co-insurers in different courts.[904] An insurer may normally be sued at any place where it has a branch if the dispute arises from an insurance contract entered into at that branch, whether or not the insurer is domiciled in a Member State or Convention State.[905]

11–344   Articles 10 and 11 create additional bases of jurisdiction against insurers. In the case of liability insurance (i.e. insurance against legal liability to third parties), jurisdiction is conferred on the courts of the State where the harmful event occurred.[906] The relevant harmful event is the event which gives rise to

---

[900] Case C–111/09 *Ceská Podnikatelska Pojistovna as, Vienna Insurance Group v Bilas* [2010] Lloyd's I.R. 734.
[901] Art.9(2).
[902] SI 2001/3929, Sch.1, para.11; 1982 Act, s.44A.
[903] Art.9(1).
[904] Schlosser, para.149. But they may be regarded as related actions, and relief granted in respect of the proceedings other than those brought first: see Art.28: Rule 38(4)(b).
[905] Arts 8 and 9(2).
[906] Art.10.

the cause of action against the insured party, and the English court will have jurisdiction if the damage occurred in England or the event which gave rise to the damage occurred in England.[907]

The court may also exercise jurisdiction in a third party claim by the **11–345** insured against an insurer domiciled in another Member State or Convention State if it is seised of an action by the injured party against the insured.[908] This would be so even if the parties to the original proceedings were both domiciled in England, but not if the insurer and insured are bound by a jurisdiction clause validly conferring jurisdiction on the courts of another Member State or Convention State.

In the case of insurance of immovable property, the court may exercise **11–346** jurisdiction if England is the place where the harmful event occurred,[909] which will in practice be the place where the immovable property is situated.

Article 11(2)–(3) deals with direct proceedings against insurers, which are **11–347** found, at least to a limited extent, in many of the Member States and Convention States.[910] In *FBTO Schadeverzekeringen NV v Odenbreit*[911] the European Court ruled that the combined effect of Arts 11(2) and 9(1)(b) of the Brussels I Regulation was that the injured third party could bring a direct action against the insurer in the court of his own domicile, and was not limited to the courts of the domicile of the policyholder, insured or beneficiary specifically mentioned in Art.9(1)(b). It was also held in that ruling that the jurisdictional rules relating to direct actions apply whether they are classified by national law as tortious or as contractual claims under the policy.

These provisions apply only "where such direct actions are permitted" **11–348** under the *lex fori*, including its rules of private international law. The policyholder or insured may be joined "if the law governing such direct actions" provides for such joinder.[912] The governing law in this context means, it seems, the law to which the private international law rules of the *lex fori* point. The Rome II Regulation (Art.18) provides that the person who suffers damage may bring the claim against the insurer of the person liable to provide compensation if the law applicable to the tort/delict or that applicable to the insurance contract so provides.[913] The question whether the policyholder or insured may be joined to such proceedings may be a question purely of procedure for the *lex fori*. In *Maher v Groupama Grand Est*[914] the view was expressed, *obiter*, that the French insured could be joined to the direct action by the English victims of a road accident in France against the French insurer.

---

[907] Case 21/76 *Bier v Mines de Potasse d'Alsace SA* [1976] E.C.R. 1735, [1978] Q.B. 708.

[908] Art.10(1); Jenard, p.32. The third party provisions do not apply to third-party proceedings between insurers based on multiple insurance: Case C–77/04 *GIE Réunion Européenne v Zurich España* [2005] E.C.R. I–4509, [2005] I.L.Pr. 456.

[909] Art.10.

[910] See, e.g. Third Parties (Rights Against Insurers) Act 1930.

[911] Case C–463/06 [2007] E.C.R. I–11321, applied in *Maher v Groupama Grand Est* [2009] EWCA Civ 1191, [2010] 1 W.L.R. 1564. But these provisions do not permit a social security institution, acting as the statutory assignee of the rights of the directly injured party in a motor accident, to bring an action directly in its own courts against the insurer: Case C–347/08 *Vorarlberger Gebietskrankenkasse v WGV-Schwäbische Allgemeine Versicherungs AG* [2009] E.C.R. I–8661.

[912] Art.11(2).

[913] paras 34–071 *et seq.*

[914] [2009] EWCA Civ 1191, [2010] 1 W.L.R. 1564.

Where there is a jurisdiction agreement valid under the restrictive provisions for such agreements in insurance contracts[915] Art.11 (as between the parties to the agreement) is superseded by the agreement.[916]

11–349   The Regulation and the Convention[917] provide that, without prejudice to the right granted by Art.10(3) to join the policyholder or insured in a direct action, an insurer may bring proceedings only in the courts of the Member State or Convention State in which the defendant is domiciled, irrespective of whether the defendant is the policyholder, the insured or a beneficiary, without prejudice to the right to bring a counterclaim in the court in which the original claim against the insurer is pending. This provision does not apply where the defendant is domiciled outside the Member States and the Convention States. In *Jordan Grand Prix Ltd v Baltic Insurance Group*[918] the House of Lords held that it applied to any insurer, whether or not domiciled in a Brussels Convention State; and that the reference to a counterclaim in the court in which the original claim against the insurer is pending meant a counterclaim against the original plaintiff. Consequently an insurer who was sued in England by an English insured could not add Irish domiciliaries as defendants to counterclaim.

11–350   **Jurisdiction clauses.** Clauses attributing jurisdiction to courts receive special treatment in the Regulation and the Convention in the case of insurance contracts, and the general provisions relating to jurisdiction agreements do not apply, although the formal requirements are applicable.[919] The position with regard to insurance contracts may be summarised as follows: (1) if there is an arbitration agreement between the parties the case will be outside the scope of the Regulation and the Convention;[920] (2) if there is a jurisdiction clause conferring jurisdiction on the courts of a particular State (perhaps even a non-Member State or non-Convention State) then it will be given effect (a) in favour of a policyholder, insured or beneficiary generally[921] (b) in favour of the insurer only if (i) it is entered into after the dispute has arisen,[922] or (ii) the agreement is between a policyholder and an insurer both domiciled[923] or habitually resident in the same Member State or Convention State and confers jurisdiction on the courts of that State,[924] or (iii) the agreement was concluded with a policyholder not domiciled in a Member State or Convention State, unless the insurance is compulsory or relates to immovable property in a Member State or a Convention State,[925] or (iv) it relates to one of the risks

---

[915] See below, para.11–350.

[916] Schlosser, para.148.

[917] Art.12. See *New Hampshire Insurance Co v Strabag Bau AG* [1992] 1 Lloyd's Rep. 361 (CA).

[918] [1999] 2 A.C. 127.

[919] Arts 13, 14, 23. *cf.* Case 201/82 *Gerling v Treasury Administration* [1983] E.C.R. 2503.

[920] Art.1(2)(d).

[921] Art.13(2).

[922] Art.13(1).

[923] This may include an insurer not domiciled in a Member State or Convention State but with a branch in a Member or Convention State in relation to a policy issued through that branch: Art.9(2).

[924] Art.13(3). A jurisdiction clause conforming with this provision cannot be relied on against a beneficiary under the insurance contract who has not expressly subscribed to that clause and is domiciled in another Member State or Convention State: Case C–112/03 *Société financière et industrielle du Peloux v Axa Belgium* [2005] E.C.R. I –3707, [2006] Q.B. 251.

[925] Art.13(4).

specified in Art.14.[926] In *Charman v WOC Offshore BV*[927] Staughton L.J. expressed the view (*obiter*, and differing from Hirst J. at first instance) that for a jurisdiction agreement to be effective under the equivalent provision in the Brussels Convention it was necessary for it to relate to one of the specified risks and no other: if it related to other risks, it was wholly ineffective and not merely to the extent it related to other risks.

The following points are worthy of note: first, it is not likely that express **11–351** agreements on choice of court after a dispute has arisen will in practice be common; secondly, an exclusive jurisdiction clause will always be effective for the benefit of a policyholder, insured or beneficiary; thirdly, the relevant time for testing the domicile or habitual residence of the insurer and the policyholder for the purposes of these provisions is the date of the contract, and not (as under the Brussels Convention) the date of commencement of the proceedings; fourthly, they apply where the policyholder is not domiciled in a Member State or a Convention State, but there are proceedings by or against an insured or beneficiary in a Member State or a Convention State on a policy containing a jurisdiction clause. The conferment of jurisdiction is to be effective unless one of two exceptions is applicable: the first is where the insurance is compulsory, in which case no departure from the basic jurisdictional provisions is permitted, even if the policyholder is domiciled outside the Member States and the Convention States.[928] The second exception is for insurance relating to immovable property, where the other applicable provisions will continue to apply even if the national law of the State in which the immovable property is situated allows jurisdiction agreements.[929]

The specified risks in Art.14 are (1) any loss of damage to (a) ships, **11–352** offshore installations or aircraft, arising from perils relating to their use for commercial purposes or (b) goods in transit, other than passengers' baggage, where the transit consists of or includes carriage by ships or aircraft; (2) any liability, other than for bodily injury to passengers or loss of or damage to their baggage (a) arising out of the use or operation of ships, etc., (b) for loss or damage caused by goods in transit as above; (3) any financial loss connected[930] with the use or operation of ships, etc., in particular loss of freight or charter-hire; (4) any risk or interest connected with any of those referred to in (1) to (3) above.[931] In addition, the jurisdiction provisions may be excluded by agreement in respect of all "large risks" as defined in Council Directive 73/239 as amended by Council Directives 88/357(EEC) and 90/618(EC), and as they may be amended in the future.

The practical effect is that an insurer in London can effectively confer **11–353** exclusive jurisdiction on the English court by the original insurance contract only in the following cases: (1) where the policyholder is domiciled in the United Kingdom at the time the insurance contract is entered into, or (2)

---

[926] Art.13(5).

[927] [1993] 2 Lloyd's Rep. 551, 557–558 (CA).

[928] See Schlosser, para.138; e.g. aviation and motor vehicle insurance.

[929] Schlosser, para.139; *sed quaere.*

[930] See *Charman v WOC Offshore BV* [1993] 2 Lloyd's Rep. 551 (CA) (jurisdiction agreement valid even if insurance covered land-based equipment, such as crawling crane, because sufficiently connected with sea-going vessels covered by insurance).

[931] See *Tradigrain SA v SIAT SpA* [2002] EWHC 106 (Comm.), [2002] 2 Lloyd's Rep. 553.

where the policyholder is not domiciled in any of the Member States or Convention States at the time the insurance contract is entered into; or (3) the insurance relates to one of the relevant major risks.

11–354   These provisions find no counterpart in the intra-United Kingdom scheme in Sch.4 to the 1982 Act. This means that where the Regulation or the Convention confer jurisdiction on the courts of the United Kingdom, a Scottish defendant will only be subject to the English jurisdiction in insurance matters where one of the general provisions in Sch.4 applies. In practice the most likely cases are where the Scottish defendant is domiciled in England or where he is sued on an obligation in an insurance contract to be performed in England.

ILLUSTRATIONS

11–355   1. X & Co and Y & Co are German companies and are participants in a joint venture for the construction of an airport in Iraq. They take out a policy of insurance through London brokers in the London market indemnifying them against certain risks in connection with the project. The leading underwriter is A & Co, an American company, but the bulk of the risk is placed with English insurers, and the contract of insurance is impliedly governed by English law. The members of the joint venture claim on the policy for corrosion damage amounting to up to £60 million. A & Co and the other insurers seek to avoid the policy for non-disclosure and commence proceedings in England against (*inter alios*) X & Co and Y & Co for a declaration that they have validly avoided the policy and are under no liability. The court has no jurisdiction.[932]

2. A, domiciled in England, takes out a policy of insurance covering his stamp collection with X & Co, a German insurance company. When the stamp collection is stolen X & Co dispute liability under the policy. A sues X & Co in England. The court has jurisdiction.[933]

3. The facts are as in Illustration 2, except that the insurance policy contains a clause providing that the German courts are to have exclusive jurisdiction over any disputes. The court has jurisdiction because the clause is ineffective.[934]

4. X, a resident of Palermo and domiciled in Italy, insures his valuable collection of antiques through a Lloyd's broker with A, a Lloyd's syndicate in London. The insurance policy provides for the exclusive jurisdiction of the English court. The antiques are stolen and A pays a substantial sum under the policy. A subsequently alleges that as a result of material non-disclosure it is entitled to avoid the policy and to have the compensation returned. A brings proceedings against X in London. The court has no jurisdiction.[935]

5. X, a Greek shipowner, insures his fleet with A, a Lloyd's syndicate. The policy provides for the exclusive jurisdiction of the English courts. A brings proceedings for rescission of the contract. The court has jurisdiction.[936]

11R–356   **(14) In proceedings concerning consumer contracts,[937]**

> **(1) the court has jurisdiction in an action against a supplier of goods, or lender, or supplier of services:**
>> **(i) if the defendant is domiciled in England;[938]**
>> **(ii) if the consumer is domiciled in England;[939]**

---

[932] Brussels I Regulation, Art.12; *New Hampshire Insurance Co v Strabag Bau AG* [1992] 1 Lloyd's Rep. 361 (CA).

[933] Brussels I Regulation, Art.9(1)(b).

[934] Brussels I Regulation, Art.13.

[935] But a London arbitration clause in the policy would have been effective.

[936] Brussels I Regulation, Arts 13(5), 14.

[937] See generally Hill, *Cross-Border Consumer Contracts* (2008).

[938] Brussels I Regulation, Art.16(1); Lugano Convention, Art.16(1); 1982 Act, Sch.4, Rule 8(1) (as substituted by SI 2001/3929, Sch.2).

[939] Brussels I Regulation, Art.16(1) (and SI 2001/3929, Sch.1, para.7(3)); Lugano Convention, Art.16(1) (and 1982 Act, s.10(3); 1982 Act, Sch.4, Rule 8(1)).

   (iii) **if the defendant has a branch, agency or establishment in England and the dispute arises out of its operations;**[940]

   (iv) **in the case of a counterclaim against the supplier, etc., where he has commenced proceedings in England arising from the same contract or facts;**[941]

   (v) **if the supplier, etc. has entered into an agreement conferring jurisdiction on the English court;**[942]

(2) the court has jurisdiction in an action against the consumer:

   (i) **if the consumer is domiciled in England;**[943]

   (ii) **in the case of a counterclaim against the consumer, where the consumer has commenced proceedings in England arising from the same contract or facts;**[944]

   (iii) **if the parties conferred jurisdiction on the English court by agreement and either (a) the agreement was entered into after the dispute arose;**[945] **or (b) the supplier, etc., and the consumer were both domiciled or habitually resident in England.**[946]

In this clause a consumer contract means a contract concluded by a person for a purpose outside his trade or profession and which is

(1) a contract for the sale of goods on instalment credit terms; or

(2) a contract for a loan repayable by instalments, or for any other form of credit, made to finance the sale of goods; or

(3) the contract has been concluded with a person who pursues commercial or professional activities in the State of the consumer's domicile or, by any means, directs such activities to that State or to several States including that State, and the contract falls within the scope of such activities.[947]

This clause does not apply to a contract of transport other than a contract which, for an inclusive price, provides for a combination of travel and accommodation.[948]

COMMENT

The objectives of the consumer contract provisions of the Brussels Convention were inspired by a desire to protect consumers; national laws, by contrast, were designed partly to protect the "weaker" party, but also to serve economic, monetary and savings policy.[949] The main change introduced by the 1978 Accession Convention was to make it clear that the provisions applied   **11–357**

---

[940] Brussels I Regulation, Arts 15(2), 5(5) (and SI 2001/3929, Sch.1, para.11); Lugano Convention, Arts 15(2), 5(5) (and 1982 Act, s.44A(2)).

[941] Regulation, Art.16(3); Convention, Art.16(3); 1982 Act, Sch.4, Rule 8(3).

[942] Regulation, Art.17(2); Convention, Art.17(2); 1982 Act, Sch.4, Rule 9(b).

[943] Regulation, Art.16(2); Convention, Art.16(2); 1982 Act, Sch.4, Rule 8(1).

[944] Regulation, Art.16(3); Convention, Art.16(3); 1982 Act, Sch.4, Rule 8(3).

[945] Regulation, Art.17(1); Convention, Art.17(1); 1982 Act, Sch.4, Rule 9(a).

[946] Regulation, Art.17(3); Convention, Art.17(3); 1982 Act, Sch.4, Rule 9(c).

[947] Regulation, Art.15(1); Convention, Art.15(1); 1982 Act, Sch.4, Rule 7(1).

[948] Regulation, Art.15(3); Convention, Art.15(3); *cf.* 1982 Act, Sch.4, Rule 7(2).

[949] Case 150/77 *Société Bertrand v Paul Ott KG* [1978] E.C.R. 1431. See generally Mennie, 1987 S.L.T. (News) 181.

only to consumer contracts, and not to all instalment sales and financing contracts irrespective of whether the buyer was a businessman or a private consumer. In *Société Bertrand v Paul Ott KG*[950] the European Court held, on the original wording of these provisions, that they applied only to private final consumers and not to those who were engaged, while buying the product, in trade or professional activities. This was confirmed in amendments to the Brussels Convention, which were influenced by the drafts of the Rome Convention on the Law Applicable to Contractual Obligations, which made special provision for choice of law in consumer contracts.[951] Further changes were introduced by the Brussels I Regulation to take account of the growth in e-commerce, and the fact that consumers might be induced to contract abroad as a result of accessing the websites of foreign sellers directed at the country of the consumer's domicile. The other change introduced by the Brussels I Regulation is the provision that the exclusion of contracts of transport from these provisions does not extend to "a contract which, for an inclusive price, provides for a combination of travel and accommodation."[952] The reference to travel packages was new.

11–358   The consumer contract provisions in clause (14) apply only where the defendant is domiciled,[953] or deemed to be domiciled, in a Member State or Convention State. Where the defendant is not so domiciled, then jurisdiction depends, under Art.4 of the Regulation and the Convention (to which the consumer contract provisions are expressly subject[954]), on the law of the Member State or Convention State where the action is brought.[955] These provisions relate to proceedings concerning a contract concluded by a person for a purpose which can be regarded as being outside his trade or profession, "the consumer."[956] They apply to contracts for the sale of goods on instalment credit terms; or contracts for a loan repayable by instalments, or for any other form of credit, made to finance the sale of goods.

---

[950] Case 150/77 [1978] E.C.R. 1431. See also Case C–269/95 *Benincasa v Dentalkit Srl* [1997] E.C.R. I–3767.

[951] See now Rome I Regulation, Art.6, Rule 235, below.

[952] Art.15(3); 1982 Act, Sch.4, Rule 7(2). See Joined Cases C–585/08 and C–144/09 *Pammer v Reederei Karl Schlüter GmbH*, December 7, 2010 (voyage by freighter involved a contract which for an inclusive price provided accommodation as well as transport for a period of more than 24 hours).

[953] Or last known domicile: Case C–327/10 *Hypotecní banka as v Lindner*, November 17, 2011.

[954] Art.15(1).

[955] Case C–318/93 *Brenner v Dean Witter Reynolds Inc* [1994] E.C.R. I–4275.

[956] They do not apply to a contract which an individual has concluded with a view to pursuing a trade in the future: Case C–269/95 *Benincasa v Dentalkit Srl* [1997] E.C.R. I–3767 (franchise agreement to sell dental hygiene products not a consumer contract). Nor do they apply to a claim by an assignee of a consumer, where the assignee is acting in pursuance of its trade or professional activity: Case C–89/91 *Shearson Lehman Hutton Inc v TVB* [1993] E.C.R. I–139. A person who concludes a contract for the purchase of goods intended for purposes which are in part within, and in part outside, his trade or profession may not rely on the consumer contract provisions, unless the trade or professional purpose is so limited as to be negligible in the overall context of the supply: Case C–464/01 *Gruber v BayWa AG* [2005] E.C.R. I–439, [2006] Q.B. 204. See also Case C–96/00 *Gabriel v Schlank & Schick GmbH* [2002] E.C.R. I–6367; Case C–167/00 *Verein für Konsumenteninformation v Henkel* [2002] E.C.R. I–8111; *Standard Bank London Ltd v Apostolakis* [2000] I.L.Pr. 766; *Standard Bank London Ltd v Apostolakis (No.2)* [2001] Lloyd's Rep. Banking 240; *Maple Leaf Marro Volatility Master Fund v Rouvray* [2009] EWHC 257 (Comm.), [2009] 1 Lloyd's Rep. 475.

The meaning of sale of goods on "instalment credit terms" was considered   **11–359**
in *Société Bertrand v Paul Ott KG*[957] where the European Court held that it
was necessary to give the expression an autonomous interpretation, and that it
meant a transaction in which the price is discharged by way of several
payments or which is linked to a financing contract. In *Mietz v Intership
Yachting Sneek BV*[958] the European Court held that taking payment by instalments from the purchaser, but where the purchase price is paid in full by the
time the purchaser takes possession, is not a sale on instalment credit
terms.

Art.15(1)(c) provides that the consumer contract provisions extend to con-   **11–360**
tracts for the supply of goods or services where "the contract has been
concluded with a person who pursues commercial or professional activities in
the Member State of the consumer's domicile or, by any means, directs such
activities to that Member State or to several States including that Member
State, and the contract falls within the scope of such activities." Art.15(1)(c)
is designed, like the other consumer contract provisions, to protect the weaker
party.[959] The concept of activity "directed to" the Member State of the
consumer's domicile is to be interpreted independently, by reference principally to the system and objectives of the Regulation, in order to ensure that it
is fully effective.[960] This provision is intended to apply to contracts concluded
as a result of marketing through e-commerce, via an interactive website
accessible in the domicile of the consumer. The criteria in the Brussels
Convention were being reframed to take account of developments in marketing techniques,[961] but they were much criticised by the e-commerce industry
on the ground that they will impose unnecessary restraints on the development
of this new form of economic activity.[962]

The Council and the Commission issued a joint declaration[963] recognizing   **11–361**
that the development of e-commerce facilitated the economic growth of
undertakings. The development of new distance marketing techniques based
on the use of the Internet depended in part on mutual confidence between
undertakings and consumers. One of the major elements in this confidence
was the opportunity offered to consumers by Art.16 of the Brussels I Regulation to bring disputes before the courts of the Member States in which they
resided, where the contract concluded by the consumer was covered by Art.15
of the Regulation. For Art.15(1)(c) to be applicable it was not sufficient for an
undertaking to target its activities at the Member State of the consumer's
residence, or at a number of Member States including that Member State; a
contract had also be concluded within the framework of its activities. The

---

[957] See Case 150/77 [1978] E.C.R. 1431.

[958] Case C–99/96 [1999] E.C.R. I–2277.

[959] Case C–180/06 *Ilsinger v Dreschers* [2009] ECR I–3961, [41]; Joined Cases C–585/08 and C–144/09 *Pammer v Reederei Karl Schlüter GmbH*, December 7, 2010, at [56].

[960] Joined Cases C–585/08 and C–144/09 *Pammer v Reederei Karl Schlüter GmbH*, December 7, 2010, at [55].

[961] Commission explanatory memorandum, COM (99) 348.

[962] See Kennett (2001) 50 I.C.L.Q.725, 728–729, and Report by the Committee on Legal Affairs and the Internal Market (Rapporteur: Diana Wallis) of the European Parliament, Sep-tember 18, 2000. See Øren (2003) 52 I.C.L.Q. 665 for discussion of consumer contracts concluded through the internet. See Farah (2008) 33 Eur. L. Rev. 257.

[963] *http://ec.europa.eu/civiljustice/docs/Reg_44-2000_joint_statement_14139_en.pdf.*

provision related to a number of marketing methods, including contracts concluded at a distance through the internet. The Council and the Commission stressed that the mere fact that an internet site was accessible was not sufficient for Art.15 to be applicable, although a factor would be that the internet site solicited the conclusion of distance contracts and that a contract had actually been concluded at a distance, by whatever means. The language or currency which a website uses did not constitute a relevant factor.

11–362   The joint declaration was relied on by the European Court in *Pammer v Reederei Karl Schlüter GmbH*.[964] The ruling involved, in the first case, an Austrian claimant who had found on a website a freighter voyage organised by a German company from Italy to the Far East and then booked by post; and in the second case, a German defendant who had found an Austrian hotel on a website and then made a reservation on the internet. In each case the question was whether the provider of the services had directed its activities to the State in which the consumer was domiciled, and in particular whether the fact that the websites could be consulted on the internet was sufficient for that activity to be regarded as such. The Court noted that internet advertising inherently had a worldwide reach, and that advertising on a website by a trader was in principle accessible in all States, and, therefore, throughout the European Union, without any need to incur additional expenditure and irrespective of the intention or otherwise of the trader to target consumers outside the territory of the State in which it was established. For Art.15(1)(c) to be applicable, the trader must have manifested its intention to establish commercial relations with consumers from one or more other Member States, including that of the consumer's domicile. The operative part of the ruling was that the following (non-exhaustive) matters were relevant: the international nature of the activity, mention of itineraries from other Member States for going to the place where the trader was established, use of a language or a currency other than the language or currency generally used in the Member State in which the trader is established with the possibility of making and confirming the reservation in that other language, mention of telephone numbers with an international code, outlay of expenditure on an internet referencing service in order to facilitate access to the trader's site or that of its intermediary by consumers domiciled in other Member States, use of a top-level domain name other than that of the Member State in which the trader was established, and mention of an international clientele composed of customers domiciled in various Member States. It was for the national courts to ascertain whether such evidence existed. But the mere accessibility of the trader's or the intermediary's website in the Member State in which the consumer was domiciled was insufficient. The same was true of mention of an email address and of other contact details, or of use of a language or a currency which were the language and/or currency generally used in the Member State in which the trader was established.[965]

---

[964] Joined Cases C–585/08 and C–144/09 [2011] 2 All E.R. (Comm.) 888.

[965] The joint declaration suggested that the language or currency which a website used did not constitute relevant factors, but the Court accepted that that was so where they corresponded to the languages generally used in the Member State from which the trader pursued its activity and to the currency of that Member State; but if the website permitted consumers to use a different language or a different currency, the language and/or currency could constitute evidence for a conclusion that the trader's activity was directed to other Member States: at [84].

Where the provisions of the Regulation or the Convention apply they **11–363** supersede national law, e.g. the Consumer Credit Act 1974, s.141.[966]

The effect of these provisions is that a consumer may bring proceedings in England if the supplier is domiciled in England or if the consumer is domiciled in England. The consumer may only be sued in England if he is domiciled in England; but a foreign consumer may be subject to a counterclaim if he sues in England, and, it seems, he may submit to the jurisdiction by voluntary appearance.[967]

Where a consumer enters into a contract with a party who is not domiciled **11–364** in a Member State or a Convention State but has a branch, agency or other establishment in one of those States, that party shall, in disputes arising out of the operations of the branch, etc., be deemed to be domiciled in that State; and the defendant is deemed to be domiciled for this purpose in the part of the United Kingdom in which the branch is situate.[968]

Jurisdiction agreements. The consumer contract provisions of the Regula- **11–365** tion and the Convention may be departed from only by an agreement (1) which is entered into after the dispute has arisen or (2) which allows the consumer to bring proceedings in courts other than those indicated in the provisions, or (3) which is entered into when the consumer and the other party are both domiciled or habitually resident in the same Member State or Convention State and which confers jurisdiction on the courts of that State, provided that such an agreement is not contrary to the law of that State.[969] The relevant date for testing domicile is that of the commencement of proceedings, subject to two points: first, if the provisions apply because of Art.15(1)(c) (advertising in the State of the consumer's domicile) then it will also be necessary to determine the consumer's domicile at the time of the conclusion of the contract; secondly, if there is a jurisdiction agreement involved it may be necessary to consider the party's domicile at the date of the conclusion of the contract. In practice, therefore, standard form consumer contracts will only be effective to confer exclusive jurisdiction on the English court if both the consumer and the supplier are domiciled, or deemed to be domiciled, in England.

These provisions apply as between the constituent parts of the United **11–366** Kingdom[970] but their application is without prejudice to the jurisdiction of the court under Rule 3(h)(ii) of Sch.4 in proceedings to enforce possessory or security rights in movable property. Thus a supplier may claim possession in the English court of goods held in England to the order of a consumer domiciled in Scotland.

---

[966] *cf.* Case 25/79 *Sanicentral v Collin* [1979] E.C.R. 3423.

[967] To this effect, see *Re Jurisdiction in a Consumer Contract* [2002] I.L.Pr. 157 (Koblenz Regional Court of Appeal, 2000).

[968] Brussels I Regulation, Art.15(2), and SI 2001/3929, Sch.1, para.11(2); Lugano Convention, Art.15(2) and 1982 Act, s.44A(2).

[969] Brussels I Regulation, Art.17; Lugano Convention, Art.17; 1982 Act, Sch.4, Rule 9.

[970] See *Waverley Asset Management Ltd v Saha*, 1989 S.L.T. (Sh Ct) 87 (provisions do not apply to sale of unit trusts).

Illustrations

11–367   1. A & Co, an English company, sells an expensive piece of household equipment to X, an individual domiciled in France. Delivery is in England, and the price is payable in England by instalments. When X defaults A & Co commences proceedings in England. The court has no jurisdiction.

2. A, an individual domiciled in England, buys a washing machine from X & Co, a French company, while he is on a visit to France. The price is payable in France by instalments. A alleges that the machine is faulty and commences proceedings in England for the return of the instalments already paid. The court has jurisdiction.

3. The facts are as in Illustration 2, except that the contract provides for the exclusive jurisdiction of the French courts. The court has jurisdiction, because the clause is ineffective.

4. A, an individual domiciled in France, buys a washing machine on instalment credit terms from X & Co, a French company. The contract provides for the exclusive jurisdiction of the French courts. A moves to England and becomes domiciled there. When the machine proves to be faulty. A commences proceedings in England against X & Co. The court has no jurisdiction.

11R–368   **(15) In matters relating to individual contracts of employment**[971]

> **(1) the court has jurisdiction in proceedings against an employer**
>> **(i) if the employer is domiciled (or deemed to be domiciled) in England;**[972]
>> **(ii) if England is the place where the employee habitually carries out his work or England was the last place where he did so;**[973]
>> **(iii) where the employee does not or did not habitually carry out his work in any one country, if England was the place where the business which engaged the employee is or was situated.**[974]
>
> **(2) An employee may only be sued in England if he is domiciled there.**[975]
>
> **(3) These provisions are without prejudice to the power of either party to bring a counterclaim.**[976]
>
> **(4) Jurisdiction agreements are, in principle, effective only if they are entered into after the dispute has arisen, or if they allow the employer to be sued in a State which would not otherwise have jurisdiction.**[977]

---

[971] For the distinction between a contract of service and a contract for services (a case involving a management consultancy) see *WPP Holdings Italy SRL v Benatti* [2007] EWCA Civ 263, [2007] 1 W.L.R. 2316. See also Rule 238, below. The contract need not be in one document or made at one time: *Samengo-Turner v J&H Marsh & McLennan (Services) Ltd* [2007] EWCA Civ 723, [2008] I.C.R. 18. This clause does not apply to collective agreements between employers and workers' representatives: Jenard-Möller, p.73. For the purposes of this clause, work carried out on installations on or above the continental shelf of a State are to be regarded as work carried out in that State: Case C–37/00 *Weber v Universal Ogden Services Ltd* [2002] E.C.R. I–2013, [2002] Q.B. 1189. For claims against employees see *Swithenbank Foods Ltd v Bowers* [2002] 2 All E.R. (Comm.) 974.

[972] Brussels I Regulation, Art.19(1); Lugano Convention, Art.19(1); 1982 Act, Sch.4, Rule 10(2)(a).

[973] Art.19(2)(a); 1982 Act, Sch.4, Rule 10(2)(b).

[974] Art.19(2)(b); 1982 Act, Sch.4, Rule 10(2)(c).

[975] Art.20(1); 1982 Act, Sch.4, Rule 10(3).

[976] Art.20(2); 1982 Act, Sch.4, Rule 10(4).

[977] Art.21; 1982 Act, Sch.4, Rule 10(5).

COMMENT

In all countries certain aspects of labour or employment law claims are **11–369**
regulated by public law, but in *Sanicentral v Collin*[978] the European Court
confirmed that employment law came within the field of application of the
Brussels Convention, and that litigation arising out of contracts of employment was subject to the Convention. It has already been seen that in *Ivenel v
Schwab*[979] the European Court held that, where claims were based on different
obligations arising under a contract of employment, the obligation to be taken
into account for the purposes of the application of Art.5(1) of the Brussels
Convention was the obligation which characterised the contract, which was
normally the obligation to carry out the work.

The Brussels Convention and the original Lugano Convention. Special **11–370**
provisions relating to contracts of employment were introduced into Art.5(1)
of the Lugano Convention, and then into Art.5(1) of the Brussels Convention
by the 1989 Accession Convention. These provisions, in slightly different
terms, defined the place of performance of the obligation for the purposes of
matters relating to individual contracts of employment. Each of them confirmed the decision in *Ivenel v Schwab* by providing that in individual
contracts of employment the place of performance of the obligation was that
where the employee habitually carried out his work. If the employee did not
carry out his work in any one country, the original Lugano Convention
provided that "this place shall be the place of business through which he was
engaged"; whereas the Brussels Convention, as amended, provided that in
such a case "the employer may also be sued in the courts for the place where
the business which engaged the employee was or is now situated."[980] In
Rutten v Cross Medical Ltd[981] it was held that where an employee carried out
his work in several Brussels Convention States, the place where he habitually
carried out his work was the place where he had established the effective
centre of his working activities. The European Court emphasised that the
purpose of these provisions was to afford protection to the employee, as the
weaker party to the contract; that protection was best assured if disputes
relating to a contract of employment fell within the jurisdiction of the courts
of the place where the employee discharged his obligations towards his
employer; that was the place where it was least expensive for the employee to

---

[978] Case 25/79 [1979] E.C.R. 3423; Jenard, p.24.

[979] Case 133/81 [1982] E.C.R. 1891. See also Case 266/85 *Shenavai v Kreischer* [1987] E.C.R.
239, 255–256, for the special characteristics of employment contracts.

[980] In relation to the unamended version of Art.5(1), the European Court had held that where
a French employee of a Belgian company worked in a number of non-Convention States, Art.5(1)
was not applicable (Case C–32/88 *Six Constructions Ltd v Humbert* [1989] E.C.R. 341), but that
where the employee carried out his activities in more than one Convention State, the place where
the obligation characterising the contract had been or had to be performed was the place where
or from which the employee mainly performed his obligations *vis-à-vis* his employer (Case
C–125/92 *Mulox IBC Ltd v Geels* [1993] E.C.R. I–4075). See also Case C–37/00 *Weber v
Universal Ogden Services Ltd* [2002] E.C.R. I–2013, [2002] Q.B. 1189 (court should take account
of whole of duration of relationship to determine the place where the employee has worked the
longest, unless the claim is more closely connected with a different place of work, which would,
in that case, be the relevant place for the purposes of Art.5(1)).

[981] Case C–383/95 [1997] E.C.R. I–57, [1997] I.C.R. 715.

engage in court proceedings. By contrast with the amended Brussels Convention, the original Lugano Convention did not expressly limit the jurisdiction based on the place where the employee was engaged to actions by the employee against the employer. As a further protection for employees the jurisdiction agreement provisions of Art.17 of each of the Conventions (now Art.23) were amended to restrict the power of employers to rely on jurisdiction agreements in contracts of employment. Schedule 4 to the 1982 Act was also amended to bring it into line with the revised Brussels Convention in relation to contracts of employment.

11–371   **Brussels I Regulation and revised Lugano Convention.** The new s.5 of Chapter II of the Brussels I Regulation (and of the revised Lugano Convention) contains similar, but not identical, provisions.[982] The object is to protect the weaker party.[983] The basic rule is that an employer may be sued (1) in the Member State or Convention State where he is domiciled; and (2) in another Member State or Convention State (a) in which the employee habitually carries out his work or which was the last place where he did so; or (b) in which the business which engaged the employee is or was situated, if the employee does not, or did not, habitually carry out his work in any one country.[984] Save in one respect, it does not affect jurisdiction over defendants domiciled outside the Member States and the Convention States, nor the rule that a defendant domiciled in another Member State or Convention State which has a branch in England may be sued in England if the dispute arises out of its operations.[985] If the employer is domiciled outside the Member or Convention States and has a branch in a Member or Convention State, the employer is deemed to be domiciled in that State in disputes arising out of the operations of the branch.[986] An employer domiciled in a Member or Convention State may be sued in the courts of the State in which he is domiciled; and may also be sued in another Member or Convention State (a) in the courts for the place where the employee habitually carries out his work or in the courts for the last place where he did so, or (b) if the employee does not or did not habitually carry out his work in any one country, in the courts for the place where the business which engaged the employee is or was situated.[987] The expression "place of business" is to be understood in a broad sense, and includes a branch or agency.[988] In *Pugliese v Finmeccanica SpA*[989] the plaintiff in German proceedings had been employed by an Italian company in the defence industry. Her employment was suspended when she went to work for a German company in the same industry in which the Italian company was a shareholder. The Italian company agreed to keep up her insurance contributions and retain her seniority and also to pay her travel costs and a rental allowance. The Italian company was taken over by the defendants, who

---

[982] 1982 Act, Sch.4, Rule 10 is modelled on the Brussels I Regulation.
[983] Recital (13); Case C–462/06 *GlaxoSmithkline v Rouard* [2008] E.C.R. I–3965, [5].
[984] Art.19.
[985] Art.18(1).
[986] Art.18(2). See also 1982 Act, s.44(2)(c); SI 2001/3929, Sch.1, para.11(2)(c).
[987] Art.19.
[988] de Almeida Cruz-Desantes Real-Jenard, p.45.
[989] Case C–437/00 [2003] E.C.R. I–4867.

terminated the suspension of employment and required her to return to work in Italy. She sued in Germany for reimbursement of rental costs and travel expenses. It was held that Germany could be regarded as the place where the employee habitually carried out her work for the purposes of the claim against the Italian company if it had an interest in the performance of the services to the German company.

The employer may bring proceedings only in the courts of the Member or Convention State in which the employee is domiciled.[990] But counterclaims may be brought in the court in which an original claim has been brought in accordance with s.5 of Chapter II.[991] In *GlaxoSmithKline v Rouard*[992] the European Court ruled that the employment provisions of s.5 were exhaustive. The employee had two joint employers in the well-known pharmaceuticals group, one French and the other English. He sued the French company in the French court and sought to join the English company under the additional defendant rule in Art.6(1).[993] The Court accepted that the sound administration of justice would be enhanced if there were jurisdiction over the English company. But because allowing the employee to rely on Art.6(1) would also mean that in other cases the employer might be able to rely on it as against an employee, the Court took the view that a literal interpretation of Art.18(1)[994] was justified and led to the conclusion that Art. 6(1) was not available.   **11–372**

The Rome I Regulation on the Law Applicable to Contractual Obligations provides that, to the extent that the law applicable to an individual employment contract has not been chosen by the parties, the contract is to be governed by the law of the country in which, or failing that, from which the employee habitually carries out his work in performance of the contract, even if he is temporarily employed in another country; or if the applicable law cannot be so determined, the contract will be governed by the law of the country where the place of business through which the employee was engaged is situated.[995] The effect of the employment contract provisions in the Brussels I Regulation and the Lugano Convention is that in many cases the State which has jurisdiction will also be the State whose law governs.[996]   **11–373**

Jurisdiction agreements. The Regulation and the Convention contain provisions limiting the right of employers to rely on jurisidction agreements.[997] Each provides that such an agreement is effective only if entered into after the dispute has arisen, or which allows the employee to bring proceedings in courts other than those specified in s.5 (Arts 18 to 21) of Chapter II of the Regulation or the Convention.   **11–374**

---

[990] Art.20(1).

[991] Art.20(2).

[992] Case C–462/06 [2008] E.C.R. I–3965 (criticised Harris (2008) 124 L.Q.R. 523; Briggs and Rees, para.2.105, "too crass to be credible").

[993] Paras 11–313 *et seq.*, above.

[994] " . . . jurisdiction shall be determined by this Section, without prejudice to Article 4 and point 5 of Article 5."

[995] Art.8, on which see Rule 238.

[996] *cf.* Jenard-Möller, p.73.

[997] Art. 21.

ILLUSTRATIONS

11–375   1. A, who is domiciled in France, is employed by X & Co, a German company, to work for a year in England. After six months A is wrongfully dismissed. A sues X & Co in England. The court has jurisdiction.[998]

2. A, who is domiciled in England, is employed through a recruitment office in London of X & Co, a French company, to work as a sales agent in Germany, France and Italy. A is wrongfully dismissed, and sues X & Co in England. The court has jurisdiction.[999]

11R–376   **(16) The court has jurisdiction in proceedings which have as their object rights *in rem* in, or tenancies of, immovable property, if the property is situated in England.**[1000]

COMMENT

11–377   This clause is based on Art.22(1) of the Brussels I Regulation and the Lugano Convention, which provides that in proceedings which have as their object rights *in rem* in, or tenancies of, immovable property, the courts of the Member State or Convention State in which the property is situated have exclusive[1001] jurisdiction. The basic principle is found in the law of most countries.[1002] The *lex situs* is paramount both from the point of view of convenience of evidence and because its law will apply.[1003] Where the court has jurisdiction under this clause, it will also be able to deal with contractual claims connected with rights *in rem*, particularly debts secured on immovable property.[1004] This clause is dealt with more fully in connection with the Rule relating to jurisdiction over immovable property.[1005]

11R–378   **(17) The court has jurisdiction in proceedings which have as their object the validity of the constitution, the nullity or the dissolution of companies or other legal persons or associations of natural or legal persons, or the validity of the decisions of their organs, if the company, legal person or association has its seat in England.**[1006]

COMMENT

11–379   This clause is based on Art.22(2) of the Brussels I Regulation and of the Lugano Convention, which applies also in intra-United Kingdom cases in a

---

[998] Brussels I Regulation, Art.19(2)(a).

[999] *ibid.* Art.19(2)(b).

[1000] Brussels I Regulation, Art.22(1); Lugano Convention Art.22(1); 1982 Act, Sch.4, Rule 11(a).

[1001] The courts of the domicile of the defendant also have jurisdiction if the proceedings have as their object tenancies of immovable property included for temporary private use for a maximum period of six consecutive months.

[1002] See Rules 130 and 131.

[1003] Case 73/77 *Sanders v Van Der Putte* [1977] E.C.R. 2383, 2390–2391. See White [1983] Conv. 180, 306.

[1004] See clause (12), and para.23–017.

[1005] Rule 131.

[1006] Brussels I Regulation, Art.22(2); Lugano Convention, Art.22(2); 1982 Act. Sch.4, Rules 4 and 11(b). These provisions do not apply to the winding-up of insolvent companies: Brussels I Regulation, Art.1(2)(b); Lugano Convention, Art.1(2)(b).

modified form. Article 22(2) provides that in proceedings which have as their object the validity of the constitution, the nullity or the dissolution of companies or other legal persons or associations of natural or legal persons, or the validity of the decisions of their organs, the courts of the Member or Convention State in which the company, legal person or association has its seat shall have exclusive jurisdiction. The English language version of Art.22(2) refers to proceedings which have "as their object" the validity etc of the constitution or the validity of the decisions of their organs. Other language versions speak of exclusive jurisdiction "in the matter of" the validity etc, or where proceedings have their "subject-matter" validity etc. The European Court has held that the divergence between the language versions is to be resolved by interpreting that provision as covering only proceedings whose "principal subject-matter" comprises the validity of the constitution, the nullity or the dissolution of the company, legal person or association or the validity of the decisions of its organs.[1007] The purpose is to avoid conflicting judgments being given as regards the existence of a company or with regard to the validity of the decisions of its organs, by providing that all proceedings should take place in the courts of the State in which the company has its seat, where information about the company will have been notified and made public.[1008] The expression "associations of natural or legal persons" includes English partnerships.[1009] Article 22(2) of the Brussels I Regulation (and the revised Lugano Convention) makes it clear (as the Brussels and original Lugano Conventions did not) that this clause is concerned with the validity of decisions of organs. It had been held in England, by reference to the French and German texts, that the phrase "the validity of" governed not only the constitution of the company, but also the decisions of its organs.[1010]

11–380 Article 22(2) has been the subject of two important rulings by the European Court. In *Hassett v South Eastern Health Board*[1011] two Irish doctors claimed in proceedings in Ireland an indemnity and/or a contribution from the Medical Defence Union (a professional association, established as a company incorporated under English law and having its registered office in the United Kingdom) in respect of any sum which, in the context of medical negligence actions brought against the health boards for which those doctors worked, either doctor might be ordered to pay by way of indemnity to the health board concerned. The Board of Management of the MDU, relying on the company's Articles of Association, under which any decision concerning a request for an indemnity comes within its absolute discretion, had refused to grant their requests. The MDU, having been joined in the Irish proceedings as a third party, maintained that, since the claims against it concerned in essence the validity of decisions adopted by its Board of Management, they fell within the scope of Art.22(2), with the result that jurisdiction lay solely with the English

---

[1007] Case C–144/10 *Berliner Verkehrsbetriebe (BVG) v JP Morgan Chase Bank NA* [2011] 1 W.L.R. 2087, [26], [44].

[1008] Jenard, p.35; Case C–372/07 *Hassett v South Eastern Health Board* [2008] E.C.R. I–7403, [20]–[21]; Case C–144/10 *Berliner Verkehrsbetriebe (BVG) v JP Morgan Chase Bank NA* [2011] 1 W.L.R. 2087, [36].

[1009] *Phillips v Symes* [2002] 1 W.L.R. 853; Schlosser, para.162.

[1010] See *Newtherapeutics Ltd v Katz* [1991] Ch. 226. See also *Grupo Torras SA v Sheikh Fahad Mohammed Al-Sabah* [1996] 1 Lloyd's Rep. 7 (CA).

[1011] Case C–372/07 [2008] E.C.R. I–7403.

courts and not with the courts of Ireland. The MDU's argument was rejected. The European Court ruled that it was not sufficient that a legal action involved some link with a decision adopted by an organ of a company, since if all disputes involving a decision by an organ of a company had to be treated as coming within the scope of Art.22(2), that would in reality mean that all legal actions brought against a company—whether in matters relating to a contract, or to tort or delict, or any other matter—would almost always come within the jurisdiction of the courts of the Member State in which the company had its seat. The effect of the decision is that Art.22(2) covers only disputes in which a party is challenging the validity of a decision of an organ of a company under the company law applicable or under the provisions governing the functioning of its organs, as laid down in its constitution (in that case, its Articles of Association).

11–381   But not every case in which such a challenge is made falls within Art.22(2). In various cases in England and elsewhere public authorities had entered into financial derivative contracts (credit default swaps) with banks containing choices of English law and English jurisdiction. The authorities resisted claims against them on the ground (inter alia) that the contracts were void because they were *ultra vires* their boards, and argued that Art.22(2) applied so that the court with exclusive jurisdiction to determine the dispute was the court in the State of incorporation. In one of the cases[1012] the bank commenced proceedings in England for a declaration that the transaction was valid and for substantial payments under the swap. The public authority subsequently commenced proceedings against the bank in Germany claiming (inter alia) a declaration that the swap was invalid. It was common ground that the issue of whether any decisions of the management and supervisory boards were *ultra vires* was a matter of German law. In England the public authority applied for an order that the English court had no jurisdiction on the ground that the proceedings had, for the purposes of Art.22(2), "as their object the validity of the decisions" of the organs of a legal person whose seat was in Germany. That application was dismissed by the Court of Appeal on the basis that the English proceedings were not principally concerned with the validity of decisions of the public authority's organs. But on an application for permission to appeal the UK Supreme Court made a reference to the European Court. Meanwhile the German court had also made a reference raising similar, but not identical, questions. The effect of the Court's answers was that the German court did not have exclusive jurisdiction, and consequently the reference by the UK Supreme Court was withdrawn.

11–382   The Court held in *Berliner Verkehrsbetriebe (BVG) v JPMorgan Chase Bank NA*[1013] that Art.22(2) applies only to proceedings whose "principal subject-matter" comprises the validity of the constitution, the nullity or the dissolution of the company, legal person or association or the validity of the

---

[1012] *JP Morgan Chase Bank NA v Berliner Verkehrsbetriebe (BVG) Anstalt des Offentlichen Rechts* [2010] EWCA Civ 390, [2010] I.L.Pr. 529. See also *Depfa Bank Plc v Provincia di Pisa* [2010] EWHC 1148 (Comm.), [2010] I.L.Pr. 903; *UBS AG v Kommunale Wasserwerke Leipzig GmbH* [2010] EWHC 2566 (Comm.), [2010] 2 C.L.C. 499.
[1013] Case C–144/10 [2011] 1 W.L.R. 2087.

decisions of its organs. In a dispute of a contractual nature, questions relating to the contract's validity, interpretation or enforceability were at the heart of the dispute and formed its subject-matter, but any question concerning the validity of the decision to conclude the contract, taken previously by the organs of one of the companies' party to it, must be considered ancillary.[1014]

These decisions are in line with previous English authority. In *New-*   **11–383**
therapeutics Ltd v Katz[1015] an English company sued two of its directors, one of whom was domiciled in the United States, and the other of whom was domiciled in France, claiming that they had acted in breach of duty, and without board authority, in signing contracts which reduced amounts payable to a French company for which the English company was performing pharmaceutical trials. Knox J. held that the English court had exclusive jurisdiction in relation to the claim that the directors had acted without the authority of the board; but not in relation to the claim that the directors were in breach of duty because they had committed the company to a transaction which was so detrimental to the interests of the company that no reasonable board could properly have assented to it. The Court of Appeal, in *Grupo Torras SA v Sheikh Fahad Mohammed Al-Sabah*,[1016] agreed with Knox J. on the first aspect, but left open the question whether he was right on the second aspect.[1017] In the *Grupo Torras* case the allegations against the directors were of a fraudulent conspiracy to misappropriate a Spanish company's funds. It was held that Art.16(2) did not apply so as to deprive the English court of jurisdiction: the subject matter of the action was the fraud which it was alleged that the defendants had practised on the company. In *Speed Investments Ltd v Formula One Holdings Ltd (No.2)*[1018] a shareholders' agreement between an English company and two Jersey companies set out terms for the appointment of directors of the English company. The claimant, a Jersey company, claimed that the appointment of two Swiss directors was invalid. It was held that, although the main area of dispute was the effect of the shareholders' agreement, the real subject matter of the dispute was the composition of the board

---

[1014] The Court distinguished Case C–4/03 *Gesellschaft für Antriebstechnik mbH & Co KG (GAT) v Lamellen und Kupplungsbau Beteiligungs KG (LuK)* [2006] ECR I–6509, para.11–391 below. In that decision the Court held that what is now Art. 22(4) applies to any proceedings in which the validity of a patent is put in issue, be it by way of an action or a plea in objection, thereby conferring exclusive jurisdiction on the courts of the State in which the patent was registered. The basis of the distinction was that the validity of the patent concerned is an essential basis in any infringement action, and it is in the interests of the sound administration of justice that exclusive jurisdiction to adjudicate upon any dispute in which the patent's validity is contested is accorded to the courts of the Member State in which deposit or registration of the patent has been applied for or has taken place, they being best placed to adjudicate upon the dispute.

[1015] [1991] Ch. 226; stated, below, Illustration 2.

[1016] [1996] 1 Lloyd's Rep. 7 (CA). See also *Papanicolaou v Thielen* [1998] 2 I.R. 42; *Grupo Torras SA v Al-Sabah* [1999] C.L.C. 1473, 1532; reversed in part on other grounds [2001] C.L.C. 221 (CA).

[1017] It is suggested that Knox J. was right on this point.

[1018] [2004] EWCA Civ 1512, [2005] 1 W.L.R. 1936, distinguishing *Ashurst v Pollard* [2001] Ch. 595 (CA), a case on Brussels Convention, Art.16(1). See also *Shahar v Tsitsekkos* [2004] EWHC 2659 (Ch.).

of the English company: although the issue was not strictly the validity of the constitution of the English company or any actual decisions of its board, determining its composition was essential for the validity of future decisions. Accordingly, since the subject matter of the dispute was, at least prospectively, the validity of its decisions, the proceedings were within Art.22(2), and the English court had exclusive jurisdiction.

11–384　　In order to determine the seat of a company for the purposes of this clause the court seised is to apply its rules of private international law.[1019] In the United Kingdom this is effected by the Civil Jurisdiction and Judgments Order 2001,[1020] and s.43 of the 1982 Act, which provide for the purposes of this clause that a corporation (or company) or association has its seat in the United Kingdom if, and only if, (a) it was incorporated or formed under the law of a part of the United Kingdom or (b) its central management and control is exercised in the United Kingdom.[1021] Thus a company incorporated under the Companies Act 2006 with its registered office in England, but with its central management and control in France, will be regarded in the United Kingdom as having its seat exclusively in England;[1022] a company incorporated in the Netherlands with its central management and control in England will be regarded as having its seat in England, and also in the Netherlands if by Netherlands law its seat is in the Netherlands.[1023]

11–385　　Under the Regulation and the Convention jurisdiction is vested *exclusively* in the courts of the Member State or Convention State of the seat of the entity concerned, but the combined effect of Rules 4 and 11(b) of Sch.4 is that although the English court will always have jurisdiction where the seat of the entity is in England, the jurisdiction will be non-exclusive as regards domiciliaries of Scotland and Northern Ireland where the proceedings have as their object a decision of an organ of the entity concerned.

Illustrations

11–386　　1. Z Ltd is a Netherlands company with its place of central management and control in England and most of its assets in England. X, Y and Z are directors and each of them is domiciled in the Netherlands. At a board meeting they resolve to transfer the assets of the company to Bermuda. A Ltd, which owns the share capital of Z Ltd, brings proceedings seeking a declaration that the board resolution is void and outside the powers of X, Y and Z. The court has jurisdiction.

2. A & Co, an English company, has a contract with a French company for the development of medicines for the treatment of AIDS. X, who is domiciled in France, is a director of A & Co.

[1019] Regulation and Convention, Art.22(2).

[1020] SI 2001/3929, Sch.1, para.10.

[1021] s.43(2); SI 2001/3929, Sch.1, para.10(2). Provision is made for allocation within the United Kingdom of jurisdiction in s.43(3)–(5). Association means an unincorporated body of persons, and corporation means a body corporate, and includes a partnership subsisting under Scots law: s.50. s.43(6)–(7) and SI 2001/3929, Sch.1, para.10(3)–(4) contain the rules for determining whether the corporation or association has its seat in another Member State or Convention State, in which case the English court will have no jurisdiction unless (as is possible) the corporation or association also has its seat in England.

[1022] SI 2001/3929, Sch.1, para.10(2), (4).

[1023] *ibid.*, para.10(2), (3). *cf. The Deichland* [1990] 1 Q.B. 361 (CA).

Shortly before he resigns as a director he executes (together with Y, another director, domiciled in the United States) a document varying the terms of A & Co's contract with the French company in a manner which A & Co claims is substantially to its disadvantage. A & Co claims (*inter alia*) that X and Y were in breach of duty by executing the variation documents in the absence of a board meeting and that it was beyond their powers as directors to sign them. The court has jurisdiction over X, but the writ is set aside since the action is bound to fail because A & Co had waived all its claims against X.[1024]

3. A & Co, a Spanish company, and its English subsidiary, B & Co, sue X, Y and Z, former directors of A & Co, claiming damages for breaches of directors' duties relating to a number of transactions entered into by them on behalf of A & Co. The English court has jurisdiction because the subject matter of the action is not the decision of the organs of A & Co, but the misappropriation of A & Co's money.[1025]

4. A & Co, a United States bank, sues a German public authority in England to enforce swap agreements which contain an English jurisdiction clause. The German public authority defends on the ground that the agreements are ultra vires its constitution and that the English court has no jurisdiction because the proceedings have as their object the validity of the decisions of its organs. The English court has jurisdiction because the principal subject matter of the proceedings is not the validity of the decisions of its organs. That question arises only as a collateral question.[1026]

(18) The court has jurisdiction in proceedings which have as their object the validity of entries in public registers, if the register is kept in England.[1027]   11R–387

COMMENT

Article 22(3) of the Regulation (and of the Convention) deals with proceedings which have as their object the validity of entries in public[1028] registers, and assigns exclusive jurisdiction to the courts of the Member State or the Convention State in which the register is kept.[1029] It corresponds to the provisions which appear in the internal laws of the original parties to the Brussels Convention and covers entries in land registers, land charges registers and commercial registers. In England it is not likely to be of practical significance except in connection with problems relating to registered land, which would in any event come within the provisions of clause (15).[1030]   11–388

(19) The court has jurisdiction in proceedings concerned with the registration or validity of patents, trade marks, designs or other similar rights required to be deposited or registered, if the deposit or registration has   11R–389

[1024] *Newtherapeutics Ltd v Katz* [1991] Ch. 226.

[1025] *Grupo Torras SA v Sheikh Fahad Mohammed Al-Sabah* [1996] 1 Lloyd's Rep. 7 (CA).

[1026] Case C–144/10 *Berliner Verkehrsbetriebe (BVG) v JP Morgan Chase Bank NA* [2011] 1 W.L.R. 2087.

[1027] Brussels I Regulation, Art.22(3); Lugano Convention, Art.22(3); 1982 Act, Sch.4, Rule 11(c).

[1028] See *Re Fagin's Bookshop Plc* [1992] B.C.L.C. 118 (register of members of company held to be public register: *sed quaere*).

[1029] Or in the particular part of the UK in which the register is kept: Sch.4, Rule 11(c).

[1030] *cf. Re Hayward* [1997] Ch. 45; *Ashurst v Pollard* [2001] Ch. 595 (CA).

been applied for or has taken place (or is deemed to have taken place) in England.[1031]

Comment

11–390   Clause (19) assigns exclusive jurisdiction in proceedings concerned with registration or validity of patents, trademarks, designs or other similar rights required to be deposited or registered, to the courts of the Member State or Convention State in which the deposit or registration has been applied for, has taken place or is under the terms of an international convention deemed to have taken place. Article 22(4) of the Regulation (and the Convention) provides that, without prejudice to the jurisdiction of the European Patent Office under the Convention of 1973 on the Grant of European Patents, the courts of each Member (or Convention State) shall have exclusive jurisdiction, regardless of domicile, in proceedings concerned with the registration or validity of any European patent granted for that State. The Lugano Convention adds "irrespective of whether the issue is raised by way of an action or as a defence."[1032]

11–391   The term "proceedings concerned with the registration or validity of patents" must be interpreted by reference to a uniform concept, and not by national law.[1033] It includes proceedings connected with the place of the grant of the right, such as proceedings[1034] relating to the validity, existence or lapse of the right, or an alleged right of priority by reason of an earlier registration.[1035] It does not apply to disputes relating to ownership.[1036] Nor does clause (18) apply in principle to proceedings for infringement.[1037] In *Gesellschaft für Antriebstechnik mbH & Co KG (GAT) v Lamellen und Kupplungsbau Beteiligungs KG (LuK)*[1038] the European Court ruled that Art.16(4)

[1031] Brussels I Regulation, Art.22(4); Lugano Convention, Art.22(4). The details of international intellectual property law, including European law, are outside the scope of this work. See Fawcett and Torremans, *Intellectual Property and Private International Law* (2nd ed. 2011), paras 1.28 *et seq.*

[1032] These words were added to take account of the decision of the European Court in Case C–4/03 *Gesellschaft für Antriebstechnik mbH & Co KG (GAT) v Lamellen und Kupplungsbau Beteiligungs KG (LuK)* [2006] E.C.R. I–6509, below. See Pocar Report, para.102.

[1033] Case 288/82 *Duijnstee v Goderbauer* [1983] E.C.R. 3663.

[1034] See, e.g. *Napp Laboratories v Pfizer Inc* [1993] F.S.R. 150 (revocation petition).

[1035] *ibid.*

[1036] *ibid.*

[1037] Case C–4/03 *Gesellschaft für Antriebstechnik mbH & Co KG (GAT) v Lamellen und Kupplungsbau Beteiligungs KG (LuK)* [2006] E.C.R. I–6509, [16]. *cf. Mölnlycke AB v Procter & Gamble Ltd* [1992] 1 W.L.R. 1112 (CA).

[1038] Case C–4/03 [2006] E.C.R. I–6509. In *Coin Controls Ltd v Suzo-International (UK) Ltd* [1999] Ch. 33, in which Laddie J. had held that an action for infringement could be within this clause if the infringement proceedings were "principally concerned" in a broad sense with validity, i.e. validity was a major feature of the litigation. This view was approved in *Fort Dodge Animal Health Ltd v Akzo Nobel NV* [1998] F.S.R. 222 (CA), but because it did not regard the question as free from doubt, the Court of Appeal made a reference to the European Court, which was withdrawn when the case was settled. See also *Prudential Assurance Co Ltd v Prudential Insurance Co of America* [2003] 1 W.L.R. 2295 (CA); *Knorr-Bremse Systems for Commercial Vehicles Ltd v Haldex Brake Products GmbH* [2008] EWHC 156 (Pat.), [2008] 2 All E.R. (Comm.) 448.

of the Brussels Convention (the equivalent of Art.22(2)) applied to all proceedings relating to the registration or validity of a patent, irrespective of
whether the issue is raised by way of an action or a defence. Although the
exclusive jurisdiction did not apply as such to infringement proceedings, in
practice the issue of a patent's validity was frequently raised as what the Court
described as a plea in objection in an infringement action, with the defendant
seeking to have the claimant retroactively denied the right on which the
claimant relied and thus have the action brought against him dismissed. The
issue could also be raised in support of a declaratory action seeking to
establish that there had been no infringement. The exclusive jurisdiction in
proceedings concerned with the registration or validity of patents conferred
upon the courts of the State in which the deposit or registration had been
applied for or made was justified by the fact that those courts were best placed
to adjudicate upon cases in which the dispute itself concerns the validity of the
patent or the existence of the deposit or registration. The exclusive jurisdiction
was also justified by the fact that the issue of patents necessitates the involvement of the national administrative authorities. The Court noted that in several
States which were parties to the Brussels Convention a decision to annul a
patent had *erga omnes* effect, and in order to avoid the risk of contradictory
decisions, it was necessary to limit the jurisdiction of the courts of a State
other than that in which the patent was issued to rule indirectly on the validity
of a foreign patent to only those cases in which, under the applicable national
law, the effects of the decision to be given were limited to the parties to the
proceedings. Such a limitation would, however, lead to distortions, thereby
undermining the equality and uniformity of rights and obligations arising for
the States and the persons concerned.

ILLUSTRATIONS

1. A petitions the High Court for revocation of a patent granted to X, the respondent, who is **11–392**
domiciled in Italy. The court has jurisdiction.

2. A is the owner of a trade mark registered in the United Kingdom. X, domiciled in the
Republic of Ireland (where the mark is not registered), uses the same mark in connection with his
business in Dublin. A commences proceedings in England for an account of the profits X has
made as a result of the passing-off and trade mark infringement. The court has no
jurisdiction.[1039]

3. A & Co, an English company, brings proceedings against X & Co, an English company, Y
& Co, a Dutch company, and Z & Co, a German company, for infringement of United Kingdom,
German and Spanish patents for a coin-dispensing machine. The defendants challenge the validity
of the patents. The court has no jurisdiction over the claims for infringement of the German and
Spanish patents because the proceedings became principally concerned with the validity of the
patents.[1040]

(20) The court has jurisdiction in proceedings concerned with the   **11R–393**
enforcement of judgments, if the judgment has been or is to be enforced
in England.[1041]

[1039] This Illustration was approved in *LA Gear Inc v Gerald Whelan & Sons Inc Ltd* [1991]
F.S.R. 670.

[1040] *Coin Controls Ltd v Suzo International (UK) Ltd* [1999] Ch. 33.

[1041] Brussels I Regulation, Art.22(5); Lugano Convention, Art.22(5); 1982 Act, Sch.4, Rule
11(d).

COMMENT

11–394   This clause is based on Art.22(5) of the Brussels I Regulation and of the Lugano Convention, and is included here only for the sake of completeness.[1042]

11R–395   **(21) The court has jurisdiction over a dispute which the parties have agreed to submit to the English court if the agreement is in writing, or evidenced in writing, or, in a form which accords with practices which the parties have established between themselves, or in international trade or commerce, in a form which accords with a usage of which the parties are or ought to have been aware and which in such trade or commerce is widely known to, and regularly observed by, parties to contracts of that type involved in the particular trade or commerce concerned.[1043]**

COMMENT

11–396   This clause is based on Art.23 of the Brussels I Regulation and of the Lugano Convention. Similar provisions (with some modifications) apply in the intra-United Kingdom cases under Rule 12 of Sch.4 to the 1982 Act. These Articles are dealt with in connection with Rule 39.[1044]

11R–397   **(22) The court has jurisdiction over a defendant who submits to its jurisdiction by appearance, except (a) where appearance was entered to contest the jurisdiction, or (b) the courts of another Member State or Convention State have exclusive jurisdiction pursuant to the terms of the Brussels I Regulation or the Lugano Convention.[1045]**

COMMENT

11–398   Article 24 of the Brussels I Regulation and of the Lugano Convention provides that, in addition to jurisdiction derived from other provisions, a court of a Member State or Convention State before whom a defendant enters an

---

[1042] See Collins, p.83, for a fuller discussion. See also Case 220/84 *AS-Autoteile Service GmbH v Malhé* [1985] E.C.R. 2267, where it was held that a court in which enforcement was sought could not take jurisdiction (by dealing with an alleged set-off against the judgment debt) over a dispute which fell within the jurisdiction of another Brussels Convention State. In Case C–261/90 *Reichert v Dresdner Bank (No.2)* [1992] E.C.R. 1–2149 it was held that what is now Art.22(5) relates to measures taken to ensure the practical implementation of judgments, and does not apply to an action to set aside a transaction in fraud of creditors. Consequently, Art.22(5) does apply to a receivership order or a freezing injunction: *Masri v Consolidated Contractors International Company SAL (No.2)* [2008] EWCA Civ 303, [2009] Q.B. 450, at [123] *et seq.* (also discussing whether Art.22(5) has "reflexive effect" in relation to non-Member States) *cf. The Filiatra Legacy* [1994] 1 Lloyd's Rep. 513n. In *Kuwait Oil Tanker Co SAK v Qabazard* [2003] UKHL 31, [2004] 1 A.C. 260 it was held that the effect of what is now Art.22(5) of the Lugano Convention was that the English court had no jurisdiction to make a garnishee order in respect of a debt situate in Switzerland.

[1043] Brussels I Regulation, Art.23; Lugano Convention, Art.23; 1982 Act, Sch.4, Rule 12.

[1044] On jurisdiction provisions in trust instruments, see above, clause (6).

[1045] Brussels I Regulation, Art.24; Lugano Convention, Art.24; 1982 Act, Sch.4, Rule 13.

appearance shall have jurisdiction. It applies only to cases within the scope of the Regulation or Convention, but if the case is within their scope appearance will confer jurisdiction even though without appearance jurisdiction could not have been taken. Clause (21) does not apply in a case which is covered by the exclusive jurisdiction provisions of Art.22.[1046] But it does apply where the parties have agreed to submit their disputes to the jurisdiction of the courts of a Member State or Convention State under Art.23. In such a case appearance by the defendant (including a defendant to a counterclaim[1047]) in the courts of another State will confer jurisdiction on the courts of the latter.[1048]

In *Elefanten Schuh GmbH v Jacqmain*[1049] the European Court drew atten-   **11–399**
tion to the fact that the French text of the Brussels Convention (unlike the English, German, Italian and Dutch texts) did not have any requirement that *solely* jurisdiction must be contested[1050] and held that a defendant did not submit by pleading to the merits as well as contesting the jurisdiction, but "only if the plaintiff and the court seised of the matter are able to ascertain from the time of the defendant's first defence that it is intended to contest the jurisdiction."[1051] If the challenge to jurisdiction was not a preliminary matter[1052] then, to avoid pleading to the merits being regarded as a submission, the challenge must not occur after the making of submissions which under national procedural law are considered to be the first defence put to the court. Article 24 of the Brussels I Regulation and of the revised Lugano Convention omit the word "solely".

In England, since 1979 (when conditional appearances were abolished) a   **11–400**
defendant who wishes to contest the jurisdiction of the English court can do so without risk of submitting. Under the Civil Procedure Rules a defendant who wishes to dispute the jurisdiction of the court, or argue that the court should not exercise its jurisdiction, must file an acknowledgment of service and apply for an order declaring that it has no jurisdiction, or should not exercise any jurisdiction which it may have. A defendant who follows this course is not treated as having submitted to the jurisdiction, and does not thereby lose any right he may have to dispute the jurisdiction of the court. If the challenge to the jurisdiction or its exercise fails, the acknowledgment of

---

[1046] It does however apply, it seems, in insurance, consumer and employment contract cases.

[1047] Case 48/84 *Spitzley v Sommer Exploitation SA* [1985] E.C.R. 787.

[1048] Case 150/80 *Elefanten Schuh GmbH v Jacqmain* [1981] E.C.R. 1671; Case 48/84 *Spitzley v Sommer Exploitation SA* [1985] E.C.R. 787.

[1049] Case 150/80 [1981] E.C.R. 1671; Case 27/81 *Rohr v Ossberger* [1981] E.C.R. 2431; Case 25/81 *CHW v GJH* [1982] E.C.R. 1189; Case 201/82 *Gerling v Treasury Administration* [1983] E.C.R. 2503; Case C–111/09 *Ceská Podnikatelska Pojistovna as, Vienna Insurance Group v Bilas* [2010] Lloyd's I.R. 734; *Kurz v Stella Musical GmbH* [1992] Ch. 196. See also *Harada Ltd v Turner* [2003] EWCA Civ 1695 (CA); *The Xing Su Hai* [1995] 2 Lloyd's Rep. 15; *Caltex Trading Pte Ltd v Metro Trading International Inc* [1999] 2 Lloyd's Rep. 724; *Maple Leaf Marro Volatility Master Fund v Rouvray* [2009] EWHC 257 (Comm.), [2009] 1 Lloyd's Rep. 475; *Clydesdale Bank Plc v Ions*, 1993 S.C.L.R. 964; *Campbell International Trading House Ltd v Van Aart* [1992] 2 I.R. 305; *Devrajan v District Judge Ballagh* [1993] 3 I.R. 377. *cf. The Atlantic Emperor (No.2)* [1992] 1 Lloyd's Rep. 624 (CA); *Toepfer International GmbH v Molino Boschi Srl* [1996] 1 Lloyd's Rep. 510 (cases on submission to jurisdiction of foreign court).

[1050] "*si la compuration a pour objet de contester la competence.*"

[1051] At p.1685.

[1052] As it is under English law.

service ceases to have effect. The defendant may then file a further acknowledgment of service, in which case he is treated as having accepted that the court has jurisdiction to try the claim.[1053]

ILLUSTRATIONS

11–401   1. A, who is domiciled in England, enters into a contract with X, who is domiciled in France. The contract is to be performed wholly in France. In proceedings by A against X, X instructs English solicitors to accept service and serve a defence. The court has jurisdiction by virtue of X's submission.

2. A, who is domiciled in England, commences proceedings against X, who is domiciled in France, in connection with a tort committed in France, and seeks a freezing injunction restraining X from removing his English assets. X files evidence resisting the injunction, in which (*inter alia*) he denies that he has committed any tort and indicates that he does not accept that the English court has jurisdiction. X's conduct does not amount to a submission.[1054]

11R–402   **(23) The court has jurisdiction to grant interim relief where proceedings have been or are to be commenced in another Member State or Convention State or in another part of the United Kingdom.**[1055]

COMMENT

11–403   Article 31 of the Brussels I Regulation and of the Lugano Convention provides that application may be made to the courts of a Member State or Convention State for such provisional measures, including protective measures, as may be available under the law of that State, even if, the courts of another Member State or Convention State have jurisdiction as to the substance of the matter. The Regulation and the Convention apply to provisional measures.[1056] Section 25 of the 1982 Act gives the English court the powers necessary to give effect to these provisions. In this case, by contrast with the other bases of jurisdiction under the Regulation and the Convention, permission is required to serve process claiming interim relief under s.25 abroad.[1057] The jurisdiction to grant interim measures is discussed in Chapter 8.

11R–404   **RULE 36—The court has no jurisdiction when the courts of another Member State or Convention State or of Scotland or Northern Ireland have exclusive jurisdiction in the cases mentioned in this Rule.**

COMMENT

11–405   The cases in this Rule are based on Art.22 of the Regulation and the Convention, and their counterparts in Sch.4 for the purposes of intra-United Kingdom

---

[1053] CPR, rr. 11(1), (2), (3), (5), (7). An application for security for costs up to and including the hearing of the application to challenge jurisdiction is not an appearance for the purposes of clause (22): *Hewden Stuart Heavy Cranes Ltd v Leo Gottwald*, unreported, 1992 (CA).

[1054] cf. *Obikoga v Silvernorth Ltd*, *The Times*, July 6, 1983, distinguished in *Esal Ltd v Pujara* [1989] 2 Lloyd's Rep. 479 (CA), para.11–130, above.

[1055] 1982 Act, s.25; Brussels I Regulation, Art.31; Lugano Convention, Art.31; 1982 Act, Sch.4, Rule 16.

[1056] Case 143/78 *De Cavel v De Cavel. (No.1)* [1979] E.C.R. 1055; Case 120/79 *De Cavel v De Cavel (No.2)* [1980] E.C.R. 731.

[1057] CPR, r.6.36 and PD6B, para.3.1(5).

jurisdiction. These provisions have been discussed in connection with the jurisdiction of the English court, i.e. where England is the place of exclusive jurisdiction for these purposes. Detailed comment is not therefore necessary in connection with this Rule. It is important to note that the exclusive jurisdiction provisions are not subject to submission or contrary agreement and apply irrespective of the domicile of the defendant.

(1) The court has no jurisdiction in proceedings which have as their object rights *in rem* in, or tenancies of, immovable property situated in another Member State or Convention State or in Scotland or Northern Ireland, unless in the case of tenancies concluded for temporary private use for a maximum period of six consecutive months the defendant is domiciled in England provided that the tenant is a natural person and the landlord and tenant are both domiciled in England.[1058]   **11R–406**

COMMENT

This case is dealt with in connection with the Rule relating to jurisdiction over foreign land.[1059]   **11–407**

(2) The court has no jurisdiction in proceedings which have as their object the validity of the constitution, the nullity or the dissolution of companies or other legal persons or associations of natural or legal persons or the validity of the decisions of their organs if the company in question (or other legal person or association) (a) does not have its seat in England and (b) has its seat in another Member State or Convention State or (except as regards proceedings relating to the validity of the decisions of organs) in Scotland or Northern Ireland.[1060]   **11R–408**

COMMENT

This clause has been discussed above.[1061] Three points should be noted. First, the version in Sch.4 differs from that in the Regulation and the Convention. Under the Sch.4 scheme the head of jurisdiction relating to decisions or organs of companies is not exclusive.[1062] Secondly, Sch.4 does not apply to winding up.[1063] Thirdly, it is possible for more than one court to have exclusive jurisdiction.[1064] This arises because Art.22 leaves it to the law of each Member State or Convention State to determine the seat of a company in   **11–409**

[1058] Brussels I Regulation, Art.22(1); Lugano Convention, Art.22(1); *cf.* 1982 Act, Sch.4, Rule 11(a).

[1059] Rule 131.

[1060] Brussels I Regulation, Art.22(2); Lugano Convention, Art.22(2), 1982 Act, Sch.4, Rules 4 and 11(b).

[1061] Rule 35(17), above.

[1062] See Sch.4, Rule 4.

[1063] Sch.5, para.1.

[1064] Where actions come within the exclusive jurisdiction of more than one court, any court other than the court first seised must decline jurisdiction in favour of the court first seised: Art.23; below, Rule 38(4).

accordance with its rules of private international law. The United Kingdom rules use the alternative tests of place of incorporation and place of central management and control. Thus, as has been seen,[1065] by United Kingdom law a Dutch company with its place of central management and control in England may have its seat in both England and the Netherlands. This problem will not arise frequently in intra-United Kingdom cases because the effect of s.43(5) of the 1982 Act is that companies incorporated under the Companies Act 2006 and its predecessors will be regarded as having their seat in the part of Great Britain (England or Scotland) in which they have their registered office even if their place of central management and control is in another part.

11R–410   **(3) The court has no jurisdiction in proceedings which have as their object the validity of entries in public registers if the register is kept in another Member State or Convention State or in Scotland or Northern Ireland.**[1066]

11R–411   **(4) The court has no jurisdiction in proceedings concerned with the registration or validity of patents, trade marks, designs, or other similar rights required to be deposited or registered, if the deposit or registration in question has been applied for, has taken place or is under the terms of an international convention deemed to have taken place in another Member State or Convention State.**[1067]

COMMENT

11–412   This provision has been discussed above.[1068]

11R–413   **(5) The court has no jurisdiction in proceedings concerned with the enforcement of judgments if the judgment has been or is to be enforced in another Member State or Convention State.**[1069]

COMMENT

11–414   This clause is based on Art.22(5) of the Brussels I Regulation and of the Lugano Convention. It does not prevent the English court from making a disclosure order relating to foreign assets situate in a Member State or Convention State where the judgment is to be enforced[1070]: the reason is that the use of CPR Pt 71 (which allows examination of a judgment debtor) in order to discover the *existence* of foreign assets, does not confer jurisdiction on the English court in relation to enforcement proceedings in any other

---

[1065] See above, para.11–384.

[1066] Brussels I Regulation, Art.22(3); Lugano Convention, Art.22(3); 1982 Act, Sch.4, Rule 11(c).

[1067] Brussels I Regulation, Art.22(4); Lugano Convention, Art.22(4).

[1068] See above, paras 11–390 *et seq.*

[1069] Brussels I Regulation, Art.22(5); Lugano Convention, Art.22(5); 1982 Act, Sch.4, Rule 11(d). See Case 220/84 *AS-Autoteile Service GmbH v Malhé* [1985] E.C.R. 2267; *The Filiatra Legacy* [1994] 1 Lloyd's Rep. 513n.

[1070] Collins, p.83.

country in which those assets may be situate.[1071] Nor does it prevent the grant of a freezing injunction relating to assets situate in another Member State or Convention State where the claimant intends to enforce a judgment.[1072] But it does prevent the making of a garnishee order in respect of a debt situate in a Member State or in a Convention State.[1073]

RULE 37—Unless the defendant submits to the jurisdiction, the court has no jurisdiction to determine a dispute which has arisen or may arise in connection with a particular legal relationship in the following circumstances: 11R–415

     (1) if one or more of the parties is domiciled in a Member State or Convention State and the parties have agreed in accordance with Article 23 of the Brussels I Regulation or the Lugano Convention that the courts of another Member State or Convention State are to have jurisdiction to settle any such dispute;

     (2) if none of the parties is domiciled in a Member State or a Convention State and the parties have agreed in accordance with Article 23 of the Brussels I Regulation or the Lugano Convention that the courts of another Member State or Convention State are to have jurisdiction to settle any such dispute and the courts chosen have not declined jurisdiction;

     (3) if proceedings are brought against a settlor, trustee or beneficiary, which involve relations between them or their rights or obligations under a trust, and the trust instrument confers jurisdiction on the courts of another Member State or Convention State.[1074]

COMMENT

This rule is based on Art.23 of the Brussels I Regulation and of the Lugano Convention, which is discussed below in connection with Rule 39.[1075] They apply in two situations where the defendant is not domiciled in a Member State or a Convention State. First, they apply where either of the parties is domiciled in a Member State or a Convention State, so that where the claimant is so domiciled the chosen court will have jurisdiction irrespective of the domicile of the defendant. Secondly, if neither of the parties is domiciled in a Member State or a Convention State, no court other than the chosen court has jurisdiction unless the chosen court declines jurisdiction. These provisions are subject to the principle of submission, so that a defendant may waive the jurisdiction agreement.[1076]   11–416

[1071] *Interpool Ltd v Galani* [1988] Q.B. 738 (CA).

[1072] *Babanaft International Co SA v Bassatne* [1990] Ch. 13, 34–35 (CA) (where it was said that in such a case the English court would have jurisdiction under what is now Art.31 of the Regulation to grant the injunction).

[1073] *Kuwait Oil Tanker Co SAK v Qabazard* [2003] UKHL 31, [2004] 1 A.C. 300.

[1074] Brussels I Regulation, Art.23; Lugano Convention, Art.23. The corresponding provisions of Sch.4 do not provide for *exclusive* jurisdiction. Their effect is that a court which would have jurisdiction but for the jurisdiction clause will have a discretion not to give the clause effect: see Rule 41(3), below.

[1075] para.12R–098.

[1076] Case 150/80 *Elefanten Schuh GmbH v Jacqmain* [1981] E.C.R. 1671.

Illustrations

11–417   1. A, who is domiciled in New York, enters into a contract with X, who is domiciled in England. The contract provides that the courts of France are to have exclusive jurisdiction. When a dispute arises A commences proceedings against X in England. The court has no jurisdiction.

2. The facts are as in Illustration 1, except that X instructs a solicitor to give notice of intention to defend and put in a defence on his behalf. The court has jurisdiction.

CHAPTER 12

FORUM NON CONVENIENS, LIS ALIBI PENDENS, ANTI-SUIT INJUNCTIONS AND JURISDICTION AGREEMENTS

1. FORUM NON CONVENIENS, ANTI-SUIT INJUNCTIONS AND LIS ALIBI PENDENS

RULE 38—(1) English courts have jurisdiction, whenever it is necessary to prevent injustice, to stay or strike out proceedings in England.[1]   12R–001

(2) Subject to the provisions of Council Regulation (EC) 44/2001 and the Lugano Convention on jurisdiction and the enforcement of judgments in civil and commercial matters ("the Brussels I Regulation" and "the Lugano Convention" respectively),[2] an English court has power to order

---

[1] The leading authorities are *Spiliada Maritime Corp v Cansulex Ltd* [1987] A.C. 460; *Connelly v RTZ Corp Plc* [1998] A.C. 854; and *Lubbe v Cape Plc* [2000] 1 W.L.R. 1545 (HL). See generally Briggs and Rees, *Civil Jurisdiction and Judgments* (5th ed. 2009); Fawcett (ed.), *Declining Jurisdiction in Private International Law* (1995); Bell, *Forum Shopping and Venue in Transnational Litigation* (2003); Kruger, *Civil Jurisdiction Rules of the EU and Their Impact on Third States* (2008); Von Mehren, *Adjudicatory Authority in Private International Law: A Comparative Study* (2007); McLachlan, *Lis Pendens in International Litigation* (2009); Schlosser (2000) 284 *Recueil des Cours*, especially pp.53–87; Von Mehren (2002) 295 *Recueil des Cours*, especially Chs 5, 6; Briggs (1983) 3 Leg. Studies 74, [1984] L.M.C.L.Q. 227, [1985] L.M.C.L.Q. 360; Schuz (1986) 35 I.C.L.Q. 374; Robertson (1987) 103 L.Q.R. 398; Slater (1988) 104 L.Q.R. 544; Juenger (1994) 16 Sydney L. Rev. 5, 28; Opeskin, *ibid.* 14; Kennett [1995] C.L.J. 552; Chalas, *L'exercice discrétionnaire de la compétence juridictionelle en droit internationale privé* (2000); Briggs, *Revue de droit suisse*, Vol.124 (2005) II 231. In 2003 the Institut de droit international adopted a Resolution on the principles for determining when the use of the doctrine of *forum non conveniens* and anti-suit injunctions is appropriate: for the Report to the Institut see Collins and Droz (2004) 71 *Ann. de l'Institut de droit international*, Vol.II, p.81.

[2] This Chapter seeks to state the law, insofar as this is derived from European materials, in accordance with the Brussels I Regulation and the revised (2007) Lugano Convention. It does not in general deal with the corresponding provisions of the Brussels Convention, as from time to time amended, or with the original (1988) Lugano Convention, which are effectively superseded (see para.11–013, above). It should be noted, however, that many of the authorities referred to in this Chapter were decided on the basis of these earlier instruments, and that where the material wording differs from that used in the instruments currently in force, particular care must be taken: this is particularly true in connection with what is now Art.23 of the Regulation on jurisdiction agreements.

a stay of proceedings on the basis that England is an inappropriate forum (*forum non conveniens*) if:

　(a)　the defendant shows there to be another court with competent jurisdiction which is clearly or distinctly more appropriate than England for the trial of the action, and

　(b)　it is not unjust that the claimant be deprived of the right to trial in England.[3]

(3) In considering whether to assume jurisdiction in any of the cases mentioned in Rule 34 (service out of the jurisdiction with the permission of the court) the court will generally require the claimant to show England to be the most appropriate forum for the trial of the claim.[4]

(4) Where the jurisdiction of the English court is derived from the Brussels I Regulation or the Lugano Convention (that is, from Rules 35 to 37, or 39(3)):

　(a)　if proceedings involving the same cause of action and between the same parties have been brought in England and in another Member State or Convention State, and the courts of that other State were seised first, the court must stay the English proceedings until such time as the jurisdiction of the court first seised is established; and where the jurisdiction of the court first seised is established, the court must decline jurisdiction;[5]

　(b)　if related actions are brought in England and in another Member State or Convention State, and the courts of that other State were seised first, the English court may decline jurisdiction if the proceedings in the court first seised are pending at first instance, that court has jurisdiction also over the English action, and its law permits the consolidation of related actions; or it may stay its proceedings;[6]

　(c)　if actions fall within the exclusive jurisdiction of the English court and of the courts of another Member State or Convention State, any court other than the court first seised shall decline jurisdiction in favour of that court.[7]

(5) Subject to the provisions of the Brussels I Regulation and the Lugano Convention, an English court may restrain a party over whom it has personal jurisdiction from the institution or continuance of proceed-

---

[3] *Spiliada Maritime Corp v Cansulex Ltd* [1987] A.C. 460, 475–478; *Connelly v RTZ Corp Plc* [1998] A.C. 854, 871–873; *Lubbe v Cape Plc* [2000] 1 W.L.R. 1545, 1553–1555 (HL).

[4] *Amin Rasheed Shipping Corp v Kuwait Insurance Co* [1984] A.C. 50, 72; *Spiliada Maritime Corp v Cansulex Ltd* [1987] A.C. 460, 478–482; *AK Investment CJSC v Kyrgyz Mobil Tel Ltd* [2011] UKPC 7, [2011] 4 All E.R. 1027. As the principles are closely related to those governing stays on the ground of *forum non conveniens*, see also the cases referred to under clauses (1) and (2) of this Rule.

[5] Brussels I Regulation, Art.27; Lugano Convention, Art.27. The European Commission has published a Proposal for the revision of the Brussels I Regulation: see COM(2009) 174 and COM(2009) 175. The main outlines of the proposal are set out in paras 11–017 *et seq.* above. For the meaning of "Member State" and "Convention State", see above, paras 11–005 and 11–017.

[6] Brussels I Regulation, Art.28; Lugano Convention, Art.28.

[7] Brussels I Regulation, Art.29; Lugano Convention, Art.29.

ings in a foreign court,[8] or the enforcement of foreign judgments,[9] where it is necessary in the interests of justice for it to do so.

COMMENT

Introduction. The principal subject matter examined under this Rule may be described as the circumstances in which an English court has a discretion to exercise,[10] or to not exercise, or to adjudicate upon a foreign court's exercise[11] of, jurisdiction. It does not specifically consider the cases where the answers to these questions will derive from a contractual agreement which designates the country or countries whose courts are to have jurisdiction to determine disputes: jurisdiction agreements conferring jurisdiction on English and foreign courts are examined under Rule 39. As a discretionary evaluation provides the principal mechanism by which the common law regulates and seeks to prevent clashes of jurisdiction which arise when proceedings take place in more than one court, it is necessary to examine it in conjunction with the very different mechanism by which the Brussels I Regulation and the Lugano Convention resolve this problem.

12–002

Though the common law material treated under this Rule covers a wide range of legal situations, the thread which links them is that, because of the wide jurisdiction exercisable by the English court, recourse to the concept of the "natural forum" for the litigation represents a principled and even-handed means of deciding whether or where jurisdiction should be exercised.[12] If the English court has been seised with jurisdiction by the service of process on the defendant, in a case involving a foreign element, a defendant who wishes to have the dispute resolved in another forum may apply for a stay of proceedings: the success of the application will depend in large measure upon the defendant showing that a foreign court is more appropriate than England for the trial of the proceedings. If the claimant requires the permission of the court to serve process on the defendant out of the jurisdiction in order to institute the proceedings, the question whether permission will be given, or will be set aside upon application by the defendant,[13] will depend in part upon the claimant showing England to be the most appropriate forum for the trial of the action. If proceedings are being brought in a foreign court but the defendant in that action applies to the English court for an injunction to restrain his

12–003

---

[8] The leading authorities are *British Airways Board v Laker Airways Ltd* [1985] A.C. 58; *Soc Nat Ind Aérospatiale v Lee Kui Jak* [1987] A.C. 871 (PC) and *Airbus Industrie GIE v Patel* [1999] 1 A.C. 119. The cases from which the principles were derived, and those which illustrate and apply these principles, are referred to in the Comment to clause (5) of this Rule. On injunctions granted in aid of a jurisdiction agreement, see clause (4) of Rule 39, below, para.12–159. On injunctions to restrain proceedings brought in breach of an arbitration agreement, see below, paras 12–166, and 16–089.

[9] *Ellerman Lines Ltd v Read* [1928] 2 K.B. 144 (CA); *ED&F Man (Sugar) Ltd v Haryanto (No.2)* [1991] 1 Lloyd's Rep. 429 (CA).

[10] By staying proceedings instituted by right, under clause (2); by denying (or setting aside) permission to serve process out of the jurisdiction, under clause (3).

[11] By injunction to restrain the proceedings, under clause (5).

[12] *cf. Airbus Industrie GIE v Patel* [1999] 1 A.C. 119, 131–133 (a case on injunctions to restrain foreign proceedings).

[13] See CPR, Pt 11.

opponent[14] from continuation of that action, it will normally be a necessary, though not sufficient, condition for the grant of an injunction that England be the most appropriate forum for the trial.

12–004   Matters stand on a different footing when the jurisdiction of the English court, or the jurisdiction of a foreign court, has been contractually agreed between the parties. The fundamental presumption is that an English court will uphold the agreement of the parties, and will generally grant such relief as will secure the performance of the jurisdictional agreement contained in the contract. The various issues which arise in this context are examined under Rule 39.

12–005   *Spiliada Maritime Corp v Cansulex Ltd,*[15] the leading case in which the common law rules were defined, referred to the English court as being "clearly or distinctly more appropriate"[16] than the competing foreign forum, or to another forum "which prima facie is clearly more appropriate for the trial of the action".[17] The test as laid down directed attention to whether a particular court was clearly more appropriate than another, and not to a search for "the natural forum" as such. But it must be acknowledged that the terminology of "the natural forum" has become irresistible, and that this convenient shorthand is now routinely used by the courts in comparing the relative strengths of connection between a court and a dispute. In the Comment to this Rule, therefore, the term "natural forum" is used as shorthand for the court identified by reference to the criteria laid down in *Spiliada Maritime Corp v Cansulex Ltd.*[18]

12–006   **Clause (1) of the Rule.** English courts have an inherent jurisdiction, reinforced by statute,[19] to stay or strike out proceedings, whenever it is

---

[14] The court must have jurisdiction *in personam* over the respondent to the application: see below, para.12–079.

[15] [1987] A.C. 460.

[16] At p.477.

[17] At p.478.

[18] [1987] A.C. 460.

[19] *Texan Management Ltd v Pacific Electric Wire & Cable Co Ltd* [2009] UKPC 46, [49]–[57]; Senior Courts Act 1981, s.49(3); Civil Jurisdiction and Judgments Act 1982, s.49. An application for a stay under clause (2) of this Rule, that is, on *forum non conveniens* grounds, is normally required to be made under CPR, Pt 11, and therefore applied for within the time limit imposed by that provision which governs applications contesting the jurisdiction of the court as well as for a stay of proceedings. However, there will be cases in which the basis for a stay of proceedings only emerges after the period fixed by CPR, Pt 11 has passed: in these, the application for a stay may be made either under the inherent jurisdiction, or by applying for an order under CPR, r.3.1(2)(f) to permit, on case management grounds, a late application under CPR, Pt 11: *Texan Management* at [77]. The period specified by CPR, Pt 11 is 14 days (but in the Commercial Court, 28 days (CPR, r.58.7)) after the acknowledgment of service; until recently it was defined indirectly, by reference to the period allowed for filing a defence. If a stay is granted, the proceedings are still pending, so that what is now called "an additional claim for contribution" (previously a contribution claim) may still be made against a defendant in relation to whom there is a stay (*Lister & Co Ltd v EG Thomson (Shipping) Ltd (No.2)* [1987] 1 W.L.R. 1614) or a defendant may be added (*Rofa Sport Management AG v DHL International (UK) Ltd* [1989] 1 W.L.R. 902). For a suggestion that the court has power to dismiss, rather than stay, proceedings, under clause (2) of the Rule, see *Haji-Ioannou v Frangos* [1999] 2 Lloyd's Rep. 337, 348 (CA); no reported case appears to have done this.

necessary to prevent injustice. The court also has an inherent power to order a stay to await the outcome of proceedings in a foreign court or arbitration in the exercise of case management.[20] The jurisdiction may be exercised in cases which have nothing to do with the conflict of laws, or with the fact that a cause of action or ground of defence arises in a foreign country. But the cases in which a party to proceedings applies to have them stayed under this jurisdiction are very often, in some way or another, connected with transactions taking place in a foreign country or with litigation being conducted abroad. In such cases, according to English notions of the conflict of laws, an English court and a court in some foreign country may both be recognised as having jurisdiction to entertain proceedings, and the English court has a discretion to determine in which forum the dispute will be resolved, by using its power to grant or refuse a stay of the proceedings by the claimant[21] in the English court, or by exercising or refusing to exercise its power to authorise the claimant to serve process out of the jurisdiction, or by using its power to enjoin a party subject to its jurisdiction, but who is or is threatening to become a plaintiff in the foreign court, from commencing or continuing proceedings in that court.[22] This topic has become of the highest importance as a result of a variety of factors including the greater ease of communication and travel; the tendency of courts in many countries to extend their jurisdiction over events and persons outside their territory; and a greater awareness of foreign laws and procedures, which in turn may lead to "forum-shopping".[23]

In certain cases jurisdiction may be conferred on an English court by an international convention dealing with particular matters. The question whether an English court may stay proceedings on the ground of *forum non conveniens* in such a case depends upon whether the operation of the common law

---

[20] *Reichhold Norway ASA v Goldman Sachs International* [2000] 1 W.L.R. 173 (CA); *Klöckner Holdings GmbH v Klöckner Beteiligungs GmbH* [2005] EWHC 1453 (Comm.) (stay of part of proceedings); *Mazur Media Ltd v Mazur Media GmbH* [2004] EWHC 1566 (Ch.), [2004] 1 W.L.R. 2966; *Prifti v Musini SA de Seguros y Reaseguros* [2005] EWHC 832 (Comm.), [2006] Lloyd's Rep. I.R. 221; *ET Plus SA v Welter* [2005] EWHC 2115 (Comm.), [2006] 1 Lloyd's Rep. 215; *Curtis v Lockheed Martin UK Holdings Ltd* [2008] EWHC 260 (Comm.), [2008] 1 C.L.C. 219; *Equitas Ltd v Allstate Insurance Co* [2008] EWHC 1671 (Comm.), [2009] Lloyd's Rep. I.R. 227; *Cooper Tire & Rubber Co Europe Ltd v Bayer Public Co Ltd* [2010] EWCA Civ 864, [2010] Bus. L.R. 1697; *Pacific International Sports Clubs Ltd v Surkis* [2010] EWCA Civ 753; *cf. Abassi v Abassi* [2006] EWCA Civ 355, [2006] 1 F.C.R. 648. For case management powers being used to forestall the need for an anti-suit injunction, see *Al-Bassam v Al-Bassam* [2004] EWCA Civ 857, [2004] W.T.L.R. 757.

[21] In exceptional cases, such as where the proceedings have been instituted to prevent time from running for limitation purposes, the stay may be granted on the application of the claimant: *Att-Gen v Arthur Andersen & Co* [1989] E.C.C. 224 (CA). See also *Ledra Fisheries Ltd v Turner* [2003] EWHC 1049 (Ch.); *Klockner Holdings GmbH v Klockner Beteiligungs GmbH* [2005] EWHC 1453 (Comm.) at [21]; *cf. The Sylt* [1991] 1 Lloyd's Rep. 240; *cf. Centro Internationale Handelsbank AG v Morgan Grenfell* [1997] C.L.C. 870. Contrast *Australian Commercial Research and Development Ltd v ANZ McCaughan Merchant Bank Ltd* [1989] 3 All E.R. 65, affirmed February 23, 1990 (CA, unreported); *Doe v Armour Pharmaceutical Co Inc* [1994] 3 I.R. 78 (Sup Ct). See Smart [1990] L.M.C.L.Q. 326.

[22] *British Airways Board v Laker Airways Ltd* [1985] A.C. 58, 80; see Comment to clause (5).

[23] This sentence was quoted with approval in *Amchem Products Inc v Workers' Compensation Board* [1993] 1 S.C.R. 897, 904 (Sup Ct Can).

doctrine is expressly or impliedly permitted by the particular convention.[24] This is true also in relation to the Brussels I Regulation and the Lugano Convention; the question in this context is dealt with in greater detail below.[25]

12–007   ***Forum non conveniens.*** The doctrine of *forum non conveniens*, i.e. that some other forum is more "appropriate"[26] in the sense of more suitable for the ends of justice, was developed by the Scottish courts in the 19th century, and was adopted (with some modifications) in the United States.[27] The Scots rule is that the court may decline to exercise jurisdiction, after giving consideration to the interests of the parties and the requirements of justice, on the ground that the case cannot be suitably tried in the Scottish court nor full justice be done there, but only in another court.[28] In England, *forum conveniens* was always a relevant factor in the exercise of the discretion to grant permission to serve out of the jurisdiction under what is now Rule 6.36 of the Civil Procedure Rules, i.e. Rule 34, but until 1984 the English courts refused to accept that the jurisdiction to stay actions commenced against defendants who were sued in England as of right could be based on *forum non conveniens* grounds.

12–008   Until the decision of the House of Lords in *The Atlantic Star*[29] a defendant who sought a stay of English proceedings had a very heavy burden. In *St Pierre v South American Stores (Gath and Chaves) Ltd*[30] Scott L.J. restated the principles on which the court acted, the effect of which was that a stay would only be granted if the continuance of the action would work an injustice in the sense that it would be "vexatious or oppressive", and if the stay would not cause an injustice to the claimant. In *The Atlantic Star* a majority of the House of Lords held that, although a plaintiff should not lightly be denied the right to sue in an English court, the words "oppressive or vexatious" should,

---

[24] See *Milor Srl v British Airways Plc* [1996] Q.B. 702 (CA); *Deaville v Aeroflot Russian International Airlines* [1997] 2 Lloyd's Rep. 67 (both Warsaw Convention 1929; held excluded); *Sepracor v Hoechst Marion Roussel Ltd* [1999] F.S.R. 746 (European Patent Convention; held excluded); *Royal & Sun Alliance Insurance Plc v MK Digital FZE Ltd* [2005] EWHC 1408 (Comm.), [2005] 2 Lloyd's Rep. 679 (C.M.R. Convention; held excluded); *Hatzl v XL Insurance Co* [2009] EWCA Civ 223, [2010] 1 W.L.R. 470 (CMR Convention: held excluded). As neither the European Patents Convention nor legislation implementing it makes express provision for a stay where there is parallel litigation in national court and European Patent Office, there is no basis for a presumption against parallel proceedings: *Glaxo Group Ltd v Genentech Inc* [2008] EWCA Civ 23, [2008] Bus. L.R. 888.

[25] See below, para.12–013.

[26] *Conveniens* does not mean "convenient": see *The Atlantic Star* [1974] A.C. 436, 475; *GAF Corp v Amchem Products Inc* [1975] 1 Lloyd's Rep. 601, 607; *Spiliada Maritime Corp v Cansulex Ltd* [1987] A.C. 460, 474–475.

[27] *Gulf Oil Corp v Gilbert*, 330 U.S. 501 (1947); *Piper Aircraft v Reyno*, 454 U.S. 235 (1981); Hay, Borchers and Symeonides, pp.551–562.

[28] *Société du Gaz de Paris v SA de Navigation "Les Armateurs Français,"* 1926 S.C. (HL) 13, (1925) 23 Ll.L.R. 209; Anton, pp.361–362.

[29] [1974] A.C. 436. Many cases decided before *The Atlantic Star*, above, would be decided differently today. The more important decisions are *McHenry v Lewis* (1882) 22 Ch.D. 397 (CA); *Peruvian Guano Co v Bockwoldt* (1883) 23 Ch.D. 225; *The Christiansborg* (1885) 10 P.D. 141 (CA); *Logan v Bank of Scotland (No.2)* [1906] 1 K.B. 141; *Jopson v James* (1908) 77 L.J. Ch. 824 (CA); *St Pierre v South American Stores Ltd* [1936] K.B. 382 (CA).

[30] [1936] 1 K.B. 382, 398 (CA).

in future, be interpreted more liberally: in considering whether a stay should be granted, the court should take into account the advantage to the plaintiff and any disadvantage to the defendant. In *MacShannon v Rockware Glass Ltd*[31] a differently constituted House of Lords went considerably further when all, except Lord Keith, were in favour of discontinuing the use of the words "oppressive or vexatious" altogether. In this decision Lord Diplock restated the governing principle as being that, in order to justify a stay, two conditions had to be satisfied, one positive and the other negative: (a) the defendant had to satisfy the court that there was another forum to whose jurisdiction he was amenable in which justice could be done between the parties at substantially less inconvenience or expense, and (b) the stay was not to deprive the plaintiff of a legitimate personal or juridical advantage which would be available to him if he invoked the jurisdiction of the English court.[32]

In *The Atlantic Star* and *MacShannon v Rockware Glass Ltd*[33] the House of Lords declined to adopt the doctrine of *forum non conveniens* as part of English law. In the latter decision, however, it was recognised that the reformulation in these decisions of the principles on which the English court acted was not far removed in practice from the Scottish doctrine of *forum non conveniens*.[34] But by 1984, when *The Abidin Daver*[35] was decided, Lord Diplock was able to say that, as a result of the successive decisions of the House of Lords commencing with *The Atlantic Star*, "judicial chauvinism has been replaced by judicial comity to an extent which I think the time is now right to acknowledge frankly is, in the field of law with which this appeal is concerned, indistinguishable from the Scottish legal doctrine of *forum non conveniens*."[36]   **12–009**

Finally, in *Spiliada Maritime Corp v Cansulex Ltd*[37] the House of Lords decided that Lord Diplock's formulation had given too great a prominence to the "legitimate personal or juridical advantage" to the plaintiff in the continuance of the proceedings: "The basic principle is that a stay will only be granted on the ground of *forum non conveniens* where the court is satisfied that there is some other available forum, having competent jurisdiction, which is the appropriate forum for the trial of the action, i.e. in which the case may be tried more suitably for the interests of all the parties and the ends of justice."[38]   **12–010**

---

[31] [1978] A.C. 795.

[32] [1978] A.C. 795, 812.

[33] Cases decided under the principles established in *The Atlantic Star* and *MacShannon v Rockware Glass Ltd* are now of sharply reduced relevance. But see *Trendtex Trading Corp v Crédit Suisse* [1980] 3 All E.R. 721, 734, affirmed [1982] A.C. 679; *European Asian Bank v Punjab Bank* [1982] 2 Lloyd's Rep. 356 (CA); *The Messiniaki Tolmi* [1984] 1 Lloyd's Rep. 267 (CA); *The Abidin Daver* [1984] A.C. 398; *The Forum Craftsman* [1985] 1 Lloyd's Rep. 291 (CA); *Muduroglu Ltd v TC Ziraat Bankasi* [1986] Q.B. 1225 (CA).

[34] See [1978] A.C. 795, at pp.812 (Lord Diplock), 822 (Lord Fraser) and *Hesperides Hotels Ltd v Aegean Turkish Holidays Ltd* [1979] A.C. 508 at pp.537 (Lord Wilberforce) and 544 (Lord Fraser). For an earlier (if premature) recognition of the same point *cf. Logan v Bank of Scotland (No.2)* [1906] 1 K.B. 141.

[35] [1984] A.C. 398.

[36] At p.411.

[37] [1987] A.C. 460.

[38] At p.476.

12–011   **Development of the principle of** *forum non conveniens* **in other jurisdictions.** It follows from what has been said that the intellectual debt to the Scottish doctrine of *forum non conveniens* is substantial; though it was also in use in the United States for many years before its adoption in England, the role there of *forum non conveniens* is slightly different[39] and the American authorities have not contributed to the development of the English doctrine. The doctrine has, to a greater or lesser extent, been adopted in several common law jurisdictions,[40] most notably in Canada (where it governs the staying of proceedings and plays a significant part in the grant of injunctions against proceedings in foreign courts[41]), New Zealand,[42] Hong Kong,[43] Singapore,[44] and India.[45] In Australia, by contrast, the High Court has reconsidered its earlier and ambivalent view[46] of the doctrine by settling instead for a much more restricted form which continues to invoke the notions of vexation and oppression,[47] According to this, a stay will not be granted unless the local court is a clearly inappropriate forum, which will be the case if continuation of the proceedings in that court would be oppressive in the sense of seriously and unfairly burdensome, prejudicial or damaging, or vexatious in the sense of productive of serious and unjustified trouble and harassment.[48]

12–012   **Abuse of the process.** Most cases involving a foreign element will be cases of competing jurisdictions in which a stay will normally be granted only if the foreign court is the natural or appropriate forum. There will be a residual category of cases in which English proceedings will be stayed even though England is the natural forum. Such cases will no doubt be rare and the onus

---

[39] It was described as a "parallel development" in *Bank of Tokyo Ltd v Karoon* [1987] 1 A.C. 45n, 61 (CA). Its role owes much to the constitutional guarantee of due process under the Fifth and Fourteenth Amendments to the Constitution of the United States: as this was interpreted in an increasingly liberal manner, so allowing a plaintiff a greater freedom in deciding where to sue (*International Shoe Co v Washington*, 326 U.S. 310 (1945)), the principle of *forum non conveniens* developed in response to allow courts to decline to exercise jurisdiction: *cf. Gulf Oil Corp v Gilbert*, 330 U.S. 501 (1947); *Piper Aircraft Co v Reyno*, 454 U.S. 235 (1981).

[40] *Airbus Industrie GIE v Patel* [1999] 1 A.C. 119.

[41] *Amchem Products Inc v British Columbia (Workers' Compensation Board)* [1993] 1 S.C.R. 897, 920–921 (Sup Ct Can). See also Pitel (2011) 7 J.Priv.Int.L. 251 for statutory codification in relation to stays.

[42] *McConnell Dowell Constructors Ltd v Lloyd's Syndicate 396* [1988] 2 N.Z.L.R. 257; *Club Mediterranée NZ v Wendell* [1989] 1 N.Z.L.R. 216 (CA); *Longbeach Holdings Ltd v Bhanabhai & Co Ltd* [1994] 2 N.Z.L.R. 28 (CA).

[43] *The Adhigina Meranti* [1988] 1 Lloyd's Rep 384 (HKCA).

[44] *JIO Minerals FZC v Mineral Enterprises Ltd* [2011] 1 Sing. L.R. 391 (CA).

[45] *cf. Airbus Industrie GIE v Patel*, above, at p.132.

[46] *Oceanic Sun Line Special Special Shipping Co Ltd v Fay* (1988) 165 C.L.R. 197; *Voth v Manildra Flour Mills Pty Ltd* (1991) 171 C.L.R. 538.

[47] *BHP Billiton Ltd v Schulz* (2004) 221 C.L.R. 400, especially at [11] (High Ct).

[48] *Henry v Henry* (1996) 185 C.L.R. 571, 587; *Régie Nationale des Usines Renault SA v Zhang* (2003) 210 C.L.R. 491. Moreover, if a claim which could be brought before an Australian court could not (for reasons of choice of law or otherwise) be "fully and properly entertained" before the foreign court, an Australian court cannot be regarded as a clearly inappropriate forum, even though it could otherwise have been so seen: *Reinsurance Australia Corp Ltd v HIH Casualty and General Insurance Ltd* (2003) 254 A.L.R. 29 (Fed Ct). The law is surveyed and summarised in *Murakami v Wiryadi* [2010] NSWCA 7, (2010) 268 A.L.R. 377.

on the defendant to prove injustice will be a heavy one,[49] but it is clear that an abuse of the process in the traditional sense, that is, resort to litigation for improper motives, such as harassment of the defendant, will justify a stay.[50]

Forum non conveniens and the Brussels I Regulation and the Lugano   12–013
Convention. The Brussels I Regulation and the Lugano Convention set out rules of jurisdiction which define and limit the jurisdiction of courts in Member and Convention States; and so far as concerns the jurisdiction of the English courts, they serve to restrict the width of jurisdiction based on service of process. It was therefore to be expected that the operation of a judicial jurisdictional discretion would play a much smaller part within this legislative system than it does as a component of the jurisdictional scheme of the common law. In addition, as will be seen in connection with the discussion of clause (4) of the Rule below,[51] these European instruments contain specific rules to deal with problem caused by actions pending in different Member and Convention States at the same time.[52] Though these instruments rest on distinct legal bases within European law,[53] and though there are minor differences between them in their wording, a common issue is whether an English court which has been given jurisdiction over the defendant to the claim by Chapter II of the Brussels I Regulation or Title II of the Lugano Convention, as the case may be, may stay its proceedings on the footing that the courts of another country are clearly more appropriate for the resolution of the dispute. Though the European Court has given rulings only in relation to the Brussels Convention, and has left much detail to be filled in, it is inevitable that the interpretation of the Brussels I Regulation and the Lugano Convention will be no different.[54]

Section 49 of the 1982 Act, as amended, provides that nothing in the Act   12–014
is to prevent the court staying its proceedings on the ground of *forum non conveniens* or otherwise "where to do so is not inconsistent with the [Brussels] Convention or, as the case may be, the Lugano Convention". As the Regulation is directly applicable in the United Kingdom, it was considered to be inappropriate for the United Kingdom to make a similar legislative statement in connection with it. But it was never in doubt that an English court would have the same power, or lack of power, to stay proceedings where jurisdiction was conferred under any of the three instruments.

Nor was it in doubt that where the Regulation or the Conventions conferred   12–015
jurisdiction on the courts of the United Kingdom, there was no power to stay

---

[49] *MacShannon v Rockware Glass Ltd* [1978] A.C. 795, 820, 826. Contrast *Spiliada Maritime Corp v Cansulex Ltd* [1987] A.C. 460, 478.

[50] See, e.g. *The Christiansborg* (1885) 10 P.D. 141 (CA); *Egbert v Short* [1907] 2 Ch. 205; *Re Norton's Settlement* [1908] 1 Ch. 471 (CA); *Lough Neagh Exploration Co v Morrice* [1999] N.I. 258.

[51] See below, paras 12–055 *et seq.*

[52] Arts 27–29 of the Brussels I Regulation and of the Lugano Convention (Arts 21 and 22 of the Brussels Convention).

[53] See Dickinson [2005] J.P.I.L. 197. But in Case C–281/02 *Owusu v Jackson* [2005] E.C.R. I–1383, [2005] Q.B. 801, Léger A.-G. concluded at paras [193]–[213] that the difference in constitutional basis as between the Brussels Convention and the Regulation was of no significance in the present context.

[54] See para.11–066, above.

or dismiss proceedings in favour of the courts of another Member or Convention State except in accordance with the express provisions of the Regulation or the Conventions.[55] As these made no reference to an independent principle of *forum non conveniens*, it would be irrelevant and inadmissible to contend that, for example, the courts of Germany were clearly more appropriate than those of England for the trial of the particular claim. Indeed, even though the justification for what is now Art.5(1) of the Regulation has been said to be that it confers special jurisdiction on a court which had a close connection to the facts and matters in dispute, it was held to be inadmissible to ask the court to decline jurisdiction under Art.5(1) where on the facts there was no such connection.[56] Subject to one important exception, a court would have power to decline to hear a case over which it had been asked to exercise, and had, jurisdiction only if the provisions of what are now Arts 27 to 29 applied to it.

12–016   The exception is for cases in which the jurisdiction of the court under the Regulation or the Convention is based on Art.4. Though the wording is not uniform,[57] Art.4 provides, in effect, that the jurisdiction of a court over a defendant who has no domicile in a Member State or Convention State, as the case may be, and who is not otherwise within the jurisdictional provisions of Chapter II of the Regulation or Title II of the Conventions, is a matter for the national law of the court seised. It was therefore the opinion of the Court of Appeal that it was not inconsistent with the Brussels Convention to stay proceedings, brought against a defendant lacking a domiciliary or other connection to the Convention States, in favour of the Greek courts which were clearly more appropriate than England for the trial of the action.[58] The difficulty caused by the fact that an English court remains seised of the proceedings which it stays[59] was answered by the court saying that it was prepared, if that bare fact would prevent the Greek courts from assuming jurisdiction, with the result that the Greek court was not available for the trial of the action, to dismiss the action instead.[60] As a decision that a court with jurisdiction under Art.4 had no power to stay its proceedings would have had

---

[55] *Re Harrods (Buenos Aires) Ltd* [1992] Ch. 72 (CA); Schlosser, pp.97–99; Collins, p.45; Kaye, pp.269, 1244; Mennie, 1989 Jur. Rev. 150. It is possible that a limited or temporary stay may be ordered under the inherent discretion of the court, or under its powers of case management, but not so as to conflict with the rules discussed in this section: *Mazur Media Ltd v Mazur Media GmbH* [2004] EWHC 1566 (Ch.), [2004] 1 W.L.R. 2966.

[56] Case C–288/92 *Custom Made Commercial Ltd v Stawa Metallbau GmbH* [1994] E.C.R. I–2913; *cf.* Case C–364/93 *Marinari v Lloyds Bank Plc* [1995] E.C.R. I–2719, 2738–2739; *Boss Group Ltd v Boss France SA* [1997] 1 W.L.R. 351, 358 (CA).

[57] Art.4 of the Regulation makes it specific, as Art.4 of the Brussels and original Lugano Conventions had not done, that jurisdiction under Art.23 of the Regulation (previously Art.17) prevails over Art.4.

[58] *Haji-Ioannou v Frangos* [1999] 2 Lloyd's Rep. 337 (CA). The conclusion was *obiter*, as the court also found that the defendant was domiciled in a Convention State, and jurisdiction over him was therefore governed by Title II of the Brussels Convention rather than by Art.4. The same conclusion had also been reached in *Sarrio SA v Kuwait Investment Authority* [1997] 1 Lloyd's Rep. 113 (CA), reversed on other grounds [1999] 1 A.C. 32.

[59] See above, para.12–006.

[60] *Haji-Ioannou v Frangos* [1999] 2 Lloyd's Rep. 337, 347–348. Even so, this would make it difficult for the claimant to proceed if, for example, an undertaking given by the defendant were to be broken. See also *The Xin Yang* [1996] 2 Lloyd's Rep. 217; *Internationale Nederlanden Aviation Lease BV v Civil Aviation Authoriity* [1997] 1 Lloyd's Rep. 80.

the unintended effect of widening jurisdiction under Art.4 still further, this was a predictable conclusion. Even so, the conclusion that the court seised with jurisdiction under Art.4 has power to stay in favour of a *forum conveniens* in another Member or Convention State has yet to be endorsed by the European Court.[61]

The most problematic case was that in which the English court had jurisdic-   **12–017** tion under the Regulation or the Conventions otherwise than on the basis of Art.4, but the *forum conveniens* was the court of a non-Member or non-Convention State. Two principles were in plain conflict. On the one hand, the Conventions contained no provision which suggested that their operation was subject to a jurisdictional discretion which was part of the common law but not generally known to civilian systems. The Schlosser Report stated that the United Kingdom had not pressed for the original Brussels Convention to be amended on its accession, which led to the perception that the doctrine remained excluded from the scheme of the Conventions and Regulation.[62] Moreover, the view of some in the original Brussels Convention States,[63] that the principle of *forum non conveniens* was unpredictable and unjust, and a means for a court to unburden itself of a case which it preferred not to be troubled by, all suggested that no room would be found for its application to a case where jurisdiction had been conferred under Chapter II. As against this, there was no reason to suppose that the question whether the Contracting States had, when they negotiated the original Brussels Convention, any proper interest in whether the courts of England or a non-Contracting State adjudicated a claim. The jurisdictional question in such a case did not touch the issue of which court within the Contracting States should entertain the proceedings, and therefore fell outside the obvious ambit of the Convention.[64] Moreover, as the doctrine of *forum non conveniens* was the mechanism[65] by which an English court gave effect to a foreign jurisdiction agreement, or dealt with a foreign *lis alibi pendens*, it was hard to see that the doctrine was liable to be excluded in its entirety from this aspect of the operation of the Convention.

In *Re Harrods (Buenos Aires) Ltd*,[66] the Court of Appeal, disapproving two   **12–018** first instance decisions to the contrary,[67] committed itself to the latter view. Proceedings had been brought by a minority shareholder in an English-registered company against the company, alleging that manner in which the business of the company was being conducted by the majority shareholder was unfairly prejudicial to him. The shareholders were Swiss;[68] and though

---

[61] See *ibid.*, at p.348.

[62] Schlosser, paras 77, 78; Case C–281/02 *Owusu v Jackson* [2005] E.C.R. I–1383, [2005] Q.B. 801, at [37].

[63] For a survey of these views, see Kennett [1995] C.L.J. 552.

[64] *Re Harrods (Buenos Aires) Ltd* [1992] Ch. 72 (CA). See Collins (1990) 106 L.Q.R. 536.

[65] Though the application of the principle to a case in which there is a breach of contract in bringing the proceedings in England is distinct from the cases in which the foreign court is otherwise the *forum conveniens*: see below, para.12–149.

[66] [1992] Ch. 72 (CA).

[67] *S&W Berisford Plc v New Hampshire Insurance Co* [1990] 2 Q.B. 631; *Arkwright Mutual Insurance Co v Bryanston Insurance Co Ltd* [1990] 2 Q.B. 649.

[68] Switzerland was, at the date of the proceedings, not a party to the original Lugano Convention.

the company was registered at Companies House, the entirety of its business was carried on in Argentina. The jurisdiction of the English courts was founded on Art.2 of the Brussels Convention,[69] but the courts of Argentina were clearly and distinctly more appropriate for the trial of the action. The court took the view that it was not inconsistent with that Convention for a stay to be ordered in favour of the Argentine courts. Leave was given to appeal to the House of Lords, which referred a series of questions to the European Court. But the dispute was resolved by agreement and the reference was withdrawn.[70]

12–019   Though subsequent decisions simply applied the law as laid down in *Re Harrods (Buenos Aires) Ltd*,[71] the correctness of the original decision remained controversial;[72] and in a subsequent case the House of Lords indicated that the question of whether *Re Harrods* was correctly decided was still one which the European Court needed to answer.[73] A reference was finally made by the Court of Appeal in *Owusu v Jackson*,[74] and the answer given by the European Court[75] was that the Brussels Convention "precludes a court of a Contracting State from declining the jurisdiction conferred on it by Art.2 of that Convention on the ground that a court of a non-Contracting State would be a more appropriate forum for the trial of the action even if the jurisdiction of no other Contracting State is in issue or the proceedings have no connecting factors to any other Contracting State".

12–020   The fact that the answer of the European Court was expressed in terms of jurisdiction which had been founded on Art.2 is of no real importance: there is no doubt that the same answer would have been given if the English court's jurisdiction had been based on (say) Art.5:[76] indeed, because where the English court has special jurisdiction there are two Member States with potential jurisdiction, it might be said that the justification for the application

---

[69] The question whether it was also founded on what is now Art.22(2) of the Brussels I Regulation was raised before the House of Lords but was not resolved.

[70] The reference was filed as Case C–314/92 *Ladenimor SA v Intercomfinanz SA*.

[71] *The Po* [1991] 2 Lloyd's Rep 206 (CA) was the first, but see also *American Motorists Insurance Co v Cellstar Corp* [2003] EWCA Civ 206, [2003] I.L.Pr. 370; *Ace Insurance SA-NV v Zurich Insurance Co* [2001] EWCA Civ 173, [2001] 1 All E.R. (Comm.) 802; *Anton Durbeck GmbH v Den Norske Bank* [2003] EWCA Civ 147, [2003] Q.B. 1160. The very long list of decisions in which the High Court was bound by *stare decisis* to accept that *Re Harrods (Buenos Aires) Ltd* was correct on this point need not be given here.

[72] *Lubbe v Cape Plc* [2000] 1 W.L.R. 1545, at 1561–1562.

[73] *Lubbe v Cape Plc* [2000] 1 W.L.R. 1545, at 1561–1562.

[74] [2002] EWCA Civ 877, [2002] I.L.Pr. 45. The Court of Appeal also made a reference raising the same issue (except that the English court had special jurisdiction rather than general jurisdiction) in *American Motorists Insurance Co v Cellstar Corp* [2003] EWCA Civ 206, [2003] I.L.Pr. 370. The question also arose in *Ace Insurance SA-NV v Zurich Insurance Co* [2001] EWCA Civ 173, [2001] 1 All E.R. (Comm.) 802, and in *Anton Durbeck GmbH v Den Norske Bank* [2003] EWCA Civ 147, [2003] Q.B. 1160, but as in each case jurisdiction was governed by the original Lugano Convention, there was no opportunity to make a reference to the European Court. In each case the Court of Appeal followed *Re Harrods (Buenos Aires) Ltd*; and further appeals to the House of Lords were later abandoned.

[75] Case C–281/02 [2005] E.C.R. I–1383, [2005] Q.B. 801; and see Peel [2005] L.M.C.L.Q. 363; Briggs, *ibid.* 378; Harris (2005) 54 I.C.L.Q. 933.

[76] *Gómez v Gómez-Monche Vives* [2008] EWHC 259 (Ch.), [2008] 3 W.L.R. 309, reversed on other aspects [2008] EWCA Civ 1065, [2009] Ch. 245 (there was no appeal on this point).

of the rule laid down in *Owusu v Jackson* would be stronger than it was in *Owusu v Jackson* itself. Even though the European Court appears to have proceeded on the footing, plainly wrong, that the doctrine of *forum non conveniens* might routinely deprive a defendant against his will of the comfort of defending in his own courts,[77] the width of the language chosen by the court to express its rejection of the principle of *forum non conveniens* makes it impossible to argue that *Re Harrods (Buenos Aires) Ltd* has not been comprehensively overruled. The argument that the court retains a procedural power to grant a stay, on the footing that the Brussels Convention did not, and that the Regulation does not, seek to harmonise rules of procedure, will be inapplicable as a stay on the ground of *forum non conveniens* will almost always jeopardise the practical effect of the Regulation and the Lugano Convention.[78] An argument that a court has a residual power to order a stay, or to put a party to his election, to prevent injustice or other unconscionable conduct, will be difficult to maintain, especially in the light of *Turner v Grovit*,[79] though it probably cannot be said that it has been completely eliminated.[80]

Even so, the reference in *Owusu v Jackson* contained a second question, but **12–021** which the European Court declined to answer.[81] Where the dispute before the court concerns a question of title to land in a non-Member State or a non-Convention State, or concerns the validity of companies which have their seat in a non-Member or non-Convention State, or the validity of the decisions of their organs, or concerns a public register in a non-Member or non-Convention State or the validity of certain forms of intellectual property right conferred under the law of a non-Member or non-Convention State,[82] or arises from a contract which contained a jurisdiction agreement for a non-Member or non-Convention State,[83] or is already the subject of proceedings before the courts of a non-Member or non-Convention State,[84] it is most improbable that an English court, seised with jurisdiction on the basis of Art.2, is obliged to exercise it if the defendant applies for a stay on the ground that a non-Member or non-Convention State is the *forum conveniens*. The language of the judgment in *Owusu*, even though emphatic, does not assist.[85] In addition to the plain common sense of the argument that a stay in these cases should be permissible, two further reasons may be offered why the court may still apply

---

[77] At [40]–[42]. Save in exceptional cases, a stay will only be granted if applied for by a defendant.

[78] The argument, and the limitation to cases which do not jeopardise the practical effect of the Convention, is in Case C–365/88 *Kongress Agentur Hagen GmbH v Zeehaghe BV* [1990] E.C.R. I–1845.

[79] Case C–159/02, [2004] E.C.R. I–3565, [2005] 1 A.C 101. See below, para.12–093.

[80] *Mazur Media Ltd v Mazur Media GmbH* [2004] EWHC 1566 (Ch.), [2004] 1 W.L.R. 2966, at [69]–[71].

[81] It considered the question to be irrelevant to the issue which the Court of Appeal had to decide.

[82] Art.22 (previously Art.16).

[83] Art.23 (previously Art.17).

[84] Arts 27, 28 (previously Arts 21 and 22).

[85] An answer to the second question referred by the Court of Appeal would have dealt with these issues.

the principle of *forum non conveniens* or an equivalent principle.[86] First, in a Brussels Convention case the European Court has previously approved the principle that a court may give effect to an agreement conferring jurisdiction on the courts of a non-Convention State if the agreement is valid under the law of the court seised in breach of contract.[87] Accordingly, if the parties have agreed that a dispute shall be submitted to the exclusive jurisdiction of the courts of New York, an English court will be entitled to apply the relevant principles of English law to an application by the defendant for a stay of proceedings. There is no reason to believe that, only four years after this decision, the European Court in *Owusu v Jackson* had changed its mind. Secondly, writing in 1972,[88] and again in 1990,[89] Droz asserted that where the facts disclosed a connection with a non-Brussels Convention State which in all other respects fell within the parameters of what is now Art.22 of the Brussels I Regulation, or involved an agreement conferring jurisdiction on the courts of a non-Convention State, it was open to a court to give a "reflexive effect" to the corresponding provision of what was then the Brussels Convention and grant such jurisdictional relief as its own law required.[90] When the authors of the Report on the original Lugano Convention[91] contradicted this, Droz was unrepentant, observing[92] that if a French judge "was fundamentally without competence to adjudicate upon German land or a German patent, one cannot see why he would be better equipped to adjudicate an Argentine agricultural lease or a Japanese patent". Despite the fact that the European Court declined to deal with the second question referred by the Court of Appeal, in the answering of which the point made by Droz would certainly have arisen, the argument for giving a "reflexive effect" to what are now Arts 22 and 23 of the Regulation (and the Lugano Convention), or to apply these provisions by analogy, is overwhelming.

12–022   Though the issue has evidently been debated on several occasions, English[93] courts have almost always been able to dispose of the matter before them in a manner which meant there was no need to rule on whether *Owusu v Jackson* would have permitted them to grant jurisdictional relief in favour of

---

[86] As a matter of common law, a court has no jurisdiction to try a question of title to foreign land (see below, para.23R–021) or (arguably) the validity of a patent (below, para.34–025); and a stay to give effect to a jurisdiction agreement is not ordered on the basis of *forum conveniens* but by way of specific performance of the contract (below, para.12–149).

[87] Case C–387/98 *Coreck Maritime GmbH v Handelsveem BV* [2000] E.C.R. I–9337, at [19]; see also *Konkola Copper Mines Plc v Coromin* [2005] EWHC (Comm.) 898, [2005] 2 Lloyd's Rep. 555, affirmed [2006] EWCA Civ 5, [2006] 1 Lloyd's Rep. 410 (there was no appeal on this point); Schlosser, para.176 (and the material there cited).

[88] Droz, *La compétence judiciaire et l'effet des jugements dans la CEE* (1972), para.164.

[89] *Rev. crit.* 1990, p.1.

[90] See also *Ace-Insurance SA-NV v Zürich Insurance Co* [2001] EWCA Civ 173, [2001] 1 Lloyd's Rep. 618 (a case pre-dating *Owusu v Jackson*).

[91] Jenard and Möller [1990] O.J. C189/35 at p.54; repeated in the Report on the 1989 Accession Convention, Almeida Cruz, Desantes Real and Jenard [1990] O.J. C189/57 at [23].

[92] *Rev. crit.* 1990, 1, at p.14.

[93] The Irish Supreme Court made a reference for a preliminary ruling in *Goshawk Dedicated Ltd v Life Receivables Ireland Ltd* [2009] IESC 7, [2009] I.L.Pr. 435 (power to stay when *lis pendens* in non-Member State), but the case settled and the reference was not proceeded with.

the courts of a non-Member state,[94] so declining to propose the answer to a question on which, eventually, the European Court will have the final word. That being so, there was no need for them to consider whether any residual power to grant relief would be derived from the common law of *forum non conveniens* or shaped by analogy with those provisions of the Regulation which remove the jurisdiction of a court in a Member State in favour of one which a superior claim to adjudicate,[95] or whether the operation of any power to grant relief is dependent upon whether the English court has general jurisdiction,[96] special jurisdiction,[97] jurisdiction designed to favour a weaker party,[98] jurisdiction by prorogation,[99] or exclusive jurisdiction regardless of domicile.[100] In the small number of cases in which a decision has been necessary, no consistent line has emerged. Though the court in *Samengo-Turner v J&H Marsh & McLennan (Services) Ltd*[101] refused a stay applied for by reference to a contractual agreement for the jurisdiction of the courts of New York, its primary justification was that the agreement was ineffective in a case where the employee invoked the jurisdictional rules in Section 5 of Chapter II of the Regulation. In *Winnetka Trading Corp v Julius Baer International Ltd*,[102] a stay was granted to give effect to a choice of court agreement in relation to a non-Member State. In *Lucasfilm Ltd v Ainsworth*,[103] the Court of Appeal expressed surprise at the contention that the Regulation might be understood to force it to rule on the validity of a US copyright in circumstances in which the court had no jurisdiction at common law to do any such thing, but the Supreme Court[104] held that there was no common law barrier to jurisdiction and did not rule on this point.

In *Catalyst Investment Group Ltd v Lewinsohn*[105] the court concluded that it was powerless to stay proceedings where the basis for the application was that proceedings between the same parties and involving the same cause of action were already pending before the courts of a non-Member State. The court was well aware of the practical disadvantages of its decision, but it

12–023

---

[94] *Antec International Ltd v Biosafety USA Inc* [2006] EWHC 47 (Comm.); *HIT Entertainment Ltd v Gaffney International Licensing Pty Ltd* [2007] EWHC 1282 (Ch.); *Masri v Consolidated Contractors International Co SAL* [2008] EWCA Civ 303, [2009] Q.B. 450; *Chaudhary v Bhatter* [2009] EWCA Civ 1176, [2010] 1 All E.R.(Comm.) 1031; *UBS AG v HSH Nordbank AG* [2009] EWCA Civ 585, [2009] 2 Lloyd's Rep. 272; *Pacific International Sports Clubs Ltd v Soccer Marketing International Ltd* [2009] EWHC 1839 (Ch.) (appeal dismissed without reference to this point: *sub nom. Pacific International Sports Clubs v Surkis* [2010] EWCA Civ 753); *Royal & Sun Alliance Insurance Plc v Rolls-Royce Plc* [2010] EWHC 1869 (Comm.), [2010] Lloyd's Rep. I.R. 637; *Sebastian Holdings Inc v Deutsche Bank AG* [2010] EWCA Civ 998, [2011] 1 Lloyd's Rep. 106; *Lucasfilm Ltd v Ainsworth* [2011] UKSC 39, [2012] 1 A.C. 208; *Abela v Baadarani* [2011] EWHC 116 (Ch.).

[95] In particular, Art.22 (exclusive jurisdiction regardless of domicile), Art.23 (jurisdiction by agreement); Art.27 (jurisdictional priority in the court first seised).

[96] Art.2.

[97] Arts.5 and 6.

[98] ss.3, 4, and 5 of Ch.II.

[99] Art.23.

[100] Art.22.

[101] [2007] EWCA Civ 723, [2008] I.C.R. 18.

[102] [2008] EWHC 3146 (Ch.), [2009] Bus. L.R. 1006.

[103] [2009] EWCA Civ 1328, [2010] 3 W.L.R. 333.

[104] *Lucasfilm Ltd v Ainsworth* [2011] UKSC 39, [2012] 1 A.C. 208.

[105] [2009] EWHC 1964, [2010] Ch. 218.

considered that despite the fact that the second question referred in *Owusu v Jackson* had gone unanswered, it could do nothing about them. By contrast, in *JKN v JCN*,[106] a matrimonial case in which jurisdiction was founded on the Brussels II Regulation but there was a *lis pendens* in New York, the court held that it was neither necessary nor desirable that *Owusu* should be held to mean that there was no power to stay where there was a *lis pendens* in a non-Member State, but that if *Catalyst* was correct in its interpretation of *Owusu*, and there really was no such power where jurisdiction was taken under the Brussels I Regulation, *Owusu* should not be permitted to spill over and into the Brussels II Regulation.

12–024   In the continuing absence of clear guidance from the English courts, or any form of guidance from the European Court, it is submitted[107] that the proper course for an English court is to use Arts 22 and 23 to identify the classes of case in which a court may continue apply its national law. It is inappropriate to go further and to insist on the Articles being applied slavishly. So, for example, it would not be necessary to show that the proceedings had as their object rights *in rem* in, or a tenancy of, land in a non-Member State; it would suffice that the case was one which required a court to rule on a question of title to foreign land or on the validity of a foreign patent. And it would not be necessary for an agreement on jurisdiction for the courts of New York to comply with the formalities specified by Art.23; it should suffice that the jurisdiction agreement is valid as a matter of English rules of the conflict of laws. Similarly, if an English court were to conclude that the case was one in which it was entitled to grant jurisdictional relief, it should be able to apply its own law to decide whether in fact the relief should be granted, and should not be driven by the analogy of Arts 22 and 23 to conclude that it had an absolute obligation to decline jurisdiction. If this is correct, then there can be no objection to an English court applying the doctrine of *forum non conveniens* in a situation of *lis alibi pendens* in a non-Member State, and in this sense applying Arts 27 and 28 of the Regulation by analogy as well. Indeed, there can be no rational justification for insisting that an English court is required to blind itself to the fact that there is a *lis alibi pendens* in a non-Member State, especially when the judgment of a court in a non-Member State may well be entitled to recognition in England.[108] The result will be that the power to apply the doctrine of *forum non conveniens* in favour of the courts of a non-Member State will be confined to cases in which Arts 22, 23, 27 and 28 of the Regulation may be applied by analogy. Where jurisdiction is founded on Art.4 of the Regulation or the Lugano Convention, there is no reason to suppose that the court's power to apply the doctrine of *forum non conveniens* in favour of the courts of a non-Member or non-Convention State is at all trammeled by the Regulation or the Convention.

12–025   In cases where the Regulation or the Convention allocates jurisdiction to the courts of the United Kingdom—or, to put it another way, where these instruments determine the international jurisdiction of the courts of the Member State, but not internal, jurisdiction—it is for the internal law of the United

---

[106] [2010] EWHC 843 (Fam.), [2011] 1 F.L.R. 826.
[107] And see also Peel [2005] L.M.C.L.Q. 363, Briggs, *ibid*. 378.
[108] See below, Ch.14.

Kingdom to allocate internal, or national, or local, jurisdiction. This is primarily done by the rules set out in Schedule 4 to the 1982 Act; but it also follows from this, as well as from the fact that Sch.4 contains no provision corresponding to Arts.27 and 28 of the Regulation, that as between the courts of the United Kingdom, the ordinary principles of *forum non conveniens* are applicable.[109] By contrast, in cases in which the Regulation allocates jurisdiction to the courts of a specific place within the United Kingdom—that is, the instrument determines international and internal jurisdiction, such as where the place for performance of the contractual obligation is England[110]—there can be no role for the principle of *forum non conveniens*, for there can be no stay in favour of a court which does not have jurisdiction, even if that court is in another part of the United Kingdom and that court, *ex hypothesi*, does not have jurisdiction according to the Regulation.[111] But where the Regulation would give jurisdiction concurrently to the courts of several places within the United Kingdom—in a newspaper libel case, for example, in which the newspaper was circulated throughout the United Kingdom and the claimant complains of all the publication in the United Kingdom, it is arguable that the principles of *forum non conveniens* may still be applied if the defendant were to seek a stay of proceedings.[112] Of course, where the subject-matter of the proceedings is outside the scope of the Regulation, jurisdiction will be governed by the traditional rules of English law, including the rules relating to *forum non conveniens*.[113]

Effect of Human Rights Act 1998.[114] In the context of rules and discretions regulating the existence and exercise of jurisdiction, it might have been expected that the European Convention on Human Rights, and in particular Art.6, would assume a distinct role in the development of the law. This has not yet happened.[115] The likely reason is, as Lord Bingham pointed out in *Lubbe v Cape Plc*,[116] that Art.6 ECHR added nothing to the common law, or, to put the point another way, the common law on the staying of actions on the

12–026

---

[109] *Cumming v Scottish Daily Record and Sunday Mail Ltd, The Times*, June 8, 1995, not following *Foxen v Scotsman (Publications) Ltd, The Times*, February 17, 1994; *Ivax Pharmaceuticals UK Ltd AKZO Nobel BV* [2005] EWHC 2658 (Pat.), [2006] F.S.R. 888. See also Collins and Davenport (1994) 110 L.Q.R. 325; Collins (1995) 111 L.Q.R. 541. The assumption that *forum non conveniens* might be applied was evidently made in *Royal Bank of Scotland v Davidson* [2009] CSOH 134, 2010 S.L.T. 92.

[110] Art.5(1).

[111] This appears to follow from Case C–386/05 *Color Drack GmbH v Lexx International Vertriebs GmbH* [2007] E.C.R. I–3699.

[112] This may have been the view preferred in *Lennon v Scottish Daily Record and Sunday Mail Ltd* [2004] EWHC 359 (QB); *Sunderland Marine Mutual Insurance Co Ltd v Wiseman (The Seaward Quest)* [2007] EWHC 1460 (Comm.), [2007] 2 Lloyd's Rep. 308. The alternative view would be that where the Regulation specifically provides that two separate courts, albeit within the one Member State, are to have jurisdiction, it is also for the Regulation (specifically Arts.27 and 28), and not for the common law, to vary that jurisdiction: *cf.* Case C–386/05 *Color Drack GmbH v Lexx International Vertriebs GmbH*, above.

[113] *Tehrani v Secretary of State for the Home Department* [2006] UKHL 47, [2007] 1 A.C. 521.

[114] See para.1–024.

[115] For a fuller analysis, see Fawcett (2007) 56 I.C.L.Q. 1.

[116] [2000] 1 W.L.R. 1545.

ground of *forum non conveniens* was and is fully compliant with the requirements of Art.6 of the European Convention on Human Rights. In that case an
application for a stay of proceedings brought by impecunious plaintiffs, who
would have had funding for their personal injury claims against an asbestos
company in England, was refused on the ground that the absence of comparable funding or other support for a claim before the courts of South Africa,
which was the natural forum for the proceedings, meant that it was unjust to
order a stay. No doubt it was true that to order a stay would have violated the
Convention principle that a fair trial requires approximate equality of arms,
but the detailed reasoning of the common law had already arrived at a
sufficient answer. Taken together with more recent developments, in which it
has become clear that proceedings will not be stayed on grounds of *forum non
conveniens* where there is a demonstrable and serious risk that justice will not
be done by the foreign court, the conclusion of Lord Bingham is plainly
correct. In all cases of this kind it will be necessary for the court to exercise
its own judgment as to whether the effect of a stay of proceedings would result
a denial of justice properly so called, as distinct from leaving the claimant to
make do with a trial in a forum in which he feels less optimistic of victory; but
the claimant has no vested right to prevail on the merits any more than the
defendant does, and as long as the natural forum offers reasonable access and
a fair trial, there will be no need to refer to Art.6 of the Human Rights
Convention. The same reasoning explains why the grant of an anti-suit
injunction to enforce an agreement conferring jurisdiction on the English
court, or in circumstances in which England is the natural forum for the trial
of the action but it would be vexatious or oppressive for the proceedings to be
brought outside England, does not implicate Art.6 of the Convention.[117]

12–027   A more difficult question arises where a claimant who is able to show that
the court has power to grant permission to serve the defendant out of the
jurisdiction, but who is unable to show that England is the natural, proper,[118]
or most appropriate,[119] forum for the proceedings, asserts that if the court
refuses to grant permission, the decision will deny him the right of access to
a court in a manner which implicates Art.6 of the Human Rights Convention.
The problem has been known for some time, but in the cases in which it might
have been raised for consideration it appears that the court was not troubled
with it. In cases in which service out was applied for in relation to a defendant
present and otherwise liable to be sued in Russia,[120] Ukraine,[121] and Kyrgyzstan,[122] in matters in which there was reason to suppose that the courts of the
foreign state in question might not approach a trial with disinterested propriety, the Court of Appeal and Privy Council authorised or approved service out

---

[117] *OT Africa Line Ltd v Hijazy (The Kribi)* [2001] 1 Lloyd's Rep. 76. For the granting of
injunctions in so-called "single forum" cases, but which issue raises no distinct issues, see below,
para.12–088.

[118] CPR, r.6.37(3).

[119] This was the formulation derived from *Spiliada Maritime Corp v Cansulex Ltd* [1987] A.C.
460.

[120] *Cherney v Deripaska* [2009] EWCA Civ 849, [2010] All E.R. (Comm.) 456.

[121] *Pacific International Sports Clubs Ltd v Surkis* [2010] EWCA Civ 753.

[122] *AK Investment CJSC v Kyrgyz Mobil Tel Ltd* [2011] UKPC 7, [2011] 4 All E.R. 1027.

of the jurisdiction without any reference to Art.6 at all. On the footing that these decisions represent settled law—that a claimant whose case falls within one of the grounds listed in the Practice Direction[123] may obtain permission to serve out on showing that there is a risk[124] that the foreign court will not even try to do justice according to the law—there will be no question of the law on service out failing to comply with Art.6. Only if it could be argued that the law fails to comply with Art.6 in a case in which it makes no provision to allow a court to authorise service out of the jurisdiction by, and hence to offer jurisdiction to, a claimant would there be any basis for the contention that the law on jurisdiction is at odds with the requirements of Art.6; and that argument will be quite hopeless, for the cases in which service out may be made are statutory. Unless Art.6 were taken to require a Contracting State to override its normal jurisdictional rules and provide what is sometimes referred to as a "forum of necessity", Art 6 would not appear to have any role to play.

The possibility of there being a violation of Art.6, and of this calling for a   **12–028**
specific judicial response, did arise in a case in which what is now Art.27 of the Brussels I Regulation prevented an Austrian court exercising jurisdiction by reason of a *lis alibi pendens* before the Italian courts: the argument was that the delay occasioned by the natural defendant instituting proceedings which would then be stranded in the Italian legal system for years on end could amount to the denial of the right of access to a court for the trial of a claim, should therefore cause the European Court to recognise a limit upon or exception to the strict rule of temporal priority in Art.27.[125] But the European Court simply observed that Art.27 meant that the Austrian court could not exercise any jurisdiction which it might have had while the matter was pending in Italy, and denied that this could be contradicted by Art.6 of the Human Rights Convention. This was a surprising result, for the requirements of the Convention are hardly anathema to the European Union, the law of which now requires it to adhere to the Convention.[126] But the court may simply have been giving a ruling on a preliminary reference made in respect of a provision of the Brussels Convention, and implicitly leaving it to the referring court to deal with any resultant incompatibility between the true interpretation of the Brussels Convention and Art.6 of the Human Rights Convention, by both of which it was bound.

Clause (2) of the Rule. *Spiliada Maritime Corp v Cansulex Ltd*[127] was a   **12–029**
case involving the discretion to grant permission to serve out of the jurisdiction under what is now Practice Direction 6B of the Civil Procedure Rules, i.e. Rule 34, but the opportunity was taken in that case to lay down common principles applicable in both service out and stay cases. The fundamental

---

[123] Practice Direction 6B, para.3.1, supplementing CPR, Pt 6.
[124] This represents the standard applied by the Privy Council in *AK Investment v Kyrgyz Mobil Tel*, above.
[125] Case C–116/02 *Erich Gasser GmbH v MISAT srl* [2003] E.C.R. I–14693.
[126] Treaty on European Union, Art.6.
[127] [1987] A.C. 460.

principle enunciated by Lord Goff of Chieveley[128] is stated in clause (2) and is based on what he described as the classic statement in the leading Scottish case.[129]

12–030   The following propositions may be derived from the speech of Lord Goff of Chieveley, which has been applied in many subsequent cases.[130] The framework which is set out in the points which follow is that which will be used on applications for a stay of proceedings: for the case in which these criteria are applied to an application for permission to serve out of the jurisdiction, they operate in a form of mirror image, which is considered under clause (3) of this Rule. First, in general the legal burden of proof rests on the defendant to persuade the court to exercise its discretion to grant a stay, although the evidential burden will rest on a party who seeks to establish the existence of matters which will assist him in persuading the court to exercise its discretion in his favour.[131] Secondly, if the court is satisfied by the defendant that there is another available forum which is clearly a more appropriate forum for the trial of the[132] action,[133] the burden will shift to the claimant to show that there are special circumstances by reason of which justice requires that the trial should nevertheless take place in England. Thirdly, the burden on the defendant is not just to show that England is not the natural or appropriate forum, but to establish that there is another forum which is clearly or distinctly more appropriate than the English forum; accordingly, where (as in some commercial disputes) there is no particular forum which can be described as the natural forum, there will be no reason to grant a

---

[128] As Stephenson L.J. said of Robert Goff J. in *European Asian Bank AG v Punjab Bank* [1982] 2 Lloyd's Rep. 356, 363: " . . . no Judge on the bench has had to study and state the principles on which proceedings in this country are stayed more often or more carefully than this learned Judge". Mr. Robert Goff Q.C. was counsel in *The Atlantic Star* [1974] A.C. 436; Robert Goff J. was the judge at first instance in *MacShannon v Rockware Glass Ltd* [1978] A.C. 795, and in *Trendtex Trading Corp v Crédit Suisse* [1980] 3 All E.R. 721, affirmed [1982] A.C. 679; and Lord Goff of Chieveley was the author of the leading speeches or opinions in *Spiliada Maritime Corp v Cansulex Ltd* [1987] A.C. 460; *de Dampierre v de Dampierre* [1988] A.C. 92; *Soc Nat Ind Aérospatiale v Lee Kui Jak* [1987] A.C. 871; *Connelly v RTZ Corp Plc* [1998] A.C. 854; and *Airbus Industrie GIE v Patel* [1999] 1 A.C. 119. See also *Bank of Tokyo v Karoon* [1987] A.C. 45n. (CA).

[129] *Sim v Robinow* (1892) 19 R. 665, 668.

[130] For stays in matrimonial proceedings, see further below, para.18R–268.

[131] In *Hindocha v Juthabhai* [2003] UKPC 77, [2004] W.T.L.R. 1119, it was suggested that where a defendant who was served out of the jurisdiction applied for a stay of proceedings, as opposed to making an application to set aside service, the burden on him is reduced from its usual level: *sed quaere*.

[132] If part of the action is bound to be retained before the English court, it will be hard to demonstrate that the English court is *forum non conveniens* for a related claim: *Crofts v Cathay Pacific Airways Ltd* [2005] EWCA Civ 599, [2005] I.C.R. 1436 (Employment Rights Act 1996 claim; claim for breach of contract of employment); appeal dismissed without reference to this point: *sub nom. Lawson v Serco Ltd* [2006] UKHL 3, [2006] I.C.R. 250.

[133] If the defendant has no defence to an application for summary judgment, so that no trial of the substantive action is called for, it has been held that the court may on that ground refuse a stay: *Bank of Credit and Commerce Hong Kong Ltd v Sonali Bank* [1995] 1 Lloyd's Rep. 227; *Standard Chartered Bank v Pakistan National Shipping Corp* [1995] 2 Lloyd's Rep. 365; *Merrill Lynch v Raffa* [2001] I.L.Pr. 437. The position may be different where the defendant intends to challenge the jurisdiction as distinct from seeking a stay: *Speed Investments Ltd v Formula One Holdings Ltd* [2004] EWHC 1772 (Ch.), [2005] 1 W.L.R. 1233.

stay.[134] Fourthly, the court will look to see what factors[135] there are which point in the direction of another forum as being the "natural forum", i.e. that with which the action has the most real and substantial connection.[136] These will include factors affecting convenience or expense (such as availability of witnesses) and such other factors as the law governing the transaction and the places where the parties reside or carry on business, and also whether the claim is part of a larger overall dispute which would be damaged by being fragmented. Fifthly, if the court concludes at that stage that there is no other available forum which is clearly more appropriate for the trial of the action, the court will ordinarily refuse a stay.[137] Sixthly, if, however, the court concludes that there is some other available forum which prima facie is clearly more appropriate,[138] it will ordinarily grant a stay unless there are circumstances by reason of which justice requires that a stay should not be granted. In that enquiry, the court will consider all the circumstances of the case, including circumstances which go beyond those taken into account when considering connecting factors with other jurisdictions.[139] Seventhly, a stay will not be refused simply because the claimant will thereby be deprived of "a legitimate personal or juridical advantage", provided that the court is satisfied that substantial justice will be done in the available appropriate forum.[140]

Most cases in which stay applications are made are in the Commercial **12–031** Court.[141] In *Spiliada*, Lord Templeman (with whom Lord Griffiths and Lord Mackay expressly agreed) observed that the factors which the court is entitled to take account in considering whether one forum is more appropriate than another are legion; the resolution of disputes about the relative merits of trial in England and abroad was pre-eminently a matter for the judge at first instance; and he expressed the hope that the judge would be referred only to the speech of Lord Goff and not to other decisions on other facts; and that

---

[134] Citing *European Asian Bank AG v Punjab and Sind Bank* [1982] 2 Lloyd's Rep. 356 (CA). See also *The Vishva Abha* [1990] 2 Lloyd's Rep. 312.

[135] The court has to consider with what forum the *issues* have the closest connection, and not simply weigh factors without reference to the likely issues: *EI du Pont de Nemours & Co v Agnew* [1987] 2 Lloyd's Rep. 585 (CA); *cf. Re Harrods (Buenos Aires) Ltd* [1992] Ch. 72 (CA). On the specific need for the application to identify issues which arise for decision, and to which the question of forum non conveniens arises, see *Limit (No.3) Ltd v PDV Insurance Co* [2005] EWCA Civ 383, [2005] Lloyd's Rep. I.R. 552, [72]; *Sawyer v Atari Interactive Inc* [2005] EWHC 2351 (Ch.), [2006] I.L.Pr. 129, [54]; *Novus Aviation Ltd v Onur Air Tasimacilik AS* [2009] EWCA Civ 122, [2009] 1 Lloyd's Rep. 576, [30].

[136] Citing *The Abidin Daver* [1984] A.C. 398, 415.

[137] Citing *European Asian Bank AG v Punjab and Sind Bank* [1982] 2 Lloyd's Rep. 356 (CA).

[138] If there are two such *fora*, both more appropriate than England, a stay may be granted: there is no requirement that one be more appropriate than the other.

[139] One of which can be the fact that the claimant will not obtain justice in the foreign jurisdiction: at p.478, citing *The Abidin Daver* [1984] A.C. 398, 411. See below, para.12–040.

[140] For Canadian authority which also holds that loss of a juridical advantage is not a separate and distinct condition, but is part of the overall assessment of which is the appropriate forum, see *Amchem Products Inc v British Columbia (Workers' Compensation Board)* [1993] 1 S.C.R. 897, 933 (Sup Ct Can) (an injunction case); *Frymer v Brettschneider* (1994) 115 D.L.R. (4th) 744 (Ont CA).

[141] As are most applications to set aside orders permitting service outside the jurisdiction.

submissions would be measured in hours and not days.[142] It is nevertheless helpful to consider how the discretion is exercised in practice and what principles have emerged in relation to matters which did not arise directly for decision in *Spiliada* itself.

12–032   **Availability of the foreign forum.** The first limb of the *Spiliada* test requires it to be shown that the foreign forum is "available" as well as being more appropriate for the trial of the action. There are three aspects of availability to consider. First, a foreign court will be considered to be "available" to a claimant if by the time of the application for a stay,[143] it would be open to him to institute proceedings against the defendant before that court.[144] If this has come about only as a result of the defendant's voluntary submission to the jurisdiction of the foreign court, this fact does not prevent the court being seen as available to the claimant. It follows that an undertaking by the defendant to submit to the jurisdiction of a foreign court can make the foreign court available even though it would not have been so without his under-taking.[145] Secondly, and despite authority which had held that the foreign court must be one in which the claimant is in practice able to bring his claim,[146] it is now irrelevant to the availability of the foreign forum under this head that the claimant will be unable to fund his action[147]: the practical difficulties which he would encounter will have their impact, if any, under the second limb of the test where the question is whether it would be unjust to deprive him of the right to a trial in England. The same is true of evidence which tends to show that it would be difficult for the claimant to manage or

---

[142] [1987] A.C. at 465; *cf. AK Investment CJSC v Kyrgyz Mobil Tel Ltd* [2011] UKPC 7, [2011] 4 All E.R. 1027, at [7]. See also, e.g. *The Nile Rhapsody* [1994] 1 Lloyd's Rep. 383, 388 (CA); *Haji-Ioannou v Frangos* [1999] 2 Lloyd's Rep. 337, 356 (CA); *Askin v Absa Bank* [1999] I.L.Pr. 471, 473 (CA). The limited powers of a court hearing an appeal, and therefore the limited grounds on which appeals could be based, were re-emphasised in *Pacific International Sports Clubs Ltd v Surkis* [2010] EWCA Civ 753, [23], where such applications were described as "jurisdictional spats". For a contradictory view, that the decision of the primary judge might not be regarded as discretionary, subject only to review if no reasonable judge could have come to it, but as involving an exercise in judgment, just as appropriately made by an appellate court, see *Murakami v Wiryadi* [2010] NSWCA 7, (2010) 268 A.L.R. 377, [32]–[34].

[143] *Lubbe v Cape Plc* [2000] 1 W.L.R. 1545 (HL), disagreeing with the view of the Court of Appeal on this point: [1999] I.L.Pr. 113 (CA). The law in the United States is to similar effect, and a foreign forum may be an available alternative forum if the defendant consents to submit to its jurisdiction as a condition of dismissal on *forum non conveniens* grounds: this was so in *Piper Aircraft Co v Reyno*, 454 U.S. 235 (1981) (see 479 F. Supp. 727, 731 (M.D. Penn. 1979)). For examples see *Re Union Carbide Gas Plant Disaster*, 809 F. 2d 195 (2d Cir. 1987); *Contact Lumber Co v PT Moges Shipping Co*, 918 F. 2d 1446 (9th Cir. 1990); *PT United Can Co v Crown Cork & Seal Co*, 138 F. 3d 65 (2d Cir. 1998).

[144] *cf. Cecil v Bayat* [2010] EWHC 641 (Comm.), [144]–[156] (a service out case), where the US court was regarded as unavailable because previous proceedings showed that the claim, which could be instituted, would be summarily dismissed. The decision was reversed without reference to this point: [2011] EWCA Civ 135, [2011] 1 W.L.R. 3086.

[145] Though if the undertaking to submit comes only after the claimant has instituted proceed-ings in England, it may be appropriate to depart from the usual costs order if a stay is eventually granted. By contrast, if the undertaking to submit is given only during the appeal, it will be irrelevant and disregarded, as the appeal lies against the order of the judge at the time he made it: *Sharab v Al-Saud* [2009] EWCA Civ 353, [2009] 2 Lloyd's Rep. 160.

[146] *Mohammed v Bank of Kuwait and the Middle East KSC* [1996] 1 W.L.R. 1483 (CA).

[147] *Connelly v RTZ Corp* [1998] A.C. 854.

supervise the process of litigation, or that he would not obtain a fair trial.[148] Thirdly, the claimant may seek to contend that the foreign court is not available to him on the ground that the claim which he makes in the English proceedings, or the remedy he seeks,[149] would be unavailable to him in the foreign court, or that because of the foreign court's choice of law rules, he would lose in the foreign court.[150] It is submitted that these matters are irrelevant to the issue of whether the foreign court is available, but that they may be taken into account under the second limb of the test in determining whether the claimant can show that it would be unjust to deprive him of a trial in England. Similarly, the impact, if any, of a time-bar which might be applied by the foreign court to preclude the claimant's proceedings is addressed under the second limb of the test.[151] That said, the line which divides the two limbs of *Spiliada* from each other is neither completely impermeable, nor drawn in such a way that there are no factors which do not appear on both sides of it: from time to time a court will locate under one limb of *Spiliada* material which, arguably at least, might more comfortably belong to the other. But when it is recalled that the overall test is one which asks what the interests of justice require, and when it is remembered that the analysis in *Spiliada* is designed to manage, rather than to constrain, that test, it will rarely be a matter of legitimate complaint that this has happened.

Identification of the natural forum. It has been seen that in *Spiliada* Lord   **12–033**
Goff of Chieveley indicated that the English court should look for the forum with which the dispute had the most real and substantial connection, and he referred in particular to factors affecting convenience or expense (such as availability of witnesses) and other factors including the law governing the relevant transaction.[152] Lord Goff could not have foreseen, however, the subsequent distortion which would be brought about by the decision of the European Court in *Owusu v Jackson*.[153] The direct effect of that case is that where proceedings in a civil or commercial matter are brought against a defendant who is domiciled in the United Kingdom, the court has no power to stay those proceedings on the ground of *forum non conveniens*. Its indirect

---

[148] *cf. Mohammed v Bank of Kuwait and the Middle East KSC*, above, which is to be doubted on this point after *Connelly v RTZ Corp Plc*, above; *Askin v Absa Bank Ltd* [1999] I.L.Pr. 471 (CA) (fugitive from justice not permitted to rely on unavailability of court to him); *Attorney-General of Zambia v Meer Care & Desai* [2006] EWCA Civ 390, [2006] 1 C.L.C. 436 (inability to attend trial in person did not make court unavailable as forum); *cf. Cherney v Deripaska* [2008] EWHC 1530 (Comm.), [2009] 1 All E.R. (Comm.) 333, affd. [2009] EWCA Civ 849, [2010] 2 All E.R. (Comm.) 456 (a service out case: inability to travel to Russia may have made Russia unavailable as alternative forum). These cases may suggest that submissions and material which go to show that the system of justice administered by the foreign court is so unsatisfactory that a sensible trial cannot take place there are better analysed under the second limb of *Spiliada*, even where it may also be said that the deficiencies are so acute that the foreign court is not available at all. See further below, para.12–040.

[149] *cf. Re Harrods (Buenos Aires) Ltd* [1992] Ch. 72 (CA: Argentine court unable to order majority shareholder to buy the shareholding of the petitioner).

[150] See below, para.12–038.

[151] See below, paras 12–037 and 12–154.

[152] [1987] A.C. at 478. See also *The Elli 2* [1985] 1 Lloyd's Rep. 107; *MacSteel Commercial Holdings (Pty) Ltd v Thermasteel (Canada) Ltd* [1996] C.L.C. 1403 (CA).

[153] Case C–281/02, [2005] E.C.R. I–1383, [2005] Q.B. 801.

effect is felt in a case in which there are multiple defendants, some of whom are not domiciled in a Member State and to whom the plea of *forum non conveniens* remains open: it is inevitable that the ability of those co-defendants to obtain a stay (or to resist service out of the jurisdiction) by pointing to the courts of a non-Member State which would otherwise represent the *forum conveniens*, will be reduced, for to grant jurisdictional relief to some but not to others will fragment what ought to be conducted as a single trial. This is not unprecedented: even before *Owusu*, if one among several defendants submitted to the jurisdiction of the English court, this will have made it more difficult for the unwilling defendant to obtain jurisdictional relief. There is no doubt, however, that the *Owusu* factor will have made things worse for a defendant who wishes to rely on the principle of *forum non conveniens* when a co-defendant cannot.[154] A court will therefore need to be astute to detect and expose abusive claims brought against defendants domiciled in a Member State but which may have been brought only in order to rely on the *Owusu* factor in relation to others.

12–034   *Governing law.* If the legal issues are straightforward, or if the competing fora have domestic laws which are substantially similar,[155] the identity of the governing law will be a factor of rather little significance.[156] But if the legal issues are complex, or the legal systems very different, the general principle that a court applies its own law more reliably than does a foreign court[157] will help to point to the more appropriate forum, whether English or foreign.[158] This will be so especially where the foreign court will disregard an express choice of English law in order to apply its own public policy or legislation,[159]

---

[154] *JSC BTA Bank v Granton Trade Ltd* [2010] EWHC 2577 (Comm.).

[155] *Marconi Communications International Ltd v PT Pan Indonesia Bank Ltd TBK* [2004] EWHC 129 (Comm.), [2004] 1 Lloyd's Rep. 594; affirmed [2005] EWCA Civ 422, [2005] 2 All E.R. (Comm.) 325.

[156] The equivalent sentence in an earlier edition was applied in *Navigators' Insurance Co v Atlantic Methanol Production Co LLC* [2003] EWHC 1706 (Comm.), at [48]. See further *The Rothnie* [1996] 2 Lloyd's Rep. 206; *Novus Aviation Ltd v Onur Air Tasimacilik AS* [2009] EWCA Civ 122, [2009] 1 Lloyd's Rep. 576; *Mujur Bakat Sdn Bhd v Uni Asia General Insurance Bhd* [2011] EWHC 643 (Comm.), [2011] Lloyd's Rep I.R. 465; *Wright v Deccan Chargers Sporting Ventures Ltd* [2011] EWHC 1307 (QB), [2011] I.L.Pr. 781.

[157] *The Eleftheria* [1970] P. 94, 105 ("a matter of common sense"). In addition, an appeal to correct errors of law is far easier to bring in the courts whose domestic law is being applied to the dispute.

[158] *Charm Maritime Inc v Kyriakou* [1987] 1 Lloyd's Rep. 433 (CA); *Muduroglu Ltd v TC Ziraat Bankasi* [1986] Q.B. 1225, 1246 (CA); *EI du Pont de Nemours & Co v Agnew* [1987] 2 Lloyd's Rep. 585 (CA); *Standard Steamship Owners' Protection and Indemnity Association (Bermuda) Ltd v Gann* [1992] 2 Lloyd's Rep. 528; *The Varna (No.2)* [1994] 2 Lloyd's Rep. 41; *Pacific International Sports Clubs Ltd v Surkis* [2010] EWCA Civ 753.

[159] *Coast Lines Ltd v Hudig & Veder Chartering NV* [1971] 2 Lloyd's Rep. 390, affirmed [1972] 2 Q.B. 34 (CA); *Sawyer v Atari Interactive Inc* [2005] EWHC 2351 (Ch.), [2006] I.L.Pr. 129, at [59]; *Cadre SA v Astra Asigurari SA* [2005] EWHC 2504 (Comm.), [2006] 1 Lloyd's Rep. 868; *Stonebridge Underwriting Ltd v Ontario Municipal Insurance Exchange* [2010] EWHC 2279 (Comm.), [2011] Lloyd's Rep. I.R. 171; *Golden Ocean Group Ltd v Salgaocar Mining Industries Pvt Ltd* [2011] EWHC 56 (Comm.), [2011] 2 All E.R. (Comm.) 95. See also *The Magnum* [1989] 1 Lloyd's Rep. 47. Contrast *Nima SARL v Deves Public Insurance Co Ltd (The Prestrioka)* [2002] EWCA Civ 1132, [2003] 2 Lloyd's Rep. 327.

or where an issue of English public policy arises.[160] That said, although the significance of the governing law as an indication of where the natural forum may lie has been raised in a large number of cases, the treatment of this factor by the courts tends to show that the weight to be given to it is case-specific, and that generalisation is not appropriate.[161] One reason for this may be that it may not always be clear, at the time of the application for a stay, which law will be applied to resolve the issues which will arise for decision. Another may be that although an English court may identify "the" *lex causae* by reference to its own rules for choice of law, it cannot be assumed that the alternative forum would apply the same choice of law rules, from which it follows that the conclusion that the identity of "the" governing law points to the natural forum should not be drawn too quickly; and in any event, there may be several issues, only some of which appear to be governed by English law.[162] A number of rules of thumb have emerged, but they fall some way short of being decisive as indicators of the natural forum.

Four particular examples may be mentioned. In cases concerned with insurance written on the London market and governed by English law, there is a strong tendency for the court to consider England as the natural forum.[163] However, the cases also show that where the insurance was written on the London market but without an express choice of law, this fact was frequently taken to indicate that English law would be the law which governs the insurance; and if that is so, it will tend to show England to be the natural forum for the resolution of disputes. It is, however, unclear that this association of the *lex contractus* with the market on which the insurance was written will remain as close where the insurance falls within Art.8 of the Rome I Regulation.[164]

---

[160] *El du Pont de Nemours & Co v Agnew* [1987] 2 Lloyd's Rep. 585; *cf. Mitsubishi Corp v Alafouzos* [1988] 1 Lloyd's Rep. 191. *cf. Britannia Steamship Insurance Association v Ausonia Assicurazioni SpA* [1984] 2 Lloyd's Rep. 98 (CA) (contract impliedly governed by English law: Italian court would not apply English law: England appropriate forum); *Midland Bank Plc v Laker Airways Ltd* [1986] Q.B. 689 (CA) (application of US anti-trust law to commercial activity in England); *Banco Atlantico SA v British Bank of the Middle East* [1990] 2 Lloyd's Rep. 504 (refusal by foreign court to apply proper law of the contract); *Irish Shipping Ltd v Commercial Union Assurance Co Plc* [1991] 2 Q.B. 206, 229–230 (CA) (preference for the conflict of laws rules of the forum); *Novus Aviation Ltd v Onur Air Tasimacilik AS* [2009] EWCA Civ 122, [2009] 1 Lloyd's Rep. 576.

[161] The High Court of Australia has gone further in suggesting that it may be a factor of low significance, though in this respect its approach is not consistent with English law: see *Puttick v Tenon Ltd* [2008] HCA 54, (2008) 238 C.L.R. 265.

[162] *cf. Middle Eastern Oil LLC v National Bank of Abu Dhabi* [2008] EWHC 2895 (Comm.), [2009] 1 Lloyd's Rep. 251, [19]–[21].

[163] e.g. *Arkwright Mutual Insurance Co v Bryanston Insurance Co Ltd* [1990] 2 Q.B. 649; *Swiss Reinsurance Co Ltd v United India Insurance Co* [2003] EWHC 741 (Comm.), [2004] I.L.Pr. 53; *CGU International Insurance Plc v Szabo* [2002] 1 All E.R. (Comm.) 83; *Lincoln National Life Insurance Co v Employers' Reinsurance Corp* [2002] EWHC 28 (Comm.), [2002] Lloyd's Rep. I.R. 853; *Markel International Insurance Co Ltd v La Republica Compania Argentina de Seguros Generales SA* [2004] EWHC 1826 (Comm.), [2005] 1 Lloyd's Rep I.R. 90. But this will not be a strong factor if there is no major issue of law or construction: *Navigators' Insurance Co v Atlantic Methanol Production Co LLC* [2003] EWHC 1706 (Comm.); *Royal & Sun Alliance Insurance Plc v Retail Brand Alliance Inc* [2004] EWHC 2139 (Comm.), [2005] 1 Lloyd's Rep I.R. 110. *cf. Royal & Sun Alliance Insurance Plc v Rolls-Royce Plc* [2010] EWHC 1869 (Comm.), [2010] Lloyd's Rep. I.R. 637.

[164] See Rules 214–216.

In cases concerned with the internal management of foreign companies, there is a strong tendency to see the place of incorporation as the natural forum.[165] In the case of defamation[166] and perhaps in the case of tort generally,[167] there is a strong tendency to see the place of the tort as the natural forum. And the natural forum for the judicial interpretation of a will governed by English law and couched in English terminology is England.[168]

12–035   *The "Cambridgeshire" factor.* But if a court has acquired a special expertise in the resolution of a particularly complex species of dispute, so that it would be in the interests of justice to allow it to resolve the present case also, this may, in exceptional cases, affect the identification of the natural forum.[169]

12–036   **Overcoming the prima facie case for a stay.** In a number of cases the English court, in deciding whether to grant a stay, took into account differences between English law and the procedural law prevailing in the competing forum, such as the more extensive discovery available to litigants in the United States and the less extensive discovery available in civil law jurisdictions. But it is clear from the decision of the House of Lords in *The Abidin Daver*[170] that in exercising the discretion it is not normally appropriate for the court to compare the quality of justice obtainable in a foreign forum which adopts a different procedural system (such as that of the civil law) with that obtainable in a similar case conducted in an English court. In *Spiliada*, Lord

---

[165] *Konamaneni v Rolls-Royce International Industrial Power (India) Ltd* [2002] 1 W.L.R. 1269; *Ceskoslovenska Obchodni Banka AS v Nomura International Plc* [2003] I.L.Pr. 321; *Smay Investments Ltd v Sachdev* [2003] EWHC 474 (Ch.), [2003] 1 W.L.R. 1973; *Reeves v Sprecher* [2007] EWHC 117 (Ch.), [2008] B.C.C. 49; to similar effect, see *Re Krug International (UK) Ltd* [2008] EWHC 2256 (Ch.), [2008] B.P.I.R. 1512 (England proper place for claim arising out of misfeasance in English insolvency). By contrast, the presumption does not apply if the companies are not being wound up compulsorily, and no other issue of corporate governance arises: *Pakistan v Zardari* [2006] EWHC 2411 (Comm.), [2006] 2 C.L.C. 667. Likewise, in relation to the supervision and regulation of a trust, the country under the law of which the trust is established, and the courts of which are in a position to give effective direction to the trustees, may well be the natural forum for such a claim: *NABB Brothers Ltd v Lloyds Bank International (Guernsey) Ltd* [2005] EWHC 405 (Ch.), [2005] I.L.Pr. 506, at [59].

[166] *Berezovsky v Michaels* [2000] 1 W.L.R. 1004 (HL) (print media); *Dow Jones & Co Inc v Gutnick* (2003) 210 C.L.R. 575 (internet). But the weaker the connection with the forum the less persuasive this argument will be: *King v Lewis* [2004] EWCA Civ 1329, [2005] I.L.Pr. 185; and in an extreme case, to rely on a miniscule local publication as giving the court proper jurisdiction may be an abuse of the process: *Jameel v Dow Jones & Co Inc* [2005] EWCA Civ 75, [2005] Q.B. 946. For similar developments in Canada, see *Bangoura v The Washington Post* (2005) 258 D.L.R. (4th) 341 (Ont CA).

[167] *The Albaforth* [1984] 2 Lloyd's Rep. 91 (CA). See para.11–217, above.

[168] *Dellar v Zivy* [2007] EWHC 2266 (Ch.), [2007] I.L.Pr. 868; see also *Jaiswal v Jaiswal* [2007] Jersey L.R. 305.

[169] *Spiliada*, at pp.484–486, where it is referred to as the *"Cambridgeshire* factor", after the ship which gave its name to the earlier litigation. But examples of cases in which this argument has been accepted are extremely rare. The issue was considered, but not given decisive effect, in *Royal & Sun Alliance Insurance Plc v Rolls-Royce Plc* [2010] EWHC 1869 (Comm.), [2010] Lloyd's Rep. I.R. 637.

[170] [1984] A.C. 398, approving the approach in *Amin Rasheed Shipping Corp v Kuwait Insurance Co* [1984] A.C. 50 (a service out case) and in *The El Amria* [1981] 2 Lloyd's Rep. 119 (CA) (an exclusive jurisdiction clause case). See also *The Traugutt* [1985] 1 Lloyd's Rep. 76, 79.

Goff of Chieveley said that injustice could not be said to be done if a party were in effect compelled to accept one of the well-recognised systems of procedural law in the appropriate foreign forum.[171] There may be cases where there is a risk that justice will not be obtained in a foreign court because of the inexperience or inefficiency of the judiciary[172] or excessive delay[173] in the conduct of the business of the courts, or the unavailability of appropriate remedies. But a claimant in the English court who wishes to resist a stay of English proceedings on such a ground must assert it candidly and support the allegation with positive and cogent evidence.[174]

If, however, the effect of a stay would be to deprive the claimant of the right **12–037** to obtain a hearing[175] of a claim which deserves to be heard, the interests of justice will rarely be served by ordering a stay of the proceedings; to put the same point another way, if practical justice requires that a trial take place in England because it is unrealistic to expect that it will be possible to obtain a sensible hearing in the alternative forum, it is improbable that a stay will be appropriate:[176] a conclusion which may today be reinforced by reference to Art.6 of the European Convention on Human Rights.[177] Thus if the claimant is able to obtain financial support for proceedings if they are brought in England, but will be unable to obtain it, or a reasonable equivalent, if the claim must be brought in the foreign court and will as a result be unable to sue at all, it will rarely be just to grant a stay of the proceedings.[178] Likewise, if the proceedings in the foreign court would be time-barred, it may be unjust to order a stay, unless the defendant undertakes to waive the time bar, or unless the claimant may be regarded as having been at fault in failing to save limitation by commencing proceedings in the foreign court.[179]

---

[171] [1987] A.C. at 482–483, citing *Trendtex Trading Corp v Crédit Suisse* [1982] A.C. 679 (stay granted in favour of Swiss forum, where plaintiffs in fraud claim would not have benefit of extensive discovery available in England); see also *Re Harrods (Buenos Aires) Ltd* [1992] Ch. 72, 126 (CA).

[172] *Lubbe v Cape Plc* [2000] 1 W.L.R. 1545 (HL).

[173] *cf. The Jalakrishna* [1983] 2 Lloyd's Rep. 628; *The Vishva Ajay* [1989] 2 Lloyd's Rep. 558; *Konamaneni v Rolls-Royce International Industrial Power (India) Ltd* [2002] 1 W.L.R. 1269; *XN Corp Ltd v Point of Sale Ltd* [2001] I.L.Pr. 525 (availability of expedited trial in England). But see also *Radhakrishna Hospitality Service Pte Ltd v EIH Ltd* [1999] 2 Lloyd's Rep. 249.

[174] *The Abidin Daver* [1984] A.C. 398, 411. See also *Muduroglu Ltd v TC Ziraat Bankasi* [1986] Q.B. 1225, 1247–1249 (CA); and *cf. Purcell v Khayat, The Times*, November 23, 1987 (CA). For further analysis of this point in the light of the most recent cases, see below, para.12–040.

[175] Including a case where the predictable delay in the foreign court is equivalent to his not obtaining a hearing at all: *The Vishva Ajay* [1989] 2 Lloyd's Rep. 558; *Pall Corp v Commercial Hydraulics (Bedford) Ltd* [1989] R.P.C. 703 (CA); *The Al Battani* [1993] 2 Lloyd's Rep. 219, 223–224; *cf. The Nile Rhapsody* [1992] 2 Lloyd's Rep. 399, 413–414, affirmed [1994] 1 Lloyd's Rep. 382 (CA).

[176] *AK Investment CJSC v Kyrgyz Mobil Tel Ltd* [2011] UKPC 7, [151], [2011] 4 All E.R. 1027.

[177] *Lubbe v Cape Plc* [2000] 1 W.L.R. 1545 (HL); *cf.* (on the potential impact of Art.6, European Convention on Human Rights): *R. (on the application of Smith) v Secretary of State for Defence* [2010] UKSC 29, [2011] 1 A.C. 1, [301]; *EM (Lebanon) v Secretary of State for the Home Department* [2008] UKHL 64, [2009] A.C. 1198 (a deportation case).

[178] *ibid.* See also *Connelly v RTZ Corp Plc* [1998] A.C. 854.

[179] *Spiliada Maritime Corp v Cansulex Ltd*, above, at pp.483–484; see below, para.12–154.

12–038   Differences between the measure of recovery (or other remedies[180]) available in England and in the foreign court will not generally overcome the prima facie case for a stay of proceedings,[181] whether this follows from different judicial approaches to the assessment of damages or from statutory limitations upon the measure of recovery.[182] Similarly, if the claimant argues that he will win if permitted to sue in England, but will lose if compelled to sue in the foreign court, there is no justification for a presumption that a claimant is entitled to win or that a defendant must be found to be liable.[183] It has been held that a claimant may overcome the case for a stay the foreign court's approach to the awarding of costs consume the fruits of recovery and render any victory largely pyrrhic,[184] but such a conclusion will tend to undermine the *Spiliada* principle, and it should be accepted, if ever,[185] only in very rare cases. It has been held that it is unjust to deprive a claimant of a judgment which he will be able to enforce overseas, with the consequence that if an English judgment would be enforceable under Chapter III of the Brussels I Regulation and Title III of the Lugano Convention, it may be unjust if he is required to sue in a court whose judgment would not be entitled to enforcement under these provisions.[186] The case for a stay may also be overcome if to grant it would adversely affect the efficient conduct of litigation: in a case with multiple defendants, if the result of one defendant obtaining a stay would be to force the claimant to bring his claim in two separate sets of proceedings, with the possible further consequence of inconsistent conclusions being reached by the two courts, it will not generally serve the interests of justice to order a stay.[187] However, no account is to be taken of factors of independent

---

[180] *Re Harrods (Buenos Aires) Ltd* [1992] Ch. 72 (CA); *cf. The Falstria* [1988] 1 Lloyd's Rep. 495; *Intermetal Group Ltd v Worslade Trading Ltd* [1998] I.L.Pr. 765 (Irish Sup Ct).

[181] *Spiliada Maritime Corp v Cansulex Ltd*, above, at 482.

[182] *The Herceg Novi* [1998] 4 All E.R. 238 (CA) (not unjust to stay proceedings in favour of Singapore where Hague Rules would limit recovery to a lower figure than available in England under the Convention on Limitation for Maritime Claims 1976). *cf. Baghlaf Al Safer Factory Co Br. for Industry Ltd v Pakistan National Shipping Corp* [1998] 2 Lloyd's Rep. 229 (CA) (reasonable for plaintiff to disregard jurisdiction agreement and sue in England where foreign court would limit liability to a fraction of the claim).

[183] *cf. Garsec v Sultan of Brunei* [2008] NSWCA 211, (2008) 250 A.L.R. 682 (stay of Australian proceedings though claim not justiciable in Brunei, though as Australian court would have applied the law of Brunei in any event, the claim was doomed).

[184] *Roneleigh Ltd v MII Exports Inc* [1989] 1 W.L.R. 619 (CA); *Agrafax Public Relations Ltd v United Scottish Society Inc* [1995] I.L.Pr. 753 (CA); *cf. The Vishva Ajay* [1989] 2 Lloyd's Rep. 558; *The Oinoussian Pride* [1991] 1 Lloyd's Rep 126; *The Al Battani* [1993] 2 Lloyd's Rep. 219.

[185] *cf. BHP Billiton Ltd v Schulz* (2004) 221 C.L.R. 400, at [258] (High Ct).

[186] *International Credit and Investment Co (Overseas) Ltd v Adham* [1999] I.L.Pr. 302 (CA); *Inter-Tel Inc v OCIS Plc* [2004] EWHC 2269 (QB); *Sharab v Al-Saud* [2009] EWCA Civ 353, [2009] 2 Lloyd's Rep. 160. But in the light of Case C–281/02 *Owusu v Jackson* [2005] E.C.R. I–1383, [2005] Q.B. 801, the court's power to grant a stay on the ground of *forum non conveniens,* in favour of the courts of a non-Member or non-Convention State, is much diminished in any event, which development will reduce the significance of this point.

[187] *Insurance Corp of Ireland v Strombus* [1985] 2 Lloyd's Rep. 138 (CA); *A-G v Arthur Andersen & Co* [1989] E.C.C. 224, 229; *Charm Maritime Inc v Kyriakou* [1987] 1 Lloyd's Rep. 433 (CA); *El du Pont de Nemours & Co v Agnew* [1987] 2 Lloyd's Rep. 585 (CA); *The Goldean Mariner* [1989] 2 Lloyd's Rep. 390, reversed on different grounds [1990] 2 Lloyd's Rep. 215 (CA); *First National Bank of Boston v Union Bank of Switzerland* [1990] 1 Lloyd's Rep. 32 (CA); *New Hampshire Insurance Co v Strabag Bau AG* [1992] 1 Lloyd's Rep. 361 (CA); *The Abidin Daver* [1984] A.C. 398, 423; *Bouygues Offshore SA v Caspian Shipping Co (Nos 1, 3, 4, 5)* [1998]

"public interest", such as the length of the queue of cases waiting to be heard, in considering whether to stay the proceedings. By contrast with the law of the United States, there is no element of public interest separate from the factors relevant to the parties, in the doctrine of *forum non conveniens*; the statement frequently found in United States judgments, to the effect that a foreign state has an interest, or a strong interest, in its law being applied, or in its courts adjudicating a claim, does not reflect English law.[188]

In determining whether, even though a foreign forum is the appropriate one, **12–039** justice requires that a stay should not be granted, the court may take account of the fact that if the stay is granted the claimant will be deprived of security, and may make the stay conditional on retention of security.[189]

Direct criticism of the foreign court. Until recently the opportunity for a **12–040** claimant to resist a stay by submitting that a trial before the foreign court, shown otherwise to be the natural forum, would be so objectively unjust that a stay should not be ordered, was restricted. Though in *The Abidin Daver*[190] Lord Diplock had accepted that such a contention might properly be advanced, he made it clear that its success would be dependent upon furnishing clear and cogent evidence that proceedings before a foreign court would fall below the minimum acceptable standards of doing what justice would require: it would not be sufficient to asperse the foreign court in general terms, or hint at criticism which was not made openly and candidly. This may have inhibited claimants who realised that if they sought to make the argument to resist a stay but did not prevail, it would be embarrassing to have to make their claim before the foreign court which they had so criticised. For while it is one thing to assert that a foreign court is inexperienced or its judiciary overworked so that delay is shocking, it is quite another to allege that it may be partial or even corrupt.

However, since 2009 claimants have been more successful in resisting stays **12–041** of proceedings, or even obtaining permission to serve out,[191] on the basis that as the foreign court cannot be trusted to do justice, the case should be allowed to proceed in England.[192] Of course, where the civil administration has utterly broken down, a stay in favour of the courts of that place cannot be granted.[193] The same principle will surely apply where the state is fully functioning, but

---

2 Lloyd's Rep. 461 (CA); *The El Amria* [1981] 2 Lloyd's Rep. 119 (CA); *The MC Pearl* [1997] 1 Lloyd's Rep. 556; *Citi-March Ltd v Neptune Orient Lines Ltd* [1996] 1 W.L.R. 1367 (the latter three cases on jurisdiction agreements); *McConnell Dowell Constructors Ltd v Lloyd's Syndicate 396* [1988] 2 N.Z.L.R. 257, 41 (CA); *cf. Soc Nat Ind Aérospatiale v Lee Kui Jak* [1987] A.C. 871, 901 (PC) (a case on injunctions).

[188] *Lubbe v Cape Plc* [2000] 1 W.L.R. 1545 (HL). For a contrary suggestion, see *James Hardie Industries Pty Ltd v Grigor* (1998) 45 N.S.W.L.R. 20, 40, 43 (CA).

[189] *Spiliada Maritime Corp v Cansulex Ltd* [1987] A.C. 460, 483; Civil Jurisdiction and Judgments Act 1982, s.26; see above, paras 8–041 *et seq.*

[190] [1984] A.C. 398.

[191] See clause (3) of this Rule, below, para.12–053.

[192] This presupposes that the court has jurisdiction over the defendant in the first place. It is not an adoption of the idea of a forum of necessity as this is found in some civilian systems.

[193] *889457 Alberta Inc v Katanga Mining Ltd* [2008] EWHC 2679 (Comm.), [2009] I.L.Pr. 175: the case may also be seen as one in which the court in the Kolwezi district of Congo was not shown by the defendant to be available to the claimant for the trial of the action.

in so depraved a fashion that the very idea that there might be a fair trial there is an absurdity.[194] But in less extreme cases, where the claimant is able to persuade the court that there is a risk[195] that the foreign court will single out the claimant or his claim for flagrantly unjust treatment, or that the foreign court is generally and seriously unreliable, it now appears that the court will not generally[196] order a stay of proceedings. The evidence required to support this contention need not be particular to the claimant or his individual claim (though it may be more persuasive if it is), but may be based on more general evidence of judicial failure or misconduct in relation to claims of the type advanced by the claimant.[197] So far, such fault has been found with certain states of the former USSR in cases in which there may be said to be a state interest in the outcome of the litigation,[198] but the modern statement of the principle is not confined to such states and such cases.[199]

12–042   *Lis alibi pendens.* There are special rules in the Brussels I Regulation, and in the Lugano Convention for simultaneous actions which are pending in different Member or Convention States between the same parties and involving the same cause of action or related causes of action.[200] Where the case is not covered by these instruments, it frequently happens that, in cases in which the English court is asked to stay English proceedings or restrain foreign proceedings, there are simultaneous actions pending in England and in a foreign

---

[194] *Oppenheimer v Louis Rosenthal & Co AG* [1937] 1 All E.R. 23; *Ellinger v Guinness Mahon & Co* [1939] 4 All E.R. 16 (Nazi court; Jewish litigants).

[195] *AK Investment CJSC v Kyrgyz Mobil Tel* [2011] UKPC 7, [2011] 4 All E.R. 1027, [92]–[95], [143].

[196] Whether this analysis applies with modification where the foreign court is one to the jurisdiction of which the claimant has submitted by contract remains to be decided, though if the claimant relies on facts and matters which were known about, or capable of being known about, when the contract was made, it should not be open to him to invoke them as reasons to resist a stay: see below, para.12–053.

[197] *ibid*, [101]. It has not been decided whether the argument may be sustained by evidence taking the form of supposed worldwide surveys of judicial quality and corruption.

[198] *Cherney v Deripaska* [2009] EWCA Civ 849, [2010] All E.R. (Comm.) 456 (Russia; inter-oligarch dispute concerning natural resources of State: service out, evidence accepted); *Pacific International Sports Clubs Ltd v Surkis* [2010] EWCA Civ 753 (Ukraine; ownership of Dinamo Kiev FC: criticism considered at length but falling just short of judicial acceptance); *AK Investment CJSC v Kyrgyz Mobil Tel* [2011] UKPC 7, [2011] 4 All E.R. 1027 (Kyrgyzstan; control of mobile telephone service: service out and foreign judgments); *Yukos Capital sarl v OJSC Rosneft Oil Co* [2011] EWHC 1461 (Comm.), [2011] 2 Lloyd's Rep. 443 (Russia; campaign to divest Yukos oil company of its assets: foreign judgments, issue regarded as res judicata by decision of Dutch court which had accepted the evidence); *Merchant International Co Ltd v NAK Naftogaz Ukrayiny* [2011] EWHC 1820 (Comm.), [2011] 2 All E.R. (Comm.) 755 (Ukraine; claim involving state energy company: foreign judgments, evidence accepted). For a case in which similar criticism has been advanced but rejected, see *OJSC Oil Co Yugraneft v Abramovich* [2008] EWHC 2613 (Comm.) (Russia).

[199] *Al-Koronky v Time-Life Entertainment Group Ltd* [2006] EWCA Civ 1123 (lack of impartiality in Sudanese court); *Korea National Insurance Co v Allianz Global Corporate and Specialty AG* [2008] EWCA Civ 1355, [2008] 2 C.L.C. 837 (North Korea; unfeasibly huge claim by state airline company against insurer, settled before the evidence was tendered for assessment: foreign judgments). The approach in *Jeyaretnam v Mahmood* (*The Times*, May 21, 1992) on this point, treating such allegations as inappropriate, is not now reliable.

[200] See clause (4) of the Rule discussed below, paras 12–055 *et seq.*

country between the same parties and involving the same or similar issues.[201]

Although it was once thought that there were special factors in cases of *lis*   **12–043**
alibi pendens, presumably because *litispendence* has always been more widely accepted as a ground for jurisdictional relief, it is now clear that the existence of simultaneous proceedings is no more than a factor relevant to the determination of the appropriate forum. In *The Abidin Daver*[202] Lord Diplock said that, where proceedings were pending in a foreign court between the parties, and the defendant in the foreign proceedings commenced proceedings as plaintiff in England, then the additional inconvenience or expense which must result from allowing two sets of legal proceedings to be pursued concurrently in two different jurisdictions, where the same facts would be in issue and the testimony of the same witnesses required, could in principle only be justified if the would-be plaintiff in England could establish objectively by cogent evidence that there was some personal or juridical advantage that would be available to him only in the English action and which was of such importance that it would cause injustice to deprive him of it. This was an application of his formula in *MacShannon v Rockware Glass Ltd*[203] to cases of *lis alibi pendens*. It was confirmed[204] that the principles enunciated in *Spiliada Maritime Corp v Cansulex Ltd*[205] apply whether or not there are other proceedings already pending in the alternative forum: the foreign proceedings may be of no relevance at all, for example, if one party has commenced them for the purpose of demonstrating the existence of a competing jurisdiction,[206] or if the proceedings have not passed beyond the stage of initiating process. But if genuine proceedings have been started and have had some impact on the dispute between the parties,[207] especially if it is likely to have a continuing effect, then this may be a relevant (but not necessarily decisive[208]) factor when considering whether the foreign jurisdiction provides the appropriate forum.

In *Australian Commercial Research and Development Ltd v ANZ*   **12–044**
McCaughan Merchant Bank Ltd[209] Sir Nicolas Browne-Wilkinson V.-C. approved the statement in the eleventh edition of this work that where the same plaintiff sues the same defendant in England and abroad it is not likely

---

[201] But patent infringement proceedings involving patents granted in several countries may be allowed to proceed at the same time, even though the cost of defending them may be difficult for the alleged infringer: *Affymetrix Inc v Multilyte Ltd* [2004] EWHC 291 (Ch.), [2005] I.L.Pr. 470.

[202] [1984] A.C. 398, 411–412.

[203] [1978] A.C. 795.

[204] *De Dampierre v De Dampierre* [1988] A.C. 92, 108.

[205] [1987] A.C. 460.

[206] As in the cases of actions for negative declarations discussed below, para.12–048. See also *Trumann Investment Group Ltd v Société Générale SA* [2004] EWHC 1769 (Ch.).

[207] See, e.g., *Cleveland Museum of Art v Capricorn International SA* [1990] 2 Lloyd's Rep. 166; *cf. Teck Cominco Metals Ltd v Lloyd's Underwriters* [2009] SCC 11, (2009) 303 D.L.R. (4th) 385; *Meridien Biao Bank GmbH v Bank of New York* [1997] 1 Lloyd's Rep. 437 (CA). In the context of jurisdiction agreements, see *Donohue v Armco Inc* [2001] UKHL 64, [2002] 1 Lloyd's Rep. 425.

[208] See *Meadows Indemnity Co Ltd v Insurance Corp of Ireland Plc* [1989] 2 Lloyd's Rep. 298 (CA).

[209] [1989] 3 All E.R. 65, affirmed February 23, 1990 (CA, unreported) See also *Racy v Hawila* [2004] EWCA Civ 209; *Al-Bassam v Al-Bassam* [2004] EWCA Civ 857.

that the court would allow, except in very unusual circumstances,[210] the continuation of proceedings in two different jurisdictions. The court would put the plaintiff to his election. In that case the Vice-Chancellor said that if the plaintiff opted to continue the foreign proceedings the English proceedings could not merely be stayed; the plaintiff would have to discontinue them. But there may be cases (e.g. where one of the actions is brought to obtain security by way of an attachment of assets) where a stay rather than an order for discontinuance of English proceedings, or an injunction requiring foreign proceedings to be discontinued, or by an order made in the context of case management,[211] would be appropriate.[212]

12–045   But there will be other cases in which the claimant may justify the bringing of proceedings in more than one court. For example, the claimant may have founded jurisdiction by the attachment of assets in two countries in circumstances where he claims to be entitled to both sets of assets; it may be necessary to bring parallel proceedings in order to prevent the cross-border infringement of an intellectual property right;[213] it may be necessary or desirable to bring proceedings in two jurisdictions, in order to be able to enforce both judgments locally, where this appears to be the only way to obtain full satisfaction of the claim against the defendant.[214] In such cases the allegation that the claimant is acting oppressively, and the submission that he should be put to his election, or other relief granted,[215] will be sufficiently answered. The same analysis is likely to be applied where the parties have agreed by contract that multiple of parallel proceedings may be brought by (say) the lender against a borrower, at least where the agreement can be shown to be commercially rational. Though there may be instances in which such a contractual right may be invoked in an inequitable way, and so be liable to restraint, the court will be likely to wish to hold the parties to their agreement and to refrain from the granting of relief which would restrict the exercise of a freely-negotiated contractual right.[216]

12–046   Where, however, the parties' contract appears to provide for the bringing of parallel proceedings before the courts of two or more Member States, it is improbable that such private agreement can displace the provisions of the Brussels I Regulation which prevent or control *lis alibi pendens*, which are mandatory in their operation, and which are examined as clause (4) of this Rule. Similarly, where the parallel proceedings are before the courts of a Member State and a non-Member State, the powers of the court to grant

---

[210] Such as where the proceedings were instituted purely to preserve the limitation position: *cf.* above, para.12–037.

[211] *Al-Bassam v Al-Bassam* [2004] EWCA Civ 857.

[212] *Walsh v Deloitte & Touche Inc* [2001] UKPC 58, (2001) 59 W.I.R. 30 (proceedings in Bahamas brought in order to obtain freezing injunction where substantive claim to be pursued in Canada). For a similar approach in the context of Art.27 of the Regulation, see *JP Morgan Europe Ltd v Primacom AG* [2005] EWHC 508 (Comm.), [2005] 2 Lloyd's Rep. 665.

[213] *Celltech R&D Ltd v MedImmune Inc* [2004] EWCA Civ 1331.

[214] *Karafarin Bank v Mansoury-Dara* [2009] EWHC 1217 (Comm.), [2009] 2 Lloyd's Rep. 289.

[215] Such as an anti-suit injunction.

[216] *Royal Bank of Canada v Cooperatieve Centrale Raiffeisen-Boerenleenbank BA* [2004] EWCA Civ 7, [2004] 1 Lloyd's Rep. 471; *Deutsche Bank AG v Highland Crusader Offshore Partners LP* [2009] EWCA Civ 725, [2010] 1 W.L.R. 1023; *TS Production LLC v Drew Pictures Pty Ltd* [2008] FCAFC 194, (2008) 252 A.L.R. 1.

jurisdictional relief are subject to the controls imposed, and therefore restricted, by the Regulation.[217]

Timing of application for a stay. Until the coming into force of the Civil   **12–047**
Procedure Rules 1998 it was generally accepted that an application for a stay of proceedings was not a challenge to the jurisdiction of the court; and that an application for a stay of proceedings was not required to be sought within the procedure, and within the time limited, for challenging the jurisdiction under RSC Order 12, r.8.[218] It was confirmed in *Texan Management Ltd v Pacific Electric Wire & Cable Co Ltd*[219] that CPR, Pt 11 now requires that an application for a stay, like a challenge to the jurisdiction of the court, be made within 14[220] days of the acknowledgment of service, and the previous sharp distinction between a challenge to the jurisdiction and an application for a stay has been removed. If the defendant wishes to apply for a stay after the expiry of that period, the court has a discretion under CPR, r.3.1(2)(a) to extend the time. In the case of an application for a stay of proceedings, where the grounds justifying the application for a stay may not emerge until some time after the defence has been served, there is no reason to suppose that the court should be reluctant to extend the time to allow the application to be made.[221] An application for a stay of proceedings on the basis of Art.28 of the Brussels I Regulation[222] may be made outside the time period limited by CPR, Pt.11.[223]

Claims for negative declarations.[224] A claim for a negative declaration is   **12–048**
for a declaration by the court that the defendant has no valid claim or right against the claimant.[225] It was once said that in England such a declaration would rarely be made, and that in most cases the person who seeks it will be left to set up his defence in the action when it is brought;[226] but this attitude of outright hostility has now been replaced by one of neutral caution.[227]

---

[217] See para.12–023, *supra*.

[218] *The Messiniaki Tolmi* [1984] 1 Lloyd's Rep. 266, 270 (CA); *cf. Ngcobo v Thor Chemicals (Holdings) Ltd, The Times*, November 10, 1995 (CA).

[219] [2009] UKPC 46.

[220] But in the Commercial Court, 28 days: CPR, r.58.7.

[221] Alternatively, the application may be made by reference to the inherent discretion of the court, though the distinct jurisdictional basis of the application has little practical significance. *cf. CNA Insurance Co v OD Inc* [2005] EWHC 456 (Comm.), [2005] Lloyd's Rep. I.R. 658 (two year delay held to be far too late).

[222] See further, clause (4) of this Rule.

[223] *Cooper Tire & Rubber Co v Shell Chemicals UK Ltd* [2009] EWHC 2609 (Comm.), [2009] I.L.Pr. 886, [96]–[103] (affd. without reference to this point: *Cooper Tire & Rubber Co Europe Ltd v Bayer Public Co Ltd* [2010] EWCA Civ 864, [2010] Bus. L.R. 1697), for otherwise a rule of English procedural law might be seen to damage the operation of the Regulation.

[224] See Collins, *Essays*, p.274; Bell (1995) 111 L.Q.R. 674.

[225] See Zamir and Woolf, *The Declaratory Judgment* (4th ed. 2011), paras 3–160, 4–167. For the procedure, see CPR, r.40.20.

[226] *Guaranty Trust Co v Hannay* [1915] 2 K.B. 536, 564–565 (CA). See also *Midland Bank Plc v Laker Airways Ltd* [1986] Q.B. 689 (CA).

[227] *Messier Dowty Ltd v Sabena SA* [2000] 1 W.L.R. 2040 (CA). For judicial confirmation of the view that such proceedings are not uncommon in other Member States, see *Andrea Merzario Ltd v International Spedition Leitner GmbH* [2001] EWCA Civ 61, [2001] 1 Lloyd's Rep. 49 (CA).

Sometimes a negative declaration has been sought in England in order to support a claim for an injunction to restrain foreign proceedings.[228]

12–049   It sometimes happens that a party seeks a negative declaration in the English court, or in the foreign court, in order to support a contention that the English court, or the foreign court (as the case may be), is the appropriate forum. This doubtless lay behind the earlier judicial view that claims for negative declarations must be viewed with great caution in all situations involving possible conflicts of jurisdiction, since they lend themselves to improper attempts at forum shopping.[229] Outside the domain of the Regulation, and the Lugano Convention,[230] it is still open to a court to take the view that proceedings have been brought by way of forum shopping, and the court will in all cases still exercise scrutiny to ensure that the declaratory procedure is not being abused. Accordingly, it may stay English proceedings for a negative declaration against defendants subject to the jurisdiction of the English court where a foreign court is the *forum conveniens*;[231] and the English court will not be disposed to authorise service out of the jurisdiction under Pt 6 of the Civil Procedure Rules, i.e. Rule 34, in a claim for a negative declaration, unless England is the appropriate forum.[232] Nor generally[233] will a claim in a foreign court for a negative declaration be of much weight in determining whether the foreign court is the appropriate forum for the purpose of staying English proceedings, or in determining whether the English court is the appropriate forum for the purposes of service out of the jurisdiction.[234] Indeed, the foreign proceedings for a negative declaration may be so artificial as to justify the grant of an injunction by the English court to restrain them.[235]

12–050   In many cases, however, there is a legitimate role for a bona fide claim for a negative declaration.[236] In modern commercial litigation, notably in the field

---

[228] e.g. *Smith Kline & French Laboratories Ltd v Bloch* [1983] 1 W.L.R. 730 (CA); *British Airways Board v Laker Airways Ltd* [1985] A.C. 58. *cf. The Rama* [1996] 2 Lloyd's Rep. 281. See para.12–081, below, for the impact of *Turner v Grovit* [2001] UKHL 65, [2002] 1 W.L.R. 107.

[229] *The Volvox Hollandia* [1988] 2 Lloyd's Rep. 361, 371 (CA).

[230] As to which, see further below.

[231] Subject to the provisions of the Regulation and the Convention (as to which, see below, para.12–051): *Camilla Cotton Oil Co v Granadex SA* [1976] 2 Lloyd's Rep. 10 (HL); *First National Bank of Boston v Union Bank of Switzerland* [1990] 1 Lloyd's Rep. 32 (CA); *New Hampshire Insurance Co v Aerospace Finance Ltd* [1998] 2 Lloyd's Rep. 539.

[232] *Insurance Co of Ireland v Strombus International Insurance Co* [1985] 2 Lloyd's Rep. 138 (CA); *The Volvox Hollandia* [1988] 2 Lloyd's Rep. 361 (CA); *Charman v WOC Offshore BV* [1993] 1 Lloyd's Rep. 378. *cf. Finnish Marine Insurance Co Ltd v Protective National Insurance Co* [1990] 1 Q.B. 1078. Contrast *Gulf Bank KSC v Mitsubishi Heavy Industries Ltd* [1994] 1 Lloyd's Rep. 323.

[233] Though it may be argued that as English law now recognises much more clearly the proper purpose of such proceedings, it should be less dismissive of similar proceedings before foreign courts.

[234] *EI du Pont de Nemours & Co v Agnew* [1987] 2 Lloyd's Rep. 585 (CA); *Arkwright Mutual Insurance Co v Bryanston Insurance Co Ltd* [1990] 2 Q.B. 649 (overruled on other grounds: *Re Harrods (Buenos Aires) Ltd* [1992] Ch. 72 (CA)); *Kawasaki Steel Corp v Owners of "Daeyang Honey"* (1993) 120 A.L.R. 109 (Fed Ct).

[235] *Sohio Supply Co v Gatoil (USA) Inc* [1989] 1 Lloyd's Rep. 588 (CA). Contrast *EI du Pont de Nemours & Co v Agnew (No.2)* [1988] 2 Lloyd's Rep. 240 (CA).

[236] See *The Rama* [1996] 2 Lloyd's Rep. 281, 291; *Akai Pty Ltd v People's Insurance Co Ltd* [1998] 1 Lloyd's Rep. 90, 106; *New Hampshire Insurance Co v Aerospace Finance Ltd* [1998]

of insurance, a party may have a genuine commercial need to obtain an early determination upon his liability to another who may seek to claim against him: an insurer who wishes to know whether he should conduct the defence of a threatened claim against his insured;[237] a supplier who needs to know whether he is obliged to continue to supply a distributor or may, instead, deal elsewhere.[238] Where a stay of proceedings for a negative declaration is sought (or there is an application to set aside service out of the jurisdiction) the court will have to consider both the question whether there is justification for seeking that form of relief and the question whether England is the appropriate forum;[239] and there will be no presumption that the proceedings are inappropriately brought.[240] If, by contrast, the court finds that such a declaration would be ignored in foreign legal proceedings between the parties and would therefore serve only to increase the risk of conflicting judgments, or if the proceedings are premature[241] in the sense that the claimant has no reasonable apprehension of being sued by the defendant,[242] or there is no sensible point in making the declaration,[243] the claimant may be regarded as abusing the process of the court.[244] The court is therefore likely to exercise its discretion to strike out the application[245] or refuse to make the order, or to stay the proceedings, or to refuse to give permission to serve process out of the jurisdiction, as the case may be.[246]

Negative declarations and the Brussels I Regulation and Lugano Convention.   12–051
Where the case is governed by the Regulation or the Convention, the ordinary jurisdictional rules of these instruments, together with their rules for preventing or controlling a situation of *lis alibi pendens* (which are examined under clause (4) of this Rule), apply to actions for negative declarations and make no distinction to reflect the fact that one set of proceedings is in the form

---

2 Lloyd's Rep. 539, 543; *Tryg Baltica International (UK) Ltd v Boston Compania de Seguros SA* [2004] EWHC 1186 (Comm.), [2005] Lloyd's Rep. I.R. 40; *Ark Therapeutics Ltd v True North Capital Ltd* [2005] EWHC 1585 (Comm.), [2006] 1 All E.R. (Comm.) 138.

[237] *cf. Booker v Bell* [1989] 1 Lloyd's Rep. 516; *HIB Ltd v Guardian Insurance Co Inc* [1997] 1 Lloyd's Rep. 412; *Gan Insurance Co Ltd v Tai Ping Insurance Co Ltd* [1998] C.L.C. 1072.

[238] *Boss Group Ltd v Boss France SA* [1997] 1 W.L.R. 351 (CA); *Smyth v Behbehani* [1999] I.L.Pr. 599 (CA).

[239] The points are separate and distinct: *New Hampshire Insurance Co v Phillips Electronics* [1998] I.L.Pr. 256 (CA).

[240] *Messier Dowty v Sabena SA* [2000] 1 W.L.R. 2040 (CA); *Bristow Helicopters Ltd v Sikorsky Aircraft Corp* [2004] EWHC 401 (Comm.), [2004] 2 Lloyd's Rep. 150.

[241] But an application for a declaration that a foreign judgment would be entitled to recognition in England was justified even though no other proceedings to seek to subvert that judgment were in prospect: *Phillips v Avena* [2005] EWHC 3333 (Ch).

[242] *Gulf Bank KSC v Mitsubishi Heavy Industries Ltd* [1994] 1 Lloyd's Rep. 323, at 329–330.

[243] *American Motorists Insurance Co Ltd v Cellstar Corp* [2003] EWCA Civ 206, [2003] I.L.Pr. 370; *cf. Standard Bank Plc v Agrinvest International Inc* [2007] EWHC 2595 (Comm.), [2008] 1 Lloyd's Rep. 532 (declarations as to jurisdiction, governing law, and non-liability, presumably to pave way for plea of estoppel).

[244] *Boss Group Ltd v Boss France SA*, above.

[245] CPR, r.3.4.

[246] *New Hampshire Insurance Co v Aerospace Finance Ltd* [1998] 2 Lloyd's Rep. 539; *Royal & Sun Alliance Plc v Retail Brand Alliance* [2004] EWHC 2139 (Comm.), [2005] 1 Lloyd's Rep. I.R. 110; *Limit (No.3) Ltd v PDV Insurance Ltd* [2005] EWCA Civ 383, [2005] Lloyd's Rep. I.R. 552.

of an action for declaratory relief. It follows from this that where the claim is founded on the jurisdictional rules in Chapter II of the Regulation or Title II of the Convention, the court may not consider that there is any element of forum shopping in the bringing of the proceedings, though it will still be permitted to find that the procedure is being used for an abusive, oppressive, or otherwise improper purpose. In *Gubisch Maschinenfabrik KG v Palumbo*[247] it was held that what is now Art.27 of the Regulation (which gives priority to the court first seised) applies where, in relation to the same contract, one party applies to a court in a Member State or Convention State for a declaration that a contract is inoperative, whilst the other institutes proceedings before the courts of another such State for its enforcement. Likewise, in *The Tatry*,[248] where proceedings were brought in the Netherlands for a declaration that the carrier had no liability for alleged cargo damage, and subsequently an action was brought in England by the cargo owner in respect of damage to the cargo, it was held that what are now Arts 27 and 28[249] were capable of applying to the proceedings in the English court: the Articles apply without regard to the nature or procedural nature of the claim and it is irrelevant, even if true, that the proceedings were instituted for the purpose of forum shopping.[250] Indeed, Tesauro A.-G. went so far as to characterise proceedings for a declaration of non-liability as being "generally allowed under the various national procedural laws and [as] entirely legitimate in every respect".[251] The result is that, in recent years, more actions for negative declaratory relief have been brought and permitted to proceed than was the case thirty years ago. *Messier Dowty v Sabena SA*[252] confirms the Court of Appeal's adoption of the new approach to such claims.

12–052   **Clause (3) of the Rule.** The role of *forum conveniens* in the exercise of the discretion to grant permission for service out of the jurisdiction under Pt 6 of the Civil Procedure Rules has already been mentioned in connection with Rule 34. The first version of what later became RSC Order 11, in 1875 required, in cases of contract, the court to take into account "the comparative cost and convenience of proceeding in England or in the place of the defendant's residence"; from the 1883 revision of Order 11 this condition applied only to defendants in Scotland and Ireland (later Northern Ireland).[253] But it was also established from the earliest years of the application of Order 11 that, in cases falling outside the express provision, *forum conveniens* was a relevant

---

[247] Case 144/86 [1987] E.C.R. 4861. *cf.* Case C–351/89 *Overseas Union Insurance Ltd v New Hampshire Insurance Co* [1991] E.C.R. I–3317, [1992] Q.B. 434; Case C–406/92; *The Tatry* [1994] E.C.R. I–5439, [1999] Q.B. 575; *Kloeckner & Co AG v Gatoil Overseas Inc* [1990] 2 Lloyd's Rep. 177.

[248] Case C–406/92 [1994] E.C.R. I–5439, [1999] Q.B. 515.

[249] See clause (4) of this Rule; below, paras 12–055 *et seq.*

[250] But there is no reason why an English court, seised with a claim for such relief, may not apply its substantive law to strike out the claim on non-jurisdictional grounds: *Boss Group Ltd v Boss France SA* [1997] 1 W.L.R. 351 (CA); *cf.* the view of Tesauro A.-G. in *The Tatry*, above, at p.5454, that it is "incumbent upon the court seised to ensure that any abuse is thwarted".

[251] At p.5455.

[252] [2000] 1 W.L.R. 2040 (CA).

[253] See now CPR, r.6.37(4).

factor.[254] Thus Scott L.J., who had in the previous year confirmed that *forum conveniens* was not a factor in the discretion to stay actions,[255] said that in Order 11 cases "if the reality of the cause of action is one which belongs to a foreign country, and not to this country, and above all, where it is a question which probably would be better tried . . . in the foreign country, leave ought not to be granted."[256]

The modern law on the role of *forum conveniens* in service out of the   **12–053** jurisdiction cases is to be found in the speeches of Lord Wilberforce in *Amin Rasheed Shipping Corp v Kuwait Insurance Co*[257] and of Lord Goff of Chieveley in *Spiliada Maritime Corp v Cansulex Ltd.*[258] The effect of the latter decision was to endorse Lord Wilberforce's statement of principle that in cases governed by Rule 34 the claimant must show good reason why service of process on a foreign defendant should be permitted, and in considering this question the court must take into account the nature of the dispute, the legal and practical issues involved, such questions as local knowledge, availability of witnesses and their evidence, and expense. Lord Goff of Chieveley added that the fundamental question (as it was in cases of staying of actions on *forum non conveniens* grounds) was to identify the forum in which the case could suitably be tried for the interests of all the parties and for the ends of justice.[259] To justify the exercise of the discretion, the claimant has to show that England is clearly the appropriate forum for the trial of the action.[260] But where the parties have contractually agreed on England as the forum which they prefer, the court will normally assume jurisdiction.[261]

A literal reading of Lord Goff's speech in *Spiliada* might have led to the   **12–054** conclusion that, just as a stay will not be granted unless another forum is shown to be available and more appropriate than England (but if it is shown,

---

[254] See *Strauss & Co v Goldsmid* (1892) 8 T.L.R. 512 (CA); *Rosler v Hilbery* [1925] Ch. 250 (CA); *Maharanee of Baroda v Wildenstein* [1972] 2 Q.B. 283, 294 (CA). See Piggott, Vol.3, pp.192–194; Collins (1972) 21 I.C.L.Q. 656. This line of authority was overlooked in *Oceanic Sun Line Special Shipping Co Inc v Fay* (1988) 165 C.L.R. 197 (criticised by Collins (1989) 105 L.Q.R. 364). The High Court of Australia subsequently ruled that in cases of service out of the jurisdiction, the plaintiff had to show that the action would not ultimately be stayed on the ground that the forum was clearly inappropriate: *Voth v Manildra Flour Mills Pty Ltd* (1990) 171 C.L.R. 538 (on which see Collins (1991) 107 L.Q.R. 182; Pryles (1991) 65 Aust. L.J. 442).

[255] *St Pierre v South American Stores Ltd* [1936] 1 K.B. 382 (CA).

[256] *Kroch v Rossell et Cie* [1937] 1 All E.R. 725, 731 (CA).

[257] [1984] A.C. 50, 72.

[258] [1987] A.C. 460, 478–482.

[259] cf. *Lopez v Chavarri* [1901] W.N. 115, 116 ("whether the true interests of justice would be best served by trying the question here, or leaving it to the foreign tribunal").

[260] [1987] A.C. at 480–482. In jurisdictions, such as New Zealand, some Australian States, and Canadian provinces, where service outside the jurisdiction is allowed without leave in specified circumstances, the court retains its discretion to set aside service, or to refuse leave to continue, on *forum conveniens* grounds: *Kuwait Asia Bank EC v National Mutual Life Nominees Ltd* [1991] A.C. 187, 217 (PC); *Singh v Howden Petroleum Ltd* (1979) 100 D.L.R. (3d) 121 (Ont CA); *Petersen v A/B Bahco Ventilation* (1979) 107 D.L.R. (3d) 49 (BC); *Canadian Commercial Bank v Carpenter* (1990) 62 D.L.R. (4th) 734 (BCCA).

[261] See below, Rule 39. But the fact that England is a *neutral* forum does not satisfy the general requirement under this clause that England be the *natural* forum; and the choice of English *law* as a neutral law is not an indication of England as a suitable forum for the solution of disputes: *Macsteel Commercial Holdings (Pty) Ltd v Thermasteel (Canada) Ltd* [1996] C.L.C. 1403 (CA).

then considerations of justice might make the stay an inappropriate order), service out will not be permitted unless England is shown to be the most appropriate forum for the trial of the claim (but if it is shown, service out may still be resisted on grounds on injustice). It now appears that this is not correct. The current formulation of the CPR requires only that England be "the proper place in which to bring the claim",[262] and this condition may be satisfied even though England is manifestly not the country with which the dispute has its closest connection, if England is, in practice, the only realistic place before the courts of which the claimant may bring the defendant to obtain a fair hearing of his claim.[263]

12–055   **Clause (4) of the Rule.** Articles 27 to 29 of the Regulation and of the Lugano Convention contain specific rules under the heading "Lis Pendens— Related Actions" to deal with the relationship between actions pending in different Member and Convention States (as the case may be) where, first, the proceedings involve "the same cause of action" and, second, where the cause of action is not the same, but the actions are related.[264] The instruments adopt a somewhat crude solution[265] to the problem of *lis alibi pendens* by requiring, in the first class of case, that any court other than the court first seised shall not exercise jurisdiction; in the second class of case they provide that any court, other than the court first seised, *may*, while the actions are pending in both courts,[266] stay its proceedings or *may* dismiss them for consolidation with the proceedings which are pending at first instance in the court first seised, or *may* choose to do neither. And in the uncommon case where actions fall within the exclusive jurisdiction of two courts, Art.29 provides that the court seised second must decline jurisdiction in favour of the court seised first.[267]

12–056   **Scope of application.** If proceedings are pending before the courts of another Member or Convention State, so that Arts 27 to 29 may apply, the proceedings must first be within the scope of the Regulation or the Convention

---

[262] CPR, r.6.37(3).

[263] *Cherney v Deripaska* [2009] EWCA Civ 849, [2010] 2 All E.R. (Comm.) 456; *AK Investment CJSC v Kyrgyz Mobil Tel Ltd* [2011] UKPC 7, [2011] 4 All E.R. 1027 (hearing in foreign court not shown to be feasible and fair); *Harty v Sabre International Security Ltd* [2011] EWHC 852 (QB) (though as the judgment treats a service out case as though it were a stay case, it may not be reliable).

[264] Previously Arts.21–23 of the Brussels Convention and the original Lugano Convention.

[265] A "tie-break rule": *Dresser UK Ltd v Falcongate Freight Management Ltd* [1992] Q.B. 502, 514 (CA).

[266] For the purpose of ordering a stay of English proceedings, where Art.28 applies, it is sufficient that the foreign action be pending at first instance or on appeal, by contrast Art.22 of the Brussels Convention, where the requirement was that the foreign action be pending at first instance.

[267] Exclusive jurisdiction in this context plainly refers to Art.22; there is no authority to support its being extended to other Articles in Ch.II of the Regulation or Title II of the Convention. In the case of related actions falling within the scope of Council Regulation (EC) 40/94, [1994] O.J. L.11/1 on the Community Trade Mark, or Council Regulation (EC) 6/2002, [2002] O.J. L.31/1 on Community Designs (as to which see also SI 2005/2339), the applicable rules are set out in Arts 100 and 91, respectively.

ratione materiae.[268] Therefore parallel actions in different Member or Convention States to enforce a judgment from a non-Member or non-Convention State are not subject to the rule, even if the same issues on the enforceability of the judgment arise in both sets of proceedings.[269] The same is true if the proceedings in the court seised second are generally or expressly excluded from the scope of the Regulation or Convention, such as where they have arbitration as their principal subject matter.[270] In principle the same analysis applies where the proceedings may be outside the Regulation or Convention *ratione temporis.* But in *Von Horn v Cinnamond*[271] the European Court interpreted Art.54 of the Brussels Convention[272] as meaning that where the proceedings in the court seised first were commenced on a date when the Convention was not in force, but those in the court seised second were instituted after[273] the coming into force of the Convention as between the two Contracting States, Art.21 would apply if it appeared to the court seised second that a judgment from the court first seised would be required to be recognised under the second paragraph of Art.54.[274] This was justified on the footing that Art.21 of the Brussels Convention was to be interpreted to forestall the non-recognition of judgments on the ground of irreconcilability

---

[268] See above, para.11–029. Where in accordance with Art.71 the court has jurisdiction under the provisions of an international convention on a particular matter, the provisions of Arts.27 to 29 are displaced by the *lis alibi pendens* provisions of the particular convention if (but evidently only if) the particular convention has such provisions, and these provisions are "highly predictable, facilitate the sound administration of justice, facilitate the sound administration of justice and enable the risk of concurrent proceedings to be minimised, and . . . ensure, under conditions at least as favourable as those provided for by the Regulation, the free movement of judgments in civil or commercial matters and mutual trust in the administration of justice in the European Union": Case C–533/08 *TNT Express Nederland BV v AXA Versicherung AG* [2010] E.C.R. I–4107. If the particular convention has no mechanism for preventing a situation of *lis alibi pendens* which measures up to this description, the provisions of the Regulation will apply by default: Case C–406/92 *The Tatry* [1994] E.C.R. I–5436; *Sony Computer Entertainment Ltd v RH Freight Services Ltd* [2007] EWHC 302 (Comm.), [2007] 2 Lloyd's Rep. 463. Where the particular convention does have provisions to regulate *lis alibi pendens*, it is difficult to say precisely when the reasoning in *TNT Express* will allow such provisions to be overridden by the "superior" provisions of the Regulation. To this extent, the reasoning in *Andrea Merzario Ltd v Internationale Spedition Leitner GmbH* [2001] 1 Lloyd's Rep. 490 may need to be reconsidered; see also *The Bergen* [1977] 1 Lloyd's Rep. 490.

[269] Case C–129/92 *Owens Bank Ltd v Bracco* [1994] E.C.R. I–117, [1994] Q.B. 509; *Dubai Bank Ltd v Abbas* [1998] I.L.Pr 391.

[270] Case C–190/89 *Marc Rich and Co AG v Soc Italiana Impianti PA* [1991] E.C.R. I–3855; *The Ivan Zagubanski* [2002] 1 Lloyd's Rep. 106. This proposition is unaffected by the reasoning in *National Navigation Co v Endesa Generacion SA (The Wadi Sudr)* [2009] EWCA Civ 1397, [2010] 1 Lloyd's Rep. 193, even if (*sed quaere*) a judgment from the court of the other Member State would be entitled to recognition under Chapter III of the Regulation, for *Owens Bank* establishes that Art.27 has no application if the proceedings before the court are outside the material scope of the Regulation.

[271] [1997] E.C.R. I–5451, [1998] Q.B. 214.

[272] As amended by Art.29 of the 1989 Accession Convention.

[273] Where the proceedings in the court seised second were also instituted before the coming into force of the Brussels Convention, *Von Horn* was inapplicable and Art.21 would not apply: *Davy International Ltd v Voest Alpine Industrieanlagenbau GmbH* [1999] 1 All E.R. 103 (CA).

[274] That is, by reason of a bilateral treaty, or because the jurisdiction of the court seised first accorded with Title II of the Brussels Convention: Art.54(2). Where the court seised second is uncertain whether this criterion would be satisfied, it should stay its proceedings until the court seised first has ruled on its jurisdiction.

with a judgment of the local court. It is to be supposed that the corresponding provisions of the Regulation will be interpreted to similar effect.[275]

12–057   Article 27 of the Regulation and the Lugano Convention provides that where proceedings involving the same cause of action and between the same parties are brought in the courts of different Regulation or Convention States, any court other than the court first seised shall of its own motion stay its proceedings until such time as the jurisdiction of the court first seised is established;[276] where the jurisdiction of the court first seised is established, any court other than the court first seised shall decline jurisdiction in favour of that court. The purpose of the Article is to prevent the courts of two Member or two Convention States from giving inconsistent judgments, and to preclude so far as possible the non-recognition of a judgment under Art.34(3) on the ground that it is irreconcilable with a judgment given by the courts of another Member or Convention State.[277]

12–058   Article 27 applies irrespective of where the defendant is domiciled. There is no reference to domicile in the text of the Article, only to proceedings; and as the aim of the provision is to limit the risk of irreconcilable judgments, it will therefore be interpreted broadly to cover, in principle, all situations of *lis pendens* before courts in Member and Convention States, irrespective of the parties' domicile. Accordingly, the English court was bound to decline jurisdiction over proceedings against an American company which had, prior to the English proceedings, commenced proceedings in France in relation to the same subject-matter.[278] But Art.27 does not apply to proceedings commenced in non-Member and non-Convention States.[279] Consequently if there are proceedings before the courts of New York involving the same parties, the English court has a discretion to stay the English proceedings, irrespective of which proceedings were commenced first and, it is submitted, whether or not the defendant in the English proceedings is domiciled in a Member State or a Convention State.[280]

---

[275] *Advent Capital Plc v GN Ellinas Imports-Exports Ltd* [2005] EWHC 1242 (Comm.), [2005] 2 Lloyd's Rep. 607.

[276] But at this stage the court still has jurisdiction, and may grant provisional or protective measures as though it were a court seised with substantive jurisdiction: *JP Morgan Europe Ltd v Primacom AG* [2005] EWHC 508 (Comm.), [2005] 2 Lloyd's Rep. 665. For the purposes of Art.27, the seisin of a court, originally seised first, is to be regarded as continuing without hiatus, even though its jurisdiction was successfully challenged at first instance, until final determination of any appeal against that dismissal: *Moore v Moore* [2007] EWCA Civ 361, [2007] 2 F.L.R. 339. See also, on the cure of irregularity and the date of seisin, *Phillips v Symes (No.3)* [2008] UKHL 1, [2008] 1 W.L.R. 180. For a straightforward illustration of the mechanism, see *Gard Marine & Energy Ltd v Tunnicliffe* [2010] EWCA Civ 1052, [2011] Bus. L.R. 839 (a case on the original Lugano Convention).

[277] Case 42/76 *De Wolf v Cox BV* [1976] E.C.R. 1759, 1767; Case 144/86 *Gubisch Maschinenfabrik KG v Palumbo* [1987] E.C.R. 4861, 4874; Case C–351/89 *Overseas Union Insurance Ltd v New Hampshire Insurance Co* [1991] E.C.R. I–3317, [1992] Q.B. 434, 457.

[278] Case C–351/89 *Overseas Union Insurance Ltd v New Hampshire Insurance Co* [1991] E.C.R. I–3317, [1992] Q.B. 434.

[279] *cf. UBS AG v Omni Holding AG* [2000] 1 W.L.R. 916 (proceedings in another Convention State but not in civil or commercial matter).

[280] On the question whether this conclusion is undermined by Case C–281/02 *Owusu v Jackson* [2005] E.C.R. I–1383, [2005] Q.B. 801, and by *Catalyst Investment Group Ltd v Lewinsohn* [2009] EWHC 1964 (Ch.), [2010] Ch. 218 (which is admittedly inconsistent with the proposition in the text), and for the submission that it is not, see above, para.12–024.

Accordingly, where Art.27 applies[281] the English court must decline juris-   **12–059**
diction if it is not the court first seised and the jurisdiction of the other court
is not challenged, or is established after it is challenged. But the court which
is seised second must not itself normally investigate the jurisdiction of the
court first seised. In *Overseas Union Insurance Ltd v New Hampshire Insurance Co*[282] it was held that in such a case the court seised second was
restricted to staying its proceedings until the court first seised had ruled on its
own jurisdiction. The European Court left open the question whether the
answer was the same if the court seised second had exclusive jurisdiction "in
particular" under what is now Art.22 of the Regulation.[283] As a result, the
exact scope of this possible exception to the application of Art.27 and remains
uncertain. There are three points to be made. First, Art.27 should be inapplicable when the court seised second has exclusive jurisdiction regardless of
domicile, under Art.22,[284] for a judgment given by the court seised first in
violation of this provision will be refused recognition in all Member and
Convention States,[285] and there is no sensible purpose in deferring to a court
whose judgment will be a nullity in England. Secondly, though the European
Court has reiterated that the court seised second has no general right to review
the jurisdiction of the court seised first,[286] this reasoning would justify extending the exception to those cases in which jurisdictional error by the court
seised first means that its judgment must not be recognised.[287] But, thirdly, the
view which had once been preferred by the Court of Appeal[288] that, even if
seised second, the English court may assume jurisdiction, notwithstanding
proceedings commenced in the court seised first, if the parties have conferred
exclusive jurisdiction on the English court by agreement, was repudiated by
the European Court in *Erich Gasser GmbH v MISAT srl*.[289] Even though the
English court, seised second, may be in the best position to give decisive
effect to the agreement of the parties, the broader scheme of the legislation has
been held to preclude it, no matter how severe or unjustified the disadvantage
for those who enter into dispute-resolution agreements. The result is that any
power which the court seised second may have to proceed notwithstanding the
prior seisin of another court certainly cannot go beyond those cases in which

---

[281] Where proceedings are before the courts of two Member States, the applicable rules are
those of the Regulation rather than the Lugano Convention, even if one party is domiciled in a
Convention State (though as Arts.27 to 30 of each are now identical, this point loses the force it
previously had): *Cooper Tire & Rubber Co Europe Ltd v Bayer Public Co Ltd* [2010] EWCA Civ
864, [2010] Bus. L.R. 1697.

[282] Case C–351/89 [1991] E.C.R. I–3317, [1992] Q.B. 434; see also Case C–163/95 *Von Horn
v Cinnamond* [1997] E.C.R. I–5451, [1998] Q.B. 214.

[283] [1991] E.C.R. I–3317, 3351–3352, [1992] Q.B. 434 at p.459, where the reply given by the
Court was stated to be "without prejudice" to this case.

[284] That is, under Section 6 of Chapter II of the Regulation and Title II of the Lugano
Convention: *Speed Investments Ltd v Formula One Holdings Ltd* [2004] EWCA Civ 1512, [2005]
1 W.L.R. 1936; and see above, para.11–376 *et seq.*

[285] Art 35(1): below, para.14–221.

[286] Case C–163/95 *Von Horn v Cinnamond* [1997] E.C.R. I–5451, [1998] Q.B. 214.

[287] Sections 3 (insurance contracts) and 4 (consumer contracts) of Ch.II of the Regulation, Title
II of the Convention: see Art.35(1).

[288] *Continental Bank NA v Aeakos Compania Naviera SA* [1994] 1 W.L.R. 588 (CA), approved
obiter: *The Angelic Grace* [1995] 1 Lloyd's Rep. 87 (CA).

[289] Case C–116/02 [2005] Q.B. 1; see Mance (2004) 120 L.Q.R. 357.

the second seised court concludes that a judgment from the court seised first would be one which Art.35(1) of the Regulation or the Convention required it to refuse to recognise. That is not the case when a court exercises jurisdiction contrary to the terms of jurisdiction agreement which Art.23 required it to give effect to.

Although Arts 27 to 29 of the Regulation and of the Convention distinguish between the concepts of declining jurisdiction, on the one hand, and staying proceedings on the other,[290] it is suggested that where the English court is required to decline jurisdiction it may do so by imposing an unconditional stay, which would enable measures of interim relief to remain in force without the need for a separate application under Art.31.[291]

12–060   **The same parties.** For the purposes of Art.27, the actions in the different States must be "between the same parties". It was held by the European Court in *The Tatry*[292] that in litigation involving multiple parties, what is now Art.27 of the Regulation applies as between pairs of plaintiff and defendant. Each *lis* between a plaintiff and a defendant has to be considered individually to determine which court was seised of it first in time, and Art.27 applied accordingly.[293] It was recognised by the Court that this may lead to an inconvenient fragmentation of litigation and it suggested that what is now Art.28,[294] which allows, but does not require, a court seised second to stay or to dismiss its proceedings, may ameliorate the consequential difficulty.

12–061   The European Court also considered the application of what is now Art.27 of the Regulation, and the requirement that the proceedings be between the same parties, in relation to English admiralty actions *in rem*. In *The Tatry* proceedings had been brought in the Netherlands between a shipowner against cargo owners for a declaration that the shipowner owed no liability for damage allegedly done to the cargo; subsequently an admiralty action *in rem* was commenced by the cargo owners' arrest of the ship. Though as a matter of English procedural law (as it was then understood) the English action was against the ship as defendant, and not against any individual, and though once the owner entered an appearance the action became one *in personam* as well, it was ruled that this procedural difference between the English and Dutch actions could not of itself preclude the operation of the Article. In *Republic of India v India Steamship Co Ltd (No.2)*[295] the House of Lords adopted the reasoning of the European Court in *The Tatry* in support of its conclusion that, as a matter of English law, an admiralty action *in rem* is to be regarded as

---

[290] Case C–351/89 *Overseas Union Insurance Ltd v New Hampshire Insurance Co*, above.

[291] *JP Morgan Europe Ltd v Primacom AG* [2005] EWHC 508 (Comm.), [2005] 2 Lloyd's Rep. 665.

[292] Case C–406/92 [1994] E.C.R. I–5439, [1999] Q.B. 515. For the reference from the Court of Appeal, see *The Maciej Rataj* [1992] 2 Lloyd's Rep. 552 (CA).

[293] For the operation of this principle in relation to amendment by joinder of defendants or by addition of new claims, see the discussion of the date of seisin, below, para.12–069.

[294] See below, para.12–072.

[295] [1998] A.C. 878. This analysis was, however, dissented from by the Full Court of the Australian Federal Court in *Comandate Marine Corp v Pan Australia Shipping Pty Ltd* (2006) 157 F.C.R. 45, [2008] 1 Lloyd's Rep. 119.

brought against the shipowner as defendant as soon as the process in the action was served[296] or was acknowledged prior to service.

Proceedings may also be regarded as being between the same parties on the ground that there is identity of interest between two parties who are, at first sight, distinct. For example, when an insurer invokes its right of subrogation to defend proceedings in the name of its insured, the insurer and the insured may be regarded as the same party for the purpose of these provisions.[297] By contrast, claims brought (i) by the insurer of the hull of a vessel against the insurer of the cargo for a contribution to general average, and (ii) by the insurer of the cargo against the owner and charterer of the vessel for a declaration that they were not liable to contribute to the general average are not between the same parties unless it is established that, with regard to the subject matter of the disputes, the interests of the insurer of the hull of the vessel are identical to and indissociable from those of its insured, the owner and the charterer of that vessel.[298] The test of identity and indissociability of interest is for the national court to apply. Thus it was held that where a claim brought in an English court was assigned to another, the assignee and assignor were to be regarded as the same party, and the claim now in the name of the assignee as having been pending, without hiatus, from the date on which the court was seised of the assignor's claim, for the interests of assignor and assignee of a claim are materially identical.[299] By contrast, the interests of the principal participant in a cartel, whose exposure to civil liability was great, and of minor participants, who were less exposed, were not identical, and they were therefore not necessarily to be regarded as the same parties, because a common interest in the defence of proceedings brought by a single claimant is not sufficient to treat the defendants to those proceedings as the same party.[300] It follows that a licensee and a licensor of intellectual property rights are not to be regarded as the same party if sued in separate proceedings by a single claimant,[301] but it has been held that a wholly-owned subsidiary may be regarded as the same party as its parent.[302]

12–062

The same cause of action. In *Gubisch Maschinenfabrik KG v Palumbo*[303] it was held that the purpose of the rules regulating *lis alibi pendens* was "to

12–063

---

[296] Approving *The Deichland* [1990] 1 Q.B. 361 (CA), and overruling *The Nordglimt* [1988] Q.B. 183.

[297] Case C–351/96 *Drouot Assurances SA v Consolidated Metallurgical Industries* [1998] E.C.R. I–3075, [1999] Q.B. 497; *Sony Computer Entertainment Ltd v RH Freight Services Ltd* [2007] EWHC 302 (Comm.), [2007] 2 Lloyd's Rep. 463 (no identity of party between insurer and insured).

[298] *ibid.*

[299] *Kolden Holdings Ltd v Rodette Commerce Ltd* [2008] EWCA Civ 10, [2008] Bus. L.R. 1051. It followed that a claim brought by the defendant against the assignee in the period between notice of the assignment and the consequent amendment of the original claim, was not to be regarded as first seised in relation to the assignee's claim (see, for similar treatment of seisin as uninterrupted during an appeal against a challenge to jurisdiction, *Moore v Moore* [2007] EWCA Civ 361, [2007] 2 F.L.R. 339.

[300] *Cooper Tire & Rubber Co Europe Ltd v Bayer Public Co Ltd* [2010] EWCA Civ 864, [2010] Bus. L.R. 1697.

[301] *Mecklermedia Corp v DC Congress GmbH* [1998] Ch. 40; *Mölnlycke Health Care AB v BSN Medical Ltd* [2009] EWHC 3370 (Pat.), [2010] I.L.Pr. 171.

[302] *Berkeley Administration Inc v McClelland* [1995] I.L.Pr. 201 (CA).

[303] Case 144/86 [1987] E.C.R. 4861.

prevent parallel proceedings before the courts of different Contracting States, and to avoid conflicts between decisions which might result therefrom. Those rules are therefore designed to preclude, in so far as is possible and from the outset, the possibility of a situation arising such as that referred to in [what is now Art.34(3) of the Brussels I Regulation], that is, the non-recognition of a judgment on account of its irreconcilability with a judgment given in a dispute between the same parties in the state in which recognition is sought".[304] It followed that concept of the "same cause of action" had to be given an independent interpretation for the purposes of the Brussels Convention, and did not depend on the procedural law of the courts concerned. In that case a German seller was suing an Italian buyer in the German court for the price; the Italian subsequently sued the German seller in the Italian court for a declaration that he was not liable on the contract, or for its rescission. The expression "the same cause of action" is a translation of what appears in the French version as "le même objet et la même cause", and the European Court held that where the same parties were suing each other in two legal proceedings in different Convention States which were based on the same contractual relationship, the "same cause of action" was involved, and it was not necessary for the two claims to be identical for them to involve the same subject matter. Accordingly, what is now Art.27 applied even if one set of proceedings was for the price, and the other was a claim for a negative declaration or rescission,[305] not least because the claims asserted in the rescission action could have been pleaded as defences to the action for the price.[306]

12–064   The test of whether two claims are based on the same cause of action is applied to the respective claims, and takes no account of the defences which will or may be raised to the claims. The European Court reached this conclusion in order to avoid the inconvenience of the answer to the question of whether proceedings have the same cause of action, and therefore the answer to whether the court has jurisdiction over the claim, undergoing changes as pleadings developed.[307]

12–065   In *The Tatry*,[308] it was held that actions have "le même objet" when the ends they have in view are the same, and "la même cause" when the facts and the rule of law relied on as the basis of the actions are the same. Consequently an action for a declaration that the owner of the vessel was under no liability

---

[304] At [8]. For application of this principle as one of wide scope and operation in an intellectual property case, see *Football Dataco Ltd v Sportradar GmbH* [2011] EWCA Civ 330, [2011] 1 W.L.R. 2044.

[305] See also Case C–351/89 *Overseas Union Insurance Ltd v New Hampshire Insurance Co* [1991] E.C.R. I–3317, [1992] Q.B. 434. However, the practice of bringing proceedings for negative declaratory relief may in certain contexts verge on the abusive: cases involving intellectual property, competition and corporate loans, where a "natural defendant" may commence proceedings purporting to determine the validity of the right or obligation which he is alleged to have infringed or disregarded. The effect of such proceedings being started first can "torpedo" the bringing of the substantive claim. Reform of the Brussels I Regulation is likely to propose amendments to the Regulation to discourage or prevent such tactical litigation: see the Report of the Commission to the Council of Ministers, April 21, 2009, COM(2009) 174 final, at paras 3.3–3.5.

[306] *Secret Hotels 2 Ltd v EA Traveller Ltd* [2010] EWHC 1023 (Ch.), [2010] I.L.Pr. 616.

[307] Case C–111/01 *Gantner Electronic GmbH v Basch Exploitatie Maatschappij BV* [2003] E.C.R. I–4207.

[308] Case C–406/92 [1994] E.C.R. I–5439, [1999] Q.B. 515.

to the cargo owner for damage to the cargo, and an action by the cargo owner against the owner of the vessel for damages in respect of damage done to the cargo, were in respect of the same cause of action for the purposes of what is now Art.27. But, as with the question whether an action is between the same parties, national procedural law will not be permitted to obscure the fact that, for the purposes of the Brussels I Regulation and the Lugano Convention, two sets of proceedings involve the same cause of action. Although it has now been established that proceedings against a shipowner to establish liability, and a limitation claim brought by that shipowner, do not involve the same cause of action,[309] there may well be other instances in which two actions, seen as a matter of English law to have distinct causes of action, could still be found to involve the same cause of action for the purposes of Art.27.[310] It will depend upon how strictly the criteria established in *The Tatry* are to be interpreted. If the predominant concern is to interpret Art.27 to avoid the possibility of courts in two Member or Convention States rendering judgments which are irreconcilable with each other, it may be correct to see actions which overlap to this degree[311] actions as falling within the provision. Similarly, if the issues raised in the two claims[312] overlap, because they have some, but not all, issues in common, there is bound to be a tension between the need to construe the Article narrowly, as was done in *The Tatry*,[313] and the incentive to interpret it more widely, the better to avoid the risk of judgments which may prove to be irreconcilable.[314] At the very least, the fact that defences are disregarded in the application of the test means that the risk of contradictory judgments has deliberately not been eliminated by the European Court's interpretation.

In any event, since the object of Art.27 is to prevent irreconcilable judgments, an application for provisional measures brought in one Member or   **12–066**

---

[309] Case C–39/02 *Maersk Olie & Gas A/S v De Haan & De Boer* [2004] E.C.R. I–9657, [2005] 1 Lloyd's Rep. 210 (limitation claim not same cause of action as claim to establish liability). See further *Eli Lilly & Co v Novo Nordisk A/S* [2000] I.L.Pr. 73 (CA) (actions to rectify contract and to interpret it not the same cause of action; a case at common law); *Glencore International AG v Shell International Trading and Shipping Co Ltd* [1999] 2 Lloyd's Rep. 692 (claim for substantive relief and interpleader claim not the same cause of action); *Re Cover Europe Ltd* [2002] EWHC 861 (Ch.) (proceedings for declaration of invalidity of guarantee same cause of action as contested claim to admit in an insolvency proof of the debt created by the guarantee).

[310] *cf. Mecklermedia Corp v DC Congress GmbH* [1998] Ch. 40 (passing off in England not the same cause of action as trademark infringement in Germany).

[311] *William Grant and Sons International Ltd v Marie-Brizard Espana SA*, 1998 S.C. 536.

[312] That is, paying no attention to the actual or proposed defences to those claims.

[313] The "individual *lis* by individual *lis*" approach of the court in that case may be considered to be a form of narrow or restrictive construction.

[314] *Evialis SA v SIAT* [2003] EWHC 863 (Comm.), [2003] 2 Lloyd's Rep. 377; *Bank of Tokyo-Mitsubishi Ltd v Baskan Gida Sanayi ve Pazarlama AS* [2004] EWHC 945 (Ch.), [2004] 2 Lloyd's Rep. 395; *Underwriting Members of Lloyd's Syndicate 980 v Sinco SA* [2008] EWHC 1842 (Comm.), [2009] Lloyd's Rep. I.R. 365; *Jacobs & Turner Ltd v Celsus sarl* 2007 S.L.T. 722. The question is whether the judgments sought would be irreconcilable, not whether the issues are raised along the way: *JP Morgan Europe Ltd v Primacom AG* [2005] EWHC 508 (Comm.), [2005] 2 Lloyd's Rep. 665; *Katsouris Brothers Ltd v Haitoglu Bros SA* [2011] EWHC 111 (Comm.).

Convention State under Art.24 will not preclude a later action on the substance in another Member or Convention State.[315] Even so, it may prevent an application for the same form of provisional relief.[316]

12–067   **Date of seisin.** According to the Brussels I Regulation, the date on which a court in a Member State is to be regarded as seised of proceedings for the purposes of Arts 27–29 of the Regulation is as set out in Art.30. According to that provision, a court is deemed to be seised *either* when the document instituting the proceedings[317] is lodged with the court, provided that the claimant has not subsequently failed to take the steps he was required to take to have service effected on the defendant, *or* if the document has to be served before being lodged with the court, it is seised at the time the document is received by the authority responsible for service, provided that the claimant has not failed to take the steps required to have the document lodged with the court.[318] As a result of this clarification, an English court will be seised on issue,[319] rather than on service, always assuming that the defendant did not fail to take the steps necessary to effect service. In this context, it is reasonable to expect that where the court is seised on issue, provided that there is no failure to take the steps to have it made, service is likely to mean substantial, as distinct from technically perfect, compliance with the rules governing service of the document in question. To put the point another way, the claimant will have "failed" to take the steps required to have service effected only where that failure is blameworthy. So a technical failure, such as the failure to include a translation of the writ with the documents served, may not be counted as a failure,[320] but a failure to pay a court fee, with the consequence that the document in question may not, and will not, be served at all, will be seen as a substantial failure on the part of the party who should have paid, with the further result that the earlier date of potential seisin is lost, and the court is not seised until the date on which the fee is paid.[321] It is important to remember, though, that, where there is no failure to arrange for service, the date of seisin is, in England, the date of issue, and not the date on which the steps necessary to arrange for service were fulfilled.[322]

---

[315] *cf. Rank Film Distributors Ltd v Lanterna Editrice Srl* [1992] I.L.Pr. 58, 68–69; *Boss Group Ltd v Boss France SA* [1997] 1 W.L.R. 351, 356 (CA). Contrast *Virgin Aviation Services Ltd v CAD Aviation Services* [1991] I.L.Pr. 79, 85–86.

[316] Case C–80/00 *Italian Leather SpA v Weco Polstermöbel GmbH & Co* [2002] E.C.R. I–6367. However it is not clear that a decision of a German court not to grant interim relief is irreconcilable with the later decision of an Italian court to grant it. Unless the first court has ruled that the relief should not be granted at all, the two judgments are factually contradictory rather than legally irreconcilable. It will be for the national court to apply the ruling.

[317] See *Nordea Bank Norge ASA v Unicredit Corporate Banking SpA* [2011] EWHC 30 (Comm.).

[318] *Bentinck v Bentinck* [2007] EWCA Civ 175, [2007] 2 F.L.R. 1.

[319] On the date stamped on the document by the Registry: CPR, r.7.2(2).

[320] *WPP Holdings Italy srl v Benatti* [2007] EWCA Civ 263, [2007] 1 W.L.R. 2316. Likewise service on a Sunday: *Weiner v Weiner* [2010] EWHC 1843 (Fam.), [2011] 1 F.L.R. 372 (though doubting that this constituted any failure at all).

[321] *Debt Collection London Ltd v SK Slavia Praha Futbol AS* [2010] EWCA Civ 1250, [2011] 1 W.L.R. 866. If the failure to serve is so lengthy that the claimant needs to apply for a extension of time for service, the court may refuse and the action will then be struck out: *Katsouris Brothers Ltd v Haitoglu Bros SA* [2011] EWHC 111 (Comm.).

[322] *Weiner v Weiner* [2010] EWHC 1843 (Fam.), [2011] 1 F.L.R. 372.

The mechanism in Art.30 works clearly in straightforward cases, but **12–068** complication may arise if the claim form as issued makes claims against a number of defendants, in respect of some, but not others, on whom it may be said that the claimant has failed to make service. A practical solution might have been to hold that so long as the claim form issued by the court has been served on at least one of the defendants, the proceedings are pending against all of them. Such an approach was suggested, though never adopted, in relation to seisin under the Brussels Convention;[323] the drawback to it was that a defendant might be wholly unaware, possibly for a substantial period, that proceedings against him were regarded as already pending before the English courts. For this reason, it seems likely that if the claimant to be blamed for not effecting service on the individual defendant, so that seisin is not established, the fact that service has been made on other defendants will not establish seisin in relation to the non-served defendant before the failure is corrected, and then seisin will only operate from the date of the correction.

Where a claim form which has been issued and served is amended by the **12–069** addition of an additional claim,[324] or by the introduction of a claim or counter-claim against another party,[325] the material question is whether the date of seisin in respect of the additional claim is the date on which the amended claim form is reissued (which may, depending on the circumstances, be only after obtaining the permission of the court), or the date of the original issue. As it is difficult to see how a court can be said to be seised of a claim which has not been made and does not appear in the claim form, it cannot be correct that as long as a claim form has been issued and served, the court already has temporal priority over any issue which may later be added by amendment. It would follow from a conclusion that the court is not seised of the new claim until the amended claim form is reissued[326] that the defendant[327] may be able to pre-empt the amendment by commencing an action of his own in another Member State.[328] The court seised with such pre-emptive proceedings will obviously be regarded as being seised later than the court before which the original action was brought,[329] but institution of the later action may serve to prevent the proposed, and now duplicative, amendment of the original action;

---

[323] *Grupo Torras SA v Sheikh Fahad Mohammed al-Sabah* [1996] 1 Lloyd's Rep. 7, 18, 21–22. See also *Fox v Taher* [1997] I.L.Pr. 441; *Glencore International AG v Metro Trading International Inc* [1999] 2 Lloyd's Rep. 632.

[324] *Underwriting Members of Lloyd's Syndicate 980 v Sinco SA* [2008] EWHC 1842 (Comm.), [2009] Lloyd's Rep. I.R. 365; *Nordea Bank Norge ASA v Unicredit Corporate Banking SpA* [2011] EWHC 30 (Comm.).

[325] *Nordea Bank Norge ASA v Unicredit Corporate Banking SpA* [2011] EWHC 30 (Comm.). But an assignee may be regarded, for this purpose, as the same party as the assignor, and the date of seisin will be unaffected: *Kolden Holdings Ltd v Rodette Commerce Ltd* [2008] EWCA Civ 10, [2008] Bus. L.R. 1051.

[326] If the court dispenses with the need for re-service, the proviso to Art.30 will be redundant.

[327] Particularly if he is notified of an application to amend the existing claim form.

[328] cf. *Kinnear v Falconfilms NV* [1996] 1 W.L.R. 920; *Molins Plc v GD SpA* [2000] 1 W.L.R. 1741.

[329] *Stribog Ltd v FKI Engineering Ltd* [2011] EWCA Civ 622, [2011] 1 W.L.R. 3264: the consequence is that the second court would be entitled to grant relief under Art.28.

and there is no basis in the Regulation for refusing to give effect to a use of the rules which might be characterised as sharp practice.[330]

12–070   The uniform rule established by Art.30 supersedes the approach which had prevailed under the Brussels and original Lugano Conventions, according to which the date on which a court in a Contracting State was seised was the date upon which the proceedings were to be regarded as "definitively pending" before it.[331] According to the European Court, the precise procedural conditions which determined this question were ascertained by reference to the national law of the particular court seised. This led to three, among many, problems. First, there was a lack of uniformity or equivalence in the laws of the various states, for whereas some courts considered themselves to be seised immediately upon the issue of process out of the court registry, others postponed the date of such seisin until the date of service of process on the defendant. The perception that this discrepancy between procedural law opened the door to forum shopping, and disreputable races to seise courts, was held by many.[332] The Court of Appeal held that an English court was not seised in such a case until service had been made,[333] with the apparent result that a defendant who got to hear that proceedings had been issued, but who had not been served, might be tempted to issue proceedings in another jurisdiction in which the conditions for seisin could be more quickly satisfied. Second, there was uncertainty whether there were exceptions to the general rule. In England, for example, it was suggested[334] that a court might be seised when it granted a freezing injunction, though a later decision did not support such a possibility.[335] Third, the fact that national procedural law varies, not only from country to country, but even from court to court, had the potential to make the ascertainment of the material dates very problematic. The uniform law put in place by Art.30 obviates many, if not all, of these perceived shortcomings.

12–071   Article 27 of the Regulation and of the Lugano Convention requires that the action be still pending in the court first seised when the proceedings are commenced in the court second seised. So if the proceedings in the first court have terminated by judgment and are no longer pending,[336] or if they have

---

[330] *Molins Plc v GD SpA* [2000] 1 W.L.R. 1741.

[331] Case C–129/83 *Zelger v Salinitri (No.2)* [1984] E.C.R. 2397.

[332] See, for example, *Knauf UK GmbH v British Gypsum Ltd* [2001] EWCA Civ 1570, [2002] 1 W.L.R. 907.

[333] *Dresser UK Ltd v Falcongate Freight Management Ltd* [1992] Q.B. 502.

[334] *Dresser UK Ltd v Falcongate Freight Management Ltd* [1992] Q.B. 502.

[335] *Neste Chemicals SA v DK Line SA (The Sargasso)* [1994] 3 All E.R. 180. In *Phillips v Symes (No.3)* [2008] UKHL 1, [2008] 1 W.L.R. 180, the majority of the House of Lords declined to reconsider *Dresser v Falcongate* on the effective ground that the coming into force of the Brussels I Regulation had so reduced its significance that there was no justification for spending time on the issue, whereas the minority would have simply overruled it.

[336] *Berkeley Administration Inc v McClelland* [1995] I.L.Pr. 201 (CA); *Tavoulareas v Tsavliris* [2005] EWHC 2643 (Comm.), [2006] 1 All E.R. (Comm.) 130 (applying this principle in a case where the English proceedings were initially stayed on the basis of Art.27, but lifting the stay and allowing the action to proceed once the court first seised had given judgment). Ch.III of the Regulation and Title III of the Lugano Convention may then require recognition of the judgment of the court seised first. Proceedings are not pending at first instance if all that remains is an appeal against an order that the claim be struck out: *Lough Neagh Exploration Co v Morrice* [1999] N.I. 258 (CA).

been discontinued,[337] or if they have been struck out on *forum non conveniens* grounds,[338] on the relevant date,[339] Art.27 will be inapplicable.

Related actions: Article 28 of the Brussels I Regulation and of the Lugano Convention. Where the actions fall outside Art.27 they may still fall within the scope of Art.28 of the Regulation or of the Convention.[340]   **12–072**

Article 28 of provides where related actions are brought in the courts of different Member or Convention States, any court other than the court first seised has the power, but not the duty, to stay its proceedings: Art.22 of the Brussels Convention limited this power to the case in which the foreign proceedings were pending at first instance. Alternatively, the court seised second may dismiss the proceedings before it to allow them to be consolidated with the action pending at first instance before the other court, always provided that the other court will have jurisdiction over both claims and its law permits the consolidation of claims. Actions are "related" for the purposes of Art.28 if they are so closely connected that it is expedient to hear and determine them together to avoid the risk of irreconcilable judgments resulting from separate proceedings.[341] The European Court has ruled[342] that the "risk of irreconcilable judgments" referred to in what is now Art.28(3) is a more flexible concept than that described by similar[343] words in Art.34(3),[344] and it covers cases where the judgments may contain conflicting decisions without necessarily giving rise to mutually exclusive legal consequences. The House of Lords in *Sarrio SA v Kuwait Investment Authority*[345] interpreted this condition as being satisfied if common issues of fact may arise and be decided in the two sets of proceedings, rejecting the narrower interpretation that the test of potential irreconcilability had to be assessed by reference to those   **12–073**

---

[337] *Internationale Nederlanden Aviation Lease BV v Civil Aviation Authority* [1997] 1 Lloyd's Rep. 80, 93–94; *cf. Gamlestaden Plc v Casa de Suecia SA* [1994] 1 Lloyd's Rep. 433.

[338] *Haji-Ioannou v Frangos* [1999] 2 Lloyd's Rep. 337 (CA).

[339] Not necessarily the date of institution of proceedings in the court seised second. A court which was prevented from proceeding with the hearing of a case because of *lis alibi pendens* will be able to exercise jurisdiction once the first seised court has given judgment and is no longer seised: *Tavoulareas v Tsavliris* [2005] EWHC 2643 (Comm.), [2006] 1 All E.R. (Comm.) 130.

[340] Which is closely modelled on, but not identical with, Art.22 of the Brussels Convention.

[341] Art.28(3). See *Watson v First Choice Holidays and Flights Ltd* [2001] EWCA Civ 972, [2001] 2 Lloyd's Rep. 339 (CA) (the reference to the European Court was withdrawn when the case was settled). For the non-related nature of claims in different Member or Convention States in respect of parallel intellectual property rights, see *Prudential Assurance Co Ltd v Prudential Insurance Co of America* [2003] EWCA Civ 327, [2003] 1 W.L.R. 2295 (CA); *Abkco Music & Records Inc v Jodorowski* [2003] E.C.D.R. 3.

[342] Case C–406/92 *The Tatry* [1994] E.C.R. I–5439, [1999] Q.B. 515; see also *Toepfer International GmbH v Molino Boschi Srl* [1996] 1 Lloyd's Rep. 510; *De Pina v MS Birka ICG* [1996] 1 Lloyd's Rep. 31; *Charterers Mutual Assurance Association Ltd v British & Foreign* [1998] I.L.Pr. 838; *The Turquoise Bleu* [1996] 1 I.L.R.M. 406.

[343] Not all language versions (see, for example the Italian language version, referred to in *The Tatry* at p.5479) use terminology which suggests that the Articles should share a common meaning.

[344] See para.14–234 below.

[345] [1999] 1 A.C. 32. See *The Happy Fellow* [1998] 1 Lloyd's Rep. 13 (CA) (limitation action related to action claiming damages for collision damage done by a ship); *Gonzalez v Mayer* [2004] 3 I.R. 326; *cf. Mecklermedia Corp v DC Congress GmbH* [1998] Ch. 40 (passing off action in England not related to trademark infringement action against licensees in Germany).

issues which the courts would be *required* to determine in order to give judgment.

12–074   By contrast with Art.27, the question whether actions are "related" is answered not just by looking at the claim, but by looking at the claims and defences, but either the granting of relief is not automatic on finding the actions to be related, or if it is not expedient that the actions be tried together, then they are not to be seen as related.[346] This makes sense, not least because the degree to which the two actions are related or connected cannot be given a sensible answer by ignoring the defences which will be raised.

12–075   The fact, however, that reference is made to defences as well as to the claim may give rise to some complexity. As with Art.27, the structure of Art.28 is straightforward if there are just two actions, one instituted earlier in time than the other: Art.28 applies to the action in the court which was not seised first; it seems that the court seised first is simply obliged to adjudicate. However, a problem arises when the action in the court first seised is amended to include matters already raised in, or related to matters raised in, the other action. If the two actions are now related—and it is hard to deny that they are—the question is which one has the power to grant relief by reference to Art.28. If the analysis were undertaken on an issue by issue basis, the answer would be that the first court would be first seised on the claim, but not of the issue added by amendment. The Court of Appeal has held, however, that the test of temporal priority which underpins Art.28 looks to the date of the actions became pending, not to the date on which issues were raised within actions. It follows that an action in a court not seised first, initially unrelated to the action in the court seised first, may find that it has become a related action, and the court seised of it may be invited to order relief under Art.28, even though no such question could have arisen when that action was instituted.[347]

12–076   The relief which may be granted under Art.28 is either a stay of proceedings, or the dismissal of the proceedings in order that they be consolidated with the proceedings pending at first instance in the court seised first. Though Jenard observed[348] that the power to stay proceedings is the primary duty of the court in a case to which what is now Art.28 applies, the approach of the House of Lords in *Sarrio SA v Kuwait Investment Authority* may mean that the more appropriate remedy would be for the court to decline jurisdiction in order that the proceedings be consolidated with those pending at first instance in the court seised first. If the court orders a stay of proceedings, it will presumably be in the situation where judgment in the action in the court first seised appears in the eyes of the court seised second to be likely to render *res judicata* issues raised for determination by it, and therefore a stay should be imposed until the court seised first gives judgment.[349] Where the English court

---

[346] *Research in Motion UK Ltd v Visto Corp* [2008] EWCA Civ 153, [2008] F.S.R. 499. See also *Prazic v Prazic* [2006] EWCA Civ 497, [2007] I.L.Pr. 381; *Prifti v Musini SA de Seguros y Reaseguros* [2005] EWHC 832 (Comm.), [2006] Lloyd's Rep. I.R. 221; *Landis & Gyr Ltd v Scaleo Chip ET* [2007] EWHC 1880 (QB), [2007] I.L.Pr. 719; *Popely v Popely* [2006] IEHC 134, [2006] I.R. 356.

[347] *Stribog Ltd v FKI Engineering Ltd* [2011] EWCA Civ 622, [2011] 1 W.L.R. 3264. The approach in *Nordea Bank Norge ASA v Unicredit Corporate Banking SpA* [2011] EWHC 30 (Comm.) may therefore have been superseded.

[348] At p.41; applied in *Virgin Aviation Services Ltd v CAD Aviation Services* [1991] I.L.Pr. 79. *cf. Centro Internationale Handelsbank AG v Morgan Grenfell* [1997] C.L.C. 870.

[349] *cf.* Droz, *op. cit.* above, para.12–021, n.88, paras 315–328.

proposes to decline jurisdiction for consolidation in the court in which the related action is pending at first instance, it is necessary that the court seised first have jurisdiction over the second action,[350] and that its law permit the consolidation of the two actions. This method of dealing with a related action will be particularly appropriate in a case where the parties to the two sets of proceedings are not identical, and it is in the interests of justice that there be a single resolution of issues by which all parties are directly bound. But it should be noted that Art.28 gives the judge in the court seised second a power to stay the proceedings, and a power to dismiss the action to allow it to be brought in, and consolidated with the proceedings brought in, the action in the first court, but it imposes no duty to do either. A judge is not precluded from considering, among other things, the likely timetable of proceedings in the court seised first, and the effect which it would have on the proceedings in the action before him, and in the light of this (and notwithstanding the view of Jenard that there is a presumption in favour of a stay of proceedings) to decline to grant any relief.[351] But once it is concluded by a court that it was not seised first, and that there is a related action before the courts of another Member State, its principal concern should be to make the order which will best avoid the risk of irreconcilable judgments which Art.28 is designed to forestall.[352]

Articles 27 to 29 have no application to *lis alibi pendens* cases where the proceedings are pending in different parts of the United Kingdom.[353]   **12–077**

Clause (5) of the Rule. English courts have long[354] exercised a jurisdiction to restrain a party from instituting or prosecuting proceedings in a foreign court.[355] As long ago as 1834 it was said that this jurisdiction is grounded "not   **12–078**

---

[350] Art.28 does not confer jurisdiction over a related action as such, but allows a court which has jurisdiction over it to consolidate with a pending action.

[351] *Cooper Tire & Rubber Co Europe Ltd v Bayer Public Co Ltd* [2010] EWCA Civ 864, [2010] Bus. L.R. 1697; *Trademark Licensing Co v Leofelis* [2009] EWHC 3285 (Ch.), [2010] I.L.Pr. 290.

[352] For illustration, *Masri v Consolidated Contractors International Co SAL* [2011] EWHC 1780 (Comm.).

[353] But the doctrine of *forum non conveniens* will be applicable: see above, para.12–025.

[354] The more significant older authorities include *Bushby v Munday* (1821) 5 Madd. 297; *Portarlington v Soulby* (1834) 3 My. & K. 104; *Carron Iron Co v Maclaren* (1855) 5 H.L.C. 416; *Hyman v Helm* (1883) 24 Ch.D. 531 (CA); *Cohen v Rothfield* [1919] 1 K.B. 410 (CA); *Orr-Lewis v Orr-Lewis* [1949] P. 347; *The Tropaioforos (No.2)* [1962] 1 Lloyd's Rep. 410; *Settlement Corporation v Hochschild* [1966] Ch. 10. For modification of these principles in the light of the developing law of *forum conveniens*, see *Castanho v Brown & Root (UK) Ltd* [1981] A.C. 557; *British Airways Board v Laker Airways Ltd* [1985] A.C. 58; *South Carolina Insurance Co v Assurantie Maatschappij "de Zeven Provincien" NV* [1987] A.C. 24; also *Smith Kline & French Laboratories Ltd v Bloch (No.1)* [1983] 1 W.L.R. 730 (CA); *Metall und Rohstoff AG v ACLI Metals Ltd* [1984] 1 Lloyd's Rep. 598 (CA); *Midland Bank Plc v Laker Airways Ltd* [1986] Q.B. 689 (CA); *Bank of Tokyo Ltd v Karoon* [1987] A.C. 45n.

[355] The modern re-statement of the rules is to be found in *Soc Nat Ind Aérospatiale v Lee Kui Jak* [1987] A.C. 871 (PC) and in *Airbus Industrie GIE v Patel* [1999] 1 A.C. 119. For Scotland see *FMC Corp v Russell*, 1999 S.L.T. 99. For development of the principles in Canada, see *Amchem Products Inc v British Columbia (Workers' Compensation Board)* [1993] 1 S.C.R. 897 (Sup Ct Can). For Australia, see *CSR Ltd v Cigna Insurance Australia Ltd* (1997) 189 C.L.R. 345; also *National Mutual Holdings Pty Ltd v Sentry Corp* (1989) 87 A.L.R. 539; *Re Siromath Pty Ltd (No.3)* (1991) 25 N.S.W.L.R. 25; *Allstate Life Insurance v ANZ Banking Group Ltd* (1996) 64 FCR 1, 44, 61 (Fed Ct). On the somewhat different practice in the United States, see *Airbus Industrie GIE v Patel* [1999] 1 A.C. 119, 136; *Laker Airways Ltd v Sabena, Belgian World*

upon any pretension to the exercise of judicial . . . rights abroad" but upon
the fact that the party to whom the order is directed is or has been made
subject to the *in personam* jurisdiction of the English court.[356] But although
the injunction operates only *in personam* against the party to the foreign
litigation, the remedy cannot avoid being seen as an indirect interference with
the process of the foreign court,[357] and the jurisdiction must therefore be
exercised with caution,[358] particularly if the overseas claimant, respondent to
the application, is suing in his own court.[359] Though some may consider the
terminology to lack elegance or even accuracy,[360] such orders are now routinely referred to as "anti-suit injunctions";[361] they may be granted on an
interlocutory[362] or final basis.

Airlines, 731 F. 2d. 909 (D.C. Cir. 1984); and for a recent discussion of the differing approaches
in the Circuit Courts of Appeal to the grant of foreign anti-suit injunctions see *Goss Intern Corp
v Man Roland Druckmaschinen AG*, 491 F.3d 355 (8th Cir. 2007). On the anti-suit injunctions
aspect of the 2003 Resolution of the Institut de droit international (above, para.12R–001, n.1) see
Collins, in *Festschrift für Erik Jayme* (ed. Mansel, *et al.* 2004), p.131; see also Raphael, *The Anti-
suit Injunction* (2008).

[356] *Portarlington v Soulby* (1834) 3 My. & K. 104, 108, *per* Lord Brougham L.C. See, e.g.,
Castanho v Brown & Root (UK) Ltd [1981] A.C. 557, 574; *ED & F Man (Sugar) Ltd v Haryanto
(No.2)* [1991] 1 Lloyd's Rep. 429 (CA).

[357] See, e.g. *British Airways Board v Laker Airways Ltd* [1985] A.C. 58, 95; *South Carolina
Insurance Co v Assurantie Maatschappij "de Zeven Provincien" NV* [1987] A.C. 24, 40. That the
foreign court may regard the English injunction as a serious interference is shown by the reaction
to the injunctions granted by the Court of Appeal in *British Airways Board v Laker Airways Ltd*
[1984] Q.B. 142 (CA) (discharged [1985] A.C. 58); see *Laker Airways Ltd v Pan American World
Airways*, 559 F. Supp. 1124, 1128 ("a direct interference") (USDC 1983), affirmed *sub. nom
Laker Airways Ltd v Sabena, Belgian World Airways*, 731 F. 2d 909 (D.C. Cir. 1984); see also 577
F. Supp. 348, 354 ("intrusive") (US D.C. 1983). For a reaction from an English court, see *General
Star International Indemnity Ltd v Stirling Cooke Browne Reinsurance Brokers Ltd* [2003]
EWHC 3 (Comm.), [2003] I.L.Pr. 314. And see, in the context of the Brussels Convention, the
reaction of the Düsseldorf Court of Appeal to the interlocutory injunctions granted in *Phillip
Alexander Securities and Futures Ltd v Bamberger* [1997] I.L.Pr. 73, affirmed *ibid.* p.104 (CA):
Re The Enforcement of an English anti-suit injunction [1997] I.L.Pr. 320. See also, para.1–008,
above, for considerations of comity.

[358] *Settlement Corp v Hochschild* [1966] Ch. 10, 15; *Castanho v Brown Root (UK) Ltd* [1981]
A.C. 557, 573; *British Airways Board v Laker Airways Ltd* [1985] A.C. 58; *Soc Nat Ind
Aérospatiale v Lee Kui Jak* [1987] A.C. 871, 892 (PC); *Airbus Industrie GIE v Patel* [1999] 1
A.C. 119.

[359] *Metall und Rohstoff AG v ACLI Metals Ltd* [1984] 1 Lloyd's Rep. 598, 613 (CA).

[360] See *Turner v Grovit* [2001] UKHL 65, [2002] 1 W.L.R. 107, at [23]. It is hard to see the
objection, as the order is an injunction to order the respondent to refrain from suing.

[361] *cf. Airbus Industrie GIE v Patel* [1999] 1 A.C. 119, 127.

[362] An interlocutory anti-suit injunction may require greater caution before it is granted than
would otherwise be demanded by the principles of *American Cyanamid Co v Ethicon Ltd* [1975]
A.C. 396: see *Apple Corps Ltd v Apple Computer Inc* [1992] R.P.C. 70, 76; *National Westminster
Bank Plc v Utrecht-America Finance Co* [2001] EWCA Civ 658, [2001] 2 All E.R. (Comm.) 7.
It is "vastly different from other forms of interlocutory relief": *CSR Ltd v Cigna Insurance
Australia Ltd* (1997) 189 C.L.R. 345, 397. For an "anti-anti-anti-suit" injunction (interlocutory
injunctions to restrain respondent from seeking order from foreign court which would purport to
restrain his application for an anti-suit injunction) such as was granted by a Philadelphia court in
relation to the litigation in *Smith Kline French Laboratories Ltd v Bloch* [1983] 1 W.L.R. 730
(CA), see *Shell UK Exploration and Production Ltd v Innes*, 1995 S.L.T. 807; *General Star
International Indemnity Ltd v Stirling Cooke Browne Reinsurance Brokers Ltd* [2003] EWHC 3
(Comm.), [2003] I.L.Pr. 314; *National Australia Bank Ltd v Idoport* [2002] NSWSC 623.

Jurisdiction to grant the injunction. As the jurisdiction is exercised *in*   **12–079**
personam, the court must have personal jurisdiction over the defendant under
Rules 31 to 37. In other words, it must be possible to serve process upon the
party against whom the order is sought.[363] Two specific points should be
noted. First, if it is necessary to serve the defendant out of the jurisdiction in
accordance with Rule 34 with the permission of the court, there is no
paragraph in Practice Direction 6B of the Civil Procedure Rules which applies
in terms to applications for an anti-suit injunction, although for those which
are sought in connection with a contractual right not to be sued,[364] there will
be no difficulty in principle. Secondly, where jurisdiction over the defendant
is governed by the Brussels I Regulation, or the Lugano Convention, the court
must have jurisdiction under the relevant instrument.[365] But where the proceedings to be restrained were commenced, or threatened to be commenced,
or apprehended, in a civil or commercial matter before the courts of another
Member State or Convention State, the power to order an anti-suit injunction
is inconsistent with the scheme of the Regulation and Convention, and the
question of personal jurisdiction does not, therefore, arise.[366]

The exercise of the discretion. The underlying principle is that the juris-   **12–080**
diction is exercised "where it is appropriate to avoid injustice",[367] or, as it was
once put, where the foreign proceedings are "contrary to equity and good
conscience".[368] Although it is possible to identify certain categories of cases
in which the jurisdiction has been exercised "the width and flexibility of
equity are not to be undermined by categorisation".[369] It was at one stage
said[370] that, as with any injunction, an anti-suit injunction could be granted
only to give effect to a legal or an equitable right not to be sued in the foreign
court, with the consequence that all applications for an anti-suit injunction
would be required to be founded on such a right.[371] But later authority
acknowledged that this formulation could not be accepted without significant

---

[363] On whether the jurisdiction of the English court over the respondent may be annulled by a
purported discontinuance (probably not), see *Castanho v Brown & Root (UK) Ltd* [1981] A.C.
557; *Fakih Bros v AP Moller (Copenhagen) Ltd* [1994] 1 Lloyd's Rep. 103; *Glencore International AG v Exter Shipping Ltd* [2002] EWCA Civ 524, [2002] C.L.C. 1090. The procedure for
discontinuance under CPR Pt 38 is less restrictive than under the previous rules, and the
authorities must be read with this in mind.

[364] See clause (4) of Rule 39. *cf. Starlight Shipping Co v Tai Ping Insurance Co Ltd* [2007]
EWHC 1893 (Comm.), [2008] 1 Lloyd's Rep. 230 (making the point that where the person to be
restrained is associated with, but not, a party to the contract, there is justification for service out
on this basis).

[365] That is, under Rule 28. For the specific jurisdictional argument in the context of an
agreement for the jurisdiction of the English courts, see Comment to Clause (4) of Rule 39,
below.

[366] Case C–159/02 *Turner v Grovit* [2004] E.C.R. I–3565, [2005] 1 A.C. 101.

[367] *Castanho v Brown & Root (UK) Ltd* [1981] A.C. 557, 573. For injunctions founded on
contractual agreements as to choice of forum, see clause (4) of Rule 39.

[368] *Carron Iron Co v Maclaren* (1855) 5 H.L.C. 416, 439.

[369] *Castanho v Brown & Root (UK) Ltd* [1981] A.C. 557, 573. *cf. Soc Nat Ind Aérospatiale v
Lee Kui Jak* [1987] A.C. 871, 892 (PC).

[370] *British Airways Board v Laker Airways Ltd* [1985] A.C. 58, 81, applying *The Siskina* [1979]
A.C. 210, 256.

[371] On the question whether choice of law principles should be developed to ascertain the
existence of an equitable right not to be sued, see Briggs [1997] L.M.C.L.Q. 90.

qualification;[372] and in the most recent authoritative formulation of the principles[373] there is no indication that the exercise of the discretion is limited by the need to demonstrate a legal or equitable right not to be sued.[374]

12–081   The English court may restrain proceedings brought abroad in breach of a contract not to sue, or in breach of a contract to be bound by the result of English proceedings, to sue only in England,[375] or to submit disputes to arbitration.[376] The court will also restrain proceedings which interfere with "the due process of the court",[377] or with the court's jurisdiction to decide cases pending before it.[378] Thus the court will enjoin proceedings taken abroad to recover foreign assets, whereby the party taking them will obtain an unfair advantage over other claimants in an English administration, or bankruptcy or winding up.[379] It will also restrain a judgment debtor from taking steps overseas which are designed to undermine the conclusiveness of an English judgment or its enforcement, because the court has jurisdiction to make ancillary orders in connection with litigation of the merits and of which it may be said to have "full possession".[380]

12–082   It is also clear that the court may restrain foreign proceedings which are "oppressive or vexatious" in the traditional sense.[381] For some years it was not clear what effect the modern development of *forum non conveniens* principles in the staying of *English* actions was to have on the exercise of the jurisdiction to enjoin *foreign* proceedings. In *Castanho v Brown & Root (UK)*

---

[372] *South Carolina Insurance Co v Assurantie Maatschappij "De Zeven Provincien" NV* [1987] A.C. 24, 40.

[373] *Airbus Industrie GIE v Patel* [1999] 1 A.C. 119. The general proposition that the grant of an anti-suit injunction violates Art.6 of the European Convention on Human Rights would be misconceived: *OT Africa Line Ltd v Hijazy* [2001] 1 Lloyd's Rep. 76.

[374] Unless an equitable "right" not to be sued is understood to mean no more than "having the basis for the grant of an equitable remedy": see *Masri v Consolidated Contractors International Co SAL (No.3)* [2008] EWCA Civ 625, [2009] Q.B. 503.

[375] Clause (4) of Rule 39.

[376] See below, paras 12–166, 16–089.

[377] *South Carolina* case [1987] A.C. 24, 41; *National Mutual Holdings Pty Ltd v Sentry Corp* (1989) 87 A.L.R. 539, 563; *CSR Ltd v Cigna Insurance Australia Ltd* (1997) 189 C.L.R. 345. If the foreign proceedings seek to prevent the English court ruling upon its own jurisdiction, this may well be oppressive, and an injunction will issue: *General Star International Indemnity Ltd v Stirling Cooke Browne Reinsurance Brokers Ltd* [2003] EWHC 3 (Comm.), [2003] I.L.Pr. 314; *Tonicstar Ltd v American Home Insurance Co* [2004] EWHC 1234 (Comm.), [2005] Lloyd's Rep. I.R. 32; *Goshawk Dedicated Ltd v ROP Inc* [2006] EWHC 1730 (Comm.), [2006] Lloyd's Rep. I.R. 711.

[378] *Turner v Grovit* [2001] UKHL 65, [2002] 1 W.L.R. 107.

[379] See *Soc Nat Ind Aérospatiale v Lee Kui Jak* [1987] A.C. 871, 893–894; *Harms Offshore AHT Taurus GmbH & Co KG v Bloom* [2009] EWCA Civ 632, [2010] Ch. 187 (restraint of foreign attachment of assets of company proposed to be sold as going concern). paras 26–032; 30–082; 31–039, below; *cf. Barclays Bank Plc v Homan* [1992] B.C.C. 757 (CA), and for parallel developments in French law, *Banque Worms v Brachot, Rev. Crit.* 2003, 816 (note Muir Watt); see also Muir Watt [2003] C.L.J. 573.

[380] *Masri v Consolidated Contractors International Co SAL (No.3)* [2008] EWCA Civ 625, [2009] Q.B. 503. This satisfies any requirement of *Turner v Grovit* [2002] UKHL 65, [2002] 1 W.L.R. 107 that the injunction protect the jurisdiction of the English court. There can be no objection to a judgment debtor taking points open to him in a foreign court when he is defendant to proceedings brought by the judgment creditor to enforce the judgment. The objection arises when the judgment debtor brings proceedings of his own which are perceived to be plainly designed to prevent the enforcement of the English judgment.

[381] *South Carolina* case [1987] A.C. 24, 41; *Aérospatiale* case [1987] A.C. 871, 893.

Ltd[382] Lord Scarman (with whom all other members of the House concurred) said that it was no longer necessary to consider case law earlier than the developments in England since *The Atlantic Star*[383] and *MacShannon v Rockware Glass Ltd.*[384] It was held that an injunction could be granted to restrain foreign proceedings in the circumstances which mirrored the conditions upon which a stay of English proceedings would be ordered: as the law then stood, that would mean that an injunction would be granted if the English court was an available forum in which justice could be done at substantially less inconvenience and expense, and the injunction would not deprive the plaintiff in the foreign proceedings of a legitimate personal or juridical advantage which would be available in the foreign jurisdiction.[385]

In the *Aérospatiale* case, however, the Privy Council (speaking through **12–083** Lord Goff of Chieveley) held that it was not right to treat the principles applicable in injunction cases as equivalent to those in *forum non conveniens* cases, as developed in *Spiliada Maritime Corp v Cansulex Ltd.*[386] If the principles were the same, it would mean a party could be restrained from proceeding in a foreign court on the sole ground that England was the natural forum. That could not be right, because it would lead to the conclusion that, in a case where there was simply a difference of view between the English court and the foreign court as to which was the natural forum, the English court could arrogate to itself, by the grant of an injunction, the power to resolve the dispute: such a conclusion would "be inconsistent with comity" and "disregard the fundamental requirement that an injunction will only be granted where the ends of justice so require."[387] The Privy Council held that where a remedy was available both in England and in the foreign court, the English court would in general only restrain the plaintiff from pursuing proceedings in the foreign court if the pursuit would be vexatious or oppressive. The English court must be the natural forum for the action, and it must take account of the injustice to the defendant if the plaintiff is allowed to pursue the foreign proceedings, and also the injustice to the plaintiff if he is not allowed to do so. The Supreme Court of Canada has broadly accepted the same principles while preferring to utilise the terminology of what is required for "the ends of justice", and by making a more direct assessment of whether the jurisdictional rules of the foreign court correspond to the Canadian principle of *forum conveniens.*[388] The High Court of Australia, by contrast, has adopted a rather narrower definition, namely that "foreign proceedings are to be regarded as vexatious or oppressive only if there is nothing which can

---

[382] [1981] A.C. 557.

[383] [1974] A.C. 436.

[384] [1978] A.C. 795.

[385] [1981] A.C. 557, 575. See also *British Airways Board v Laker Airways Ltd* [1985] A.C. 58, 80; *South Carolina* case [1987] A.C. 24, 40.

[386] [1987] A.C. 460.

[387] [1987] A.C. at 495. See also *EI du Pont de Nemours & Co v Agnew (No.2)* [1988] 2 Lloyd's Rep. 240, 244–245 (CA).

[388] *Amchem Products Ltd v British Columbia (Workers' Compensation Board)* [1993] 1 S.C.R. 897. See also *OT Africa Line Ltd v Magic Sportswear Corp* [2005] EWCA Civ 710, [2005] 2 Lloyd's Rep. 170, at [25] (for further proceedings, see *OT Africa Line Ltd v Magic Sportswear Corp* (2006) 273 D.L.R. (4th), [2007] 1 Lloyd's Rep. 85 (Can Fed Ct)).

be gained by them over and above what may be gained in local proceedings",[389] but it also characterised as oppressive proceedings which were instituted in one court after an action had been begun in another court and which appeared to be brought for the dominant purpose of preventing the first action from continuing.

12–084   In the result, although there may still be some cases which do not fit within this framework yet call for and justify the grant of an injunction, an injunction may be granted if England is the natural forum for the resolution of the dispute and the proceedings in the foreign court are vexatious or oppressive. English courts have refrained from giving a comprehensive or limiting definition of these expressions; indeed, they have deliberately refrained[390] from marking the outer extent of their power to act to restrain conduct which may give rise to injustice or, if the need for caution is given its due weight, serious injustice. It has been held that vexation or oppression may be indicated by the following: subjecting the other party to oppressive procedures in the foreign court,[391] especially a party with no substantial connection with that jurisdiction;[392] bad faith in the institution of the proceedings,[393] or the institution of proceedings which are bound to fail;[394] extreme inconvenience caused by the foreign proceedings;[395] multiplicity of actions, especially where the foreign action

---

[389] *CSR Ltd v Cigna Insurance Australia Ltd* (1997) 189 C.L.R. 345, 393; approving *Bank of Tokyo Ltd v Karoon* [1987] A.C. 45n. (CA). It follows from this decision that objection may not be taken to the form of the foreign proceedings, nor to the nature of the relief available from that court, so that the more unlike Australian law the foreign procedure will be, the less likely it will be to be restrained. The accuracy of this evaluation of Australian law was questioned in *TS Production LLC v Drew Pictures Pty Ltd* [2008] FCAFC 194, (2008) 252 A.L.R. 1, [32], and in *Sunland Waterfront (BVI) Ltd v Prudentia Investments Pty Ltd (No.2)* [2010] FCA 312, (2010) 267 A.L.R. 46, [22], but the material difference lies less in the wording of the respective tests than in the results of their application.

[390] *McHenry v Lewis* (1882) 22 Ch.D. 397, 407–408 (CA); *Re Connelly Bros Ltd* [1911] 1 Ch. 731, 746 (CA); *Aérospatiale*, at p.896.

[391] *A/S D/S Svendborg v Wansa* [1996] 2 Lloyd's Rep. 559, affirmed [1997] 2 Lloyd's Rep. 183 (CA) (threats of personal violence and power to manipulate the judges in the foreign forum); *cf. South Carolina Insurance Co v Assurantie Maatschappij "De Zeven Provincien" NV* [1987] A.C. 24 (application for discovery under U.S.C., s.1782: not oppressive or an interference with the due process of the court); *Royal Bank of Scotland Plc v Hicks* [2011] EWHC 287 (Ch.); contrast *Bankers Trust International Plc v PT Dharmala Sakti Sejahtera* [1996] C.L.C. 252 (application for discovery under U.S.C., s.1782 restrained); *Allstate Life Insurance Cov. ANZ Banking Corp Ltd* (1996) 64 F.C.R. 61 (Aust Fed Ct) (application for discovery under US law; restrained); *Omega Group Holdings Ltd v Kozeny* [2002] C.L.C. 132 (application for discovery under US law; restrained).

[392] *cf. British Airways Board v Laker Airways Ltd* [1985] A.C. 58 with *Midland Bank Plc v Laker Airways Ltd* [1986] 1 Q.B. 689 (CA) (US anti-trust pre-trial procedure). See also *Simon Engineering Plc v Butte Mining Plc (No.2)* [1996] 1 Lloyd's Rep. 91; *cf. Simon Engineering Plc v Butte Mining Plc* [1996] 1 Lloyd's Rep 104n. (claim for treble damages under RICO (the US Racketeer Influenced and Corrupt Organisations Act) may not be legitimate advantages in light of Protection of Trading Interests Act 1980).

[393] *McHenry v Lewis* (1882) 22 Ch.D. 397, 414 (CA); *Re Connolly Bros Ltd* [1911] 1 Ch. 731 (CA); *Midland Bank Plc v Laker Airways Ltd* [1986] 1 Q.B. 689 (CA).

[394] *Smith Kline & French Laboratories v Bloch* [1983] 1 W.L.R. 730 (CA), as explained in *British Airways Board v Laker Airways Ltd* [1985] A.C. 58, 86; *Shell International Petroleum Co Ltd v Coral Oil Co Ltd* [1999] 2 Lloyd's Rep. 606.

[395] *Logan v Bank of Scotland (No.2)* [1906] 1 K.B. 141 (CA); *cf. Albon v Naza Motor Trading Sdn Bhd* [2007] EWCA Civ 1124, [2008] 1 Lloyd's Rep. 1 (restraint of parallel arbitration).

might spawn further consequential litigation which might not be reconcilable with the foreign decision;[396] bringing proceedings which interfere with or undermine the control of the English court of its own process;[397] bringing proceedings which seek to undermine, or frustrate the enforcement of, an English judgment given in proceedings in which the respondent played a full part;[398] bringing proceedings which seek to undermine or hamper the enforcement of an English arbitral award;[399] bringing proceedings which could and should have formed part of an English action brought earlier;[400] bringing proceedings for no good reason in a court which will disregard an express choice of English law.[401]

If a prima facie case of oppression or vexation has been made out by the applicant the respondent will be entitled to show why it would nevertheless be unjust for an injunction to be granted: the interests of both parties must be borne in mind.[402] The respondent may point to substantive or procedural advantages, available to him in the foreign court, which will be lost if the injunction is granted. But if these advantages are available to him only in a

12–085

---

[396] *Australian Commercial Research and Development Ltd v ANZ McCaughan Merchant Bank Ltd* [1989] 3 All E.R. 65, affirmed February 23, 1990 (CA, unreported); *Racy v Hawila* [2004] EWCA Civ 209; *Soc Nat Ind Aérospatiale v Lee Kui Jak* [1987] A.C. 871 (consequential action for contribution would not necessarily accept the foreign court's assessment of liability as *res judicata*); *Tracomin SA v Sudan Oil Seeds Co Ltd (No.2)* [1983] 1 W.L.R. 1026 (CA); *Sohio Supply Co v Gatoil (USA) Inc* [1989] 1 Lloyd's Rep. 588 (CA) (jurisdiction clause case). But where the parties have contracted to provide for the right to being proceedings in more than one court, it will be difficult to show wrongdoing, still less oppression or vexation: *Royal Bank of Canada v Cooperatieve Centrale Raiffeisen-Boerenleenbank* [2004] EWCA Civ 7, [2004] 1 Lloyd's Rep. 471 (CA); *Deutsche Bank AG v Highland Crusader Offshore Partners LP* [2009] EWCA Civ 725, [2010] 1 W.L.R. 1023; *TS Production LLC v Drew Pictures Pty Ltd* [2008] FCAFC 194, (2008) 252 A.L.R. 1. In the particular context of claims involving intellectual property rights, in which the validity of the right may be in dispute, it may make sense to give separate competence to separate courts: *Celltech R&D Ltd v MedImmune Inc* [2004] EWCA Civ 1331.

[397] *South Carolina Insurance Co v Assurantie Maatschappij "De Zeven Provincien" NV* [1987] A.C. 24, 41, 44–45; *Bank of Tokyo Ltd v Karoon* [1987] A.C. 45n. (CA); *Bankers Trust International Plc v PT Dharmala Sakti Sejahtera* [1996] C.L.C. 252; *Glencore International AG v Exter Shipping Ltd* [2002] EWCA Civ 524, [2002] C.L.C. 1090 (complex litigation under close case management); *Star Reefers Pool Inc v JFC Group Co Ltd* [2010] EWHC 3003 (Comm.), [2011] 2 Lloyd's Rep. 215; *Morris v Davies* [2011] EWHC 1272 (Ch.) (probate dispute); *Weinstock v Sarnat* [2005] NSWSC 744, (2005) 3 I.E.T.L.R. 141 (administration of estate).

[398] *Masri v Consolidated Contractors International Co SAL (No.3)* [2008] EWCA Civ 625, [2009] Q.B. 503.

[399] *Noble Assurance Co v Gerling-Konzern General Insurance Co-UK Branch* [2007] EWHC 253 (Comm.), [2008] Lloyd's Rep. I.R. 1; *C v D* [2007] EWCA Civ 1282, [2008] 1 Lloyd's Rep. 239 (see also *Shashoua v Sharma* [2009] EWHC 957 (Comm.), [2009] 2 All E.R. (Comm.) 477).

[400] By extension of the principle in *Henderson v Henderson* (1843) 3 Hare 100: *Zeeland Navigation Co Ltd v Banque Worms, The Times*, December 26, 1995 (*obiter*; injunction refused).

[401] *Cadre SA v Astra Asigurari SA* [2005] EWHC 2626 (Comm.), [2006] 1 Lloyd's Rep. 560; *Standard Bank Plc v Agrinvest International Inc* [2007] EWHC 2595 (Comm.), [2008] 1 Lloyd's Rep. 532; *cf. Trafigura Beheer BV v Kookmin Bank Co* [2006] EWHC 1921, [2007] 1 Lloyd's Rep. 669 (injunction granted: even though English law not expressly chosen, it was the law with the closest connection to the contractual claims).

[402] *Soc Nat Ind Aérospatiale v Lee Kui Jak* [1987] A.C. 871 (PC).

forum which is not the natural forum, they will be given little weight, and may even be themselves seen as evidence of oppression.[403]

12–086   It was also indicated in *Aérospatiale* that before the English court was justified in granting an injunction to restrain vexatious or oppressive conduct, it was generally required that the court conclude that it provides the natural forum for the action.[404] This was reiterated in *Airbus Industrie GIE v Patel*[405] where it was said that this requirement—which was elevated to the status of a general rule requiring to be satisfied before the court may act—was necessary in order to respect the limits placed by comity upon the power of an English court to grant orders in relation to proceedings in foreign courts.[406] In the absence of such a connection with England it will be a rare case in which the English court would be justified in granting an injunction against a defendant whose conduct was oppressive or vexatious. In that case French aircraft manufacturers were refused an injunction restraining English defendants from pursuing proceedings in Texas arising out of an aircraft accident in India. Although the English court had *in personam* jurisdiction over the defendants, it was contrary to comity to restrain the Texas proceedings because the English forum did not have a sufficient interest in, or connection with, the matter.

12–087   In *Turner v Grovit*,[407] when giving reasons for referring to the European Court the general question whether it was consistent with the Brussels Convention for a court to issue an anti-suit injunction against parties who had brought proceedings before the Spanish court, the House of Lords indicated that an injunction could be granted only if the applicant had a "legitimate interest" in making the application. Such an interest would exist if the applicant had a legal right not to be sued, or if it was necessary to protect the jurisdiction of the English court over proceedings which were already pending before the court. Lord Hobhouse implied that outside these two instances a court would not grant an anti-suit injunction. It is submitted that Lord Hobhouse was not endeavouring to give an exhaustive statement of the circumstances in which the injunction will be granted,[408] that the law is not be so confined, and that the power to restrain by an injunction should be capable of adapting to new circumstances. The requirement that there be pending proceedings on the merits of a claim was not mentioned as a limitation on the court's broad power to restrain vexatious or oppressive behaviour in *Aérospatiale* or in *Airbus*, and this would not be a desirable restriction on the power

---

[403] *Smith Kline & French Laboratories v Bloch* [1983] 1 W.L.R. 730 (CA); *Simon Engineering Plc v Butte Mining Plc* [1996] 1 Lloyd's Rep. 104n.; *(No.2)* [1996] 1 Lloyd's Rep. 91. It is open to a respondent to undertake not to rely on or invoke such procedures in the foreign court, and thereby defeat the allegation of oppression: *Soc Nat Ind Aérospatiale v Lee Kui Jak* [1987] A.C. 871 (PC).

[404] [1987] A.C. 871, 896. For the case where the action may be brought only in the foreign forum, a so-called "single forum" case, see below, para.12–088.

[405] [1999] 1 A.C. 119.

[406] At pp.134–140. For the case where the application for an injunction is founded on breach of a jurisdiction agreement, and to which the rule laid down in *Airbus* (see p.138) was not directed, see Clause (4) of Rule 39.

[407] [2001] UKHL 65, [2002] 1 W.L.R. 107, at [27]. See also *Glencore International AG v Exter Shipping Ltd* [2002] EWCA Civ 524, [2002] C.L.C. 1090, at [42].

[408] In particular, he plainly did not have in mind the "single forum" cases referred to below: para.12–088.

of the court, not least because it will encourage applicants to institute unwanted substantive proceedings simply in order to satisfy a precondition for the grant of an injunction. It is not necessary for a claimant who seeks an injunction to restrain foreign proceedings to seek any relief in England on the substance of the dispute. Although the claimant in English proceedings has sometimes sought a negative declaration (i.e. a declaration that he is not liable to the defendant),[409] this is not a pre-condition of the right to seek an injunction. It was said as early as 1915 that a respondent could be restrained from instituting or continuing proceedings in a foreign court if a proper case of injustice were made out without any declaration of right.[410] This was justified on the footing that anti-suit injunctions of this kind can be sought by defendants who are not seeking to assert any independent cause of action but who simply claim to have a right, whether legal or equitable, not to be sued in a foreign court.[411] Thus when Midland Bank was granted an injunction restraining the liquidator of Laker Airways Ltd from joining the bank in the United States anti-trust proceedings, the bank was refused a declaration that it was not liable to Laker Airways under English law.[412] It is submitted that the correct position is that an injunction may be granted if there is a legal or an equitable right not to be sued in the foreign jurisdiction, or if it is otherwise unconscionable for the proceedings to be brought in the foreign jurisdiction, or if the order is necessary to protect the jurisdiction of the court.[413]

"Single forum" cases. The principles upon which the court exercises its   **12–088** discretion may be modified in relation to cases where, if the foreign proceedings are discontinued in obedience to an injunction, the party claiming in the foreign proceedings will not be able to bring a successful claim elsewhere. This situation arises when the cause of action relied on in the foreign court cannot be advanced in England,[414] and there is no cause of action available (as a matter of English domestic or private international law) to the claimant to allow him to win before the English courts.[415] The House of Lords, in *British*

---

[409] As in *Smith Kline & French Laboratories v Bloch* [1983] 1 W.L.R. 730 (CA); and in *British Airways Board v Laker Airways Ltd* [1985] A.C. 58.

[410] *Guaranty Trust Co of New York v Hannay & Co* [1915] 2 K.B. 536, 556 (CA).

[411] *Associated Newspapers Ltd v Insert Media Ltd* [1988] 1 W.L.R. 509, 514.

[412] *Midland Bank Plc v Laker Airways Ltd* [1986] Q.B. 689 (CA).

[413] *Royal Bank of Canada v Cooperatieve Centrale Raiffeisen-Boerenleenbank BA* [2004] EWCA Civ 7, [2004] 1 Lloyd's Rep 471; *Seismic Shipping Inc v Total E&P UK Plc* [2005] EWCA Civ 985, [2005] 2 All E.R. (Comm.) 515 (holding that an injunction cannot be ordered to prevent a party to a maritime claim proceeding in a court on the basis that it is uncertain whether the foreign judge will give effect to an English limitation decree). See also *Standard Bank Plc v Agrinvest International Inc* [2007] EWHC 2595 (Comm.), [2008] 1 Lloyd's Rep. 532, where non-parties to an agreement on jurisdiction and choice of law were restrained from bringing foreign proceedings designed to frustrate or subvert the English proceedings between the parties to the agreement.

[414] The most usual reason being that it arises under a foreign statute which is territorial in its operation or which creates a cause of action which is excluded from application in England by English choice of law rules.

[415] cf. *Simon Engineering Plc v Butte Mining Plc (No.2)* [1996] 1 Lloyd's Rep. 91, 95 (RICO affords a remedy, as distinct from providing a cause of action; therefore not a single forum case); cf. *Société Commerciale de Réassurance v Eras International Ltd* [1995] 2 All E.R. 278, 308–312.

Airways Board v Laker Airways Ltd[416] and the Court of Appeal, in *Midland Bank Plc v Laker Airways Ltd*,[417] have considered those cases where an injunction may be granted to restrain foreign proceedings even where the would-be plaintiff in the foreign proceedings has no remedy in England.[418] Both cases arose from the anti-trust proceedings brought, or threatened, in the United States against (among other defendants) certain British airlines and banks by the English liquidator of Laker Airways Ltd in connection with an alleged conspiracy to drive Laker Airways Ltd out of business. In *British Airways Board v Laker Airways Ltd* the House of Lords held that an injunction might be granted to restrain foreign proceedings even if the plaintiff in those proceedings had no remedy in England, but only if the bringing of the action in the foreign court were in the circumstances so unconscionable that it could be regarded as an infringement of an equitable right.[419] In the circumstances the British airlines were not entitled to an injunction, since by carrying on their business in the United States they had accepted that they were subject to US law, including US anti-trust law.[420] In the subsequent case of *Midland Bank Plc v Laker Airways Ltd* the Court of Appeal held that two British banks were entitled to an injunction restraining the liquidator from joining them in the US proceedings. They had been the bankers to Laker Airways Ltd, and it was alleged that they had joined in a conspiracy to deprive Laker Airways Ltd of the benefits of a financial rescue package. It was held that for an English plaintiff to sue them in the United States on the basis of the extra-territorial application of US anti-trust law to activities in England, intended to be governed by English law, was unconscionable and unjust.[421]

12–089   The suggestion that "single forum" cases represent a separate category of case, having its own distinctive rules, is open to question, for it is not obvious that a claimant has a right to bring a claim in the only court in which he may prevail, any more than a defendant has a contradictory right to defend in the one place which his defence may be successful. The correct analysis appears to be that for a court to grant an injunction to restrain a respondent, in circumstances in which to do so will mean, in effect, that the substantive claim will not be brought to court for a hearing, is a strong thing, and that a court should require a more than usually compelling basis for finding that the making of such an order is what justice demands. It may be that the strength of this point is reinforced by Art.6 of the European Convention on Human Rights. However, if the true analysis is, as it is submitted that it is, that the claimant is free and entitled to bring the case before an English court, but that

---

[416] [1985] A.C. 58.

[417] [1986] Q.B. 689 (CA).

[418] e.g. *Oceanconnect UK Ltd v Angara Maritime Ltd* [2010] EWCA Civ 1050, [2011] 1 Lloyd's Rep. 399 (claim in US for maritime lien could not really be brought anywhere else: not oppressive or vexatious): cf. *CSR v Cigna Insurance Australia Ltd* (1997) 189 C.L.R. 345 (holding not oppressive or vexatious to seek relief in foreign court not available from court in Australia).

[419] [1985] A.C. 58, 81, 95.

[420] See also *Smith Kline & French Laboratories Ltd v Bloch (No.2)*, *The Times*, November 13, 1984 (CA).

[421] [1986] Q.B. 689 (CA), distinguished in *Barclays Bank Plc v Homan* [1992] B.C.C. 757 (CA). cf. *Masri v Consolidated Contractors International Co SAL (No.3)* [2008] EWCA Civ 625, [2009] Q.B. 503, [56], indicating that such an injunction will be difficult to justify against a non-English party, both jurisdictionally and substantively.

if he does so, the defendant will defeat his claim on its merits, no infringement of Art.6 of the Convention could possibly be alleged.

The timing of the application. In principle, the sooner the application for   **12–090** an injunction is made the better its chances of success, for the amount of wasted time and money will increase the longer the application is delayed,[422] and a combination of delay and participation before the foreign court might well lead to the conclusion that it is too late for the applicant to ask for relief from the English court.[423] Moreover, the application may well be defeated if the applicant has already submitted to the jurisdiction of the foreign court.[424] There is some support for the view that an application is premature if it has not been preceded by an application for jurisdictional relief in the foreign court:[425] as an anti-suit injunction will interfere with the procedures of the foreign court, it may be preferable that the foreign court be asked not to exercise jurisdiction. It would follow that the practice of applying to the foreign court first is appropriate, at least in cases where the foreign proceedings are not themselves vexatious: this has been described as the "normal" procedure,[426] and it has been said that there must be some good reason why the application is made in England first.[427] But this approach, though discussed, was not specifically approved in *Airbus Industrie*,[428] and was specifically disapproved in *The Angelic Grace*.[429] It is submitted that there is no

---

[422] *Toepfer International GmbH v Molino Boschi srl* [1996] 1 Lloyd's Rep. 510; *A/S D/S Svendborg v Wansa* [1996] 2 Lloyd's Rep. 559, 571–572, 573, affirmed [1997] 2 Lloyd's Rep. 183 (CA); *REC Wafer Norway AS v Moser Baer Photo Voltaic Ltd* [2010] EWHC 2581 (Comm.), [2011] 1 Lloyd's Rep. 410 (delay not sufficient to overcome expectation of relief). The point is also supported by *Donohue v Armco Inc* [2001] 1 Lloyd's Rep. 579 (CA), reversed without reference to this point: [2001] UKHL 64, [2002] 1 Lloyd's Rep. 425.

[423] *REC Wafer Norway AS v Moser Baer Photo Voltaic Ltd* [2010] EWHC 2581 (Comm.), [2011] 1 Lloyd's Rep. 410.

[424] *Schiffahrtsgesellschaft Detlev von Appen GmbH v Voest Alpine Intertrading GmbH* [1997] 2 Lloyd's Rep. 279, 288 (CA); see also *Tracomin SA v Sudan Oil Seeds Co Ltd (No.2)* [1983] 1 W.L.R. 1026 (CA); *Sohio Supply Co v Gatoil (USA) Inc* [1989] 1 Lloyd's Rep. 588 (CA); *Advent Capital Plc v GN Ellinas Importers-Exporters Ltd* [2003] EWHC 3320 (Comm.), [2004] I.L.Pr. 377. Likewise, an application for an anti-suit injunction may strengthened if the respondent has already submitted to the jurisdiction of the English court but now seeks to change his mind and bring proceedings elsewhere: *CNA Insurance Co v OD Inc* [2005] EWHC 456 (Comm.), [2007] Lloyd's Rep. I.R. 89 at [27].

[425] *Pan American World Airways Inc v Andrews*, 1992 S.L.T. 268; *First Security National Bank Association v Air Gabon* [1999] I.L.Pr. 617.

[426] *Barclays Bank Plc v Homan* [1992] B.C.C. 757, 762 (Hoffmann J.), affirmed *ibid.* 777 (CA); *Shell UK Exploration and Production Ltd v Innes*, 1995 S.L.T. 807, 825 (Ct of Sess); *Deaville v Aeroflot Russian International Airlines* [1997] 2 Lloyd's Rep. 67; *Charterers Mutual Assurance Association Ltd v British & Foreign* [1998] I.L.Pr. 838. It also appears to be the view of the Supreme Court of Canada: *Amchem Products Inc v British Columbia (Workers' Compensation Board)* [1993] 1 S.C.R. 897, 930–931, distinguished (in relation to interlocutory injunctions) in *CSR v Cigna Insurance Australia Ltd* (1997) 189 C.L.R. 345, 395–397.

[427] *Arab Monetary Fund v Hashim (No.6)*, *The Times*, July 24, 1992. See also *Metall und Rohstoff AG v ACLI (Metals) London Ltd* [1984] 1 Lloyd's Rep. 598 (CA); *Bank of Tokyo Ltd v Karoon* [1987] A.C. 45n (CA).

[428] [1999] 1 A.C. 119: an anti-suit injunction had already been obtained in India, and dismissal in Texas on *forum conveniens* grounds was at that time unobtainable: p.128.

[429] [1995] 1 Lloyd's Rep. 87, 95, 96 (CA) where it was pointed out that to order an injunction after the foreign court has specifically confirmed its jurisdiction may constitute a rather greater affront to comity.

general requirement that an application be first made to the foreign court. Certainly, the demands of comity must be respected before the English court may make such an order, but that if the court has already ascertained that England is clearly the natural forum for the resolution of the dispute, comity will have been respected.[430] It should not therefore be seen as "normal" for an application for jurisdictional relief to be required to be made to the foreign court before an English court is asked to issue an injunction.

12–091   **Anti-suit injunctions under the Brussels I Regulation and Lugano Convention.** The impact of the Brussels I Regulation and the Lugano Convention raises (as the impact of the Brussels Convention raised) a number of inter-connected problems. First, as it is incumbent on the applicant for relief to establish personal jurisdiction over the respondent, it will be necessary to take account of these jurisdictional rules when the party to be restrained is domiciled in a Member or Convention State. In principle, and always assuming that the respondent is to be regarded as being "sued" in the sense of Art.2, a respondent who is entitled to object to the jurisdiction of the English courts does not lose this right when he is respondent to an application for an anti-suit injunction. However, there are some instances—for example, where an injunction is sought against a defendant to proceedings already before the English court, and to the jurisdiction of which the defendant has already submitted—in which the application for an injunction, made in the course of those proceedings, does not involve "suing" the respondent, and the provisions of Chapter II of the Regulation and Title II of the Lugano Convention have no part to play.[431]

12–092   More problematic is the question of whether it is open to an applicant to apply for an anti-suit injunction when the proceedings to which the application relates are pending or anticipated to become pending before the courts of another Member State or Convention State. In *Continental Bank NA v Aeakos Compania Naviera SA*,[432] the parties had bound themselves by contract to the exclusive jurisdiction of the English courts but the respondent borrower, having defaulted on the agreement and anticipating legal proceedings, launched proceedings against the applicant bank before the Greek courts. The Court of Appeal acknowledged little difficulty in granting the bank an injunction. So far as concerned any possible jurisdictional objection, it held that jurisdiction under what is now Art.23 of the Brussels I Regulation "prevailed over" what is now Art.27, so that even though the English court was seised second, it was not obliged to decline jurisdiction in favour of the Greek court seised first: though the court did not use the language, it proceeded as though wrongful seisin was incapable of establishing the jurisdiction of the court seised first. Having concluded that it had personal jurisdiction to restrain the respondent, the court granted the injunction on the orthodox ground that damages for breach of contract[433] were insufficient as a remedy. No significance was attached to the fact that the proceedings which were indirectly

---

[430] And may for this reason not have been respected by the foreign court.

[431] *Masri v Consolidated Contractors International Co SAL (No.3)* [2008] EWCA Civ 625, [2009] Q.B. 503, [55]–[59].

[432] [1994] 1 W.L.R. 588 (CA).

[433] The court did not elaborate on how damages would be assessed. See below, para. 12–164.

to be restrained were before the courts of a State which was equally bound to apply the provisions of the Brussels Convention. In subsequent cases, the Court of Appeal applied the principle in *Continental Bank*, extending it to cases where the wrongful behaviour of the respondent lay in the breach of an agreement to arbitrate,[434] and in vexatious or oppressive behaviour in bringing proceedings before the foreign court.[435]

Despite the obvious commercial attraction of being able to grant a summary remedy against wrongdoers, there were problems with this approach. First, there was nothing in the text of the Brussels Convention which could be read as giving a court power to grant such relief; and to the extent that it required an English court to reach the conclusion that the court first seised was or would be wrong to conclude that it had no jurisdiction, there was the authority of the European Court[436] that such a finding was not one which a court seised second was entitled to make. Secondly, it became clear that courts in other Convention States were notably hostile to the proposition that an English court had the right, even if the English court maintained that it was only doing so indirectly, to interfere with proceedings pending before them.[437] Thirdly, there was little doubt that the granting of anti-suit injunctions had the potential to complicate the free circulation of judgments. As against that, the argument that an English court was granting a remedy to restrain a wrongdoer, and passing no judgment, even indirectly, against the exercise of jurisdiction by a foreign court, was and is accurate, at least in a technical sense,[438] and the European Court had previously[439] accepted the principle that equity operates *in personam*. In *Turner v Grovit*[440] the Court of Appeal granted an injunction to restrain the respondents from bringing proceedings before the Spanish courts in circumstances where the English courts had been seised first and saw the granting of an injunction as essential to protect the integrity of their proceedings, and saw the behaviour of the respondent as being abusive, vexatious and oppressive. On appeal to the House of Lords[441] a reference was made to the European Court, which ruled that the Brussels Convention "is to be interpreted as precluding the grant of an injunction whereby a court of a Contracting State prohibits a party

12–093

---

[434] *The Angelic Grace (No.2)* [1995] 1 Lloyd's Rep. 87 (CA) But *Phillip Alexander Securities & Futures Ltd v Bamberger* [1997] I.L.Pr. 73, affirmed 104, and in *Toepfer International GmbH v Soc Cargill France* [1998] 1 Lloyd's Rep. 379, 387–388 (CA) it was accepted that in the context of the Brussels Convention, additional restraint was appropriate.

[435] *Turner v Grovit* [2000] Q.B. 345 (CA).

[436] Case C–351/89 *Overseas Union Insurance Ltd v New Hampshire Insurance Co* [1991] E.C.R. I–3317.

[437] For a German judicial view, see *Re The Enforcement of an English anti-suit injunction* [1997] I.L.Pr. 320; for a French judicial view, see Case C–24/02 *Marseilles Frêt SA v Seatrano Shipping Co Ltd* [2002] E.C.R. I–3383 (reference rejected as court lacked jurisdiction to make it).

[438] See, e.g. *Turner v Grovit* [2001] UKHL 65, [2002] 1 W.L.R. 107 at [26]; *Through Transport Mutual Insurance Association (Eurasia) Ltd v New India Assurance Co Ltd* [2004] EWCA Civ 1598, [2005] 1 Lloyd's Rep. 67 at [87]–[92]; *OT Africa Line Ltd v Magic Sportswear Corp* [2005] EWCA Civ 710, [2005] 2 Lloyd's Rep. 170 at [36]–[38]. But see para.12–078, above, for the more realistic view that the injunction is an indirect interference with the proceedings in the foreign court.

[439] Case C–294/92 *Webb v Webb* [1994] E.C.R. I–1717.

[440] [2000] Q.B. 345 (CA).

[441] [2001] UKHL 65, [2002] 1 W.L.R. 107.

to proceedings pending before it from commencing or continuing legal proceedings before a court of another Contracting State, even where that party is acting in bad faith with a view to frustrating the existing proceedings".[442] The Court explained that this conclusion followed from the fact that the courts of Contracting States owed each other obligations of trust,[443] and the anti-suit injunction could not be reconciled with that duty. The result is that an English court has no power to make an order restraining the respondent from bringing a claim in a civil or commercial matter before the courts of another Member or Convention State, and that the question[444] of whether there is personal jurisdiction over the respondent is irrelevant. No exception was made for cases in which the English court is seised first,[445] or has exclusive jurisdiction,[446] or is the only court actually seised, or is exercising jurisdiction over a matter which is entirely concerned with arbitration and therefore outside the material scope of the Regulation.[447] The essential point is that the English court has no power to restrain a person who is bringing or who threatens to bring civil or commercial proceedings before the courts of another Member State from doing so; if the bringing of those proceedings is objectionable, it is for the court before which they are brought to deal with the objection and grant any relief.

ILLUSTRATIONS

12–094

1. A, a Scotsman living in Scotland, is injured in an accident while employed by X, an English company, at its Scottish factory. A is medically treated in Scotland, and all witnesses of fact live and work in Scotland. Medical and other expert witnesses are available in Scotland. A's action in England against X for negligence is stayed.[448]

2. A Turkish ship, owned by X, a Turkish state corporation, and a Cuban ship, owned by A, a Cuban state corporation, collide in Turkish territorial waters. Both ships are damaged in the collision. X sues A in the Turkish courts. Subsequently A arrests in England another ship owned by X and commences an action *in rem* against X in England. The Turkish court is the natural and appropriate forum, and A is unable to establish that there is some personal or juridical advantage which would be available only in England and which is of such importance that it would cause injustice to deprive A of it. The action in England is stayed.[449]

3. A & Co, a Liberian company, insure their cargo vessel with X & Co, a Kuwaiti insurance company, against war and marine risks under a Lloyd's standard form of marine insurance, which excludes loss caused by infringement of customs regulations. The vessel is detained by Saudi Arabian officials on the ground that it is engaged in smuggling oil. A & Co sue in England, claiming that the vessel is a constructive total loss. The court has jurisdiction to grant leave under what is now CPR, PD6B, para.3.1 because the applicable law of the contract is English law, but the court will not exercise its jurisdiction because England is not the *forum conveniens*: the central

---

[442] C–159/02 [2004] E.C.R. I–3565, [2005] 1 A.C. 101.

[443] See Blobel and Späth (2005) 30 Eur. L.R. 528.

[444] Discussed above, para.12–079.

[445] As it was in *Turner v Grovit*.

[446] Even if the English court has exclusive jurisdiction regardless of domicile under Art.22, it is possible that the foreign proceedings are not within Art.22, so there is no question of an injunction being permitted here. The effect of Case C–116/02 *Erich Gasser GmbH v MISAT srl* [2003] E.C.R. I–14693, [2005] Q.B. 1 is that a court seised second may not exercise jurisdiction even where it has exclusive jurisdiction by prorogation; and it must follow that there is no power to grant an injunction in this case either; see below, para.12–163.

[447] Case C–185/07 *West Tankers Inc v Allianz SpA* [2009] E.C.R. I–663, [2009] 1 A.C. 1138.

[448] *MacShannon v Rockware Glass Ltd* [1978] A.C. 795.

[449] *The Abidin Daver* [1984] A.C. 398.

issue is one of fact, whether the vessel was engaged in smuggling in the Gulf, and there is an available forum in Kuwait.[450]

4. A & Co, Liberian ship-owners, charter a carrier, *The Spiliada*, to Y & Co, an Indian **12–095** company, for the carriage of sulphur from Vancouver, British Columbia, to Indian ports. X & Co, a Canadian company engaged in the export of sulphur, ship a cargo of sulphur on *The Spiliada* from Vancouver under bills of lading whose applicable law is English law. A & Co sues X & Co in England claiming that the sulphur was wet when loaded and caused severe corrosion. There is already a substantial trial proceeding in England arising out of similar allegations against X & Co by a different shipowner concerning a cargo loaded at Vancouver for carriage to South Africa and Mozambique: there is, therefore, an accumulated expertise of the lawyers and experts in the other case, many of whom are also involved in the case of *The Spiliada*. The court has jurisdiction to grant permission to serve process under what is now CPR, PD6B, para.3.1 because the applicable law of the contract is English law, and will exercise its jurisdiction because England is the *forum conveniens*.[451]

5. A, a Portuguese citizen residing in Portugal, is employed by X, a Panamanian company, on one of its ships. While the ship is in an English port A is injured by what he alleges is the negligence of X and of Y, an English company, which provided shore services for the ship. Both X and Y are subsidiaries of Z, a Texan company. A brings an action in England against X and Y and by consent an interim payment of damages is made, and subsequently X admits liability. A is approached by an American firm of lawyers who persuade him to enforce his claim in the United States against X, Y and Z with legal fees to be on a contingency basis. A gives notice to discontinue the proceedings in England, and X and Y apply in England for an injunction to restrain A from pursuing the United States proceedings. The injunction is refused because the prospect of higher damages is a legitimate personal or juridical advantage and the Texas court was no less natural or appropriate a forum than England.[452]

6. A brings proceedings against X in England in circumstances where the claim and the parties are more closely connected to a particular foreign country and to the application of its law than they are to England and English law. A may resist a stay of proceedings by showing cogent evidence that there is a risk that the courts of the foreign country will not do justice to his claim against X.[453]

7. A brings proceedings against X in England in respect of a claim arising out of an alleged contract said by A to have been made within the jurisdiction. Even though the parties, the dispute, and the subject matter of the dispute have practically nothing to do with England or English law, A believes that he will not obtain a fair trial before the courts of the country which would otherwise represent the natural forum. It is open to the court to accept the evidence put forward by A, and to find that England is therefore the proper place to bring the claim.[454]

8. Proceedings are brought by A against X in England. A later assigns its business to Y, and gives notice of an application to amend the proceedings to substitute Y as the claimant. Before the application can be heard, X commences proceedings against Y before the Cypriot courts, with the result that when the application to amend the English proceedings is heard, X argues that the Cypriot courts were (are) first seised in relation to the claim. The amendment is allowed; the interests of A and Y as assignee and assignor are identical and indissociable, and after the amendment is made, the claim of A against X will be regarded as dating or relating back to the original formulation of the claim as one by A.[455]

9. Proceedings are brought by A against X before the English courts, and proceedings are brought by X against A before the courts of another Member State. The two sets of proceedings are quite distinct. But A then amends the proceedings to include claims which in substance relate to those already raised in the proceedings before the other Member State. The English court is the first court seised, and the argument that it is to be regarded as second seised, for the purposes of Art.28 of the Regulation, in respect of the issues raised in the amendment is wrong.[456]

---

[450] *Amin Rasheed Shipping Corp v Kuwait Insurance Co* [1984] A.C. 50.

[451] *Spiliada Maritime Corp v Cansulex Ltd* [1987] A.C. 460.

[452] *Castanho v Brown & Root (UK) Ltd* [1981] A.C. 557. But the reasoning in the decision is now to be regarded as unreliable.

[453] See *AK Investment CJSC v Kyrgyz Mobil Tel* [2011] UKPC 7, [2011] 4 All E.R. 1027.

[454] *Cherney v Deripaska* [2009] EWCA Civ 849, [2010] All E.R. (Comm.) 456.

[455] *Kolden Holdings Ltd v Rodette Commerce Ltd* [2008] EWCA Civ 10, [2008] Bus. L.R. 1051.

[456] *Stribog Ltd v FKI Engineering Ltd* [2011] EWCA Civ 622, [2011] 1 W.L.R. 3264.

10. A, domiciled in England, sustains personal injuries while on holiday in Jamaica. Among the six defendants whom he sued for damages is one (X) who is domiciled in England, and five who are domiciled only in Jamaica. As jurisdiction over him is founded on Art.2 of the Brussels I Regulation, X may not seek a stay of proceedings against him in favour of the courts of Jamaica.[457]

11. X, an airline incorporated in Jersey, and in liquidation with an English liquidator, commences an action in the United States against A and B, two British airlines, and various other airlines and aircraft manufacturers. X claims in the United States action treble damages for breach of the United States anti-trust laws, arising out of (inter alia) allegedly anti-competitive fares fixed by the airline defendants. A and B commence an action in England against X claiming a declaration that they are not liable to X and an injunction restraining X from continuing with the United States proceedings. The injunction is refused because, although the court has jurisdiction to grant an injunction to restrain foreign proceedings in the circumstances, X has no remedy in England for the alleged wrong, and A and B do not show that A's conduct in bringing the United States proceedings is unconscionable.[458]

12-096   12. A is a passenger in a helicopter manufactured by X & Co, a French company, and operated by Y & Co, an English company. A is killed in a crash in England. His widow and administrators sue X & Co and Y& Co both in England and in Texas. The Texas court has jurisdiction because X & Co carries on business there, but the case otherwise has no connection with Texas. Under Texas law X & Co cannot claim contribution from Y & Co. The court grants an injunction restraining the Texas proceedings.[459]

13. After a fatal accident at an Indian airport, X, who is resident in England, institutes proceedings in India against A, the French corporation which manufactured the aircraft. The proceedings make slow progress. X later commences proceedings against A in the courts of Texas. An Indian court orders X to discontinue the Texas proceedings on the ground of *forum conveniens*, but X is not within its personal jurisdiction and ignores the order. A seeks an injunction from the English courts to restrain X from continuing the Texas proceedings. The court refuses the injunction as England is not the natural forum for the litigation and to interfere with proceedings pending in Texas in such a case would be incompatible with the requirements of comity.[460]

14. X, a British citizen, enters into an English contract with A. He breaks it and by fraud obtains a Turkish judgment against A. The court grants an injunction restraining X from enforcing the judgment.[461]

15. A & Co, an English company, sells furniture to X & Co, an Italian company. The price is payable in England; delivery is to take place in Italy. After the goods are delivered, X & Co sues A Co for damages in Italy, claiming that the furniture is not in conformity with the contract. Subsequently A Co sues X & Co in England for the price. The court must decline jurisdiction.[462]

12-097   16. A & Co, an American insurance company with a place of business in England, reinsure with X & Co, a Singapore insurance company, and Y & Co and Z & Co, English insurance companies. The reinsurance is of insurance placed with A & Co in connection with five warranties on products sold by a French company. A & Co sues X & Co, Y & Co and Z & Co in France, claiming monies due under the reinsurance policies. The defendants challenge the jurisdiction of the French court. Subsequently, X & Co, Y & Co and Z & Co bring proceedings against A & Co in England for a declaration that they have lawfully avoided the policies for non-disclosure. The English court must stay its proceedings until the French court has decided whether it has jurisdiction.[463]

17. A, an employee of company controlled by X, brings proceedings in England claiming damages for unfair and wrongful dismissal. While the proceedings are pending in England, X causes proceedings to be brought against A in Spain by other companies under his control, alleging that A has caused them loss. The Spanish court appears to be unaware of the English proceedings. A

---

[457] Case C–281/02 *Owusu v Jackson* [2005] E.C.R. I–1383, [2005] Q.B. 801 (a case on the Brussels Convention).

[458] *British Airways Board v Laker Airways Ltd* [1985] A.C. 58. Contrast *Midland Bank Plc v Laker Airways Ltd* [1986] Q.B. 689 (CA).

[459] cf. *Soc Nat Ind Aérospatiale v Lee Kui Jak* [1987] A.C. 871.

[460] *Airbus Industrie GIE v Patel* [1999] 1 A.C. 119.

[461] *Ellerman Lines Ltd v Read* [1928] K.B. 144 (CA).

[462] Art.27, Brussels I Regulation; Case 144/86 *Gubisch Maschinenfabrik KG v Palumbo* [1987] E.C.R. 4861.

[463] Art.27, Brussels I Regulation; cf. Case C–351/89 *Overseas Union Insurance Co v New Hampshire Insurance Co* [1991] E.C.R. I–3317, [1992] Q.B. 434.

applies in England for an anti-suit injunction to restrain the vexatious or oppressive behaviour of X and his companies. As the injunction is aimed at interfering with the proceedings before the courts of a Member State, the English court has no power to grant it.[464]

2. JURISDICTION AGREEMENTS

RULE 39—(1) Where a contract provides that all disputes between the parties are to be referred to the jurisdiction of the English courts, the court normally has jurisdiction to hear and determine proceedings in respect thereof.[465]   12R–098

(2) Subject to clause (3) of this Rule, where a contract provides that all disputes between the parties are to be referred to the exclusive jurisdiction of a foreign tribunal, the English court will stay proceedings instituted in England in breach of such agreement[466] **(or, as the case may be, refuse to give permission to serve process out of the jurisdiction**[467]**) unless the claimant satisfies the court that strong cause exists to allow them to continue.**[468]

---

[464] Case C–159/02 *Turner v Grovit* [2004] E.C.R. I–3565, [2005] 1 A.C. 101.

[465] CPR, r.6.11; CPR, PD6B, para.3.1(6)(d); Brussels I Regulation, Art.23; Lugano Convention, Art.23; 1982 Act, Sch.4, Rule 12 (inserted by SI 2001/3929, Sch.2, para.4). In addition to the works cited in n.1 to para.12–001, above, see Briggs, *Agreements on Jurisdiction and Choice of Law* (2008); Joseph, *Jurisdiction and Arbitration Agreements and their Enforcement* (2nd ed, 2010). On possible options for reform, Briggs (2010) 12 Yb.P.I.L. 311.

[466] The leading modern case on the effect of exclusive jurisdiction clauses at common law is *Donohue v Armco Inc* [2001] UKHL 64, [2002] 1 Lloyd's Rep. 425 at [23] *et seq.* On this part of the Rule see *Gienar v Meyer* (1796) 2 H.Bl. 603; *Law v Garrett* (1878) 8 Ch.D. 26 (CA); *Austrian Lloyd SS Co v Gresham Life Assurance Society Ltd* [1903] 1 K.B. 249 (CA); *Kirchner & Co v Gruban* [1909] 1 Ch. 413; *The Cap Blanco* [1913] P. 130 (CA); *The Media* (1931) 41 Ll.L.Rep. 80; *The Eleftheria* [1970] P. 94; *The Sindh* [1975] 1 Lloyd's Rep. 372 (CA); *The Makefjell* [1976] 2 Lloyd's Rep. 29 (CA); *The Kislovodsk* [1980] 1 Lloyd's Rep. 183; *The Star of Luxor* [1981] 1 Lloyd's Rep. 139; *Trendtex Trading Corp v Crédit Suisse* [1980] 3 All E.R. 721, affirmed [1982] A.C. 679; *The Biskra* [1983] 2 Lloyd's Rep. 59; *The Sennar (No.2)* [1985] 1 W.L.R. 490 (HL); *The Benarty (No.2)* [1985] Q.B. 325 (CA); *The Iran Vojdan* [1984] 2 Lloyd's Rep. 380; *The Pioneer Container* [1994] 2 A.C. 324 (PC); *The Mahkutai* [1996] A.C. 650 (PC); *The Nile Rhapsody* [1994] 1 Lloyd's Rep. 382 (CA); *The Havhelt* [1993] 1 Lloyd's Rep. 523; *ZI Pompey Industrie v ECU-Line NV* [2003] 1 S.C.R. 450; *Leigh & Mardon Pty Ltd v PRC Inc* (1993) 44 F.C.R. 88 (Fed Ct); *Williams v Society of Lloyd's* [1994] 1 V.R. 274; *Francis Travel Marketing Pty Ltd v Virgin Atlantic Airways* (1994) A.T.P.R. 41–332; *FAI General Insurance Co Ltd v Ocean Marine Mutual Protection and Indemnity Association* (1996) 41 N.S.W.L.R. 117. See Cowen and Mendes da Costa (1965) 43 Can.Bar.Rev. 453; Kahn-Freund (1977) 26 I.C.L.Q. 825; Briggs [1984] L.M.C.L.Q. 227, 241–9; Morse (1989) 1 African J. Int. Comp. L. 551; Peel [1998] L.M.C.L.Q. 182; Bell (1996) 10 J. Contract. Law 53, 97. For the United States see *M/S Bremen v Zapata Offshore Co*, 407 U.S. 1 (1972), [1972] 2 Lloyd's Rep. 315; *Carnival Cruise Lines, Inc v Shute*, 499 U.S. 585 (1991); Hay, Borchers and Symeonides, pp.537–541.

[467] See para.12–146, below.

[468] The leading case is *Donohue v Armco Inc* [2001] UKHL 64, [2002] 1 Lloyd's Rep. 425. Earlier decisions, which are to be read in the light of this decision, include *The Athenée* (1922) 11 Ll. L. Rep. 6 (CA), *The Vestris* (1932) 43 Ll. L. Rep. 86; *The Fehmarn* [1957] 1 W.L.R. 815; [1958] 1 W.L.R. 159 (CA); *The Adolf Warski* [1976] 2 Lloyd's Rep. 241 (CA); *Carvalho v Hull Blyth (Angola) Ltd* [1979] 1 W.L.R. 1228 (CA); *The Vishva Prabha* [1979] 2 Lloyd's Rep. 286; *The Panseptos* [1981] 1 Lloyd's Rep. 152; *The El Amria* [1981] 2 Lloyd's Rep. 119 (CA); *The Atlantic Song* [1983] 2 Lloyd's Rep. 394; *The Pia Vesta* [1984] 1 Lloyd's Rep. 169; *Standard Chartered Bank v Pakistan National Shipping Corp* [1995] 2 Lloyd's Rep. 365; *Citi-March Ltd v Neptune Orient Lines Ltd* [1996] 2 All E.R. 545; *The MC Pearl* [1997] 1 Lloyd's Rep. 566; *Bouygues Offshore SA v Caspian Shipping Co (Nos 1, 3, 4, and 5)* [1998] 2 Lloyd's Rep. 461 (CA); *Akai Pty Ltd v People's Insurance Co* (1997) 188 C.L.R. 418; *Apple Computer Inc v Apple Corps SA* [1990] 2 N.Z.L.R. 598; *ZI Pompey Industrie v ECU-Line NV* [2003] SCC 27, [2003]

(3) Where the case falls within the scope of the Brussels I Regulation, or the Lugano Convention, unless the defendant submits to the jurisdiction, the court has no jurisdiction to determine a dispute

    (a) if one or more of the parties is domiciled in a Member State or a Convention State and the parties have agreed in accordance with Article 23 of the Brussels I Regulation or of the Lugano Convention, as the case may be, that the courts of a Member or Convention State other than the United Kingdom are to have jurisdiction to settle any such dispute and that the courts of the United Kingdom are not to have jurisdiction; or

    (b) if none of the parties is domiciled in a Member State or a Convention State and the parties have agreed in accordance with Article 23 of the Brussels I Regulation or of the Lugano Convention, as the case may be, that the courts of a Member or Convention State other than the United Kingdom are to have jurisdiction to settle any such dispute and the courts chosen have not declined jurisdiction.[469]

(4) An English court may restrain a party over whom it has personal jurisdiction from the institution or continuance of proceedings in a foreign court in breach of a contract to refer disputes to an English (or, *semble*, another foreign) court, or to arbitration, unless the foreign proceedings in question are in a civil or commercial matter brought, or to be brought, before the courts of a Member State or a Convention State.[470]

COMMENT

12–099   **Introductory.** Rule 39 deals with the common case where parties[471] to a contract, frequently but not necessarily in international trade or commerce,[472] agree in advance on the forum which is to have jurisdiction to determine disputes which may arise between them.[473] Three issues may arise in connection with such clauses. First, the contract may purport to confer jurisdiction on the English courts, and the claimant may seek to invoke that jurisdiction. Whether (and if so, how) he may do so will be determined in part by whether the Brussels I Regulation, or the Lugano Convention, applies to the agreement: if they do, they regulate the form, and to some extent the content, of the

---

1 S.C.R. 450. See also *OT Africa Line Ltd v Magic Sportswear Corp* [2005] EWCA Civ 710, [2005] 2 Lloyd's Rep. 170.

[469] Brussels I Regulation, Art.23; Lugano Convention, Art.23 (*cf.* Brussels Convention, Art.17).

[470] Case C–185/07 *West Tankers Inc v Allianz SpA* [2009] E.C.R. I–663, [2009] 1 A.C. 1138.

[471] For the position of third parties who may be bound by an agreement entered into between others, see *The Pioneer Container* [1994] 2 A.C. 324 (PC) (jurisdiction agreement between bailee and sub-bailee binding on bailor who had consented to the bailee sub-contracting the carriage "on any terms"); *cf. The Mahkutai* [1996] A.C. 650 (PC) (sub-contractor not entitled to rely on agreement between owner and principal contractor as jurisdiction agreement not within scope of "Himalaya" clause). For the same issue in the context of Art.23 of the Regulation and the Convention, see below, para.12–139.

[472] For a very early example see *Gienar v Meyer* (1796) 2 Hy.Bl. 603.

[473] For jurisdiction clauses in trust instruments see above, para.11–305.

agreement; and the question whether permission is required to serve process out of the jurisdiction will be determined by whether the agreement is one to which the Regulation or the Convention applies. The entitlement of an English court to exercise jurisdiction on the basis of a contractual agreement for the English courts is examined in clause (1) of the Rule. Secondly, the contract may purport to confer jurisdiction upon the courts of another country, and yet a claimant may commence,[474] or seek to commence,[475] proceedings in England. Whether the court will permit the action to proceed as a matter of common law, is examined in clause (2) of the Rule; whether it is obliged by the Regulation or the Convention to dismiss the action is examined in clause (3) of the Rule. Thirdly, proceedings may be brought in a foreign court in breach of an agreement that they be brought in an English or in another foreign court or before an arbitral tribunal. The principles which govern when such proceedings may be restrained by injunction are examined in clause (4) of the Rule. A number of inter-connected arguments have to be considered. The approach adopted here is first to examine the case in which there is no dispute as to the validity and existence of a contract between the parties, but the parties disagree about the jurisdiction agreement. This will be followed by examination of the issues which arise when it is argued by one party that the contract and hence the jurisdiction agreement is void or otherwise ineffective. This is followed by an examination of how the Regulation and the Convention affect the validity of a jurisdiction agreement.

Proposed legislative reform. It is to be expected that during the lifetime of this edition, significant reform to the law on jurisdiction agreements will take place. The project to amend the Brussels I Regulation[476] appears likely to make significant alterations to the manner in which jurisdiction (and possibly also arbitration[477]) clauses operate within the broader framework of the Regulation. The principal aim of such reform will be to give greater support to the designated court (or arbitral tribunal) as the body which will take the decision whether the proceedings proposed to be brought fall within the scope of the jurisdiction clause (or arbitration agreement) in question. One perceived shortcoming of the Regulation as currently drafted is that it is too easy for a party to frustrate an opponent, who has the advantage of an agreed dispute resolution clause, by bringing proceedings outside the designated court or tribunal.[478] The existence of these blocking, or "torpedo", proceedings will, so long as they remain pending before the courts of a State other than that designated by the agreement, prevent the designated court being seised with proceedings (or if that court is seised, those proceedings will be required to be

12–100

---

[474] By service of process without the permission of the court.

[475] By service of process with the permission of the court.

[476] See Ch.11, where the general nature of the programme of reform is described.

[477] The proposed reforms, so far as they relate to arbitration, are discussed in greater detail in Ch.16. The complication arises from the fact that national laws are not uniform on the issue whether it is the arbitral tribunal itself, or the courts at the seat of the arbitration, which correspond to the "designated court" for the purpose of the reform to the law on jurisdiction agreements.

[478] See further, para.12–158, below.

stayed).[479] It may require disproportionate time and expense to defeat these blocking proceedings, which is manifestly contrary to the policy of the Regulation which aims to respect the autonomy of the parties,[480] and within which the use of jurisdiction agreements can only promote legal certainty. Even if the result of allowing the "designated" court or tribunal to make the decision carries the risk that decisional primacy will turn out to have been given to a court or tribunal which, as one party had maintained all along, had not actually been chosen or designated, the price paid in such cases is generally considered to be one worth paying to underpin the effectiveness of jurisdiction agreements for the courts of a Member State.

12–101   The Brussels I Regulation confines its legislative treatment to agreements conferring jurisdiction on the courts of a Member State. There is, therefore, still some uncertainty as to how the Regulation accommodates jurisdiction agreements referring to the courts of a non-Member State. For as the European Union has no power to legislate for such courts to exercise or not exercise[481] jurisdiction, it was impossible for the Regulation to say anything about them. This almost certainly means that the effect of jurisdiction agreements in relation to non-Member States will fall to be decided by the law of the Member State seised with proceedings,[482] and this will therefore be liable to vary from State to State as each court applies its own rules of the conflict of laws, in default of any other, to an issue on which the Regulation abstains from providing a solution. Partly in order to reduce this risk of diversity of treatment and outcome, the European Court confirmed[483] that the European Union was entitled to take further steps towards the harmonising of civil jurisdiction by signing[484] the Hague Convention on Choice of Court Agreements of 2005. This instrument came about after the comprehensive failure at The Hague to settle the terms of a worldwide convention modelled on the Brussels and Lugano scheme. The 2005 Hague Convention aims to put in place rules which would govern some of the effects and consequences of exclusive[485] jurisdiction agreements. Viewed from a purely English perspective, the 2005 Convention would do little to alter existing law, but if it were to take root in other legal systems, whose laws would become accordingly more respectful of jurisdiction agreements, it will be beneficial. The largest challenge will be to accommodate the rules which the EU proposes to extract from the 2005 Hague Convention alongside the changes which have

---

[479] *JP Morgan Europe Ltd v Primacom AG* [2005] EWHC 508 (Comm.), [2005] 2 Lloyd's Rep. 665.

[480] Recital (14) to the Regulation.

[481] For example, on grounds equivalent to those provisions of the Regulation which limit or exclude the effectiveness of such agreements, in the context of insurance, consumer, or employment contracts.

[482] Case C–387/98 *Coreck Maritime GmbH v Handelsveem BV* [2000] E.C.R. I–9337.

[483] Opinion 1/03: *Opinion under Art 300(6) of the EC Treaty as to whether the conclusion of a new Lugano Convention falls within the sphere of exclusive competence of the Community* [2006] E.C.R. I–1145.

[484] That is to say, in place of the Member States who had participated in the negotiations leading up to the adoption of the Hague Convention.

[485] For non-exclusive jurisdiction agreements, and their relationship to the 2005 Convention, see Art.22 of the Convention.

been identified as desirable to improve the working of the Brussels I Regulation.[486]

The varieties of jurisdiction agreement. The chosen court may be a court   **12–102** in the country of one or both of the parties, or it may be a neutral forum.[487] The jurisdiction clause may provide for a submission to the courts of a particular country,[488] or to a court identified by a formula in a printed standard form,[489] such as a bill of lading referring disputes to the courts of the carrier's principal place of business.[490] Some jurisdiction clauses provide for the courts of a particular country to have *exclusive* jurisdiction; others provide for the courts of one or more countries to have non-exclusive jurisdiction, i.e. they confer jurisdiction on the courts of one or more countries without prejudice to the right of the parties to institute proceedings in any other court which may have jurisdiction. But, as will be seen below, others may not clearly do either, or do one to the exclusion of the other, and as a result, a rigid division into exclusive and non-exclusive jurisdiction agreements may sometimes be misleading.

The law which governs a jurisdiction agreement. A jurisdiction agree-   **12–103** ment is almost invariably part of a wider contract. The rules governing choice of law in contract are now contained in the Rome I Regulation on the law applicable to contractual obligations,[491] which for present purposes is to the same effect as its predecessor instrument, the Rome Convention on the law applicable to contractual obligations.[492] The Rome I Regulation is dealt with in detail in Chs 32 and 33. Article 1(2)(e) of the Rome I Regulation[493] provides that the rules of the Regulation are not to apply to "agreements on

---

[486] See Brand and Jablonski, *Forum Non Conveniens: History, Global Practice and Future under the Hague Convention on Choice of Court Agreements* (2007); Brand and Herrup, *The 2005 Hague Convention on Choice of Court Agreements*; Kessedjian, 2006 *Clunet* 813; Spigelman (2009) 83 A.L.J. 386. Distinct from any decision to incorporate the Hague Convention into the framework of the Brussels I Regulation is the possibility, which is under active consideration, that the Regulation might be amended to make specific and uniform provision for a court, seised with jurisdiction under the Regulation, to grant relief on the ground that effect ought to be given to a jurisdiction agreement for the courts of a non-Member State. Though such a rule could not require a court in a non-Member State to exercise jurisdiction, it could remove the question whether and when to grant relief from the realm of national rules of the conflict of laws by imposing a uniform provision for staying or dismissing proceedings. See also see the Report of the Commission to the Council of Ministers, April 21, 2009, COM(2009) 174 final, at para.3.3.

[487] As in *The Chaparral* [1968] 2 Lloyd's Rep. 158, 163–164 (CA); see also *Attock Cement Co Ltd v Romanian Bank for Foreign Trade* [1989] 1 W.L.R. 1147, 1161 (CA).

[488] On the effect of a change in the identity of the foreign country see *Carvalho v Hull, Blyth (Angola) Ltd* [1979] 1 W.L.R. 1228 (CA). *cf. The Panseptos* [1981] 1 Lloyd's Rep. 152.

[489] Whether the agreement is standard form, or has been individually negotiated, may be relevant to the weight to be accorded to it: *The Bergen (No.2)* [1997] 2 Lloyd's Rep. 710, 715.

[490] As in *The Eleftheria* [1970] P. 94; *The El Amria* [1981] 2 Lloyd's Rep. 119 (CA); *The Ruben Martinez Villena (No.2)* [1988] 1 Lloyd's Rep. 435; *The Sylt* [1991] 1 Lloyd's Rep. 240; *The Rewia* [1991] 2 Lloyd's Rep. 325 (CA).

[491] Regulation (EC) 593/2008.

[492] Given effect by Contracts (Applicable Law) Act 1990, and appearing as Sch.1 to that Act.

[493] Art.1(2)(d) of the Rome Convention was identically worded.

the choice of court".[494] Consequently, the English court is not required by the Rome I Regulation to apply its rules to jurisdiction agreements. But as a matter of common law, normally a jurisdiction agreement (like arbitration agreements, which are also excluded by Art.1(2)(e) from the application of the Rome I Regulation) is governed by the law applicable to the contract of which it forms a part. Accordingly, and as a matter of the common law principles of the conflict of laws, the law which governs the contract will also generally govern the jurisdiction agreement. This means, as will be seen below, that this law governs the construction and interpretation of the agreement; it will also, in principle at least, govern the original validity of the agreement.[495] Difficulty arises in cases in which it is necessary to take a preliminary decision[496] as to whether there is a jurisdiction clause in a contract in order to help identify the law which governs that contract. It has been held, and appears to be correct, that this preliminary assessment has to be undertaken by reference to English domestic law principles. But it should follow that once the law governing the contract has been identified by these means, it is that law which must be used to make the definitive assessment whether the jurisdiction agreement in question is in fact one of the terms of the contract.

12–104   **Incorporation of jurisdiction agreement from another instrument.** It is sometimes argued that a jurisdiction agreement contained in express terms in one contract, or contained in another document, such as the membership rules of a trade association, has been incorporated by reference into another contract by a form of words contained in the second agreement. In principle, any dispute as to the content of the second agreement will be determined by the law which governs that second agreement, which will either be its applicable law or by a combination of that law and (in cases falling within their scope) the Brussels I Regulation or the Lugano Convention. Where English law governs the second agreement, the usual rule, which was until recently, taken to be well established in cases of insurance and reinsurance,[497] and also applicable to charterparties and bills of lading,[498] is that general words of incorporation of one set of provisions from another contract will not incorporate a jurisdiction agreement from the first contract. The justification usually given is that because a jurisdiction agreement is not germane to but ancillary to the risk insured, or to the adventure, it will not be presumed from mere general words that it was intended to be incorporated into one contract from

---

[494] For the reasons for the exclusion see Giuliano-Lagarde Report [1980] O.J. C282, at pp.11–12.

[495] For the effect of an agreement on choice of court when it is alleged that the contract is void or voidable, or when the action is bought to have the contract declared unenforceable or a nullity, see below, para.12–113.

[496] But, it is submitted, not to *decide*.

[497] *AIG Europe (UK) Ltd v The Ethniki* [2000] 2 All E.R. 566 (CA); *AIG Europe SA v QBE International Insurance Ltd* [2001] 2 Lloyd's Rep. 268; *Assicurazioni Generali SpA v Ege Sigorta A/S* [2002] Lloyd's Rep. I.R. 480; *Welex AG v Rosa Maritime Ltd* [2003] EWCA Civ 938, [2003] 2 Lloyd's Rep. 509. *Dornoch Ltd v Mauritius Union Assurance Co Ltd* [2005] EWHC 1887 (Comm.), [2006] EWCA Civ 389, [2006] 2 Lloyd's Rep. 475 (which also supports the view that the English approach applies even though the second contract is governed by a foreign law: *sed quaere*).

[498] *TW Thomas & Co Ltd v Portsea Steamship Co Ltd* [1912] A.C. 1; *Siboti K/S v BP France SA* [2003] EWHC 1278 (Comm.), [2003] 2 Lloyd's Rep. 364.

another, but requires a clear and specific reference to be made to it in the second contract.[499] However, more recently, the view that general words will not incorporate a jurisdiction agreement has been questioned, some decisions preferring instead to say that the question is one of construction of the words of the second contract, and that this is should not be prejudiced by any presumption against the effect of general words.[500] One possible reconciliation of the cases is that where the incorporation is from another (first) contract to which the parties to the second contract had also been party, general words will be likely to be sufficient, but that where the jurisdiction clause is to be taken from a contract to which they were not, such as in the context of charterparties and bills of lading, the test for incorporation will be stricter, and general words will be less likely to suffice.[501]

Where the Brussels I Regulation or the Lugano Convention is applicable to the jurisdiction agreement, it is not clear whether the question of incorporation is answered by sole reference to the rules governing formality, or is, or is also, regulated as a matter of substantive law by the *lex contractus* of the agreement into which it is alleged the term was incorporated.[502] But if the second contract contains words which satisfy the "clear and specific" requirement of the common law, it is unlikely that the result will be different.[503]

Exclusive, non-exclusive, and hybrid jurisdiction clauses. It is a question   **12–105** of interpretation, governed by the law applicable to the contract, or more accurately, the law governing the jurisdiction agreement,[504] whether a jurisdiction clause is exclusive or non-exclusive, i.e. whether it requires proceedings to be brought in a particular forum, or simply records the parties' agreement, or the absence of objection, to the jurisdiction of courts of a particular country without requiring proceedings to be brought there.[505] The question may be relevant to the question whether the English court should exercise jurisdiction, though it will certainly be important if an application is made for an injunction to restrain a party who, as it is contended, has brought foreign proceedings in breach of an exclusive jurisdiction clause. Some authorities suggest that the clause must provide in terms that the jurisdiction

---

[499] For the effect of deletion of a jurisdiction agreement in the course of negotiation, see *Brotherton v Aseguradora Colseguros SA (No.1)* [2002] Lloyd's Rep. I.R. 848.

[500] *Axa Re v Ace Global Markets Ltd* [2006] EWHC 216 (Comm.), [2006] Lloyd's Rep. I.R. 683; *Sea Trade Maritime Corp v Hellenic Mutual War Risks Association (Bermuda) Ltd (The Athena) (No.2)* [2006] EWHC 2530 (Comm.), [2007] 1 Lloyd's Rep. 280.

[501] *Habaş Sinai ve Tibbi Gazlar Isthisal Endustri AS v Sometal SRL* [2010] EWHC 29 (Comm.), [2010] Bus. L.R. 880 (distinguished *Stellar Shipping Co LLC v Hudson Shipping Lines* [2010] EWHC 2985 (Comm.)).

[502] See para.12–128, below.

[503] *Prifti v Musini SA de Seguros y Reaseguros* [2003] EWHC 2797 (Comm.), [2004] Lloyd's Rep. I.R. 528 (a case on Art.23 of the Brussels I Regulation); *Merkel International Insurance Co Ltd v La Republica Compania Argentina de Seguros Generales SA* [2004] EWHC 1826 (Comm.), [2005] 1 Lloyd's Rep. I.R. 90; *Nestorway Ltd v Ambaflex BV* [2006] IEHC 235, [2007] I.L.Pr. 633.

[504] *cf. Mackender v Feldia AG* [1967] 2 Q.B. 590, 598, *per* Lord Denning M.R., and the cases on arbitration clauses, see below, paras 16–011 *et seq.*

[505] See *Evans Marshall & Co Ltd v Bertola SA* [1973] 1 W.L.R. 349, 361–362. *cf. Commercial Bank of the Near East Plc v A* [1989] 2 Lloyd's Rep. 319; *Green v Australian Industrial Investment Ltd* (1989) 90 A.L.R. 500. See also Kahn-Freund (1977) 26 I.C.L.Q. 825, 828–829.

of the chosen court be exclusive,[506] but the true question is whether on its proper construction the clause *obliges* the parties to resort to the relevant jurisdiction, irrespective of whether the word "exclusive" is used.[507] Where the agreement is governed by English law, and in the absence of explanation to the contrary, the court may conclude that if the nominated court would have had jurisdiction by right in the absence of the agreement, the agreement would be idle unless it conferred *exclusive* jurisdiction on the nominated court.[508] But the parties may have provided for jurisdiction without realising that this principle of interpretation exists, and it is submitted that the point should not be pressed too far. Surprisingly, perhaps, this and similar questions of construction have not tended to rely on the application of more general contractual principles, such as the rule that ambiguity in contractual wording is resolved by construction *contra proferentem*,[509] though there appears to be no reason why such an approach should be applicable here as it is elsewhere in the law of contract.[510] By contrast, an occasionally-used rule of construction,[511] that a clause is exclusive if transitive in form (i.e. the parties submit disputes), but non-exclusive if intransitive (i.e. the parties submit (themselves), would appear to have practically nothing to recommend it.[512]

---

[506] *Hoerter v Hanover, etc. Works* (1893) 10 T.L.R. 103 (CA); *Westcott v Alsco Products of Canada Ltd* (1960) 26 D.L.R. 281 (Nfld CA); *Harrington v Industrial Sales Ltd* [1973] 2 W.W.R. 330, affirmed [1973] 5 W.W.R. 577 (Sask CA); *Khalij Commercial Bank Ltd v Woods* (1985) 17 D.L.R. (4th) 358 (Ont); *Contractors Ltd v MTE Control Gear Ltd* [1964] S.A.S.R. 47. cf. *Compagnie Commerciale André SA v Artibell Shipping Co Ltd*, 1999 S.C.L.R. 349.

[507] This sentence was treated as correctly stating the law in *Sohio Supply Co v Gatoil (USA) Inc* [1989] 1 Lloyd's Rep. 588, 591 (CA); *British Aerospace Plc v Dee Howard Co* [1993] 1 Lloyd's Rep. 368; *Continental Bank NA v Aeakos Compania Naviera SA* [1994] 1 W.L.R. 588 (CA). See also *Ocarina Marine v Macard Stein & Co* [1994] 2 Lloyd's Rep. 524; *FAI General Insurance Co Ltd v Marine Mutual Protection and Indemnity Assn* (1996) 41 N.S.W.L.R. 117; *Middle Eastern Oil LLC v National Bank of Abu Dhabi* [2008] EWHC 2895 (Comm.), [2009] 1 Lloyd's Rep. 251; *Bank of New York Mellon v GV Films Ltd* [2009] EWHC 2338 (Comm.), [2010] 1 Lloyd's Rep. 365; *General Motors Corp v Royal & Sun Alliance Insurance Plc* [2007] EWHC 2206 (Comm.), [2007] 2 C.L.C. 507. See also *Breitenbücher v Wittke* [2008] CSOH 145 (persons affected by jurisdiction clause to be determined by governing law).

[508] *Sohio Supply Co v Gatoil USA Inc*, above; *A/S D/S Svendborg v Wansa* [1997] 2 Lloyd's Rep. 368, 373 (CA); *British Aerospace Plc v Dee Howard Corp* [1993] 1 Lloyd's Rep. 368; *FAI General Insurance Co Ltd v Ocean Marine Mutual Protection and Indemnity Assn*, above; *Ace Insurance Ltd v Moose Enterprise Pty Ltd* [2009] NSWSC 724. But for the view that the question is one of construction by close attention to the words actually used, unaided by any such presumption, see *McGowan v Summit at Lloyd's*, 2002 S.L.T. 1258 (IH). On service of suit clauses, see *Ace Insurance SA-NV v Zürich Insurance Co* [2001] EWCA Civ 173, [2001] 1 Lloyd's Rep. 618 (CA). Whether the agreement also applies to applications for provisional or protective relief is also a matter of construction: *Bankgesellschaft Berlin AG v First International Shipping Corp Ltd* [2001] C.P. Rep. 62.

[509] cf. *Noble v Carnival Corp* (2006) 80 O.R. (3d) 392. The possibility of construction *contra proferentem* was raised, but did not need to be relied on, in *Sebastian Holdings Inc v Deutsche Bank AG* [2010] EWCA Civ 998, [2011] 1 Lloyd's Rep. 106.

[510] *Ace Insurance Ltd v Moose Enterprise Pty Ltd* [2009] NSWSC 724, [33].

[511] See *Austrian Lloyd SS Co v Gresham Life Assurance Soc Ltd* [1903] 1 KB 249; *British Aerospace Ltd v Dee Howard Corp* [1993] 1 Lloyd's Rep 368; *Sabah Shipyard (Pakistan) Ltd v Islamic Republic of Pakistan* [2002] EWCA Civ 1643, [2003] 2 Lloyd's Rep 571, esp. at [30]–[35].

[512] Not least because if the parties submit, they only do so for the purpose of having disputes resolved, with the result that the distinction may be grammatical but is practically illusory. The suggestion that the parties drafting the contract, who may not have had English as their first or second language, were alert to this supposed rule is not credible.

Where the court finds that the agreement confers non-exclusive jurisdiction   **12–106**
on the designated court (whether England or a foreign court), it is more
difficult to argue that the institution of proceedings is a breach of contract; and
on that footing, an application for a stay of proceedings in favour of that
foreign court will be determined on the basis of *Spiliada Maritime Corp v
Cansulex Ltd.*[513] But the fact that a court was contractually chosen by the
parties will be taken as clear evidence that it is an available forum, and that,
in principle at least, it is not open to either party to object to the exercise of
its jurisdiction at least on grounds which should have been foreseeable when
the agreement was made.[514]

However, the position is sometimes more complex. It may be that, on its   **12–107**
true construction, though the court was given non-exclusive jurisdiction, the
parties agreed that if either were to invoke it, the other would submit to the
jurisdiction of the named court for the sole determination of the dispute.[515] It
would follow that proceedings taken in a foreign court would breach such a
jurisdiction agreement if they sought to prevent the other party from invoking
the jurisdiction agreement, or if they aimed to frustrate or prevent the other
party having recourse to it. The question is therefore whether the effect of
instituting proceedings in the foreign court, or doing so and refusing to appear
to defend the claim made in England, may, on a true construction of the
jurisdiction agreement, be seen as a breach of it.[516] Certainly the question of
exclusivity or non-exclusivity is a guide to the answer, but it is not always
definitive.

In sum, there is no reason why the parties may not, if so advised, make an   **12–108**
agreement for the resolution of disputes which is more complex, and better
suited to their needs, than would be provided by a plain and simple "exclusive
or non-exclusive" template.

Scope and reach of jurisdiction clause. In cases in which there is no   **12–109**
dispute as to the validity of a jurisdiction clause, the principal question is
likely to be to determine that the dispute in question falls within the material
scope of the clause, or the within the jurisdiction clause *ratione materiae*. As

---

[513] [1987] A.C. 460; see clause (2) of Rule 38, above. The same will apply when it is
complained that the bringing of proceedings in a foreign court is wrongful and should be
restrained see clause (4) of Rule 39, below.

[514] *S&W Berisford Plc v New Hampshire Insurance Co* [1990] 2 Q.B. 631 (disapproved on
other grounds in *Re Harrods (Buenos Aires) Ltd* [1992] Ch. 72 (CA)); *Standard Steamship
Owners Protection and Indemnity Association (Bermuda) Ltd v Gann* [1992] 2 Lloyd's Rep. 528;
British Aerospace Plc v Dee Howard Co [1993] 1 Lloyd's Rep. 368; *The Rothnie* [1996] 2
Lloyd's Rep. 206; *Mercury Communications Ltd v Communications Telesystems International*
[1999] 2 All E.R. (Comm.) 33; *JP Morgan Securities Asia Pte Ltd v Malaysian Newsprint
Industries Sdn Bhd* [2001] 2 Lloyd's Rep. 41 (CA); *Antec International Ltd v Biosafety USA Inc*
[2006] EWHC 47 (Comm.); *BP Plc v Aon Ltd* [2005] EWHC 2554 (Comm.), [2006] 1 Lloyd's
Rep. 549.

[515] *cf. Breams Trustees Ltd v Upstream Downstream Simulation Services Ltd* [2004] EWHC
211 (Ch.).

[516] *Sabah Shipyard (Pakistan) Ltd v Government of Pakistan* [2002] EWCA Civ 1643, [2003]
2 Lloyd's Rep. 571; *Standard Bank Plc v Agrinvest International Inc* [2007] EWHC 2595
(Comm.), [2008] 1 Lloyd's Rep. 532; *Antec International Ltd v Biosafety USA Inc* [2006] EWHC
47 (Comm.); *HIT Entertainment Ltd v Gaffney International Licensing Pty Ltd* [2007] EWHC
1282 (Ch.).

the common law regards these clauses as ordinary contractual terms, the question is one of construction and interpretation.[517] In principle, where it is a matter of dispute, the construction and interpretation of a jurisdiction clause is a matter to be referred to the law which governs the jurisdiction clause, which will usually[518] be the law governing the contract of which it forms a part, albeit a separable part. The account which follows explains the approach to construction and interpretation as this will be applied to a jurisdiction clause which is governed by English law, or which is not governed by a law demonstrated to be materially different from English law. Prior to 2007 the case law had allowed a minute examination of the comparative scope of clauses framed in terms of their being applicable to claims "arising from", or "arising under", or "arising under or in connection with" a contract, etc.[519] This was undertaken with a view to determining how each of these verbal formulae might or might not apply if a claim were brought to enforce a contract, or to assert the right to have rescinded a contract, or to allege the legal nullity of a supposed contract, as well as where the claimant formulated a claim as one in tort (for example, for fraud[520] or other misrepresentation), or for restitution,[521] or as a claim for breach of fiduciary duty, etc. In *Fiona Trust & Holding Corp v Privalov*,[522] the House of Lords decisively repudiated the authority which had held that there were material differences between claims "arising under", "arising in connection with", etc. stating that the "fussy distinctions"[523] made in those cases "reflect no credit upon English commercial law".[524] Henceforth, as a matter of English law the proper approach to such clauses was to treat the parties as rational commercial actors who would have had no reason to prescribe jurisdiction over some parts, but not over other parts, of what might be a claim which advanced alternative causes of action, some but not other parts of which were plainly contractual.[525]

---

[517] *The Sindh* [1975] 1 Lloyd's Rep. 372, 374 (CA); *The Sennar (No.2)* [1984] 2 Lloyd's Rep. 142 (CA), affd. [1985] 1 W.L.R. 490 (HL); *Youell v Kara Mara Shipping Co Ltd* [2000] 2 Lloyd's Rep. 102; *Francis Travel Marketing Pty Ltd v Virgin Atlantic Airways* (1996) 39 N.S.W.L.R. 160; *cf.* Case C–214/89 *Powell Duffryn Plc v Petereit* [1992] E.C.R. I–1745.

[518] But not always, as, for example, where the jurisdiction clause is the subject of a self-contained agreement about the resolution of disputes, such as in *A v B* [2006] EWHC 2006 (Comm.), [2007] 1 Lloyd's Rep. 237 (freestanding arbitration agreement).

[519] e.g. *Heyman v Darwins Ltd* [1942] A.C. 356 ("arising under" narrower than "arising out of"); *Fillite (Runcorn) Ltd v Aqua-Lift* (1989) 26 Con. L.R. 66 ("under a contract" did not apply to obligations not created by the contract itself).

[520] *Cavell USA Inc v Seaton Insurance Co* [2009] EWCA Civ 1363, [2009] 2 C.L.C. 991.

[521] *Mackays Stores v Topward Ltd* 2006 S.L.T. 716.

[522] [2007] UKHL 40, [2007] Bus. L.R. 1719 (also reported as *Premium Nafta Products Ltd v Fili Shipping Co Ltd*). To the same effect, see *Comandate Marine Corp v Pan Australia Shipping Pty Ltd* (2006) 157 F.C.R. 45, [2008] 1 Lloyd's Rep. 119.

[523] *Fiona Trust & Holding Corp v Privalov*, at [27].

[524] *ibid*, at [12].

[525] *Ashville Investments Ltd v Elmer Contractors Ltd* [1989] Q.B. 488; *AWB Geneva SA v North America Steamships Ltd* [2007] EWCA Civ 739, [2007] 1 C.L.C. 749; *Brave Bulk Transport Ltd v Spot On Shipping Ltd* [2009] EWHC 612 (QB), [2009] 2 Lloyd's Rep. 115 (applied in *Vitol SA v Capri Marine Ltd (No.2)* [2010] EWHC 458 (Comm.), [2011] 1 All E.R. (Comm.) 366); *Oceanconnect UK Ltd v Angara Maritime Ltd* [2010] EWCA Civ 1050, [2011] 1 Lloyd's Rep. 399; *Louis Dreyfus Commodities Kenya Ltd v Bolster Shipping Co Ltd* [2010] EWHC 1732 (Comm.), [2011] All E.R. (Comm.) 540.

Material scope and concurrent jurisdiction clauses. Where a complex   **12–110**
financial or other commercial transaction is put in place by means of a number
of interlinked contracts, and each has its own provision for the resolution of
disputes, the point of departure will be that it is improbable that a jurisdiction
clause in one contract even if expressed in ample terms, was intended to
capture disputes more naturally seen as arising under a related contract.[526] In
some cases the court called upon to disentangle such provisions has guided
itself by seeking to identify the particular contract out of which the dispute
most naturally arises, or to locate the centre of gravity of the dispute; in others
it has preferred to ask whether the claim brought by the claimant was one
which a jurisdiction agreement permitted the claimant to bring, whatever else
may also have been permitted by other jurisdiction agreements,[527] though
these are simply two aspects of the single issue, which is one of contractual
interpretation. Even if the effect is that there will be a risk of fragmentation of
the overall process for the resolution of disputes, this is not by itself sufficient
to override the construction, and consequent giving of effect to the complex
agreements for the resolution of disputes which the parties have made.[528]

Personal scope. A separate aspect of the scope of a jurisdiction agreement   **12–111**
is the question of its scope *ratione personae*, its personal scope. In *Donohue
v Armco Inc*,[529] Lord Scott specifically considered a question which had been
raised, but not answered, in a previous case:[530] whether a dispute-resolution
agreement could be framed according to which A promised B not to bring
proceedings against C except in a designated court in such a way as gave some
form of protection to C, and what would happen if it was. It is apparent that
there are two points to consider. The first is whether, on a true construction of
the language in which the clause is expressed, it represents such a promise
made to B.[531] Those courts which have been called upon to deal with this
point have frequently had to struggle with drafting which is wordy and

---

[526] *Satyam Computer Services Ltd v Upaid Services Ltd* [2008] EWCA Civ 487, [2008] 2 All
E.R. (Comm.) 465; *UBS AG v HSH Nordbank AG* [2009] EWCA Civ 585, [2009] 2 Lloyd's Rep.
272. See also *ACP Capital Ltd v IFR Capital Plc* [2008] EWHC 1672 (Comm.), [2008] 2 Lloyd's
Rep. 665; *ACE Capital Ltd v CMS Energy Corp* [2008] EWHC 1843 (Comm.), [2008] 2 C.L.C.
318; *Choil Trading SA v Addax Energy SA* [2009] EWHC 2742 (Comm.); *Douglas v Glenvarigill
Co Ltd* [2009] CSOH 17, 2009 S.C.L.R. 379.
[527] *Sebastian Holdings Inc v Deutsche Bank AG* [2010] EWCA Civ 998, [2011] 1 Lloyd's Rep.
106.
[528] *BP Plc v Aon Ltd* [2005] EWHC 2554 (Comm.), [2006] 1 Lloyd's Rep. 549; *Deutsche Bank
AG v Highland Crusader Offshore LP* [2009] EWCA Civ 725, [2010] 1 W.L.R. 1023; *Morgan
Stanley & Co International Plc v China Haisheng Juice Holdings Ltd* [2009] EWHC 2409
(Comm.), [2010] 1 Lloyd's Rep. 265; *Skype Technologies SA v Joltid Ltd* [2009] EWHC 2783
(Ch.), [2011] I.L.Pr. 103; *Brave Bulk Transport Ltd v Spot On Shipping Ltd* [2009] EWHC 612
(QB), [2009] 2 Lloyd's Rep. 115; *Dubai Islamic Bank PJSC v PSI Energy Holding Co BSC*
[2011] EWHC 1019 (Comm.).
[529] [2001] UKHL 64, [2002] 1 Lloyd's Rep. 425.
[530] *Credit Suisse First Boston (Europe) Ltd v MLC (Bermuda) Ltd* [1999] 1 All E.R. (Comm.)
237. The decision pre-dated the Contracts (Rights of Third Parties) Act 1999; the court was
reluctant to interpret a contract as conferring a benefit which the common law of privity would
not then allow the third party, supposed beneficiary, to enforce.
[531] In this section the discussion is based on the assumption that the law which governs the
agreement is English law. If it is not, the corresponding provisions of whatever other law applies
to the jurisdiction agreement will apply instead.

opaque, and have come to a variety of conclusions, though as the question is one of construction, and no more, this is not surprising.[532] The second is whether such a promise gives rights to B, or to C, or to both. In principle, the answer is provided by the ordinary rules of privity of contract.[533] If the promisee, B, seeks to enforce the promise made by A, by applying for a stay or dismissal of the proceedings brought against C, there is no obvious reason why relief should be denied, unless it can be said that he has no legitimate interest in A's proceedings against C.[534] Whether C may seek relief in his own right will depend on whether the benefit of the jurisdiction agreement was one which A and B purported to confer on him: if it was, and if the contract is governed by English law, the Contracts (Rights of Third Parties) Act 1999 will, in principle at least, allow C to assert and enforce the benefit of the jurisdiction agreement. If the contract between A and B makes it clear that C is not to have this right,[535] C certainly cannot claim any contractual entitlement to apply for relief, though it has been suggested that where A has promised B not to sue C in the forum court, C, though having no contractual right to relief, may still contend that the bringing of proceedings against him in that court is vexatious or oppressive, or otherwise unconscionable, presumably on the ground that if A has made a clear statement on which reliance has been placed, it should not be open to A to proceed as if that statement had never been made, and the court's inherent power to stay proceedings, for example, on the footing that they are oppressive or vexatious, or that the court is, in the light of the promise made, a *forum non conveniens*, may still available to justify jurisdictional relief.[536]

12–112   *Jurisdiction clauses associated with voidable contracts.* Closely associated with the question of material scope is the issue whether a jurisdiction clause is applicable when a contract, the original making of which is not in dispute, has been rescinded, or avoided, or frustrated, or terminated.[537] Such a case

---

[532] *Morgan Stanley & Co International Plc v China Haisheng Juice Holdings Ltd* [2009] EWHC 2409 (Comm.), [2010] 1 Lloyd's Rep. 265; *Whitesea Shipping & Trading Corp v El Paso Rio Clara Ltda (The Marielle Bolten)* [2009] EWHC 2552, [2010] 1 Lloyd's Rep. 648; *Global Partners Fund Ltd v Babcock & Brown Ltd (In Liquidation)* [2010] NSWCA 196. But where the promise is only worded to apply to proceedings against A, associates of A have no rights in relation to it, and any attempt to be joined as claimants "in order to give effect to the jurisdiction clause" by obtaining an injunction for themselves will be rejected: *Donohue v Armco Inc* [2001] UKHL 64, [2002] 1 Lloyd's Rep. 425.

[533] Assuming the contract to be governed by English law. Where it is governed by a foreign law, that law will provide the answer to the question whether non-parties may take advantage of the contract, and if so, how.

[534] If, for example, the contract provides that B will indemnify C (or "hold C harmless"), a sufficient interest will be likely to be present. *cf. Gore v Van Der Lann* [1967] 2 Q.B. 31 (CA); *Beswick v Beswick* [1968] A.C. 58; *Snelling v John G Snelling Ltd* [1973] Q.B. 87; *Global Partners Fund Ltd v Babcock & Brown Ltd (In Liquidation)* [2010] NSWCA 196.

[535] For example, by expressly excluding the Contracts (Rights of Third Parties) Act 1999.

[536] *Global Partners Fund Ltd v Babcock & Brown Ltd (In Liquidation)* [2010] NSWCA 196, [73]: perhaps by analogy with the reasoning in *Norwich CC v Harvey* [1989] 1 All E.R. 1180 (CA).

[537] Quite apart from the case in which fault is found with the substantive contract, and the question is as to the effect on the jurisdiction agreement, it is clear that a jurisdiction clause can itself be repudiated, so freeing the other party from the obligation to comply with it: *Dubai Islamic Bank PJSC v PSI Energy Holding Co BSC* [2011] EWHC 1019 (Comm.).

presented itself in *Fiona Trust & Holding Corp v Privalov*,[538] in which a shipowner sought to avoid a charterparty, which contained a jurisdiction agreement, on the ground that as the substantive contract had been procured by bribery, and that once the bribery had come to light the entire contract had been rescinded, the shipowner had been freed from the constraint of the jurisdiction clause. In *Fiona Trust and Holding Co v Privalov*,[539] the House of Lords decisively rejected the contention that where a claimant had rescinded, or had purported to rescind, an admitted commercial contract the validity of which was governed by English law, the dispute-resolution clause was nullified together with everything else. This conclusion was justified by aligning the common law of jurisdiction clauses with the developed law of arbitration,[540] and adopting the idea that, at least where the matter was governed by English law,[541] a jurisdiction clause was legally separable from the substantive contract in which it was recorded, with the result that its validity was unaffected by the rescission of the substantive contract. A dispute resolution clause would only be deprived of intrinsic[542] effect if the fact or factor which was relied on to impugn the agreement was one specifically referable to or targeted at the dispute-resolution agreement itself.[543] In *Fiona Trust* itself, a contention that the charterparty had been rescinded when it had been discovered that it had been procured by bribery was held insufficient to impugn the dispute-resolution clause in the charter itself, for the allegation of bribery was not one specifically targeted at the dispute-resolution agreement.

Jurisdiction clauses associated with "void contracts". It is important to observe that the context in which *Fiona Trust* re-stated the law was that there was no dispute about the original validity of the contract. It does not follow   **12–113**

---

[538] [2007] UKHL 40, [2007] Bus. L.R. 1719. To the same effect, see *Comandate Marine Corp v Pan Australia Shipping Pty Ltd* (2006) 157 F.C.R. 45, [2008] 1 Lloyd's Rep. 119. For earlier cases proposing this approach, see *FAI General Insurance Co Ltd v Ocean Marine Mutual Protection and Indemnity Association* (1997) 41 NSW.L.R. 559, [1998] Lloyd's Rep. I.R. 24; *IFR v Federal Trade SpA*, September 19, 2001; *Harbour Assurance Co (UK) Ltd v Kansa General International Insurance Co Ltd* [1993] Q.B. 701 (CA). For an analogous approach in French law, see *Monster Cable Products Inc v Audio Marketing Services* (Cass. civ. I, October 22, 2008) [2009] I.L.Pr. 158.

[539] To the same effect, see *Comandate Marine Corp v Pan Australia Shipping Pty Ltd* (2006) 157 F.C.R. 45, [2008] 1 Lloyd's Rep. 119.

[540] Arbitration Act 1996, s.7, though it had been widely accepted in the law of arbitration long before that.

[541] Where English law is not the law which governs the jurisdiction agreement, this approach will not apply as a rule, though it is to be supposed that it will be presumed to be consistent with the relevant foreign law unless the contrary is convincingly shown.

[542] As distinct from legal effect (such as by reason of overriding mandatory law, whether domestic or resulting from European harmonization, such as the Unfair Terms in Consumer Contracts Regulations 1999 (SI 1999/2083): Case C–240/98 *Océano Grupo Editorial SA v Quintero* [2000] E.C.R. I–4941). Likewise, rules which require particular notice to be given in respect of onerous terms may apply to a dispute resolution clause: *Kaye v Nu Skin UK Ltd* [2009] EWHC 3509 (Ch.), [2011] 1 Lloyd's Rep. 40 (applying the rule in *J Spurling Ltd v Bradshaw* [1956] 1 W.L.R. 461 to an arbitration agreement).

[543] This will be the case where, for example, there was a misrepresentation on the very question whether a written document contained a jurisdiction clause. The question of how to proceed where the contention is that a contract never came into existence in the first place is entirely distinct from the issues examined and resolved in *Fiona Trust*, which was a case in which the original contract was not denied.

that the same approach, of detaching the jurisdiction agreement from the rescission or avoidance or termination of the substantive contract, can be justified where the contention of one of the parties is that no contract ever came into existence in the first place. This may arise (taking the examples, for convenience of illustration only, from English domestic law) where there is an allegation of failure to reach material agreement, or an absence of consideration, or mistake (including perhaps forgery[544] and *non est factum*), and perhaps some varieties of illegality.[545] The question whether the parties agreed upon the jurisdiction of a court as one of the terms of a contract must in principle be governed by the law which governs the broader issue of contractual formation.[546] As to that, the general approach of the common law has been to refer to the question to the putative proper law, or governing law, for two reasons. The first is that any question whether a contract contains a particular term is a matter for its governing law; and if that is so, the same law should also determine whether there was any agreement at all; the second is that if negotiating parties allowed themselves to come close to the point where a rationally-connected legal system might conclude that they had reached contractual agreement, each can fairly be regarded as being at risk of the court arriving at such a conclusion.

12–114   *Standard of proof.* As was explained in Chapter 11, where an English court is called on to exercise jurisdiction in circumstances in which the material jurisdictional facts are not agreed, the party who wishes to invoke the jurisdiction will be required to have the better of the argument that the facts which support its invocation of the jurisdiction are satisfied.[547] It is likely that the same principle applies in mirror image when a party challenges the exercise of jurisdiction by pointing to an agreement providing for the jurisdiction of the courts of a foreign country. If the court is required to decide who, on the material before it, has the better of the argument on the facts and matters relevant to the existence and exercise of jurisdiction, the question of who has

---

[544] See Lord Hoffmann in *Fiona Trust*, at [17]; *cf.* at [34], where Lord Hope appeared to suggest that contentions of forgery of document or signature fell under the voidable, rather than under the void, category of objection, and that they therefore did not impeach the dispute-resolution agreement.

[545] The answer will depend, in principle at least, on whether the illegality in question is said to make the contract a complete nullity, or makes it an unenforceable agreement, or affects the substantive contract but not the provision for the resolution of disputes. For an illustration of the difficulty see *Mackender v Feldia AG* [1967] 2 Q.B. 590.

[546] *Midgulf International Ltd v Groupe Chimiche Tunisien* [2010] EWCA Civ 66, [2010] 1 C.L.C. 113; *Rimpacific Navigation Inc v Daehan Shipbuilding Co Ltd* [2009] EWHC 2941 (Comm.), [2010] 2 Lloyd's Rep. 236 (a service out case). There may be rare cases in which the parties have agreed that a particular court is to have jurisdiction to determine whether the contract between them is void: *cf. UR Power GmbH v Kuok Oils & Grains Pte Ltd* [2009] EWHC 1940 (Comm.), [2009] 2 Lloyd's Rep. 495, [40] (an arbitration case).

[547] *Bols Distilleries BV v Superior Yacht Services Ltd* [2006] UKPC 45, [2007] 1 W.L.R. 12 (a case on the Brussels I Regulation, but upon which point, English procedural law is applicable). On the relationship between "the better of", "much the better of", and "clearly the better of" the argument, see *Global 5000 Ltd v Wadhawan* [2011] EWHC 853 (Comm.), [2011] 2 All E.R. (Comm.) 190 and the cases discussed therein.

the burden of proof will be the ordinary one, that the party who seeks to establish a fact bears the burden of establishing it.[548]

The Brussels I Regulation. The account of the common law given above is applicable where the jurisdiction agreement is not one governed by Art.23 of the Brussels I Regulation or of the Lugano Convention. The function of a jurisdiction agreement, and the approach in cases in which the agreement is contested, within the distinctive jurisdictional scheme of the Regulation, is, as will be shown below, quite distinct from that of the common law, and cross-fertilisation is not conducive to clarity of thought. The effect of jurisdiction agreements within the scope of the Brussels I Regulation is therefore examined separately below.

12–115

Legal effect of valid jurisdiction clause. As a general rule, but subject to important exceptions, English courts (in common with the courts of other countries) will give effect to a choice of jurisdiction. If the English court is the chosen forum, the jurisdiction clause will be effective to confer jurisdiction on the English court; in certain circumstances, the court will have discretion not to exercise it. If a foreign court is the chosen forum, then the English court will give effect to the choice by staying proceedings brought in breach of the jurisdiction clause or by refusing to give permission to serve process outside the jurisdiction; but (except in cases within the scope of Art.23 of the Regulation or the Convention) the English court has a discretion to override the choice of jurisdiction.[549]

12–116

The effectiveness of jurisdiction agreements is, in most countries, limited to a lesser or greater degree. In general, though English law accords to the parties a high degree of autonomy to choose the forum, it may override the parties' expressed choice, and the courts are not obliged to uphold and enforce the parties' choice to confer jurisdiction on an English or a foreign court.[550] But where the Regulation, or the Convention, governs the case, the position is different.[551] So, for example, an employee cannot contract out of the jurisdiction of an employment tribunal by agreeing in a contract of employment that

12–117

---

[548] See, with specific reference to jurisdiction agreements, *Knauf UK GmbH v British Gypsum Ltd* [2001] EWCA Civ 1570, [2002] 1 W.L.R. 907, [61]; *Bank of Tokyo-Mitsubishi Ltd v Baskan Gida Sanayi ve Pazarlama AS* [2004] EWHC 945 (Ch.), [2004] 2 Lloyd's Rep. 395, [193]–[194]; *Konkola Copper Mines Ltd v Coromin Ltd* [2006] EWCA Civ 5, [2006] 1 Lloyd's Rep. 410; *Astrazeneca UK Ltd v Albemarle International Corp* [2010] EWHC 1028 (Comm.), [2010] 2 Lloyd's Rep. 61.

[549] *Donohue v Armco Inc* [2001] UKHL 64, [2002] 1 Lloyd's Rep 425; for the position under the Regulation and Convention, see *Hough v P&O Containers Ltd* [1999] Q.B. 834; *Emilceramica v Jannier, Gendry*, Cass. Civ. I [2004] I.L.Pr. 693. See also *OT Africa Line Ltd v Magic Sportswear Corp* [2005] EWCA Civ 710, [2005] 2 Lloyd's Rep 170 (where, however, the jurisdiction clause seems to have been within the scope of Art.23 of the Regulation, so precluding any discretion not to give effect to it: see below, para.12–135).

[550] *Bouygues Offshore SA v Caspian Shipping Co (Nos 1, 3, 4, 5)* [1998] 2 Lloyd's Rep. 461 (CA). In *Donohue v Armco Inc* [2001] UKHL 64, [2002] 1 Lloyd's Rep. 425, the House of Lords set aside the injunction which had been ordered to give effect to the English jurisdiction clause, as other persons not party to the jurisdiction agreement could not be prevented from bringing proceedings in the courts of their choice.

[551] *Hough v P&O Containers Ltd* [1999] Q.B. 834.

all claims by him must be brought in a foreign tribunal,[552] but where the agreement is one to which the Regulation or the Convention applies and which conforms to the requirements imposed by it, the agreement may not be invalidated on such grounds derived from national law.[553] These instruments contain severe limitations on the effectiveness of jurisdiction agreements in insurance contracts, consumer contracts, and employment contracts, but these limitations are apparently exhaustive.[554]

12–118   At common law, a jurisdiction agreement cannot be regarded as effective unless it is valid by reference to its applicable law,[555] which for the reasons already given will normally be the law applicable to the contract of which it forms a part; and a jurisdiction agreement which is void or ineffective under the law which governs it law will therefore not be given effect in England. Nor will effect be given to a jurisdiction agreement which, although valid by the applicable law, offends against a mandatory rule of English law,[556] or which, it is submitted, would not be regarded as effective under the law of the State of the chosen court.

12–119   **Article 23 of the Brussels I Regulation and of the Lugano Convention.** In the form which it had at the date of the accession of the United Kingdom to the Brussels Convention, Art.17 of the Brussels Convention provided that where parties, one or more of whom is domiciled in a Contracting State, have agreed[557] that a court or the courts of a Contracting State are to have

---

[552] Employment Rights Act 1996, s.203(1); see also, e.g., Consumer Credit Act 1974, s.141(1); Carriage of Goods by Sea Act 1971, Sch.1, Art.III.8; in Australia, Carriage of Goods by Sea Act 1991 (Cth.), s.11(2)(b); Insurance Contracts Act 1984 (Cth.) (applied in *Akai Pty Ltd v People's Insurance Co* (1997) 188 C.L.R. 418).

[553] Case 25/79 *Sanicentral GmbH v Collin* [1979] E.C.R. 3423.

[554] See above, paras 11–350 (insurance), 11–365 (consumer contracts), and 11–374 (employment). On insurance contracts, see Case C–112/03 *Soc financière et industrielle de Peloux v AXA Belgium* [2005] E.C.R. I–3707, [2006] Q.B. 251; on consumer contracts, see *Standard Bank London Ltd v Apostolakis (No.2)* [2001] Lloyd's Rep. Banking 240 (and for subsequent proceedings in Greece, see [2003] I.L.Pr. 342); Case C–240/98 *Océano Grupo Editorial SA v Quintero* [2000] E.C.R. I–4941. It appears to have been held in *Samengo-Turner v J&H Marsh & McLennan (Services) Ltd* [2007] EWCA Civ 723, [2008] I.C.R. 18 that the restrictions which the Regulation places on jurisdiction for the courts of other Member States which are contained in contracts of employment apply equally to jurisdiction agreements for the courts of a non-Member State, and that an employer who brings proceedings in the court so designated may even be restrained by injunction: for criticism see Briggs (2007) 78 B.Y.I.L. 615.

[555] *Mackender v Feldia AG* [1967] 2 Q.B. 590, 602; *The Iran Vojdan* [1984] 2 Lloyd's Rep. 380; *The Frank Pais* [1986] 1 Lloyd's Rep. 529; Kahn-Freund (1977) 26 I.C.L.Q. 825, 827–833. For treatment of inconsistent jurisdiction agreements, see *Sinochem International Oil (London) Co Ltd v Mobil Sales & Supply Corp* [2000] 1 Lloyd's Rep. 670.

[556] *The Hollandia* [1983] 1 A.C. 565, see below, para.12–151. Agreements on jurisdiction may be invalidated by Unfair Terms in Consumer Contracts Regulations 1999 (SI 1999/2083): Case C–240/98 *Océano Grupo Editorial SA v Quintero* [2000] E.C.R. I–4941.

[557] An assignee from one of the contracting parties clearly falls within Art.17: Case 71/83 *The Tilly Russ* [1984] E.C.R. 2417, [1985] Q.B. 931; Case C–159/97 *Soc Trasporti Castelletti Spedizioni Internazionali SpA v Hugo Trumpy SpA* [1999] E.C.R. I–1597. But it has been held that the relationship between an owner of goods and a sub-bailee is not to be regarded as an agreement to a jurisdiction agreement contained in the contract between the owner and the bailee for the purposes of what is now Art.23, for Art.23 requires the agreement to be contained in a contract, and between owner and sub-bailee there is none: *Dresser (UK) Ltd v Falcongate Freight Management Ltd* [1992] Q.B. 502 (CA). However on this point, see further below, para.12–136.

jurisdiction to settle any disputes which have arisen or which may arise in connection with a particular legal relationship, that court or those courts shall have exclusive jurisdiction. Article 23 of the Brussels I Regulation, and now also the revised Lugano Convention, is cast in very similar terms, though it provides that the chosen jurisdiction will be exclusive "unless the parties have agreed otherwise". In principle, and subject to the rules about dates of commencement,[558] the Regulation will apply when the chosen court is that of a Member State; and the Lugano Convention to a choice of the courts of Iceland, Norway, or Switzerland. It is a characteristic of Art.23 of the Brussels I Regulation and the Lugano Convention (as it was for Art.17 of the Brussels Convention) that the formal requirements[559] for a clause to be valid are to be interpreted strictly[560] because their purpose is to ensure that parties have indeed consented to a jurisdiction agreement derogating from the ordinary jurisdictional rules and that it is therefore necessary that this consent is clearly and precisely demonstrated.[561] This requirement, when applied to the incorporation of jurisdiction agreements from an earlier contract, echoes the requirements of the common law that clear and precise language is required to demonstrate the agreement or consent of the parties to a dispute to be bound by a jurisdiction clause contained in a separate contract or other document.[562] As will be seen, the relationship between the requirements of form set out in the Articles, and the rules of national law as these determine the validity or invalidity of an agreement, is not straightforward.

Burden of proof in relation to Article 23. The question whether there is **12–120** an agreement conferring jurisdiction on the courts of a Member State, which satisfies the requirements of Art.23, may arise before an English court in two ways: when the alleged agreement designates the English court, but the defendant to proceedings is domiciled in another Member State and denies that the jurisdiction agreement is valid and effective; and where proceedings are brought before the English court on the basis that there is no jurisdiction agreement for the courts of another Member State, but the defendant contends that there is such an agreement. The European Court has confirmed that, where dealing with this kind of jurisdictional challenge, the court should use its own procedural law;[563] and according to the settled view of the courts in

---

[558] See above, para.11–013.
[559] See below, para.12–134.
[560] *cf. IP Metal Ltd v Ruote OZ SpA* [1993] 2 Lloyd's Rep. 60.
[561] Case 26/76 *Salotti v RUWA* [1976] E.C.R. 1831; Case 25/76 *Galeries Segoura Sprl v Bonakdarian* [1976] E.C.R. 1851; Case 71/83 *The Tilly Russ* [1984] E.C.R. 2417, [1985] Q.B. 931; Case 221/84 *Berghoefer GmbH v ASA SA* [1985] E.C.R. 2699; Case 313/85 *Iveco Fiat SpA v Van Hool* [1986] E.C.R. 3337; Case C–106/95 *Mainschiffahrts-Genossenschaft eG v Les Gravières Rhénanes SARL* [1997] E.C.R. I–911; [1997] Q.B. 731; Case C–159/97 *Soc Trasporti Castelletti Spedizioni Interazionali SA v Hugo Trumpy SpA* [1999] E.C.R. I–1597.
[562] *AIG Europe (UK) Ltd v The Ethniki* [2000] 2 All E.R. 566 (CA); *AIG Europe SA v QBE International Insurance Ltd* [2001] 2 Lloyd's Rep. 268.
[563] Subject to the proviso that the rule of procedural law must not jeopardise the practical effect of the Regulation: Case C–68/93 *Shevill v Presse Alliance SA* [1995] E.C.R. I–415, [1995] 2 A.C. 18.

the most recent cases, the test to be applied requires the party who alleges that there to be an applicable agreement on jurisdiction to have the better of the argument on the materials before the court at the time of the challenge.[564]

12–121   There is a question, not yet resolved by the European Court, as to the time at which the requirement that one of the parties be domiciled in a Member State (or a Convention State) must be fulfilled. It is generally accepted that Art.23 will apply if at the time of the conclusion of the jurisdiction agreement one of the parties is domiciled in a Member State or a Convention State, even if by the time proceedings are commenced neither party is so domiciled. But there is more controversy about the converse situation, where neither is so domiciled at the time of the conclusion of the contract, but at least one has become so domiciled by the time proceedings are commenced. It is suggested that the relevant Article should apply to that case also, and that the provision about domicile be treated as a rule of alternative validity. Article 23 also provides that, where none of the parties is domiciled in a Member State (or a Convention State), the courts of other such States are to have no jurisdiction over the dispute unless the chosen court or courts have declined jurisdiction.

12–122   It was sometimes said that of Art.17 of the Brussels Convention that it only applied in cases with an international character.[565] The example used to illustrate the point was where parties who were domiciled in one Convention State might seek to confer jurisdiction on the courts of another State, such as where two French domiciliaries agreed that the English courts should have exclusive jurisdiction for their disputes. It is now certain that Art.17 would have applied to such a case,[566] and the same will be true of the Regulation which is, in any event, not expressed to be restricted in its operation to cases of international jurisdiction.

12–123   Where the court has jurisdiction by virtue of an international convention, whose precedence over the Regulation, is provided for by Art.71,[567] the question whether proceedings should be stayed or jurisdiction must be exercised is a matter governed by the particular convention and (if permitted by the particular convention) by national law. Accordingly where the English court has jurisdiction under Art.7 of the Arrest Convention,[568] and it is

---

[564] *Bols Distilleries BV v Superior Yacht Services Ltd* [2006] UKPC 45, [2007] 1 W.L.R. 12; *Knorr-Bremse Systems for Commercial Vehicles Ltd v Haldex Brake Products GmbH* [2008] EWHC 156 (Pat.); *Deutsche Bank AG v Asia Pacific Broadband Wireless Communications Inc* [2008] EWCA Civ 1091, [2008] 2 Lloyd's Rep. 619; *Kolmar Group AG v Visen Industries Ltd* [2009] EWHC 3765 (QB), [2010] I.L.Pr. 449.

[565] Jenard, pp.37–38.

[566] *ibid.* p.38. According to the French Cour de cassation, the requirement of internationality was required to be satisfied at the date of the agreement: *Soc Keller Grundbau v Electricité de France*, 2006 Rev Crit 413, [2007] I.L.Pr. 8. Internationality did not mean inter-Contracting State (Case C–281/02 *Owusu v Jackson* [2005] E.C.R. I–1383, [2005] Q.B. 801 (England, Jamaica), but the decision in *Snookes v Jani-King (GB) Ltd* [2006] EWHC 289 (QB), [2006] I.L.Pr. 433, that Art.23 applied to a dispute which was wholly internal to the United Kingdom must be wrong.

[567] See above, paras 11–053 *et seq.*

[568] International Convention for Unification of Certain Rules relating to the Arrest of Sea-going Ships, 1952.

contended that an agreement conferring jurisdiction on the courts of Germany requires the court to stay its proceedings, the applicable principles are those of the common law, as modified by the particular convention, and not Art.23 of the Regulation.[569]

Article 23 of the Brussels I Regulation and of the Lugano Convention, like **12–124** Art.17 of the Conventions before them, refer only to the choice of a forum in a Member or a Convention State. Where the parties have agreed to a forum which is outside these States, it is almost certainly correct that an English court, seised with general or special jurisdiction over the defendant, may stay its proceedings, in accordance with its own rules of the conflict of laws, in order to give effect to the agreement on jurisdiction.[570] The Regulation should not be thought of as deficient in this regard: as the European Union could not legislatively determine the jurisdiction of non-Member States, it would have been inappropriate for the Regulation to specify the conditions under which such an agreement on jurisdiction might be given legal effect. The European Court stated that the validity of a jurisdiction agreement for a non-Member State is a matter to be assessed by reference to the law of the court seised:[571] this appears to be distinct from a rival approach, which would be to apply Art.23 by analogy, or to give it "reflexive effect". There is nothing in the decision of the Court in *Owusu v Jackson*[572] to suggest that the Court has resiled from this position. If the validity of the clause is a matter for the national law, including conflicts rules, of the court seised, it may well follow from this that the effectiveness of a jurisdiction agreement for a non-Member State is not dependent on its complying with the formality provisions of Art.23 (though insofar as the jurisdiction agreement may displace the jurisdiction of a court which is conferred by the Regulation, there is a basis for requiring no lesser a degree of formal validity as a precondition to any question of validity being referred to national law). The reasoning in *Coreck* also indicates that the decision whether to give effect to the agreement in the individual case by staying English proceedings is a matter for English law, according to which the decision is a discretionary one: this may be contrasted with the non-discretionary nature of Art.23 if applied by strict analogy. However, it is to be supposed that such an agreement will not be permitted to override exclusive jurisdiction regardless of domicile established under Art.22; it is less clear whether such an agreement may override the jurisdiction which protects the weaker party to contracts of insurance, certain consumer contracts, and employment cases in those circumstances in which, *mutatis*

---

[569] *The Bergen* [1997] 1 Lloyd's Rep. 380; *The Bergen (No.2)* [1997] 2 Lloyd's Rep. 710; *cf. Milor Srl v British Airways Plc* [1996] Q.B. 702 (CA); *Deaville v Aeroflot Russian International Airlines* [1997] 2 Lloyd's Rep. 67. For discussion of the question whether a court with jurisdiction under such a Convention is permitted to exercise it even though there are proceedings in the courts of another Member State, see above, para.12–059.

[570] See *Konkola Copper Mines Ltd v Coromin Ltd* [2005] EWHC 898 (Comm.), [2005] Lloyd's Rep. 555 (affd. [2006] EWCA Civ 5, [2006] 1 Lloyd's Rep. 410, where there was no appeal on this point), and para.12–021, above.

[571] Case C–387/98 *Coreck Maritime GmbH v Handelsveem BV* [2000] E.C.R. I–9337, [19]. The reference to the law of the court seised will include its conflicts rules.

[572] Case C–281/02, [2005] E.C.R. I–1383, [2005] Q.B. 801.

mutandis, a jurisdiction agreement for the courts of a Member State would not be effective.[573]

12–125   In *Powell Duffryn Plc v Petereit*[574] the European Court held that the concept of an "agreement conferring jurisdiction" under what is now Art.23 should be regarded as an independent concept. The question arose in the context of whether the administrator of a German company could sue an English shareholder for the return of dividends which, it was alleged, had been wrongly paid. The statutes of the company provided, in effect, that the German court would have exclusive jurisdiction in relation to all disputes between shareholders and the company. The English company argued that the jurisdiction clause in the statutes did not amount to an "agreement" because the statutes were regulations which the shareholder could not dispute. A comparative survey of the legal systems of the Contracting States showed that in some legal systems the relationship between a company and its shareholders was regarded as contractual, and in others it was classified as institutional, regulatory or *sui generis*. The European Court held that an autonomous interpretation of the expression "agreement conferring jurisdiction" led to the conclusion that the ties between the shareholders and a company were comparable to those between the parties to a contract, and that the statutes of the company must be regarded as a contract governing relationships between the shareholders *inter se* and between the shareholders and the company. By becoming and remaining a shareholder the member submits to all the provisions of the statutes and to company resolutions, irrespective of whether he agrees with them or even knows of them.

12–126   **Allocation of authority between Regulation and national law.** Perhaps the most difficult question to answer is to define and describe the line which separates those questions upon which a national court is permitted and required to apply rules of substantive national law from those issues on which a court is required to derive its answer from the text of Art.23, as interpreted by the European Court, without regard to the rules of national law which might otherwise have contributed to the answer. For if the application of Art.23 is to be uniform across the Member States, there must be a tight limit on the extent to which a national court may have recourse to individual rules of national law when answering the question whether Art.23 applies in a given case. The aim of the Regulation is that a court should be able to apply Art.23 to determine whether it has or does not have jurisdiction, without the need for detailed or complex analysis of a kind better undertaken at trial. The more a court has to answer that question by making reference to rules of substantive law (and the point is all the more telling if the rules of substantive national law are foreign, identified by the court's rules for choice of law), the less predictable, and maybe the less reliable, its answer will be. The proposition that a

---

[573] *Samengo-Turner v JH Marsh & McLennan (Services) Ltd* [2007] EWCA Civ 723, [2008] I.C.R. 18 holds that a jurisdiction agreement in an employment contract for New York will be ineffective in circumstances in which such an agreement for the courts of a Member State would not be effective.

[574] Case C–214/89 [1992] E.C.R. I–1745; see also *Re Jurisdiction in Internal Company Matters* [1995] I.L.Pr. 424 (German Fed Sup Ct, 1993). *cf. Copin v Adamson* (1875) 1 Ex. D. 17; *Re Schintz* [1926] Ch. 710 (CA).

question arising in relation to Art.23 is one to be referred to national law is, therefore, one to be considered with care before it is accepted.

A starting point is the decision in *Powell Duffryn* where the European **12–127** Court, having ruled that the autonomous interpretation of "agreement conferring jurisdiction" covered a provision in a the constitutional documents of a company, directed the national court that it was the task of the national court to interpret the clause before it to determine whether the claim brought fell within its scope.[575] The European Court did not purport to direct the national court as to how it was to discharge the task laid upon it, but it is usually understood that this required the court to interpret the scope of the clause by reference to the substantive law which governed the contract of which it was a part, treating it, in effect, as a matter of contractual construction.[576] But though construction and scope may be a matter for national law, issues of validity (as will be seen below) are not; and it is not always easy to tell whether a particular question is one of construction or one of validity.[577] For example, if there is a rule of national law that specific words are required to bring a claim for fraud, or deliberate wrongdoing, within a jurisdiction agreement, the question for a court may be seen as one of ascertaining the meaning of the words used, or of applying a rule of national law to limit the effectiveness of a clause which satisfies the requirements of Art.23. Only if the court concludes that it is doing the former rather than the latter will it be entitled to apply this particular rule of national law to assess the scope of the agreement on jurisdiction.[578]

Likewise, if it is contended that a jurisdiction agreement in one contract has **12–128** been incorporated into another contract, it is not certain whether the issue for decision is one which is entirely governed by Art.23 or by the substantive law of the second contract. In principle, if the issue is understood as one which is essentially contractual in nature, recourse to the law governing the second contract, to identify its terms as including, or not, a jurisdiction agreement is appropriate. If instead the issue is not seen as an essentially contractual one,[579] but is conceived as one which asks whether the party to be bound by it indicated his agreement to the jurisdiction of the particular court, the question is not one for a contractual governing law, but one which is to be determined

---

[575] Or whether a person fell within its scope: *Breitenbücher v Wittke* [2008] CSOH 145.

[576] *British Sugar Plc v Fratelli Babbini di Lionello Babbini* [2004] EWHC 2560 (TCC), [2005] 1 Lloyd's Rep. 332. See also *Nursaw v Dansk Jersey Eksport* [2009] I.L.Pr. 63.

[577] See, e.g. *Knorr-Bremse Systems for Commercial Vehicles Ltd v Haldex Brake Products GmbH* [2008] EWHC 156 (Pat.), [2008] I.L.Pr. 326. It was held in *Antonio Gramsci Shipping Corp v Stepanovs* [2011] EWHC 333 (Comm.), [2011] 1 Lloyd's Rep. 647 that a court may apply rules of national company law which allow the corporate veil to be lifted, in order to find that a hidden non-signatory, non-contracting party, had agreed to the jurisdiction of a court by means of an agreement which had been made in writing by a company.

[578] *Roche Products Ltd v Provimi Ltd* [2003] EWHC 961 (Comm.), [2003] 2 All E.R. (Comm.) 683.

[579] Art.23 speaks of the parties as having *agreed*, not as having *contracted*. However, where the dispute is of the "battle of the forms" kind, and it has to be decided whether there was, by reference to the document, agreement to the jurisdiction of the court, there may be no practical alternative to a traditional, contractual, offer and acceptance analysis to determine whether there was (clearly and distinctly) agreement to the jurisdiction of the court: *Claxton Engineering Services Ltd v TXM Olaj-és Gázkutató KFT* [2010] EWHC 2567 (Comm.), [2011] 1 Lloyd's Rep. 252.

by recourse only to the formal requirements set out in Art.23 itself.[580] A practical solution may be to conclude that a test which asks whether the material before the court shown that the jurisdiction was accepted clearly and precisely by the party who is proposed to be held to it will satisfy whichever test is the correct one.[581] In principle, if the agreement on jurisdiction is said to have been incorporated into the second contract, it must be shown that the formalities prescribed for the second contract, by Art.23, have been complied with. In practice, if they are satisfied, it is improbable that there is any further requirement which national law would impose.[582]

12–129   The European Court has held that the provisions of what is now Art.23 cannot be supplemented or overridden by national law. As has been seen, the law of the United Kingdom, in common with the law of other countries, prevents employees working in England for foreign employers from contracting out of the jurisdiction of employment tribunals.[583] But the European Court held in *Sanicentral GmbH v Collin*[584] that a jurisdiction clause in an employment contract providing for the jurisdiction of the German courts had to be given effect in France, notwithstanding French legislation of a type similar to that in the United Kingdom. The principle in that decision remains valid, but as regards contracts of employment it has been superseded by Article 21 of the Regulation (and of the Lugano Convention), which provides that the jurisdiction agreement will be valid only if it is entered into after the dispute has arisen, or if it allows the employee to bring proceedings in courts other than those indicated in Section 5 of Chapter II (or Title II). It is probable that a jurisdiction clause which is to be validated by Art.21 must still comply with the formal and other requirements of Art.23.[585]

12–130   The principle that national laws may not supplement or override the provisions of Art.23 was applied in the context of national laws which purported to override an actual or admitted agreement.[586] But a distinct issue arises where one party contends that he simply did not consent to the jurisdiction agreement. For example, if it is alleged that apparent consent to the agreement was procured by misrepresentation or duress, or was entered into under mistake,[587] the agreement on jurisdiction may fully comply with the requirements of form, yet if the national court is not entitled to examine

---

[580] Examined below.

[581] *Bols Distilleries BV v Superior Yacht Services Ltd* [2006] UKPC 45, [2007] 1 W.L.R. 12; *Knauf UK GmbH v British Gypsum Ltd* [2001] EWCA Civ 1570, [2002] 1 W.L.R. 907, [61]; *Africa Express Line Ltd v Socofi SA* [2009] EWHC 3223 (Comm.), [2010] 2 Lloyd's Rep. 181.

[582] See above, para.12–126.

[583] See above, para.12–117.

[584] Case 25/79 [1979] E.C.R. 3423. *cf.*, on the formal requirements, Case 150/80 *Elefanten Schuh GmbH v Jacqmain* [1981] E.C.R. 1671.

[585] It was held in *Samengo-Turner v J&H Marsh & McLennan (Services) Ltd* [2007] EWCA Civ 723, [2008] I.C.R. 18, that this provision also applied to invalidate a jurisdiction agreement for the courts of New York, and that an anti-suit injunction would go to reinforce the invalidity by restraining the proceedings in New York: for criticism see Briggs (2007) 78 B.Y.I.L. 615.

[586] The decision in *Snookes v Jani-King (GB) Ltd* [2006] EWHC 289 (QB), [2006] I.L.Pr. 433, that the Unfair Contract Terms Act 1977 (as distinct from the Unfair Terms in Consumer Contracts Regulations 1999, for which Art.67 makes provision) could invalidate a jurisdiction agreement otherwise valid according to Art.23, must be taken as wrong.

[587] An argument that the clause should not be given effect because the writing was too feint, or illegible or otherwise incomprehensible may also be accommodated here.

the essential validity of the agreement, the fundamental purpose of the Article may be frustrated.[588] Whether any such examination should be founded on national law, or derived from an autonomous interpretation of the concept of agreement, is not clear. In *Benincasa v Dentalkit Srl*[589] the European Court ruled out any role for the *lex contractus* in assessing the validity of a jurisdiction agreement, and stated that the formal requirements of what is now Art.23 were sufficient to ensure that there was a consensus; the same view, rejecting the argument that the validity of the clause may be tested by reference to any law other than what is now Art.23 itself, was expressed in *Soc Trasporti Castelletti Spedizioni Internazionali SpA v Hugo Trumpy SpA*.[590] But recourse only to the formality provisions of Art.23 cannot provide a sufficient response to the use of fraud or duress. It is submitted that it should be held to be contrary to the requirements of good faith for one party to seek to invoke a jurisdiction agreement procured by such means,[591] whether in writing or otherwise formally compliant with Art.23 or not. An alternative approach, which is particularly appropriate when there is an allegation that the jurisdiction agreement was never accepted by one of the parties and so did not constitute an *agreement*, would be to consider that whether there has been a sufficient consensus which could satisfy Art.23 is a predominantly a question of fact for the court seised, and that, as suggested above,[592] it is to be answered without specific recourse to rules of national law.

It follows from *Benincasa v Dentalkit srl* that an agreement on jurisdiction   **12–131** may[593] be effective for the purpose of Art.23, even though the claimant contends that the substantive contract in which it may have been contained was rescinded or has come to an end.[594] This may be derived from a principle of separability, though if, as the European Court has said, the validity of a jurisdiction agreement is legally independent of the question whether there is a binding contract between the parties, it may be that no separation is called for: instead, all that is required is that the court find that claimant had agreed, in writing, to accept the jurisdiction of the designated court,[595] which is

---

[588] Which is to give effect to the intentions of the parties: Case 22/85 *Anterist v Credit Lyonnais* [1986] E.C.R. 1951. The perception that national courts may be adopting divergent solutions to this problem of disputed validity, on which it is at least arguable that the Regulation currently gives no sufficiently clear and firm answer, means that this is one of the issues with which the proposed legislative reform of the Regulation may be expected to deal: see the Report of the Commission to the Council of Ministers, April 21, 2009, COM(2009) 174 final, at para.3.3.

[589] Case C–269/95 [1997] E.C.R. I–3767. See also the Opinion of Lenz A.-G. in Case C–288/92 *Custom Made Commercial Ltd v Stawa Metallbau GmbH* [1994] E.C.R. I–2913.

[590] Case C–159/97 [1999] E.C.R. I–1597.

[591] *cf.* Case 221/84 *Berghöfer v ASA SA* [1985] E.C.R. 2699.

[592] See above, para.12–128.

[593] Though a jurisdiction agreement may, in an appropriate case, be found to have been repudiated: *Dubai Islamic Bank PJSC v PSI Energy Holding Co BSC* [2011] EWHC 1019 (Comm.).

[594] *AP Moller-Maersk A/S v Sonaec Villas Cen Sad Fadoul* [2010] EWHC 355 (Comm.), [2011] 1 Lloyd's Rep. 1 (Jurisdiction clause allows English court to declare that it has exclusive jurisdiction even if substantive contract has come to an end).

[595] *Deutsche Bank AG v Asia Pacific Broadband Wireless Communications Inc* [2008] EWCA Civ 1091, [2008] 2 Lloyd's Rep. 619; *Maple Leaf Macro Volatility Master Fund v Rouvroy* [2009] EWHC 257 (Comm.), [2009] 1 Lloyd's Rep. 475; *Ryanair Ltd v Bravofly* [2009] IEHC 41, [2009] I.L.Pr. 701; *cf. Andromeda Marine SA v OW Bunker & Trading A/S* [2006] EWHC 777 (Comm.), [2006] I.L.Pr. 739.

something which may be done in the form of a contractual term, but which may also be done outside any contract.

12–132   A jurisdiction agreement in an insurance contract, consumer contract, or contract of employment is only effective to the extent allowed by Arts 13, 17 and 21 of the Brussels I Regulation and the Lugano Convention. The result is to limit severely the effectiveness of clauses conferring jurisdiction on English courts where the defendant is an insured (or policyholder or beneficiary), or a consumer,[596] or an employee, domiciled in another Member State or Convention State. Conversely, where the insured, consumer or employee is domiciled in the United Kingdom, the effectiveness of a choice of a foreign[597] court would be correspondingly limited.[598] Nor is a jurisdiction agreement effective if it purports to exclude the jurisdiction of a court which has exclusive jurisdiction regardless of domicile under Art.22 of the Regulation or of the Lugano Convention.[599]

12–133   **Effect of Article 23.** The broad effect of Art.23 of the Brussels I Regulation and of the Lugano Convention, as with Art.17 of the Brussels Convention before them, where clause (1) or Rule 39 applies, is to confer jurisdiction on the English court if the parties have agreed to give it jurisdiction notwithstanding that the defendant is domiciled in another Member or Convention State or, where neither party is domiciled in such a State, notwithstanding that the courts of another Member or Convention State may have, under its law, jurisdiction over the dispute. Where clause (3) of Rule 39 applies, its effect is to deny jurisdiction to the English court if the parties have chosen to submit their disputes to the jurisdiction of the courts of another Member or Convention State. Article 17 of the 1968 and the original Lugano Conventions[600] also provided that if the jurisdiction agreement had been concluded for the benefit of only one of the parties, that party retained the right to sue in any other court which had jurisdiction under the Conventions. In *Anterist v Crédit Lyonnais*[601] the European Court held that this provision applied only where it was clear from the wording of the jurisdiction clause, or from evidence therein, or from the surrounding circumstances, that there was a common intention to confer

---

[596] *Standard Bank London Ltd v Apostolakis (No.2)* [2001] Lloyd's Rep Banking 240.

[597] including a jurisdiction agreement in relation to the courts of a non-Member State: *Samengo-Turner v J&H Marsh & McLennan (Services) Ltd* [2007] EWCA Civ 723, [2008] I.C.R. 18.

[598] See above, paras 11–350, 11–365 and 11–374 *et seq.*

[599] *cf.* Art.16 of the Brussels Convention. The relationship between Art.22 and Art.23, in circumstances in which a company party to an agreement on jurisdiction contends that the *lex incorporationis* denied it legal power to enter into the substantive contract, and contends that this raises a question which means that the substantive dispute falls within the material scope of Art.22(2), so excluding the jurisdiction designated by Art.23, see C–144/10 *Berliner Verkehrsbetriebe (BVG) v JP Morgan Chase Bank NA* [2011] 1 W.L.R. 2087 (narrow interpretation of Art.22 in order to give fullest effect to parties' exercise of autonomy in choice of jurisdiction); see also *JP Morgan Chase Bank NA v Berliner Verkehrsbetriebe BVG* [2010] EWCA Civ 390, [2011] 3 W.L.R. 1353; *UBS AG v Kommunale Wasserwerke Leipzig GmbH* [2010] EWHC 2566 (Comm.), [2010] 2 C.L.C. 499; *Depfa Bank Plc v Provincie di Pisa* [2010] EWHC 1148 (Comm.), [2010] I.L.Pr. 930.

[600] Brussels Convention, Art.17, penult. para.; Lugano Convention, Art.17(4).

[601] Case 22/85 [1986] E.C.R. 1951; *cf. Ocarina Marine Ltd v Macard Stein & Co* [1994] 2 Lloyd's Rep. 524; *Soc Edmond Coignet SA v Banca Commerciale Italiana* [1992] I.L.Pr. 450 (French Cour de cassation, 1990).

an advantage on one of the parties only. Clauses which expressly stated the name of the party for whose benefit they were concluded and those which, while specifying the courts in which either party might sue the other, gave one of them a wider choice of courts must be regarded as clauses which were agreed for the exclusive benefit of one of the parties. An agreement conferring jurisdiction would not be regarded as having been concluded for the benefit of only one of the parties where all that was established was that the parties had agreed that the courts of the State in which that party was domiciled were to have jurisdiction. So if a contract between X, domiciled in England, and A, domiciled in France, provided that all claims by X against A should be brought in France, A could sue X in England under the general rules.[602] But Art.23 of the Brussels I Regulation does not reproduce this rule, probably because it makes express provision for a clause to be exclusive or non-exclusive according to the choice made by the parties.

Formal requirements. A jurisdiction agreement, to be given legal validity   **12–134**
by Art.23 of the Regulation or or the Convention must be

"(a) in writing or evidenced in writing, or (b) in a form which accords with practices which the parties have established between themselves, or (c) in international trade or commerce, in a form which accords with a usage of which the parties are or ought to have been aware and which in such trade or commerce is widely known to, and regularly observed by, parties to contracts of the type involved in the particular trade or commerce concerned."

Article 23 goes on to add that any communication by electronic means which provides a durable record of the agreement shall be the equivalent of "writing".

The formal requirement in the original version of the Brussels Convention   **12–135**
was that the jurisdiction agreement be "in writing or evidenced in writing". But this requirement, especially as it was very strictly interpreted by the European Court,[603] did not fit at all easily with the needs of international commerce, where the use of printed standard conditions, and communication

---

[602] No such contortions are required in the context of Art.23 of the Regulation.

[603] See Case 24/76 *Salotti v RUWA* [1976] E.C.R. 1831; Case 25/76 *Galeries Segoura Sprl v Bonakdarian* [1976] E.C.R. 1851. Some measure of liberalisation could be seen in Case 71/83 *The Tilly Russ* [1984] E.C.R. 2417, [1985] Q.B. 931 (on which see North [1985] L.M.C.L.Q. 177), decided under the original wording. See also *Credit Suisse Financial Products v Soc Gen. d'Entreprises* [1997] I.L.Pr. 165 (CA) (signature on document referring to printed conditions containing jurisdiction agreement); *O'Connor v Masterwood Ltd* [2009] IESC 49. The highest courts in the original Contracting States had in the past applied Art.17 restrictively: see, e.g. *Itier v Soc Genovesi*, French Cour de cassation, 1985, Digest I– 17.1.2.–B32; *Lejeune v Soc FIAS*, French Cour de cassation, 1989, in 1990 *Rev. Crit.* 358, note Gaudemet-Tallon, and 1991 *Clunet* 158, note Huet; *Luz v Bertram*, Italian Corte di cassazione, 1991, in [1992] I.L.Pr. 202. See also *Jeumont-Schneider SA v Gruppo Industriale Ercole Marelli SpA* [1994] I.L.Pr. 12 (Italian Corte di cassazione, 1990); *Re A Purchase of Yarn* [1995] I.L.Pr. 479 (German Fed Sup Ct, 1994); *cf. Fulgurit v Cie d'Assurances PFA* [1996] I.L.Pr. 495 (French Cour de cassation, 1996); *Richard SA v Pavan* [1998] I.L.Pr. 193 (illegible writing) (French Cour de cassation, 1996).

by instantaneous means are common. As a result, the 1978 Accession Convention added that the agreement could be in a form which accorded with practices in international trade or commerce of which the parties were or ought to have been aware.[604] This amendment was elaborated into its present form in the course of the negotiations for the original Lugano Convention, and in turn the equivalent provision in the Brussels Convention was brought into line with it in the 1989 Accession Convention.[605] The Brussels I Regulation adopts the same form of words, but adds an elaboration of "writing" to deal with the increasingly common use of electronic means of communication. Thus there are now three (plus one more, under the Regulation) ways in which a jurisdiction clause may be effective. First, it may be in writing or evidenced in writing. The effect of the decisions on the unamended Brussels Convention was that this requirement would not normally be fulfilled by the sending of standard printed conditions unless the recipient signed a document which expressly referred to the conditions[606]: in other words, the agreement to jurisdiction, rather than the identity of the court, was required to be in written form. In *Iveco Fiat SpA v Van Hool NV*[607] the European Court considered the effect of a jurisdiction clause in a written agreement, which expressly provided that it could be renewed only in writing. The agreement expired, but continued in effect for another 20 years without any written extension. The European Court held that if the applicable law (i.e. the law governing the original contract) allowed the contract to be renewed without complying with the express provision that the renewal had to be in writing, then the conditions of Art.17 of the Brussels Convention would be fulfilled: there would be an agreement on jurisdiction in writing or evidenced in writing. But if the applicable law did require the express provision to be complied with, the formal requirements of Art.17 would be complied with if one of the parties had confirmed in writing either the jurisdiction clause or the contractual terms which had been tacitly renewed (of which the jurisdiction clause formed a part) without any objection from the other party: in those circumstances the written confirmation would evidence the jurisdiction agreement.

12–136   Where the requirement of written evidence is applicable, it is not always necessary that the party alleged to be bound by the jurisdiction clause be the party who has executed the written document. In *The Tilly Russ*[608] the European Court held that a jurisdiction clause in a bill of lading would be

---

[604] Schlosser, para.179.

[605] Jenard-Möller, p.76; d'Almeida Cruz, etc., p.47. The amendments are based on the Vienna Convention on International Contracts for the Sale of Goods, 1980, Art.9(2).

[606] For the conclusion that signature on a document which refers to terms which include a jurisdiction agreement is sufficient to comply with Art.23(1)(a), see *Coys of Kennington Automobiles Ltd v Pugliese* [2011] EWHC 655 (QB), [2011] 2 All E.R. (Comm.) 664.

[607] Case 313/85 [1986] E.C.R. 3337. See also *IP Metal Ltd v Ruote OZ SpA* [1993] 2 Lloyd's Rep. 60, affirmed [1994] 2 Lloyd's Rep. 560; *Zamakona SA v MacKinnons* 2002 S.L.T. 1206 (no need to apply Art.17 strictly where consent is not in doubt).

[608] Case 71/83 [1984] E.C.R. 2417, [1985] Q.B. 931. See also Case 221/84 *Berghöfer GmbH v ASA SA* [1985] E.C.R. 2699; *Ocarina Marine Ltd v Macard Stein & Co* [1994] 2 Lloyd's Rep. 524; *Firswood Ltd v Petra Bank* [1996] C.L.C. 608 (CA). And see, for analysis of cases on imposing the burden of a jurisdiction agreement on non-parties, below, para.12–139.

effective if the agreement of both the shipper and the carrier to the conditions had been expressed in writing; or if the jurisdiction clause had been the subject of an oral agreement between the shipper and the carrier, and the carrier had signed the bill of lading; or the bill of lading came within the framework of a continuing business relationship between the parties. As regards bills of lading, which are typical of the instruments to which the revised wording of Art.17 of the Brussels Convention was intended to apply, this decision is superseded, but it remains of assistance on the nature of the requirement of writing. Even as between the original parties to the agreement, it may be the party relying on Art.23 who alone has signed the document said to evidence the agreement. Thus in the latter case the European Court held that the formal requirements of Art.17 of the Brussels Convention would be satisfied if there were an express oral agreement on jurisdiction between A and X, and if A wrote to X confirming the agreement and X raised no objection within a reasonable time of receipt of the letter. In these circumstances X would be bound by the jurisdiction agreement even though the only written document was signed by A.[609] The conclusion therefore is that the question is whether the writing, or the written and writing-related evidence, demonstrates, clearly and precisely, the agreement or consent of the party who is to be held to the jurisdiction of the designated court;[610] and the evaluation of the answer to that question is principally a factual matter for the court seised with the claim. If that is correct, then previous decisions are properly understood as illustrative of the application of the legal principle, rather than as authorities properly so called.

It has already been seen that in *Powell Duffryn Plc v Petereit*[611] the **12–137** European Court held that a jurisdiction clause in the statutes of a company was binding on its shareholders. It was also held that the requirement of writing was satisfied by the fact that the statutes were invariably in writing, irrespective of how the shares were acquired, or whether the shareholder actually knew of them, provided that the statutes were lodged at a place which was accessible to shareholders (such as the company's registered office) or were kept in a public register. But it is improbable that the argument which was accepted by the European Court, that the shareholder was bound because he had the means of knowledge and was therefore deemed to be bound by what he should have known, will be extended to cases concerning invoices and printed conditions of business.[612]

The second way in which a jurisdiction clause may be effective is if it is in **12–138** a form which accords with practices which the parties have established

---

[609] *cf.* Case C–106/95 *Mainschiffahrts-Genossenschaft eG v Les Gravières Rhénanes SARL* [1997] E.C.R. I–911, [1997] Q.B. 731.

[610] For further, mainly illustrative, examples, see *7E Communications Ltd v Vertex Antennentechnik GmbH* [2007] EWCA Civ 140, [2007] 1 W.L.R. 2175; *Polskie Ratownictwo Okretowe v Rallo Vito & C snc* [2009] EWHC 2249 (Comm.), [2010] 1 Lloyd's Rep. 384, [55]–[62]; *Kolmar Group AG v Visen Industries Ltd* [2009] EWHC 3765 (QB), [2010] I.L.Pr. 449; *Coys of Kennington Automobiles Ltd v Pugliese* [2011] EWHC 655 (QB).

[611] Case C–214/89 *Powell Duffryn Plc v Petereit* [1992] E.C.R. I–1745; see above, para.12–127.

[612] See also *Ryanair Ltd v Billigfluege.de GmbH* [2010] IEHC 47, [2010] I.L.Pr. 439.

between themselves.[613] The third way is, in international trade or commerce,[614] in a form which accords with a usage of which the parties are or ought to be aware; in addition, this usage must be widely known to, and regularly observed by, parties to contracts of the type involved in the particular trade or commerce concerned. The European Court gave general guidance in *Mainschiffahrts-Genossenschaft eG v Les Gravières Rhénanes SARL*.[615] As a result of that decision, and adapting the ruling in the light of Art.23, the third category of formal validity will be satisfied if the conduct is consistent with a usage in force in the field of international trade or commerce in which the parties in question operate and the latter are aware or ought to be aware of the usage in question. It will be for the national court to determine whether such a usage exists and whether the parties to the contract were aware of it. A usage will exist in a branch of international trade or commerce in particular where a particular course of conduct is generally followed by contracting parties operating in that branch when they conclude contracts of a particular type. The fact that the contracting parties were aware of that usage will be made out in particular where they had previously had trade or commercial relations between themselves or with other parties operating in the branch of trade or commerce in question or where, in that branch, a particular course of conduct is generally and regularly followed when concluding a certain type of contract.

12–139   A third party beneficiary may take advantage of a jurisdiction clause between the actual parties to the contract and an assignee of a contract may be entitled to take advantage of a jurisdiction clause contained in it. Thus the European Court has held that a beneficiary of an insurance policy may rely, as against the insurer, on a jurisdiction clause in the insurance policy taken out by the insured;[616] and that a third party who has acquired a bill of lading may be entitled to rely upon a jurisdiction clause in it if, under the relevant national law, the third party has succeeded to the rights and obligations of the shipper.[617] But it is different where it is contended that the burden of a jurisdiction

---

[613] *cf.* Case 25/76 *Galeries Segoura Sprl v Bonakdarian* [1976] E.C.R. 1851. *Jurisdiction in the Case of a Sale Involving the Carriage of Goods* [2010] I.L.Pr. 583 (Stuttgart OLG); they will not have satisfied this if each side has customarily used its own contractual documentation, this containing inconsistent terms: *Lafarge Plasterboard Ltd v Fritz Peters & Co KG* [2000] 2 Lloyd's Rep. 689. See also *OT Africa Line Ltd v Hijazy* [2001] 1 Lloyd's Rep. 76; *SSQ Europe SA v Johann & Backes OHG* [2002] 1 Lloyd's Rep. 465; *Calyon v Wytwornia Sprzetu Komunikacynego PZL Swidnik SA* [2009] EWHC 1914 (Comm.), [2009] 2 All E.R. (Comm.) 603.

[614] Which expression includes insurance associated with that trade or commerce: *Standard Steamship Owners P&I Association (Bermuda) Ltd v GIE Vision Bail* [2004] EWHC 2919 (Comm.), [2005] 1 All E.R. (Comm.) 618.

[615] Case C–106/95 [1997] E.C.R. I–911, [1997] Q.B. 731: the decision was based on the 1978 version of Art.17, which merely required the agreement to be "in a form which accords with practices in that trade or commerce of which the parties are or ought to have been aware". The decision was applied in Case C–159/97 *Soc Trasporti Castelletti Spedizioni Internazionali SpA v Hugo Trumpy SpA* [1999] E.C.R. I–1597, also dealing with the 1978 version of Art.17. *cf.* Case C–288/92 *Custom Made Commercial Ltd v Stawa Metallbau GmbH* [1994] E.C.R. I–2913, 2934, *per* Lenz A.-G.

[616] Case 201/82 *Gerling v Treasury Administration* [1983] E.C.R. 2503.

[617] Case 71/83 *The Tilly Russ* [1984] E.C.R. 2417, [1985] Q.B. 931; Case C–159/97 *Soc Trasporti Castelletti Spedizioni Internazionali SpA v Hugo Trumpy SpA* [1999] E.C.R. I–1597. *cf. The Rewia* [1991] 2 Lloyd's Rep. 325, 336 (CA): contract contained in bill of lading issued for goods on a chartered ship is normally with the owner.

clause has been imposed on a stranger to the original contract. If as a matter of national law the stranger has succeeded to the obligations of the contract, as well as the rights under it, he will be bound without the need for a separate signature or other acceptance of his own.[618] But where burdens are to be assumed or imposed on a non-party otherwise than by way of such succession, it has been held that a non-party may not be deprived of the protection given to him by the formality provisions of Art.23[619] even if otherwise taking advantage of the contract; and accordingly, a separate act of acceptance will be required from him before the agreement on jurisdiction is binding upon him.[620]

The parties may, by agreeing orally the place of performance, achieve an **12–140** object very similar to that of a choice of court under Art.23, but only if the place agreed on is genuine and is not solely chosen to establish a court as having jurisdiction. In *Zelger v Salinitri (No.1)*[621] the plaintiff was a Munich merchant and the defendant was a merchant in Sicily. The plaintiff alleged an express oral agreement that Munich was to be the place of performance for repayment, and the German Federal Supreme Court asked the European Court whether the informal agreement was sufficient to found jurisdiction under Art.5(1)[622] of the Brussels Convention or whether the form in what was then Art.17 was necessary. It was held that an informal agreement was sufficient; the jurisdiction of the court for the place of performance and that of the selected court were two distinct concepts and only agreements selecting a court were subject to the requirements of form prescribed by Art.17. By contrast, in *Mainschiffahrts-Genossenschaft eG v Les Gravières Rhénanes SARL*,[623] the designated place of performance was described by the national court as being "abstract": it was a place at which contractual performance was impossible in fact, and which had been nominated with the sole aim of specifying a court with jurisdiction over the defendant. The European Court ruled that in such a case Art.5(1) of the Brussels Convention was inapplicable, and that to be effective the clause was required to comply with the formalities

---

[618] Case C–378/98 *Coreck Maritime GmbH v Handelsveem BV* [2000] E.C.R. I–9337.

[619] All the more so where the protection intended to be applicable to insureds or beneficiaries of insurance contracts is concerned: Case C–112/03 *Soc financière et industrielle de Peloux v AXA Belgium* [2005] E.C.R. I–3707, [2005] Q.B. 251.

[620] *Hapag Lloyd Container Line GmbH v La Réunion Européenne*, Cass. Civ. I, 4 March 2003, [2003] I.L.Pr. 779 (no rule of French law provides for succession to rights and obligations of shipper under bill of lading, so holder must accept the jurisdiction agreement); cf. *Soc CMA-CGM v Soc BNP Paribas Suisse* (Cass I Civ, 16.12.2008); *Deutsche Afrika Linien GmbH v Soc Dole France* (Cass Ch Com, 16.12.2008) (joined cases): 2009 *Rev. Crit.* 524 (note Jault-Seseke); see also Gaudemet-Tallon, *Compétence et execution des jugements en Europe* (4th ed. 2010), pp.149–150. *Soc financière et industrielle de Peloux v AXA Belgium*, above (jurisdiction agreement in group policy of insurance cannot bind beneficiary unless he specifically subscribes to it). This appears to exclude the possibility of arguing, in this context, that a party acts in bad faith if he blows hot and cold: cf. Case 221/84 *Berghöfer GmbH v ASA SA* [1985] E.C.R. 2699. On whether a jurisdiction clause in a chain of contracts is effective against a sub-buyer, and if so, on what conditions, see Case C–543/10 *Refcomp SpA v Axa Corporate Solutions Assurance SA* (pending).

[621] Case 56/79 [1980] E.C.R. 89.

[622] See above, Rule 35(2).

[623] Case C–106/95 [1997] E.C.R. I–911; cf. *Sarl Noge v Götz GmbH* [1998] I.L.Pr. 189 (French Cour de cassation, 1996).

of Art.17. The same must be true in relation to Art.23 of the Brussels I Regulation.

12–141   **Contents of the agreement.** Although Art.23 speaks of an agreement to the jurisdiction of a court or courts of a Member State or a Convention State, they also apply if the courts of more than one such State are contemplated by the contract as each having exclusive jurisdiction. In *Meeth v Glacetal Sarl*[624] a contract provided that if a German buyer were to sue a French seller, the French courts alone would have jurisdiction, and if the French seller were to sue the German buyer the German courts alone would have jurisdiction. The French seller sued the German buyer in Germany, in accordance with the jurisdiction clause, for failure to pay for deliveries. The European Court held that, although Art.17 of the Brussels Convention referred to a court in the singular, it could not be interpreted as intended to exclude the right to agree on two or more courts in a form which was based on widespread commercial practice. If the parties designate a court by description rather than by country, this may be valid if it is sufficiently clear to allow the court to identify the country concerned.[625]

12–142   Article 23 of the Regulation and the Convention now provides that the jurisdiction is to be exclusive unless the parties have agreed otherwise, and therefore an express agreement that a court is to have non-exclusive jurisdiction will be given effect according to its terms.

12–143   Where a jurisdiction agreement is within the scope of Art.23, the chosen court will have jurisdiction (both as regards claims and counterclaims).[626] The defendant may waive the benefit of a jurisdiction clause and voluntarily submit to the jurisdiction of another court,[627] and if the defendant voluntarily enters a plea to the merits in the foreign court, he will be taken to have submitted to its jurisdiction.[628] But Art.23 each prevails over the special jurisdiction conferred by Art.6, which is permissive rather than exclusive.[629] Accordingly, if A brings proceedings against B, and B wishes to make a third party claim against C, C is entitled to rely on a jurisdiction agreement between him and B and, if this is the true construction of the agreement, to insist that any claim against him be brought in the designated court.[630]

12–144   **Intra-United Kingdom cases.** The modified version of the European texts which appears in Sch.4 to the 1982 Act[631] deals with jurisdiction agreements

---

[624] Case 23/78 [1978] E.C.R. 2133.

[625] Case C–387/98 *Coreck Maritime GmbH v Handelsveem BV* [2000] E.C.R. I–9337 ("carrier's principal place of business"; no dispute as to who the carrier was).

[626] On set-off and counterclaim see Case 23/78 *Meeth v Glacetal Sarl* [1978] E.C.R. 2133 (where an unusual clause was involved: see Collins, pp.89–90); Case 48/84 *Spitzley v Sommer Exploitation SA* [1985] E.C.R. 787.

[627] Case 150/80 *Elefanten Schuh GmbH v Jacqmain* [1981] E.C.R. 1671.

[628] *The Atlantic Emperor (No.2)* [1992] 1 Lloyd's Rep. 624, 633 (CA); *Toepfer International GmbH v Molino Boschi Srl* [1996] 1 Lloyd's Rep. 510, 515; and see above, para.11R–397.

[629] *cf. Deforche SA v Tomacrau SA* [2007] I.L.Pr. 367 (French Cour de cassation, 2006).

[630] *Hough v P&O Containers Ltd* [1999] Q.B. 834.

[631] Rule 12 of the Schedule. Provision is also made for jurisdiction agreements in relation to consumer contracts by Rule 9, and employment contracts (Rule 10(5)). There are no special provisions in Sch.4 for contracts of insurance, which will therefore be governed by the general rules.

which confer jurisdiction on the courts of a particular part of the United Kingdom. It is designed for cases in which the defendant is domiciled in another part of the United Kingdom. It differs in certain respects from Art.23 of the Regulation, in the light of which it was drafted. It imposes no formal requirements for the agreement to be valid; and there is no reason to suppose that it is not subject other rules of English law which might override its effectiveness. The clause confers jurisdiction, as opposed to exclusive jurisdiction, on the chosen court and consequently the chosen court may decline jurisdiction, and a court other than the chosen court may, if it otherwise has jurisdiction, override the clause in accordance with clause (2) of Rule 39.[632]

Discretion. Where Art.23 applies, the chosen court has no discretion to decline jurisdiction, and other courts have no power to override the jurisdiction agreement.[633] But where it does not apply, the exercise of jurisdiction under clause (1) of Rule 39 is in theory subject to the discretion of the court, although (as will be seen) it is only infrequently that the court would be likely refuse to exercise it by staying an action or refusing permission to serve out of the jurisdiction.[634] The court has a discretion under clause (2) of Rule 39 to override the choice of a foreign court.   **12–145**

Clause (1) of the Rule. At common law the mere agreement of the parties that the High Court would have jurisdiction to determine disputes arising out of a contract between them was insufficient by itself to give the court jurisdiction, because the defendant could not effectively be served with a writ if he were outside England.[635] But if one party nominated an agent resident in England to accept service of process on his behalf, he was deemed to submit to the jurisdiction, and service could be effected on the agent in accordance with the contract.[636] Part 6 of the Civil Procedure Rules[637] provides that where a contract contains a term providing that, in the event of a claim being issued in relation[638] to the contract the claim form may be served by a method   **12–146**

---

[632] *cf. British Steel Corp v Allivane International Ltd*, 1989 S.L.T. (Sh Ct) 57 (Scots court may override English jurisdiction clause if no real dispute). This decision was misunderstood in *Jenic Properties Ltd v Andy Thornton Architectural Antiques*, 1992 S.L.T. (Sh Ct) 5. See also *McCarthy v Abowall (Trading) Ltd*, 1993 S.L.T. (Sh Ct) 65; *Morrison v Panic Link Ltd*, 1993 S.C. 631 (English jurisdiction clause held non-exclusive).

[633] A point which appears to have been overlooked in *OT Africa Line Ltd v Magic Sportswear Corp* [2005] EWCA Civ 710, [2005] 2 Lloyd's Rep. 170, and in *Dubai Islamic Bank PJSC v PSI Energy Holding Co BSC* [2011] EWHC 1019 (Comm.) (though the domicile of the parties to the jurisdiction agreement was not examined in detail, so the application of Art.23 may not be wholly clear). *cf. Microsoft Ireland Operations Ltd v EIM International Electronics Ltd* [2010] IEHC 228.

[634] Though see *Bouygues Offshore SA v Caspian Shipping Co (Nos 1, 3, 4, 5)* [1998] 2 Lloyd's Rep. 461 (CA).

[635] See *British Wagon Co v Gray* [1896] 1 Q.B. 35 (CA).

[636] *Tharsis Sulphur Co v Société des Métaux* (1889) 58 L.J.Q.B. 435; *Montgomery, Jones & Co v Liebenthal Co* [1898] 1 Q.B. 487 (CA); *Reversionary Interest Society Ltd v Locking* [1928] W.N. 227.

[637] CPR, r.6.11.

[638] CPR, r.6.11 applies only to actions "in respect of a contract" and there is no jurisdiction to allow service out of the jurisdiction where the parties have agreed to submit in respect of a tort: *The Anna L* [1994] 2 Lloyd's Rep. 379, 382.

specified in the contract, the claim form is deemed to be served on the defendant if it is served by a method specified in the contract. If the place of service specified is within the jurisdiction, permission of the court for issue and service of process is not necessary. But (except where the case comes within Art.23 of the Brussels I Regulation or of the Lugano Convention or of Sch.4 to the 1982 Act[639]) if the contract provides for service outside the jurisdiction, or contains no provision for service and the defendant is outside the jurisdiction, permission to serve outside the jurisdiction is required. Permission can be obtained under what is now CPR, PD6B, para.3.1(6)(d), the effect of which is that service outside the jurisdiction is permissible where the claim is brought in respect of a contract which contains a term to the effect that the High Court shall have jurisdiction to hear and determine any action in respect of the contract.

12–147   The provision which is now found in CPR, PD6B, para.3.1(6)(d), had its origin in 1920,[640] when it was introduced to allow service out of the jurisdiction in cases where there was a contractual submission but where no other head of what was then RSC Order 11, r.1(1) was applicable. Today cases will be rare in which CPR, PD6B, para.3.1(6)(d), would be the only available head of jurisdiction, especially since, in the absence of an express choice of some other law, it will normally be inferred from the jurisdiction clause that English law is the governing law of the contract.[641] Although permission to serve outside the jurisdiction may be required in cases outside the scope of Art.23 of the Regulation or the Convention, where the parties have agreed to an English forum it would require strong grounds for one of the parties to resist the exercise of jurisdiction by the English court.[642]

12–148   Where there is an agreement within the scope of Art.23 of the Brussels I Regulation or of the Lugano Convention or of Sch.4 to the 1982 Act conferring jurisdiction on the English court, permission to serve process out of the jurisdiction is not necessary, and, in the case of such an agreement, no question of the exercise of a discretion arises.

12–149   **Clause (2) of the Rule.** "Where plaintiffs sue in England in breach of an agreement to refer disputes to a foreign court, and the defendants apply for a stay, the English court, assuming the claim to be otherwise within its jurisdiction, is not bound to grant a stay but has a discretion whether to do so or not."[643] The court will exercise its discretion to grant a stay unless the

---

[639] In which event service is permitted without permission under CPR, rr. 6.32 and 6.33.

[640] Ord.11, r.2(a).

[641] See below, para.32–061.

[642] *The Chaparral* [1968] 2 Lloyd's Rep. 158, 163–164 (CA); *Attock Cement Co Ltd v Romanian Bank for Foreign Trade* [1989] 1 W.L.R. 1147, 1161 (CA); *Gulf Bank KSC v Mitsubishi Heavy Industries Ltd* [1994] 1 Lloyd's Rep. 323; *Egon Oldendorff v Libera Corp* [1995] 2 Lloyd's Rep. 64; *BAS Capital Funding Corp v Medfinco Ltd* [2003] EWHC 1798 (Ch), [2004] 1 Lloyd's Rep 652. On the power to stay proceedings brought in England as the contractual forum, see *UBS AG v Omni Holding AG* [2000] 1 W.L.R. 916; *Marubeni Hong Kong & South China Ltd v Mongolian Government* [2002] 2 All E.R. (Comm.) 873. On the power of the court to restrain foreign proceedings brought in breach of a jurisdiction agreement see clause (4) of the Rule, below, para.12–159.

[643] *The El Amria* [1981] 2 Lloyd's Rep. 119, 123 (CA) approving *The Eleftheria* [1970] P. 94, 99; applied in *The Pioneer Container* [1994] 2 A.C. 324, 347 (PC); also *Donohue v Armco Inc* [2001] UKHL 64, [2002] 1 Lloyd's Rep. 425.

claimant shows strong reasons, certainly requiring more than that he show England to be the *forum conveniens*, why the English proceedings should not be stayed. This is because the underlying principle is that the court makes people abide by their contracts. There is an even heavier burden on a claimant who applies to serve a foreign defendant out of the jurisdiction than on a claimant who institutes proceedings in England against a defendant present in England.[644] In this respect, the approach of the court to jurisdiction agreements does not draw significant distinctions according to whether they relate to the English court or to a foreign court:[645] a strong case will be required to justify the grant of relief which has the effect of allowing a party to a contract to resile from its terms. Where the defendant is present in England, or a ship is arrested in England in an action *in rem*, and the action is brought in breach of a jurisdiction agreement, the application by the defendant is to stay proceedings, and not to have them set aside.[646]

Clause (2) of Rule 39 is subject to the effect of Art.23 of the Brussels I Regulation and of the Lugano Convention under clause (3). Rule 12 of Sch.4 to the 1982 Act, which deals with jurisdiction agreements in intra-United Kingdom cases, does not give conclusive effect to an exclusive jurisdiction clause and therefore falls within the general principle of clause (2). **12–150**

English law as the *lex fori* determines the effect which will be given to the jurisdiction clause, and, in particular, the circumstances in which the court has a discretion to override it.[647] A stay will be refused if the choice of jurisdiction is contrary to a statutory rule against ousting the jurisdiction of the court[648] or against referring a dispute to the courts and law of a foreign country. Thus in *The Hollandia*[649] it was held that the effect of the Hague-Visby Rules, scheduled to the Carriage of Goods by Sea Act 1971, was to prohibit the submission of a dispute to the courts of a foreign country which would give effect to a limitation of the liability of the carrier under the original Hague Rules. On the other hand, the fact that, under the law of another country, an agreement providing for the jurisdiction of the English courts would be denied effect furnishes no ground for the English court to refrain from giving the **12–151**

---

[644] *Evans Marshall & Co Ltd v Bertola SA* [1973] 1 W.L.R. 349, 362. For other cases of service out of the jurisdiction involving foreign jurisdiction clauses see *Hoerter v Hanover, etc. Works* (1893) 10 T.L.R. 103 (CA); *Re Schintz* [1926] Ch. 710 (CA); *Ellinger v Guinness Mahon & Co* [1939] 4 All E.R. 16; *Mackender v Feldia* [1967] 2 Q.B. 590 (CA); *YTC Universal Ltd v Trans Europa SA* [1973] 1 Lloyd's Rep. 480n. (CA); *Standard Steamship Owners' Protection and Indemnity Assn (Bermuda) Ltd v Gann* [1992] 2 Lloyd's Rep. 528; *Citi-March Ltd v Neptune Orient Lines* [1996] 1 W.L.R. 1367; *Northern Sales Co Ltd v Government Trading Corp of Iran* (1991) 81 D.L.R. (4th) 316 (BCCA); *Ash v Corporation of Lloyd's* (1992) 94 D.L.R. (4th.) 378 (Ont CA); *Lewis Construction Co Ltd v M. Tichauer SA* [1966] V.R. 341.

[645] *Donohue v Armco Inc* [2001] UKHL 64, [2002] 1 Lloyd's Rep. 425.

[646] *The Fehmarn* [1958] 1 W.L.R. 159 (CA); *The Eleftheria* [1970] P. 94; *The Pia Vesta* [1984] 1 Lloyd's Rep. 169.

[647] See Kahn-Freund (1977) 26 I.C.L.Q. 825, 833–836.

[648] See, e.g. Consumer Credit Act 1974, s.141(1); Employment Rights Act 1996, s.203(1).

[649] [1983] 1 A.C. 565, distinguished in *The Benarty (No.2)* [1985] Q.B. 325 (CA). The actual decision would now be different under Art.23, because the conventions which enact the Hague and Hague-Visby Rules are not within Art.71. See also *Messageries Maritimes v Wilson* (1954) 94 C.L.R. 577; *Kim Meller Imports Pty Ltd v Eurolevant SpA* (1986) 7 N.S.W.L.R. 269; *Akai Pty Ltd v People's Insurance Co Ltd* (1997) 188 C.L.R. 418.

jurisdiction agreement its full effect, which may also mean enforcement by anti-suit injunction.[650]

12–152   In exercising its discretion whether to grant a stay, the court considers all the circumstances of the case, and the following formulation[651] of the particular factors to be taken into account has been much relied upon: (1) in which country the evidence is available, and the effect of that on the relative convenience and expense of a trial in England or abroad; (2) whether the contract is governed by the law of the foreign country in question, and if so, whether it differs from English law in any material respect; (3) with what country either party is connected, and how closely; (4) whether the defendants genuinely desire trial in a foreign country, or are only seeking procedural advantages; (5) whether the claimants would be prejudiced by having to sue in the foreign court because they would be deprived of security for their claim,[652] or be unable to enforce the judgment in their favour, or be faced with a time-bar not applicable in England, or for political, racial, religious or other reasons be unlikely to get a fair trial.[653] Until recently it could be confidently stated that if the making of an order to give effect to a jurisdiction clause— whether a stay of local proceedings, or permission to serve out of the jurisdiction, or even an anti-suit injunction—would have the effect that there would be concurrent legal proceedings, with different parties, that factor will cause the court to exercise its discretion against the making of the order; and subject to what is said below, that approach is still sound. In *The El Amria*,[654] a stay of English proceedings in favour of the chosen court would have meant that the claim for damages for spoiling of a cargo would be tried partly in Alexandria against the sea carrier, and partly in England against the Mersey Docks and Harbour Board. The risk of irreconcilable judgments, and the duplication of time and expense, justified the decision not to stay the English proceedings. In *Donohue v Armco Inc*[655] the House of Lords declined to enforce an English jurisdiction clause, by refusing to restrain parties who were bringing proceedings in the United States courts in breach of their promise, because there were other claimants in the United States proceedings who were under no contractual obligation to sue in England, and whose actions against

---

[650] *Akai Pty Ltd v The People's Insurance Co Ltd* [1998] 1 Lloyd's Rep. 90; *OT Africa Line Ltd v Magic Sportswear Corp* [2005] EWCA Civ 710, [2005] 2 Lloyd's Rep. 170.

[651] *The Eleftheria* [1970] P. 94, 100, *per* Brandon J., approved in the *The El Amria* [1981] 2 Lloyd's Rep. 119, 123–124, *per* Brandon L.J. (CA); *The Sennar (No.2)* [1985] 1 W.L.R. 490, 500, *per* Lord Brandon (HL).

[652] Where the claimant would be entitled to security in England, but not in the foreign court, the stay may be made conditional on the claimant retaining the security: *The Eleftheria*, above; Civil Jurisdiction and Judgments Act 1982, s.26. *cf. The Sylt* [1991] 1 Lloyd's Rep. 240; above, para.8–036.

[653] On the effect of delay in the chosen forum see *Evans Marshall & Co Ltd v Bertola* [1973] 1 W.L.R. 349 (CA); *The Vishva Prabha* [1979] 2 Lloyd's Rep. 286; *The El Amria*, above; *The Nile Rhapsody* [1994] 1 Lloyd's Rep. 382 (CA).

[654] [1981] 2 Lloyd's Rep. 119. See also *Citi-March Ltd v Neptune Orient Lines Ltd* [1996] 1 W.L.R. 1367; *The MC Pearl* [1997] 1 Lloyd's Rep. 566; *Soc Nat Ind Aérospatiale v Lee Kui Jak* [1987] A.C. 871 (not a jurisdiction clause case).

[655] [2001] UKHL 64, [2002] 1 Lloyd's Rep. 425. See also *Bouygues Offshore SA v Caspian Shipping Co (Nos 1, 3, 4, 5)* [1998] 2 Lloyd's Rep. 461 (CA).

the claimants were not open to criticism.[656] The general principle is that a court, while it will give great weight to a jurisdiction agreement, will not allow the parties to a contract to insist on the strict enforcement of their contractual agreement at the cost of damage being done to the orderly and efficient resolution of complex disputes or of the resolution of the controversy by "a single tribunal which is best fitted to make a reliable, comprehensive judgment on all matters in issue",[657] especially where this would risk exposing non-parties to serious prejudice.

Where the parties, however, have agreed to the jurisdiction of the English   **12–153**
court, they are to be taken to be aware that the Brussels I Regulation removes any judicial discretion to not give effect to that agreement, and that a concentration of jurisdiction by declining to exercise English jurisdiction may therefore be impossible to achieve. In those circumstances, the court may be more willing to enforce the jurisdiction agreement according to its terms, including by anti-suit injunction if appropriate.[658] Likewise, if the parties have made an agreement on jurisdiction which was incomplete, or have entered into a series of contracts which contain a number of jurisdiction clauses[659] and which, if all enforced according to their terms, would result in the fragmentation of proceedings, it will not lie in the mouth of one of them to ask the court to withhold effect from one or another of the clauses on the ground that to give it effect will be to risk the fragmentation of a complex dispute. Where a party may be said to have subscribed to jurisdiction clauses which now show it to have brought its jurisdictional misfortune upon itself,[660] it may face an uphill struggle to persuade the court to exercise its discretion to allow it to depart from the terms of an agreement.[661] It will certainly need to do a good deal more than to assert that there is an abstract risk, as opposed to a real and present danger, of fragmentation.

Effect of time bar. Where a claimant sues in England in breach of a foreign   **12–154**
jurisdiction clause it frequently happens that, by the time the defendant's application for a stay comes before the court, any action in the contractually-chosen forum is time-barred. If the existence of a time bar is taken into account in favour of the claimant in refusing a stay, it would deprive the defendant of an accrued defence in the chosen forum; if it is taken into

---

[656] *cf. Horn Linie GmbH v Panamericana Formas e Impresos SA* [2006] EWHC 373 (Comm.), [2006] 2 Lloyd's Rep. 44; *Starlight Shipping Co v Tai Ping Insurance Co Ltd* [2007] EWHC 1893 (Comm.), [2008] 1 Lloyd's Rep. 230.

[657] *Donohue v Armco Inc* [2001] UKHL 64, [2002] 1 Lloyd's Rep. 425, [34].

[658] Though there is certainly no requirement that an injunction be granted; it remains a matter for the discretion of the court: *Skype Technologies SA v Joltid Ltd* [2009] EWHC 2783 (Ch), [2011] I.L.Pr. 103; *Bank of New York Mellon v GV Films Ltd* [2009] EWHC 2328 (Comm.).

[659] Or clauses which envisage the bringing of parallel claims in different courts.

[660] That could not be said of the claimant in *The El Amria*, who had had no reason to make a jurisdiction agreement with anyone other than the sea carrier. However, if the risk of being deprived of a fair trial in the designated court is significant, it would not be right to blindly enforce the jurisdiction agreement and blame the parties for their own predicament: see above, para.12–040.

[661] *Konkola Copper Mines Plc v Coromin Ltd (No.2)* [2006] EWHC 1093 (Comm.), [2006] 2 Lloyd's Rep. 446; *Deutsche Bank AG v Highland Crusader Offshore LP* [2009] EWCA Civ 725, [2010] 1 W.L.R. 1023.

account in favour of the defendant, the claimant may be left with no remedy at all.

12–155   In *Spiliada Maritime Corp v Cansulex Ltd*[662] Lord Goff of Chieveley, said that if[663] the plaintiff acted reasonably in commencing proceedings in England (and did not act unreasonably in failing to commence proceedings in the other forum, e.g. by issuing a protective writ) it would not be just to deprive the plaintiff of the benefit of having started proceedings in England within the applicable limitation period;[664] but it may be a rare case in which the claimant is able to say that allowing time to run in an expressly-chosen court was not unreasonable. Where it grants a stay, the court may make it a condition that the defendant should waive the time bar in the foreign jurisdiction.[665]

12–156   But, as in the *forum non conveniens* cases, the court will not take into account in favour of a claimant who seeks to avoid a foreign jurisdiction clause a submission that the procedure in the foreign court is less favourable or less efficient than English procedure. Where the foreign court follows the civil law system and adopts the inquisitorial method without full discovery or cross-examination, it is not appropriate (otherwise than in wholly exceptional cases) for the English court to make a general comparison between the merits and demerits of the two systems.[666] Where the parties have agreed to submit their dispute to the jurisdiction of a court whose procedure does not allow full discovery, the parties have chosen that procedure, and the fact that a procedure which is generally applicable in the chosen jurisdiction is not helpful to a claimant is not a reason for refusing to give effect to the contractual choice of forum.[667]

12–157   **Clause (3) of the Rule. The effect of the Brussels I Regulation, and Lugano Convention.** The material provisions of the Brussels I Regulation and of the Lugano Convention relating to jurisdiction clauses have been

---

[662] [1987] A.C. 460, 483–484; see also *The Pioneer Container* [1994] 2 A.C. 324, 347–349 (PC).

[663] *The Blue Wave* [1982] 1 Lloyd's Rep. 151; *The Pioneer Container* [1994] 2 A.C. 324 (PC); *Citi-March Ltd v Neptune Orient Lines* [1996] 1 W.L.R. 1367; *The M C Pearl* [1997] 1 Lloyd's Rep. 566; *The Bergen (No.2)* [1997] 2 Lloyd's Rep. 710, 719; *Baghlaf al Safer Factory Co Br. for Industry v Pakistan National Shipping Corp* [1998] 2 Lloyd's Rep. 229 (CA); *BMG Trading Ltd v McKay* [1998] I.L.Pr. 691, (CA); *Nima SARL v Deves Public Insurance Co Ltd* [2002] EWCA Civ 1132, [2003] 2 Lloyd's Rep. 327 at [77]–[80]. See also *The Adolf Warski* [1976] 1 Lloyd's Rep. 107, 113–114, affirmed on different grounds [1976] 2 Lloyd's Rep. 241 (CA); *cf. The Vishva Prabha* [1979] 2 Lloyd's Rep. 286; *The Sennar (No.2)* [1984] 2 Lloyd's Rep. 142, 155, 160 (CA), affirmed [1985] 1 W.L.R. 490, 501 (HL); *The Indian Fortune* [1985] 1 Lloyd's Rep. 344.

[664] The effect of Foreign Limitation Periods Act 1984 may, of course, make the law of the chosen forum applicable (above, para.7–058), but if the claimant has commenced proceedings only in England, he may still be faced with a time-bar in the foreign court. Where Art.23 applies, the effect of suing in the wrong forum may be that the claimant is faced with a time-bar in the chosen forum, with the result that the remedy is lost irrevocably: *The Rewia* [1991] 2 Lloyd's Rep. 325, 335 (CA).

[665] And lift the stay if this is not done or cannot be done: *Baghlaf Al Zafer Factory Co Br. for Industry v Pakistan National Shipping Co (No.2)* [2000] 1 Lloyd's Rep. 1 (CA).

[666] *The El Amria* [1981] 2 Lloyd's Rep. 119, 127 (CA), approved in *Amin Rasheed Shipping Corp v Kuwait Insurance Co* [1984] A.C. 50 (a service out case).

[667] *Trendtex Trading Corp v Crédit Suisse* [1980] 3 All E.R. 721, 736–737, affirmed [1982] A.C. 679.

discussed above in detail.[668] Where they apply the court will not have discretion to override the jurisdiction clause, so that it will almost always have to set aside or stay its proceedings where a claimant sues in England in breach of a jurisdiction clause which conforms with the requirements of the Regulation or the Convention. It should be noted that the English court may make an order for interim relief notwithstanding that the substance of the matter has been referred to the courts of another Member State or Convention State.[669] The English court may disregard a foreign jurisdiction clause if it does not meet the requirements for validity of the Regulation or Convention, or is otherwise ineffective; and where the validity is in dispute the court will apply the test of asking "who has the better of the argument" on the validity of the agreement on jurisdiction. But it may not disregard the agreement, and must decline jurisdiction, if the chosen foreign court has first been seised of the proceedings between the parties; if the jurisdiction of the court first seised is being contested by the defendant, then the English court may only stay its proceedings pending the outcome of the contest over jurisdiction in the foreign court.[670]

It may happen that the English court is the chosen court, but one of the **12–158** parties first commences proceedings in another Member or Convention State in alleged breach of the jurisdiction clause. In such a case, even though the institution of proceedings before the foreign court is wholly unjustified, and has been done in bad faith to oppress the party who wishes to sue in England in accordance with the agreement, the English court must stay its proceedings and await the outcome in the court seised first. This was the decision of the European Court in *Erich Gasser GmbH v MISAT srl*,[671] and it had the effect of overruling a line of authority in the Court of Appeal to the effect that a valid agreement on jurisdiction prevailed over the provisions of the Conventions on *lis alibi pendens*.[672] *Erich Gasser* was about as strong a case as could be imagined; and the Austrian court, which had been prorogated with exclusive jurisdiction and from which the reference was made, even raised the possibility that the effect of its being obliged to stay its proceedings would be to deprive the claimant of his right of access to a court under Art.6 of the European Convention on Human Rights. The arguments were to no avail: the European Court proceeded on the basis that the rules regulating situations of *lis alibi pendens* did not yield to the contradictory demands of commercial sense, or respond to the public interest in giving the greatest effect possible to dispute-resolution agreements. On the other hand, while the jurisdiction of the court seised first and wrongly is being challenged, it has been held that the English court remains seised of the claim, and may order provisional or

---

[668] See above, paras 12–119 *et seq*.

[669] Brussels I Regulation, Art.31; Lugano Convention, Art.31; 1982 Act, s.25(1) (as amended by SI 2001/3929 Sch.2, para.10).

[670] Art.27, see above, paras 12–059 *et seq*.

[671] Case C–116/02 [2003] E.C.R. I–14693, [2005] Q.B. 1.

[672] *Kloeckner & Co AG v Gatoil Overseas Inc* [1990] 1 Lloyd's Rep. 177; *Denby v Hellenic Mediterranean Lines Co Ltd* [1994] 1 Lloyd's Rep. 320; *Continental Bank NA v Aeakos Compania Naviera SA* [1994] 1 W.L.R. 588 (CA); *Bankers Trust International Plc v RCS Editori SpA* [1996] C.L.C. 899; *Bank of Scotland v Banque Nationale de Paris*, 1996 S.L.T. 103. On whether an English court may order an injunction to restrain the proceedings in the court seised first, see clause (4) of the Rule, below, para.12–159.

protective measures by way of interim relief, without needing to rely on Art.31 of the Regulation or of the Lugano Convention.[673]

12–159   **Clause (4) of the Rule.** The general principles upon which an English court may order a party who is subject to its personal jurisdiction not to institute, or to discontinue, proceedings in a foreign court have been examined above.[674] But where the basis for the exercise of the court's discretion is that the defendant has bound himself by contract not to bring the proceedings which he threatens to bring, or has brought, in the foreign court, the principles which guide the exercise of the discretion of the court are distinct from those which were examined under clause (5) of Rule 38. In summary, (i) the English court must have personal jurisdiction over the defendant, but this will almost always be available under Art.23 of the Brussels I Regulation or of the Lugano Convention, or through personal presence, or under CPR, PD6B, para-a.3.1(6)(d); (ii) there is no need to show that there is oppression or vexation, nor that England is the natural forum for the claim; and (iii) there is no obligation[675] upon the applicant to seek relief from the foreign court first. But there is no power to grant an injunction if the proceedings to be indirectly restrained are or will be brought in a civil or commercial matter before the courts of another Member State or Convention State.[676]

12–160   The requirement that the party to be restrained be subject to the personal jurisdiction of the court is unaffected by whether the claim is based on a contractual right not to be sued in the foreign court. Where the claim is within the material scope of the Regulation or the Convention, the jurisdiction of the English court will be established in accordance with Rule 35.[677] Where there is an agreement conferring jurisdiction on the English court but which is not within the Regulation or the Convention,[678] permission to serve process out of the jurisdiction may be sought under CPR, PD6B, para.3.1(6)(d).[679] If the claim for an injunction is founded upon a legal right not to be sued in the foreign court, but the basis of the right is something other than a contractual right to be sued in the English courts,[680] permission to serve out, if this is required, will have to sought upon another ground; but if it amounts to a breach of the jurisdiction agreement for a foreign court for the applicant to seek relief in the English court, it would be surprising if permission were to be granted.

---

[673] *JP Morgan Europe Ltd v Primacom AG* [2005] EWHC 508 (Comm.) [2005] 2 Lloyd's Rep. 665.

[674] Clause (5) of Rule 38, see above, para.12–078.

[675] Though it is far from being established that there is such a requirement in cases discussed under Clause (5) of Rule 38.

[676] Case C–159/02 *Turner v Grovit* [2004] E.C.R. I–3565, [2005] 1 A.C. 101.

[677] See above, para.11R–247.

[678] Where neither party is domiciled in a Member or Convention State.

[679] See above, para.11–188.

[680] Such as a contractual right to be sued in the courts of a third country, or to submit differences to arbitration, or to bring no proceedings in respect of a dispute which has been settled. For an injunction to enforce a contractual right to have the dispute governed by English law, see *Shell International Petroleum Co Ltd v Coral Oil Co Ltd* [1999] 1 Lloyd's Rep. 72. *cf. Ace Insurance Ltd v Moose Enterprise Pty Ltd* [2009] NSWSC 724 (held no such right on the facts of the case; injunction granted on other grounds).

The manner in which the court will exercise its discretion to grant the   **12–161** injunction where the claimant in England has a legal right not to be sued by the respondent[681] in the foreign court reflects the legal character of the right which is sought to be enforced. Dealing with the substance of the discretion, Lord Diplock in *British Airways Board v Laker Airways Ltd*[682] spoke of cases in which the claimant had a legal right not to be sued in the foreign court[683] which may be enforced by an injunction. Those cases in which the courts have refined the criteria of vexation and oppression as the basis for an injunction,[684] and in which it has been stated that an English court should only act if it would be the natural forum for the trial of the action,[685] or that an equivalent interest in the forum must be shown to exist in order that the principles of comity are respected,[686] do not extend the requirement to cases where the court is asked to enforce a legal right not to be sued.[687]

If the applicant demonstrates that the respondent, plaintiff in the foreign   **12–162** proceedings, is acting in breach of the applicant's legal right not to be sued, the court will be likely to order an injunction: it has been said that there must be shown to be a good reason why in such a case an injunction should not be ordered.[688] It will be rare for an action for damages to be a sufficient response to a defendant who has instituted proceedings in a foreign court in breach of a contractual promise not to do so.[689] If the application is promptly brought

---

[681] Where he is sued by others, the contractually-bound respondent doing nothing to impede the proceedings, the relevant principles are in principle those in clause (5) of Rule 38: *Mamidoil-Jetoil Greek Petroleum Co SA v Okta Crude Oil Refinery AD* [2003] 1 Lloyd's Rep. 1, especially at [200] *et seq.*

[682] [1985] A.C. 58, 81.

[683] See also *Pena Copper Mines v Rio Tinto Co* (1912) 105 L.T. 846; *Ellerman Lines Ltd v Read* [1928] 2 K.B. 144 (CA); *Tracomin SA v Sudan Oil Seeds Co Ltd (No.2)* [1983] 1 W.L.R. 1026 (CA); *South Carolina Insurance Co v Assurantie Maatschappij "de Zeven Provincien" NV* [1987] A.C. 24, 40; *Schiffahrtsgesellschaft Detlev von Appen GmbH v Voest Alpine Intertrading GmbH* [1997] 2 Lloyd's Rep. 279, 286 (CA); *Charterers Mutual Assurance Assn Ltd v British & Foreign* [1998] I.L.Pr. 838.

[684] See above, para.12–082.

[685] *Soc Nat Ind Aérospatiale v Lee Kui Jak* [1987] A.C. 871 (PC).

[686] *Airbus Industrie GIE v Patel* [1999] 1 A.C. 119.

[687] *ibid.* p.138. A "legal right not to be sued" may be founded upon something other than a jurisdiction agreement, such as (1) a "no action" clause: *Elektrim SA v Vivendi Holdings 1 Corp* [2008] EWCA Civ 1178, [2009] 1 Lloyd's Rep. 59; (2) a right not to be brought before an arbitral tribunal, it having been found that the contract did not contain an agreement to arbitrate: *Claxton Engineering Services Ltd v TXM Olaj-és Gázkutato KFT* [2011] EWHC 345 (Comm.), [2011] 1 Lloyd's Rep. 510; *Excalibur Ventures LLC v Texas Keystone Inc* [2011] EWHC 1624 (Comm.), [2011] 2 Lloyd's Rep. 289; (3) a choice of law agreement which a foreign court would not respect: *Ace Insurance Ltd v Moose Enterprise Pty Ltd* [2009] NSWSC 724; (4) an Article of the Regulation which specifies the Member State in which proceedings must be brought: *Samengo-Turner v J&H Marsh & McLennan (Services) Ltd* [2007] EWCA Civ 723, [2008] I.C.R. 18 (criticised Briggs (2007) 78 B.Y.I.L. 615).

[688] *Standard Chartered Bank v Pakistan National Shipping Corp* [1995] 2 Lloyd's Rep. 365; *Akai Pty Ltd v Peoples' Insurance Co Ltd* [1998] 1 Lloyd's Rep. 90.

[689] *Castanho v Brown & Root (UK) Ltd* [1980] 1 W.L.R. 833, 865–866 (CA), affirmed [1981] A.C. 557; *Continental Bank NA v Aeakos Compania Naviera SA* [1994] 1 W.L.R. 588, 598 (CA). On the effectiveness of a claim for damages for breach of a jurisdiction or arbitration agreement see *The Lisboa* [1980] 2 Lloyd's Rep. 546 (CA); *Mantovani v Carapelli SpA* [1980] 1 Lloyd's Rep. 375 (CA); *Tracomin SA v Sudan Oil Seeds Co Ltd (No.2)* [1983] 1 W.L.R. 1026 (CA); *The Eastern Trader* [1996] 2 Lloyd's Rep. 585; *The Angelic Grace* [1995] 1 Lloyd's Rep. 87 (CA); *Skype Technologies SA v Joltid Ltd* [2009] EWHC 2783 (Ch.), [2011] I.L.Pr. 103, [33]. *Compagnie des Messageries Maritimes v Wilson* (1954) 94 C.L.R. 577, 587; *Anderson v GH Mitchell*

and the injunction granted, it may mean that the foreign court has no need to investigate the propriety of proceedings brought before it;[690] there is no reason to suppose that application must first be made to the foreign court.[691] Moreover, the fact that the foreign court has been applied to and has declined to grant jurisdictional relief,[692] or would be bound to refuse the relief because it regards the agreement as legally ineffective,[693] does not preclude the English court from granting an injunction. The fact that under law of the other country the agreement conferring jurisdiction on the English courts is ineffective generally furnishes no ground for the English court to refrain from enforcing the jurisdiction agreement by anti-suit injunction.[694] Nor does the fact that there are related proceedings before the courts of the foreign State in circumstances in which the court disapproves of the motivation behind them.[695]

12–163   If the foreign proceedings are brought in a Member State or a Convention State, there was until 2004 a live question of whether it was consistent with the overall scheme of the Regulation or the Brussels/Lugano Conventions for an English court to grant an injunction by way of enforcement of a jurisdiction agreement, where the objection was to proceedings pending in the courts of another Member or Convention State. Though it was noted that European Court had held that a court in one Brussels Convention State had no right to make its own assessment of the jurisdiction of the court of another Convention State over a pending action,[696] the English courts still took the view that they, even if seised after proceedings had been commenced in another Convention State, were entitled to order an injunction by way of enforcement of an English jurisdiction or arbitration agreement.[697] The Court of Appeal took the view that Art.17 of the Brussels Convention had mandatory effect, and even if proceedings had been commenced first in another Convention State, Art.17 took priority over the *lis alibi pendens* provisions of Arts 21 and 22 (now Arts 27 and 28), with the result that the English court was not bound to decline jurisdiction or consider whether to grant a stay under the latter provisions. This was justified on the ground that the principle of the autonomy of the

---

& *Sons Ltd* (1941) 65 C.L.R. 543, 548; *Adelaide Steamship Industries Pty Ltd v Commonwealth* (1974) 8 S.A.S.R. 425, 437. And see, on the availability of damages, below, para.12–164.

[690] *The Angelic Grace* [1995] 1 Lloyd's Rep. 87 (CA); *cf. Verity Shipping SA v NV Norexa* [2008] EWHC 213 (Comm.), [2008] 1 C.L.C. 45.

[691] *cf.* see above, para.12–090. But for a more cautious view, see *Credit Suisse First Boston (Europe) Ltd v MLC (Bermuda) Ltd* [1999] 1 Lloyd's Rep. 767.

[692] *Donohue v Armco Inc* [2001] UKHL 64, [2002] 1 Lloyd's Rep 425; *Akai Pty Ltd v People's Insurance Co Ltd* [1998] 1 Lloyd's Rep. 90; *REC Wafer Norway AS v Moser Baer Photo Voltaic Ltd* [2010] EWHC 2581 (Comm.), [2011] 1 Lloyd's Rep. 410.

[693] *OT Africa Line Ltd v Magic Sportswear Corp* [2005] EWCA Civ 710, [2005] 2 Lloyd's Rep. 170.

[694] *Akai Pty Ltd v The People's Insurance Co Ltd* [1998] 1 Lloyd's Rep. 90; *OT Africa Line Ltd v Magic Sportswear Corp* [2005] EWCA Civ 710, [2005] 2 Lloyd's Rep. 170.

[695] *Horn Linie GmbH v Panamericana Formas e Impresos SA* [2006] EWHC 373 (Comm.), [2006] 2 Lloyd's Rep. 44; *Starlight Shipping Co v Tai Ping Insurance Co Ltd* [2007] EWHC 1893 (Comm.), [2008] 1 Lloyd's Rep. 230.

[696] See Case 351/89 *Overseas Union Insurance Ltd v New Hampshire Insurance Co* [1991] E.C.R. I–3317; [1992] Q.B. 434; above, para.12–059.

[697] For example, *Continental Bank NA v Compania Aeakos Naviera SA* [1994] 1 W.L.R. 588 (CA); *Bankers Trust Plc v RCS Editori SpA* [1996] C.L.C. 899; *cf.* (for a more cautious view) *Phillip Alexander Securities & Futures Ltd v Bamberger* [1997] I.L.Pr. 73, affirmed *ibid.* 104 (CA); *Toepfer International GmbH v Soc Cargill France* [1998] 1 Lloyd's Rep. 379, 387–388 (CA).

parties, enshrined in Art.17 of the Brussels Convention, could not counte-
nance the conclusion that a party would be able to override and frustrate the
commercial purpose of an exclusive jurisdiction agreement by pre-emptively,
and wrongfully, suing in the courts of another Convention State, for the
commercial utility of such summary and effective enforcement of agreements
is obvious. Nor would there be any risk of irreconcilable judgments if the
relief were granted and the order obeyed. But the European Court disagreed,
and in *Turner v Grovit*[698] it ruled that it was not consistent with the Brussels
Convention for the courts of one Convention State to grant an injunction to
prevent a respondent from bringing a claim before the courts of another. In
fact, the conclusion was inevitable once the decision in *Erich Gasser GmbH
v MISAT srl*[699] had refused to allow the court prorogated with jurisdiction to
act upon it, but it was based upon the broader principle that the courts of what
are now Member and Convention States are obliged to demonstrate mutual
trust in each other's judicial institutions. For court in one Member State to
assert a right to interfere, even if indirectly, with civil or commercial proceedings before[700] the courts of another Member State is inconsistent with the
broad scheme of the Regulation. The same principle explains why it is
inconsistent with the Regulation for a court at the seat of an arbitration, seised
with a matter wholly relating that arbitration, to grant an injunction to restrain
one of the parties to the arbitration agreement from bringing proceedings
before the courts of another Member or Convention State. As a result of the
decision of the European Court in *West Tankers Inc v Allianz SpA*,[701] if the
proceedings brought before a court in another such state are brought in a civil
or commercial matter,[702] the rule of general application which requires the
demonstration of mutual trust is applicable, and no injunction may be
ordered.

Damages for breach of jurisdiction agreements. On the footing that an   **12–164**
agreement on jurisdiction represents a contractual promise supported by
consideration,[703] and is not otherwise invalid as a source of legal obligation,
the question arises whether a party who is the victim of a breach of that
agreement may in principle maintain a claim[704] for damages for breach of

---

[698] Case C–159/02 [2004] E.C.R. I–3565, [2005] 1 A.C. 101.

[699] Case C–116/02 [2003] E.C.R. I–14693, [2005] Q.B. 1.

[700] Whether pending or not.

[701] Case C–185/07, [2009] E.C.R. I–663, [2009] 1 A.C. 1138. The original reference by the
House of Lords, which also sets out the reasons which might be thought to support the availability
of an injunction, is at [2007] UKHL 4, [2007] 1 Lloyd's Rep. 319. For further consideration of
the effect of *Allianz SpA*, see *National Navigation Co v Endesa Generacion SA (The Wadi Sudr)*
[2009] EWCA Civ 1397, [2010] 1 Lloyd's Rep. 193; and for further proceedings, see *West
Tankers Inc v Allianz SpA* [2011] EWHC 829 (Comm.), [2011] 2 Lloyd's Rep. 117.

[702] It is quite different if the proceedings to be restrained are those of an arbitral tribunal with
its seat in a Member State: *Claxton Engineering Services Ltd v TXM Olaj-és Gázkutato KFT*
[2011] EWHC 345 (Comm.), [2011] 1 Lloyd's Rep. 510.

[703] If the contract is governed by English law this will be required. It is not necessarily required
if the contract is governed by foreign law.

[704] Or, if the English court exceptionally refuses a stay of proceedings brought in breach of
contract, a counterclaim. In *Incitec Ltd v Alkimos Shipping Corp* (2004) 206 A.L.R. 588 (Fed Ct)
it was suggested that instead of a counterclaim, the breach of contract could be reflected in the
costs order made. Whether a counterclaim may be made in the substantive proceedings will also
depend in part on when the cause of action is deemed to have arisen.

contract.[705] One argument may be disposed of at the outset: it is plainly no answer to a claim for damages for breach of contract that a court declined to grant specific or other procedural relief[706] to the victim of the breach. The decision of a court to refuse to enforce a contract by injunction or decree of specific performance does not entail a conclusion that there is no breach.[707] Damages for breach of contract are a common law right, at least where the contract is governed by English law.[708]

12–165   Surprisingly, perhaps, there was little judicial authority[709] on the subject until 2001, when the Court of Appeal approved, in principle at least, the proposition that damages could be obtained in an action for breach of contract.[710] The ruling was a narrow one: the defendant had brought proceedings before an American court; the American court had dismissed them on jurisdictional grounds; it had made no order for costs because it lacked the procedural power to make such an order; and the claimant sought only to recover in damages only the loss represented by the expense it had incurred in defeating the proceedings wrongly brought in America on jurisdictional grounds. Since then, the principle has been accepted as correct by the House of Lords.[711] But there has been no clear decision[712] about the degree to which the principle may be extended, especially in cases in which the claimant has been unsuccessful in contesting the jurisdiction of the foreign court. The rules on *res*

---

[705] Briggs and Rees, para.5.57 *et seq*; Briggs (2001) 72 B.Y.B.I.L. 446. See also Tan and Yeo [2003] L.M.C.L.Q. 435; Tham [2004] L.M.C.L.Q. 46 (who argues that a distinction is to be drawn between arbitration and jurisdiction clauses, and that the basis for a claim may be found to lie more easily in tort, on the footing that there was wrongful interference with a contract, or a wrong equivalent to abuse of the process of the foreign court). See further for an analysis based on tortious interference with contractual rights, *The Kallang* [2008] EWHC 2761 (Comm.), [2009] 1 Lloyd's Rep. 124; *The Duden* [2008] EWHC 2762 (Comm.), [2009] 1 Lloyd's Rep. 145. For the position in the United States, see Tan (2005) 40 Tex. Int. L.J. 623.

[706] Such as a stay of proceedings.

[707] *Incitec Ltd v Alkimos Shipping Corp* (2004) 206 A.L.R. 588 (Fed Ct).

[708] If the law governing the agreement on jurisdiction does not consider that damages are available for its breach, or (if the argument is advanced as in tort) if the *lex delicti* does not allow damages, an English court cannot make any such award.

[709] In *The Lisboa* [1980] 2 Lloyd's Rep. 546, 552 (CA) Dunn L.J. accepted that there was a remedy in damages, by analogy with damages for breach of an arbitration agreement (on which see, e.g. *Mantovani v Carapelli SpA* [1980] 1 Lloyd's Rep. 375 (CA); *The Eastern Trader* [1996] 2 Lloyd's Rep. 585). See Collins, *Essays*, pp.71–72.

[710] *Union Discount Co Ltd v Zoller* [2001] EWCA Civ 1755, [2002] 1 W.L.R. 1517.

[711] *Donohue v Armco Inc* [2001] UKHL 64, [2002] 1 Lloyd's Rep. 425. But the acceptance was of a concession made by counsel in argument, and the point did not require to be ruled on.

[712] *A/S D/S Svendborg v Akar* [2003] EWHC 797 (Comm.) followed *Union Discount*, but does not go any further towards elucidating the principle. *Union Discount* was applied at first instance in *A/S D/S Svendborg v Akar* [2003] EWHC 797 (Comm.), and in *National Westminster Bank Plc v Rabobank Nederland* [2007] EWHC 1056 (Comm.): in *National Westminster Bank Plc v Rabobank Nederland* [2007] EWHC 1742 (Comm.) the court assessed damages be reference to an award of costs on the indemnity basis. The court appears to have regarded a claim as properly pleadable in *Underwriting Members of Lloyd's Syndicate 980 v Sinco SA* [2008] EWHC 1842 (Comm.), [2009] Lloyd's Rep. I.R. 365. The principle was approved in *Sunrock Aircraft Corp Ltd v SAS Denmark-Norway-Sweden* [2007] EWCA Civ 882, [2007] 2 Lloyd's Rep. 612, and was referred to without discussion in *C v D* [2007] EWCA Civ 1282, [2008] Bus. L.R. 843. See also Takahashi (2008) 10 Yb.P.I.L. 57. For damages for breach of an agreement to arbitrate, see *CMA CGM SA v Hyundai Mipo Dockyard Co Ltd* [2008] EWHC 2791 (Comm.), [2009] 1 Lloyd's Rep. 213 (doubted, but not on this point: *National Navigation Co v Endesa Generacion SA (The Wadi Sudr)* [2009] EWCA Civ 1397, [2010] 1 Lloyd's Rep. 193).

judicata, as well as considerations of public policy, will need to be examined carefully in order to prevent avoidable satellite litigation, but the principle that a civil wrong sounds in damages is fundamental to the common law. For while it is objectionable to allow litigation to undermine a foreign judgment, a party who has breached his contract has no proper expectation of being allowed to profit from his wrong; and a victim who chooses to defend a claim in proceedings wrongly brought before a foreign court could also be seen to be mitigating his loss. Proof and quantification of loss may not be straightforward, but English law provides that a breach of contract, or a tort, sounds in damages; and it is difficult see the principled basis for refusing damages in this area of contractual breach or wrongful interference with contracts.[713]

Injunctions to restrain foreign proceedings in breach of arbitration **12–166**
agreement. The English court exercises a jurisdiction *in personam*[714] to restrain by injunction foreign proceedings brought in breach of an agreement to refer disputes to arbitration. The exercise of this jurisdiction, and the extent to which it is affected by the Brussels I Regulation and the Lugano Convention is considered in Chapter 16.[715]

ILLUSTRATIONS

1. A, an English company, and X, an American company, enter into a contract which provides **12–167**
that the parties submit to the jurisdiction of the High Court and that N of London should be the
agent of X to accept service of process on its behalf. A brings an action against X for breach of
contract. Process is served upon N. The court has jurisdiction.[716]
2. A, a Japanese company, and X, a United States company, enter into a contract whereby A's
tug will tow X's oil rig from the United States to Italy. The contract provides that "any dispute
arising must be treated before the London Court of Justice," but does not make any provision for
service. The tug and tow are forced to take refuge in Tampa, Florida, each alleging that this was
the other's fault. X brings an action against A in Florida, and A brings an action against X in
England. The court may assume jurisdiction and give permission to serve process on X in the
United States.[717]
3. The facts are as in Illustration 2, except that A is a German company. The court has
jurisdiction and permission to serve out of the jurisdiction is not required.[718]
4. A & Co is the holder of bills of lading in respect of plywood shipped from Roumania to
England on board a Turkish ship. The bills of lading provide that disputes shall be decided in
Turkey in accordance with Turkish law. A & Co brings an action *in rem* against the ship claiming
damages for breach of contract. Most of the evidence is available in England; but Turkish law

---

[713] For damages to be recoverable for breach of a choice of law agreement, it would first be
necessary to find that the expression of a choice of law was or embodied a promissory obligation.
In *Ace Insurance Ltd v Moose Enterprise Pty Ltd* [2009] NSWSC 724 the court was sceptical as
to the possibility.
[714] Which can be exercised, even if the defendant is not in England, where among other cases,
the arbitration agreement is governed by English law.
[715] See below, para.16–088.
[716] CPR, r.6.11; *cf. Tharsis Sulphur Co v Société des Métaux* (1889) 58 L.J.Q.B. 435.
[717] CPR, PD6B, para.3.1(6)(d); *cf. The Chaparral* [1968] 2 Lloyd's Rep. 158 (CA). For the
sequel in the United States courts see *M/S Bremen v Zapata Offshore Co*, 407 U.S. 1 (1972),
[1972] 2 Lloyd's Rep. 315; Collins, *Essays*, p.253; Kahn-Freund (1977) 26 I.C.L.Q. 825,
845–848.
[718] Brussels I Regulation, Art.23.

differs materially from English law in the relevant respects. The factors tending to rebut and reinforce the prima facie case for a stay are nicely balanced. The court stays the action.[719]

5. By a contract governed by Israeli law between A, an English company, and X, an Israeli company with a branch in London. A is appointed to be the sole distributor in the United Kingdom of wine produced by X. The contract contains a clause submitting all disputes to the exclusive jurisdiction of the courts of Tel Aviv. X purports to terminate the contract on the ground that A has not used proper efforts to market the wine in the United Kingdom, and appoints Y to be its distributor in place of A. A commences proceedings in England against X for breach of contract and conspiracy and against Y for unlawful interference with contract and conspiracy. The substance of the case is about the proper marketing of wine in the United Kingdom; all the essential witnesses are in the United Kingdom; Israeli law does not differ from English law in any material respect; the action is properly brought against Y and a stay would result in two sets of proceedings. The court declines to stay the action.[720]

12–168

6. A enters into a contract with X which provides for the exclusive jurisdiction of the courts of a foreign country. When A discovers that the terms of the contract are so disadvantageous, and that the probable explanation was that X had bribed A's agent to agree to the terms, A rescinds the contract and brings proceedings before the English courts for a declaration of non-liability to X. The jurisdiction clause remains binding on A notwithstanding any rescission of the contract, and unless there is a strong reason for doing otherwise, the court will stay the proceedings in order to allow the claim to be brought before the designated court.[721]

7. The facts are as in Illustration 6, except for the fact that A argues that the agent who purported to bind A to the contract had no authority to do so. A is bound by the agreement on jurisdiction.[722]

8. The facts are as in Illustration 6, except for the fact that the person who purported to bind A was not A's agent, even though he held himself out as being A's agent. *Semble* that A is not bound by the jurisdiction clause.[723]

9. The facts are as in Illustration 6, except that A or his representative signed the contract which contained the jurisdiction agreement as a result of X's misrepresentation. A is bound by the jurisdiction clause.[724]

10. The facts are as in Illustration 6, except that A or his respresentative signed the contract on being told by X, in response to a specific question, that it did not contain an agreement on jurisdiction. *Semble* that A is not bound by the jurisdiction clause.[725]

11. X enters into a contract with A which provides that the courts of a foreign country are to have exclusive jurisdiction over any claims arising out of the contract. Y, an entity associated with X, is mentioned in the contract and has the benefit of an indemnity from X in respect of its participation in the commercial arrangement; but the contract expressly provides that Y does not have the benefit of the jurisdiction clause. When A brings proceedings in England against X and Y, X is entitled to a stay of the proceedings against X. If on a true construction of the contract, A had promised X not to sue Y in England, X may, as the indemnity gives him a sufficient interest in the matter, obtain a stay of A's proceedings against Y. *Semble*, Y may also apply for a stay of proceedings in its own right: not as a third party having a right to enforce a contract made for its benefit, but on the ground that the existence of the contract supports its assertion that England is *forum non conveniens*.[726]

12. Potatoes are shipped from Alexandria in Egypt to Liverpool on an Egyptian ship, The El Amria. A & Co, an English company controlled by an Egyptian businessman, is the holder of bills

---

[719] *cf. The Eleftheria* [1970] P. 94, where the ship was Greek.

[720] These are the facts of *Evans Marshall & Co Ltd v Bertola SA* [1973] 1 W.L.R. 349 (CA), except that the foreign company in that case did not have a branch in England. The court declined to set aside service out of the jurisdiction.

[721] *Fiona Trust & Holding Corp v Privalov* [2007] UKHL 40, [2007] Bus.L.R. 1719 (where, however, the agreement was for arbitration).

[722] *Fiona Trust & Holding Corp v Privalov*, above.

[723] *Fiona Trust & Holding Corp v Privalov*, above.

[724] *Fiona Trust & Holding Corp v Privalov*, above.

[725] *Fiona Trust & Holding Corp v Privalov*, above.

[726] Derived from *Global Partners Fund Ltd v Babcock & Brown Ltd (In Liquidation)* [2010] NSWCA 196.

of lading. When the potatoes are unloaded, A & Co alleges that they have deteriorated as a result of the breach of contract and/or negligence of X & Co, the Egyptian owner of The El Amria, and brings an action *in rem* in England. Subsequently A & Co also sues Y, the harbour authority, for damages for delay in discharging the cargo. The effect of the bills of lading is to provide that all claims against the carriers should be decided in Egypt according to Egyptian law. The connection of the parties and of the evidence with Egypt is closer than that with England, but similar issues are involved in the actions against X & Co and against Y and there is a danger of conflicting decisions. The court refuses to stay the action against X & Co.[727]

13. A, domiciled in England, sells goods to X, domiciled in France. The price is payable in England. X's purchase order, which A has seen in previous transactions, provides in printed conditions on the back that the French courts are to have exclusive jurisdiction over any disputes. X refuses to pay, claiming that the goods are not in conformity with the contract. A brings an action in England. The court has no jurisdiction.[728]

14. A & Co, an American bank with a branch in London, lends money to X and Y, one-ship Panamanian and Liberian companies, owned and managed by Greek nationals, who guarantee the loan. The loan agreement provides that the English court is to have jurisdiction over all disputes arising under it. X, Y and Z bring proceedings in Greece for damages for breach of business morality; A & Co then institutes proceedings and applies for an anti-suit injunction from the English courts. The English court has no jurisdiction by reason of Art.27 of the Brussels I Regulation, and no power to grant an injunction either.[729]

15. A & Co enters into a contract with X & Co, an Italian company, which provides that the English courts are to have exclusive jurisdiction over all disputes arising under or connection with the contract. Apprehending that A & Co is about to institute proceedings in England for breach of contract, X & Co commences proceedings before the Italian courts. A & Co issues and serves a claim form for damages for breach of contract. The English court must stay its proceedings until the jurisdiction of the Italian courts has been established, but may in the interim grant relief in the form of a freezing injunction.[730]

16. The facts are as in Illustration 9, except that X & Co is incorporated in Texas, and the proceedings which it brings are in Texas. The English court has jurisdiction, and is not prevented from hearing A & Co's claim by the existence of the proceedings in Texas.

17. The facts are as in Illustration 9, but A & Co brings a claim for an injunction to restrain X & Co from prosecuting the proceedings in Italy. The injunction may not be granted.[731]

18. A Co and X enter into a contract which provides for the exclusive jurisdiction of the English courts. A Co considers that X has perpetrated a fraud, and together with B, an entity associated with A Co but not a party to the contract with X, brings proceedings against X in the United States. X applies for an injunction to restrain A Co and B from bringing the US proceedings. The court refuses to grant the injunction against A Co. The proceedings brought by B against X are genuine and would not be liable to any form of restraint by the English court, even if B were to have been subject to the personal jurisdiction of the English courts, which it was not. It would be contrary to the interests of justice to enforce the jurisdiction agreement by injunction and leave the English action between A Co and X to run in parallel with the US proceedings between B and X. *Semble* if A Co were to advance a claim before the US courts which it would not have been entitled to run before the English courts, it would be liable in an action for damages for breach of contract.[732]

---

[727] *The El Amria* [1981] 2 Lloyd's Rep. 119 (CA).

[728] Brussels I Regulation, Art.23, reversing the effect of Case 24/76 *Salotti v RÜWA* [1976] E.C.R. 1831.

[729] *Continental Bank NA v Aeakos Compania Naviera SA* [1994] 1 W.L.R. 588 (CA), but which is for all practical purposes overruled by a combination of Case C–116/02 *Erich Gasser GmbH v MISAT srl* [2003] E.C.R. I–14693, [2005] Q.B. 1 and Case C–281/02 *Turner v Grovit* [2004] E.C.R. I–3565, [2005] 1 A.C. 101.

[730] Case C–116/02 *Erich Gasser GmbH v MISAT srl* [2003] E.C.R. I–14693, [2005] Q.B. 1 (where the original proceedings were in Austria); *JP Morgan v Primacom AG* [2005] EWHC 508 (Comm.), [2005] 2 Lloyd's Rep. 665.

[731] Case C–281/02 *Turner v Grovit* [2004] E.C.R. I–3565, [2005] 1 A.C. 101.

[732] *Donohue v Armco Inc* [2001] UKHL 64, [2002] 1 Lloyd's Rep. 425.

19. A makes an agreement with X which provides for any disputes to be settled by arbitration in London. A, who considers that he should not be bound to arbitrate, brings proceedings against X before the New York courts, which find that the arbitration agreement is binding on X and dismiss the proceedings. As a matter of New York law the court has no power to award X its costs. X may bring proceedings in England against A for damages for breach of the contractual agreement to arbitrate.[733]

---

[733] *Union Discount Co v Zoller* [2001] EWCA Civ 1755, [2002] 1 W.L.R. 1517.

CHAPTER 13

JURISDICTION IN ADMIRALTY CLAIMS IN REM[1]

RULE 40—[2] (1) Subject to the provisions of the Senior Courts Act 1981[3]   13R–001
and to Clause (2) of this Rule, the High Court has jurisdiction to entertain
an Admiralty claim *in rem* if the process is served on the *res* in
England.[4]

(2)(a) Where the defendant is not domiciled in the United Kingdom,
but is domiciled in a State to which Council Regulation (EC) 44/2001
("the Brussels I Regulation") applies (a "Member State"),[5] the High
Court does not have jurisdiction to entertain an Admiralty claim *in rem*
(even if the process is served on the *res* in England) unless it has jurisdic-
tion under the Brussels I Regulation or under a convention "on a partic-
ular matter" within the terms of Article 71 of the Brussels I
Regulation.

(b) Where the defendant is not domiciled in the United Kingdom, and
is domiciled in a State which is party to the Lugano Convention on
jurisdiction and the enforcement of judgments in civil and commercial

---

[1] See generally Ruiz Abou-Nigm, *Arrest of Ships in Private International Law* (2011). The Admiralty jurisdiction of the High Court comprises jurisdiction both *in rem* and *in personam*. See CPR, Pt 61 and *Practice Direction—Admiralty Claims* (CPR PD 61); Tsimplis and Gaskell [2002] L.M.C.L.Q. 520. "Admiralty claim" is defined in Senior Courts Act 1981, s.20. See also the Admiralty and Commercial Courts Guide (2011). Admiralty claims which are not *in rem* may be brought in the Admiralty court (CPR, r.61.1(2)). Such claims must be brought in accordance with CPR, Pt 58 (Commercial Court). Hence, they remain Admiralty claims but, subject to CPR PD 61, para.12, they are processed as ordinary commercial claims. Jurisdiction *in personam* is discussed in Ch.11. This Chapter deals only with Admiralty claims *in rem*. On Admiralty jurisdiction and practice, see Jackson, *Enforcement of Maritime Claims* (4th ed. 2005); McGuffie, *Admiralty Practice* (1964); Meeson, *Admiralty Jurisdiction and Practice* (4th ed. 2011).

[2] This Rule must be read subject to Rules 26, 60 and 61, and to the provisions of ss.6–10 of Chapter II of the Brussels I Regulation and of Title II of the Lugano Convention in particular: Art.23 of the Brussels I Regulation and the Lugano Convention (jurisdiction agreements); Art.24 of the Brussels I Regulation and the Lugano Convention (submission to jurisdiction); Art.27 of the Brussels I Regulation and the Lugano Convention (*lis alibi pendens*); and Art.28 of the Brussels I Regulation and the Lugano Convention (related actions). As to the power of the court to stay an action, see above, Ch.12. On the arrest of a ship as a means of securing satisfaction of a judgment or arbitration award, see paras 8–042 *et seq*.

[3] Supreme Court Act 1981 was renamed Senior Courts Act 1981: Constitutional Reform Act 2005, s.59 and Sch.11, in force October 1, 2009.

[4] *Castrique v Imrie* (1869–70) L.R. 4 H.L. 414, 448; *The Nautik* [1895] P. 121; Senior Courts Act 1981, ss.20, 21; CPR PD 61, para.3.6.

[5] For these purposes, Denmark is treated as a Member State. See the Agreement between the European Community and Denmark [2005] O.J. L299/62 (approved [2006] O.J. L120/22 with effect from July 1, 2007: SI 2007/1655) (above, para.11–013), which applies the provisions of the Brussels I Regulation to Denmark, subject to certain modifications.

matters (but is not subject to the Brussels I Regulation),[6] the High Court does not have jurisdiction to entertain an Admiralty claim *in rem* (even if the process is served on the *res* in England) unless it has jurisdiction under the Lugano Convention or under a convention "on a particular matter" within the terms of Article 67 of the Lugano Convention.[7]

(3) For the purposes of this Rule, the domicile of a party is to be determined according to Rule 30.[8]

COMMENT

13–002   **Introduction.** The only claim *in rem* which exists in English law is an Admiralty claim brought in the Queen's Bench Division of the High Court.[9] The *res* is normally a ship, though, as will be seen below, it can sometimes be something else. The precise nature of a claim *in rem* in English law has been a matter of controversy,[10] but it may be distinguished from a claim *in personam* on the basis of two characteristics. First, if the judgment is solely *in rem*, it may be enforced only against the *res*; consequently, it does not affect anyone who does not have an interest in the *res* and, if he does have such an interest, affects him only to the extent of that interest. Secondly, it is binding, to the extent of his interest in the *res*, on anyone who has such an interest, even if he was not served with process or otherwise informed of the proceedings, and even if he took no part in the proceedings. In view of these characteristics, it has sometimes been said that an action *in rem* is against the *res*, rather than against an individual.[11] Since the idea that a ship can be a defendant in legal proceedings was always a fiction,[12] this should be regarded as a metaphor rather than as a literal statement of the legal position.[13] In *Republic of India v India Steamship Co Ltd (No.2)*[14] the House of Lords rejected the personification theory, that an action *in rem* is brought against a ship, and held that the

---

[6] The defendant must also not be domiciled in one of the few territories in which the Brussels Convention still applies: see above, para.11–013, n.19.

[7] For the revised text of the Lugano Convention, see [2007] O.J. L339/1. It entered into force between the Member States of the European Union (including Denmark) and Norway on January 1, 2010 and is also now in force in Iceland and Switzerland.

[8] *The Deichland* [1990] 1 Q.B. 361 (CA); *The Po* [1991] 2 Lloyd's Rep. 206 (CA); Brussels I Regulation, Arts 3 and 71; Lugano Convention, Arts 3 and 67.

[9] The Admiralty jurisdiction of the High Court was transferred from the Probate, Divorce and Admiralty Division to the Queen's Bench Division in 1970. A special Admiralty court is constituted as part of the Queen's Bench Division: Senior Courts Act 1981, s.6(1)(b).

[10] See *Republic of India v India Steamship Co Ltd (No.2)* [1998] A.C. 878; Teare [1998] L.M.C.L.Q. 33.

[11] See, for example, *The Burns* [1907] P. 137, 149–150; *The Nordglimt* [1988] Q.B. 183; *The Mawan* [1988] 2 Lloyd's Rep. 459, 460; *The Al Tawwab* [1991] 1 Lloyd's Rep. 201, 205 (CA).

[12] *Republic of India v India Steamship Co Ltd (No.2)* [1998] A.C. 878, 907, *per* Lord Steyn.

[13] *The Deichland* [1990] 1 Q.B. 361 (CA); *The Sylt* [1991] 1 Lloyd's Rep. 240, 244–245.

[14] [1998] A.C. 878. A somewhat different view has been adopted in Australia, see *The Elusive* [2010] NSWSC 525, at [37]; *Comandate Marine Corp v Pan Australia Shipping Pty Ltd* (2006) 157 F.C.R. 45, [2008] 1 Lloyd's Rep. 119, at [99] and [120]–[128]. See also, on the distinction between foreign judgments *in rem* and *in personam*, *Cambridge Gas Transportation Corp v Official Committee of Unsecured Creditors of Navigator Holdings Plc* [2006] UKPC 26, [2007] 1 A.C. 508; *Pattni v Ali* [2006] UKPC 51, [2007] 2 A.C. 85.

owners are parties to an action *in rem*. If the claim results in a judgment for a sum of money, such judgment (if not satisfied voluntarily) can be enforced only through the sale of the *res* by order of court. The *res* may be arrested by the court,[15] thus providing security for the claim, but (apart from the Lugano Convention) the jurisdiction of the court is not dependent on its arrest.

These characteristics of a claim *in rem* are obscured by the fact that the owner of the *res* (or someone else with an interest in it) will almost invariably defend the claim. If he defends on the merits, he is considered by English law to have submitted to the jurisdiction *in personam* of the court.[16] The result is that the court can give a judgment *in personam* against him, provided that he is liable *in personam* on the claim.[17] That judgment is not then limited to the value of the *res* and can be enforced against him in the normal way.[18] Moreover, if the *res* has been arrested, the person defending the action will usually obtain its release by putting up security. However, the claimant will normally accept security only if the defendant submits to the jurisdiction *in personam* of the court, in which case the defendant's liability is not limited either to the amount of the security or the value of the *res*.[19] For these reasons, the characteristic features of a claim *in rem* are apparent only if it is not defended, a rare occurrence. This, however, does not alter its essential nature.

13–003

Admiralty jurisdiction. The Admiralty jurisdiction of the High Court, whether *in rem* or *in personam*,[20] is defined by s.20 of the Senior Courts Act 1981,[21] which lists "questions and claims" of a maritime nature in paragraphs (a) to (s) of subs.(2) and three further types of proceedings in subs.(3), together with the residuary jurisdiction of the former High Court of Admiralty.[22] For example, the High Court has Admiralty jurisdiction in relation to

13–004

---

[15] Although process may be served by the claimant, arrest is effected only by the marshal or his substitute (after the claimant has obtained a warrant of arrest from the court). Arrest may take place at the same time as service of process (in which case the marshal or his substitute may serve the process along with the warrant of arrest) or at a later date.

[16] *The Gemma* [1899] P. 285 (CA); see also *The August 8* [1983] 2 A.C. 450, 456 (PC); *The Dictator* [1892] P. 304. If process was properly served on the *res*, the court would also have jurisdiction *in rem*; the claim *in rem* is not merged in the action *in personam* and the two claims continue side by side: *The Nordglimt* [1988] Q.B. 183; *The Maciej Rataj* [1992] 2 Lloyd's Rep. 552 (CA). If process was never served on the *res* (for example, where solicitors accept service on behalf of the owner), the claim is *in personam* only: *The Tuyuti* [1984] 1 Q.B. 838, 842 (CA). See also *The Oakwell* [1999] 1 Lloyd's Rep. 249.

[17] *The Nordglimt* [1988] Q.B. 183, 200–201.

[18] *The Gemma*, above.

[19] *The Dictator* [1892] P. 304; *The Gemma* [1899] P. 285 (CA); *The Dupleix* [1912] P. 8; *The August 8* [1983] 2 A.C. 450 (PC). See also *The Good Herald* [1987] 1 Lloyd's Rep. 236; *The Linda* [1988] 1 Lloyd's Rep. 175. *cf. The Dagmara* [1988] 1 Lloyd's Rep. 431. If the owner voluntarily gives bail to prevent the ship's arrest, or if he acknowledges the issue of the claim form, he is deemed to have submitted to the jurisdiction of the court: *The Prinsengracht* [1993] 1 Lloyd's Rep. 41.

[20] The term "Admiralty claims *in personam*" is no longer used: CPR PD 61, para.12.1.

[21] Merchant Shipping Act 1995, s.314(2), Sch.13, para.59; Merchant Shipping and Maritime Security Act 1997, s.29(1), Sch.6, para.2.

[22] The claims which must be started in the Admiralty court are stated in CPR, r.61.2.

claims for damage received by a ship,[23] for loss or damage to goods carried in a ship[24] and for damage done by a ship;[25] the High Court also has jurisdiction for any claim arising out an agreement relating to the carriage of goods in a ship or to the use or hire of a ship.[26] Some of the claims so listed are in practice obsolete, e.g. claims arising out of bottomry.[27] Although a claim *in personam* may be brought in all cases within the court's Admiralty jurisdiction,[28] the court's jurisdiction *in rem* is more limited.[29] For example, a claim *in rem* cannot be brought to enforce a claim for damage done by a ship falling within s.20(2)(e).

13–005   The *res* against which Admiralty claims *in rem* can be brought are as follows: ships;[30] cargo in or landed from a ship and still identifiable as cargo; freight; aircraft and their cargo; and the proceeds of sale of ships, cargo or aircraft. Not all the claims listed in the Act may be brought against all these *res*. For instance, a collision claim may be brought against a ship but not against cargo; a claim can only be brought against an aircraft[31] if the claim is for towage or pilotage while the aircraft is waterborne, or for salvage.[32] In practice, claims *in rem* against aircraft or their cargo are virtually unknown.

13–006   **Service of claim form and warrant of arrest.** The process by which a claim *in rem* is begun will be regarded as having been effectively served if a claim form *in rem* is served on any solicitor authorised to accept service,[33] or

---

[23] Senior Courts Act 1981, s.20(2)(d).

[24] *ibid.*, s.20(2)(g).

[25] *ibid.*, s.20(2)(e). Compare, in Australia, *Elbe Shipping SA v The Ship "Global Peace"* [2006] FCA 954, (2006) 232 A.L.R. 694, at [80]; considering, in particular *The Eschersheim* [1976] 1 W.L.R. 430.

[26] *ibid.*, s.20(2)(h). In *The Bumbesti* [2000] Q.B. 559, Aikens J. declined to follow *The St Anna* [1983] 1 W.L.R. 895 and decided that he was bound by the decision of the Court of Appeal in *The Beldis* [1936] P. 51 (CA). Where a dispute arising out of a charterparty is referred to arbitration, a claim to enforce the resulting arbitration award is not to be regarded as a "claim arising out of any agreement relating to . . . the use or hire of a ship." In *Heilbrunn v Lightwood Plc* [2007] FCA 1518, (2007) 243 A.L.R. 343, the Federal Court of Australia held that an obligation could arise "out of an agreement relating to the carriage of goods or persons by a ship or to the use or hire of a ship" within the meaning of the Admiralty Act 1988 (Cth), s.4(3)(f) even where there was no contract between the parties and the claim was in tort or bailment if there was a reasonably direct connection between the claim and an agreement for use of a ship or carriage by ship; see also *Beluga Shipping GmbH & Co v Headway Shipping Ltd (No.2)* [2008] FCA 1770; *The Catur Samudra* [2010] SGHC 18, [2010] 1 Lloyd's Rep. 305 (High Court of Singapore).

[27] Bottomry (*respondentia*) bonds were originally given by the master of a ship as security for a loan needed when the ship was in distant parts of the world. Modern methods of communication have made them unnecessary.

[28] Senior Courts Act 1981, s.21(1).

[29] s.21(2)–(4). See below and paras 13–009 *et seq.*

[30] The term "ship" as used in this chapter includes any description of vessel (including hovercraft) used in navigation, whether British or not and whether registered or not and wherever the residence or domicile of the owners may be: Senior Courts Act 1981, ss.20(7), 24(1).

[31] See *The Glider Standard Austria SH 1964* [1965] P. 463.

[32] Senior Courts Act 1981, s.20(2)(j), (k) and (l) and s.24(1).

[33] CPR PD 61, para.3.6(5). Where a P&I club issues a letter of undertaking in which it undertakes to appoint solicitors for the service of process in return for the claimants refraining from arresting the ship in question (or a sister-ship), the court can order specific enforcement of this undertaking and require the club to make the appointment and to file acknowledgment of service: *The Juntha Rajprueck* [2003] EWCA Civ 378, [2003] 2 Lloyd's Rep. 107.

if the owner acknowledges service before service has actually been effected,[34] or if there has been compliance with a contractually agreed method of service.[35] In the absence of one of these methods of service, process must normally be served on the property against which the claim is brought.[36] Service of an *in rem* claim form is made by fixing it on the outside of the property proceeded against in a position which may reasonably be expected to be seen.[37] However, if the property is freight, process must be served on the cargo in respect of which the freight is payable or on the ship in which that cargo was carried;[38] and, if the property has been sold and the proceeds of sale paid into court, process must be served by filing the claim form at the court.[39] If the property to be served is in the custody of a person who will not permit access to it, service is effected by leaving the claim form with that person.[40] If there is a notice against arrest, service should be made on the person named in the notice as authorised to accept service.[41] The court has power to order an alternative method of service.[42] If the claim form is served in any other way, e.g. by leaving a copy with the master,[43] the service is invalid and will be set aside, because other persons with an interest in the ship would not be sufficiently notified of the proceedings.

A claim form must be served by the claimant or his solicitor.[44] But a   **13–007** warrant of arrest may only be executed by the marshal or his substitute.[45] No arrest of proceeds of sale in court is necessary or permitted.

Unlike process beginning a claim *in personam*, process beginning an action   **13–008** *in rem* cannot be served out of the jurisdiction.[46] Therefore, unless it is deemed to have been duly served on the defendant under the CPR Admiralty Practice Direction,[47] the *res* must be in England at the time when the process is served, though it need not be in England at the time when process is issued;

---

[34] CPR, r.61.3(6).

[35] CPR PD61, para.3.6(6). In these situations the action will be *in personam* and not *in rem*: *The Tuyuti* [1984] Q.B. 838, 842 (CA).

[36] CPR PD61, para.3.6(1).

[37] para.3.6(1)(a).

[38] para.3.6(1)(b).

[39] para.3.6(3).

[40] para.3.6(2).

[41] para.3.6(4).

[42] para.3.6(7), (but only if the *res,* or part thereof, is situated in England).

[43] *The Prins Bernhard* [1964] P. 117, 130–132.

[44] CPR PD61, para.3.8.

[45] CPR, r.61.5(8); see also CPR PD61, para.3.7.

[46] *Aichorn & Co KG v The Talabut* (1974) 132 C.L.R. 449; *General Motors-Holdens v The Northern Highway* (1982) 29 S.A.S.R. 138. An English court will not restrain a party to an English arbitration agreement from arresting a vessel in a foreign jurisdiction if the sole purpose of the arrest is to obtain reasonable security for the claim to be arbitrated in England: *Kallang Shipping SA Panama v AXA Assurances Senegal ("The Kallang")* [2008] EWHC 2761 (Comm.), [2009] 1 Lloyd's Rep. 124. See also the judgment handed down simultaneously in *Sotrade Denizcilik Sanayi Ve Ticaret AS v Amadou LO ("The Duden")* [2008] EWHC 2762 (Comm.), [2009] 1 Lloyd's Rep. 145. *The Kallang* was followed in *Ispat Industries Ltd v Western Bulk PTE Ltd* [2011] EWHC 93 (Comm.), at [44]–[47]; and *Oceanconnect UK Ltd v Angara Maritime Ltd* [2010] EWCA Civ 1050, [2011] 1 Lloyd's Rep. 399.

[47] CPR PD61, para.3.6(5); para.3.6(6); CPR, r.61.3(6); and see para.13–006, above.

and it is immaterial that the ship leaves the jurisdiction after the service of the claim form but before the execution of the warrant of arrest.[48]

13–009   **Senior Courts Act 1981, s.21.** Section 21(1) to (4) sets out the three types of case in which a claimant may invoke the court's Admiralty jurisdiction by bringing a claim *in rem*. The predecessor of s.21(4) of the Senior Courts Act 1981 was enacted to implement the Brussels Convention of 1952 on the Arrest of Seagoing Ships.[49] In interpreting the Act recourse may be had not only to the Brussels Arrest Convention itself,[50] but also to its *travaux préparatoires*, the proceedings of the conference which led to it.[51]

13–010   Section 21(2) provides that in the cases mentioned in s.20(2)(a) to (c) and (s) an action *in rem* may be brought in the High Court against the ship or property in question.

Section 21(3) provides that in any case in which there is a maritime lien[52] or other charge on any ship, aircraft or other property for the amount claimed, an action *in rem* may be brought in the High Court against that ship, aircraft or property.[53]

13–011   A maritime lien permits a claim form to be served on the *res*, and the *res* to be arrested, no matter who is the owner at the time of the arrest or the issue or service of process.[54] A claimant who has a maritime lien on a ship may thus proceed under s.21(3) by a claim *in rem* against the ship, even though it may have changed hands since the cause of action arose.[55] In English law, a maritime lien arises for claims for collision damage, salvage, wages of the master and crew, and master's disbursements.[56] It attaches from the time the cause of action accrues. In English law, a claim supported by a maritime lien enjoys priority over certain other maritime claims, such as a mortgage, if the proceeds of the sale of the *res* are insufficient to meet all claims against it.[57]

---

[48] *The Nautik* [1895] P. 121.

[49] Text in Cmnd. 8954 (1953) and in Singh, *International Maritime Law Conventions* (1983), Vol.4, pp.3101–3107. It is replaced by the International Convention on Arrest of Ships 1999 from September 14, 2011 for States which have ratified the 1999 Convention. The United Kingdom has not signed or ratified the 1999 Convention. For consideration of the 1999 Arrest Convention see Berlingieri, *Arrest of Ships* (5th ed. 2011); Gaskell and Shaw [1999] L.M.C.L.Q. 470. For comparison of the 1952 and 1999 Conventions, see Berlingieri [2005] L.M.C.L.Q. 327.

[50] *The Eschersheim* [1976] 1 W.L.R. 430 (HL). On resort to the French text see *The Antonis P Lemos* [1985] A.C. 711, 731.

[51] *Gatoil International Inc v Arkwright-Boston Manufacturers Mutual Insurance Co* [1985] A.C. 255. See also *The River Rima* [1988] 1 W.L.R. 758 (HL).

[52] See also the International Convention on Maritime Liens and Mortgages 1993 (in force from September 5, 2004 but not ratified by the United Kingdom).

[53] On the distinction between a maritime lien and a statutory right *in rem* and the implications for choice of law purposes, see *World Fuel Services Corporation v The Ship "Nordems"* [2011] FCA 73; see also *JP Morgan Chase Bank v Mystras Maritime Corp* [2008] FCA 399, (2008) 305 D.L.R. (4th) 442.

[54] A maritime lien will, however, be lost if the *res* is sold by order of the court.

[55] *The St Merriel* [1963] P. 247, 251.

[56] There is also a maritime lien for claims on bottomry (*respondentia*) bonds, but these are now obsolete.

[57] Questions of priorities are decided by the *lex fori*: *The Union* (1860) Lush. 128; *The Colorado* [1922] P. 102. See, further, para.7–041, above.

The words "other charge" in s.21(3) are not defined in the Act and their **13–012**
meaning is not free from doubt. They do not refer to charges in the nature of
a mortgage, because these are specifically referred to in s.21(2) above. They
probably refer to certain charges imposed by the Merchant Shipping Acts. At
any rate they do not include a possessory lien for repairs.[58]

Section 21(4) provides as follows: **13–013**

"In the case of any such claim as is mentioned in section 20(2)(*e*) to (*r*),
where (a) the claim arises in connection with a ship; and (b) the person who
would be liable on the claim in an action *in personam* ('the relevant
person') was, when the cause of action arose, the owner or charterer of, or
in possession or control of, the ship, an action *in rem* may (whether or not
the claim gives rise to a maritime lien on that ship) be brought in the High
Court against (i) that ship, if at the time when the action is brought the
relevant person is either the beneficial owner of that ship as respects all the
shares in it or the charterer of it under a charter by demise; or (ii) any other
ship of which, at the time when the action is brought, the relevant person
is the beneficial owner as respects all the shares in it."

At first sight it might appear that s.21(4) has a restrictive effect on the   **13–014**
jurisdiction of the court and cuts down the unqualified right conferred by
s.21(3). For s.21(3) says that a claimant with a maritime lien on a ship can
proceed by action *in rem* against that ship, irrespective of a change of
ownership; and then s.21(4), particularly the words in brackets "(whether or
not the claim gives rise to a maritime lien on that ship)," seems to say that he
cannot do so if the ship has changed hands after the cause of action arose and
before the issue of process. But the effect of s.21(4) is in reality an enlarging
and not a restricting one.[59] The two subsections have to be read disjunctively,
so that a claimant who has a maritime lien on a ship and is content to proceed
against that ship can do so under s.21(3). It is only when the claimant has no
maritime lien, or (whether he has a maritime lien or not) when he wishes to
proceed against some other ship than the one in respect of which the cause of
action arose, that s.21(4) (which creates what is sometimes referred to as "the
statutory lien") comes into operation. Before 1956 an action *in rem* could not
be brought against any ship other than the one in respect of which the cause
of action arose.[60] But under s.21(4) such an action may be brought against a
sister ship owned (at the time of the issue of the claim form[61]) by the person
who (at the time when the cause of action arose) would have been liable on
the claim in an action *in personam*.[62] There is no requirement that the sister
ship must have been owned by that person at the time when the cause of action

---

[58] *The St Merriel* [1963] P. 247. Compare *Elbe Shipping SA v The Ship "Global Peace"* [2006]
FCA 954, (2006) 232 A.L.R. 694; *Heilbrunn v Lightwood Plc* [2007] FCA 1518, (2007) 243
A.L.R. 343; *CSL Australia Pty Limited v Formosa* [2009] NSWCA 363; *The Altair II* [2009]
NZHC 734.
[59] *The St Elefterio* [1957] P. 179, 185.
[60] *The Beldis* [1936] P. 51 (CA).
[61] *The Andria* [1984] Q.B. 477, 489 (CA).
[62] For the position under Irish law see *The Kapitan Labunets* [1995] I.R. 164.

arose. Section 21(4) does not allow a claim *in rem* to be brought against a ship owned by a "sister company", i.e. a company with the same shareholders and directors as the company owning the ship in relation to which the claim arises.[63]

13–015   Soon after the passing of the Administration of Justice Act 1956 (the predecessor of the relevant provisions of the Senior Courts Act 1981) a practice grew up of issuing process against the ship in respect of which the cause of action arose and against sister ships in the same ownership, and serving it on one ship as soon as a suitable one (i.e. one whose value was sufficient to provide adequate security for the claim) came within the jurisdiction. The validity of this practice was approved (*obiter*) by a majority of the Court of Appeal in *The Banco*,[64] and confirmed by s.21(8) of the 1981 Act, which provides that once a ship has been served with a writ (now called a claim form) or arrested in an action *in rem* brought to enforce a claim within s.20(2)(e) to (r), no other ship may be served with a writ or arrested in that or any other action *in rem* brought to enforce that claim;[65] but this provision does not prevent the issue of process naming more than one ship or of two or more claim forms each naming a different ship.[66] In addition, s.21(8) does not preclude a ship being arrested in England in connection with English proceedings *in rem* notwithstanding that the ship[67] or a sister ship[68] has previously been arrested and released in foreign proceedings involving the same maritime claim. However, the court has a discretion to order the ship's release if the arrest is vexatious or oppressive or otherwise an abuse of the process of the court.[69]

13–016   The relationship between the "relevant person" and the ship, which for convenience one may call "ownership", is not quite the same in the different provisions of s.21(4). It refers to two points in time: when the cause of action arises and when the claim is brought. When the cause of action arises the relevant person may be either "the owner or charterer[70] of, or in possession[71] or in control of, the ship".[72] Here "owner" means "registered owner".[73] When the claim is brought, if it is brought against the same ship,[74] the relevant

---

[63] *The Evpo Agnic* [1988] 1 W.L.R. 1090 (CA). See also *The Mawan* [1988] 2 Lloyd's Rep. 459.

[64] [1971] P. 137, 153, 158–159.

[65] For the position in Scotland see *The Afala* [1995] 2 Lloyd's Rep. 286 (OH).

[66] See also *The Stephan J* [1985] 2 Lloyd's Rep. 344.

[67] *The Tjaskemolen (No.2)* [1997] 2 Lloyd's Rep. 477.

[68] *The Kommunar (No.2)* [1997] 1 Lloyd's Rep 8.

[69] *The Tjaskemolen (No.2)*, above.

[70] It was established in *The Span Terza* [1982] 1 Lloyd's Rep. 225 that the term "charterer" includes a "time charterer". In *The Tychy* [1999] 2 Lloyd's Rep. 11 (CA), the Court of Appeal held that it also included a "voyage charterer" or a "slot charterer".

[71] See also *The Catur Samudra* [2010] SGHC 18, [2010] 1 Lloyd's Rep. 305 (High Court of Singapore), at [60].

[72] s.21(4)(b).

[73] *The Evpo Agnic* [1988] 1 W.L.R. 1090 (CA). *cf. Tisand Ltd v Owners of the Ship MV Cape Moreton* [2005] F.C.A.F.C. 68. See also *The Tian Sheng (No.8)* [2000] 2 Lloyd's Rep. 430 (Hong Kong CFA).

[74] s.21(4)(i).

person must be either (a) the "beneficial owner"[75] of the ship as respects all the shares in it or (b) the demise charterer;[76] if, on the other hand, it is brought against a sister ship, alternative (b) does not exist: it must be shown that the relevant person is the beneficial owner of the ship as respects all the shares in it. The statute does not define "beneficial owner".[77] Under the predecessor of this section it was held by Brandon J. in *The Andrea Ursula*[78] that for the purposes of determining the beneficial ownership of the ship in respect of which the cause of action arose the expression included the interest of a charterer by demise and any other person with a similar complete possession and control over the ship who might thereby become liable on a claim within what are now paragraphs (e) to (r) of s.20(2) of the Act. But this decision was not followed by Robert Goff J. in *The I Congreso del Partido*,[79] where it was held that the expression means equitable ownership, whether or not accompanied by legal ownership, and does not include possession and control (however full and complete) without ownership. Robert Goff J.'s interpretation, which was made in the context of a case involving the determination of the beneficial ownership of a sister ship, where the question remains relevant, was followed by the Court of Appeal in *The Nazym Khikmet*.[80]

The onus of showing that the beneficial ownership is the same at the time **13–017** when the claim is brought as it was when the cause of action arose rests on the claimant. The court will look behind the registered owner to determine the beneficial ownership.[81] Where a ship is transferred by the relevant person to a new owner after the cause of action has arisen but before the institution of

---

[75] Contrast the position under s.17(b) of the Australian Admiralty Act 1988, which simply refers to "the owner of the ship or property", without defining the nature of the ownership in question. It has been held to include the beneficial owner of the ship: *Kent v SS Maria Luisa (No.2)* [2003] F.C.R. 12. But in *Tisand Ltd v Owners of the Ship MV Cape Moreton* [2005] F.C.A.F.C. 68, it was held that the registered owner of the property was not necessarily the owner within the meaning of s.17(b). That person must be the owner in a proprietary sense, with the power honestly and lawfully to dispose of the property. On the interpretation of the Australian Admiralty Act 1988, see *Elbe Shipping SA v The Ship "Global Peace"* [2006] FCA 954, (2006) 232 A.L.R. 694, at [74]; *The Ship "Gem of Safaga" v Euroceanica (UK) Ltd* [2010] FCAFC 14; *Brisbane Slipways Operations Pty Ltd v Pantaloni* [2010] FCA 654.

[76] *The Giuseppe di Vittorio* [1998] 1 Lloyd's Rep. 136 (CA); cf. *Laemthong International Lines Co Ltd v BPS Shipping Ltd* (1997) 190 C.L.R. 181.

[77] On the law applicable to the question of beneficial ownership, see *The Nazym Khikmet* [1996] 2 Lloyd's Rep 362 (CA); *Bridge Oil Ltd v Owners and/or Demise Charterers of the Ship Guiseppe di Vittorio* [1998] 1 Lloyd's Rep. 136 (CA); *The Kapitan Temkin* [2002] 4 S.L.R. 978; *Vostok Shipping Co Ltd v Confederation Ltd* [2000] 1 N.Z.L.R. 37 (CA); *Tisand Ltd v Owners of the Ship MV Cape Moreton* [2005] F.C.A.F.C. 68.

[78] [1973] Q.B. 265, not following *The St Merriel* [1963] P. 247, 258. These decisions are obsolete since s.21(4) provides that the ship in respect of which the cause of action arose may be arrested if the person liable *in personam* is either the beneficial owner *or* the charterer by demise. See also *The Father Thames* [1979] 2 Lloyd's Rep. 364, 366–367.

[79] [1978] Q.B. 500, 537–542, revd. on other grounds [1983] 1 A.C. 244; applied in *The Father Thames* [1979] 2 Lloyd's Rep. 364; *The Permina 3001* [1979] 1 Lloyd's Rep. 327 (Singapore CA).

[80] [1996] 2 Lloyd's Rep. 362 (CA). See also *Vostok Shipping Co Ltd v Confederation Ltd* [2000] 1 N.Z.L.R. 37 (CA). On the law applicable to ownership of a ship, see below, paras 22E–057 *et seq.* See also *Thor Shipping A/S v The Ship "Al Duhail"* [2008] FCA 1842.

[81] *The Aventicum* [1978] 1 Lloyd's Rep. 184; *The Saudi Prince* [1982] 2 Lloyd's Rep. 255; *The Convenience Container* [2007] HKCA 302 (with corrigendum [2007] HKCA 379).

proceedings *in rem*, the court may conclude that the transfer is a sham if, rather than serving a commercial purpose, it is designed simply to prevent the arrest of the ship in question.[82] In such a case, the relevant person remains the beneficial owner.

13–018   If the claimant has a statutory right of action *in rem* not amounting to a maritime lien (i.e. a statutory lien), and the ship is sold after the cause of action arose but before the issue of process, he cannot proceed *in rem* against the ship.[83] But he can do so if the ship is sold after the issue of process but before service thereof or arrest of the ship.[84]

13–019   In determining for the purposes of s.21(4) whether a person would be liable on a claim in an action *in personam*, it is to be assumed that he has his habitual residence or a place of business in England.[85] This statutory assumption is necessary because proceedings *in personam* for damage, loss of life or personal injury arising out of a collision or other like navigational incident between two or more ships lie only if that collision or incident occurred in English inland waters or in an English port, or is or has been the subject-matter of proceedings in the court, or if the defendant has his habitual residence or a place of business in England.[86] The effect of the assumption is to render the person who incurred the claim notionally liable in an action *in personam*, even if he habitually resides abroad and has no place of business in England, but only for the limited purposes of the court's jurisdiction in an action *in rem* under s.21(4). The reference to "the person who would be liable on the claim in an action *in personam*" does not mean that the claimant must prove at the outset that he has a cause of action sustainable in law;[87] as long as the claimant's case is not bound to fail he is entitled to proceed with it.[88] The purpose of the words is merely to identify the person whose ship may be arrested in relation to the right of arresting a sister ship.[89]

13–020   Section 21(5) provides that in the case of a claim in the nature of towage or pilotage in respect of an aircraft, the Admiralty jurisdiction of the court may be invoked by an action *in rem* against that aircraft if at the time when the action is brought it is beneficially owned by the person who would be liable on the claim in an action *in personam*. The same assumption applies as it does under s.21(4) that the person who would be liable on the claim in an action *in personam* has his habitual residence or a place of business in England.[90] But there is no provision for such claims against an aircraft when a mere charterer has incurred the claim, nor for such claims against another aircraft in the same ownership.

---

[82] *The Tjaskemolen* [1997] 2 Lloyd's Rep. 465.

[83] *The Henrich Björn* (1886) 11 App. Cas. 270.

[84] *The Monica S.* [1968] P. 741; *The Helene Roth* [1980] Q.B. 273.

[85] Senior Courts Act 1981, s.21(7).

[86] *ibid.* s.22; and see Rule 30.

[87] *The St Elefterio* [1957] P. 179. See also *Ocean Industries Pty Ltd v Owners of the Ship MV "Steven C"* [1994] 1 Qd.R. 69; *"Iran Amanat" v KMP Coastal Oil Pte Limited* (1999) 196 C.L.R. 130 (High Ct).

[88] *The Yuta Bondarovskaya* [1998] 2 Lloyd's Rep. 357.

[89] *The St Elefterio* [1957] P. 179, 186; *The St Merriel* [1963] P. 247, 258.

[90] s.21(7).

Section 22 of the Act, which defines the jurisdiction of the court in claims **13–021** *in personam* for damage, loss of life or personal injury arising out of a collision between two or more ships,[91] does not apply to claims *in rem*.[92] But s.23, which excludes the jurisdiction of the court in cases certified by the Secretary of State to fall within the provisions of the Rhine Navigation Convention,[93] applies equally to claims *in personam* and claims *in rem*.

Effect of the Brussels I Regulation and the Lugano Convention. Admi- **13–022** ralty claims *in rem* fall within the scope of the Brussels I Regulation and the Lugano Convention; it follows, therefore, that an English court cannot take jurisdiction in such a claim if this is precluded by the provisions of the Regulation or the Convention.[94] If the defendant is domiciled (for the purposes of the Regulation) in the United Kingdom, the court will have jurisdiction under Art.2 of the Regulation. If the defendant is not domiciled in the United Kingdom, a Member State or a Contracting State to the Lugano Convention (a "Convention State"), Art.4 of either the Regulation or the Lugano Convention allows the English court to take jurisdiction under the provisions of English law. Where, however, the defendant is not domiciled in the United Kingdom, but is domiciled in a Member State or a Convention State, the provisions of the Regulation or the Convention must be satisfied. Which instrument applies depends on the domicile of the defendant: if he is domiciled in a Member State, the Regulation applies; if the defendant is not domiciled in another Member State,[95] but is domiciled in a State which is a party to the Lugano Convention (i.e. Iceland, Norway, or Switzerland), the Lugano Convention is to be applied.[96]

Where the defendant is not domiciled in the United Kingdom, but is **13–023** domiciled in another Member State or Convention State, Art.3 of the Regulation and the Convention provides that the English court may take jurisdiction only by virtue of the rules set out in ss.2 to 7 of Chapter II of the Regulation or the Lugano Convention (Arts 5 to 24). However, Art.71 of the Brussels I Regulation[97] provides that it does not prevent the court of a Member State (or Convention State) from assuming jurisdiction in accordance with a convention "on a particular matter" to which the Member State (or Convention State) is a party, even where the defendant is domiciled in another Member State (or Convention State). Consequently, where the Brussels I Regulation (or Lugano Convention) applies, the English court must have jurisdiction under the

---

[91] See below, para.15–039.

[92] *Conocophillips (UK) Ltd v Partnereederei Ms Jork* [2010] EWHC 1214 (Comm.), at [38].

[93] See below, para.15–051.

[94] *The Deichland* [1990] 1 Q.B. 361 (CA). The scope of the Regulation and the Lugano Convention as regards subject matter is defined by Art.1, by which they apply in civil and commercial matters, whatever the nature of the court or tribunal. This is subject to certain exceptions, none of which concerns proceedings *in rem*.

[95] Or one of the very few territories to which the Brussels Convention is still applicable: see above, para.11–013, n.19.

[96] Lugano Convention, Art.64(2).

[97] Somewhat similar provisions are contained in Art.67 of the Lugano Convention; and were contained in Art.57 of the Brussels Convention. But see para.13–026, below.

provisions of the Regulation (or the Lugano Convention) or under the provisions of a convention on a particular matter.

13–024   **Meaning of "defendant".** It has not yet been definitively determined who would be regarded as a defendant in a claim *in rem* for the purposes of the Brussels I Regulation and the Lugano Convention, but the owner of the res or anyone with an interest in it whose interest would be affected by the claim would probably be so regarded. In *The Deichland*,[98] which was approved by the House of Lords in *Republic of India v India Steamship Co Ltd (No.2)*,[99] a company which was the demise charterer of the ship at the time when the process was issued (though the charter had ended by the time it was served) was regarded as the defendant for the purposes of the Brussels Convention.

13–025   **Sections 2 to 7 of Chapter II of the Brussels I Regulation; Sections 2 to 6 of Title II of the Conventions.** With two exceptions, none of these provisions is specifically concerned with Admiralty claims. The first exception is Art.7 of the Regulation (which corresponds to Art.6A of the Conventions), which deals with limitation claims. This has already been discussed.[100] The second exception is Art.5(7), which deals with claims for remuneration for the salvage of cargo or freight, but not ships. It provides that such claims may be brought in the court under whose authority the cargo or freight (a) has been arrested or (b) could have been arrested, but bail or other security has been given. The reason why this very narrow head of jurisdiction is included in the Regulation is explained below.

13–026   **Conventions on particular matters.** The question of Admiralty jurisdiction *in rem* was discussed in the negotiations preceding the United Kingdom's accession to the Brussels Convention. The solution adopted was to rely on Art.57 of the Brussels Convention.[101] Article 71 of the Brussels I Regulation, reproduces this provision[102] but with one important difference. Article 71 of the Brussels I Regulation preserves the application of conventions on particular matters to which Member States are already party. However, in contrast to Art.57 of the Brussels Convention, it does not provide that new Conventions on particular matters will not be affected by the Brussels I Regulation.[103] Article 67 of the Lugano Convention defers to conventions on "particular matters" by which Convention States "are bound"; but goes on to say that "Without prejudice to obligations resulting from other agreements between

---

[98] [1990] 1 Q.B. 361 (CA).
[99] [1998] A.C. 878.
[100] See Rule 35(8), above.
[101] Amended and consolidated by the 1989 Accession Convention.
[102] In its amended and consolidated form.
[103] On the differences between Art.71 of the Brussels I Regulation and Art.57 of the Brussels Convention, see Case C–533/08 *TNT Express Nederland BV v AXA Versicherung AG* [2010] I.L.Pr. 663, at [38]. The European Court ruled that, pursuant to Art.71 of the Brussels I Regulation, the rules of an international convention apply only if they are "highly predictable, facilitate the sound administration of justice and enable the risk of concurrent proceedings to be minimised"; and on condition "that they ensure, under conditions at least as favourable as those provided for by the regulation, the free movement of judgments in civil and commercial matters and mutual trust in the administration of justice in the European Union."

certain Contracting Parties, this Convention shall not prevent Contracting Parties from entering into such conventions."[104]

Conventions on particular matters are conventions which fall within the   **13–027** general scope of the Regulation (and the Lugano Convention) because they deal with jurisdiction or the enforcement of judgments, but which concern only particular issues (by contrast with the Regulation and the Lugano Convention, which deal with these matters in a general way).[105] Conventions dealing specifically with Admiralty actions *in rem* fall into this category.

Article 71(2)(a) of the Regulation (and Art.67(2) of the Lugano Conven-   **13–028** tion) makes clear that a court of a Member State (or Convention State) which is a party to a convention on a particular matter may assume jurisdiction in accordance with that convention, even if the defendant is domiciled in another Member State (or in a Convention State) and that State is not a party to the convention on a particular matter.[106] Moreover, it is not necessary for the claimant to be domiciled in, or a national of, a Member State (or Convention State), nor is it necessary—unless this is required by the convention on a particular matter—for him to be domiciled in, or a national of, a State party to the convention on a particular matter.[107] A judgment given by an English court in these circumstances must be recognised by all Member States (and the Contracting States to the Lugano Convention), even if such State is not a party to the convention on a particular matter.[108]

This means that if the United Kingdom is a party to a convention on a   **13–029** particular matter, and if an English court assumes jurisdiction in a claim *in rem* in accordance with the provisions of that convention, the bar imposed by Art.3 of the Regulation and the Lugano Convention is lifted. Where there is conflict between provisions, the jurisdictional provisions of a convention on a particular matter prevail over those contained in the Brussels I Regulation and the Lugano Convention (as the case may be); and there is no reason for thinking that the convention on a particular matter should be interpreted narrowly in order that it should impinge as little as possible on the Brussels I Regulation and the Lugano Convention.[109] Article 71 of the Regulation (and

---

[104] See also Protocol 3 to the Lugano Convention on the interpretation of Art.67. Article1 of Protocol 3 states that "provisions which, in relation to particular matters, govern jurisdiction or the recognition or enforcement of judgments and which are or will be contained in acts of the institutions of the European Communities shall be treated in the same way as the conventions referred to in Article 67(1)."

[105] For a list of such conventions, which is not complete, see Schlosser Report [1979] O.J. C59/71, para.238, n.59.

[106] Art.26 of the Brussels I Regulation and the Lugano Convention must nevertheless be applied. Each provision requires the court in certain cases to declare of its own motion that it has no jurisdiction; it also makes provision for the defendant to be served in sufficient time to enable him to arrange for his defence. See also Case C–148/03 *Nürnberger Allgemeine Versicherungs AG v Portbridge Transport International BV* [2004] E.C.R. I–10327.

[107] *The Po* [1991] 2 Lloyd's Rep. 206 (CA).

[108] Art.71(2)(b) of the Brussels I Regulation. For the Lugano Convention, see Art.67(3); but see Art.67(4), which provides that a Convention State need not enforce such a judgment against a person domiciled in its territory if that State is not bound by the convention on a particular matter, or, if the State addressed is a Member State of the European Community in respect of conventions which would have to be concluded by the European Community, unless the judgment may otherwise be recognised or enforced under any rule of law in the State addressed. See also Art.67(5) of the Lugano Convention.

[109] *The Anna H* [1995] 1 Lloyd's Rep. 11 (CA).

Art.67 of the Lugano Convention) does not, however, make the convention on a particular matter part of English law, nor does it positively grant jurisdiction to the English court.[110] It is not necessary that United Kingdom legislation should expressly provide that the convention on a particular matter is to have force of law in England,[111] but, if it does not, the English court must have jurisdiction under some other provision of English law. In other words, the requirements of Rule 40(1) must be satisfied, in addition to those of the convention on a particular matter.

13–030   Two conventions on particular matters need to be considered. The first is the Brussels Arrest Convention of 1952.[112] This provides that a ship flying the flag of a Contracting State (to the Arrest Convention) may be arrested for a "maritime claim", but not for any other claim;[113] a ship flying a flag of a non-Contracting State, on the other hand, may be arrested for a maritime claim or for any other claim for which it may be arrested under the law of the Contracting State in which the arrest takes place.[114] The Convention then provides that the courts of the country where the arrest took place will have jurisdiction to hear the claim if they have such jurisdiction under their domestic law.[115] This means that, in the case of a ship flying the flag of a Contracting State, the court has jurisdiction only with regard to a "maritime claim". This is defined in the Convention[116]: the definition covers largely the same ground as s.20 of the Senior Courts Act 1981, but is not identical to it.

13–031   The result is that, where the English court has jurisdiction under Rule 40(1), it will normally have jurisdiction under the Arrest Convention. There are, however, two important exceptions. The first results from the fact that the Arrest Convention provides for the arrest only of ships; consequently, it grants jurisdiction *in rem* only against ships. Section 20 of the Senior Courts Act 1981, on the other hand, makes provision for claims *in rem* against certain other kinds of property. One such case is a salvage action against cargo or freight. Article 5(7) of the Brussels Convention (and later the Lugano Convention and the Brussels I Regulation) was adopted to allow such a claim.

---

[110] *The Po* [1991] 2 Lloyd's Rep. 206 (CA).

[111] *ibid.*

[112] The International Convention Relating to the Arrest of Seagoing Ships, signed in Brussels on May 10, 1952. The text is set out in Cmnd. 8954 (1953) and in Singh, *International Maritime Law Conventions* (1983), Vol.4, pp.3101–3107. It has been recognised as being a "convention on a particular matter" in terms of Art.57 of the Brussels Convention: Schlosser [1979] O.J. C59/71, para.238, n.59; *The Deichland* [1990] 1 Q.B. 361 (CA). See also *Kallang Shipping SA Panama v AXA Assurances Senegal ("The Kallang")* [2008] EWHC 2761 (Comm.), [2009] 1 Lloyd's Rep. 124, at [72]–[73]. It was replaced by the International Convention on Arrest of Ships 1999 with effect from September 14, 2011 in States which have ratified the 1999 Convention. The United Kingdom has not signed or ratified the 1999 Convention. See further Berlingieri, *Arrest of Ships* (5th ed. 2011); Berlingieri [2005] L.M.C.L.Q. 327; Gaskell and Shaw [1999] L.M.C.L.Q. 470.

[113] Art.2.

[114] Art.8(2).

[115] Art.7(1). For the meaning of domestic law see *The Anna H* [1995] 1 Lloyd's Rep. 11 (CA). This also gives additional grounds of jurisdiction, but, since Art.7(1) as a whole applies only if the ship has been arrested, and the jurisdictional requirements of English law must in any event be satisfied, these additional grounds appear to be of little relevance. See also *The Juntha Rajprueck* [2003] EWCA Civ 378, [2003] 2 Lloyd's Rep. 107.

[116] Art.1(1).

The second exception is that the Arrest Convention grants jurisdiction only   **13–032**
when the ship has been arrested. It is not sufficient that the ship *could have
been* arrested, but was not (because security was given).[117] Once the ship has
been arrested within the jurisdiction of the English court, the court will not
lose its jurisdiction if the ship is then released.[118] It is, therefore, necessary
both to serve the process on the ship (to fulfil the requirements of English law)
and to arrest it (to fulfil the requirements of the Arrest Convention).[119] Once
this has been done, security may be accepted for its release. The court is able
to claim jurisdiction under the Arrest Convention even if the defendant has put
up security for the claim prior to the arrest and the ship is released immediately afterwards.[120] Although the Arrest Convention defines arrest as "the
detention of a ship by judicial process to secure a maritime claim",[121] it has
been held that to qualify as an arrest for the purposes of the Convention all
that is required is that the legal consequence of judicial detention of the ship
is that it becomes security for a maritime claim; there is no requirement that
the claimant's motive for the arrest should be to obtain security.[122]

The second convention is the Brussels Collision Convention,[123] which   **13–033**
concerns claims for collision between seagoing vessels or between seagoing
vessels and inland navigation craft.[124] Article 1(1) confers jurisdiction in such
claims on (a) the court where the defendant has his habitual residence or a
place of business; (b) the court of the place where arrest has been effected of
the defendant ship or of any other ship belonging to the defendant which can
lawfully be arrested, or where arrest could have been effected and bail or other
security has been furnished; or (c) the court of the place of collision when the
collision has occurred within the limits of a port or in inland waters.[125] The
most important of these grounds is that set out in Art.1(1)(b). To some extent
it covers the same ground as the Arrest Convention.[126] However, it goes
further in one important respect: it is sufficient if arrest could have been

---

[117] *The Deichland* [1990] 1 Q.B. 361 (CA). The court will, however, have jurisdiction in
personam over the defendant if he voluntarily submits to its jurisdiction, for example by giving
bail to prevent the ship's arrest or by acknowledging the issue of the claim form. See *The
Prinsengracht* [1993] 1 Lloyd's Rep. 41.

[118] *The Anna H* [1995] 1 Lloyd's Rep. 11 (CA).

[119] If the defendant submits to the jurisdiction of the English court in terms of Art.23 of the
Brussels I Regulation or the Lugano Convention (jurisdiction agreements) or Art.24 of the
Regulation or the Lugano Convention (defending on the merits) arrest will not of course be
necessary.

[120] *The Anna H* [1995] 1 Lloyd's Rep. 11 (CA).

[121] Art.1(2).

[122] *The Anna H*, above.

[123] International Convention on Certain Rules Concerning Civil Jurisdiction in Matters of
Collision, May 10, 1952. The text is set out in Cmnd. 8954 (1953). This has been recognised as
a convention on a particular matter: Schlosser [1979] O.J. C59/71, para.238, n.59; *The Po* [1991]
2 Lloyd's Rep. 206 (CA).

[124] It also concerns certain other actions: see Art.4.

[125] At first sight, Art.8 might be thought to limit the application of the Collision Convention to
cases where all the vessels concerned fly the flag of a Contracting State, but this view was rejected
by the Court of Appeal in *The Po*, above, where it was held that the action before the court was
covered by the Collision Convention, even though the plaintiff's vessels flew the flag of a non-
Contracting State. The correct interpretation of Art.8 may perhaps be that it does no more than
preclude additional grounds of jurisdiction where the vessels concerned fly the flag of a Contracting State.

[126] See Art.1(1)(a) and Art.7(1) of the Arrest Convention.

effected and bail or other security was furnished. This means that in collision cases the arrest of the defendant vessel is not essential.[127]

13–034   **Jurisdictional issues not regulated by conventions on particular matters.** Although it is provided that the operation of conventions on particular matters is not to be affected either by the Brussels I Regulation or the Lugano Convention,[128] this principle was glossed by the European Court in *The Tatry*.[129] The European Court ruled that the provisions of a convention on a particular matter prevail over the Brussels Convention only to the extent that there is a conflict; in a case where a specific jurisdictional issue was not covered by a convention on a particular matter the provisions of the Brussels Convention continued to apply. So, even where the court has obtained jurisdiction *in rem* by virtue of an arrest under the Arrest Convention, Arts 27 and 28 of the Brussels I Regulation are applicable if there are concurrent proceedings in another Member State. This is because the Arrest Convention does not contain provisions dealing with *lis pendens* or related actions.

13–035   The European Court's decision in *The Tatry* was distinguished in *The Bergen*,[130] a case in which the defendant challenged the court's jurisdiction *in rem* on the basis that the parties had agreed to the exclusive jurisdiction of the German courts. The defendant argued that, since the Arrest Convention was silent as to the effect of a jurisdiction agreement, the case was governed by Art.17 of the Brussels Convention,[131] according to which the English court had no jurisdiction. Clarke J. distinguished *The Tatry* on the ground that Art.17 (which has the effect of depriving all courts other than those chosen of the jurisdiction which they otherwise would have had) is different from Art.21[132] (which does not deprive courts of jurisdiction but merely requires them not to exercise it); if the court were required to give effect to Art.17 it would have been deprived of jurisdiction under the Arrest Convention, something expressly excluded by Art.57 of the Brussels Convention.[133]

13–036   **Defendant domiciled in Scotland or Northern Ireland.** As was said above, Art.2 of the Regulation (and of the Lugano Convention) confers jurisdiction on the courts of the Member State (or Convention State) in which the defendant is domiciled; consequently, if the defendant is domiciled in the United Kingdom, the courts of the United Kingdom have jurisdiction in terms of the Regulation. It is provided by s.16 of the Civil Jurisdiction and Judgments Act 1982 that, where the defendant is domiciled in the United Kingdom, the provisions of Sch.4[134] determine whether the courts of any part of

---

[127] *The Po*, above.

[128] Brussels I Regulation, Art.71(1); Lugano Convention, Art.67(1).

[129] Case C–406/92 [1994] E.C.R. I–5439, [1999] Q.B. 515. See also Case C–148/03 *Nürnberger Allgemeine Versicherungs AG v Portbridge Transport International BV* [2004] E.C.R. I–10327; 592; Case C–522/03 *Scania Finance France SA v Rockinger Spezialfabrik für Anhängerkupplungen GmbH & Co* [2006] I.L.Pr. 11.

[130] [1997] 1 Lloyd's Rep. 380.

[131] The equivalent of Art.23 of the Brussels I Regulation.

[132] The equivalent of Art.27 of the Brussels I Regulation.

[133] The proceedings were subsequently stayed under the court's inherent jurisdiction: *The Bergen (No.2)* [1997] 2 Lloyd's Rep. 710. See also Baatz [2011] L.M.C.L.Q. 208.

[134] As substituted by SI 2001/3929, Sch.2.

the United Kingdom have jurisdiction in any given case. However, para.6(a) of Sch.5 (read with s.17) provides that Sch.4 does not apply to proceedings brought in pursuance of a statutory provision which implements a convention on a particular matter or which makes provision with respect to jurisdiction in any field to which the convention relates. Under para.6(b), the same applies to proceedings brought in pursuance of a rule of law which has the effect of implementing such a convention. If one regards the "field" to which the Brussels Arrest Convention relates as being Admiralty claims *in rem*, such claims would seem to be exempt from the requirements of Sch.4.[135] It would seem therefore that, as long as the defendant is domiciled in some part of the United Kingdom, compliance with Rule 40(1) is all that is required.

ILLUSTRATIONS

1. By a contract of sale made in London, an English company, on behalf of the Russian Government, purports to sell to an Italian company a Russian ship which, prior to the promulgation of a Russian decree nationalising the Russian mercantile marine, had belonged to A & Co, a Russian company. A & Co, which has removed its business to France, issues a claim form *in rem* claiming possession of the ship and a declaration that it is the owner thereof. The claim form is served on the ship in an English port. The court has jurisdiction, although the dispute is between foreigners and relates exclusively to a foreign ship.[136]   **13–037**

2. Y & Co, charterers by demise of X & Co's German ship, order repairs to be done to her by A. A issues a claim form *in rem* against the ship claiming £5,180 in respect of the repairs. The claim form is served on the ship in England. At the date of the service of the claim form Y & Co are still charterers by demise. The court has jurisdiction. There is no maritime lien, so the case is not within s.21(3) of the Senior Courts Act 1981.[137] But the requirements of s.21(4) are met, because at the time when the cause of action arose and at the time when the claim form was issued, Y & Co was the charterer by demise.[138]

3. The circumstances are the same as in Illustration 2, except that A brings a claim *in rem* against another ship beneficially owned at the time of the issue of the proceedings by Y & Co. The court has jurisdiction.[139]

4. The circumstances are the same as in Illustration 2, except that A brings a claim *in rem* against another ship of which Y & Co is, at the time of issue of the proceedings, the charterer by demise. The court has no jurisdiction.[140]

5. A collision occurs on the high seas between A's ship and X's ship. After the collision, X's ship is transferred to Y. A then issues a claim form *in rem* against that ship and serves it on the ship in England. The court has jurisdiction.[141]

6. The circumstances are the same as in Illustration 5, except that A issues a claim form against another ship beneficially owned at the time of the issue by X and serves it on that ship in England.   **13–038**

---

[135] The statutory provision would be s.20 of the Senior Courts Act 1981 together with such other statutory provisions as may be relevant. Common law rules which have the effect of implementing the Arrest Convention would be covered by para.6(b). If the "field" to which the Convention relates is regarded as being restricted to claims in rem against ships, proceedings in which the res is something other than a ship would have to comply with the requirements of Sch.4. In salvage cases, Rule 3(g) of Sch.4 would be relevant; in other cases, Rule 3(h)(ii) might possibly be applicable.

[136] *The Jupiter (No.2)* [1925] P. 69 (CA). As to notifying the consul of the State to which the ship belongs, see CPR, r.61.5(5).

[137] *The St Merriel* [1963] P. 247.

[138] Senior Courts Act 1981, s.21(4).

[139] Senior Courts Act 1981, s.21(4).

[140] *The I Congreso del Partido* [1978] Q.B. 500, 537–542, reversed on other grounds [1983] 1 A.C. 244.

[141] Senior Courts Act 1981, s.21(3).

The court has jurisdiction, even though X habitually resides abroad and has no place of business in England.[142]

7. A's Spanish ship collides with an oil jetty in the River Thames because of the negligent navigation of the *Banco*, a British ship belonging to X. The oil catches fire and A is faced with claims amounting to several million pounds from those who suffered damage in the collision. A brings an Admiralty action *in rem* against the *Banco* and six sister ships owned by X. The court sets aside the service of the claim form on the six sister ships.[143]

8. A, the owner of cargo damaged while carried on a ship belonging to (or demise chartered by) X & Co, brings a claim *in rem* under the Senior Courts Act 1981. The claim form is served on the ship in an English port, but the ship is not arrested because contractual security is given by X & Co, a company domiciled in a State to which the Brussels I Regulation applies. X & Co challenges the jurisdiction of the court. On the facts of the case the court does not have jurisdiction under Arts 5–24 of the Brussels I Regulation. Since the ship was not arrested, the court has no jurisdiction to hear the action under the Brussels Arrest Convention.[144]

9. The circumstances are the same as in Illustration 8, but the ship is arrested. Although the court does not have jurisdiction under the Brussels I Regulation, it does have jurisdiction under the Brussels Arrest Convention.[145]

10. The circumstances are the same as in Illustration 8, but X & Co puts up security by means of a bail bond. The court has jurisdiction to determine the claim because, by giving bail, X & Co is deemed to have submitted to the court's jurisdiction.[146]

11. A ship owned by the United States is damaged in Rio de Janeiro harbour as a result of a collision with a ship owned by X & Co, a company domiciled in Italy (a State to which the Brussels I Regulation applies). The United States Government brings proceedings *in rem* in England to obtain damages, serving the claim form in an English port on the ship owned by X & Co. The ship could have been arrested, but is not, since security is given. On the facts of the case, the English court does not have jurisdiction under the provisions of Arts 5–24 of the Brussels I Regulation; nevertheless, it has jurisdiction to hear the proceedings, since it has jurisdiction under Art.1(1)(b) of the Brussels Collision Convention of 1952.[147]

12. A, the owners of cargo carried in a ship owned by X & Co, a Polish shipping company, alleges that in the course of the voyage the cargo was contaminated. X & Co starts proceedings against A in the Netherlands for a declaration of non-liability. A issues English proceedings *in rem* under the Senior Courts Act 1981, the claim form is served and the ship is arrested. Although the court's jurisdiction is derived from the Brussels Arrest Convention, the court must decline jurisdiction under Art.27 of the Brussels I Regulation.[148]

---

[142] *ibid.* s.21(4)(7).

[143] *The Banco* [1971] P. 137 (CA).

[144] *The Deichland* [1990] 1 Q.B. 361 (CA) (decided under the Brussels Convention).

[145] *ibid.*

[146] *The Prinsengracht* [1993] 1 Lloyd's Rep. 41.

[147] *The Po* [1991] 2 Lloyd's Rep. 206 (CA) (decided under the Brussels Convention).

[148] Case C–406/92 *The Tatry* [1994] E.C.R. I–5439; [1999] Q.B. 515. The case was decided on the basis of the Brussels Convention and before Poland became party to the Lugano Convention and subsequently joined the European Union (and became subject to the Brussels I Regulation). The result would still be the same.

CHAPTER 14

FOREIGN JUDGMENTS[1]

---

[1] See Patchett, *Recognition of Commercial Judgments and Awards in the Commonwealth* (1984), Pt I; Read, *Recognition and Enforcement of Foreign Judgments* (1938); Piggott, *Foreign Judgments* (1908); Briggs & Rees, *Civil Jurisdiction and Judgments* (5th ed. 2009), Ch.7; Barnett, *Res Judicata, Estoppel and Foreign Judgments* (2001); Schlosser (2000) 284 *Receuil des Cours* 9, pp.31–53, 200–214; Restatement, Ch.5; Von Mehren, *Adjudicatory Authority in Private International Law: A Comparative Study* (2007); Briggs, *Agreements on Jurisdiction and Choice of Law* (2008), Ch.9; Restatement Third, *Foreign Relations Law*, 1987, ss.481–483; Scoles, Hay, Borchers and Symeonides, Ch.24. Proposals at the Hague Conference for a worldwide Convention on jurisdiction and the enforcement of judgments foundered, and the resulted only in a limited Convention on Choice of Court Agreements which will, even if brought into force in England, have very little impact upon the recognition of foreign judgments in England. Art.8 of the Convention will establish that a judgment given by a court designated by an exclusive choice of court agreement may be denied recognition and enforcement only on the limited grounds set out, principally in Art.9. However, Art.9(1) provides for non-recognition if "the agreement was null and void under the law of the State of the chosen court, unless the chosen court has determined that the agreement is valid": a rule in these terms has no direct counterpart in the common law on the recognition of judgments. On the Hague Conference process, see Spigelman (2009) 83 A.L.J. 386; Garnett (2009) 5 J. Priv. Int. L. 161. For a response to the failure of the process see American Law Institute, *Recognition and Enforcement of Foreign Judgments: Analysis and Proposed Federal Statute* (2006), on which, and on US law generally, see Silberman (2008) 19 King's L.J. 235. This Chapter deals with judgments of foreign municipal courts. International tribunals set up by treaty are variously described as courts and arbitral tribunals, but their judgments or awards do not fall within the scope of this chapter. See below, Rule 72 (International Centre for Settlement of Investment Disputes); and Schachter (1960) 54 A.J.I.L. 1, 12–14; Schreuer (1975) 24 I.C.L.Q. 153; Giardina (1979) *Recueil des Cours*, IV, p.233.

1. INTRODUCTORY

14R–001 **Rule 41—A judgment of a court of a foreign country (hereinafter referred to as a foreign judgment) has no direct operation in England but may**

(1) **be enforceable by claim or counterclaim at common law or under statute, or**

(2) **be recognised as a defence to a claim or as conclusive of an issue in a claim.**

Comment

14–002 **The distinction between enforcement and recognition.** A foreign judgment has no direct operation in England. It cannot be immediately enforced by execution. This follows from the circumstance that the operation of legal systems is, in general, territorially circumscribed. Nevertheless, a foreign judgment may be recognised or enforced in England. It is plain that, while a court must recognise every foreign judgment which it enforces, it need not enforce every foreign judgment which it recognises.[2]

14–003 Such questions may arise in various ways but may be grouped into three categories. In the first place, the person in whose favour such a judgment is pronounced may seek to have that judgment executed or otherwise carried out as against the person against whom it is given. The claimant is then seeking to *enforce* the judgment. The case is not different when the plaintiff in the original or foreign proceedings, being subsequently made a defendant in English proceedings in the same or a related matter, sets up the foreign judgment by way of counterclaim or other cross-proceedings of a positive sort. Not every type of judgment is capable of enforcement in this way. A judgment dismissing a claim or counterclaim is obviously not capable of enforcement, unless it orders the unsuccessful party to pay costs, as it frequently does; nor is a declaratory judgment, e.g. one declaring the status of a person or the title to a thing; nor is a decree of divorce. There may, however, be orders ancillary to a decree of divorce which, because they order the payment of money, are capable of enforcement. Examples are an order that the husband should pay maintenance to his wife, or vice versa, or that the unsuccessful party should pay the other's costs.

14–004 A judgment *in rem* determining the title to a foreign immovable is equally obviously incapable of enforcement in England. A foreign judgment *in rem* decreeing the sale of a ship or other chattel to meet the claim does not normally require enforcement in England, because this can usually be satisfied out of the proceeds of sale of the *res*, or out of the bail or other security which the owner gave to avoid the arrest of the *res*. But if the security given in the foreign court is insufficient, it has been held that an action *in rem* may be brought in England against the ship to enforce the foreign decree if it is necessary to complete the execution of the judgment, provided that the ship

---

[2] As Lord Rodger put it: "The logic of the law is that recognition is the necessary primary concern": *Clarke v Fennoscandia Ltd* [2007] UKHL 56, 2008 S.C. (HL) 122, [21].

remains the property of the judgment debtor at the time of arrest.[3] It has also been accepted that a foreign judgment which would not be entitled to be enforced in England as a judgment *in rem* may be given effect, and enforced, as a judgment *in personam* if it satisfies the distinct conditions for such enforcement, at least where to do so is consistent with the substance of the judgment.[4]

Secondly, the person in whose favour a judgment is given in a foreign country may seek on its basis merely to resist a claim here in the same or a connected matter. In this case the type of judgment involved is largely immaterial. For instance, A may sue X in England for a debt and X successfully defend the action by showing that the matter has already been litigated in a foreign court, which has found that the alleged debt does not exist and has in consequence given judgment for X.[5] In such a case the situation indeed is that a party to English proceedings is relying directly upon a foreign judgment, but he is doing so merely to establish a negative proposition and seeks that *recognition* alone be accorded to that judgment. There is no question of *enforcement*. Again, if a foreign judgment *in rem* decrees the sale of a ship or other chattel in favour of A, A may resist proceedings in England by the owner of the ship or chattel in reliance on the foreign judgment,[6] or he may bring a claim *in personam* for wrongful interference against one who denies his title. In neither case is he seeking to enforce the judgment; he is relying on the foreign judgment to prove his title, and the judgment is recognised *qua* an assignment of property rather than *qua* a judgment. For A is relying on the title created by the foreign judgment rather than on the judgment itself.[7]   **14–005**

Thirdly, the party against whom a judgment was given may seek to use that judgment, or the fact that he has satisfied that judgment, to resist a further claim by the party in whose favour the judgment was given. For example, a claimant may have brought proceedings in a foreign court but have obtained a judgment for less than he had sought. If he brings a second set of proceedings upon the same claim, the defendant may seek to rely on the foreign judgment in support of either of two answers to the claim. He may seek *recognition* of the judgment if it contained a discrete ruling in his favour dismissing part of the claim, just as in the previous example. But he may also rely upon the existence, or the satisfaction, of the judgment as a bar to further proceedings on the same claim,[8] or on a separate claim but which should have been advanced, if at all, in the proceedings in the foreign court.[9] This also involves *recognition* of a foreign judgment, but its effect is to treat the foreign judgment as a final adjudication of the issues which arose between the parties, and to preclude the bringing of further proceedings *ab initio*, as distinct from establishing that the findings in favour of the party relying on the foreign   **14–006**

---

[3] *The Despina GK* [1983] Q.B. 214; see also *The City of Mecca* (1879) 5 P.D. 28, reversed on other grounds (1881) 6 P.D. 106 (CA). See below, para.14–112.

[4] *Pattni v Ali* [2006] UKPC 51, [2007] 2 A.C. 85.

[5] *cf. Barber v Lamb* (1860) 8 C.B. (N.S.) 95.

[6] See *Castrique v Imrie* (1870) L.R. 4 H.L. 414.

[7] See below, para.14–110.

[8] *cf.* Civil Jurisdiction and Judgments Act 1982, s.34; *Republic of India v India Steamship Co Ltd* [1993] A.C. 410. See below, paras 14–041 *et seq.*

[9] *Henderson v Henderson* (1843) 3 Hare 100. See below, para.14–043.

judgment are conclusive upon issues which will arise for adjudication in the English proceedings.

14–007   **The bases of enforcement and recognition.** English courts have recognised and enforced foreign judgments from the 17th century onwards.[10] It was at one time supposed that the basis of this enforcement was to be found in the doctrine of comity. English judges believed that the law of nations required the courts of one country to assist those of any other, and they feared that if foreign judgments were not enforced in England, English judgments would not be enforced abroad.[11] But later this theory was superseded by what is called the doctrine of obligation, which was stated by Parke B. in *Russell v Smyth*[12] and *Williams v Jones*[13] and approved by Blackburn J. a generation later in *Godard v Gray*[14] and *Schibsby v Westenholz*[15] in the following words: "We think that . . . the true principle on which the judgments of foreign tribunals are enforced in England is . . . that the judgment of a court of competent jurisdiction over the defendant imposes a duty or obligation on the defendant to pay the sum for which judgment is given, which the courts in this country are bound to enforce; and consequently that anything which negatives that duty, or forms a legal excuse for not performing it, is a defence to the action."[16] It followed that provided the foreign court had jurisdiction to give the judgment according to the English rules of the conflict of laws, the judgment is conclusive in England (unless it is impeachable for reasons of fraud, public policy or the like) and not merely prima facie evidence of the defendant's liability as had at one time been supposed.[17]

14–008   In *Adams v Cape Industries Plc*[18] Scott J. accepted Blackburn J.'s restatement of the obligation doctrine as being the basis on which English courts would recognise and enforce foreign judgments *in personam*.[19] The Court of Appeal, however, gave some support to the idea that the obligation doctrine was purely theoretical, since it has no practical value in identifying the foreign judgments which give rise to the obligation. The Court of Appeal accepted that at common law foreign judgments were enforced, not through considerations of comity, but on the basis of the principle that a legal obligation arises to satisfy a judgment of a court of competent jurisdiction;[20] but in a later passage it also expressed the view that some notion of comity lay behind the recognition of judgments, but "this cannot be comity on an individual nation-to-nation basis, for our courts have never thought it necessary to investigate what reciprocal rights of enforcement are conceded by the foreign country, or

---

[10] See Sack in *Law, A Century of Progress*, 1835–1935 (1937), Vol.3, pp.342, 382–384. *cf.* Holdsworth, *History of English Law*, Vol.11, pp.270–273.
[11] See *Roach v Garvan* (1748) 1 Ves.Sen. 157, 159; *Wright v Simpson* (1802) 6 Ves. 714, 730; *Alves v Bunbury* (1814) 4 Camp. 28.
[12] (1842) 9 M. & W. 810, 819.
[13] (1845) 13 M. & W. 628, 633.
[14] (1870) L.R. 6 Q.B. 139, 149–150.
[15] (1870) L.R. 6 Q.B. 155.
[16] (1870) L.R. 6 Q.B. 155, 159. For criticism, see Ho (1997) 46 I.C.L.Q. 443.
[17] See below, Rule 48.
[18] [1990] Ch. 433 (Scott J. and CA).
[19] *ibid.* p.457.
[20] [1990] Ch. 433, 513. See also *Owens Bank Ltd v Bracco* [1992] 2 A.C. 443, 484.

to limit their exercise of jurisdiction to that which they would recognise in others. The most one can say is that the duty of positive law first identified in *Schibsby v Westenholz* ... must stem from an acknowledgement that the society of nations will work better if some foreign judgments are taken to create rights which supersede the underlying cause of action, and which may be directly enforced in countries where the defendant or his assets are to be found."[21]

In *Adams v Cape Industries Plc* the basis for the recognition of judgments **14–009** was considered to be relevant by the Court of Appeal in deciding the issue whether the federal court in Texas had jurisdiction under Rule 43(1) by virtue of the alleged presence of the judgment debtor in another State of the American Union, Illinois: was the relevant "country", for the purposes of the enforcement of the Texas court, the United States (in which event presence in Illinois would be regarded as giving the court jurisdiction) or Texas (in which event it would not be so regarded)? Scott J. took as the starting point the suggestion in *Schibsby v Westenholz*[22] that the basis of the jurisdiction of a foreign court over resident aliens was that they had the benefit of the protection of the laws of that country or owed temporary allegiance to it. Scott J. concluded that the relevant "country" was the United States because the source of authority of the Federal court was in the sovereign power which established it, namely the United States.[23] The Court of Appeal was sceptical about the application of the idea of "allegiance" as being the basis of the obligation, and saw the judgment debtor's duty to abide by the foreign judgment as deriving from the fact that "by going to a foreign place he invests himself by tacit consent with the rights and obligations stemming from the local laws as administered by the local court."[24] In the event, it was not necessary to decide this issue, because (like Scott J.) the Court of Appeal held that the judgment debtor had not been present or resident in Illinois; but the Court of Appeal indicated that if it had been necessary to decide the question, it would have agreed with Scott J. that the relevant "country" was the United States rather than Texas.

Judgments in insolvency proceedings. Where the foreign judgment is **14–010** given by a court exercising insolvency jurisdiction, the judgment may be enforced at common law, or registered under the Foreign Judgments (Reciprocal Enforcement) Act 1933,[25] as the case may be, if it satisfies the requirements of those schemes. But it has been held that effect may also be given to it outside the ordinary provisions of the law for the enforcement of foreign judgments, as these are explained in this Chapter, if the foreign court requests the English court to co-operate with its exercise of insolvency jurisdiction.

---

[21] [1990] Ch. 433, 552.

[22] (1870) L.R. 6 Q.B. 155, 161.

[23] [1990] Ch. 433, 490–491.

[24] *ibid.* at p.555.

[25] *New Cap Reinsurance Corp Ltd) v Grant* [2011] EWCA Civ 971, [2011] B.P.I.R. 1428. For the 1933 Act, see Rule 54, below. It is likely that the position under the Administration of Justice Act 1920 (as to which, see Rule 53, below) is the same.

The request for cooperation may be made pursuant to the Insolvency Act 1986,[26] the Cross-Border Insolvency Regulations 2006,[27] or under the general common law;[28] it may ask the English court to make orders which have the effect, as a matter of practicality, of treating the foreign order or request as though it were, as far as the defendant is concerned, enforceable as a foreign judgment.[29] In such a case, a defendant, not otherwise subject to the international jurisdiction of the foreign court in the sense of Rule 43 or 54,[30] may be deprived of the shield from being adversely affected which that fact would otherwise have afforded him, if the court were to exercise its discretion to cooperate with the foreign court. To put it another way, an order from a foreign court which would not qualify for enforcement under the rules which govern the enforcement of foreign judgments may still have an effect in England. These cases are dealt with in Chapter 30 below.

14–011   **Enforcement at common law.** A judgment creditor seeking to enforce a foreign judgment in England at common law cannot do so by direct execution of the judgment. He must bring an action on the foreign judgment.[31] But he can apply for summary judgment under what is now Part 24 of the Civil Procedure Rules 1998, previously Order 14 of the Rules of the Supreme Court, on the ground that the defendant has no real prospect of successfully defending the claim;[32] and if his application is successful, the defendant will

---

[26] Section 426: see para.30–107, below.

[27] SI 2006/1030, implementing the UNCITRAL Model Law, on which see further, para.30–353, below.

[28] *Cambridge Gas Transportation Corp v Official Committee of Unsecured Creditors of Navigator Holdings Plc* [2006] UKPC 26, [2007] 1 A.C. 508; *Re HIH Casualty and General Insurance Ltd* [2008] UKHL 21, [2008] 1 W.L.R. 852; *Rubin v Eurofinance SA* [2010] EWCA Civ 895, [2011] Ch. 133; *New Cap Reinsurance Corp Ltd v Grant* [2011] EWCA Civ 971, [2011] B.P.I.R. 1428.

[29] *Cambridge Gas Transportation Corp v Official Committee of Unsecured Creditors of Navigator Holdings Plc* [2006] UKPC 26, [2007] 1 A.C. 508 (request for cancellation and reissue of shares: common law); *Re HIH Casualty and General Insurance Ltd* [2008] UKHL 21, [2008] 1 W.L.R. 852 (request for remission of assets: common law, also under Insolvency Act 1986 s.426); *Rubin v Eurofinance SA* [2010] EWCA Civ 895, [2011] Ch. 133 (request for enforcement of judgment for repayment of preferences: at common law; effect of Cross-Border Insolvency Regulations 2006, SI 2006/1030, not decided); *New Cap Reinsurance Corp Ltd (In Liquidation) v Grant* [2011] EWCA Civ 971 (order for return of preferential payment: at common law and under 1933 Act: the foreign court had seen fit to "proceed with confidence" that the English court would accede to the request: *New Cap Reinsurance Corp Ltd v Grant* [2009] NSWSC 662, (2009) 257 A.L.R. 740).

[30] It is unclear whether the participation of a defendant in insolvency proceedings before a foreign court, by the submission of a claim or otherwise, may be found to have submitted to the jurisdiction of that court if it makes orders against him which do not derive directly from the claim which he has submitted: see *New Cap Reinsurance Corp Ltd (In Liquidation) v Grant* [2011] EWCA Civ 971; *Ex p. Robertson, In re Morton* (1875) 22 Eq. 733.

[31] The judgment creditor may serve a statutory demand in terms of the foreign judgment, just as with any other unpaid debt. But if the validity of the debt is contested, the issue will have to be resolved as in an ordinary action to establish the enforceability of the judgment and hence the existence, as a matter of English law, of the debt.

[32] *Grant v Easton* (1883) 13 Q.B.D. 302 (CA); *Colt Industries Inc v Sarlie (No.2)* [1966] 1 W.L.R. 1287 (CA). See below, para.14–028.

not be allowed to defend at all.[33] The speed and simplicity of this procedure, coupled with the tendency of English judges narrowly to circumscribe the defences that may be pleaded to a claim on a foreign judgment, mean that foreign judgments are in practice enforceable at common law much more easily than they are in many foreign countries.[34]

Enforcement under statute. A foreign judgment may be enforceable **14–012** under statute by a more direct process of registration. The first step in this direction was taken as long ago as 1801, when the Crown Debts Act provided for the reciprocal enrolment and enforcement of English and Irish Exchequer orders and Chancery decrees. This early innovation was broadened and applied also in relation to Scotland by the Judgments Extension Act 1868. This enactment dispensed with the necessity for an action upon a judgment to which it applied. A certificate of such a judgment obtained in one part of the United Kingdom was registrable as of right in another such part, and thereupon acquired exactly the force and effect of a local judgment.

The Judgments Extension Act 1868[35] was followed by the Administration **14–013** of Justice Act 1920 ("the 1920 Act") wherein provision is made for the reciprocal enforcement of the judgments of superior courts within the United Kingdom, on the one hand, and corresponding courts of other territories within the Commonwealth on the other.[36] Before the 1920 Act could be extended to a country in the Commonwealth Her Majesty had to be satisfied that reciprocal provisions had been made in the country concerned for the enforcement therein of United Kingdom judgments;[37] and it has been extended by Order in Council to very many such countries.[38] Registration of a foreign judgment under the 1920 Act is discretionary and not as of right, since it can be refused unless the registering court considers that it is "in all the circumstances of the case . . . just and convenient that the judgment should be enforced in the United Kingdom."[39] Registration is, moreover, not to be ordered if the original court acted without jurisdiction (though no attempt is made to give a comprehensive definition of this term), or if the defendant establishes any of a limited number of defences which are very similar to those available at common law.[40] Where, however, a judgment has

---

[33] As to any question of security for costs, it would normally be open to the defendant to make an application for security. However, if the foreign court plainly had jurisdiction over the defendant, and the issue in the English proceedings is whether the defendant can raise a substantive defence to the recognition and enforcement, the defendant is the effective claimant, and in principle, an order for security should not be made against the claimant: *Relational LLC v Hodges* [2011] EWCA Civ 774, [24].

[34] For a comparative study on the recognition and enforcement of foreign judgments see Delaume, *Law and Practice of Transnational Contracts* (1988), Ch.7. See also Report of the Foreign Judgments (Reciprocal Enforcement) Committee, Cmd. 4213 (1932), paras 2, 9, 10, 14.

[35] The Inferior Courts Judgment Extension Act 1882 provided for enforcement of judgments of lesser tribunals. The 1868 and 1882 Acts are replaced by the Civil Jurisdiction and Judgments Act 1982, Pt II.

[36] See Rule 53.

[37] 1920 Act, s.14.

[38] See below, para.14–181.

[39] s.9(1).

[40] s.9(2).

been duly registered it is to have the same force and effect as a judgment of the registering court.[41] Although the person entitled under a judgment registrable under the Act is not deprived of the possibility of suing thereon at common law, the employment of this alternative is discouraged by a provision that it should ordinarily involve sacrifice of the costs of the claim.[42] The Act still remains generally in force[43] but its application to territories to which it had not already been applied was excluded by an Order in Council made under the Foreign Judgments (Reciprocal Enforcement) Act 1933,[44] the intention being that the wider scheme elaborated in the latter enactment should ultimately replace that of the 1920 Act.

14–014   The basis of the system of enforcement of foreign judgments introduced by the Foreign Judgments (Reciprocal Enforcement) Act 1933 ("the 1933 Act") is still reciprocity of treatment. But the scheme of the 1933 Act is wider than that of the 1920 Act in that it is capable of application to countries completely foreign in the political sense. So far it has been applied only to Austria, Belgium, France, Germany, Israel, Italy, the Netherlands, Norway and Suriname among countries of this category and, of countries within the Commonwealth, only to Australia, Canada, India, Pakistan, Tonga, Guernsey, Jersey and the Isle of Man.[45] But as regards Austria, Belgium, France, Germany, Italy, and the Netherlands, the 1933 Act is almost entirely superseded by Chapter III of the Brussels I Regulation,[46] and in the case of Norway, by Pt I of the Civil Jurisdiction and Judgments Act 1982.[47] The 1933 Act permits the registration of judgments of courts of countries to which it applies within a period of six years of their pronouncement.[48] Registration is available as of right instead of merely at discretion as under the 1920 Act, provided that any judgment sought to be registered has not been wholly satisfied and is enforceable by execution in the country of the original court.[49] Registration, however, may or must be set aside if the judgment debtor shows certain grounds and execution may not issue until the time has passed within which an application for setting it aside may be made.[50] The 1933 Act contains detailed rules[51] on when foreign courts are deemed to have jurisdiction for the purposes of its provisions; these rules are modelled very closely on those of the common law. The grounds for the setting aside of a registered judgment correspond, broadly, to those upon which a foreign judgment is impeachable at common law or upon which registration of a judgment under the 1920 Act is to be refused and are discussed in detail hereafter.[52] The effect of registration is in general, as under the earlier Acts, to assimilate a foreign judgment

---

[41] s.9(3).

[42] s.9(5).

[43] For the territories to which the Act applies, see below, para.14–181.

[44] See the Foreign Judgments (Reciprocal Enforcement) Act 1933, s.7(1), and S.R. & O. 1933/1073. And see para.14–175, below.

[45] See Rule 54.

[46] Council Regulation (EC) 44/2001, [2001] O.J. L12. The Regulation took effect from March 1, 2002. See further, Rule 55, below.

[47] As amended by SI 2009/3131; see Rule 55, below.

[48] s.2(1).

[49] *ibid.* proviso.

[50] ss.4(1), 2(2), proviso.

[51] s.4(2).

[52] See paras 14R–173 *et seq.*

to a judgment of the registering court.[53] No proceedings upon the judgment itself other than proceedings for its registration may be brought in any court in the United Kingdom.[54]

Judgments from courts in Europe[55] are recognised and enforced according to an increasingly complex set of schemes. The Civil Jurisdiction and Judgments Act 1982 provides for the recognition and enforcement of judgments emanating from Scotland, Northern Ireland, and Gibraltar.[56] Where they are given in civil and commercial matters, judgments from Member States of the European Union are now governed by Chapter III of the Brussels I Regulation,[57] having earlier been provided for by Part I of the Civil Jurisdiction and Judgments Act 1982, which gave effect to the Brussels Convention on jurisdiction and judgments in civil and commercial matters.[58] The Brussels I Regulation took effect on March 1, 2002, save in respect of the States which acceded to membership of the EU after that date.[59] Its transitional provisions[60] mean that the Regulation may also apply to the recognition and enforcement of judgments given after the date on which the Regulation took effect in relation to the State in question, even though the proceedings were instituted in the courts of the State of origin prior to that date. Judgments from Iceland, Norway and Switzerland, which are parties (together with the European Union[61]) to the Lugano Convention take effect under Part I of the Civil Jurisdiction and Judgments Act 1982, though the substantive provisions of the Lugano Convention are practically indistinguishable from those of the Brussels I Regulation. As regards judgments of States which are parties to or bound by any of these schemes, the system under the 1933 Act is effectively superseded. The common basis of these European systems is that, in general, it is for the court in which the judgment is given to determine whether it has jurisdiction under the relevant instrument, and it is not generally open to the English court to make that assessment for itself in the proceedings for enforcement. The judgment may be impeached only on a limited number of

14–015

---

[53] s.2(2).

[54] s.6. See *New Cap Reinsurance Corp Ltd (In Liquidation) v Grant* [2011] EWCA Civ 971, [2011] B.P.I.R. 1428.

[55] But judgments from Andorra, Liechtenstein, and Monaco, and from certain states in eastern Europe, remain outside these statutory schemes and are governed by the common law.

[56] See Rule 56, below.

[57] Council Regulation (EC) 44/2001.

[58] For the Brussels Convention, see Ch.11, above. For the purpose of recognition of judgments it is effectively superseded by the Brussels I Regulation, save in respect of those territories of Member States to which the Brussels Convention had been applied or extended, but which are not within the definition of "Member State" for the purpose of the Brussels I Regulation: see further below, para.14–199.

[59] Also, the Regulation did not initially apply to Denmark, which had exercised its right to opt out, with the result that the Brussels Convention had continued to apply to judgments from that country. However, by an Agreement given effect in the United Kingdom by SI 2007/1655, the Regulation was applied to Denmark with effect from July 1, 2007, and Art.1(3) of the Regulation has ceased to have effect.

[60] Art.66(2).

[61] The European Union, rather than the Member States, is party to the Lugano Convention. This is different from the position under the 1988 (original) Lugano Convention, to which only States were party.

grounds; enforcement is by way of registration;[62] and the schemes extend beyond final money judgments to encompass non-money judgments (such as injunctions) and interlocutory judgments. Indeed, the recent procedure for a European Enforcement Order,[63] will simplify the process even further, by removing the courts of the State in which enforcement is sought from the procedure of enforcement.

14–016   The European Communities (Enforcement of Community Judgments) Order 1972[64] makes provision for the enforcement by registration in the United Kingdom of "community judgments," i.e. decisions or orders of the European Court of Justice and of certain other organs of the European Communities.

14–017   The State Immunity Act 1978[65] makes provision for the recognition of judgments rendered against the United Kingdom in countries which are parties to the European Convention on State Immunity.

14–018   **Common law and statute.** The statutes which deal with enforcement of foreign judgments are of limited geographical application and the judgments of very many foreign countries are not within their scope. There thus remains a considerable area within which enforcement at common law is the only process possible, and it remains of practical importance because several important foreign countries (including the United States) do not yet have treaties with the United Kingdom for the reciprocal enforcement and recognition of judgments and thus do not come within the statutory schemes.

14–019   **Scope and arrangement of this chapter.** The arrangement of this chapter is as follows: it is divided into four sections. The first contains the present introductory rule. The second deals with enforcement and recognition of foreign judgments at common law, including the jurisdiction of foreign courts to pronounce judgments capable of enforcement (or recognition)[66] in England, and the extent to which a foreign judgment is conclusive in England and the extent to which it may be impeached in English proceedings in which its recognition or enforcement is sought.[67] The third section deals with enforcement and recognition under statute, by which is meant the 1920, 1933 and 1982 Acts, as well as the Brussels I Regulation and the Lugano Convention,[68] and enforcement of Community judgments and foreign judgments against the Crown.[69] The fourth section deals with the effect of the Protection of Trading Interests Act 1980 on the enforceability of foreign judgments for multiple damages.[70] The chapter does not deal, however, except incidentally, with the effect given in England to foreign judgments relating to the administration of

---

[62] See below, paras 14–224 and 14–239.
[63] See below, Rule 55(2).
[64] SI 1972/1590; below, Rule 57.
[65] ss.18–19; below, Rule 58.
[66] Rules 42 to 47.
[67] Rules 48 to 52.
[68] Rules 53 to 56.
[69] Rules 57 to 58.
[70] Rule 59.

estates, foreign decrees of dissolution or nullity of marriage, foreign adjudications in bankruptcy[71] or orders for the winding up of companies, or foreign maintenance orders, which because of their special character are dealt with in the context of the matters to which they relate.[72]

2. ENFORCEMENT AND RECOGNITION AT COMMON LAW

A. *Enforcement and recognition*

RULE 42—(1) Subject to the Exceptions hereinafter mentioned and to Rule 62 (international conventions), a foreign judgment[73] *in personam* given by the court of a foreign country with jurisdiction to give that judgment in accordance with the principles set out in Rules 43 to 46, and which is not impeachable under any of Rules 49 to 54, may be enforced by a claim or counterclaim for the amount due under it if the judgment is   14R–020

   (a)   **for a debt, or definite sum of money[74] (not being a sum payable in respect of taxes or other charges of a like nature[75] or in respect of a fine or other penalty[76]); and**

   (b)   **final and conclusive,[77]**

---

[71] For the relationship between the material examined in this Chapter and judgments given by foreign courts exercising insolvency jurisdiction see para.14–010, above, and paras 30–109, below.

[72] See Rules 86–90 (divorce and nullity); 102 (maintenance orders); 144 (administration of estates); 179 (winding up); 188–194 (bankruptcy).

[73] As to what is a judgment, see *Berliner Industriebank AG v Jost* [1971] 2 Q.B. 463 (CA) (ascertainment of a debt in German bankruptcy proceedings); *Midland International Trade Services Ltd v Sudairy, Financial Times*, May 2, 1990 (judgment of court as distinct from administrative tribunal).

[74] *Sadler v Robins* (1808) 1 Camp. 253. The historical explanation of this limitation is that the form of action appropriate for the enforcement of a foreign judgment was originally debt, though some authorities allow assumpsit. The rule that enforcement of foreign judgments is confined to final judgments for a fixed sum in money was repudiated by the Supreme Court of Canada in *Pro-Swing Inc v Elta Golf Inc* [2006] 2 S.C.R. 612 (on which see also *Minera Aquiline Argentina SA v IMA Exploration Inc* [2007] 10 W.W.R. 648 (BCCA); *USA v Yemec* (2010) 320 D.L.R. (4th) 96, and it was rejected in Jersey (*Brunei Investment Agency v Fidelis Nominees Ltd* [2008] Jersey L.R. 337). However, if the non-money judgment of the foreign court is entitled to recognition as *res judicata*, the fact that it cannot be enforced as a debt may be of limited practical significance, for if proceedings which have to be brought on the original cause of action can be cut short by showing the issues of substance to be *res judicata*, with only the question of remedy left for the original decision of the English court, the technical unenforceability of the foreign judgment is merely a detail.

[75] *Government of India v Taylor* [1955] A.C. 491, 514; *Rossano v Manufacturers' Life Insurance Co Ltd* [1963] 2 Q.B. 352, 376–378; *Att–Gen for Canada v Schulze*, (1901) 9 S.L.T. 4; *USA v Harden* (1963) 41 D.L.R. (2d) 721 (Sup Ct Can); *Commissioner of Taxes v McFarland*, 1965 (1) S.A. 470. See Stoel (1967) 16 I.C.L.Q. 663.

[76] *Huntington v Attrill* [1893] A.C. 150 (PC); *US v Inkley* [1989] Q.B. 255 (CA). See Restatement, s.120.

[77] *Nouvion v Freeman* (1889) 15 App.Cas. 1; *Plummer v Woodburne* (1825) 4 B. & C. 625; *Paul v Roy* (1852) 15 Beav. 433; *Patrick v Shedden* (1853) 2 E. & B. 14; *Frayes v Worms* (1861) 10 C.B.(N.S.) 149; *Blohn v Desser* [1962] 2 Q.B. 116; *Berliner Industriebank AG v Jost* [1971] 2 Q.B. 463 (CA); *Gauthier v Routh* (1842) 6 U.C.Q.B.(O.S.) 602; *Graham v Harrison* (1889) 6 Man.L.R. 210; Read, pp.64–86; Restatement, ss.107–109.

but not otherwise.

Provided that a foreign judgment may be final and conclusive, though it is subject to an appeal, and though an appeal against it is actually pending in the foreign country where it was given.[78]

(2) A foreign judgment given by the court of a foreign country with jurisdiction to give that judgment in accordance with the principles set out in Rules 43 to 46, which is not impeachable under any of Rules 49 to 54 and which is final and conclusive on the merits,[79] **is entitled to recognition at common law and may be relied on in proceedings in England.**[80]

(3) No proceedings may be be brought by a person on a cause of action in respect of a judgment which has been given in his favour in proceedings between the same parties or their privies in a court in another part of the United Kingdom or in a court in an overseas country unless that judgment is not enforceable according to clause (1), or not entitled to recognition according to clause (2), of this Rule.[81]

This Rule must be read subject to Rule 59.

COMMENT

14–021   **Introduction.** Until after 1933 there was no mode of directly enforcing a foreign judgment in England (unless it were a Scottish or Northern Irish judgment or the judgment of a court of some country of the Commonwealth overseas[82]) by execution, but a foreign judgment for a debt or definite sum of money might be enforced by an action *in personam* on the part of the person in whose favour the judgment was given (generally[83] the plaintiff in the foreign proceedings) for the sum due under the judgment. Enforcement was not dependent on the reciprocal treatment of English judgments in the foreign country. Nor was it necessary that the judgment should be given as the result of investigation of the merits of the case; if the court were one which in the view of English law had jurisdiction over the defendant, and he failed to defend, the court's judgment might be enforced in England as fully as if he

---

[78] *Nouvion v Freeman* (1889) 15 App.Cas. 1, 13; *Nouvion v Freeman* (1887) 37 Ch.D. 244, 255 (CA); *Scott v Pilkington* (1862) 2 B. & S. 11; *Colt Industries Inc v Sarlie (No.2)* [1966] 1 W.L.R. 1287; *Barned's Banking Co Ltd v Reynolds* (1875) 36 U.C.Q.B. 256; *Howland v Codd* (1894) 9 Man.L.R. 435; *Wilcox v Wilcox* (1914) 16 D.L.R. 491 (Man CA); *Campbell v Morgan* [1919] 1 W.W.R. 644 (Man); *Pan American World Airways v Varghese* (1984) 7 D.L.R. (4th) 499, app. dismissed (1985) 15 D.L.R. (4th) 768 (Ont CA); *Four Embarcadero Center Venture v Mr Greenjeans* (1988) 64 O.R. (2d) 746, app. dismissed (1988) 65 O.R. (2d) 160 (CA).

[79] *Harris v Quine* (1869) L.R. 4 Q.B. 653; *Black-Clawson International Ltd v Papierwerke Waldhof-Aschaffenburg AG* [1975] A.C. 591; *The Sennar (No.2)* [1985] 1 W.L.R. 490 (HL); *Tracomin SA v Sudan Oil Seeds Co Ltd (No.1)* [1983] 1 W.L.R. 662, affirmed [1983] 1 W.L.R. 1026 (CA); contrast *Charm Maritime Inc v Kyriakou* [1987] 1 Lloyd's Rep. 433, 441, 450 (CA); *Desert Sun Loan Corp v Hill* [1996] 2 All E.R. 847 (CA).

[80] See Read, pp.101–106, and Gutteridge (1932) 13 B.Y.I.L. 49, 60–64.

[81] Civil Jurisdiction and Judgments Act 1982, s.34.

[82] See Rules 53, 56, below.

[83] But not invariably: an order for payment of costs made against an unsuccessful claimant may be enforced under this Rule.

had defended the case on the merits.[84] The foregoing remains the law in the sense that a foreign judgment is still enforceable by action, but since 1933 the more direct enforcement of certain foreign judgments has become possible under the 1933 and 1982 Acts and the Brussels I Regulation and the Lugano Convention.

Clause (1) of the Rule. For a claim to be brought to enforce a foreign   **14–022** judgment, the judgment must be for a definite sum of money, which expression includes a final order for costs, e.g. in a divorce suit.[85] It must order X, the defendant in the English action, to pay to A, the claimant, a definite and actually ascertained[86] sum of money; but if a mere arithmetical calculation is required for the ascertainment of the sum it will be treated as being ascertained;[87] if, however, the judgment orders him to do anything else, e.g. specifically perform a contract, it will not support an action,[88] though it may be *res judicata* as to the issues of substance, with the consequence that there may be summary judgment as to liability on a fresh claim brought on the original cause of action.[89] The judgment must further be for a sum other than a sum payable in respect of taxes or the like, or in respect of a fine or other penalty. It is well settled[90] that an English court will not entertain an action for the enforcement, either directly or indirectly, of a penal[91] or revenue[92], or other public[93] law of a foreign country. Since "the essential nature and real foundation of a cause of action are not changed by recovering judgment upon it,"[94] it follows that the court cannot entertain an action for the enforcement, either directly or indirectly,[95] of a foreign judgment ordering the payment of taxes,[96] fines or other contributions or penalties. A penalty in this sense normally means a sum payable to the State, and not to a private claimant,[97] so that an award of punitive or exemplary damages is not penal.[98] But it is possible that an award of multiple damages, e.g. in an anti-trust action, might

---

[84] *Russell v Smyth* (1842) 9 M. & W. 810; *Boyle v Victoria Yukon Trading Co* (1902) 9 B.C.R. 213.

[85] *Russell v Smyth* (1842) 9 M. & W. 810; *cf. Ruf v Walter* [1990] 6 W.W.R. 661 (Sask).

[86] *Sadler v Robins* (1808) 1 Camp. 253. Compare *Hall v Odber* (1809) 11 East 118.

[87] *Beatty v Beatty* [1924] 1 K.B. 807 (CA).

[88] *cf. Church of Scientology of California v Miller, The Times*, October 15, 1987, affirmed *The Times*, October 23, 1987 (CA); and see n.85, above.

[89] Wolff, s.243; see *Duke v Andler* [1932] 4 D.L.R. 529 (Sup Ct Can). But see White (1982) 9 Sydney L.Rev. 630.

[90] See Rule 3.

[91] See, e.g. *Huntington v Attrill* [1893] A.C. 150 (PC); *US v Inkley* [1989] Q.B. 255 (CA).

[92] See, e.g. *Government of India v Taylor* [1955] A.C. 491.

[93] *United States Securities and Exchange Commission v Manterfield* [2009] EWCA Civ 27, [2010] 1 W.L.R. 172 (not enforcement of penal or public law).

[94] *Wisconsin v Pelican Insurance Co*, 127 U.S. 265, 292 (1888). See Hay, Borchers and Symeonides pp.1476–1478, for subsequent developments in the United States. For subsequent development and analysis, see Finch (2002) 86 Minn.L.R. 497.

[95] *Rossano v Manufacturers' Life Insurance Co Ltd* [1963] 2 Q.B. 352, 376–378.

[96] *Att-Gen for Canada v Schulze*, (1901) 9 S.L.T. 4; *USA v Harden* (1963) 41 D.L.R. (2d) 721 (Sup Ct Can); *Commissioner of Taxes v McFarland*, 1965 (1) S.A. 470.

[97] See also *Robb Evans v European Bank Ltd* (2004) 61 N.S.W.L.R. 75 (applying this principle to the category of other public laws).

[98] *cf. S.A. Consortium General Textiles v Sun & Sand Agencies Ltd* [1978] Q.B. 279, 309, *per* Lord Denning M.R., *obiter* (a case on the 1933 Act).

nevertheless be regarded as penal at common law.[99] If the purpose of the damages as awarded by the foreign court is to punish the defendant, enforcement of the judgment may be found to be against English public policy, with which the rule against enforcing foreign penal laws will overlap.[100] If the foreign judgment imposes a fine on the defendant and also orders him to pay compensation to the injured party (called the "*partie civile*" in French proceedings), the latter part of the judgment can be severed from the former and enforced in England.[101]

14–023   No foreign judgment will be recognised or enforced in England at common law unless it is "final and conclusive." The expression is repetitive but, having been rendered familiar by many judicial statements, is reproduced in the 1933 Act.[102] The test of finality is the treatment of the judgment by the foreign tribunal as a *res judicata*. "In order to establish that [a final and conclusive] judgment has been pronounced, it must be shown that in the court by which it was pronounced, it conclusively, finally, and forever established the existence of the debt of which it is sought to be made conclusive evidence in this country, so as to make it *res judicata* between the parties":[103] it follows that the possibility of an appeal to a higher court does not alter the finality of the judgment.[104] A foreign judgment which is liable to be abrogated or varied by the court which pronounced it is not a final judgment.[105] But a default judgment may, in this sense, be final and conclusive, even though it is liable to be set aside in the very court which rendered it.[106] Otherwise, the clearer the

---

[99] *cf. Jones v Jones* (1889) 22 Q.B.D. 425 (a case not involving a foreign judgment). The effect of the Protection of Trading Interests Act 1980 is that such judgments are not enforceable at common law or otherwise, though where there are judgments on separate causes of action, a judgment under one for compensatory damages may still be enforced notwithstanding that judgment under another is for multiple damages and so unenforceable: *Lewis v Eliades* [2003] EWCA Civ 1758, [2004] 1 W.L.R. 692: see Rule 59.

[100] In *Schnabel v Lui* [2002] NSWSC 15, the court regarded (at [177]) damages which had been awarded to punish the defendant for his wrongdoing as being penal, and enforcement as precluded by Rule 3. The precise application of Rule 3 in these circumstances is therefore unsettled. But Art.11 of the Hague Convention on Choice of Court Agreements (above, n.1) provides for the non-enforcement of judgments "if and to the extent that the judgment awards damages, including exemplary or punitive damages, that do not compensate a party for actual loss or harm suffered".

[101] *Raulin v Fischer* [1911] 2 K.B. 93; *cf. Black v Yates* [1992] Q.B. 526.

[102] s.1(2)(a), as substituted by 1982 Act, Sch.10, para.1.

[103] *Nouvion v Freeman* (1889) 15 App. Cas. 1, 9.

[104] A judgment is also still final if separate (but related) proceedings which may be brought in same court may result in a judgment which may then be set off against, or otherwise used to abate the sums due under, the original judgment: *Bussoleno Ltd v Kelly* [2011] IEHC 220.

[105] *Nouvion v Freeman* (1889) 15 App. Cas. 1, 13; *Re Macartney* [1921] 1 Ch. 522, 531, 532; *Westfal-Larsen AS v Ikerigi Naviera SA* [1983] 1 All E.R. 382, 389; *cf. Charm Maritime Inc v Kyriakou* [1987] 1 Lloyd's Rep. 433, 442, 450 (CA); see also *M'Donnell v M'Donnell* [1921] 2 I.R. 148; and in the context of judgments on arbitration awards, *Svenska Petroleum Exploration AB v Government of Republic of Lithuania* [2005] EWHC 9 (Comm.), [2005] 1 Lloyd's Rep. 515.

[106] *Vanquelin v Bouard* (1863) 15 C.B.(N.S.) 341, 367–368; *Boyle v Victoria Yukon Trading Co* (1902) 9 B.C.R. 213; *Barclays Bank Ltd v Piacun* [1984] 2 Qd.R. 476; *Minkler and Kirschbaum v Sheppard* (1991) 60 B.C.L.R. (2d) 360; *Re Dooney* [1993] 2 Qd.R. 362; *cf. Four Embarcadero Center Venture v Mr Greenjeans* (1988) 64 O.R. (2d) 746, app. dismissed (1988) 65 O.R. (2d) 160 (CA). For criticism of dicta in *Nouvion v Freeman* see Read, pp.85–86.

claimant's case, the more useless his judgment would be. The test has been stated as whether the default judgment was "entirely floating as a determination, enforceable only as expressly provided and in the course of that enforcement subject to revision", in which case it will not be final, or "given the effect of finality unless subsequently altered", in which case it will be final.[107]

If the judgment is given by a court of a law district forming part of a larger **14–024** federal system, e.g. an American State, the finality and conclusiveness of the judgment in the law district where it was given are alone relevant in England; its finality and conclusiveness in other parts of the federal system, e.g. in other American States, are irrelevant.[108]

The class of foreign judgments in relation to which it is most difficult to **14–025** decide whether or not they are "final and conclusive" are maintenance orders, providing for periodical payments. The principle applicable to such orders is, however, the same as that applying to all other foreign judgments. If they are incapable of alteration by the court which made them, then they are actionable in England.[109] But if they are capable of variation by the court which made them, as are orders for periodical payments made by the Family Division of the High Court, no action is maintainable upon them,[110] just as no action in the Queen's Bench Division will lie upon an order of the Family Division.[111] Yet an order variable in respect of future payments may be invariable in so far as arrears are concerned in which case an action may be brought for the recovery of the arrears.[112] Statutory means exist for the enforcement in England of maintenance orders made by Scottish or Northern Irish courts, and by the courts of certain foreign countries outside the United Kingdom.[113]

Proviso. At common law, a foreign judgment may be final and conclusive **14–026** even though an appeal is actually pending in the foreign country where it was

---

[107] *Ainslie v Ainslie* (1927) 39 C.L.R. 318, 389–390, applied in *Schnabel v Lui* [2002] NSWSC 15, at [97]; *CLE Owners Inc v Wanlass* [2005] 8 W.W.R. 559 (Man.CA); *Re Cavell Insurance Co* (2006) 269 D.L.R. (4th) 663 (Ont.CA). But if the default judgment is set aside (and there is no sustainable objection to the order by which it is set aside: *cf. Merchant International Co Ltd v AK "Naftogaz Ukrayiny"* [2011] EWHC 1820 (Comm.), [2011] 2 All E.R. (Comm.) 755, it ceases to be entitled to recognition, and a local judgment will be set aside on application: *Benefit Strategies Group Ltd v Prider* (2007) 211 F.L.R. 113 (SASC).

[108] *Colt Industries Inc v Sarlie (No.2)* [1966] 1 W.L.R. 1287.

[109] *cf. McLean v McLean* [1979] 1 N.S.W.L.R. 620; *Holt v Thomas* (1987) 38 D.L.R. (4th) 117 (Alb).

[110] *Harrop v Harrop* [1920] 3 K.B. 386; *Re Macartney* [1921] 1 Ch. 522; *M'Donnell v M'Donnell* [1921] 2 I.R. 148; *Maguire v Maguire* (1921) 64 D.L.R. 180 (Ont CA); *Davis v Davis* (1922) 22 S.R.N.S.W. 185; *Estate H v Estate H*, 1952 (4) S.A. 168; *Ashley v Gladden* [1954] 4 D.L.R. 848 (Ont CA); *Smith v Smith* [1955] 1 D.L.R. 229 (BC); *Re Paslowski and Paslowski* (1957) 11 D.L.R. (2d) 180 (Man). The rule is criticised by Grodecki (1959) 8 I.C.L.Q. 18, 32–40, and has been rejected by some American state courts: see Restatement, s.109.

[111] *Bailey v Bailey* (1884) 13 Q.B.D. 855 (CA); *Robins v Robins* [1907] 2 K.B. 13.

[112] *Beatty v Beatty* [1924] 1 K.B. 807 (CA); *G v G* [1984] I.R. 368; *Splatt v Splatt* (1889) 10 N.S.W.L.R. 227; *Hadden v Hadden* (1898) 6 B.C.R. 340; *Robertson v Robertson* (1908) 16 O.L.R. 170; *Wood v Wood* (1916) 28 D.L.R. 367 (Ont CA); *Patton v Reed* (1972) 30 D.L.R. (3d) 494 (BC); *Lear v Lear* (1974) 51 D.L.R. (3d) 56 (Ont CA).

[113] See below, Rule 102.

given.[114] "In order to its receiving effect here, a foreign decree need not be final in the sense that it cannot be made the subject of appeal to a higher court; but it must be final and unalterable in the court which pronounced it; and if appealable the English court will only enforce it, subject to conditions which will save the interests of those who have the right of appeal."[115] So in a proper case a stay of execution would no doubt be ordered pending a possible appeal.[116]

14–027   It has also been held that a judgment which was final in the court which pronounced it may be recognised and enforced even though it was later set aside by an appellate court if the appellate judgment is refused recognition on the basis of one of the defences in Rules 50 to 52.[117] When a party successfully appeals against the judgment of a lower court, there is no doubt that, so far as the foreign system is concerned, the appellate judgment entirely supersedes the judgment of the court below. However, if it is only the appellate judgment which is shown to have been tainted by fraud, it is only the appellate judgment which may be refused recognition.

14–028   **Enforcement.** Where the statement of case[118] in proceedings on a foreign judgment has been served on the defendant and the defendant has acknowledged service or filed a defence, the claimant may apply for summary judgment on the ground that the defendant has no real prospect of successfully defending the claim.[119] Unless the defendant satisfies the court that there is an issue or question in dispute which ought to be tried—for instance, on the ground that the judgment was obtained by fraud[120]—the court may give judgment for the claimant.[121] Where the defendant does not appear the claimant may enter judgment at once.[122] The proceedings upon such an action may thus have a largely formal character. The English court must have *in personam* jurisdiction over the judgment debtor, and the process in a claim to enforce a judgment at common law must be served on him in England, unless permission is obtained to serve him outside. But even where the judgment

---

[114] *Scott v Pilkington* (1862) 2 B. & S. 11; *Colt Industries Inc v Sarlie (No.2)* [1966] 1 W.L.R. 1287. Contrast the position under the 1920 Act, s.9(2)(e), the 1933 Act, ss.1(3), 5(1) and the 1982 Act, Sch 1, Art.38, and Schs 6 and 7, para.3, and the Brussels I Regulation and Lugano Convention, Art.46, below, paras 14–177, 14–187, 14–215 and 14–261.

[115] *Nouvion v Freeman* (1889) 15 App. Cas. 1, 13.

[116] *Scott v Pilkington* (1862) 2 B. & S. 11, 41; *Colt Industries Inc v Sarlie (No.2)* [1966] 1 W.L.R. 1287; *Four Embarcadero Center Venture v Mr Greenjeans*, above, n.91; *Arrowmaster Inc v Unique Farming Ltd* (1993) 17 O.R. (3d) 407; *cf. The Varna (No.2)* [1994] 2 Lloyd's Rep. 41, 46.

[117] *Merchant International Co Ltd v AK "Naftogaz Ukrayiny"* [2011] EWHC 1820 (Comm.), [2011] 2 All E.R. (Comm.) 755.

[118] Under the practice prior to the CPR, the statement of claim usually contained a specific assertion that the foreign court had jurisdiction: there is nothing in the CPR which requires any change in the practice.

[119] CPR, r.24.2, replacing RSC Ord.14, r.1; *Grant v Easton* (1883) 13 Q.B.D. 302 (CA); *Colt Industries Inc v Sarlie (No.2)* [1966] 1 W.L.R. 1287 (CA).

[120] *Manger v Cash* (1889) 5 T.L.R. 271; *Codd v Delap* (1905) 92 L.T. 510 (HL); *Israel Discount Bank of New York v Hadjipateras* [1984] 1 W.L.R. 137 (CA); *Jet Holdings Inc v Patel* [1990] 1 Q.B. 335, 347 (CA); *House of Spring Gardens Ltd v Waite* [1991] 1 Q.B. 241, 250 (CA); *Jacobs v Beaver* (1908) 17 O.L.R. 496.

[121] CPR, r.24.2.

[122] CPR Pt 12.

debtor has no connection with England process may be issued, with permission, for service outside the jurisdiction, solely on the basis that the claim is to enforce a foreign judgment.[123]

It is immaterial that the debtor dies before judgment is pronounced by the foreign court and that the judgment is pronounced against his personal representatives.[124]

14–029

Since *Miliangos v George Frank (Textiles) Ltd*[125] there is no reason why a claim for enforcement of a foreign judgment may not be for the amount of the judgment in the currency in which it was rendered.

A foreign judgment *in personam* cannot be enforced in England by a claim *in rem*.[126]

Clause (2) of the Rule. A foreign judgment may be relied on in English proceedings otherwise than for the purpose of its enforcement. A claimant who has brought proceedings abroad and lost may seek to bring a similar claim in England; or in proceedings on a different claim an issue may be raised which has been decided abroad. In such cases a foreign judgment entitled to recognition may give rise to *res judicata*, i.e. to a cause of action estoppel, which prevents a party to proceedings from asserting or denying, as against the other party, the existence of a cause of action, the nonexistence or existence of which has been determined by the foreign court, or to an issue estoppel, which will prevent a matter of fact or law necessarily decided by a foreign court from being re-litigated in England.[127]

14–030

Thus a foreign judgment which is final and conclusive on the merits in favour of the defendant is at common law[128] a good defence to a claim in

14–031

---

[123] CPR, PD6B, para.3.1(10), which replaces CPR, r.6.20(9), which in turn replaced RSC, Ord.11 r.1(1)(m). The effect of *Perry v Zissis* [1977] 1 Lloyd's Rep. 607 (CA) is therefore reversed. There is no requirement that there be shown to be assets in England when the application is made: *Tasarruf Mevduati Sigorta Fonu v Demirel* [2007] EWCA Civ 799, [2007] 1 W.L.R. 2508 (which appears not to have been cited to the Court of Appeal in a decision to the contrary effect, *Linsen International Ltd v Humpuss Transportasi Kimia* [2011] EWCA Civ 1042: see *Parbulk II AS v PT Humpuss Intermoda Transportasi TBK* [2011] EWHC 3143 (Comm.), at [80]). But this jurisdictional rule will not apply unless and until a final judgment has been rendered by the foreign court: *Mercedes-Benz AG v Leiduck* [1996] 1 A.C. 284, 289–299 (PC); and proceedings to obtain freezing and delivery up orders against a respondent implicated in the concealment of assets do not fall within this jurisdictional rule unless judgment has been given against those respondents, or has been given against other persons but steps are now being taken to enforce it against these respondents: *Belletti v Morici* [2009] EWHC 2316 (Comm.), [2010] 1 All E.R. (Comm) 412.

[124] *Re Flynn (No.2)* [1969] 2 Ch. 403.

[125] [1976] A.C. 443. See Rule 261. *cf.* the position under the 1933 Act, below, para.14–187.

[126] *The City of Mecca* (1881) 6 P.D. 106 (CA); *The Sylt* [1991] 1 Lloyd's Rep. 240, 244.

[127] In an appropriate case the court may declare, in advance, that a foreign judgment is entitled to be recognised in England: *Phillips v Avena* [2005] EWHC 3333 (Ch.). A decision by a foreign court that it has no jurisdiction to entertain a claim to enforce a foreign revenue law is not a decision, but an abstention from decision, on the merits of the claim in question, and no estoppel arises from it: *Relfo Ltd v Varsani* [2009] EWHC 2297 (Ch.) (not challenged on appeal: *Varsani v Relfo Ltd* [2010] EWCA Civ 560, [2011] 1 W.L.R. 1402).

[128] See also 1933 Act, s.8 (below, para.14–195), 1982 Act, s.19, and Brussels I Regulation and Lugano Convention, Art.33, (below, para.14–241).

England for the same matter.[129] There is no cause of action estoppel against a different remedy,[130] although there may be an issue estoppel if a relevant issue has been decided directly in the foreign action. Where two conflicting foreign judgments, each of which would satisfy the criteria for recognition, have determined issues which arise in the English proceedings, the general rule is that the one given first in time is to be recognised, to the exclusion of the latter.[131]

14–032   It was established by a majority of the House of Lords in *Carl Zeiss Stiftung v Rayner & Keeler Ltd (No.2)*[132] that a foreign judgment could give rise to an issue estoppel, i.e. prevent a party from denying any matter of fact or law necessarily decided by the foreign court. For there to be such an issue estoppel, three requirements must be satisfied[133]: first, the judgment of the foreign court must be (a) of a court of competent jurisdiction in relation to the party who is to be estopped, (b) final and conclusive and (c) on the merits; secondly, the parties to the English litigation must be the same parties (or their privies) as in the foreign litigation;[134] and, thirdly, the issues raised must be identical. A decision[135] on the issue must have been necessary for the decision of the foreign court and not merely collateral.[136] But Lord Reid emphasised that special caution is required before a foreign judgment can be held to give rise to an issue estoppel: English courts are unfamiliar with modes of procedure in many foreign countries, and it may be difficult to see whether a particular issue has been decided or that a decision was a basis of a foreign

---

[129] *Ricardo v Garcias* (1845) 12 Cl. & F. 368; *Jacobson v Frachon* (1927) 138 L.T. 386 (CA). *cf. Booth v Leycester* (1837) 1 Keen 579. It is irrelevant which proceedings were commenced first. It used to be said that the foreign judgment only gave rise to the estoppel if the English proceedings were subsequent to the foreign judgment: but see *Lee v Citibank NA* [1981] Hong Kong L.R. 470 (CA), following *Bell v Holmes* [1956] 1 W.L.R. 1359 and *Morrison Rose & Partners v Hillman* [1961] 2 Q.B. 266 (CA) and not following *The Delta* (1876) 1 P.D. 393; *Houstoun v Sligo* (1885) 29 Ch.D. 448, 454.

[130] *Callandar v Dittrich* (1842) 4 M. & G. 68. On the other hand, a mere change in form to proceedings *in rem* is immaterial: *The Griefswald* (1859) Swab. 430, 435. But the same relief may be asked based on a different case giving rise to a new equity: *Hunter v Stewart* (1861) 4 De G.F. & J. 168; contrast *Henderson v Henderson* (1843) 3 Hare 100, 115. See *Michado v The Hattie and Lottie* (1904) 9 Exch.C.R. 11.

[131] *Showlag v Mansour* [1995] 1 A.C. 431 (PC). But if the party holding the earlier judgment is himself estopped from relying on it, the general rule will be displaced.

[132] [1967] 1 A.C. 853, 917, 925, 967.

[133] *The Sennar (No.2)* [1985] 1 W.L.R. 490, 499 (HL) See also *Vervaeke v Smith* [1983] 1 A.C. 145; *Tracomin SA v Sudan Oil Seeds Co Ltd (No.1)* [1983] 1 W.L.R. 662, 673, affirmed [1983] 1 W.L.R. 1026 (CA); *The Jocelyne* [1984] 2 Lloyd's Rep. 569; *ED&F Man (Sugar) Ltd v Haryanto (No.2)* [1991] 1 Lloyd's Rep. 429; *cf. Westfal-Larsen A/S v Ikerigi Compania Naviera SA* [1983] 1 All E.R. 382; *El du Pont de Nemours v Agnew (No.2)* [1988] 2 Lloyd's Rep. 240 (CA); *Black v Yates* [1992] Q.B. 526; *Desert Sun Loan Corp v Hill* [1996] 2 All E.R. 847 (CA).

[134] *Carl Zeiss Stiftung v Rayner & Keeler Ltd (No.2)* [1967] 1 A.C. 853, 910–911, 928–929, 936–937, 944–946.

[135] But where what was decided by the foreign court cannot be determined, e.g. where judgment is entered in default of appearance, this principle will be inapplicable: *Masters v Leaver* [2000] I.L.Pr. 387 (CA); *Baker v Ian McCall International Ltd* [2000] C.L.C. 189.

[136] *Good Challenger Navegante SA v Mineralexportimport SA* [2003] EWCA Civ 1668, [2004] 1 Lloyd's Rep 67 (CA); *Air Foyle Ltd v Center Capital Ltd* [2002] EWHC 2325 (Comm.), [2003] 2 Lloyd's Rep. 753; *Sun Life Assurance Association of Canada v Lincoln National Life Insurance Co* [2004] EWCA Civ 1660, [2005] 1 Lloyd's Rep. 606; *H J Heinz Co Ltd v EFL Inc* [2010] EWHC 1203 (Comm.), [2010] 2 Lloyd's Rep. 727.

judgment and not merely collateral or obiter; and it might be unjust for a litigant to be estopped from putting forward his case in England because he failed to do so in an earlier case of a trivial character abroad.[137]

The question of who is estopped by the decision of a foreign court may be more complex than the "same parties (or their privies)" formula suggests. For example, if a foreign court has decided an issue against one, but not both, of the parties to the English action, it may be an abuse of process for the other to seek to litigate the point already decided against his co-party.[138] In *House of Spring Gardens Ltd v Waite*[139] it was held that a foreign judgment was enforceable against a judgment debtor who (unlike his co-defendants) had stood aside from proceedings in the foreign country to have the original judgment set aside for fraud. As he knew of the proceedings, which were brought by the co-defendants whose interest in the matter was joint, he should be seen as privy to the proceedings and the judgment, but if there were a technical objection to that reasoning, it would still be an abuse of process to allow the party to ask the English court to re-examine the point already adjudicated by the foreign court.

14–033

Likewise, the question whether a person was a party and is liable on that account to be estopped may require careful examination. For example, persons may be "represented" in proceedings before a foreign court in circumstances in which the foreign court has ordered them to be joined or deems them to be bound according to local procedure (for example, in class action proceedings), even though they have not made or given any expression of assent. Even if it is correct to regard a person in such a case as party to the proceedings, on the footing that whether a person is a party to proceedings is principally[140] a matter for the procedural law of the foreign court to determine, estoppel will only arise against them if the foreign court is regarded as one of competent jurisdiction so far as the individual person is concerned. In the absence of what English law will accept as having been a submission to the adjudicatory jurisdiction of the foreign court, a person who is involuntarily made a party to foreign proceedings, or who is placed by the foreign court in an analogous position, will not be estopped by the decision of the foreign court.[141]

14–034

---

[137] [1967] 1 A.C. 853 at p.918, *per* Lord Reid. But *cf. The Sennar (No.2)* [1985] 1 W.L.R. 490, 500 (HL).

[138] *Rayner v Bank für Gemeinwirtschaft AG* [1983] 1 Lloyd's Rep. 462 (CA).

[139] [1991] 1 Q.B. 241; *Bussoleno Ltd v Kelly* [2011] IEHC 220. See also *Owens Bank Ltd v Etoile Commerciale SA* [1995] 1 W.L.R. 44 (PC), which shows that the abuse of process doctrine extends more generally to those whose contention that they are not estopped is devoid of merit.

[140] The correct analysis should be that the foreign system determines the precise relationship of the individual to the proceedings, and the incidents of that relationship, but it is ultimately for English law to determine whether that makes the individual a party for the purpose of the doctrine of estoppel by *res judicata*.

[141] *cf. Currie v McDonald's Restaurants of Canada Ltd* (2005) 250 D.L.R. (4th) 224 (Ont.CA) (on which, see Monestier (2010) 45 Tex.Int.L.J. 537), finding a non-participant person may in principle be bound and estopped by a judgment or settlement in class action proceedings on the basis of "passive submission". Neither this decision nor the analyses proposed by Dixon (1997) 46 I.C.L.Q. 134 or Stiggelbout (2011) 52 Harvard Int. L.J. 435 is consistent with English law as it has so far been developed or declared. French law comes to the same conclusion that a non-participant person is not bound (Lemontey & Michon, 2009 *Clunet* 535), though by a different route; Dutch law, by contrast, evidently does not rule out the possibility that a non-participant who

14–035   The requirement that the judgment must be final and conclusive applies when it is relied on by the defendant as a defence,[142] just as it does when it is relied upon by the claimant seeking enforcement. The judgment must be "on the merits." In *The Sennar (No.2)*[143] Lord Diplock seems to have thought this added nothing to the condition that the judgment must be final and conclusive, but Lord Brandon suggested that "a decision on the merits is a decision which establishes certain facts as proved or not in dispute; states what are the relevant principles of law applicable to such facts; and expresses a conclusion with regard to the effect of applying those principles to the factual situation concerned."[144] The issue determined by the foreign court in *The Sennar (No.2)*, was that a jurisdiction agreement bound the claimant to bring his claim in Sudan, and as such may have been considered as being procedural in nature. But it was the final conclusion of the foreign court on the point which it had been asked to decide, namely, whether the exclusive jurisdiction agreement applied to a claim framed in tort; and it was on this account held capable of supporting an estoppel against the claimant[145] upon the issue. In *Desert Sun Loan Corp v Hill*[146] the Court of Appeal accepted in principle that issue estoppel could arise from an interlocutory judgment of a foreign court on a procedural, non-substantive issue where there was express submission of the issue in question to the foreign court, and the specific issue of fact was raised before and decided, finally and not just provisionally, by the court. It was emphasised that before according preclusive effect to any such finding by a foreign court the need for caution should be borne in mind.[147] Consequently, if the decision of the foreign court is a non-reviewable but clear decision upon an issue submitted to it for its determination,[148] it is unneces-

---

did not take steps to opt out of the class may be bound by the judgment or settlement (*Re Royal Ahold NV* (June 23, 2010) (Amsterdam Dist Ct)); and for the possibility that there may yet be a distinction to be drawn between "non-parties and non-parties", in relation to whom the law is not identical, see *Global Partners Fund Ltd v Babcock & Brown Ltd* [2010] NSWCA 196, [73]. On intra-Canada recognition of class action judgments, see *Canada Post Corp v Lépine* [2009] 1 S.C.R. 549.

[142] *Plummer v Woodburne* (1825) 4 B. & C. 625; *Frayes v Worms* (1861) 10 C.B. (N.S.) 149; *Carl Zeiss Stiftung v Rayner & Keeler Ltd (No.2)* [1967] 1 A.C. 853. See also *Charm Maritime Inc v Kyriakou* [1987] 1 Lloyd's Rep. 433 (CA).

[143] [1985] 1 W.L.R. 490, 494 (HL).

[144] *ibid*. p.499.

[145] Who was necessarily taken to be bound by findings made by a court to the jurisdiction of which he had unquestionably submitted.

[146] [1996] 2 All E.R. 847 (CA).

[147] This represents the view of the majority, Evans and Stuart-Smith L.JJ; Roch L.J. dissented. The decision is problematic, for it suggests that issue estoppel may arise against a defendant who appears before a foreign court for the sole purpose of contesting its jurisdiction over him, in circumstances in which Civil Jurisdiction and Judgments Act 1982, s.33, would appear to make it clear that the appearance does not constitute submission, with the consequence that the foreign court is not one of competent jurisdiction for the purpose of deriving issue estoppel from its decision (*cf. A/S D/S Svendborg v Wansa* [1997] 2 Lloyd's Rep. 183). This point seems to have been overlooked in *Armacel Pty Ltd v Smurfit Stone Container Corp* [2008] FCA 592, (2008) 248 A.L.R. 573.

[148] For further consideration of the separate question whether it is open to the losing party to contend that he did not submit to the jurisdiction of the foreign court, so that its ruling is not to be recognised as against him, notwithstanding that he sought a determination on the point in question, see below, para.14–071.

sary for the purposes of issue estoppel to characterise the issue so decided as being substantive rather than procedural.

Other cases can be more difficult. Estoppel can arise from a decision of a **14–036** foreign court refusing to recognise a judgment from a third state,[149] even though it is generally understood that a foreign judgment which recognises the judgment of a third country does not become a judgment for the purposes of recognition and enforcement in England. Estoppel may also, in principle at least, arise from an implied determination by a foreign court.[150] It has even been suggested that in cases in which a finding made by a foreign court does not meet the strict requirement of having been a final determination on the merits, a degree of deference may still be given to the finding.[151] It is, however, far from clear that there is any stable legal principle which could explain whether, and to what extent, this is to be done.

It has been held that at common law and under the 1933 Act a judgment **14–037** given in favour of the defendant on the ground that the action is barred by a statute of limitation was not on the merits.[152] But the effect of these decisions is reversed by s.3 of the Foreign Limitation Periods Act 1984, by which a foreign judgment determining any matter by reference to limitation is deemed to be on the merits. A judgment in default or by consent may, however, be a judgment on the merits.[153]

By the Civil Liability (Contribution) Act 1978 "any person liable" in **14–038** respect of any damage may recover from any other person liable in respect of the same damage. It has been held that the equivalent provision in Scots law (which is in different terms and refers to liability found in an action) applies to the liability of the party seeking contribution established in an action in Scotland, and not in a foreign country.[154] The view has been expressed that a foreign judgment gives no right to seek contribution under the 1978 Act.[155] This question was left open in the Privy Council in *Soc Nat Ind Aerospatiale v Lee Kui Jak*,[156] but it indicated that the argument that the 1978 Act did not apply to foreign judgments had some substance.[157] It is suggested that these doubts are well-founded, unless a foreign judgment, in proceedings to which the person from whom contribution is sought is a party, has held him liable and is entitled to recognition as against him.

---

[149] *Yukos Capital Sarl v OJSC Rosneft Oil Co* [2011] EWHC 1461 (Comm.), [2011] 2 Lloyd's Rep. 443 (estoppel arising from decision of Dutch court to refuse recognition of Russian judicial decision annulling arbitral award).

[150] *Republic of Kazakhstan v Istil Group Inc (No.2)* [2006] EWHC 448 (Comm.), [2006] 2 Lloyd's Rep. 370 (affd [2007] EWCA Civ 471, [2008] Bus. L.R. 878).

[151] *Deutsche Bank AG v Highland Crusader Offshore Partners LP* [2009] EWCA Civ 725, [2010] 1 W.L.R. 1023, [22]–[29] (findings made on motion to dismiss on jurisdictional grounds).

[152] *Harris v Quine* (1869) L.R. 4 Q.B. 653; *Black-Clawson International Ltd v Papierwerke-Aschaffenburg AG* [1975] A.C. 591.

[153] See Read, p.101; but on the need for caution in the case of default judgments see *Carl Zeiss Stiftung v Rayner & Keeler Ltd (No.2)* [1967] 1 A.C. 853, 916–917, 926, 946.

[154] *Comex Houlder Diving Ltd v Colne Fishing Co Ltd*, 1987 S.L.T. 443 (HL).

[155] Clerk and Lindsell, *Torts* (20th ed. 2010), para.4–013.

[156] [1987] A.C. 871.

[157] *ibid.* at p.902, *per* Lord Goff of Chieveley, who was a party to both decisions, as was Lord Keith who delivered the leading speech in the former case.

14–039   A distinct question arises when a foreign judgment is relied on as the basis of a consequential contractual claim. Where an insurer has been adjudged liable to an insured, and claims reimbursement from his reinsurer, the judgment of the foreign court will be recognised as the foundation for the claim if the foreign court was one of competent jurisdiction in relation to the claim against the insurer; judgment was not obtained by the insured in breach of a jurisdiction agreement or other contractual obligation not to proceed in that court; the insured took all proper defences; and the judgment was not manifestly perverse. To this extent the reinsurer is bound by the findings of a court in proceedings to which he was not party,[158] provided that there is no express term to the contrary in the contract of reinsurance.

14–040   **Clause (3) of the Rule.** Clause (2) of the Rule deals with the case in which issues determined by a foreign court are recognised as being *res judicata* for the purpose of proceedings properly brought in an English court in which those issues also arise. The party in whose favour the relevant finding was made relies on the foreign judgment to prevent his being at risk for a second time. The situation is different when a claimant has succeeded in a foreign court, but, dissatisfied with the measure of his recovery, sues again on the original cause of action. In this case there may have been no finding in favour of the defendant which may be recognised in his defence,[159] and clause (2) will furnish no answer to the second claim. A foreign judgment in favour of a claimant was at one time no bar to a subsequent action in England based on the original cause of action. But s.34 of the 1982 Act provides that no proceedings may be brought by a person on a cause of action[160] in respect of which a foreign judgment has been given in his favour in proceedings between the same parties, or their privies,[161] unless the judgment is not enforceable or entitled to recognition in England.[162] This displaces in part the rule of the common law that a foreign judgment does not extinguish the original cause of action in respect of which the judgment was given: a rule which was described by Lord Wilberforce as a rule "which, if surviving at all, is an illogical survival".[163]

14–041   Section 34 does not enact a statutory rule of merger[164] (by which the original cause of action would cease to exist), but provides that "no proceedings shall be brought". This form of words was held by the House of Lords

---

[158] *Commercial Union Assurance Co Plc v NRG Victory Reinsurance Ltd* [1998] 2 All E.R. 434 (CA). But if the insured's claim has been settled, this principle cannot be applied, and the reinsurer may require the insurer to demonstrate its legal liability to the insured; see also *Enterprise Oil Ltd v Strand Insurance Co Ltd* [2006] EWHC 58 (Comm.), [2006] 1 Lloyd's Rep. 500; *Korea National Insurance Corp v Allianz Global Corporate & Specialty AG* [2007] EWCA Civ 1066, [2008] Lloyd's Rep. I.R. 413.

[159] If there has been, and if the defendant succeeded in part and obtained a determination of certain issues in his favour, recognition of that part of the judgment under clause (2) of this Rule will provide him with the necessary defence.

[160] For the meaning of the same cause of action, see *Black v Yates* [1992] Q.B. 526; *Republic of India v India Steamship Co Ltd* [1993] A.C. 410, 419–421. It means the factual situation which confers a remedy, and not the evidence to support it, nor the nature of the remedy itself.

[161] *cf. Black v Yates*, above; *House of Spring Gardens v Waite* [1991] 1 Q.B. 241 (CA); para.14–033, above.

[162] *Karafarin Bank v Mansoury-Dara* [2009] EWHC 1217, [2009] 2 Lloyd's Rep. 289.

[163] *Carl Zeiss Stiftung v Rayner & Keeler Ltd (No.2)* [1967] 1 A.C. 853, 966.

[164] [1993] A.C. 410, 423–424.

in *Republic of India v India Steamship Co Ltd*[165] to debar the claimant from bringing proceedings, as distinct from removing the jurisdiction of the court to hear the claim. Accordingly it would be open to the claimant to demonstrate that reasons existed, such as prior agreement between the parties to litigate a claim in two separate parts, or estoppel by representation, acquiescence or convention, why the claimant should not be prevented from proceeding in the circumstances of the particular case. In *Republic of India v India Steamship Co Ltd*, cargo owners sued shipowners in India for damages for short delivery of a small part of a cargo which had been jettisoned en route; after the Indian proceedings had been commenced, but before judgment, the parties agreed that the claim for the total loss of the whole cargo would be subject to English law and jurisdiction. The cargo owners recovered damages in their action in India, but when they sued in England for damages for loss of the whole cargo, the shipowners succeeded in an argument that s.34 debarred the cargo owners' action. Though the House of Lords held that s.34 might not apply in the case of waiver, estoppel or agreement to exclude it, and remitted the matter to the Admiralty judge for his determination, it ruled in *Republic of India v India Steamship Co Ltd (No.2)*[166] that there was no basis on the facts for lifting the bar to proceedings constituted by s.34.

Where the proceedings in the foreign court were brought in the form of an **14–042** action *in personam*, but the subsequent English proceedings are brought as an Admiralty claim *in rem*, the two sets of proceedings are to be regarded as being between the same parties, for a claim *in rem* is a claim against the owners of the vessel from the moment the Admiralty Court is seised with jurisdiction.[167] The fact that the proceedings are differently constituted as a matter of procedural law is insufficient by itself to displace the operation of s.34. The section may also apply even though the foreign court has not given judgment by the date of institution of the English proceedings.[168] It is unclear what the position would be if the English proceedings were commenced first and the foreign action second, but the foreign court were to give judgment before the English court did. If the policy behind s.34 is to prevent the institution of a second set of proceedings, there is no reason why it should have any application to the proceedings which were commenced first.

Section 34 has no application when the English claim is in respect of a **14–043** different cause of action from that litigated in the foreign proceedings. But the principle in *Henderson v Henderson*[169] may be applied to prevent the subsequent raising of a claim which could and should have been brought and included in the proceedings before the foreign court; alternatively (though to the same effect) it may be an abuse of process for the second action to brought.[170]

---

[165] [1993] A.C. 410.
[166] [1998] A.C. 878.
[167] *ibid.*, at pp.906–910.
[168] *ibid.*, at p.912.
[169] (1843) 3 Hare 100. See also *Desert Sun Loan Corp v Hill* [1996] 2 All E.R. 847, 863 (CA); the point was left open in *Republic of India v India Steamship Co Ltd (No.2)*, above, at p.916.
[170] *cf. Desert Sun Loan Corp v Hill*, above, at pp.859, 863–4.

Illustrations

(1) Enforcement

14–044
1. A recovers judgment against X in a Jamaican court, that X should pay A £3,000, after first deducting thereout X's costs, to be taxed by the proper officer. The costs have not been taxed. The judgment is not a judgment for a fixed sum. No claim is maintainable.[171]

2. A agrees with X in California to sell to X land situate in England. The land is conveyed to X in accordance with English law. A sues X in California to set aside the conveyance because of X's fraud. The Californian court orders X to reconvey the land to A and on X's refusal to do so the clerk of the court purports to reconvey in X's name. A cannot obtain in England a declaration that he is the owner of the land on the sole ground of the Californian decision.[172]

3. X, a British subject, is arrested in Florida on fraud charges. He is released on bail on condition that he enters into an "appearance bond". He is given permission to leave the United States for 30 days, but fails to return. The United States Government obtains a judgment on the bond in a civil action. No claim on the judgment is maintainable, because the purpose of the claim is the enforcement of the criminal process.[173]

14–045
4. X, while recklessly galloping her horse in a foreign country, ran into A, and seriously injured him. X was prosecuted for her criminal negligence by the foreign authorities, and A intervened in the prosecution and claimed damages from X as allowed by the foreign law. The court convicted X, fined her 100 francs, and ordered her to pay 15,000 francs to A by way of damages, and also costs. A was held entitled to recover the sterling equivalent of the damages and costs in England.[174]

5. A took certain summary or "executive" proceedings against X in a Spanish court for the recovery of a debt, and obtained a so-called *remate* judgment for £10,000. In these executive proceedings X could set up certain limited defences, but could not dispute the validity of the contract under which the debt arose. Either party, if unsuccessful in the executive proceedings, might in the same court and in respect of the same matter take ordinary or (so-called) plenary proceedings in which all defences might be set up, and the merits of the matter could be gone into. In the plenary proceedings a *remate* judgment could not be set up as *res judicata* or otherwise, and a plenary judgment rendered the *remate* judgment inoperative. The *remate* judgment was not final and conclusive. No action was maintainable on the *remate* judgment.[175]

14–046
6. A, in an action in New York, recovers judgment against X for the equivalent of £900,000. X appeals against the judgment to the New York Court of Appeals. An appeal under the law of New York is not a stay of execution. While the appeal is pending A brings a claim in England against X on the judgment. The claim is maintainable, and it is immaterial that the judgment may not be enforceable in other American States until the appeal has been dismissed.[176]

7. X, who resided in England, was a sleeping partner in a firm carrying on business in Vienna. A obtained judgment against the firm in Vienna on a bill of exchange. By Austrian law, although the firm had no separate legal personality, the judgment was not enforceable against the partners personally unless a further action was brought against them individually, when various personal defences not concluded by the judgment against the firm would be available. A brought an action in England against X on the judgment. The action was not maintainable because the Austrian judgment against the firm was not final and conclusive as against X.[177]

8. W obtains a maintenance order against H in a foreign court. The court has power under its law to vary the amount of the payments, both in respect of past and future instalments. W cannot bring a claim in England on the judgment of the foreign court, as that judgment is not final and conclusive.[178]

---

[171] *Sadler v Robins* (1808) 1 Camp. 253.

[172] cf. *Duke v Andler* [1932] 4 D.L.R. 529 (Sup Ct Can); cf. *Haspel v Haspel* [1934] 2 W.W.R. 412 (Alta): see below, para.14–114.

[173] *US v Inkley* [1989] Q.B. 255 (CA).

[174] *Raulin v Fischer* [1911] 2 K.B. 93.

[175] *Nouvion v Freeman* (1889) 15 App. Cas. 1.

[176] *Colt Industries Inc v Sarlie (No.2)* [1966] 1 W.L.R. 1287; cf. *Scott v Pilkington* (1862) 2 B. & S. 11, 41.

[177] *Blohn v Desser* [1962] 2 Q.B. 116 (a case on the law prior to the Brussels Convention). As to whether the Austrian court had jurisdiction over X, see below, para.14–079.

[178] *Harrop v Harrop* [1920] 3 K.B. 386; cf. *M'Donnell v M'Donnell* [1921] 2 I.R. 148. Contrast *Beatty v Beatty* [1924] 1 K.B. 807 (CA). Compare *Re Macartney* [1921] 1 Ch. 522.

(2) RECOGNITION

9. A brings an action in a Victorian court against X for breach of contract. X denies the breach.   **14–047**
A judgment which is final and conclusive in Victoria is given in favour of X. The judgment is a
defence to a claim in England against X by A for the same breach of contract.[179]

10. In 1865 A brought an action against X in the Isle of Man to recover a debt. Under a Manx
statute no action could be brought to recover a debt more than three years after the cause of action
accrued. The statute did not extinguish the debt. The Manx court gave judgment for X on the
ground that the action was statute-barred. A then sued X for the debt in England. The Manx
judgment was not a defence to the action.[180] But today it would be a defence.[181]

11. A sued X in England for the return of a sum of money, and obtained judgment that X was
constructive trustee of the money and liable to return it. A brought similar proceedings in Jersey;
as the English judgment was recognised under Jersey law, X's defence was struck out. An
Egyptian court later gave a judgment that X had received the money by way of gift and not as
trustee; and X applied to amend his defence, contending that the Egyptian judgment was *res
judicata*. Both judgments would in principle have qualified for recognition in Jersey. The Jersey
court would recognise the first, and therefore not the second, judgment.[182]

12. In proceedings by the Zeiss Foundation of East Germany against X in England, X denies   **14–048**
the authority of Zeiss' solicitors to bring the action, relying (in part) on a decision of a West
German court in proceedings between Zeiss and X that Zeiss was not properly before the West
German court because the East German organ which purported to act on its behalf had no
authority. The decision of the West German court does not give rise to an issue estoppel because
there is no identity of parties or identity of interest, since the relevant parties in England on the
issue are X and Zeiss' solicitors and not X and Zeiss.[183]

13. A sues X in the Netherlands. The Dutch court decides that the parties have agreed that the
dispute should be heard exclusively by the Sudanese courts. A then sues X in England. A is bound
by the determination of the Dutch court on the issue of the applicability of the jurisdiction
clause.[184]

14. H, an Englishman, was killed in Spain by the negligent driving of X, on whose motorcycle
H was a passenger. W, his widow, gave a power of attorney to a Spanish lawyer to represent her
and their children in Spanish criminal proceedings (in which civil damages may also be awarded).
The Spanish lawyer failed to reserve the right under Spanish law to seek damages elsewhere than
in Spain. The Spanish court ordered the defendant to pay damages. In a subsequent action in
England, W could not sue on her own behalf because the English proceedings were brought on
a cause of action in respect of which the Spanish judgment had been given; but she could sue on
behalf of the estate, because no claim on behalf of the estate had been made in Spain, and she
could sue on behalf of the children because the actions taken on their behalf in Spain were
contrary to their interests, and there was no evidence that they were able to give informed consent
to the power of attorney.[185]

(3) DEBARRING PROCEEDINGS

15. A brings an action in New York against X, a resident of New York, and recovers judgment   **14–049**
for $100,000. Part of the judgment debt is paid by X. Thereupon A brings a claim in England
against X for the same debt. The claim on the debt will fail;[186] A's remedy is to enforce the
balance of the judgment.

16. A brings proceedings in New York against X, a resident of New York, and recovers
judgment for $100,000, which is far less than he had claimed. He later brings a claim in England

---

[179] 1982 Act, s.34. *cf. Plummer v Woodburne* (1825) 4 B. & C. 625. See also *Ricardo v Garcias*
(1845) 12 Cl. & F. 368. Contrast *Frayes v Worms* (1861) 10 C.B.(N.S.) 149.

[180] *Harris v Quine* (1869) L.R. 4 Q.B. 653.

[181] Foreign Limitation Periods Act 1984, s.3.

[182] *Showlag v Mansour* [1995] 1 A.C. 431 (PC).

[183] *Carl Zeiss Stiftung v Rayner & Keeler Ltd (No.2)* [1967] 1 A.C. 853.

[184] *The Sennar (No.2)* [1985] 1 W.L.R. 490 (HL), a case on the law prior to the Brussels
Convention.

[185] *Black v Yates* [1992] Q.B. 526, a case on the law prior to the Brussels Convention.

[186] 1982 Act, s.34.

against X in respect of the same cause of action, giving credit for the $100,000 already recovered. In the absence of grounds for an estoppel or the like, the proceedings must be struck out.[187]

14E–050   *Exception 1*—**No proceedings may be entertained by any court in the United Kingdom for the recovery of a sum payable under a foreign judgment capable of registration in accordance with the provisions of**

    (1) Part I of the Foreign Judgments (Reciprocal Enforcement) Act 1933;

    (2) Part I of the Civil Jurisdiction and Judgments Act 1982;

    (3) Parts II and IV of the Civil Jurisdiction and Judgments Act 1982; and

    (4) Chapter III of Council Regulation (EC) 44/2001,

other than proceedings for registration in the manner described in Rules 54 to 56.

COMMENT

14–051   The various schemes which provide for the enforcement of qualifying judgments to be undertaken by registration also have the effect that the alternative of proceeding by action at common law is not available. Under the 1933 Act, it is expressly provided that no action may be brought at common law upon a judgment capable of direct enforcement by registration under the Act.[188] For judgments which are recognised and enforced under the various statutory mechanisms which implement or supplement European legislation—Part I of the Civil Jurisdiction and Judgments Act 1982 for judgments falling under the Brussels[189] and Lugano[190] Conventions, Parts II and IV of the 1982 Act for judgments from other parts of the United Kingdom and Gibraltar, and the Civil Jurisdiction and Judgments Order 2001 for judgments from Member States covered by Chapter III of the Brussels I Regulation[191]—the same is assumed to be true. Though neither the Act nor the Order provides in express terms that the possibility of registering the judgment entails the impossibility of suing on the judgment at common law, the Conventions and the Brussels I Regulation have the force of law in the United Kingdom, and the European Court has held that where a judgment is entitled to be recognised under what is now Chapter III of the Brussels I Regulation, it is not open to a judgment creditor to proceed with alternative forms of enforcement.[192] Accordingly, where the judgment is one which may be registered pursuant to these statutory schemes, enforcement by registration is the exclusive mode of enforcement.

---

[187] 1982 Act, s.34. *cf. Republic of India v India Steamship Co Ltd* [1993] A.C. 410.

[188] 1933 Act, s.6. However, s.6 only prevents enforcement of the judgment by common law action brought by the judgment creditor. It does not prevent the giving of assistance at common law to a foreign court exercising insolvency jurisdiction which has requested it, even where the assistance given at common law would take the form of enforcing the foreign judgment: *New Cap Reinsurance Corp Ltd v Grant* [2011] EWCA Civ 971, [2011] B.P.I.R. 1428. Neither may a claim be brought on the original cause of action: para.14–194, below.

[189] 1982 Act, s.4.

[190] 1982 Act, s.4A.

[191] SI 2001/3929, Sch.1, para.2.

[192] Case C–42/76 *De Wolf v Cox* [1976] E.C.R. 1759 (not permitted to sue on original cause of action as cheaper alternative than registration of judgment).

As regards judgments of courts of other parts of the United Kingdom, the 1982 Act provides expressly that they shall not be enforced otherwise than in accordance with the registration procedures of the Act.[193] Where a judgment is registrable under the 1920 Act[194] the judgment creditor is not deprived of the possibility of suing to enforce it at common law, but the employment of this alternative is discouraged by a provision that it should ordinarily involve sacrifice of the costs of the action.[195]

***Exception 2*—No proceedings may be entertained in any court in the United Kingdom for the recovery of any sum alleged to be payable under a judgment given in a court of a country to which section 9 of the Foreign Judgments (Reciprocal Enforcement) Act 1933 has been applied by Order in Council.[196]**   14E–052

COMMENT

Section 9(1) of the 1933 Act provides that if it appears to Her Majesty that the treatment in respect of recognition and enforcement accorded by the courts of any foreign country to judgments given in the courts of the United Kingdom is substantially less favourable than that accorded by the courts of the United Kingdom to judgments of the courts of that country, Her Majesty may apply that section to that country, with the consequences stated in Exception 2 above. The object of this enactment was to strengthen the hand of HM Government in negotiating conventions with foreign counries for the reciprocal enforcement of foreign judgments.[197] No Order in Council has yet been made under the section. The section refers to "any foreign country." It is thus not limited to foreign countries to which Pt I of the 1933 Act applies, but is of general application. However, the term "foreign country" is limited to countries foreign in the political sense: it does not extend to countries forming part of the Commonwealth.[198]   14–053

B. *Jurisdiction of foreign courts at common law*

(1) JURISDICTION IN PERSONAM

RULE 43—Subject to Rules 44 to 46, a court of a foreign country outside the United Kingdom has jurisdiction to give a judgment *in personam* capable of enforcement or recognition as against the person against whom it was given in the following cases[199]:   14R–054

---

[193] 1982 Act, s.18(8).

[194] Rule 53.

[195] 1920 Act, s.9(5). But a claim on the original cause of action may not be brought: para.14–179, below.

[196] 1933 Act, s.9, as amended by 1982 Act, Sch.10, para.2.

[197] See the Report of the Foreign Judgments (Reciprocal Enforcement) Committee, Cmd. 4213 (1932), Annex V, para.14.

[198] This is made clear in s.7.

[199] See generally *Adams v Cape Industries Plc* [1990] Ch. 433, 512–525 (CA). See also *Schibsby v Westenholz* (1870) L.R. 6 Q.B. 155, 161; *Rousillon v Rousillon* (1880) 14 Ch.D. 351, 371; *Emanuel v Symon* [1908] 1 K.B. 302, 309 (CA).

First Case[200]—**If the person against whom the judgment was given was, at the time the proceedings were instituted, present in the foreign country.**

Second Case[201]—**If the person against whom the judgment was given was claimant, or counterclaimed, in the proceedings in the foreign court.**

Third Case[202]—**If the person against whom the judgment was given, submitted to the jurisdiction of that court by voluntarily appearing in the proceedings.**

Fourth Case[203]—**If the the person against whom the judgment was given, had before the commencement of the proceedings agreed, in respect of the subject matter of the proceedings, to submit to the jurisdiction of that court or of the courts of that country.**

COMMENT

14–055   A fundamental requirement for the recognition or enforcement of a foreign judgment in England at common law[204] is that the foreign court should have had jurisdiction according to the English rules of the conflict of laws. "All jurisdiction is properly territorial," declared Lord Selborne,[205] "and *extra territorium jus dicenti, impune non paretur.* . . . In a personal action, . . . a

---

[200] *Carrick v Hancock* (1895) 12 T.L.R. 59; *Littauer Glove Corporation v FW Millington (1920) Ltd* (1928) 44 T.L.R. 746; *Vogel v RA Kohnstamm Ltd* [1973] Q.B. 133; *Adams v Cape Industries Plc* [1990] Ch. 433 (CA); *cf. Sfeir & Co v National Insurance Co of New Zealand* [1964] 1 Lloyd's Rep. 330 (a case on the 1920 Act); Read, pp.148–151.

[201] Cases cited in n.199 above, and *Burpee v Burpee* [1929] 3 D.L.R. 18 (BC); Read, p.160.

[202] *De Cosse Brissac v Rathbone* (1861) 6 H. & N. 301, as explained in *Schibsby v Westenholz* (1870) L.R. 6 Q.B. 155, 162; *Voinet v Barrett* (1885) 55 L.J.Q.B. 39 (CA); *Guiard v de Clermont* [1914] 3 K.B. 145; *SA Consortium General Textiles v Sun & Sand Agencies Ltd* [1978] Q.B. 279 (CA) (a case under the 1933 Act); *Jet Holdings Inc v Patel* [1990] 1 Q.B. 335, 341 (CA); *Re Overseas Food Importers & Brandt* (1981) 126 D.L.R. (3d) 422; (BCCA); *Canada Trustco Mortgage Co v Rene Management & Holdings Ltd* (1988) 53 D.L.R. (4th) 222 (Man CA); *575225 Saskatchewan Ltd v Boulding* [1988] 6 W.W.R. 738 (BCCA); *First National Bank of Houston v Houston E&C Inc* [1990] 5 W.W.R. 719 (BC); *Gourmet Resources International Inc v Paramount Capital Corp* [1993] I.L.Pr. 583 (Ont); and *cf. The Atlantic Emperor (No.2)* [1992] 1 Lloyd's Rep. 624, 633 (CA); Read, pp.161–171; Clarence Smith (1953) 2 I.C.L.Q. 510; on the effect of an appearance to protest the jurisdiction of the foreign court see 1982 Act, s.33, and paras 14–070, *et seq.*, below.

[203] *Feyerick v Hubbard* (1902) 71 L.J.K.B. 509; *Copin v Adamson* (1875) 1 Ex. D. 17 (CA); *Jeannot v Fuerst* (1909) 25 T.L.R. 424; *Bank of Australasia v Harding* (1850) 9 C.B. 661; *Bank of Australasia v Nias* (1851) 16 Q.B. 717; *Kelsall v Marshall* (1856) 1 C.B.(N.S.) 241; *Vallée v Dumergue* (1849) 4 Exch. 290; *Blohn v Desser* [1962] 2 Q.B. 116; *Vogel v RA Kohnstamm Ltd* [1973] Q.B. 133; *SA Consortium General Textiles v Sun & Sand Agencies Ltd* [1978] Q.B. 279 (CA) (a case on the 1933 Act); *First City Capital Ltd v Winchester Computer Corp* (1987) 44 D.L.R. (4th) 301 (Sask CA); *Bank of Credit & Commerce International (Overseas) Ltd v Gokal* [1995] 2 W.W.R. 240 (BCCA); Read, pp.171–177; Restatement, ss.32, 43.

[204] And under the 1920 and 1933 Acts. The power of the English court to review the jurisdiction of the foreign court under the 1982 Act and the Brussels I Regulation is more limited. See Rule 55, below.

[205] *Sirdar Gurdyal Singh v Rajah of Faridkote* [1894] A.C. 670, 683–684 (PC).

690

decree pronounced *in absentem* by a foreign court, to the jurisdiction of which the defendant has not in any way submitted himself, is by international law an absolute nullity. He is under no obligation of any kind to obey it; and it must be regarded as a mere nullity by the courts of every nation, except (when authorised by special local legislation) in the country of the forum by which it was pronounced." Thus, in an early leading case[206] upon the subject, the plaintiff brought an action in England on a judgment of a court in the island of Tobago. The defendant had never been in the island, nor had he submitted to its jurisdiction. There had been a substituted service, valid by the law of Tobago, effected by nailing a copy of the writ to the court-house door. In refusing to recognise the judgment, Lord Ellenborough said "Can the Island of Tobago pass a law to bind the rights of the whole world? Would the world submit to such an assumed jurisdiction?"

In *Adams v Cape Industries Plc*,[207] the leading modern authority, it was said **14–056** that "in determining the jurisdiction of the foreign court. . . . , our court is directing its mind to the competence or otherwise of the foreign court to summon the defendant before it and to decide such matters as it has decided"[208] and "we would . . . regard the source of the territorial jurisdiction of the court of a foreign country to summon a defendant to appear before it as being his obligation for the time being to abide by its laws and accept the jurisdiction of its courts while present in its territory."[209]

It has already been seen[210] that the identification of the relevant "country" **14–057** can present a problem in the case of a federal system, whose constituent States (like those in the United States) retain some degree of legislative sovereignty. But while not deciding the issue, the Court of Appeal inclined to agree with Scott J. that the relevant country (or law district) for the purposes of the recognition and enforcement of the judgment of a federal court sitting in Texas (and applying Texan substantive law) was the United States and not Texas.

In that case the Court of Appeal indicated, first, that foreign judgments were **14–058** enforced in England only if the foreign court was one of "competent jurisdiction";[211] second, in deciding whether the foreign court was one of competent jurisdiction, the English court would apply, not the law of the foreign court, but English rules of the conflict of laws.[212] Those rules were developed in the 19th century, and were restated in the frequently cited judgment of Buckley L.J. in *Emanuel v Symon*[213]: "In actions *in personam* there are five cases in which the courts of this country will enforce a foreign judgment: (1) where the defendant is a subject of the foreign country in which the judgment has been obtained; (2) where he was resident in the foreign country when the action

---

[206] *Buchanan v Rucker* (1808) 9 East 192, 194.

[207] [1990] Ch. 433, 517–518 (CA).

[208] Citing *Pemberton v Hughes* [1899] 1 Ch. 781, 790 (CA).

[209] [1990] Ch. at pp.517–519.

[210] *Williams v Jones* (1845) 13 M. & W. 628, 633; *Godard v Gray* (1870) L.R. 6 Q.B. 139, 147; *Schibsby v Westenholz* (1870) L.R. 6 Q.B. 155, 159.

[211] *ibid.*

[212] See below, para.14–129.

[213] [1908] 1 K.B. 302, 309 (CA), which (as he acknowledged) was taken verbatim from the judgment of Fry J. in *Rousillon v Rousillon* (1880) 14 Ch.D. 351, 371. The Supreme Court of Canada has said that Buckley L.J.'s summary "bears a remarkable resemblance to a Code": *Morguard Investments Ltd v De Savoye* [1990] 3 S.C.R. 1077, 1087.

began; (3) where the defendant in the character of plaintiff has selected the forum in which he is afterwards sued;[214] (4) where he has voluntarily appeared; and (5) where he has contracted to submit himself to the forum in which the judgment was obtained." The actual issue in the case was whether the possession of property in the foreign country was sufficient to give jurisdiction to the foreign court,[215] and none of the heads of jurisdiction enumerated by Buckley L.J. was subjected to scrutiny in that case. As will be seen later,[216] the first case mentioned in Buckley L.J.'s statement can no longer be relied on. The second case was adopted in the 1933 Act, but was stated without reference to those cases which led to the conclusion that mere presence, without residence, would be sufficient to confer jurisdiction and which were approved by the Court of Appeal in *Adams v Cape Industries Plc.*[217] The other three cases are examples of the principle of submission and correspond respectively to the Second, Third and Fourth Cases of Rule 43. All four cases (including residence, rather than presence) were adopted (and slightly altered) in the 1933 Act, and in their altered and re-arranged form they are set out in Rule 54.

14–059   The provisions of the 1933 Act were deliberately framed so as to reproduce the rules of the common law as closely as possible,[218] though, as the Foreign Judgments (Reciprocal Enforcement) Committee conceded, it was found desirable to make one or two departures from the common law rules in order to secure international agreements which would be likely to operate satisfactorily in practice.[219] The question therefore arises whether the provisions of the 1933 Act as to the jurisdiction of foreign courts, and as to the scope of the defences, can legitimately be invoked by a court which is asked to enforce a foreign judgment at common law, even though the 1933 Act has not been extended by Order in Council to the foreign country in question. Although the Act has been used[220] to negative arguments that there are additional bases for recognition at common law,[221] the Court of Appeal has held that it is wrong to use the Act to ascertain the common law "by arguing backwards from the provisions of the statute."[222]

14–060   **The first case. Presence.** There is divergence of authority on the question whether presence, as distinct from residence, is a sufficient basis of jurisdiction. The older cases acknowledge that the residence of a defendant in the

---

[214] i.e. where a counterclaim is brought.

[215] See below, para.14–083.

[216] See below, para.14–085.

[217] [1990] Ch. 433 (CA).

[218] Report of the Foreign Judgments (Reciprocal Enforcement) Committee, Cmd. 4213 (1932), paras 2, 16, 18 and Annex V, para.7.

[219] *ibid.* para.18 and Annex V, para.7.

[220] See *Re Trepca Mines Ltd* [1960] 1 W.L.R. 1273, 1282 (CA); *Rossano v Manufacturers' Life Insurance Co Ltd* [1963] 2 Q.B. 352, 383.

[221] In *Owens Bank Ltd v Bracco* [1992] 2 A.C. 443, 489, it was held that, because the 1920 Act adopted the common law approach to fraud in relation to foreign judgments (below, para.14–145), it would be wrong for the courts now to alter the common law rule.

[222] *Henry v Geoprosco International* [1976] Q.B. 726, 751. *cf. Société Co-opérative Sidmetal v Titan International Ltd* [1966] 1 Q.B. 828, 845–846.

country at the time when proceedings are commenced gives that court jurisdiction over him at common law.[223] The position is the same under the 1920
Act[224] and the 1933 Act,[225] except that the former requires "ordinary residence", which in this context probably does not differ much from residence
simpliciter[226] and the latter contains special rules for corporations. But some
of the older cases also suggest that presence, rather than residence, is a
sufficient basis,[227] and presence as a basis of jurisdiction is strengthened by
those authorities which suggested that "temporary allegiance" to the local
sovereign was one of the reasons why a defendant might be under an
obligation to comply with the judgments of its courts.[228] For this reasoning is
no less applicable where a defendant is merely present within the foreign
country concerned. It is also supported by the authorities on the jurisdiction of
the English court over persons present in England: the temporary presence of
an individual defendant in England gives the English court jurisdiction at
common law[229] and the test for the presence of corporations in that context[230]
is the same as that for corporations in the context of the jurisdiction of foreign
courts, although in the latter context it is described as residence rather than
presence.[231] It may be questioned, however, whether casual presence, as
distinct from residence, is a desirable basis of jurisdiction if the parties are
strangers and the cause of action arose outside the country concerned. For the
court is not likely to be the *forum conveniens*, in the sense of the appropriate
court most adequately equipped to deal with the facts or the law.[232] The 1920
and 1933 Acts adopted residence rather than presence as the basis of jurisdiction over individuals, and presence (at least as regards domiciliaries of
Member and Convention States) is regarded as an exorbitant basis of jurisdiction over individuals for the purposes of the Brussels I Regulation, and the
Lugano Conventions.[233] Whilst it is true that the test for corporations in
relation to foreign judgments is equivalent to that for the "presence" of
corporations in the context of the jurisdiction of the English court, the test for
"presence" of corporations involves some fixed place of business in the
foreign country,[234] and is not comparable to what may be the fleeting presence

---

[223] *Schibsby v Westenholz* (1870) L.R. 6 Q.B. 155, 161; *Emanuel v Symon* [1908] 1 K.B. 302,
309 (CA). In *State Bank of India v Murjani Marketing Group Ltd*, unreported, March 27, 1991
(CA), Sir Christopher Slade inclined to the view that residence (in the sense of principal home)
would be a sufficient basis of jurisdiction, even if the judgment debtor was not present in the
foreign country at the date of commencement of proceedings.

[224] s.9(2)(b).

[225] s.4(2)(a)(iv).

[226] *cf.* above, para.6–160.

[227] *Carrick v Hancock* (1895) 12 T.L.R. 59; *Herman v Meallin* (1891) 8 W.N. (NSW) 38;
Forbes v Simmons (1914) 20 D.L.R. 100 (Alta); *cf. General Steam Navigation Co v Guillou*
(1843) 11 M. & W. 377. Contrast *Australian Assets Co Ltd v Higginson* (1897) 18 L.R. (NSW)
Eq. 189, 193.

[228] *Schibsby v Westenholz* (1870) L.R. 6 Q.B. 155, 161; *cf. Sirdar Gurdyal Singh v Rajah of
Faridkote* [1894] A.C. 670, 683–684 (PC).

[229] *Colt Industries Inc v Sarlie* [1966] 1 W.L.R. 440 (CA); *Maharanee of Baroda v Wildenstein*
[1972] 2 Q.B. 283 (CA) above, para.11–108; *cf.* Restatement, s.28.

[230] See above, paras 11–113 *et seq.*

[231] See below, para.14–065.

[232] *cf.* Dodd (1929) 23 Ill.L.Rev. 427, 437–438.

[233] See above, para.11–257.

[234] See below, para.14–065.

of an individual, even in the extreme case where the place of business is established for a very short period.[235]

14–061   In *Adams v Cape Industries Plc*[236] the Court of Appeal reviewed the authorities on presence and residence in the context of the jurisdiction of foreign courts over corporations, but took the opportunity to express general views on the issue. The First Case of the Rule is framed in terms of presence rather than residence in the light of this decision but the issue remains open in the Supreme Court.

14–062   In *Carrick v Hancock*[237] the plaintiff was an Englishman domiciled in Sweden who had acted in Sweden as an agent on commission for the defendant, an Englishman. The defendant was served with Swedish proceedings during a short visit to Sweden, and he subsequently defended the Swedish proceedings. Accordingly, the case had a significant connection with Sweden, and in any event the defendant had clearly submitted to the jurisdiction of the Swedish courts. But in an unreserved judgment Lord Russell of Killowen C.J. decided that the Swedish judgment was enforceable because of the defendant's presence in Sweden, and "the question of the time the person was actually in the territory was wholly immaterial".[238]

14–063   This decision (among others[239]) was relied on by the Court of Appeal in *Adams v Cape Industries Plc* as supporting the principle that, in the absence of submission to the jurisdiction of the foreign court, the competence of a foreign court to summon the defendant before it depended on the physical presence of the defendant in the country concerned at the time of suit: "So long as he remains physically present in that country, he has the benefit of its laws, and must take the rough with the smooth, by accepting his amenability to the process of its courts. In the absence of authority compelling a contrary conclusion, we would conclude that the voluntary presence of an individual in a foreign country, whether permanent or temporary and whether or not accompanied by residence, is sufficient to give the courts of that country territorial jurisdiction over him under our rules of private international law."[240]

14–064   The Court of Appeal referred to the "voluntary" presence of the defendant as being one not induced by compulsion, fraud or duress, but it is clear from the context[241] that it was not finally decided that the presence of these factors would negative jurisdiction. There is no decision in England on what the position is when the defendant is forcibly brought, or fraudulently induced to

---

[235] As in *Dunlop Pneumatic Tyre Co Ltd v AG Cudwell & Co* [1902] 1 K.B. 342 (CA).

[236] [1990] Ch. 433 (CA).

[237] (1895) 12 T.L.R. 59.

[238] *ibid.* at p.60.

[239] *Sirdar Gurdyal Singh v Rajah of Faridkote* [1894] A.C. 670, 683–684; *Employers' Liability Assurance Corp v Sedgwick Collins & Co Ltd* [1927] A.C. 95, 114–115.

[240] [1990] Ch. 433 at p.519. The Court of Appeal indicated that dicta (in cases on the jurisdiction of the *English* court) indicated that the relevant time was *service* of proceedings, rather than *issue*, but expressed no final view. The Court of Appeal (at p.518) also left open the question whether residence without presence would be a sufficient basis of jurisdiction, but *cf. State Bank of India v Murjani Marketing Group Ltd*, above, which suggests that it does suffice, para.14–060.

[241] See *ibid.* pp.518–519.

come, into the jurisdiction of the foreign court and there served with process.[242] But in the United States the view is held that in such a case jurisdiction exists but may or should be disclaimed by the court for reasons of equity if the plaintiff is privy to the force or fraud.[243] In this case also, it is clear, the defendant has the benefit of the laws of the State concerned and owes temporary allegiance thereto. The question whether at common law a foreign court has jurisdiction over an individual who is neither resident or present within the foreign jurisdiction but who carries on business regularly there through an agent has been raised but not decided,[244] although it is a basis of jurisdiction under the 1920 Act.[245]

Where a corporation is concerned neither residence nor presence has, of **14–065** course, any real meaning. But there is a long line of cases dealing with the question whether a foreign corporation does or does not carry on business in England so as to render itself amenable to the jurisdiction of the English courts at common law.[246] The principle of these cases applies also to the question whether a corporation is present in a foreign country so as to give its courts jurisdiction over it.[247] In *Adams v Cape Industries Plc*[248] the Court of Appeal held that in the case of corporations the test of jurisdiction is satisfied if the corporation is carrying on business at a definite and fixed place. The basic principle is that a trading corporation will be regarded as present within the jurisdiction of the courts of a foreign country if (a) it has established and maintained a fixed place of business and for more than a minimal time has carried on its own business there, *or* (b) its representative has for more than a minimal period of time been carrying on the corporation's business in that country at or from some fixed place of business. In the latter case it will be necessary to consider a number of factors (already mentioned in connection with the jurisdiction of the English court[249]) to determine whether the business being carried on is that of the corporation or its representative. In deciding whether a company is present in a foreign country as a result of the acts of a subsidiary present there, the court must consider whether the subsidiary was acting as agent, and if so, on what terms; it may also treat the subsidiary as the *alter ego* of the parent if special circumstances exist which indicate that there is a "mere façade concealing the true facts".[250] If the local agent has authority

---

[242] See *Stein v Valkenhuysen* (1858) E.B. & E. 65 and *Watkins v North American Lands, etc., Co* (1904) 20 T.L.R. 534 (HL), above, para.11–108, which suggest that in appropriate circumstances English process might be set aside if the defendant was fraudulently lured into the jurisdiction.

[243] Restatement, s.82, comments b, d and f.

[244] *Blohn v Desser* [1962] 2 Q.B. 116, 123, on which see below, para.14–079. The mere fact that the defendant contracted through an agent in the foreign country is not of itself sufficient: *cf. Seegner v Marks* (1895) 21 V.L.R. 491.

[245] 1920 Act, s.9(2)(b). On the jurisdiction of the English court in such a case see above, para.11–109.

[246] See above, paras 11–114 *et seq.*

[247] *Littauer Glove Corporation v FW Millington (1920) Ltd* (1928) 44 T.L.R. 746; *Vogel v RA Kohnstamm Ltd* [1973] Q.B. 133; *Adams v Cape Industries Plc* [1990] Ch. 433 (CA); see also *Moore v Mercator Enterprises Ltd* (1978) 90 D.L.R. (3d) 590 (N.S.).

[248] [1990] Ch. 433, 530–544. *cf. Akande v Balfour Beatty Construction Ltd* [1998] I.L.Pr. 110 (a case on the 1920 Act).

[249] See above, para.11–120.

[250] [1990] Ch. at p.539, citing *Woolfson v Strathclyde Regional Council*, 1978 S.L.T. 159, 161 (HL) (a case not involving the conflict of laws).

to enter into contracts on behalf of the corporation without seeking the prior approval of the corporation, this is a powerful indicator that the corporation is present; if the agent does not have this authority, this fact points powerfully in the opposite direction.[251]

14-066   In the case of companies which carry on or promote their business by placing advertisements or other invitations or information on an internet website which is accessible from, or even targeted at customers in, the foreign country in which the judgment was given, there is no English support for the view that this should be regarded as, or as equivalent to, presence in that jurisdiction, or as conduct which connoted temporary allegiance to the foreign state.[252] There is a distinction to be drawn between "carrying on business in" and carrying on business from a fixed place of business in the foreign country.[253] Though the former expression may have some jurisdictional relevance in some systems, it is the latter which establishes presence for the purpose of the First Case of the Rule. And this latter has not yet been held to be demonstrated or satisfied by a "presence in cyberspace".

14-067   Under the 1920 Act the principle of the cases on the jurisdiction of the English court applies also to the question whether a corporation carries on business in the jurisdiction of the original court within the meaning of the Act. Thus it has been held that a New Zealand insurance company does not carry on business in Ghana merely because it maintains agents there with limited powers to settle claims.[254] The 1933 Act[255] requires that the corporation must have its principal place of business (and not merely carry on business) in the foreign country.

14-068   **The second case. Appearance as claimant or counter-claimant.** It is obvious that a person who applies to a tribunal as claimant is bound to submit to its judgment, should that judgment go against him, if for no other reason than that fairness to the defendant demands this. It is no less obvious that a claimant exposes himself to acceptance of jurisdiction of a foreign court as regards any set-off, counterclaim or cross-action which may be brought against him by the defendant.[256] By the same token, a defendant who resorts

---

[251] *F&K Jabbour v Custodian of Israeli Absentee Property* [1954] 1 W.L.R. 139, 146; *Adams v Cape Industries Plc* [1990] Ch. 433, 531 (CA).

[252] *Lucasfilm Ltd v Ainsworth* [2009] EWCA Civ 1328, [2010] 3 W.L.R. 333. The point was not discussed on further appeal to the Supreme Court: [2011] UKSC 39, [2012] 1 A.C. 208.

[253] An Irish court has held that when a company is in liquidation and is no longer carrying on business, it is not to be regarded as present within the jurisdiction in question: *Re Flightlease (Ireland) Ltd* [2006] IEHC 193, [2008] 1 I.L.R.M. 53.

[254] *Sfeir & Co v National Insurance Co of New Zealand* [1964] 1 Lloyd's Rep. 330.

[255] s.4(2)(a)(iv).

[256] *Schibsby v Westenholz* (1870) L.R. 6 Q.B. 155, 161; *Burpee v Burpee* [1929] 3 D.L.R. 18 (BC); Westlake, ss.324, 325. It may, however, be otherwise where the action instituted after the claimant has submitted to the foreign jurisdiction is brought by someone other than the defendant against whom the original claim was made: see *Murthy v Sivajothi* [1999] 1 W.L.R. 467, discussed further below, para.14–075. Indeed, if a cross-action brought by the original defendant has nothing whatever to do with the subject matter of the original claim, but is permitted by the foreign court in accordance with its procedural law, it may still be arguable that the submission of the claimant should not be regarded as a matter of English law (whatever the foreign law may say, which is of no significance on this point) as automatically extending to proceedings and judgment in the cross-action.

to a counterclaim or like cross-proceeding in a foreign court clearly submits to the jurisdiction thereof.

The third case. Appearance. This case rests on the simple and universally admitted principle that a litigant who has voluntarily submitted himself to the jurisdiction of a court by appearing before it cannot afterwards dispute its jurisdiction. Where such a litigant, though a defendant rather than a claimant, appears and pleads to the merits without contesting the jurisdiction there is clearly a voluntary submission. The same is the case where he does indeed contest the jurisdiction[257] but nevertheless proceeds further to plead to the merits,[258] or agrees to a consent order dismissing the claims and cross-claims,[259] or where he fails to appear in proceedings at first instance but appeals on the merits.[260] If the defendant takes no part in the proceedings and allows judgment to go against him in default of appearance, and later moves to set the default judgment aside, the application to set aside may be a voluntary appearance if it is based on non-jurisdictional grounds, even if the application is unsuccessful.[261] There is no English authority directly in point; in *Guiard v De Clermont*[262] the defendant applied successfully to have a default judgment set aside and to have judgment entered in his favour at first instance, but the original judgment was restored by an appeal court; he was held to have voluntarily submitted.

14-069

Where the defendant contests the jurisdiction of a foreign court, the position is regulated by s.33 of the Civil Jurisdiction and Judgments Act 1982. If his challenge to the jurisdiction of the foreign court is successful, no question of submission arises. If it is unsuccessful and he goes on[263] to contest the case on the merits, he will have submitted to the jurisdiction of the foreign court. But if he takes no further part in the proceedings and judgment in default is entered against him, will he be regarded as having voluntarily submitted? Common sense would suggest that a defendant who has been vigorously protesting that a court has no jurisdiction should not be regarded as having voluntarily submitted.[264] Under the 1933 Act an appearance for the purpose of (inter alia) contesting the jurisdiction is not to be regarded as a voluntary

14-070

---

[257] But a defendant who wishes to enter an appearance but fails to succeed in doing so does not submit: *De Santis v Russo* [2002] 2 Qd.R 230 (Qd CA).

[258] *cf. Boissière v Brockner* (1889) 6 T.L.R. 85, criticised by Clarence Smith (1953) 2 I.C.L.Q. 510, 517–520; *McFadden v Colville Ranching Co* (1915) 8 W.W.R. 163 (Alta); *Richardson v Allen* (1916) 28 D.L.R. 134 (Alta CA).

[259] *Adams v Cape Industries Plc* [1990] Ch. 433, 461, *per* Scott J., affd. on other grounds *ibid.* p.503 (CA).

[260] *SA Consortium General Textiles v Sun & Sand Agencies Ltd* [1978] Q.B. 279 (CA) (a case on the 1933 Act).

[261] This may be an explanation for *Desert Sun Loan Corp v Hill* [1996] 2 All E.R. 847, where the application to set aside was based on the construction or validity of a power of attorney: a non-jurisdictional issue which had jurisdictional consequences.

[262] [1914] 3 K.B. 145.

[263] This expression was adopted and relied on at first instance in *AES Ust-Kamenogorsk Hydropower Plant LLP v AES Ust-Kamenogorsk Hydropower Plant JSC* [2010] EWHC 772 (Comm.), [2010] 2 Lloyd's Rep. 493, [47]–[51], affd. [2011] EWCA Civ 647, [2011] 2 C.L.C. 51.

[264] *Re Dulles' Settlement (No.2)* [1951] Ch. 842, 850 (CA), *per* Denning L.J. See also *Daarnhouwer & Co NV v Boulos* [1968] 2 Lloyd's Rep. 259.

appearance.[265] But in *Harris v Taylor*,[266] decided at common law, a defendant who had entered a conditional appearance in the Isle of Man court in order to set aside the proceedings on jurisdictional grounds was held to have submitted to the jurisdiction of the Manx Court, even though he took no further part in the proceedings after his application to set aside was unsuccessful. This decision was followed in *Henry v Geoprosco International*,[267] where the Court of Appeal held that there was a voluntary appearance where the defendant appeared before the foreign court to invite that court in its discretion not to exercise a jurisdiction which it had under its local law; and that there was also a voluntary appearance if the defendant merely protested against the jurisdiction of the foreign court if the protest took the form of a conditional appearance which was converted automatically by operation of law into an unconditional appearance if the decision on jurisdiction went against the defendant. The court left open the question whether an appearance the sole purpose and effect of which was to protest against the jurisdiction of the foreign court would be a voluntary appearance. The criticism to which this decision was subjected led to considerable pressure for its reversal by legislation, and this was effected by s.33 of the 1982 Act.

14–071   Section 33 provides that a judgment debtor shall not be regarded as having submitted by reason only of the fact that he appeared (conditionally or otherwise) in the foreign proceedings (a) to contest the jurisdiction of the court; (b) to ask the court to dismiss or stay the proceedings on the ground that the dispute in question should be submitted to arbitration[268] or to the determination of the courts of another country; or (c) to protect, or obtain the release of, property seized or threatened with seizure in the proceedings. If the defendant in the foreign court fails on any of these issues, but nevertheless goes on to defend the case on the merits, he will be regarded as having submitted. It follows that s.33 will be relevant if, but only if, the defendant has, apart from anything mentioned in the section, submitted to the jurisdiction of the foreign court, for if he has, the judgment against him will, in accordance with this Rule, be liable to be recognised and may be enforced: it is to this possibility that s.33 provides a defence.[269] If, by contrast, his participation before the foreign court would not constitute submission for the

---

[265] 1933 Act, s.4(2)(a)(i).

[266] [1914] 3 K.B. 580 (CA); followed in *Kennedy v Trites* (1916) 10 W.W.R. 412 (BC); not followed in *Dovenmuehle v Rocca Group Ltd* (1981) 34 N.B.R. (2d) 444, app. dismissed (1982) 43 N.B.R. (2d) 359 (Sup Ct Can); *WSG Nimbus Pte Ltd v Board of Control for Cricket in Sri Lanka* [2002] 3 Sing. L.R. 603 (HC). See also *Re McCain Foods and Agricultural Publishing Co Ltd* (1979) 103 D.L.R. (3d) 734 (Ont CA); *Mid-Ohio Imported Car Co v Tri-K Investments Ltd* (1995) 129 D.L.R. (4th) 181 (BCCA).

[267] [1976] Q.B. 726 (CA), criticised by Collins (1976) 92 L.Q.R. 268 (reprinted in Collins, *Essays*, p.313); Carter (1974–75) 47 B.Y.I.L. 379; Solomons (1976) 25 I.C.L.Q. 665.

[268] As in *Tracomin SA v Sudan Oil Seeds Co Ltd (No.1)* [1983] 1 W.L.R. 662, affirmed [1983] 1 W.L.R. 1026 (CA). If the applicant does not proceed to have his challenge heard and ruled on, it will be taken as waived and his appearance will be denied the protection of s.33: *Starlight International Inc v Bruce* [2002] EWHC 374 (Ch.), [2002] I.L.Pr. 617.

[269] The apparent suggestion in *AES Ust-Kamenogorsk Hydropower Plant LLP v AES Ust-Kamenogorsk Hydropower Plant JSC* [2011] EWCA Civ 647, [2011] 2 Lloyd's Rep. 233, [151], that even though the defendant has submitted to the jurisdiction of the foreign court, the English court is not bound to recognise or enforce the foreign judgment, because s.33 does not contain a specific instruction to that effect, is insupportable.

purpose of the English rules of the conflict of laws, s.33 has no role to play.[270]

If a defendant makes an appearance in order to argue that the court seised   **14–072** has no international jurisdiction over him according to its law, the section plainly applies to protect him from the contention that he submitted by appearance. But if he appears to argue that the particular court has no local jurisdiction because the claim exceeds its internal competence, or because the court in a different judicial district alone has jurisdiction, it is less clear that an appearance to make this objection this would be protected by s.33(1)(a). Certainly it was not the problem which was presented by *Henry v Geoprosco International*, and which the section was immediately designed to remedy. It is submitted that if the whole of the relief sought by the defendant from the foreign court is a decision by the court that it has no international jurisdiction, the appearance will be protected from being regarded as a submission by s.33(1)(a);[271] but that a contention that a different court (but in the same country) has jurisdiction is not to be seen as contesting the jurisdiction within the meaning of s.33(1)(a), for it is implicit in the contention that the courts of the country do not lack jurisdiction.

Some systems of law require or allow a defendant to plead to the merits at   **14–073** the same time as, and as an alternative to, an objection to the jurisdiction. In *Boissière & Co v Brockner*[272] a plea on the merits put forward in this way was regarded as a submission at common law. But it should not now be so regarded, provided at least that, having lost on the issue of jurisdiction, the defendant does not put forward his case on the merits. This conclusion is supported by two decisions on submission as a basis of jurisdiction in the original court, and by two decisions on foreign judgments. In *Elefanten Schuh GmbH v Jacqmain*[273] the European Court held, in the context of Art.18 of the Brussels Convention, that pleading to the merits as an alternative to an objection to the jurisdiction would not be a submission. The House of Lords has held, in the context of submission to the jurisdiction of the English court,[274] that a step in the proceedings only amounts to a submission when the defendant has taken some step which is only necessary or only useful if the objection to the jurisdiction has been waived.[275] In *Adams v Cape Industries Plc*[276] defendants to United States proceedings objected to the jurisdiction of

---

[270] cf. *AES Ust-Kamenogorsk Hydropower Plant LLP v AES Ust-Kamenogorsk Hydropower Plant JSC* [2010] EWHC 772 (Comm.), [2010] 2 Lloyd's Rep. 493 (no submission, as it could not be said that the defendant had lost his jurisdictional challenge but then gone on to defend: the defendant contested jurisdiction at all times, so there was neither room nor need for s.33 to be applied). This analysis is to be preferred to that of the Court of Appeal.

[271] In *Desert Sun Loan Corp v Hill* [1996] 2 All E.R. 847 (CA), the defendant appeared before the foreign court to contend that he had not authorised his attorney to accept service of the writ. The majority (Evans and Stuart-Smith L.JJ.) did not appear to consider s.33(1)(a) to be relevant to the case; by contrast, Roch L.J. interpreted such a contention as falling squarely within the section.

[272] (1889) 6 T.L.R. 85.

[273] Case 150/80 [1981] E.C.R. 1671.

[274] See above, para.11–128.

[275] *Williams & Glyn's Bank v Astro Dinamico* [1984] 1 W.L.R. 438 (HL), applied in *Akai Pty Ltd v People's Insurance Co Ltd* [1998] 1 Lloyd's Rep. 90.

[276] [1990] Ch. 433, 461 *per* Scott J., affirmed on other grounds *ibid.* p.503 (CA); *The Eastern Trader* [1996] 2 Lloyd's Rep. 585, 600; *Akai Pty Ltd v People's Insurance Co Ltd*, above *cf. Canada Trustco Mortgage Co v Rene Management & Holdings Ltd* (1986) 32 D.L.R. (4th) 747

the court, but also participated in pre-trial discovery on the merits of the case. These steps were accompanied, expressly or impliedly, by a re-assertion of the jurisdictional objection, and under Federal law the steps taken did not amount to a submission. It was held that steps not regarded by the foreign court as a submission should not be regarded as a submission for the purposes of enforcement in England. More importantly, perhaps, in *AES Ust-Kameno-gorsk Hydropower Plant LLP v AES Ust-Kamenogorsk Hydropower Plant JSC*[277] it was held, correctly, that even if the foreign court might regard the defendant as having submitted to its jurisdiction, it was still open to an English court to find that there had been no submission as a matter of the English rules of the conflict of laws. In *Marc Rich & Co AG v Soc Italiana Impianti PA (No.2)*[278] it was held that s.33 should not be construed narrowly: an objection to the jurisdiction of the Italian court, accompanied by a defence on the merits, did not amount to a submission, even though it was not necessary under Italian law for an alternative defence on the merits to be put forward. But after the Italian court had ruled that the parties had not agreed to arbitrate in London, and that it therefore had jurisdiction over the merits of the dispute, the defendants in the Italian proceedings lodged a defence on the merits. The consequence was that they thereby submitted to the jurisdiction of the Italian court, and were bound by the decision that the contract did not contain an arbitration clause. The general thrust of the authorities, which were all examined in *AES Ust-Kamenogorsk Hydropower Plant LLP v AES Ust-Kameno-gorsk Hydropower Plant JSC*[279] is that for so long as the defendant asserted, and is obviously[280] still asserting, as his primary defence that the court has no jurisdiction over him in relation to the merits of the claim, then even if he also takes steps which are purposeful in relation to the merits of the claim, his doing so should not be taken to mean that he has submitted to the jurisdiction for the purposes of the common law of submission, and has abandoned his challenge for the purpose of s.33. The real question for the English court should not be whether the defendant has taken a step in proceedings which prepare for the trial of the merits, but whether he has chosen to abandon his challenge to the jurisdiction. In answering this, the English court is not bound to follow the law of the foreign court on whether a defendant has succumbed to its jurisdiction; and if the defendant had "no real option but to act as it did", as it was put in *AES Ust-Kamenogorsk Hydropower Plant LLP v AES Ust-Kamenogorsk Hydropower Plant JSC,*[281] the court may be reluctant to find that it has submitted to the jurisdiction.

14–074   Where the property of the defendant is attached in foreign proceedings and he intervenes to obtain its release, a similar question of submission arises. The

---

(Man); *Gourmet Resources International Inc v Paramount Capital Corp* [1993] I.L.Pr. 583 (Ont).

[277] [2010] EWHC 772 (Comm.), [2010] 2 Lloyd's Rep. 493, [42]–[52]. The decision of the Court of Appeal ([2011] EWCA Civ 647, [2011] 2 Lloyd's Rep. 233) at [186] did not disturb this conclusion.

[278] [1992] 1 Lloyd's Rep. 624 (CA); *The Eastern Trader*, above, at pp.598–602.

[279] [2011] EWCA Civ 647, [2011] 2 Lloyd's Rep. 233.

[280] And perhaps rationally: it will not be open to a defendant to give himself a lifeline by complaining about the jurisdiction in circumstances where there is no basis for making a challenge to it.

[281] [2011] EWCA Civ 647, [2011] 2 Lloyd's Rep. 233, [200].

1933 Act provided, for cases within its scope, that an appearance for the purpose of protecting, or obtaining the release of, property seized or threatened with seizure in the foreign proceedings was not to be regarded as a voluntary appearance.[282] There was some doubt as to the extent to which this represented the common law rule,[283] but the 1982 Act[284] makes this principle one of general application. The common law authorities may still be helpful in considering the extent to which the defendant may go in taking steps to preserve his property. Thus it is clear that an appearance was not involuntary at common law merely because it was motivated by the fact that the defendant had property within the jurisdiction of the foreign court on which execution might be levied in the event of judgment going against him by default;[285] still less was an appearance involuntary when it was made because, although the defendant had no property within the jurisdiction of the foreign court, his business often took him there, so that the judgment might be made effective against him.[286] Secondly, an appearance is not involuntary when it is made after execution has been levied under the judgment in order to rescue the property which is the subject-matter of the execution.[287] Thirdly, if property is seized and the defendant appears and defends the case on the merits, the appearance is not involuntary.[288] But there may be cases in which the defendant may appear to oppose the seizure on jurisdictional grounds, e.g. where he denies he has property within the jurisdiction or where he challenges the validity of the seizure.[289] In such cases the effect of s.33 of the 1982 Act is that the appearance will not be voluntary.

The defendant, by an appearance which is voluntary in the sense explained, **14–075** renders himself subject to the jurisdiction of the foreign court with respect not only to the original claim but also to such further claims as the court allows to be added by the plaintiff. But this does not mean that he subjects himself also to claims by new claimants.[290] In principle, a submission will extend to claims concerning the same subject-matter, and to related claims which ought to be dealt with in the same proceedings, but (in either case) only if advanced

---

[282] 1933 Act, s.4(2)(a)(i).

[283] *Voinet v Barrett* (1885) 55 L.J.Q.B. 39, 41 (CA); *Schibsby v Westenholz* (1870) L.R. 6 Q.B. 155, 162 (CA); *Guiard v De Clermont* [1914] 3 K.B. 145, 155; *Henry v Geoprosco International* [1976] Q.B. 726, 746–747 (CA).

[284] 1982 Act, s.33(1)(c).

[285] *De Cosse Brissac v Rathbone* (1861) 6 H. & N. 301 (the third plea).

[286] *Voinet v Barrett* (1855) 55 L.J.Q.B. 39 (CA).

[287] *Guiard v De Clermont* [1914] 3 K.B. 145; *Poissant v Poissant* [1941] 3 W.W.R. 646, 650 (Sask).

[288] *Clinton v Ford* (1982) 137 D.L.R. (3d) 281 (Ont CA); *cf. Re Low* [1894] 1 Ch. 147, 160 (CA).

[289] As he may do in the United States on constitutional grounds: see *Shaffer v Heitner*, 433 U.S. 186 (1977). It is to be noted that although s.33(1)(c) is not expressly limited to appearances to protect property on jurisdictional grounds, such a limitation should be read it to avoid the absurdity of the sub-section providing a shield against recognition to every defendant who asserts, truthfully, that the only reason he defended on the merits was to protect property which had been seized or which had been threatened with seizure if judgment on the merits was given against him.

[290] See Restatement, s.26, comment e and Illustration 8, and *Re Indiana Transportation Co*, 244 U.S. 456 (1917) (submission to jurisdiction in respect of death of one passenger held not to involve submission in other claims). And see, by analogy, *Jordan Grand Prix Ltd v Baltic Insurance Group* [1999] 2 A.C. 127.

by parties who were such at the date of the defendant's submission to the jurisdiction of the court; the decision of the foreign court to allow the new claim is not decisive.[291]

14–076   **The fourth case. Agreement to submit.** If a contract provides that all disputes between the parties shall be referred to the exclusive[292] jurisdiction of a foreign tribunal, not only will proceedings brought in England in breach of such agreement usually be stayed,[293] but also the foreign court is deemed to have jurisdiction over the parties.[294] A contractual submission to a particular court is not of itself a submission generally to the jurisdiction of all courts of that country;[295] the question is one of construction of the contract.[296]

14–077   An agreement to submit may also take the form of an agreement to accept service of process at a designated address. Thus, if a person takes shares in a foreign company, the articles of association or statutes of which provide that all disputes shall be submitted to the jurisdiction of a foreign court, and that every shareholder must "elect a domicile" at a particular place for service of process, and that in default the officers of the company may do so for him, then he is deemed to have agreed to submit to the jurisdiction of the foreign court, even if he never does elect a domicile.[297] And a member of a foreign company is bound by a statute enacted in the country of its incorporation providing that the particular company may sue and be sued in the name of its chairman and that execution on any judgment against the company may be issued against the property of any member in like manner as if the judgment had been obtained against him personally.[298] But English courts have stopped short of inferring an agreement to submit from a mere general provision in the foreign law (and not in the articles of association or in a statute specifically referring to the particular company) that the shareholder must "elect a domicile" for the service of process,[299] unless he does in fact elect such a domicile.[300]

14–078   It would seem that a judgment based on a "cognovit clause," which gives a claimant or his lawyer power to enter judgment against the defendant in a

---

[291] *Murthy v Sivajothi* [1999] 1 W.L.R. 467 (CA), in which the text to n.290 was approved. The principle in *Murthy* was applied in *Whyte v Whyte* [2005] EWCA Civ 858.

[292] The same will be true where the jurisdiction agreement is non-exclusive, though proceedings brought in England in breach of such an agreement be less likely to be stayed.

[293] Rule 40(2). A non-exclusive jurisdiction agreement (see above, para.12–105) will also be regarded as a submission: *First Capital Ltd v Winchester Computer Corp* (1987) 44 D.L.R. (4th) 301 (Sask CA).

[294] *Feyerick v Hubbard* (1902) 71 L.J.K.B. 509; *Jeannot v Fuerst* (1909) 25 T.L.R. 424.

[295] *SA Consortium General Textiles v Sun & Sand Agencies Ltd* [1978] Q.B. 279 (CA) (a case on the 1933 Act).

[296] See Briggs (2004) 8 Sing. Yb. Int. L. 1.

[297] *Copin v Adamson* (1874) L.R. 9 Ex. 345; (1875) 1 Ex. D. 17 (CA) (the first replication).

[298] *Bank of Australasia v Harding* (1850) 9 C.B. 661; *Bank of Australasia v Nias* (1851) 16 Q.B. 717; *Kelsall v Marshall* (1856) 1 C.B.(n.s.) 241.

[299] *Copin v Adamson* (1874) L.R. 9 Ex. 345 (the second replication). The point was reserved in the Court of Appeal: see 1 Ex D. 17, 19. See also *Risdon Iron & Locomotive Works v Furness* [1906] 1 K.B. 49, 57; *Allen v Standard Trusts Co* (1920) 57 D.L.R. 105 (Man CA); *Veco Drilling v Armstrong* [1982] 1 W.W.R. 177 (BC); *Jamieson v Robb* (1881) 7 V.L.R. 170, on which see Read, pp.176–177.

[300] *Vallée v Dumergue* (1849) 4 Exch. 290.

specified court in the event of a default in payment, would be enforceable on the basis that the defendant has agreed thereby to submit,[301] at any rate if the clause is valid by the law applicable to the contract. Such clauses are common in the United States, where they are subject to widespread criticism because of their potential abuse, and where their validity varies from state to state.[302]

It may be laid down as a general rule that an agreement to submit to the **14–079** jurisdiction of a foreign court must be express: it cannot be implied.[303] If the parties agree, expressly or by implication, that their contract shall be governed by a particular foreign law, it by no means follows that they agree to submit to the jurisdiction of the courts which apply it.[304] Nor can any such agreement be implied from the fact that the cause of action arose within a foreign country or from the additional fact that the defendant was present there when the cause of action arose.[305] In *Emanuel v Symon*,[306] the Court of Appeal held that a defendant did not submit to the courts of a foreign country merely because he became a member of a partnership firm which carried on business there. But in *Blohn v Desser*,[307] Diplock J. held that where a person resident in England became a sleeping partner in an Austrian firm she did submit to the jurisdiction of the Austrian courts. These cases can perhaps be reconciled on the basis that *Emanuel v Symon* was concerned with the liability of the partners *inter se*, while *Blohn v Desser* was concerned with the liability of a partner to an outside creditor. In other words, there was an element of holding out in *Blohn v Desser* which was absent from *Emanuel v Symon*. It is submitted that on this point *Blohn v Desser* cannot be supported. It was not followed in *Vogel v RA Kohnstamm Ltd*,[308] and in *Adams v Cape Industries Plc*[309] Scott J. said that he did not think it was right that an agreement to submit could be implied: but he accepted that an alleged consent which was not contractually enforceable could be treated as a representation by the defendant of a willingness to submit to the jurisdiction if acted upon by the plaintiff, provided that the representation was intended to be acted upon, or at least be one which the

---

[301] See *Re Hughes & Sharp* (1968) 70 D.L.R. (2d) 298, reversed on other grounds (1969) 5 D.L.R. (3d) 760 (BCCA); *Batavia Times Publishing Co v Davis* (1977) 82 D.L.R. (3d) 247, app. dismissed (1979) 102 D.L.R. (3d) 192 (Ont CA); Read, p.172.

[302] See Hay, Borchers and Symeonides, p.1467; Restatement, s.32.

[303] *Sirdar Gurdyal Singh v Rajah of Faridkote* [1894] A.C. 670 (PC); *Emanuel v Symon* [1908] 1 K.B. 302 (CA); *Vogel v RA Kohnstamm Ltd* [1973] Q.B. 133 and *New Hampshire Insurance Co v Strabag Bau AG* [1992] 1 Lloyd's Rep. 361, 371–372 (CA), not following dicta in *Blohn v Desser* [1962] 2 Q.B. 116, 123 and in *Sfeir & Co v National Insurance Co of New Zealand* [1964] 1 Lloyd's Rep. 330, 339–340.

[304] *Sfeir & Co v National Insurance Co of New Zealand* [1964] 1 Lloyd's Rep. 330, 340 (a case on the 1920 Act); *Mattar and Saba v Public Trustee* [1952] 3 D.L.R. 399 (Alta CA); *Dunbee Ltd v Gilman & Co* (1968) 70 S.R.N.S.W. 219; also reported [1968] 2 Lloyd's Rep. 394.

[305] *Sirdar Gurdyal Singh v Rajah of Faridkote* [1894] A.C. 670 (PC); *Emanuel v Symon* [1908] 1 K.B. 302 (CA); *Mattar and Saba v Public Trustee* [1952] 3 D.L.R. 399 (Alta CA); *Gyonyor v Sanjenko* [1971] 5 W.W.R. 381 (Alta).

[306] [1908] 1 K.B. 302 (CA).

[307] [1962] 2 Q.B. 116, 123, criticised Lewis (1961) 10 I.C.L.Q. 910; Cohn (1962) 11 I.C.L.Q. 583; Carter (1962) 38 B.Y.I.L. 493.

[308] [1973] Q.B. 133.

[309] [1990] Ch. 433, 465–466, *per* Scott J., affirmed on other grounds *ibid.* p.503 (CA).

plaintiff reasonably believed was intended to be acted upon. But in that case no such representation could be inferred.[310]

14–080   If the defendant agrees to submit to the jurisdiction of a foreign court, and agrees (or is deemed to agree) to a particular method of service, it is immaterial at common law that he does not receive actual notice of the proceedings if service is effected in the agreed manner.[311] It was suggested in earlier editions of this work[312] that, even if there is no agreement as to method of service, it is immaterial that the defendant did not receive sufficient notice of the proceedings to enable him to defend them; but it is submitted that there is no rule to this effect: the ultimate question is whether there has been substantial injustice, and the court may take into account (inter alia) whether the foreign law provides an opportunity for the judgment to be set aside.[313]

14–081   The 1920 and 1933 Acts both contain provisions, separate and distinct from their provisions as to jurisdiction, which require respectively that the defendant must have been duly served[314] or must have received notice of the proceedings in sufficient time to enable him to defend.[315]

14–082   **What does not give jurisdiction.** The rules of common law (by contrast with those under the 1933 Act, which are exhaustive[316]) as to jurisdiction are not necessarily exclusive. Like any other common law rules, they are no doubt capable of judicious expansion to meet the changing needs of society. However, English courts have decided that certain jurisdictional bases are inadequate, though some of them are quite commonly relied upon by foreign courts. These are as follows:

14–083   (1) *Possession by the defendant of property in the foreign country.* This is relied upon in Scotland[317] but has been rejected in England.[318] As early as the Judgments Extension Act 1868 the registration in England or Northern Ireland of a Scottish judgment based on this ground was specifically excluded.

14–084   (2) *Presence of the defendant in the foreign country at the time when the cause of action arose.* Though a dictum of Lord Blackburn favours this

---

[310] In particular, it was held that a submission in one set of proceedings could not be regarded as a submission in another set of (related) proceedings.

[311] *Vallée v Dumergue* (1849) 4 Exch. 290; *Bank of Australasia v Harding* (1850) 9 C.B. 661; *Bank of Australasia v Nias* (1851) 16 Q.B. 509; *Copin v Adamson* (1875) 2 Ex. D. 17 (CA). *cf. Jamieson v Robb* (1881) 7 V.L.R. 170.

[312] 11th ed., p.446. *cf. Feyerick v Hubbard* (1902) 71 L.J. K.B. 509; and the Canadian cases on "cognovit clauses", above, n.301.

[313] *Adams v Cape Industries Plc* [1990] Ch. 433, 563–571; *cf. Jeannot v Fuerst* (1909) 25 T.L.R. 424. See below, Rule 52.

[314] 1920 Act, s.9(2)(c).

[315] 1933 Act, s.4(1)(a)(iii).

[316] *Société Co-opérative Sidmetal v Titan International Ltd* [1966] 1 Q.B. 828; *Sharps Commercials Ltd v Gas Turbines Ltd* [1956] N.Z.L.R. 819 (a decision on the identically worded New Zealand Act).

[317] See Anton, paras 9.32–9.33.

[318] *Schibsby v Westenholz* (1870) L.R. 6 Q.B. 155, 163; *Rousillon v Rousillon* (1880) 14 Ch.D. 351, 371; *Sirdar Gurdyal Singh v Rajah of Faridkote* [1894] A.C. 670 (PC); *Emanuel v Symon* [1908] 1 K.B. 302 (CA).

head,[319] the Privy Council and the Court of Appeal have since rejected it.[320]

(3) *Defendant a national of the foreign country.* There is a long chain of **14–085** dicta extending from 1828 to 1948 suggesting that the courts of a foreign country might have jurisdiction over a person if he was a subject or citizen of that country.[321] But there is no actual decision which supports this proposition. *Douglas v Forrest*[322] goes nearest to a decision to this effect. But that is a very old case, and the judgment dwells also on the fact that the defendant retained property in the foreign country—an alternative basis of jurisdiction which would not now be acknowledged as adequate. It is evident that nationality is quite inappropriate as a basis of jurisdiction when the defendant is, e.g. a British citizen[323] or an American citizen,[324] or an Australian citizen since in these cases the political unit (or State) does not coincide with the law district (or country). Citizenship does not serve to identify them with any particular law district, such as England or New York or Victoria, within a composite State such as the United Kingdom, the United States or Australia. Moreover, the question whether a person is a national of a given state is a matter for the law of that State.[325] As a connecting factor, therefore, nationality is not subject to the control or definition of the *lex fori*; and as the law of the given State may deem a person to be a national, or deny nationality, on grounds which are objectionable in English eyes, nationality would constitute too unpredictable a basis for jurisdiction. Nationality as a basis of jurisdiction has been doubted by three High Court judges,[326] and definitely rejected by the Irish High Court.[327] It cannot therefore safely be relied upon today.[328] It is not mentioned as a basis of jurisdiction in the 1933 Act.

(4) *Defendant domiciled (but not resident or present) in the foreign country.* **14–086** There are dicta in English cases[329] which suggest (though rather faintly) the

---

[319] *Schibsby v Westenholz* (1870) L.R. 6 Q.B. 155, 161.

[320] *Sirdar Gurdyal Singh v Rajah of Faridkote* [1894] A.C. 670 (PC); *Emanuel v Symon* [1908] 1 K.B. 302 (CA); *cf. Mattar and Saba v Public Trustee* [1952] 3 D.L.R. 399 (Alta CA); *Gyonyor v Sanjenko* [1971] 5 W.W.R. 381 (Alta).

[321] *Douglas v Forrest* (1828) 4 Bing. 686; *Schibsby v Westenholz* (1870) L.R. 6 Q.B. 155, 161; *Rousillon v Rousillon* (1880) 14 Ch.D. 351, 371; *Emanuel v Symon* [1908] 1 K.B. 302, 309 (CA); *Gavin Gibson & Co v Gibson* [1913] 3 K.B. 379, 388; *Harris v Taylor* [1915] 2 K.B. 580, 591 (CA); *Forsyth v Forsyth* [1948] P. 125, 132 (CA). *cf.* Restatement, s.31, comment c. Contrast *Independent Trustee Services Ltd v Morris* [2010] NSWSC 1218.

[322] (1828) 4 Bing. 686.

[323] See *Gavin Gibson & Co v Gibson* [1913] 3 K.B. 379.

[324] See *Dakota Lumber Co v Rinderknecht* (1905) 6 Terr.L.R. 210, 221–224.

[325] See above, para.6–167.

[326] *Blohn v Desser* [1962] 2 Q.B. 116, 123; *Rossano v Manufacturers' Life Insurance Co Ltd* [1963] 2 Q.B. 352, 382–383; *Vogel v RA Kohnstamm Ltd* [1973] Q.B. 133; see also *Patterson v D'Agostino* (1975) 58 D.L.R. (3d) 63 (Ont).

[327] *Rainford v Newell-Roberts* [1962] I.R. 95.

[328] The observations in *British Nylon Spinners Ltd v Imperial Chemical Industries* [1953] Ch. 19, 25 (CA) relate, it is submitted, to nationality as a basis of legislative rather than curial jurisdiction.

[329] *Turnbull v Walker* (1892) 67 L.T. 767, 769; *Emanuel v Symon* [1908] 1 K.B. 302, 308, 314 (CA); *Jaffer v Williams* (1908) 25 T.L.R. 12, 13; *Gavin Gibson & Co v Gibson* [1913] 3 K.B. 379, 385.

recognition of domicile in the common law sense[330] as a basis of jurisdiction, but no English decision supports this, though one Canadian decision does.[331] It is not claimed as a ground of jurisdiction by the Scottish courts.[332] It is not mentioned in the 1933 Act. Despite the Canadian decision referred to above, Dean Read concluded that "domicile alone, unaccompanied by either residence or presence, will not yet suffice."[333]

14–087   (5) *Reciprocity.* Reciprocity is used in two distinct senses in connection with the recognition and enforcement of foreign judgments. Firstly, it is used to describe the view, once espoused by the United States Supreme Court[334] but which has been largely abandoned in the United States,[335] that a judgment rendered by the court of a foreign country will not be enforced unless that country would enforce a comparable judgment of the requested court. That view of reciprocity forms part of the law of many civil law countries,[336] but has never been the law in England. Secondly, reciprocity is used to describe the view that the English court should recognise the jurisdiction of the foreign court if the situation is such that, *mutatis mutandis*, the English court might have exercised jurisdiction, e.g. under CPR, r.6.36 and Practice Direction 6B.[337] On the present state of the authorities, the jurisdiction of the foreign court will not be recognised on such a basis.

14–088   In *Schibsby v Westenholz*[338] the plaintiff brought an action in England on a French judgment. The defendant was not in France when the writ was issued, nor did he appear or submit to the jurisdiction. The writ was served on him in England. The Court of Queen's Bench was much pressed with the argument that, under what were then ss.18 and 19 of the Common Law Procedure Act 1852 and is now CPR, r.6.36[339] the English court would have had power to order service out of the jurisdiction on converse facts, and therefore it should enforce the French judgment. In rejecting this argument Lord Blackburn observed[340] that "if the principle on which foreign judgments were enforced was that which is loosely called 'comity,' we could hardly decline to enforce a foreign judgment given in France against a resident in Great Britain under circumstances hardly, if at all, distinguishable from those under which we, *mutatis mutandis*, might give judgment against a resident in France; but it is quite different if the principle be that which we have just laid down" (i.e. the doctrine of obligation quoted earlier in this chapter[341]). This was followed in *Turnbull v Walker*,[342] where Wright J. refused to enforce a New Zealand

---

[330] Domicile in the sense of the 1982 Act would for most purposes be within the First Case.

[331] *Marshall v Houghton* [1923] 2 W.W.R. 553 (Man CA). *cf.* Restatement, s.29.

[332] *Kerr v Ferguson*, 1931 S.C. 736, overruling *Glasgow Corporation v Johnston*, 1915 S.C. 555.

[333] Read, p.160.

[334] *Hilton v Guyot*, 159 U.S. 113 (1895).

[335] Restatement Third, *Foreign Relations Law*, s.481, Rep. Note 1.

[336] e.g. Germany: Code of Civil Procedure, para.328.

[337] See Rule 34, above.

[338] (1870) L.R. 6 Q.B. 155.

[339] i.e. Rule 34, above.

[340] At p.159.

[341] See above, para.14–006.

[342] (1892) 67 L.T. 767. *cf. Phillips v Batho* [1913] 3 K.B. 25, 29–30; *Wendel v Moran*, 1993 S.L.T. 44 (fact that delict occurred in the US insufficient to give jurisdiction).

judgment based on provisions for the service of writs out of the jurisdiction which were identical with the English provisions.

In spite of these decisions, it was suggested by Denning L.J.[343] that an **14–089** English court would recognise that a court in the Isle of Man had jurisdiction to give a judgment based on service of the writ out of the jurisdiction if the English court would have assumed jurisdiction in converse circumstances. And in *Travers v Holley*[344] the Court of Appeal recognised a New South Wales divorce granted in the absence of domicile on the ground that "it would be contrary to principle and inconsistent with comity if the courts of this country were to refuse to recognise a jurisdiction which *mutatis mutandis* they claimed for themselves." The width and generality of this statement led to suggestions being made extra-judicially[345] that the principle of reciprocity might be applicable to foreign judgments *in personam*. But it has since been held that this is not so and that English courts do not concede jurisdiction in the international sense *in personam* to foreign courts merely because English courts would, in converse circumstances, have power to order service out of the jurisdiction.[346] "The decision in *Travers v Holley* was a decision limited to a judgment *in rem* in a matter affecting matrimonial status, and it has not been followed in any case except a matrimonial case."[347] "Comity has never been the basis on which we recognise or give effect to foreign judgments."[348] "I am unwilling to accept . . . that the law of foreign divorce (still less other) jurisdiction must be a mirror image of our own law."[349] Indeed, in *Amin Rasheed Shipping Corp v Kuwait Insurance Co*[350] (which was not a case involving foreign judgments) Lord Diplock went so far as to say that the jurisdiction exercised under what is now CPR, r.6.36 and PD6B, para.3.1 is an exorbitant jurisdiction, in the sense that "it is one which, under general English conflict rules, an English court would not recognise as possessed by any foreign court in the absence of some treaty providing for such recognition." Although Lord Diplock was wrong to describe what is now CPR, r.6.36 and PD6B, para.3.1 as an exorbitant jurisdiction,[351] he was certainly expressing the orthodox view on recognition of foreign judgments in cases where the debtor was neither within the foreign jurisdiction nor had submitted to it. Thus, none of the following facts by itself gives international jurisdiction to the courts of a foreign country: that the cause of action arose out of a contract made or broken there or which was to be governed by the law thereof, or out of a tort committed there; or that the defendant is a necessary or proper party

---

[343] *Re Dulles' Settlement (No.2)* [1951] Ch. 842, 851 (CA).

[344] [1953] P. 246, 257, *per* Hodson L.J.

[345] Kennedy (1954) 32 Can.Bar Rev. 359, 373–383; (1957) 35 *ibid.* 123; Cheshire, 7th ed., pp.557–558.

[346] *Re Trepca Mines Ltd* [1960] 1 W.L.R. 1273, 1280–1282 (CA); *Société Co-opérative Sidmetal v Titan International Ltd* [1966] 1 Q.B. 828; *Sharps Commercials Ltd v Gas Turbines Ltd* [1956] N.Z.L.R. 819, 823; *Crick v Hennessy* [1973] W.A.R. 74.

[347] *Re Trepca Mines Ltd*, above, at pp.1281–1282, *per* Hodson L.J., approved in *Henry v Geoprosco International* [1976] Q.B. 726, 745 (CA). *cf. Schemmer v Property Resources Ltd* [1975] Ch. 273, 287.

[348] *Indyka v Indyka* [1969] 1 A.C. 33, 58, *per* Lord Reid, citing *Schibsby v Westenholz* (1870) L.R. 6 Q.B. 155 at p.159.

[349] *ibid.*, at p.106, *per* Lord Wilberforce.

[350] [1984] A.C. 50, 65.

[351] See above, para.11–142, n.404.

to an action properly brought against a person duly served. This has led some to say that in proceedings *in personam*, English courts claim a wider jurisdiction than they are prepared to concede to foreign courts. But it is submitted that such an observation involves playing with words and is apt to mislead. For there is no obvious need for there to be symmetry between the jurisdiction which is exercised by an English court which is asked to adjudicate (but which does not do so with any concern for whether its judgment may be enforced outside the jurisdiction), and that "jurisdiction" of a foreign court which means that, as far as the common law is concerned, its judgment may be recognised as *res judicata* in England. The word "jurisdiction" is used in each case, but it is being used in two distinct different senses. Insofar as the point can be made at all, the similarity is linguistic rather than substantial.

14–090   (6) *Real and substantial connection.* In *Indyka v Indyka*[352] the House of Lords held that foreign divorce decrees should be recognised, not only on the basis of reciprocity under the doctrine in *Travers v Holley*, but also wherever a real and substantial connection was shown between the petitioner and the country whose court granted the decree. There is no authority in England which suggests that this is the appropriate test for the recognition and enforcement of foreign judgments *in personam*. But in 1990 the Supreme Court of Canada held in *Morguard Investments Ltd v De Savoye*[353] that, as regards the enforcement of judgments between the Canadian provinces, it was no longer appropriate to apply the 19th century rules developed in England for the recognition and enforcement of wholly foreign judgments. It was held that courts in one province should give full faith and credit (a phrase borrowed from the United States Constitution) to judgments given by a court in another province or territory "so long as that court has properly, or appropriately, exercised jurisdiction in the action". That condition was met when the defendant was present in the foreign jurisdiction at the time of the action, or submitted to its judgment by agreement or appearance: in other cases, the test to be applied was not that of reciprocity in the sense discussed above,[354] but whether the foreign jurisdiction had a real and substantial connection with the claim.

14–091   The decision of the Supreme Court of Canada involved the enforcement of an Alberta judgment in British Columbia, and rested in part on the federal structure of the Constitution, including the strong need for the enforcement throughout the country of judgments given in one province; the fact that there were no concerns about differential quality of justice in the various provinces; and the existence of the Supreme Court of Canada as a court of final review, which could determine when the courts of one province have appropriately

---

[352] [1969] 1 A.C. 33.
[353] [1990] 3 S.C.R. 1077, on which see Black and Swan (1991) 12 Advocates' Q. 489. *cf.* Briggs (1987) 36 I.C.L.Q. 240.
[354] Which was the basis on which the judgment had been recognised in the lower court: [1988] 5 W.W.R. 650 (BCCA), on which see Blom (1989) 68 Can.B.Rev. 359; Black (1989) 4 Oxford J. Leg. Stud. 547; Law Reform Commission, British Columbia, *The Enforcement of Judgments Between Canadian Provinces* (1989).

exercised jurisdiction. Despite these doubts, in *Beals v Saldanha*[355] the Supreme Court extended the principle to permit the recognition of a judgment from the courts of Florida entered in default of defence. It thereby confirmed that this test will be applied to the recognition of foreign judgments generally, though this will be in addition to the traditional grounds of presence and submission, rather than as replacement of them.

(7) *Judgment in personam ancillary to divorce decree.* In *Phillips v Batho*,[356] it was held that a judgment of an Indian divorce court awarding damages to a husband against a co-respondent could be enforced in England, although the co-respondent had left India before the commencement of the proceedings for divorce and did not submit to the jurisdiction. The decision is in terms confined to a foreign country which is part of the Commonwealth. It is submitted that this decision is wrong and that a foreign judgment for damages or costs against a co-respondent cannot be enforced in England unless the foreign court had jurisdiction over him under Rule 44. The decision has been severely criticised extra-judicially,[357] it has not been followed in New Zealand,[358] and there is a later English case which undermines its reasoning.[359]

14–092

ILLUSTRATIONS[360]

THE FIRST CASE

1. 462 Individuals bring personal injury actions in the federal court in Texas against (inter alia) X & Co, an English company which is the holding company of two other defendants: Y & Co, an English company, which is engaged in the worldwide marketing of asbestos, and Z & Co, an Illinois corporation, which is engaged in the marketing of asbestos in the United States. X & Co and Y & Co object to the jurisdiction of the federal court, but the actions are settled under a consent order by a payment to the plaintiffs to which X & Co and its subsidiaries contribute. Subsequently a further 206 individuals commence similar proceedings in Texas. X & Co, Y & Co and Z & Co take no part in these proceedings. Z & Co ceases to carry on business, and the United States marketing is carried on by two new subsidiaries of X & Co, one incorporated in Illinois and the other in Liechtenstein, whose shares are held by nominees. Subsequently default judgments are entered in the Texas court. The default judgments are not recognised because, among other reasons,[361] the federal court in Texas has no jurisdiction: the consent order in the first set of actions is a submission to the jurisdiction of the court in that set of actions, but not in the second set of actions; whether or not presence in Illinois was sufficient for the purposes of the enforcement of the judgment of a Federal court sitting in Texas, X & Co and Y & Co were not present in Illinois through their Illinois subsidiaries.[362]

14–093

---

[355] [2003] 3 S.C.R. 416, (2003) 234 D.L.R. (4th) 1; *King v Drabinsky* (2008) 92 O.R. (3d) 616 (Ont.CA); *Disney Enterprises Inc v Click Enterprises Inc* (2006) 267 D.L.R. (4th) 291 (Ont.); *Canada Post Corp v Lépine* [2009] SCC 16, [2009] 1 S.C.R. 549. See also Briggs (2004) 8 Sing. Yb. Int. L. 1.

[356] [1913] 3 K.B. 25.

[357] Read, pp.262–267.

[358] *Redhead v Redhead* [1926] N.Z.L.R. 131 (costs).

[359] *Jacobs v Jacobs and Ceen* [1950] P. 146, where dicta in *Phillips v Batho* were dissented from. See below, para.18–088.

[360] See also the Illustration to Rule 49, below, para.14–136.

[361] See below, para.14R–128, on natural justice.

[362] *Adams v Cape Industries Plc* [1990] Ch. 433 (CA).

2. X, an English traveller, is staying for a few days in an hotel in Massachusetts when there is issued and served upon him a summons commencing an action against him in the Massachusetts court. The Massachusetts court has jurisdiction.[363]

3. Y is the director of X & Co, an English company. Y visits New York and while he is there A, a New York firm, takes out a summons against X & Co and serves process upon Y. X & Co has no branch in New York and does not carry on business there. The New York court has no jurisdiction.[364]

4. X & Co, an English company, employs Y, a resident of Israel, as its representative there to elicit orders from customers for X & Co.'s goods. Y has no authority from X & Co to make contracts on its behalf. Y introduces an Israeli customer, A, who contracts with X & Co for the purchase of X & Co.'s goods. A sues X & Co in Israel for damages for breach of contract. X & Co takes no part in the proceedings and has no office or place of business in Israel. The Israeli court has no jurisdiction at common law.[365]

The Second Case

14–094   5. A, an Englishman residing in England, brings an action against X in Tel Aviv for breach of a contract made and broken in England. The court gives judgment for costs against A. The Israeli court has jurisdiction.

The Third Case

14–095   6. A brings an action in a New York court against X, an Englishman. X appears and defends the action because his business transactions frequently involve his presence in New York, so that judgment might be executed against him there. His appearance is voluntary and the New York court has jurisdiction over him.[366]

7. The circumstances are the same as in Illustration 6 save that X has valuable property in the United States upon which execution might be levied. X appears and defends the action in order to protect that property. The New York court has jurisdiction.[367]

8. The circumstances are the same as in Illustration 6 save that X does not appear until after judgment has been given against him in default and execution has been levied, when he appears and secures the reopening of the proceedings in order to recover property upon which execution has been levied. The New York court has jurisdiction.[368]

9. A brings an action in a foreign court against X and obtains a judgment against X in default of appearance. X's application to the foreign court for leave to appeal out of time is dismissed, but X also appeals to the Court of Appeal for the relevant district on the basis that he was not in fact out of time to appeal. The appeal is not expressed to be on jurisdictional grounds. The foreign court has jurisdiction.[369]

10. A brings an action in a foreign country against X, an Englishman, jurisdiction being founded solely upon the arrest of property of X in the country concerned. X appears in order to recover the property arrested. *Semble*, the foreign court has no jurisdiction.[370]

11. A brings an action against X in a foreign court. X enters a conditional appearance in order to contest the jurisdiction. The conditional appearance becomes unconditional automatically when X's application to contest the jurisdiction fails, but X takes no further part in the proceedings. The foreign court has no jurisdiction.[371]

---

[363] *Carrick v Hancock* (1895) 12 T.L.R. 59.

[364] *Littauer Glove Corporation v FW Millington* (1920) *Ltd* (1928) 44 T.L.R. 746.

[365] *Vogel v RA Kohnstamm Ltd* [1973] Q.B. 133 (decided before the 1933 Act was extended to Israel).

[366] *cf. Voinet v Barrett* (1885) 55 L.J.Q.B. 39 (CA).

[367] *cf. De Cosse Brissac v Rathbone* (1861) 6 H. & N. 301 (the third plea).

[368] *cf. Guiard v De Clermont* [1914] 3 K.B. 145. Although the language of Civil Jurisdiction and Judgments Act 1982, s.33(1)(c) might appear to cover the case, the view taken here is that it does not apply to cases in which the intervention in the foreign proceedings is not based on jurisdictional grounds. But no case has yet so held.

[369] *SA Consortium General Textiles v Sun & Sand Agencies Ltd* [1978] Q.B. 279 (CA) (a case on the 1933 Act).

[370] *Guiard v De Clermont*, above, at p.155. *cf. Re Low* [1894] 1 Ch. 147 (CA).

[371] 1982 Act, s.33(1)(a), reversing the effect of *Harris v Taylor* [1915] 2 K.B. 580 (CA).

12. A brings an action against X in a foreign court. X applies to the foreign court to set aside the proceedings on the grounds that the foreign court is not the *forum conveniens*. The foreign court has no jurisdiction.[372]

13. A brings an action against X in a foreign court. X merely contests the jurisdiction. The foreign court has no jurisdiction.[373]

14. A brings an action against X in a foreign court. X applies to challenge the jurisdiction, but the court decides that rather than ruling on the jurisdictional challenge it will hear the merits of the claim and rule on jurisdiction at the end of that process, giving a ruling on the merits only if it concludes that there is jurisdiction. X calls evidence. The court rules that it has jurisdiction, and gives judgments on the merits in favour of A. As the purpose of X in appearing before the foreign court was to contest the jurisdiction, the judgment against him will, in principle at least, not be recognised.[374]

THE FOURTH CASE

15. A is a New York firm carrying on business in New York. X is a British citizen resident in   **14–096**
England. By a contract made in New York X agrees to assign certain patent rights to A, the contract providing inter alia that "all disputes as to the present agreement and its fulfilment shall be submitted to the New York jurisdiction." In an action by A in the appropriate New York court for breach of the contract, judgment is given for A for $1 million. The New York court has jurisdiction.[375]

16. X, who was resident in England, held shares in a French company. The statutes or articles of association of the company provided that every dispute should be subject to the jurisdiction of the French courts and that every shareholder must "elect a domicile" in France for service of process and that in default the officers of the company might do so for him. X never elected a domicile. The company went into liquidation and A brought an action in France against X for moneys not paid up on X's shares. Notice was duly served on X at his statutory domicile. X, however, had no knowledge of the proceedings. Judgment was given against X. The French court had jurisdiction.[376]

17. The circumstances are the same as in Illustration 16, except that the provisions about disputes being referred to the jurisdiction of the French courts and about "electing a domicile" were general provisions of French law applicable to all French companies. The French court had no jurisdiction.[377]

18. X, who is resident in England, is a member of an Australian company. By an Australian statute referring to this particular company the chairman of the company is capable of suing or being sued in place of the company and may act and be treated as the agent of the members. A recovers judgment against the chairman, and therefore against, *inter alios*, X, in an action in an Australian court of which X has no notice. The Australian court has jurisdiction.[378]

19. X, a British citizen, when resident and carrying on business in Western Australia, there entered into partnership with A for the working of a gold mine there situate. The partnership was dissolved and an account was taken under decree of a Western Australian court. A deficiency appearing, A sued X therefor in the same court. X had ceased to be resident in Western Australia and the writ was served upon him in England. X did not appear. The Western Australian court had no jurisdiction.[379]

---

[372] 1982 Act, s.33(1)(b), reversing the effect of *Henry v Geoprosco International*, above.

[373] 1982 Act, s.33(1)(a).

[374] See *AES Ust-Kamenogorsk Hydropower Plant LLP v AES Ust-Kamenogorsk Hydropower Plant JSC* [2010] EWHC 772 (Comm.), [2010] 2 Lloyd's Rep. 493, affirmed [2011] EWCA Civ 647, [2011] 2 Lloyd's Rep. 233.

[375] cf. *Feyerick v Hubbard* (1902) 71 L.J.K.B. 509. See also *Jeannot v Fuerst* (1909) 25 T.L.R. 424.

[376] *Copin v Adamson* (1874) L.R. 9 Ex. 345; 1 Ex. D. 17 (CA) (the first replication).

[377] *Copin v Adamson*, above (the second replication). Contrast *Vallée v Dumergue* (1849) 4 Exch. 290, where X did "elect a domicile" though he had no notice of the proceedings. cf. Case C–214/89 *Powell Duffryn Plc v Petereit* [1992] E.C.R. I–1745.

[378] *Bank of Australasia v Harding* (1850) 9 C.B. 661. See also *Bank of Australasia v Nias* (1851) 16 Q.B. 717.

[379] *Emanuel v Symon* [1908] 1 K.B. 302 (CA). Contrast *Blohn v Desser* [1962] 2 Q.B. 116.

(2) WHERE JURISDICTION DOES NOT EXIST

14R–097   **RULE 44—A court of a foreign country outside the United Kingdom has no jurisdiction under the First Case of Rule 43 if the bringing of the proceedings in that court was contrary to an agreement under which the dispute in question was to be settled otherwise than by proceedings in the courts of that country and the judgment debtor did not agree to the proceedings being brought in that court nor counterclaim in the proceedings, or otherwise submit to the jurisdiction of that court.[380]**

COMMENT

14–098   This Rule is based on s.32 of the 1982 Act, which adopted and extended a similar provision in the 1933 Act[381] on which there was no authority at common law.[382] Section 32 provides that a judgment of a foreign court shall not be recognised or enforced in the United Kingdom if (a) the bringing of the proceedings in that court was contrary to an agreement under which the dispute in question was to be settled otherwise than by proceedings in the courts of that country; and (b) those proceedings were not brought in that court by or with the agreement of, the person against whom the judgment was given; and (c) that person did not counterclaim in the proceedings or otherwise submit to the jurisdiction of that court. Section 32 is therefore subject to the principle of submission. Consequently, where an action was brought in a foreign country in breach of an arbitration agreement and the defendant defended the action on the merits after the foreign court had dismissed an objection to its jurisdiction, the defendant was held to have submitted to the jurisdiction of the foreign court; it could not therefore rely on s.32.[383] The principal object of s.32 is to counteract those systems of law which disregard[384] arbitration clauses or clauses providing for the jurisdiction of the English courts on the ground (for example) that an exchange of telexes or faxes or printed forms incorporating an arbitration or jurisdiction clause is not in "writing." The section does not apply where the agreement was illegal, void or unenforceable or was incapable of being performed for reasons not attributable to the fault of the party bringing the proceedings in which the

---

[380] 1982 Act, s.32.

[381] 1933 Act, s.4(3)(b).

[382] But for Canada, see *Old State Brewing Co v Newlands Service Inc* (1998) 155 D.L.R. (4th) 250 (BCCA).

[383] *Marc Rich & Co AG v Soc Italiana Impianti PA (No.2)* [1992] 1 Lloyd's Rep. 624 (CA); see also *The Eastern Trader* [1996] 2 Lloyd's Rep. 585; *Akai Pty Ltd v People's Insurance Co Ltd* [1998] 1 Lloyd's Rep. 90. The suggestion (*obiter*) in *AES Ust-Kamenogorsk Hydropower Plant LLP v AES Ust-Kamenogorsk Hydropower Plant JSC* [2011] EWCA Civ 647, [2011] 2 Lloyd's Rep. 233, [2011] 2 Lloyd's Rep. 233, [149], that if the defendant has, as a matter of English law, submitted to the jurisdiction of the foreign court, the English court may, but is not bound to, recognise or enforce the foreign judgment, is not supportable. If proceedings are brought in a foreign court contrary to a jurisdiction agreement, but the defendant submits to the jurisdiction of the foreign court, he loses the shield which s.32 might otherwise have afforded him; and the judgment is to be recognised by reason of his submission to the jurisdiction of the court.

[384] For an extreme example see *Deutsche Schachtbau v Shell International Petroleum Co Ltd* [1990] 1 A.C. 295, 310–311 (CA), reversed on other grounds, p.329.

judgment was given, but in determining whether a judgment given by the foreign court should be recognised or enforced a court in the United Kingdom is not bound by any decision of the overseas court relating to any of these matters.[385] English law (including its rules of the conflict of laws) would apply to determine whether the agreement was illegal, void or unenforceable, etc., without regard to the determination of the foreign court.

Section 32(4) provides that s.32 does not apply to judgments which are **14–099** required to be recognised under the Brussels or Lugano Conventions,[386] or under the Brussels I Regulation.[387]

ILLUSTRATION

A New York company buys peanuts from a company connected with the Government of the **14–100** Sudan. The contract form provides for English law to govern and for London arbitration. In breach of the arbitration clause the New York buyers bring an action in the New York courts because the sellers had some assets there whereas they had none in England. The sellers apply to the New York court for a stay on the ground that the parties had agreed to arbitration in London; the New York courts hold that the arbitration clause is not binding. In proceedings in England in which the buyers challenge the validity of the appointment of an arbitrator the English court will not recognise the New York judgment.[388]

RULE 45—A court of a foreign country outside the United Kingdom has **14R–101** **no jurisdiction to give a judgment capable of enforcement or recognition in England against a person who under the rules of public international law was entitled to immunity from the jurisdiction of the courts of that country and did not submit thereto.**

COMMENT

This Rule is based on a provision of the 1933 Act,[389] which (although there **14–102** is no direct authority) probably reflects the position at common law. Section 31 of the 1982 Act deals comprehensively with one class of defendant entitled to immunity under public international law, namely States. The effect of the

---

[385] 1982 Act, s.32(2), (3). The apparent suggestion in *AES Ust-Kamenogorsk Hydropower Plant LLP v AES Ust-Kamenogorsk Hydropower Plant JSC* [2011] EWCA Civ 647, [2011] 2 Lloyd's Rep. 233, [2011] 2 Lloyd's Rep. 233, [163], that because the Kazakh court had (by reference to English law) misconstrued an arbitration agreement, by which judgment s.32(3) provides that the English court is not bound in any event, there was "no reason why" its judgments (*sc.* as to other matters) should be recognised or enforced, is not persuasive.

[386] That is, recognition and enforcement under Rule 55. For the question whether these instruments require the recognition or enforcement of judgments rendered in breach of arbitration agreements, see below, paras 14–206 *et seq.*

[387] SI 2001/3929, Sch.2, para.14.

[388] *cf. Tracomin SA v Sudan Oil Seeds Co Ltd (No.1)* [1983] 1 W.L.R. 662, affirmed [1983] 1 W.L.R. 1026 (CA).

[389] 1933 Act, s.4(3)(c).

section[390] is that a foreign judgment against a State, other than the United Kingdom or the State to which the court which pronounced the judgment belongs, is to be recognised and enforced in the United Kingdom if it would be so recognised and enforced if it had not been given against a State and the foreign court would have had jurisdiction in the matter if it had applied rules corresponding to those applicable to such matters in the United Kingdom in accordance with ss.2 to 11 of the State Immunity Act 1978.[391] For this purpose judgments against a State include judgments against a government, a department of the government, against the sovereign or head of State in his public capacity, but not judgments against an entity which is distinct from the executive organs or government, except in proceedings relating to anything done by it in the exercise of the sovereign authority of the State; in the case of a federal State, State includes any of its constituent territories. A foreign judgment against a State will be capable of enforcement in England, if both of the following conditions are fulfilled: first, that the foreign court would have had jurisdiction if it had applied the United Kingdom rules on sovereign immunity set out in Sections 2 to 11 of the State Immunity Act 1978, the effect of which is that a State is not immune (inter alia) where it submits to the jurisdiction or where the proceedings relate to a commercial transaction; second, that under United Kingdom law the State is not immune from the processes of execution. Section 31(4) of the 1982 Act gives to judgments against foreign States the benefit of (inter alia) the immunities from execution contained in ss.13 and 14(3), (4) of the 1978 Act; their effect is that there can be no execution against sovereign property without the written consent of the foreign State unless the property is in use or intended for use for commercial purposes.[392]

14–103   The foregoing statement of the law was approved in *NML Capital Ltd v Argentina*,[393] in which a New York court had given judgment against the Republic of Argentina, based on its non-payment of sums due on a bond issue. As to the enforcement of the New York judgment in England, it was held that this could not be shown to be justified by reference to the commercial transactions exception in s.3 of the State Immunity Act 1978, for the English proceedings were not to be seen as "proceedings relating to . . . a commercial transaction": they related to a foreign judgment, and therefore not to the commercial transaction of issuing a bond. But as the bonds had contained an express and very broadly-worded submission to the jurisdiction of the New York court, in which the proceedings had been brought, in the form of a waiver of immunity, and which meant that the exercise of jurisdiction by the New York court was consistent with English law on state immunity, the action

---

[390] 1982 Act, s.31(3) provides that s.31 is not to affect the recognition or enforcement in the United Kingdom of judgments to which the 1933 Act applies by virtue of the Carriage of Goods by Road Act 1965, s.4; Nuclear Installations Act 1965, s.17(4); Merchant Shipping Act 1995, s.166(4); Merchant Shipping Act 1995, s.314(2) and Sch.13; Carriage by Railway Act 1972, s.5 (replaced by International Transport Conventions Act 1983, s.6); Carriage of Passengers by Road Act 1974, s.5 (not yet in force).

[391] Rule 19, Exceptions 1 to 11, above.

[392] See above, paras 10–015 *et seq.*

[393] [2011] UKSC 31, [2011] 2 A.C. 495, at [54]. See also *Svenska Petroleum Exploration AB v Government of the Republic of Lithuania* [2006] EWCA Civ 1529, [2007] Q.B. 886.

on the New York judgment fell within s.31(1) of the 1982 Act.[394] In addition, the waiver of immunity was, independently, wide enough to amount to a submission to the jurisdiction of the English court for the purposes of an action on the judgment at common law.

Section 31 does not deal with other persons entitled to immunity such as diplomats and international organisations. In these cases the general principle in this Rule will apply.   **14–104**

ILLUSTRATIONS

The Argentine Republic issues bonds governed by New York law which provide that a New York   **14–105**
judgment on the bonds may be enforced in any other courts to the jurisdiction of which the
Republic is or may be subject by a suit upon such judgment; and also that it waives state immunity
in any such court. The Republic defaults on the bonds. A buys bonds and obtains a New York
judgment on them, and sues in England on the bonds. The Republic is not entitled to immunity,
because (among other reasons) the New York court would have had jurisdiction in the matter if
it had applied rules corresponding to those applicable to such matters in the United Kingdom in
accordance with ss.2 to 11 of the State Immunity Act 1978, namely the rule in s.2 that a State is
not immune if it has submitted to the jurisdiction.

**RULE 46—A court of a foreign country outside the United Kingdom has   14R–106
no jurisdiction to give a judgment in proceedings regulated by certain
international conventions which have been given effect in the law of the
United Kingdom unless the jurisdictional requirements of the convention
concerned are fulfilled.**

COMMENT

The scope of this Rule extends to international conventions relating to such   **14–107**
matters as carriage of goods by road, carriage by railway, third party liability
in the field of nuclear energy, and oil pollution damage. The jurisdictional
rules of these conventions, and their provisions relating to enforcement of
judgments, are dealt with in Chapter 15.

(3) JUDGMENTS IN REM

**RULE 47[395]—(1) A court of a foreign country has jurisdiction to give a   14R–108
judgment *in rem* capable of enforcement or recognition in England if the
subject-matter of the proceedings wherein that judgment was given was
immovable or movable property which was at the time of the proceedings
situate in that country.**

---

[394] s.31 does not apply to foreign judgments against a State from the courts of that State: *AIC v Federal Republic of Nigeria* [2003] EWHC 1357 (QB).

[395] *Castrique v Imrie* (1870) L.R. 4 H.L. 414; *Meyer v Ralli* (1876) 1 C.P.D. 358; *The City of Mecca* (1879) 5 P.D. 28, reversed on other grounds (1881) 6 P.D. 106 (CA); *Re Trufort* (1887) 36 Ch.D 600; *Minna Craig Steamship Co v Chartered, etc. Bank* [1897] 1 Q.B. 460; *McKie v McKie* [1933] I.R. 464; Read, pp.133–144; Restatement, ss.56, 59–65. See also 1933 Act, s.4(2)(b).

(2) A court of a foreign country has no jurisdiction to adjudicate upon the title to, or the right to possession of, any immovable situate outside that country.[396]

COMMENT

14–109   **Introduction.**   A judgment *in rem* is a judgment whereunder either (1) possession or property in a thing is adjudged to a person, or (2) the sale of a thing is decreed in satisfaction of a claim against the thing itself. The term is used also to describe (3) an adjudication as to status such as a decree of nullity or dissolution of marriage,[397] and (4) a judgment ordering property to be sold by way of administration in bankruptcy[398] or on death, but judgments of these last two categories are outside the scope of this chapter. The question whether a foreign judgment is *in personam* or *in rem* is sometimes a difficult one on which English judges have been divided in opinion.[399] But unless the foreign judgment claims to operate *in rem*, it cannot be recognised in England as a judgment *in rem*.[400] By contrast, if the judgment might be construed as a judgment *in rem*, but in which quality it would not qualify for recognition, yet also contains orders which require a person to pay money or otherwise perform acts, it may be recognised or enforced to that extent as a judgment which binds the parties *in personam* if it satisfies the requirements of Rule 43.[401]

14–110   Foreign judgments *in rem* are freely recognised in England but rarely call for enforcement. If, for instance, a foreign judgment *in rem* determines the title to an immovable, either the immovable is within the country of the foreign court, in which case no question of enforcement can arise;[402] or it is elsewhere, in which case that court had no jurisdiction. Again, if the person entitled under a foreign judgment *in rem* vesting in him the title to some movable thing brings an action for wrongful interference in England against a person who denies that title, he is in reality relying on his title rather than the source of it—the judgment. He is, in other words, relying on the foreign judgment *qua* an assignment rather than *qua* a judgment. So also is the purchaser of a ship sold by foreign judicial sale who sets up the foreign

---

[396] *Boyse v Colclough* (1854) 1 K. & J. 124; *Re Hoyles* [1911] 1 Ch. 179, 185–186 (CA); *Re Trepca Mines Ltd* [1960] 1 W.L.R. 1273, 1277 (CA); *Duke v Andler* [1932] 4 D.L.R. 529 (Sup Ct Can); *Haspel v Haspel* [1934] 2 W.W.R. 412 (Alta); *cf. Tezcan v Tezcan* (1987) 46 D.L.R. (4th) 176 (BCCA); *Chapman Estate v O'Hara* [1988] 2 W.W.R. 275 (Sask CA); Read, pp.135–137.

[397] *Von Lorang v Administrator of Austrian Property* [1927] A.C. 641, 662.

[398] For the broader question of the recognition and enforcement of judgments made by a foreign court exercising insolvency jurisdiction, see para.14–010, above.

[399] See *Cammell v Sewell* (1858) 3 H. & N. 617 (*in rem*); (1860) 5 H. & N. 728 (*in personam*); *Castrique v Imrie* (1860) 8 C.B.(N.S.) 1 (*in personam*); *Imrie v Castrique* (1860) 8 C.B.(N.S.) 405 (*in rem*); *Castrique v Imrie* (1870) L.R. 4 H.L. 414 (*in rem*).

[400] *Air Foyle Ltd v Center Capital Ltd* [2002] EWHC 2535 (Comm.), [2003] 2 Lloyd's Rep. 752 (but if regarded as a decree *in personam* which operates *erga omnes*, the rule in *Cammell v Sewell* (1860) 5 H.&N. (as to which, see Rule 133, below) will produce much the same effect.

[401] *Pattni v Ali* [2006] UKPC 51, [2007] 2 A.C. 85

[402] It has been held in New Zealand that an action *in personam* to recover instalments of purchase money due under a sale of land is not an action of which the subject-matter is immovable property within the meaning of the 1933 Act, s.4(2)(b): *Re a Judgment, McCormac v Gardner* [1937] N.Z.L.R. 517.

judgment by way of defence to the original owner's proceedings for wrongful interference. All that is involved is, at most, recognition of the foreign judgment, and, at that, recognition *qua* an assignment. As Lord Blackburn put it,[403] "In the case of *Cammell v Sewell*[404] a more general principle was laid down, viz. that 'if personal property is disposed of in a manner binding according to the law of the country where it is, that disposition is binding everywhere.' This, we think, as a general rule is correct, though no doubt it may be open to exceptions and qualifications; and it may very well be said that the rule commonly expressed by English lawyers, that a judgment *in rem* is binding everywhere, is in truth but a branch of that more general principle."

The degree of recognition to be accorded to such a judgment, therefore, **14–111** falls to be determined not so much by the rules governing the recognition of foreign judgments as by the rules governing the validity of assignments of property.[405] The distinction is important because while a foreign judgment is in general impeachable for fraud,[406] the validity of an assignment of property depends almost entirely upon the *lex situs*;[407] though it is conceivable that recognition of a foreign judgment *qua* an assignment may be refused on grounds of public policy.

There are two reported cases of a foreign judgment *in rem* being enforced **14–112** in England by an action *in rem*. In *The City of Mecca*,[408] a collision occurred on the high seas between a Spanish ship and a British ship. The owners of the Spanish ship brought an action in Portugal against the British ship, then lying in Lisbon, and obtained a judgment against the owners for damages. The ship returned to England before the judgment was satisfied. On the assumption that the Portuguese judgment was *in rem*, Sir Robert Phillimore allowed an action *in rem* in the Admiralty Division of the High Court against the ship on the unsatisfied judgment. His ground for doing so was that international law requires courts of admiralty to act in aid of each other,[409] although Blackburn J. had categorically denied in *Godard v Gray*[410] that it was "an admitted principle of the law of nations that a State is bound to enforce within its territories the judgment of a foreign tribunal." On the production of further evidence to the effect that Portuguese law had abolished actions *in rem*, Sir Robert Phillimore's decision was reversed by the Court of Appeal.[411] In the *Despina GK*[412] Sheen J. applied Sir Robert Phillimore's decision in an action *in rem* in England in which cargo owners claimed the balance of a sum outstanding on a judgment which they had obtained in an action *in rem* in the Swedish admiralty court in respect of the cargo. It was held that a judgment

---

[403] *Castrique v Imrie* (1870) L.R. 4 H.L. 414, 429.
[404] (1860) 5 H. & N. 728, 746.
[405] See Rules 133–134.
[406] See Rule 43. *cf. Ellerman Lines v Read* [1928] 2 K.B. 144 (CA).
[407] See Rules 133–134.
[408] (1879) 5 P.D. 28.
[409] *ibid.* p.32.
[410] (1870) L.R. 6 Q.B. 139, 148.
[411] (1881) 6 P.D. 106.
[412] [1983] Q.B. 214. See also *Pacific Star v Bank of America National Trust and Savings Association* [1965] W.A.R. 159.

creditor who has obtained a final judgment against a shipowner by proceedings *in rem* in a foreign admiralty court can bring an action *in rem* in England against the ship to enforce the decree of the foreign court if that is necessary to complete the execution of the judgment, provided that the ship is the property of the judgment debtor when she is arrested. The correctness of this decision was open to doubt, since nothing in the Senior Courts Act 1981, s.21, justified the exercise of jurisdiction *in rem* in relation to such a claim. There seems to be no reason why a judgment *in rem* should not be registrable under the 1920 or 1933 Acts provided that a sum of money was payable thereunder, or under Parts I and II of the 1982 Act, or under Chapter III of the Brussels I Regulation.

14–113   Clause (1) of Rule 47 reproduces almost exactly a provision of the 1933 Act;[413] and there is also ample support for it at common law. Hence it is essential to the recognition or enforcement in England of a foreign judgment *in rem* that the *res* should have been situate in the foreign country concerned at the time of the proceedings. If it was, jurisdiction probably exists even though the owner of the *res* did not consent to its being there, e.g. when a ship puts into a foreign port through stress of weather, or a yacht is stolen and abandoned in a foreign port.[414]

14–114   Clause (2) of the Rule rests on a very slender basis of precedent, and its exact scope is a matter of some doubt. It is a corollary of the principle that English courts have no jurisdiction to determine the title to, or the right to the possession of, any immovable situate outside England.[415] But though this principle is subject to exceptions,[416] Rule 47(2) is not; or, to put it more precisely, none have yet been formulated. It is therefore an illustration of the proposition that English courts sometimes claim for themselves a wider jurisdiction than they are prepared to concede to foreign courts as being sufficient for the judgment of that court to be recognised in England as *res judicata*. Thus, English courts do not admit the jurisdiction of any foreign court to determine a person's title, under a will or otherwise, to English immovables,[417] even though English courts sometimes determine the validity of wills dealing with foreign land.[418] Again, the Supreme Court of Canada has held that a foreign equitable degree *in personam* relating to land in British Columbia, though based on the fraud of a defendant personally subject to the jurisdiction of the foreign court and therefore within the rule in *Penn v Lord Baltimore*,[419] will not be enforced in Canada.[420] Section 30 of the 1982 Act abrogates the rule that an English court has no jurisdiction to entertain proceedings for torts to foreign land.[421] This change does not directly affect

---

[413] s.4(2)(b).
[414] *Cammell v Sewell* (1860) 5 H. & N. 728, 745. Contrast Read, pp.139–142.
[415] *British South Africa Co v Companhia de Moçambique* [1893] A.C. 602.
[416] See below, Rule 131.
[417] *Boyse v Colclough* (1854) 1 K. & J. 124; *Re Hoyles* [1911] 1 Ch. 179, 185–186 (CA).
[418] *Nelson v Bridport* (1846) 8 Beav. 547; *Re Piercy* [1895] 1 Ch. 83; *Re Stirling* [1908] 2 Ch. 344; *Re Ross* [1930] 1 Ch. 377; *Re Duke of Wellington* [1948] Ch. 118 (CA); below, para.23–052.
[419] (1750) 1 Ves.Sen. 444; see below, paras 23–042 *et seq.*
[420] *Duke v Andler* [1932] 4 D.L.R. 529 (Sup Ct Can); *cf. Haspel v Haspel* [1934] 2 W.W.R. 412 (Alta); *Fall v Eastin*, 215 U.S. 1 (1909). See Restatement, s.102, comment d.
[421] See below, para.23–040.

Rule 47(2) but its adoption makes it unlikely that a foreign court would be regarded as not having jurisdiction to entertain proceedings for torts to land outside the country in which it sits. The 1933 Act provides[422] that the courts of a foreign country shall not be deemed to have jurisdiction if the subject-matter of the proceedings is immovable property outside that country. The precise scope of this enactment is not very clear; but it is not likely that it affects this conclusion in cases within its scope. However, where the judgment is otherwise entitled to be registered for enforcement under the Brussels I Regulation or the Lugano Convention, it is improbable that registration may be denied on the basis of this clause of the Rule.[423]

14–115 The jurisdiction of the courts of the *situs* to give a judgment *in rem* affecting a movable is not necessarily exclusive. For example, English courts recognise that the courts of a foreign country have jurisdiction to determine the succession to all movables wherever locally situate of a testator or intestate dying domiciled in such country.[424] For this reason clause (2) of Rule 47 is limited to immovables.

ILLUSTRATIONS

14–116 1. A, an Englishman, is owner of a British ship. Whilst the ship is at a foreign port, the foreign court, honestly exercising its jurisdiction, pronounces in a proceeding *in rem* a judgment under which the ship is ordered to be sold for the payment of necessaries supplied to M, the master, and is sold to X, a British citizen. The court has acted under a misconception of English law, and in consequence has not recognised the rights of A as owner. The foreign court has jurisdiction.[425]

2. A foreign Admiralty court gives a judgment *in rem* against a British ship owned by A, an Englishman. The judgment is obtained by the fraud of B, the plaintiff. The ship is, under the judgment, sold to X, an innocent purchaser, and comes into an English port. A claims the vessel and seeks to show that the foreign judgment was obtained by fraud. *Semble*, X's title prevails.[426]

3. A British ship is seized as prize by a Russian vessel, on the ground of attempted breach of blockade, and taken to a Russian port for adjudication as prize by a prize court. The goods on board the ship are sold under the order of the court to X. It is ultimately decided by the prize court that the ship was not lawfully captured. The Russian court has jurisdiction.[427]

4. Cargo was consigned on a Greek vessel to A in Malta. It was damaged en route while the ship was in a Greek port, and a Greek court authorised the hypothecation of the cargo and the execution thereon of a bottomry bond to cover the cost of transhipment. The Greek court was held to have jurisdiction.[428]

14–117 5. A & Co, cargo-owners, bring an action *in rem* in the Admiralty Court of Stockholm against a Liberian ship, from which their cargo has been dumped at sea. A & Co. obtain judgment against X, the shipowners, who pay part of the sum awarded by the Swedish court. When the ship enters an English port, A & Co. issue proceedings *in rem* claiming the sum outstanding on the Swedish judgment and apply for a warrant of arrest of the ship. *Semble*, the proceedings may not be

---

[422] s.4(3)(a).

[423] If recognition of the judgment is precluded by Art.34(1), this clause of the Rule will be irrelevant.

[424] See Rule 147. *cf.* Rule 216 (bankruptcy).

[425] *Castrique v Imrie* (1870) L.R. 4 H.L. 414.

[426] See *Castrique v Imrie* (1870) L.R. 4 H.L. 414, 433; *Simpson v Fogo* (1863) 1 H. & M. 195, 248. See also *Castrique v Behrens* (1861) 30 L.J.Q.B. 163.

[427] See *Stringer v English, etc., Insurance Co* (1870) L.R. 5 Q.B. 599, especially 606; *Hughes v Cornelius* (1681) 2 Show.K.B. 232.

[428] *Messina v Petrococchino* (1872) L.R. 4 P.C. 144; *Dent v Smith* (1869) L.R. 4 Q.B. 414.

brought and A & Co. must proceed by enforcing their judgment by registration under Rule 48, or by proceedings on the judgment at common law.[429]

6. T, by his will executed in 1842, devised all his real and personal estate to A. He had real estate in Ireland and also in England. The Irish courts, it was held, had no jurisdiction to adjudicate upon the validity of the will as related to the real estate in England; and a decree of the Irish Court of Chancery did not determine the validity or invalidity of the will so far as the lands in England are concerned, and could not be pleaded in bar to a suit in the English Court of Chancery.[430]

7. A agrees with X in California to sell to X land in England. A and X are residents of California. The land is conveyed to X in accordance with English law. A sues X in California to set aside the conveyance because of X's fraud. The Californian court orders X to reconvey the land to A and on X's refusal to do so the clerk of the court purports to reconvey in X's name. A sues X in England for a declaration that he (A) is the owner of the land. The Californian decree will not be recognised in England.[431]

C. *Conclusiveness of foreign judgments: defences*

14R–118   **Rule 48[432]—A foreign judgment which is final and conclusive[433] on the merits and not impeachable under any of Rules 49 to 52 is conclusive as to any matter thereby adjudicated upon, and cannot be impeached for any error either**

    (1) of fact;[434] or

    (2) of law.[435]

Comment

14–119   During the 18th century and the first part of the 19th century it was much debated whether a foreign judgment given by a court of competent jurisdiction could be re-examined on its merits when recognition or enforcement of that judgment was sought in England. In 1834 Lord Brougham said in the House of Lords "a foreign judgment is only prima facie, not conclusive, evidence of a debt."[436] In 1863 Page Wood V.-C. refused to recognise a Louisiana judgment on the ground that it showed on its face "a perverse and deliberate

---

[429] 1982 Act, s.34, reversing *The Despina GK* [1983] Q.B. 214. Sweden is now subject to the Brussels I Regulation.

[430] *Boyse v Colclough* (1854) 1 K. & J. 124.

[431] *cf. Duke v Andler* [1932] 4 D.L.R. 529 (Sup Ct Can).

[432] *Godard v Gray* (1870) L.R. 6 Q.B. 139; *Bank of Australasia v Nias* (1851) 16 Q.B. 717; *Ellis v M'Henry* (1871) L.R. 6 C.P. 228, 238; *Carl Zeiss Stiftung v Rayner & Keeler Ltd (No.2)* [1967] 1 A.C. 853, 917, 925, 965–966; *Page v Phelan* (1844) 1 U.C.Q.B. 254; *Kingsmill & Davis v Warrener & Wheeler* (1852) 13 U.C.Q.B. 18; *Four Embarcadero Center Venture v Kalen* (1988) 65 O.R. (2d) 551; Read, pp.87–93. See also 1933 Act, s.8(1), below, para.14–195.

[433] See Rule 42, where the meaning of this expression is elucidated, and below, para.14–125.

[434] *Henderson v Henderson* (1844) 6 Q.B. 288; *De Cosse Brissac v Rathbone* (1861) 6 H. & N. 301 (the third plea).

[435] *Castrique v Imrie* (1870) L.R. 4 H.L. 414; *Godard v Gray* (1870) L.R. 6 Q.B. 139; *Scott v Pilkington* (1862) 2 B. & S. 11; *De Cosse Brissac v Rathbone* (1861) 6 H. & N. 301 (the third plea); *Minna Craig Steamship Co v Chartered, etc., Bank* [1897] 1 Q.B. 460 (CA); *cf. Dallal v Bank Mellat* [1986] Q.B. 441. See Restatement, s.106.

[436] *Houlditch v Donegal* (1834) 2 Cl. & F. 470, 477. *cf. Smith v Nicolls* (1839) 5 Bing.N.C. 208, 221.

refusal to recognise the law" of England.[437] But meanwhile it had been decided in a series of cases that a foreign judgment could not be re-examined on the merits provided the foreign court had jurisdiction according to the English rules of the conflict of laws.[438] And finally, in *Godard v Gray*[439] it was held that this was so even if the foreign court made an obvious mistake of English law which appeared on the face of the judgment. Since that decision, the principle of Rule 48 has never been questioned.[440] It is consistent with the maxims *interest reipublicae ut sit finis litium* (it is in the public interest that there should be an end to litigation) and *nemo debet bis vexari pro eadem causa* (no one should be sued twice on the same ground).

Rule 48 holds good whether the judgment is relied upon by the claimant[441] **14–120** or by the defendant.[442] It applies whether the judgment is *in personam* or *in rem*[443] (including a judgment affecting status[444]). The only difference in this respect between a judgment *in personam* and a judgment *in rem* is that the former is conclusive only between the parties and their representatives, while the latter is conclusive against all the world.[445] A foreign judgment *in rem* is within the scope of Rule 48 even though there may be only one original party thereto.

It is unlikely, however, that "judgment" in this sense extends to a decision **14–121** of a foreign court that the judgment of a court of a third country is entitled to be enforced under the law of the foreign country, even where the proceedings in the foreign court were contested by parties who submitted to its jurisdiction in relation to this issue. The civil law principle that *exequatur sur exequatur ne vaut*[446] is sometimes used to help explain why a judgment from the third state is not converted into an enforceable foreign judgment by virtue its recognition or endorsement by another court. Though no English case expressly so holds,[447] the principle is sound for at least three reasons: the effect of the foreign proceedings will often only be to declare the third country judgment to be enforceable or executable within the territory of the foreign court, an order which by its very terms can have no effect in England; the foreign judgment will not usually be on the merits of the claim; and because of the confusion liable to result if both the judgment of the third country and

---

[437] *Simpson v Fogo* (1863) 1 H. & M. 195, 247. The correctness of this decision was doubted in *Luther v Sagor* [1921] 3 K.B. 532, 558 (CA) and in *Carl Zeiss Stiftung v Rayner & Keeler Ltd (No.2)* [1967] 1 A.C. 853, 917–918, 922, 978, and it may be of only historical interest today.

[438] *Henderson v Henderson* (1844) 6 Q.B. 288; *Bank of Australasia v Harding* (1850) 9 C.B. 661; *Bank of Australasia v Nias* (1851) 16 Q.B. 717; *De Cosse Brissac v Rathbone* (1861) 6 H. & N. 301.

[439] (1870) L.R. 6 Q.B. 139. *cf. Castrique v Imrie* (1870) L.R. 4 H.L. 414.

[440] It is not clear whether *AES Ust-Kamenogorsk Hydropower Plant LLP v AES Ust-Kamenogorsk Hydropower Plant JSC* [2011] EWCA Civ 647, [2011] 2 Lloyd's Rep. 233, esp. at [163], questions the proposition in the text, but if it does, it should be understood to be confined to foreign judgments on the point mentioned in 1982 Act, s.32(2),(3).

[441] Cases above.

[442] *Ricardo v Garcias* (1845) 12 Cl. & F. 368. See Rule 42, above.

[443] *Castrique v Imrie* (1870) L.R. 4 H.L. 414.

[444] *Harvey v Farnie* (1882) 8 App.Cas. 43 (divorce); *Von Lorang v Administrator of Austrian Property* [1927] A.C. 641 (nullity).

[445] *Castrique v Imrie*, above; *Von Lorang v Administrator of Austrian Property*, above.

[446] A judgment on a judgment is not valid.

[447] 1933 Act, s.1(2A) (1982 Act, Sch.10) makes express provision to exclude such orders from the category of judgments which may be registered under the Act.

the foreign (enforcement) judgment were to be separately enforceable in England.[448] However, there is no reason why issue estoppel may not, in an appropriate case, arise from rulings made by the foreign court in such cases.[449] In *Yukos Capital Sarl v OJSC Rosneft Oil Co*,[450] a decision of a Dutch court that a Russian judgment would be refused recognition in the Netherlands on the ground that it was the product of a "partial and dependent" judicial process, was treated as conclusive when the same substantive issue arose in considering whether to recognise the Russian judgment in England. The court was not asked to recognise the Dutch judgment as such, but confirmed that issue estoppel was capable of arising, and did arise, from the Dutch court's findings of bias on the part of the Russian court, and this dictated the outcome of the English proceedings.

14–122   Rule 48 in effect applies to foreign judgments the principles well known in English domestic law under the name of estoppel *per rem judicatam*. This doctrine has two branches: "cause of action estoppel," which precludes a party from relitigating the existence of the same cause of action, and "issue estoppel," which precludes a party from denying any matter of fact or law necessarily decided by the earlier judgment.[451] Most of the cases applying the doctrine to foreign judgments have been concerned with cause of action estoppel. A foreign judgment may be *res judicata* whether it is given in favour of the claimant or defendant. The judgment of an English court of record extinguishes the original cause of action, which merges in the judgment.[452] If A in an English court recovers judgment for £10,000 against X for breach of contract or for a tort he can issue execution on the judgment, but he cannot bring proceedings against X for the breach of contract or for the tort. But at common law a foreign judgment did not extinguish the original cause of action, so that if A recovered judgment in a New York court for $10,000 against X he could bring an action in England on the judgment but he could also, if he chose, bring an action for the debt, in which case the foreign judgment would be merely evidence of the debt. This anomaly has been removed by s.34 of the 1982 Act, which has been discussed in connection with Rule 42, and which provides that no proceedings may be brought by a person in England on a cause of action in respect of which a judgment has been given in his favour in proceedings between the same parties, or their privies, in a foreign court,[453] unless the judgment is not enforceable or entitled to recognition in England.

---

[448] *Cortés v Yorkton Securities Inc* (2007) D.L.R. (4th) 740, [49] (making the point that the judgment creditor may have to enforce his judgment in more than one jurisdiction; *Owen v Rocketinfo Inc* (2008) 305 D.L.R. (4th) 370; *cf. Morgan Stanley & Co International Ltd v Pilot Lead Investments Ltd* [2006] 4 H.K.C. 93 (on which, Smart (2007) 81 A.L.R. 349).

[449] See *Owens Bank Plc v Bracco* [1992] 1 A.C. 443, 470–471 (CA); *House of Spring Gardens Ltd v Waite* [1991] 1 Q.B. 241. It is not clear whether observations in *Clarke v Fennoscandia Ltd* [2007] UKHL 56, 2008 S.C. (HL) 122, [23]–[24], that a declaration by a Scottish court that foreign judgment was obtained by fraud would not have any effect *in rem*, but only in Scotland, is intended to contradict this suggestion, but it is submitted that the statement should be regarded as *obiter*.

[450] [2011] EWHC 1461 (Comm.), [2011] 2 Lloyd's Rep. 443.

[451] See above, para.14–030.

[452] Halsbury's *Laws of England*, 5th ed. Vol.12, para.1190.

[453] Or in a court of another part of the UK.

In *Carl Zeiss Stiftung v Rayner & Keeler Ltd (No.2)*,[454] a majority of the   **14–123** House of Lords held that issue estoppel can be based on a foreign judgment, and this decision was applied by a unanimous House in *The Sennar (No.2)*.[455] Three conditions must be fulfilled before the doctrine can be applied[456]: (1) The judgment of the foreign court must be of a court of competent jurisdiction, and must be final and conclusive on the merits in the sense of Rule 42; (2) there must be identity of parties;[457] (3) there must be identity of subject-matter, that is to say, the issues must be the same. In the *Carl Zeiss* case it was not expressly laid down that the foreign judgment must not be impeachable on any of the grounds referred to in Rule 48, i.e. under any of Rules 49 to 52. But in *The Sennar (No.2)* it was made clear that the foreign court must be competent in the sense of its having jurisdiction in the international sense over the party to be bound, and it can hardly be supposed that an estoppel could be based, e.g. on a foreign judgment which had been obtained by fraud.[458]

Closely parallel to the rule that a foreign judgment is conclusive is the rule   **14–124** that the defendant must take all available defences in the foreign court, and that, if he does not do so, he cannot be allowed to plead them afterwards in England.[459] But neither of these rules applies if the judgment was obtained by fraud.[460] It has even been held that it is no defence to plead that since the date of the judgment the defendant has discovered new evidence which he could not with reasonable diligence have discovered earlier and which shows that the judgment is erroneous.[461] But it would be a mistake to conclude from this one decision that in no circumstances can a foreign judgment be impeachable at common law on the ground that fresh evidence has been discovered. For the plea was much less precise than a statement of case would have to be in an action to review an English judgment on this ground;[462] it did not even allege that if the fresh evidence had been produced to the foreign court, it must have led to the opposite result. Since an English judgment can be set aside, even in the absence of fraud, if the unsuccessful party discovers new and material evidence after the trial,[463] there seems no reason why a foreign judgment should be in a different position.

The meaning of the word "conclusive" in Rule 48 must be carefully   **14–125** distinguished from the meaning of the term "final and conclusive" in Rule 42.

---

[454] [1967] 1 A.C. 853.

[455] [1985] 1 W.L.R. 490 (HL).

[456] [1967] 1 A.C. 853, 909–910, 935, 942, 967–971; [1985] 1 W.L.R. 490, 499. See above, para.14–032.

[457] Of course this condition does not apply to judgments *in rem*: see n.445, above.

[458] See, e.g. *Von Lorang v Administrator of Austrian Property* [1927] A.C. 641, which does not appear to have been cited in *Carl Zeiss Stiftung v Rayner & Keeler Ltd (No.2)*, above.

[459] *Henderson v Henderson* (1844) 6 Q.B. 288; *De Cosse Brissac v Rathbone* (1861) 6 H. & N. 301; *Ellis v M'Henry* (1871) L.R. 6 C.P. 228; *Israel Discount Bank of New York v Hadjipateras* [1984] 1 W.L.R. 137 (CA).

[460] Below, Rule 50. Contrast *House of Spring Gardens Ltd v Waite* [1991] 1 Q.B. 241 (CA), where judgment debtors were estopped from raising fraud by a judgment in a separate action in the foreign court to set aside the original judgment.

[461] *De Cosse Brissac v Rathbone* (1861) 6 H. & N. 301 (the fifth plea).

[462] *Boswell v Coaks* (1894) 6 R. 167, 170–172; 86 L.T. 365n., 366n. (HL); D.M. Gordon (1961) 77 L.Q.R. 358, 533, especially at pp.549–554.

[463] Halsbury's *Laws of England*, 5th ed. Vol.12, para.1204; Gordon (1961) 77 L.Q.R. 358, 533 especially at pp.371, 536.

For clearly the word "conclusive" is used in these two Rules in two quite different senses. In this Rule the reference is to a rule of English law whereby a foreign judgment given by a court of competent jurisdiction, and not impeachable on a number of strictly limited grounds, is conclusive and not merely prima facie evidence of the matters therein decided. But in Rule 42 the reference is to a quality which the foreign judgment must possess by the law of the foreign country concerned, without which quality it cannot be recognised or enforced in England.

ILLUSTRATIONS

14–126   1. A sued X in a French court for breach of an English charterparty, in which was a clause, "penalty for the non-performance of this agreement, estimated amount of freight." The foreign court, under an erroneous view of the English law, treated this clause as fixing the amount of damages recoverable, and therefore gave judgment in favour of A for £700, the amount of the freight. The judgment, though given under a mistaken view of English law, was conclusive.[464]

2. A brings an action in England for £200 due to A from X under a judgment of a New York court. The judgment is founded on a mistaken view of the law of New York. The judgment is conclusive.[465]

3. A obtains a judgment for a debt against X in a Canadian court. X, at the time when the action is brought in Canada, has been made bankrupt in England, and might have pleaded his discharge in the bankruptcy in defence to the action. The Canadian judgment is conclusive.[466]

14–127   4. A obtains a judgment on a guarantee against X and Y in a New York court. X seeks to resist enforcement in England on the ground that the guarantee was executed under the undue influence of Y, but X had deliberately refrained from making that allegation in the New York proceedings. The judgment is conclusive.[467]

5. A sues X for a debt in a foreign court. X pleads that he has paid the debt but lost the receipt. The court disbelieves him and gives judgment for A. Subsequently, X finds the missing receipt and applies to the foreign court for leave to appeal out of time against the judgment. The foreign court dismisses his application. A brings an action on the judgment against X in England. *Semble*, the action will fail.[468]

6. A Russian court awards salvage in respect of a Russian ship. The decision probably rests on a misinterpretation of maritime law. The judgment is conclusive in an English court in a claim by an owner who has paid against an insurance company.[469]

7. A sues X in Russia and the Russian court gives judgment against X. Proceedings brought by A to enforce the judgment against X in the Netherlands are dismissed, the Dutch court finding that the Russian judgment was obtained by a "partial and dependent" procedure. In proceedings by A to enforce the Russian judgment in England the ruling of the Dutch court against A is entitled to recognition as *res judicata*, and as a result the Russian judgment may not be recognised in England.[470]

---

[464] *Godard v Gray* (1870) L.R. 6 Q.B. 139. See also *Castrique v Imrie* (1870) L.R. 4 H.L. 414.

[465] *Scott v Pilkington* (1862) 2 B. & S. 11. *cf. De Cosse Brissac v Rathbone* (1861) 6 H. & N. 301; and contrast *Meyer v Ralli* (1876) 1 C.P.D. 358 which (*semble*) is wrongly decided, unless it can be sustained on the score of the consent of the parties to recognise the incorrectness of the foreign court's view of the law.

[466] *Ellis v M'Henry* (1871) L.R. 6 C.P. 228.

[467] *Israel Discount Bank of New York v Hadjipateras* [1984] 1 W.L.R. 137 (CA).

[468] See para.14–124, above. Contrast *De Cosse Brissac v Rathbone* (1861) 6 H. & N. 301 (the fifth plea).

[469] *cf. Dent v Smith* (1869) L.R. 4 Q.B. 414.

[470] *Yukos Capital Sarl v OJSC Rosneft Oil Co* [2011] EWHC 1461 (Comm.), [2011] 2 Lloyd's Rep. 443.

RULE 49—(1) **A foreign judgment is impeachable if the courts of the**   14R–128
foreign country did not, in the circumstances of the case, have jurisdiction
to give that judgment in the view of English law in accordance with the
principles set out in Rules 43 to 47 inclusive.[471]

(2) A foreign judgment cannot, in general, be impeached on the ground
that the court which gave it was not competent to do so according to the
law of the foreign country concerned.[472]

COMMENT

Clause (1) of the Rule. Lack of jurisdiction on the part of the foreign court   14–129
is the objection which can most frequently be raised in answer to a party who
relies on a foreign judgment in English proceedings. It is not enough, it must
be again emphasised, that the foreign court is duly invested with jurisdiction
under the foreign legal system. It must also have jurisdiction according to the
English rules of the conflict of laws. These rules have already been considered
in Rules 43 to 47 and there is no need to repeat here what is there said. Clause
(1) of the present Rule is thus in a sense merely mechanical, in that it merely
refers to other Rules.

But a foreign judgment, whatever its jurisdictional basis, is prima facie   14–130
capable of enforcement or, as the case may be, recognition in England.[473] In
Adams v Cape Industries Plc[474] the Court of Appeal accepted that no specific
assertion need be made that the foreign court was competent in terms of
foreign law, because whether the foreign court was competent was irrelevant.
But there was a legal burden on a claimant seeking to enforce a foreign
judgment to prove that the foreign court was competent in the sense recognised by English law to assume jurisdiction over him: the evidentiary burden
might shift at trial.

There is a rule similar to Rule 49 under the 1920 Act[475] and the 1933 Act.[476]   14–131
But where recognition of the judgment falls under Chapter III of the Brussels
I Regulation, or under Title III of the Lugano Convention, the right of the
English court to examine the jurisdiction of the court which gave judgment is
very restricted. Under Pts II and IV of the 1982 Act, the English court has no
power to examine the jurisdiction of the Scottish or Northern Irish court, and
a restricted power to examine the jurisdiction of a Gibraltar court.[477]

---

[471] *Buchanan v Rucker* (1808) 9 East 192; *Schibsby v Westenholz* (1870) L.R. 6 Q.B. 155;
Sirdar Gurdyal Singh v Rajah of Faridkote [1894] A.C. 670 (PC); *Emanuel v Symon* [1908] 1
K.B. 302 (CA).

[472] *Vanquelin v Bouard* (1863) 15 C.B. (N.S.) 341; *Pemberton v Hughes* [1899] 1 Ch. 781 (CA);
Adams v Cape Industries Plc [1990] Ch. 433, 513–514, 550 (CA); Read, pp.93–100; *cf.*
Restatement, s.105.

[473] *Alivon v Furnival* (1834) 1 C.M. & R. 277; *Bank of Australasia v Nias* (1851) 16 Q.B. 717;
Henderson v Henderson (1844) 6 Q.B. 288; *Robertson v Struth* (1844) 5 Q.B. 941; *Taylor v Ford*
(1873) 29 L.T. 392.

[474] [1990] Ch. 433, 450 (CA).

[475] 1920 Act, s.9(2)(a).

[476] 1933 Act, ss.4(1)(a)(ii), 8(1)(2).

[477] See below, paras 14–221 and 14–261.

14–132   **Clause (2) of the Rule.** If a judgment is pronounced by a court of a foreign country whose courts have jurisdiction in the view of English law, but the particular foreign court is not the proper court in terms of the domestic rules of the foreign legal system, is the judgment capable of enforcement or recognition in England? This question must almost certainly be answered in the affirmative, at any rate so far as judgments *in personam* are concerned; but the authorities are at first sight in a state of some confusion.

14–133   In *Vanquelin v Bouard*[478] the defendant was sued in England on a French judgment in respect of a bill of exchange. The French court had jurisdiction according to the English rules of the conflict of laws and the subject-matter of the action (bills of exchange) was within its internal competence. But the defendant pleaded that the particular French court had no internal competence over him because he was not a trader. This plea was held bad.

14–134   On the other hand, in *Castrique v Imrie*[479] (a case on a foreign judgment *in rem*) Blackburn J. regarded it as material "whether the sovereign authority of that State has conferred on the court jurisdiction to decide as to the disposition of the thing, and the court has acted within its jurisdiction." This could be taken to mean that a foreign judgment *in rem*, in order to be recognised in England, must have been pronounced by a court having local competence as well as international jurisdiction. Further, in *Papadopoulos v Papadopoulos*,[480] one reason for refusing to recognise a Cypriot decree of nullity of marriage was that the court had no internal competence to annul a marriage under the Order in Council which established it. And in *Adams v Adams*,[481] a Rhodesian divorce was not recognised because the judge who pronounced it had not taken the oath of allegiance and the judicial oath in the prescribed form.

14–135   The difficulties of the question raised and the apparent differences of opinion between judges may be reduced by the following considerations. When, e.g. a New York court, which from an international point of view is a court of competent jurisdiction, delivers a judgment in excess of the authority conferred upon the court by New York law, the judgment, though obviously not pronounced by a court having local competence, may bear one of two characters. It may be irregular, but have validity in New York until it is set aside; or it may be a complete nullity, and have no legal effect whatever in New York. In the former case the judgment ought to be held valid in England unless and until it is set aside in New York.[482] The latter case is doubtful, but most unlikely to occur in practice. A judgment pronounced by a foreign court is far more likely to be irregular than void. The practical result, therefore, is that such a judgment is generally unimpeachable in England, even though not pronounced by a court having local competence.[483]

---

[478] (1863) 15 C.B.(N.S.) 341, approved in *Pemberton v Hughes* [1899] 1 Ch. 781, 791 (CA). See also *Brijlal Ramjidas v Govindram Seksaria* [1943] I.L.R.(Bom.) 366; (1947) L.R. 74 Ind.App. 203, and Monroe (1950) 3 Int.L.Q. 444.

[479] (1870) L.R. 4 H.L. 414, 429. Blackburn J.'s statement was approved by Lord Chelmsford at p.448.

[480] [1930] P. 55.

[481] [1971] P. 188.

[482] *cf. SA Consortium General Textiles v Sun & Sand Agencies Ltd* [1978] Q.B. 279 (CA) (a case on the 1933 Act).

[483] See further *Macalpine v Macalpine* [1958] P. 35, 41, 45; *Merker v Merker* [1963] P. 283, 297–299.

ILLUSTRATION[484]

A, a Danish subject resident in France, obtained judgment in a French court for £460 against X, a Danish subject resident and carrying on business in England. X was not present in France when the writ was issued, nor did he appear or submit to the jurisdiction of the French court. He was served with the writ in England. The judgment was impeachable for lack of jurisdiction.[485]   **14–136**

RULE 50[486]—**A foreign judgment relied upon as such in proceedings in England, is impeachable for fraud.**   **14R–137**
Such fraud may be either
(1) fraud on the part of the party in whose favour the judgment is given; or
(2) fraud on the part of the court pronouncing the judgment.

COMMENT

Any judgment whatever, and therefore any foreign judgment, is, if obtained by fraud, open to attack. A party against whom an English judgment has been given may bring an independent action to set aside the judgment on the ground that it was obtained by fraud; but this is subject to very stringent safeguards, which have been found to be necessary because otherwise there would be no end to litigation and no solemnity in judgments.[487] The most important of these safeguards is that the second action will be summarily dismissed unless the claimant can produce evidence newly discovered since the trial, which evidence could not have been produced at the trial with reasonable diligence, and which is so material that its production at the trial would probably have affected the result, and (when the fraud consists of perjury) so strong that it would reasonably be expected to be decisive at the rehearing and if unanswered must have that result.[488] But it does not matter whether the fraud is extrinsic, e.g. consists in bribing witnesses, or intrinsic, e.g. consists in giving or procuring of perjured or forged evidence.[489]   **14–138**

---

[484] See also the Illustrations to Rule 43, above, paras 14–093 *et seq.*

[485] *Schibsby v Westenholz* (1870) L.R. 6 Q.B. 155.

[486] As to the effect of fraud upon judgments generally, see *Duchess of Kingston's Case* (1776) 2 Sm.L.C. (13th ed.) 644; upon foreign judgments *in personam, Ochsenbein v Papelier* (1873) L.R. 8 Ch.App. 695; *Abouloff v Oppenheimer* (1882) 10 Q.B.D. 295 (CA); *Vadala v Lawes* (1890) 25 Q.B.D. 310 (CA); *Syal v Heyward* [1948] 2 K.B. 433 (CA); *Blohn v Desser* [1962] 2 Q.B. 116; *Jet Holdings Ltd v Patel* [1990] 1 Q.B. 335 (CA); *House of Spring Gardens Ltd v Waite* [1991] 1 Q.B. 241 (CA); *Owens Bank Ltd v Bracco* [1992] 2 A.C. 443; on foreign judgments *in rem, Castrique v Behrens* (1861) 30 L.J.Q.B. 163; *Castrique v Imrie* (1870) L.R. 4 H.L. 414, 433; *Ellerman Lines Ltd v Read* [1928] 2 K.B. 144 (CA); on foreign decrees of divorce and nullity, see below, para.18–127; under statute, 1920 Act, s.9(2)(d); 1933 Act, s.4(1)(a)(iv). See, generally, Read, pp.273–281; Restatement, s.115.

[487] See *Hunter v Chief Constable of the West Midlands Police* [1982] A.C. 529; D. M. Gordon (1961) 77 L.Q.R. 358, 533.

[488] Gordon (1961) 77 L.Q.R. 358, 376–377, and cases there cited; see for a recent example *Kuwait Airways Corp v Iraq Airways Corp* [2005] EWHC 2524 (Comm.). Contrast *Toubia v Schwenke* [2002] NSWCA 34, (2002) 54 N.S.W.L.R. 46 (doubting whether, where the allegation is of fraud, the limitation to evidence which could not have been discovered with reasonable diligence is well-founded).

[489] Gordon, *ibid.* at pp.535–546, and cases there cited.

14–139   A foreign judgment, on the other hand, can be impeached for fraud even though no newly discovered evidence is produced and even though the fraud might have been, and was, alleged in the foreign proceedings. This was first laid down in *Abouloff v Oppenheimer*,[490] where the Court of Appeal had some difficulty in reconciling its decision with the then recently established principle that foreign judgments are conclusive on the merits and cannot be impeached for any errors of fact or law.[491] Lord Coleridge C.J. and Brett L.J. solved the difficulty by holding that the issue whether a foreign court had been deliberately misled was not, and never could be, one on which that court had passed.[492] Hence to examine the judgment in subsequent English proceedings was not to re-open the merits of the judgment pronounced by the foreign court. The technical nature of this hypothesis was admitted in *Vadala v Lawes*,[493] where the evidence necessary to establish the fraud was precisely the same as that which had been rejected by the foreign court. But Lindley L.J. refused to "fritter away" the judgment in *Abouloff v Oppenheimer*; and he observed that "if the fraud upon the foreign court consists in the fact that the plaintiff has induced that court by fraud to come to a wrong conclusion, you can re-open the whole case even although you will have in this court to go into the very facts which were investigated and which were in issue in the foreign court."[494] It has even been held to be immaterial that the facts relied upon to establish a prima facie case of fraud were known to the party relying on them at all material times and could thus have been raised by way of defence in the foreign proceedings.[495] Thus, the rule that foreign judgments can be impeached for fraud stands in square opposition to the principle of conclusiveness and also to the principle that English judgments can only be impeached for fraud if new evidence of a decisive character has since been discovered. Objections to the doctrine as thus established have been advanced by various writers and a different approach has been adopted in Canada.[496] It may be observed, however, that if fraud is alleged in relation to an English judgment,

---

[490] (1882) 10 Q.B.D. 295 (CA), stated below, para.14–150, Illustration 1. By demurring to the plea of fraud, the plaintiff conceded that the foreign judgment had been so obtained, and rendered it unnecessary to prove the fraud by evidence.

[491] See Rule 48.

[492] (1882) 10 Q.B.D. 295, 302, 306.

[493] (1890) 25 Q.B.D. 310 (CA); stated below para.14–150, Illustration 2. *cf. Ellerman Lines Ltd v Read* [1928] 2 K.B. 144 (CA); contrast *Blohn v Desser* [1962] 2 Q.B. 116. The reasoning in *Abouloff v Oppenheimer* was described as illogical in *Westacre Investments Inc v Jugoimport SDPR Holding Co Ltd* [1999] Q.B. 740, 782 (a case on arbitral awards).

[494] (1890) 25 Q.B.D. 310 at pp.316–317. The principle laid down in these two cases was mentioned, with apparent approval, in *R. v Humphrys* [1977] A.C. 1, 21, 30, 46.

[495] *Syal v Heyward* [1948] 2 K.B. 443 (CA); stated below, para.14–150, Illustration 4; *Svirskis v Gibson* [1977] 2 N.Z.L.R. 4.

[496] Cheshire (1st ed.), pp.521–524; Wolff, s.247; Read, pp.279–293, and in (1930) 8 Can.Bar Rev. 231–237; Cowen (1949) 65 L.Q.R. 82. In *Beals v Saldanha* [2003] 3 S.C.R. 416, (2003) 234 D.L.R. 4th 1, at [50]–[52], a majority of the court preferred the view that for the merits of a foreign judgment to be impugned on the ground of fraud, so as to defeat a plea of *res judicata*, the evidence relied on must be something which could not have been discovered and brought to the attention of the foreign court if reasonable diligence had been exercised, even if the foreign judgment were given in default: see also *Lapp v Lapp* [2010] BCCA 517, [2011] 3 W.W.R. 694. The requirement of due diligence was not applicable to allegations of fraud going to the jurisdiction of the foreign court (as to which, see also *Consolidated Contractors International Co SAL v Masri* [2011] UKPC 29, [2]).

its effect will be to destroy the judgment and prevent its enforcement anywhere. By contrast, when fraud is alleged in relation to a foreign judgment, the effect is only to prevent enforcement in England; no impact will be felt in the State whose courts produced the judgment nor (issues of estoppel aside) in any third country.[497] As such, the effect of a finding of fraud in relation to a foreign judgment is more limited than in the case of an English judgment, and it is not difficult to argue that the nature of the evidence required to justify these two discrete results need not be identical in quality.[498]

In *Keele v Findley*[499] the New South Wales Supreme Court rejected the **14–140** English authorities and preferred the Canadian authorities. It was held that the current state of English law reflected an historical error: the authorities had failed to take proper account of the developments in the law relating to domestic judgments. Consequently, fraud was a defence to an action on a foreign judgment only if there had been a new discovery of material evidence which would establish fraud and make it reasonably probable that the opposite result would have been reached. But the Federal Court of Australia considered *Keele v Findley* to have been wrongly decided, preferring the traditional English approach to the doctrine of fraud.[500] The English authorities have now been reaffirmed by the Court of Appeal in *Jet Holdings Inc v Patel*[501] and by the House of Lords in *Owens Bank Ltd v Bracco*,[502] in each of which it was confirmed that the defence of fraud was not limited to fraud which was extraneous or collateral to the dispute which the foreign court determined, and applied equally to fraud which was intrinsic in the sense mentioned above. The latter decision was on s.9(2)(d) of the 1920 Act, under which no judgment can be registered if it was obtained by fraud. The House of Lords held it had to be construed with reference to the common law as understood when the 1920 Act was enacted. It was recognised that there was a strong case for according to overseas judgments the same finality as was accorded to English judgments, but the House of Lords considered that to overrule *Abouloff v Oppenheimer* and *Vadala v Lawes* would produce the absurd result that a judgment creditor, denied statutory enforcement under the 1920 Act or the 1933 Act on the ground that he had obtained his judgment by fraud, could succeed in a common law action to enforce his judgment because the evidence on which the judgment debtor relied did not satisfy the English rule for

---

[497] cf. *Clarke v Fennoscandia Ltd* [2007] UKHL 56, 2008 S.C. (H.L.) 122, [23]–[24].

[498] See also *Soleimany v Soleimany* [1999] Q.B. 785 (CA).

[499] (1991) 21 N.S.W.L.R. 444. See also *Wentworth v Rogers (No.5)* (1986) 6 N.S.W.L.R. 534, 541. But in *Close v Arnot*, unreported, November 21, 1997 (NSW), the Common Law Division distinguished *Keele v Findley* and applied the traditional English standard of fraud in respect of a foreign judgment in a case where the defendant had, for good reason, allowed foreign proceedings to go undefended.

[500] *Ki Won Yoon v Young Dung Song* (2000) 158 F.L.R. 295 (Fed. Ct); to the same effect *Close v Arnot*, unreported, November 21, 1997 (NSW); *Santis v Di Russo* (2001) 27 Fam. L.R. 414 (Qd) (appeal allowed without reference to this point: [2001] QCA 457). The Irish courts continue to follow the traditional common law: *Bussoleno Ltd v Kelly* [2011] IEHC 220. The approach in *Keele v Findley* was adopted in *Hong Pian Tee v Les Placements Germain Gauthier Inc* [2002] 2 Sing. L.R. 81 (Sing CA), though without reference to the contrary Australian decisions. See also Garnett (2002) 1 J. Int. Comm. L. 1.

[501] [1990] 1 Q.B. 335 (CA).

[502] [1992] 2 A.C. 443. See also *Commercial Innovation Bank Alfa Bank v Kozeny* [2002] UKPC 66, (2002) 61 W.I.R. 34.

domestic judgments. "Accordingly", said Lord Bridge (with whom all the other members concurred), "the whole field is effectively governed by statute and, if the law is now in need of reform, it is for the legislature, not the judiciary, to effect it."[503] This reasoning is, it is suggested, unconvincing: first, the whole field is *not* governed by statute, since the legislation applies to two countries only (Israel and Suriname) outside the Commonwealth and Western Europe;[504] secondly, as has been seen, under the 1933 Act no action may be brought at common law upon a judgment capable of direct enforcement by registration under the Act.[505]

14–141   In *Jet Holdings Inc v Patel* the Court of Appeal also reaffirmed that it was irrelevant that in the view of the foreign court there was no fraud. But in *House of Spring Gardens Ltd v Waite*[506] some of the judgment debtors commenced a fresh action in the foreign country to set aside the original foreign judgment on the ground of fraud. That action failed after a 22 day trial. It was held that the judgment debtors (including one who had not been a party to the fresh action) were estopped by the decision of the foreign court that there had been no fraud. This decision has been held to lay down a general principle that a decision by a foreign court that a judgment from the courts of that country was, or was not, obtained by fraud can create an estoppel in English proceedings to enforce that judgment.[507]

14–142   The decision of the Court of Appeal in *House of Spring Gardens Ltd v Waite*, that the decision of a foreign court on the allegation of fraud given in fresh proceedings instituted by the judgment debtor may found an estoppel upon that issue in subsequent English enforcement proceedings, is consistent with recent authority on issue estoppel.[508] The fact that the judgment debtor elected[509] to seise the foreign court[510] distinguishes the case from *Jet Holdings Inc v Patel*. But the court went on to hold[511] that if it was wrong in its analysis of fraud, it was nevertheless an abuse of the process of the court to raise for a second (or third) time an argument which had been raised and disposed of in the foreign court. Subsequent authorities support the suggestion that the concept of abuse of process may be capable of circumscribing the common law rule that, as long as there can be shown to be a prima facie

---

[503] [1992] 2 A.C. 443, 489.

[504] See below, paras 14R–183 and 14–184 and see Collier [1992] C.L.J. 441 for criticism on this ground (the criticism was noted, without dissent, in *Owens Bank Ltd v Etoile Commerciale SA* [1995] 1 W.L.R. 44, 50 (PC)).

[505] 1933 Act, s.6, Exception 1 to Rule 42, above.

[506] [1991] 1 Q.B. 241 (CA).

[507] *Owens Bank Ltd v Bracco* [1992] 2 A.C. 443, 474 (CA) (where the foreign court in question was not in the country of the original judgment, but another country in which enforcement was sought). The point was not addressed by the House of Lords.

[508] For issue estoppel in relation to foreign judgments, see generally Rule 42, above, paras 14R–020 *et seq*.

[509] It should be noted that this may not be uncontroversial: the judgment debtor may not have had a free and unconstrained choice to bring the second action if, for example, he had assets within the jurisdiction of the foreign court which were threatened with seizure by way of execution. *cf.* 1982 Act, s.33(1)(c), and para.14–071, above, for the possibility that an appearance in such circumstances may not be a submission to the jurisdiction of the court applied to.

[510] With the consequence that he has submitted to the jurisdiction, and the court in the second action had, as a matter of the English rules of the conflict of laws, jurisdiction to bind him.

[511] [1991] 1 Q.B. 241, 254 (CA).

case[512] for investigation, a foreign judgment may be impeached for fraud. In *Owens Bank Ltd v Etoile Commerciale SA*[513] a French court had given judgment in favour of Etoile on a bank guarantee, rejecting the bank's allegation of fraud and forgery on the part of the plaintiff. A claim brought by the bank in St Vincent against Etoile for damages for fraud was struck out by the court; in subsequent proceedings in St. Vincent to enforce the French judgment, the Privy Council struck out, as an abuse of process, the bank's attempt to plead fraud as a defence.[514]

In *AK Investment CJSC v Kyrgyz Mobil Tel Ltd*[515] the Privy Council held **14–143** that it was not appropriate on an interlocutory hearing on jurisdiction to review the line of authority from *Abouloff v Oppenheimer.* In that case, a judgment from the courts of Kyrgyzstan had been obtained in circumstances best described as extremely unsatisfactory. The court suggested that if *Aboul-off* were to be departed from, it would not be correct to treat all foreign judgments said to have been procured by fraud as if they were judgments of an English court. Instead, a "nuanced approach . . . depending on the reliability of the foreign legal system, the scope for challenge in the foreign court, and the type of fraud alleged"[516] to the fraud defence might be preferred. However, as the Kyrgyz judgment was not liable to be recognised in any event, there was no need to consider the matter further. In practice, it may be that objections of the kind raised in *AK Investment*, to the effect that the foreign judicial process was so deficient that it is unjust to recognise its judgment,[517] will in future be more easily, or less controversially, formulated under the defence that recognition would be contrary to public policy, or inconsistent with the duty of the English court to apply Art.6 of the European Convention on Human Rights.[518]

The fraud which vitiates a judgment must generally be fraud of the party in **14–144** whose favour the judgment is obtained, but it may (conceivably, at any rate) be fraud on the part of the foreign court giving the judgment,[519] as where a court gives judgment in favour of A, because the judges are bribed by some person, not the plaintiff, who wishes judgment to be given against X, the defendant. In such a case the defence of fraud tends to merge with the defence that the proceedings were opposed to natural justice.[520]

---

[512] The question is whether there is a prima facie that the particular foreign court was defrauded in the particular case. According to *Habib Bank Ltd v Ahmed* [2001] EWCA Civ 1270, [2002] 1 Lloyd's Rep. 444, an allegation of fraud has eventually to be proved "to a high degree of probability". There must, therefore, be a prima facie case that this demanding standard can be reached at trial.

[513] [1995] 1 W.L.R. 44 (PC). Lord Templeman stated that the Privy Council did not "regard the decision in *Abouloff*'s case . . . with enthusiasm". *cf. Desert Sun Loan Corp v Hill* [1996] 2 All E.R. 847, 859, 863–864 (CA).

[514] A submission that issue estoppel arose from the first St. Vincent action was not addressed.

[515] [2011] UKPC 7, [109]–[119]. Though the case was an appeal from the Isle of Man, there is no reason to doubt the judgment as a statement of English law.

[516] At [116].

[517] See also *Korea National Insurance Co v Allianz Global Corporate & Specialty AG* [2008] EWCA Civ 1355, [2008] 2 C.L.C. 837.

[518] See Rule 51, below.

[519] *Price v Dewhurst* (1837) 8 Sim. 279; *Korea National Insurance Co v Allianz Global Corporate & Specialty AG* [2008] EWCA Civ 1355, [2008] 2 C.L.C. 837.

[520] See Rule 52, below.

14–145   The doctrine that fraud vitiates a judgment does not necessarily apply to foreign judgments of every class. It is clearly applicable to a judgment *in personam*,[521] where, be it noted, the rights in question are the rights of the litigants or of their representatives. Evidence raising a triable issue of fraud suffices for permission to be given to defend a claim if the claimant applies for summary judgment on the ground that the defendant has no real prospect of successfully defending the claim.[522] It has already been seen that the 1920 Act provides[523] that no judgment can be registered under that Act if it was obtained by fraud and that in *Owens Bank Ltd v Bracco*[524] it was held that the reference to fraud in the 1920 Act must be construed by reference to the common law principles. It has been assumed that the same is so under the 1933 Act,[525] which provides[526] that the registration of a judgment under that Act must be set aside if the registering court is satisfied that the judgment was obtained by fraud. And under that Act a foreign judgment, whether registered or not and whether registrable or not, will not be recognised as conclusive between the parties thereto in English proceedings founded on the same cause of action if it was obtained by fraud.[527]

14–146   But fraud as such is not a ground for refusal to enforce or recognise a judgment under Pt I of the 1982 Act,[528] because neither the Brussels I Regulation nor the Lugano Convention (nor the Brussels Convention before them) makes provision for a defence of fraud. They do contain a defence of public policy. In continental European law fraud in this context generally falls within the exception of public policy,[529] and it is for this reason that international conventions on the recognition of judgments[530] and arbitration awards[531] commonly omit the defence of fraud as such. In *Interdesco SA v Nullifire Ltd*[532] and in *Société d'Informatique Service Réalisation Organisation v Ampersand Software BV*[533] it was confirmed that the defence of fraud had only a very limited scope under the Brussels Convention. It was accepted that it could come within the public policy exception.[534] But if means of redress against the alleged fraud were available in the country of judgment, it

---

[521] *Vadala v Lawes* (1890) 25 Q.B.D. 310 (CA).

[522] See para.14–028, n.120, above.

[523] s.9(2)(d).

[524] [1992] 2 A.C. 443.

[525] *Syal v Heyward* [1948] 2 K.B. 443 (CA).

[526] s.4(1)(a)(iv).

[527] s.8(1)(2).

[528] See below, para.14–227.

[529] *cf.* Gaudemet-Tallon, *Compétence et Exécution des Jugements en Europe* (4th ed. 2010), p.422; Schlosser [1979] O.J. C.59/71, para.192.

[530] e.g. Hague Convention on the Recognition of Divorces and Legal Separations (1968), implemented by the Family Law Act 1986, as to which see below, paras 18–127 *et seq.* In *Kendall v Kendall* [1977] Fam. 208 it was held that recognition of a foreign divorce decree obtained by fraud would be refused because it was manifestly contrary to public policy within the meaning of what is now s.51(3) of the Family Law Act 1986, notwithstanding that there was no separate basis for non-recognition on the ground of fraud in the Act.

[531] Geneva Convention (1927) and New York Convention (1958), implemented by the Arbitration Act 1950, Pt II, and the Arbitration Act 1975, as to which see Rules 68 and 69.

[532] [1992] 1 Lloyd's Rep. 180.

[533] [1994] I.L.Pr. 55 (CA).

[534] For approval of the reasoning in *Interdesco v Nullifire SA*, but refusal to allow it to contradict the public policy of upholding the finality of arbitral awards, see *Westacre Investments Inc v Jugoimport SDPR Holding Co Ltd* [1999] Q.B. 740.

would not be contrary to English public policy to recognise and register a judgment which was subject to those means of redress.

Because of the absolute terms of Pt II of the 1982 Act,[535] no Scottish or Northern Irish judgment registrable in England can be impeached on the ground that it was obtained by fraud. In such a case the defendant's remedy would be to attack the judgment in Scotland or Northern Ireland by appeal out of time or by an application to set it aside.   **14–147**

The doctrine may apply as between the litigants to a judgment *in rem*.[536] But it is questionable whether the fraud which, as between the litigants, appears to vitiate a judgment *in rem* affects the rights of third persons, e.g. bona fide purchasers, who, in ignorance of the fraud, acquire under or in consequence of the judgment a title to the *res*, e.g. a ship, affected thereby.[537] The reason why there is a question in this last case is that such third persons are relying on the judgment merely *qua* an assignment rather than *qua* a judgment and are entitled to the benefit of the rule that an assignment of movables is wholly governed in its proprietary aspects by the *lex situs*.[538] As Blackburn J. put it,[539] "Fraud will indeed vitiate everything; though we may observe that there is much force in what [counsel] suggested in the course of his argument in this case, that even if there had been fraud on the part of the litigants, or even of the tribunal, it would be very questionable whether it could be set up against a bona fide purchaser who was quite ignorant of it." The recognition of foreign decrees affecting status is not within the scope of this chapter, and the position in relation to those decrees has been touched on merely because of the connection it has with the effect of fraud on judgments properly *in rem*. It may be that only foreign judgments *in personam*, or which, despite being judgments *in rem* are relied on as imposing obligations *in personam*,[540] are impeachable for fraud.   **14–148**

It is equally possible to adduce fraud in opposition to a claim based on a foreign judgment and to a defendant's defence based on a similar source.[541]   **14–149**

ILLUSTRATIONS

1. A obtains in a Russian court judgment against X that X shall either deliver to A certain goods of A's, then, as alleged, in X's possession, or pay A a sum equivalent to £1,050. The judgment,   **14–150**

---

[535] See below, para.14–262.

[536] *Messina v Petrococchino* (1872) L.R. 4 P.C. 144, 157. In *AK Investment CJSC v Kyrgyz Mobil Tel Ltd* [2011] UKPC 7, at [120]–[121], the Privy Council held that the fraud defence may apply to prevent recognition of the foreign judgment, even where the foreign judgment was or purported to operate *in rem*, when the claim between the parties before the English court was *in personam* (wrongful misappropriation, or unjust enrichment). It was also arguable that if the foreign judgment were simply relied on as an effective assignment of movable property, its recognition might still be prevented on grounds of public policy.

[537] *Castrique v Behrens* (1861) 30 L.J.Q.B. 163, stated below, para.14–151, Illustration 8; *Castrique v Imrie* (1870) L.R. 4 H.L. 414, 433. See Rule 47.

[538] See Rule 133.

[539] *Castrique v Imrie*, above, at p.433.

[540] *Pattni v Ali* [2006] UKPC 51, [2007] 2 A.C. 85.

[541] See Westlake, s.335, though *Henderson v Henderson* (1843) 3 Hare 100, 117 is not conclusive; *Manolopoulos v Pnaiffe* [1930] 2 D.L.R. 169 (NSCA). See also *Merchant International Co Ltd v AK "Naftogaz Ukrayiny"* [2011] EWHC 1820 (Comm.), [2011] 2 All E.R. (Comm.) 755 (appellate judgment tainted and not entitled to recognition; judgment of court below entitled to be enforced despite having been set aside by appellate court in the country in which it was given).

which is affirmed on appeal to a superior Russian court, is obtained by A's fraudulently concealing from the court that at the very moment when the action is brought the goods are in the possession of A. The judgment is impeachable in England.[542]

2. A brings an action in New York against X to recover money alleged to be due on certain bills of exchange. A obtains judgment against X by fraudulently representing to the New York court that the bills of exchange were given under the authority of X and for mercantile transactions, whereas they were given without X's authority for gambling debts. The judgment is impeachable in England.[543]

3. A, an Indian moneylender, obtains judgment against X for 20,000 rupees alleged to be due on a loan. The writ is served upon X in India, but he fails to appear. A registers his judgment in the High Court under the 1933 Act. X applies to set aside the registration of the judgment on the ground of fraud. He alleges that the amount of the loan was only 10,800 rupees and that A has concealed from the Indian court the possibility that X might have a defence under the Indian Usurious Loans Act. The court will direct the trial of an issue whether X's allegations are true and, if they are, will set aside the registration of the judgment.[544]

4. A & Co sue X in California to recover sums allegedly misappropriated by X. X defends the proceedings on the ground that representatives of A & Co had been violent towards him and that X had, under further threats from them, to pay substantial amounts to A & Co X is too frightened to attend depositions in California, and judgment in default is given against him after A & Co's lawyers represent to the Californian court that X's account of violence and threats is untrue. X has an arguable defence that the judgment was obtained by fraud, and leave to defend is given.[545]

14–151   5. A & Co sue X, Y and Z in the Republic of Ireland for misuse of confidential information and breach of copyright, and obtain judgment for £3 million. X, Y and Z appeal unsuccessfully to the Supreme Court of Ireland. X and Y (but not Z) bring a fresh action in Ireland to set aside the judgment on the ground of fraud. After a 22 day trial, the allegation of fraud is rejected. The original judgment is enforceable in England, not only against X and Y, but also against Z, who is estopped from alleging fraud: he is privy to the second Irish judgment because the original judgment was obtained against X, Y and Z jointly and severally and because he was well aware of the proceedings to set aside the original judgment.[546]

6. A foreign court gives judgment for A against X. X had argued that A's evidence is perjured and based on falsified documents. The defence is rejected at trial and also on appeal. When A seeks to enforce the judgment in England the court is not bound to recognise the decision of the foreign court on perjury and forgery but, if the evidence put forward by X appears to raise a prima facie case of fraud, may try for itself the allegation of fraud raised by X.[547]

7. A foreign court gives judgment for A against B, but on appeal B the judgment at first instance is set aside. A contends that the judgment of the appeal court was obtained by fraud and is not entitled to recognition in England. The contention is liable to succeed, and if it does, the judgment of the appellate court will be denied recognition, with the result that the judgment of the first instance court may be recognised and enforced in England.[548]

8. B. is the owner of a British ship. He mortgages her to A and later goes bankrupt. While the ship is at Melbourne M, the master, draws a bill of exchange on B for necessaries supplied to the ship by X. The bill is never accepted and is dishonoured at maturity. During the ship's return voyage to Europe X conspires with Y, and indorses the bill to Y (but not for value) in order that Y may take advantage of a provision of foreign law whereby the bona fide holder of such a bill can take proceedings *in rem* against the ship in the foreign court. When the ship is in the foreign

---

[542] *cf. Abouloff v Oppenheimer* (1882) 10 Q.B.D. 295 (CA).

[543] *cf. Vadala v Lawes* (1890) 25 Q.B.D. 310 (CA). Contrast *Blohn v Desser* [1962] 2 Q.B. 116.

[544] *Syal v Heyward* [1948] 2 K.B. 443 (CA).

[545] *Jet Holdings Inc v Patel* [1990] 1 Q.B. 335 (CA).

[546] *House of Spring Gardens Ltd v Waite* [1991] 1 Q.B. 241 (CA). The proceedings were instituted before the Brussels Convention had come into force in the United Kingdom and Ireland.

[547] *Owens Bank Ltd v Bracco* [1992] 2 A.C. 443 (a case on registration under the 1920 Act).

[548] *cf. Merchant International Co Ltd v AK "Naftogaz Ukrayiny"* [2011] EWHC 1820 (Comm.), [2011] 2 All E.R. (Comm) 755, where the basis for non-recognition was Art.6 of the European Convention on Human Rights, though the reasoning must be equally applicable to the defence of fraud.

port Y brings proceedings *in rem* against her which result in the court ordering the sale of the ship in order to pay the bill. In an action by A against X in England for conspiracy to defraud, A cannot impeach the foreign judgment for fraud.[549]

RULE 51[550]—A foreign judgment is impeachable on the ground that its enforcement or, as the case may be, recognition, would be contrary to public policy.   14R–152

COMMENT

Until recently, there were very few reported cases in which foreign judgments *in personam*[551] had been denied enforcement or recognition for reasons of public policy at common law.[552] In *Re Macartney*,[553] a foreign judgment awarding the mother on behalf of an illegitimate child perpetual maintenance against the estate of the deceased putative father was refused enforcement on three grounds: (1) it was contrary to public policy to enforce an affiliation order not limited to minority; (2) the cause of action—a posthumous affiliation order—was unknown to English law; and (3) the judgment was not final and conclusive.[554] Under the second head the court relied heavily on an American case[555] in which a French judgment awarding maintenance to a French son-in-law against his American father-in-law and mother-in-law was refused enforcement in the United States. Both these cases were disapproved or distinguished in *Burchell v Burchell*[556] and *Phrantzes v Argenti*.[557]   14–153

In *Burchell v Burchell* an Ontario court enforced a judgment of an Ohio divorce court for a lump-sum payment by a wife for the support of her husband, although by the law of Ontario a husband could not have obtained alimony from his wife. In *Phrantzes v Argenti* (which was not a case upon a foreign judgment), the English court refused to enforce a claim by a Greek   14–154

---

[549] *Castrique v Behrens* (1861) 30 L.J.Q.B. 163; approved in *Bater v Bater* [1906] P. 209, 219, 228 (CA). Compare *Castrique v Imrie* (1870) L.R. 4 H.L. 414, 433.

[550] *Re Macartney* [1921] 1 Ch. 552; *SA Consortium General Textiles v Sun & Sand Agencies Ltd* [1978] Q.B. 279 (CA); *Israel Discount Bank of New York v Hadjipateras* [1984] 1 W.L.R. 137 (CA); *ED&F Man (Sugar) Ltd Haryanto (No.2)* [1991] 1 Lloyd's Rep. 429 (CA); *Mayo-Perrott v Mayo-Perrott* [1958] I.R. 336; *Holt v Thomas* (1987) 38 D.L.R. (4th) 117 (Alta); *Honolulu Savings and Loan Ass'n v Robinson* (1989) 64 D.L.R. (4th) 551, affirmed (1990) 76 D.L.R. (4th) 103 (Man CA); *Minkler and Kirschbaum v Sheppard* (1991) 60 B.C.L.R. (2d) 360; *Resorts International Hotel Inc v Auerbach* (1991) 89 D.L.R. (4th) 688 (Que CA); *Boardwalk Regency Corp v Maalouf* (1992) 88 D.L.R. (4th) 612 (Ont CA); *Union of India v Bumper Development Corp* [1995] 7 W.W.R. 80 (Alta); *Connor v Connor* [1974] 1 N.Z.L.R. 632; Read, pp.292–295; Restatement, s.117. In *Adams v Cape Industries Plc* [1990] Ch. 433, 496, affirmed *ibid.* 503, Scott J. suggested that the principles in Rules 51 and 52 might overlap in the sense that, if a foreign judgment were obtained in breach of natural justice, it would also be contrary to public policy to enforce it.

[551] For non-recognition of foreign divorce and nullity decrees see below, Rule 91.

[552] There is also a public policy in favour of accepting the finality of litigation: *cf.*, in the context of arbitral awards, *Westacre Investments Inc v Jugoimport SDPR Holding Co Ltd* [1999] Q.B. 740.

[553] [1921] 1 Ch. 522.

[554] See Rule 42, above. This third ground would clearly have been sufficient by itself to dispose of the case.

[555] *De Brimont v Penniman* (1873) 10 Blatchford Circuit Court Reports 436.

[556] [1926] 2 D.L.R. 595 (Ont).

[557] [1960] 2 Q.B. 19, 31–34.

daughter against her father for the provision of a dowry on her marriage as required by Greek law, not on the ground that the cause of action was unknown to English law, but on the ground that English law had no remedy for awarding a dowry, the amount of which in Greek law was within the discretion of the court and varied in accordance with the wealth and social position of the father and the number of his children. On the other hand, in *Mayo-Perrot v Mayo-Perrot*[558] the Supreme Court of the Republic of Ireland refused to enforce an English order for costs in favour of a wife against her husband which was ancillary to an English divorce decree. The grounds of this decision were partly that the cause of action was of such a character that it could not have supported an action in the Republic, where divorce was then not allowed, and partly that to enforce an order ancillary to a divorce decree was contrary to Irish public policy.

14–155   In *Israel Discount Bank of New York v Hadjipateras*[559] it was suggested that it might be contrary to public policy to enforce a judgment based on a contract which had been executed as a result of undue influence. But the decision has been convincingly criticised[560] on the grounds that it is the recognition of the judgment which must be contrary to public policy, and not the underlying contract on which the cause of action is based;[561] and that as a matter of domestic English law the enforcement of a contract obtained by undue influence is not contrary to public policy, although it may be rescinded in equity.

14–156   It will in principle be contrary to public policy to recognise or enforce a judgment which has been obtained in disobedience of an injunction not to proceed with the action in a foreign court.[562] In *AK Investment CJSC v Kyrgyz Mobil Tel Ltd*[563] it was said to be arguable that a foreign judgment obtained in breach of an arbitration agreement for a tribunal in a third country,[564] and in disregard of an injunction issued by the courts of a fourth country, and in circumstances of evidently discreditable behaviour on the part of the court might be refused recognition on grounds of public policy. However, where a husband obtained a decree of divorce from a Russian court in defiance of an order that no step be taken in those proceedings until after the hearing of a matrimonial matter before the English court, the Court of Appeal held in *Golubovich v Golubovich*[565] that the statutory obligation to recognise the

---

[558] [1958] I.R. 336.

[559] [1984] 1 W.L.R. 137 (CA).

[560] Collier [1984] C.L.J. 47. The narrowness of the defence was reaffirmed in *Society of Lloyd's v Meinzer* (2002) 210 D.L.R. (4th) 519 (Ont CA) (a decision on the Ontario equivalent of the 1933 Act), which restricted it to cases affecting essential principles of justice or moral interests in the receiving court. See also *Great America Leasing Corp v Yates* (2003) 68 O.R. (3d) 566 (Ont CA).

[561] But *cf.* 1920 Act, s.9(2)(f).

[562] *Phillip Alexander Securities & Futures Ltd v Bamberger* [1997] I.L.Pr. 73, at p.103 (Waller J.) affirmed *ibid.* 104, at p.115 (CA); *WSG Nimbus Pte Ltd v Board of Control for Cricket in Sri Lanka* [2002] 3 Sing. L.R. 603. *cf. Fakih Bros v AP Moller (Copenhagen) Ltd* [1994] 1 Lloyd's Rep. 103; *Cocoon Data Holdings Pty Ltd v K2M3 LLC* [2011] VSC 355 (strike out of defence for breach of anti-suit injunction).

[563] [2011] UKPC 7, [2011] 4 All E.R. 1027, [121].

[564] As the Privy Council was sitting on an appeal from the Isle of Man, Civil Jurisdiction and Judgments Act 1982, s.32 was inapplicable to the case.

[565] [2010] EWCA Civ 810, [2011] Fam. 88. See also *A v L* [2010] EWHC 460 (Fam.).

divorce prevailed over the contention that the wrongful behaviour of the husband meant that recognition would be manifestly contrary to public policy.[566] It may be that that there is a distinction in this respect between judgments *in rem* and *in personam*.[567] It is now established that a foreign judgment will not be recognised if it is inconsistent with a previous decision of a competent English court in proceedings between the same parties (or their privies). In *Vervaeke v Smith*[568] it was held that the principle of *res judicata* in English law was a rule of public policy, and that it would therefore be contrary to public policy to recognise a foreign decree of nullity which was inconsistent with an earlier decision of the English court that the marriage was valid. This principle was applied to a foreign judgment *in personam* in *ED&F Man (Sugar) Ltd v Haryanto (No.2)*,[569] where the English court had dismissed the defendant's action for a declaration that he was not bound by contracts for the purchase of sugar, and an Indonesian court had subsequently decided that the contracts were illegal and contrary to Indonesian public policy. The Indonesian judgment was denied recognition.

The question whether enforcement of a judgment may be refused on **14–157** grounds of public policy when the judgment is for exemplary, punitive, or manifestly excessive damages remains undecided. In *SA Consortium General Textiles v Sun & Sand Agencies Ltd*[570] Lord Denning M.R. considered that there was no such objection at common law, but the element of the overall damages which was allegedly punitive was a modest figure awarded in respect of the manner in which the defendant had exposed the claimant to greater expense by the abusive manner in which he had defended the claim. An Australian court[571] has refused to enforce a judgment which ordered payment of damages which had been described by the awarding court as "punitive". A Canadian court[572] refused to order summary judgment in respect of an application to enforce a US judgment awarding a massive sum of damages for "emotional distress", but in *Beals v Saldanha*[573] a majority of the Supreme Court of Canada declined to accept a submission that to enforce a Florida judgment for quite extraordinary sums could offend against Canadian public policy. In the English context it is arguable that to enforce a judgment for a sum which is manifestly excessive, when measured against what an English

---

[566] Family Law Act 1986, s.53(1)(c).

[567] Though as recognition of the Russian divorce would not affect the English court's jurisdiction over the claim for matrimonial relief, there was little practical reason to withhold recognition.

[568] [1983] 1 A.C. 145. For a similar rule under the Brussels I Regulation and the Lugano Convention see below, para.14–235.

[569] [1991] 1 Lloyd's Rep. 429 (CA), stated below, Illustration, para.14–161. The decision in that case is discussed in *Masri v Consolidated Contractors International Co SAL (No.3)* [2008] EWCA Civ 625, [2009] Q.B. 503, but with a focus on the restraint of a party bound by an English judgment who is taking steps before the courts of another country to obtain a judgment with which to seek to undermine the English judgment.

[570] [1978] Q.B. 279, at p.299.

[571] *Schnabel v Lui* [2002] NSWSC 15. But if the true basis for the decision was the principle in Rule 3, that a foreign penal law will not be enforced, it is unclear that this may be applied to a case awarding damages to a claimant: *cf. Ontario Harness Horse Association v Ontario Racing Commission* (2003) 62 O.R. (3d) 26 (Ont CA).

[572] *Kidron v Green* (2000) 48 O.R. (3d) 775 (Ont).

[573] [2003] 3 S.C.R. 416, (2003) 234 D.L.R. (4th) 1.

court would have awarded by way of compensation, would be contrary to the European Convention on Human Rights.[574] It has been held in New Zealand that, although the court will not directly or indirectly enforce a foreign public law,[575] the enforcement of a foreign judgment for costs is not contrary to public policy merely because the costs if recovered would be payable to a foreign legal aid fund.[576] The 1933 Act contains a separate provision[577] excluding from its registration provisions a foreign judgment for taxes or for a fine or other penalty.

14–158   The 1920 Act excludes from registration a judgment "which was in respect of a cause of action which for reasons of public policy or for some other similar reason could not have been entertained by the registering court."[578] The 1933 Act provides that registration may be set aside if "the enforcement of the judgment would be contrary to public policy in the country of the registering court."[579] It will be observed that there is an important difference between the 1920 and 1933 Acts in this connection. The 1920 Act excludes enforcement of a judgment on the basis that the original cause of action is contrary to public policy. The 1933 Act lays down the more limited principle that enforcement or recognition must be withheld if enforcement or recognition would be contrary to public policy. The effect of Art.27 of the Brussels Convention was that enforcement or recognition under Pt I of the 1982 Act might be refused if recognition was "contrary to public policy" in the United Kingdom.[580] The corresponding provision of the Brussels I Regulation and Lugano Convention Art.34(1), is in the same terms except for the addition of the word "manifestly", which appears to add little. Enforcement or recognition of Scottish or Northern Irish judgments cannot be refused on the ground of public policy. Any such objection is precluded by the terms of Pt II of the 1982 Act.[581]

14–159   **Human Rights Act 1998.** The 1998 Act gave the force of law to the European Convention on Human Rights. If the enforcement of a foreign judgment would be contrary to the European Convention, enforcement will in principle be refused.[582] Indeed, such a case is not really an example of recognition or enforcement being refused on grounds of public policy, but is rather because primary legislation produces that result. On the other hand, in cases which fall under the 1982 Act, or under the Brussels I Regulation and

---

[574] See below, para.14–159. See also decisions in New Zealand to the effect that public policy is not triggered by the fact that the foreign judgment is substantially different from that which would have been given by a local court, but may require non-recognition where recognition would offend a reasonable New Zealander's sense of morality: *Reeves v One World Challenge LLC* [2006] N.Z.L.R. 184, [50]–[67]; *Questnet v Lane* [2008] NZHC 710.

[575] Rule 3.

[576] *Connor v Connor* [1974] 1 N.Z.L.R. 632.

[577] s.1(2)(b).

[578] 1920 Act, s.9(2)(f).

[579] 1933 Act, ss.4(1)(a)(v), 8(1)(2).

[580] See below, para.14–225.

[581] See below, para.14R–258.

[582] Where recognition or enforcement is required by the terms of legislation which cannot be interpreted in a manner consistent with the European Convention, recognition or enforcement will be upheld, but the legislation which required it will be declared to be incompatible with the European Convention: Human Rights Act 1998, ss.3, 4.

the Lugano Convention, the application of the European Convention is not specifically provided for, and any non-recognition has to be accommodated under the rubric of public policy.[583]

Suppose a foreign judgment has been obtained in proceedings which fall **14–160** short of the guarantee of fair trial in Art.6 of the Convention. Where the judgment comes from the courts of a State party to the European Convention, little difficulty arises if the English court refuses recognition by reference to Art.6 of the European Convention.[584] The position is less clear where the original judgment was obtained in the courts of a State not party to the European Convention. In an early decision, the European Court of Human Rights held that a French court was permitted to recognise a judgment from a non-Contracting State without regard to Art.6.[585] But in *Pellegrini v Italy*[586] it ruled that an Italian court was not permitted to recognise a judgment from the Vatican City where the act of recognition by the Italian courts would itself violate the guarantees of the European Convention, notwithstanding that Italy had a prior treaty with the Vatican which required the recognition of such judgments. The difference between the result in *Pellegrini* and treating a non-Contracting State as though it were party to and bound by the European Convention is elusive. The House of Lords in *Government of USA v Montgomery (No.2)*[587] held that the enforcement of a United States judgment could only be refused by reference to the European Convention where the shortcomings in the foreign proceedings were "flagrant". This conclusion avoids treating the United States as though it were a party to the European Convention, but is not easily reconciled with *Pellegrini*.[588] However, to the extent that the notion of flagrancy lacks real precision, any problem may be made to dissolve if the court is willing to characterise the shortcomings in the foreign proceedings as "flagrant".[589] The European Court of Human Rights has since affirmed the principle in *Pellegrini* without significant further comment, though subject to the qualification that where a State has acted in compliance

---

[583] See below, para.14–225.

[584] Case C–7/98 *Krombach v Bamberski* [2000] E.C.R. I–1935, [2001] Q.B. 709; *Maronier v Larmer* [2002] EWCA Civ 774, [2003] Q.B. 620.

[585] *Drozd & Janousek v France and Spain* (1992) 14 E.H.R.R. 745. See also *Prince Hans-Adam II of Liechtenstein v Germany* (2001) 11 B.H.R.C. 526.

[586] (2002) 35 E.H.R.R. 44.

[587] [2004] UKHL 37, [2004] 1 W.L.R. 2241.

[588] See Kinsch, in Einhorn and Siehr (eds.), *Intercontinental Cooperation Through Private International Law* (2004), p.197.

[589] In *Merchant International Co Ltd v AK "Naftogaz Ukrayiny"* [2011] EWHC 1820 (Comm.), [2011] 2 All E.R. (Comm.) 755 the court had no apparent difficulty in characterising the defects in the Ukraine proceedings, which were essentially errors of Ukraine procedural law, as "flagrant" or glaring. The trend may be for the traditional defences to lose their separate identity and to merge into the principles established by Art.6 (*cf. Merchant International Co Ltd v AK "Naftogaz Ukrayiny"*, above). The principle that it is a breach of the principle of legal certainty, and hence of Art.6, for a court to remit a case to a lower court for reconsideration generally, rather than for reconsideration on the specific basis which was found to justify the remission (*Lizanets v Ukraine* [2007] ECHR 555), or to remit the case for reconsideration of the evidence when there has been no new discovery of evidence (*Pravednaya v Russia*, [2004] ECHR 641), may have an impact on the traditional rule that, in relation to foreign judgments, the domestic fresh evidence rule does not apply.

with its legal obligations under EU law, there will be a presumption that it has not acted contrary to the European Convention.[590]

ILLUSTRATION

14–161   A & Co, sugar traders, sell sugar to X, an Indonesian citizen, for $200 million under contracts governed by English law. Disputes arise and X seeks a declaration in England that he is not bound by the contracts. His action is dismissed, and the judgment is confirmed by the Court of Appeal, which also dismisses his application to raise an issue that the contracts are illegal by reason of a prohibition on importation of sugar into Indonesia. Further English proceedings ensue which are settled by an agreement governed by English law, under which X agrees to pay A & Co $27 million. Subsequently, X commences proceedings in Indonesia against A & Co, and the Indonesian court decides that the settlement agreement is illegal because it arises out of illegal contracts, and that it is contrary to Indonesian public policy to recognise the English judgment. A & Co. then seek a declaration in England that the settlement agreement is valid and binding on X. The Indonesian judgment is not recognised because the real issue in those proceedings was the validity of the underlying agreements which had already been the subject of a decision of the English court.[591]

14R–162   **Rule 52—A foreign judgment may be impeached if the proceedings in which the judgment was obtained were opposed to natural justice.[592]**

COMMENT

14–163   In a celebrated passage[593] in his judgment in *Pemberton v Hughes*[593] (a case on the recognition of a foreign divorce decree), Lord Lindley observed: "If a judgment is pronounced by a foreign court over persons within its jurisdiction and in a matter with which it is competent to deal, English courts never investigate the propriety of the proceedings in the foreign court, unless they offend against English views of substantial justice." This passage refers to irregularity in the proceedings, for it is clear that a foreign judgment, which is manifestly wrong on the merits or has misapplied English law or foreign law, is not impeachable on that ground.[594] Nor is it impeachable because the

[590] *Bosphorus Hava Yollari Turizm ve Ticaret AS v Ireland* (2006) 42 E.H.R.R. 1.

[591] *ED&F Man (Sugar) Ltd v Haryanto (No.2)* [1991] 1 Lloyd's Rep. 429 (CA).

[592] *Buchanan v Rucker* (1808) 9 East 192; *Sheehy v Professional Life Assurance Co* (1857) 2 C.B.(N.S.) 211; *Crawley v Isaacs* (1867) 16 L.T. 529; *Pemberton v Hughes* [1899] 1 Ch. 781, 790 (CA); *Robinson v Fenner* [1913] 3 K.B. 835; *Bergerem v Marsh* (1921) 91 L.J.K.B. 80; *Richardson v Army, Navy and General Assurance Association Ltd* (1925) 21 Ll.L.R. 345; *Jacobson v Frachon* (1927) 138 L.T. 386 (CA); *Adams v Cape Industries Plc* [1990] Ch. 433 (CA); *Beals v Saldanha* [2003] 3 S.C.R. 416, (2003) 234 D.L.R. (4th) 1; Read, pp.281–288; Restatement, s.25.

[593] [1899] 1 Ch. 781, 790 (CA). Canadian law places more emphasis on the principle of natural justice to control the recognition of foreign judgments as a consequence of its wider approach to rules of jurisdictional competence as these were established by the Supreme Court: see *Oakwell Engineering Ltd v Evernorth Industries Inc* (2007) 81 O.R. (3d) 88 (CA); *United States of America v Shield Development Co* (2004) 74 O.R. (3d) 585; *CLE Owners Inc v Wanlass* [2005] 8 W.W.R. 559 (Man.CA); *United States of America v Yemec* (2010) 320 D.L.R. (4th) 96 (Ont. CA). On whether the objection needs to be taken before the foreign court, see *Cortés v Yorkton Securities Inc* (2007) 278 D.L.R. (4th) 740; *Marx v Balac* [2008] BCSC 195.

[594] See *Jacobson v Frachon* (1927) 138 L.T. 386, 390, 393 (CA); *Adams v Cape Industries Plc* [1990] Ch. 433, 569 (CA).

court admitted evidence which is inadmissible in England[595] or did not admit evidence which is admissible in England[596] or otherwise followed a practice different from English law.[597] In *Jacobson v Frachon*[598] Atkin L.J., after referring to the use of the expression "principles of natural justice,"[599] said: "Those principles seem to me to involve this, first of all that the court being a court of competent jurisdiction, has given notice to the litigant that they are about to proceed to determine the rights between him and the other litigant; the other is that having given him that notice, it does afford him an opportunity of substantially presenting his case before the court."[600]

Adams v Cape Industries Plc[601] appears to have been the first English case **14–164** in which the defence of breach of natural justice was established in relation to a judgment *in personam*.[602] The Court of Appeal held that the defence of breach of natural justice was not limited to the requirements of due notice of the hearing to a litigant and opportunity to put a case to the foreign court. It confirmed that the basic question was that stated in *Pemberton v Hughes*,[603] namely whether there was a procedural defect which constituted a breach of the English court's view of substantial justice,[604] which would depend on the nature of the proceedings under consideration. The principle was applied in *Masters v Leaver*,[605] where the Court of Appeal considered that a substantial failure to follow its own procedure for an assessment of damages meant that proceedings before a Texas court had led to a judgment in denial of substantial justice.

A mere procedural irregularity would not offend English concepts of **14–165** substantial justice.[606] In *Adams v Cape Industries Plc* the foreign judgment was for damages in default of appearance, and notice was given to the defendants of the application for a default judgment on an unliquidated claim. Under United States law (as under English law) the assessment of damages is effected (even in cases of default) by the court, but the United States judge did not hold any form of hearing, and the judgment was not based on an objective assessment by the judge of the evidence.[607] The Court of Appeal did not decide that a lack of judicial assessment of damages is *per se* a breach of natural justice; but it is a breach where the foreign legal system contains provision for judicial assessment and the judgment debtor therefore has a reasonable expectation that there will be a judicial assessment.

---

[595] *De Cosse Brissac v Rathbone* (1861) 6 H. & N. 301 (the sixth plea).

[596] *Scarpetta v Lowenfeld* (1911) 27 T.L.R. 509; *Robinson v Fenner* [1913] 3 K.B. 835.

[597] *Boissière v Brockner* (1899) 6 T.L.R. 85.

[598] (1927) 138 L.T. 386 (CA).

[599] By Lord Hanworth M.R. *ibid.* at p.390.

[600] *ibid.* at p.392.

[601] [1990] Ch. 433, at 564–566. *cf. Leaton Leather & Trading Co v Ngai Tak Kong* (1997) 147 D.L.R. (4th) 377 (BC).

[602] On foreign decrees of divorce and nullity see below, para.18–125; *Shaw v Att-Gen* (1870) L.R. 2 P. & D. 156; *Rudd v Rudd* [1924] P. 72 (divorce); *Gray v Formosa* [1963] P. 259 (CA); *Lepre v Lepre* [1965] P. 52 (nullity). See also Family Law Act 1986, s.51(3).

[603] [1899] 1 Ch. 781; *Jacobson v Frachon* (1927) 138 L.T. 386, 392 (CA), *per* Atkin L.J.

[604] The terms "natural justice" and "substantial justice" appear to be used interchangeably in this context.

[605] [2000] I.L.Pr. 387.

[606] [1990] Ch. 433, at 567, citing *Pemberton v Hughes* [1899] 1 Ch. 781.

[607] *Masters v Leaver* [2000] I.L.Pr. 387.

14–166   The case is therefore an example of a breach of natural justice outside the categories of notice and opportunity to be heard, because the judgment debtors were given notice and had an opportunity to contest the quantum of damages; they did not take the opportunity because they did not wish to submit to the jurisdiction of the foreign court. This decision also puts into context those decisions which were thought to be the authority for the view that, if the defendant agrees to the jurisdiction of the foreign court, he cannot take the objection that he did not receive sufficient notice.[608] If the defendant has agreed, or is deemed to agree, a particular method of service (such as service at an address in the foreign country notified to a company of which he is a member) then it is immaterial that he did not receive actual notice.[609] If the defendant has agreed to submit to the jurisdiction of the foreign court, and service has been effected in accordance with the foreign law, but actual notice has not been given, then the question will be whether substantial injustice has been caused by the lack of notice, including consideration of whether the defendant had a remedy in the foreign court.[610] The objection that the defendant did not receive sufficient notice of the foreign proceedings to enable him to defend them tends to become confused with the objection that the foreign court had no jurisdiction. If the defendant is resident in the foreign country at the time when the proceedings were commenced, or if he voluntarily appears in the proceedings, it is difficult for him to take the objection that he did not receive sufficient notice, for in such circumstances any notice is sufficient which is in accordance with the law of the foreign country,[611] provided that the foreign procedure does not offend against English views of substantial justice.[612] If the defendant agrees in advance to submit to the jurisdiction of the foreign court and service is effected in accordance with the method of service to which he has agreed (or is deemed to have agreed) he cannot complain if he did not receive actual notice.[613] "It is not contrary to natural justice that a man who has agreed to receive a particular mode of notification of legal proceedings should be bound by a judgment in which that particular mode of notification has been followed, even though he may not have had actual notice of them."[614]

14–167   May the defence of breach of natural justice be raised before the English court if the objection could have been taken before the foreign court? In *Jet Holdings Inc v Patel*[615] Staughton L.J. said, *obiter*, that logically the foreign court's view should be neither conclusive nor relevant as to the propriety of its own proceedings. In *Adams v Cape Industries Plc*[616] the evidence was that the judgment debtors had the right to apply in the United States to set aside

---

[608] See above, para.14–080.

[609] *Vallée v Dumergue* (1849) 4 Exch. 290; *Copin v Adamson* (1875) 1 Ex.D. 17 (CA). *cf. Bank of Australasia v Harding* (1850) 9 C.B. 661; *Bank of Australasia v Nias* (1851) 16 Q.B. 717 (chairman of company deemed agent of shareholders); *Jamieson v Robb* (1881) 7 V.L.R. 170.

[610] [1990] Ch. at 570. *cf. Jeannot v Fuerst* (1909) 25 T.L.R. 424. Contrast *Feyerick v Hubbard* (1902) 71 L.J.K.B. 509.

[611] Dicey, 3rd ed., p.441.

[612] See above, para.14–080.

[613] *ibid.*

[614] *Vallée v Dumergue* (1849) 4 Exch. 290, 303.

[615] [1990] 1 Q.B. 335, 345 (CA).

[616] [1990] Ch. 433, 569 (CA).

the default judgment on the ground that the assessment of damages was irregular, and it was recognised that such an application would have been allowed if made in due time. The Court of Appeal thought that where the objection came within the two categories mentioned by Atkin L.J., want of notice or lack of opportunity to be heard, the judgment debtor may raise the objection in England even if there is a remedy in the foreign country.[617] But in other categories (as in the one under consideration in that case) the existence of a remedy in the foreign court is not wholly irrelevant in determining whether the proceedings in the foreign court, viewed as a whole, offend against English views of substantial justice: it would be anomalous if the English court were obliged to disregard the existence of a remedy under a foreign system of procedure in considering whether the defective operation of that procedure had led to a breach of natural justice. The judgment debtor cannot justify a failure to avail himself of the remedy by reference to his unwillingness to submit to the jurisdiction of a foreign court. But in that case the defendants had no way of knowing from the judgment served on them that the judgment had been entered without a judicial assessment of damages, since the recitals in the judgment indicated there had been a hearing. In *Masters v Leaver*,[618] the Court of Appeal held that, on the evidence before it, it was not incumbent on the judgment debtor to have pursued his complaint before the foreign court. It appears that there is no general answer, and that in each case the plea that the judgment debtor should have complained to the foreign court will be assessed in the context of the broader merits. But where the issue or procedural error has been raised before the foreign court and rejected, it is less likely that an English court will entertain arguments concerning natural or substantial justice which are based on it.[619]

The 1920 and 1933 Acts contain specific provisions dealing with service **14–168** and notice. The 1920 Act provides[620] that registration of a foreign judgment must be refused if the defendant was not duly served with the process of the original court and did not appear, notwithstanding that he was ordinarily resident or was carrying on business within the jurisdiction of that court or agreed to submit to its jurisdiction. There is some doubt as to what "duly served" means in this connection. In one case[621] it was assumed that it means duly served according to the law of the original court. However, some limit must no doubt be imposed on the width of this principle. In *Buchanan v Rucker*,[622] nailing a copy of the writ to the court-house door was no doubt "due service" according to the law of Tobago, but it could hardly constitute due service within the meaning of the 1920 Act. Probably due service must involve actual notice, but not necessarily service within the jurisdiction of the

---

[617] Contrast *Jeannot v Fuerst* (1909) 100 L.T. 816, 818. In *Leaton Leather & Trading Co v Ngai Tak Kong* (1997) 147 D.L.R. (4th) 1377 (BC) a failure to exercise a right to appeal was held not to make enforceable a judgment rendered contrary to natural justice.

[618] [2000] I.L.Pr. 387.

[619] cf. *Minmetals Germany GmbH v Fercosteel Ltd* [1999] C.L.C. 647 (a case on setting aside an arbitral award).

[620] s.9(2)(c).

[621] *Sfeir & Co v National Insurance Co of New Zealand* [1964] 1 Lloyd's Rep. 330, 341.

[622] (1809) 9 East 192; above, para.14–055.

original court.[623] The 1933 Act provides[624] that registration of a foreign judgment must be set aside if the defendant did not receive notice of the proceedings (i.e. of the initiation of the action[625]) in sufficient time to enable him to defend and he did not appear, even if process may have been duly served on him in accordance with the applicable foreign law. And under the 1933 Act a foreign judgment, whether registered or not and whether registrable or not, will not be recognised as conclusive between the parties thereto in English proceedings founded on the same cause of action if the defendant did not receive such notice and did not appear.[626] This ground for setting aside the registration of a judgment is quite independent of and distinct from the ground that the foreign court had no jurisdiction. Hence it follows that the common law authorities suggesting that a defendant who agrees to submit to the jurisdiction of a foreign court also agrees to waive actual notice of the proceedings[627] have no application.

14–169   The effect of Art.34(2) of the Brussels I Regulation and the Lugano Convention is that judgments in default of appearance, falling within their scope, will not be entitled to recognition, and may not be enforced, in the United Kingdom, if the defendant was not served with the document which instituted the proceedings or with an equivalent document in sufficient time and in such a way as to allow him to arrange for his defence.[628] But if he had the opportunity of instituting proceedings to challenge the judgment when he learned of it, yet failed to do so, he forfeits the protection of Art.34(2) and the judgment will be liable to be recognised after all. Article 34(2) therefore differs in two respects from its counterpart in the Brussels Convention, which contained an express requirement that the defendant be *duly* served, and omitted the provision which penalised the defendant's failure to institute proceedings to challenge the judgment. Lack of notice or service, or failure to observe natural justice, are not grounds for refusal of recognition or enforcement of Scottish and Northern Irish judgments under Pt II of the 1982 Act.[629]

14–170   **Human Rights Act 1998.** For a court to recognise or enforce a foreign judgment, in circumstances in which this would give effect in England to a decision which given or obtained in breach of the rules of natural justice, would be almost certain to involve the court in a violation of Art.6 of the European Convention on Human Rights.[630] It therefore seems that the material which naturally falls within the scope of this Rule will also be liable to be dealt with by the application of Art.6, though it is improbable that this will make a substantial difference to the outcome of cases.

---

[623] *cf. Re Gacs and Maierovitz* (1968) 68 D.L.R. (2d) 345 (BC).

[624] s.4(1)(a)(iii).

[625] *Brockley Cabinet Co Ltd v Pears* (1972) 20 F.L.R. 333.

[626] s.8(1), (2). See below, para.14–195.

[627] See above, para.14–080.

[628] See below, para.14–229.

[629] See above, para.14–262. But this fact cannot oust the application of the Human Rights Act 1998 to the recognition and enforcement of judgments from these parts of the United Kingdom.

[630] On which see further above, para.14–159.

ILLUSTRATIONS

1. X, who was resident in England, held shares in a French company. The articles of association **14–171** of the company provided that all disputes between the company and its shareholders should be subject to the jurisdiction of the French courts and that service of process on each shareholder should be at a designated address in France. The company went into liquidation and A brought an action against X in France for moneys not paid up on X's shares. Process was served on X at the designated address, but he received no notice of the proceedings. The French court gave judgment against X before 1937 (when the 1933 Act was extended to France). A brought an action on the judgment against X in England. The judgment was not impeachable.[631]

2. The circumstances were the same as in Illustration 1, except that the French judgment was given after 1937, and that A registered the judgment in England under the 1933 Act. Registration would be set aside.[632]

3. X, a merchant of Lyons, contracted to sell silk to A, a merchant of London. A dispute having **14–172** arisen about the quality of the silk, X brought an action against A in a court at Lyons. The court appointed an expert to examine the goods and report on their quality. The expert made no proper examination of the goods; he refused to listen to A's witnesses; and his report (described by the English court as "the erroneous and uncandid production of a biased and prejudiced mind") was wholly in favour of X. The French court gave judgment in favour of X. When A sued X in England, X pleaded the French judgment as a defence. The judgment was not impeachable because the French court was not obliged to accept the report, and because A attacked it unsuccessfully in France.[633]

4. 206 plaintiffs sue X & Co and Y & Co, both English companies, in an action for personal injuries, in the Federal Court in Texas. X & Co and Y & Co, not wishing to submit to the jurisdiction of the United States court, take no part in the proceedings. X & Co and Y & Co are given notice of a hearing to assess damages in default of appearance, but again take no part. On the application of the plaintiffs the United States judge signs a default judgment for $15 million, but without holding any hearing. No evidence of damage or injury to the plaintiffs is placed before the judge; the judgment is signed before the judge has an opportunity to consider the medical records or summaries of each plaintiff's case; the damages awarded are quantified on a global basis or as an average per plaintiff, and are arbitrary. The judgment is not enforceable.[634]

3. ENFORCEMENT AND RECOGNITION UNDER STATUTE

(1) ADMINISTRATION OF JUSTICE ACT 1920

RULE 53—When Part II of the Administration of Justice Act 1920 is **14R–173** **extended to any part of the Commonwealth outside the United Kingdom,[635] a judgment creditor who has obtained a judgment in a Superior Court in such part of the Commonwealth under which a sum of money is made payable, may apply to the High Court,[636] at any time within twelve months (or such longer period as may be allowed by the court) after the date of the judgment, to have the judgment registered in the court, and,**

---

[631] *Copin v Adamson* (1875) 1 Ex.D. 17 (CA).

[632] 1933 Act, s.4(1)(a)(iii).

[633] *Jacobson v Frachon* (1927) 138 L.T. 386 (CA).

[634] *Adams v Cape Industries Plc* [1990] Ch. 433 (CA).

[635] The Act has been extended to almost the whole of the Commonwealth. Apart from countries to which the 1933 Act has been extended (as to which see below, para.14–184), the most important exceptions are South Africa and Bangladesh. The Act no longer applies to Hong Kong as it is no longer a member of the Commonwealth; and it does not apply to Gibraltar judgments given after February 1, 1998: see below, para.14–181. For the countries to which the 1920 Act has been extended see below, para.14–181.

[636] Or, as the case may be, the Court of Session in Scotland or the High Court of Northern Ireland.

if the court thinks it is just and convenient that the judgment should be enforced in the United Kingdom, it may order the judgment to be registered accordingly,[637] **and from the date of registration the judgment will be of the same force and effect, and proceedings may be taken upon it,**[638] **as if it were a judgment of the court in which it is registered.**

Provided that no judgment will be ordered to be registered if the judgment debtor satisfies the High Court either that an appeal is pending, or that he is entitled and intends to appeal against the judgment.[639]

This Rule must be read subject to Rule 59.

COMMENT

14–174   This Rule, which closely follows the terms of the Administration of Justice Act 1920, is the outcome of proposals for the reciprocal enforcement of judgments and arbitration awards throughout the Empire which were brought forward at the Imperial Conference of 1911.[640] It was enacted in s.14 that the Act could come into operation only by the issue of an Order in Council extending it to some part of the Commonwealth outside the United Kingdom in which reciprocal provision had been made for the recognition of judgments obtained in the Superior Courts of the United Kingdom.

14–175   The 1933 Act empowers the Crown in Council to extend Pt I of that enactment to all parts of the Commonwealth outside the United Kingdom. It is provided that upon the application of the later Act in this manner the 1920 Act shall cease to have effect except in relation to such territories to which it extends at the date of such Order.[641] The effect of this provision, which has been acted upon,[642] is merely to prevent the further extension of the system of enforcement envisaged by the 1920 Act. Its effect is not to apply instead the scheme of the 1933 Act. For Pt I of the latter to come into operation in relation to any particular territory, a further and specific Order in Council is required.[643] The making of such an Order, which has occurred only in relation to India,[644] Pakistan,[645] Canada (apart from Quebec)[646] and Australia,[647] is, however, to revoke the application of the 1920 Act, if it has any application, in relation to the territory concerned.[648]

14–176   The judgments to which the Rule applies are any judgments or orders in any civil proceedings providing for the payment of a sum of money, and include

---

[637] 1920 Act, s.9(1).

[638] *ibid.* s.9(3)(a).

[639] *ibid.* s.9(2)(e).

[640] See Sumner Committee Report, 1919, Cmd. 251.

[641] s.7(1).

[642] S. R. & O. 1933/1073.

[643] *Yukon Consolidated Gold Corporation v Clark* [1938] 2 K.B. 241 (CA); *Jamieson v Northern Electricity Supply Corporation Ltd*, 1970 S.L.T. 113.

[644] SI 1958/425.

[645] SI 1958/141. The Act formerly applied also to Burma.

[646] SI 1987/468, SI 1987/2211, SI 1988/1304, SI 1988/1853, SI 1989/987, SI 1991/1724, SI 1992/1731.

[647] SI 1994/1901.

[648] s.7(2) of the 1933 Act. As to the status of a judgment already given upon the making of such an Order, see the Administration of Justice Act 1956, s.51; and see para.14R–183.

awards in arbitration proceedings if these can, under the law in force where they are made, be enforced in the same manner as judgments.[649] Rules of court provide that an application for registration may be made without notice (ex parte). It must be supported by a verified or certified or otherwise duly authenticated copy of the judgment, and by evidence that the judgment does not fall within any of the cases in which a judgment may not be registered under the Act. The judgment may, and perhaps must, be registered for an amount expressed in the currency in which it was rendered.[650] The order granting permission to register the judgment must be served on the judgment debtor. If he is out of the jurisdiction, the notice can be served on him without special permission.[651] The High Court, moreover, has the same control and jurisdiction over the execution of the judgment as it has over judgments given by itself.[652] Registration is not to be ordered if "the original court acted without jurisdiction."[653] No attempt is made to give a comprehensive definition of this term, but s.9(2)(b) provides that a judgment shall not be registered under the Act if the judgment debtor was "neither carrying on business nor ordinarily resident within the jurisdiction of the original court, did not voluntarily appear or otherwise submit or agree to submit to the jurisdiction of that court." This differs from the common law principles in Rule 43[654] only in minor respects and there is little room for additional objection on jurisdictional grounds on the basis of s.9(2)(a). Under the 1920 Act "carrying on business" is used as an alternative to residence not only in the case of corporations but also in the case of individuals. The principle of the cases on the jurisdiction of the English court[655] applies also to the question whether a corporation carried on business in the jurisdiction of the original court within the meaning of the 1920 Act. Thus it was held that a New Zealand insurance company did not carry on business in Ghana merely because it maintained agents there with limited powers.[656] The 1920 Act includes, as a basis of jurisdiction additional to carrying on of business, ordinary residence, while under the 1933 Act residence simpliciter is required, but there is not likely to be any significant difference.[657] Rules 44 to 46 on where jurisdiction does not exist apply also to registration under the 1920 Act.[658]

The other grounds for non-registration are that (i) the judgment debtor was **14–177** not duly served with the process of the original court and did not appear; (ii) the judgment was obtained by fraud; (iii) the judgment debtor satisfies the

---

[649] 1920 Act, s.12(1); see para.16–167. A judgment against a State obtained in the courts of that State cannot be enforced under the 1920 Act or the 1933 Act: *AIC Ltd v Federal Government of Nigeria* [2003] EWHC 1357 (QB). It has been held in Scotland that an order of a Commonwealth court setting aside an assignment of property by a husband to his wife is not registrable under the Act: *Platt v Platt*, 1958 S.C. 95.

[650] See para.14–187, below.

[651] CPR Part 74: rr.3 (applications), 4 (evidence in support), 6 (registration orders).

[652] 1920 Act, s.9(3)(b).

[653] 1920 Act, s.9(2)(a).

[654] 1982 Act, s.33 (what constitutes a voluntary appearance) applies to judgments under the 1920 Act.

[655] See above, paras 11–114 *et seq.* See also *Akande v Balfour Beatty Construction Ltd* [1998] I.L.Pr. 110.

[656] *Sfeir & Co v National Insurance Co of New Zealand* [1964] 1 Lloyd's Rep. 330.

[657] See above, paras 14–063 *et seq.*; *cf. Re Duncan & Hirsch* [1952] 3 D.L.R. 850 (Alta).

[658] See above, paras 14R–097 *et seq.*

court that an appeal is pending, or that he is entitled and intends to appeal, against the judgment; or (iv) the judgment was in respect of a cause of action which for reasons of public policy or for some other similar reason could not have been entertained by the English court. The defence of fraud under the Act is to be decided by reference to the common law principles discussed in connection with Rule 50.[659] There is no general ground for impeachment on the basis of lack of natural justice. Instead, the 1920 Act provides[660] that registration must be refused if the defendant was not duly served with the process of the original court and did not appear, notwithstanding that he was ordinarily resident or was carrying on business within the jurisdiction of the foreign court or agreed to submit to its jurisdiction. As has been seen,[661] it was assumed in one case[662] that "duly served" meant served according to the law of the foreign court whose document it was. At common law (and under the 1933 and 1982 Acts) the public policy exception relates to enforcement and recognition of the judgment itself, whereas the 1920 Act excludes from registration any judgment in respect of a cause of action which for reasons of public policy or some other similar reason could not have been entertained by the registering court.[663] Finally it should be noted that the pendency of an appeal is a ground for non-registration, even though at common law that does not prevent the judgment being "final and conclusive."[664]

14–178   The 1920 Act also provides that registration is within the discretion of the court and will only be allowed if the court thinks it just and convenient that the judgment should be enforced here.[665] The Act does not specifically provide that judgments for taxes or fines or other penalties are not registrable under its provisions. Since it is clear that a foreign judgment for fines or other penalties cannot be enforced at common law or under the 1933 and 1982 Acts, it seems safe to conclude that it would not be enforced under the 1920 Act, either because it would be contrary to public policy or because the court would exercise its discretion not to register the judgment.

14–179   The judgment creditor remains free to bring an action at common law on the foreign judgment, subject to the rule that, unless the court otherwise orders, the claimant will not be entitled to recover any costs of the action, unless he has previously applied for registration of his judgment and has been refused, in any case in which such registration is permissible under the terms of the Act.[666]

14–180   The 1920 Act contains no provisions dealing with recognition, as opposed to enforcement, of judgments within its scope. Recognition will, therefore, depend on common law principles.[667]

14–181   The list of States and territories to which the Act applies was consolidated by statutory instrument,[668] and has since been amended by deletion. It now

---

[659] *Owens Bank Ltd v Bracco* [1992] 2 A.C. 443.
[660] s.9(2)(c).
[661] See above, para.14–176.
[662] *Sfeir & Co v National Insurance Co of New Zealand*, above.
[663] s.9(2)(f).
[664] See above, para.14–023.
[665] s.9(1).
[666] 1920 Act, s.9(5).
[667] See above, paras 14–002 *et seq.*
[668] SI 1984/129 as amended.

applies to many of the States of the Commonwealth, but it should be noted that it does not apply to Australia,[669] Bangladesh,[670] Canada,[671] Gibraltar,[672] Hong Kong,[673] India,[674] Pakistan[675] and South Africa.[676]

ILLUSTRATIONS

1. A & Co, who carry on business in Ghana, bring an action in Ghana against X & Co, a New Zealand insurance company, for a loss under a policy of marine insurance issued by X & Co in Beirut. X & Co do not carry on business in Ghana or have any assets there or connection therewith except that they maintain agents there with limited power to settle claims. The policy contains a clause stating that claims are payable by X & Co's agents in Ghana to whom notice of loss must be given. The writ is served on X & Co at their branch office in London by leave of the Ghana court. X & Co take no part in the Ghana proceedings and judgment is given against them in default of appearance. A & Co now seek to register their judgment in England under the Act of 1920. Although X & Co were duly served with the process of the court under the law of Ghana, the judgment will not be registered in England, because X & Co neither carried on business in Ghana nor submitted to the jurisdiction of the Ghana court.[677]

2. A & Co, bankers, bring proceedings against X, an Italian citizen, and Y & Co, an Italian company, in the courts of St Vincent and the Grenadines, on agreements providing for a loan to Y & Co, to be guaranteed by X. X and Y & Co allege that the agreements are forgeries, but their defence is rejected by the St Vincent court. A & Co bring enforcement proceedings in England (where the defendants have assets) and in Italy. Registration of the judgment is set aside because there is a prima facie case of fraud, and an issue is directed to be tried as to whether the judgment was obtained by fraud.[678]

14–182

(2) FOREIGN JUDGMENTS (RECIPROCAL ENFORCEMENT) ACT 1933

RULE 54[679]—(1) When Part I of the Foreign Judgments (Reciprocal Enforcement) Act 1933 is extended to any foreign country outside the United Kingdom, a judgment creditor under a judgment[680] to which the

14R–183

---

[669] SI 1994/1901, which extends the 1933 Act to Australia and to the Australian States and territories.

[670] Enforcement of judgments from Bangladesh is governed by the common law.

[671] The 1933 Act applies to Canada and to all provinces and territories except Quebec; judgments from Quebec are recognised and enforced under the common law.

[672] SI 1997/2601. Judgments from Gibraltar are enforced under regulations made under Pt IV of the 1982 Act: Rule 56(3), below, para.14–259.

[673] Which is no longer a member of the Commonwealth; judgments will be recognised and enforced in accordance with the common law.

[674] SI 1958/425.

[675] SI 1958/141.

[676] Judgments from South Africa are enforced under the common law.

[677] *Sfeir & Co v National Insurance Co of New Zealand* [1964] 1 Lloyd's Rep. 330.

[678] *Owens Bank Ltd v Bracco* [1992] 2 A.C. 443. The European Court ruled (Case C–129/92 [1994] E.C.R. I–117, [1994] Q.B. 509) that as the enforcement of judgments from non-Contracting States was not within the scope of the Brussels Convention, Arts 21 and 22 (now Arts 27 and 28 of the Brussels I Regulation) had no application to proceedings which were part of that process.

[679] See Report of the Foreign Judgments (Reciprocal Enforcement) Committee, 1932, Cmd. 4213. In case of ambiguity resort may be had to the Report of the Committee to determine the mischief the Act was intended to remedy: *Black-Clawson International Ltd v Papierwerke Waldhof-Aschaffenburg AG* [1975] A.C. 591.

[680] Including an arbitration award enforceable as a judgment in the place where it is given: 1933 Act, s.10A (added by 1982 Act, s.35(1), Sch.10, para.4). See para.16–167, below.

Act applies may apply to the High Court[681] at any time within six years[682] after the date of such judgment to have the judgment registered in the High Court, and on any such application the court will order the judgment to be registered.

Provided that no judgment will be ordered to be registered if—

(a) it has been wholly satisfied; or

(b) it could not be enforced by execution in the country of the original court.[683]

(2) Subject to the provisions of the 1933 Act with respect to the setting aside of registration, a registered judgment will be of the same force and effect as if the judgment had been a judgment originally given in the High Court and entered on the date of registration.[684]

(3) Any judgment of a recognised court of a country to which the Act applies given after the application of the Act to such country is capable of registration in accordance with this Rule if—

(a) it is final and conclusive as between the judgment debtor and the judgment creditor or requires the former to make an interim payment to the latter; and

(b) there is payable thereunder a sum of money (not being a sum payable in respect of taxes or other charges of a like nature or in respect of a fine or other penalty).[685]

This Rule must be read subject to Rule 59.

COMMENT

14–184   The scheme of direct enforcement of foreign judgments provided for in the 1933 Act upon which this Rule is based and the wording of which it follows closely, is designed to apply in relation not only to countries foreign in the political sense, but also to countries of the Commonwealth outside the United Kingdom. It would clearly be redundant as regards the latter to have two systems of enforcement of judgments, and the Act therefore provides for the restriction and replacement of the system set up earlier by the 1920 Act.[686] In pursuance of this provision the later Act was extended to India,[687] Pakistan,[688] Australia and the States and territories of Australia,[689] the Federal Court of

---

[681] For Scotland and Northern Ireland, see 1933 Act, ss.12 and 13.

[682] A judgment of a court of a country which forms part of the Commonwealth given before the application of the 1933 Act to that country is registrable within twelve months of the date thereof or within such longer period as the court may allow. And any judgment of any such country registered under the 1920 Act is to be deemed to have been registered under the 1933 Act: Administration of Justice Act 1956, s.51.

[683] 1933 Act, ss.1(2), 2(1).

[684] 1933 Act, s.2(2).

[685] *ibid.* s.1(2), as amended by 1982 Act, s.35(1) and Sch.10, para.1.

[686] See above, para.14–175.

[687] SI 1958/425.

[688] SI 1958/141; Pakistan Act 1990, Sch., para.8.

[689] SI 1994/1901.

Canada and the Canadian provinces except Quebec,[690] Tonga,[691] Guernsey,[692] Jersey,[693] and the Isle of Man.[694] Of countries foreign in the political sense, only Austria,[695] Belgium,[696] Germany,[697] France,[698] Israel,[699] Italy,[700] the Netherlands,[701] Norway,[702] and Suriname[703] so far come within the Act for general purposes. For almost all practical purposes the 1933 Act is superseded by the Brussels I Regulation as regards Austria, Belgium, France, Germany, Italy and the Netherlands, and as regards Norway, which is party to the Lugano Convention, by Pt I of the 1982 Act. In addition, the 1933 Act extends to any country which is a party to certain international conventions dealt with in connection with Rule 62, but only in relation to proceedings arising under those conventions.[704] The basis of the application of the 1933 Act in regard to any territory is the existence of a substantial measure of reciprocity. The specific rules applicable to the foreign judgment will be those set out in the particular bilateral treaty as given force by the statutory instrument made under the authority of the 1933 Act.

A judgment is defined as meaning a judgment or order given or made by a **14–185** court in any civil proceedings[705] or a judgment or order given or made by a court in any criminal proceedings for the payment of a sum of money in respect of compensation or damages to an injured party.[706] Thus, under the

---

[690] SI 1987/468 (Federal Court, British Columbia, Manitoba, New Brunswick, Nova Scotia, Ontario) as amended by SI 1987/2211 (Yukon Territory), SI 1988/1304 (Prince Edward Island) and 1853 (Saskatchewan), SI 1989/987 (Northwest Territories), SI 1991/1724 (Newfoundland) and SI 1992/1731 (Alberta). For amendment of the UK-Canada Convention, see SI 1995/2708.

[691] SI 1980/1523.

[692] SI 1973/610.

[693] SI 1973/612.

[694] SI 1973/611.

[695] SI 1962/1339.

[696] S.R. & O. 1936/1169.

[697] SI 1961/1199.

[698] S.R. & O. 1936/609.

[699] SI 1971/1039, as amended by SI 2003/2618.

[700] SI 1973/1894.

[701] SI 1969/1063, as amended by SI 1977/2149.

[702] SI 1962/636.

[703] SI 1981/735.

[704] See below, paras 15R–053 *et seq.*

[705] This expression includes awards in arbitration proceedings if these have become enforceable in the same manner as judgments; includes judgments ordering interim payments; but excludes "judgments on judgments", that is, judgments given by foreign courts enforcing the judgments of courts of third States: 1933 Act, s.1(2A), as inserted by 1982 Act, s.35(1) and Sch.10, para.1. It has been held to include orders made by a court exercising insolvency jurisdiction which require the recipient of an unfair preference to repay it: *New Cap Reinsurance Corp Ltd v Grant* [2011] EWCA Civ 971, [2011] B.P.I.R. 1428 (on which, see further above, para.14–010): the Supreme Court of New South Wales had tended to the opposite interpretation of the 1933 Act: *New Cap Reinsurance Corp Ltd (In Liquidation) v Grant* [2009] NSWSC 662, (2009) 257 A.L.R. 740. It will exclude judgments against States: *AIC Ltd v Federal Government of Nigeria* [2003] EWHC 1357 (QB). For the proposition that the definition of "judgment" in the UK-Canada treaty includes a judicially-approved scheme of arrangement under what is now Companies Act 2006, ss.895–896, see *Re Cavell Insurance Co* (2006) 269 D.L.R. (4th) 663 (CA) (though the judgment does not resolve the extent to which such an order may be recognised as binding on creditors).

[706] 1933 Act, s.11.

Act, as at common law, it was possible to enforce a judgment of e.g. a French court awarding compensation to the *"partie civile"* or injured victim of a crime, even though the judgment also imposes a fine or penalty on the defendant which is not enforceable.[707]

14–186   As a result of amendments made by the 1982 Act, the 1933 Act applies to judgments of "recognised courts" of the foreign country, i.e. courts to which the 1933 Act is extended by Order in Council, and not only, as before, to superior courts of that country.[708] In the case of any country to which the 1933 Act had been extended before its amendment by the 1982 Act, superior courts of that country are deemed to be recognised courts. As from January 1, 1987 the 1933 Act has applied, not only to judgments which are "final and conclusive", but also to judgments for interim payments.[709]

14–187   As at common law, a judgment is deemed to be final and conclusive notwithstanding that an appeal is pending or that it may still be subject to appeal.[710] But the court has a discretionary power to set aside the registration of a judgment on such terms as it thinks fit, if the applicant satisfies the court that an appeal is pending or that he is entitled and intends to appeal.[711] And if upon an application for registration it appears that part or parts only of the judgment are capable of registration, then such part or parts may be registered alone.[712] Registration is for the sum payable under the original judgment, plus interest due under the law of the original court up to the date of registration, plus reasonable costs incidental to registration.[713] The judgment may, and perhaps must, be registered for an amount expressed in the currency in which it was rendered.[714] Where the judgment has been partially satisfied, registration is for the unsatisfied balance.[715]

14–188   An application for registration in accordance with the Act may be made without notice. It must be supported by a verified or certified or otherwise duly authenticated copy of the judgment, and by a certified translation thereof, as well as by a witness statement or affidavit stating that the applicant believes himself entitled to enforce the judgment and that registration is not liable to be set aside. The order granting permission to register the judgment must be served on the judgment debtor. If he is out of the jurisdiction, the notice can be served on him without permission.[716] There is no requirement that the judgment debtor be subject to the personal jurisdiction of the English court.[717]

---

[707] s.1(2). For the meaning of penalty, see above, para.14–022. See also Rule 59, below. But see Isle of Man Act 1979, s.4.

[708] Judgments from courts which are not "recognised courts" will be capable of enforcement and recognition under the common law. A court may require and receive expert evidence to determine whether the judgment is one from a recognised court: *Habib Bank Ltd v Ahmed* [2001] EWCA Civ 1270, [2002] 1 Lloyd's Rep. 444.

[709] s.1(2)(a), as amended by 1982 Act, s.35(1) and Sch.10, para.1(2).

[710] s.1(3).

[711] s.5. See *SA Consortium General Textiles v Sun and Sand Agencies Ltd* [1978] Q.B. 279 (CA); *Hunt v BP Exploration Co (Libya)* [1980] 1 N.Z.L.R. 104.

[712] s.2(5).

[713] s.2(6).

[714] Administration of Justice Act 1977, s.4.

[715] s.2(4).

[716] See CPR Pt 74: rr.3 (applications), 4 (evidence in support), 6 (registration orders).

[717] See in this sense *Hunt v BP Exploration Co (Libya) Ltd* (1980) 144 C.L.R. 565; *Hunt v BP Exploration Co (Libya)* [1980] 1 N.Z.L.R. 104.

Enforcement is by registration, and not by action, and the judgment debtor need have no connection with England, although in practice registration will be of little value unless he has assets in England.

The effect of registration of a foreign judgment under the 1933 Act is to render it for purposes of execution of the same force and effect as if it were a judgment of the High Court. Thus, a stay of execution will not be ordered merely because an English action is pending between the same parties which raises similar issues.[718] Execution may not, however, issue so long as it is open to any party to make an application for the setting aside of the judgment or until the final determination of any such application. The High Court has the same control over execution as it has over the execution of its own judgments. Proceedings may be taken upon a registered judgment exactly as if it were a judgment of the High Court.[719] Thus a statutory demand under the Insolvency Act 1986 may be served upon it.[720] The sum for which a foreign judgment is registered carries interest in the same manner as an English judgment debt.[721]   **14–189**

Jurisdiction of the foreign court. Registration must be set aside under the 1933 Act if "the courts of the country of the original court had no jurisdiction in the circumstances of the case."[722] Except in the case of judgments within the scope of the international conventions referred to above,[723] the original court is deemed to have had jurisdiction in an action *in personam*[724]: (i) if the judgment debtor submitted by voluntarily appearing;[725] or (ii) if the judgment debtor was plaintiff in, or counterclaimed in, the proceedings in the original court; or (iii) if the judgment debtor had before the commencement of the proceedings agreed, in respect of the subject matter of the proceedings, to submit to the jurisdiction of that court or of the courts of the country of that court; or (iv) if the judgment debtor was at the time when the proceedings were instituted resident in, or being a body corporate, had its principal place of business in, the country of that court; or (v) if the judgment debtor had an office or place of business in the country of that court and the proceedings in that court were in respect of a transaction effected through or at that office or place. Rules 44 and 45 on where jurisdiction does not exist also apply to cases within the 1933 Act. The grounds of jurisdiction in the 1933 Act were deliberately framed so as to reproduce the rules of the common law as closely as possible,[726] though it was found desirable to make some slight departures from the common law rules in order to secure international agreements which   **14–190**

---

[718] *Wagner v Laubscher Bros & Co* [1970] 2 Q.B. 313 (CA).

[719] s.2(2).

[720] *Re a Judgment Debtor (No.2176 of 1938)* [1939] Ch. 601 (CA), a case under the Bankruptcy Act 1914; *Re McGilvray* (1986) 66 A.L.R. 181.

[721] s.2(2)(c); *cf.* Private International Law (Miscellaneous Provisions) Act 1995, s.1.

[722] s.4(1)(a)(ii).

[723] In these cases the jurisdictional rules depend on the Conventions as incorporated by legislation discussed in connection with Rule 62.

[724] s.4(2)(a).

[725] See also 1982 Act, s.33, paras 14–070 *et seq.*, above, which was derived from the original version of 1933 Act, s.4(2)(a)(i), and applies to judgments under the 1933 Act.

[726] Report of the Foreign Judgments (Reciprocal Enforcement) Committee, Cmd. 4213 (1932), paras 2, 16, 18 and Annex V, para.7.

would be likely to operate satisfactorily in practice.[727] The provisions of the 1933 Act as to the jurisdiction of foreign courts are exclusive, i.e. no judgment can be registered under the 1933 Act unless the jurisdiction of the foreign court can be brought under one of these heads.[728] The main differences between the common law and the 1933 Act are as follows: first, the 1933 Act does not treat the foreign court as having jurisdiction over an individual by virtue of the mere presence of the defendant, whereas the First Case of Rule 43[729] now states, on the authority of *Adams v Cape Industries Plc*,[730] that presence is a head of jurisdiction at common law. Secondly, under the 1933 Act there is jurisdiction over a corporation only if either (a) it has its principal place of business in the foreign country or (b) where it has an office or place of business which is not its principal place of business and the cause of action arose from a transaction effected through that office. At common law it is sufficient that there be a place of business irrespective of its status or how the cause of action arose.[731] Thirdly, like the 1920 Act, the 1933 Act contemplates jurisdiction over an individual with a place of business in the foreign country, provided (in the case of the 1933 Act) that the cause of action is connected with that place.

14–191   Complete satisfaction of the foreign judgment, or the circumstance that it could not be enforced by execution in the place where it was given, are absolute bars to registration under the Act.[732] Registration is liable to be set aside on certain specified grounds upon the application of any party against whom it is enforceable made within a time specified in the registration order.[733] Registration *must* be set aside[734] if the court is satisfied (i) that the judgment is incapable of registration under the Act or has been registered in contravention of it; or (ii) that the courts of the country of the original court had no jurisdiction in the circumstances of the case; or (iii) that the judgment debtor, being the defendant in the original proceedings, did not receive sufficient notice to enable him to defend and he did not appear; or (iv) that the judgment was obtained by fraud; or (v) that the enforcement of the judgment would be contrary to English public policy; or (vi) that the rights under the judgment are not vested in the applicant for registration, which expression includes any person in whom the rights under the judgment have become vested by succession or assignment or otherwise.[735] Of these grounds (i) calls

---

[727] *ibid.* para.18, and Annex V, para.7.

[728] *Société Co-opérative Sidmetal v Titan International Ltd* [1966] 1 Q.B. 828; *Sharps Commercials Ltd v Gas Turbines Ltd* [1956] N.Z.L.R. 819 (a decision on the identically worded New Zealand Act). In *New Cap Reinsurance Corp Ltd (In Liquidation) v Grant* [2011] EWCA Civ 971, [2011] B.P.I.R. 1428, it was held that that even though the foreign court could not be shown to have had jurisdiction by reference to any of the jurisdictional grounds in the Act, if a judgment were nevertheless registered and an application made to set it aside, that application could be resisted if the judgment was the subject of a request for assistance in insolvency, following *Rubin v Eurofinance SA* [2010] EWCA Civ 895, [2011] Ch. 133. See para.14–010, above, and paras 30–109 *et seq.*, below.

[729] See above, para.14R–054.

[730] [1990] Ch. 433 (CA).

[731] See above, para.14–065.

[732] s.2(1), Proviso.

[733] ss.4, 5. For the practice, see CPR, r.74.7.

[734] s.4(1)(a).

[735] s.11.

for no comment, and (ii) has been discussed in the previous paragraph. The provision with regard to notice of the proceedings has been mentioned in connection with the common law principle of natural justice.[736] where it was pointed out that under the 1933 Act a waiver of notice of proceedings by a defendant who submits to the jurisdiction of a foreign court will not be implied. The provisions with regard to fraud and public policy are the same as the common law rules.[737] In particular, the common law rule that a foreign judgment can be impeached for fraud even though no newly discovered evidence is produced, and even though the fraud was alleged in the foreign proceedings, applies to enforcement and recognition under the 1933 Act. In *Owens Bank Ltd v Bracco*[738] the House of Lords held that the fraud exception in the 1920 Act was subject to the same rule, and indicated (*obiter*) that the same must be so under the 1933 Act.

Registration *may* be set aside if the court is satisfied that the matter in dispute in the original proceedings had previously to the date of judgment in those proceedings been the subject of a final and conclusive judgment by a court having jurisdiction in the matter.[739]   **14–192**

Where registration is set aside on the ground that an appeal is pending or that the applicant is entitled and intends to appeal the right to apply again later for registration is not prejudiced.[740] The same is the case where registration is set aside on the sole ground either that the judgment was not enforceable by execution in the country of the original court[87] or that, having been registered for the whole sum payable thereunder, it has been partially satisfied.[741] In all other cases the setting aside of registration would presumably be a bar to a second application for registration. An application to set aside registration is made under Pt 23 of the Civil Procedure Rules 1998 supported by witness statement or affidavit.[742]   **14–193**

The 1933 Act introduced what was then a striking innovation in that it provided that no proceedings for the recovery of a sum payable under a foreign judgment capable of registration in accordance with its provisions, other than proceedings for such registration, might be entertained by any court.[743] This provision does not of course limit in any way the taking of proceedings upon a registrable judgment after its registration. Neither does it prevent other effects being ascribed to the foreign judgment, so long as these do not amount to its enforcement by bringing an action at common law to collect the debt constituted by the judgment: it has been held that the judgment may be made the subject of a request for assistance in insolvency by the court   **14–194**

---

[736] Rule 52. A Canadian court has held that if the defendant was not served in accordance with English law, an English default judgment is precluded from registration in Canada under the terms of the UK–Canada Treaty, but as in that case the defendant did not otherwise have notice of the proceedings, the decision rests on the absence of notice as much as on the irregularity in service: *Bank of Scotland Plc v Wilson* (2008) 295 D.L.R. (4th) 128 (BC).

[737] Rules 50 and 51.

[738] [1992] 2 A.C. 443. See also *Syal v Heyward* [1948] 2 K.B. 443 (CA).

[739] s.4(1)(b). See Illustration 2, below, para.14–196.

[740] s.5(2).

[741] s.5(3).

[742] CPR, r.74.7.

[743] s.6. The position is the same under the 1982 Act, Pts I and II and the Brussels I Regulation, Rules 55–56, below.

which gave it.[744] For it is elsewhere specifically provided that proceedings may be taken upon a registered judgment as if it had been originally given by the High Court.[745] As has been seen above,[746] no proceedings may be brought on the original cause of action.

14–195   **Recognition.** The 1933 Act[747] saves the common law rule as to conclusiveness which is discussed above.[748] But it also contains a tortuously drafted provision which states that a judgment to which Pt I of the Act applies, or would have applied if a sum of money had been payable thereunder, whether it can be registered or not, and whether it is registered or not, "shall be recognised in any court in the United Kingdom as conclusive between the parties thereto in all proceedings founded on the same cause of action and may be relied on by way of defence or counterclaim in any such proceedings."[749] This provision, however, is expressed not to apply where the registration of a judgment has been set aside or could be set aside (whether it could have been registered or not) on any of the grounds on which registration under the 1933 Act must be set aside (i.e. lack of jurisdiction, fraud, lack of notice of the proceedings, public policy).[750] The expression "a judgment to which Pt I of this Act ... would have applied if a sum of money had been payable" is obscure. The House of Lords held by a majority in *Black-Clawson International Ltd v Papierwerke Waldhof-Aschaffenburg AG*[751] that the section applies to judgments in favour of a defendant dismissing the plaintiff's claim. Under the 1933 Act, as at common law, the judgment is only conclusive as regards the question adjudicated upon, so that a judgment which was not on the merits, because it was given in the defendant's favour on the ground that the action was time-barred, was not a bar to a subsequent action in England.[752] Whether the provision applies to judgments as to status is a question on which differing views have been expressed. The extrinsic material, namely the Report of the Foreign Judgments (Reciprocal Enforcement) Committee[753] and the Conventions which were negotiated prior to the enactment of the 1933 Act, suggests that s.8 was not intended to be confined to judgments *in personam*.[754] A literal interpretation of the sub-section, in conjunction with the definition of judgment in s.1(2), suggests that judgments as to status are within the scope of s.8(1), and this view had the support of Sir John Arnold, P. in *Vervaeke v Smith*.[755] But in the same decision Eveleigh L.J.[756] (with

---

[744] *New Cap Reinsurance Corp Ltd (In Liquidation) v Grant* [2011] EWCA Civ 971, [2011] B.P.I.R. 1428, on which, see further above, para.14–010.

[745] s.2(2)(b).

[746] 1982 Act, s.34, above, para.14–040.

[747] s.8(3).

[748] See above, paras 14–030 *et seq.*

[749] s.8(1).

[750] s.8(2).

[751] [1975] A.C. 591 at pp.619 (Lord Dilhorne), 635 (Lord Diplock), and 652 (Lord Simon). Lord Reid dissented.

[752] [1975] A.C. 591. But the result would be different under the Foreign Limitation Periods Act 1984, s.3. See above, para.14–037.

[753] Cmd. 4213, para.4.

[754] Patchett, at p.179, *op. cit.* above, p.663, n.1. See also Lipstein [1981] C.L.J. 201.

[755] [1981] Fam. 77, 126 (CA). The point was left open in the House of Lords: [1983] 1 A.C. 145.

[756] [1981] Fam. 77, at pp.126–127.

whom Cumming-Bruce L.J. agreed) shared the doubts of Lord Reid[757] and thought that s.8(1) did not apply to decrees in matrimonial cases concerning status (as opposed to money judgments). In *Maples v Maples*[758] Latey J. preferred the majority view that the 1933 Act in general, and s.8(1) in particular, did not apply to judgments relating to marital status.

ILLUSTRATIONS

1. A obtains a judgment for 1 million shekels against X from an Israeli Court. The judgment has not been registered. No action lies upon the judgment in England.   **14–196**

2. A, a French company, sells clothing from its Lille branch and its Paris branch to X & Co, an English company. The invoices for the goods from Lille provide for the jurisdiction of the Lille court and the invoices for the goods from Paris provide for the jurisdiction of the Paris court. When X & Co refuses to pay for either sets of goods, A sues in the Lille court for the total amount outstanding, plus 10,000 francs as "résistance abusive," a head of claim for unreasonable refusal to pay. X & Co initially ignores the Lille proceedings and judgment in default is awarded against it for the amount claimed. X & Co subsequently applies to appeal out of time from the Lille judgment. The appeal proceedings are a submission to the jurisdiction of the Lille court, even for the Paris goods, although there has been no contractual submission to the Lille court in respect of those goods. The judgment for "résistance abusive" is not a fine or penalty, or contrary to public policy. The judgment is registrable.[759]

(3) THE BRUSSELS I REGULATION, THE LUGANO CONVENTION AND COUNCIL REGULATION (EC) 805/2004[760]

RULE 55—(1) Subject to clause (2) of this Rule, a judgment given by a court in a State to which Council Regulation (EC) 44/2001 ("the Brussels I Regulation") applies, or which is a party to the Lugano Conventions on jurisdiction and the recognition and enforcement of judgments in civil and commercial matters, and which falls within the scope of the relevant instrument has, on registration in the appropriate court[761] in the United Kingdom, the same force and effect as a judgment of the court in which it is registered, and proceedings for or with respect to its enforcement may be taken, as if the judgment had been originally given by the registering court.[762]   **14R–197**

(2) Where the judgment has been certified with a European Enforcement Order it may be enforced without the need to apply for registration of the judgment.

---

[757] *Black-Clawson International Ltd v Papierwerke Waldhof-Aschaffenburg AG* [1975] A.C. 591, 617 (a dissenting judgment).

[758] [1988] Fam. 14.

[759] *SA Consortium Textiles v Sun & Sand Agencies Ltd* [1978] Q.B. 279 (CA). This case would now fall within Rule 55.

[760] Collins, pp.105–125; Hartley, pp.82–100; Briggs & Rees, Ch.7; Kaye, Pt 8; Layton & Mercer, Chs 26–28. For the States to which they apply, see paras 11–013 *et seq.*

[761] The High Court in England; the Court of Session in Scotland; the High Court in Northern Ireland: Art.39 of, and Annex II to, the Regulation; and Civil Jurisdiction and Judgments Order 2001 (SI 2001/3929), Sch.1, para.2.

[762] SI 2001/3929, Sch.1, para.2(2); in relation to the Convention, see 1982 Act, s.4A. For the recognition of such judgments without the need for registration, see below, para.14–224.

Comment

14–198   **Introduction.** The jurisdictional provisions of the Brussels I Regulation[763] and the Lugano Convention[764] have been fully discussed in Chapter 11; and Rule 55 states the essence of the judgment recognition and enforcement aspects of these two instruments. The provisions dealing with the recognition and enforcement of judgments are set out in Chapter III of the Regulation,[765] and Title III of the Convention.[766] Save where it would be positively misleading to do otherwise, the discussion of this Rule does not deal with the corresponding provisions of the 1968 Brussels Convention, as from time to time amended, or with the original Lugano Convention of 1988, which are effectively superseded.[767] It should be noted, however, that many of the authorities referred to in this Chapter were decided on the basis of these earlier instruments, and that in several important respects their material wording differs from that found in the instruments currently in force. The trend of legislative reform, so far as this applies to the provisions for the recognition and enforcement of judgments from Member and Contracting States, is to abridge or reduce, as far as possible, the judicial process required before a judgment from another Member or Contracting State may be enforced, and earlier decisions need to be read with this in mind. The substantive provisions of the Brussels I Regulation and the Lugano Convention are very closely similar, and for this reason, the discussion in this Chapter will place its principal focus on the provisions of Chapter III of the Regulation. It is likely that further legislative reform of the Brussels I Regulation in general, and of Chapter III in particular, will take place. There is a desire on the part of the European Commission to reduce still further the objections which may be raised to the enforcement in one Member State of judgments handed down by the courts of another Member State.[768]

14–199   Recognition and enforcement under the instruments is restricted to judgments in civil and commercial matters. If the judgment is in a civil or commercial matter, the question of which instrument applies to its recognition and enforcement is determined by the Member State or Convention State from which the judgment comes. So far as concerns judgments from the courts of states which were Member States on March 1, 2002, the Brussels I Regulation governs the recognition and enforcement of such judgments if the proceedings were instituted on or after March 1, 2002,[769] save in the case of Denmark, for

---

[763] Regulation (EC) 44/2001.

[764] [2007] O.J. L339/3,

[765] As supplemented by Sch.1 para.1 of the Civil Jurisdiction and Judgments Order 2001, SI 2001/3929 and CPR Pt 74.

[766] As supplemented by Civil Jurisdiction and Judgments Act 1982, s.4A (inserted by Civil Jurisdiction and Judgments Regulations Order 2009, SI 2009/3131, reg.5) and CPR Pt 74.

[767] For the territories in respect of which the Brussels Convention remains in force, because they are outside the territorial scope of the Brussels I Regulation, see para.11–013, above. For a full treatment of the Brussels Convention see Ch.14 of the 13th edition (2000) of this work.

[768] See Commission Proposal on the Brussels I Regulation: COM(2010) 748 (December 14, 2010).

[769] Art.66(1). For judgments from those few territories of Member States to which the Brussels Convention had been extended, but to which the Brussels I Regulation does not apply, the recognition and enforcement of the judgment will continue to be governed by the Brussels Convention.

which the material date is July 1, 2007.[770] However, for judgments given by the courts of these Member States after, but in proceedings which were instituted before, March 1, 2002,[771] the transitional provisions of the Regulation provide that it will govern the recognition of the judgment if the Brussels Convention was in force in the Contracting State of origin when the proceedings were commenced.[772]

For judgments from the courts of those Member States which acceded to **14–200** membership of the European Union after March 1, 2002, the Brussels I Regulation will govern the recognition and enforcement of judgments if the proceedings were instituted in the Member State in question after the Regulation came into effect in that Member State.[773] However, in cases in which the proceedings were instituted before, but the judgment was given after, that date, the transitional provisions of the Brussels I Regulation[774] provide for the recognition of the judgment if the jurisdiction was founded on upon rules which accorded with those provided for in the Brussels I Regulation.[775]

For judgments from Iceland, Norway and Switzerland, which together with **14–201** the Member States of European Union are bound by the Lugano Convention,[776] the Lugano Convention[777] provides for the recognition and enforcement of the judgment if the proceedings were instituted after the Lugano Convention came into effect as between the state bound by the Lugano Convention and the EU.[778] However, in the case of judgments given in proceedings instituted in these courts prior to such coming into effect, the transitional provisions of the Lugano Convention provide for the recognition and enforcement of judgments under the Lugano Convention if the proceedings were brought in the court in accordance with the original Lugano Convention.[779] In effect, the Lugano Convention governs the recognition and enforcement of judgments from the courts of Iceland, Norway and Switzerland.

The most notable features of enforcement under the Regulation, and in **14–202** which respect it and the Brussels and Lugano Conventions differ from the regime established by the common law and the 1920 and 1933 Acts, are that enforcement under the Regulation or the Conventions is not limited to money judgments, or to final judgments, and that in principle (but subject to certain limitations) the court in which enforcement is sought is not entitled to investigate the jurisdiction of the court which gave the judgment. It is also important to note that the effect of the Regulation and the Lugano Convention is that the enforcement procedures apply to all judgments within their scope,

---

[770] Until that date, Denmark had opted not to be bound by the Brussels I Regulation: see SI 2007/1655. As from this date, Art.1(3) of the Brussels I Regulation is inapplicable.

[771] Or, in the case of Denmark, July 1, 2007.

[772] Art.66(2).

[773] Art.66(1) as applied by the accession agreement for the Member State in question.

[774] Art.66(2).

[775] See, e.g. *Advent Capital Plc v GN Ellinas Imports-Exports Ltd* [2005] EWHC 1242 (Comm.), [2005] 2 Lloyd's Rep. 607; *T v L* [2008] IESC 48, [2009] I.L.Pr. 46.

[776] Though it is the European Union, rather than the Member States, which is party to the Lugano Convention.

[777] In this context, the reference is to the revised (2007) Lugano Convention.

[778] Art.63(1).

[779] Art.63(2).

whether or not they are against persons domiciled in a Member State or Convention State. Thus an English default judgment against a New York resident in a case where the jurisdiction of the English court was based on the temporary presence of the defendant in England will be enforceable in France; and a French judgment against a New York resident in a case where the jurisdiction of the French court was based on the French nationality of the plaintiff under Art.14 of the Civil Code will be enforceable in England. Article 59 of the Brussels Convention and the original (1988) Lugano Convention allowed a Contracting State to assume in relation to a non-Contracting State the obligation not to recognise judgments given in other Contracting States against defendants domiciled or habitually resident in the non-Contracting State where the basis of jurisdiction could only be one of the "exorbitant" bases of jurisdiction set out in Art.3(2) of the Conventions (which include the jurisdiction in England based on temporary presence and the jurisdiction in France based on nationality). Such bilateral treaties were negotiated by the United Kingdom with Australia[780] and with Canada.[781] These remain effective where recognition is governed by the Regulation and the Lugano Convention,[782] but there is no provision for such bilateral treaties to be negotiated in the future.

14–203   Even so, the free circulation of judgments within the Member States, to which the Regulation aspires, is impeded by the right of the judgment debtor to raise certain defences to the application for recognition of the judgment. These have been gradually reduced, but still give a stalling defendant opportunity to delay the enforcement of a judgment against him. To overcome this, the European Union has implemented a rather different procedure for the largely automatic enforcement of certain judgments which are exempted from the procedure for obtaining an order for registration under Chapter III of the Regulation. The European Enforcement Order for uncontested claims applies to a class of judgments otherwise within the material scope of the Regulation, and provides, in effect, for a certified judgment to be enforceable in other Member States (with the exception of Denmark) without the need to go through the procedure in, (or without the protection offered by) Chapter III of the Regulation.[783] It is discussed in detail under clause (2) of this Rule, together with the additional proposals of the European Commission for simplifying the enforcement of judgments in particular cases.

14–204   **Clause (1) of the Rule.** Article 32 of the Regulation (and of the Lugano Convention) provides that "judgment" means any judgment given by a court or tribunal of a Member (or Convention) State, whatever the judgment may be called, including a decree, order, decision, or writ of execution, as well as the determination of costs by an officer of the court.[784] It does not include

---

[780] SI 1994/1901.

[781] See para.14–224, n.845.

[782] Art.72 of the Regulation; Art.68 of the Convention.

[783] See Crifò (2005) 24 C.J.Q. 200.

[784] SI 2001/3929, Sch.1, para.1(1) provides that "judgment" has the meaning given to it by Article 32 of the Regulation. For maintenance orders see Rule 102.

judicially approved settlements, but does include judgments by consent,[785] as well as a judgment entered when a defendant is debarred from defending, even though there is no actual judicial consideration of the merits of the claim.[786] The expression includes not only judgments ordering the payment of money,[787] orders for costs[788] and for interest,[789] but also non-money judgments and judgments which are not final and which are interlocutory or provisional in nature.[790] This is because there is no requirement that the judgment be "final and conclusive": it may be an interim order providing for periodical payments or a provisional order freezing assets.[791] It may be an order made under Art.31 of the Regulation or the Convention, made by a court which has no jurisdiction over the substance of the case, provided that it is properly to be seen as a provisional, including protective, measure,[792] and that is not granted ex parte and intended to be executed without notice.[793] Thus, for example, the English court may be required to enforce German injunctions. But the mode of enforcement (e.g. sequestration or committal) will in principle be a matter for English law,[794] which will determine the procedural

---

[785] *Landhurst Leasing Plc v Marcq* [1998] I.L.Pr. 822 (CA). On the enforcement of authentic instruments and of settlements approved by courts in the course of proceedings, see Arts 57 and 58 of the Regulation and of the Lugano Convention, below, para.14–244. For the distinction between court-approved settlements and judgments by consent see Case C–414/92 *Solo Kleinmotoren GmbH v Boch* [1994] E.C.R. I–2237, 2255, and especially at p.2245, *per* Gulmann A.-G.

[786] Case C–394/07 *Gambazzi v Daimler Chrysler Canada Inc* [2009] E.C.R. I–2563.

[787] Including the order to pay under the "*Zahlungsbefehl*" procedure of German law: Case 166/80 *Klomps v Michel* [1981] E.C.R. 1593, and the order to pay made under the "*decreto ingiuntivo*" procedure of Italian law: Case C–474/93 *Firma Hengst Import BV v Campese* [1995] E.C.R. I–2113.

[788] SI 2001/3929, Sch.1, para.5.

[789] SI 2001/3929, Sch.1, para.5.

[790] e.g. *The Tjaskemolen (No.2)* [1997] 2 Lloyd's Rep. 476, 478–479; *Normaco v Lundman* [1999] I.L.Pr. 381.

[791] *cf.* Case 143/78 *De Cavel v De Cavel (No.1)* [1979] E.C.R. 1055; Case 125/79 *Denilauler v SNC Couchet Frères* [1980] E.C.R. 1553; *Babanaft International Co SA v Bassatne* [1990] Ch. 13, 31 (CA); *cf.* Case 258/83 *Brennero v Wendel GmbH* [1984] E.C.R. 3971; *The Atlantic Emperor (No.2)* [1992] 1 Lloyd's Rep. 624 (CA); *Barren International Resorts Ltd v Martin*, 1994 S.L.T. 434.

[792] Case C–391/95 *Van Uden Maritime B.V. v Deco-Line* [1998] E.C.R. I–7091; Case C–99/96 *Mietz v Intership Yachting Sneek BV* [1999] E.C.R. I–2277; and see *Comet Group Plc v Unika Computer SA* [2004] I.L.Pr. 10 (party obtaining an order which could not be justified by reference to what is now Art.31, and which was obtained in breach of contract, may be required by mandatory injunction to have it set aside by the foreign court).

[793] Case 125/79 *Denilauler v SNC Couchet Frères* [1980] E.C.R. 1553; *EMI Records Ltd v Modern Music GmbH* [1992] Q.B. 115. But orders for discovery and the taking of evidence are not within its scope: see *CFEM Façades v Bovis Construction SA* [1992] I.L.Pr. 561; see also Schlosser, paras 184–187; Collins, p.106.

[794] Schlosser, paras 212–213; Collins, p.116. For an illustration of the manner in which a German court enforced an English worldwide freezing injunction, by making that German order which appeared to be closest in effect to the English order, see Zuckerman and Grunert, *Zeitschrift für Zivilprozess International*, 1996, 89. For a decision of the Swiss Federal Tribunal, ordering measures by way of enforcement under the original Lugano Convention of the worldwide freezing order made by the High Court in *Motorola Credit Corp v Uzan (No.2)* [2003] EWCA Civ 752, [2004] 1 W.L.R. 113 (CA), see BGE/ATF 129 III 626. The French Cour de cassation has also authorised the enforcement of an English worldwide freezing order: *Stolzenberg v Daimler Chrysler Canada Inc* (Cass. Civ. I, July 30, 2003) [2005] I.L.Pr. 266, 2005 *Clunet* 112 (note Cuniberti).

requirements (such as the endorsement of a penal notice on the order) and also the extent of the court's discretion to commit or fine.

14–205   It is obvious that a judgment must fall within the scope of the Regulation or the Convention if it is to fall within Chapter III or Title III, as the case may be, and qualify for recognition and enforcement under this Rule.[795] But these provisions do not extend to "judgments on judgments". Accordingly, a judgment from the courts of State A enforcing a judgment of State B would not constitute a judgment within Art.32.[796] A similar result is reached when the courts of Member State A enforce the judgment of a non-Member State, and the judgment creditor then seeks to enforce the "judgment" of State A under Chapter III of the Regulation in Member State B. The European Court held, in *Owens Bank Ltd v Bracco*,[797] that in such circumstances the judgment of State A fell outside the scope of the Brussels Convention altogether, presumably because the merits of the dispute will have been adjudicated upon by a judge in a non-Contracting State, and that such a decision fell outside the framework of mutual recognition established by the Convention. The effect of the Regulation will, in this respect, be identical. It should also follow, for example, that a decision of a court in a Member State recognising the preclusive effect of a judgment or settlement in class action proceedings made by a court in the United States will not be seen as a judgment from the courts of that Member State for the purpose of Chapter III of the Regulation.[798]

14–206   **Effect of exclusion of arbitration.** Article 1(2)(d) of the Regulation and of the Convention, like Art.1(4) of their predecessors, excludes "arbitration" from its scope. This exclusion has been considered earlier,[799] and in the

---

[795] A fine for contempt of court and payable to the state, imposed in civil proceedings for non-compliance with an order of the court falls within the material scope of the Regulation, and may be enforced under Chapter III of the Regulation: Case C–406/09 *Realchemie Nederland BV v Bayer Crop Science BV* [2012] I.L.Pr. 17. For the approach in cases where the judgment on a matter prima facie within the scope of the Regulation is closely connected to matters which are excluded from the scope of the Regulation, see Case 145/86 *Hoffmann v Krieg* [1988] E.C.R. 645 (status); Case C–22/95 *Van Den Boogaard v Laumen* [1997] E.C.R. I–1147 (status); Case C–267/97 *Coursier v Fortis Bank SA* [1999] E.C.R. I–2543 (insolvency). For cases where the judgment was given between parties who had agreed to arbitrate their differences, see below, paras 14–206 *et seq*. It has also been held that a foreign judgment will not be recognised when its recognition would have (by way of estoppel) an effect in proceedings over which the English court has exclusive jurisdiction regardless of domicile under what is now Art.22 of the Regulation: *Prudential Assurance Co Ltd v Prudential Insurance Co of America* [2003] EWCA Civ 32, [2003] 1 W.L.R. 2295 (CA).

[796] Droz, para.437; *cf.* 1982 Act, s.18(7). See also *Clarke v Fennoscandia Ltd*, 2004 S.C. 197 (appeal dismissed on other grounds: [2007] UKHL 56, 2008 S.C. (HL) 122).

[797] Case C–129/92 [1994] E.C.R. 1–117, [1994] Q.B. 509; *Dubai Bank Ltd v Abbas* [1998] I.L. Pr. 391.

[798] To be distinguished from the case in which Dutch law applies its own original procedure for imposing a class action settlement, usually in relation to those persons over whose claim the US court would find it had no jurisdiction, and who are therefore excluded from the US class: see, for illustration, *Re Royal Dutch Shell* (May 29, 2009, Amsterdam CA); *Re Royal Ahold NV* (June 23, 2010, Amsterdam Dist. Ct.). Orders made in such procedures may constitute judgments or court-approved settlements, and their effect outside the Netherlands will be governed by Chapter III or Chapter IV of the Brussels I Regulation.

[799] paras 11–041—11–048. And see also (2001) 18 J. Arb. L. 13–39.

present context arises in relation to the recognition or enforcement of judgments of Member States rendered in connection with disputes which the parties have agreed, or are alleged to have agreed, should be resolved exclusively by arbitration.

It is clear from the Jenard Report[800] and the Schlosser Report[801] that the recognition and enforcement of arbitral awards will be outside the scope of the Regulation and the Convention. It has been held that a French judgment making a French award enforceable was not entitled to enforcement under the Brussels Convention for that reason;[802] the same will certainly apply to the Regulation. There are two more controversial questions.   **14–207**

The first question is whether a judgment deciding that an arbitration agreement is valid, or invalid or ineffective, is entitled to recognition under the Regulation or the Convention. The second question is whether a decision of a court in another Member State or Convention State that there is no valid arbitration agreement, or giving judgment in disregard of what English law would regard as a valid arbitration agreement, is entitled to recognition or enforcement under the Regulation or the Convention. As has been seen, the United Kingdom's position in the accession negotiations was that, because the exclusion covered all disputes which the parties had agreed should be settled by arbitration, such judgments would not come within the scope of the Brussels Convention. As has been seen, it was agreed that no amendment should be made to the original text, and that the new Contracting States could deal with the problem in their implementing legislation. The effect of the Civil Jurisdiction and Judgments Act, s.32(1), is that foreign judgments given in breach of arbitration agreements were not to be recognised and enforced in the United Kingdom, but it is also provided that nothing in s.32(1) is to affect the recognition or enforcement of judgments which are required to be recognised or enforced under (inter alia) the Brussels I Regulation or the Lugano Convention.[803]   **14–208**

As has been seen, the Jenard Report expressed the view that the Brussels Convention did not apply to the recognition of judgments in litigation relating to arbitration, and the Schlosser Report also indicated that the Brussels Convention did not apply to a judgment determining whether an arbitration agreement was valid or not. But the Evrigenis-Kerameus Report on the 1982 Accession Convention[804] expressed the view that the verification, as an incidental question, of the validity of an arbitration agreement which was relied on by a litigant in order to contest the jurisdiction of the court before which he was being sued pursuant to the Brussels Convention, fell within the scope of the Convention.   **14–209**

---

[800] p.13, referred to with approval in Case C–190/89 *Marc Rich & Co AG v Soc Italiana Impianti PA* [1991] E.C.R. I–3855, 3900.

[801] para.65(c), referred to with approval in Case C–391/95 *Van Uden Maritime BV v Firma Deco-Line* [1998] E.C.R. I–7091, [1999] Q.B. 1225, at para.32.

[802] *ABCI v Banque Franco-Tunisienne* [1996] 1 Lloyd's Rep. 495; affirmed on other aspects [1997] 1 Lloyd's Rep. 531 (CA). See Hascher (1996) 12 Arb. Int. 233, who suggests that the decision is supportable on the basis that the French order was not in fact a judgment on the award, but simply an execution order.

[803] s.32(4)(a).

[804] [1986] O.J. C298/1/10, para.35.

14–210   One of the questions referred by the English court to the European Court in the *Marc Rich* case[805] was whether the exclusion applied to judgments where the initial existence of an arbitration agreement was in issue. Darmon A.-G.[806] was of the opinion that, where the main issue in a proceeding before a national court related to whether an arbitration agreement existed between the parties, the dispute did not fall within the Brussels Convention, since a dispute as to the existence of an arbitration agreement fell outside the scope of the Convention. The Court did not rule expressly on this question: the actual ruling was the narrow one that the exclusion extended to litigation pending before a national court concerning the appointment of an arbitrator even if the existence or validity of the arbitration agreement was a preliminary issue in that litigation. But it did expressly reject the argument that the exclusion in respect of arbitration did not apply where the existence or validity of an arbitration agreement was being disputed before different courts, regardless of whether the issue was raised as a main issue or preliminary one. In *National Navigation Co v Endesa Generacion SA (The Wadi Sudr)*[807] consignees arrested a ship in Spain in respect of a claim for late delivery of a cargo of coal. The owners commenced court proceedings in England, but also sought a stay from the Spanish court in the ground that the consignees were bound by an arbitration clause incorporated by reference to a charterparty in the bill of lading, alternatively on the ground that the English court was first seised. The Spanish court decided that no arbitration clause was incorporated in the contract. The Court of Appeal decided that a judgment given in a Member State (Spain) which ruled, as a preliminary issue in proceedings on the substance of the dispute, that an arbitration clause had not been incorporated in a bill of lading, was a judgment which had to be recognised and enforced under the Brussels I Regulation. It was the subject matter of the proceedings which dictated whether the proceedings were within the Regulation or not. A judgment on a preliminary issue in proceedings within the Regulation would be a judgment within the Regulation, even if, when looked at in isolation, the subject of the preliminary issue fell within the ambit of arbitration. Nor was there any basis for refusing to recognise the foreign judgment on public policy grounds.[808]

14–211   There has not yet been any decision on whether a judgment of a court of a Member or Convention State on the merits of the claim, but given in breach of an arbitration agreement, may be refused recognition or enforcement. But

---

[805] n.800, above.

[806] At 3876, citing the Schlosser Report, and Kaye, p.150.

[807] [2009] EWCA Civ 1397, [2010] 1 Lloyd's Rep. 193. The point had been left open in *Through Transport Mutual Insurance Association (Eurasia) Ltd v New India Assurance Co Ltd* [2004] EWCA Civ 1598, [2005] 1 Lloyd's Rep. 67, [50]–[51].

[808] Waller L.J. distinguished *Phillip Alexander Securities and Futures Ltd v Bamberger* [1997] I.L.Pr. 73, affd *ibid.* 104, in which he had at first instance suggested, *obiter*, that it might be contrary to public policy to recognise such a judgment, at any rate if the objection to arbitration was not bona fide or if the English court (even subsequently) granted an injunction restraining continuation of the proceedings and/or granted a declaration that the proceedings were covered by the arbitration agreement. The Court of Appeal decided that the issue did not arise, and that if it had arisen, it would have been appropriate to make a reference to the European Court. In *The Wadi Sudr* Waller L.J. said (at [61]) that the *Phillip Alexander Securities* case was pre-*West Tankers* and that he had been dealing with a situation in which it was clear that there was an arbitration agreement: see also Moore-Bick L.J. at [132].

in two decisions at first instance the court has made an order under the Arbitration Act 1996, s.66, giving leave to enforce an award as a judgment in order to pre-empt, by reference to Art.34(3) of the Regulation (refusal of recognition on ground of irreconcilable judgments), an attempt to register in England a subsequent judgment from another Member State which had failed to respect the arbitration agreement.[809]

Effect of submission. Of course, if the defendant disputes the jurisdiction **14–212** of the foreign court, on the ground that it has no jurisdiction because the parties have agreed to arbitrate,[810] but having lost, goes on to contest the merits of the dispute, any possible[811] defence to recognition of the judgment which may have been open to him based on the law of arbitration, will have been waived and abandoned.[812]

In the *Marc Rich* proceedings, prior to the ruling of the European Court, the **14–213** effect of which was that the provision which is now Art.27 of the Regulation[813] did not prevent English proceedings for the appointment of arbitrators, the Italian Corte di Cassazione had decided that the Italian courts had jurisdiction and that there was no binding arbitration agreement. While the ruling of the European Court was pending, the Swiss buyers lodged a pleading on the merits in the Italian proceedings. On their application for an injunction to restrain the Italian proceedings, it was held by the English Court of Appeal that the effect of their pleading in the Italian court was that they had submitted to the jurisdiction of the Italian court to deal with the merits of the claim; that submission covered the whole proceedings, including the prior interlocutory decision by the Italian court that there was a valid arbitration agreement.[814]

Proposals for change. The European Commission has recognised that the **14–214** current legal framework does not sufficiently protect the effectiveness of arbitration agreements in the EU. The Commission has accepted that the ruling in *West Tankers Inc v Allianz SpA*[815] creates a real risk of the abuse of litigation tactics and has put forward proposals for changes to the Brussels I Regulation as part of the general review of the Regulation. It has put forward

---

[809] Further proceedings in *West Tankers Inc v Allianz SpA* [2011] EWHC 829 (Comm.), [2011] 2 All E.R. (Comm.) 1; *African Fertilisers & Chemicals Nig Ltd v BD Shipsnavo GmbH & Co Reederei KG* [2011] EWHC 2452 (Comm.), [2011] 2 Lloyd's Rep 531.

[810] *cf.* Case C–391/95 *Van Uden Maritime BV v Deco-Line* [1998] E.C.R. I–7091, [1999] Q.B. 1225.

[811] But if *The Wadi Sudr* is correct, there will not be such a defence, and this paragraph may be disregarded.

[812] Civil Jurisdiction & Judgments Act 1982, s.32(1). On the interpretation of s.32(1), as it applies to a party who unsuccessfully pleads an arbitration agreement but who then plays a part in the proceedings on the merits but who is able to show that this was practically necessary to maintain its assertion that the parties were obliged to proceed to arbitration rather than to the courts, see *AES Ust-Kamenogorsk Hydropower Plant LLP v AES Ust-Kamenogorsk Hydropower Plant JSC* [2011] EWCA Civ 647, [2011] 2 Lloyd's Rep. 233.

[813] Art.21 of the Brussels Convention.

[814] *The Atlantic Emperor (No.2)* [1992] 1 Lloyd's Rep. 624 (CA).

[815] Case C–185/07 [2009] E.C.R. I–663, [2009] 1 A.C. 1138, and see above, para.11–048.

a solution designed to ensure that a national court should stay its proceedings in favour of the courts of the seat of the arbitration, or in favour of the arbitral tribunal.[816]

14–215   **Appeals.** The pendency of an appeal in the foreign court will not prevent registration of a judgment capable of enforcement,[817] but once it is registered the court may stay[818] enforcement proceedings if an "ordinary" appeal has been lodged against the judgment in the State in which it was given;[819] enforcement may also be stayed if the time for appeal has not yet expired, and an appeal has not been lodged, subject to the power of the English court to specify the time within which the appeal must be lodged.[820] In seeking a stay, the judgment debtor is not entitled to rely on the likelihood of success of his pending appeal in the foreign court, since the enforcing court is not permitted to examine, directly or indirectly, the substance of the case.[821]

14–216   Article 46(3) provides that the court may also make *enforcement* conditional on the provision of such security as it shall determine.[822] This is primarily designed to ensure that the judgment *debtor* does not find that he is unable to recover the judgment debt from the judgment creditor if the original judgment is overturned. But it has been held that a stay of enforcement may

---

[816] COM(2010) 748 Final. See also Report to the European Parliament on the Application of the Brussels I Regulation, April 21, 2009 (COM (2009) 174, para.3.7; Green Paper, April 21, 2009 (COM (2009) 175, para.7; Hess, Pfeiffer, Schlosser, *The Brussels I-Regulation (EC) No.44/2001* (2008), at paras 106–136. A draft report of the Committee on Legal Affairs of the European Parliament proposes that the exclusion of arbitration should be widened to include judicial procedures ruling on the validity or extent of arbitral competence as a principal issue or as an incidental or preliminary question. 2010/0383(COD), p.13, and also pp.6, 9.

[817] Art.38 provides that a judgment may be enforced when it is has been declared enforceable in the State of origin; for the meaning of "enforceable" see Case C–267/97 *Coursier v Fortis Bank SA* [1999] E.C.R. I–2843. The fact that the judgment might be enforceable only in a restricted sense does not prevent its satisfying the requirement that it be enforceable. In C–420/07 *Apostolides v Orams* [2009] E.C.R. I–3571, the fact that a Cypriot judgment ordering the return of land situated in the occupied northern part of Cyprus could not in practice be specifically enforced by execution at that place did not mean that the judgment, which imposed several obligations on the defendant, was not enforceable in Cyprus. The consequence was that it could be registered under Chapter III.

[818] *DHL GBS (UK) Ltd v Fallimento Finmatica SpA* [2009] EWHC 291 (Comm.), [2009] 1 Lloyd's Rep. 430. Where it is uncertain whether or to what extent the foreign judgment is enforceable, the application may be adjourned to allow for clarification obtained by procedural methods available in the foreign court: *La Caisse Régionale du Credit Agricole de France v Ashdown* [2007] EWCA Civ 574.

[819] Art.46 confers this power on the first instance court (Art.43) and also on the court hearing the further appeal under Art.44. In this respect it is wider than, and an improvement on, Art.38 of the Brussels Convention, which limited this power to the first instance court: under the Convention there may be no appeal against its refusal to order a stay: Case C–183/90 *Van Dalfsen v Van Loon* [1991] E.C.R. I–4743. Nor may the court hearing an appeal on a point of law under what is now Art.44 impose such a stay for itself: Case C–432/93 *Société d'Informatique Service Réalisation Organisation v Ampersand Software BV* [1995] E.C.R. I–2269; [1996] Q.B. 127. Art.37 contains corresponding provisions relating to recognition.

[820] *cf.* 1933 Act, s.5, and para.14–193.

[821] Case C–183/90 *Van Dalfsen v Van Loon* [1991] E.C.R. I–4743.

[822] This order may only be made when, or after, the High Court confirms the registration: Case 258/83 *Brennero SAS v Wendel GmbH* [1984] E.C.R. 3971.

be made conditional on the provision of security by the judgment debtor, so that the judgment *creditor* is not prejudiced by the delay.[823]

The distinction between ordinary and extraordinary appeals has no counter-part in the United Kingdom, and although the distinction is found in the civil law Member and Convention States it is not applied uniformly. The European Court, in *Industrial Diamond Supplies v Riva*,[824] held that (a) whether an appeal was ordinary or extraordinary depended on an autonomous inter-pretation rather than on the procedural law of the court of origin; (b) the expression "ordinary appeal" must be understood as meaning any appeal which forms part of the normal course of an action and which, as such, constitutes a procedural development which any party must reasonably expect; (c) any appeal bound by the law to a specific period of time which starts to run by virtue of the actual decision whose enforcement is sought constitutes such a development. Consequently, any appeal which might be dependent on events which were unforeseeable at the date of the original judgment or upon action taken by persons who were extraneous to the judgment would not be an "ordinary appeal". Thus an application for a re-trial after new evidence had come to light or an application for a re-hearing would not be an "ordinary appeal". Article 46(2)[825] of the Regulation (and of the Convention) provides that where the judgment is given in the United King-dom or the Republic of Ireland any form of appeal available under their law shall be treated as an ordinary appeal for the purposes of Art.46(1). The special provisions relating to the United Kingdom and Ireland apply only to the enforcement of their judgments in other Member or Convention States. Therefore the English court may still be required to consider whether an ordinary appeal is pending in another Member or Convention State in order to decide whether to grant a stay of enforcement proceedings.

14–217

No review of substance. Article 36 provides that "under no circumstances may a foreign judgment be reviewed as to its substance".[826] The grounds for non-recognition or non-enforcement of judgments are very limited.[827] The English court has no right, except within very confined limits, to question the jurisdiction of the court which gave the judgment. There are grounds, such as public policy or lack of notice, which bear some distant resemblance to the rules at common law and under the 1920 and 1933 Acts,[828] but these have no effect whatever on the true construction of the Regulation.

14–218

---

[823] *Petereit v Babcock International Ltd* [1990] 1 W.L.R. 350. The inter-relationship of the powers conferred on the court by Arts 38 and 39 of the Brussels Convention was considered in *William Grant & Sons International Ltd v Marie-Brizard Espana SA*, 1998 S.C. 536, and various questions referred to the European Court. The reference was subsequently withdrawn; and as the provisions of Art.46 of the Regulation are somewhat different from those of Art.39 of the Brussels Convention, this case must now be applied with care. See also below, para.14–240.

[824] Case 43/77 [1977] E.C.R. 2175, applied in *Interdesco SA v Nullifire Ltd* [1992] 1 Lloyd's Rep. 180 (*recours en revision* in France not an ordinary appeal; stay refused).

[825] Art.31 of the Conventions is identical to Art.38 of the Brussels I Regulation.

[826] But a court must be able to review the substance to the extent necessary to determine whether Art.34 requires that the judgment be not recognised: *cf.* Case C–78/95 *Hendrickman v Magenta Druck & Verlag GmbH* [1996] E.C.R. I–4943.

[827] They are drawn more tightly than the corresponding provisions of the Brussels Convention.

[828] See paras 14R–183 *et seq.* and below, paras 14–225 *et seq.*

14–219   It has not been finally determined whether the court in which recognition or enforcement is sought would be precluded from deciding for itself whether the judgment fell within the scope of the Regulation or the Convention (that is, was given in a civil or commercial matter and was not otherwise excluded from the scope of the relevant instrument), but it is submitted that it must have this right and duty.[829] Article 36 does not cover the point, for though it precludes jurisdictional review for judgments which are within the scope of the Regulation or the Convention, it does not apply to the distinct question whether a judgment falls within the perimeter of the Regulation or the Convention in the first place: only if it does do the obligations imposed by Art.36 affect the court addressed. It follows that the English court must be free to decide this question for itself, not being bound to accept the view of the adjudicating court upon whether the case fell within the scope of the Regulation or the Convention. If the judgment is outside the scope of the relevant instrument, recognition and enforcement may be sought under the common law or the 1933 Act.

14–220   **Nature and effect of recognition.** According to the European Court in *Hoffmann v Krieg*,[830] the duty of a court which is required to recognise a judgment under Chapter III of the Regulation, is, in principle at least, to accord to the judgment the authority and effectiveness which it has in the Member State of origin. This principle forms the point of departure for the decision by the recognising court in selecting the order which it will make which will most closely correspond with that which was made in the state of origin.[831] But in other respects, such as the effect the judgment will have in relation to non-parties,[832] it is suggested that recognition of a foreign judgment means treating it as though it were an English judgment given in identical terms, rather than a judgment defined in all its aspects by the law of the Member State of origin and received into English law as such.[833] Nor is the enforcing court bound to give to the foreign judgment effects which an equivalent local judgment would not have.[834] However, a court may not refuse to recognise a judgment on the ground that it has already been satisfied, for such an objection, which may be taken in accordance with national law as an objection to execution, is not provided for by Chapter III.[835]

---

[829] *cf.* Case 29/76 *LTU GmbH v Eurocontrol* [1976] E.C.R. 1541; Case 133/78 *Gourdain v Nadler* [1979] E.C.R. 733; and Case C–172/91 *Sonntag v Waidmann* [1993] E.C.R. I–1963, where the court in which recognition was sought apparently undertook this inquiry for itself.

[830] Case C–156/86, [1988] E.C.R. 645.

[831] See para.14–204, n.794, above.

[832] Such as a surety, when the original proceedings were between creditor and debtor: see Schlosser, para.191.

[833] *cf. Calyon v Michailidis* [2009] UKPC 34 (Greek judgment in proceedings between A and B determining whether property formed part of a deceased estate was as a matter of English law not binding on C, who had known nothing of the proceedings).

[834] Case C–420/07 *Apostolides v Orams* [2009] E.C.R. I–3571, [66].

[835] Case C–139/10 *Prism Investments BV v Van Der Meer* (October 13, 2011). Likewise, it is probably not open to the court which recognises a judgment in accordance with Chapter III to vary it in the way it would be able to vary a judgment of its own, or to treat the parties as if it had done so: if the judgment is to be varied, the power to do it may lie with original court, and not with the recognising court: *D'Hoker v Tritan Enterprises Ltd* [2009] EWHC 949 (QB).

Jurisdiction of the foreign court. The jurisdiction of the foreign court may   **14–221**
only be investigated by the English court if the case may fall within Sections
3 (insurance contracts), 4 (certain consumer contracts) or 6 (exclusive jurisdiction) of Chapter II of the Regulation[836]: if it is found that the adjudicating
court violated these important jurisdictional provisions, recognition must be
denied. But even in those cases the English court is bound by the findings of
fact on which the foreign court based its judgment.[837] No explanation is given
for the failure to include Section 5 of Chapter II of the Regulation, which deals
with contracts of employment,[838] in this list of instances where the jurisdiction
of the adjudicating court may be reviewed, but it does not appear possible to
argue that Art.35 should read as if such cases were there included. In addition
to these cases, if the order of which recognition is sought is one where the
court which made it purported to base, or may have based, its jurisdiction on
Art.31, the court asked to recognise or enforce the order is obliged to ascertain
for itself whether the order is of the type which is authorised to be made by
reason of Art.31: that is to say, that it was an order which properly fell within
the material scope of this Article.[839] This is not, therefore, a review of the
jurisdiction of the court which made the order.

Because the English court cannot investigate the jurisdiction of the foreign   **14–222**
court, it is no objection to enforcement that the foreign court took jurisdiction
wrongly, e.g. where it is alleged that the parties had agreed to the exclusive
jurisdiction of the English court or that the defendant had not voluntarily
appeared before the foreign court.[840] These questions must be raised at the
outset of proceedings before the foreign court and cannot be raised *de novo*,
or re-opened, in England at the point or recognition of the judgment. It is for
the court in which the proceedings are begun to rule on whether another court
has exclusive jurisdiction by virtue of an agreement under Art.23.[841] If the
foreign court decides that the agreement is invalid or inoperative, or decides
for any other reason that the alleged jurisdiction agreement is inapplicable and
that it has jurisdiction, then any resulting judgment will be enforceable in the
United Kingdom. This is so notwithstanding the terms of s.32 of the 1982 Act
(which would otherwise entitle the United Kingdom court to disregard a
foreign judgment given in disregard of a jurisdiction agreement) since that
section is expressly subject to the Regulation and the Convention.[842]

---

[836] Title II of the Lugano Convention.

[837] Art.35. For examples see German Federal Supreme Court, 1979, in *Digest* I–28–B3
(insurance); *Tonnoir v Vanherf SA* (Ct.App. Douai, 1989), 1991 *Clunet* 161 (consumer contract).
The court may also investigate the jurisdiction of the foreign court over a defendant domiciled or
habitually resident in a non-Member State with which there is a Treaty under Art.72 of the
Regulation (Art.67, Lugano Convention): see below, para.14–224; and it may also do so if the
judgment is to be recognised under the transitional provisions: Case C–163/95 *Van Horn v
Cinnamond* [1997] E.C.R. I–5451, [1998] Q.B. 214.

[838] And which has no direct precursor in the Brussels and original Lugano Conventions.

[839] *cf.* Case C–99/96 *Mietz v Intership Yachting Sneek BV* [1999] E.C.R. I–2277.

[840] Or that the foreign court misapplied the *lis alibi pendens* provisions of Art.27: *cf. Société
Brasserie du Pêcheur v Kreissparkasse Main-Spessart* [1997] I.L.Pr. 173 (French Cour de
cassation, 1996).

[841] See generally Case C–351/89 *Overseas Union Insurance Ltd v New Hampshire Insurance
Co* [1991] E.C.R. I–3317, [1992] Q.B. 434.

[842] On 1982 Act, s.32 (as amended by SI 2001/3929, Sch.2, para.14) see above, Rule 44; for
further discussion of s.32 in this context, see above, paras 14–206 *et seq.*

14–223   Where the defendant has appeared to protest the jurisdiction of the court of another Member or Convention State, Art.24 provides that the appearance is not a submission. If the foreign court holds that it has jurisdiction under the Regulation or the Convention (i.e. the defendant loses on the question of jurisdiction) and the defendant then contests the proceedings, any resulting judgment against the defendant will be enforceable in England because the foreign court found that it had jurisdiction under the Regulation (or the Convention) and the defendant submitted to its jurisdiction; if, however, the defendant takes no further steps in the proceedings and the foreign court enters a judgment in default of defence, it should only do so if it finds that it has jurisdiction in accordance with Art.26 and should not do so merely on the basis of the appearance to contest the jurisdiction; but if it finds it has jurisdiction the resulting judgment will be enforceable in England. There will be no room for refusal to enforce the judgment on the basis of s.33 of the 1982 Act on the theory that the defendant submitted only for the purpose of contesting the jurisdiction.[843]

14–224   **Grounds for refusal to recognise or enforce.** The other grounds for non-recognition and non-enforcement are set out in Arts 34 and 35 of the Regulation and the Lugano Convention, which correspond to, but do not exactly reproduce, Arts 27 and 28 of the Brussels Convention.[844] In addition, the effect of Art.35(1) is that the English court does not have to recognise or enforce a judgment of a Member or Convention State to the extent that it conflicts with an obligation of the United Kingdom assumed vis-à-vis a third State not to recognise "exorbitant" judgments given against domiciliaries or residents of that State.[845]

14–225   **Public policy.** The first ground is that recognition of the foreign judgment would be manifestly contrary to public policy in the State where its recognition or enforcement is sought. The public policy exception is to operate only in exceptional circumstances,[846] a fact which is reinforced by the incorporation of the word "manifestly" into Art.34(1). The European Court, in interpreting the corresponding provision in Art.27(1) of the Brussels Convention, provided a definition of when recognition may be said to be contrary to public policy: whereas the content of English public policy is a matter of English law alone, the role of that public policy within the framework of the Regulation and the Convention is a matter for the European Court. Before it may find recognition contrary to public policy, the court addressed must conclude that recognition would conflict, to an unacceptable degree, with the legal order in

---

[843] s.33 (as amended by SI 2001/3929, Sch.2, para.15, and on which see para.14–070) is not intended to affect enforcement under the Regulation or the Convention: s.33(2).

[844] Another ground not expressly mentioned is that the judgment is not enforceable in the State of the original court: see Jenard, p.50; Schlosser, para.220.

[845] Under Art.59 of the Brussels and original Conventions, which is applied in the Regulation by Art.72 and the Lugano Convention by Art.67. See above, para.14–202.

[846] Jenard, p.44; Case 145/86 *Hoffmann v Krieg* [1988] E.C.R. 645, 668; Case C–78/95 *Hendrickman v Magenta Druck & Verlag GmbH* [1996] E.C.R. I–4943; *cf. Klopp v Holder*, Cour de cassation, France, 1984, in 1985 *Rev. Crit.* 131, note Mezger; *Hupprichs v Dorthu*, Supreme Court, Netherlands, 1986 in [1990] I.L. Pr. 180. Contrast *Vanclef v Soc TTI*, Cour de cassation, France, in 1979 *Clunet* 380, note Holleaux.

the State of recognition because it would infringe a fundamental principle, or would involve a manifest breach of a rule of law which is regarded as fundamental within that legal order. Accordingly, where the adjudicating court had refused to hear a defendant who had placed himself in contempt of court, the recognising court was entitled to consider this to be a violation of Art.6 of the European Convention on Human Rights, and to refuse to recognise the judgment.[847] By contrast, where the adjudicating court had misapplied European competition law, the effect could not be regarded as the manifest breach of a fundamental right, serious enough to raise issues of public policy, especially as the adjudicating court had a proper procedure for the correction of errors by appeal or review.[848]

The European Court has held that a judgment entered after the defendant   **14–226** has been debarred from defending as a result of continued defiance of orders made by the court will be liable to be denied recognition only if the order was manifestly disproportionate to the aim of preventing a defiant defendant from bringing about a denial of justice, or involved a manifest and disproportionate denial of the right to be heard.[849] The fact that the English court had not identified any fundamental rule of English law which would be infringed if the court were to recognise a Cypriot judgment requiring the transferee of title to land in the occupied northern part of Cyprus meant that there was no basis in public policy for refusing to recognise the Cypriot judgment: speculation that such recognition might "complicate" efforts to reach a political settlement to the Cypriot problem furnished no possible basis for the application of Art.34(1).[850] National court decisions have applied this approach.[851] It is therefore plain that a mere difference between the substantive law (or the rules

---

[847] Case C–7/98 *Krombach v Bamberski* [2000] E.C.R. I–1935. For the proceedings before the European Court of Human Rights which found the French proceedings to have violated the defendant's right to a fair trial, see *Krombach v France*, February 13, 2001, noted (2001) 12 H.R. Case Digest 76. See Lowenfeld, in Einhorn and Siehr (eds.), *Intercontinental Cooperation Through Private International Law* (2002), p.229. The failure to notify a defendant that proceedings against him have been revived by a claimant after a delay of several years will also violate the right to a fair trial under Art.6 E.C.H.R., and recognition of the resultant judgment will conflict with public policy: *Maronier v Larmer* [2002] EWCA Civ 774, [2003] Q.B. 620 (CA). For the view that an English order for security for costs led to the claimant being denied access to justice, with the consequence that an English costs order would not be enforced in France on grounds of public policy, see *Pordea v Times Newspapers Ltd* [2000] I.L.Pr. 763 (France, Cour de cass., March 16, 1999).

[848] Case C–38/98 *Régie Nationale des Usines Renault SA v Maxicar SpA* [2000] E.C.R. I–2973.

[849] Case C–394/07 *Gambazzi v Daimler Chrysler Canada Inc* [2009] E.C.R. I–2563.

[850] Case C–420/07 *Apostolides v Orams* [2009] E.C.R. I–3571. See further *Apostolides v Orams* [2010] EWCA Civ 9, [2011] Q.B. 519 (rejecting the surprising contention that the European Court had overlooked the existence of a separate "international public policy" which might also be relevant to Art.34(1)).

[851] See further *National Navigation Co v Endesa Generacion SA (The Wadi Sudr)* [2009] EWCA Civ 1397, [2010] 1 Lloyd's Rep. 193 (fact that a foreign court has given judgment contrary to a contractual agreement to arbitrate will not make the recognition of judgment contrary to public policy unless the rule of English law set out in 1982 Act, s.32, is regarded as of fundamental importance within the English legal system, which s.32(4) shows it is not). A Greek court (*Case 1829/2006* [2008] I.L.Pr. 608) has refused to recognise an English costs order on the ground that its disproportion to the sum at stake in the proceedings made its recognition manifestly contrary to public policy. *cf. Tolstoy Miloslavsky v United Kingdom* (1995) 20 E.H.R.R. 442.

of private international law) of the original court and that of the court in which enforcement is sought is not sufficient to justify non-recognition or non-enforcement.[852] Moreover, recourse to public policy is inappropriate when the issue must be resolved on the basis of another provision of Art.34,[853] such as Art.34(2)[854] or Art.34(3).[855] In many countries, including England, a default judgment does not contain reasons, and the mere fact that a foreign judgment does not contain reasons should be insufficient for public policy to be invoked to deny recognition. But it appears that the French courts may not recognise a default judgment from another Member State if that judgment does not give reasons.[856] It is on the basis of evidence of a similar practice in other European States that the Commercial Court[857] is prepared, in effect, to conduct a trial (in the absence of the defendant) before giving judgment against a defendant who has not acknowledged service, so as to ensure that the judgment creditor would not be impeded in enforcing the judgment in other Member States.[858]

14–227   In England fraud is a ground for refusal of recognition or enforcement of a foreign judgment, and in this context fraud has a very wide meaning.[859] In civil law countries fraud is not a distinct reason for non-recognition, and neither the Regulation nor the Convention contains a special provision for fraud. But in civil law countries a judgment procured by fraud may be refused recognition on grounds of public policy, and this is reflected in the bilateral treaties, now superseded, between the United Kingdom and France and Germany. Under the Regulation and the Convention, though it is theoretically possible that the recognition of a judgment procured by fraud may be held to offend against the public policy of the court in which enforcement is sought,[860] it will in practice be very difficult. In *Interdesco SA v Nullifire Ltd*[861] it was held that the English court would not refuse enforcement of a French judgment on the ground of alleged fraud, even if there were newly discovered evidence, if the judgment debtor had a remedy in the French courts. That was because the public policy ground of recognition ought to

---

[852] See also *Re Enforcement of a Guarantee* (Case IX ZB 2/98) (German Fed Sup Ct) [2001] I.L.Pr. 425.

[853] Case C–78/95 *Hendrickman v Magenta Druck & Verlag GmbH* [1996] E.C.R. I–4943, 4968, citing Jenard, p.44.

[854] *ibid.*, below, para.14–229.

[855] Case 145/86 *Hoffmann v Krieg* [1988] E.C.R. 645, below, para.14–217.

[856] *Sarl Polypetrol v Soc Gen Routière* [1993] I.L.Pr. 107 (Cour de cassation, 1991); *Soc Transports Internationaux Dehbashi v Ceding* [1996] I.L.Pr. 104 (Cour d'App., Poitiers, 1991); *X Ltd v Y SA* (Swiss Federal Sup Ct, 2001), noted *Int. Lit. News* (International Bar Assn), October, 2001; *Masson v Ottow, Union Discount Ltd v Casamata*, 2007 *Clunet* 543; *Material Auxiliare d'Informatique v Printed Forms International* [2006] I.L.Pr. 803; *Society of Lloyd's v X* [2009] I.L.Pr. 161 (French Cour de cassation, 2008); and see Cuniberti (2008) 57 I.C.L.Q. 25.

[857] Acting under the inherent jurisdiction.

[858] *Berliner Bank v Karageorgis* [1996] 1 Lloyd's Rep. 426, followed in *Bhatia Shipping and Agencies Pvt Ltd v Alcobex Metals Ltd* [2004] EWHC 2323 (Comm.), [2005] 2 Lloyd's Rep. 336; *Habib Bank Ltd v Central Bank of Sudan* [2006] EWHC 1767 (Comm.), [2007] 1 W.L.R. 470.

[859] See para.14–138.

[860] *cf.* para.14–139 and *Kendall v Kendall* [1977] Fam. 208 (foreign divorce obtained by fraud refused recognition on grounds of public policy).

[861] [1992] 1 Lloyd's Rep. 180; *Société d'Informatique Service Réalisation Organisation v Ampersand Software BV* [1994] I.L.Pr. 55 (CA).

operate only in exceptional circumstances,[862] and the court in the State in which enforcement was sought should always consider whether the judgment debtor could seek a remedy in the foreign court.[863] On the footing that the legal systems in the Member States and Convention States all do allow a party who claims that he has suffered judgment as a result of fraud to bring proceedings to challenge the judgment, albeit that this may be subject to restrictive conditions, it is difficult to see when it will be manifestly contrary to public policy for a judgment obtained from the courts of such a system to be recognised.

Article 35(1) expressly provides that public policy cannot be used to re-open the question of jurisdiction of the original court. This would prevent, for example, an English court from invoking public policy in order to refuse to recognise a French judgment based on Art.14 of the Civil Code, in a case where the party suing was French, the defendant was domiciled in a non-Member State, and the case had nothing to do with France,[864] or a German court from refusing to enforce a judgment in favour of a civil party who intervened in criminal proceedings in a French court, and which had been founded on the nationality of the victim of the alleged offence.[865] But if the judgment was obtained by the claimant in defiance of an injunction ordering him not to institute or proceed with the foreign action, it will be contrary to public policy for the judgment to be recognised in England.[866] **14–228**

Right to defend. Article 34(2) is derived from Art.27(2) of the Brussels Convention, but places additional limits on its scope and effect. According to Art.27(2), a judgment is to be denied recognition if the judgment is in default of appearance, and either the defendant was not duly served with the document instituting the proceedings[867] (or an equivalent document), or was duly served, but not in sufficient time to arrange for his defence. Article 34(2) departs from this in two respects: it omits the word "duly" as a quality of the service, and adds a further element: that the defendant is to lose his shield if he failed to commence proceedings to challenge the judgment when it was possible for him to do so. The purpose of this provision (which is particularly **14–229**

---

[862] Jenard, p.44; *cf.* Case C–78/95 *Hendrickman v Magenta Druck & Verlag GmbH* [1996] E.C.R. I–4943.

[863] Schlosser, para.192. In *SA Marie Brizard et Roger International v William Grant & Sons Ltd*, 2002 S.L.T. 1365 (OH) it was held that where a foreign court's appellate procedure provided a sufficient safeguard against the possibility of bias or incompetence in the lower courts, it would be rare for recognition to be contrary to Scottish public policy.

[864] *cf.* Case C–7/98 *Krombach v Bamberski* [2000] E.C.R. I–1935.

[865] Case C–7/98 *Krombach v Bamberski* [2000] E.C.R. I–1935 (*cf.* Art.5(4) for the special jurisdictional basis for such claims).

[866] *Phillip Alexander Securities & Futures Ltd v Bamberger* [1997] I.L.Pr. 73; affirmed *ibid.* 104 (CA); *cf. Fakih Bros v AP Mailer (Copenhagen) Ltd* [1994] 1 Lloyd's Rep. 103. But contrast *Golubovich v Golubovich* [2010] EWCA Civ 810, [2011] Fam. 88 (Russian divorce recognised notwithstanding breach of English order restraining taking of steps in Russian proceedings); *National Navigation Co v Endesa Generacion SA (The Wadi Sudr)* [2009] EWCA Civ 1397, [2010] 1 Lloyd's Rep. 193, at [60] *et seq.* where the position was reconsidered in the light of Case C–185/07 *West Tankers Inc v Allianz SpA* [2009] E.C.R. I–663, [2009] 1 A.C. 1138).

[867] See Case C–14/07 *Ingenierbüro Weiss & Partner GbR v Industrie- und Handelskammer Berlin* [2008] E.C.R. I–3367 (material documents and requirement of service according to the Service Regulation).

important in relation to default judgments entered following substituted service on a defendant) is to safeguard the interests of the defendant and to ensure that he has sufficient time to defend himself.[868] But the Regulation and the Convention place the onus on the defendant, when he finds out about the entry of judgment, to take such steps as may be open to him to challenge it, in the absence of which the defence is withdrawn.

14–230   The defence applies only to judgments given in default of appearance,[869] but this expression has been held to have an autonomous meaning, rather than being defined by strict reference to the law of the adjudicating court. In *Hendrickman v Magenta Druck & Verlag GmbH*[870] a German court gave judgment against a defendant in circumstances where a legal representative purported to be authorised to represent the defendant but where, according to the defendant, no such authorisation had been given.[871] As a matter of German law the judgment was not entered in default of appearance, but the European Court accepted that the judgment was to be seen as one in default of appearance, for the defendant had been "quite powerless to defend himself" and was on that account to be regarded as a defendant in default of appearance. It is unlikely that the consequent extension of the scope of Art.34(2) will be wide, but in some circumstances the argument that a defendant lacked a proper opportunity to be heard may now be accommodated under Art.34(2), whether or not the judgment was technically in default of appearance.[872]

14–231   A judgment in default of appearance may retain this character even if the defendant later seeks, unsuccessfully, to set it aside.[873] The opportunity to apply for a legal remedy after the making of the order may not be equivalent, but may instead be inferior, to having the right to be heard before the order is made. If, however, the defendant has had and has exercised the opportunity to challenge the judgment, was under no handicap in doing so, and was entitled as part of that challenge to argue that he had not been served in time to make his defence, Art.34(2) will no longer be available, and the question whether the judgment is still to be regarded as one given in default of appearance is without substance.[874] The overriding question is whether the procedure of the foreign court was sufficient to protect the rights of the defendant to defend.

Article 34(2) applies whether or not the defendant is domiciled or resident in the State of the court of origin.[875]

14–232   The court in which enforcement of a default judgment is sought must consider the manner in which service was effected and whether, following

---

[868] Case 166/80 *Klomps v Michel* [1981] E.C.R. 1593, 1605; Case 228/81 *Pendy Plastic Products v Pluspunkt* [1982] E.C.R. 2723.

[869] Which excludes appearance for the sole purpose of contesting the jurisdiction of the court: Case C–39/02 *Maersk Olie & Gas A/S v De Haan & De Boer* [2004] E.C.R. I–9657.

[870] Case C–78/95 [1996] E.C.R. I–4943.

[871] This will be a matter for the recognising court to determine for itself: see p.4967.

[872] This reasoning, however, was not applied to the defendant in Case C–7/98 *Krombach v Bamberski* [2000] E.C.R. I–1935, even though he had no opportunity to be heard as a direct result of the order of the court.

[873] Case C–123/91 *Minalmet GmbH v Brandeis Ltd* [1992] E.C.R. I–5661; Case C–78/95 *Hendrickman v Magenta Druck & Verlag GmbH* [1996] E.C.R. I–4943.

[874] Case C–420/07 *Apostolides v Orams* [2009] E.C.R. I–3571.

[875] Case 49/84 *Debaecker and Plouvier v Bouwman* [1985] E.C.R. 1779; *cf.* Case 166/80 *Klomps v Michel* [1981] E.C.R. at p.1621, *per* Reischl A.-G.

service, the defendant had sufficient time to arrange for his defence.[876] So far as concerns the manner of service, Art.27(2) of the Brussels Convention was understood to allow and require an English court to re-open and consider for itself whether service was effected in accordance with the law of the court of origin,[877] provided that the court of origin has not been seised of this question in adversary proceedings.[878] If service was not made in accordance with that law, it could not be said to have been *duly* made, and it was not open to an English court to purport to cure by reference to its own procedural law, or to overlook, the defect in service.[879] The omission of the word "duly" in the corresponding provision of the Brussels I Regulation and revised Lugano Convention was deliberate and was designed to change the law: the fact that service on the defendant may not have been made in strict compliance with the procedural law of the state in which judgment was given will not automatically mean that the door to the defence in Art.34(2) will be opened.[880] But there must still be some form of service which may be regarded as having been sufficient to protect the rights of the defence; by contrast, if there is an irregularity so gross that the purported or failed service was not sufficient to secure the rights of the defence, the case will fall within Art.34(2).[881] Of course, if the defendant is well aware that there has been purported service, and that judgment has been entered, but has taken no step to challenge the

---

[876] Case 166/80 *Klomps v Michel* [1981] E.C.R. 1593, applied in Case 228/81 *Pendy Plastic Products v Pluspunkt* [1982] E.C.R. 2733. Both conditions must be fulfilled: Case C–305/88 *Isabelle Lancray SA v Peters und Sickert KG* [1990] E.C.R. I–2725; Case C–123/91 *Minalmet GmbH v Brandeis Ltd* [1992] E.C.R. I–5661. See also *Artic Fish Sales Co Ltd v Adam (No.2)*, 1996 S.L.T. 970; *Selco Ltd v Mercier*, 1996 S.L.T. 1247.

[877] Though a German court has held that even though service may have been made in accordance with the law of the State of origin, this is not due service, as it is an unlawful discrimination on grounds of nationality, proscribed by what is now Art.18, TFEU. In *Re the Enforcement of a French Interlocutory Order* [2001] I.L.Pr. 208 (Case 9W 67/97) the court refused to regard as effective service by delivery to the court office (remise au parquet) for onward transmission to the defendant, as it was considered to discriminate against non-French defendants on grounds which could not be objectively justified. Subsequently, a different German court made a reference to the European Court in relation to the same points. By its judgment in Case C–522/03 *Scania Finance France SA v Rockinger Spezialfabrik für Anhängerkupplungen GmbH & Co* [2005] E.C.R. I–8639 the Court confirmed that service of the document instituting the proceedings was required to have been made in accordance with Art.IV of the Protocol annexed to the Brussels Convention; and it refrained from answering the question concerned with discrimination in methods of service. See, for elaborate discussion on how service is required to be made, *Ólafsson v Gissurarson (No.2)* [2008] EWCA Civ 152, [2008] 1 W.L.R. 2016, [167].

[878] See also Case 49/84 *Debaecker and Plouvier v Bouwman* [1985] E.C.R. 1779. On service under the Hague Convention, see *Noirhomme v Walklate* [1992] 1 Lloyd's Rep. 427.

[879] Case C–305/88 *Isabelle Lancray SA v Peters & Sickert KG* [1990] E.C.R. I–2725. Breaches of the law of the court of origin other than those relating to due service may not be relied on to impugn the quality or effectiveness of service: Case C–474/93 *Hengst Import BV v Campese* [1995] E.C.R. I–2113.

[880] Case C–283/05 *ASML Netherlands BV v Semiconductor Industry Services GmbH* [2006] E.C.R. I–12041; Case C–14/07 *Ingenierbüro Weiss & Partner GbR v Industrie- und Handelskammer Berlin* [2008] E.C.R. I–3367; Case C–420/07 *Apostolides v Orams* [2009] E.C.R. I–3571. Judgments from territories still covered by the Brussels Convention will continue to require service to have been *duly* made: see *Ólafsson v Foreign and Commonwealth Office* [2009] EWHC 2608 (QB) (a case on the original (1988) Lugano Convention).

[881] Case C–420/07 *Apostolides v Orams* [2009] E.C.R. I–3571; see also *Tavoulareas v Tsavliris (No.2)* [2006] EWCA Civ 1772, [2007] 1 W.L.R. 1573.

judgment, the effect of Art.34(2) is that the judgment will be recognised, regardless of the quality of service; by contrast, under the Brussels Convention, where service had not been *duly* made, Art.27(2) treated this as sufficient to deny recognition to the judgment[882] (though if the defect in service might have been, and had been, cured according to the law of the court of origin, service could be treated as duly made[883]).

14–233   The question whether service was effected in sufficient time is a question of fact, which is not to be determined on the basis of the law of the court of origin or of English law as the law of the court in which enforcement is sought. Thus the fact that service was properly effected under the law of the court of origin does not preclude re-examination of whether it was effected in sufficient time.[884] As a general rule the court in which enforcement is sought may confine its examination to ascertaining whether the period reckoned from the date on which service was effected allowed the defendant sufficient time to arrange for his defence. Nevertheless the court must consider whether, in the particular case, there are exceptional circumstances which warrant the conclusion that although service was effected, it was, however, inadequate for the purpose of enabling the defendant to take steps to arrange for his defence (because it did not in fact come to his notice until some time later) and accordingly could not cause the time stipulated by Art.34(2) to begin to run. In considering whether it is confronted with such a case, the English court may take account of all the circumstances (including those occurring after service is effected[885]) such as the means employed for effecting service, the relations between the claimant and the defendant or the nature of the steps which had to be taken in order to prevent judgment from being given in default.[886] If, for example, the dispute concerns commercial relations and if the document which instituted the proceedings was served at an address at which the defendant carries on his business activities, the mere fact that the defendant was absent at the time of service should not normally prevent him from arranging his defence, especially if the action necessary to avoid a judgment in default may be taken informally and by a representative. A question which arose in *Klomps v Michel*,[887] and which has considerable practical importance with regard to certain forms of judgment was whether a *Zahlungsbefehl*, or order to pay, under German law was the document instituting the proceedings for the purposes of enforcement. The European Court ruled that a measure such as the order for payment in German law, service of which on the defendant enables the plaintiff, where no objection to the order is made, to obtain an enforceable decision was to be understood as being

---

[882] *Ólafsson v Foreign and Commonwealth Office* [2009] EWHC 2608 (QB).

[883] Case C–123/91 *Minalmet GmbH v Brandeis Ltd* [1992] E.C.R. I–5661.

[884] Case 49/84 *Debaecker and Plouvier v Bouwman*, above.

[885] For a list of possible circumstances see VerLoren van Theemat A.-G. in Case 49/84 *Debaecker and Plouvier v Bouwman*, above; see also *Re A Belgian Default Judgment* [1992] I.L.Pr. 528 (German Fed Sup Ct 1991).

[886] See *Jurgens v TSN Kunststoffrecycling GmbH* [2002] EWCA Civ 11, [2002] 1 W.L.R. 2459 (CA).

[887] Case 166/80 [1981] E.C.R. 1593; in Case C–474/93 *Hengst Import BV v Campese* [1995] E.C.R. I–2113 it was held that the Italian *decreto ingiuntivo*, together with the application instituting the proceedings, was "the document which instituted the proceedings". See also Case C–39/02 *Maersk Olie & Gas A/S v De Haan & De Boer* [2004] E.C.R. I–9657.

covered by the words "the document which instituted the proceedings". The enforcement order, issued following service of an order for payment and which is, in itself, enforceable, was not the relevant document.[888]

The defendant will lose the protection of Art.34(2) if he failed to commence **14–234** proceedings to challenge the judgment when it was possible for him to do so. This aims to overcome the sense of disquiet at the behaviour of a defendant who knows perfectly well of the proceedings which have been commenced against him, but who elects to do nothing about them, and who then relies on a shortcoming in the service of process. If it is not possible for him to challenge the judgment, Art.34(2) will not penalise the failure. Moreover, it would accord with principle that the defendant should not be penalised either unless the steps which were open to him to take were not, in effect, steeper and more difficult than would have been the case if he had been properly notified of the institution of proceedings and had had an opportunity to participate. This submission is consistent with the judgment of the European Court in *Apostolides v Orams*,[889] and is inherent in the proposition that the underlying purpose of Art.34(2) is to safeguard the rights of the defence.

Incompatibility with a judgment from the courts of the State in which **14–235** **recognition is sought.** Article 34(3) provides that a judgment[890] irreconcilable with a judgment given[891] in a dispute between the same parties in the State in which recognition is sought shall not be recognised. Its practical importance will be limited by Arts 27 to 30 which in effect give priority to the court first seised.[892] The court which is second to be seised with the same cause of action must give up its jurisdiction or stay its proceedings,[893] and must recognise the judgment of the first court under Art.33. It is not necessary under Art.28 for the same cause of action to be involved. But where (for whatever reason) there are irreconcilable judgments, then the English court may refuse to recognise or enforce the foreign judgment even if it was rendered before the conflicting English judgment, and even if the English judgment is outside the scope of the Regulation or the Convention.[894]

Judgments are irreconcilable when they entail consequences which are **14–236** mutually exclusive.[895] A judgment awarding damages for breach of contract

---

[888] Case C–14/07 *Ingenierbüro Weiss & Partner GbR v Industrie- und Handelskammer Berlin* [2008] E.C.R. I–3367; *British Seafood Ltd v Kruk* [2008] EWHC 1528 (Comm.).

[889] Case C–420/07 [2009] E.C.R. I–3571.

[890] The rule applies to judgments, but not to authentic instruments or to settlements approved in the course of judicial proceedings: Case C–414/92 *Solo Kleinmotoren GmbH v Boch* [1994] E.C.R. I–2237; see also Arts 57 and 58 of the Regulation. But it does also apply to judgments granting or refusing to grant interim measures where such decisions from the courts of two States are irreconcilable, it being irrelevant that the irreconcilability arises from divergent perceptions of the need for the orders sought before each court or from other differences of procedural law: Case C–80/00 *Italian Leather SPA v WECO Polstermoebel GmbH & Co* [2002] E.C.R. I–4995. See also above, para.12–066, n.316.

[891] If there are proceedings pending in England but no judgment which has yet been given, Art.34(3) has no application: *Landhurst Leasing Plc v Marcq* [1998] I.L.Pr. 822 (CA).

[892] See above, Rule 38(3).

[893] But only until the jurisdiction of the first court is established; when this happens it must dismiss its proceedings.

[894] Case 145/86 *Hoffmann v Krieg* [1988] E.C.R. 645.

[895] Case 145/86 *Hoffmann v Krieg* [1988] E.C.R. 645; *Macaulay v Macaulay* [1991] 1 W.L.R. 179.

would be irreconcilable with one declaring that the contract had been rescinded; and a declaration of non-liability of one party to the other may[896] be irreconcilable with a judgment awarding damages. But a judgment awarding an unpaid seller the price would not be irreconcilable with a judgment awarding damages to the buyer for breach of warranty.

14–237   **Preliminary questions as to status.** Article 27(4) of the Brussels Convention provided for the non-recognition of a judgment where the original court, in order to arrive at its judgment, decided a preliminary question concerning the status of legal capacity of natural persons, rights in property arising out of a matrimonial relationship, wills or succession in a way that conflicts with a rule of the private international law of the court in which recognition or enforcement is sought, unless the same result would have been reached by the application of the rules of private international law of the latter. But this provision is not reproduced in the Regulation and the revised Lugano Convention and, formally at least, this ground of non-recognition is no longer available when they apply. But the effect of the deletion is much less than this would suggest: as the status or legal capacity of natural persons, rights in property arising out of a matrimonial relationship, wills and succession are excluded from their material scope by Art.1(2)(a) in any event, a judgment whose recognition would require the State addressed to give effect to the ruling of a foreign court which contradicted its own view on status, etc., will fall outside the scope of the Regulation and the Convention.[897]

14–238   **Conflicts with foreign judgments which qualify for recognition.** Article 34(4)[898] provides that a judgment shall not be recognised if it is irreconcilable with an earlier judgment given in a Member State or a non-Member State[899] involving the same cause of action and between the same parties, provided that this latter judgment fulfils the conditions necessary for its recognition in the State addressed. No further explanation is necessary: as long as the prior judgment qualifies for recognition in the State addressed, whether under the

---

[896] It will depend on the breadth or basis of the declaration and its compatibility with the basis for the damages award. The question whether an order to constitute a limitation fund is irreconcilable with a judgment made in proceedings to establish liability is now pending before the European Court: Case C–39/02 *Maersk Olie & Gas A/S v De Haan and De Boer* [2004] E.C.R. I–9657.

[897] In *T v L* [2008] IESC 48, [2009] I.L.Pr. 46, the Irish Supreme Court interpreted the Regulation as leading to the same result as in *Hoffmann v Krieg*, which supports the view that the disappearance of Art.27(4) of the Brussels Convention from the text of the Regulation has had little effect. *cf. Navigation Co v Endesa Generacion SA (The Wadi Sudr)* [2009] EWCA Civ 1397, [2010] 1 Lloyd's Rep. 193.

[898] Lugano Convention, Art.34(4). By contrast, Art.27(5) of the Brussels Convention applied only to prior judgments from non-Convention States, and neither it nor any other Article made provision for cases in which two Convention State judgments were irreconcilable. It is to be supposed that the solution in Art.34(4) of the Regulation will be applied to fill the gap; and for the position at common law, see *Showlag v Mansour* [1995] 1 A.C. 431 (PC).

[899] Even though a solution has now been given, it is to be noted that it is the earlier judgment, as distinct from the judgment in the proceedings which were instituted earlier in time, which is given the right to be recognised.

Regulation (if it is a judgment from a Member State which falls within the scope of the Regulation) or under the conflict of laws rules of the State addressed (if it is not), this fact precludes recognition of the subsequent Member State judgment.

Procedure. The combined effect of Art.38 and of Sch.1 to the Civil Jurisdiction and Judgments Order 2001[900] is that enforcement of a judgment under the Regulation is by way of registration.[901] The judgment creditor cannot bring an action on the original cause of action.[902] Nor, it seems, can he proceed by way of enforcement at common law; this follows from the decision in *De Wolf v Cox*[903] where it was held that it would be incompatible with the enforcement provisions of the Brussels Convention to allow an action on the original cause of action, even though it might be cheaper to obtain summary judgment on the original cause of action than to enforce a foreign judgment. Interest is payable on a registered judgment debt at the rate applicable under the law of the court of origin, not only for the period prior to registration[904] but also until satisfaction of the judgment.[905] It is implicit in the Regulation system that judgments should be registered in their original currency.

14–239

The procedure for registration is regulated by Arts 39 to 52, as supplemented by the Civil Procedure Rules.[906] Initial registration of the judgment is made by application without notice to the judgment debtor,[907] and the judgment debtor, who has no right to be heard on the initial application, is notified only after registration is effected.[908] By contrast with the position under the Brussels Convention, which permitted the registering court power to refuse registration if it considered that there was a defence to recognition, Art.41 removes any such right from the court when dealing with an application for

14–240

---

[900] SI 2001/3929, paras 2 to 6.

[901] The same procedure applies to judgments recognised and enforced under the Conventions: in the case of judgments recognised and enforced under the Lugano Convention, the effect of registration is provided by the 1982 Act, as amended by SI 2009/3131. The procedures are substantially identical. The application is made by an "interested party": for the case where the initial application is made by the judgment creditor, but who dies before the application is heard, see *Haji-Ioannou v Frangos* [2009] EWHC 2310 (QB), [2009] I.L.Pr. 936.

[902] Case 42/76 *De Wolf v Cox* [1976] E.C.R. 1759; *B v R* [2009] EWHC 2026 (Fam.), [2010] 1 F.L.R. 563; 1982 Act, s.34.

[903] See above.

[904] As under the 1933 Act.

[905] SI 2001/3929, Sch.1, para.5 (1982 Act, s.7).

[906] CPR, r.74.1–11. In relation to what is now Art.40(2) see Case 198/85 *Carron v Germany* [1986] E.C.R. 2437; *Rhatigan v Textiles Confecciones Europeas SA* [1990] I.L.R.M. 825.

[907] But as the Regulation (and the Lugano Convention) provides for the enforcement of non-money judgments as well, this terminology, though convenient, is not completely accurate.

[908] Art.42, to which CPR, r.74.6 applies. For the documents required to make the application, see Art.53 and Annex V and CPR, r. 74.4(6). For defects in the documents, and the power of the recognising court to cure the defect, see Case C–275/94 *Van der Linden v BFE* [1996] E.C.R. I–1393; Case C–3/05 *Verdoliva v J M Van der Hoeven BV* [2006] E.C.R. I–1579. However, both authorities, which are concerned with the Brussels Convention, may need to be read in the light of the less rigid approach of the Regulation: it may be sufficient that the service be sufficient to inform the judgment debtor that a judgment has been registered.

registration of a judgment: all it may do is ascertain that the formal requirements set out in Art.53[909] have been complied with. If registration is ordered,
the judgment debtor may appeal[910] to a judge[911] against registration of the
judgment, though the time limits on bringing of the appeal are strict;[912] if
registration was refused,[913] the judgment creditor may likewise appeal.[914]
According to Art.45(1), the appeal against registration may only be founded
on the grounds listed in Arts 34 and 35, but this must be an error on the part
of the drafters: an appellant must be entitled to question whether the judgment
falls within the scope of the Regulation or the Convention,[915] or that the
provisions of some other law or international treaty preclude its recognition.[916] The decision on the first appeal may be itself appealed by the losing
party one further time, but only on a point of law.[917] Before the expiry of the
time for appealing against the order for registration has expired, or before such
appeal has been determined, the execution of the judgment is not possible,[918]
although protective measures may be taken:[919] the policy is that measures
should be available to prevent the judgment debtor from being able to frustrate
a later enforcement, and there is therefore a strong presumption in favour of

---

[909] That is to say, that there is an authenticated copy of the judgment, and a completed
certificate in the form set out in Annex V. See also Case C–619/10 *Trade Agency Ltd v Seramico
Investments Ltd* (pending) (judgment debtor contradicting the content of the certificate from the
court in which judgment was given which states that he was served).

[910] See Art.43 of and Annex III; CPR, r.74.8. It is the judgment debtor alone who has standing
to appeal against the order for registration (and, presumably, the judgment creditor who may
appeal against a refusal to order registration): see Case 148/84 *Deutsche Genossenschaftsbank v
Brasserie du Pêcheur SA* [1985] E.C.R. 1981; Case C–172/91 *Sonntag v Waidmann* [1993]
E.C.R. I–1963; C–167/08 *Draka NK Cables Ltd v Omnipol Ltd* [2009] E.C.R. I–3477. But the
Art.43 appeal procedure is concerned with appeals against the authorisation of enforcement, and
do not permit an appeal from a decision refusing a stay of enforcement under Art.46 while there
is an appeal pending in the State of origin: Case C–183/90 *Van Dalfsen v Van Loon* [1991] E.C.R.
4743; see also Case 258/83 *Brennero SAS v Wendel GmbH* [1984] E.C.R. 3971.

[911] The court which will hear the appeal is listed in Annex III of the Regulation (as amended
by Council Regulation (EC) 280/2009, [2009] O.J. L93/13) and of the Lugano Convention.

[912] Art.43(5): one month after service of the notice of registration, though if the judgment
debtor is domiciled in a Member or Convention State other than that of enforcement, this is
extended to a fixed period of two months. Where he is not domiciled in a Member or Convention
State, the period is two months, but which may, in an appropriate case, be extended: CPR,
r.74.8(3). See *Citibank NA v Rafidain Bank* [2003] EWHC 1950 (QB), [2003] I.L.Pr. 758.

[913] Which will be rare, at least if the formal requirements have been met.

[914] Also under Art.43.

[915] Under Art.1; also that it does not fall within its temporal scope (Art.66).

[916] e.g. Arts 67 and 71(2)(b), second paragraph.

[917] Art.44, to the court identified in Annex IV of the Regulation (as amended by Council
Regulation (EC) 280/2009, [2009] O.J. L93/13) and of the Lugano Convention. This is the
exclusive remedy: Case 145/86 *Hoffmann v Krieg* [1988] E.C.R. 645.

[918] Art.47.

[919] Art.47. The measures may last only until the expiry of the appeal period: *Citoma Trading
Ltd v Republic of Brazil* [1999] C.L.C. 1847. The nature and availability of these protective
measures otherwise depends on national procedural law, and there is no question of there being
a *right* to any particular form of protective measure: *Banco Nacional de Comercio Exterior SNC
v Empresa de Telecomunicaciones de Cuba SA* [2007] EWCA Civ 662, [2008] 1 W.L.R. 1936,
[2008] Bus. L.R. 1265. See also *Elwyn (Cottons) Ltd v Pearle Designs Ltd* [1989] I.R. 9 (further
proceedings: *Elwyn (Cottons) Ltd v Master of the High Court* [1989] I.R. 14). See generally
Lipstein (1987) 36 I.C.L.Q. 873.

their being granted.[920] If the judgment is still subject to appeal in the State of origin, the court hearing the first appeal under Art.43, or the further appeal under Art.44 may[921] stay the proceedings before it to await the outcome in the State of origin, or may grant enforcement conditional upon the giving of security, so as to preserve a proper balance between the parties.[922]

Recognition. Article 33 of the Regulation[923] distinguishes between recog-   **14–241**
nition and enforcement and provides that: (a) a judgment given in a Member State shall be recognised in the other Member States without any special procedure being required.[924] This was designed to abolish special procedures for recognition existing in some countries, such as Italy; (b) any interested party who raises the recognition of a judgment as the principal issue in a dispute may apply for a decision that the judgment be recognised.[925] This is designed to deal with a situation where a person who is not a party to the action in which a judgment was given wishes to raise the judgment as a defence, e.g. a bank in Member State B presented with a bill of exchange which has already been declared invalid in Member State A. In this case the jurisdiction of the court which gave the original judgment does not have to be verified by the court of the Member State in which the recognition is sought unless the matter in question falls within the scope of provisions relating to insurance, contracts, consumer contracts, or exclusive jurisdiction; (c) if the outcome of the proceedings in a court of a Member State depends on the determination of an incidental question of recognition that court shall have jurisdiction over the question.

The object of Art.33 is to confer on judgments the authority and effective-   **14–242**
ness accorded to them in the Member State in which they were given,[926] and accordingly a foreign judgment which is to be recognised under Art.33 must in principle have the same effect in the Member State in which recognition is sought as it does in the Member State in which it is given.[927] The grounds for

---

[920] Case 119/84 *Capelloni v Pelkmans* [1985] E.C.R. 3147 (where it was also held that national law cannot require a separate judicial proceeding for protective measures; or require them to be taken before the appeal procedure under what is now Art.43 of the Regulation is exhausted; or make an order for protective measures subject to a confirmatory hearing).

[921] But is not obliged to: *DHL GBS (UK) Ltd v Fallimento Finmatica SpA* [2009] EWHC 291 (Comm.), [2009] 1 Lloyd's Rep. 430.

[922] Art.46, departing from the corresponding provisions in Art.38 of the Brussels Convention which was held to confer these powers only on the court hearing the first appeal: Case C–432/93 *Société d'Informatique Service Réalisation Organisation v Ampersand Software BV* [1995] E.C.R. I–2269; see also Case 258/83 *Brennero SAS v Wendel GmbH* [1984] E.C.R. 3971; *Petereit v Babcock International Ltd* [1990] 1 W.L.R. 350; *Banco Nacional de Comercio Exterior SNC v Empresa de Telecomunicaciones de Cuba SA* [2007] EWHC 2322 (Comm.).

[923] Art.33 of the Lugano Convention is materially identical.

[924] Recognition involves according to the judgment the same effects in the State in which enforcement is sought as it does in the State in which the judgment was given: Case 145/86 *Hoffmann v Krieg* [1988] E.C.R. 645. See also *Berkeley Administration Inc v McClelland* [1995] I.L.Pr. 201 (CA); and see further the discussion at para.14–220, above.

[925] See CPR, r.74.10 for the procedure.

[926] Jenard, p.43.

[927] Case 145/86 *Hoffmann v Krieg* [1988] E.C.R. 645, 666 (an enforcement case); *Boss Group Ltd v Boss France SA* [1997] 1 W.L.R. 351 (CA) (finding made in provisional proceedings in France not binding).

non-recognition are the same as those for refusal to enforce.[928] The effect of Art.33 is that the English court will have to recognise judgments of Member States within the scope of the Regulation and will have very limited power to examine the jurisdiction of the foreign court.[929] Neither the Regulation, nor the Conventions or their Official Reports, gives an answer to the difficult question of the scope of the estoppel which arises when the foreign judgment dismisses a case on grounds which are regarded in some countries as procedural and in others as substantive.[930]

14–243   **Orders made to assist the enforcement of English judgments.** The orders may be sought or made against persons (whether the judgment debtor, or those associated with him) domiciled in other Member (or Convention) States, or may relate in some respect to assets located in other Member or non-Member States (or Convention or non-Convention States). In three judgments, the Court of Appeal considered various orders which might be made, after final judgment had been given against a defendant which had submitted to the jurisdiction of the English courts, to assist the judgment debtor in enforcing the English judgment. In essence, it held that where the court had exercised jurisdiction to try the merits of the claim against a defendant who had submitted to the jurisdiction of the court, the jurisdictional rules of the Regulation were no obstacle to the making of orders (i) requiring the judgment debtor to refrain from bringing proceedings before the courts of non-Member States which were designed to frustrate the enforcement of the judgment, including by seeking to relitigate the question of original liability;[931] (ii) appointing a receiver by way of equitable execution;[932] and (iii) requiring a director of the judgment debtor to attend for examination as to the assets of the judgment debtor.[933] In all three cases, the court understood its power to derive from the fact that the defendant had submitted to its jurisdiction over the merits of the claim, and that this fact allowed it to make any and all such orders as were necessary to the effective exercise of that jurisdiction.[934] It is nevertheless to be inferred that if the court had had jurisdiction on some basis other than submission, the conclusions would have been the same, on the ground that it was the existence of jurisdiction under Chapter III of the Regulation, rather than the particular Article which gave the court that jurisdiction, which formed the basis for its power to make the orders applied for. Two limitations subsequently emerged. The House of Lords held that the power to summon an office-holder for examination was not, as a matter of

---

[928] Art.34.

[929] See, e.g. *The Atlantic Emperor (No.2)* [1992] 1 Lloyd's Rep. 624 (CA) (judgment of Italian court that contract did not incorporate arbitration clause).

[930] See Schlosser, para.191. This is not likely to arise frequently in practice since the Foreign Limitation Periods Act 1984: see para.14–037.

[931] *Masri v Consolidated Contractors International Co SAL (No.3)* [2008] EWCA Civ 625, [2009] Q.B. 450.

[932] *Masri v Consolidated Contractors International Co SAL (No.2)* [2008] EWCA Civ 303, [2009] Q.B. 503.

[933] Under CPR, r.71.2: *Masri v Consolidated Contractors International Co SAL (No.4)* [2008] EWCA Civ 876, [2010] 1 A.C. 90.

[934] Case C–391/95 *Van Uden Maritime BV v Deco-Line* [1998] E.C.R. I–7091.

English law, exercisable against a person out of the jurisdiction[935] and the
Court of Appeal subsequently held that it was an infringement of the principle
of comity for an English court to direct a person appointed to hold office as
judicial administrator of a foreign company to cooperate with the receiver on
pain of being found to be in contempt where there was a real risk that this
might place the administrator in breach of the law under which he had been
appointed.[936]

Authentic instruments and court-approved settlements. Chapter III of   **14–244**
the Regulation,[937] deals with the recognition and enforcement of judgments.
Though the category is broad enough to include, and does encompass, judgments by consent,[938] it does not extend to certain other procedural measures,
found under the law of certain other Member States, by which a dispute may
be brought to an end. The recognition and enforcement of two such measures
is dealt with in Chapter IV.

An authentic instrument is a document which has been formally drawn up   **14–245**
or registered as such. It must be drawn up by a public official, usually a civil
law notary.[939] Under the law of certain Member States, such as Germany, the
instrument takes effect as an express, conclusive, and enforceable, statement
of a party's indebtedness, but which is obtained without the institution of court
proceedings. Authentic instruments may be enforced in another Member State
in accordance with the procedures in Arts 38 *et seq.* of the Regulation;[940] the
application for enforcement may be refused or a declaration of enforceability
revoked only if enforcement of the instrument is manifestly contrary to the
public policy of the Member State in which enforcement is sought.

A settlement which has been approved by a court in the course of proceed-   **14–246**
ings is not regarded as a judgment within the scope of Chapter III, for it
derives its authority from the parties' agreement, and not from the adjudication of a court; for this reason it does not enjoy the authority of *res judicata*.[941]

---

[935] *Masri v Consolidated Contractors International Co SAL (No.4)* [2009] UKHL 43, [2010]
1 A.C. 90.

[936] *Joujou v Masri* [2011] EWCA Civ 746.

[937] And Title III of the Lugano Convention. For the procedure which governs the enforcement
in England of authentic instruments and court settlements from other Member States, see SI
2001/3928, which makes minor adaptations to the provisions of SI 2001/3929.

[938] *cf.* Case C–414/92 *Solo Kleinmotoren GmbH v Boch* [1994] E.C.R. I–2237, at 2245, *per*
Gulmann A.-G., drawing a distinction between this and a court-approved settlement.

[939] For examples, see German Code of Civil Procedure, Art.794; *Office de Prevoyance v
Grand*, 1991 *Clunet* 162 (Cour d'App. Paris, 1990); *Tonon v Office Cantonal de la Jeunesse de
Tutlingen* [1995] I.L.Pr. 23 (French Cour de cassation, 1991). But if the law of the State in
question does not require the participation of, and authentication by, a public official, the
document drawn up will not be an authentic instrument for these purposes: Case C–260/97
Unibank A/S v Christensen [1999] E.C.R. I–3715: promissory note formally drawn up and
enforceable under Danish law not authentic instrument as authentication by public official, even
though this was not required by Danish law for the instrument to be enforceable. See also Fitchen
(2011) 7 J.Priv.Int.L. 33.

[940] See *Re Baden-Württembergische Bank AG* [2009] CSIH 47.

[941] An English judgment by consent, though not an adjudication, has the authority of *res
judicata*: *Landhurst Leasing Plc v Marcq* [1998] I.L.Pr. 822 (CA). See para.14–204, above, n.785,
per Gulmann A.-G. Contrast the English "Tomlin order", whereby proceedings are stayed except
for the purpose of putting into effect the terms of settlement scheduled to the order: that is not a
judgment.

But if it is enforceable in the Member State in which it was concluded, it may be enforced under the same conditions as govern the enforcement of authentic instruments.

14–247   **Clause (2) of the Rule.** In further pursuit of its aim of making the enforcement of judgments across the Member States as subject to as little judicial scrutiny as possible, Regulation (EC) 805/2004[942] of the European Parliament and Council creates the "European Enforcement Order" for judgments given on uncontested claims. The Regulation, applicable from October 21, 2005[943] to all judgments given after that date,[944] provides that where judgment has been given on a claim for a specific sum of money, and the defendant did not contest the claim, the adjudicating court may certify the judgment for enforcement under an European Enforcement Order, which the judgment creditor may thereupon present for enforcement in any Member State.[945] There is no right of appeal against issue of the certificate,[946] and very little opportunity is allowed for the judgment debtor to object to enforcement in the receiving court.[947] It is to be expected that once the principle of the European Enforcement Order has been established, it will be extended to judgments in respect of other forms of claim, whether for unliquidated sums or for other relief, and whether the claim is contested or not. The eventual aim is that the substantive law on recognition and enforcement of judgments should be replaced by a system in which any judicial order from a judge in a Member State has the force of law in every other Member State and is equivalent in effect to an order made by a local judge.[948]

14–248   The procedure applies to judgments in civil and commercial matters, which expression has the same definition as that in the Brussels I Regulation save for the specific further exclusion of "the liability of a State for acts and omissions in the exercise of state authority (*'acta jure imperii'*)".[949] The definition of judgment is the same as in the Brussels I Regulation;[950] the certificate may not be issued unless the judgment is enforceable in the State of origin.[951] The original court must not have violated Sections 3 and 6 of Chapter II of the Brussels I Regulation, and there are further jurisdictional restrictions where

---

[942] 2004 O.J. L143/15 [2004]. The procedural rules supplementing the Regulation form Section V of CPR Pt 74 (which is supplemented by Practice Direction 74B). See also Crifò, *Cross-Border Enforcement of Debts in the EU* (2009).

[943] Art.33.

[944] Art.26: the date on which the proceedings were instituted is therefore irrelevant. The EEO Regulation applies equally to court-approved settlements, and to documents formally drawn up or registered as authentic instruments: Art.3(2).

[945] Art.5. "Member State" means a Member State other than Denmark: Art.1(3).

[946] Art.10(4). For making objection to the issue of the certificate by an English court, see CPR, r.74.30.

[947] For the procedure in England, see CPR Pt 74, Section V.

[948] See Council and Commission, *Action Plan implementing the Hague Programme on strengthening freedom, security and justice in the European Union* [2005] O.J. C198/1, at pp.20–21. In the process of review of the Brussels I Regulation, the European Commission has made the reduction or abolition of what remains of the *exequatur* procedure a high priority, though it is as yet unclear whether Member States are prepared to abandon all judicial control over the judgments from other Member States which may be enforced within their territory.

[949] Art.2.

[950] Art.4(1).

[951] Art.6(1)(a).

the judgment is against a consumer.[952] The claim must have been one for payment of a specific[953] sum of money which has fallen due or the date for which is indicated in the judgment. The procedure therefore excludes claims for unliquidated or general damages or for damages to be assessed.

The critical definitional element is that the claim be regarded as uncon-   **14–249**
tested.[954] A claim is regarded as uncontested if (a) the debtor expressly agreed to it by admission or by means of a court approved settlement or in a settlement in the course of proceedings, or (b) the debtor never objected to it, in compliance with the relevant procedural requirements under the law of the Member State or origin in the course of court proceedings, or (c) the debtor did not appear and was not represented at a court hearing regarding that claim after having initially objected to the claim in the course of court proceedings, provided that such conduct amounts to a tacit admission of the claim or of the facts alleged by the creditor under the law of the Member State of origin, or (d) the debtor expressly agreed to it in an authentic instrument. It appears to follow that a defendant to proceedings in England who ticks the boxes to show that he acknowledges service and denies that he is admitting the claim[955] will take the claim against him outside the scope of the Regulation. But if this is all he does, there is a risk that the claim, though initially contested, will become regarded as an uncontested one.[956] It is to be supposed that the filing of a defence will prevent the claim being seen as uncontested, for no question will normally arise of the claim being admitted, even though the further defence of the claim is absent. On the other hand, the basic principle under-pinning the procedure is that judgment on a claim which is expressly or tacitly admitted should be enforceable, and the failure to oppose an application for summary judgment, or to appear at the trial, risks being seen as a tacit consent to the judgment, making the judgment one on an uncontested claim.

The certificate, the form of which is prescribed in the Regulation,[957] is   **14–250**
issued by the court which gives judgment. The procedure for obtaining an order for the enforcement of the judgment set out in Chapter III of the Brussels I Regulation is thereupon redundant.[958] The certificate may be issued if the judgment is enforceable in the State of origin. The issuing court must also certify that it did not violate the provisions on exclusive jurisdiction regardless of domicile, or the provisions on insurance contracts and contracts made by consumers; and where the judgment is against a consumer domiciled in a Member State the judgment must be from the court of his domicile unless the consumer expressly agreed to the claim.[959] The Regulation prescribes in some detail procedural "minimum standards" which must have been observed

---

[952] Art.6(1)(c), (d). But any objection based on these provisions must be taken before the original court, and may not be raised before the receiving court: see below. For the procedure in England, see CPR, rr.74.28 and 74.29.

[953] Which presumably includes a claim for a sum which may be made specific by arithmetic.

[954] Art.3(1).

[955] Or who does the equivalent in answer to a foreign claim form.

[956] Art.6(1)(c).

[957] Art.9 and Annex I.

[958] Art.5.

[959] Art.6.

and which guarantee the defendant's right to notification of the claim and his right to be heard on it.[960]

14–251   A claim that there is a material error in the certificate, or that it was "clearly wrong" to grant it may be made to the court which issued it, but there is no right of appeal, and no right to raise these matters before any other court.[961] Only if the certificate is irreconcilable with an earlier judgment from the courts of another State, given in proceedings between the same parties and on the same cause of action, and then only if this irreconcilability neither was nor could have been raised before the original court, may enforcement be resisted.[962] The apparent fact that an English court is deprived of all right to find that the enforcement of the judgment is in manifest conflict with its public policy, or is given no the opportunity to conclude that the proceedings in the original court violated Art.6 of the European Convention on Human Rights,[963] is perplexing; the proposition that the rights of the defendant[964] are sufficiently secured by allowing him to be heard before, and only before, the original court is unconvincing.[965]

14–252   The procedure does not affect bilateral treaties preserved by Art.72 of the Brussels I Regulation,[966] and does not otherwise affect that Regulation[967] or the Service Regulation.[968]

14–253   **Further enforcement of orders made in specific debt recovery procedures.** Building on the foundation of the European Enforcement Order, the European Union has developed a number of schemes for improving the recovery of debts: most of these contain provision for the simplification of enforcement measures for orders made within their scope. The European Order for Payment ("EOP") Regulation[969] provides for order made pursuant to it to be certified in order for them to be enforced: the grounds on which the certification may be opposed are restricted.[970] The European Small Claim Procedure ("ESCP") Regulation[971] provides for orders made in the procedure to be certified and enforced.[972] The Mediation Directive[973] makes provision

---

[960] Ch.III, Arts 12–19.

[961] Art.10.

[962] Art.21.

[963] *cf. Maronier v Larmer* [2002] EWCA Civ 774, [2003] Q.B. 620 (Dutch judgment held to have violated Art.6, ECHR).

[964] Especially if the defendant is a consumer.

[965] But a very similar argument was rejected by the European Court in two cases concerned with judgments concerning the removal and return of children under the Brussels IIa Regulation (Case C–491/10 PPU *Aguirre Zarraga v Pelz* [2011] I.L.Pr. 659, and Case C–211/10 PPU *Povse v Alpago* [2011] 3 W.L.R. 164), where the issue arises in much more acute form, and there is no realistic prospect of its being permitted to oppose enforcement of a judgment certified under the EEO procedure.

[966] Art.22.

[967] Art.27.

[968] That is, Council Regulation (EC) 1348/2000: Art.28.

[969] Regulation (EC) 1896/2006, [2006] O.J. L399/1.

[970] Enforcement in England is governed by CPR, Pt 78.

[971] Regulation (EC) 861/2007, [2007] O.J. L199/1.

[972] Enforcement in England is governed by CPR, Pt 78.

[973] Council Directive 2008/52/EC, [2008] O.J. L136/3, partially given effect in England by Cross-Border Mediation Directive Regulations 2011, SI 2011/1133. Enforcement in England is governed by CPR, Pt 78, Section III.

for certain agreements resulting from cross-border mediation to be enforced as though they were judgments. In additions, proposals for the attachment of bank accounts[974] and for the disclosure of debtors' assets[975] are envisaged.

ILLUSTRATIONS

1. A, a Frenchman, obtains a judgment against X, an Englishman, for €500,000 in a French court. The judgment is registrable in England under the Brussels I Regulation and the Civil Jurisdiction and Judgments Order 2001.[976]

2. A obtains a final order from the French court ordering X to return a chattel to A. X brings the chattel to England. The order is registrable under the Brussels I Regulation and the Civil Jurisdiction and Judgments Order 2001.

3. The facts are as in Illustration 2, except that the order is a provisional one pending trial of the merits in France. The provisional order is registrable.

4. A, a Frenchman, sues in France X, who is resident in New York, for €1,000,000 for breach of a contract to be performed in New York. X does not appear in the French court, which assumes jurisdiction on the basis of A's French nationality under Art.14 of the Civil Code. A obtains a default judgment. The judgment is registrable in England. The position would be different if the United Kingdom and the United States were to have entered into a treaty requiring non-enforcement of judgments rendered by third States on the basis of exorbitant provisions such as Art.14 of the French Civil Code, or if references to New York and the United States had been to Ontario and Canada, respectively.[977]

5. A & Co, a German company, obtains from a German court, without notice to the respondent, X & Co, an English company, an injunction, which restrains X & Co from various acts in relation to tapes made by a pop music group. The order is not registrable in England.[978]

6. A, a French public authority, obtains a default judgment in France against X, an Englishman who is not present or resident in France, and who has not submitted to the jurisdiction of the French courts. The judgment is registrable under the Brussels I Regulation and the 2001 Order if the matter is a "civil or commercial matter" but not otherwise.[979]

7. A, a Frenchman, sues in France X, an Englishman, who is not resident in France, for breach of contract. X does not submit to the French jurisdiction. The French court assumes jurisdiction on the mistaken view that the contract was to be performed in France, and A obtains a default judgment. The judgment is registrable.

8. The facts are as in Illustration 7 except that X appears in the French proceedings to contest the jurisdiction but his objection fails and he takes no further part in the proceedings and judgment is entered in default of appearance. The judgment is registrable, not because of the appearance but because the French court has found that it has jurisdiction.

9. The facts are as in Illustration 7, except that service on X under French law is not effected. Without proof of more, the judgment, is not registrable. But if X has since learned of the judgment, but taken no steps before the French court to challenge it, it will be registrable.[980]

10. A, a Frenchman, obtains a judgment in France against X, an Englishman. X appeals the judgment in France. A is entitled to register the judgment, but the English court may stay enforcement pending the appeal.[981]

11. A Frenchman obtains a judgment in France against X, a Frenchman with assets in England, and obtains an order for its registration. X appeals to the judge in chambers against the registration. Pending the appeal, A cannot execute the judgment, but the English court may order X not to remove his assets from the jurisdiction.[982]

14–254

14–255

14–256

---

[974] COM(2011) 455 Final, July 25, 2011.
[975] COM(2008) 128 Final, March 6, 2008.
[976] SI 2001/3929.
[977] Art.59 of the Brussels Convention, which is carried across into the Regulation by Art.72.
[978] *EMI Records Ltd v Modern Music GmbH* [1992] Q.B. 115.
[979] Case 29/76 *LTU GmbH v Eurocontrol* [1976] E.C.R. 1541.
[980] Art.34(2).
[981] Art.46.
[982] Art.47.

12. A & Co, a French company, obtain a judgment in France for damages to be assessed against X & Co, an English company. X & Co's appeal fails, and judgment is entered for 7 million euros. A & Co register the judgment in England. X & Co institute a special form of procedure before the Court of Appeal in Paris to set aside the judgment on the ground that it was obtained by fraud. X & Co also seek to set aside the registration in England on the ground that recognition would be manifestly contrary to public policy. Registration is confirmed because X & Co have a sufficient remedy in the French court, and no stay of enforcement can be ordered because the application to the Court of Appeal in Paris is not an "ordinary appeal" within the meaning of Art.46.[983]

14–257   13. A, the receiver of a German company, obtains a judgment in Germany against X & Co, an English company. X & Co appeal against the judgment. A registers the judgment in England. The court stays execution conditionally on X & Co providing security pending the outcome of the appeal in Germany.[984]

14. A, a Belgian, brings proceedings in Belgium against X, an Englishman, who has left his residence without leaving a forwarding address. Substituted service pursuant to Belgian law is effected on X at a Belgian police station. Subsequently X informs A's lawyer of his new address, but service is not effected at the new address, and A obtains a judgment in default. In considering whether service was effected on X in sufficient time for him to arrange for his defence, the English court may take into account the fact that A was informed of X's new address, and also the fact that X contributed to the failure of the document originating the proceedings to reach him. But if X has learned of the judgment and has not taken steps before the Belgian court to challenge it, it will be entitled to recognition by reason of his default.[985]

15. The facts are as in Illustration 14, except that the substituted service was not in accordance with Belgian law. Without proof of more, the judgment is not registrable.[986] But if X has learned of the judgment but not taken steps before the Belgian court to challenge it, it will be registrable.[987]

16. A French court gives judgment against X, having partially debarred X from participation on the ground of his failure to comply with orders made by the court. On an application to set aside registration of the judgment in Germany, a German court is entitled to find that Art.6 of the European Convention on Human Rights furnishes a reason why recognition would be manifestly incompatible with German public policy.[988]

17. An English court gives judgment against X when X is debarred from defending by reason of his contempt. On X's application to set aside registration of the judgment in Italy, the Italian court is entitled to find that recognition would be manifestly contrary to Italian public policy only if the debarring order made by the English court was a manifest and disproportionate infringement of the right to be heard.[989]

18. A court in a Member State gives judgment against X in circumstances in which the court may be seen to have misapplied a provision of European competition law. Registration of the judgment in another Member State may not be set aside on the ground that the error by the original court renders recognition manifestly contrary to public policy.[990]

19. A Cypriot court gives judgment against X in a dispute over title to land in the occupied north of Cyprus. The judgment is given in default of appearance, but X is served with the judgment and applies to have it set aside. After a full hearing, the application is rejected. The judgment may be registered in England, even though it had originally been given in default of appearance; the fact that the judgment was, in practice, not capable of being performed in the place where the land was did not mean that it was not enforceable according to Cypriot law.[991]

---

[983] *Interdesco SA v Nullifire Ltd* [1992] 1 Lloyd's Rep. 180.

[984] *Petereit v Babcock International Ltd* [1990] 1 W.L.R. 350.

[985] Case 49/84 *Debaecker and Plouvier v Bouwman* [1985] E.C.R. 1779 (a case on Art.27(2) of the Brussels Convention, and which would therefore be reasoned differently under Art.34(2) of the Regulation).

[986] Case C–305/88 *Isabelle Lancray SA v Peters und Sickert KG* [1990] E.C.R. 1–2725 (a case on Art.27(2) of the Brussels Convention).

[987] As a result of the changes brought about by Art.34(2) of the Regulation.

[988] Case C–7/98 *Krombach v Bamberski* [2000] E.C.R. I–1935.

[989] Case C–394/07 *Gambazzi v Daimler Chrysler Canada Inc* [2009] E.C.R. I–2563.

[990] Case C–38/98 *Régie Nationale des Usines Renault SA v Maxicar SpA* [2000] E.C.R. I–2973.

[991] Case C–420/07 *Apostolides v Orams* [2009] E.C.R. I–3571.

20. A judgment is given against X by a Belgian court. The judgment is registered for enforcement in the Netherlands, but the order for registration is appealed against on the ground that the judgment has now been satisfied. The appeal is inadmissible as no such ground for setting aside registration is given in the Regulation; an objection of this kind is instead to be taken within the framework of the Dutch procedure for execution.[992]

21. A and X have entered into a contract which, according to X, requires them submit any disputes to arbitration. In proceedings claiming damages brought by A before a Spanish court, the court rules that there is no obligation to arbitrate. Even if the judgment of the Spanish court is to the opposite effect from that which an English court would have given, the judgment was a judgment given in a civil and commercial matter, in relation to which the ruling on arbitration was incidental to the claim for damages, and it is therefore required to be recognised in England.[993]

(4) PARTS II AND IV OF THE CIVIL JURISDICTION AND JUDGMENTS ACT 1982

RULE 56—(1) A money judgment of a court in any part of the United Kingdom has, on a certificate being duly registered in a Superior Court of any other part of the United Kingdom, the same force and effect as a judgment of the court in which the certificate is registered, and proceedings for or with respect to its enforcement may be taken, as if the certificate had been a judgment originally given in the court in which the certificate is registered.[994]   **14R–258**

(2) A non-money judgment of a court in any part of the United Kingdom has, on being duly registered in a Superior Court of any other part of the United Kingdom, the same force and effect as a judgment of the court in which it is registered, and proceedings for or with respect to its enforcement may be taken, as if it had been a judgment originally given in the court in which the judgment is registered.[995]

The term "Superior Court"[996] means in this Rule,

(a) as applied to England, the High Court of Justice in England;

(b) as applied to Northern Ireland, the High Court of Justice in Northern Ireland;

(c) as applied to Scotland, the Court of Session in Scotland.

(3) A judgment from a territory in respect of which provision has been made for the recognition and enforcement of judgments on grounds corresponding to those of the Brussels Convention may be enforced or, as the case may be, recognised, according to the terms of that provision.[997]

COMMENT

Clauses (1)–(2) of the Rule. Until the 1982 Act came into force the enforcement of judgments of the courts of a part of the United Kingdom in   **14–259**

---

[992] Case C–139/10 *Prism Investments BV v JA Van Der Meer qq Arilco Holland BV*, October 13, 2011.

[993] *National Navigation Co v Endesa Generacion SA (The Wadi Sudr)* [2009] EWCA Civ 1397, [2010] 1 Lloyd's Rep 193. The correctness of the decision is, however, open to question.

[994] 1982 Act, s.18 and Sch.6.

[995] 1982 Act, s.18 and Sch.7.

[996] Schs 6 and 7, para.5(2).

[997] 1982 Act, s.39.

other parts was regulated by the antiquated and limited procedure of the Judgments Extension Act 1868 and the Inferior Courts Judgments Extension Act 1882. The main defect of the dual system under the 1868 and 1882 Acts was that enforcement was limited to money judgments. An important difference between the 1868 Act and the 1920 and 1933 Acts was that, subject to one exception, under the 1868 Act the enforcing court was not entitled to investigate the jurisdiction of the original court and could not disregard its judgment on the ground that it lacked international jurisdiction. The exception was where a Scots judgments was founded on arrestment and entered in default. Under the 1882 Act there were stringent jurisdictional requirements. The 1982 Act makes the international jurisdiction of the original court irrelevant. If the judgment has been pronounced by a court in the United Kingdom, a court in another part of the United Kingdom cannot question the exercise of its jurisdiction.

14–260　　Section 18 applies the provisions of Schedules 6 and 7 to the enforcement in one part of the United Kingdom of money and non-money judgments given by a court in another part. Judgments are widely defined.[998] The extension of the enforcement system to non-money judgments is novel.[999] But it does not apply to interlocutory orders.[1000] "Judgments on judgments" cannot be enforced,[1001] at least where they are judgments registered under the statutory provisions for enforcement of foreign judgments, including the 1982 Act itself. So if a French judgment is registered in Scotland under the 1982 Act, it will be the French judgment which the judgment creditor will have to register in England and not the Scottish registration.

14–261　　The procedure by way of registration is the exclusive procedure.[1002] In the case of money judgments, the party who wishes to enforce applies for a certificate from the original court, and, in the case of non-money judgments, for a certified copy of the judgment. Once registered, the judgment of the original court has effect as a judgment of the court in which it is registered. A certificate (or certified copy) is not to be issued unless under the law of the part of the United Kingdom in which the judgment was given two conditions are fulfilled: first, either (i) the time for bringing an appeal against the judgment has expired, no such appeal having been brought within that time; or (ii) such an appeal having been brought within that time, that appeal has finally been disposed of; and, secondly, enforcement of the judgment is not for the time being stayed or suspended, and the time available for its enforcement has not expired. If the conditions are fulfilled, the officer of the original court issues a certificate, in the case of a money judgment, stating the sum or aggregate of sums (including any costs or expenses) payable under the money provisions contained in the judgment, the rate of interest, if any, payable thereon and the date or time from which any such interest began to accrue; and

---

[998] See s.18(2), (4) for a full list of the judgments to which it applies. See also Proceeds of Crime Act 2002, s.443; see also SI 2002/3133.

[999] For the procedure in the High Court see CPR, rr.74.15 and 16.

[1000] 1982 Act, s.18(5)(d).

[1001] 1982 Act, s.18(7).

[1002] 1982 Act, s.18(8). See *Clarke v Fennoscandia Ltd*, 1998 S.C. 464 (no injunction to restrain enforcement of English costs order).

stating that the conditions concerning the absence of an appeal or enforce-ability of a judgment are satisfied. In the case of a non-money judgment he issues a certified copy of the judgment. Where a certificate (or certified copy of a judgment) has been issued any interested party may, within six months from the date of its issue, in the case of money judgments (there is no time limit for non-money judgments) apply to the proper officer of the Superior Court in any other part of the United Kingdom for the certificate (or judgment) to be registered. Where application is made to the proper officer, he registers the certificate in court. Where a certificate or judgment is registered the reasonable costs of obtaining the certificate and its registration are recover-able. In the case of money judgments, provision is made for interest from registration at the rate, if any, stated in the certificate.

The registering court may, if it is satisfied that any person against whom it   **14–262** sought to enforce the certificate is entitled and intends to apply under the law of the part of the United Kingdom in which the judgment was given for any remedy which would result in the setting aside or quashing of the judgment, stay proceedings for the enforcement of the certificate (or judgment). A certificate or registered judgment must be set aside by the registering court if it is satisfied that registration was contrary to the provisions of Sch.6 or 7; and may set aside the registration if it is satisfied that the matter in dispute in the proceedings in which the judgment in question was given had previously been the subject of a judgment by another court or tribunal having jurisdiction in the matter. But fraud is not a ground for setting registration aside.[1003]

Clause (3) of the Rule. Section 39 of the 1982 Act[1004] provides that   **14–263** provision may be made corresponding[1005] to that in the Brussels Convention for the recognition and enforcement of judgments from any colony. Provision has been made under the section for judgments from Gibraltar;[1006] these will be treated for the purposes of English law[1007] as if Gibraltar were a Contract-ing State to the Convention. Such a judgment may therefore be registered for enforcement under s.4 of the 1982 Act,[1008] and the only permitted grounds of objection to the registration will be those set out in Rule 55.

(5) COMMUNITY JUDGMENTS

RULE 57—A Community judgment to which the Secretary of State has   **14R–264**
appended an order for enforcement must be registered in the High Court,

---

[1003] See *Parkes v MacGregor* [2008] CSOH 43, 2008 S.C.L.R. 345.

[1004] As amended by SI 1990/2591, Art.10.

[1005] Modifications are permitted: s.39(1).

[1006] SI 1997/2602 (in force February 1, 1998). As a result of SI 1997/2601, the 1920 Act will no longer apply to Gibraltar. Judgments from the Isle of Man, Jersey, and Guernsey are at present governed by the 1933 Act; those from Akrotiri and Dhekelia by the 1920 Act.

[1007] But for the purposes of the Brussels I Regulation, judgments of the courts of Gibraltar will take effect in Member States other than the United Kingdom as though they were judgments of the courts of the United Kingdom. The Spanish Supreme Court was hostile to the proposition that judgments from the courts of Gibraltar may be recognised or enforced in Spain under the Brussels Convention: see [2003] I.L.Pr. 9.

[1008] It is not expressly so provided by the Order. But if Gibraltar is to be regarded as if Art.31 of the Brussels Convention applied to it, s.4(1) of the 1982 Act will mean that the judgment may be registered for enforcement.

whereupon it has for all purposes of execution the same force and effect as if it had been a judgment or order made by the High Court.[1009]

COMMENT

14–265 The European Communities (Enforcement of Community Judgments) Order 1972 provides that a Community judgment[1010] to which the Secretary of State has appended an order for enforcement[1011] shall, upon application duly made by the person entitled to enforce it, be registered in the High Court.[1012] A "Community judgment" means a judgment of the European Court of Justice or of the Arbitration Committee of the European Atomic Energy Community, or a decision of the Council or Commission of the European Communities imposing a pecuniary obligation on persons other than States, or a decision of the High Authority of the European Coal and Steel Community which includes a pecuniary obligation on undertakings.

14–266 If the judgment has been partly satisfied, the judgment is registered only for the unpaid balance.[1013] The effect of registration is that the judgment has for all purposes of execution the same force and effect as if it had been a judgment or order given or made by the High Court; and proceedings may be taken on it and any sum payable under it carries interest accordingly.[1014] The Order in Council is not confined to judgments under which a sum of money is payable.

14–267 An order of the European Court that the enforcement of a registered Community judgment be suspended must be registered and has the same force and effect as if the order had been made by the High Court staying the execution of the judgment.[1015] No steps to enforce the judgment can then be taken while the order remains in force.

14–268 If a Euratom inspection order[1016] is registered, the High Court may make such order as it thinks fit against any person for the purpose of ensuring that effect is given to the order.[1017]

[1009] European Communities (Enforcement of Community Judgments) Order, SI 1972/1590, amended by Administration of Justice Act 1977, Sch.5, Pt I. The 1972 Order is further amended by SI 1998/1259, to make provision for Council Regulation (EC) 40/94 on the Community Trade Mark, and by SI 2003/3204 to make provision for Council Regulation (EC) 6/2002 on Community Designs. CPR, r.74.19 is amended accordingly.

[1010] Any decision, judgment or order which is enforceable under Art.187 or 192 of the EEC Treaty (now Arts 280, 299, TFEU); Art.18, 159 (no longer in force) or 164 of the Euratom Treaty; Art.44 or 92 of the ECSC Treaty (no longer in force).

[1011] Defined as an order by or under the authority of the Secretary of State that the Community judgment to which it is appended is to be registered for enforcement in the United Kingdom: *ibid.*

[1012] *ibid.* Art.3(1): or in the Court of Session or the High Court in Northern Ireland: *ibid.* Art.2(1).

[1013] *ibid.* Art.3(4).

[1014] *ibid.* Art.4.

[1015] *ibid.* Art.5.

[1016] Defined as an order made by or in the exercise of the functions of the President of the European Court or by the Commission of the European Communities under Art.81 of the Euratom Treaty: *ibid.* Art.2(1).

[1017] *ibid.* Art.6.

(6) JUDGMENTS AGAINST THE UNITED KINGDOM

**RULE 58—A judgment given against the United Kingdom by a court in a   14R–269
State which is a party to the European Convention on State Immunity
will be recognised in the United Kingdom, if it was given in proceedings
in which the United Kingdom was not entitled to immunity by virtue of
provisions corresponding to sections 2 to 11 of the State Immunity Act
1978 and if it is final in the sense that it is not subject to appeal or liable
to be set aside.**[1018]

Provided that no judgment will be recognised under this Rule if
**(a)   it would be manifestly contrary to public policy or if any party to
the proceedings in which the judgment was given had no adequate
opportunity to present his case;**[1019] **or**
**(b)   the judgment was given without proper notice having been given
to the United Kingdom and the United Kingdom has not entered
an appearance or applied to have the judgment set aside;**[1020] **or**
**(c)   prior proceedings between the same parties are pending in the
United Kingdom or another State party to the Convention;**[1021]
or
**(d)   the judgment is inconsistent with a prior judgment of a court in
the United Kingdom or of a court in another State party to the
Convention;**[1022] **or**
**(e)   the judgment is in respect of proceedings relating to an interest of
the United Kingdom in movable or immovable property arising by
way of succession, gift or *bona vacantia*, and either (i) the foreign
court would not have had jurisdiction if it had applied rules of
jurisdiction corresponding to those applicable to such matters in
the United Kingdom; or (ii) the foreign court applied a law other
than that indicated by the United Kingdom rules of private international law and would have reached a different conclusion if it
had applied the law so indicated.**[1023]

COMMENT

Sections 18 and 19 of the State Immunity Act 1978 are designed to give effect,   **14–270**
in part, to Arts 20–22 of the European Convention on State Immunity of
1972,[1024] which set out the circumstances in which a Contracting State is
bound to give effect to a judgment given against it in another Contracting
State in circumstances where it is not immune from the jurisdiction. The broad

---

[1018] State Immunity Act 1978, s.18(1).
[1019] s.19(1)(a).
[1020] s.19(1)(b).
[1021] s.19(2)(a).
[1022] s.19(2)(b).
[1023] s.19(3). There are no unified rules of jurisdiction and choice of law in these matters in the
United Kingdom, but English and Scots law are similar.
[1024] For Text see Cmnd. 7742. See Sinclair (1973) 22 I.C.L.Q. 254, 266–267, 273–276. A
certificate of the Secretary of State is conclusive as to whether a State is party to the Convention:
State Immunity Act 1978, s.21(c).

effect of ss.18 and 19 is to provide for *recognition* (but not enforcement[1025]) of judgments given in other Contracting States against the United Kingdom in circumstances where a foreign government would not have been immune from similar proceedings in the United Kingdom.[1026] Recognition may be refused on grounds of public policy, but only where it is manifestly contrary to public policy. Proviso (e) is concerned with judgments relating to interests in movable or immovable property arising by way of succession, gift or *bona vacantia*, and follows closely the wording of Art.20(3) of the Convention.

4. PROTECTION OF TRADING INTERESTS ACT 1980

14R–271   **Rule 59—No judgment given in a court of a country outside the United Kingdom will be enforced under any of Rules 42, 53 or 54 if it is**
   (a)   a judgment for multiple damages, or
   (b)   a judgment based on a provision or rule of law specified by the Secretary of State as concerned with the prohibition of restrictive trade practices.

COMMENT

14–272   This Rule is based upon s.5 of the Protection of Trading Interests Act 1980, which prohibits the enforcement under the common law, and under the 1920 and 1933 Acts,[1027] of foreign judgments for multiple damages and other foreign judgments specified by statutory instrument as concerned with restrictive trade practices. It was enacted in order to counteract what was perceived by the United Kingdom to be an excessive exercise of jurisdiction by United States courts in anti-trust actions.[1028] Similar (but not identical) legislation has been enacted in Australia, Canada, and South Africa.[1029]

14–273   A judgment for multiple damages is defined as a judgment for an amount arrived at by doubling, trebling or otherwise multiplying a sum assessed as compensation for the loss or damage sustained by the judgment creditor.[1030]

[1025] Presumably an action on a relevant foreign judgment could be brought against the Crown as for a debt, although process of execution would not lie: Crown Proceedings Act 1947, ss.1, 25.

[1026] See Exceptions to Rule 26, above.

[1027] If an attempt were made to register in England a judgment from another Member State which fell within the definition of judgments to which the Act applies, its recognition in England would be manifestly contrary to public policy, and Art.34(1) of the Brussels I Regulation would mean that recognition would be forbidden: see above, Rule 55.

[1028] The exercise of anti-trust jurisdiction by United States courts gave rise to misgivings in the United Kingdom for many years: see, e.g. *British Nylon Spinners Ltd v Imperial Chemical Industries* [1953] Ch. 19 (CA); *Re Westinghouse Uranium Contract Litigation MDL Docket No.235* [1978] A.C. 547; *cf. British Airways Board v Laker Airways Ltd* [1985] A.C. 58, 78; *Midland Bank Plc v Laker Airways Ltd* [1986] Q.B. 689 (CA). See also Lowe (1981) 75 A.J.I.L. 257, *Extraterritorial Jurisdiction* (1983), pp.176–192; Lowenfeld (1981) 75 A.J.I.L. 629; and generally Jennings (1957) 33 B.Y.I.L. 153; FA Mann, *Studies in International Law* (1973), pp.82–94; Collins [1986] J.B.L. 372 and 542 (reprinted in Collins, *Essays*, Ch.8).

[1029] Foreign Proceedings (Excess of Jurisdiction) Act 1984 (Aus); Foreign Extraterritorial Measures Act 1984 (Can) (amended 1996 Statutes, Ch.28); Protection of Businesses Act 1978 (SA).

[1030] s.5(3).

But where a foreign court has given judgment in respect of several causes of action, and the multiplication of damages has been applied to some but not to others of them, the judgment may be severed and the prohibition imposed by s.5 confined to those causes of action for which damages were multiplied, leaving the others unaffected.[1031] The scope of judgments whose enforcement is prohibited may be extended by the Secretary of State to any judgment based on a provision or rule of law which appears to him to be concerned with the prohibition or regulation of agreements, arrangements or practices designed to restrain, distort or restrict competition in the carrying on of business of any description or to be otherwise concerned with the promotion of such competition.[1032]

The judgments most likely to be affected by the Act are judgments in **14–274** United States anti-trust actions,[1033] but the Act applies to judgments of all overseas countries[1034] whether rendered before or after the passage of the Act.[1035] Judgments caught by section 5 are wholly unenforceable, and not merely as regards that part of the judgment which exceeds the damages actually suffered by the judgment creditor.

Section 6 of the Protection of Trading Interests Act 1980 goes further and **14–275** gives British citizens, corporations incorporated in the United Kingdom, and persons carrying on business in the United Kingdom against whom multiple damages have been awarded the right to recover from persons in whose favour the judgment was rendered so much of the damages as exceeds the sum assessed by the foreign court as compensation for the loss or damage sustained. This section does not apply in favour of an individual who was ordinarily resident, or of a corporation which had its principal place of business, in the foreign country where the proceedings in which the judgment was given were instituted; nor does it apply to judgments concerned with activities exclusively concerned with a branch or establishment carried on by the defendant in the foreign proceedings in that country.[1036] The section contains the unusual provision that proceedings under it may be brought notwithstanding that the plaintiff in the foreign proceedings is not within the jurisdiction of the United Kingdom court.[1037] Permission to serve the proceedings is not required.[1038]

The effect of s.6 is that where a United States corporation obtains a **14–276** judgment for treble damages against an English company and is able to

---

[1031] *Lewis v Eliades* [2003] EWCA Civ 1758, [2004] 1 W.L.R. 692.

[1032] s.5(4). The power of the Secretary of State is exercisable by statutory instrument: s.5(5).

[1033] For claims under the US Racketeer Influenced and Corrupt Organisations Act (RICO), see also *Société Commerciale de Réassurance v Eras International Ltd (No.2)* [1995] 2 All E.R. 278, 307–312; *Simon Engineering Plc v Butte Mining Plc* [1996] 1 Lloyd's Rep. 104n, at 111. But for the possibility of severance of RICO awards from other causes of action, see *Lewis v Eliades* [2003] EWCA Civ 1758, [2004] 1 W.L.R. 692.

[1034] Defined by s.7(2) to mean any country outside the UK other than one for whose international relations the UK Government is responsible.

[1035] But it does not apply to judgments which had actually been registered under the 1920 or 1933 Acts, or where judgment had been obtained at common law on the foreign judgment, before its passage: s.5(6).

[1036] s.6(3), (4).

[1037] s.6(5).

[1038] This is because proceedings under the Act covered by CPR, rr.6.32(2), 6.33(2).

execute the judgment in the United States against the English company's assets there, the English company may sue in England to recover the punitive element. English proceedings in these circumstances will only be of assistance to the English company if either the United States corporation has assets in the United Kingdom (e.g. a branch or shares in a subsidiary) or in a country which will recognise the English judgment. The Australian, Canadian and South African legislation goes further. The Australian Foreign Proceedings (Exercise of Jurisdiction) Act 1984 provides[1039] that any corporation which is related to the foreign plaintiff is liable to repay the relevant part of the judgment given in the foreign anti-trust proceedings. The Canadian Foreign Extraterritorial Measures Act 1984 provides[1040] that the Canadian court which gives judgment for the recovery of damages paid under a foreign anti-trust judgment may order the seizure and sale of shares of any Canadian corporation in which the foreign plaintiff has a direct or indirect beneficial interest. The South African Protection of Businesses Act 1978,[1041] as amended in 1984, makes corporations which control, or are controlled by, the foreign plaintiff jointly and severally liable to repay damages.

14–277   By s.7 of the 1980 Act[1042] provision may be made by Order in Council for the reciprocal enforcement in the United Kingdom of foreign judgments which are given pursuant to foreign laws designed to counteract multiple damages awards. This power may be exercised if the following conditions are met: (a) the law of the foreign country provides for the enforcement of United Kingdom judgments given under s.6 of the 1980 Act; (b) the foreign judgment is given under a provision of the foreign law relating to the recovery of sums paid or obtained pursuant to a judgment for multiple damages within the meaning of the 1980 Act. The Australia–United Kingdom Agreement of 1990 provides for the reciprocal recognition and enforcement of such "clawback" judgments.[1043]

[1039] s.10(5).

[1040] s.9(2). But the Canadian legislation is restricted to anti-trust judgments, is not automatically applicable, and unless it is made applicable by the Federal Attorney-General, a judgment for treble damages may be enforced in Canada: *Old North State Brewing Co v Newlands Services Inc* [1999] 4 W.W.R. 573 (BCCA).

[1041] s.1B(4).

[1042] As amended by Civil Jurisdiction and Judgments Act 1982, s.38. This amendment made it unnecessary for the foreign law to "correspond" with s.6.

[1043] SI 1994/1901, Art.6 (*cf.* Foreign Proceedings (Excess of Jurisdiction) Act 1984, s.10 (Aus.)). No such provision is to be found in the Canada–United Kingdom Agreement 1984, SI 1987/468.

CHAPTER 15

JURISDICTION AND ENFORCEMENT OF JUDGMENTS UNDER MULTILATERAL CONVENTIONS

**RULE 60—The Court has jurisdiction to entertain a claim under enact-   15R–001
ments giving effect in the law of the United Kingdom to certain international conventions if and only if the respective jurisdictional
requirements of those enactments are fulfilled.**

COMMENT

Introduction. There are a number of international conventions which, in   15–002
relation to the particular subject-matter of the convention, establish special
rules as to the courts which are to have jurisdiction to hear and determine
disputes. Many of these conventions also contain provisions as to the recognition and enforcement of judgments.[1] The special jurisdictional rules derived
from these conventions and given effect by statutory enactment in the law of
England are examined in the present Rule. The enactments concerned are the
Carriage by Air Act 1961, the Carriage by Air (Supplementary Provisions)
Act 1962, the Carriage of Goods by Road Act 1965, the Carriage by Air Acts
(Application of Provisions) Order 2004,[2] the Consular Relations Act 1968 (in
respect of certain proceedings relating to members of the crew of aircraft and
ships), the Carriage by Air and Road Act 1979[3] (the relevant provisions of
which are not yet in force), the Carriage of Passengers and their Luggage by
Sea (Interim Provisions) Order 1980,[4] s.22 of the Senior Courts Act 1981
(dealing with certain claims arising out of collisions at sea), certain provisions
of the Civil Aviation Act 1982[5] dealing with claims in respect of air navigation services, the Merchant Shipping (Liner Conference) Act 1982, ss.152 to
171 of the Merchant Shipping Act 1995 (dealing with oil pollution), s.182B
of the Merchant Shipping Act 1995 (which concerns claims for damage
arising from the carriage of hazardous and noxious substances by sea),[6]
s.183(1) of the Merchant Shipping Act 1995 (which deals with the carriage of

---

[1] See below, Rule 62.

[2] SI 2004/1899, as amended by SI 2004/1974.

[3] Carriage of Passengers by Road Act 1974 Act (which did not enter into force) was repealed
by Statute Law (Repeals) Act 2004.

[4] SI 1980/1092 as amended by SI 1987/670.

[5] As amended by the Civil Aviation (Eurocontrol) Act 1983.

[6] No order has yet been made under this section to give effect to the convention in
question.

passengers and their luggage by sea)[7] and the Railways (Convention on International Carriage by Rail) Regulations 2005 (dealing with carriage by rail).[8] They are examined below, grouped by subject-matter.

15–003   In principle, these jurisdictional rules are affected neither by Council Regulation (EC) 44/2001 ("the Brussels I Regulation")[9] nor by the Lugano Convention[10] on jurisdiction and the enforcement of judgments in civil and commercial matters. Article 71 of the Brussels I Regulation provides that it is not to affect any conventions to which the Member States are parties and which, in relation to particular matters, govern jurisdiction or the recognition or enforcement of judgments.[11] Article 67 of the Lugano Convention states that it does not affect any such conventions by which the Contracting States are bound, although it shall not prevent Contracting Parties from entering into such conventions.[12]

In *The Tatry*,[13] however, the European Court held that what is now Art.71 of the Brussels I Regulation did not have the effect of excluding the Regulation entirely in matters falling within the scope of a convention which, in relation to particular matters, governs jurisdiction. The Brussels I Regulation is excluded only to the extent that it conflicts with a convention on a particular matter; if the latter does not cover a specific jurisdictional issue the provisions of the Brussels I Regulation continue to apply.[14] Accordingly, in a case where the court has jurisdiction under an international convention which does not

---

[7] On the jurisdiction of English courts in relation to claims for limitation of liability under the Convention on Limitation of Liability for Maritime Claims 1976 (enacted by Merchant Shipping Act 1995, s.185, and set out in Sch.7 to the Act, as amended) and the service of proceedings outside the jurisdiction pursuant to CPR, r.61.11(5), see *ICL Shipping Ltd v Chin Tai Steel Enterprise Co Ltd* [2003] EWHC 2320 (Comm.), [2004] 1 Lloyd's Rep. 21; *Seismic Shipping Inc v Total E&P UK Plc* [2005] EWCA Civ 985, [2005] 2 Lloyd's Rep. 359. See also para.7–047.

[8] SI 2005/2092 entered into force on July 1, 2006 and repealed the relevant sections of International Transport Conventions Act 1983. See also SI 2010/1504.

[9] There is an Agreement between the European Community and Denmark [2005] O.J. L299/62 (approved [2006] O.J. L120/22 with effect from July 1, 2007: SI 2007/1655), in substantially the same terms as the Brussels I Regulation. See above, para.11–013.

[10] The revised Lugano Convention ([2007] O.J. L339/1) entered into force on January 1, 2010 between the Member States of the European Union (including Denmark) and Norway on January 1, 2010. It is now also in force for Iceland and Switzerland.

[11] For the interpretation of this provision, see Art.71(2).

[12] For the interpretation of this provision, see Arts 67(1)–(5).

[13] [1994] E.C.R. 1–5439; [1999] Q.B. 515. Contrast *The Bergen* [1997] 1 Lloyd's Rep. 380. See also *Andrea Merzario Ltd v Internationale Spedition Leitner Gesellschaft GmbH* [2001] EWCA Civ 61, [2001] 1 Lloyd's Rep. 490 (CA), disapproving *Frans Maas Logistics (UK) Ltd v CDR Trucking BV* [1999] 2 Lloyd's Rep. 179. See above, paras 13–034—13–035.

[14] The European Court, however, ruled in Case C–148/03 *Nürnberger Allgemeine Versicherungs AG v Portbridge Transport International BV* [2004] E.C.R. I–10327 (a case decided in respect of the Brussels Convention) that the courts of a Member State in which a defendant domiciled in another Member State was sued could take jurisdiction pursuant to a specialised convention containing rules of jurisdiction to which the former State was a party (in this case, the CMR Convention), even where the defendant did not enter a plea on the merits. What are now Art.26(1) and Art.71(2)(a), final sentence, of the Brussels I Regulation did not deny the court jurisdiction, since the application of a specialised convention was expressly sanctioned by the Regulation and so ultimately derived from the Regulation itself (para.17). See also Case C–522/03 *Scania Finance France SA v Rockinger Spezialfabrik für Anhangerkupplungen GmbH & Co* [2006] I.L.Pr. 11.

contain provisions dealing with *lis pendens* or related actions,[15] the court should apply Arts 27 and 28 of the Brussels I Regulation if there are concurrent proceedings in another Brussels I Regulation State.[16] The position under Arts 27 and 28 of the Lugano Convention is the same.[17]

A further limitation to the application of Art.71 of the Brussels I Regulation   **15–004** was expounded by the European Court in *TNT Express Nederland BV v AXA Versicherung AG*.[18] It held that the overarching aims of the Brussels I Regulation cannot be compromised by an international convention. Hence, pursuant to Art.71 of the Brussels I Regulation, the rules of an international convention can only prevail, for matters also falling within the ambit of the Brussels I Regulation, if they are "highly predictable, facilitate the sound administration of justice and enable the risk of concurrent proceedings to be minimised"; and on condition "that they ensure, under conditions at least as favourable as those provided for by the regulation, the free movement of judgments in civil and commercial matters and mutual trust in the administration of justice in the European Union."[19]

Jurisdictional rules derived from international conventions are not affected   **15–005** by those provisions of the Civil Jurisdiction and Judgments Act 1982 based upon the Brussels I Regulation which regulate the allocation of jurisdiction between the various parts of the United Kingdom.[20] Where a special jurisdictional rule derived from an international convention confers jurisdiction on the courts of the United Kingdom without specifying the relevant part whose courts are to have jurisdiction, the allocation of jurisdiction as between the various parts of the United Kingdom has to be resolved by traditional jurisdiction rules (including the doctrine of *forum non conveniens*).[21]

It is provided in the Brussels I Regulation that it shall not prejudice the   **15–006** application of provisions which, in relation to particular matters, govern jurisdiction or the recognition or enforcement of judgments and which are[22] contained in Community instruments or in national legislation harmonised in implementation of such instruments.[23] The Brussels Convention contained a similar provision, but applied to provisions which "are *or will be contained*" in Community instruments.[24] Article 67 of the Lugano Convention defers to

---

[15] Or where the international convention contains an incomplete set of rules on *lis alibi pendens*: see *Royal & Sun Alliance Insurance Plc v M.K. Digital FZE (Cyprus) Ltd* [2005] EWHC 1408 (Comm.), [2005] 2 Lloyd's Rep. 679, reversed on other grounds [2006] EWCA Civ 629, [2006] 2 Lloyd's Rep. 110.

[16] *cf. Deaville v Aeroflot Russian International Airlines* [1997] 2 Lloyd's Rep. 67.

[17] See also *Moubarak el Dousri v EIG Airbus Industrie* [2011] I.L.Pr. 71 (Cour de cassation, France, 2009), in respect of jurisdiction over co-defendants.

[18] Case C–533/08 [2010] I.L.Pr. 663.

[19] *ibid.*, at [56]. See also below, paras 15–026 and 15–055.

[20] Civil Jurisdiction and Judgments Act 1982, ss.16 and 17, Sch.4, and Sch.5, para.6 (as amended: see SI 2001/3929).

[21] See *Abnett v British Airways Plc*, 1996 S.L.T. 529 (OH). For further proceedings not involving this point see *ibid.* (I.H.) and *Sidhu v British Airways Plc* [1997] A.C. 430.

[22] Future Community instruments are not expressly addressed.

[23] Art.67.

[24] Art.57(3) (emphasis added). "By use of the words 'or will be', Art.57(1) of the Brussels Convention made it clear that the rules contained in that convention did not preclude the application of different rules to which the Contracting States would agree in the future through the conclusion of specialised conventions. Those words were not reproduced in Art.71(1) of Regulation 44/2001. Accordingly, that provision does not enable the Member States to introduce,

conventions on "particular matters" by which Contracting States "are bound"; but then states that "Without prejudice to obligations resulting from other agreements between certain Contracting Parties, this Convention shall not prevent Contracting Parties from entering into such conventions." The Lugano Convention has an annexed Protocol which provides that provisions which, in relation to particular matters, govern jurisdiction or the recognition or enforcement of judgments and which are or will be contained in acts of the institutions of the European Communities are to be treated in the same way as the conventions referred to in Art.67(1).[25]

15–007 In many of the cases here examined, service of process out of the jurisdiction will be permissible without the permission of the court by virtue of CPR, r.6.33(3) the claims being claims which, by virtue of an enactment, the High Court has power to hear and determine notwithstanding that the person against whom the claim is made is not within the jurisdiction of the Court or that the wrongful act, neglect or default giving rise to the claim did not take place within the jurisdiction.[26]

15–008 **Carriage by air.** The Carriage by Air Act 1961 gives binding force in the United Kingdom to an international convention on carriage by air known as the Warsaw Convention 1929, as amended at The Hague in 1955. The Act has also been amended so as to give effect to the Montreal Convention 1999.[27] This creates a complex hierarchy between the various Conventions.[28] Within the scope of its subject matter, the English court should apply the most recent Convention in force in the State of departure and the State of destination.[29]

15–009 The Warsaw Convention applies to the carriage of passengers, baggage and cargo,[30] provided that it falls within the definition of "international carriage," that is, carriage in which, according to the agreement between the parties, the place of departure and the place of destination, whether or not there be a break in the carriage or a transhipment, are situated either within the territories of two High Contracting Parties, or within the territory of a single High Contracting Party, if there is an agreed stopping place within the territory of another State.[31] The United Kingdom and its dependencies are a single High Contracting Party; thus while a flight between London and Dublin, or between London and Paris, will be "international carriage" for the purposes of the Act, a flight

---

by concluding new specialised conventions or amending conventions already in force, rules which would prevail over those of Regulation 44/2001": Case C–533/08 *TNT Express Nederland BV v AXA Versicherung AG* [2010] I.L.Pr. 663, at [38].

[25] Protocol No.3, para.1.

[26] See above, Rule 33.

[27] For a full account of "the Warsaw system," see Shawcross and Beaumont, *Air Law* (4th ed. Re-Issue) Division VII.

[28] The application of these Conventions is subject to Council Regulation (EC) 2027/97 [1987] O.J. L285/1, as amended by Council Regulation (EC) 889/02 [2002] O.J. L140/2. See Carriage by Air Act 1961, s.1(2); Carriage by Air Acts (Application of Provisions) Order 2004, SI 2004/1899, art.3(2). See also Regulation (EC) 261/2004 [2004] O.J. L46/1.

[29] *Laroche v Spirit of Adventure (UK) Ltd* [2009] EWCA Civ 12, [2009] Q.B. 778.

[30] But not of mail or postal packets. Such carriage is governed for the purposes of English law by Sch.1 to Carriage by Air Acts (Application of Provisions) Order 2004, SI 2004/1899, as amended by SI 2004/1974: *American Express Co v British Airways Board* [1983] 1 W.L.R. 701.

[31] Carriage by Air Act 1961, Sch.1, Art.1(2).

between London and Gibraltar will not be (in the absence of an agreed stopping place in, e.g. France or Spain).

An Order in Council made under the Carriage by Air Act 1961[32] gives **15–010** binding force in the United Kingdom both to the unamended text of the Warsaw Convention 1929 in respect of international carriage within the terms of that unamended Convention and to the Warsaw Convention, as amended by additional Protocol No.1 of Montreal 1975.[33] These provisions deal with cases where the 1955 Hague Protocol is inapplicable. Whether the carriage falls within the scope of the amended or unamended[34] texts is a matter largely determined by the identity of the High Contracting Parties concerned. So, Indonesia is a party to the unamended text only, never having ratified the 1955 Hague Protocol; a flight from London to Jakarta does not, therefore, fall within the amended text as given effect by the Carriage by Air Act 1961, but does fall within the provisions of the unamended Convention given effect by the Order in Council.

The High Contracting Parties to both versions of the Convention are **15–011** certified from time to time by Order in Council, which is conclusive evidence of the matters certified.[35]

Under the different versions of the Warsaw Convention, the same special **15–012** jurisdictional rules are prescribed.[36] These rules are designed to provide a claimant with a limited choice of competent and appropriate jurisdictions in which to bring his claim. An action for damages must be brought, at the option of the plaintiff, in the territory of one of the High Contracting Parties either before the court having jurisdiction where the carrier is ordinarily resident, or has his principal place of business, or has an establishment by which the contract has been made, or before the court having jurisdiction at the place of destination. The court's inherent jurisdiction to stay proceedings on the basis of *forum non conveniens* in favour of the courts of another High Contracting Party is inconsistent with the option conferred on the claimant by the Convention; once the claimant has chosen the courts of a particular Contracting Party as his forum the defendant has no basis on which to challenge that choice.[37] However, since the Convention's jurisdictional rules identify the High Contracting Parties whose courts are to have jurisdiction without addressing the allocation of jurisdiction as between various parts of a Contracting Party (e.g. as between England and Scotland),[38] it is not inconsistent with the Convention for proceedings commenced in England under the Convention to be stayed on the ground that the courts of Scotland or Northern Ireland provide a more

---

[32] Carriage by Air Acts (Application of Provisions) Order 2004, SI 2004/1899, arts 3, 5 and 6; Schs 2 and 3.

[33] See below.

[34] i.e. the texts which do not incorporate the 1955 Hague amendments.

[35] Carriage by Air Act 1961, s.2(1)(3). See Carriage by Air (Parties to Convention) Order 1999, SI 1999/1313; and Carriage by Air (Parties to Protocol No.4 of Montreal 1975) Order 2000, SI 2000/3061. See *Philippson v Imperial Airways Ltd* [1939] A.C. 332 for the position where the text of the Warsaw Convention is incorporated by contractual term.

[36] Carriage by Air Act 1961, Sch.1, Art.28(1); Carriage by Air Acts (Application of Provisions) Order 2004, SI 2004/1899, Sch.2, Art.28(1); Sch.3, Art.28(1).

[37] *Milor Srl v British Airways Plc* [1996] Q.B. 702 (CA). cf. *Aircrash Disaster near New Orleans, Louisiana, on 9 July 1982, Re*, 821 F.2d 1147 (5th Cir. 1987).

[38] *Abnett v British Airways Plc*, 1996 S.L.T. 529 (OH).

appropriate forum. Any clause in the contract of carriage, and all special agreements entered into before the damage occurred by which the parties purport to alter the rules as to jurisdiction are null and void; but in the carriage of cargo arbitration clauses are allowed if the arbitration is to take place within one of the jurisdictions referred to.[39] It would seem that an agreement as to jurisdiction made after the occurrence of the damage would be valid, and that submission by the defendant would also give the court jurisdiction.[40] Where the claimant has a claim for damages which falls within the scope of the Warsaw Convention, the Convention provides the claimant with his only remedy.[41] If recovery is not available under the Warsaw Convention, e.g. because of the limitation provisions contained in Art.29, the claimant cannot rely on any alternative cause of action.[42]

15–013   Carriers by air are almost invariably corporations, and their ordinary residence will generally coincide with their principal place of business; the mere existence of a branch office within the jurisdiction will not support a finding of ordinary residence.[43] There is no English authority on the precise relationship which need exist between the carrier and the "establishment by which a contract has been made." It is submitted that the establishment need not be in the exclusive ownership of the carrier, but that more than a mere agency is required; a sales organisation maintained by the carrier, even if in co-operation with another carrier, would suffice.[44] The "place of destination" in the case of a round trip will be identical with the place of departure.[45]

15–014   Further amendments to the Warsaw Convention were agreed in a series of Protocols drawn up at Montreal in 1975. The new text creates an additional basis for jurisdiction: in respect of damage resulting from the death, injury or delay of a passenger, or the destruction, loss, damage or delay of baggage, the action may also be brought in the territory of one of the High Contracting Parties before the court within the jurisdiction of which the carrier has an establishment if the passenger has his ordinary or permanent residence in that territory.[46] Provisions are made in the Carriage by Air and Road Act 1979 to give binding force in the United Kingdom to the Convention as so amended,

---

[39] Carriage by Air Act 1961, Sch.1, Art.32; Carriage by Air Acts (Application of Provisions) Order 2004, SI 2004/1899, Sch.2, Art.32; Sch.3, Art.32.

[40] *Rothmans of Pall Mall (Overseas) Ltd v Saudi Arabian Airlines Corp* [1980] 3 All E.R. 359; *Vertzyas v Singapore Airlines Ltd* (2000) 50 N.S.W.L.R. 1; *Ashad v Deutsche Lufthansa Aktiengesellschaft*, 2009 Carswell Ont 7251, at [45]–[49].

[41] See *Moubarak el Dousri v EIG Airbus Industrie* [2011] I.L.Pr. 71 (Cour de cassation, France, 2009).

[42] *Sidhu v British Airways Plc* [1997] A.C. 430. See also *Emery Air Freight Corporation v Nerine Nurseries Ltd* [1997] 3 N.Z.L.R. 723 (CA); *Thibodeau v Air Canada*, 2011 FC 876.

[43] *Rothmans of Pall Mall (Overseas) Ltd v Saudi Arabian Airlines Corp* [1981] Q.B. 368; *Roberts v Guyana Airways Corp* (1998) O.R.(3d) 653.

[44] See *Qureshi v KLM Royal Dutch Airlines* (1979) 102 D.L.R. (3d) 205 (N.S.); *Berner v United Airlines Inc*, 3 A.D. 2d 9, 157 N.Y.S. 2d 884 (1956), affirmed 3 N.Y. 2d 1003, 147 N.E. 2d 732 (1957). *cf. Eck v United Arab Airlines Inc*, 360 F. 2d 804 (2d Circ. 1966); *Orchestre Symphonique de Vienne v TWA* (1972) 35 R.G.A.E. 202.

[45] *Grein v Imperial Airways Ltd* [1937] 1 K.B. 50; *Qureshi v KLM Royal Dutch Airlines* (1979) 102 D.L.R. (3d) 205 (N.S.); *Ashad v Deutsche Lufthansa Aktiengesllschaft*, 2009 Carswell Ont 7251; *Vertzyas v Singapore Airlines Ltd* (2000) 50 N.S.W.L.R. 1; *Gulf Air Company GSC v Fattouh* [2008] NSWCA 225.

[46] Carriage by Air and Road Act 1979, Sch.1, Art.28(2) (not yet in force).

but the provision introducing the additional basis of jurisdiction is not yet in force.[47]

The Carriage by Air Act 1961 (and the corresponding provisions in the Carriage by Air and Road Act 1979) are enactments within CPR, r.6.33(3),[48] and permission is not required to serve process out of the jurisdiction. The Act contemplates that the defendant carrier may itself be a High Contracting Party, that is a foreign government.[49] A High Contracting Party is deemed to have submitted to the jurisdiction of the court, and s.12 of the State Immunity Act 1978 provides for serving process upon the foreign government with the assistance of the Secretary of State;[50] these provisions do not, however, authorise the issue of execution against the property of any High Contracting Party.[51]

15–015

The Carriage by Air (Supplementary Provisions) Act 1962 gives binding force in the United Kingdom to a supplementary convention known as the Guadalajara Convention 1961. It deals with the problems which arise when, as is very frequently the case, the "actual carrier" who performs carriage by air is not the carrier with whom the original contract of carriage was made (the "contracting carrier").[52] An action for damages in relation to carriage performed by the actual carrier may be brought, at the option of the plaintiff, against that carrier or the contracting carrier, or against both together or separately.[53] Such an action must be brought, again at the option of the plaintiff, either before a court in which an action may be brought against the contracting carrier as provided by Art.28 of the different versions of the Warsaw Convention, or before the court having jurisdiction at the place where the actual carrier is ordinarily resident or has his principal place of business.[54] Permission of the court is not required for service of process out of the jurisdiction when a claim is brought under this Act.[55]

15–016

A further Convention for the Unification of Certain Rules for International Carriage by Air was concluded at Montreal in 1999.[56] It entered into force on November 4, 2003 and came into force in the United Kingdom on June 28,

15–017

---

[47] Additional Protocols Nos 1 and 2 (which, *inter alia*, establish a new unit of account for the Warsaw Convention) are implemented by SI 1997/2565 (which brings into force various provisions of Carriage by Air and Road Act 1979) and SI 2004/1899. S.3(1) of the 1979 Act was brought into force by SI 1998/2562 to allow for the implementation of Additional Protocol No.4, which was, in turn, brought into force by SI 1999/1312. The text of the amended Warsaw Convention, together with the further amendments made by Protocol No.4 of 1975, as they apply in the UK, appear as Sch.1(A) to Carriage by Air Act 1961. For the parties to Additional Protocol No.4, see SI 2000/3061. S.3(2) of the 1979 Act was brought into force by SI 2000/2768.

[48] See above, Rule 33.

[49] Carriage by Air Act 1961, s.8. (as amended by SI 2002/263). This is applied to carriage within the Second Schedule to Carriage by Air Acts (Application of Provisions) Order 2004, SI 2004/1899 by Art.5(3) of the Order.

[50] See also CPR, r.6.44 which is however limited to cases in which permission to serve the process has been obtained from the court.

[51] Carriage by Air Act 1961, s.8(3) (as amended by SI 2002/263).

[52] The Act is also applied to carriage falling within Schs 2 and 3 to Carriage by Air Acts (Application of Provisions) Order 2004, SI 2004/1899, i.e. carriage under the unamended Warsaw Convention.

[53] Carriage by Air (Supplementary Provisions) Act 1962, Sch., Art.VII.

[54] *ibid.* Sch., Art.VIII.

[55] CPR, r.6.33(3); see above, Rule 33.

[56] See Cheng (2004) 53 I.C.L.Q. 833.

2004.[57] The Montreal Convention of 1999 seeks to modernise the rules on carriage by air and to streamline them. It combines existing instruments into a single set of provisions which States should accept or reject in their entirety. As more and more States become parties to the 1999 Convention, the importance of the earlier carriage by air Conventions will necessarily diminish. The scope of the Convention is defined in Art.1(2) and is in similar terms to the Warsaw Convention.[58] However, the application of the Convention is subject to the Regulation on air carrier liability in respect of the carriage of passengers and their baggage by air.[59] As well as implementing the provisions of the Montreal Convention, the Regulation extends their application to carriage by air within a single Member State.[60]

15–018　　　The jurisdictional provisions of the 1999 Convention[61] largely mirror those of the earlier Conventions.[62] Under Art.33 of the 1999 Convention (which corresponds to Art.28 of the Warsaw Convention, as amended), an action for damages may be brought in a State Party (i) where the carrier is domiciled or (ii) where the carrier has its principal place of business or (iii) where the carrier has a place of business through which the contract was made or (iv) the place of destination[63] In relation to damage resulting from the death or injury of a passenger, an additional ground of jurisdiction is provided: an action may also be brought in the State Party in which at the time of the accident the passenger has his principal and permanent residence as long as the carrier (i) operates services for the carriage of passengers by air to or from that place and (ii) conducts its business from premises leased or owned by the carrier or by another carrier with which it has a commercial agreement.[64] For the purposes

---

[57] Provision was made for the 1999 Convention to come into force in the UK when the Convention had entered into force internationally: Carriage by Air Acts (Implementation of the Montreal Convention 1999) Order 2002, SI 2002/263, Art.1. The 2002 Order makes various amendments to Carriage by Air Act 1961 and Carriage by Air (Supplementary Provisions) Act 1962. In *Ashad v Deutsche Lufthansa Aktiengesllschaft*, 2009 Carswell Ont 7251, it was held that the 1999 Convention would be inapplicable where a State was not party to the Convention at the time when the alleged cause of action accrued but had subsequently become a party before the proceedings were heard.

[58] Carriage by Air Act 1961, Sch.1(B), Art.1(2). The provisions of the Montreal Convention are extended to non-international carriage, with some modifications, by Carriage by Air Acts (Application of Provisions) Order 2004, SI 2004/1899, Sch.1.

[59] Council Regulation (EC) 2027/97 [1987] O.J. L285/1, as amended by Regulation (EC) 889/02 OJ 2002 L140/2. See Carriage by Air Act 1961, s.1(2); Carriage by Air Acts (Application of Provisions) Order 2004, SI 2004/1899, s.3(2). See also Regulation (EC) 261/2004 [2004] O.J. L46/1.

[60] Art.1, second sentence.

[61] In Case C–204/08 *Rehder v Air Baltic Corp* [2009] E.C.R. I–6073, the European Court ruled that a passenger's claim for a standardised and lump-sum payment following the cancellation of a flight, which was based on Regulation (EC) 261/2004 of the European Parliament and Council establishing common rules on compensation and assistance to passengers in the event of denied boarding and of cancellation or long delay of flights, was independent of a claim for compensation for damage under the Montreal Convention, Art.19 (relying upon Case C–344/04 *IATA and ELFAA* [2006] E.C.R. I–403). Accordingly, the claim was subject to the jurisdiction rules in the Brussels I Regulation, rather than those in the Montreal Convention. See also Case C–173/07 *Emirates Airlines Direktion fur Deutschland v Schenkel* [2008] E.C.R. I–5237, [2009] 1 Lloyd's Rep. 1; Case C–402/07 *Sturgeon v Condor Flugdienst GmbH* [2009] E.C.R. I–10923.

[62] On the use of arbitration, see Art.34.

[63] Art.33(1).

[64] Art.33(2).

of this rule, it makes no difference whether the carrier uses its own aircraft or those of another carrier pursuant to a commercial agreement. Article 46 of the 1999 Convention follows Art.VIII of the Guadalajara Convention: where the actual carrier is not the contracting carrier, the plaintiff may bring proceedings against the actual carrier either in the State Party where the contracting carrier may be sued (under Art.33) or where the actual carrier has its domicile or principal place of business. Permission is not required to serve process out of the jurisdiction.[65]

The provisions of the Carriage by Air Act 1961 as to actions against foreign governments are applied equally to actions under the 1962 Act.[66]   **15–019**

Carriage by rail. The Berne Convention concerning International Carriage by Rail 1980 (COTIF) was designed to replace the earlier international conventions on carriage by rail which it consolidates with amendments.[67] It was given the force of law in the United Kingdom by the International Transport Conventions Act 1983. The COTIF Convention was modified by a Protocol[68] in 1990 and the Act was amended[69] to implement it.[70] The Convention was modified by the Vilnius Protocol of 1999. The Railways (Convention on International Carriage by Rail) Regulations 2005[71] repealed the provisions of the International Transport Conventions Act 1983 which gave the force of law to the 1980 Convention. These are largely replicated in the Regulations. The Regulations gave the 1999 Protocol the force of law upon its ratification and entry into force in the United Kingdom with effect from July 1, 2006.[72] Subsequently, an Agreement between the European Union and the Intergovernmental Organisation for International Carriage by Rail on the Accession of the European Union to the COTIF Convention, as amended by the Vilnius Protocol, was signed[73] and entered into force on July 1, 2011.[74]   **15–020**

---

[65] CPR, r.6.33(3).

[66] Carriage by Air (Supplementary Provisions) Act 1962, s.3(3) (as amended by Statute Law (Repeals) Act 2004).

[67] For the text of the Convention, see Cmnd. 8535 (1982).

[68] 43 Cm. 1689 (1991).

[69] SI 1992/237; repealed by SI 2005/2092.

[70] For the consolidated text of the Convention as amended by the 1990 Protocol see Cm. 2312.

[71] SI 2005/2092. It was modified by Rail Passengers' Rights and Obligations Regulations 2010 (SI 2010/1504, in force June 25, 2010), which provide for the implementation of Regulation (EC) 1371/2007 of the European Parliament and of the Council on rail passengers' rights and obligations [2007] O.J. L315/14. The European Regulation harmonises the rules regarding the rights and obligations of rail passengers in the European Union. Where there is a conflict between the European Regulation and the COTIF Convention (as modified by the Vilnius Protocol of 1999), the former prevails. The European Regulation, however, largely replicates the COTIF Convention, as modified. The European Regulation does not contain rules on jurisdiction and arbitration. Where there is no incompatibility with the European Regulation, the United Kingdom must continue to apply the COTIF Convention, as modified by the Vilnius Protocol.

[72] Any subsequent amendments to COTIF will automatically have the force of law: SI 2005/2092, Reg.2(2). For detailed discussion of the Berne Convention prior to the Vilnius Protocol, see the 13th edition of this work, paras 15–013–15–015.

[73] On June 23, 2011.

[74] In accordance with Art.9 of the Agreement.

15–021   The revised Convention incorporates a number of sets of Uniform Rules,[75] many of which contain rules on the jurisdiction of courts.[76] Appendix A deals with Contracts of International Carriage of Passengers by Rail (CIV).[77] Article 57(1) stipulates that actions based upon these Rules may be brought in the courts or tribunals of the Member States designated by agreement between the parties, or where the defendant has his domicile or habitual residence, its principal place of business or the branch or agency which concluded the contract of carriage. Where such an action is pending before a competent court or tribunal, or a judgment of a competent court or tribunal has been delivered, no new action may be brought between the same parties on the same cause of action, unless the judgment of the State of origin is not enforceable in the State where the new action is instigated.[78]

15–022   Appendix B addresses the Uniform Rules Concerning the Contract of International Carriage of Goods by Rail (CIM).[79] Art.46(1) states that actions based upon these Rules may be brought either in the courts or tribunals of the Member States designated by agreement between the parties, or where the defendant has his domicile or habitual residence, its principal place of business or the branch or agency which concluded the contract of carriage, or in the place where the goods were taken over by the carrier or the place designated for delivery is situated. Article 46(2) contains a provision in similar terms to Art.57(2) of the CIV convention on the prevention of parallel proceedings.

15–023   Appendix D deals with Contracts of Use of Vehicles in International Rail Traffic (CUV). Article 11 provides that actions based upon contacts concluded in accordance with these Uniform Rules may be brought before the courts chosen by the parties.[80] Otherwise the courts of the Member State where the defendant has its place of business have jurisdiction; and if there is no place of business, the action should be brought where the loss or damage occurred.[81]

15–024   Appendix C on the International Carriage of Dangerous Goods by Rail (RID) does not presently contain rules of jurisdiction.[82] The United Kingdom entered a declaration at the time of ratification of the Vilnius Protocol[83] that

---

[75] Appendices A to G shall have effect in the UK: see SI 2005/2092, Reg. 2(2)(c). See also the Protocol on the Privileges and Immunities of the Intergovernmental Organisation for International Carriage by Rail (OTIF), to be given effect by Reg. 2(2)(b).

[76] On the use of arbitration, see Title V, Arts 28–32 to the Convention. Title V makes provision for the use of an arbitration tribunal as an alternative to the ordinary courts and regulates the composition and procedure of such a tribunal.

[77] These are mandatory rules, although the carrier may assume greater responsibilities and burdens than those stipulated in the Rules: Art.5.

[78] Art.57(2). On the enforcement of judgments, see below, para.15–058.

[79] These lay down a mandatory minimum level of responsibilities for the carrier: Art.5.

[80] Art.11(1).

[81] Art.11(2).

[82] There is to be an Annex to the Rules. The Expert Committee for the Carriage of Dangerous Goods has yet to produce the Annex. See also SI 2009/1348 (as amended by SI 2011/1885) implementing, inter alia, Directive 2008/68/EC of the European Parliament and of the Council of September 24, 2008 on the inland transport of dangerous goods: [2008] O.J. L260/13.

[83] Although SI 2005/2092 does not make reference to this declaration and instead refers in reg.2(2)(c) to Appendices A–G having the force of law.

Appendices E,[84] F[85] and G[86] of the Convention would not enter into force in the United Kingdom, at the instigation of the European Community.[87]

Carriage by road. The Carriage of Goods by Road Act 1965 gives binding force in the United Kingdom to the Geneva Convention on the Contract for the International Carriage of Goods by Road, of May 19, 1956, generally known as the CMR Convention.[88] The Convention applies to every contract for the carriage of goods by road in motor vehicles for reward, when the place of taking over the goods and the place designated for delivery, as specified in the contract, are situated in two different countries, of which at least one is a Contracting country.[89] It also applies if part of the journey is by sea, rail, inland waterways or air, provided that the goods are not unloaded from the vehicle.[90] It does not apply to traffic between the United Kingdom and the Republic of Ireland.[91] High Contracting Parties are specified from time to time by Orders in Council which are conclusive for the purposes of English law.[92] Any legal proceedings arising out of carriage under the Convention[93] must be brought in a court or tribunal of a Contracting country[94] designated by agreement between the parties, or in the courts or tribunals of a country within

15–025

---

[84] The Uniform Rules concerning the Contract of Use of Infrastructure in International Rail Traffic (CUI). Article 24 states that actions based on these Rules may be brought in the courts chosen by the parties to the contract; and otherwise, the competent courts are those of the Member State where the manager has his place of business.

[85] Uniform Rules concerning the Validation of Technical Standards and the Adoption of Uniform Technical Prescriptions applicable to Railway Material intended to be used in International Traffic (APTU).

[86] Technical Admission of Railway Material used in International Traffic (ATMF). Article 19 allows for two or more Contracting States to refer certain disputes to the Committee of Technical Experts if not resolved by direct negotiation, or to an arbitration tribunal in accordance with Art.5 and Title V, Arts 28 to 32 of the Convention.

[87] This reflects possible inconsistencies between the rules in the Vilnius Protocol and rules of Community law: see COM(2009) 441 final, Annex 3. The rules of Community law prevail in the case of any such inconsistencies.

[88] For text see Cmnd. 3455; for commentary see Hill and Messent, *CMR: Contracts for the International Carriage of Goods by Road* (3rd. ed. 2000, Messent and Glass). An Additional Protocol concerning the Electronic Consignment Note was concluded in 2008 and entered into force on June 5, 2011 but has not yet been ratified by the United Kingdom.

[89] Carriage of Goods by Road Act 1965, Sch., Art.1(1). See *Gefco (U.K.) Ltd v Mason* [1998] C.L.C. 1468; *Aqualon (UK) Ltd v Vallana Shipping Corp* [1994] 1 Lloyd's Rep. 669; *Lukoil-Kaliningradmorneft Plc v Tata Ltd & Global Marine Transportation Inc* [1999] 2 Lloyd's Rep. 129; *Royal & Sun Alliance Insurance Plc v MK Digital FZE (Cyprus) Ltd* [2005] EWHC 1408 (Comm.), [2005] 2 Lloyd's Rep. 679, reversed (but not on this point) [2006] EWCA Civ 629, [2006] 2 Lloyd's Rep. 110; *Datec Electronic Holdings Ltd v United Parcels Service Ltd* [2007] UKHL 23, [2007] 1 W.L.R. 1325. For the applicability of Carriage of Goods by Road Act 1965 in cases where the contract involves more than one type of carriage see *Quantum Corp Inc v Plane Trucking Ltd* [2002] EWCA Civ 350, [2002] 1 W.L.R. 2678.

[90] *ibid.* Sch., Art.2.

[91] Protocol of Signature.

[92] Carriage of Goods by Road Act 1965, s.2. The current Order is the Carriage of Goods by Road (Parties to Convention) Order 1967, SI 1967/1683, as amended by SI 1980/697.

[93] Including "extra-contractual claims" under Art.28.

[94] On the relationship between the Geneva Convention's jurisdiction rules and the Brussels I Regulation, see Case C–148/03 *Nürnberger Allgemeine Versicherungs AG v Portbridge Transport International BV* [2004] E.C.R. I–10327 (decided in respect of the relationship to the Brussels Convention).

whose territory (a) the defendant is ordinarily resident, or has his principal place of business,[95] or the branch or agency through which the contract of carriage was made; or (b) the place where the goods were taken over by the carrier or the place designated for delivery[96] is situated.[97] The designation of a court by agreement can take place in the contract, or after the cause of action has arisen; if the designation is in the original contract it would seem to be binding on the consignee of the goods the subject of the contract as the consignee's rights are those "arising from the contract."[98] An arbitration clause is permitted, so long as it expressly provides that the arbitral tribunal must apply the Convention.[99] Where jurisdiction is based upon the presence in England of a "branch or agency" through which the contract was made, it must be shown that it was "his," i.e. the defendant's, branch or agency; but the precise meaning of this requirement, especially in the agency case, is far from clear. If the goods were "taken over" by a carrier in England the English court will have jurisdiction, even if the defendant carrier was the actual carrier only in respect of a later stage of the journey, provided that the carrier can be regarded as a carrier for the purposes of the contract as a whole.[100]

15–026   The CMR Convention provides that where, in respect of a claim, an action is pending before a court or tribunal of a contracting country no new action shall be started between the same parties on the same grounds. It is also provided that no new action shall be started where a judgment has been entered by a court or tribunal of a contracting country unless the judgment is not enforceable in the country in which the fresh proceedings are brought.[101] In *Andrea Merzario Ltd v Internationale Spedition Leitner Gesellschaft GmbH*[102] it was held that, for the purposes of the CMR Convention, proceedings should not be regarded as pending until they were served. As, on the facts of the case, the claim form in the English action had been issued and served before proceedings had been served in Austria, the English proceedings were not stayed. In *Royal & Sun Alliance Insurance Plc v MK Digital FZE (Cyprus) Ltd*[103] proceedings were issued in England but had not yet been served and were, accordingly, not "pending" in England. Between the time of issue and

---

[95] An assignee who is resident in England cannot be sued in England on this basis where the assignor who was party to a carriage by road contract was not itself resident in England: *Hatzl v XL Insurance Co Ltd* [2009] EWCA Civ 223, [2010] 1 W.L.R. 470.

[96] See *Royal & Sun Alliance Insurance Plc v MK Digital FZE (Cyprus) Ltd* [2005] EWHC 1408 (Comm.), [2005] 2 Lloyd's Rep. 679, reversed (but not on this point) [2006] EWCA Civ 629, [2006] 2 Lloyd's Rep. 110.

[97] Carriage of Goods by Road Act 1965, Sch., Art.31(1). For actions between carriers, see *ibid.*, Sch., Art.39 and *Cummins Engine Co Ltd v Davis Freight Forwarding (Hull) Ltd* [1981] 1 W.L.R. 1363 (CA).

[98] *ibid.*, Sch., Art.13(1).

[99] *ibid.*, Sch., Art.33; *AB Bofors-UVA v AB Skandia Transport* [1982] 1 Lloyd's Rep. 410 (where the court recognised the existence of divergent views on the point in foreign courts).

[100] *Moto Vespa SA v MAT (Britannia Express) Ltd* [1979] 1 Lloyd's Rep. 175.

[101] Carriage of Goods by Road Act 1965, Sch., Art.31(2).

[102] [2001] EWCA Civ 61, [2001] 1 Lloyd's Rep. 490 (CA).

[103] [2005] EWHC 1408 (Comm.), [2005] 2 Lloyd's Rep. 679. The decision was reversed, without consideration of this point, on the basis that the contract did not fall within the scope of the CMR Convention: [2006] EWCA Civ 629, [2006] 2 Lloyd's Rep. 110.

service in England, it was argued that proceedings had become pending in France. The court ruled that the CMR Convention was silent as to the English court's jurisdiction in such circumstances.[104] The question was therefore answered by applying the court first seised rule in Art.27 of the Brussels I Regulation. As the English court was first seised within the meaning of that Regulation,[105] the English court could hear the case. The CMR Convention conferred no discretion on the court to stay such proceedings on *forum non conveniens* grounds. The court also held[106] that these principles applied equally to a declaration of non-liability as to an action for substantive relief.

In *Sony Computer Entertainment Ltd v RH Freight Services Ltd*,[107] Sony sought to bring claims against various companies in England for the loss of a consignment of its goods during its carriage by road from England to the Netherlands. One of the companies, K, issued Dutch proceedings seeking a declaration of non-liability or, alternatively, a declaration limiting its liability under the CMR Convention. Sony's insurers were named as a defendant in those proceedings; but Sony itself was not named. When Sony subsequently brought English proceedings, K then sought the same relief in the Dutch proceedings against Sony itself. The English court ruled[108] that, as the CMR Convention was silent on the treatment of related actions, Art.28 of the Brussels I Regulation was applicable. It then held that the Dutch court was first seised, since the action became pending as a matter of Dutch law when it was issued, considerably before the English action became pending and the English court should decline jurisdiction pursuant to Art.28 of the Brussels I Regulation.   **15–027**

Permission of the court is not required for service of process out of the jurisdiction when the claim is brought under this Act.[109] The Act contemplates that the defendant carrier may itself be a High Contracting Party, that is a foreign government.[110] A High Contracting Party is deemed to have submitted to the jurisdiction of the court, and s.12 of the State Immunity Act 1978 provides for serving process upon the foreign government with the assistance of the Secretary of State;[111] these provisions do not, however, authorise the issue of execution against the property of any High Contracting Party.[112]   **15–028**

The Carriage of Passengers by Road Act 1974 was enacted so as to give effect to the Geneva Convention on the Contract for the International Carriage   **15–029**

---

[104] Rejecting the view (*obiter*) of Rix L.J. in *Andrea Merzario Ltd v Internationale Spedition Leitner Gesellschaft GmbH* [2001] EWCA Civ 61, [2001] 1 Lloyd's Rep. 490 (CA) that only the first court before which proceedings were pending had jurisdiction.

[105] See Brussels I Regulation, Art.30.

[106] Approving the *obiter* remarks of the majority in *Andrea Merzario Ltd v Internationale Spedition Leitner Gesellschaft GmbH* [2001] EWCA Civ 61, [2001] 1 Lloyd's Rep. 490 (CA).

[107] [2007] EWHC 302 (Comm.), [2007] 2 Lloyd's Rep. 463.

[108] At [27].

[109] CPR, r.6.33(3); above, Rule 33.

[110] Carriage of Goods by Road Act 1965, s.6.

[111] See also CPR, r.6.44 which is however limited to cases in which permission to serve the claim form has been obtained from the court.

[112] Carriage of Goods by Road Act 1965, s.6.

of Passengers and Luggage 1973 (CVR). The Act never entered into force, and was repealed by the Statute Law (Repeals) Act 2004.[113]

15–030   **Carriage of passengers and luggage by sea.** Section 183(1) of the Merchant Shipping Act 1995 (which replaced s.14(1) of the 1979 Act) gives the force of law in the United Kingdom to the Athens Convention relating to the Carriage of Passengers and their Luggage by Sea 1974. The Convention, which is reproduced in Pt I of Sch.6 to the Act, applies to any international carriage (defined as meaning any carriage in which, according to the contract of carriage, the place of departure and the place of destination are situated in two different States, or in a single State if, according to the contract of carriage or the scheduled itinerary, there is an intermediate port of call in another State[114]) if the ship is flying the flag of or is registered in a State which is a party to the Convention, or if the contract of carriage has been made in such a State, or if the place of departure or destination according to the contract of carriage is in such a State.[115] Carriage which is not for reward is excluded.[116] The Act makes provision for Orders in Council declaring States to be contracting parties to the Convention,[117] but such an Order does not preclude evidence that additional States are in fact parties.[118]

15–031   Any action arising under the Convention must be brought, at the option of the claimant, in one of the following courts, provided that the court is located in a State which is a party to the Convention. The courts are (a) the court of the place of permanent residence or principal place of business of the defendant; (b) the court of the place of departure or that of the destination according to the contract of carriage; (c) a court of the State of the domicile or permanent residence of the claimant, if the defendant has a place of business and is subject to jurisdiction in that State; or (d) a court of the State where the contract of carriage was made, if the defendant has a place of business and is subject to jurisdiction in that State.[119] However, after the occurrence of the incident which has caused the damage, the parties may agree that the claim for damages shall be submitted to any jurisdiction or to arbitration.[120] Any contractual provision concluded before the occurrence of the incident which has caused the death of or personal injury to a passenger or the loss of or damage to his luggage purporting to restrict the claimant's choice of forum under Art.17(1) is null and void.[121]

---

[113] For further discussion of the jurisdictional rules of this Convention, see the 13th ed. of this work, paras 15–018—15–019.

[114] Merchant Shipping Act 1995, Sch.6, Pt I, Art.1(9).

[115] *ibid.*, Sch.6, Pt I, Art.2(1).

[116] *ibid.*, s.183(2) and Sch.6, Pt II, para.9. The provisions of the Convention are also excluded in two further situations: (*a*) by its own terms in certain cases of combined transport, where an international convention relating to another mode of transport has mandatory effect (Art.2(2)), and (*b*) by virtue of the Merchant Shipping Act 1995, s.183(2) and Sch.6, Pt II, para.2, if such other convention is declared to be mandatory in the contract of carriage.

[117] *ibid.*, Sch.6, Pt II, para.10. See Carriage of Passengers and their Luggage by Sea (Parties to Convention) Order 1987, SI 1987/931.

[118] *cf.* the more usual formula, found, e.g. in the Carriage by Air Act 1961, s.2(1)(3).

[119] Merchant Shipping Act 1995, Sch.6, Pt I, Art.17(1).

[120] *ibid.*, Sch.6, Pt I, Art.17(2).

[121] *ibid.*, Sch.6, Pt I, Art.18.

Section 184(1) of the Merchant Shipping Act 1995 (replacing s.16(2) of the   **15–032**
1979 Act) enables a modified version of the Convention to be applied by
Order in Council to domestic carriage, i.e. carriage where the place of
departure and the place of destination under the contract are within the British
Islands and there is no intermediate port of call outside those Islands. The
power conferred by s.16(2) of the 1979 Act was exercised.[122] The jurisdictional requirements under the modified text are as in the Convention itself, but
without the requirement that the court chosen must be located in a State which
is party to the Convention.[123]

Permission is not required for the service of process out of the jurisdiction   **15–033**
when the claim is brought under the Convention as given effect by section
183(1) of the Merchant Shipping Act 1995 or (in its modified form) by Order
in Council.[124]

The United Nations Convention on Contracts for the International   **15–034**
Carriage of Goods Wholly or Partly By Sea (the Rotterdam Rules). On
December 11, 2008, the General Assembly of the United Nations adopted the
UN Convention on Contracts for the International Carriage of Goods Wholly
or Partly by Sea. The Rotterdam Convention will enter into force once it has
been adopted by at least twenty States. It will replace the Hague Rules, the
Hague-Visby Rules and the Hamburg Rules, and establish a single international set of rules. Unlike the Hague and Hague-Visby Rules, the Rotterdam
Rules contain detailed provisions on jurisdiction[125] and arbitration.[126] These,
however, will only apply if a Contracting State declares its intention to be
bound by either or both sets of rules[127] and such a declaration may be
withdrawn at any time.[128] The Rules have not been signed or ratified by the
United Kingdom.

Claims in respect of air navigation services. The Civil Aviation Act   **15–035**
1982,[129] as amended, contains rules as to the provision of air navigation
services. The supply of air navigation services is an obligation imposed upon
Contracting States by the Chicago Convention on International Civil Aviation

---

[122] Carriage of Passengers and their Luggage by Sea (Interim Provisions) Order 1980, SI
1980/1092 as amended by SI 1987/670. Merchant Shipping Act 1979, s.16(1) (which was
repealed by the 1995 Act) also enabled a modified version of the Convention to be applied, in
respect of contracts made during the period before the relevant provisions of the 1979 Act came
into force, to any contract of carriage for international carriage which was made in the UK, or
under which a place in the UK was the place of departure or destination. This power was
exercised by Carriage of Passengers and their Luggage by Sea (Interim Provisions) Order 1980,
SI 1980/1092.

[123] Art.17(1) as modified by SI 1980/1092, Sch., para.3.

[124] CPR, r.6.33(3); above, Rule 33.

[125] In Ch.14 of the Rules.

[126] Ch.15 of the Rules.

[127] Pursuant to Art.91 of the Rules.

[128] For discussion, see Baatz (2008) 14 J.I.M.L. 608; Baatz, in Thomas (ed.), *The Carriage of
Goods by Sea Under the Rotterdam Rules* (2010), Ch.16; Baatz [2011] L.M.C.L.Q. 208; Alvarez-
Rubio (2009) 11 Yb. P.I.L. 171. See also Berlingieri [2010] L.M.C.L.Q. 583; Diamond [2008]
L.M.C.L.Q. 135, at pp.183–186; [2009] L.M.C.L.Q. 445; Sturley (2008) 14 J.I.M.L. 461.

[129] See also Civil Aviation Act 2006, in force from March 1, 2007.

1944.[130] It is discharged through agencies such as the Civil Aviation Authority in the United Kingdom, through international arrangements applying to particular routes, and through international agencies such as Eurocontrol. The latter, known more formally as the European Organisation for the Safety of Air Navigation, was established by the Brussels Convention relating to Co-operation for the Safety of Air Navigation of December 13, 1960,[131] which was extensively revised by a Protocol of 1981.[132]

15–036   In relation to charges payable to Eurocontrol, jurisdictional rules are contained in the Multilateral Agreement Relating to Route Charges (1981). This contained rules of jurisdiction and rules on the recognition and enforcement of foreign judgments. As to jurisdiction, the Agreement provides that proceedings for the recovery of such charges shall be instituted in the territory of the Contracting State where the debtor has his residence or registered office; or, if there is no such residence or office in a Contracting State, in the territory of a Contracting State where the debtor has a place of business; or if none of the preceding grounds of jurisdiction are available, in the territory of a Contracting State in which the debtor has assets; or, if no other ground is available, in Belgium, the country in which Eurocontrol has its headquarters.[133] But s.74(6) of the Civil Aviation Act 1982, which would have allowed effect to be given in the United Kingdom to these jurisdictional rules, was repealed by the Transport Act 2000.[134]

15–037   Schedule 4 to the Civil Aviation Act 1982 provides[135] that a court in any part of the United Kingdom shall have jurisdiction to hear and determine a claim against Eurocontrol for damages in respect of any wrongful act, neglect or default, notwithstanding that the act, neglect or default did not take place within the jurisdiction of the court or that Eurocontrol is not present within the jurisdiction of the court; but a court does not have jurisdiction under this provision in respect of damage or injury sustained wholly within or over a country to which the provisions of the Act relating to Eurocontrol do not extend.[136] Permission of the court is not required for the service of process out of the jurisdiction in respect of claims brought against Eurocontrol under these provisions.[137]

15–038   Under s.73 of the Civil Aviation Act 1982, the Secretary of State for Transport was given power to make regulations establishing charges to be paid in respect of air navigation services. Section 74(6) contained rules on the jurisdiction of a court in any part of the United Kingdom to hear and

---

[130] Cmd. 8742. See, in particular, Art.28.

[131] For text, see Cmnd. 1373 (1962).

[132] For text, see Cmnd. 8662 (1982).

[133] Art.13.

[134] ss.97, 274, Sch.8, Pt III, para.4, Sch.31, Pt I(2). But provision is made to give effect to the Agreement in respect of the enforcement of foreign judgments in Civil Aviation (Eurocontrol) Act 1983, s.1, which inserts s.74A in Civil Aviation Act 1982. S.74A remains in force. See para.15–064, below.

[135] para.3(1), as amended by Civil Aviation (Eurocontrol) Act 1983, s.2 and Transport Act 2000.

[136] Civil Aviation Act 1982, Sch.4, para.3(2). See also para.1(4B)(4C) inserted by Civil Aviation (Eurocontrol) Act 1983, s.2.

[137] CPR, r.6.33(3); above, Rule 33.

determine a claim for charges or interest payable to the Secretary of State or the Civil Aviation Authority or Eurocontrol.[138] But ss.73 and 74 were repealed by the Transport Act 2000.[139]

Collisions at sea. Section 22 of the Senior Courts Act 1981 contains   **15–039** provisions based upon those of the Brussels International Convention on Certain Rules concerning Civil Jurisdiction in Matters of Collision, 1952.[140] The provisions apply to any claim, whether or not it is within the Admiralty jurisdiction of the High Court,[141] for damage, loss of life or personal injury, arising out of a collision between ships, or the carrying out of, or omission to carry out, a manoeuvre in the case of one or more of two or more ships, or non-compliance on the part of one or more such ships, with the collision regulations. The High Court has jurisdiction to entertain an action to enforce such a claim if, but only if, the defendant has his habitual residence or place of business in England, or the cause of action arose within inland waters of England or within the limits of a port of England, or an action arising out of the same incident or series of incidents is proceeding in the court or has been heard and determined in the court,[142] or if the defendant submits or has agreed to submit to the jurisdiction of the court.[143] Permission is required for the service of process out of the jurisdiction in claims brought under these provisions.[144]

Disputes as to liner conferences. The Geneva Convention on a Code of   **15–040** Conduct for Liner Conferences 1974 was negotiated under the auspices of UNCTAD (the United Nations Conference on Trade and Development). The United Kingdom acceded to the Convention with reservations made in accordance with the agreed policy of the EC Member States.[145] The Code contains provisions for the settlement of disputes.[146] The Merchant Shipping (Liner

---

[138] Claims for the payment of charges due to Eurocontrol are not within the Brussels I Regulation: Case 29/76 *LTU GmbH & Co v Eurocontrol* [1976] E.C.R. 1541. See above, para.11–030.

[139] ss.97, 274, Sch.8, Pt III, para.4, Sch.31, Pt I(2).

[140] For text see Cmd. 8954 (1952); Singh, *International Maritime Law Conventions* (1983), Vol.4, pp.3107–3111.

[141] Senior Courts Act 1981, s.22(8).

[142] *ibid.* s.22(1)(2)(6). "Inland waters" and "port" are defined in s.22(2). See *The World Harmony* [1967] P. 341.

[143] Senior Courts Act 1981, s.22(5).

[144] On the possible differences between the jurisdiction provisions applicable to collisions between ships, on the one hand, and collision by a ship with an oil platform, on the other, see *Conocophillips (UK) Ltd v Partnereederei Ms Jork* [2010] EWHC 1214 (Comm.), at [38].

[145] Council Regulation 954/79 of May 15, 1979 [1979] O.J. L121/1.

[146] Ch.VI (Arts 23 to 46). These include a provision (Art.23(2)) that disputes between shipping lines of the same flag, as well as those between organisations belonging to the same country, shall be settled within the framework of the national jurisdiction of that country, unless this creates serious difficulties in the fulfilment of the provisions of the Code. The Act provides that proceedings arising out of a dispute to which this provision applies shall not be entertained by the High Court except as permitted by that provision: Merchant Shipping (Liner Conferences) Act 1982, s.7(2) (which remains in force).

Conferences) Act 1982, which gave effect to the Code,[147] has now been repealed in part. The mandatory provisions of the Code, as implemented by the 1982 Act,[148] are no longer in force.[149]

15–041   **Employment of crew of aircraft and ships.** An Order in Council made under s.4 of the Consular Relations Act 1968 may exclude or limit the jurisdiction of any court in the United Kingdom to entertain proceedings relating to the remuneration or any contract of service of the master or commander or a member of the crew of any ship or aircraft belonging to a State specified in the Order, except where a consular officer of that State has been notified of the intention to invoke the jurisdiction of the court and does not object within a period of two weeks from the date of such notification.[150] A provision of this nature is included in the European Convention on Consular Functions 1967,[151] but can also be included in bilateral arrangements between the United Kingdom and other States.

15–042   **Oil pollution by ships.** Sections 152 to 171 of the Merchant Shipping Act 1995 give effect to the International Convention on Civil Liability for Oil Pollution Damage 1992.[152] Civil liability is imposed on the owner of a ship from which persistent oil has been discharged or has escaped[153] and, where there is a grave and imminent threat of damage being caused if oil were to be discharged or to escape from a ship, the owner is liable for the cost of measures taken to prevent or minimise such damage and for any damage caused by such measures.[154] The Act provides for compulsory insurance

---

[147] The Merchant Shipping (Liner Conferences) Act 1982 designates the Secretary of State to perform certain functions in order to give effect to the Code: see s.10 (still in force). SI 1985/405 and 406, which enabled the Secretary of State to make by regulation appropriate provision to give effect to the Code, have both been repealed by SI 2008/163. See also CPR PD74A, paras 10–14.

[148] ss.2–4, 11–13.

[149] They were repealed by Merchant Shipping (Liner Conferences) Act 1982 (Repeal) Regulations 2008, SI 2008/163. Council Regulation (EC) 1419/2006, [2006] O.J. L269/1 repealed Council Regulation (EEC) 4056/86, and removed the block exemption from Arts 101 and 102 of the EC Treaty granted to liner shipping conferences. Accordingly, Council Regulation (EEC) 954/79, [1979] O.J. L121/1, which gave effect to the Code within the European Union, became inapplicable. The 2008 Regulations repeal the provisions giving effect to Regulation 954/79. Other provisions of the 1982 Act remain in force.

[150] For Orders in Council under s.4, see *Halsbury's Laws of England*, Vol.18, para.1594.

[151] Art.35(3).

[152] The 1992 Convention is the Brussels International Convention on Civil Liability for Oil Pollution Damage 1969 (Cmnd. 4403 (1970)) as amended by the Protocols of November 19, 1976 and December 2, 1992. A further amendment raising the limits for compensation was adopted on October 18, 2000 and entered into force on November 1, 2003. See Merchant Shipping (Oil Pollution Compensation Limits) Order 2003, SI 2003/2559. The Merchant Shipping (Pollution) Act 2006, which is in force, enables effect to be given to the Supplementary Fund Protocol 2003 and to future revisions of the international arrangements relating to compensation for oil pollution from ships.

[153] s.153(1). See *The Sea Empress* [2003] EWCA Civ 65, [2003] 1 Lloyd's Rep. 327.

[154] s.165 (as amended by SI 2006/1244 and to be amended by Third Parties (Rights against Insurers) Act 2010, Sch.2, para.3 (not yet in force)).

against liability for oil pollution damage[155] and for direct action against the insurer.[156] Under the Convention,[157] actions can be brought only in the courts of the contracting State or States in which the damage occurred. This is reflected in s.166(2) of the Act in its negative aspect: no court in the United Kingdom is to entertain an action (whether *in rem* or *in personam*) to enforce any claim arising from damage caused in another Convention country by contamination resulting from the discharge or escape of persistent oil from a ship or arising from the cost of measures taken in another Convention country to prevent or minimise such damage if no damage is caused or no measures are taken in the United Kingdom. Convention countries may be certified from time to time by Orders in Council, which are conclusive for the purposes of English law.[158]

Permission of the court is required for the service of process outside the   **15–043**
jurisdiction in respect of a claim under s.153 of the Act.[159] The Act contemplates the possibility of actions against Convention States.[160] A Convention State is deemed to have submitted to the jurisdiction of the court, and section 12 of the State Immunity Act 1978 and CPR, r.6.44 provide for service of process upon the foreign government with the assistance of the Secretary of State; these provisions do not, however, authorise the issue of execution against the property of any State.[161]

The International Convention on Civil Liability for Bunker Oil Pollution   **15–044**
2001[162] entered into force on November 21, 2008.[163] Merchant Shipping Act 1995, ss.152–71 have been amended accordingly.[164] The Convention is designed to fill a gap in the international regime for dealing with oil spillage,[165] as the 1992 Convention does not include bunker oil spills from vessels other than tankers. Article 9(1) of the 2001 Convention provides: "Where an incident has caused pollution damage in the territory, including the territorial sea, or in an area referred to in article 2(a)(ii) of one or more States Parties, or preventive measures have been taken to prevent or minimise pollution damage in such territory, including the territorial sea, or in such area, actions for compensation against the shipowner, insurer or other person providing security for the shipowner's liability may be brought only in the courts of any such States Parties." The Regulations introduce a new s.153A into Merchant

---

[155] s.163.

[156] s.165 (as amended).

[157] Art.IX(1).

[158] Merchant Shipping Act 1995, s.152(2).

[159] CPR PD6B, para.3.1(19)(b).

[160] s.167(3).

[161] Merchant Shipping Act 1995, s.167(3).

[162] For discussion, see Tsimplis [2005] L.M.C.L.Q. 83, especially pp.97–98; Jacobsson (2009) 15 J.I.M.L. 21.

[163] Member States of the European Union were authorised to ratify the Convention and urged to do so: see Council Decision 2002/762/EC, [2005] O.J. L256/7, Arts 1(1), 3(2).

[164] By Merchant Shipping (Oil Pollution) (Bunkers Convention) Regulations 2006, SI 2006/1244.

[165] On other forms of pollution, see Merchant Shipping (Prevention of Pollutions by Sewage and Garbage from Ships) Regulations 2008 (SI 2008/3257), Reg.45 (in force February 1, 2009).

Shipping Act 1995 and supplement[166] the rules on jurisdiction and registration of foreign judgments in s.166 of the 1995 Act.[167]

15–045   **Claims for damage arising from the carriage of hazardous and noxious substances by sea.**   Section 182B of the Merchant Shipping Act 1995 (inserted by the Merchant Shipping and Maritime Security Act 1997) makes provision for the implementation of the International Convention on Liability and Compensation for Damage in Connection with the Carriage of Hazardous and Noxious Substances by Sea 1996.[168] The text of the 1996 Convention is set out in Schedule 5A to the 1995 Act.[169] It is expressly provided that the 1996 Convention has no application to pollution damage as defined in the International Convention on Civil Liability for Oil Pollution Damage.[170]

15–046   Where a person has a claim, other than a claim arising out of a contract for the carriage of goods and passengers,[171] as a result of damage arising from the carriage of hazardous and noxious substances (HNS) by sea, the Convention imposes liability on the owner of the ship carrying the HNS[172] and requires the owner to maintain insurance or other financial security for such claims.[173] A claim may be brought against the owner only in accordance with the Convention.[174] The Convention also establishes the International Hazardous and Noxious Substances Fund (HNS Fund),[175] the purpose of which is to pay compensation to any person who suffers damage and who is unable to obtain adequate compensation from the owner.[176] Accordingly, the Convention contemplates claims being brought against either the owner of the ship carrying the HNS or, in appropriate circumstances, the HNS Fund.

15–047   Where a claim against an owner arises out of an incident which causes damage in the territory (including the territorial sea) of a State Party or which leads to the taking of preventative measures in the territory of a State Party, an action for compensation may be brought against the owner only in the courts of that State; if damage is caused in more than one State Party, the

---

[166] See Reg.20.

[167] Section 166(3A) of the Act provides that: "Where— (a) there is a discharge or escape of bunker oil falling within section 153A(1) which does not result in any damage caused by contamination in the territory of the United Kingdom and no measures are reasonably taken to prevent or minimise such damage in that territory, or (b) any relevant threat of contamination falling within section 153A(2) arises but no measures are reasonably taken to prevent or minimise such damage in the territory of the United Kingdom, no court in the United Kingdom shall entertain any action (whether *in rem* or *in personam*) to enforce a claim arising from any relevant damage or cost– (i) against the owner of the ship, or (ii) against any person to whom section 156(2A) (ii) applies, unless any such damage or cost resulted from anything done or omitted to be done as mentioned in that provision."

[168] No order has yet been made under s.182B to implement the 1996 Convention. A Protocol was adopted in 2010 which will supersede the 1996 Convention but it is not yet in force.

[169] Inserted by Merchant Shipping and Maritime Security Act 1997, s.14(2); Sch.3.

[170] Art.4(3)(a).

[171] Art.4(1).

[172] Arts 7–11.

[173] Art.12.

[174] Art.7(4).

[175] Arts 13–36.

[176] Art.14(1).

plaintiff may sue the owner in the courts of any of the State Parties concerned.[177] If the incident causing damage (or leading to the taking of preventative measures) does not cause damage in the territory of any State Party (or does not cause preventative measures to be taken in any State Party), an action may be brought against the owner in (i) the State Party in which the ship is registered (or, if unregistered, the State Party whose flag the ship is entitled to fly), or (ii) the State Party where the owner is habitually resident or in which his principal place of business is established, or (iii) the State Party in which the owner has established a limitation fund.[178] Where a limitation fund has been established in a State Party the courts of that State have exclusive jurisdiction over the apportionment and distribution of the fund.[179] Where a claim for compensation is brought against the HNS Fund the action must be brought in the court which had jurisdiction in respect of the action against the owner (or which would have had jurisdiction in respect of an action against an owner if an owner had been liable).[180]

ILLUSTRATIONS

1. A, resident in England, makes a contract with X & Co in Jakarta for a return air flight Jakarta–London–Jakarta. X & Co is an Indonesian company with a branch office in London. A is injured in an accident as the aircraft lands in London. He wishes to claim damages from X & Co The English courts have no jurisdiction; London is not the place of destination, nor does the presence of a branch office render X & Co ordinarily resident in England.[181]   **15–048**

2. A, resident in England, makes a contract with X & Co in Stockholm for a return air flight Stockholm–London–Stockholm. X & Co is a Swedish company with a branch office in London. A is injured in an accident as the aircraft lands in London. He wishes to claim damages from X & Co The English courts have jurisdiction. London is not the place of destination, nor does the presence of a branch office render X & Co ordinarily resident in England.[182] However, the claim concerns injury to a passenger resident in England and the carrier operates services for the carriage of passengers by air to England.[183]

3. A, resident in England, purchases a railway ticket from the English branch of B Co, a Belgian carrier, from London to Brussels. A is injured during transit. A may bring proceedings against B Co in England.[184]

4. A makes a contract with B & Co, a Spanish company, for the carriage of goods by road from Birmingham to Madrid. B & Co sub-contracts the carriage of the goods from Birmingham to Paris to C & Co, and only carries the goods itself from Paris to Madrid. The goods are damaged during the Paris–Madrid carriage, and A claims damages from B & Co. The English court has

---

[177] Art.38(1).

[178] Art.38(2). Limitation of liability is governed by Art.9, which provides that the fund may be established only in a State Party where an action against the owner has been (or could be) brought under Art.38.

[179] Art.38(5).

[180] Art.39(1).

[181] Carriage by Air Acts (Application of Provisions Order) 2004, SI 2004/1899, Sch. 2, Art.28(1); *Grein v Imperial Airways Ltd* [1937] 1 K.B. 50; *Qureshi v KLM Royal Dutch Airlines* (1979) 102 D.L.R. (3d) 205 (N.S.); *Rothmans of Pall Mall (Overseas) Ltd v Saudi Arabian Airlines Corp* [1981] Q.B. 368 (CA).

[182] Carriage by Air Act 1961, Sch.1B, Art.33(1).

[183] *ibid.*, Art.33(2).

[184] Vilnius Protocol 1999 modifying the Berne Convention concerning International Carriage by Rail 1980 (COTIF); Appendix A (Uniform Rules concerning the Contract of International Carriage of Passengers (CIV)), Art.57(1).

jurisdiction as the goods were taken over by the carrier in England. The sub-contracting of the first part, or the whole, of the actual carriage is immaterial.[185]

5. S seeks to bring a claim against certain companies in respect of the loss of a consignment of its goods carried by road from England to the Netherlands. One of the companies, K, issues proceedings in the Netherlands against S's insurers for a declaration that it has no liability, or limited liability under the CMR Convention. S then starts proceedings against K in England. Subsequently, K seeks to bring proceedings for the same declaratory relief against S in the Netherlands. The English court declines jurisdiction in favour of the Dutch court pursuant to Art.28 of the Brussels I Regulation.[186]

6. A, an English resident, makes a contract in England with X & Co, a French company, for the carriage by sea of himself and his luggage from Cork to Bordeaux. The luggage is damaged during the carriage. A wishes to claim damages from X & Co. The English court has jurisdiction if X & Co has a place of business in England and the claim form is served upon the persons authorised to accept service on behalf of the company.[187]

15R–049 **Rule 61—English courts have no jurisdiction to determine any claim or question certified under statutory powers by the Secretary of State to be a claim or question which under an international convention falls to be determined by a court in some foreign country.**[188]

COMMENT

15–050   The jurisdictional requirements of international conventions to which the United Kingdom is a party are commonly incorporated in the enactment giving the convention the force of law in the United Kingdom; these cases were examined in Rule 60. In certain cases, however, a different technique is used, the enactment merely providing for the exclusion of jurisdiction by the grant of a certificate by the Secretary of State that the claim is one which falls, in accordance with the relevant convention, to be determined by the courts of some foreign country.

15–051   Thus, s.23 of the Senior Courts Act 1981 provides that the High Court[189] shall not have jurisdiction to determine any claim or question certified by the Secretary of State to be a claim or question which, under the Rhine Navigation Convention,[190] falls to be determined in accordance with the provisions

---

[185] Carriage of Goods by Road Act 1965, Sch., Art.31(1); *Moto Vespa SA v MAT (Britannia Express) Ltd* [1979] 1 Lloyd's Rep. 175; *Ulster-Swift Ltd v Taunton Meat Haulage Ltd* [1977] 1 W.L.R. 625 (CA).

[186] *Sony Computer Entertainment Ltd v RH Freight Services Ltd* [2007] EWHC 302 (Comm.), [2007] 2 Lloyd's Rep. 463. See also *Andrea Merzario Ltd v Internationale Spedition Leitner Gesellschaft GmbH* [2001] EWCA Civ 61, [2001] 1 Lloyd's Rep. 490 (CA); *Royal & Sun Alliance Insurance Plc v M.K. Digital FZE (Cyprus) Ltd* [2005] EWHC 1408 (Comm.), [2005] 2 Lloyd's Rep. 679, reversed on other grounds [2006] EWCA Civ 629, [2006] 2 Lloyd's Rep. 110.

[187] In accordance with the Companies Act 2006 and CPR, r.6. See Merchant Shipping Act 1995, Sch.6, Pt I, Art.17(1); Carriage of Passengers and their Luggage by Sea (Interim Provisions) Order 1980, SI 1980/1092, as amended by SI 1987/670.

[188] Senior Courts Act 1981, s.23; Nuclear Installations Act 1965, s.17(1).

[189] For Scotland, see Administration of Justice Act 1956, s.46; for Northern Ireland, see Sch.1, Pt. I, para.6. For county courts, see County Courts Act 1984, s.27(9).

[190] Defined in Senior Courts Act 1981, s.24(1) as the Convention of October 17, 1868 as revised by any subsequent convention. See *British and Foreign State Papers*, Vol.59, p. 470. The 7th October, is evidently a mistake for 17th October. An amending Convention (to which the United Kingdom is a party) was signed at Strasbourg on November 20, 1963, and came into force on April 14, 1967. See Cmnd. 3371 (1967).

thereof. The United Kingdom is not a party to that Convention. But Pt I of the Administration of Justice Act 1956 (since replaced by ss.20 to 24 of the Senior Courts Act 1981) was passed in order to implement two Conventions signed at Brussels in 1952,[191] to which the United Kingdom is a party, and which contain savings for the Rhine Navigation Convention. The section is unlikely to be invoked very often, partly because of its restricted scope and partly because various British shipping and insurance associations have stated that they will not seek the Secretary of State's certificate in claims for death or personal injuries brought by British citizens against the owners of British ships owned or insured by members of those associations.[192]

Again, s.17(1) of the Nuclear Installations Act 1965 provides that no court   **15–052** in the United Kingdom or any part thereof shall have jurisdiction to determine any claim or question under that Act certified by the Secretary of State[193] to be a claim or question which, under any relevant international agreement,[194] falls to be determined by a court of some other country which is bound by that agreement or of some other part of the United Kingdom. The Act gives effect to various international conventions (to which the United Kingdom is a party) on civil liability for nuclear "occurrences."[195] The Act imposes absolute liability on the operators (including certain foreign operators) of nuclear installations for nuclear occurrences which cause injury to any person or damage to any property of any person other than the operator.[196] Under the Conventions,[197] jurisdiction prima facie lies only with the courts of the Contracting Party within whose territory the nuclear incident occurred. But if the nuclear incident occurred outside the territory of any Contracting Party, or if the place of the nuclear incident cannot be determined with certainty, jurisdiction lies with the courts of the Contracting Party in whose territory the nuclear installation of the operator liable is situated. If jurisdiction lies with the courts of more than one Contracting Party, then if the nuclear incident occurred partly outside the territory of any Contracting Party and partly within

---

[191] Convention on Certain Rules Concerning Civil Jurisdiction in Matters of Collision, and Convention Relating to the Arrest of Sea-going Ships, Cmnd. 8954 (1952); reprinted in Singh, *International Maritime Law Conventions* (1983), Vol.4, pp.3107, 3101.

[192] Marsden, *Collisions At Sea* (13th ed. 2003), para.2–50.

[193] The functions under s.17(1) are transferred, in so far as they are exercisable in or as regards Scotland, to the Scottish Ministers, by SI 1999/1750, Sch.1, Art.2.

[194] A "relevant international agreement" is one with respect to third-party liability in the field of nuclear energy (excluding liability in respect of nuclear reactors comprised in means of transport): s.26(1).

[195] The Paris Convention on Third Party Liability in the Field of Nuclear Energy (1960) (as amended), Cmnd. 2514 (1964); and the Convention (1963) Supplementary to the Paris Convention, Cmnd. 2515 (1964), as amended (1982). A 2004 Protocol to amend the Paris Convention was concluded between Contracting States. Part M of the 2004 Protocol inserts more detailed provisions on jurisdiction. The 2004 Protocol has yet to enter into force. *cf.* the Vienna Convention (1963), Cmnd. 2333 (1964), not yet ratified by the United Kingdom and the Joint Protocol relating to the Application of the Vienna Convention and the Paris Convention (1988), Cmnd. 774, signed but not yet ratified by the United Kingdom. See also Protocol to Amend the 1963 Vienna Convention (which entered into force on October 4, 2003 but which has not been signed by the United Kingdom); and the Supplementary Compensation Convention 1997 (which has yet to enter into force and which has not been signed by the United Kingdom). See further Blanchard [2011] 2 I.B.L.J. 131; and see below, paras 15–068—15–071.

[196] ss.7–10, 12. See Street and Frame, *Law Relating to Nuclear Energy* (1966).

[197] Vienna Convention, Art.XI; Paris Convention, Art.13(a)(b) and (c).

the territory of a single Contracting Party, jurisdiction lies with the courts of the latter; in any other case jurisdiction lies with the courts of one of the relevant Contracting Parties, under the Vienna Convention that chosen by agreement between the Contracting Parties and under the Paris Convention that identified by an arbitral tribunal as being the Contracting Party most closely related to the case in question. The Secretary of State's certificate will in appropriate cases reflect the agreement reached, or the ruling of the arbitral tribunal, as to the proper forum.

The certificate of the Secretary of State under s.17(1) of the Nuclear Installations Act 1965 is conclusive,[198] and the same is no doubt true under s.23 of the Senior Courts Act 1981.

15R–053   **Rule 62—A judgment of a court of a foreign country outside the United Kingdom in proceedings regulated by certain international conventions which have been given effect in the law of the United Kingdom will be recognised and enforced if the jurisdictional requirements of the convention concerned are fulfilled.**

Comment

15–054   A number of international conventions dealing with particular matters contain provisions as to the recognition and enforcement of judgments, and these are reflected in the United Kingdom legislation giving effect to the conventions. The United Kingdom legislation concerned[199] is the Carriage of Goods by Road Act 1965, ss.152 to 171 of the Merchant Shipping Act 1995,[200] s.182B of the Merchant Shipping Act 1995,[201] certain provisions of the Civil Aviation Act 1982 dealing with air navigation charges, and the Railways (Convention on International Carriage by Rail) Regulations 2005.[202] The legislation commonly provides for the application to judgments given in accordance with the relevant convention of a modified version of Pt I of the Foreign Judgments (Reciprocal Enforcement) Act 1933. Where the judgment is given by a court in a Member State bound by the Brussels I Regulation, the position is affected by Art.71 of the Regulation. If both the United Kingdom and the Member State in which the judgment was given are parties to a convention on a particular matter, and that convention lays down conditions for the recognition or enforcement of judgments, those conditions continue to apply.[203] In any event, the procedures of the Brussels I Regulation may be applied.[204] Similar

---

[198] s.17(2).

[199] Carriage of Passengers by Road Act 1974 never entered into force and was repealed by Statute Law (Repeals) Act 2004.

[200] As amended by SI 2006/1244, with effect from November 21, 2008. See entry at para. 15–044, above.

[201] See above, n.169.

[202] SI 2005/2092. The Regulations repeal the relevant provisions of International Transport Conventions Act 1983.

[203] Art.71(2)(b).

[204] *ibid.* On the requirements for service for where the State of origin and the State of recognition are party to an international convention on the service of documents, see Case C–522/03 *Scania Finance France SA v Rockinger Spezialfabrik für Anhängerkupplungen GmbH & Co* [2005] E.C.R. I–8639.

principles apply where the State in which judgment is given and the United Kingdom are both Contracting States to the Lugano Convention.[205]

Certain conventions, e.g. the Warsaw Convention of 1929 and the Montreal   **15–055** Convention 1999 dealing with carriage by air, contain no express provisions as to the recognition and enforcement of judgments but do contain provisions as to the allocation of jurisdiction. If a judgment is given in another State to which the Brussels I Regulation applies, or a Contracting State to the Lugano Convention in the exercise of jurisdiction provided for in such a convention, e.g. as being the court having jurisdiction at the place of destination in carriage by air, its recognition and enforcement will be governed in the United Kingdom by the Brussels I Regulation,[206] or by the Lugano Convention. It follows that a judgment given by the courts of a state bound by the Brussels I Regulation, or a Contracting State to the Lugano Convention[207] under the Warsaw Convention 1929 or the Montreal Convention 1999 may be denied recognition or enforcement only on the grounds set out in the Brussels I Regulation or the Lugano Convention (as the case may be).[208] When a judgment is given in a Lugano Convention Contracting State under a particular convention, recognition or enforcement may be refused not only on the grounds provided for in Arts 34 and 35,[209] but also if the State addressed is not a contracting party to the convention in question and the person against whom recognition or enforcement is sought is domiciled in that State, or, if the State addressed is a Member State of the European Community and judgment is given in a Contracting State in respect of a convention which would have to be concluded by the European Community, if the person against whom recognition or enforcement is sought is domiciled in any Member State, unless the judgment may otherwise be recognised or enforced under any rule of the State addressed.[210] If such a judgment is given in a foreign court to whose judgments Pt I of the Foreign Judgments (Reciprocal Enforcement) Act 1933 applies, it is submitted that the foreign court will be deemed to have jurisdiction, this exercise of jurisdiction being one recognised by the United Kingdom legislation; but there seems no clear authority to this effect. If recognition and enforcement is sought at common law a similar argument can be advanced, that the jurisdiction of the foreign court is recognised in English law; again, there is no clear authority.[211] United Kingdom legislation to which these arguments apply includes the Carriage by Air Act 1961, the Carriage by Air (Supplementary Provisions) Act 1962, the Carriage by Air Acts (Application of Provisions) Order 2004,[212] s.183(1) of the Merchant Shipping Act 1995, and the Carriage of Passengers and their Luggage by Sea (Interim Provisions) Order 1980.[213]

---

[205] Art.67(5).

[206] Art.71(2)(b).

[207] Art.67(5).

[208] Arts 34 and 35 of the Brussels I Regulation and the Lugano Convention.

[209] See above, paras 14–221—14–237.

[210] Lugano Convention, Art.67(4).

[211] This is not an argument based upon "reciprocity" (see paras 14–087—14–089); it does not rest upon the assertion of jurisdiction by the English courts but upon its allocation to the courts of various countries by a convention having effect in English law.

[212] SI 2004/1899, as amended by SI 2004/1974).

[213] SI 1980/1092 as amended by SI 1987/670.

15–056   In *TNT Express Nederland BV v AXA Versicherung AG*,[214] the European Court held that Art.71(2)(b) of the Brussels I Regulation had the effect that rules on the enforcement of foreign judgments in an international convention to which a Member State was party would prevail over the rules in the Brussels I Regulation; but on condition that they did not compromise the fundamental aims of free movement and the sound administration of justice in the Brussels I Regulation; and, in particular, provided that the rules on enforcement of foreign judgments in the international convention were not less favourable than those in the Brussels I Regulation.[215]

The various cases falling within the scope of the Rule are examined below, grouped by subject-matter.

15–057   **Carriage by air.** There are no provisions as to the recognition and enforcement of judgments in any version of the Warsaw Convention 1929 nor in the supplementary Guadalajara Convention 1961, nor in the Montreal Convention 1999, nor in the United Kingdom legislation giving effect to those Conventions.[216] There are however provisions as to jurisdiction enabling actions to be brought only in certain courts[217] and, for the reasons stated above,[218] it is submitted that a judgment given in a foreign court under these provisions is entitled to recognition and enforcement in England.

15–058   **Carriage by rail.** Part I of the Foreign Judgments (Reciprocal Enforcement) Act 1933, with the omission of s.4(2) and (3), applies to any judgment given by a court in a country which is a party to the Berne Convention concerning International Carriage by Rail (COTIF), as modified by the Vilnius Protocol 1999, in accordance with the jurisdictional rules of the modified Convention and its related Uniform Rules,[219] and which has become enforceable under the law applied by that court.[220] The effect of the omission of s.4(2) and (3) is that while the registration of the foreign judgment must be set aside if the courts of the country concerned had no jurisdiction in the circumstances

---

[214] Case C–533/08 [2010] I.L.Pr. 663.

[215] The European Court relied upon Recitals 6, 16 and 17 of the Brussels I Regulation and Case C–283/05 *ASML Netherlands BV v Semiconductor Industry Services GmbH (Semis)* [2006] E.C.R. I–12041, [2007] 1 All E.R. (Comm.) 949, [2007] I.L.Pr. 4, at [23]; Case C–185/07 *West Tankers Inc v Allianz SpA* [2009] E.C.R. I–663, [2009] 1 A.C. 1138, [24]; and Case C–420/07 *Apostolides v Orams* [2009] E.C.R. I–3571, [2011] Q.B. 519, at [73]. See further above, paras 15–003 and 15–056.

[216] For the Conventions and the legislation (the Carriage by Air Act 1961, the Carriage by Air (Supplementary Provisions) Act 1962, and the Carriage by Air Acts (Application of Provisions) Order 2004, SI 2004/1899, as amended by SI 2004/1974), see above, paras 15–008 *et seq.*

[217] See Carriage by Air Acts 1961, Sch.1, Art.28(1); Sch.1A, Art.28(1); Sch.1B, Art.33, Carriage by Air (Supplementary Provisions) Act 1962, Sch., Art.VIII and Carriage by Air Acts (Application of Provisions) Order 2004, SI 2004/1899, Sch.2, Art.28(1); Sch.3, Art.28(1).

[218] See above, para.15–055.

[219] For discussion of the Convention, see above, paras 15–020 *et seq.*

[220] Railways (Convention on International Carriage by Rail) Regulations 2005, SI 2005/2092, reg.8; Convention, Art.12. See also Civil Jurisdiction and Judgments Act 1982, ss.31(3) and 32(4)(b), both as amended by reg.9(2), Sch.3, para.2. These provisions, which give the force of law to the 1999 Protocol (which entered into force in respect of the United Kingdom on July 1, 2006), replace the corresponding provisions in International Transport Conventions Act 1983, s.6; Convention, Art.18(1).

of the case,[221] the existence of jurisdiction is to be gathered from the terms of the Convention.

Carriage by road. Part I of the Foreign Judgments (Reciprocal Enforce-   **15–059** ment) Act 1933, with the omission of section 4(2) and (3), applies to any judgment given by a court or tribunal in a country which is a party to the Geneva Convention on the Contract for the International Carriage of Goods by Road 1956 (the CMR Convention),[222] which was given in accordance with the jurisdictional provisions of the Convention, and which has become enforceable in the country in which it was given; this is the case whether or not that Part has been extended to the country concerned, and whether or not the judgment is given by a court specified for the purposes of that Part.[223] In effect jurisdiction will exist if, and only if, the courts of the foreign country were designated by agreement between the parties, or the defendant was ordinarily resident in that country or had his principal place of business there or the branch through which the contract was made was situated there, or the place where the goods were taken over by the carrier or the place designated for delivery was situated there.[224]

In *TNT Express Nederland BV v AXA Versicherung AG*,[225] the question   **15–060** arose whether a Dutch court, which was first seised of proceedings under the CMR Convention (and whose judgment was the subject of a pending appeal) was required to enforce a German judgment ostensibly given in defiance of the court first seised rule in Art.31(2) of the CMR Convention. TNT alleged that the Dutch court could decline to enforce the German judgment on public policy grounds. AXA argued that this would be incompatible with Art.35(3) of the Brussels I Regulation, which precludes the use of the public policy defence in Art.34(1) of the Brussels I Regulation to review the jurisdiction of the court of origin. This, in turn, gave rise to questions as to the meaning of Art.71(2)(b) of the Brussels I Regulation and the extent to which the rules on the enforcement of foreign judgments in the CMR Convention could prevail over rules in the Brussels I Regulation. The European Court ruled that the effect of Art.71(2)(b) of the Brussels I Regulation was that the CMR rules on enforcement of foreign judgments would prevail, provided that they did not compromise the key requirements of free movement and sound administration of justice in the Brussels I Regulation. This required, in particular, that the rules on enforcement of foreign judgments in the CMR Convention were not less favourable than those in the Brussels I Regulation. The European Court declined to determine whether this was the case, on the basis that it lacked competence to interpret the CMR Convention.[226]

---

[221] Foreign Judgments (Reciprocal Enforcement) Act 1933, s.4(1)(a)(ii).

[222] For the Convention, and parties to it, see above, para.15–025.

[223] Carriage of Goods by Road Act 1965, s.4. See also the exclusion of judgments to which this provision applies from the scope of Civil Jurisdiction and Judgments Act 1982, ss.31 (judgments against States) and 32 (judgments in breach of agreement for settlement of disputes).

[224] Carriage of Goods by Road Act 1965, Sch., Art.31(1) and (3). See above, para.15–025.

[225] Case C–533/08 [2010] I.L.Pr. 663; see, in particular, [51].

[226] At [51]. See also entries at paras 15–004 and 15–056, above.

15–061   The Carriage of Passengers by Road Act 1974, which contained provisions on the recognition and enforcement of foreign judgments, did not enter into force and was repealed by the Statute Law (Repeals) Act 2004.

15–062   **Carriage of passengers and luggage by sea.** There are no provisions as to the recognition and enforcement of judgments in the Athens Convention relating to the Carriage of Passengers and their Luggage by Sea 1974, nor in s.183(1) of the Merchant Shipping Act 1995 (which gives effect to the Convention), nor in the Carriage of Passengers and their Luggage by Sea (Interim Provisions) Order 1980.[227] There are however provisions as to jurisdiction enabling actions to be brought only in certain courts,[228] and, for the reasons stated above,[229] it is submitted that a judgment given in a foreign court under these provisions is entitled to recognition and enforcement in England.

15–063   **The United Nations Convention on Contracts for the International Carriage of Goods Wholly or Partly By Sea (the Rotterdam Rules).** The Rotterdam Rules[230] (not yet in force) contain provisions on the recognition and enforcement of foreign judgments.[231] These Rules would only apply if the State of origin and the State where recognition was sought were both Contracting States that had declared their intention to be bound by the chapter on jurisdiction[232] in the Rules.

15–064   **Claims in respect of air navigation services.** The Civil Aviation (Eurocontrol) Act 1983 contains provisions as to the recognition and enforcement of determinations by a relevant authority in a Contracting State to the Multilateral Agreement relating to Route Charges 1981 as to whether or not any sum is due to Eurocontrol in respect of air navigation services.[233] Certain provisions of the Foreign Judgments (Reciprocal Enforcement) Act 1933[234] are applied, but there are more elaborate further provisions than in the other cases considered in this Rule. "Relevant authority" includes courts and tribunals, and also administrative authorities if their determinations are subject to appeal to or review by a court or tribunal.[235] The relevant authority has jurisdiction for the purposes of recognition and enforcement if the proceedings are brought (a) in the Contracting State (if any) in which there is situated the residence or, as the case may be, the registered office of the person liable

---

[227] SI 1980/1092 (amended by SI 1987/670).
[228] Convention, Art.17(1), applied by the 1980 Order with the omission of the requirement that the court be located in a Contracting State.
[229] See above, para.15–055.
[230] Considered above, at para.15–034.
[231] Art.73.
[232] Ch.14.
[233] Civil Aviation (Eurocontrol) Act 1983, s.1 adding a new s.74A to the Civil Aviation Act 1982. For the Multilateral Agreement and Eurocontrol, see above, paras 15–035–15–038. Although the jurisdiction rules in the 1983 Act, which were contained in s.74(6) of Civil Aviation Act 1982, were repealed by Transport Act 2000, s.74A of the 1982 Act on the recognition and enforcement of foreign judgments was preserved.
[234] ss.2, 3, 5(3), with modifications to s.5(2).
[235] Civil Aviation Act 1982, s.74A(8) as inserted by Civil Aviation (Eurocontrol) Act 1983, s.1.

to pay the charges; (b) if his residence or registered office is not situated in a Contracting State, in any Contracting State in which he has a place of business; (c) if his residence or registered office is not situated in a Contracting State and he has no place of business in any Contracting State, in any Contracting State in which he has assets; (d) if his residence or registered office is not situated in a Contracting State and he has neither a place of business nor any assets in a Contracting State, in Belgium (being the country in which Eurocontrol has its headquarters).[236]

Oil pollution by ships. Part I of the Foreign Judgments (Reciprocal   **15–065**
Enforcement) Act 1933 applies, with the omission of section 4(2) and (3), to any judgment given by a court in a country which is a party to the International Convention on Civil Liability for Oil Pollution Damage 1992[237] to enforce a claim in respect of liability incurred under any provision of foreign legislation corresponding to section 153 of the Merchant Shipping Act 1995; this is the case whether or not that Part has been extended to the country concerned, and whether or not the judgment is of a court specified for the purposes of that Part.[238] The effect of omitting Section 4(2) and (3) of the 1933 Act is that while the registration of the foreign judgment must be set aside if the courts of the country concerned had no jurisdiction in the circumstances of the case,[239] the existence of jurisdiction is to be gathered from the terms of the Convention. In effect, jurisdiction will exist if damage was caused or preventive or remedial measures were taken in the foreign country, including its territorial waters.[240] The International Convention on Liability and Compensation for Damage in Connection with the Carriage of Hazardous and Noxious Substances by Sea 1996, which may be implemented by Order in Council under section 182B of the Merchant Shipping Act 1995,[241] deals with the recognition and enforcement of judgments.[242] Where the courts of a Contracting State assume jurisdiction in accordance with the Convention, the ensuing judgment is entitled to recognition and enforcement in other Contracting States provided that the judgment is enforceable in the State of origin and is "no longer subject to ordinary forms of review".[243] The only exceptions to recognition and enforcement countenanced by the Convention are where the judgment was obtained by fraud and where the defendant was not given reasonable notice and fair opportunity to present his case. In no circumstances may the merits of the case be reopened.[244]

The International Convention on Civil Liability for Bunker Oil Pollution   **15–066**
2001[245] entered into force on November 21, 2008. It contains provisions on the recognition and enforcement of judgments. Article 10(1) states that a

---

[236] *ibid.* s.74A(5) as inserted by 1983 Act, s.1.
[237] For the Convention, see above, para.15–042.
[238] Merchant Shipping Act 1995, s.166(4).
[239] Foreign Judgments (Reciprocal Enforcement) Act 1933, s.4(1)(a)(ii).
[240] See above, para.15–042.
[241] See above, n.169.
[242] Art.40.
[243] Art.40. For consideration of the analogous wording in Art.37 of the Brussels I Regulation see above, para.14–215.
[244] Art.40(2).
[245] See Tsimplis [2005] L.M.C.L.Q. 83, especially 97–98.

judgment from a Contracting State's court with jurisdiction under Art.9 of the Convention shall be recognised in another State Party, provided that the judgment is enforceable in the State of origin. There are exceptions laid down where the judgment was obtained by fraud or the defendant was not given reasonable notice and a fair opportunity to present his or her case. The merits of the case may not be re-opened in the State of recognition.[246] Where the judgment is delivered in a European Union Member State, another Member State which is party to the Convention is required to recognise the judgment in accordance with the Community rules on the subject.[247] Merchant Shipping (Oil Pollution) (Bunkers Convention) Regulations 2006[248] amends s.166(4) of the Merchant Shipping Act 1995 so as to extend Part I of the Foreign Judgments (Reciprocal Enforcement) Act 1933 to relevant judgments given by courts in Bunker Convention countries.

15R–067   **RULE 63—(1) A court in a foreign country outside the United Kingdom which is a party to the Paris Convention on Third Party Liability in the Field of Nuclear Energy (1960) (as amended in 1964)[249] has no jurisdiction to give judgment in proceedings in which the plaintiff claims damages for injury to his person or for damage to his property in respect of a nuclear occurrence unless the Secretary of State certifies that the judgment is a relevant foreign judgment for the purposes of the Nuclear Installations Act 1965.[250]**

(2) No judgment given in a court of a country outside the United Kingdom will be enforced in England against a person who shows that—

(a) **the sum payable under the judgment was awarded in respect of injury or damage which is the subject of an international convention with respect to liability in the field of nuclear energy to which the United Kingdom is a party; and**

(b) **the country of the foreign court is not a party to such convention; and**

(c) **the sum was not awarded in pursuance of any international convention referred to in the Carriage by Air Act 1932,[251] the Carriage by Air Act 1961, the Carriage by Air (Supplementary Provisions) Act 1962, or the Carriage of Goods by Road Act 1965,[252]**

unless the judgment in question is enforceable in the United Kingdom in pursuance of an international agreement.[253]

---

[246] Art.10(2).

[247] That is, the rules in the Brussels I Regulation. See Council Decision 2002/762/EC, [2005] O.J. L56/7, Art.2.

[248] SI 2006/1244, Regulation 20(4).

[249] Cmnd. 2514 (1964).

[250] Nuclear Installations Act 1965, s.17(4).

[251] Now repealed.

[252] Nuclear Installations Act 1965, s.17(5) as amended by Energy Act 1983, s.31. See also Nuclear Installations Act 1965, s.12(4).

[253] Nuclear Installations Act 1965, s.17(5A), inserted by Energy Act 1983, s.31.

COMMENT

Clause (1) of the Rule. The Nuclear Installations Act 1965 gives effect to   **15–068**
various international conventions (to which the United Kingdom is a party) on
civil liability for nuclear occurrences.[254] Section 17(4) of the Act provides that
Pt I of the Foreign Judgments (Reciprocal Enforcement) Act 1933 shall apply
to any judgment given in a court of any foreign country which is certified by
the Secretary of State[255] to be a relevant foreign judgment for the purposes of
the Act, and shall have effect as if in s.4 of that Act subs.(1)(a)(ii), (2) and (3)
were omitted. A "relevant foreign judgment" means a judgment of a court of
a relevant territory other than the United Kingdom which, under a relevant
international agreement, is to be enforceable anywhere within the relevant
territories. A "relevant international agreement" means an international
agreement with respect to third-party liability in the field of nuclear energy to
which the United Kingdom is a party. A "relevant territory" means a country
for the time being bound by a relevant international agreement.[256]

The effect of omitting parts of s.4 of the 1933 Act is that the court cannot   **15–069**
address itself to the question whether the foreign court had jurisdiction. The
matter is determined by the Secretary of State, whose certificate is presumably
conclusive. He will base his decision on the jurisdictional rules in the Conventions, which are not set out in the Nuclear Installations Act 1965.[257]

Clause (2) of the Rule. This clause is based upon s.17(5) of the Nuclear   **15–070**
Installations Act 1965,[258] which provides that it shall be a sufficient defence
to proceedings in the United Kingdom against any person for the recovery of
a sum alleged to be payable under a judgment given in a country outside the
United Kingdom for that person to show the three things mentioned in sub-
clauses (a), (b) and (c) of the Rule. However this provision does not apply
where the judgment in question is enforceable in the United Kingdom in
pursuance of an international agreement.[259] "International agreement" will
include any bilateral or multilateral convention to which the United Kingdom
is a party; the phrase is not to be confused with "relevant international
agreement" which has a special meaning for the purposes of the Nuclear
Installations Act 1965.[260]

The 1965 Act and the Conventions aim to channel all liability to the   **15–071**
operator of the nuclear installation in which the occurrence happened, and to
limit his liability.[261] Both these objects would have been frustrated, and a
plaintiff suing in a country which is not a party to the Conventions might be
in a better position than a plaintiff suing in a country which is such a party had

---

[254] See entry at para.15–052, n.196, above. The 2004 Protocol, which further amends the Paris
Convention on Third Party Liability in the field of Nuclear Energy (1960), is not yet in force.

[255] The functions under s.17(4) are transferred, in so far as they are exercisable in or as regards
Scotland, to the Scottish Ministers, by SI 1999/1750, Sch.1, Art 2.

[256] s.26.

[257] For these jurisdictional rules, see above, para.15–052.

[258] As amended by Energy Act 1983, s.31.

[259] Nuclear Installations Act 1965, s.17(5A) inserted by Energy Act 1983, s.31.

[260] s.26(1); see above, para.15–049.

[261] The original limit of £5 million has since been raised; the current limit is £140 million,
except for licensees for whom it is £10 million: Energy Act 1983, s.27; SI 1994/909.

it not been for s.17(5). For the plaintiff could have brought his action in a non-contracting country against a person who would be under no liability to him under the Conventions, or might have recovered a sum in excess of the upper limit imposed by the Act, and could then have enforced his judgment in England. Section 17(5) therefore provides that no such judgment shall be enforceable here.[262] This principle cannot, however, prevail against treaty obligations of the United Kingdom requiring the enforcement of judgments, and this was recognised by an amendment made to the Act in 1983.[263] The original text of the 1965 Act made it clear that the principle did not affect the application of certain international conventions in the field of transport. These are listed in the Rule; the Carriage of Goods by Road Act 1965 is there specified, the Nuclear Installations Act 1965 (which was passing through Parliament at the same time) referring to "any Act which may be passed to give effect to" the CMR Convention.[264] Subsequent international transport conventions expressly save the provisions of conventions dealing with nuclear damage.[265]

---

[262] See also s.12(4).

[263] i.e. the insertion of s.17(5A), above.

[264] The future tense in the words cited in the text is not thought to preclude reference to the Carriage of Goods by Road Act 1965 which has an earlier chapter number than the Nuclear Installations Act 1965.

[265] e.g. Carriage of Goods by Sea Act 1971, Sch., Art.IX; Merchant Shipping Act 1995, Sch.6, Art.20.

CHAPTER 16

ARBITRATION AND FOREIGN AWARDS

1. GOVERNING LAW

RULE 64—(1) The material validity, scope and interpretation of an arbitration agreement are governed by its applicable law, namely: 16R–001

    (a) the law expressly or impliedly chosen by the parties; or,

    (b) in the absence of such choice, the law which is most closely connected with the arbitration agreement, which will in general be the law of the seat of the arbitration.[1]

(2) In general, arbitral proceedings are governed by the law of the seat of the arbitration.[2]

(3) The substance of the dispute is governed by either:

    (a) the law chosen by the parties; or

    (b) if the parties so agree, such other considerations as are agreed by the parties or determined by the tribunal; or

---

[1] There are many authorities supporting Rule 64(1), although the result in some of the decisions prior to the Arbitration Act 1996 would now be different. See especially *Hamlyn & Co v Talisker Distillery* [1894] A.C. 202; *NV Kwik Hoo Tong Handel Maatschappij v James Finlay & Co Ltd* [1927] A.C. 604; *Whitworth Street Estates (Manchester) Ltd v James Miller & Partners Ltd* [1970] A.C. 583, 616; *Nova (Jersey) Knit Ltd v Kammgarn Spinnerei* [1977] 1 W.L.R. 713 (HL); *Naviera Amazonica Peruana SA v Cia Internacional de Seguros del Peru* [1988] 1 Lloyd's Rep. 116, 119 (CA); *Paul Smith Ltd v H&S International Holdings Inc* [1991] 2 Lloyd's Rep. 127, 129–130; *Union of India v McDonnell Douglas Corp* [1993] 2 Lloyd's Rep. 48, 49–50; *Sumitomo Heavy Industries Ltd v Oil and Natural Gas Commission* [1994] 1 Lloyd's Rep. 45; *Oldendorff v Libera Corp* [1995] 2 Lloyd's Rep. 64, 69; *XL Insurance Ltd v Owens Corning* [2000] 2 Lloyd's Rep. 500, 506–507; *C v D* [2007] EWCA Civ 1282, [2008] 1 Lloyd's Rep. 239; Arzandeh and Hill (2009) 5 J. Priv. Int. L. 425; *cf.* Bantekas (2010) 27 J. Int. Arb. 1.

[2] 1996 Act, ss.2, 3, 4, and Sch.1 (and *cf.* s.103(2)(e)); *Lesotho Highlands Development Authority v Impregilo SpA* [2005] UKHL 43, [2006] 1 A.C. 221, at [20]; *Dubai Islamic Bank PJSC v Paymentech Merchant Services Inc* [2001] 1 Lloyd's Rep. 65; *Viking Insurance Co v Rossdale* [2002] 1 W.L.R. 1323. See also, for the law governing arbitral proceedings outside England, *Whitworth Street Estates (Manchester) Ltd v James Miller & Partners Ltd* [1970] A.C. 583, at 616–617; *Dalmia Dairy Industries Ltd v National Bank of Pakistan* [1978] 2 Lloyd's Rep. 223, 270 (CA). See below, paras 16–029 *et seq.*

(c)   **if there is no such choice or agreement, the law determined by the conflict of laws rules which the arbitral tribunal considers applicable.**[3]

Comment

16–002   **Scope of this Chapter.** Chapter 16 is concerned with those issues of the English conflict of laws arising in the course of international commercial arbitration.[4] The first topic (Rule 64) is the set of rules for the determination, in arbitration, of the law governing the arbitration agreement, the arbitral procedure, and the substance of the dispute. Here, developments in English law unique to arbitration require a separate consideration to that accorded to choice of law in other parts of the work. The second topic (Rule 65) brings together two issues concerned with the inter-relationship of judicial and arbitral proceedings in the same dispute: the extent to which an English action may, or must, be stayed in favour of arbitration; and the circumstances in which an English court will restrain by injunction a party from proceeding with a foreign action in breach of an arbitration agreement. The third topic (Rules 66–72) is that of the enforcement of foreign arbitral awards pursuant to the various regimes provided for such enforcement under English law. This topic requires separate treatment, as the legal regime for the enforcement of arbitral awards is, in general, founded upon different legal rules and sources from those applicable to foreign judgments.[5]

16–003   The law relating to the conduct of international commercial arbitration, including the conflict of laws issues discussed here, has been profoundly influenced by international developments. Of these, the most notable in terms of their influence on current English law have been two instruments prepared under the auspices of the United Nations: the New York Convention on the Recognition and Enforcement of Foreign Arbitral Awards 1958 ("the New York Convention")[6] and the United Nations Commission on International

---

[3] Arbitration Act 1996 (the "1996 Act") s.46.

[4] On international commercial arbitration see generally Redfern and Hunter, *International Arbitration* (5th ed. Blackaby and Partasides, 2009); Poudret and Besson, *Comparative Law of International Arbitration* (2nd ed. 2007); Lew, Mistelis and Kröll, *Comparative International Commercial Arbitration* (2003), especially Chs 6, 17 and 26; Mustill and Boyd, *Commercial Arbitration* (2nd ed. 1989, and Companion volume 2001); Craig, Park and Paulsson, *International Chamber of Commerce Arbitration* (3rd ed. 2000); Fouchard, Gaillard, Goldman, *International Commercial Arbitration* (ed. Gaillard and Savage, 1999); Rubino-Sammartano, *International Arbitration Law* (2nd ed. 2001); Born, *International Commercial Arbitration* (2009); Petrochilos, *Procedural Law in International Arbitration* (2004).

[5] In particular, the Brussels I Regulation, the Brussels Convention and the Lugano Convention on jurisdiction and the enforcement of judgments in civil and commercial matters exclude arbitration from their scope: Art.1; see above, paras 11–041—11–048. For the effect of this exclusion on the power of the English courts to restrain by injunction foreign proceedings in breach of an arbitration agreement see below, Rule 65(2).

[6] UKTS 20 (1976), Cmnd. 6419. The New York Convention is now given effect in English law by the 1996 Act. See especially ss.5, 9 and 100–104. For judicial decisions on the construction and application of the New York Convention see van den Berg, *New York Arbitration Convention of 1958* (1981) and his Commentaries and national court decisions reported in the *Yearbook of Commercial Arbitration*; Gaillard and Di Pietro, *Enforcement of Arbitration Agreements and International Arbitral Awards: The New York Convention in Practice* (2008); Kronke, Nacimiento, Otto and Port, *Recognition and Enforcement of Foreign Arbitral Awards: A Global Commentary on the New York Convention* (2010).

Trade Law Model Law on International Commercial Arbitration ("the Model Law").[7] The New York Convention now represents the dominant tool for the enforcement of arbitral awards internationally, and also underpins the law on the staying of judicial proceedings in favour of arbitration. The Model Law has been adopted as the arbitration law in Scotland[8] and in a number of Commonwealth countries.[9]

In England, the Model Law was not adopted *en bloc*. However, it had in the   **16–004** end a considerable influence on the content of the Arbitration Act 1996 ("the 1996 Act").[10] The law relating to arbitration, including the law on the conflict of laws issues discussed here, was comprehensively reformed and restated in the 1996 Act, which was adopted after a prolonged period of close consulta-tion with arbitration practitioners and users.[11] The extent of the reform achieved by this Act is such that it must now be regarded as the *terminus a quo* for many of the issues which are discussed in this Chapter, and earlier authorities can no longer be assumed to be good law.[12]

This work does not deal with the procedural rules which are to be applied   **16–005** in arbitration, following a determination of which legal system governs such matters. That is a matter of substantive arbitration law. Nor does it, in general, deal with the conflict of law rules applicable in arbitration in cases where that question is not itself governed by English law.

Governing law in international commercial arbitration. Many transna-   **16–006** tional commercial contracts contain clauses by which the parties choose to submit their disputes to international commercial arbitration, rather than to adjudication by a national court. Such a choice has a significant effect on the applicable law. It takes the regulation of such disputes outside the operation of the ordinary rules of law applicable to private law disputes (including those of the conflict of laws described in this work). Instead, it subjects them to a separate regime, which is partly the product of private regulation, and partly the result of developments in international treaties and national law, which themselves permit a considerable scope for party autonomy in arbitration. In English law, the principal legislation is the 1996 Act.

Three distinct issues of governing law may arise in international commer-   **16–007** cial arbitration: the law governing the arbitration agreement itself; the law

---

[7] *Yearbook of the United Nations Commission on International Trade Law 1985*, Pt 1, sect. A.

[8] Arbitration (Scotland) Act 2010.

[9] See, e.g. New Zealand: Arbitration Act 1996; Australia: International Arbitration Act 1974 (Cth), Pt III, with effect from June 12, 1989. For the current status of adoption of the Model Law see *http://www.uncitral.org*.

[10] The first report of the Departmental Advisory Committee on Arbitration Law (the "D.A.C."), under the chairmanship of Mustill L.J., had recommended against adoption of the Model Law. However, in the process of drafting the 1996 Act, the Model Law came to have progressively greater influence. See the two reports on the Act prepared by the D.A.C.: (1997) 13 Arb. Int. 275 (reprinting paras 1–276 only); and (1997) 13 Arb. Int. 317.

[11] The Act came into force on January 31, 1997. It superseded Arbitration Act 1950, Pt I, and Arbitration Act 1975, Arbitration Act 1979, and Consumer Arbitration Agreements Act 1988.

[12] *Lesotho Highlands Development Authority v Impregilo SpA* [2005] UKHL 43, [2006] 1 A.C. 221, at [19], approving *Seabridge Shipping AB v AC Orssleff's Eftf's A/S* [1999] 2 Lloyd's Rep. 685, 690.

governing the arbitral procedure; and the law governing the substance of the dispute.[13]

16–008   *Law governing the arbitration agreement.* Which law governs the validity, scope and interpretation of the agreement to arbitrate? This issue is one of great practical importance, since the jurisdiction of the arbitrator is limited to those matters submitted to him by agreement of the parties. If the arbitrator proceeds on the basis of an agreement to arbitrate, which is invalid or ineffective, or if the arbitrator exceeds the scope of his mandate, the award would in principle be unenforceable. An agreement to arbitrate may be found in a *compromis*, or submission agreement, submitting a present dispute to arbitration. But, much more commonly, it will be found in a clause in a contract, by which the parties bind themselves to submit future disputes arising under their contract to arbitration. In both cases, English law treats the agreement to arbitrate as a separate and distinct agreement, whose validity is not *ipso facto* affected by the invalidity, non-existence or ineffectiveness of any other agreement of which it forms part. As such, the arbitration agreement is subject to its own governing law. The determination of that law is the subject of Rule 64(1).

16–009   *Law governing the arbitration procedure.* Which law governs the arbitral proceedings (the *lex arbitri*)? A valid arbitration agreement need specify neither the venue for the arbitration nor the applicable procedural rules. Commonly, however, the parties will, when drafting the arbitration agreement either choose ad hoc arbitration or arbitration under the auspices of an international arbitration institution. In the case of ad hoc arbitration, the parties may choose to draft their own procedural rules, or they may nominate a standard set of rules for use in such cases, of which the most well-established are UNCITRAL Arbitration Rules.[14] If institutional arbitration is chosen, there are a number of well-known institutions around the world which supervise the conduct of arbitrations, most notably the International Chamber of Commerce Court of Arbitration (ICC) and the London Court of International Arbitration (LCIA). Each of these institutions has its own set of procedural rules, which have themselves been the subject of extensive interpretation by arbitral tribunals.[15] However, it is still always necessary to connect the conduct of the arbitral proceedings to a national legal system, which will regulate, for example, the extent of autonomy which the parties are permitted to exercise in selecting the arbitral procedure (and any mandatory rules from which the parties cannot derogate); the assistance which the national courts will provide to the arbitration in the grant of provisional measures, collection of evidence, etc.; and procedures for the review of

---

[13] *Channel Tunnel Group Ltd v Balfour Beatty Construction Ltd* [1993] A.C. 334, 357, *per* Lord Mustill; *Naviera Amazonica Peruana SA v Cia Internacional de Seguros del Peru* [1988]1 Lloyd's Rep. 116, 119 (CA).

[14] *Yearbook of the United Nations Commission on International Trade Law 1976*, Pt 1, Ch.II, sect. A. There is an official commentary on the Rules: *ibid.*, Pt 2, Ch.III, sect. 2; Caron, Caplan and Pellonpää, *The UNCITRAL Arbitration Rules: A Commentary* (2006).

[15] For the ICC practice see Craig, Park and Paulsson, *op. cit.* above, n.4; Derains and Schwartz, *A Guide to the ICC Rules of Arbitration* (2nd ed. 2005). For the text of the ICC Rules (2010) see *http://www.iccwbo.org/ICCDRSRules/*.

awards. National arbitration laws will also typically provide (as does the 1996 Act) a set of directory rules on arbitral procedure which will apply in the absence of express derogation by the parties. However, determination of which set of such rules is applicable may present problems. The parties may not have chosen a venue for the conduct of the arbitration. Even where they have done so, the choice may well have been dictated by convenience, or by the desire to find a neutral venue, than by any necessary connection with the subject-matter of the dispute or the parties. The arbitral tribunal itself may make a choice of venue for its hearings which is dictated by administrative convenience. National laws differ considerably in the manner and extent to which they regulate arbitration. In these circumstances, it is important to be able to determine which law governs the arbitral procedure. That is the subject of Rule 64(2).

Law governing the substance of the dispute. The third clause of Rule 64 **16–010** deals with the approach which the arbitrator is to take to the determination of the law governing any issue of substantive law (the *lex causae*). Since international commercial arbitration concerns disputes which by definition involve more than one country, it will be necessary in every case to determine the law applicable to the substance of the dispute. Until 1996, it was assumed that any arbitrator conducting an arbitration in England was bound to apply English law, including the English rules of the conflict of laws, to any dispute before the arbitral tribunal; and that every dispute submitted to arbitration in England had to be determined by reference to some system of national law.[16] Thus, there would have been no need for a separate Rule in this work on the law applicable to the substance of the dispute in arbitration. However, the position was different in the practice of international arbitration as it had developed outside England, and in particular in the practice of the major arbitral institutions, where a much greater freedom for the parties to choose non-national systems of law was increasingly recognised.[17] There was criticism of a rigid rule which required the arbitrator to apply the conflict of law rules of the seat of the arbitration, since the place of arbitration might be fortuitous.[18] Rule 64(3) reflects the substantial reform of the approach to this issue embraced by English law in the 1996 Act.[19]

---

[16] For the pre-1996 Act position see Collins, in Lew (ed.), *Contemporary Problems in International Arbitration* (1986), p.126. The leading authority was *Czarnikow v Roth, Schmidt & Co* [1922] 2 K.B. 478, 488, *per* Scrutton L.J. See F.A. Mann, *Lex facit arbitrum*, in Sanders (ed.), *International Arbitration: Liber Amicorum for Martin Domke* (1967), p.167.

[17] See e.g. ICC Rules, Art.21, on which see Craig, Park and Paulsson, Ch.17. See also Grigera Naon (2001) 289 *Recueil des Cours* 9, at pp.210 *et seq.*

[18] For summaries of the criticisms see Lew, Mistelis and Kröll, paras 17–51—17–55 and Born, pp.2123–6.

[19] Section 46. *cf.* Model Law, Art.28. For commentary see D.A.C. Report (1997) 13 Arb. Int. 275, paras 222–225. The fact that the choice of law rules in contractual and non-contractual matters are now contained in EU Regulations, the Rome I Regulation and the Rome II Regulation (Chaps 32–36, below), does not affect the power of an arbitral tribunal sitting in England to choose the law applicable to the substance of the dispute according to the provisions of s.46: see Dickinson, *Rome II Regulation: A Commentary* (2009) paras 3.77–3.84; *contra*, Yuksel (2011) 7 J. Priv. Int. L. 149.

16–011   **Law governing arbitration agreement.** It is "part of the very alphabet of arbitration law"[20] that an arbitration agreement, even if (as is usually the case) it is contained in an arbitration clause within the body of a larger contract, forms a separate and distinct agreement.[21] Accordingly its validity, scope and interpretation falls to be considered separately from that of the main contract, and is not necessarily affected by the invalidity or avoidance of the main contract.[22] In *Fiona Trust and Holding Corp v Privalov*,[23] the House of Lords upheld the principle of separability, finding that it applied even in a case where it was alleged that the main contract was invalid, having been procured by bribery. There has to be some special reason for saying that the bribery impeaches the arbitration clause in particular to remove the question from the competence of the arbitral tribunal. Allegations that are parasitical to a challenge to the validity of the main agreement will not suffice.

16–012   It follows from the autonomy of the arbitration agreement that the law applicable to it must be determined separately from that applicable to the main contract.[24] Although, in many cases, the law applicable to the main contract will have a strong influence on the law applicable to the arbitration agreement, this will not be so in every case.[25] Rule 64(1) is specifically concerned with material validity, scope and interpretation. However, in view of the existence of the arbitration agreement as a separate contract, it may also be necessary to determine the law applicable to issues of formal validity and capacity to contract, discussed further below.

16–013   Issues as to the validity and interpretation of arbitration agreements commonly arise in international commercial arbitration, since such agreements form the root of the jurisdiction of every arbitral tribunal. As a result, the validity and extent of the arbitration agreement will determine: whether the arbitrators may assume jurisdiction; whether a court is obliged to stay its

---

[20] *Lesotho Highlands Development Authority v Impregilo SpA* [2005] UKHL 43, [2006] 1 A.C. 221, at [21], *per* Lord Steyn.

[21] This is a general principle of international commercial arbitration. For the main English decisions prior to the 1996 Act see *Heyman v Darwins Ltd* [1942] A.C. 356; *Bremer Vulkan Schiffbau und Maschinenfabrik v South India Shipping Corp Ltd* [1981] A.C. 909; *Paul Smith Ltd v H&S International Holdings Inc* [1991] 2 Lloyd's Rep. 127; *Harbour Assurance Co (UK) Ltd v Kansa General Insurance Co Ltd* [1993] Q.B. 701. The principle has been approved by the United States Supreme Court: *Buckeye Check Cashing Inc v Cardegna,* 546 U.S. 440 (2006); and by the Full Court of the Federal Court of Australia: *Comandate Marine Corp v Pan Australia Shipping Pty Ltd* [2006] FCAFC 192, (2006) 157 F.C.R. 45. For a full account of the international practice see Fouchard, Gaillard, Goldman, paras 388–419; Born, Ch.3; Poudret and Besson, paras 162–182. See also Schwebel, *International Arbitration: Three Salient Problems* (1987), pp.1–60.

[22] 1996 Act, s.7. For recent examples see *Vee Networks Ltd v Econet Wireless International Ltd* [2004] EWHC 2909 (Comm.), [2006] 1 Lloyd's Rep. 181 at [16]–[22]; *Svenska Petroleum Exploration AB v Republic of Lithuania (No.2)* [2005] EWHC 2437 (Comm.), [2005] 1 Lloyd's Rep. 192 at [75].

[23] *sub nom. Premium Nafta Products Ltd v Fili Shipping Co Ltd* [2007] UKHL 40, [2008] 1 Lloyd's Rep. 254, affirming [2007] EWCA Civ 20, [2007] 2 Lloyd's Rep. 267; applied *El Nasharty v J Sainsbury Plc* [2007] EWHC 2618 (Comm.), [2008] 1 Lloyd's Rep. 360.

[24] Collins, in Lew (ed.), *Contemporary Problems in International Arbitration* (1986), p.126, at 127–131.

[25] *Deutsche Schachtbau v Shell International Petroleum Co Ltd* [1990] 1 A.C. 295, 309–310 (CA), reversed on other grounds *ibid.* p.329; *Naviera Amazonica Peruana SA v Cia Internacional de Seguros del Peru* [1988] 1 Lloyd's Rep. 116, 119 (CA).

proceedings in favour of arbitration;[26] and whether the resulting award is enforceable.[27] The consequence of this necessary link between the arbitration agreement and jurisdiction is that, in this context, party autonomy often requires a careful scrutiny according to the applicable national law.[28] The arbitral tribunal is free to determine its own jurisdiction[29] (a process often referred to as "*Kompetenz-Kompetenz*").[30] However, it will need to found its jurisdiction upon the validity of the arbitration agreement judged according to the external standards of the law which governs that agreement.

There is, however, no international consensus on the choice of law rule **16–014** applicable to an arbitration agreement.[31] The New York Convention provides that the recognition and enforcement of an award may be refused where "the said agreement is not valid under the law to which the parties have subjected it or, failing any indication thereon, under the law of the country where the award was made."[32] In the light of the pervasive reach of the New York Convention in modern times, this rule, although not itself prescribing a choice of law rule of general application, nevertheless provides a strong indication of one, since invalidity of the arbitration agreement under the applicable law may render the resulting award unenforceable.[33] Thus, in *Dallah Real Estate and Tourism Holding Co v Ministry of Religious Affairs, Government of Pakistan,*[34] on an application for enforcement of a New York Convention award in England, the question whether a valid arbitration agreement had been entered into between the parties was determined according to French law, the award having been made in France.

For most other purposes, the choice of law rules applicable to contracts in **16–015** England are subject to the uniform provisions of the Rome I Regulation.[35] The

---

[26] New York Convention, Art.II(3); 1996 Act s.9; see below, Rule 65(1).

[27] New York Convention, Art.V(1)(a) and (c); 1996 Act s.103(2)(a), (b) and (d); below, Rule 69(1)(b).

[28] The Supreme Court of Canada has upheld the primacy of the autonomy of the parties in both arbitration and jurisdiction clauses, subject to operation of mandatory rules of the forum and the construction of the clause itself: *GreCon Dimter Inc v J R Normand Inc* [2005] 2 S.C.R. 401. The law governing the arbitration agreement must be that of a national legal system: *Halpern v Halpern* [2006] EWHC 603 (Comm.), [2006] 2 Lloyd's Rep. 83, at [47]–[58] (reversed in part, but not on this point [2007] EWCA Civ 291, [2008] Q.B. 195).

[29] 1996 Act s.30. The English court now has only limited powers to determine the jurisdiction of an arbitral tribunal itself: s.32, see below, para.16–076. However, there is a right to challenge an arbitral award on jurisdiction in the court, where the seat of the tribunal is in England: s.67 (a mandatory provision).

[30] Lew, Mistelis and Kröll, paras 14–13—14–18; Fouchard, Gaillard, Goldman, paras 650–660; Born, Ch.6; Poudret and Besson, paras 457–477.

[31] See Lew, Mistelis and Kröll, paras 6–25—6–74; Redfern and Hunter, paras 3.09–3.33; Born, Ch.4; Poudret and Besson, paras 291–303. See also van den Berg (ed.), *ICCA Congress Series No.9* (1999).

[32] Art.V(1)(a). See below, Rule 69(1)(b). Art.36(1)(a)(i) of the Model Law is to like effect.

[33] This view is also taken by Born, pp.460–463 and Poudret and Besson, para.299.

[34] [2010] UKSC 46, [2011] 1 A.C. 763. The English courts determined that, according to the applicable principles of French law, no such agreement had been validly concluded. A different view on the facts was subsequently taken by the French courts: *Gouvernement du Pakistan—Ministère des Affaires Religieuses v Société Dallah Real Estate and Tourism Holding Company* (CA, Paris, February 17, 2011) [2011] Rev. arb. 286.

[35] The Rome I Regulation (Regulation (EC) 593/2008 of the European Parliament and of the Council of June 17, 2008 on the law applicable to contractual obligations) which replaced the Rome Convention when it came into force on December 17, 2009: [2008] O.J. L177/6. It applies to contracts concluded as from that date. See below, Ch.32.

Regulation however, does not apply to arbitration agreements.[36] Accordingly, its rules will only have indirect impact on the present issue.

16–016   It is submitted that in most cases the correct solution will be found in the construction of the agreement as to the parties' choice of law. This respects the fact that what is in issue is a contractual question, on which the parties enjoy autonomy of choice of law, whether under the common law or under the Rome I Regulation. If no such choice, express or implied, can be discerned, then it will often be the case that the arbitration agreement will be found to be most closely connected with the law of the place where the arbitration has its seat, which is also the place where the award is to be treated as "made" for the purpose of the New York Convention.[37]

16–017   *The law chosen by the parties.* If there is an express choice of law to govern the arbitration agreement, that choice will be effective, irrespective of the law applicable to the contract as a whole.[38] If there is an express choice of law to govern the contract as a whole, the arbitration agreement may also be governed by that law.[39]

16–018   But the parties' express choice of a governing law for the main contract may be held not to apply to the arbitration agreement, where there are, as a matter of construction, contrary indications in favour of the law of the seat. Thus, for example, where the parties had chosen New York law to govern their substantive obligations, the arbitration agreement was nevertheless found to be governed by English law, since the parties had not merely designated London as the seat, but had also expressly provided that the provisions of the 1996 Act would apply to their arbitration, and had not opted out of the provisions regarding the validity of the arbitration agreement.[40]

16–019   *Applicable law in the absence of choice.* If there is no express choice of law, and no choice of the seat of the arbitration, the applicable law of the main contract will be determined in accordance with the principles in the Rome I Regulation, and the arbitration agreement will be governed by the law so determined.[41] If there is no express choice of the law to govern either the

---

[36] Art.1(2)(e).

[37] 1996 Act, s.53. The Act in this respect reverses *Hiscox v Outhwaite* [1992] 1 A.C. 562, in which it had been held that an award was made where it was signed. The equivalent passage in earlier editions of this work was applied in *Musawi v R E International (UK) Ltd* [2007] EWHC 2981 (Ch.), [2008] 1 Lloyd's Rep. 326).

[38] *Naviera Amazonica Peruana SA v Cia Internacional de Seguros del Peru* [1988] 1 Lloyd's Rep. 116, 119 (CA); *Tamil Nadu Electricity Board v ST-CMS Electric Co Pvt Ltd* [2007] EWHC 1713 (Comm.), [2008] 1 Lloyd's Rep. 93.

[39] *International Tank & Pipe SAK v Kuwait Aviation Fuelling Co KSG* [1975] Q.B. 224 (CA); *Qatar Petroleum v Shell International Petroleum* [1983] 2 Lloyd's Rep. 35 (CA); *The Marques de Bolarque* [1984] 1 Lloyd's Rep. 652; *Paul Smith Ltd v H&S International Holdings Inc* [1991] 2 Lloyd's Rep. 127; *Union of India v McDonnell Douglas Corporation* [1993] 2 Lloyd's Rep. 48; *Sumitomo Heavy Industries Ltd v Oil and Natural Gas Commission* [1994] 1 Lloyd's Rep. 45; *Sonatrach Petroleum Corp v Ferrell International Ltd* [2002] 1 All E.R. (Comm.) 627; *Svenska Petroleum Exploration AB v Government of the Republic of Lithuania (No.2)* [2005] EWHC 2437 (Comm.), [2006] 1 Lloyd's Rep. 181.

[40] *XL Insurance Ltd v Owens Corning* [2000] 2 Lloyd's Rep. 500; and see *C v D* [2007] EWCA Civ 1282, [2008] 1 Lloyd's Rep. 239.

[41] The equivalent passage in an earlier edition of this work was quoted with approval in *The Star Texas* [1993] 2 Lloyd's Rep. 445, 448 (CA).

contract as a whole or the arbitration agreement, but the parties have chosen the seat of the arbitration, the contract will frequently (but not necessarily) be governed by the law of that country on the basis that the choice of the seat is to be regarded as an implied choice of the law governing the contract.[42] In each of these cases, the main contract and the arbitration agreement will be governed by the same law. The parties are free, under s.46(1)(b) of the 1996 Act, to choose a non-national system of law to govern the substance of their contract. The arbitration agreement, on the other hand, must be governed by a national legal system.[43] This may lead to a different applicable law for the arbitration agreement, even where the parties have made an express choice of law to govern the substantive contract.

If there is no choice of law to govern the contract as a whole, and the selection of the seat of the arbitration is not treated as an implied choice of the law of that place to govern the contract,[44] the question arises whether the arbitration agreement is governed by the law applicable to the contract or by the law of the seat of the arbitration. It has been held that to determine the governing law, it is not permissible to look at the arbitration agreement in isolation; regard should be had to the surrounding circumstances, including the law governing the substantive contract. Nevertheless, the law of the seat of the arbitration will apply if the circumstances point to an implied intention to choose the law of that place to govern the arbitration agreement.[45] In such cases the law governing the arbitration agreement will be different from the law governing the substantive contract. In *Deutsche Schachtbau v Shell International Petroleum Co Ltd*[46] it was held that an arbitration agreement providing for arbitration in Geneva under the auspices of the ICC was governed by Swiss law, notwithstanding that the contract, which was to be performed in R'As Al Khaimah, had been held by the arbitral tribunal to be governed by general principles of law.

16–020

Even if the choice of the seat does not point to an implied intention to choose the law governing the arbitration agreement, there is an argument for saying that the arbitration agreement should nonetheless be governed by the law of the seat; an arbitration agreement is severable from the contract of

16–021

---

[42] *Egon Oldendorff v Libera Corp* [1995] 2 Lloyd's Rep. 64; *(No.2)* [1996] 2 Lloyd's Rep. 380. See also the cases decided at common law: *Hamlyn & Co v Talisker Distillery* [1894] A.C. 202; *NV Kwik Hoo Tong Handel Maatschappij v James Finlay & Co Ltd* [1927] A.C. 604; *The Njegos* [1936] P. 90; *NV "Vulcaan" v A/S J. Ludwig Mowinckels Rederi* [1938] 2 All E.R. 152 (HL); *The SLS Everest* [1981] 2 Lloyd's Rep. 389 (CA); *The Parouth* [1982] 2 Lloyd's Rep. 351 (CA); *The Mariannina* [1983] 1 Lloyd's Rep. 12 (CA); *Steel Authority of India Ltd v Hind Metals Inc* [1984] 1 Lloyd's Rep. 405; *The Elli 2* [1985] 1 Lloyd's Rep. 107 (CA).

[43] *Halpern v Halpern* [2006] EWHC 603 (Comm.), [2006] 2 Lloyd's Rep. 83 (reversed in part, but not on this point [2007] EWCA Civ 291, [2008] Q.B. 195, applied in *Musawi v R E International (UK) Ltd* [2007] EWHC 2981 (Ch.), [2008] 1 Lloyd's Rep. 326); *Dallah Real Estate and Tourism Holding Co v Ministry of Religious Affairs, Government of Pakistan* [2010] UKSC 46, [2011] 1 A.C. 763, affirming [2009] EWCA Civ 755, [2010] 2 W.L.R. 805.

[44] See, e.g. *Atlantic Underwriting Agencies Ltd v Compagnie di Assicurazione di Milano* [1979] 2 Lloyd's Rep. 240 (arbitration in Geneva, contract governed by Italian law); *The Castle Alpha* [1989] 2 Lloyd's Rep. 383 (arbitration in London, contract governed by Japanese law).

[45] *C v D* [2007] EWCA Civ 1282, [2008] Lloyd's Rep. 239.

[46] *Deutsche Schachtbau v Shell International Petroleum Co Ltd* [1990] 1 A.C. 295 (CA), reversed on other grounds, at p.310. cf. *Black-Clawson International Ltd v Papierwerke Waldhof-Aschaffenberg AG* [1981] 2 Lloyd's Rep. 446, 456.

which it forms a part and is normally more closely connected with the country of the seat than with any other country.

16–022   All questions relating to the formation of an arbitration agreement are governed by the law which would govern if it were validly concluded, i.e. by its putative applicable law.[47] The law governing the arbitration agreement will determine its validity, effect and interpretation. The question whether the arbitration agreement is wide enough to cover the dispute between the parties is a question of interpretation and therefore depends on the law governing the arbitration agreement.[48] That law will normally[49] determine whether the clause remains binding on the parties although one of them alleges that the contract is void, voidable or illegal,[50] or that it has been discharged by breach or frustration.[51] The governing law will also determine whether an arbitration agreement can be imported by implication into a different contract between the same parties, or between one of them and a third party.[52]

16–023   *Formal validity.*[53] The New York Convention supplies in Art.II(2) only a non-exhaustive definition of what constitutes an "agreement in writing" for the purpose of its obligation to recognise arbitration agreements. The term is defined to "include an arbitral clause in a contract or an arbitration agreement, signed by the parties or contained in an exchange of letters or telegrams."[54] That this is merely a maximum standard is further confirmed by Art.VII(1) which provides that the Convention's provisions shall not "deprive any interested party of any right he may have to avail himself of an arbitral award in the manner and to the extent allowed by the law or the treaties of the country where such award is sought to be relied upon." Thus, the New York Convention's provisions as to form do not impose an internationally uniform standard. On the contrary, they leave open the possibility that arbitration

---

[47] *The Heidberg* [1994] 2 Lloyd's Rep. 287; *Midgulf International Ltd v Groupe Chimiche Tunisien* [2010] EWCA Civ 66, [2010] 2 Lloyd's Rep. 543, at [56].

[48] *Nova (Jersey) Knit Ltd v Kammgarn Spinnerei* [1977] 1 W.L.R. 713 (HL); *Dalmia Dairy Industries Ltd v National Bank of Pakistan* [1978] 1 Lloyd's Rep. 223 (CA); *The Marques de Bolarque* [1984] 1 Lloyd's Rep. 652; *Abu Dhabi Investment Co v H Clarkson & Co Ltd* [2006] EWHC 1252 (Comm.), [2006] 2 Lloyd's Rep. 381; *ET Plus SA v Welter* [2005] EWHC 2115 (Comm.), [2006] 1 Lloyd's Rep. 251; *Midgulf International Ltd v Groupe Chimiche Tunisien* [2010] EWCA Civ 66, [2010] 2 Lloyd's Rep. 543, at [56]. In *Emmott v Michael Wilson & Partners Ltd* [2008] EWCA Civ 184, [2008] 1 Lloyd's Rep. 616, at [84], [110], the tentative view was expressed *obiter* that the extent and scope of any obligation of confidentiality in an arbitration were matters of substance, which were governed by the law applicable to the arbitration agreement (and ought therefore to be determined by the arbitral tribunal, rather than by application to court).

[49] Subject to overriding legislation which applies irrespective of the governing law, such as Carriage of Goods by Road Act 1965: *A/B Bofors v A/B Skandia Transport* [1982] 1 Lloyd's Rep. 410.

[50] *Dalmia Dairy Industries Ltd v National Bank of Pakistan*, above; *cf. Mackender v Feldia* [1967] 2 Q.B. 590 (CA); Kahn-Freund (1977) 26 I.C.L.Q. 825, 838–841.

[51] *Black-Clawson International Ltd v Papierwerke Waldhof-Aschaffenburg AG* [1981] 2 Lloyd's Rep. 446.

[52] *Kianta Osakeyhtio v Britain and Overseas Trading Co Ltd* [1953] 2 Lloyd's Rep. 569; *The Elizabeth H* [1962] 1 Lloyd's Rep. 172; *Datronics Engineers Inc v Hardeman-Monier-Hutcherson* [1966] W.A.R. 55.

[53] See Lew, Mistelis and Kröll, paras 6–37 *et seq.*; Born, pp.535–552.

[54] See van den Berg (2003) 28 Yb. Comm. Arb. 562, 584–598.

agreements concluded with less formality than Art.II contemplates may be enforceable in some States, but not in others.

In practice, however, at least in English law, the potential problems of **16–024** choice of law as to form which would thus arise have been ameliorated by a uniform definition of the formal requirements of an arbitration agreement. This is applicable in all cases where the seat of the arbitration is in England[55] (save where the parties have expressly agreed otherwise) and also to the enforcement of foreign awards pursuant to the New York Convention.[56] For all of these purposes, s.5 of the 1996 Act provides:

"(2) There is an agreement in writing—   **16–025**

(a) if the agreement is made in writing (whether or not it is signed by the parties),

(b) if the agreement is made by exchange of communications in writing, or

(c) if the agreement is evidenced in writing.

(3) Where the parties agree otherwise than in writing by reference to terms which are in writing, they make an agreement in writing.

(4) An agreement is evidenced in writing if an agreement made otherwise than in writing is recorded by one of the parties, or by a third party, with the authority of one of the parties to the agreement.

(5) An exchange of written submissions in arbitral or legal proceedings in which the existence of an agreement otherwise than in writing is alleged by one party against another party and not denied by the other party in his response constitutes as between those parties an agreement in writing to the effect alleged.

(6) References in this Part to anything being written or in writing include its being recorded by any means."[57]

Save in the rare cases where the parties have expressly excluded the **16–026** operation of this section, it will be applied (either by an arbitrator sitting in England or by an English court) to cure defects in formal validity alleged to arise under, for example, the law applicable to the merits.[58]

Capacity. There is little authority on the law applicable to the capacity of **16–027** the parties to enter into an arbitration agreement.[59] The New York Convention

---

[55] 1996 Act, s.5.

[56] 1996 Act, s.100(2).

[57] See further below, paras 16–068—16–069.

[58] *XL Insurance Ltd v Owens Corning* [2000] 2 Lloyd's Rep. 500.

[59] Redfern and Hunter, paras 2.28–2.38; Fouchard, Gaillard, Goldman, paras 453–470; Born, pp.552–561. On the important practical question whether, and under what law, a foreign State may invoke its incapacity under its own law to submit to international arbitration see Redfern and Hunter, paras 2.34–2.38; van den Berg, pp.278–282; Delaume, *Law and Practice of Transnational Contracts*, 1988, pp.354–359; Paulsson (1986) 2 Arb. Int. 90. The Swiss Private International Law Act of 1987, Art.177(2), provides that a State cannot rely on its own law to contest its capacity to be a party to arbitration. The answer should depend on the law governing the arbitration agreement, rather than the law of the State concerned, but Arbitration Act 1996, s.103(2)(a) (and the corresponding provision in the New York Convention) suggest otherwise in the context of enforcement: below, para.16–138. In *Svenska Petroleum Exploration AB v Lithuania (No.2)* [2006] EWCA Civ 1529, [2007] Q.B. 886, the Court of Appeal applied the law governing the arbitration agreement to the question. The choice of law clause in the agreement

merely provides obliquely that it will be a ground for refusal of enforcement that "the parties to the agreement . . . were, *under the law applicable to them,* under some incapacity."[60] It is submitted that in principle the same rules which are applicable to capacity to contract generally[61] are also applicable to capacity to enter into arbitration agreements.

16–028   The 1996 Act expressly determines the scope of each of the provisions of Pt I, thus delineating the borderline between issues of substance determined by the law governing the arbitration agreement and issues of procedure governed by the *lex arbitri.*[62] Although the general rule is that Pt I applies in cases where England is the seat of the arbitration,[63] it is also expressly provided[64] that, where the seat is outside England or where the seat has not been determined or designated, s.7 (which provides, subject to the parties' contrary agreement, that an arbitration agreement is to be treated as distinct from any contract of which it forms a part) and s.8 (which provides that, unless the parties agree otherwise, an arbitration agreement is not discharged by the death of a party) are applicable if English law is the law governing the arbitration agreement.

16–029   **Law governing arbitration procedure.** *The function of the procedural law.*[65] The concept of the procedural law of an arbitration (or *lex arbitri*) is not adequately explained as merely synonymous with procedural law in litigation, and is not to be circumscribed by the same rules which apply to distinguish procedure from substance in the conflict of laws generally. In essence, the procedural law of an arbitration deals with two sets of issues: (a) the *internal* procedure of the arbitration itself: commencement of the arbitration, appointment of arbitrators, pleadings, provisional measures, evidence, hearings and awards; and (b) the *external* intervention of national courts in the arbitral process. Such intervention may itself have two distinct purposes: (i) *supportive:* by which the court assists the arbitration, such as by the appointment of arbitrators in default of agreement, or the ordering of provisional measures or collection of evidence where the arbitral tribunal is unable to do so; and (ii) *supervisory:* being those rules of national law which define the extent to which a court may intervene in an arbitration, or review an award on grounds of procedural or substantive error.

---

provided for the application of the law of Lithuania ". . . supplemented, where required, by rules of international business activities generally accepted in the petroleum industry if they do not contradict the laws of the Republic of Lithuania". The Republic of Lithuania sought to rely on general principles of law applied by international tribunals, rather than its own law, as grounds for a submission that it was not bound by an arbitration agreement. The court held that effect had to be given to both parts of the clause in interpreting the arbitration agreement. It upheld the finding at first instance that the agreement did bind the State as a matter of Lithuanian law, and found no general principle of law applied by international tribunals which was inconsistent with that conclusion.

[60] Art.V(1)(a) (emphasis added); 1996 Act, s.103(2)(a).

[61] Rule 175 in the case of corporations and Rule 228 in the case of individuals.

[62] See D.A.C. Supplementary Report (1997) 13 Arb. Int. 317, 318–322.

[63] 1996 Act, s.2(1).

[64] *ibid.*, s.2(5).

[65] See generally Petrochilos, *Procedural Law in International Arbitration* (2004); Redfern and Hunter, paras 3.34–3.87; Born, pp.1310–1347; Poudret and Besson, Ch.2.

This dual character of procedural law in arbitration is reflected in the dual **16–030** source of procedural rules. All of the major international arbitral institutions have their own procedural rules, which will apply to arbitrations conducted under their auspices (save to the extent that the parties expressly provide otherwise). From the perspective of the parties to an international arbitration (and of the arbitral institution) these rules will form the primary procedural code. Even where the parties have chosen ad hoc rather than institutional arbitration, the parties may select a set of procedural rules such as the UNCITRAL Arbitration Rules.

The other source of procedural law for arbitration is those provisions of **16–031** national law which deal specifically with arbitration—the *lex arbitri* properly so called. Such rules may perform one of three functions: (a) *directory*: they may provide a source of arbitral rules which may be applied to the extent that the parties have not expressly chosen their own rules of procedure (whether by drafting specific rules into their arbitration agreement, or, more commonly, by choosing a set of standard procedural rules, such as those of the ICC or LCIA or the UNCITRAL Arbitration Rules); (b) *mandatory*: national law may also, however, place mandatory limits on the autonomy of the parties in arbitration, by prescribing certain matters of arbitral procedure from which no contracting out is permitted; (c) *supportive:* national law may extend the support of national court processes to arbitration, by making available to the parties certain judicial procedures to deal with matters which are outside the scope of the arbitrators' authority, since they require the coercive powers of the State. This arises especially where the procedural measures affect the position of third parties, who are not subject to the jurisdiction of the arbitrators, such as, for example, in the taking of evidence under compulsion or the ordering of provisional measures. It also arises after an award has been rendered and enforcement is sought.

In the latter half of the 20th century, there was considerable debate between **16–032** those who favoured state control of arbitration, and the proponents of "de-localised arbitration", a concept which would give the greatest possible scope for party autonomy by disconnecting international commercial arbitration altogether from the control of national law, both as to procedure and as to applicable substantive law.[66] England was traditionally seen as a country

---

[66] The literature is very considerable. See especially Redfern and Hunter, paras 3.71–3.87; Lew, Mistelis and Kröll, paras 4–46—4–59; Fouchard, Gaillard, Goldman, paras 1444 *et seq.*; Gaillard, *Legal Theory of International Arbitration* (2010); Poudret and Besson, paras 120–131; *Lex Mercatoria and Arbitration*, ed. Carbonneau (rev. ed. 1998); Fragistas, *Rev. Crit.* 1960, 1; Goldman (1963) *Recueil des Cours*, II, p.347; Lalive (1967) *Recueil des Cours*, I, p.571; F.A. Mann, *Lex facit arbitrum*, in Sanders (ed.), *International Arbitration: Liber Amicorum for Martin Domke* (1967), p.167; Lew, *Applicable Law in International Commercial Arbitration* (1978); Wetter, *International Arbitral Process* (1979), Vol.2, pp.403–404, 526–531; Paulsson (1981) 30 I.C.L.Q. 358, (1983) 32 I.C.L.Q. 53; Park (1983) 32 I.C.L.Q. 21; Collins, in *Basle Symposium on the Law Governing Contractual Obligations* (ed. Klein and Vischer, 1983), pp.70–79; Mustill, in *Liber Amicorum for Lord Wilberforce* (1987), pp.149–184, reprinted in (1988) 4 Arb. Int. 86; Strenger (1991) *Recueil des Cours*, II, p.207; Kerr (1993) 2 Am. Rev. Int. Arb. 377; Rivkin (1993) 9 Arb. Int. 67; Gaillard, 1995 *Clunet* 5; Gaillard (1995) 10 ICSID Rev.-FILJ 208; Gaillard, in *Liber Amicorum Claude Reymond—Autour de l'arbitrage* (2004), p.83. See also *SA Coppée Lavalin NV v Ken-Ren Chemicals and Fertilizers Ltd* [1995] 1 A.C. 38, 51–52, *per* Lord Mustill.

which favoured closer state control of arbitration. Certainly before the abolition of the case stated procedure by the Arbitration Act 1979, English law did permit considerable scrutiny of arbitration by the courts. Even after the reforms of 1979, the courts continued to hold that English law "does not recognise the concept of arbitral procedures floating in the transnational firmament, unconnected with any municipal system of law."[67] By contrast in France, the idea of delocalised arbitration has received the support of the courts. The French Cour de cassation has held that " . . . an international arbitral award—which is not anchored to any national legal order—is an international judicial decision whose validity must be ascertained with regard to the rules applicable in the country where its recognition and enforcement is sought."[68] Powerful support to the delocalisation theory has also been given recently by the Supreme Court of Canada which has held that: "[a]rbitration is part of no state's judicial system . . . The arbitrator has no allegiance or connection to any single country. . . In short, arbitration is a creature that owes its existence to the will of the parties alone."[69]

16-033   The arbitral process is an exercise of party autonomy, which nevertheless can only proceed (and subsequently be enforced) to the extent permitted by national law. Two trends in modern arbitration law have led to a convergence between party autonomy and state control. The first has been an acceptance in many modern arbitration laws of a much wider scope for the operation of party autonomy to choose the procedures applicable to an international commercial arbitration. This trend is exemplified by the Model Law, and is reflected in the 1996 Act. The second element has been a renewed explicit acceptance of the rule set out in Rule 64(2), namely that it is the law of the seat of the arbitration which governs the arbitral procedure.[70] This measure of convergence is also promoted by human rights law. It is now well recognised that according the parties a wide degree of party autonomy to resolve their disputes is not inconsistent with their human right of access to a court (for instance under Art.6 of the European Convention on Human Rights), provided the domestic courts of the seat retain some measure of control of the arbitration proceedings.[71]

16-034   Where, as in the case of the 1996 Act (or other Commonwealth legislation giving effect to the Model Law), the law of the seat in fact accords considerable freedom to the parties to choose their procedure and imposes few mandatory provisions upon it, the control of the law of the seat will be in practice limited, and its provisions are unlikely to be brought into conflict with arbitration procedures chosen by the parties. Nevertheless, the law of the seat will still perform vital functions: in supplementing the procedural rules chosen by the parties where these are incomplete; in supporting the arbitral procedure when the coercive powers of the State are needed; and in providing a forum

---

[67] *Bank Mellat v Helliniki Techniki SA* [1984] Q.B. 291, 301.

[68] *PT Putrabali Adyamulia v Est Epices* (June 29, 2007) (2008) 24 Arb. Int. 293, 295.

[69] *Dell Computer Corp v Union des consommateurs* 2007 SCC 34, (2007) 284 D.L.R. (4th) 577, at [51].

[70] See Petrochilos, paras 3.31–3.72; Redfern and Hunter, paras 3.51–3.59; Poudret and Besson, paras 130–131, 134–135, 145–147; Goode (2001) 17 Arb. Int. 19.

[71] *Sumukan Ltd v Commonwealth Secretariat* [2007] EWCA Civ 243, [2007] 2 Lloyd's Rep. 87, at [57]; followed *Kaye v Nu Skin UK Ltd* [2009] EWHC 3509 (Ch.), [2011] 1 Lloyd's Rep. 40.

for challenging arbitral awards, especially where they are said to exceed the jurisdiction vouchsafed to the arbitrators by the parties under the arbitration agreement, or where there has been a serious irregularity in the arbitral procedure. Finally, it is the law of the seat which endows the arbitral award with its binding character upon which enforcement may be sought internationally under the provisions of the New York Convention. The international arbitral institutions, which have developed to a considerable extent the autonomy of the arbitral procedure, also recognise the ultimately controlling function of the law of the seat.[72]

Determination of the seat. Party autonomy in the choice of the law to govern arbitral procedure (the *lex arbitri*) is expressed in the choice of a seat for the arbitration. This "seat" is in most cases sufficiently indicated by the country chosen as the place of the arbitration. For such a choice of place not to be given effect as a choice of seat, there will need to be clear evidence that the parties (or the arbitrators, if so authorised by the parties) agreed to choose another seat for the arbitration; and that such a choice will be effective to endow the courts of that country with jurisdiction to supervise and support the arbitration. The concept of the "seat" of the arbitration is a juridical concept. The legal "seat" must not be confused with the geographically convenient place chosen to conduct particular hearings.[73]   **16–035**

The courts of the seat will have the sole supervisory and primary supportive function in relation to the conduct of the arbitration, save where there has been an express and effective choice of a different *lex arbitri*, in which event the role of the courts of the seat will be limited to those matters specified by their own law as internationally mandatory, i.e. non-derogable, even where an express choice of a different *lex arbitri* has been made by the parties. Where the parties have expressly chosen the seat of their arbitration, it is the courts at the seat which have exclusive supervisory jurisdiction to determine claims for a remedy going to the existence or scope of the arbitrator's jurisdiction, or to allegations of bias. Proceedings seeking to determine these issues in a court elsewhere than the seat would amount to a breach of the arbitration agreement and should be stayed. Thus, where a claim has been brought in England on the grounds that the arbitration agreement is liable to be avoided, but the parties have chosen foreign law to govern their arbitration agreement and a foreign seat of the arbitration, the English court will, as necessary, refuse to grant an injunction restraining the arbitrator from determining his own jurisdiction on the principle of *Kompetenz-Kompetenz*;[74] grant a stay of English proceedings against the arbitrator personally in the exercise of the court's inherent powers;[75] and make an award of damages or of indemnity costs against the party   **16–036**

---

[72] See, e.g., ICC Rules, Art.34(6).

[73] A paragraph to this effect in the previous edition of this work was applied in *Shashoua v Sharma* [2009] EWHC 957 (Comm.), [2009] 2 Lloyd's Rep. 87, at [32]. See *Naviera Amazonica Peruana SA v Cia. Internacional de Seguros del Peru* [1988] 1 Lloyd's Rep. 116, 117 (CA); *cf. Bay Hotel and Resort Ltd v Cavalier Construction Co Ltd* [2001] UKPC 34, [2001] 5 L.R.C. 376. See ICC Rules, Art.18; LCIA Rules, Art.16; Model Law, Art.20.

[74] *Weissfisch v Julius* [2006] EWCA Civ 218, [2006] 1 Lloyd's Rep. 716.

[75] *A v B* [2006] EWHC 2006 (Comm.), [2007] 1 Lloyd's Rep. 237.

bringing proceedings otherwise than in the courts of the seat.[76] By the same token, where the parties have expressly chosen England as the seat of their arbitration, the English court will restrain by injunction foreign court proceedings seeking to challenge, vacate or review an English arbitral award.[77] Choice of the seat of the arbitration confers upon the courts of that country exclusive jurisdiction for remedies seeking to attack the award (other than in the course of its enforcement in other countries under the New York Convention or otherwise) even if the arbitration agreement itself is governed by another law.[78] The same approach applies where the foreign proceedings are before an arbitral review tribunal, rather than a judicial forum.[79]

16–037   The "seat" of the arbitration is a term which is adopted by the 1996 Act. The seat is an important concept in that the scope of the legislation is largely determined by reference to it: the general principle is that Pt I of the Act (which effectively deals with all aspects of arbitration law other than the recognition and enforcement of foreign awards) applies where the seat of the arbitration is in England.[80] The seat is defined by s.3 of the 1996 Act to mean the juridical seat of the arbitration designated (a) by the parties to the arbitration agreement, or (b) by any arbitral or other institution or person vested by the parties with powers to fix the seat, or (c) by the arbitral tribunal if so authorised by the parties, or determined, in the absence of any such designation, having regard to the parties' agreement and all the relevant circumstances. These provisions are more complex and comprehensive than the corresponding provision of the Model Law, which states simply that the parties are free to agree on the place of arbitration and that, in the absence of such agreement, the place of arbitration shall be determined by the arbitral tribunal.[81] In practice, the choice of a place of arbitration by contract is common. In the absence of choice by the parties, arbitral rules may provide for its determination by the arbitral institution (as in the ICC Rules) or by the tribunal (as in the UNCITRAL Arbitration Rules).

16–038   The 1996 Act prescribes the seat of the arbitration as the primary connecting factor for the application of its provisions by distinguishing between mandatory provisions of the Act, and all other ("non-mandatory") provisions. Mandatory provisions apply notwithstanding any agreement to the contrary. Non-mandatory provisions apply only where the parties have not made their own arrangements. The choice of another law to govern any such non-mandatory provision is relegated by s.4(5) of the Act to being equivalent to an agreement about the matter. Section 4(5) requires a choice of law with regard to the specific provision of the Act which the parties agree is not to apply. Where the parties have chosen England as the seat of the arbitration, and English law as the *lex arbitri,* it will therefore not be sufficient to engage

---

[76] *A v B (No.2)* [2007] EWHC 54 (Comm.), [2007] 1 Lloyd's Rep. 358, at [15]–[19].

[77] *C v D* [2007] EWCA Civ 1282, [2008] 1 Lloyd's Rep. 239.

[78] *Shashoua v Sharma* [2009] EWHC 957 (Comm.), [2009] 2 Lloyd's Rep. 87.

[79] *Sheffield United Football Club Ltd v West Ham United Football Club Plc* [2008] EWHC 2855 (Comm.), [2009] 1 Lloyd's Rep. 167.

[80] *ibid.,* s.2; *Lesotho Highlands Development Authority v Impregilo SpA* [2005] UKHL 43, [2006] 1 A.C. 221, at [20]. See further paras 16–042 *et seq.,* below.

[81] Art.20(1).

s.4(5) that they have chosen a different law to govern the arbitration agreement, still less the main contract.[82]

Where there has been no express designation of the seat of the arbitration, the court is empowered to determine its seat having regard to the parties' agreement and all the relevant circumstances.[83] These circumstances include any connections in relation to the parties, the dispute, the arbitral procedures, and the place of hearings, as indicated at the time when the arbitration began. Once determined, the seat will not be peripatetic. It can only change if the conditions specified in s.3 are met.[84]   **16–039**

Although s.3 of the 1996 Act is in form only a self-limiting provision indicating the scope of the English legislation, it is submitted that the test propounded by that section also correctly encapsulates the multilateral conflicts rule.[85] As it was put in a recent Australian decision, the provision, though not replicated in the Australian legislation, "appears to state accurately how the 'seat' or 'place' of an arbitration is identified and its essential function as a 'juridical' concept. The concept has particular importance for an arbitration where the conduct or enforcement may have international dimensions."[86]   **16–040**

As indicated above,[87] the determination of the seat must be distinguished from the place chosen, as a matter of convenience, for any hearings. Where the parties have expressly chosen a place for the arbitration, its law will govern the procedure, even if another law has been chosen to govern the substance of the dispute, and the arbitration hearings have in fact been conducted in another country for convenience. Thus in *Bay Hotel and Resort Ltd v Cavalier Construction Co Ltd*[88] the Privy Council decided, on appeal from the Turks and Caicos Islands Court of Appeal, that the holding of arbitration hearings in Miami had been simply for convenience, and that the addition to the contract of an agreed term that disputes were to be resolved by the laws of the Turks and Caicos Islands amounted to an express choice of the same curial law as the proper law of the contract. Although the reasoning is   **16–041**

---

[82] *C v D* [2007] EWCA Civ 1282, [2008] 1 Lloyd's Rep. 239, at [19].

[83] *Arab National Bank v El Abdali* [2004] EWHC 2381 (Comm.), [2005] 1 Lloyd's Rep. 541, at [14].

[84] *Dubai Islamic Bank PJSC v Paymentech Merchant Services Inc* [2001] 1 Lloyd's Rep. 65.

[85] In any event the existence of such a rule is put beyond doubt by the many decisions at common law which refer questions of procedure to the law of the place of arbitration or the "curial law." See e.g. *Naviera Amazonica Peruana SA v Cia Internacional de Seguros del Peru* [1988] 1 Lloyd's Rep. 116, 119 (CA); *Paul Smith Ltd v H&S International Holdings Inc* [1991] 2 Lloyd's Rep. 127; *Sumitomo Heavy Industries Ltd v Oil and Natural Gas Commission* [1994] 1 Lloyd's Rep. 45; *Bay Hotel and Resort Ltd v Cavalier Construction Co Ltd* [2001] UKPC 34, [2001] 5 L.R.C. 376.

[86] *Raguz v Sullivan* [2000] NSWCA 240, (2000) 50 N.S.W.L.R. 236 at [95].

[87] Text at n.73, above.

[88] [2001] UKPC 34, [2001] 5 L.R.C. 376. So, too, where the parties had by their contract expressly decided that their arbitration was to be held in Glasgow, but it was clear from all of the other express terms that they wished English law to be the *lex arbitri*, Glasgow was treated as a convenient place for hearings only, and not as a choice of Scots law as the *lex arbitri*: *Braes of Doune Wind Farm (Scotland) Ltd v Alfred McAlpine Business Services Ltd* [2008] EWHC 426 (TCC), [2008] 1 Lloyd's Rep. 608.

not cast in terms of the "seat" of the arbitration being in the Turks and Caicos Islands, that is the effect of the decision.

16–042   *Scope of the 1996 Act.* Section 2 of the 1996 Act determines the scope of Pt I of the Act. The basic rule in s.2(1) is that the provisions contained in Pt I apply where the seat of the arbitration is in England. The general principle in s.2(1) is subject to four qualifications which extend the scope of various statutory provisions to cases where the seat of the arbitration is outside England or where no seat has been designated or determined. First, certain provisions apply regardless of the seat of the arbitration,[89] namely those relating to the stay of proceedings[90] and the enforcement of arbitral awards.[91] Secondly, some powers are exercisable by the English court in relation to foreign arbitrations and in cases where the seat of the arbitration has not been determined.[92] The specific powers are the power to secure the attendance of witnesses who are in the United Kingdom in cases where the arbitral proceedings are being conducted in England[93] and powers exercisable in support of arbitral proceedings[94] (in particular, the power to grant interim injunctions[95]). These powers are discretionary and the court may refuse to exercise any of them if, in the opinion of the court, the fact that the seat of the arbitration is outside England makes it inappropriate to do so. The court must be careful to avoid coming into conflict with the courts of other countries, in particular the courts of the seat. In a case where another country is the seat of the arbitration, the courts of that country are the natural forum for the granting of interim relief; if, in such a case, an application for interim relief is made in English proceedings, it is for the claimant to show why the English court should prefer itself to the natural forum.[96] Thirdly, the English court may exercise any other power under the Act for the purpose of supporting the arbitral process where the seat of the arbitration has not been designated or determined and, by reason of a connection with England, the court is satisfied that it is appropriate to do so.[97] For example, in a case where the seat of the arbitration has yet to be determined, the court may exercise its power to extend agreed time limits or to appoint an arbitrator if the arbitration agreement is governed by English law or if it is likely that, once determined, the seat will be in England.[98] Fourthly, as already noted, the provisions relating to the separability of the arbitration agreement and the death of a party[99] also apply where English law

---

[89] 1996 Act, s.2(2).

[90] *ibid.*, ss.9–11 (because the power to stay proceedings is exercisable wherever the arbitration is being, or is to be, held).

[91] *ibid.*, s.66 (because the powers are exercisable in relation to foreign awards).

[92] *ibid.*, s.2(3).

[93] *ibid.*, s.43. See *Commerce and Industry Insurance Co of Canada v Certain Underwriters at Lloyd's* [2002] 1 W.L.R. 1323.

[94] 1996 Act, s.44.

[95] *ibid.*, s.44(2)(e).

[96] *cf. Channel Tunnel Group Ltd v Balfour Beatty Construction Ltd* [1993] A.C. 334, 368, *per* Lord Mustill.

[97] 1996 Act, s.2(4).

[98] For the position under the 1950 Act see *International Tank & Pipe SAK v Kuwait Aviation Fuelling Co KSC* [1975] Q.B. 224 (CA).

[99] 1996 Act, ss.7, 8.

is the law applicable to the arbitration agreement, regardless of the seat of the arbitration.[100]

Although s.2 determines the circumstances in which the various provisions of Pt I of the 1996 Act are prima facie applicable, it is important to note that most of these provisions may be excluded by the agreement of the parties.[101] The scheme of the Act is to divide the provisions of Pt I into two groups: those which are mandatory and those which are non-mandatory (or "directory").[102] To the extent that they are rendered applicable by the terms of s.2, the mandatory provisions cannot be excluded. Some of the most important of the mandatory provisions relate to the court's powers of supervision (in particular, the power to set aside or remit an award for lack of jurisdiction or serious irregularity and the power to remove an arbitrator). Where England is the seat of the arbitration, the parties cannot contract out of the supervisory role of the court altogether. However, s.69 of the 1996 Act, which provides that a party to arbitral proceedings may appeal to the court on a question of law arising out of an award, and s.45, which allows questions of law arising out of arbitral proceedings to be referred to the court, are non-mandatory provisions which may be excluded by the parties' agreement. By contrast with the provisions of the 1979 Act which it replaces, the 1996 Act does not limit the parties' freedom to exclude the right to appeal on a point of law in cases falling within the so-called special categories; nor does it draw a distinction between domestic and non-domestic arbitration agreements.[103] Some of the provisions which relate to the court's support of the arbitral process (for example, the duty to stay proceedings brought in breach of an arbitration agreement, the power to extend agreed time limits and the power to secure the attendance of witnesses) are mandatory. Certain of the mandatory provisions relate to the general duties of the parties, the duty of the arbitral tribunal to act fairly and impartially and the immunity of the arbitral tribunal and arbitral institutions. It should also be noted that s.13, which provides that the English Limitation Acts (including the Foreign Limitation Periods Act 1984[104]) apply to any arbitration whose seat is in England, is a mandatory provision.

16–043

The non-mandatory provisions are in effect "fall-back" provisions, which apply only to the extent that the parties have not made their own arrangements.[105] Parties may make their own arrangements in one of a number of ways. As regards specific provisions—such as s.69, which enables parties to appeal to the court on a question of law arising out of an award—the parties may simply exclude them by an agreement in writing and not put anything else in their place. More generally, the parties may enter into an ad hoc arbitration agreement which regulates many of the issues covered by the non-mandatory provisions or they may incorporate a set of arbitration rules (such as the LCIA Rules or the UNCITRAL Arbitration Rules) into their arbitration

16–044

---

[100] *ibid.*, s.2(5).

[101] See *Re Q's Estate* [1999] 1 Lloyd's Rep. 931.

[102] 1996 Act, s.4 and Sch.1.

[103] The restrictions in the 1979 Act were intended as a temporary measure and the responses to the D.A.C.'s consultation exercise led to the conclusion that the restrictions should not be preserved.

[104] 1996 Act, s.13(4).

[105] *ibid.*, s.4(2).

agreement, with the consequence that the non-mandatory provisions of the 1996 Act are replaced by the corresponding arbitration rules agreed by the parties.[106] Finally, the parties may specifically agree that foreign law is to apply to one or more of the non-mandatory provisions of the 1996 Act, such a choice being treated as an agreement between them about that matter.[107]

16–045   The procedure to be adopted by the High Court for applications to court under the 1996 Act is dealt with by CPR Pt 62, Section I, and its Practice Direction. These rules contain special requirements for the contents of an arbitration claim form.[108] Where a foreign defendant to an arbitration in England has instructed solicitors or other representatives to act for him in the arbitration, the court will ordinarily order substituted service of any application to court in relation to that arbitration on such representatives in England.[109] In any case in which it is not possible to serve such a form upon the defendant within the jurisdiction,[110] it will be necessary to apply to the court for permission to serve the claim form outside the jurisdiction under CPR, r.62.5. The provisions of this rule apply only to applications by and against parties to an arbitration agreement. The rule does not apply to proceedings against non-parties.[111] The heads of jurisdiction provided under this rule essentially mirror the scope of the 1996 Act. The primary basis for jurisdiction is where the seat of the arbitration is within the jurisdiction.[112] The other heads of jurisdiction follow the exceptions, and supplemental provisions, in respect of the scope of the Act.[113] Of these, the most important extension in practical terms is that provided by CPR, r.62.5(1)(b), which applies where an order is sought under s.44 of the 1996 Act for interim orders in support of arbitration. These powers apply even where the seat of the arbitration is not in England and Wales,[114] and this provision in the rules permits the court to exercise those

---

[106] *ibid.*, s.4(3). An agreement to arbitrate under ICC Rules has the effect of excluding the right to appeal to the court on a point of law because the rules provide that the parties waive their right to any form of recourse insofar as such waiver can validly be made: ICC Rules, Art.34(6): *Arab African Energy Corporation Ltd v Olieprodukten Nederland BV* [1983] 2 Lloyd's Rep. 419; *Marine Contractors Ltd v Shell Petroleum Development Co of Nigeria Ltd* [1984] 2 Lloyd's Rep. 77. An agreement to arbitrate under the statute of an international organisation may have the same effect: *Sumukan Ltd v Commonwealth Secretariat* [2007] EWCA Civ 243, [2007] 2 Lloyd's Rep. 87.

[107] 1996 Act, s.4(5); *C v D* [2007] EWCA Civ 1282, [2008] 1 Lloyd's Rep. 239 , at [19].

[108] CPR, r.62.4.

[109] CPR, PD 62, para.3.1; *Kyrgyz Republic Ministry of Transport Department of Civil Aviation v Finrep GmbH* [2006] EWHC 1722 (Comm.), [2006] 2 C.L.C. 402.

[110] Either under CPR Pt 6 or pursuant to CPR PD 62, para.3.1.

[111] *The Cienvik* [1996] 2 Lloyd's Rep. 395; *Vale do Rio Doce Navegacao SA v Shanghai Bao Steel Ocean Shipping Co Ltd* [2000] 2 Lloyd's Rep. 1 (both cases under previous rules). There is special provision made for notice to be given to arbitrators, who are defendants to claims under 1996 Act, ss.24, 28 or 56: CPR, r.62.6.

[112] CPR, r.62.5(1)(c)(ii).

[113] Thus, CPR, r.62.5(1) provides that the court has jurisdiction for challenges to, or appeals from, arbitral awards, where they were made in the jurisdiction, but states that such place is to be determined by the 1996 Act, s.53. S.53 provides that an award is made at its seat, unless the parties have otherwise agreed. CPR, r.62.5(1)(c)(ii) also permits the court to exercise jurisdiction in cases where the conditions in the 1996 Act, s.2(4), are satisfied. This applies where no seat has been designated or determined and there is a connection with England.

[114] 1996 Act, s.2(3).

powers, even where the defendant is not within the *in personam* jurisdiction of the court.[115]

CPR, r.62.5 does not contain an express provision requiring the court to be satisfied that the case is a proper one in which to give permission for service out of the jurisdiction. However, the grant of permission still remains a matter within the court's discretion. It is therefore considered that the same requirements which apply to the exercise of that discretion generally, including a serious issue to be tried on the merits and a finding that England is the appropriate forum for the hearing of the matter will continue to apply to arbitration applications.[116] However, in view of the care taken to define the territorial scope of the application of the provisions of the 1996 Act, it is likely that, where the court is satisfied that the Act is applicable, as for example because the seat of the arbitration is in England, the requirement of *forum conveniens* will be satisfied.[117] Similarly, the Act itself provides that the court may refuse to exercise its powers to order interim measures under s.44 in support of arbitrations outside England and Wales when the fact that the seat is foreign makes it inappropriate to do so.[118]   **16–046**

Law governing substance of the dispute. The question of the appropriate approach which an arbitrator should take to the determination of the applicable rules to govern the substance of the dispute has been a matter of great controversy internationally.[119] In England, prior to the 1996 Act, it was axiomatic that an English arbitrator was bound to apply English law, including the English conflict of laws rules to decide the substance of any dispute, and many of the most important cases in the conflict of laws arose by way of appeal on matters of law from arbitral awards.[120] The other consequence of this approach was that, just as in the English courts, an English arbitrator could only apply a national legal system, designated as applicable by the relevant choice of law rule. The tribunal could not apply non-national rules, still less decide the dispute "*ex aequo et bono*" or as an "*amiable compositeur*", on the basis of general principles of justice and fairness.[121]   **16–047**

By contrast, other legal systems permitted the development of much greater flexibility in the approaches of arbitrators to determining the applicable substantive law.[122] This trend was another aspect of the development of   **16–048**

---

[115] See below, paras 16–085—16–086.

[116] See Rule 34 and paras 11–143—11–148. For cases prior to the 1996 Act and CPR Pt 62 approving this approach see *The Atlantic Emperor* [1989] 1 Lloyd's Rep. 548, 553 (CA); *Sokana Industries Inc v Freyre & Co Inc* [1994] 2 Lloyd's Rep. 57; *The John C. Helmsing* [1990] 2 Lloyd's Rep. 290 (CA).

[117] *Kyrgyz Republic Ministry of Transport Department of Civil Aviation v Finrep GmbH* [2006] EWHC 1722 (Comm.), [2006] 2 C.L.C. 402.

[118] 1996 Act, s.2(3).

[119] See generally Redfern and Hunter, paras 3.88–3.223; Lew, Mistelis and Kröll, Ch.17; Fouchard, Gaillard, Goldman, Pt V; Born, Ch.18; Poudret and Besson, Ch.7; Blessing (1997) 14(2) J. Int. Arb. 39; Lew, *Applicable Law in International Commercial Arbitration* (1978); Grigera Naon (2001) 289 *Recueil des Cours* 9.

[120] For the former English law position see the 12th edition of this work, p.584, and Collins, in Lew (ed.), *Contemporary Problems in International Arbitration* (1986) 126, at pp.136–8.

[121] See, e.g. *Orion Compania Espanola de Seguros v Belfort* [1962] 2 Lloyd's Rep. 257.

[122] See, e.g. Art.1496 (1), French New Code of Civil Procedure (1981), discussed in Fouchard, Gaillard, Goldman, paras 1540 *et seq.*

"delocalised arbitration", which saw the mandatory application of the choice of law rules of the forum as an unnecessary fetter on party autonomy. The fullest expression of this approach was found in the development of a doctrine of a new "*lex mercatoria*". This doctrine contemplated that there was a set of rules developed from the practice of merchants and from international codifications, which might be applied directly by the arbitrators, either as a result of an express choice by the parties, or in the absence of any express choice of law.[123]

16–049   This approach was sanctioned, to a greater or lesser extent, by the major international arbitral rules. Thus, most notably, the ICC Rules provide that: "The parties shall be free to agree upon the *rules of law* to be applied by the arbitral tribunal to the merits of the dispute. In the absence of any such agreement, the arbitral tribunal shall apply the *rules of law* which it determines to be appropriate."[124] The reference to "rules of law" means that neither the parties nor the arbitrator is restricted to choosing a given national legal system. Moreover, the arbitrator is not limited to using the techniques of a set of conflict of law rules to determine the applicable law in the absence of choice. In practice, a great variety of different techniques and approaches have been adopted by ICC arbitrators.[125] The revised text of the UNCITRAL Arbitration Rules (2010)—widely used in *ad hoc* arbitration—adopts a *via media* by providing that: "The arbitral tribunal shall apply the rules of law designated by the parties as applicable to the substance of the dispute. Failing such designation by the parties, the arbitral tribunal shall apply the law which it determines to be appropriate."[126] Under this formulation, the parties have considerable flexibility to choose "rules of law". In the absence of express choice, the arbitral tribunal is directed to apply "the law", but it is not (in contrast to the formulation in the previous text of the Rules[127]) directed to find the applicable law by first identifying the conflict of law rules which it considers appropriate.

16–050   The Model Law permits the parties to choose *rules* of law. But, in the absence of choice, it provides that: " . . . the arbitral tribunal shall apply the law determined by the conflict of laws rules which it considers applicable."[128] In the event, therefore, that the parties have not exercised their right to make an express choice of law, the arbitrator is bound to apply a national legal system to the resolution of the dispute, and is bound to apply such legal system as is designated by a system of conflict of laws rules. In England, the 1996 Act substantially adopts the solution to determination of applicable law preferred by the Model Law.

---

[123] See Fouchard, Gaillard, Goldman, paras 1443–1499; Lew, Mistelis and Kröll, paras 18–41—18–70; Berger, *The Creeping Codification of the New Lex Mercatoria* (2nd ed. 2010). See also Goldman, in Lew (ed.), *Contemporary Problems in International Arbitration* (1986) 113; Lando (1985) 34 I.C.L.Q. 747; Mustill (1988) 4 Arb. Int. 86; Goode (2005) 54 I.C.L.Q. 539, at pp.545–552.
[124] Art.21(1) (emphasis added). To like effect LCIA Rules, Art.22.3.
[125] Craig Park and Paulsson, Ch.17; Grigera Naon (2001) 289 *Recueil des Cours* 9.
[126] Art.35(1).
[127] UNCITRAL Arbitration Rules 1976, Art.33.
[128] Model Law, Art.28.

Section 46 of the 1996 Act provides: 16–051

"(1) The arbitral tribunal shall decide the dispute—
  (a) in accordance with the law chosen by the parties as applicable to the substance of the dispute, or
  (b) if the parties so agree, in accordance with such other considerations as are agreed by them or determined by the tribunal. ...
(3) If or to the extent that there is no such choice or agreement, the tribunal shall apply the law determined by the conflict of laws rules which it considers applicable."

Applicable rules chosen by the parties. Section 46(1) thus presents the 16–052 parties with two options by way of an express choice. In the first place, under s.46(1)(a), they may choose an applicable legal system to govern their dispute. That legal system may be either a national legal system or public international law. When the parties have made a choice of applicable law under s.46(1), the arbitrators are bound to apply that law.[129] Such a choice denotes substantive law and not conflict of laws rules.[130] This rule does not, however, affect the approach which the arbitral tribunal is entitled to take to the ascertainment of the content of the *lex causae*. Thus, an arbitral tribunal sitting in England may, if there is no suggestion by the parties that there is an issue under the applicable system of law which is different from English law, or the tribunal does not itself raise a specific issue, decide the matter under English law. Equally (and subject to the contrary agreement of the parties and to the requirements of due process) it may decide to take the initiative in ascertaining the contents of the law chosen by the parties.[131]

Pursuant to s.46(1)(b), the parties may also choose to subject the determina- 16–053 tion of their dispute to "such other considerations as are agreed by them or determined by the tribunal." This option allows the parties the freedom to apply a set of rules or principles which do not in themselves constitute a legal system. Such a choice may thus include a non-national set of legal principles (such as the 1994 UNIDROIT Principles of International Commercial Contracts[132]), or, more broadly, general principles of commercial law or the *lex mercatoria*. Equally, the parties may choose a mixed system of law. Thus, in *Channel Tunnel Group Ltd v Balfour Beatty Construction Ltd*[133] the parties to the construction contract to build the cross-Channel rail link had inserted a governing law clause into their contract, requiring its interpretation "in accordance with the principles common to both English law and French law, and in the absence of such common principles by such general principles of international trade law as have been applied by national and international tribunals ... ". This choice of law was treated as valid and enforceable by the

---

[129] *Peterson Farms Inc v C&M Farming Ltd* [2004] EWHC 121 (Comm.), [2004] 1 Lloyd's Rep. 603, where it was held that the defect was one of jurisdiction under 1996 Act, s.67.
[130] s.46(2).
[131] *Hussman (Europe) Ltd v Al Ameen Development & Trade Co* [2000] 2 Lloyd's Rep. 83; 1996 Act, s.34(2)(g). See generally ILA Committee on International Commercial Arbitration *Ascertaining the Contents of the Applicable Law in International Commercial Arbitration* (2010) 26 Arb. Int. 191.
[132] See Berger (1998) 46 Am. J. Comp. Law 129; Gaillard (2001) 17 Arb. Int. 59.
[133] [1993] A.C. 334.

House of Lords.[134] In that case, the seat of the arbitration was Belgium.[135] Under the 1996 Act, such a choice would be equally valid where the seat of the arbitration is England.[136] Finally, the parties may simply invite the arbitral tribunal to decide the dispute *ex aequo et bono,* according to general principles of equity and fairness.[137]

16–054   Although the 1996 Act is generally applicable to arbitrations commenced on or after January 31, 1997, s.46(1)(b) is applicable only in cases where the arbitration agreement was concluded on or after that date.[138]

16–055   *Applicable law in the absence of choice.* If there is no choice of the applicable law, and no agreement to the application of other considerations, the tribunal is to "apply the law determined by the conflict of laws rules which it considers applicable."[139] This formulation is identical to that found in Art.28(2) of the Model Law. Its effect is that, in the context of an arbitration whose seat is in England, an arbitral tribunal is not bound to apply English conflict of laws rules. For example, if the dispute is between parties neither of whom has any connection with Europe, it may not be appropriate for the tribunal to apply the Rome I Regulation in order to determine the applicable law. Although in cases falling within the scope of s.46(3) considerable discretion is conferred on the arbitrators, it should be observed that the arbitral tribunal is obliged to apply the *law* determined by the applicable conflict of laws rules. In the absence of agreement by the parties, there is no scope for the arbitrators to apply the *lex mercatoria* or general principles of law, because neither constitutes "law", which can mean only a specific system of law.[140]

16–056   Section 46 is not a mandatory provision; it applies only to the extent that the parties have not made their own arrangements by agreement. If the parties have agreed to arbitration in accordance with a set of arbitration rules (such as the ICC Rules or the LCIA Rules) which includes a choice of law provision, the arbitral tribunal should have regard to the rules agreed by the parties rather than to s.46(3).

16–057   As discussed above, such rules typically confer upon the arbitral tribunal the ability to apply "the rules of law which it determines to be appropriate".[141]

---

[134] *ibid.* at p.368, *per* Lord Mustill.

[135] For other recent examples of mixed choice of law agreements see: *Channel Tunnel Group Ltd v Secretary of State for Transport of the United Kingdom of Great Britain and Northern Ireland* (2007) 132 I.L.R. 1; *Svenska Petroleum Exploration AB v Lithuania (No.2)* [2006] EWCA Civ 1529, [2007] Q.B. 886.

[136] But see Redfern and Hunter, paras 3.155–3.159 for an account of the practical difficulties posed in the application of this hybrid clause. See also, on this decision Rubino-Sammartano (1993) 10 J. Int. Arb. 59; Reymond (1993) 109 L.Q.R. 337.

[137] D.A.C. Report (1997) 13 Arb. Int. 275, 310.

[138] SI 1996/3146, Sch.2, para.4. As regards arbitrations arising from agreements concluded before January 31, 1997 the effect of an equity clause or a clause expressly adopting the *lex mercatoria* continues to be governed by the common law, under which it is generally assumed that an English arbitrator is bound to apply the choice of law rules which would be binding on an English court: see pp.584–585 of the 12th edition of this work. *cf. Deutsche Schachtbau v Shell International Petroleum Co Ltd* [1990] 1 A.C. 295 (CA), reversed on other grounds, *ibid.* p.329; Lando (1998) 47 I.C.L.Q. 394, 403–404.

[139] 1996 Act, s.46(3).

[140] See D.A.C. Report (1997) 13 Arb. Int. 275, 310; *cf.* Shackleton (1997) 13 Arb. Int. 375.

[141] ICC Rules, Art.21(1); LCIA Rules, Art.22.3.

Thus, the selection by the parties of the rules of an arbitral institution to govern their dispute, even if not accompanied by an express choice of applicable substantive law, would amount to an agreement under s.46(1), delegating to the arbitrators such additional flexibility as is offered by the institution's procedural rules, beyond that contemplated by s.46(3).

Section 46(3) gives no guidance to the arbitrator as to the manner of **16–058** determination of which conflict of laws rules are appropriate. The section invites a preliminary step in the choice of law process in which the arbitrator must first determine the applicable conflicts rules, and then apply those rules to determine the applicable law.[142] However, the section supplies no connecting factor by reference to which that first step is to be carried out. Possible options are: (a) *The conflicts rules of the seat.* It is submitted that this approach (which was mandatory in England until the 1996 Act) will continue to be appropriate in cases, where the parties have made an express choice of seat and there is a real connection between the parties to the dispute and the nominated seat. This will be especially so if there are no other factors (such as choice of a more liberal set of arbitral rules) suggesting that the parties did not wish to have the seat's conflicts rules applied to their dispute. Nevertheless, the arguments in favour of flexibility convinced the D.A.C., and prevailed in the legislation.[143] The D.A.C. declined the invitation to give more guidance in this field, but considered that "it is not our remit to lay down principles in this highly complex area".[144] (b) *The conflicts rules most closely connected with the subject-matter.* Whilst superficially attractive, this approach risks circularity, since it merely restates the ultimate goal of most choice of law rules in contract. (c) *The cumulative application of relevant conflict of laws rules.* This approach may be suitable, especially if, and to the extent that it demonstrates common ground, and identifies false conflicts between legal systems, either because both relevant legal systems share the same conflicts rule, or because the application of different conflicts rules nevertheless leads to the same applicable law being designated by both systems. (d) *General principles of the conflict of laws.* This approach may also be appropriate, provided that such a general principle can safely be identified to apply to the particular problem. The progressive codification of some aspects of the conflict of laws by unification bodies such as the Hague Conference on Private International Law may yield suitable guidance. But such codification remains very partial in its scope, both as to subject-matter and as to geographical acceptance. Otherwise, national legal systems continue to vary widely in their solutions to choice of law. An arbitrator should be wary of assuming that solutions adopted, for example, within the European Union, are necessarily a safe guide to the determination of applicable conflicts rules for a dispute where the parties and the subject-matter are outside the European Union.

Much of the discussion in the literature has tended to focus on the arbi- **16–059** trator's selection of the law applicable to the *contract* in the absence of an express choice by the parties. However, s.46(3) provides for selection of the appropriate conflicts rules "if *or to the extent* that there is no such choice or

---

[142] See Lew, Mistelis and Kröll, paras 17–38—17–78; Wortmann (1998) 14 Arb. Int. 97.
[143] D.A.C. Report (1997) 13 Arb. Int. 275, 310, para.225.
[144] *ibid.*

agreement" (emphasis added). This statutory language denotes the important point that not all aspects of applicable law are necessarily questions of contract law, amenable to selection by the parties, even in international arbitration. Thus, for example, an arbitrator, in the course of an arbitration, may have to determine the law applicable to the constitution and internal management of a corporation. Or the arbitrator may have to decide other matters which are not clearly subject to the *lex causae*, such as the appropriate period of limitation, the right to, or rate of, interest and the effect of assignment.[145] In each case, s.46(3) will require the arbitrator to consider which choice of law rules are applicable to the issue presented.

16–060   Where the matters are, or may be regarded as, procedural for the purpose of the conflict of laws generally, it is not the case that the *lex fori* at the seat of the arbitration will necessarily be the appropriate applicable law. This will be so especially where the rules in question were principally developed in the context of court proceedings. The 1996 Act makes express provision for some of the more common of these issues. Thus it provides that the Limitation Acts, including the Foreign Limitation Periods Act 1984, apply to arbitral proceedings as they apply to legal proceedings.[146] The general effect of this is to subject issues of limitation to the *lex causae*.[147] Further, the 1996 Act furnishes a wide discretion to the arbitrators as to the award of interest in the absence of the parties' agreement.[148]

16–061   The approach taken to the applicable law by arbitrators is most unlikely to come under the purview of the English courts following the reforms of the 1996 Act. In the first place, the formula set out in s.46(3) confers on the arbitrator significant discretion in determination of the applicable law. Secondly, a mistake by the arbitrator in the application of the applicable law will not be treated by the English court as a significant procedural irregularity permitting an appeal as of right under the mandatory provisions of s.68.[149] Thirdly, the parties may exclude by agreement the possibility of appeals to the courts on points of law, and selection of the rules of a number of the major arbitral institutions has this effect.[150] Fourthly, even if such a right has not been excluded by the parties, an error of foreign law is not subject to appeal under s.69, as "law" for this purpose means English law.[151] Thus, the courts have on a number of occasions declined to entertain appeals, where the law applied by the arbitral tribunal to the substance of the dispute was other than

---

[145] See Veeder, in van den Berg (ed.) *ICCA Congress Series No.7* (1996) 268.

[146] 1996 Act, s.13. This rule is mandatory: Sch.1.

[147] See further, above, paras 7–054—7–060.

[148] s.49. See *Lesotho Highlands Development Authority v Impregilo SpA* [2005] UKHL 43, [2006] 1 A.C. 221, at [35]–[40].

[149] *Lesotho Highlands Development Authority v Impregilo SpA* [2005] UKHL 43, [2006] 1 A.C. 221; *B v A* [2010] EWHC 1626 (Comm.), [2010] 2 Lloyd's Rep. 681 (where it was suggested that a conscious disregard of the provisions of the chosen law would be a necessary, but not sufficient, requirement to challenge an award under s.68(2)(b) for excess of powers in the determination of the applicable law). It is no ground for review under s.68 that the arbitrator might have expressed his conclusions on foreign law at greater length: *ABB AG v Hochtief Airport GmbH* [2006] EWHC 388 (Comm.), [2006] 2 Lloyd's Rep. 1.

[150] See. e.g. ICC Rules, Art.34(6); LCIA Rules, Art.26.9.

[151] 1996 Act, s.82(1).

English law, even where there was no material difference between the applicable law and English law.[152]

ILLUSTRATIONS

1. A, the owner of a vessel, enters into a charterparty with X, the charterer, containing an arbitration agreement. A alleges that the charters were procured by bribery and claims that it is entitled to rescind them. It further claims that, as a result, the arbitration agreement is not binding upon it. The allegation of bribery does not vitiate the arbitration agreement, which is separable from the main contract, unless the facts are such as to impeach the arbitration agreement specifically.[153]   **16–062**

2. A, a Saudi company, enters into an arbitration agreement with X, a legal entity under the law of country Y, providing for ICC arbitration in Paris. A claims that the Government of Y is a party to the agreement. The ICC arbitral tribunal agrees and renders an award against the Government of Y. The question whether the arbitration agreement binds the Government of Y is governed by the law of the arbitration agreement, which, in the absence of express choice, is the law of the seat of the arbitration, namely French law. It is for French law to determine the content of the principles applicable to a transnational contract of this kind.[154]

3. A, a Bermudian insurance company, contracts to insure X, a Delaware corporation, on terms which provide for New York law to govern the contract, but stipulate for arbitration in London "under the provisions of the Arbitration Act 1996". The validity of the arbitration agreement is governed by English law.[155]

4. A contract concluded by A, a Japanese corporation, and X, an Indian entity, provides that disputes arising out of the contract shall be subject to the laws of India and that such disputes shall be referred to arbitration, the proceedings of which shall be held in London. Although England is the seat of the arbitration, as a consequence of which English law governs the arbitration, the arbitration agreement is governed by Indian law.[156]

5. A & Co, a Scottish firm of builders, agree to carry out conversion work at the factory in Scotland of X & Co, an English company. The contract contains an arbitration clause providing for the appointment of an arbitrator by the President of the Royal Institute of British Architects. The President appoints a Scottish architect as arbitrator and the arbitration proceedings take place in Scotland. Although the law governing the contract is English law, the seat of the arbitration is in Scotland. The parties to the arbitration may not appeal to the High Court on a question of law arising out of the award.[157]   **16–063**

6. A, a Dubai bank, contract with X Inc, for the provision of credit card processing services under the terms of the VISA International Operating Regulations, which provide for arbitration. No seat of the arbitration is chosen by the parties. The original arbitration is conducted on the papers, but there is an internal appeal to the VISA International Board of Directors, considered at a board meeting, which happens to take place in London. The seat of the arbitration is California, where the arbitration was administered, and not England, the venue for the subsequent

---

[152] *Egmatra AG v Marco Trading Corp* [1999] 1 Lloyd's Rep. 862; *Sanghi Polyesters Ltd (India) v International Investor (KCFC) (Kuwait)* [2000] 1 Lloyd's Rep. 480; *Reliance Industries Ltd v Enron Oil and Gas India Ltd* [2002] 1 Lloyd's Rep. 645; *Athletic Union of Constantinople v National Basketball Association* [2002] 1 Lloyd's Rep. 305. See also *Re Independent State of Papua New Guinea (No.2)* [2001] 2 Qd. R. 162.

[153] *Fiona Trust and Holding Corp v Privalov sub nom. Premium Nafta Products Ltd v Fili Shipping Co Ltd* [2007] UKHL 40, [2008] 1 Lloyd's Rep. 254.

[154] *Dallah Real Estate and Tourism Holding Co v Ministry of Religious Affairs, Government of Pakistan* [2010] UKSC 46, [2011] 1 A.C. 763.

[155] *XL Insurance Ltd v Owens Corning* [2000] 2 Lloyd's Rep. 500.

[156] *Sumitomo Heavy Industries Ltd v Oil and Natural Gas Commission* [1994] 1 Lloyd's Rep. 45.

[157] 1996 Act, s.2; *cf. Whitworth Street Estates (Manchester) Ltd v James Miller & Partners Ltd* [1970] A.C. 583 (a case at common law).

appeal being fortuitous. The jurisdiction of the English court under Pt I of the 1996 Act is limited accordingly.[158]

16–064   7. An oil agreement between A and the Government of X provides for the application of the law of X supplemented, where required, by rules of international business activities generally accepted in the petroleum industry if they do not contradict the laws of the Republic of X. The parties agree to submit their dispute to international arbitration. The arbitral tribunal may apply such a hybrid set of rules to the substance of the dispute, where the parties have expressly so chosen.[159]

8. A contract between A & Co, a company incorporated in Nigeria, and X & Co, a company incorporated in Delaware, provides that X & Co shall lay a pipeline in Nigeria for A & Co. The contract provides for arbitration in London according to the Rules of the International Chamber of Commerce. The Rules exclude the right of recourse to any court. The right to appeal to the court on a question of law under s. 69 of the 1996 Act, a non-mandatory provision, is excluded by the parties' agreement; the right to challenge the award for lack of jurisdiction or serious irregularity under ss.67 and 68, which are mandatory provisions, is not.[160]

2. STAYING OF PROCEEDINGS AND INJUNCTIONS TO RESTRAIN FOREIGN PROCEEDINGS

16R–065   **RULE 65[161]—(1) Upon application by a party to an arbitration agreement[162] against whom legal proceedings are brought (whether by way of claim or counterclaim) in respect of a matter which under the agreement is to be referred to arbitration, the court shall grant a stay of the proceedings so far as they concern that matter unless satisfied that the arbitration agreement is null and void, inoperative, or incapable of being performed.**

(2) The English court has jurisdiction *in personam* to restrain by injunction foreign proceedings in breach of an arbitration agreement, save where those proceedings are brought in the courts of a State to which the Brussels I Regulation or the Lugano Convention applies.

COMMENT

16–066   **Staying English actions.** Clause (1) of this Rule states the effect of s.9 of the 1996 Act. Section 9, which replaced s.1 of the 1975 Act, gives effect (with some modifications) to Art.II of the New York Convention.[163] Article I limits

---

[158] 1996 Act, s.3; *Dubai Islamic Bank PJSC v Paymentech Merchant Services Inc* [2001] 1 Lloyd's Rep. 65.

[159] 1996 Act, s.46; *Svenska Petroleum Exploration AB v Lithuania (No.2)* [2006] EWCA Civ 1529, [2007] Q.B. 886.

[160] 1996 Act, ss.2(1), 4(1) and Sch.1; *cf. Marine Contractors Ltd v Shell Petroleum Development Co of Nigeria Ltd* [1984] 2 Lloyd's Rep. 77 (a case under the 1979 Act).

[161] 1996 Act, s.9.

[162] A party to an arbitration agreement includes any person claiming under or through a party to the agreement: 1996 Act, s.82(2).

[163] For the text of the Convention, see e.g. Redfern and Hunter, App.A. On the Convention see van den Berg, *New York Arbitration Convention of 1958* (1981). The Convention (and its *travaux préparatoires*) may be referred to in aid of the interpretation of the Act in so far as the provisions of the latter are ambiguous: *Government of Kuwait v Sir Frederick Snow and Partners* [1984] A.C. 426, 436; *The Tuyuti* [1984] Q.B. 838, 852 (CA); *Hiscox v Outhwaite* [1992] 1 A.C. 562, 593; above, para.1–031. International arbitration practice is documented in the volumes of *Yearbook Commercial Arbitration* (Yb. Comm. Arb.), the first of which was published in 1975; a special section of each volume since 1982 (Vol.7) is devoted to court decisions on the Convention and includes a consolidated commentary (by van den Berg) on the case law of the Contracting States.

the Convention's scope to awards made in another State and to those which are regarded as non-domestic awards under the law of the forum, but there is no equivalent provision which expressly limits the scope of the rules which deal with arbitration agreements to cases with a foreign element. Nevertheless, it is generally accepted that it was not intended that Contracting States should be required to enforce arbitration agreements in wholly domestic cases.[164] However, the 1996 Act applies the same provisions to domestic and non-domestic awards. As a result, a mandatory stay is in principle available in any case where proceedings are brought in breach of an agreement to refer a dispute to arbitration.[165]

It is provided that, "[n]o appeal shall lie to the Court of Appeal . . . except   **16–067** as provided by Part I of the Arbitration Act 1996, from any decision of the High Court under that Part".[166] In *Inco Europe Ltd v First Choice Distribution*[167] it was argued that, as the 1996 Act makes no provision for appeals against decisions under s.9, there was no mechanism whereby decisions of the High Court (whether to grant a stay under s.9 or to refuse a stay, such as on the basis that the alleged arbitration agreement is null and void) could be reviewed. The House of Lords held that, in view of the legislative history, the amended s.18(1)(g) of the Senior Courts Act 1981 should be read as not excluding appeals from decisions of the High Court under s.9 of the 1996 Act.

Arbitration agreements in writing. Rule 65(1) applies only to arbitration   **16–068** agreements "in writing", an expression which is exhaustively defined by s.5 of the 1996 Act. The effect of s.5 is considerably wider than that of the equivalent Art.7 of the Model Law. The 1989 D.A.C. Report recommended against the adoption of Art.7, because it would have excluded most bills of

---

[164] See Cohn (1962) 25 M.L.R. 449, 451. During the reform process which led to the enactment of the 1996 Act, the D.A.C. recommended that consideration should be given to abolishing the distinction between domestic and non-domestic agreements. However, because there had not been adequate opportunities to take soundings, special provisions relating to domestic arbitration agreements (ss.85–87) were included in the 1996 Act. Shortly before the Act received the Royal Assent, the Court of Appeal decided, in the context of Consumer Arbitration Agreements Act 1988 (repealed by the 1996 Act), that the distinction between domestic and non-domestic arbitration agreements was incompatible with European Community law because it amounted to a restriction on the freedom to provide services contrary to what is now Art.56, TFEU and/or unlawful discrimination contrary to what is now Art.18, TFEU: *Phillip Alexander Securities and Futures Ltd v Bamberger* [1997] I.L.Pr. 73 (Waller J. and CA). After a short consultation exercise it was decided to abolish the distinction and the special provisions of the 1996 Act relating to domestic arbitration agreements were not brought into force: SI 1996/3146.

[165] Although the 1996 Act does not generally apply to proceedings pursuant to the Washington Convention for the Settlement of Investment Disputes (ICSID), it is expressly provided that legal proceedings brought in breach of an agreement to arbitrate under the auspices of ICSID shall be stayed in accordance with s.9 of the 1996 Act: Arbitration (International Investment Disputes) Act 1966, s.3 (as amended by Arbitration Act 1996, s.107(1) and Sch.3, para.24). On ICSID arbitration, see Rule 72. For special provision for consumer arbitration agreements see Arbitration Act 1996, ss.89–91 (the effect of which is to apply Unfair Terms in Consumer Contracts Regulations 1999, SI 1999/2083 to arbitration agreements) and SI 1999/2167 (the effect of which is that, for the purposes of 1996 Act, s.91, as long as the other conditions are satisfied, an arbitration agreement is unfair under those Regulations if it relates to a claim for a pecuniary remedy which does not exceed £5,000).

[166] Senior Courts Act 1981, s.18(1)(g), as amended.

[167] [2000] 1 W.L.R. 586 (HL).

lading, many brokers' contract notes and many other important categories of contract.[168] Although the definition in the 1996 Act goes beyond the Model Law, the D.A.C. considered that it was consistent with Art.II(2) of the New York Convention.[169]

16–069   For the purposes of the 1996 Act there is an agreement in writing (a) if the agreement is made in writing (whether or not it is signed by the parties), (b) if the agreement is made by exchange of communications in writing, or (c) if the agreement is evidenced in writing.[170] So, an oral acceptance of a written quotation containing an arbitration clause constitutes an agreement in writing.[171] Where parties agree otherwise than in writing by reference to terms which are in writing, they make an agreement in writing.[172] The reference in an agreement to a written form of arbitration clause or to a document containing an arbitration clause constitutes an arbitration agreement if the reference is such as to make that clause part of the agreement.[173] The effect is to cover extremely common situations such as salvage operations where parties orally agree to a set of written terms (such as Lloyd's Open Form) which include an arbitration agreement.[174] An agreement is evidenced in writing if an agreement made otherwise than in writing is recorded by one of the parties, or by a third party, with the authority of the parties to the agreement.[175] An exchange of written submissions in arbitral or legal proceedings in which the existence of an agreement otherwise than in writing is alleged by one party against another party and not denied by the other party in his response constitutes as between those parties an agreement in writing to the effect alleged.[176] Although based on Art.7(2) of the Model Law, this rule is more stringent in that an agreement in writing cannot arise where one party alleges an arbitration agreement and the other party fails to respond at all.[177] References to anything being written or in writing, include its being recorded by other means,[178] though it is doubtful whether this extends to recorded speech as opposed to recorded text.[179]

16–070   *The court's duty to stay.* Under the 1996 Act an application for a stay may be made only by a party to an arbitration agreement against whom legal

---

[168] (1990) 6 Arb. Int. 3, 52. See also Kaplan (1996) 12 Arb. Int. 27.

[169] D.A.C. Report (1997) 13 Arb. Int. 275, 282. In the shipping context, it is sufficient if the arbitration agreement is contained in a telex exchange prior to issue of the bill of lading, even if no formal charter-party has been executed: *Welex AG v Rosa Maritime Ltd (The Epsilon Rosa)* [2003] EWCA Civ 938, [2003] 2 Lloyd's Rep. 509.

[170] 1996 Act, s.5(2).

[171] See *Zambia Steel & Building Supplies Ltd v Clark & Eaton Ltd* [1986] 2 Lloyd's Rep. 225 (decided under the 1975 Act).

[172] 1996 Act, s.5(3).

[173] 1996 Act, s.6(2). See *The Federal Bulker* [1989] 1 Lloyd's Rep. 103; *Sea Trade Maritime Corp v Hellenic Mutual War Risks Assn (Bermuda) Ltd (No.2)* [2006] EWHC 2530 (Comm.), [2007] 1 Lloyd's Rep. 280.

[174] D.A.C. Report (1997) 13 Arb. Int. 275, 282–283.

[175] 1996 Act, s.5(4).

[176] *ibid.*, s.5(5).

[177] See D.A.C. Report (1997) 13 Arb. Int. 275, 283.

[178] 1996 Act, s.5(6).

[179] *cf.* Model Law, Art.7(2).

proceedings are brought.[180] The duty to grant a stay applies both to claims and counterclaims.[181] However, the court can only grant a stay in respect of a counterclaim which is within the scope of the arbitration agreement (which includes cases where the counterclaim amounts to a defence of a transactional set-off to the original claim.)[182] It is quite possible for a situation to arise in which, although the defendant's counterclaim falls within the terms of the parties' arbitration agreement, the claim made by the claimant does not. In these circumstances only the counterclaim will be referred to arbitration. But if, in that case, the cross-claim which is subject to an arbitration agreement amounts, under the law governing the claim, to a substantive defence to the claim, the cross-claim will not be stayed.[183]

The court's duty to grant a stay does not depend on the parties being able   **16–071** to proceed to arbitration as soon as the proceedings are stayed; a stay must be granted even where other dispute resolution procedures must be followed before reference of the parties' dispute to arbitration.[184] It is not necessary that the arbitration agreement should have been entered into before the court proceedings were commenced.[185] But the party wishing to enforce the arbitration agreement loses the right to a stay if he takes a step in the proceedings to answer the substantive claim.[186] Where a party to an alleged arbitration agreement brings proceedings for a declaration that the arbitration agreement is non-existent, the right to a stay is not lost if the proceedings are unsuccessful.[187] The duty to grant a stay under s.9 applies in cases where the arbitration agreement takes the form of a *Scott v Avery* clause (i.e. a contractual provision which makes an award a condition precedent to the bringing of legal proceedings); if, however, the court refuses to stay proceedings brought in breach of a *Scott v Avery* clause (for example, because the arbitration clause is unworkable) it is provided that the clause ceases to have effect,[188] thereby permitting the parties' dispute to be litigated.

---

[180] 1996 Act, s.9(1). Although s.1 of the 1975 Act referred simply to "any party" this was interpreted as meaning a party to the arbitration agreement: *Etri Fans Ltd v NMB (UK) Ltd* [1987] 1 W.L.R. 1110 (CA); *cf. Marine Expeditions Inc v The Ship Akademik Shuleykin* [1995] 2 N.Z.L.R. 743.

[181] 1996 Act, s.9(1).

[182] *Metal Distributors (UK) Ltd v ZCCM Investment Holdings Plc* [2005] EWHC 156 (Comm.), [2005] 2 Lloyd's Rep. 37. See also *Ronly Holdings Ltd v JSC Zestafoni G Nikoladze Ferroalloy Plant* [2004] EWHC 1354 (Comm.), [2004] 1 C.L.C 1168.

[183] See *Aectra Refining and Manufacturing Inc v Exmar NV* [1994] 1 W.L.R. 1634; *Benford Ltd v Lopecan SL (No.2)* [2004] EWHC 1897 (Comm.), [2004] 2 Lloyd's Rep. 618; *Prekons Insaat Sanayi AS v Rowlands Castle Contracting Group Ltd* [2006] EWHC 1367 (Comm.), [2007] 1 Lloyd's Rep. 98. Where, by their arbitration agreement, the parties have limited the tribunal's jurisdiction over defences of set-off to counterclaims arising out of the same contract, the court will give effect to the limitation: *Econet Satellite Services Ltd v VEE Networks Ltd* [2006] EWHC 1664 (Comm.), [2006] 2 Lloyd's Rep. 423 (construing Art.19(3) LCIA Rules to this effect).

[184] 1996 Act, s.9(2). This provision resolves doubts in dicta of Lord Mustill in *Channel Tunnel Group Ltd v Balfour Beatty Construction Ltd* [1993] A.C. 334 at p.354, on which see Reymond (1993) 109 L.Q.R. 337.

[185] *The Tuyuti* [1984] Q.B. 838, 852 (CA).

[186] 1996 Act, s.9(3). See *Patel v Patel* [2000] Q.B. 551; *Queensland Sugar Corp v The Hanjin Jedda* [1995] 7 W.W.R. 237 (BC) (a case concerning Model Law, Art.8). The time-limits in CPR, Pt. 11 (see para.11–073) do not apply to applications under s.9: *Bilta (UK) Ltd (In Liquidation) v Nazir* [2010] EWHC 1086 (Ch.), [2010] Bus. L.R. 1634.

[187] See *Metal Scrap Trade Corp v Kate Shipping Co Ltd* [1990] 1 W.L.R. 115 (HL).

[188] 1996 Act, s.9(5).

16–072   Section 12 of the 1996 Act permits a party to make an application to the court for an extension of time in which to commence arbitral proceedings, where the arbitration agreement imposes a time limit and any available arbitral process for an extension has been exhausted. In implementing this section, the court will strive to give priority to s.9 of the Act. Thus, even where one party disputes the valid existence of an arbitration agreement (as, for example where it is submitted that the operation of such an agreement has become time-barred), the court will normally stay an application for an extension of time under s.12 until the arbitrators have determined that prelimi- nary point.[189]

16–073   A party who has initiated an application for a stay pending arbitration has not taken a "step" in the proceedings for the purposes of s.9(3) of the 1996 Act if that party, either simultaneously or subsequently, invokes or accepts the court's jurisdiction, provided that it is done so only conditionally on the stay application failing.[190]

16–074   Although the service of a statutory demand is an essential prerequisite for the commencement of a certain type of legal proceeding, it does not itself constitute a legal proceeding for the purposes of s.9; only the issue of a bankruptcy petition constitutes legal proceedings and gives rise to the court's duty to grant a stay if the bringing of such proceedings is in breach of an arbitration clause.[191]

16–075   Once the party seeking the stay has established that the parties agreed to arbitration and that their dispute falls within the scope of that agreement, the court must grant a stay unless the other party satisfies the court that there is a good reason why a stay should be refused (for example, because the arbitration agreement is null and void).[192] The question whether an arbitration agreement is wide enough to cover the dispute between the parties depends on the principles of interpretation of the law applicable to the arbitration agree- ment.[193] Before granting a stay under s.9, the court must be satisfied that there is an arbitration agreement between the parties and that the subject of the action is within the scope of the agreement.[194]

---

[189] See *Grimaldi Compagnia di Navigazione SpA v Sekihyo Lines Ltd* [1999] 1 W.L.R. 708, where the relationship between ss.12 and 9 is fully discussed. See also *Thyssen Inc v Calypso Shipping Corp SA* [2000] 2 Lloyd's Rep. 243, [2001] C.L.C. 805.

[190] *Capital Trust Investments Ltd v Radio Design TJ AB* [2002] EWCA Civ 135, [2002] 2 All E.R. 159.

[191] *Shalson v DF Keane Ltd* [2003] EWHC 599 (Ch.), [2003] B.P.I.R. 1045.

[192] *The Lapad* [2004] EWHC 1273 (Comm.), [2004] 2 Lloyd's Rep. 109. Factors usually relevant to *forum conveniens* (such as the existence of legal proceedings in a foreign country) are not relevant to the court's duty to grant a stay to enforce an arbitration agreement.

[193] See, Rule 64(1) and paras 16–011—16–022; and *The Paola d'Alesio* [1994] 2 Lloyd's Rep. 366. This principle is supported by analogous cases concerning the interpretation of jurisdiction clauses: see paras 12–090 *et seq.*, above. For the approach to construction of arbitration clauses in English law see *Fiona Trust and Holding Corp v Privalov* [2007] UKHL 40, [2007] Bus. L.R. 1179, [13]. For a recent example see *Deutsche Bank AG v Tongkah Harbour Plc* [2011] EWHC 2251 (Comm.).

[194] *Law Debenture Trust Corp Plc v Elektrim Finance BV* [2005] EWHC 1412 (Ch.), [2005] 2 Lloyd's Rep. 755. The court may refuse to grant a stay when the validity of the clause or the jurisdiction of the arbitrators is a question properly answered by the courts, as under s.72, where the party has not taken part in the arbitral proceedings.

There is a general principle of the law of international arbitration that the   **16–076**
arbitral tribunal has the power to determine its own jurisdiction. This is known
as the principle of *Kompetenz-Kompetenz* or *compétence-compétence*.[195] But
the principle does not require that the tribunal has the exclusive power to
determine its jurisdiction, nor that the court may not determine whether the
tribunal has jurisdiction before the tribunal has ruled on its jurisdiction.[196]
Where there is an application to stay proceedings under s.9 of the 1996 Act,
both in international and domestic cases, the court may examine the issue of
whether there ever was an agreement to arbitrate.[197] If an application for a stay
is resisted on the basis that no arbitration agreement exists, the court may
determine (1) to decide on the evidence before the court that such an agreement does exist in which case (if the disputes fall within the terms of that
agreement) a stay must be granted; (2) to stay the proceedings on the basis that
it will be left to the arbitrators to determine their own jurisdiction pursuant to
s.30 of the 1996 Act;[198] (3) not to decide the issue but to make directions for
an issue to be tried as to whether an arbitration agreement exists; (4) to decide
that no arbitration agreement exists and to dismiss the application to
stay.[199]

Grounds for refusal of stay. Neither Art.II of the Convention nor s.9 of the   **16–077**
1996 Act indicates what law is to decide whether the arbitration agreement is
null and void, inoperative or incapable of being performed. The validity of the

---

[195] For a full discussion see *Dallah Real Estate and Tourism Co v Ministry of Religious Affairs of the Government of Pakistan* [2010] UKSC 46, [2011] 1 A.C. 763, [79]–[98]; and also *AES Ust-Kamenogorsk Hydropower Plant LLP v Ust-Kamenogorsk Hydropower Plant JSC* [2011] EWCA Civ 647, [78] *et seq*. For the general principle see also *Dell Computer Corp v Union des consommateurs* 2007 SCC 34, (2007) 284 D.L.R. (4th) 577, [84]–[87].

[196] *Dallah Real Estate and Tourism Holding Co v Ministry of Religious Affairs, Government of Pakistan* [2010] UKSC 46, [2011] 1 A.C. 763, at [84].

[197] At [97].

[198] Which gives the arbitral tribunal (in the case of an arbitration with its seat in England) the power to rule on its own jurisdiction, including whether there is a valid arbitration agreement and what matters have been submitted to arbitration.

[199] *Al-Naimi v Islamic Press Agency Inc* [2000] 1 Lloyd's Rep 522, a case of an English arbitration, approving *Birse Construction v St David Ltd* [1999] BLR 194, 196–197; *Albon v Naza Trading Sdn Bhd (No.4)* [2007] EWCA Civ 1124, [2008] 1 Lloyd's Rep. 1 (Malaysian arbitra-tion). See also *Accentuate Ltd v ASIGRA Inc* [2009] EWHC 2655 (QB), [2009] 2 Lloyd's Rep. 599, [69]–[71]; *JSC BTA Bank v Ablyazov* [2011] EWHC 587 (Comm.); *Claxton Engineering Services Ltd v TXM Olaj-és Gázutató KFT* [2010] EWHC 2567 (Comm.), [2011] 1 Lloyd's Rep. 252.This approach may be contrasted with that favoured in a number of other countries where a stay is granted where the applicant can show a prima facie case of a valid arbitration agreement applying to the dispute; and the court only intervenes to decide the issue for itself where it is clear that the arbitration agreement is invalid. See Fouchard, Gaillard, Goldman, paras 671–682; Lew, Mistelis & Kröll, paras 14–49—14–64. This approach has been adopted, e.g. in India: *Shin-Etsu Chemical Co Ltd v M/S Aksh Optifibre Ltd* [2005] INSC 402 (Indian Sup Ct), where authorities in other countries are considered. In Canada, the Supreme Court held in *Dell Computer Corp v Union des consommateurs* 2007 SCC 34, (2007) 284 D.L.R. (4th) 577, [84]–[87], that a court should in general refer challenges to an arbitral tribunal's jurisdiction to the tribunal first. It should only depart from this approach in cases where the challenge is based solely on a question of law (or involves questions of fact requiring only a superficial consideration from the record).

arbitration agreement is a matter for its governing law.[200] But in practice the English court is likely to determine the other matters mentioned for itself, uninfluenced by foreign law. "Null and void" means "devoid of legal effect."[201] The words "incapable of being performed" presumably refer to cases where there is no mechanism for constituting the arbitral tribunal or putting the arbitral procedure in motion. For example, if it is impossible for a party to find a person who has the necessary qualifications to act as arbitrator in the case and who is prepared to act at the place where the parties have agreed that the arbitration is to be conducted, it is arguable that the arbitration agreement is incapable of being performed.[202]

16–078   An arbitration agreement, however, is not inoperative or incapable of being performed simply because it fails to specify the seat of the arbitration or the method by which the arbitral tribunal is to be appointed. An arbitration agreement should be regarded as incapable of being performed only if gaps in the parties' agreement cannot be filled by any arbitral institution chosen by the parties or by a court of competent jurisdiction exercising its powers. If, for example, a named arbitrator refuses to act, there will normally be a court with the power to appoint a replacement. Also, an arbitration agreement is not incapable of being performed because it refers to a non-existent arbitral institution or to non-existent arbitration rules. In such a case the law of the seat of the arbitration will furnish the applicable procedural rules and, in the event of the parties failing to reach agreement, the local courts will normally be competent to appoint an arbitrator and to exercise other powers to support the arbitral process. The fact that the claimant cannot afford the deposit for the costs of the arbitration,[203] or that the defendant would be financially incapable of satisfying the award in full[204] is no reason for refusing a stay. Moreover, the mere fact that if the dispute goes to arbitration, the claimant will be met by a plea that his claim is out of time, is no reason for regarding the arbitration agreement as "inoperative."[205] Otherwise, the claimant could avoid a stay by waiting until the time for arbitration had expired and then bringing an action. But an arbitration agreement may become inoperative by reason of some further agreement between the parties (for example, by a contractual agreement settling the dispute[206] or by a jurisdiction agreement which supersedes the original arbitration clause). The arbitration agreement may also become "inoperative" where one party has repudiated the arbitration agreement and

---

[200] See above, Rule 64(1) and paras 16–011—16–022. *cf. A/B Bofors v A/B Skandia* [1982] 1 Lloyd's Rep. 410 (where a mandatory rule of English law invalidated an arbitration agreement governed by foreign law).

[201] *Albon v Naza Motor Trading Sdn Bhd* [2007] EWHC 665 (Ch.), [2007] 2 All E.R. 1075, [18], applying *Rhone Mediterranée v Achille Lauro*, 712 F.2d 50 (3d Cir. 1983). See also *JSC BTA Bank v Ablyazov* [2011] EWHC 587 (Comm.), [34].

[202] *Gatoil International Plc v National Iranian Oil Co* (1992) 17 Yb. Comm. Arb. 587 (Gatehouse J.); *The Independent*, March 13, 1990 (CA).

[203] *Paczy v Haendler and Natermann GmbH* [1981] 1 Lloyd's Rep. 302 (CA). For controversial decisions in Germany to a different effect see Lew, Mistelis and Kröll, para.14–48.

[204] *The Rena K* [1979] Q.B. 377, 391–393.

[205] *The Merak* [1965] P. 223, 239. Nor is the fact that there is a risk of inconsistent findings as a result of other pending litigation: *Lonrho Ltd v Shell Petroleum Co Ltd*, *The Times*, February 1, 1978.

[206] *Shanghai Foreign Trade Corp v Sigma Metallurgical Co Pty Ltd* (1996) 133 F.L.R. 417 (NSW); *Cangene Corp v Octapharma AG* [2000] 9 W.W.R. 606 (Man).

that repudiatory breach has been accepted by the other party by the issue and service of legal proceedings.[207] There is also no room for the argument, which was unsuccessfully raised in *The Merak*,[208] that there is no obligation to stay the proceedings unless and until arbitrators have been appointed.

The mere fact that some issues between the parties fall outside the scope of the arbitration agreement does not render the agreement inoperative or incapable of being performed.[209] In this type of case the court must grant a stay in respect of the part of the claim which is covered by the arbitration agreement.[210] Also, an arbitration agreement can still be performed even if some parties to the dispute are not parties to the agreement[211]; as between the parties to the agreement the dispute must be referred to arbitration even though, in the interest of the efficient administration of justice, it might well be preferable if related issues were resolved in a single set of proceedings.[212] In a case involving multiple parties, only some of whom are bound by the arbitration agreement, the court may, under its inherent jurisdiction, stay proceedings against litigants who are not parties to the arbitration agreement.[213] But it need not do so (and may permit the joinder of both parties to the arbitration agreement in the court proceedings) where the dispute is not between those parties.[214]   **16–079**

The 1975 Act qualified the defendant's right to a stay by providing that the court need not order a stay if satisfied that "there [was] not in fact any dispute between the parties with regard to the matter agreed to be referred."[215] The 1975 qualification, which does not appear in Art.II of the Convention, was successfully relied upon by plaintiffs to enable them to resist a stay of English proceedings in cases where, although the defendant did not admit the plaintiff's claim, the defendant had no real defence.[216] By contrast, in those countries which implemented Art.II of the Convention (or the similar Art.8 of the Model Law) without the addition of an equivalent of the 1975 qualification, it is well established that the court has no power to investigate the reality   **16–080**

---

[207] *Downing v Al Tameer Establishment* [2002] EWCA Civ 721, [2002] 2 All E.R. (Comm.) 545. The issue of Admiralty proceedings *in rem* does not, without more, amount to the repudiation of an arbitration agreement between the owner and charterer, since the arrest of the ship may be maintained as a provisional measure pending the outcome of the arbitration: *Comandate Marine Corp v Pan Australia Shipping Pty Ltd* [2006] FCAFC 192, (2006) 157 F.C.R. 42.

[208] See above, n.305.

[209] *Kaverit Steel and Crane Ltd v Kone Corp* (1992) 87 D.L.R. (4th) 129 (Alta CA).

[210] *The Tuyuti* [1984] Q.B. 838, 849 (CA); *ET Plus SA v Welter* [2005] EWHC 2115 (Comm.), [2006] 1 Lloyd's Rep. 251; *Hi-Fert Pty Ltd v Kiukiang Maritime Carriers* (1996) 150 A.L.R. 54.

[211] *BWV Investments Ltd v Saskferco Products Inc* [1995] 2 W.W.R. 1 (Sask CA).

[212] See *Wealands v CLC Contractors Ltd* [1999] 2 Lloyd's Rep. 739 (CA), affirming [1998] C.L.C. 808.

[213] *Roussel-Uclaf v GD Searle Ltd* [1978] 1 Lloyd's Rep. 225. That part of the decision which holds that a stay may be granted under s.9 against non-parties was overruled in *City of London v Sancheti* [2008] EWCA Civ 1283, [2009] 1 Lloyd's Rep. 117.

[214] *Carvill America Inc v Camperdown UK Ltd* [2005] EWCA Civ 645, [2005] 2 Lloyd's Rep. 457.

[215] s.1(1). The words are taken from Arbitration (Foreign Awards) Act 1930, s.8 which amended Arbitration Clauses (Protocol Act) 1924. They were reproduced in the 1975 Act on the recommendation of the Private International Law Committee: Fifth Report, Cmnd. 1515 (1961).

[216] For a review of the position under the 1975 Act see *Channel Tunnel Group Ltd v Balfour Beatty Construction Ltd* [1993] A.C. 334.

of the dispute with a view to refusing a stay in cases where there is no answer to the claim.[217]

16–081   The 1975 qualification was not reproduced in s.9 of the 1996 Act. In *Halki Shipping Corp v Sopex Oils Ltd*,[218] the first reported case decided under s.9, the question arose whether this omission necessarily entailed a change in the practice of the courts. The plaintiffs claimed demurrage which was allegedly due under a charterparty which included an arbitration clause. The defendants did not admit liability. When the plaintiffs applied for summary judgment under RSC Order 14 (now Pt 24 of the Civil Procedure Rules), the defendants sought a stay under s.9 of the 1996 Act. It was held (by a majority, Henry and Swinton Thomas L.JJ., Hirst L.J. disssenting) that the word "dispute" should not be narrowly and artificially construed so as to be restricted to those disputes which cannot be resolved by the summary judgment procedure (i.e. cases in which there is an arguable defence to the claim);[219] there is a dispute wherever a claim is made by one party against another and the claim has not been admitted.[220] Although the decision has been criticised on the ground that arbitrators are less well equipped than courts to decide disputes summarily,[221] there is no reason to doubt the correctness of the majority's decision, which is consistent with the principle of party autonomy, one of the cornerstones of the 1996 Act.[222]

16–082   Thus the inherent jurisdiction has been used to justify a stay pending the decision of the arbitral tribunal on its own jurisdiction when the court was not satisfied that there was an arbitration agreement.[223] So also it has been held that the High Court has an inherent power to stay proceedings brought in disregard of an arbitration agreement if for some reason the statutory requirements are not met.[224] For example, the court may stay proceedings brought in breach of an oral arbitration agreement under its inherent jurisdiction.[225]

---

[217] See e.g. *Baltimar Aps Ltd v Nalder & Biddle Ltd* [1994] 3 N.Z.L.R. 129 (CA).

[218] [1998] 1 W.L.R. 726 (CA).

[219] Under CPR Pt 24 the question is whether the defendant has a real prospect of successfully defending the claim: CPR, r.24.2(a)(i).

[220] At p.761, *per* Swinton Thomas L.J. See, e.g. *Ellerine Bros (Pty) Ltd v Klinger* [1982] 1 W.L.R. 1375; *Hayter v Nelson* [1990] 2 Lloyd's Rep. 265. "Dispute" also includes admitted but unpaid claims: *Exfin Shipping (India) Ltd v Tolani Shipping Co Ltd* [2006] EWHC 1090 (Comm.), [2006] 2 Lloyd's Rep. 389.

[221] Duncan Wallace [1998] I.C.L.R. 371, 395–397. See also *Glencore Grain Ltd v Agros Trading Co* [1999] 2 Lloyd's Rep. 410 (CA).

[222] s.1(b).

[223] *Al-Naimi v Islamic Press Agency Inc* [2000] 1 Lloyd's Rep 522, at 528; *A v B* [2006] EWHC 2006 (Comm.), [2007] 1 Lloyd's Rep. 237; *Albon v Naza Motor Trading SDN Bhd (No.3)* [2007] EWHC 665 (Ch.), [2007] 2 All E.R. 1075. See also *ET Plus SA v Welter* [2005] EWHC 2115 (Comm.), [2006] 1 Lloyd's Rep. 251.

[224] *Roussel-Uclaf v GD Searle Ltd* [1978] 1 Lloyd's Rep. 25 (overruled on other grounds: *City of London v Sancheti* [2008] EWCA Civ 1283, [2009] 1 Lloyd's Rep. 117); *Etri Fans Ltd v NMB (UK) Ltd* [1987] 1 W.L.R. 1110 (CA); *Nissan (UK) Ltd v Nissan Motor Co Ltd*, 1991, unreported (CA); *Channel Tunnel Group Ltd v Balfour Beatty Construction Ltd* [1993] A.C. 334; *Reichhold Norway ASA v Goldman Sachs International* [2000] 1 W.L.R. 173 (CA). See also *T&N Ltd v Royal and Sun Alliance Plc* [2002] EWHC 2420 (Ch.), [2002] C.L.C. 1342; *Kaverit Steel and Crane Ltd v Kone Corp* (1992) 87 D.L.R. (4th) 129 (Alta CA). Contrast *Mount Cook (Northland) Ltd v Swedish Motors Ltd* [1986] 1 N.Z.L.R. 720.

[225] The common law as to the effect of oral arbitration agreements is expressly preserved by the 1996 Act, s.81(1)(b).

The court's inherent jurisdiction to grant a stay of proceedings is also **16–083** relevant in cases where the parties have agreed to refer their dispute to other types of alternative dispute resolution process. In *Cable & Wireless Plc v IBM United Kingdom Ltd*,[226] the contract provided for disputes to be resolved by an ADR procedure to be recommended to the parties by a particular dispute resolution service. When one party commenced litigation, the other sought to enforce the ADR clause. It was held that the ADR clause was analogous to an arbitration agreement and that the court should enforce it, by granting a stay of proceedings, unless there was a strong cause for not doing so.

Provisional measures. May a party who has agreed to arbitration retain a **16–084** form of security, or obtain interlocutory relief, from the court[227] pending the outcome of the arbitration and satisfaction of the award? If the claim is *in personam*, the question will normally arise in the context of an application for a freezing injunction or other form of interim remedy. If the claim is *in rem*, it will arise in the context of retention of the arrested property. Where, however, the claimant takes action in a foreign court which goes beyond simply seeking reasonable security for the arbitration proceedings, and seeks instead to secure the jurisdiction of the court in breach of the arbitration agreement, the court will, if necessary, restrain the claimant by injunction from further pursuit of the foreign proceedings.[228] The modern international trend is to recognise that, whether or not the seat of the arbitration is within the jurisdiction of the court which is asked to grant interim remedies, a court which grants a mandatory stay of proceedings on the basis of an arbitration agreement between the parties is entitled to grant interim measures of protection, including pre-award attachments or injunctions to secure the eventual award.[229]

The 1996 Act adopts the modern position.[230] Where there is a mandatory **16–085** stay under the 1996 Act, the court has the power to make orders in support of

---

[226] [2002] EWHC 2059 (Comm.), [2002] 2 All E.R. (Comm.) 1041.

[227] On the power of the arbitral tribunal to order interim measures see 1996 Act, s.39(1); UNCITRAL Model Law, Art.17.

[228] *Sotrade Denizcilik Sanayi Ve Ticaret AS v Amadou Lo* [2008] EWHC 2762 (Comm.), [2009] 1 Lloyd's Rep. 145.

[229] See Fouchard, Gaillard, Goldman, paras 1325 *et seq.*; *cf.* Model Law, Art.9, and e.g. *Katran Shipping Co Inc v Amalgamated Mill Supplies Ltd* [1992] 1 H.K.C. 538 (Kaplan, J.); *Trade Fortune Inc v Amalgamated Mill Supplies Ltd* (1994) 113 D.L.R. (4th) 116 (BC). For the position generally in the US see *Borden Inc v Meiji Milk Products Co Ltd*, 919 F. 2d 822 (2d Cir. 1990), cert. denied, 500 U.S. 953 (1991); *cf. Pilkington Bros Plc v AFG Industries Inc*, 581 F. Supp. 1039 (D.Del. 1984). There has been considerable discussion in the US in relation to whether it is incompatible with the New York Convention for a court to grant pre-judgment attachments: see McDonnell (1984) 22 Col. J. Trans. L. 273; Becker (1985) 1 Arb. Int. 40; Brower and Tupman (1986) 80 A.J.I.L. 24; Marchac (1999) 10 Am.Rev.Int.Arb. 123; and many cases, especially *McCreary Tire and Rubber Co v CEAT SpA*, 501 F. 2d 1032 (3d Cir. 1974) (attachment incompatible with Convention); *Carolina Power and Light Co v Uranex*, 451 F. Supp. 1044 (ND Cal. 1977); *China National Metal Products Import/Export Co v Apex Digital Inc*, 155 F. Supp. 2d 1174 (CD Cal. 2001) (attachment compatible with Convention). The United States authorities are reviewed in *Bahrein Telecommunications Co v Discoverytel, Inc*, 476 F. Supp. 2d 176 (D. Conn. 2007). See Collins, *Essays*, pp.48–67; McLachlan (2005) 7 *International Law FORUM du droit international* 5.

[230] The court's power to grant interim injunctions under 1950 Act, s.12(6)(h), was limited to cases involving English arbitrations, though it had been held that the court could grant injunctions in support of foreign arbitrations under the general law if the defendant was amenable to the *in*

arbitral proceedings, in particular the power to grant interim injunctions under s.44(2)(e). The 1996 Act seeks to ensure that the court is not able to interfere with or usurp the arbitral process.[231] It is provided that, unless the case is one of urgency, the court shall act under s.44 only where the application is made with the permission of the tribunal or the written agreement of the other parties.[232] If the court is to act without the permission of the parties in a case of urgency, it is only permitted to do so for the purpose of preserving evidence or assets.[233] Furthermore, the court is permitted to act only to the extent that the arbitral tribunal has no power or is unable for the time being to act effectively.[234]

16–086   Subject to the contrary agreement of the parties, the powers conferred by s.44 may be exercised not only in cases where England is the seat of the arbitration, but also where the seat is abroad or even if no seat has been determined or designated. The court may, however, refuse to exercise the power if the fact that the seat is outside England (or when designated or determined it is likely to be outside England) makes it inappropriate to do so.[235] If the grant of the injunction sought by the claimant would largely preempt any decision to be made by the arbitrators, it would not be appropriate for the court to exercise the power conferred by s.44.[236] In addition, the European Court has ruled that, in a case where the court does not have jurisdiction over the substance of the dispute between the parties, the grant of provisional measures is conditional on the existence of a real connecting link between the subject-matter of the measures and the territorial jurisdiction of the court.[237]

16–087   In Admiralty proceedings *in rem*, the question whether the arrested property or security may be retained even if proceedings are stayed is regulated by s.11 of the 1996 Act.[238] Section 11(1) provides that where proceedings are stayed on the ground that the dispute should be referred to arbitration (whether in

---

personam jurisdiction of the court: *Channel Tunnel Group Ltd v Balfour Beatty Construction Ltd* [1993] A.C. 334. No legislative action was taken to bring into force of Civil Jurisdiction and Judgments Act 1982, s.25(3), which would have provided for the grant of interim relief in relation to any arbitral proceedings, and which was repealed by the 1996 Act, which superseded it. Consequently, 1996 Act, s.25, does not otherwise apply to the grant of interim relief in aid of arbitration; specific provision for this having been made by s.44: *ETI Euro Telecom International NV v Bolivia* [2008] EWCA Civ 880, [2009] 1 W.L.R. 665 (s.25 cannot be used in support of foreign judicial proceedings, which were themselves only for interim relief in aid of arbitration).

[231] D.A.C. Report (1997) 13 Arb. Int. 275, 308–309.

[232] 1996 Act, s.44(4).

[233] 1996 Act, s.44(3); *Cetelem SA v Roust Holdings Ltd* [2005] EWCA Civ 618, [2005] 1 W.L.R. 3555 (overruling *Hiscox Underwriting Ltd v Dickson Manchester & Co Ltd* [2004] EWHC 479 (Comm.), [2004] 2 Lloyd's Rep. 438).

[234] *ibid.*, s.44(5).

[235] *ibid.*, s.2(3); *Commerce and Industry Insurance Co of Canada v Certain Underwriters at Lloyd's* [2002] 1 W.L.R. 1323; *Econet Wireless Ltd v VEE Networks Ltd* [2006] EWHC 1568 (Comm.), [2006] 2 Lloyd's Rep. 428 (injunction refused in both cases). *cf.* the position under Civil Jurisdiction and Judgments Act 1982, s.25, above, paras 8–027 *et seq.*

[236] *cf. Channel Tunnel Group Ltd v Balfour Beatty Construction Ltd* [1993] A.C. 334.

[237] Case C–391/95 *Van Uden Maritime BV v Firma Deco-Line* [1998] E.C.R. I–7091, [1999] Q.B. 1225. See *Mobil Cerro Negro Ltd v Petroleos de Venezuela SA* [2008] EWHC 532 (Comm.), [2008] 1 Lloyd's Rep. 684, [119], [135].

[238] Which, as regards cases which are stayed on the basis of an arbitration agreement, replaced Civil Jurisdiction and Judgments Act 1982, s.26. See *The Tuyuti* [1984] Q.B. 836 (CA); *The*

England or abroad), the court may (a) order that property arrested be retained as security for the satisfaction of any award, or (b) order that the stay of proceedings be conditional on the provision of equivalent security. Potential problems surround the second alternative form of order in cases falling within the scope of the New York Convention. The wording of s.11(1)(b) suggests that, if a defendant who is ordered to provide equivalent security fails to do so, the proceedings *in rem* will proceed, a result which would be inconsistent with the mandatory nature of the stay under s.9 of the 1996 Act and with the New York Convention. For this reason, in *The World Star*[239] Sheen J. indicated that only the first form of order is available in cases where a stay is mandatory. But the same result is reached by the exercise of the power to release a vessel from arrest. That power is normally exercised only if security is provided by guarantee or otherwise for the claim, interest and costs.[240]

Injunctions to restrain foreign actions.[241] The English court has, since at least 1911,[242] exercised a jurisdiction *in personam*[243] to restrain by injunction foreign proceedings brought in breach of an agreement to refer disputes to arbitration. The injunction is granted on the basis that without it the claimant will be deprived of its contractual right to have disputes settled by arbitration in a situation in which damages are manifestly an inadequate remedy.[244] In   **16–088**

Bazias 3 [1993] Q.B. 673 (CA). For the position under New Zealand law (which has no equivalent to 1996 Act, s.11) see *The Irina Zharkikh* [2001] 2 Lloyd's Rep. 319 (NZ).

[239] [1986] 2 Lloyd's Rep. 274.

[240] CPR, r.61.8(4); *The Bazias 3* [1993] Q.B. 673 (CA): see above, paras 8–042—8–045. In Australia, where an action *in rem* is stayed on account of an arbitration agreement, the arrested property may be retained, or released on condition of provision of equivalent security, pending the outcome of the arbitration: *Comandate Marine Corp v Pan Australia Shipping Pty Ltd* [2006] FCAFC 192, (2006) 157 F.C.R. 42.

[241] See generally Gaillard (ed.), *Anti-suit Injunctions in International Arbitration* (2005); Gaillard, in *Pervasive Problems in International Arbitration* (ed. Mistelis and Lew, 2006), p.201; Raphael, *The Anti-suit Injunction* (2008), Ch.6; McLachlan, *Lis Pendens in International Litigation* (2009), Ch.3.

[242] *Pena Copper Mines Ltd v Rio Tinto Co Ltd* (1911) 105 L.T. 846 (CA). See also *The Maria Gorthon* [1976] 2 Lloyd's Rep. 720; *Marazura Navegacion SA v Oceanus Mutual Underwriting Assn* [1977] 1 Lloyd's Rep. 283; *Tracomin SA v Sudan Oil Seeds Co Ltd (No.2)* [1983] 1 W.L.R. 1026 (CA); *The Golden Anne* [1984] 2 Lloyd's Rep. 489 (CA); *Marc Rich & Co AG v Soc Italiana Impianti PA (No.2)* [1992] 1 Lloyd's Rep. 624; *Sokana Industries Inc v Freyre & Co Inc* [1994] 2 Lloyd's Rep. 57; and other English cases cited in the following notes.

[243] Which (in cases not governed by the Brussels I Regulation or the Lugano Convention) can be exercised, even if the defendant is not in England, where, among other cases, the arbitration agreement is governed by English law. See para.11–181, above. The application must be made without delay and before the proceedings in the foreign court are too far advanced: *The Angelic Grace* [1995] 1 Lloyd's Rep. 87, 96; *Toepfer International GmbH v Molino Boschi srl* [1996] 1 Lloyd's Rep. 510; *Verity Shipping SA v NV Norexa* [2008] EWHC 213 (Comm.), [2008] 1 Lloyd's Rep. 652; *REC Wafer Norway AS v Moser Baer Photo Voltaic Ltd* [2010] EWHC 2581 (Comm.), [2011] 1 Lloyd's Rep 410. An injunction may be granted to restrain declaratory proceedings in the foreign court as to the validity of the arbitration agreement (*Midgulf International Ltd v Groupe Chimique Tunisien* [2010] EWCA Civ 66, [2010] 1 C.L.C. 113) or to restrain foreign proceedings designed to challenge or nullify an English award (*C v D* [2007] EWCA Civ 1282, [2008] 1 Lloyd's Rep. 239; *Noble Assurance Co v Gerling-Konzern General Insurance Co* [2007] EWHC 253 (Comm.), [2007] 1 C.L.C. 85).

[244] *The Angelic Grace* [1995] 1 Lloyd's Rep. 87, 96, *per* Millett L.J. (CA).

1994, in *The Angelic Grace*,[245] Millett L.J. (with whom Neill L.J. expressly agreed) said that the time had come to lay aside the ritual incantation that this was a jurisdiction which should be exercised only sparingly and with great caution, and said that there was no reason for diffidence in granting an injunction to restrain foreign proceedings brought in breach of an arbitration agreement, on the clear and simple ground that the defendant had promised not to bring them.

16–089   The court also has power to grant an injunction restraining foreign arbitral proceedings, although it is a power that is only exercised in exceptional circumstances and with caution.[246]

16–090   Special rules were enacted in section 44 of the 1996 Act relating to the powers of the court exercisable in support of arbitral proceedings, including the power to grant an interim injunction.[247] The question has arisen whether the powers of the court to grant an injunction to restrain a foreign action brought in breach of an arbitration agreement now derive from the general terms of section 37 of the Senior Courts Act 1981, or are limited by the narrower terms of s.44. As indicated above,[248] the powers under s.44 apply even if the seat of the arbitration is outside England, but in such a case the court may refuse to exercise the power if the fact that the seat is outside England makes it inappropriate to do so. The power in s.44(2)(e) of the 1996 is more limited than that in s.37 of the Senior Courts Act: the power in s.44(2)(e) is limited to interim injunctions, and under s.44, if the case is not urgent, the court is to act only on the application of a party (upon notice to the other parties and to the tribunal) made with permission of the tribunal and the agreement in writing of the other parties; the court is only to act if and to the extent the arbitral tribunal (or any arbitral institution) has no power, or is unable, to act.[249] The question of the relationship between s.44 of the 1996 Act and s.37 of the Senior Courts Act 1981 has arisen at first instance in cases involving injunctions to restrain proceedings in a foreign court or to restrain one of two competing arbitral proceedings, where it has been assumed that

---

[245] [1995] 1 Lloyd's Rep. 87; *Through Transport Mutual Insurance Assn (Eurasia) Ltd v New India Assurance Assn Co Ltd* [2004] EWCA Civ 1598, [2005] 1 Lloyd's Rep. 67, at [87]–[91]; Gross [2005] L.M.C.L.Q. 10.

[246] *Black Clawson International Ltd v Papierwerke Waldhof-Aschaffenberg AG* [1981] 2 Lloyd's Rep. 446, 458; *Weissfisch v Julius* [2006] EWCA Civ 218, [2006] 1 Lloyd's Rep 716; *Intermet FZCO v Ansol Ltd* [2007] EWHC 226 (Comm.); *Elektrim SA v Vivendi Universal SA (No.2)* [2007] EWHC 571 (Comm.), [2007] 2 Lloyd's Rep. 8; *Albon v Naza Motor Trading Sdn Bhd* [2007] EWCA Civ 1124, [2008] 1 Lloyd's Rep. 1; *Republic of Kazakhstan v Istil Group Inc (No.2)* [2007] EWHC 2729 (Comm.), [2008] 1 Lloyd's Rep. 382; *Claxton Engineering v TXM (No.2)* [2011] EWHC 345 (Comm.), [2011] 1 Lloyd's Rep 510; *Excalibur Ventures LLC v Texas Keystone Inc* [2011] EWHC 1624 (Comm.). Thus an injunction may be granted, e.g. (a) where the arbitral tribunal's determination of its jurisdiction has already been reviewed by the court of the seat, and that court has decided that the tribunal lacked jurisdiction, yet one party is still claiming the right to pursue the arbitration: *Republic of Kazakhstan v Istil Group Inc (No.2)*, above; and (b) where the essence of the challenge to the arbitral tribunal's jurisdiction is that the arbitration agreement is a forgery, and it has been agreed that the English court may determine that question: *Albon v Naza Motor Trading Sdn Bhd*, above. In these cases the essential claim was that there was no arbitration agreement at all, and the English court either had determined, or was entitled to determine, that point. Such cases are likely to be very rare.

[247] s.44(2)(e).

[248] Para.16–086.

[249] s.44(4), (5).

s.37 can still be used as the basis of the injunction,[250] and left open in several decisions in the Court of Appeal not involving anti-suit injunctions.[251] In *AES Ust-Kamenogorsk Hydropower Plant LLP v Ust-Kamenogorsk Hydropower Plant JSC*[252] it was held that the court had jurisdiction to grant an anti-suit injunction under s.37 to restrain foreign proceedings brought in breach of an arbitration agreement, even where there were no actual or intended arbitration proceedings (and thus s.44 did not apply). Rix L.J., after a lengthy review of the authorities, expressed the view that, where s.44 applied, it would be wrong in principle to utilise s.37 to get round the limitations in s.44.[253] It is suggested that s.44 of the 1996 Act was not intended to limit the long-standing power under s.37 of the Senior Courts Act 1981, and its predecessors, to grant interim or final injunctions to restrain court proceedings brought in breach of an agreement to arbitrate.

In *Van Uden Maritime BV v Firma Deco-Line*[254] the European Court said   **16–091** that where the parties had validly excluded the jurisdiction of the courts in a contractual dispute and had referred the dispute to arbitration, there were no courts of any Contracting State which had jurisdiction for the purposes of the Brussels Convention. The important question then arose whether these rulings affected the jurisdiction of the English court to restrain the continuance of proceedings which have been commenced in another Regulation State in breach of an arbitration agreement.

In *The Angelic Grace*[255] an injunction was granted to restrain proceedings   **16–092** in Italy which had been commenced shortly after the proceedings in England for a declaration that the dispute was subject to arbitration, and for an injunction to restrain the commencement of proceedings in Italy. There was no discussion of the question whether it was consistent with the Brussels Convention for the English court to entertain a claim for an injunction to restrain proceedings in another Contracting State. The point arose in several subsequent cases, where the foreign proceedings were commenced before the English claim for an injunction. The question depended primarily on (a) whether the English proceedings were outside the scope of what is now the Brussels I Regulation because of the provision in Art.1(2)(d) that it shall not apply to "arbitration"; and (b) whether the claim for injunctive relief involved the same cause of action as the claim in the foreign proceedings for the purposes of what is now Art.27. In *Toepfer International GmbH v Cargill*

---

[250] *Elektrim SA v Vivendi Universal SA (No.2)* [2007] EWHC 571 (Comm.), [2007] 2 Lloyd's Rep. 8, at [67]–[79] (a case of an anti-arbitration injunction); *Starlight Shipping Co v Tai Ping Insurance Co Ltd Hubei Branch* [2007] EWHC 1893 (Comm.), [2008] 1 Lloyd's Rep. 230, [19] (in which Cooke J. held that, in exercising its discretion, the court would have regard to the factors enumerated in s.44). See also *REC Wafer Norway AS v Moser Baer Photo Voltaic Ltd* [2010] EWHC 2581 (Comm.), [2011] 1 Lloyd's Rep 410.

[251] *Cetelem SA v Roust Holdings Ltd* [2005] EWCA Civ 618, [2005] 1 W.L.R. 3555, [74]; *Emmott v Michael Wilson & Partners Ltd* [2008] EWCA Civ 184, [2008] 1 Lloyd's Rep. 616, [110], [123]; and *ETI Euro Telecom International NV v Bolivia* [2008] EWCA Civ 880, [2009] 1 W.L.R. 665, [97].

[252] [2011] EWCA Civ 647.

[253] At [96].

[254] Case C–391/95 [1998] E.C.R. I–7091, [1999] Q.B. 1225, para.24.

[255] [1995] 1 Lloyd's Rep. 87 (CA).

France SA[256] the Court of Appeal referred to the European Court the questions (a) whether the claim for a declaration that French proceedings were in breach of an arbitration agreement and the injunction sought in support were excluded from the operation of what is now the Brussels I Regulation by Art.1(2)(d); and (b) whether the English proceedings constituted the same cause of action as the challenge to the jurisdiction of the French court for the purposes of what is now Art.27. The Court of Appeal expressed doubt as to whether a dispute about jurisdiction could be a "cause of action" at all for the purposes of what is now Art.27, but added that it seemed to be in fundamental conflict with the scheme of the Brussels Convention that the defendant in the French proceedings should, without entering a challenge to jurisdiction in the French court, be able to commence proceedings in the English court to challenge the jurisdiction of the court first seised. The case was settled, and the reference was withdrawn.

16–093   In *Through Transport Mutual Insurance Assn (Eurasia) Ltd v New India Assurance Assn Co Ltd*[257] the Court of Appeal decided that there was nothing in the Brussels I Regulation to prevent an English court from granting an injunction to restrain the defendant from pursuing proceedings in a Member State which would be in breach of the arbitration agreement.

16–094   In *West Tankers Inc v Allianz SpA*[258] a vessel owned by A and chartered to X collided with a jetty owned by X. The charterparty provided for arbitration of disputes in London. While X began arbitration to recover the losses not covered by their insurers, the insurers exercised their statutory right of subrogation under Italian law to commence proceedings against A in Italy for the insured losses. A responded with proceedings in England, seeking a declaration that, as the dispute being litigated in Italy arose out of the charterparty, the insurers inherited the obligation to refer it to arbitration. A sought an injunction that the insurers not pursue the claim further except by way of arbitration, and in particular that they discontinue the Italian proceedings.

16–095   Colman J.[259] held that the insurers' claim was subject to the arbitration clause and that the court had jurisdiction to grant the injunction because arbitration was excluded from the Brussels I Regulation. The House of Lords referred to the European Court the question whether it was consistent with the Brussels I Regulation for a court of a Member State to make an order to restrain a person from commencing or continuing proceedings in another Member State on the ground that such proceedings were in breach of an arbitration agreement. Lord Hoffmann (with whom all other members agreed) expressed the view that an injunction would be consistent with the Regulation.[260] But the European Court ruled that it was incompatible with the Brussels I Regulation for a court of a Member State to make an order to

---

[256] [1998] 1 Lloyd's Rep. 379 (CA).

[257] [2004] EWCA Civ 1598, [2005] 1 Lloyd's Rep. 67.

[258] Case C–185/07 [2009] E.C.R. I–663, [2009] 1 A.C. 1138; on a reference from the House of Lords *sub nom. West Tankers Inc v Ras Riunione Adriatica di Sicurta SpA (The Front Comor)* [2007] UKHL 4, [2007] 1 Lloyd's Rep. 391.

[259] [2005] EWHC 454 (Comm.) [2005] 2 Lloyd's Rep. 257. Colman J. certified the case as suitable for a direct appeal to the House of Lords under Administration of Justice Act 1969, s.12, because the Court of Appeal would have been bound by the *Through Transport* case, above.

[260] [2007] 1 Lloyd's Rep. 391, [16].

restrain a person from commencing or continuing proceedings before the courts of another Member State on the ground that such proceedings would be contrary to an arbitration agreement.

The European Court accepted that the English proceedings as a whole, **16–096** which sought declaratory as well as injunctive relief, did not come within the scope of the Brussels I Regulation because their subject matter was arbitration. But the proceedings before the Italian court came within the scope of the Regulation. Since they did, the effect of the arbitration agreement, including its validity, was an incidental question, which also came within the scope of the Regulation.²⁶¹ Consequently it was the Italian court which had the exclusive power under the Regulation to rule on the effect of the arbitration agreement on its jurisdiction. Proceedings, such as the English proceedings, which did not come within the scope of the Brussels I Regulation, might have consequences which undermined its effectiveness, in particular where such proceedings prevented a court of another Member State from exercising the jurisdiction conferred on it by the Regulation. The use of an anti-suit injunction to prevent a court of a Member State, which normally had jurisdiction to resolve a dispute under Article 5(3) of the Regulation, from ruling, on the applicability of the Regulation to the dispute brought before it necessarily amounts to stripping that court of the power to rule on its own jurisdiction under the Regulation. The proceedings for the anti-suit injunction were contrary to the general principle that it was every court seised to determines for itself whether it had jurisdiction to resolve the dispute before it,²⁶² and that in general the Brussels I Regulation did not authorise the jurisdiction of a court of a Member State to be reviewed by a court in another Member State.²⁶³ In no case was a court of one Member State in a better position to determine whether the court of another Member State had jurisdiction.²⁶⁴ In obstructing the court of another Member State in the exercise of the powers conferred on it by the Brussels I Regulation to decide whether the Regulation was applicable, the anti-suit injunction also ran counter to the trust which the Member States accorded to one another's legal systems and judicial institutions and on which the system of jurisdiction under the Regulation was based.²⁶⁵ If, by means of an anti-suit injunction, the Italian court were prevented from examining itself the preliminary issue of the validity or the applicability of the arbitration agreement, a party could avoid the proceedings merely by relying on that agreement and the applicant, which considered that the agreement is void, inoperative or incapable of being performed, would thus be barred from access to the court before which it brought proceedings under Art.5(3) of the Regulation and would therefore be deprived of a form of judicial protection to which it is entitled. The conclusion was said to be supported by Article II(3)

---

²⁶¹ At [26], citing the Evrigenis and Kerameus report on the Greek Accession Convention: [1986] O.J. C298/1, para.35.

²⁶² Citing Case C–116/02 *Erich Gasser GmbH v MISAT Srl* [2003] E.C.R. I–14693, [2005] Q.B. 1, [48]–[49].

²⁶³ Case C–351/89 *Overseas Union Insurance Ltd v New Hampshire Insurance Co* [1991] E.C.R. I–3317, [1992] Q.B. 434, [24] and Case C–159/02 *Turner v Grovit* [2004] E.C.R. I–3565, [2005] 1 A.C. 101, [26].

²⁶⁴ Case C–351/89 *Overseas Union Insurance Ltd v New Hampshire Insurance Co*, at [23], and Case C–116/02 *Erich Gasser GmbH v MISAT Srl*, at [48].

²⁶⁵ Case C–159/02 *Turner v Grovit*, at [24].

of the New York Convention, under which it was the court of a Contracting State, when seised of an action in a matter in respect of which the parties had made an arbitration agreement, which would, at the request of one of the parties, refer the parties to arbitration, unless it found that the agreement was null and void, inoperative or incapable of being performed.[266]

16–097   The European Commission has accepted that the ruling in the *West Tankers* case creates a real risk of the abuse of litigation tactics and has put forward proposals for changes to the Brussels I Regulation as part of the general review of the Regulation.

ILLUSTRATIONS

16–098   1. A contract between A & Co and X & Co, two English companies, provides for arbitration in Switzerland. The English court must stay proceedings brought in England, if the requirements of Rule 65(1) are met.

2. A contract between A & Co, a Greek company, and X & Co, a French company, provides for arbitration in England. A & Co applies for summary judgment against X & Co in English proceedings under CPR, Pt 24. When X & Co applies for a stay of the proceedings, A & Co seeks to resist the stay on the ground that X & Co has no real defence to the claim. The English court must stay the proceedings.[267]

3. A, a Norwegian company, commences concurrent arbitration proceedings in Norway and court proceedings in London. The proceedings are against unrelated defendants, but arise out of the sale of the same business. The English court has inherent discretion to stay the English action pending the outcome of the arbitration in Norway.[268]

4. A & Co, a Panamanian company, owns a ship which it lets to X & Co, United States charterers, for the carriage of grain from New York to Italy. The charter is governed by English law, and provides for arbitration in London. The cargo is discharged into an unpowered open "floating elevator", which is owned by X & Co when there is a collision between both vessels which are moored alongside each other for the purpose of the discharging operation. X & Co indicates that it will sue A & Co in New York. A & Co claims in England a declaration that X & Co is bound by the arbitration clause, and an injunction to restrain the commencement of proceedings in New York. The English court will grant an injunction.[269]

5. The facts are as in Illustration 4, except that the New York proceedings are commenced prior to the English proceedings for an injunction. The English court will grant an injunction.

6. *The Front Comor*, a vessel owned by A, is chartered to Y, an Italian company, under a charterparty containing a London arbitration clause. It collides with a jetty in Sicily owned by Y. X, which is Y's insurer, relying on its rights of subrogation under the Italian Civil Code, commences proceedings in Syracuse against A for the amount which it has paid to Y. A commences proceedings against X in England for a declaration that X is bound by the arbitration clause and for an injunction to restrain the Italian proceedings. A is not entitled to an injunction in England because the Italian court has the exclusive power to rule on the applicability of the arbitration agreement to X's claim, and the English proceedings undermine the effectiveness of the Brussels I Regulation.[270]

---

[266] But nothing in the *West Tankers* ruling affects the power of the English court to grant an injunction to restrain proceedings in a court outside the Member States (or the Convention States): *Shashoua v Sharma* [2009] EWHC 957 (Comm.), [2009] 2 Lloyd's Rep. 87, at [39].

[267] *Halki Shipping Corp v Sopex Oils Ltd* [1998] 1 W.L.R. 726 (CA).

[268] *Reichhold Norway ASA v Goldman Sachs International* [2000] 1 W.L.R. 173.

[269] *cf. The Angelic Grace* [1995] 1 Lloyd's Rep. 87 (CA).

[270] Case C–185/07 *West Tankers Inc v Allianz SpA* [2009] E.C.R.I–663, [2009] 1 A.C. 1138.

7. The facts are as in Illustration 6, except that the proceedings by X are in the United States. The English court may grant an injunction to restrain the court proceedings.

3. ENFORCEMENT OF FOREIGN AWARDS

Introduction. This Part of Chapter 16 sets out all of the means by which a foreign arbitral award may be recognised and enforced in England. These methods include enforcement at common law (Rules 66–67), which is in principle available for an award rendered in any country,[271] and a number of more specific mechanisms, which present alternative options for enforcement in defined cases (Rules 70–71). There is also a discrete regime for investment arbitral awards rendered under the auspices of the International Centre for the Settlement of Investment Disputes ("ICSID"): Rule 72. In contrast, however, to the position in relation to foreign judgments, the enforcement of arbitral awards is dominated by the uniform provisions of an international convention: the New York Convention of 1958 (Rules 68–69). Indeed, the popularity of arbitration as a means of resolving trans-national commercial disputes is in no small measure attributable to the conclusion and subsequent wide acceptation of this Convention.   **16–099**

Early efforts to achieve international co-operation in the enforcement of arbitral awards yielded the Geneva Protocol of 1923 and the Geneva Convention of 1927, which were framed under the auspices of the League of Nations. Both of these instruments were given effect in England by Pt II of the Arbitration Act 1950. This Part of the 1950 Act remains in force in England.[272] But, for almost all practical purposes, it is of historic interest only.[273] That is because the New York Convention expressly provides that it supersedes the earlier instruments as between those States which are contracting parties to both.[274] There are now more than 140 States party to the New York Convention, and very few remaining States who are parties only to the earlier instruments.[275]   **16–100**

The preparation of the New York Convention after World War II represents a very significant achievement in international co-operation. The parties now   **16–101**

---

[271] A party seeking to enforce a New York Convention award may do so by proceedings at common law (i.e. under Rule 66) if he so prefers. 1996 Act, s.104, provides that nothing in Pt III affects any right to rely upon or enforce a New York Convention award at common law or under s.66. s.40(a) of the 1950 Act contains a similar saving. This is in accordance with Art.VII.1 of the New York Convention.

[272] But not in Scotland: Arbitration (Scotland) Act 2010, s.29, Sch.2.

[273] For a detailed statement of the provisions of these instruments see 13th edition of this work, Rule 62.

[274] Art.VII.2 of the New York Convention provides that the Geneva Convention shall cease to have effect between Contracting States on their becoming bound by the later Convention. This provision is implemented not by the repeal of Pt II of Arbitration Act 1950 (because it may still be required as between the UK and States which are parties to the Geneva Convention but not to the New York Convention), but by s.99 of the 1996 Act which provides that Pt II of the 1950 Act applies to foreign awards within the meaning of that Part only if they are not also New York Convention awards.

[275] States which are parties to the earlier instruments, but not to the New York Convention, are (at September 1, 2011) The Democratic Republic of the Congo, The Gambia, Guyana, Iraq and Myanmar.

include most of the world's great trading nations, such as the United States (1970); Japan (1961); China (1987); Russia (1960); and Germany (1961). It has found favour in every continent, including amongst States which had been traditionally less receptive to international arbitration, such as Argentina (1989); Brazil (2002); Pakistan (2005) and Saudi Arabia (1994). The United Kingdom became a party in 1975, and has been joined by many Commonwealth countries, including Australia (1975), Canada (1986), and New Zealand (1983).

16–102   Apart from its very wide (though not universal) acceptance, the New York Convention also has the merit of simplicity. Its operative provisions are found in just six articles, the substance of which are reflected in Rules 68 and 69. In particular, the Convention limits the grounds for the refusal of enforcement of a Convention award to the seven cases listed in Art.V (Rule 69). The twin advantages of relative simplicity and wide adherence mean that today, for most practical purposes, any consideration of the enforcement of a foreign arbitral award in England should begin with the question whether it was made in another State party to the New York Convention. If it was, then enforcement by that route is likely to furnish the most effective and straight-forward option. It will normally only be necessary to consider the alternative mechanisms described in other rules in this Part if the award does not fall within the scope of the Convention.

A. *At common law*

16R–103   **RULE 66—(1) Subject to Rule 67, a foreign arbitral award will be enforced in England, or recognised as a defence to a claim, if the award is**

(a) in accordance with an agreement to arbitrate which is valid by its applicable law; and

(b) valid and final according to the law governing the arbitration proceedings.[276]

(2) The award will be enforced by a claim or, by leave of the High Court, under the more summary procedure of section 66 of the Arbitration Act 1996.[277]

(3) A foreign arbitral award will be enforced in England whether or not the law governing the arbitration proceedings requires a judgment or order of a court to make the award enforceable.[278]

---

[276] *Norske Atlas Insurance Co Ltd v London General Insurance Co Ltd* (1927) 43 T.L.R. 541, 542; 28 Ll.L.R. 104, 106; *Oppenheim & Co v Mahomed Haneef* [1922] 1 A.C. 482 (PC); *Bankers and Shippers Insurance Co of New York v Liverpool Marine and General Insurance Co Ltd* (1926) 24 Ll.L.R. 85 (HL); *Dalmia Cement Ltd v National Bank of Pakistan* [1975] Q.B. 9; *Dalmia Dairy Industries Ltd v National Bank of Pakistan* [1978] 2 Lloyd's Rep. 223 (CA); *cf. Union Nationale des Coopératives Agricoles v Catterall* [1959] 2 Q.B. 44 (CA).

[277] *Dalmia Cement Ltd v National Bank of Pakistan*, above; below, paras 16–114 *et seq.* In view of this decision, enforcement at common law must be taken to mean "as reinforced by s.66 of the Arbitration Act 1996."

[278] *Union Nationale des Coopératives Agricoles v Catterall* [1959] 2 Q.B. 44 (CA).

COMMENT

Although English courts have enforced foreign judgments from the 17th **16–104**
century onwards,[279] the earliest reported case of the enforcement of a foreign
arbitral award was in 1927.[280]

What is it which is enforced? It is sometimes necessary to determine the **16–105**
nature of the claim to enforce a foreign arbitral award, and, in particular,
whether a party who seeks to enforce a foreign award is suing on the award,
or on the contract containing the arbitration agreement, or on the arbitration
agreement itself. The question has arisen in decisions (involving both English
and foreign awards) in several different contexts, and there is a clear tendency
to give the answer which will make the award enforceable. Thus in *Norske
Atlas Insurance Co Ltd v London General Insurance Co Ltd*[281] the unsuccessful respondents to an arbitration in Norway arising out of a reinsurance
contract made in London sought to resist enforcement of the Norwegian
award on the ground that the action was brought to enforce a reinsurance
contract which had not been validly stamped. It was held that the plaintiffs
were suing not on the reinsurance contract, but on the award, and the action
was therefore maintainable. In *Bremer Oeltransport v Drewry*[282] the defendants, who were unsuccessful respondents to an award made in Hamburg
arising out of a charterparty made in London, sought to set aside proceedings
served on them outside the jurisdiction to enforce the award. Leave to serve
the proceedings abroad had been granted on the basis that the action was for
the enforcement of a contract made within the jurisdiction, i.e. the submission
to arbitration contained in the charterparty. In this case, therefore, by contrast
with *Norske Atlas Insurance*, it was the defendant who argued that the action
was on the award, for in that event there would at that time[283] have been no
basis for service outside the jurisdiction. The Court of Appeal, however, held
that for this purpose the plaintiffs were suing "on the agreement to submit the
difference of which the award is the result" or "on the charterparty made in
London and more particularly on the submission to arbitration therein contained" or on the "agreement containing a term to refer disputes."[284] It was
therefore an action for the enforcement of a contract made within the jurisdiction and accordingly an appropriate case for service outside the jurisdiction.
The Court of Appeal left open the question whether the action could also be
regarded as being solely on the award.[285]

---

[279] See above, para.14–007.

[280] *Norske Atlas Insurance Co Ltd v London General Insurance Co Ltd* (1927) 28 Ll.L.R.
104.

[281] (1927) 28 Ll.L.R. 104.

[282] [1933] 1 K.B. 753 (CA). See also *Brali v Hyundai Corp* (1988) 84 A.L.R. 176.

[283] See now CPR, PD6B, para.3.1(10), above, paras 11R–222 *et seq.*

[284] At pp.764–765, *per* Slesser L.J.

[285] The court does not, however, have jurisdiction *in rem* under Senior Courts Act 1981,
s.20(2)(h), to enforce an arbitral award. The action for enforcement, being based on the agreement
to arbitrate, is not "arising out of any agreement relating ... to the use or hire of a ship": *The
Bumbesti* [2000] Q.B. 559, applying *The Beldis* [1936] P. 51 (CA), not following *The St Anna*
[1983] 1 W.L.R. 895.

16–106   In *Agromet Motoimport Ltd v Maulden Engineering Co (Beds) Ltd*[286] the unsuccessful respondents to a Zurich arbitration resisted enforcement of the award on the ground that the limitation period (six years from the date on which the cause of action accrued) had expired; they argued that the relevant cause of action was the breach of the underlying contract on which the award was based and that the breach had occurred more than six years before the action to enforce the award. This unmeritorious argument was rejected on the ground that the action was an action on the award or on an implied term in the submission agreement that the award would be honoured. Accordingly, the action was not time-barred. The effect of these authorities is that the claimant must plead and prove both the arbitration agreement and the award and that depending on the context, the proceedings may be classified as a claim on the award itself or on the submission agreement.

16–107   The definition of that which is being enforced, i.e. the choice between the view that the claimant is seeking to enforce the agreement to arbitrate and the view that he is seeking to enforce the award, is in England exclusively a matter of English law as the *lex fori*.[287] The attitude to this question of the law governing the arbitration agreement is irrelevant and so is the attitude of the law governing the arbitration proceedings. The question, however, whether the claimant may, instead of suing on the arbitration agreement or on the award, go back to the original cause of action and sue on the contract itself is, it is submitted, determined by the law which governs the arbitration proceedings. This includes the question whether the claim made before the arbitrators is merged in the award.

16–108   An English award may give rise to a cause of action estoppel or an issue estoppel,[288] and if the award is a final award under the law governing the arbitration proceedings the claimant in the arbitration should not be entitled to sue on the original cause of action.[289] There is no reason of legal policy why

---

[286] [1985] 1 W.L.R. 762. See also *Northern Sales Co Ltd v Compania Maritima Villa Nova SA* [1992] 1 F.C. 550 (Fed CA).

[287] *cf.* Kahn (1930) 12 Jo.Comp.Leg. (3rd series) 228, 245; Lorenzen, pp.520–524.

[288] *Fidelitas Shipping Co Ltd v V/O Exportchleb* [1966] Q.B. 630, 643 (CA); *Arnold v National Westminster Bank Plc* [1991] 2 A.C. 93 (HL); *Associated Electric and Gas Insurance Services Ltd (AEGIS) v European Reinsurance Co of Zurich* [2003] 1 W.L.R. 1041 (PC); *Noble Assurance Company v Gerling-Konzern General Insurance Company–UK Branch* [2007] EWHC 253 (Comm.), [2007] 1 C.L.C. 85; *Laughland v Stevenson* [1995] 2 N.Z.L.R. 474 (HC). The broader principle of English law, derived from *Henderson v Henderson* (1843) 3 Hare 100, preventing subsequent re-litigation of issues which should have been raised, but were not, in prior proceedings cannot, however, be applied to arbitral awards, at least without significant qualifications arising from the fact that the arbitral tribunal's jurisdiction is limited to the matters entrusted to it by the parties' arbitration agreement: Mustill and Boyd, *The Law and Practice of Commercial Arbitration in England* (2nd ed. 1989), 412; *Associated Electric and Gas Insurance Services Ltd (AEGIS) v European Reinsurance Co of Zurich*, above.

[289] In *The Rena K* [1979] Q.B. 377, 405, Brandon J. assumed (without deciding) that this was so in the case of an English award. *East India Trading Co Inc v Carmel Exporters and Importers Ltd* [1952] 2 Q.B. 439 has been taken to suggest the contrary in the case of a foreign award, but the decision does not bear this out. On the question whether, in cases where there is an unsatisfied award in the claimant's favour, the claimant may, in appropriate circumstances, bring proceedings *in rem* on the same cause of action see *The Irina Zharkikh* [2001] 2 Lloyd's Rep. 319 (NZ). See also West [2002] L.M.C.L.Q. 259.

the same should not be true in the case of a foreign award.[290] In relation to foreign judgments the non-merger rule has been abolished by statute,[291] and there is no reason of policy or principle why the obsolete and anomalous rule of non-merger in relation to foreign judgments should be extended to foreign awards. Indeed the consensual and contractual character of arbitration means that parties to an arbitration agreement impliedly promise to perform a valid award,[292] and it should follow that they also promise not to take any action inconsistent with their submission to arbitration. Bringing proceedings on the original cause of action would be wholly inconsistent with the obligation under the submission and the subsequent award. If, therefore, under the law governing the arbitration proceedings the original cause of action is merged in the award, a claimant should not be entitled to rely on the original contract.

This question should not be confused with the very different question   **16–109** whether, in the event of a judgment having been obtained abroad on the award, the award is merged in that judgment: as in other cases of enforcement of foreign judgments this is a matter for the *lex fori* of the court asked to enforce it. In England a local award may be enforced under s.66 of the Arbitration Act 1996, under which leave of the court may be obtained to enforce the award in the same manner as a judgment, and also, if the claimant applies, to enter judgment in terms of the award. In most countries a local award may be enforced by a similar or analogous procedure, varying from mere deposit of the award with the court which gives it executory effect, to a formal order giving the award executory effect or entering judgment in terms of the award. If enforcement measures of this kind are taken in the foreign country, is it the award or the foreign judgment which is to be enforced in England, or does the claimant have an option? There is no doubt that, provided it fulfils the requirements for enforcement, a foreign judgment on a foreign award is regarded as a judgment for the purposes of the rules relating to enforcement of foreign judgments.[293] Nor, where the foreign order has merely the effect of rendering the award executory, is there any reason why the award should not be enforced as such.[294]

May, however, an award be enforced as such after entry of judgment on it   **16–110** in the foreign country? The mere fact that the claimant has taken enforcement proceedings involving entry of judgment abroad should as a matter of policy be no bar to enforcement of the award, but it is possible that the abolition of

---

[290] *Good Challenger Navegante SA v Metalexportimport SA (The Good Challenger)* [2003] EWCA Civ 1668, [2004] 1 Lloyd's Rep 67 (considering issue estoppel when a foreign court has refused to enforce an award and the claimant is seeking to enforce that same award in England); *Weizmann Institute of Science v Neschis*, 421 F. Supp. 2d 654 (SDNY 2005) (enforcement of foreign award at common law). See generally ILA Committee on International Commercial Arbitration, *Interim Report:* 'Res Judicata' *and Arbitration* (2004) 71 ILA Conf. Rep. 826.

[291] Civil Jurisdiction and Judgments Act 1982, s.34, above, paras 14–040 *et seq.*

[292] See *Bremer Oeltransport v Drewry* [1933] 1 K.B. 753 (CA).

[293] *East India Trading Co Inc v Carmel Exporters and Importers Ltd* [1952] 2 Q.B. 439; *International Alltex Corp v Lawler Creations Ltd* [1965] I.R. 264; *Union Nationale des Coopératives Agricoles v Catterall* [1959] 2 Q.B. 44, 54 (CA); *Uniforêt Pâte Port-Cartier Inc v Zerotech Technologies Inc* [1998] 9 W.W.R. 688 (BC); *cf. Stolp & Co v Browne & Co* [1930] 4 D.L.R. 703 (Ont); see Rule 71(1).

[294] *cf.* Lorenzen, p.523; Kahn (1930) 12 Jo.Comp.Leg. (3rd series) 228, 246; Hascher (1996) 12 Arb. Int. 233; *cf. ABCI v Banque Franco-Tunisienne* [1996] 1 Lloyd's Rep. 485, affirmed on other aspects [1997] 1 Lloyd's Rep. 531 (CA).

the doctrine of non-merger in relation to foreign judgments[295] may have had the unintended result that, provided the judgment is enforceable in England, then it will be the foreign judgment, and not the award, which will be enforceable in England. This anomalous result could only apply to enforcement at common law, since (it is suggested) the provision in s.101 of the Arbitration Act 1996 that Convention awards "shall" be recognised as binding on the parties would apply even if judgment on the award had been entered abroad.[296]

16–111   **Conditions for enforcement.** The cases support the proposition, stated in the Rule, that a foreign award can be enforced or recognised in England, provided that it fulfils two fundamental requirements. These are (1) that the parties have submitted to the arbitration by an agreement which is valid by its governing law; and (2) that the award is valid and final according to the law which governs the arbitration proceedings. The principles governing those questions have been discussed in Rule 64. The jurisdiction of the tribunal to render the award is governed by the law governing the arbitration agreement, and the validity of the award depends on the law governing the arbitration proceedings.

16–112   The English court will not refuse to recognise or enforce a foreign award merely because the arbitrators (in its view) misapplied the law. There is no authority to this effect, but it is a reasonable deduction from the similar rule applicable to the recognition and enforcement of foreign judgments.[297] Nor should it be of any concern to the English court that the arbitrators applied no law at all if this is permissible under the law governing the arbitration proceedings.

16–113   To be enforceable in England, the award must be final and binding on the parties in the English sense, i.e. it must fulfil one of the conditions for the enforcement of foreign judgments.[298] This is one of the most important

---

[295] 1982 Act, s.34, above, n.291. In England a domestic award is merged in a judgment entered on it. The prior non-merger rule prevailing in relation to foreign judgments was used to justify the ability to enforce the award: Mustill and Boyd, above n.288, p.423; *Brali v Hyundai Corp* (1988) 84 A.L.R. 176, 178–181; *Oilcakes and Oilseeds Trading Co v Sinason-Teicher Inter American Grain Corp*, 170 N.Y.S. 2d 378, affirmed 8 N.Y. 2d 852, 203 N.Y.S. 2d 904 (1960). See also van den Berg, *op. cit.*, para.16–003, n.6; Patchett, *Recognition of Commercial Judgments and Awards in the Commonwealth* (1984), pp.233, 296; Note (1975) 124 U.Pa.L.Rev. 223. In Canada it was held that where a foreign judgment was entered on a foreign award, only the judgment was enforceable: *Stolp & Co v Browne & Co* [1930] 4 D.L.R. 703 (Ont), not followed in *Schreter v Gasmac Inc* (1992) 7 O.R. (3d) 608, a case on the enforcement provisions of the Model Law. The question was left open in *Oppenheim & Co v Mahomed Haneef* [1922] 1 A.C. 482 (PC). 1920 Act, s.12(1) and 1933 Act, s.10A (added by 1982 Act, Sch.10, para.4) below, para.16–169, strongly suggest that the award remains enforceable as such under those Acts, even if judgment has been entered on it in the foreign country.

[296] See below, para.16–132, for the position under the 1996 Act and US decisions on the New York Convention.

[297] See above, paras 14R–118 *et seq.*

[298] See Rule 42. The difference between finality and enforceability under the foreign law is discussed in the Comment to Rule 66(3) below, at paras 16–118—16–119. *Uniforêt Pâte Port-Cartier Inc v Zerotech Technologies Inc* [1998] 9 W.W.R. 688 (BC). indicates that, at least in the inter-provincial context in Canada, a judgment which confirms an interim arbitral award is, in principle, enforceable in other provinces notwithstanding the fact that the judgment is not a monetary judgment. But sufficient certainty in the terms of the award is necessary if the award (and thus any judgment thereon) is to be regarded as final and conclusive.

requirements for the recognition or enforcement of foreign awards in England. Whether the award is final in the English sense must, it is submitted, depend on the law governing the arbitration proceedings. The question to be answered is "Has it become final, as we understand that phrase, in the country in which it was made? Of course the question whether it is final in [that country] will depend no doubt upon [the foreign] law, but the [foreign] law is directed to showing whether it is final as that word is understood in English."[299] These remarks were made in a case where the award was enforced under statute; but it is submitted that they are equally applicable to the enforcement of awards at common law. However, it is far from clear whether the pendency of proceedings contesting the validity of the award in the country in which it was made prevents the enforcement of a foreign award at common law. On the analogy of the enforcement of foreign judgments at common law,[300] it is suggested that it would not. However, it is reasonable to suppose that, in appropriate circumstances, enforcement proceedings in England may be stayed[301] pending the outcome of any foreign proceedings challenging the award.

Mode of enforcement. In order to enforce an arbitral award it is always necessary to apply to a court. This applies to foreign, as it applies to English, awards. The party seeking to enforce the award has the choice between bringing proceedings on it and applying for permission to enforce it by a summary procedure under s.66 of the 1996 Act. In practice, the s.66 procedure is used in most cases.[302] Section 66 provides a means by which the award creditor may obtain the benefit of his award. Normally this will be when it is sought to obtain execution of a monetary award over assets of the award debtor in England. But where there is a real advantage in granting enforcement of a declaratory award (as where it may afford the creditor priority over an inconsistent judgment), the court has power to use the s.66 procedure for this purpose as well.[303] The court may also order a freezing injunction in support of a s.66 application for enforcement of an arbitral award.[304] An application to enforce an award under s.66 may be made without notice,[305] though the court may direct that the application is to be served on the relevant parties.[306] Service of the application out of the jurisdiction may be effected with the permission of the court, whether the award is made in England or

16–114

---

[299] *Union Nationale des Coopératives Agricoles v Catterall* [1959] 2 Q.B. 44, 53 (CA).

[300] Rule 42, proviso.

[301] For the position under the 1996 Act see s.103(5) and *Soleh Boneh International Ltd v Government of Uganda* [1993] 2 Lloyd's Rep. 208, which is discussed at para.16–146, below.

[302] *The Amazon Reefer* [2009] EWCA Civ 1330, 1 Lloyd's Rep. 222 (holding that the same limitation period is applicable to an action on award as to an application on the award under s.66); *Sovarex S.A v Romero Alvarez S.A* [2011] EWHC 1661 (Comm.), [2011] 2 Lloyd's Rep. 320.

[303] *West Tankers Inc v Allianz SpA (The Front Comor)* [2011] EWHC 829 (Comm.), [2011] 2 Lloyd's Rep 117.

[304] Such an injunction will ordinarily contain an ordinary course of business exception: *Mobile Telesystems Finance SA v Nomihold Securities Inc* [2011] EWCA Civ 1040, [2012] 1 All E.R. (Comm.) 223.

[305] CPR, r.62.18(1).

[306] CPR, r.62.18(2).

abroad.[307] The summary procedure is available for the enforcement of awards provided that the arbitration agreement is in writing as required by s.5 of the 1996 Act. The summary procedure can be employed unless there is a real ground for doubting the validity of the award.[308]

16–115 If the award provides for payment of money out of the jurisdiction, it cannot be enforced under s.66, though it can be enforced by action on the award.[309]

16–116 An award may be expressed in foreign currency, and such an award can be enforced under s.66.[310] But, whether enforced by proceedings or under s.66, it must be converted into sterling before it can be enforced in England by any process of execution. The date for conversion will be the date when the court authorises enforcement of the judgment or when permission to enforce the award in sterling under s.66 is given.[311]

16–117 **Recognition.** The conditions under which a foreign award may be enforced in England at common law apply, it is submitted, also to its recognition otherwise than by enforcement.[312] A valid award duly made in pursuance of a valid agreement to arbitrate is a defence to proceedings on the original cause of action.[313] More difficult questions arise if the foreign award was not based on the underlying merits, e.g. because the notice to arbitrate was out of time. There is a tendency in cases not involving a foreign element for the English court to construe contractual time-barring provisions as barring the claim if the arbitral machinery is not invoked in time. Thus it was held that an action on the same cause of action was barred by an award holding that the arbitration was out of time.[314] In that case the arbitrators held that they had jurisdiction and the claim was dismissed on the basis that the claim (as

---

[307] CPR, r.62.18(4). Permission to serve out of the jurisdiction on a foreign defendant may be given even if there is no jurisdictional connection with England (e.g. assets in England): *Rosseel NV v Oriental Commercial & Shipping Co (UK) Ltd* [1991] 2 Lloyd's Rep. 625; *cf. ABCI v Banque Franco-Tunisienne* [1996] 1 Lloyd's Rep. 485, affirmed [1997] 1 Lloyd's Rep. 531 (CA).

[308] *Re Boks & Co and Peters, Rushton & Co Ltd* [1919] 1 K.B. 491 (CA), as explained in *Middlemiss & Gould v Hartlepool Corp* [1972] 1 W.L.R. 1643, 1647 (CA). In *Union Nationale des Coopératives Agricoles v Catterall* [1959] 2 Q.B. 44, 52 (CA), the same test was adopted and applied to the enforcement of a foreign award under Pt II of the Arbitration Act 1950. S.36 of the 1950 Act makes the summary procedure under s.66 of the 1996 Act applicable to the enforcement of foreign awards which come within Pt II of the 1950 Act and the same summary procedure is available in cases involving the enforcement of New York Convention awards under s.101 of the 1996 Act (CPR, r.62.18(1)). See below, para.16–134.

[309] *Dalmia Cement Ltd v National Bank of Pakistan* [1975] Q.B. 9, 23–27; *cf. Bank Mellat v GAA Development and Construction Co* [1988] 2 Lloyd's Rep. 44.

[310] *Jugoslavenska Oceanska Plovidba v Castle Investment Co Inc* [1974] Q.B. 292 (CA). See Rule 261.

[311] In the *Jugoslavenska* case, above, the date of the award was chosen: see at pp.300, 302, 305, 306. But in *Miliangos v George Frank (Textiles) Ltd* [1976] A.C. 443, 469, Lord Wilberforce could see no reason why this date should not be adjusted so as to allow conversion to be made at the date stated in the text. See also Administration of Justice Act 1977, s.4, repealing Arbitration (International Investment Disputes) Act 1966, s.1(3).

[312] For the analogous question under the 1996 Act, see Rule 68(1).

[313] See the discussion *supra* at para.16–108 and the authorities there cited.

[314] See *Ayscough v Sheed, Thomson & Co Ltd* (1924) 40 T.L.R. 707 (HL). *cf.* the position with regard to foreign judgments, above, para.14–037, and Foreign Limitation Periods Act 1984, s.3, which does not apply to foreign awards.

opposed to the remedy) was barred by the claimant's failure to invoke the arbitral machinery in time. A foreign award to the effect that a claim was barred by a contractual time limitation would be entitled to recognition in England, for the decision would be "on the merits."[315]

No requirement for foreign judgment on award. The enforcement in England of foreign awards, like the enforcement of foreign judgments, is governed by English law. Foreign law regulating the enforcement of awards and in particular the need for obtaining judgments thereon does not apply in England. Hence a foreign award may be enforced in England though it has not been made enforceable by judgment in its country of origin and though the law of that country requires a judgment of a court to make the award enforceable. If the English court insisted on a foreign judgment in order to make the award enforceable in England, it would "not be enforcing the award but the judgment,"[316] i.e. the foreign award as such might be deprived of all effect in England. The English technique of enforcing an award applies to all proceedings for the enforcement of arbitral awards in England, whether the awards are English or foreign. How the award can be made enforceable under its own law is of no concern to the English court. All doubts concerning this important principle were removed by the decision of the Court of Appeal in *Union Nationale des Coopératives Agricoles v Catterall.*[317] As Lord Evershed M.R. pointed out,[318] the opposite view leads to the result that a foreign award as such would never be enforceable in an English court, a conclusion clearly incompatible with the rule established at least since the decision in the *Norske Atlas Insurance* case. **16–118**

Since, to be enforced in England, a foreign arbitral award must be valid and final in accordance with the law which governs the arbitration proceedings, a distinction must be made between conditions which under that law must be fulfilled to render the award valid and final, and conditions which must be fulfilled to render it enforceable. This line may sometimes be difficult to draw.[319] But the distinction between "validity" and "finality" on the one side and "enforceability" on the other is, it is submitted, familiar in English domestic law and the difficulties which arise are not insuperable. **16–119**

---

[315] *cf. The Sennar (No.2)* [1984] 2 Lloyd's Rep. 142 (CA), affirmed [1985] 1 W.L.R. 490 (HL). If the foreign arbitral tribunal decides merely that it has no jurisdiction because notice of arbitration was not given within the contractual time, the unsuccessful claimant may be able to bring proceedings in England on the original cause of action: *cf. Pinnock Brothers v Lewis & Peat Ltd* [1923] 1 K.B. 690, a case involving an English arbitration.

[316] *Union Nationale des Coopératives Agricoles v Catterall* [1959] 2 Q.B. 44, 54 (CA) (a Geneva Convention case, but the principle is of general application). The earlier contrary decision of *Merrifield, Ziegler & Co v Liverpool Cotton Association Ltd* (1911) 105 L.T. 97 is no longer good law: *Dalmia Dairy Industries Ltd v National Bank of Pakistan* [1978] 2 Lloyd's Rep. 223, 249 (there was no appeal from this part of Kerr J.'s judgment).

[317] [1959] 2 Q.B. 44.

[318] *ibid.*, p.54; see also Pearce L.J. at p.56.

[319] For a succinct formulation of the problem, see *Bankers and Shippers Insurance Co of New York v Liverpool Marine and General Insurance Co Ltd* (1924) 19 Ll.L.R. 335, 338. This decision was affirmed by the House of Lords: (1926) 24 Ll.L.R. 85, stated, para.16–120, Illustration 2.

ILLUSTRATIONS

16–120   1. A, a Norwegian company, and X, an English company, enter into a reinsurance contract containing an agreement to arbitrate in Oslo. The reinsurance contract (but not the arbitration clause) is void according to English law because it is not embodied in a stamped policy. A dispute arises, and A appoints an arbitrator, but X refuses to do so. In accordance with the agreement to arbitrate a second arbitrator is appointed by a Norwegian judge at A's request. The arbitrators make an award in favour of A which is valid by Norwegian law. A can enforce the award by proceedings in England.[320]

2. A, a New York company, and X, an English company, enter into a reinsurance contract containing an agreement to arbitrate in New York. A dispute arises, and A appoints an arbitrator, but X fails to do so and revokes the submission. In accordance with the agreement to arbitrate A appoints a second arbitrator and the arbitrators appoint an umpire. An award is made in favour of A. According to a New York statute an order of the New York court is required to allow the arbitration to proceed without an arbitrator appointed by X. This statute is interpreted by the New York Court of Appeals as establishing a condition for the validity of the award. The award is a nullity and A cannot in England recover the amount of the award.[321]

3. A contract for the sale of skins made between A, a foreign buyer, and X, an English seller, provides for arbitration in the foreign country. A dispute having arisen as to the quality of the skins, A proceeds to arbitration and appoints an arbitrator, but X, although he has notice of the proceedings, fails to do so. The arbitrator appointed by A proceeds with the arbitration in the absence of X and makes an award in favour of A. This award is valid and final according to the law of the foreign country. A can enforce it by proceedings in England.[322]

16–121   4. A contract for the sale of wheat seed made between A, French buyers, and X, English sellers, contains a clause referring all disputes to the Arbitration Chamber of Copenhagen. A dispute having arisen, A obtains an award from the committee of the Copenhagen Arbitration Chamber ordering X to pay £183,000. Under the rules of the Chamber, awards made by the committee are final. But by Danish law, the award is not enforceable in Denmark until a judgment of a Danish court has been obtained. However, only objections of a formal nature can be taken in the proceedings to obtain a judgment, which are in no sense a rehearing. *Semble*, A can enforce the award by proceedings in England at common law or under s.66 of the Arbitration Act 1996, even though no judgment has been obtained in Denmark, because the award is by Danish law final and binding in the English sense.[323]

16R–122   RULE 67—**A foreign arbitral award which complies with Rule 66 will (*semble*) not be recognised or enforced in England if**

     (1) **under the arbitration agreement and the law applicable thereto the arbitrators had no jurisdiction to make it;**[324] **or**

     (2) **it was obtained by fraud;**[325] **or**

---

[320] *Norske Atlas Insurance Co Ltd v London General Insurance Co Ltd* (1927) 28 Ll.L.R. 104.

[321] *Bankers and Shippers Insurance Co of New York v Liverpool Marine and General Insurance Co Ltd* (1926) 24 Ll.L.R. 85 (HL).

[322] *cf. Oppenheim & Co v Mahomed Haneef* [1922] 1 A.C. 482 (PC).

[323] *cf. Union Nationale des Coopératives Agricoles v Catterall* [1959] 2 Q.B. 44 (CA). This case was decided under Arbitration Act 1950, Pt II, but it is submitted that the result would have been the same at common law.

[324] See *Kianta Osakeyhtio v Britain and Overseas Trading Co Ltd* [1954] 1 Lloyd's Rep. 247 (CA); *Dalmia Dairy Industries Ltd v National Bank of Pakistan* [1978] 2 Lloyd's Rep. 223 (CA). Compare Rule 49(1), and Rule 69(1)(d), (e) (which reproduces s.103(2)(d), (e) of the 1996 Act).

[325] *Oppenheim & Co v Mahomed Haneef* [1922] 1 A.C. 482, 487 (PC), *obiter*. For a discussion of the effect of fraud in the context of the New York Convention (Rule 69) (where it is not a separate defence, but is subsumed under public policy) see *Westacre Investments Inc v Jugoimport-SPDR Holding Co Ltd* [2000] Q.B. 288, 305–310, below, at paras 16–150—16–151. *cf.* Rule 50.

(3) **its recognition, or as the case may be enforcement, would be contrary to public policy;**[326] **or**

(4) **the proceedings in which it was obtained were opposed to natural justice.**[327]

COMMENT

Defences to enforcement. There is very little authority on the circum-   **16–123**
stances in which a foreign award can be challenged in England at common
law, notwithstanding that it was made in accordance with a valid agreement to
arbitrate as required by Rule 66(1), and is valid and final according to the law
governing the arbitration proceedings as required by Rule 66(2). Rule 67 must
therefore be regarded as somewhat speculative. But it will be observed that it
follows closely the grounds on which a foreign judgment can be impeached in
England at common law. It can hardly be supposed that foreign arbitral awards
will be more readily enforced or recognised in England than are foreign
judgments. Hence the existence at least of these grounds of opposition can, it
is submitted, be taken for granted.

In one sense the jurisdiction of the arbitrators raises less complicated   **16–124**
problems than does the jurisdiction of a foreign court to give a judgment
capable of recognition or enforcement in England.[328] This is because the
agreement of the parties to submit their dispute to arbitration is the sole
ground of the arbitrators' jurisdiction, and not one of several grounds as is an
agreement to submit to the jurisdiction of a foreign court. But a court which
is asked to enforce or recognise an award will require to be satisfied that the
arbitrators acted within the terms of the agreement to arbitrate. It is for the
claimant seeking enforcement to prove that the award is covered by the terms
of the arbitration agreement. It is a "fundamental principle which is . . .
equally applicable to the case of English law and of foreign law that it is for
the party who is setting up the award to prove that the arbitrators acted within
the terms of the authority which was given to them."[329] If, however, the
claimant produces "a document which appears to be regular and made with
jurisdiction, . . . the onus may pass to the defendant to prove, if he can do so,
that the award which appeared to be regular is defective in that it deals with
matters beyond the scope of the agreement for arbitration."[330]

There are very few reported cases in which foreign judgments *in personam*   **16–125**
have been denied recognition or enforcement in England on grounds of public
policy,[331] no doubt because this concept is narrowly interpreted in the English

---

[326] Compare Rule 51, and Rule 69(2) (which reproduces 1996 Act, s.103(3)).

[327] Compare Rule 52, and the more limited provisions of Rule 69(1)(c) (which reproduces 1996 Act, s.103(2)(c)).

[328] See Rule 43.

[329] *Kianta Osakeyhtio v Britain and Overseas Trading Co Ltd* [1953] 2 Lloyd's Rep. 569, 573, affirmed [1954] 1 Lloyd's Rep. 247 (CA). *cf. Dalmia Dairy Industries Ltd v National Bank of Pakistan* [1978] 2 Lloyd's Rep. 233 (CA).

[330] [1954] 1 Lloyd's Rep. 247, 250–251 (CA). *cf.* Rule 69(1)(d),(e) (which reproduces 1996 Act, s.103(2)(d), (e)).

[331] See above, Rule 51.

883

conflict of laws;[332] and the refusal to recognise or enforce a foreign arbitral award on this ground is likely to be an equally rare event. Nor can there be any doubt that the rule that a foreign judgment may be denied recognition or enforcement because the proceedings in which it was obtained were opposed to natural justice[333] applies also to foreign awards.[334] It is a general principle of law, applicable to international arbitration, that "[t]he parties shall be treated with equality and each party shall be given a full opportunity of presenting his case."[335] An award based upon an arbitral procedure which fails to accord these rights will be liable to be annulled,[336] and, for the same reason, may be denied recognition and enforcement.[337]

ILLUSTRATIONS

16–126   1. A, Finnish sellers, contract with X, English buyers, for the sale of timber. The contract contains an arbitration clause for disputes to be settled in Helsinki. Part delivery only is made under the contract and a compromise "compensation" agreement without an arbitration clause is entered into. No deliveries are made under the latter agreement and A institute arbitration proceedings in Finland, X refusing to participate. An award is made in favour of A. *Semble*, A cannot enforce the award by action in England at common law, because under the "compensation" agreement the arbitrators had no jurisdiction to make it.[338]

2. Arbitration proceedings take place in a foreign country between A, a foreign buyer, and X, an English seller. The arbitrator admits evidence which is inadmissible by the law of the foreign country. He refuses to adjourn the proceedings in order to give X an opportunity of rebutting this evidence. Throughout the proceedings he shows bias against X. His award is in favour of A. In these circumstances an English arbitrator could have been removed by the court for misconduct,[339] but there is no such power of removal under the foreign law, according to which the award is valid and final. *Semble*, it will not be enforced in England, for the proceedings were opposed to natural justice.

16–127   3. Arbitration proceedings arising out of a collision on the high seas between a Norwegian and a Portuguese ship take place in a foreign country. During the course of the proceedings the arbitrator makes remarks indicating that he holds preconceived ideas about the veracity of

---

[332] See Rule 2; *Westacre Investments Inc v Jugoimport-SDPR Holding Co Ltd* [2000] Q.B. 288; *Soinco SACI v Novokuznetsk Aluminium Plant* [1998] C.L.C. 730 (CA). See also Comment to Rule 69(2). On fraud see *Westacre Investments Inc v Jugoimport-SDPR Holding Co Ltd*, above, at 309 (normally necessary to show either that the evidence of fraud was not available to the party alleging it at the time of the arbitration hearing or, if perjury is alleged, that the evidence for it is so strong that it would reasonably be expected to be decisive at a hearing).

[333] See above, Rule 52.

[334] *cf. Dalmia Dairy Industries Ltd v National Bank of Pakistan* [1978] 2 Lloyd's Rep. 223, 270 (where it was argued, unsuccessfully, that the arbitrator's refusal to hear witnesses was contrary to public policy or to principles of natural justice); *Weizmann Institute of Science v Neschis*, 421 F. Supp. 2d 654 (S.D.N.Y. 2005) (parties to be afforded a full and fair opportunity to be heard on the relevant issue in the arbitration).

[335] UNICTRAL Model Law, Art.18; 1996 Act, s.33; Fouchard, Gaillard, Goldman, paras 1638–1644; Poudret and Besson, paras 546–554; Born, pp.2582–3; *Maritime International Nominees Establishment (MINE) v Guinea*, Decision on Annulment (1989), 4 ICSID Rep. 79, para.5.06; *Fraport AG Frankfurt Airport Services Worldwide v The Philippines*, Decision on Annulment, ICSID Case No.ARB/03/25 (December 23, 2010), paras 197–208.

[336] *Fraport AG Frankfurt Airport Services Worldwide v The Philippines*, above.

[337] *cf.* Rule 69(1)(c), applying New York Convention, Art.V(1)(b).

[338] *cf. Kianta Osakeyhtio v Britain and Overseas Trading Co Ltd* [1954] 1 Lloyd's Rep. 247 (CA). This case was decided under Pt II of the Arbitration Act 1950, but it is submitted that the result would have been the same at common law. The right to proceed at common law is preserved by s.40(a) of the Act.

[339] *Re Enoch and Zaretsky, Bock & Co* [1910] 1 K.B. 327 (CA).

Portuguese witnesses. In such circumstances an English arbitrator would be removed by the court for misconduct.[340] The owners of the Portuguese ship apply to the foreign court to remove the arbitrator, but the court declines to interfere. The arbitrator makes an award in favour of the owners of the Norwegian ship. *Semble*, it will not be enforced in England.

4. A, an Indian company, sells a cement factory in Pakistan to B, a resident of Pakistan. The contract (which is governed by Indian law) provides for arbitration in Geneva under the rules of the International Chamber of Commerce. X, a Pakistan bank, unconditionally and irrevocably guarantees the payment of the price. Before the price can be paid, war breaks out between India and Pakistan. Under the Rules of the International Chamber of Commerce, the arbitrator can determine his own jurisdiction. The arbitrator makes his award in favour of A, who seeks enforcement against X in England. The Court of Appeal holds that though the arbitrator cannot determine his own jurisdiction, by Indian law the arbitration clause was not abrogated by the outbreak of war, and it was not contrary to English public policy to enforce the award.[341]

B. *New York Convention awards*

RULE 68—(1) A New York Convention award[342] **(a) shall be recognised as binding on the persons as between whom it was made, and may accordingly be relied on by those persons by way of defence, set-off or otherwise in any legal proceedings in England,**[343] **and (b) may be enforced either by proceedings at common law or under the provisions of section 66 of the Arbitration Act 1996, i.e. by leave of the High Court, in the same manner as a judgment or order of the court to the same effect,**[344] **subject to the grounds for refusal in Rule 69.**   **16R–128**

(2) A party seeking the recognition or enforcement of a New York Convention award must produce

(a) **the duly authenticated original award or a duly certified copy of it; and**

(b) **the original arbitration agreement or a duly certified copy of it; and**

(c) **if the award or agreement is in a foreign language, a translation of it certified by an official or sworn translator or by a diplomatic or consular agent.**[345]

COMMENT

Enforcement of Convention Award. This Rule states the effect of sections 100 to 102 of the Arbitration Act 1996, the language of which it closely   **16–129**

---

[340] *Catalina (Owners) v Norma (Owners)* (1938) 61 Ll.L.R. 360.

[341] *Dalmia Dairy Industries Ltd v National Bank of Pakistan* [1978] 2 Lloyd's Rep. 223 (CA).

[342] i.e. an award made in pursuance of an arbitration agreement in the territory of a State, other than the UK, which is a party to the New York Convention on the Recognition and Enforcement of Foreign Arbitral Awards of June 10, 1958. For parties to the Convention see *http://www.uncitral.org*. The UK declared upon accession, pursuant to Art.I(3), that it would only apply the Convention to awards made in other Convention States.

[343] 1996 Act, ss.100(1), (4), 101(1). These provisions apply to Northern Ireland as well as England. The court's jurisdiction to recognise and enforce a New York Convention award is limited strictly to the party against whom the award was made. Save in the case of a slip or a change of name, the court has no discretion to change the respondents as named in the award: *Norsk Hydro ASA v State Property Fund of Ukraine* [2002] EWHC 2120 (Comm.), [2009] Bus. L.R. 558.

[344] *ibid.*, s.101(2).

[345] *ibid.*, s.102. See *Proctor v Schellenberg* [2002] 7 W.W.R. 287 (Man CA).

follows. These sections replace the equivalent provisions of the Arbitration Act 1975, which was passed to enable the United Kingdom to accede to the New York Convention on the Recognition and Enforcement of Foreign Arbitral Awards of June 10, 1958.[346]

16–130   *Definition.* A Convention award is defined[347] as "an award made in pursuance of an arbitration agreement[348] in the territory of a State, other than the United Kingdom, which is a party to the New York Convention". For this purpose an award made in a Contracting State before it became a party to the Convention is a Convention award.[349] To be entitled to recognition and enforcement under Rule 68 the decision of the arbitrator must constitute an arbitral award. An interlocutory order made by an arbitrator is not an award for these purposes, but an interim award may be, provided that it is binding on the parties.[350] It is also permissible to enforce part of a Convention award, provided that the part to be enforced can be ascertained from the face of the award and judgment can be given in the same terms as the award.[351] Whether awards granted under the Italian form of arbitration known as *arbitrato irrituale* fall within the scope of the Convention has yet to be considered by the English courts,[352] though it is suggested that they do not.[353]

16–131   The Arbitration Act 1996 provides that, as a matter of law, an award is made at the seat of the arbitration: where the seat of the arbitration is located in a State which is a party to the New York Convention the award is a New York Convention award;[354] if England is the seat of the arbitration the award is treated as made in England, regardless of where it was signed.[355]

---

[346] For the text of the New York Convention and its current status see: *http://www.uncitral.org/ uncitral/en/uncitral_texts/arbitration/NYConvention.html*, and for literature on enforcement under the Convention, van den Berg, *New York Arbitration Convention of 1958* (1981); Gaillard and Di Pietro, *Enforcement of Arbitration Agreements and International Arbitral Awards: The New York Convention in Practice* (2008); Kronke, Nacimiento, Otto and Port, *Recognition and Enforcement of Foreign Arbitral Awards: A Global Commentary on the New York Convention* (2010).

[347] 1996 Act, s.100(1).

[348] Which must be in writing as defined by s.5: s.100(2)(a). On the requirement of an arbitration agreement see *Peter Cremer GmbH v Co-operative Molasses Traders Ltd* [1985] I.L.R.M. 564.

[349] *Government of Kuwait v Sir Frederick Snow and Partners* [1984] A.C. 426. *cf. Dallal v Bank Mellat* [1986] 1 Q.B. 441 (award of international claims tribunal sitting in the Netherlands under Iran–US treaty not a New York Convention award) with *Ministry of Defense of Islamic Republic of Iran v Gould Inc*, 887 F. 2d 1357 (9th Cir. 1989), cert. denied 494 U.S. 1016 (1990) (award enforced under New York Convention).

[350] *Svenska Petroleum Exploration AB v Government of the Republic of Lithuania (No.2)* [2005] EWHC 2437 (Comm.), [2006] 1 Lloyd's Rep. 181; *Re Resort Condominiums International Inc* [1995] 1 Qd. 406. See Kojovic (2001) 18 J. Int. Arb. 511.

[351] *Nigerian National Petroleum Corp v IPCO (Nigeria) Ltd (No.2)* [2008] EWCA Civ 1157, [2009] 1 Lloyd's Rep. 89.

[352] It is an informal method of arbitration; it results in an award which is enforceable as a contract. See Patocchi and Schiavello [1998] Arb. & Dispute Res. L.J. 132. See *Europcar Italia SpA v Maiellano Tours Inc*, 156 F. 3d 310 (2d Cir. 1998), for an inconclusive discussion of Italian and German decisions on the application of the New York Convention to this form of arbitration.

[353] Sanders and van den Berg (1979) 4 Yb. Comm. Arb. 231, 232–233; Gaillard and Di Pietro, *op. cit.* n.346, 145–8.

[354] s.100(2)(b).

[355] s.53, reversing the effect of *Hiscox v Outhwaite* [1992] 1 A.C. 562.

It has been seen[356] that there is controversy at common law whether, when **16–132** a foreign judgment has been entered on an award, it is the judgment or award which is enforceable. Courts in other countries have regularly enforced awards under the New York Convention which have been declared enforceable by judgments in the country in which they were made, and it is suggested that in such cases the award may be enforced under the 1996 Act.[357] Exceptionally, a judgment on the award may be enforced at common law.[358]

Recognition. Any New York Convention award must be recognised as **16–133** binding on the persons as between whom it was made, and may accordingly be relied upon by way of defence, set-off or otherwise in any legal proceedings in England.[359] Hence, a valid New York Convention award in favour of the defendant is a defence to an action on the original cause of action.[360]

Mode of enforcement. A party who has obtained a New York Convention **16–134** award may, at his option, enforce it either by action or by an application for leave to enforce the award summarily under s.66 of the 1996 Act, as if it were a judgment or order of the court.[361] The provision in s.101(3) to the effect that judgment may be entered "in terms of the award" does not preclude the court from requiring the payment of interest at the judgment rate from the date upon which judgment has been entered on the award, even if the arbitral tribunal did not provide for the payment of interest in its award.[362]

Article III of the New York Convention provides that "[e]ach Contracting **16–135** State shall recognise arbitral awards as binding and enforce them in accordance with the rules of procedure of the territory where the award is relied upon, under the conditions laid down in the following articles. There shall not be imposed substantially more onerous conditions or higher fees or charges on

---

[356] See above, Comment under Rule 66.

[357] *ABCI v Banque Franco-Tunisienne* [1996] 1 Lloyd's Rep. 485, 489, affirmed on other aspects [1997] 1 Lloyd's Rep. 531 (CA).

[358] See Rule 71(1) and para.16–162, below. This has been decided in Ontario in relation to the Model Law: *Schreter v Gasmac Inc* (1992) 7 O.R. (3d) 608. The trend in the US is in a similar direction, although there is no clear decision in this sense: *Island Territory of Curacao v Solitron Devices Inc*, 489 F. 2d 1313 (2d Cir. 1973); *Fotochrome Inc v Copal Co Ltd*, 517 F. 2d 512, 518 (2d Cir. 1975); *Waterside Ocean Navigation Co, Inc v International Navigation Ltd*, 737 F. 2d 150 (2d Cir. 1984); *Victrix Steamship Co v Salen Dry Cargo AB*, 825 F. 2d 709 (2d Cir. 1987); *Seetransport Wiking Trader v Navimprex Cetrala Navara*, 29 F. 3d 79 (2d Cir. 1994). *cf. Oriental Commercial & Shipping Co (UK) Ltd v Rosseel NV*, 769 F. Supp. 514, (SDNY 1991); Roth (2007) 92 Cornell L. R. 573. However, the German Federal Supreme Court, reversing its earlier jurisprudence, decided in 2009 that only the award should be enforceable, since otherwise the review standards of the New York Convention could be subverted: (2010) 35 Yb. Comm.Arb. 374; and see Einhorn (2010) 12 Ybk. P.I.L 43. In *ABCI v Banque Franco-Tunisienne*, above, it was held that a French judgment making a French award enforceable was not entitled to enforcement under the Brussels Convention because the enforcement of arbitral awards is outside its scope. Hascher (1996) 12 Arb. Int. 233, 239–240 supports the result, but on the basis that the French order was not a judgment on the award, but an execution order.

[359] 1996 Act, s.101(1).

[360] See further above, paras 16–108 and 16–117 on the scope of recognition.

[361] See above, paras 16–114—16–116.

[362] *Gater Assets Ltd v Nak Naftogaz Ukrainiy (No.3)* [2008] EWHC 1108 (Comm.), [2008] 2 Lloyd's Rep. 295.

the recognition or enforcement of arbitral awards to which this Convention applies than are imposed on the recognition or enforcement of domestic arbitral awards." The Limitation Act 1980, s.7 provides: "An action to enforce an award, where the submission is not by an instrument under seal, shall not be brought after the expiration of six years from the date on which the cause of action accrued." The imposition of this requirement at the place of enforcement is not inconsistent with Art.III, s.7 being a rule of procedure of the territory where the award is relied on.[363]

16R–136   RULE 69—Recognition or enforcement of a New York Convention award may be refused only if (1) the person against whom it is invoked proves

(a) **that a party to the arbitration agreement was (under the law applicable to him) under some incapacity;[364] or**

(b) **that the arbitration agreement was not valid under the law to which the parties subjected it or, failing any indication thereon, under the law of the country where the award was made;[365] or**

(c) **that he was not given proper notice of the appointment of the arbitrator or of the arbitration proceedings or was otherwise unable to present his case;[366] or**

(d) **that the award deals with a difference not contemplated by or not falling within the terms of the submission to arbitration or contains decisions on matters beyond the scope of the submission to arbitration; provided that an award which contains decisions on matters not submitted to arbitration may be recognised or enforced to the extent that it contains decisions on matters submitted to arbitration which can be separated from those on matters not so submitted;[367] or**

(e) **that the composition of the arbitral authority or the arbitral procedure was not in accordance with the agreement of the parties or, failing such agreement, with the law of the country in which the arbitration took place;[368] or**

(f) **that the award has not yet become binding on the parties, or has been set aside or suspended by a competent authority of the country in which, or under the law of which, it was made.[369]**

(2) the award is in respect of a matter which is not capable of settlement by arbitration, or if it would be contrary to public policy to recognise or enforce the award.[370]

---

[363] *Yugraneft Corp v Rexx Management Corp* [2010] SCC 19, [2010] 1 S.C.R. 649 (considering the same point by reference to s.3 Alberta Limitations Act 2000).

[364] 1996 Act, s.103(2)(a); New York Convention, Art.V(1)(a).

[365] 1996 Act, s.103(2)(b); New York Convention, Art.V(1)(a).

[366] 1996 Act, s.103(2)(c); New York Convention, Art.V(1)(b).

[367] 1996 Act, s.103(2)(d), (4); New York Convention, Art.V(1)(c).

[368] 1996 Act, s.103(2)(e); New York Convention, Art.V(1)(d).

[369] 1996 Act, s.103(2)(f); New York Convention, Art.V(1)(e).

[370] *ibid.*, s.103(3).

Grounds for refusal of enforcement. Rule 69 sets out the grounds enu-   **16–137**
merated under s.103(2) of the 1996 Act for refusal of the enforcement of a
New York Convention award, which in turn give effect to the provisions of
Art.V of the Convention itself. These grounds, which have also been closely
followed in the provisions of the Model Law,[371] operate as a code, and their
consistent interpretation and application across more than 140 Contracting
States is therefore of the greatest possible importance for the successful
operation of the modern system of international commercial arbitration.[372] A
challenge to an award invoking one of the grounds under s.103 (Rule 69) is
by way of rehearing not review, and the court will determine the question
anew, irrespective of whether a different view on the relevant issues may have
been reached by the arbitral tribunal. On the contrary, though the court would
examine the tribunal's reasoning and conclusions, its decision on the relevant
issue has no legal or evidential value.[373] The grounds on which recognition
and enforcement may be refused, listed in Rule 69, are exhaustive.[374] So, the
court before which recognition or enforcement of a New York Convention
award is sought may not review the merits of the award because a mistake of
fact or law by the arbitrator is not one of the available grounds of review.[375]
However, the power to *refuse* recognition under s.103(2) of the 1996 Act is
discretionary.[376] That discretion is not, however, open-ended, and the court
will be unlikely to exercise its discretion to enforce an award which is subject
to a fundamental or structural defect. So, where one of the grounds stated
under s.103 has been made out, the court would normally only enforce the
award if the right to rely upon one of the stated grounds had been lost, for
example by another agreement or estoppel, or on some other recognizable
legal principle.[377]

---

[371] Arts 34 and 36.

[372] Detailed commentaries on Art.V, with citation to comparative authority, may be found in
van den Berg, *The New York Arbitration Convention of 1958* (1981), Ch.3; Gaillard and Di Pietro,
*Enforcement of Arbitration Agreements and International Arbitral Awards: The New York Con-
vention in Practice* (2008), Pt V; Kronke, Nacimiento, Otto and Port, *Recognition and Enforcement of Foreign Arbitral Awards: A Global Commentary on the New York Convention* (2010),
pp.205–414; Born, pp.2732–2872.

[373] *Dallah Real Estate and Tourism Holding Co v Ministry of Religious Affairs, Government of
Pakistan* [2010] UKSC 46, [2011] 1 A.C. 763; and, to like effect in French law: *République
tchèque v Nreka* (CA, Paris, September 25, 2008) [2009] *Rev. arb.* 337, 339, note Fadlallah.

[374] *Rosseel NV v Oriental Commercial & Shipping Co (UK) Ltd* [1991] 2 Lloyd's Rep. 625. See
also *M&C Corp v Erwin Behr GmbH & Co KG*, 87 F. 3d 844 (6th Cir. 1996).

[375] See *Corporacion Transnacional de Inversiones SA de CV v STET International SpA* (1999)
45 O.R. (3rd) 183 (app. dismissed (2000) 49 O.R. (3d) 414 (Ont CA)), a case concerning an
application to set aside an award under Model Law, Art.34, which reproduces the grounds for
refusing recognition and enforcement under the New York Convention.

[376] *Svenska Petroleum Exploration AB v Government of the Republic of Lithuania* [2005]
EWHC 9 (Comm.), [2005] 1 Lloyd's Rep. 515.

[377] *Dardana Ltd v Yukos Oil Co* [2002] EWCA Civ 543, [2002] 2 Lloyd's Rep. 326; *Kanoria
v Guinness* [2006] EWCA Civ 222, [2006] 1 Lloyd's Rep. 701; *Dallah Real Estate and Tourism
Holding Co v Ministry of Religious Affairs, Government of Pakistan* [2009] EWCA Civ 755,
[2010] 2 W.L.R. 805, affirmed [2010] UKSC 46, [2011] 1 A.C. 763 (where it was added *obiter*
that it might be necessary to revisit the question whether the discretion to permit enforcement
might be broader in a case under Rule 69(1)(f)—award set aside by the supervisory court).

16–138   (1) *Incapacity.* The first ground under clause (1) of the Rule is that a party
to the arbitration agreement was (under the law applicable to him) under some
incapacity. The Convention does not state what that law is, and therefore the
court is thrown back on its own conflict rule for capacity to contract. This is
by no means an easy question in the English conflict of laws. The Rome I
Regulation does not apply to arbitration agreements, and its general choice of
law rules do not apply to the legal capacity of natural persons or of corporations.[378] Consequently the common law rules of the conflict of laws on
capacity will apply, but the content of these rules is controversial.[379] It is to be
noted that the defence is not limited to cases where the defendant was under
some incapacity. It extends to cases where a party to the arbitration agreement
(including apparently the claimant seeking enforcement) was so incapable.

16–139   (2) *Invalidity.* The second ground is that the arbitration agreement was not
valid under the law to which the parties subjected it or, failing any indication
thereon, under the law of the country where the award was made.[380] This
ground also applies where a party claims that the agreement is not binding
upon it because it never was a party to the arbitration agreement.[381] Where the
parties have not chosen the law applicable to the arbitration agreement, the
reference to the law of the country where the award was made denotes the
substantive law rules of that country, and not its conflict of law rules.[382] Thus,
in *Dallah Real Estate and Tourism Holding Co v Ministry of Religious Affairs,
Government of Pakistan,*[383] the Government of Pakistan resisted enforcement
of a French arbitration award against it in England on the ground that it had
never been a party to the arbitration agreement with the claimant. The arbitral
tribunal had decided that the arbitration agreement did extend to the Government because, though it was not a signatory, the factual elements as a whole
showed that it was a true party. The Supreme Court, affirming the courts
below, held that the English court, as a court from which enforcement under
the New York Convention was sought, was entitled to examine for itself
whether there was a valid arbitration agreement binding upon the relevant
party. The law applicable to that question, in the absence of express choice by
the parties, was French substantive law, France being the country where the
award was made. The French substantive law applicable to an international
arbitration agreement (being rules which French law itself described as
"transnational") required consideration of the common intention of the parties
derived from the objective evidence. Applying that rule of French law, the
Supreme Court considered that the Government was not a party to the

---

[378] Rome I Regulation, Art.1(2)(a) (natural persons, subject to Art.13), Art.1(2)(f) (corporations). See below paras 32–169 *et seq.*

[379] See below, paras 32R–168 *et seq.*

[380] See *Deutsche Schachtbau v Shell International Petroleum Co Ltd* [1990] 1 A.C. 295,
309–310 (CA), reversed on other grounds, *ibid.* p.329; and Rule 64(1).

[381] *Dardana Ltd v Yukos Oil Co* [2002] EWCA Civ 543, [2002] 2 Lloyd's Rep. 326; *Dallah
Real Estate and Tourism Holding Co v Ministry of Religious Affairs, Government of Pakistan*
[2010] UKSC 46, [2011] 1 A.C. 763, at [77].

[382] *Dallah Real Estate,* above, at [123]–[125].

[383] *ibid.*

arbitration agreement, and accordingly the judge had been right to refuse enforcement.[384]

(3) *Natural justice.* The third ground is in substance a defence of absence   **16–140** of natural justice: that there was no proper notice of the appointment of the tribunal or of the arbitration proceedings, or that otherwise the party resisting recognition or enforcement was unable to present his case. This ground gives effect to a general principle of law, applicable to international arbitration, that "[t]he parties shall be treated with equality and each party shall be given a full opportunity of presenting his case."[385] An award based upon an arbitral procedure which fails to accord these rights will be liable to be annulled,[386] and, for the same reason, may be denied recognition and enforcement.[387] This does not mean, however, that the parties to an international arbitration may seek refusal of enforcement on the ground that the process adopted by the arbitral tribunal does not accord with the procedures of the English court, or any other national court. Although parties to an arbitration are often entitled to a hearing, it does not follow from the fact that the arbitral tribunal determines the dispute solely on the basis of the parties' documentary evidence that there has been a procedural irregularity.[388] A party who resists recognition or enforcement of an award on the ground of inability to present its case must point to matters outside its control and cannot rely on its own failure to take advantage of an opportunity to participate in the arbitral proceedings.[389] A breach of natural justice may occur if, for example, it is established either that the arbitrator's decision was influenced by pressure brought to bear by a third party; or that the award was based on information which was not available to one of the parties and, therefore, on which that party was unable to comment;[390] or that one party was not informed of the case which he was called upon to meet.[391]

(4) *Excess of jurisdiction.* The fourth ground is that the award deals with a   **16–141** difference not contemplated by or not falling within the terms of the submission to arbitration or contains decisions on matters beyond the scope of the submission to arbitration. Construction of the scope of the arbitration agreement is a matter for its applicable law.[392] But it is expressly provided that

---

[384] Subsequently, the French court, from which recourse on annulment was sought as the court of the seat, declined to annul the award against the Government: *Gouvernement du Pakistan—Ministère des Affaires Religieuses v Société Dallah Real Estate and Tourism Holding Company* (CA, Paris, February 17, 2011) [2011] Rev. arb. 286.

[385] UNICTRAL Model Law, Art.18; 1996 Act, s.33; *Fouchard, Gaillard, Goldman,* paras 1638–1644; Poudret and Besson, paras 546–554; Born, pp.2582–3; *cf. Maritime International Nominees Establishment (MINE) v Guinea,* Decision on Annulment (1989), 4 ICSID Rep 79, para.5.06; *Fraport AG Frankfurt Airport Services Worldwide v The Philippines* (Decision on Annulment, ICSID Case No. ARB/03/25 (December 23, 2010), paras 197–208.

[386] *Fraport AG Frankfurt Airport Services Worldwide v The Philippines,* above.

[387] Born, pp.2737–2764.

[388] *Dalmia Dairy Industries Ltd v National Bank of Pakistan* [1978] 2 Lloyd's Rep. 223 (a case decided at common law).

[389] *Minmetals Germany GmbH v Ferco Steel Ltd* [1999] C.L.C. 647.

[390] *Irvani v Irvani* [2000] 1 Lloyd's Rep. 412 (CA).

[391] *Kanoria v Guinness* [2006] EWCA Civ 222, [2006] 1 Lloyd's Rep. 701.

[392] *Dallah Real Estate and Tourism Holding Co v Ministry of Religious Affairs, Government of Pakistan* [2010] UKSC 46, [2011] 1 A.C. 763; see Rule 64(1) above.

matters properly submitted may be separated from matters not so submitted.[393] Rule 69(1)(d) is to be construed narrowly and should never lead to a re-examination of the merits of the award.[394]

16–142   (5) *Breach of procedural law.* The fifth ground is that the composition of the arbitral authority or the arbitral procedure was not in accordance with the agreement of the parties, or, failing such agreement, with the law of the country where the arbitration took place.[395] The wording of the New York Convention represented a compromise between those countries who wished arbitration to be subject to the procedural law of the place of arbitration and those countries who wished the parties to be free from legal control.[396] The parties are free to choose the arbitral procedure, and, in the absence of such choice, the proceedings are governed by the law of the country where the arbitration takes place. It follows that for the purposes of clause (1)(e) it is no defence that the award was not rendered in accordance with the law of the country where the arbitration was conducted, provided that it was rendered in accordance with the procedural law chosen by the parties. Potential problems arise, however, if there is a conflict between the procedure chosen by the parties and the mandatory requirements of the procedural law of the seat. If the arbitrator applies the former, thereby failing to comply with the latter, the award may be set aside by the courts of the country in which it was made, as a consequence of which recognition or enforcement may be refused under clause (1)(f) of the Rule. Although the arbitrator's failure to follow the agreed procedure provides a ground on which recognition or enforcement may be refused under clause (1)(e), the parties' freedom to choose the arbitral procedure must be understood as being subject to the mandatory rules of the law of the seat.[397] If the arbitrator diverges from the procedure agreed by the parties in order to comply with the mandatory procedural rules of the law of the seat the court should, in the exercise of its discretion, not refuse to recognise or enforce the award under clause (1)(e).[398] Where the agreed arbitral procedure has not been complied with, a party who has waived the procedural irregularity is not able to rely on clause (1)(e).[399]

16–143   (6) *Award not binding.* The sixth ground is that the award has not yet become binding on the parties,[400] or has been set aside or suspended by a

---

[393] 1996 Act, s.103(2)(d), (4). See *Deutsche Schachtbau v Shell International Petroleum Co Ltd*, above, at pp.311–312.

[394] *Lesotho Highlands Development Authority v Impregilo SpA* [2005] UKHL 43, [2006] 1 A.C. 121, at [30].

[395] See, e.g. *China Agribusiness Development Corp v Balli Trading* [1998] 2 Lloyd's Rep. 76; *Encyclopaedia Universalis SA v Encyclopeaedia Britannica Inc,* 403 F. 3d 85, (2005) 30 Yb. Comm. Arb. 1136; Decision of German Federal Sup Ct, May 21, 2007, (2009) 34 Yb. Comm. Arb. 504.

[396] See Contini (1959) 8 Am.J.Comp. L. 283, 301–303; Quigley (1961) 70 Yale L.J. 1049, 1068–1069.

[397] *cf.* Rule 64(2); 1996 Act, s.4; Poudret and Besson, para.915; but *cf.* Born, p.2768 *contra.*

[398] See van den Berg (1989) 5 Arb. Int. 2, 9–10.

[399] *Minmetals Germany GmbH v Ferco Steel Ltd* [1999] C.L.C. 647.

[400] See *Rosseel NV v Oriental Commercial & Shipping Co (UK) Ltd* [1991] 2 Lloyd's Rep. 625 (agreement that any proceedings to confirm or vacate New York award would be brought in the US did not prevent enforcement in England; it was not an agreement which deprived the award of its binding character, and it did not amount to an agreement not to enforce).

competent authority of the country in which, or under the law of which, it was made. The wording of this ground omits the word "final" which appears in the Geneva Convention and caused difficulty in interpretation.[401] It is clear that the Conference which approved the New York Convention chose the word "binding" rather than "final" in order to avoid a double *exequatur* of arbitral awards, one in the country where the award was made and the other in the country where it is sought to be enforced. The Private International Law Committee in its Fifth Report[402] suggested that an award is to be regarded as "binding" if no further recourse may be had to another arbitral tribunal (e.g. an appeals tribunal); and the fact that recourse may be had to a court of law does not prevent the award from being binding.[403]

Rule 69(1)(f) gives effect in English law to Art.V(1)(e) of the New York **16–144** Convention.[404] The paradigm case which brings clause (1)(f) into play is one where an award is set aside in the country where the seat of the arbitration was located, regardless of whether the grounds on which the award was set aside would have constituted good grounds in the enforcing court.[405] In addition, this ground is intended to encompass the exceptional cases where, an arbitration having been conducted in one country under the law of another country, the award is set aside by the courts of the latter. The reference to the law of the country under which the award was made signifies the *lex arbitri* and not the substantive law governing the contract out of which the dispute arose nor the law governing the arbitration agreement.[406] So, where a dispute arising out of a contract governed by Pakistani law is referred to arbitration in Switzerland, if the resulting award were set aside by the Pakistani courts,[407] that would not provide a basis for refusal of enforcement of the award under clause (1)(f).

A question arises whether the court may refuse to enforce a New York **16–145** Convention award in a case where, as a result of the bringing of proceedings to have the award set aside in the country where it was made, the award is automatically suspended. Since the ground provided by clause (1)(f) refers to an award being suspended *by a competent authority*, it would seem that automatic suspension under the law of the country where the award was made does not entitle the courts of other countries to refuse to recognise or enforce

---

[401] See above, para.16–113 for discussion of "final" in the context of enforcement of arbitral awards at common law.

[402] Cmnd. 1515 (1961), para.14.

[403] See, e.g. *IPCO (Nigeria) Ltd v Nigerian National Petroleum Corp* [2005] EWHC 726 (Comm.), [2005] 2 Lloyd's Rep. 326, at [12]; *Dowans Holding SA v Tanzania Electric Supply Co Ltd* [2011] EWHC 1957 (Comm.); *Fertilizer Corp of India v IDI Management Inc*, 517 F. Supp. 948 (SD Ohio 1981). There was an apparent concession in *Svenska Petroleum Exploration AB v Government of the Republic of Lithuania (No.2)* [2005] EWHC 2437 (Comm.), [2006] 1 Lloyd's Rep. 181 at [57], that finality depended on whether the award *could* be challenged. This was incorrect.

[404] 1996 Act, s.103(2)(f).

[405] *TermoRio SA v Electranta SP*, 487 F. 3d 928 (D.C. Cir. 2007).

[406] Decisions to this effect in several countries are discussed in *International Standard Electric Corp v Bridas Sociedad Anonima Petrolera, Industrial y Comercial*, 745 F. Supp. 172 (SDNY 1990).

[407] As in *Rupali Polyester Ltd v Bunni* [1995] 3 L.R.C. 617 (in which the Supreme Court of Pakistan held that the Pakistani courts have supervisory jurisdiction over an award made in another country if the arbitration agreement is governed by the law of Pakistan).

the award.[408] This analysis is consistent with the framework of the Convention which draws a distinction between grounds on which recognition or enforcement may be *refused* and circumstances in which proceedings for the recognition or enforcement of an award may be *adjourned*. Although a court may refuse to recognise or enforce an award which has been suspended by a competent authority, it may adjourn proceedings in which an award is relied upon if the award is automatically suspended as a result of proceedings challenging the award being brought in the country in which the award was made. It is provided that where an application for setting aside or suspension of a New York Convention award has been made to a competent authority of the country in which, or under the law of which, it was made, the court which is asked to recognise or enforce the award may adjourn the proceedings and may, on the application of a party seeking recognition or enforcement of the award, order the other party to give security.[409] Where, however, a severable part of the award is not subject to credible challenge in the courts of the seat, the enforcing court may enter judgment for that part of the award, maintaining a stay in respect of the balance.[410]

16–146   In *Soleh Boneh International Ltd v Government of Uganda*[411] it was held that there are two important factors in the exercise of the discretion to order security in enforcement cases. The first is the strength of the argument that the award is invalid, as perceived on a brief consideration by the court which is asked to enforce the award while proceedings to set aside are pending elsewhere. If the award is manifestly invalid there should be an adjournment and no order for security; if it is manifestly valid there should either be an order for immediate enforcement or else an order for substantial security. In between there are various degrees of plausibility in the argument for invalidity; and the judge must be guided by his preliminary conclusion on the point. The second factor is that the court must consider the ease or difficulty of enforcement of the award, and whether it will be rendered more difficult, for example, by movement of assets or improvident trading, if enforcement is delayed. If this is likely to occur the case for security is stronger; if, on the other hand, there are and always will be insufficient assets within the jurisdiction, the case for security is necessarily weakened. Although the court will normally act under s.103(5) of the 1996 Act on the application of one of the parties, the power to stay enforcement proceedings under s.103(5) can be exercised by the court of its own motion.[412] Can an award debtor obtain security for costs against an award creditor, seeking enforcement of his award in England under the New York Convention? Although the question has not

---

[408] van den Berg, p.352; *AB Götaverken v General National Maritime Transport Co* (1981) 6 Yb. Comm. Arb. 237 (Swedish Sup Ct, 1979); Decision of Swiss Federal Sup Ct, December 9, 2008, (2009) 34 Yb. Comm. Arb. 810; but *cf. Creighton Ltd v Government of Qatar* (1996) 21 Yb. Comm. Arb. 751 (DDC 1995).

[409] 1996 Act, s.103(5). See Tupman (1987) 3 Arb. Int. 209; *Apis AS v Fantazia Kereskedelmi KFT* [2001] 1 All E.R. (Comm.) 348. *cf. Hallen v Angledal* [1999] NSWSC 552. See also *IPCO (Nigeria) Ltd v Nigerian National Petroleum Corp* [2005] EWHC 726 (Comm.), [2005] 2 Lloyd's Rep. 326.

[410] *IPCO (Nigeria) Ltd v Nigerian National Petroleum Corp* [2008] EWHC 797 (Comm.), affirmed [2008] EWCA Civ 1157, [2009] 1 Lloyd's Rep. 89.

[411] [1993] 2 Lloyd's Rep. 495 (CA). See also *Dalimpex Ltd v Janicki* (2003) 228 D.L.R. (4th) 179 (Ont CA).

[412] *Dardana Ltd v Yukos Oil Co* [2002] EWCA Civ 543, [2002] 2 Lloyd's Rep. 326.

been finally decided, the better view is that no security may be awarded against the award creditor. No such provision is made in the Convention itself, and to insert such a requirement would be to impose upon a Convention creditor a more onerous requirement than applies in the case of domestic awards, contrary to Art.III.[413]

Rule 69(1)(f), in common with the other grounds for refusal, is permissive **16–147** only, and the question has arisen as to whether the court in which enforcement is sought may enforce an award notwithstanding that it has been set aside by the court of the seat of the arbitration. The prevailing view is that the courts of the seat are best placed to decide on the setting aside of an award, and that the courts of other countries should in general respect the decisions of the court of the seat. In some countries (notably France), the view has been taken that the enforcing court, not being bound to follow the decision of the court of the seat, should not do so, respecting the international character of the arbitral award itself.[414] These decisions rest upon the power of the enforcing court under Art.VII(1) of the Convention to apply laws which are more generous to enforcement than the rules of the Convention.[415]

In the absence of direct authority in England[416] it is suggested that where **16–148** it has been set aside in the court of the seat, an arbitral award should be enforced only if recognition of the order setting aside the award would be impeachable for fraud or as being contrary to natural justice, or otherwise contrary to public policy, in accordance with Rules 50 to 52.[417]

---

[413] In *Gater Assets Ltd v Nak Naftogaz Ukrainiy* [2007] EWCA Civ 988, [2007] 2 Lloyd's Rep. 588, Moses L.J. held in the terms submitted in the text. Rix L.J. did not decide the question of the court's jurisdiction to make such an order, but held (disapproving *Dardana Ltd v Yukos Oil Co (No.2)* [2002] 2 Lloyd's Rep. 261 on the point) that the court should, in the exercise of its discretion, be reluctant to order security against an award creditor, save in an exceptional case. Buxton L.J. dissented.

[414] See *Hilmarton Ltd v Omnium de Traitement et de Valorisation* (1995) 20 Yb. Comm. Arb. 663 (Cour de cassation, France, 1994); *Arab Republic of Egypt v Chromalloy Aeroservices Inc* (1997) 22 Yb. Comm. Arb. 691 (Cour d'appel, Paris, 1997); *PT Putrabali Adyamulia v Est Epices* (Cour de cassation, France, June 29, 2007), (2008) 24 Arb. Int. 293; see Petrochilos, Ch.7; Fouchard, Gaillard, Goldman, paras 1595 *et seq.*; Paulsson (1998) 9 (1) ICC Arb. Bull. 14; van den Berg (1998) 9 (2) ICC Arb. Bull. 15; Gaillard (1999) 14 ICSID Rev.-FILJ 16; Lastenouse (1999) 16 (2) J. Int. Arb. 25; Wahl (1999) 16 (4) J. Int. Arb. 131; Freyer (2000) 17(2) J. Int. Arb. 1; Arfazadeh (2001) 17 Arb. Int. 73.

[415] *Dallah Real Estate and Tourism Holding Co v Ministry of Religious Affairs, Government of Pakistan* [2010] UKSC 46, [2011] 1 A.C. 763, at [129]; Born, pp.2677–2680; *Yukos Capital S.a.r.L v OAO Rosneft* (Dutch CA, April 28, 2009) (2009) 34 Yb. Comm. Arb. 703.

[416] In *Yukos Capital S.a.r.L v OJSC Rosneft Oil Co* [2011] EWHC 1461 (Comm.), the court held that the award debtor was estopped, by the decision of the Dutch Court of Appeal of April 28, 2009 (2009) 34 Yb. Comm. Arb. 703, from denying that decisions of the Russian courts to annul an arbitral award were the result of a partial and dependent judicial process.

[417] *cf.* Petrochilos, paras 7.56 *et seq.* There may be a concern that the courts of the seat have not acted in an impartial manner in setting aside an award, especially where one of the parties is the State itself, or a State-owned entity. *Yukos Capital S.a.r.L v OAO Rosneft* (Dutch CA, April 28, 2009)(2009) 34 Yb. Comm. Arb. 703; *Yukos Capital S.a.r.L v OJSC Rosneft Oil Co* [2011] EWHC 1461 (Comm.). *cf.* the approach in the US: *Chromalloy Aeroservices Inc v Arab Republic of Egypt*, 939 F. Supp. 907 (DDC 1996); *Karaha Bodas Co LLC v Perusahaan Pertambangan Minyak Dan Gas Bumi Negara*, 335 F. 3d 357 (5th Cir. 2003). Contrast *Baker Marine (Nigeria) Ltd v Chevron Corp Inc* 191 F. 3d. 194 (2d. Cir. 1999); *Spier v Calzaturificio Tecnica SpA*, 71 F. Supp. 2d 279 (S.D.N.Y. 1999), application for re-argument dismissed, 77 F. Supp. 2d 405 (SDNY 1999).

16–149   *Public policy.* It is for the law of England to decide what matters are capable of settlement by arbitration,[418] and it is English public policy which is meant. This is not explicit in s.103(3) of the Act, but it is explicit in Art.V.2 of the Convention.[419] In *Deutsche Schachtbau v Shell International Petroleum Co Ltd*[420] it was held that it was not contrary to English public policy to enforce a Swiss award, valid under Swiss law, in which the arbitrators applied general principles of law; the arbitrators' choice of the governing law (in the absence of a choice by the parties) was not outside the scope of the choice which the parties left to the arbitrators. Sir John Donaldson M.R. emphasised that public policy could never be exhaustively defined, and that it should be approached with extreme caution: for an argument based on public policy to succeed it has to be shown that there is some element of illegality or that recognition or enforcement of the award would be clearly injurious to the public good, or, possibly, that recognition or enforcement would be wholly offensive to the ordinary reasonable and fully informed member of the public on whose behalf the powers of the State are exercised.[421]

16–150   English law recognises an important public policy in the enforcement of arbitral awards, and the courts will only refuse to do so under Rule 69(2) in a clear case. A controversial question, which has been the subject of several recent decisions, is the extent to which it may be contrary to English public policy to enforce a foreign arbitral award rendered on the basis of an underlying contract the enforcement of which (as distinct from enforcement of the arbitral award) might be contrary to English public policy. The following principles can be derived from the authorities.[422] First, it is legitimate for the

---

[418] This is made clear by the wording of the Convention, Art.V(5)(a). As to what matters are capable of settlement by arbitration by the law of England, see Mustill and Boyd, pp.149–150. See *G v G* [2000] 7 W.W.R. 363 (Alta) (a dispute arising out of a prenuptial agreement which purported to exempt the parties from the provisions of the Matrimonial Property Act 1980 (Alta.) was not incapable of settlement by arbitration.); *Desputeaux v Editions Chouette (1987) Inc* (2002) 223 D.L.R. (4th) 407 (Sup Ct) (in a domestic case, ownership of copyright is arbitrable). *cf. Metrocall Inc v Electronic Tracking Systems Pty Ltd* (2000) 52 N.S.W.L.R. 1 (the power of the Industrial Relations Commission in Court Session to declare contracts void or varied under Industrial Relations Act 1996 (NSW) was a matter which was incapable of settlement by arbitration). See also *Mitsubishi Motors Corp v Soler Chrysler-Plymouth Inc*, 473 U.S. 614 (1985); *Shearson/American Express Inc v McMahon*, 482 U.S. 220 (1989); *Rodriguez de Quijas v Shearson/American Express Inc*, 490 U.S. 477 (1989); *PPG Industries Inc v Pilkington Plc*, 825 F. Supp. 1465 (D.Ariz. 1993).

[419] See generally: ILA Committee on International Commercial Arbitration, *Final Report on Public Policy as a Bar to Enforcement of International Arbitral Awards*, in (2002) 70 ILA Conf. Rep. 352; *cf. World Duty Free Co Ltd v Kenya* (2007) 46 Int. Leg. Mat. 339, at para.138; Radicati di Brozolo (2005) 315 *Recueil des Cours* 265.

[420] [1990] 1 A.C. 295 (CA), reversed on other grounds, *ibid.* p.329. On alleged procedural unfairness see *Minmetals Germany GmbH v Ferco Steel Ltd* [1999] 1 All E.R. (Comm.) 315.

[421] At p.316. It is widely accepted that the public policy ground should be given a restrictive application: see, e.g. *Renusager Power Co Ltd v General Electric Co* (1995) 20 Yb. Comm. Arb. 681 (Indian Sup Ct); *Paklito Investment Ltd v Klöckner (East Asia) Ltd* [1993] 2 H.K.L.R. 39; *Waterside Ocean Navigation Co Inc v International Navigation Ltd*, 737 F. 2d 150 (2d Cir. 1984); *Inter Maritime Management SA v Russin & Vecchi* (1997) 22 Yb. Comm. Arb. 789 (Swiss Federal Tribunal, 1995). See also *Amaltal Corp Ltd v Maruha (NZ) Corp Ltd* [2003] 2 N.Z.L.R. 92.

[422] See *Soleimany v Soleimany* [1999] Q.B. 785 (CA); *R v V* [2008] EWHC 1531 (Comm.), [2009] 1 Lloyd's Rep. 97 (cases involving English awards); *Westacre Investments Inc v Jugoimport-SPDR Holding Co Ltd* [2000] Q.B. 288 (CA); *Omnium de Traitement de Valorisation SA v Hilmarton Ltd* [1999] 2 Lloyd's Rep. 222.

court, in considering whether a foreign arbitral award should not be enforced on the ground of public policy, to take account of the underlying contract on which the award is based. Second, if that contract is in itself contrary to public policy (e.g. the classic case of a contract to share the proceeds of crime) the award may be refused enforcement on the ground of public policy.[423] Third, it is important to distinguish between domestic public policy in English law; and considerations of international public policy applied by the English courts so as to disapply foreign law or refuse to enforce an arbitral award, as the case may be.[424] Thus the mere fact that English law would have arrived at a different result does not of itself justify the application of English public policy.[425] Fourth, the mere fact that the performance of the contract may be illegal in the place of performance, without more, will not render an award on the basis of such a contract unenforceable in England, where the contract is legal by its applicable law and by the *lex arbitri*.[426] Fifth, if it is apparent on the face of the award that the contract was made with the intention of violating the law of a foreign friendly State, then the enforcement of an award rendered on the basis of such a contract may be contrary to English public policy.[427] Sixth, the court has to perform a balancing exercise between the finality that should prima facie exist particularly for those that agree to have their disputes arbitrated, against the policy of ensuring that the enforcement power of the English court is not abused: the nature of, and strength of the case for, the illegality, and the extent to which it can be seen that the asserted illegality was addressed by the arbitral tribunal are factors in the balancing exercise between the competing public policies of finality and illegality.[428]

Where fraud is alleged, the English court has declined to extend to arbitration the approach taken in relation to the enforcement of foreign judgments. It will normally be necessary to show either that the evidence of fraud was not available to the party alleging it at the time of the arbitration hearing; or, if perjury is alleged, that the evidence for it is so strong that it would reasonably be expected to be decisive at a hearing;[429] or, in the case of suppression of relevant evidence, that the award creditor dishonestly intended to deceive in a way that contributed substantially to obtaining an award in his favour.[430]

16–151

---

[423] *Soleimany v Soleimany* [1999] Q.B. 785, at 800 (CA); *cf. World Duty Free Co Ltd v Kenya* (2007) 46 Int. Leg. Mat. 339; and see Sayed, *Corruption in International Trade and Commercial Arbitration* (2004).

[424] See above, paras 5–003 *et seq.*; and below, paras 32R–181 *et seq.*; *Westacre Investments Inc v Jugoimport-SPDR Holding Co Ltd*, at 305.

[425] *Omnium de Traitement et de Valorisation SA v Hilmarton Ltd*, at 224; *Bad Ass Coffee Company of Hawaii Inc v Bad Ass Enterprises Inc* 2008 ABQB 404, [2009] 1 W.W.R. 289.

[426] *Westacre Investments Inc v Jugoimport-SPDR Holding Co Ltd*, at 304–305. See further Recommendation 3(a) of the ILA Committee on International Commercial Arbitration in their Final Report on Public Policy above n.419 at p.365.

[427] *Foster v Driscoll* [1929] 1 K.B. 470 (CA) and *Regazzoni v KC Sethia Ltd* [1958] A.C.301 (below, paras 32–191 *et seq.*); applied in *Soleimany v Soleimany*, at 794.

[428] *Westacre Investments Inc v Jugoimport-SPDR Holding Co Ltd*, above, at 314; applied in *R v V* [2008] EWHC 1531 (Comm.), [2009] 1 Lloyd's Rep. 97; *cf. Soleimany v Soleimany*, above, at 800.

[429] *Westacre Investments Inc v Jugoimport-SPDR Holding Co Ltd*, above, at 309. *cf.* the position with regard to foreign judgments, above, paras 14R–137 *et seq.* See also Gee (2006) 22 Arb. Int. 337.

[430] *Gater Assets Ltd v Nak Naftogaz Ukrainiy* [2008] EWHC 237 (Comm.), [2008] 1 Lloyd's Rep. 479.

16–152   For the purposes of Rule 69(2), public policy should be interpreted as including EC public policy. In *Eco Swiss China Time Ltd v Benetton International NV*[431] a dispute arising out of a licensing agreement had been referred to arbitration in the Netherlands under Dutch law. The arbitral tribunal ordered the defendant to pay damages to the plaintiff. The defendant applied to the court to have the award set aside on the ground that, because the licensing contract was a nullity under what is now Art.101, TFEU, the award was contrary to public policy. During the arbitration proceedings neither the parties nor the arbitrators had raised the point that the licensing contract might be contrary to EC law. In response to the questions posed by the Dutch court, the European Court ruled that a national court to which an application is made for annulment of an arbitral award on grounds of public policy must grant that application if it considers that the award in question is in fact contrary to Art.101. The Court also observed that the provisions of Art.101 may be regarded as a matter of public policy within the meaning of the New York Convention. Accordingly, in a case where enforcement of an arbitral award is resisted in England on the basis of public policy, if the underlying contract between the parties is contrary to Art.101 enforcement of the award should be refused.

16–153   In a case where the defendant alleges that a New York Convention award has been obtained by fraud and this allegation has been considered (and rejected) by a foreign court, the foreign judgment may be treated as creating an issue estoppel on the question of fraud.[432]

16–154   Even in cases which do not fall within clause (1)(c) or (e), recognition or enforcement of an award may be refused on the ground of public policy if it is established that the award is contrary to English requirements of substantial justice.[433] Where, however, an award has been challenged on procedural grounds before the courts of the seat of arbitration, and the challenge has been dismissed, the court must, when deciding whether or not to refuse to recognise or enforce the award on grounds of public policy, give appropriate weight to the policy of upholding New York Convention awards; normally, the English court will not re-investigate an alleged procedural defect which has been ruled on by the courts of the seat of arbitration.[434]

---

[431] Case C–126/97 [1999] E.C.R. I–3055 (discussed by de Groot (2003) 20(4) J. Int. Arb. 365; von Mehren (2003) 19 Arb. Int. 465). See also Case C–168/05 *Claro v Centro Móvil Milenium* [2006] E.C.R. I–10421 (the court's duty to annul an award rendered in breach of mandatory EU consumer protection law); *Accentuate Ltd v ASIGRA Inc* [2009] EWHC 2655 (QB), [2009] 2 Lloyd's Rep. 599. The French Cour de cassation has held that a breach of a mandatory provision of European law may constitute a ground of international public policy upon which a French court may refuse to enforce an arbitral award. But the court is entitled to limit its review to an examination of whether the arbitral tribunal considered the issue of European law. Where it did so, the court should only refuse to enforce the resulting award if the tribunal misapplied European law in a flagrant manner: *SNF v Cytec Industries BV*, Bull.Civ. I, No. 162 (French Cour de cassation, 2008).

[432] On this point, see *ABCI v Banque Franco-Tunisienne* [2002] 1 Lloyd's Rep. 511, 538–541, affirmed without reference to this point [2003] EWCA Civ 205, [2003] 2 Lloyd's Rep. 146.

[433] *Adams v Cape Industries Plc* [1990] Ch. 433 (CA) (a case concerning the enforcement of a foreign judgment at common law).

[434] *Minmetals Germany GmbH v Ferco Steel Ltd* [1999] C.L.C. 647.

ILLUSTRATIONS

1. A & Co enters into a contract, on behalf of a consortium of oil companies, with the R'as Al   **16–155**
Khaimah National Oil Company (Raknoc) for exploration for oil in R'as Al Khaimah, one of the
United Arab Emirates. The contract provides for arbitration in Geneva under the Rules of the
International Chamber of Commerce, but contains no choice of law to govern the contract. When
disputes arise, A & Co commences an arbitration. Raknoc takes no part in the proceedings. The
arbitral tribunal makes a substantial award of damages. In arriving at their award, the arbitrators
decide that the law governing the contractual relations of the parties is "internationally accepted
principles of law". The award is valid under Swiss law. Raknoc fails to comply with the award.
Some years later A & Co discovers that Raknoc has sold a quantity of oil to Shell Petroleum,
London, and that consequently Shell Petroleum owes a large sum of money to Raknoc. A & Co
is granted leave to enforce the award, and obtains an injunction restraining Raknoc from
removing outside the jurisdiction the proceeds of the debt due to it from Shell Petroleum. Raknoc
applies to set aside the leave to enforce the award, on the ground (inter alia) that it is contrary to
English public policy to enforce an award based on general principles of law. The award is held
to be enforceable, because the parties intended to create legally enforceable rights and liabilities,
and the arbitrators' choice of law was not outside the scope of the choice left to the arbitrators.
Subsequently A & Co obtains a garnishee order nisi in relation to the debt owed by Shell
Petroleum to Raknoc. But the Government of R'as al Khaimah sues Shell Petroleum in the courts
of R'as Al Khaimah for the same debt (in breach of an agreement providing for arbitration in
London), and arrests a ship belonging to an affiliated company. The garnishee order absolute is
discharged, because it would be unjust to subject Shell Petroleum to the risk of having to pay
twice.[435]

2. A, a Saudi company, enters into an arbitration agreement with X, a legal entity under the law   **16–156**
of country Y, providing for ICC arbitration in Paris. A claims that the Government of Y is a party
to the agreement. The ICC arbitral tribunal agrees and renders an award against the Government
of Y. The Government of Y resists enforcement of a New York Convention arbitration award
against it in England on the ground that it had never been a party to the arbitration agreement. The
English court is entitled to examine for itself whether there was a valid arbitration agreement
binding upon the relevant party. The law applicable to that question, in the absence of express
choice by the parties, will be the law of the country where the award was made.[436]

3. A Corp, a Chinese corporation, and X & Co, an English company, enter a contract which
provides for arbitration in China under the provisional rules of procedure of FETAC (Foreign
Trade Arbitration Commission). A dispute is referred to arbitration; the arbitration is conducted
under the auspices of FETAC's successor, CIETAC (China International Economic and Arbitration Commission) and the arbitration is conducted in accordance with CIETAC's new arbitration
rules. An award is made in A Corp's favour. X & Co has no defence to enforcement of the award
in England under clause (1)(e) of the Rule because, as a matter of construction, the parties agreed
that the arbitration would be conducted under the rules of the relevant institution (i.e. CIETAC)
at the time when arbitration was invoked; even if the defence under clause (1)(e) were established,
enforcement of the award would be ordered as the difference between FETAC's provisional rules
of procedure and CIETAC's new rules is insubstantial.[437]

4. A enters into a contract with X the purpose of which is to smuggle carpets out of Iran, which
is contrary to Iranian law. The contract provides for arbitration in Paris under Jewish law. The
arbitrator finds that such a contract is not illegal under Jewish law, and therefore enters an award
in favour of A. The award is unenforceable by the English courts. It is contrary to English public
policy to enforce an award given on the basis of a contract, the purpose of which is to violate the
laws of a foreign friendly State.[438]

5. A appoints X Ltd as a consultant in relation to the procurement of contracts in Algeria, under
a contract providing for Swiss law and arbitration in Switzerland. Under Algerian law, such a
contract is illegal. Under Swiss law it is legal, unless there is evidence of bribery or corruption.

---

[435] *Deutsche Schachtbau v Shell International Petroleum Co Ltd* [1990] 1 A.C. 295 (CA and
HL).

[436] *Dallah Real Estate and Tourism Holding Co v Ministry of Religious Affairs, Government of
Pakistan* [2010] UKSC 46, [2011] 1 A.C. 763.

[437] *China Agribusiness Development Corp v Balli Trading* [1999] 2 Lloyd's Rep. 76.

[438] *cf. Soleimany v Soleimany* [1999] Q.B. 785 (a case involving an English award).

The arbitral tribunal finds that there is no such evidence and renders an award in favour of A. The award is enforceable in England. It is not contrary to English public policy to enforce an award which is legal by its proper law and by the law of the seat, simply on the basis that its performance is illegal under the *lex loci solutionis*.[439]

C. *Intra-United Kingdom enforcement*

16R–157   **RULE 70—An arbitral award which has become enforceable in one part of the United Kingdom in the same manner as a judgment given by a court of law in that part is enforceable by registration in other parts of the United Kingdom under Schedules 6 or 7 to the Civil Jurisdiction and Judgments Act 1982.**

COMMENT

16–158   **Enforcement of awards within the United Kingdom.** This Rule stems from the definition of "judgment" in s.18(2)(e) of the Civil Jurisdiction and Judgments Act 1982. It means that an arbitral award made, e.g. in Scotland or Northern Ireland, which has become enforceable there in the same manner as a judgment given there by a court of law can be registered in England as a judgment under Sch.6 of the 1982 Act (if it orders payment of a sum or sums of money) or under Sch.7 (if it orders any relief or remedy not requiring payment of a sum of money) and then enforced accordingly. The provisions of Schs 6 and 7 have been discussed above[440] and here it is only necessary to state that the application for a certificate (which is the necessary prerequisite to registration) must be made to the court which gave the judgment or made the order by virtue of which the award has become enforceable as a judgment.[441]

16–159   Registration of a Scottish or Northern Irish judgment in England is normally the only way in which it can be enforced there. But this does not apply to arbitral awards within this Rule,[442] and accordingly such an award may be enforced in England at the option of the claimant either by registration or by the summary procedure of s.66 of the Arbitration Act 1996, where it is available.

16–160   Section 19 of the 1982 Act provides that a judgment within s.18 given in one part of the United Kingdom shall not be refused recognition in another part of the United Kingdom solely on the ground that the court which gave the judgment was not a court of competent jurisdiction according to the rules of private international law in force where it is sought to be registered. But this does not apply to arbitral awards falling within s.18(2)(e).

---

[439] *Omnium de Traitement et de Valorisation SA v Hilmarton Ltd* [1999] 2 Lloyd's Rep. 222.
[440] See above, paras 14R–258 *et seq.*
[441] Schs 6 and 7, para.2(2)(e).
[442] 1982 Act, s.18(8).

D. *Enforcement as foreign judgment*

RULE 71—(1) If a party obtains a foreign judgment by which a foreign   **16R–161**
arbitral award is made enforceable, he may enforce that judgment in
England in accordance with Rules 42, 53, 54 and 56.[443]

(2) An arbitral award made in a country outside the United Kingdom
to which Part II of the Administration of Justice Act 1920 or Part I of the
Foreign Judgments (Reciprocal Enforcement) Act 1933 applies is enforce-
able in the same manner as a judgment given by a court in that country,
provided that the award has, in pursuance of the law in force in the
country where it was made, become enforceable in the same manner as a
judgment given by a court in that country.[444]

(3) An arbitral award made in a country outside the United Kingdom
which is a party to the Geneva Convention on the International Carriage
of Goods by Road of May 19, 1956, is enforceable by registration under
the Foreign Judgments (Reciprocal Enforcement) Act 1933, if
  (a)   the award has become enforceable in that country;[445] **and**
  (b)   the clause in the contract of carriage conferring competence on the
        arbitral tribunal provided that the tribunal should apply the
        Convention.[446]

COMMENT

Enforcement of judgment on award. Clause (1) of the Rule sets forth the   **16–162**
traditional rule at common law. As stated in Rule 66, the common law does
not require the award creditor to obtain a judgment on the award. On the
contrary, the award itself may be enforced directly in England, whether or not
the law governing the arbitration proceedings requires a judgment or order of
the court to make the award enforceable. However, Rule 71(1) provides an
award creditor, who has obtained a judgment on that award from the courts of
the place where the award was made, with the additional option of enforcing
the judgment rather than the award.[447] In order to do so, the creditor must
meet the ordinary conditions for the enforcement of a foreign judgment at
common law, as provided in Rules 42, 53, 54 and 56. The courts of the seat
of the arbitration will ordinarily have jurisdiction for the purpose of enforcement of any such judgment under Rule 43 (*fourth case*), since, by submitting
to arbitration, the parties also submit to the jurisdiction of the courts of the seat
for enforcement purposes.[448]

---

[443] *East India Trading Co Inc v Carmel Exporters and Importers Ltd* [1952] 2 Q.B. 439;
International Alltex Corp v Lawler Creations Ltd [1965] I.R. 264; see also above,
para.16–109.

[444] Administration of Justice Act 1920, s.12(1); Foreign Judgments (Reciprocal Enforcement)
Act 1933, s.10A (added by Civil Jurisdiction and Judgments Act 1982, Sch.10, para.4). *cf. Brali
v Hyundai Corp* (1988) 84 A.L.R. 176.

[445] Carriage of Goods by Road Act 1965, ss.4(1), 7(1).

[446] *ibid.* Sch., Art.33.

[447] *East India Trading Co Inc v Carmel Exporters and Importers Ltd* [1952] 2 Q.B. 439, stated
below, Illustration 2; *International Alltex Corp v Lawler Creations Ltd* [1965] I.R. 264; *ED & F
Man Sugar Ltd v Lendoudis* [2007] EWHC 2268 (Comm.), [2007] 2 Lloyd's Rep. 579.

[448] *International Alltex Corp, ibid.*

16–163   *Distinction between foreign judgment and exequatur.* Clause (1) provides for the enforcement of a foreign judgment, which orders the judgment debtor to pay a sum of money in the amount of an award. It does not apply to a foreign *exequatur* (the equivalent to the English procedure under s.66 of the Arbitration Act 1996) under which the leave of the foreign court is given to execute the award as if it were a judgment.[449]

16–164   *No enforcement under Brussels I Regulation or Lugano Convention.* Clause (1) provides for enforcement of the judgment on an arbitral award at common law only. The Brussels I Regulation and the Lugano Convention each exclude (by Art.1(2)(d) of each instrument) arbitration from their scope.[450] Accordingly, not only are the recognition and enforcement of arbitral awards outside the scope of these instruments, but so also is a judgment on an award.[451]

16–165   *Effect of New York Convention.* The question that remains is the extent to which it is permissible to enforce at common law a foreign judgment on an award made in a New York Convention country.[452] As has been seen,[453] this is a controversial question. It has not been the subject of authoritative decision in England, and authority in other common law countries is divided.[454] In 2009, the German Federal Supreme Court, reversing its previous jurisprudence, decided that only the award should be enforceable, since otherwise the review standards of the New York Convention, which provide a closed list of defences to enforcement, could be subverted.[455] In almost all cases, the proper course will be direct enforcement of the New York Convention award itself. It is suggested that, save in an exceptional case, it is likely to be contrary to public policy to enforce a judgment (particularly a default judgment) on an award, where there are proven grounds to refuse enforcement of the award itself under the provisions of Art.V of the New York Convention (set out in Rule 69). However, there may exceptionally be a valid basis for proceeding to enforce the judgment, as, for example, where an action on the award would be barred by limitation in England, but an action on the judgment would not.[456]

16–166   **Enforcement of award as judgment.** As we have seen,[457] the Administration of Justice Act 1920 provides for the direct enforcement in the United Kingdom of judgments of superior courts of countries of the Commonwealth

---

[449] *ED & F Man Sugar Ltd v Lendoudis* [2007] EWHC 2268 (Comm.), [2007] 2 Lloyd's Rep. 579, at [33]; see above para.16–109.

[450] See above, paras 11–041 *et seq.*

[451] See above, para.14–206; *ABCI v Banque Franco-Tunisienne* [1996] 1 Lloyd's Rep. 495, affirmed on other aspects [1997] 1 Lloyd's Rep. 531 (CA); *cf.* Hascher (1996) 12 Arb. Int. 233.

[452] See generally Einhorn (2010) 12 Yb. P.I.L. 43.

[453] See above, para.16–132.

[454] See the cases cited *ibid* at n.358 and Roth (2007) 92 Cornell L.R. 573.

[455] (2010) 35 Ybk. Comm. Arb. 374.

[456] As in *ED & F Man Sugar Ltd v Lendoudis* [2007] EWHC 2268 (Comm.), [2007] 2 Lloyd's Rep. 579. The rules of limitation are a matter for the enforcing court and are not regulated by the New York Convention itself: *Yugraneft Corp v Rexx Management Corp* [2010] SCC 19, [2010] 1 S.C.R. 649.

[457] See Rule 53.

to which the Act has been extended by Order in Council.[458] The Act provides that any such judgment may be registered in the High Court in England, if that court thinks it is just and convenient that the judgment should be enforced in the United Kingdom;[459] and that a judgment so registered shall be of the same force and effect as if it had been a judgment of the High Court.[460] The Act defines a judgment so as to include an arbitral award if the award has, in pursuance of the law in force in the place where it was made, become enforceable in the same manner as a judgment given by a court in that place.[461] The judgment creditor remains free to bring an action on the award in accordance with Rule 66, but he may be deprived of his costs.[462]

It was the intention of Parliament that the system introduced by the **16–167** Administration of Justice Act 1920 should gradually be replaced by that introduced by the Foreign Judgments (Reciprocal Enforcement) Act 1933,[463] since it would clearly be redundant to have two different systems of registration of judgments, one for countries of the Commonwealth and one for politically foreign countries. Accordingly, no further extension of the 1920 Act to countries of the Commonwealth can now take place;[464] and the 1933 Act has been extended to India,[465] Pakistan,[466] Australia,[467] Canada,[468] Tonga,[469] Guernsey,[470] Jersey[471] and the Isle of Man.[472] It was found that the replacement of the 1920 Act by the 1933 Act was impeded by various circumstances, one of which was that in the 1920 Act the definition of judgments includes arbitral awards, while in the 1933 Act it did not. The 1933 Act was therefore amended so that it also applies to awards which are made enforceable in the same manner as a judgment by an order of the court of the country in which the award was made.[473]

To be registrable under the 1920 Act or the 1933 Act the award must have **16–168** become enforceable in the same manner as a judgment according to the law in force in the place where it was made. This requirement would appear to be satisfied if leave to enforce has been given in terms equivalent to those in s.66 of the Arbitration Act 1996.[474] It would seem that all the provisions of Pt II

---

[458] For those countries, see above, para.14R–173, n.635.
[459] Administration of Justice Act 1920, s.9(1).
[460] *ibid.*, s.9(3)(a).
[461] *ibid.* s.12(1).
[462] *ibid.* s.9(5).
[463] See above, para.14–175.
[464] Foreign Judgments (Reciprocal Enforcement) Act 1933, s.7(1); S.R.&O. 1933/1073.
[465] SI 1958/425.
[466] SI 1958/141.
[467] SI 1994/1901.
[468] SI 1987/468, as amended.
[469] SI 1980/1523.
[470] SI 1973/610.
[471] SI 1973/612.
[472] SI 1973/611.
[473] Civil Jurisdiction and Judgments Act 1982, Sch.10, para.4. which added s.10A to the 1933 Act. For an earlier extension of the 1933 Act to arbitral awards made in Commonwealth countries see Administration of Justice Act 1956, s.51(a).
[474] If the award has actually been entered as a judgment in the country where it was made, the judgment itself will be enforceable under the 1920 and 1933 Acts, since the parties would be regarded as having submitted to the jurisdiction of the foreign court: see above, Rule 67(1) and also para.16–124.

of the 1920 Act and of Pt I of the 1933 Act as to what judgments are registrable and as to the setting aside of registration[475] apply *mutatis mutandis* to arbitral awards registrable as judgments under those Acts. In addition, the English court which is asked to register the award as a judgment would no doubt require to be satisfied that the agreement to arbitrate was valid by its applicable law and that the arbitration tribunal acted within the terms of the agreement.

16–169   Where an award is enforceable by registration under the 1933 Act, it will remain enforceable at common law or under s.66 of the Arbitration Act 1996. This is because s.10A of the 1933 Act provides that s.6 of the 1933 Act, which makes registration the exclusive method of enforcement, is not to apply to the enforcement of awards under the 1933 Act.

16–170   The Carriage of Goods by Road Act 1965, which (as we have seen[476]) enacts as part of the law of the United Kingdom the provisions of the Geneva Convention on the International Carriage of Goods by Road (1956), provides in s.4(1) that Pt I of the Foreign Judgments (Reciprocal Enforcement) Act 1933[477] shall apply to any judgment given by any court or tribunal of a foreign country which is a party to the Convention[478] in proceedings arising out of carriage under the Convention, provided that the judgment has become enforceable in that country. Section 7(1) of the Act provides that any reference in the preceding provisions of the Act to a court includes a reference to an arbitral tribunal acting by virtue of Art.33 of the Convention. Art.33 provides that the contract of carriage may contain a clause conferring competence on an arbitral tribunal if the clause provides that the tribunal shall apply the Convention. It would appear, therefore, that if the above conditions are satisfied, an arbitral award is registrable as a judgment under the Foreign Judgments (Reciprocal Enforcement) Act 1933.

ILLUSTRATIONS

16–171   1. A obtains an arbitral award in New York ordering X to pay a sum of money. A obtains a judgment against X in New York to enforce the award. A can bring proceedings in England against X on the judgment.[479] *Quaere*, whether A could, had he so chosen, have sued X on the award instead of suing on the judgment.[480]

2. A, a Dutch firm, obtains an arbitral award in Holland against X, a Canadian firm. A deposits the award in the competent court at Amsterdam which, by endorsing the award, gives it executory force. No notice of these proceedings is given to X, nor is this required by Dutch law. Although notice of analogous proceedings would have been required according to the law of Ontario, the Dutch award, as endorsed by the Dutch court, can be enforced in Ontario as a foreign judgment.[481]

---

[475] See above, Rules 53 and 54.

[476] See above, para.15–025.

[477] Except s.4(2) and (3) thereof, which relate to jurisdiction: Carriage of Goods by Road Act 1965, s.4(2).

[478] SI 1967/1683, as amended by SI 1980/697, states who are parties to the Convention.

[479] *East India Trading Co Inc v Carmel Exporters and Importers Ltd* [1952] 2 Q.B. 439.

[480] See above, para.16–110 and *cf. Oppenheim & Co v Mahomed Haneef* [1922] 1 A.C. 482 (PC).

[481] *Stolp & Co v Browne & Co* [1930] 4 D.L.R. 703 (Ont).

E. *Arbitration and investment disputes*

**RULE 72—An arbitral award rendered under the auspices of the Inter-   16R–172
national Centre for the Settlement of Investment Disputes (an "ICSID
Award")[482] may be registered in the High Court, and shall thereupon, as
respects the pecuniary obligations which it imposes, be of the same force
and effect for the purposes of execution as if it had been a judgment of the
High Court.[483]**

Development of arbitration in international investment disputes.[484] The   16–173
protection of the property rights of foreign nationals has been one of the
central concerns of the law of diplomatic protection.[485] Traditionally, such
disputes, if they could not be resolved diplomatically, were the subject of
inter-State arbitration on the plane of public international law. However, the
resolution of disputes at this level has a number of serious shortcomings.
These include the frequent absence of compulsory adjudication, restrictive
rules as to nationality for the exercise of diplomatic protection,[486] and the
absence of any duty on the part of the State of nationality to espouse a
claim.[487] Commercial arbitration could also provide a forum for the resolution
of disputes involving a sovereign State, but only where the State had consented to arbitration by contract. Such consent was typically granted in the
context of concessions, and rarely extended to the many other ways in which
an investment could be made in a host State. Otherwise, a foreign investor was
left to pursue litigation, with the special difficulties which that posed against
a defendant State as regards jurisdiction and immunity.[488]

---

[482] Pursuant to the provisions of the Convention on the Settlement of Investment Disputes
between States and Nationals of other States, Washington, 1965 (575 U.N.T.S. 159) (the Washington Convention). The Convention is scheduled to the Arbitration (International Investment
Disputes) Act 1966. See Schreuer, Malintoppi, Reinisch and Sinclair, *The ICSID Convention: A
Commentary* (2nd ed. 2009); Reed, Paulsson and Blackaby, *Guide to ICSID Arbitration* (2nd ed.
2010). Arbitral awards and decisions rendered by ICSID tribunals are reported in the *ICSID
Reports* (ICSID Rep.) Awards may also be accessed in unreported form at: *http://italaw.com/*.

[483] Arbitration (International Investment Disputes) Act 1966, ss.1 and 2. Such an award is not
subject to challenge or appeal to the High Court: 1966 Act, s.3(2) (excluding the operation of the
1996 Act); Washington Convention, Art.53.

[484] See generally Bishop, Crawford and Reisman, *Foreign Investment Disputes* (2005).
McLachlan, Shore and Weiniger, *International Investment Arbitration: Substantive Principles*
(2007); Muchlinski, Ortino and Schreuer, *The Oxford Handbook of International Investment Law*
(2008); Newcombe and Paradell, *Law and Practice of Investment Treaties: Standards of Treatment* (2009); Dolzer and Schreuer, *Principles of International Investment Law* (2008); Douglas,
The International Law of Investment Claims (2009).

[485] Oppenheim, *International Law* (9th ed. Jennings and Watts, 1992), Vol.1, ss.403–411.
International Law Commission, *Diplomatic Protection: Text of the Draft Articles with Commentaries thereto* (2006) Supp. No.10, UN Doc. A/61/10, 22–100.

[486] *Case concerning the Barcelona Traction, Light and Power Co Ltd (Belgium v Spain)* 1970
I.C.J. Rep. 3, on which see *Occidental Exploration & Production Co v Republic of Ecuador*
[2005] EWCA Civ 1116, [2005] 2 Lloyd's Rep. 707, at [20] *et seq.* See also: *Ahmadou Sadio
Diallo (Republic of Guinea v Democratic Republic of Congo)* 2007 I.C.J. Rep. 582 (Preliminary
Objections); (2011) 50 I.L.M. 37 (Merits).

[487] Oppenheim, above, n.485, s.410.

[488] See Ch.10.

16–174   Two developments have increased considerably the practical ability of foreign investors to seek to vindicate claims against a sovereign State through arbitration. The first is the conclusion in 1965, under the auspices of the World Bank, of the Washington Convention on the Settlement of Disputes between Contracting States and Nationals of other Contracting States.[489] This Convention created the International Centre for the Settlement of Investment Disputes (ICSID), an arbitral institution with its own set of rules and procedures, specifically designed for arbitrations between foreign nationals and sovereign States. The success of the Convention, which has been ratified by more than 140 States, is in part attributable to two factors, which also constitute limitations on its scope. First, the Convention creates only a dedicated set of procedures for investment arbitration. It does not attempt to codify substantive rules of international investment law, on which it has proved impossible to achieve multilateral agreement.[490] Second, the jurisdiction is limited to hearing those cases in which both parties have given their consent in writing to the exercise of jurisdiction.[491]

16–175   **Bilateral investment treaties.** Each of these limitations has now been significantly addressed by the enormous growth in the conclusion of bilateral investment treaties ("BITs").[492] The United Kingdom is one of the States which has been particularly active in this field.[493] Although the bilateral nature of such treaties gives rise to wide diversity, the typical outline of such treaties is broadly constant. Indeed many States, including the United Kingdom, have published a preferred model form BIT.[494] These treaties generally include guarantees of national treatment, most favoured nation treatment, fair and equitable treatment, and protection against expropriation without compensation.[495] They also typically provide for a direct right of recourse by the investor who is a national of one Contracting State against the other Contracting State. Such a right may be exercised through arbitration. The treaty may simply provide for ICSID arbitration alone, or it may grant the investor the right to choose from a set of dispute resolution options, which include litigation in the courts of the host State, as well as a variety of international arbitration options. ICSID arbitral tribunals have held that, where a State

---

[489] See the references above at n.482.

[490] See generally Muchlinski, *Multinational Enterprises and the Law* (2nd ed. 2007); Lowenfeld, *International Economic Law* (2nd ed. 2008), Pt VI; Sornarajah, *International Law on Foreign Investment* (3rd ed. 2010).

[491] Art.25.

[492] See generally the works cited above at n.484; Vandevelde, *Bilateral Investment Treaties: History, Policy and Interpretation* (2010). More than 2,800 BITs have been concluded. For details see *Investment Instruments Online*: *http://www. unctadxi.org/templates/DocSearch____779.aspx*. For discussion see *Occidental Exploration & Production Co v Republic of Ecuador* [2005] EWCA Civ 1116, [2005] 2 Lloyd's Rep. 707, at [14] *et seq.*

[493] Details of bilateral investment treaties (referred to in UK practice as Investment Promotion and Protection Agreements or "IPPAs") currently in force between the UK and other countries, together with copies of the agreements may be accessed at: *http://www.fco.gov.uk/en/publications-and-documents/treaties/treaty-texts/ippas-investment-promotion/*.

[494] The UK model form is reprinted in UNCTAD, *International Investment Instruments* (Vol.3, 1996) at p.185, and McLachlan, Shore and Weiniger, App.4.

[495] See the works cited above at nn.484 and 490.

agrees to ICSID arbitration by a bilateral treaty, that is sufficient to constitute the State's consent in writing for the purpose of the conditions for invoking the jurisdiction of the Centre.[496] Thus, it has been possible for foreign investors to bring disputes for the vindication of treaty rights before ICSID. This development accounts for the considerable growth in the case-load of the Centre in recent years.

Nevertheless, the future of BITs entered into by Member States of the **16–176** European Union has been called into question by two important developments in Europe. First, the European Court was called upon to consider the compatibility of BITs with Member States' obligations under European law in three cases decided in 2009.[497] Prior to their accession to the European Union, the Respondent States had entered into BITs with third states, containing free transfer of capital provisions. The European Court held that these provisions were incompatible with the powers of the European Council to impose restrictions on the free transfer of capital. Accordingly the Respondent States were in breach of the obligations which they had assumed under EC Treaty, Art.307, to take all appropriate steps to eliminate incompatibilities with Community law found in agreements with third states entered into prior to accession to the Union. Second, under Art.207 of the TFEU, the Member States transferred to the Union competence in investment matters. On July 7, 2010, the European Commission issued a Communication and a Proposal for a Regulation as to implementation of Art.207.[498] The proposed Regulation would, during a transitional period of five years, authorise Member States to maintain existing BITs in force, provided that they have been notified to the Commission. But it would give the Commission the power to decide whether to authorise negotiation and conclusion of future BITs in light of their compatibility with European law. In its policy statement, the Commission proposes that the European Union should negotiate investment agreements directly with third states. The statement endorses investor-state arbitration as a means of dispute settlement and supports EU accession to the ICSID Convention (noting that this would require an amendment to the 1CSID Convention).

ICSID arbitration. ICSID arbitrations have two characteristics which **16–177** distinguish them from international commercial arbitration *simpliciter*, and which arise from their mixed or hybrid nature. The first is the law applicable

---

[496] See, e.g. *Goetz v Burundi* (1996), 6 ICSID Rep. 3, at 25; *American Manufacturing & Trading Inc v Zaire* (1997), 5 ICSID Rep. 11, at 25–26; *Ceskoslovenska Obchodni Banka AS v Slovakia*, Decision on Objections to Jurisdiction (1999), 5 ICSID Rep. 330, at 344; *Olguin v Paraguay*, Decision on Jurisdiction (2000), 6 ICSID Rep. 154, at 161–162.

[497] Case C–205/06 *Commission of the European Communities v Republic of Austria* [2009] E.C.R. I–1301; Case C–249/06 *Commission of the European Communities v Kingdom of Sweden* [2009] E.C.R. I–1335; Case C–118/07 *Commission of the European Communities v Republic of Finland* [2009] E.C.R. I–10889.

[498] European Commission, *Towards a comprehensive European international investment policy*, COM (2010) 343; *Proposal for a Regulation of the European Parliament and of the Council establishing transitional arrangements for bilateral investment agreements between Member States and third countries*, COM (2010) 344.

to the substance of the dispute. The second is the limit on the role of national courts in the arbitral procedure.

16–178   *Applicable law.*[499] Outside the context of ICSID, the mere fact that one of the parties to an arbitration agreement is a State does not of itself affect the ordinary operation of the rules of the conflict of laws which determine the law applicable to the substance of the dispute.[500] Thus, the parties are at liberty to choose to govern their contract: the law of the State involved;[501] or the law of the State of which the private party is a national; or the law of an unconnected third State; or public international law or a hybrid set of rules.[502] If no express choice is made, the arbitral tribunal must proceed to determine the applicable law by the same process as is applicable to a private contract. However, the content of the applicable law may be affected by the fact that one of the parties to the contract is a State. First, the parties may by contract agree to circumscribe the operation of the applicable national law, either by including a stabilisation clause providing that the law chosen is that in force at the date of entry into force of the agreement;[503] or by agreeing to subject their contract to a given national legal system to be supplemented by international law;[504] or by choosing a combination of host State law in force at the date of the agreement and international law.[505]

16–179   Article 42 of the Washington Convention provides:

> "(1) The Tribunal shall decide a dispute in accordance with such rules of law as may be agreed between the parties. In the absence of such agreement, the Tribunal shall apply the law of the Contracting State party to the dispute (including its rules on the conflict of laws) and such rules of international law as may be applicable.
>
> (2) The tribunal may not bring a finding of *non liquet* on the ground of silence or obscurity of the law.
>
> (3) The provisions of paragraphs (1) and (2) shall not prejudice the power of the Tribunal to decide a dispute *ex aequo et bono* if the parties so agree."

---

[499] On applicable law in investment arbitration see generally Douglas, *The International Law of Investment Claims* (2009) Ch.2; McLachlan (2009) 14 ICCA Congress Series 95.

[500] See, below, para.32–044; See generally Brownlie, *Principles of Public International Law* (7th ed., 2008) pp 546 *et seq.*; F.A. Mann (1960) 54 A.J.I.L. 572, reprinted in *Studies in International Law* (1973), p.302, at pp.313–4. See also Begic, *Applicable Law in International Investment Disputes* (2005).

[501] For a recent example of a choice of host State law see *Lesotho Highlands Development Authority v Impregilo SpA* [2005] UKHL 43, [2006] 1 A.C. 121.

[502] For recent examples of hybrid choices of law to govern State contracts see *Svenska Petroleum Exploration AB v Lithuania (No.2)* [2006] EWCA Civ 1529, [2007] Q.B. 886 and *cf.* also *Channel Tunnel Group Ltd v Secretary of State for Transport of the United Kingdom of Great Britain and Northern Ireland* (2007) 132 I.L.R. 1.

[503] See Schreuer, para.42.117 *et seq.*; Delaume (1997)12 ICSID Rev.-FILJ 1; Hansen (1988) 28 Virg. J.I.L. 1015; and *cf. AGIP SpA v Congo* (1979) 1 ICSID Rep. 306, at 324; *LETCO v Liberia* (1986), 2 ICSID Rep. 343, 368; and other arbitral awards referred to below, para.32–051.

[504] See e.g. *AGIP SpA v Congo*, above, at 313.

[505] As in *Kaiser Bauxite Co v Jamaica*, Decision on Jurisdiction (1975), 1 ICSID Rep. 296, at 301.

Article 42 respects party autonomy by permitting the parties the freedom to **16–180** choose[506] the rules of law applicable to the substance. If the parties exercise such a choice, the tribunal is bound to respect it, and to apply the chosen rules. Further, the parties may agree that the tribunal can decide the dispute *ex aequo et bono*. Failure to apply the rules or law chosen by the parties,[507] or, in the absence of choice, to apply the default provisions of Art.42(1)[508] may constitute an excess of the tribunal's powers, providing grounds for annulment of the award.[509] Where the claim is brought pursuant to the provisions of a BIT (or a multilateral convention which provides for ICSID arbitration), the rules of law chosen by the parties for the purpose of Art.42 in order to determine liability for the claim will be those stipulated in the treaty under international law.[510]

If no choice has been made, however, Art.42(1) provides its own choice of **16–181** law rule, requiring the application of host State law "(*including* its rules on the conflict of laws) *and* such rules of international law as may be applicable."[511] This provision does not leave the ICSID tribunal with liberty to choose the applicable set of conflict of laws rules. It requires the tribunal to apply the law of the host State and includes a *renvoi* provision should the conflict of laws

---

[506] See Schreuer, para.42.21 *et seq.* and Begic, *op. cit.* above, at pp.57 *et seq.* for the question whether implied choice is sufficient. *cf. LETCO v Liberia* (1986), 2 ICSID Rep. 343, 358–359. The choice may be a choice of international law. On the application of Art.42 in investment treaty claims see further: Douglas, *op. cit.* n.484, Rule 14; McLachlan (2009) 14 ICCA Congress Series 95.

[507] *Maritime International Nominees Establishment v Guinea*, Decision on Annulment (1989) 4 ICSID Rep. 79, at 87; *Wena Hotels Ltd v Egypt*, Decision on Annulment (2002), 6 ICSID Rep. 129, at 135.

[508] *Klöckner Industrie-Anlagen GmbH v Cameroon*, Decision on Annulment (1985), 2 ICSID Rep. 95, at 118 *et seq.*; *Amco Asia Corp v Indonesia*, Decision on Annulment (1986), 1 ICSID Rep. 509, at 515. See also *Amco Asia Corp v Indonesia*, Decision on Annulment and Partial Annulment (1992), 9 ICSID Rep. 3, at 39.

[509] Under Art.52(1)(b), below, para.16–189.

[510] On the relationship between the obligations in the treaty and those of general international law in the context of a defence of necessity see: *CMS Gas Transmission Co v Argentine Republic*, Decision on Annulment (2007), 14 ICSID Rep. 251; *LG&E Energy Corp v Argentina* (2006) 18 World Trade & Arb. Mat. 199; *Continental Casualty Co v Argentina* (ICSID Case No. ARB/03/9, September 5, 2008) but *cf. Enron Corp v Argentine Republic* (ICSID Case No.ARB/01/3, May 22, 2007); *Sempra Energy International v Argentine Republic* (2008) 20 World Trade & Arb. Mat. 117. On the relationship between investment treaties and general international law in investment treaty arbitration see McLachlan (2008) 57 I.C.L.Q. 361; Alvarez (2009) 42 N.Y.U. J.Int. L.& Pol. 17. For an example of a provision in a BIT for the application of the principles of international law, see *Occidental Exploration & Production Co v Republic of Ecuador* [2005] EWCA Civ 1116, [2006] 1 W.L.R. 70, at [6]. So also major multilateral treaties provide for ICSID arbitration in accordance with international law: e.g. the North American Free Trade Agreement, Art.1131, in (1993) 32 Int.Leg.Mat. 605; and the Energy Charter Treaty, Art.26(6), in (1995) 34 Int.Leg.Mat. 381. For proceedings involving the latter see *Plama Consortium Ltd v Bulgaria*, Decision on Jurisdiction (2005) 20 ICSID Rev.-FILJ 262 and *Yukos Universal Ltd (Isle of Man) v Russian Federation* (Interim Award on Jurisdiction and Admissibility, PCA, November 30, 2009, (2010) 22 World Trade & Arb. Mat. 279). In the latter decision (following *Kardassopoulos v Georgia*, Decision on Jurisdiction (ICSID Case No.ARB/05/18, July 6, 2007)), the Tribunal applied Energy Charter Treaty ("ECT"), Art.45, so as to find that it had jurisdiction over the Russian Federation in respect of a dispute which had arisen during the period within which the ECT was provisionally applied in Russia and before Russia had formally notified its intention not to ratify the ECT.

[511] Emphasis added.

rules of the host State indicate that the law of another State is more appropriate.[512] The reference to international law is intended to be a reference to all of the sources of international law referred to in Art.38 of the Statute of the International Court of Justice.[513] Varying formulations of the role of international law have been adopted by ICSID tribunals, but the predominant trend is for international law to be relied upon in a supplementary or complementary manner to fill gaps, or in a corrective manner where the law of the host State does not conform with international law.[514] It has been decided that the law of the host State can be applied in conjunction with international law if this is justified, and that international law can be applied by itself if the appropriate rule of decision is to be found in international law.[515] International law may also be applied if the law of the host State is chosen and that law incorporates international law and makes it directly applicable.[516]

16–182   When the national of one State invokes the jurisdiction of ICSID on the basis of the reference to arbitration contained in a BIT, the claim must be founded upon breach of a right protected by the BIT, and not otherwise.[517] The fact that the contract between the investor and the host State contains a choice of the law of the host State, or a submission to the jurisdiction of its courts, will not prevent a claim in international law under the BIT.[518]

16–183   *Umbrella clause.* The distinction between a BIT claim and a contract claim may be affected by a clause (found in a number of BITs) pursuant to which the host State agrees to observe any undertakings which it has entered into with

---

[512] See Schreuer, at paras 42.138–42.142; Shihata and Parra (1994) 9 ICSID Rev.-FILJ 183.

[513] Report of the Executive Directors (March 18, 1965), para.40, 1 ICSID Rep. 23, at 31.

[514] *Klöckner Industrie-Anlagen GmbH v Cameroon*, above, at 122. See also *Amco Asia Corp v Indonesia*, Decision on Annulment (1986), 1 ICSID Rep. 509, at 515; Second Award (1990), *ibid.* 569 at 580; *LETCO v Liberia* (1986), 2 ICSID Rep. 343, 358–359. See also *CME Czech Republic BV v Czech Republic*, Partial Award (2001), 9 ICSID Rep.113, at 348–352.

[515] See *Wena Hotels Ltd v Egypt*, Decision on Annulment (2002), 6 ICSID Rep. 129, at 138; *CMS Gas Transmission Co v Argentina* (2005), in (2005) 14 ICSID Rep. 158, at paras 115–118 (partially annulled (2007) 14 ICSID Rep. 251, but not on this point).

[516] *Goetz v Burundi* (1996), 6 ICSID Rep. 3, at 33–34 (BIT provided for application by tribunal of host State law (including its rules of the conflict of laws), the provisions of the BIT, the agreement between the investor and the State, and "the generally admitted principles of international law").

[517] *Compañia de Aguas del Aconquija SA and Vivendi Universal SA v Argentina*, Decision on Annulment (2002), 6 ICSID Rep. 340, at 365–366; *Salini Costruttori SpA v Morocco*, Decision on Jurisdiction (2001), 6 ICSID Rep. 398, at 415; *SGS Soc Gen de Surveillance SA v Pakistan*, Decision on Objections to Jurisdiction (2003), 8 ICSID Rep. 384, at 436–441; *Joy Mining Machinery Ltd v Egypt* (2004), 19 ICSID Rev.-FILJ 486, at 505 *et seq*. See also *Wena Hotels Ltd v Egypt*, Decision on Annulment (2002), 6 ICSID Rep. 129, at 137–138, applied in *CMS Gas Transmission Co v Argentina* (2005), in (2005) 14 ICSID Rep. 158, at paras 115–118 (partially annulled (2007) 14 ICSID Rep. 251, but not on this point); *Impregilo SpA v Pakistan* (2005), in (2005) 12 ICSID Rep. 245, at 296; *Azurix Corp v Argentina*, Decision on Annulment (ICSID Case No.ARB/01/12, September 1, 2009), [146]–[147].

[518] *Compañia de Aguas del Aconquija SA and Vivendi Universal SA v Argentina*, Decision on Annulment (2002), 6 ICSID Rep. 340, at 367; *Salini Costruttori SpA v Morocco*, Decision on Jurisdiction (2001), 6 ICSID Rep. 398, at 415; *Joy Mining Machinery Ltd v Egypt*, above, at 510 *et seq.*; *cf. SGS Soc Gen de Surveillance SA v Pakistan*, Decision on Objections to Jurisdiction (2003), 8 ICSID Rep. 384, at 439. But contrast *SGS Soc Gen de Surveillance SA v Philippines* (2004), 8 ICSID Rep. 515, at 556–561.

regard to investments (sometimes referred to as an "umbrella clause"). The proper construction of such a clause is a controversial question. Subject to the specific wording of the clause, the following general observations may be advanced. First, such a clause is generally effective to confer jurisdiction upon the investment arbitral tribunal in relation to contractual claims.[519] Second, however, where the parties have by contract chosen a specific forum to resolve their contractual dispute (for example, the courts of the host State), the arbitral tribunal should ordinarily hold the parties to that part of their contractual bargain as *lex specialis* and stay its proceedings pending a determination of the contractual dispute in the parties' chosen forum.[520] Third, nevertheless, if the State has, in the exercise of its sovereign authority (*jure imperii*), subsequently altered fundamentally the nature of the contractual bargain, such conduct could constitute a free-standing claim in international law under the umbrella clause, irrespective of any contractual submission clause. Fourth, an umbrella clause which protects "any obligations it may have entered into with regard to investments" protects specific consensual obligations arising independently of the BIT itself. It does not cover general requirements of host state law. Fifth, such a clause does not change the proper law of the contract or the content of the obligation in question, nor confer benefits on persons other than the parties to that obligation.[521]

Arbitration procedure. The second respect in which ICSID arbitration may be distinguished from other forms of arbitration involving States is in the self-contained nature of the arbitration procedure. Where the arbitration takes place pursuant to the provisions of the Washington Convention itself, the arbitral procedure is, to the greatest possible extent, self-contained and insulated from intervention by national courts. This is to be contrasted with the position of arbitrations conducted outside the ICSID framework pursuant to BITs,[522] and also with the position where an arbitral tribunal is constituted pursuant to ICSID's Additional Facility for those States which are not parties to the Washington Convention.[523]   **16–184**

The *lex arbitri* of an ICSID arbitration is exclusively the Washington Convention and the ICSID Arbitration Rules (which are themselves subject to   **16–185**

---

[519] *Siemens AG v Argentina* (2007), 14 ICSID Rep. 518, at para.204.

[520] SGS *Soc Gen de Surveillance SA v Philippines* (2004) 8 ICSID Rep. 515, at pp.557–558.

[521] *CMS Gas Transmission Co v Argentine Republic*, Decision on Annulment (2007), 14 ICSID Rep. 251, at [95]. See further: McLachlan, Shore and Weiniger, Ch.4, especially at paras 4.93–4.116; Crawford (2008) 24 Arb. Int. 351.

[522] See *Occidental Exploration & Production Co v Republic of Ecuador* [2005] EWCA Civ 1116, [2006] 1 W.L.R. 70, below, para.16–187.

[523] This includes claims submitted to ICSID under the North American Free Trade Agreement, as Mexico and Canada are not parties to the Washington Convention. For examples of applications for judicial review of ICSID Additional Facility awards in Canadian courts see *United Mexican States v Metalclad Corp*, British Columbia (2001), 5 ICSID Rep. 236, and *United Mexican States v Karpa* (2005) 248 D.L.R. (4th) 443 (Ont CA). For an example of the enforcement of an ICSID Additional Facility award under NAFTA in the United States see *International Thunderbird Gaming Corp v United Mexican States,* 473 F. Supp. 2d 80 (D.D.C. 2007).

international law) and not the law of the seat of the arbitration.[524] The
Convention provides its own internal annulment procedure.[525] It excludes the
right of recourse to domestic courts.[526] Provisional measures may be sought
only from the ICSID tribunal itself, and not from national courts, unless the
parties agree otherwise.[527]

16–186   Thus, ICSID arbitrations may only be the subject of proceedings in the
English court, if it proves necessary to stay court proceedings brought in
breach of an agreement to arbitrate, or where the assistance of the court is
sought to enforce the award. ICSID awards are the subject of the Arbitration
(International Investment Disputes) Act 1966 ("the 1966 Act"). This Act was
not replaced by the Arbitration Act 1996 (although the later Act did make
some consequential amendments to it). It is the enforcement obligation under
the 1966 Act which is the subject of Rule 72.

16–187   **Investment arbitration outside ICSID.** Where, however, the investment
arbitration does not take place under the aegis of ICSID, the provisions of the
1966 Act will not apply. In *Occidental Exploration & Production Co v
Republic of Ecuador*[528] the arbitration was founded upon a BIT between
Ecuador and the United States. The Treaty provided for several dispute
resolution options. The option selected by Occidental was ad hoc arbitration
under UNCITRAL Arbitration Rules. The Treaty expressly provided that the
Contracting States gave their consent to submit any dispute to arbitration, and
that such consent should, together with the consent of the investor satisfy the
requirement of an "agreement in writing" for the purpose of the New York

---

[524] Washington Convention Arts 26, 44 and 53; Schreuer, p.672 *et seq.*; Broches (1987) 2
ICSID Rev.- FILJ 287, 288; *Fraport AG Frankfurt Airport Services Worldwide v Philippines*,
Decision of *ad hoc* Annulment Committee on Application for Disqualification of Counsel (2009)
24 ICSID Rev-FILJ 216, at [36]. The revised Arbitration Rules, effective April 10, 2006, are
available at: *http://icsid.worldbank.org/ICSID/StaticFiles/basicdoc/CRR_English-final.pdf.*

[525] Art.52. See below, para.16–188.

[526] Art.53.

[527] Washington Convention, Art.47 and ICSID Arbitration Rule 39(6). See *ETI Euro Telecom
International NV v Republic of Bolivia* [2008] EWCA Civ 880, [2009] 1 W.L.R. 665, at [108], and
Amco Asia Corp v Indonesia, Decision on Provisional Measures (1983), 1 ICSID Rep. 376, at
410; *Maritime International Nominees Establishment v Guinea* (1988), 4 ICSID Rep. 54, at 69;
Tanzania Electric Supply Co Ltd v Independent Power Tanzania Ltd, Decision on Request for
Provisional Measures (1999), 8 ICSID Rep. 220, at 239–242; and Lalive (1980) 51 B.Y.I.L. 123
(on the *Holiday Inns v Morocco* proceedings). *cf. SGS Soc Gen de Surveillance SA v Pakistan*,
Procedural Order No.2 (2002), 8 ICSID Rep. 384, at 388, on which see Kerameus, in Gaillard
(ed.), *Anti-Suit Injunctions in International Arbitration* (2005), p.131. On resort to national courts
without agreement and the practice prior to the change in Rule 39 in 1984 see *Atlantic Triton Co
v Guinea* (1987) 12 Yb. Comm. Arb. 184 (French Cr. de cass., November 18, 1986) and Collins,
Essays, pp.73–79; Fouchard, Gaillard, Goldman, para.1309.

[528] [2005] EWCA Civ 1116, [2006] 1 W.L.R. 70. *cf. Dallal v Bank Mellat* [1986] 1 Q.B. 441:
Hobhouse J. was invited to recognise an award rendered by the Iran/US Claims Tribunal, so as
to strike out an attempt at re-litigation of the same issue before the English court. He held that the
award could not be recognised under the New York Convention. The jurisdiction of the arbitral
tribunal was not founded upon an agreement between the parties. It derived from the mandatory
provisions of a treaty, the Algiers Accords, between the United States and Iran, which had
established the Iran/US Claims Tribunal (with its seat in The Hague) and removed private
disputes within its remit from the jurisdiction of the national courts of either State. He nevertheless found that the court should recognise and give effect to the award, the competence of the
tribunal being derived from international law.

Convention.[529] The seat of the arbitration was London. The losing party, the Republic of Ecuador, applied to the English court to set the arbitral award for want of jurisdiction under s.67 of the 1996 Act. Occidental, the successful party in the arbitration, argued that the proceedings were non-justiciable because the arbitration proceedings were held under the provisions of an international treaty. The Court of Appeal held that the proceedings were not precluded by the principles of non-justiciablity.[530] The 1996 Act applied to the award, and the proceedings to set aside the award were justiciable in the English courts. The Treaty conferred direct rights in international law in favour of investors.[531] English rules of the conflict of laws would recognise an arbitration agreement concluded under public international law, and would also recognise the validity of a choice of public international law to govern the substance of the dispute.[532] The court should therefore give effect to the intention of the Contracting States to create a binding and enforceable arbitration agreement between the State and a foreign investor.[533] The result of this decision is that where the seat of the arbitral tribunal is in England, the fact that the tribunal is dealing with an investment dispute under the provisions of a treaty will not insulate it from the provisions of the 1996 Act relating to the supervisory jurisdiction of the English court. An application for a stay of court proceedings on the grounds of submission to non-ICSID arbitration under a BIT will therefore fall to be dealt with under s.9 of the 1996 Act.[534] Once an award has been rendered, the court hearing a challenge to the jurisdiction of the arbitral tribunal under s.67 of the 1996 Act will determine whether the arbitral tribunal was correct in its decision on jurisdiction, not whether it was entitled to reach the decision that it did.[535]

Enforcement of ICSID awards. The position is different as regards ICSID   **16–188**
awards, as a result of the special provisions of the Washington Convention, the effect of which in England is reflected in Rule 72. Article 53(1) of the Convention provides that: "The award shall be binding on the parties and shall not be subject to an appeal or to any other remedy except those provided for in this Convention. Each party shall abide by and comply with the terms

---

[529] Art.VI.4(b) of the Treaty.

[530] See above, para.5–052.

[531] *ibid.*, at [18].

[532] *ibid.*, at [33], approving a passage to this effect in a previous edition of this work.

[533] *ibid.*, [32], [37], [40].

[534] *City of London v Sancheti* [2008] EWCA Civ 1283, [2009] 1 Lloyd's Rep. 117 (where the stay application failed because the parties to the English litigation and the BIT claim were not the same).

[535] *Republic of Ecuador v Occidental Exploration & Production Co (No.2)* [2007] EWCA Civ 656, [2007] 2 Lloyd's Rep. 352; followed *Czech Republic v European Media Ventures SA* [2007] EWHC 2851 (Comm.), [2008] 1 Lloyd's Rep. 186. The same approach applies in France: *République tchèque v Nreka* (CA, Paris, September 25, 2008) [2009] Rev. arb. 337, 339, note Fadlallah. In the United States, the Court will review such an award for excess of powers, applying the test in *Stolt-Nielsen SA v Animal Feeds International Corp,* 130 S. Ct. 1758 (2010) namely whether the "arbitrator stray[ed] from interpretation and application of the agreement and effectively dispense[d] his own brand of industrial justice": *Republic of Argentina v BG Group Plc* 715 F. Supp. 2d 108 (DDC 2010); award upheld 764 F. Supp. 2d 21 (D.D.C. 2011). See also *Argentine Republic v National Grid Plc* 637 F. 3d 365 (D.C. Cir. 2011). For a comparison of national court review of non-ICSID BIT awards with annulment under the ICSID Convention see Verhoosel (2009) 14 ICCA Congress Series 285.

of the award except to the extent that enforcement shall have been stayed pursuant to the relevant provisions of this Convention." Article 54(1) provides that each Contracting State shall recognise an ICSID award as binding and enforce the pecuniary obligations imposed by the award as if it were a final judgment of a court in that State.

16–189   These articles take ICSID awards outside the normal regime for the enforcement of arbitral awards, including the New York Convention regime, which enables recognition to be refused by national courts on specified grounds. Instead, the Washington Convention contains its own internal procedures for the interpretation, revision and annulment of awards. In particular, an award may only be annulled on the grounds[536]: "(a) that the Tribunal was not properly constituted; (b) that the Tribunal has manifestly exceeded its powers; (c) that there was corruption on the part of a member of the Tribunal; (d) that there has been a serious departure from a fundamental rule of procedure; or (e) that the award has failed to state the reasons on which it is based." A request for annulment is dealt with by an ad hoc Committee. If the award is annulled, the dispute is, at the request of either party, to be submitted to a new Tribunal.[537] Unless an ICSID award is annulled pursuant to this procedure, the courts of Contracting States are bound to recognise it and enforce it in accordance with Art.54(1), to which effect is given in England by ss.1 and 2 of the 1966 Act.[538] The Convention does not, however, affect the law in relation to state immunity from execution.[539] Thus, the question of the property in respect of which an ICSID award may be enforced must be determined by the law on immunity from execution.[540]

---

[536] Art.52(1). See annulment decisions cited in nn.507, 508, and 517; *MTD Equity Sdn. Bhd. v Chile*, Decision on Annulment (2007) 13 ICSID Rep. 500; *Rumeli Telekom A/S v Kazakhstan*, Decision on Annulment, ICSID Case No. ARB/05/16 (March 25,2010); *Fraport AG Frankfurt Airport Services Worldwide v The Philippines*, Decision on Annulment, ICSID Case No. ARB/03/25 (December 23, 2010); Gaillard and Banifatemi (eds.), *Annulment of ICSID Awards* (2004).

[537] Art.52(6), and see Schreuer, pp.1083 *et seq.*

[538] The relevant procedural rules are in CPR, r.62.21. On the enforcement of ICSID awards see: Baldwin, Kantor and Nolan (2006) 23 J. Int. Arb. 1; Verhoosel (2009) ICCA Congress Series No.14, 285.

[539] Art.55. See *AIG Capital Partners Inc v Republic of Kazakhstan* [2005] EWHC 2239 (Comm.), [2006] 1 All E.R. 284.

[540] See paras 10–014—10–015, above.

INDEX

Abduction
  see **International child abduction**
Access
  see **Contact**
Acquiescence
  international child abduction,
    19–133—19–135
Act of state
  exclusion of foreign law
    examples, 5–051—5–053, 5–057
    generally, 5–043
    meaning, 5–044—5–046
    scope, 5–048—5–049n
    use of, 5–047
    validity of foreign law, 5–050
  property
    ability to be recognised by English
      court, 25–004
    compensation for seizure of property,
      25–010—25–011
    examples, 25–015—25–016
    extra-territorial property,
      25–006—25–008
    generally, 25–002
    intention of government, 25–004
    interim governments, 25–005
    location of property, 25–004
    mergers of companies, 25–013
    nationalisation, 25–014
    public policy, 25–009
    recognition of transfer of title by state,
      25–012
    rule, 25R–001
    scope of rule, 25–003
  Rome II Regulation, 34–015
Acts of Parliament
  general choice of law clauses,
    1–047—1–048
  interpretation of statutes implementing
    international conventions
    generally, 1–028—1–029
    language, 1–032—1–033
    modern approach, 1–035
    purpose, 1–030
    travaux preparatoires, 1–034
    wording of Convention, 1–031
  introduction, 1–036
  no indication of application,
    1–037—1–041
  overriding statutes, 1–053—1–062
  particular choice of law clauses,
    1–042—1–046

Acts of Parliament—*cont.*
  self-denying statutes, 1–063—1–064
  self-limiting statutes, 1–049—1–052
Administration
  see **Insolvency proceedings**
Administration of estates
  see also **Succession; Wills**
  choice of law
    examples, 26–035
    generally, 26–031—26–034
    rule, 26R–030
  claims *in personam*, 11R–232
  foreign personal representatives
    effect of appointment,
      26R–036—26–041
    liability in England, 26R–042—26–046
  foreign property
    real property, 23–042—23–051,
      23–058—23–059
  grants of representation
    Colonial Probates Act 1892, 26R–019,
      26–021
    consular grants, 26–016—26–017
    effect of, 26R–022—26–029
    EU law proposal, 26–006
    examples, 26–007
    foreign domiciles, 26R–008—26–018
    history, 26–002—26–004
    Northern Ireland domicile,
      26R–019—26–020
    recovery of property, 26R–026—26–029
    rule, 26R–001
    Scottish domicile, 26R–019 —26–020
    separate wills, 26–005
    vesting of property, 26R–022—26–025
Administration of Justice Act 1920
  recognition and enforcement of foreign
    judgments, 14R–173—14–182
Administrative receivers
  insolvency proceedings, 30–139—30–141
Administrators
  insolvency proceedings, 30–142—30–146
Admiralty claims
  see also **Claims *in personam***
  claims *in rem*
    admiralty jurisdiction, 13–004—13–005
    Brussels I Regulation, 13–022—13–023
    conventions on particular matters,
      13–026—13–035
    defendant, meaning of, 13–034
    examples, 13–037—13–038
    introduction, 13–002—13–003

I

Index

Index

Personal representatives
see also **Administration of estates**
foreign personal representatives
effect of appointment,
26R–036—26–041
liability in England, 26R–042—26–046
Place of performance
claims *in personam*, 11R–260—11–283
Pledges
moveable property, 33R–001, 33–013
Polygamy
divorce, 18–018—18–020
judicial separation, 18–018—18–020
Powers of attorney
choice of law
mental capacity, 21–020
Prescription
choice of law
real property, 23–075, 23–079
contracts, 32–156—32–161, 32–167
Rome II Regulation, 34–064
Presumption of death orders
dissolution of marriage on,
18R–158—18–164
Presumptions
domicile of choice, 6–047
evidence, 7–036—7–037
Priorities
lex fori, 7–041—7–042, 7–079
Prisoners
domicile of choice, 6–059
Privacy
breach of confidence, 35–141
defamation claims
contribution, 35–132
damages, 35–131
defences, 35–128
double actionability, 35–106—35–117
generally, 35–101—35–105
indemnities, 35–132
lex delciti, 35–112—35–117
lex fori, 35–112—35–117
limitations, 35–129
parties, 35–127
place of commission, 35–118—35–125
procedure, 35–130
renvoi, 35–126
rule, 35R–099
substance, 35–130
introduction, 35–100
Rome II Regulation, 34–011, 34–035,
34–091—34–092
rule, 35R–099
**Private International Law (Miscellaneous
Provisions) Act 1995**
choice of law, 35–014—35–018
non-Rome II Regulation torts, 35–133
Rome II Regulation, and, 35–019
Probate
see also **Administration of estates**
claims *in personam*, 11R–233—11–234

Procedure
arbitration
Arbitration Act 1996, 16–042—16–044
Civil Procedure Rules 1998,
16–045—16–046
determination of seat, 16–035—16–041
function of procedural law,
16–029—16–032
generally, 16–009
ICSID, 16–184—16–186
party autonomy, 16–033—16–034
defamation, 35–130
lex fori
counterclaims, 7–039—7–040, 7–078
damages, 7–043—7–053, 7–080
evidence, 7–022—7–038, 7–077
examples, 7–075—7–081
generally, 7–002—7–005
limitations, 7–054—7–070, 7–081
method of enforcement, 7–011—7–016,
7–075
miscellaneous cases, 7–071—7–074
nature of remedy, 7–011—7–016, 7–075
parties, 7–017—7–021, 7–076
priorities, 7–041—7–042, 7–079
Rome I and Rome II Regulations,
7–006—7–009
set-off, 7–039—7–040, 7–078
recognition and enforcement of foreign
judgments
EU law, 14–239—14–240
Rome II Regulation, 34–037
Product liability
escape clause, 35–050
examples, 35–051
foreseeability, 35–046—35–047
habitual residence, 35–049
hierarchy of rule, 35–045
introduction, 35–039
liable persons, 35–041
meaning of damage, 35–042
meaning of marketed, 35–044
meaning of product, 35–043
rule, 38R–038
scope of rule, 35–040
timing, 35–049
Prohibited steps orders
jurisdiction
orders relating to children,
19–029—19–043
Promissory notes
acceptance, 33R–342
choice of law, 33–332—33–333
contracts connected to, 33–334
discharge, 33R–344, 33–356—33–357
drawing, 33R–342
duties of holder, 33R–366—33–372
enforcement, 33R–346
examples, 33–355, 33–365
face of instrument, 33R–343
generally, 33–328—33–331